THE CAMBRIDGE DICTIONARY OF PSYCHOLOGY

The Cambridge Dictionary of Psychology is the first and only dictionary that surveys the broad discipline of psychology from an international, cross-cultural, and interdisciplinary focus. This focus was achieved in several ways. The managing and consulting editorial boards comprise world-renowned scholars in psychology from many different countries, not just the United States. They reviewed and edited all of the keyword entries to make them lively and applicable across cultural contexts, incorporating the latest knowledge in contemporary international psychology. Thus entries related to culture, as well as those from all domains of psychology, are written with the broadest possible audience in mind. Also, many keywords central to contemporary psychology were incorporated that are not included by many competitors, including the Oxford and American Psychological Association dictionaries.

David Matsumoto is an internationally acclaimed author and psychologist. He received his B.A. from the University of Michigan in 1981 with high honors in psychology and Japanese. He subsequently earned his M.A. (1983) and Ph.D. (1986) in psychology from the University of California at Berkeley. He is currently Professor of Psychology and Director of the Culture and Emotion Research Laboratory at San Francisco State University, where he has been since 1989. He has studied culture, emotion, social interaction, and communication for 20 years. His books include well-known titles such as *Culture and Psychology: People Around the World*, *The Intercultural Adjustment Potential of Japanese*, *The Handbook of Culture and Psychology*, and *The New Japan*. He is the recipient of many awards and honors in the field of psychology, including being named a G. Stanley Hall lecturer by the American Psychological Association. He is the Series Editor for Cambridge University Press's Culture and Psychology series. He is also Editor of the *Journal of Cross-Cultural Psychology* and for the Culture and Diversity section of *Social and Personality Psychology Compass*. He has appeared on numerous television and radio shows and has worked in more than 40 countries around the world.

THE CAMBRIDGE DICTIONARY OF
PSYCHOLOGY

General Editor

David Matsumoto

San Francisco State University

CAMBRIDGE
UNIVERSITY PRESS

CAMBRIDGE UNIVERSITY PRESS

Cambridge, New York, Melbourne, Madrid, Cape Town, Singapore,
São Paulo, Delhi, Dubai, Tokyo

Cambridge University Press
32 Avenue of the Americas, New York, NY 10013–2473, USA

www.cambridge.org
Information on this title: www.cambridge.org/9780521671002

First published 2009

Printed in the United States of America

A catalog record for this publication is available from the British Library.

Library of Congress Cataloging in Publication data
The Cambridge dictionary of psychology / edited by David Matsumoto.
   p.   cm.
ISBN 978-0-521-85470-2 (hardback) – ISBN 978-0-521-67100-2 (pbk.)
1. Psychology – Dictionaries.   I. Matsumoto, David Ricky.   II. Title.
BF31.C28 2009
150.3–dc22   2008037677

ISBN 978-0-521-85470-2 Hardback
ISBN 978-0-521-67100-2 Paperback

This book is dedicated to all of the pioneers and scholars of psychology who have contributed to the field as it is today, and to those who will mold it into what it will be tomorrow.

CONTRIBUTORS TO THE CAMBRIDGE DICTIONARY OF PSYCHOLOGY

Icek Aizen
University of Massachusetts

Dolores Albarracin
University of Florida

Jeanette Altarriba
SUNY – Albany

Bob Altemeyer
University of Manitoba

Drew A. Anderson
SUNY – Albany

Alfredo Ardila
Florida International University

Evelyn W. M. Au
University of Illinois – Urbana-Champaign

Ozlem N. Ayduk
University of California, Berkeley

Amy Badura-Brack
Creighton University

Mahzarin R. Banaji
Harvard University

Albert Bandura
Stanford University

Lisa M. Bauer
Pepperdine University

Veronica Benet-Martinez
University of California, Riverside

Kathy R. Berenson
Columbia University

Peter Borkenau
Martin-Luther University

Marc A. Brackett
Yale University

Laura A. Brannon
Kansas State University

Linda Brannon
McNeese State University

Jonathan Brown
University of Washington

Jennifer Bruce
Purdue University

Susan Burns
Morning Side College

Gustavo Carlo
University of Nebraska, Lincoln

Dana R. Carney
Harvard University

David W. Carroll
University of Wisconsin – Superior

Jose Centeno
St. John's University

Edward C. Chang
University of Michigan

Rita Chang
University of Michigan

Shirley Y. Y. Cheng
University of Illinois – Urbana-Champaign

Chi Yue Chiu
University of Illinois – Urbana-Champaign

Andrew Christopher
Albion College

Austin Timothy Church
Washington State University

Mark Costanzo
Claremont McKenna College

Thomas S. Critchfield
Illinois State University

Frances Daniel
University of Illinois, Chicago

Sharon Danoff-Burg
SUNY – Albany

Mark Dechesne
University of Maryland

Filip De Fruyt
Ghent University

Ken DeMarree
Texas Tech University

Nicholas DiFonzo
Rochester Institute of Technology

Kristen A. Diliberto-Macaluso
Berry College

Dale Dinnel
Western Washington University

Stephen Dollinger
Southern Illinois University

G. William Domhoff
University of California, Santa Cruz

Christina A. Downey
University of Michigan

Geraldine Downey
Columbia University

Andrew Elliot
University of Rochester

Robert A. Emmons
University of California, Davis

Erica Fanning
CUNY Graduate Center

Eva M. Fernandez
City University of New York

Steve Franconeri
University of British Columbia

David Gard
San Francisco State University

Michele Gelfand
University of Maryland

Jennifer L. Gianico
SUNY – Albany

Howard Giles
University of California, Santa Barbara

Anna Gladkova
Australian National University

Normaris Gonzalez-Miller
New York Medical College

Donald Graves
SUNY – Albany

William Graziano
Purdue University

Jeffrey Greenberg
University of Arizona

Maria Rosario T. De Guzman
University of Nebraska, Lincoln

Curtis Hardin
Brooklyn College

Sam A. Hardy
University of Virginia

Trevor A. Harley
Dundee University

Rachel Hayes
University of Nebraska, Lincoln

Marlone D. Henderson
University of Chicago

E. Tory Higgins
Columbia University

Allyson L. Holbrook
University of Illinois – Chicago

Ying-yi Hong
University of Illinois – Urbana-Champaign

Tim Johnson
University of Illinois – Chicago

John T. Jost
New York University

Janice M. Juraska
University of Illinois – Urbana-Champaign

Lee Jussim
Rutgers University

Todd Kahan
Bates College

Yoshi Kashima
University of Melbourne

Anatoliy V. Kharkhurin
American University of Sharjah

John F. Kihlstrom
University of California, Berkeley

Young-Hoon Kim
University of Illinois – Urbana-Champaign

Suzanne Kirschner
College of the Holy Cross

Jason W. Kisling
Sun Lake Shimane Prefecture Youth Center, Japan

Arie Kruglanski
University of Maryland

John Kurtz
Villanova University

Nicole Landi
Haskins Laboratories

Ellen Langer
Harvard University

Jennifer Langhinrichsen-Rohling
University of South Alabama

Heidi Lary
Stony Brook University

Patrick R. Laughlin
University of Illinois – Urbana-Champaign

Greg Lehne
Johns Hopkins Medical Center

Hong Li
University of Florida

Elizabeth F. Loftus
University of California, Irvine

Kevin MacDonald
California State University, Long Beach

David MacKinnon
Arizona State University

B. Jean Mandernach
Park University

Viorica Marian
Northwestern University

Todd Jason McCallum
Case Western Reserve University

Michael McCaslin
Ohio State University

Robert R. McCrae
National Institute on Aging

Kathleen C. McCulloch
Idaho State University

Rodolfo Mendoza-Denton
University of California, Berkeley

Tanya Menon
University of Chicago

Felicity Miao
University of Virginia

Joshua Miller
University of Georgia

Arlen C. Moller
University of Rochester

Sik-hung Ng
City University of Hong Kong

Kim Noels
University of Alberta

J. Farley Norman
University of Western Kentucky

Shigehiro Oishi
University of Virginia

Sumie Okazaki
University of Illinois – Urbana-Champaign

Margaret R. Ortmann
University of Nebraska, Lincoln

Nansook Park
University of Rhode Island

Marc Patry
St. Mary's University

Sam Paunonen
University of Western Ontario

Chris Peterson
University of Michigan

Tiamoyo Peterson
University of California, Irvine

Richard Petty
Ohio State University

Cynthia L. Pickett
University of California, Davis

Valerie K. Pilling
Kansas State University

Jason Plaks
University of Washington

Gary E. Raney
University of Illinois – Chicago

Neal Roese
University of Illinois – Urbana-Champaign

Glenn Roisman
University of Illinois – Urbana-Champaign

Jerome Rossier
University of Lausanne

Kelly A. Sauerwein
University of California, Davis

Virginia Saunders
San Francisco State University

Anne R. Schutte
University of Nebraska, Lincoln

William G. Shadel
RAND Corporation

Dikla Shmueli
University of California, San Francisco

Jessica Sim
University of Chicago

Peter Smith
University of Sussex

Emily G. Soltano
Worcester State College

Amy Summerville
University of Illinois – Urbana-Champaign

William B. Swann
University of Texas

Carmit Tamar Tadmor
University of California, Berkeley

Howard Tennen
University of Connecticut Health Center

Philip E. Tetlock
University of California, Berkeley

Abraham Tresser
University of Georgia

Harry Triandis
University of Illinois – Urbana-Champaign

Yaacov Trope
New York University

Chi-Shing Tse
SUNY – Albany

Jim Uleman
New York University

Johanneke van der Toorn
New York University

Joseph A. Vandello
University of South Florida

Patrick Vargas
University of Illinois – Urbana-Champaign

Brendan Weekes
University of Sussex

Neil D. Weinstein
Rutgers University

Kipling D. Williams
Purdue University

Jessie Wilson
San Francisco State University

Katie M. Wood
University of South Alabama

Robert S. Wyer
Hong Kong University of Science and Technology

PREFACE

dictionary *n*. A book containing a selection of the words of a language, usually arranged alphabetically, giving information about their meanings, pronunciations, etymologies, and the like.

psychology *n*. The study of the mind including consciousness, perception, motivation, behavior, the biology of the nervous system in its relation to mind, scientific methods of studying the mind, cognition, social interactions in relation to mind, individual differences, and the application of these approaches to practical problems in organization and commerce and especially to the alleviation of suffering.

It is perhaps most fitting that a dictionary of psychology begins with definitions of the terms *dictionary* and *psychology*. This is the definition of psychology presented in this work, and it highlights several important points concerning this dictionary. First, psychology is broad. Its contents range from the microlevel neural processes that form the building blocks of thought, feeling, and action to the macrolevel social and cultural processes that bind us with our primate relatives in our evolutionary history and define our collectives. For that reason, a dictionary of psychology needs to include terms and concepts related to neural structures, chemicals, transmitters, genes, and anatomy, as much as it needs to include social processes, network analysis, and cultural norms and artifacts. It also needs to include concepts related to the array of abnormal behaviors and methods related to their treatment.

Second, psychology is a science. Knowledge in psychology is generated through empirical research, a conglomeration of methods that allow for the generation of theories of human behavior and the testing of hypotheses derived from those theories. This set of methods includes both qualitative and quantitative approaches, case studies as well as carefully controlled experiments, and rigorous statistical procedures and inferential decision making. All knowledge in psychology is based on such research. Thus, understanding the meaning, boundaries, and limitations of psychological knowledge *requires* students to have a working knowledge of psychological research methods, statistics, probability, and inference.

Third, because the discipline of psychology is broad, and because it is based on science, it is a *living* discipline. That means that the theories, concepts, and terminology used in psychology are never static but often are in flux, changing across time as theories, methodologies, and knowledge change. Terms that had a certain meaning in previous years, such as *borderline personality*, *homosexuality*, and *self*, have different meanings today and will likely mean different things in the future. Additionally, new terms and concepts are continually being invented (e.g., *psychoneuroimmunology*), in keeping with the contemporary and evolving nature of psychology as a science.

This dictionary captures these characteristics of psychology as a living, scientific discipline by focusing on several defining characteristics. It is *comprehensive*, capturing the major terms and concepts that frame the discipline of psychology, from the level of neurons to social structures and as a science. It is *interdisciplinary*, highlighting psychological concepts that cut behavior at its joints, whether the joints refer to social cognitive neuroscience (a term defined in this dictionary) or the interactions among culture, personality, and genes. And it is *international and cross-cultural*, owing to the growth of psychology around the world, the interaction between American and international approaches and perspectives, and the education of American psychology by the study and practice of psychology in other countries and cultures.

In this digital age, when information concerning psychology and many other disciplines is already readily available online and in various reference texts, a relevant question is, Why produce another? The answer is very simple: because no other reference work on the field of psychology captures the characteristics described previously. Many, for example, do not do justice to psychology as a science and therefore do not include references to research methodologies and statistics. This work does. Many reference works present psychology from a more clinical orientation and do not present psychology as an interdisciplinary science. This work does. And many other works present psychology mainly from an American perspective and do not present it as the global, international discipline that it is. This work does.

These characteristics were accomplished in several ways, the most important of which were the recruitment and active participation of a stellar Editorial Advisory Board (EAB). Each of these individuals is an accomplished scholar in his or her own right, and we were very fortunate indeed to gain their participation in the project. They guided me in every single aspect of the production, and I was fortunate to gain many insights their wisdom and guidance provided.

Next, the entire work was reviewed not only by the EAB but also by an equally stellar cast of Managing Editors. Like the EAB, all of these individuals are accomplished scholars in their own right, and indeed are some of the leading researchers in the world in their respective areas of expertise. Equally important, they are from many different countries, cultures, and perspectives and have been able to create the interdisciplinary, international, and cross-cultural flavor in the book, not only in the selection of the keyword entries but also in their writing.

Finally, we were very fortunate to have so many authors contribute their time and expertise to the project (see pages ix–xiii). All of them are excellent researchers, teachers, and scholars in psychology, and all brought their expertise to bear in making the discipline of psychology come to life in their entries. They also made their entries relevant to a global perspective, not just an American one, and accessible to the educated lay reader.

These three groups of individuals worked seamlessly as a team to deliver the product you see today. The work started with the creation of the keyword list. For any reference work of this type, the selection of the keyword entries is crucial to the success of the final product, and I believe that the process by which they were selected for inclusion in this work was exemplary. First, the Editorial Advisory Board and I reviewed all of the keyword entries in the various psychology dictionaries that currently exist, as well as a number of the leading textbooks used in introductory psychology. This accomplished two goals. While of course it led to an identification of keywords that we could deem "standard" in the field of psychology – by being cross-listed in multiple sources – it also allowed us to identify what was *not* included elsewhere, or that which was idiosyncratic to its source. It was at this point that the EAB and I were able to add keyword terms that we felt could accomplish the goal of making this work comprehensive and timely, terms that specifically addressed our goal of being international, cross-cultural, and interdisciplinary.

In addition, many contemporary dictionaries do not focus on the scientific aspects of psychology and consequently do not include terms concerning research methods or statistics. In this dictionary, however, we have made a point of including many of the terms that students of psychological science will encounter, especially concerning the numerous types of reliability and validity, various types of statistics and probability, and various experimental designs.

Finally, after the EAB and I had completed our initial selection of keywords, our distinguished group of Managing Editors and authors provided us with yet additional levels of expertise, proposing new keywords within their areas of interests. For example, these are a sampling of the keywords included in the *Cambridge Dictionary* that are *not* included in many of the other dictionaries on the market:

Behavioral endocrinology
Collective self
Configurative culture
Culture assimilator training
Dialectical reasoning
Differential item functioning
Distributive justice
Ecological fallacy
Ecological-level analysis
Effect size
Emotion theory
Eta squared
Face (concept of)
False uniqueness effect
Filial piety
Fourfold point correlation
Front horizontal foreshortening theory
Gene expression
Hardiness
Hierarchical linear modeling
Implicit communication
Indigenous healing
Individual-level analysis
Intercultural adaptation
Intercultural adjustment
Intercultural communication
Intercultural communication competence
Intercultural sensitivity
Item reliability
Lay theories of behavioral causality
Naikan therapy
National character
Need for cognition
Neural imaging
Neurocognition
Normality
Norm group
Omega squared
Omnibus test
Outgroup homogeneity bias
Ranked distribution
Regression weight
Response sets
Retributive justice
Social axiom

Social network analysis
Standardization sample
Statistical artifact
Statistical inference
Tacit communication
Terror management theory
Tetrachoric correlation
Ultimatum game

A quick perusal of the list makes it clear that all of these terms are widely used in contemporary psychology today, owing to its interdisciplinary and cross-cultural ties and its existence as a scientific discipline. These entries, along with the way they were written, make this text unique and timely in the field.

ACKNOWLEDGMENTS

I give special thanks to the EAB for spearheading this project from its inception, for guiding me through the years that the project was active, and for helping to generate keywords, to recruit the stellar authors we have on board, and to review all of the entries. This work could not have been done without your hard work and dedication, and the many users of this work and I thank you.

I give thanks also to the Managing Editors, who carefully reviewed the entries, made incredibly helpful suggestions, added new entries, and wrote entries themselves. Your work went above and beyond, and the users and I are grateful to you for your careful review and guidance.

I give thanks to the amazing authors who wrote entries for us – in most cases, many entries. The project has gone through many changes from its inception, and you stuck with the project and me throughout, and I am eternally grateful for your doing so.

I am indebted to many at Cambridge University Press for making this happen. Former editor Phil Laughlin first approached me about this dictionary in 2001 or so, and we tinkered around with the idea for about 3 years before, in 2004, we finally agreed to launch this project. When Phil left the Press, the project and I were handed over to the able hands of Eric Schwartz, with whom I worked closely on bringing the project to fruition and who helped me manage the enormous tasks that composed the work and supported me in every way possible. Throughout these years, Frank Smith has been an incredible behind-the-scenes supporter and advocate, and I am grateful for the support he has given to the project.

Back at home, I have been supported by many of my own staff who have helped in some way with this project. I thank Stephanie Hata, Shannon Pacaoa, Hyi-Sung Hwang, and Mina Park for their clerical help in managing the project. I am indebted to my colleagues, students, and assistants at the Culture and Emotion Research Laboratory at San Francisco State University, many of whom wrote entries, especially Jeff LeRoux. I also thank two of my faculty colleagues in the Department of Psychology at San Francisco State University who helped out by writing entries – David Gard and Virginia Saunders. I thank my research collaborators and friends for keeping me on my toes and keeping me current with the field – Paul Ekman, Mark Frank, Dacher Keltner, Deborah Krupp, Maureen O'Sullivan, Yohtaro Takano, Jessica Tracy, Bob Willingham, Toshio Yamagishi, and Susumu Yamaguchi. I thank my wife, Mimi, for giving me the freedom to take on crazy projects such as creating a dictionary of psychology.

It is virtually impossible to produce a work such as this completely without errors, especially of omissions of keywords that should be included, or of mistakes in definitions. I encourage all readers to let me know of keywords that they feel should be included, or of potential mistakes in the entries. Just as the discipline of psychology itself is a living entity, a dictionary of psychology should be a living work, changing across time to describe the ever-changing and dynamic nature of the field and its contents. Consequently, this work should change across time as well, and I embrace suggestions for such change to improve it. Nevertheless, although it is quite clear that this work is the culmination of the efforts, hard work, and dedication of a lot of people, the errors and omissions in the work are solely mine.

David Matsumoto
San Francisco, California
July 2008

THE CAMBRIDGE DICTIONARY OF

PSYCHOLOGY

A

abasement

n. Unfavorable comparison to some other person or some standard. Henry Murray suggested abasement was a basic human need to lower one's self relative to those other people a person considers superior to himself or herself, to give power to that superior person, or to atone for perceived errors or sins.

abasia

n. The state of being unable to walk due to an absence or deficiency in motor coordination. There are numerous causes of abasia including muscle, joint, nerve, or bone problems in the legs; damage or malformation of the spinal cord; and damage or malformation of the brain.

aberration

n. **1.** A deviation from what is normal or expected. **2.** A temporary deviation in behavior by an individual from what is usual for him or her. **3.** An astigmatism, dioptric variation, or any other defect of the lens of the eye which brings about a scattering of light so that it does not appropriately project on the retina. **4.** A chromatic aberration is one caused when the lens differently refracts different wavelengths of light so that their projection on the retina does not perfectly overlap, causing blurred perception. **5.** A spherical aberration is one in which the lens is imperfectly shaped, causing light from different parts of the lens to have different focal lengths, leading to blurred perception.

ability

n. A capacity to accomplish a task at the present moment. This implies that any learning or developmental process necessary to the task has already been accomplished. Ability often contrasts with aptitude or potential or inherent but unrealized capacity which needs further learning or development to become an ability. Intelligence tests measure ability and are sometimes used to infer aptitude for future learning.

ability test

n. Any test which measures a mental or physical competence to perform certain actions and is used to infer native capacity to learn or to perform. Such tests are usually referenced to specific age or group norms and are sometimes used to predict future academic or vocational achievement. Examples include all intelligence tests, the Scholastic Aptitude Test (SAT), and the Raven Progressive Matrices Test.

ablation

n. The surgical removal of part of an organ. Ablation of portions of the brain was often used as a method of investigating brain function in the 20th century.

Abney effect

n. **1.** A perceptual distortion that occurs when a large surface is suddenly illuminated such that the center appears to be lighted before the edges. When a large surface which has been illuminated is suddenly darkened, the center appears to be illuminated longer than do the edges. **2.** A perceived change in the hue of light when white light is added to monochromatic light, thus increasing total illumination.

abnormal

adj. Differing from the usual, expected, or mean. In psychology this term is used both in the statistical sense of deviation from the central tendency of a distribution and in the sense of behavioral deviation from the social norm. Confusion often arises as a result of failing to specify which use of the term is meant. So a person with a very high IQ is abnormal in the statistical sense but not the pathological one.

abnormal psychology

n. The study of persons whose behavior causes significant distress to them or others; the behavior's cause is believed to be the pathological functioning of the mind. This field includes the development, classification,

1

diagnosis, treatment, and prevention of mental disorders. The term *abnormal psychology* is not applied in a statistical sense to both the highest and lowest functioning persons but only to the lowest functioning ones, and so the term is usually used in a pejorative sense rather than a statistical one, causing significant confusion among laypersons.

abortion
n. The early termination of a pregnancy by means of either a surgical procedure or biological processes. A slight majority of first human pregnancies are aborted by biological processes and referred to as spontaneous abortions or miscarriages.

abreaction
n. A psychoanalytic term used to describe the release of anxiety and tension after completely remembering or reliving a repressed memory. This was important in early psychoanalytic treatment and several modern therapies.

absolute error
n. In psychophysics absolute error refers to the difference between a consensual measurement and the judgment of it by a subject without respect to whether the error is above or below the consensual measure.

absolute limen
n. The lowest level of a sensory stimulus to which a subject can give any indication of perception of a stimulus. Originally psychophysicists believed there was some absolute level which corresponded with human consciousness which defined this limit, but close study revealed variability in subject responses which were partially random and partially dependent on the instructions given to the subject. Subsequent study revealed that there is a gradual onset of stimulus detection which is usually described using signal detection methods which give probabilities of response to a stimulus at different intensities or levels of the stimulus.

absolute pitch
n. The human capacity to recognize and name any given pure tone without reference to another tone. It is also called perfect pitch or perfect ear in music.

absolute refractory period
n. **1.** A brief period while an electric impulse is traveling down the axon in which the neuron is completely unable to generate another such impulse. **2.** A short period after orgasm in which the organism is unresponsive to sexual stimuli or even finds such stimuli aversive.

absolute scale
n. Another name for a ratio scale. An absolute scale has a meaningful zero point, unlike nominal, ordinal, and interval scales.

absolute thinking
n. A cognitive error in which events are interpreted in total or absolute ways; thus failure at a particular task might lead to the thought "I cannot do anything right." Absolute thinking is assumed to be a cause of errors in judgment about the self which lead to depression, anxiety, and other psychological problems.

absolute threshold
n. The lowest level of a sensory stimulus to which a subject can give any indication of perception of a stimulus. Originally psychophysicists believed there was some absolute level which corresponded with human consciousness which defined this limit, but close study revealed variability in subject responses which were partially random and partially dependent on the instructions given to the subject. Subsequent study revealed that there is a gradual onset of stimulus detection which is usually described using signal detection methods which give probabilities of response to a stimulus at different intensities or levels of the stimulus. ▶ *See also* **ABSOLUTE LIMEN**

absolute value
n. The difference between a value and zero regardless of whether the difference is above or below zero. The absolute value of −3 is 3 and the absolute value of +3 is 3.

absolute zero
n. **1.** The complete absence of a thing or a characteristic. **2.** In the measurement of

temperature absolute zero is the point at which something can get no colder and at which Brownian motion ceases; 0 degrees Kelvin, −273.15 degrees Celsius, and −459.67 degrees Fahrenheit.

abstract attitude

n. The capacity to use conceptual categories to classify objects or ideas by means of their particular characteristics. The ability to think abstractly and to move between thinking about particular things and things in general.

abstract intelligence

n. The capacity to make meaning out of experience as opposed to the kind of intelligence that allows the recall or juxtaposition of previously learned material. It is also called fluid intelligence.

abuse

n. Abuse refers to harmful and/or injurious treatment by one individual toward another. It is commonly accepted that specific instances of abuse can result from deliberate intent, ignorance, or negligence. The study of abuse began in the 1950s with regard to children; it is now widely understood that adults also experience violence. Both children and adults suffer various types of abuse including physical, sexual, verbal, and emotional/psychological abuse; recently, intellectual/spiritual abuse has also been identified. Different categories of abuse often serve as umbrella terms and include various types of actions. The most common categories are child abuse, elder abuse, partner abuse, wife abuse, financial abuse, workplace violence, stalking, and abusive professional relationships.

Theories regarding the causes and/or risk factors for abuse are usually specific to the category of abuse in question. Proposed causal factors across the various categories include sociocultural explanations including cultural values and belief systems, individual personality and/or psychopathological factors, economic stressors, and, increasingly, biological factors.

Effects of abuse can be life-altering and, in extreme cases, deadly. Nonfatal effects include physical, neurobiological, cognitive, emotional, social, and educational repercussions.

It is widely recognized that treatment options for abused individuals must be tailored to individual needs and can include medical, psychological, and legal interventions.

Psychologists are increasingly seeking ways both to intervene in and to prevent various types of violence. Changing underlying attitudes in communities and educational, societal, and legal systems is central to prevention and intervention efforts.   – HLa

ABX paradigm

n. An experimental method in psychophysics in which two stimuli (A and B) that are different are presented to someone, followed by a third (X), which is the same as either of the first two and, the subject is then asked whether the third stimulus matches A or B. This is usually used in a series to find out how much difference there has to be between the first two stimuli for a person to recognize the difference.

academic achievement tests

n. Tests designed to measure knowledge acquisition after a specific course of study. Because the goal of academic achievement tests is to determine whether or not students have gained the knowledge targeted by a specific course of instruction, content validity is the primary focus. Academic achievement tests are valid when the items selected for the test adequately represent the complete subject domain. For example, an academic achievement test in math may be concerned with students' understanding of basic mathematical calculations; therefore to sample the content domain completely, it is important to include questions targeting addition, subtraction, multiplication, and division. While there are standardized academic achievement tests (such as the Stanford Achievement Test or the Metropolitan Achievement Test), most academic achievement tests are nonstandardized measures developed explicitly for a class, topic, or training module (such as most classroom tests).   – BJM

academic aptitude tests

n. Tests designed to measure an individual's potential for learning. In contrast to academic achievement tests, which examine what a student already knows, academic aptitude tests target what a student is capable of learning under the appropriate instructional conditions. As such, academic aptitude tests cover a more variable range of topics, experiences, and abilities. Since the goal of academic aptitude tests is to measure potential for knowledge acquisition, they are primarily concerned with predictive criterion validity. For example, college entrance exams (such as the American College Test) are often considered academic aptitude tests as they are designed to predict a student's success in college as a function of his or her intellectual capacity for understanding advanced material.

– BJM

academic skills disorders (now known as learning disorders, LDs)

n. Learning disorders are diagnosed when an individual's achievement, as determined by the administration of standardized tests in reading, mathematics, or writing, is substantially below what would be expected for the age, schooling, and level of intelligence of that individual. Learning problems must significantly interfere with academic achievement or activities of daily living that require academic skills. "Substantially below" is usually defined as a discrepancy of two standard deviations between IQ and achievement. There are three types of learning disorders: reading disorders, mathematics disorders, and disorders of written expression. The DSM-IV-TR states that if a child meets the criteria for more than one learning disorder, he or she should be diagnosed with all of them. It is important to note that LD differs from mental retardation in that the achievement deficit is not due to a lack of intelligence. The idea is that the individual is intellectually capable of achieving higher than he/she currently is. It is also necessary to take background into account, as LD is not diagnosed if the deficit is due to lack of opportunities to learn.

– EF

academic underachievement

n. Academic underachievement results when a student is not academically performing to the best of his/her abilities. This can be due to failure to complete assignments and/or lack of motivation. In addition, heightened levels of anxiety may interfere during tests, and poor organization or study skills may also lead to problems. Depression and low self-esteem have also been found to affect academic performance. This phenomenon can occur in gifted students and/or in students who have a disability. In addition, it has been noted that minority students often underachieve in the academic arena. Among other possibilities, this may be due to lack of opportunity, stereotype threat, discrimination, or possible cultural differences. Once it has been discovered that a student is underachieving academically, it is necessary to determine the cause to apply the appropriate treatment or intervention.

– EF

acalculia

n. Impairment in numerical abilities as a result of brain pathology. It is also known as acquired dyscalculia. The developmental defect in the normal acquisition of numerical abilities is usually referred to as developmental dyscalculia or simply dyscalculia. Two major types of acalculia can be distinguished: primary acalculia (also referred to as anarithmetia) and secondary acalculia. Primary acalculia represents a fundamental defect in understanding the numerical system. Patients present a loss of numerical concepts, inability to understand quantities, defects in using syntactic rules in calculation (e.g., "to borrow"), and deficits in correctly understanding numerical signs. The failure in calculation tasks has to be found in both oral and written operations. Secondary acalculia, on the other hand, refers to the calculation defects resulting from a different cognitive deficit (such as language defects or attention impairments). Several subtypes of secondary acalculia can be distinguished: aphasic acalculia, alexic acalculia, agraphic acalculia, spatial acalculia, and frontal acalculia.

– AA

accessibility of knowledge in memory

n. Knowledge accessibility is the ease with which a unit of previously acquired knowledge comes to mind. This knowledge could consist of a single concept or a configuration of interrelated concepts (a schema), a proposition or social norm, a past experience and the affect associated with the experience, or a procedure for attaining a particular goal. The accessibility of a particular unit of knowledge can be inferred from the time required to perform a task in which the knowledge is required or, alternatively, the likelihood that it is used rather than other knowledge that is equally or more applicable.

The importance of knowledge accessibility derives from the fact that when individuals are called upon to make a judgment or decision, they rarely consider all of the knowledge they have accessible in memory that potentially bears on it. Rather, they typically use the subset of relevant knowledge that comes to mind most easily without considering other, less accessible concepts and information that might also be applicable. Thus, when several units of knowledge are equally applicable for accomplishing a particular purpose (interpreting a piece of information, making a judgment, performing a certain task, etc.), the knowledge that is most accessible in memory is most likely to be used.

Theoretical underpinnings. Conceptualizations of the impact of knowledge accessibility are rooted in more general theories of memory. These theories are typically metaphorical and do not pretend to describe how knowledge is actually represented in memory. Connectionist models, which assume that knowledge is distributed throughout the memory system rather than stored in a specific location, may ultimately provide more valid descriptions of knowledge accessibility phenomena. At this writing, however, these models have not been sufficiently well developed to generate clear a priori predictions.

One conceptualization of knowledge accessibility is based on a spreading activation model of associative memory. According to this model, units of knowledge are connected in memory by associative pathways, with the length of the path (an indication of the strength of the association) decreasing with the number of times that the units have been thought about in relation to one another. When one knowledge unit is activated (i.e.,

thought about), excitation spreads from the unit along the pathways that connect it to other units, and when the excitation that accumulates at one of these locations exceeds a given activation threshold, it is activated as well. When a unit of knowledge is no longer thought about, the excitation that has accumulated at the unit gradually dissipates. However, as long as some residual excitation still exists, less excitation from other sources is required to reactivate it. Thus, it is more likely to come to mind.

A second conceptualization assumes that units of knowledge about a particular referent are stored in memory in a stack (e.g., a bin) pertaining to this referent. Whenever a unit of knowledge about the referent is used, a copy of it is deposited in the bin that pertains to its referent. Thus, the more often it is used, the more copies of it exist. Moreover, recently deposited copies are on top of the stack. When information about the referent is required, the bin is identified and a probabilistic, top-down search is performed. Thus, the more recently deposited knowledge units are more likely to be retrieved. Because the search is imperfect, however, relevant units of knowledge can often be missed. Therefore, the number of times a unit of knowledge has been used in the past (and thus the number of copies that are contained in the bin) is also a determinant of the likelihood of retrieving it.

Determinants. Two determinants of knowledge accessibility are implied by the theories of memory just described: the recency with which a unit of knowledge has been used in the past and the frequency with which it has been used. First, concepts or units of knowledge that have been used a short time before people are called upon to make a judgment or decision may influence this judgment, whereas other cognitive material, although equally applicable, may be ignored. To give an example, people who are asked to form an impression of someone who wants to cross the Atlantic in a sailboat are more likely to interpret the behavior as foolhardy, and to evaluate the person unfavorably, if they have recently encountered the term *reckless* in the course of performing an unrelated activity than if they have encountered the term *adventurous*.

The effect of recency is short lived, however, whereas the effects of frequency are more enduring. Concepts and knowledge that have been drawn upon frequently can become chronically accessible in memory and thus may have a disproportionate influence on judgments and behavior in situations in which they are applicable. Cultural and social factors that influence the frequency of encountering a concept or normative standard may increase the likelihood of applying it in making judgments and decisions despite the fact that alternative criteria are available in memory and equally applicable. The effect of recently activated knowledge can override the effect of chronic accessibility a short time after the knowledge has been activated. However, activation frequency is likely to predominate after time has elapsed.

Other factors can also influence the accessibility of knowledge in memory. For example, thinking extensively about stimuli at the time they are encountered, because of their novelty, vividness, or inconsistency with expectations, can increase the ease with which they later come to mind.

Effects. The accessibility of concepts and knowledge can affect judgments and decisions through their mediating influence at several stages of processing. When new stimulus information is received, an existing concept whose features are similar to those of the information is likely to be retrieved from memory for use in interpreting it. When more than one such concept is applicable, however, the one that is most easily accessible is the more likely to be used. Similarly, people who are asked to report their belief about an event or the existence of a particular state of affairs, or to indicate their attitude toward a person, object, or event, may often search memory for information with implications for this judgment. In these cases, the first relevant information that one identifies is most likely to be applied, and other, equally relevant but less accessible information may have less effect. (As a simple example, people are more likely to report that drinking coffee is desirable if they are asked in the morning, when thoughts about the desirability of being alert are likely to be activated, than if they are asked late at night when they are trying to fall asleep. Alternatively, they are more likely to evaluate a U.S. president favorably if they are asked a short time after hearing a speech in which he/she has espoused a position they like than if time has elapsed and other, less desirable positions come to mind.)

The use of various cognitive procedures (e.g., the disposition to focus on positive as opposed to negative consequences of a behavior when deciding whether or not to engage in it) can also depend on the accessibility of these procedures in memory. On the other hand, concepts that happen to be accessible in memory can have a direct impact on behavior. John Bargh and his colleagues, for example, found that exposing college-age participants to concepts associated with the elderly led them to walk more slowly to the elevator after leaving the experiment.

Demonstrations of the effects of knowledge accessibility have generally focused on the impact of semantic concepts and knowledge. However, the affective reactions that are associated with this knowledge can have similar effects. For example, people who feel happy or unhappy as a result of recalling a pleasant or unpleasant past experience might misattribute these feelings to a stimulus they encounter subsequently, leading them to evaluate the stimulus either more favorably or more unfavorably than they otherwise would.

The role of awareness. People who are called upon to make a judgment or decision typically assume that the knowledge that comes to mind is determined by the type of judgment or decision they have to make and do not consider the possibility that other, objectively irrelevant factors might also have an influence. In some cases they may not be aware of these factors at all. Several studies show that subliminally exposing participants to a specific set of concepts, thereby increasing the concepts' accessibility in memory, increases the likelihood that these concepts are applied to information they later encounter in an unrelated situation. Even when people are aware of the concepts they have employed in a situation, however, they may not attribute the accessibility of these concepts to this situation when they come to mind at a later point in time. Consequently, for example, experimental participants report stronger beliefs in a hypothetical event if they have previously encountered a statement about the event in an opinion questionnaire they completed some time earlier. Alternatively, they are more likely to judge a fictitious name to be that of a well-known public figure if they have encountered the name in a different experiment 24 hours earlier. In each case, people may attribute the ease of retrieving this knowledge to having encountered it in other, nonlaboratory contexts, thus inferring that the event or name is generally well known. In fact, people may often base their judgment of the frequency of occurrence of an event on the ease with which an instance of the event comes to mind, independently of other considerations. By the same token, experiencing difficulty in retrieving knowledge in support of a particular proposition may be used as an indication that the proposition is invalid.

When people are aware that the accessibility of knowledge in memory might be due to factors that are irrelevant to a stimulus they are judging, they may sometimes discount it or seek alternative bases for the judgment. However, this may occur only if they are both motivated and able to conduct this search. Individuals who are aware they have used a trait concept in performing an initial task might sometimes avoid using the concept to interpret the information they receive in an unrelated task they perform subsequently. If they are distracted from thinking about the judgment they are asked to make, however, or if they are chronically unmotivated to devote thought to the task, they might use the activated concept as a basis for judgment despite their awareness that its use may be biased by extraneous factors.   – RSW

accessibility, principle of

n. A unit of knowledge cannot be activated, or brought to a person's mind, unless it is present in that person's memory. Knowledge *availability* refers to whether or not a knowledge unit is actually stored in memory. Knowledge *accessibility* refers to the activation potential of an available knowledge unit. The term *potential* in the definition of accessibility

captures the fact that accessible knowledge is capable of being activated (and then used), but it exists in a latent rather than in an active state. The word *potent*, the root of *potential*, captures the property of accessibility that it contributes to the likelihood that the knowledge will be used in judgments, inferences, and other responses. The term *potential* also includes notions of energy or effectiveness from chemical or electrical properties or from the position of a piece of matter in an arrangement, and these notions cover the major models that have been proposed for understanding the nature and functions of accessibility.

Two basic types of models have been used to understand the nature of knowledge accessibility and its effects – mechanistic models and excitation transmission models. Mechanistic models understand accessibility in terms of the arrangement and the working of stored component parts. In contrast, excitation transmission models understand accessibility in terms of the heightening and the dissipation of excitation (or energy levels) from stimulation and decay. These models differ in their assumptions about the interrelations among accessibility, activation, and stimulus input.

In mechanistic models, a knowledge unit that has been recently or frequently activated has a position within the structural arrangement of categories that makes it likely to be retrieved first. Once activated, the knowledge unit is then compared to the stimulus input and its use in judgment or inference depends on there being a reasonably good fit between the knowledge unit and the input. In excitation transmission models, the accessibility of the knowledge unit and the input features that match the category both contribute to the excitation level of the knowledge unit, which determines whether it becomes activated in the first place. If a knowledge unit has very low accessibility, then the fit between it and the input must be very good for it to become activated. On the other hand, if a knowledge unit has very high accessibility, then the fit between it and the input need not be good for it to become activated because the accessibility will compensate for the poor fit.

The accessibility of an available knowledge unit can be increased temporarily by priming or recently activating the unit prior to the situation in which the knowledge might be used. Many studies have found that prior exposure to a knowledge-related word in one situation, even subliminally, increases the likelihood that the knowledge will be used several minutes later to make a judgment in a different situation. Such priming effects on judgment can occur automatically outside people's conscious awareness.

A stored knowledge unit can also be primed frequently over an extended period, causing it to have relatively high accessibility for a long time afterward – a property called high *chronic accessibility*. There are personality, developmental, and cultural differences in chronic accessibility. The most common measure of individuals' chronically accessible social knowledge involves asking a person to list the traits or characteristics of a type of person whom he or she likes, dislikes, seeks out, avoids, and frequently encounters. Chronic accessibility is defined in terms of output primacy and/or frequency. A person has high chronic accessibility for a given knowledge unit if he or she lists that unit first in response to one or more questions and/or lists it frequently in response to the questions. A person has low chronic accessibility for a given knowledge unit (i.e., nonchronic) if he or she does not list the category in response to any question. Studies have found that chronically accessible social knowledge units can be relatively stable for months or even years, and they influence memory, impressions, and behavior. Another important kind of knowledge is attitudes, which also vary in their chronic accessibility. The most common measure of attitude accessibility involves asking people about their attitudes, such as asking them to evaluate whether each attitude object is "good" or "bad" and measuring the speed with which each person responds to the inquiry. The faster the response, the higher the accessibility. Higher attitude accessibility, in turn, predicts greater consistency between a person's attitude toward some object and his or her behavior toward that object.   – ETH

accessory nerve

n. The 11th of the 12 pairs of nerves which leave the skull independently of the spinal cord. The accessory nerve has two branches, one of which controls the large muscles on the side (sternocleidomastoid) of the neck and upper back (trapezeus) and another which joins with the vagus nerve.

accommodation

n. A term used by Jean Piaget to explain one way in which we confront new information. Accommodation occurs when we are faced with new information that we cannot incorporate in our existing knowledge or schemes. Thus, we must alter our existing knowledge to integrate this new information. Accommodation is a process that works in conjunction with the process of assimilation.   – SRB

accountability

n. Accountability is the implicit or explicit pressure to justify one's beliefs and actions to others. Unlike most research on cognition, the accountability literature posits that individuals do not operate in a social vacuum but rather are immersed in interdependent relationships and pressures to adhere to culturally shared norms and practices. As such, accountability can be viewed as a critical norm enforcement mechanism – the social-psychological link between individuals and social systems. Failure to act in ways for which one can construct acceptable explanations will lead to varying degrees of censure and punishment. Accountability pressure is rooted in people's fundamental need for social approval, whether as an end in itself or as a way to procure power over scarce resources. Different kinds of accountability motivate distinctive social and cognitive coping strategies. Ultimately, the benefits of accountability depend on the interpersonal and institutional goals that people are trying to achieve.   – CTT, PET

acculturation

n. Acculturation refers to the process of change in a person as a result of extended contact with another cultural group. At some point or another in their lives, virtually all people have contact with people from other cultural groups and hence can potentially undergo cultural change. Some groups of people, however, are more likely to experience acculturation than others. To distinguish these groups, John Berry provides a useful classification system which employs three dimensions: **(1)** the mobility of the group, **(2)** the voluntariness of the intercultural contact, and **(3)** the permanence of the intercultural contact. Various models have been proposed to capture the pattern of change experienced by acculturating individuals. Acculturation is a process that occurs over time, and hence longitudinal research designs, consisting of several assessments at multiple points in time, are the ideal method to understand the experience.

– KN

acculturative stress

n. Stress caused among migrants or other long-term sojourners by having to deal with a culture different than one's own. Humans, like most organisms, react with stress to uncertain situations, and new cultures present many situations in which both the social definition of the situation and appropriate behavior are unknown to the individual new to the culture.

accuracy motivation

n. A need or desire to make no or few errors in accomplishing a task. This is important to subjects in psychology experiments asked to perform tasks in which accuracy is used as a dependent measure. A subject who lacks the motivation to do the task accurately may skew results. This is particularly important in boring and/or repetitive tasks.

accuracy test

n. A test in which the score is derived from the accuracy of answers rather than from the speed at which answers are given. Also called a power test by some. An accuracy test is in some ways the opposite of a speed test, in which the primary measure is the speed at which a subject performs a task up to a predetermined level of accuracy.

acetylcholine

n. (ACh) The first neurotransmitter to be scientifically identified. ACh is the primary neurotransmitter secreted by efferent (motor) axon terminals in the central nervous system. ACh is active in an ionic form at nicotinic receptors, including the neuromuscular junction, and in a metabolic form at muscarinic receptors in the postganglionic parasympathetic system, such as in the activity of the vagus nerve affecting the heart, as well as at sympathetic ganglia in the spinal cord.

In the brain itself, most cholinergic neurons (neurons using acetylcholine as a neurotransmitter) have excitatory muscarinic metabotropic sites, initiating actions such as rapid eye movement (REM) sleep (dream sleep). ACh in the forebrain facilitates learning, while ACh in the limbic system facilitates memory functions.

– VS

acetylcholinesterase

n. (AChE) The enzyme present at neuromuscular synaptic junctions, in the parasympathetic system and in the brain, which inactivates excess acetylcholine (ACh). AChE thus reduces or halts the activity of ACh by breaking it down into choline and acetate, which are not neurotransmitters. Because of the presence of AChE at the synapse, cholinergic-initiated activity is brief in duration, easily interrupted, rather than prolonged, as with adrenergic (epinephrinergic) transmission. When AChE is pharmacologically blocked, cholinergic activity is more robust and prolonged.   – VS

achievement motivation

n. A desire to achieve social status, recognition, and rewards through the accomplishment of difficult goals, competition, and independent effort which has been linked with academic and vocational success in the United States and some other cultures. This has been found to be correlated with a combination of high parental support, high parental demand, and childhood autonomy training.

achievement motive

n. An inferred drive to accomplish difficult tasks at a high standard of competence and overcoming all obstacles. A desire to master tasks, to manipulate and control objects and other human beings, and to do so better than others are able to do. A desire to surpass one's previous accomplishments and to be recognized as better than others. It includes a need to increase one's self-esteem by the successful exercise of one's own talents.

achievement need

n. An inferred drive to accomplish difficult tasks at a high standard of competence and overcoming all obstacles. A desire to master tasks, to manipulate and control objects and other human beings, and to do so better than others are able to do. A desire to surpass one's previous accomplishments and to be recognized as better than others. It includes a need to increase one's self-esteem by the successful exercise of one's own talents.

achievement test

n. Any test which measures a mental or physical competence to perform certain actions and is used to infer learning, usually in a particular setting such as a school or vocational training program. Such tests are usually referenced to specific age or group norms and are sometimes used to predict future academic or vocational achievement. The Iowa Tests of Basic Educational Skills are an example. Achievement tests may measure ability/competence or performance.

achromat

n. A person or other organism that is able to see no color and is unable to distinguish either color or saturation of colored light. This is also called total color blindness.

achromatic

adj. **1.** Without color (hue) or saturation, containing only black, white, and shades of gray. **2.** The capacity to refract light without separating the colors of the spectrum. **3.** An achromatic color is a neutral shade of gray without any admixture of other hue or color.

achromatic interval

n. **1.** Eyes are able to see light at a lower level than they can see the color of light. The achromatic interval is the difference between the

brightness a light of a particular wavelength needs to have to be seen and the brightness it needs for a subject to be able to recognize the color of the light. **2.** In hearing it is the difference between the minimal loudness at which sound can be detected and the loudness at which the tone of the sound can be recognized.

achromatism

n. **1.** Lack of both hue and saturation of color. **2.** Total color blindness; in human beings it is a lack of the capacity to perceive either color or saturation of color. Many species lack this capacity.

achromatopsia

n. Inability to distinguish colors (color blindness). It is also known as monochromatism. Congenital achromatopsia (daltonism or *maskun*) is a hereditary vision defect found in 1/33,000 persons in the United States (incidence is different in different world areas). People may have congenital achromatopsia as a result of having a low number of cells, an absence of cells, or morphologically malformed cone cells. Individuals who have achromatopsia may be either totally color-blind or almost totally color-blind; visual acuity is poor. Different subtypes are distinguished: complete rod monochromats, incomplete rod monochromats, and blue cone monochromats. Achromatopsia appearance requires two recessive genes and it is more frequently found in men than in women. Achromatopsia can also be due to an acquired brain condition (acquired or cerebral achromatopsia), associated with stroke, trauma, or some other cause. Persons who develop cerebral achromatopsia report that they only can see shades of gray. Usually, ventro-medial occipital lobe damage involving the lingual and fusiform gyri is observed in patients who have acquired achromatopsia.   – AA

acoustic

adj. Of or about sound or pressure waves in air or other mediums.

acoustic confusion

n. Any confusion in perception or memory related to similarities in sound, as in hearing or remembering *bat* when *hat* has been said. This is contrasted with confusion resulting from inattention or confusion as to the meaning of something.

acoustic cue

n. **1.** Any acoustic characteristic of speech that is used in understanding what has been said. As an example, a chief difference between the sounds for the *t* and *d* in *die* and *tie* is primarily voice onset time, or the interval of time that passes before sound starts from the vocal cords; in *t* it is delayed and in *d* it is almost immediate. **2.** Any acoustic character used as an aid in remembering; particularly remembering a word.

acoustic filter

n. Any device or mechanism that blocks or selectively deadens some sounds while allowing others to pass through. Many acoustic filters block particular frequencies or tones while others partially block the amplitude or loudness of very loud sounds regardless of tone.

acoustic generalization

n. The tendency to react to one sound as one has previously learned to react to another, similar sound. Dogs conditioned to salivate to one bell will salivate (although somewhat less) when bells of similar but different tones are heard.

acoustic nerve

n. Also known as the vestibulocochlear or auditory nerve is nerve VIII of the 12 cranial nerves. This cranial nerve includes two different branches: a cochlear branch (hearing information) and a vestibular branch (balance and head position information). The VIII cranial nerve emerges from the medulla oblongata and enters into the internal acoustic canal in the temporal bone, along with the facial nerve (V cranial nerve). The cochlear branch arises from bipolar cells in the spiral ganglion of the cochlea. The nerve passes along the internal acoustic canal and terminates in the cochlear nucleus. The vestibular branch arises from bipolar cells in the vestibular ganglion.   – A A

acoustic store

n. An inferred memory that contains all sound information heard within the last second or so which allows integration of sound over time into comprehensible wholes and the association of these wholes with immediately subsequent wholes. So we are able to create a perception of the first syllable of the word layer and then retain it until the word is completely said and so hear the entire word as a comprehensible whole instead of a series of sounds shorter than those meaningful to us, which might prevent formation of a meaningful perception of either syllable or word.

acquiescence bias

n. A tendency to go along with what one believes to be the opinion or desire of others. In testing, it is the tendency to answer yes on yes/no questions regardless of the content of the question. This is counteracted in test construction by counterbalancing the meaning of test questions so that saying yes to one question means the opposite or nearly the opposite of saying yes to another question.

acquired drives

n. In learning theory it is usually assumed that organisms are born with some drives to act. Drives to act are inferred in organisms which have had opportunities to learn from the environment which are not initially observed in the organism. It is believed that acquired drives are learned as intermediaries which were originally linked in some way with either original drives or the satisfaction of those original drives and become functionally autonomous drives in their own right.

acquired dyslexia

n. As opposed to genetic dyslexia, acquired dyslexia is some major disturbance in reading capacity which appears in an individual who has had normal capacity to read. It is usually attributable to brain damage in the left hemisphere.

acquisition

n. Usually a synonym for *learning*, as in the acquisition of a behavior. Gaining or incorporating something new, usually a behavior, into one's repertoire of possible behaviors. It is also used to denote a significant increase in the frequency of a behavior up to some standard.

acquisition trial

n. A trial in a learning experiment in which stimuli are presented which are intended to lead the organism in the trial to acquire a particular behavior. The number of acquisition trials before acquisition of a behavior to a predetermined criterion determines the difficulty of learning.

acromegaly

n. A chronic disease caused by excessive production of growth hormone in the pituitary gland leading to elongation of the bones and tissues of the head and face, legs, feet, arms, and hands. It is sometimes called cerebral gigantism.

acroparesthesia

n. Chronic pain or numbness in the hands and feet usually described as tingling or pins and needles. It is often caused by compression of local nerve fibers. It is particularly common in middle-aged and older people.

acting out

1. *n.* In psychoanalysis acting on an impulse instead of reporting it during the course of treatment. **2.** *v.* A defense mechanism in which unconscious impulses are expressed through actions which are often inappropriate and uncharacteristic as a way of expressing the energy of an impulse while keeping the impulse itself unconscious. **3.** *v.* In common usage it has come to denote any negatively valued or socially inappropriate enactment of inferred unconscious impulses and especially those considered immature by the observer.

action

n. **1.** Any process of doing something usually involving complex motor behaviors intended to accomplish a goal, as in the action of eating. **2.** A natural process such as the action of a drug on the nervous system. **3.** The initiation of a legal proceeding. **4.** A particular military

conflict or combat, as in "He saw action in Vietnam." **5.** An operating mechanism, as in the action of a rifle. **6.** Sexual interaction, as in the phrase "looking for some action." **7.** The important activity in a particular field, as in the phrase "where the action is."

action potential

n. A change in voltage potential across the surface membrane of the axon of a neuron caused by an influx of sodium ions, which can build into a wave of the action potential down the axon, leading to the release of neurotransmitters at the end of the axon in the synaptic cleft, which, in turn, may cause a change in the action potential for the next axons in a nerve fiber.

action research

n. Applied research in the form of use of research techniques in programs of social action in order to bring about positive social change and to understand the processes involved in social change.

activation theory of emotion

n. A theory of emotion in which physiological arousal is the key element which is given direction by situational and/or cognitive considerations. Early versions of arousal theory focused on autonomic arousal in order to explain the energy mobilization in emotion; the focus has shifted to arousal centered on the reticular activating system (RAS) in more recent years.

active analysis

n. A form of psychoanalysis in which the therapist is more active in offering interpretations than is usual in psychoanalysis, in which the therapist generally spends the vast majority of the time listening in complete silence.

active avoidance

n. Engaging in physical activity so as to avoid punishment. A dog may jump over a barrier to avoid getting shocked. A child may hide from a parent to avoid being spanked.

active avoidance conditioning

n. In learning experiments, putting an animal in a situation in which it must act in order to avoid punishment. For example, a rat may be placed in a box with an electric grid on the floor and must learn to jump across a water barrier when a buzzer sounds in order to avoid having its feet shocked by the electric grid.

active vocabulary

n. The words a person actually uses in normal speech or writing as opposed to the words a person knows but seldom uses in actual speech or writing. In contemporary society most adults can identify the meaning of the word *heretofore* but almost never actually use the word in speaking or writing. From early language acquisition on, the total number of words a person can understand is much larger than the number of words he/she typically uses.

activity wheel

n. A drum usually made of thin bars or wire which is suspended horizontally so that an animal may walk continually up the drum, which rotates as the animal walks in it. This is common in cages and enclosures for small pets such as hamsters and mice and is also used to measure the activity levels of animals in experiments.

actor-observer difference

n. In attribution theory, this is a pair of biases in which the observer tends to attribute the actions of the actor to the actor's character or inherent tendencies while actors tend to attribute their own behavior to circumstances. There is much debate about the cause of this difference: some suggest the cause is a difference in information available to actor and observer, and others suggest the cause is motivational as actors wish to attribute their own behavior to socially desirable motives.

actor-observer effect

n. The predictable difference in attribution of motivation for behavior by actors and observers. ▶ *See also* **ACTOR-OBSERVER DIFFERENCE**

actual neurosis

n. In psychoanalysis, anxiety and maladaptive behavior that arise from pressures in the real world rather than from repressed childhood memories, as is usually the case. For example, a person who is given more work than he/she can do by the boss may have difficulty sleeping and may begin forgetting to do things which are necessary to do his/her work, such as a carpenter's forgetting to buy nails.

actual self

n. The person as he or she actually is rather than as he or she believes himself/herself to be. In several branches of psychology it is believed that there are often differences between the way a person perceives and reacts to an experience and the way he or she believes that he/she perceives and reacts. This is most likely to occur when a person believes it is socially desirable to be a way that he or she actually is not. For example, a person may believe he or she lacks sexual desire when he/she actually does react with arousal to sexual stimulation.

acuity

n. The capacity to distinguish fine details and small differences. This term is usually used with regard to a particular sense or aspect of a sense. For example, visual acuity is the capacity to see small differences and distinguish small parts of things and particularly at a distance. Auditory acuity may be the capacity to hear noises that are not very loud or to distinguish between two tones that have nearly the same wavelength.

acuity, auditory

n. The capacity to hear very weak sounds and to make fine distinctions and notice small differences in sound. A person with a high degree of auditory acuity can hear very weak sounds, recognize small differences in tone, and notice when a sound changes key very slightly. People with very good auditory acuity are sometimes said to have perfect pitch.

acuity grating

n. A grating of black bars on a white background such that both the width of the bars and the width of the white strips separating them can be reduced until the capacity to see the bars as separate objects disappears and the whole is seen as a single gray object. It is used as a measuring device to test visual acuity.

acuity, sensory

n. The capacity to distinguish fine details and small differences in one of the five senses. For example, a person who has good gustatory or taste acuity will be able to notice small differences in tastes. A good chef can tell the difference between small differences of amount of a spice in a particular dish while a wine connoisseur can tell the difference between wines made with grapes from the same vineyard in different years.

acuity, visual

n. The capacity to distinguish fine details and notice small differences in light patterns. For example, a person with good visual acuity can read road signs which are too far away for others to read. Good fighter pilots are noted for their capacity to be able to see other airplanes when they are far away as well as to tell in what direction and how fast they are moving.

acupuncture

n. An ancient Chinese technique of inserting very thin metal needles into the body at precise points to alter the flow of spiritual or biological energies in the body in order to block pain or to produce better health. In traditional Chinese medicine there is a complex system of energy channels or meridians in the body with connections to all the organs. By inserting needles and heating or twisting them, the energy flow along the meridians is affected. Acupuncture has been recognized by Euro-American medicine as having significant pain reducing properties, but other claims have been less substantiated, in part because Euro-American medicine and traditional Chinese medicine have very different ideas of what constitutes good health and different conceptions of the mechanisms by which the body functions.

acute pain

n. Pain which appears relatively quickly and does not last a very long time. Acute pain is opposed to chronic pain, which may last for years or for the lifetime of the person. An example of acute pain is the pain of a broken leg, which usually appears nearly instantaneously in an accident and lasts only until the leg begins to heal.

acute schizophrenic episode

n. A brief period of one of the sorts of psychotic behaviors usually associated with schizophrenia, which lasts from a few hours to a few days to a few months. These may appear in people previously diagnosed with schizophrenia whose symptoms have partially or completely disappeared or in people with no previous symptoms of schizophrenia. Symptoms can include disorganized thought, paranoid delusions, hallucinations, inappropriately extreme emotions, or the absence of normal emotion. When a person who has no previous experience with psychosis has an acute schizophrenic episode, it is usually after prolonged stress, and he or she usually recovers with few long-term effects.

acute stress disorder

n. Acute stress disorder (ASD) was first included as an anxiety disorder in the fourth edition of the *Diagnostic and Statistical Manual of Mental Disorders* (DSM-IV-TR, 2000). The specified etiology of ASD is a traumatic event that was severe enough to generate intense fear, helplessness, or horror in the victim. In addition, the traumatic event must have involved actual or threatened harm to oneself or others. ASD symptoms include dissociative, anxiety, and avoidance components, such as a lack of emotional responsiveness, a sense of numbing or detachment, persistent re-experiencing of the event through recurring images, and/or thought, dreams, or flashbacks of the event. To meet criteria for ASD, the symptoms must have persisted for a minimum of 2 days and have occurred within a month of the trauma. If the symptoms persist longer than 4 weeks, the diagnosis is typically changed to post-traumatic stress disorder (PTSD). Although symptom severity in the first few days following the trauma is not predictive of the eventual development of PTSD, ASD symptom severity 1 to 2 weeks post trauma is highly correlated with the eventual development of PTSD. Other negative prognostic signs include catastrophic appraisal of the symptoms that are being experienced, as well as attributions of shame or self-blame about the traumatic event. To date, cognitive behavioral therapy appears to be the treatment of choice for individuals diagnosed with ASD.   – JL-R

acute stress reaction

n. Anxiety and inappropriate physical arousal which appear shortly after an event which is stressful and which begin to subside within a few hours. The anxiety and physical arousal may lead the person to act in inappropriate or self-destructive ways while they last.

adaptation

n. Adaptation is an individual or group's ability to process new or modified information and the consequent psychological, physiological, or behavioral response that allows for effective functioning or goal attainment in a constantly changing environment.
                                              – JW, DM

adaptation level

n. A theoretical level of adaptation of a single dimension of a sensory system against which new levels of stimulation are judged. Thus a bucket of water is judged as warm at 50 degrees Fahrenheit if a person has just removed his or her hand from a bucket of ice water. In this theory all dimensions of sensory perception have adaptation levels which change, resulting in differing perceptions of the same stimulus by the same person depending on the immediately preceding experience.

adaptation level theory

n. A theory of sensory contexts developed by Harry Helson in which background stimulation provides a basis of comparison for all new stimulation. This theory was developed with sensory systems in mind but has been applied to a wide variety of fields such as attitudes and beliefs. ▶ *See also* **ADAPTATION LEVEL**

adaptation, selective

n. Alteration of a sensory or learning system to a particular stimulus so that the stimulus

produces less and less reaction but a new stimulus will produce a reaction at the original level of the first stimulus. For example, a person who hears traffic going by will soon show little reaction to it as long as it does not change intensity but will react to the sound of a voice equal in loudness to the traffic at the same level as if he/she had not been accustomed to the traffic noise.

adaptation syndrome

n. A three-stage description of reaction to continuing stress in which there is an immediate alarm reaction in which physiological and mental arousal rises, a resistance stage in which mental and physical arousal remain high and the body adapts to the high stress level, and then an exhaustion phase in which mental and physical resistance to stress collapses. ▶ *See also* **GENERAL ADAPTATION SYNDROME**

adaptive testing

n. A testing process in which each item, after an initial set of items, is selected on the basis of the correctness of a response to the previous item. So a person is given an item on a test and if he/she answers correctly, he/she is then given a more difficult item but is given an easier item if he/she has answered incorrectly.

ADD ▶ *See* **ATTENTION DEFICIT DISORDER**

addiction

n. A dependence on a drug or other substance, especially one in which the person feels pleasure or release from tension in using the substance and anticipates negative future consequences from its use, as in cigarette smoking. Previously the term denoted a physiological dependence in which the person needed increasing doses to reach a given level of reaction (tolerance) and unpleasant and sometimes dangerous consequences when the substance was withdrawn. However, governmental agencies have continuously expanded the use of the term for political purposes so that the term *addiction* is now used in a much broader sense and people speak of being addicted to chocolate or exercise, which produce high levels of bodily chemicals associated with pleasurable sensations.

additive color mixture

n. A color composed of a mixture of primary colors to produce a noticeably different mixed color with properties of both or all original colors. For example, purple is an additive mixture of red and blue with some perceptual characteristics of both red and blue.

additive counterfactual

n. A mental event in which a person mentally adds an action to what has actually occurred. For example, a spurned lover might think, "If only I had given her roses, then she would have gone out with me." Additive counterfactuals function to lessen the negative emotions after failure and to plan for future and, ideally, successful courses of action.

additive model

n. A statistical or other mathematical model in which multiple variables are used to predict another variable by means of a weighted sum. The most commonly used form of additive modeling is multiple regression, in which a linear model is used to assign weights to the values of predictor variables so that there is the least possible error when compared with other possible linear models.

address modes

n. **1.** In computer software an address mode is the manner in which the structure or architecture of the software creates procedures which allow the program to perform useful tasks. **2.** In art a general way of presenting a picture or other form. In realistic painting, for example, linear perspective is an address mode in which nearer objects are portrayed as larger than more distant ones.

adenine

n. One of four bases which compose all deoxyribonucleic acid (DNA) and ribonucleic acid (RNA), which are the chemical building blocks of genetic inheritance and body functioning ($C_5H_5N_5$). Adenine also is a component of adenosine triphosphate (ATP), which stores energy in the

mitochondria of cells, and of adenosine diphosphate (ADP).

adenohypophysis

n. The front or anterior portion of the pituitary gland.

adenosine triphosphate

n. (ATP) A nucleotide synthesized in the mitochondria of all living cells which functions to store energy ($C_{10}H_{16}N_5O_{13}P_3$). Energy is released when adenosine triphosphate loses a phosphate group and is converted into adenosine diphosphate (ADP) in the Krebs cycle. ATP in neurons is sometimes converted by adenosine triphosphatase (ATPase) into cyclic adenosine monophosphate (AMP), which serves to help change the electric potential across the membrane of a cell during a nerve impulse.

adenylate cyclase

n. An enzyme which begins the conversion of adenosine triphosphate (ATP) into cyclic adenosine monophosphate (AMP) in the membrane of a neuron.

adequate stimulus

n. Anything which provokes a response in a sensory organ. The correct kind of stimulus of an appropriate intensity for any sense in its current state of adaptation. Light, for example, is an adequate stimulus for the visual system when it has a wavelength within the visible spectrum and is bright enough for the person to detect it in a particular background of brightness.

adiadochokinesia

n. Difficulty or inability to perform rapid rhythmic alternate movements such as tapping or drumming the fingers against a solid object. Also called dysdiadochokinesia.

adipose

adj. Of or relating to fat or fatty tissue in the body. Adipose tissue makes up structures in mammalian bodies composed of fat cells.

adipsia

n. The absence of thirst or refraining from drinking. Chronic adipsia is sometimes produced by lesions in the lateral hypo-thalamus.

adjective checklist

n. **1.** Any list of adjectives with whose accuracy in describing a user agrees or disagrees, which is used to describe the self, ideal self, other people, a relationship, a culture or population, an idea, or an object. Ad hoc adjective checklists are widely used in consumer psychology, relationship counseling, studies of interpersonal behavior, and personality assessment. **2.** The Adjective Checklist (ACL) is a list of 300 adjectives scored on 37 scales which measure needs, goal states, creativity and intelligence, typical response styles, and 9 topical scales.

adjustment

n. Adaptation to function better in a particular environment. Changing thought or actions to interact in more satisfying ways with one's physical, social, and cultural environment. Adjustment, in the discipline of psychology, is generally conceived of as learning to deal better with changes in life.

adjustment disorder

n. An unusually strong reaction to a specific external source of stress that impairs functioning in one or more areas of life in a usually normal person. Symptoms can include almost any emotional and behavioral ones that affect personal, social, marital, or vocational functioning as long as they arise as a reaction to a specific source of stress and endure less than 6 months longer than the stressor itself, which may persist for any length of time. This is one of the most commonly used diagnostic categories in the DSM-IV-TR as it encompasses a wide variety of symptoms, bears little social stigma, and can be used to obtain insurance payments for psychotherapy.

adjustment method

n. An experimental method used in psychophysics to determine perceptual thresholds, in which a subject is given a set of stimuli and asked to adjust each stimulus to match a standard stimulus. The differences between the adjustments and the original standard are used to estimate the sensitivity of perception.

Adlerian

adj. Of or relating to Alfred Adler (1870–1937) or the psychological system or therapeutic methods he developed. *See also* **ADLERIAN PSYCHOLOGY** *and* **ADLERIAN PSYCHOTHERAPY**

Adlerian psychology

n. The psychological system developed by Alfred Adler (1870–1937), in which it is assumed that humans have two basic motivations: to have a sense of connectedness with others (social interest) and to use one's creative abilities to overcome obstacles and achieve a respected place in society (striving for superiority). Goals are chosen consciously at an early age to achieve the two main motivations, and a person creates a lifestyle around the chosen goals, the methods he/she uses to attain them, and the various ideals, thoughts, memories, and emotions which arise as a result of trying to reach those goals. Pathology arises only when a person chooses a style of life that prevents her/him from having a sense of closeness with others or becomes discouraged and fails to keep trying to solve her/his problems (inferiority complex). Adlerian psychology is often called individual psychology, as Adler emphasized that each person becomes the individual he or she is through a creative interaction with the environment and can only be understood in relationship to the environment as experienced by the individual.

Adlerian psychotherapy

n. The psychotherapy techniques developed by Alfred Alder (1870–1937), in which a person is urged to examine his or her goals and the methods he/she uses to achieve them and to use his/her own courage and creative potential to alter them in ways that lead to more satisfaction in life and a greater contribution to society. Pathology arises only when a person chooses a style of life that prevents her/him from having a sense of closeness and ability to cooperate with others or when he/she becomes discouraged and fails to keep trying to solve her/his problems (inferiority complex). Adler pioneered couples and family therapy as well as therapy for working-class persons.

adolescence

n. The period of transition from childhood to adulthood and all the physical, mental, social, and cultural changes that mark it, including the maturation of the sexual organs and secondary sexual characteristics, the development of behavioral sexual interaction patterns appropriate for adults within a given culture, the incorporation of sexuality into self-concepts and alterations in role expectations, and the enacting of them, which typically differ among children, adolescents, and adults.

adolescent development

n. The set of physical, mental, social, and cultural changes that mark the period of transition from childhood to adulthood. It includes maturation of the sexual organs and secondary sexual characteristics, the development of behavioral sexual interaction patterns, the incorporation of sexuality into self-concepts and alterations in role expectations, and enaction as well as identity formation.

adolescent identity formation

n. The process of forming a relatively stable sense of self including commitment to social and sexual roles and beliefs about the purpose and meaning of life. This usually takes place primarily in late adolescence after a period of personal and philosophical questioning and trying out of a variety of different roles and perspectives, which results in the moodiness, changeability, and sometimes rebellious social behavior of persons during their teenage years.

adoption study

n. A method used in trying to distinguish between the effects of genetics and environment in which children separated from their parents shortly after birth and raised in an adopted family are compared with genetic relatives and with other members of the family in which the children are raised. If the genetic influence on a specific trait is high, it is assumed that there will be a higher correlation between the children and their biological relatives, while if the genetic influence is weak, there will be a greater correlation with the families in which the children have been raised. Among the many difficulties in such studies is the lack of randomness of both selection of children to be adopted and the households which adopt them and the fact that most children are not separated from their biological families at birth but after a significant amount of time has elapsed since birth.

adrenal cortex

n. The external portion of the adrenal gland produces mineralocorticosteroids, androgens, and glucocorticosteroids, all of which contribute to bodily homeostasis. Of particular importance is the glucocorticosteroid cortisol, which is released when the adrenal cortex is stimulated by adrenocorticotropic hormone from the pituitary gland. The release of cortisol is a response to stress.   – vs

adrenal gland

n. Located atop (*ad*) the kidney (*renal*), the adrenal gland is composed of the adrenal cortex and the adrenal medulla. This gland produces hormones which regulate bodily homeostasis and energy expenditure.   – vs

adrenaline

n. A hormone ($C_9H_{13}NO_3$) and neurotransmitter created in the adrenal glands which acts primarily as an arousal agent. Adrenaline causes an increase in heart rate and heart stroke volume, dilates the pupils, increases blood sugar levels, reduces blood flow to the skin and digestive tract, increases blood flow to the muscles, and suppresses immune function. Adrenaline is used to stimulate the heart in cases of cardiac arrest and sometimes in cardiac arrhythmias. Adrenaline is one of the main neurotransmitters in the fight-or-flight response and in activation of the reticular activating system (RAS). Its action is mimicked by amphetamines, caffeine, and Ritalin. ▶ *See also* **EPINEPHRINE**

adrenal medulla

n. The internal portion of the adrenal gland, which secretes the catecholamine hormones epinephrine (adrenaline) and norepinephrine (noradrenaline) in response to sympathetic nervous system stimulation. These actions are catabolic: the production of these hormones leads to the immediate availability of physical energy for work, heat, or energy storage.   – vs

adrenergic neurons

n. Also known as catecholaminergic neurons in neural transmission. The transmitters in these neurons are the catecholamines dopamine, norepinephrine (noradrenaline), and epinephrine (adrenaline). Adrenergic neurons are part of the central nervous system's regulation of attention, mood, movement, and reinforcement (reward). In addition, in the autonomic nervous system, the postganglionic sympathetic neurons compose an adrenergic response system active in stress, increasing blood flow to the skeletal muscles, increasing heart rate, and raising blood sugar levels, for a fight-or-flight response.   – vs

adrenocorticotropic hormone (ACTH)

n. A hormone produced in the anterior portion of the pituitary gland. ACTH stimulates neurons in the cortex of the adrenal gland, subsequently leading to the secretion of cortisol and other glucocorticosteroids. ACTH is regulated by corticotropic releasing factor (CRF) released from neurosecretory cells in the periventricular hypothalamus. ACTH is part of an important feedback loop, the hypothalamic pituitary adrenal (HPA) axis. This HPA axis takes part in the regulation of stress. In the presence of emotional, physiological, or psychological stress, ACTH responds to CRF and releases cortisol from the adrenal cortex to support a continuation of the organism's response to stress.   – vs

adult attachment interview schedule

n. A structured interview designed for use with adults and particularly with parents to assess the attachment style or styles the adults had with their caregivers as children. The interview has been used widely in research on the relationship of attachment styles between parents and children.

adult development

n. **1.** The field of study within psychology addressing changes in human functioning across the decades of adult life. **2.** A style of education in which adult pupils learn by participation rather than through lecture or other more traditional pedagogic methods.

adulthood

n. The period in which physical and mental growth slows and nears its peak. This point is quite variable in different cultures, with technologically simple cultures usually considering persons to arrive at adulthood shortly after sexual maturity, whereas in advanced technological societies adulthood tends to be seen as occurring many years later than sexual maturity.

adult intelligence

n. **1.** In psychometrics, intelligence from the point at which growth in intelligence becomes very small in contrast to childhood, during which intelligence grows rapidly. **2.** The average level of intelligence of an adult population.

adventitious reinforcement

n. Reward delivered independently of any response by the subject. This can lead to superstitious behavior in which the subject acts as if there were a cause and effect relationship between the adventitious reward and past responses.

aerophagia

n. The swallowing of air. In humans it is a nervous habit which can result in belching and stomach discomfort. It is a method of obtaining oxygen in some species.

aesthesiometer

n. A device for measuring sensitivity to pressure. It can measure sensitivity by total pressure necessary for threshold perception, as is commonly done in corneal surgery, or by measuring the distance between points necessary for discrimination between the points on the skin.

aetiology ▶ *See* ETIOLOGY

affect

1. *n.* A transient neurophysiological response to a stimulus that excites a coordinated system of bodily and mental responses including facial expressions that inform us about our relationship to the stimulus and prepare us to deal with it in some way. The basic affects are anger, fear, surprise, happiness, disgust, and contempt. **2.** *n.* The subjective feeling or evaluative component of human experience or thought. **3.** *v.* To have an effect upon.

affect display
n. Facial expressions, gestures, postures, or other bodily movements that demonstrate an emotional state. These may be spontaneous reactions without intention or social acts with the intention of persuading the receiver. Every culture has social rules for the appropriateness of the display of different emotions.

affect infusion model
n. A theory of the relationship between emotional states and cognition or judgment in which it is supposed that emotion affects thinking more when quick, heuristic judgments or long involved chains of reasoning are involved than in quick judgments involving direct access of previous conclusions or when strong goal motivation is involved.

affective cognitive consistency
n. The idea that persons are comfortable when their attitudes are consistent with the information they have about the world and that part of attitudes is affective in nature and this affective component can change along with the cognitive component when new information is encountered. Attitudes can be changed by first changing either the affective or cognitive component with the other following.

affective disorder
n. Any of several mental disorders whose primary characteristic is extreme or pathologically unchanging emotion or mood. Affective disorders include depression, bipolar disorder, dysthymic disorder, and cyclothymic disorder.

affective forecast
n. A prediction of how one will feel should a particular course of events occur. As an example, one might say, "I would love a vanilla ice cream cone," in which one predicts one will have a positive experience if he or she eats a vanilla ice cream cone.

affective intensity
n. **1.** The level of arousal or experience of an emotion. One of the three major dimensions of emotion along with positive-negative evaluation and the direction of impulse, toward or away from.

affective primacy
n. A hypothesis that basic emotional responses can occur with minimal stimulation and outside conscious cognitive processing. Rapidly presented and emotionally charged stimuli are often presented in order to prime or affect subsequent emotional judgments.

affective priming
n. The presentation of emotion laden stimuli in an attempt to affect or control subsequent reactions or judgments.

afferent
adj. Leading to the center, as some nerve fibers send impulses toward the central nervous system and veins lead blood back to the heart. This contrasts with efferent, in which nerve impulses go toward the periphery or arteries lead blood from the heart or lungs toward the rest of the body.

affiliation
n. **1.** A sense of joining or social connection. **2.** A need to seek and enjoy close and cooperative relationships with others and to adhere to and remain loyal in those relationships.

affiliation need
n. A need to seek and enjoy close and cooperative relationships with others and to adhere to and remain loyal in those relationships.

affordance
n. An environmental resource allowing or stimulating an organism to interact with the environment in a particular way. Thus a flat surface affords a person the opportunity to sit or to lay something down without its falling

and an ice cream cone affords the opportunity to eat.

aftereffect

n. Any effect that lasts longer than the cause and particularly in a sensory system. Thus the aftereffect of a camera flash is momentary blindness.

afterimage

n. A visual perception after the actual stimulus is gone which is usually in attenuated or altered form. A Hering afterimage is a brief image similar to the original image but not as bright, while a Perkinje image is of complementary or opposite color to the original one.

afterimage, movement

n. The perception of motion following fixating the eyes on moving objects such that motion in the opposite direction is usually perceived. Thus staring at a small, moving circle and then at a stationary one will often lead a person to perceive motion in the stationary circle.

afterimage, negative ▶ *See* NEGATIVE AFTERIMAGE

afterimage, positive ▶ *See* POSITIVE AFTERIMAGE

aftersensation

n. Any sensory perception that persists after the stimulus for the sensation has gone. Afterimages and aftertastes are the most common ones.

age, chronological

n. The most common of numerous ways to define age. Chronological age is measured in units of time that have elapsed since the date of one's birth, usually days, months, or years. Age can also be defined functionally, biologically, psychologically, or socially.   – TJM

age, developmental

n. A measure of one's development expressed in terms of age norms. Common units of developmental measurement include body size, motor skill, and psychological function. Developmental tasks also often serve as the anchors by which developmental age is measured. Developmental age has most often been used to describe infant and early childhood development but can also be applied to adolescence, early adulthood, middle adulthood, and later adulthood.   – TJM

age-equivalent score

n. A raw score that corresponds to the chronological age of the norm group who obtained a similar score. Age-equivalent scores should only be used for relative comparisons of performance on a given assessment measure, not for diagnostic or placement purposes. Because most abilities and skills are acquired more rapidly during the early years than during later years of development, age-equivalent scores do not have equal intervals. For example, the difference in language/vocabulary of a 4- and a 7-year-old is considerably different from the difference in language/vocabulary between a 24- and a 27-year-old despite the fact that both are characterized by a 3-year chronological age difference. Because age-equivalent scores lack the properties of ratio or interval scales, they cannot be mathematically manipulated.   – BJM

age, mental

n. Level of intellectual development as measured through a range of cognitive tasks and through comparison with chronological age peers. Mental age is most commonly used for the assessment of children and those with cognitive impairments, but also increasingly with older adults. Mental age can be expressed as the age at which that level of development is typically attained.

Alfred Binet, a French psychologist, developed a test to predict academic success accurately when the French government asked him to help them determine which children in the public schools would have difficulty with formal education. He and his colleague, Theodore Simon, found that tests of practical knowledge, memory, reasoning, vocabulary, and problem solving were better predictors of school success than the sensory tests that had been used previously. Participants were asked to perform simple commands and gestures, repeat spoken numbers, name objects in pictures, define common words, tell how two objects are different, and define abstract terms.

Assuming that children all follow the same pattern of development but develop at different rates, Binet and Simon created the concept of mental age, whereby, for example, a child of any age who scored as well as an average 12-year-old was said to have a mental age of 12. The intelligence test score also gives a clue to the child's readiness to assume social responsibility by getting along with others, to his or her ability to care for himself/herself, and to the level of play behavior he or she might be expected to show.   – TJM

agency

n. Agents are actors who shape their environments, affect their surroundings, and simply do things. According to Kant, they possess autonomy, the power to exert their internal will rather than to be controlled by external forces. Dworkin argues that as self-governing entities, their behavior is not determined by external forces such as luck or another person's will.

Philosophers often characterize autonomous agency as the competence to articulate goals and intentions that are truly one's own. Mackenzie and Stoljar identify various requirements for autonomous agency, for example:

Rationality: According to Taylor, a rational agent knows, plans, and acts deliberately and intentionally.

Self-control: Frankfurt states that agents must have mastery over desires (e.g., the impulse for alcohol) that conflict with their core values (a basic goal such as living a happy and productive life).

Self-trust and self-reflection: According to Sandel, self-reflection enables people to "work out" their basic values such that they will not simply act on impulse.

A person who fulfills these conditions has intentions that flow from an authentic self – rather than from impulse, weakness, ignorance, or incompetence.   – TM, JS

age scale

n. Age scales group measurement items according to the age at which the average test taker can correctly complete the item (as opposed to simply ordering items according to increasing difficulty). The age scale concept is based on age differentiation theory, which states that children of increasing age have greater intellectual capabilities. As such, while age scales are effective measures for children whose abilities vary widely from year to year, they are generally ineffective for use on adult populations, who show little variability in intellectual capabilities as a function of age. Popularized by Binet in the development of the 1908 Binet-Simon intelligence scale, age scales are now commonly used in educational and clinical assessments.   – BJM

age score

n. In psychometrics a score on a test of skill or ability with reference to the average age at which a population achieves that score. Thus a child of 10 years may read at the 12-year-old level and so obtain an age score of 12 years on a reading test.

ageusia

n. Disturbance in taste recognition. When there is only a partial disturbance in taste recognition, the term *hypogeusia* is used; when there is a distortion in tasting, the term *dysgeusia* is used. Ageusia is typically associated with anosmia (disturbance in smell recognition), because a significant proportion of what is considered taste is derived from the olfactory information. Diverse conditions can affect taste recognition: during normal aging a decrease in taste recognition especially for bitter and salty is observed. Smoking also affects taste recognition. Local damage affecting the taste buds also interferes with taste. Certain neurological conditions, such as Bell's palsy and multiple sclerosis, can also affect taste recognition. Vitamin B_3 and zinc deficiencies can also be associated with taste recognition defects. In some specific disorders of the endocrine system such as Cushing's syndrome and diabetes mellitus, disturbances in taste are also found.   – AA

▶ *See also* **HYPOGEUSIA**

aggregation
n. **1.** A collection of several individual parts into a whole. **2.** The process of collecting parts into a whole. **3.** The characteristic of an object of being composed of a collection of individual parts.

aggression
n. A general term for behavior with the intention of harming another or controlling another for one's own needs and to the other's detriment. The term has been used with widely different theoretical points of view in psychology. Freud viewed aggression as an expression of thanatos, the death wish. Adler regarded aggression as a flawed expression of superiority striving. Murray supposed there was a basic need for aggression. Dollard supposed it was the outcome of frustration. Ethologists have subcategorized aggression in many ways, including predation, territorial defense, play, status competition, and altruistic or protection. Hormone theory proposes that hormones, such as testosterone, lead to an increased tendency to show toss and tumble behavior in pre- and adolescent development and more physical as opposed to verbal aggression in males as compared to females.

aggression, displaced
n. Behavior with the intention of harming another or controlling another for one's own needs and to the other's detriment toward another who is not the original object of hostility. Thus a man who is angry with his boss may go home and act hostilely toward his spouse.

aggression, fear-induced
n. Behavior with the intention of harming another or controlling another for one's own needs and to the other's detriment resulting from fear. This can take the form of an attack upon the cause of the fear or be displaced onto a safer target or scapegoat.

aggression, instrumental
n. Behavior with the intention of harming another or controlling another for one's own needs and to the other's detriment for the purpose of obtaining some desired object or state. Thus a robber may act aggressively toward a victim for the purpose of obtaining money, or an employer may verbally abuse employees for the purpose of getting more work from them.

aggression, territorial
n. In naturalistic studies of animal behavior, hostile and/or threatening actions taken toward another for the purpose of gaining or protecting a territory for predation or breeding purposes.

aggressiveness
n. A trait or characteristics of acting with the intention of harming another or controlling another for one's own needs and to the other's detriment. Asserting one's own needs or status above that of others and in disregard for the others.

aging and intelligence
n. The relationship between performance on tests of ability and chronological age through adulthood. Generally speaking, speeded tests find a decrement in intelligence after middle school, while power tests find a slow increase throughout adulthood until physical ailments begin to interfere with performance. In practice cross-sectional studies of intelligence across age groups have found a downward trend in intelligence scores after early middle age, while longitudinal studies have found an upward trend until physical illness affects individuals. Fluid intelligence decreases with age, whereas crystallized intelligence (accumulated knowledge and skills, language) rises slowly or stays the same after middle age.

aging, behavior changes
n. Behavior changes associated with aging in the absence of disease are commonly linked to principles of life span development. Because not all behavioral change is developmental, certain criteria must be met to define

a given behavior change as such. These criteria include behavior changes which

> direct individuals toward a state of maturity,
> exhibit qualitative and quantitative or stagelike change,
> display relative robustness or irreversibility of change, and
> support movement toward greater complexity and differentiation.

The area of behavioral gerontology emphasizes behavior as modifiable, reversible, and contextually driven. From this perspective the primary goal is to assess the causes of behavior change and create appropriate interventions to eradicate behaviors deemed problematic to the elder or others. Numerous other behavior changes are associated with diseases common among older adults, but these should be defined in relation to each disorder, not in relation to aging per se.   – TJM

agitated depression

n. A prolonged period of sadness, gloominess, pessimistic beliefs, belief in one's helplessness and worthlessness, guilt, sleep disturbance, diminished capacity for focused attention and cognitive ability in general, accompanied by high levels of anxiety manifest in pacing, fidgeting, wringing one's hands, or performing some other behavior whose only purpose is an expression of or distraction from anxiety.

agitation

n. A state characterized by anxiety manifest in pacing, fidgeting, wringing one's hands, or performing some other behavior whose only purpose is an expression of or distraction from anxiety.

agnosia

n. Inability to recognize and understand external information in the absence of decreased sensory acuity. It implies an impairment in the ability to transform simple sensations in perceptions, and as a result, the individual cannot recognize the stimuli. Agnosia supposes a – at least partially – primary sensory integrity and absence of global intellectual deterioration.

Agnosias are observed in cases of damage in the parietal, temporal, and occipital association areas. Cortical association areas participate in the analysis, integration, and interpretation of the incoming sensory information. Different types of agnosia can be distinguished: visual, spatial, auditory, tactile, and body schema (somatoagnosias or asomatoagnosias) agnosias. Perceptual difficulties can also potentially exist in other sensory systems, such as taste and smell. Usually, however, taste and smell are not supposed to be involved in cognitive processing. Some reports of gustatory agnosia are currently available.   – AA

agonist

n. (Greek *agon* = contest). In neuropharmacology, a drug which facilitates synaptic transmission at the receptor site and facilitates the receptor's response. A direct agonist drug attaches to the same binding site as does the neurotransmitter. An indirect agonist attaches to another binding site at the receptor and facilitates action of the neurotransmitter binding site. An agonist operates in contrast to an antagonist, which blocks synaptic transmission.

In muscle physiology, an agonist is a contractile skeletal muscle opposed by another muscle, the antagonist.   – VS

agoraphobia

n. An irrational and generalized fear of being in open places or of leaving one's home, being in a crowded place, traveling alone, being in a place from which quick exit is difficult or in which panic or other strong emotions would be very embarrassing. Agoraphobia is among the most common of phobias.

agrammatism

n. Oral expressive impairment characterized by short, structurally simple utterances lacking morphosyntactic elements (e.g., articles, prepositions, auxiliaries, verb endings). Agrammatic patients speak in halting, non-fluent, effortful speech, relying on the most meaning-carrying words (i.e., verbs, nouns, and adjectives) as in "Girl eat apple" or "Eat apple" for "The girl is eating/ate/has eaten the apple." They prefer simple rather than complex verbs (e.g., *go* and *going* instead of *goes*, *would go*, or *have gone*). This fragmented expression has been described as telegraphic. Symptomatology varies, and not all patients exhibit the same symptoms to the same degree. Though similar morphosyntactic impairments may be present in other language modalities (i.e., comprehension, reading, and writing), agrammatic patients can understand everyday conversation but have difficulty understanding grammatically complex sentences (e.g., passive sentences: The apple was eaten by the girl). Agrammatism is found in Broca's aphasia and transcortical motor aphasia.   – JGC

agraphia
n. Impairment in the ability to write usually due to neurological damage and usually to recognized speech centers in the brain. There are many forms of agraphia including inability to form letters without models, inability to spell, inability to write numbers, inability to write irregularly spelled words, and inability to write in a spatially organized form.

agreeableness
n. Agreeableness is one of the dimensions of the five factor model. It contrasts individuals who are good-natured, compliant, modest, gentle, and cooperative with those who are irritable, ruthless, suspicious, and inflexible. Persons higher in agreeableness differ systematically from their peers not only in their evaluations of others but also in emotional responsiveness, empathic responding, and reports of feeling connected and similar to others. Lower levels of agreeableness are associated with negative evaluations of people in general and of outgroups in particular. These evaluative processes are linked to overt behavior, including refusal of interpersonal interaction with outgroup members. Processes responsible for these individual differences may be present in "effortful control," an early childhood temperament tied to frustration regulation.   – JBru, WG

agrypnia
n. Insomnia or disturbance in normal sleep. Agrypnia includes difficulty in falling asleep, difficulty in remaining asleep, and early awakening.

aha experience
n. The subjective experience in the moment of achieving an insight. It has been described as a flash of light, a clearing of mind or vision, and a relief from tension.

ahedonia
n. A state of being in which pleasure and interest are lacking. It often occurs in depression and is the disappearance of interest and pleasure in things usually pleasurable. In sociopathy it is the normal state of the individual.

AIDS dementia complex
n. Cognitive impairment attributable to human immunodeficiency virus (HIV). HIV directly invades neural tissue and causes cell death, leading to typical dementia symptoms such as cognitive impairment, mood disturbance, personality change, and sensory and motor difficulties. Its incidence is reduced by about 60% with the use of antiretroviral medication.

air crib
n. A soundproof cabinet with a large window, air conditioning, and a moving sheet to remove waste, built as an ideal crib by B. F. Skinner to teach babies not to cry for attention while having their physical needs met.

akinesia
n. Inability to initiate voluntary movements. Akinetic mutism is a condition in which the person is both akinetic and mute. In akinetic mutism the patient is awake, but immobile (akinetic), mute, and unresponsive to commands. It is generally associated with frontal lobe damage, usually bilateral mesial frontal pathology involving the cingulate gyrus, but has also been reported as a result of damage in other brain areas, such as the basal ganglia, or the fornix, the medial nuclei of the thalamus, and as a result of diffuse white

matter disease. Differential diagnoses include locked-in state and catatonia. Different etiologies have been reported in cases of akinesia, including toxic (e.g., carbon monoxide intoxication), infectious (e.g., encephalitis), vascular (e.g., infarcts of the anterior cerebral artery), degenerative (e.g., frontal-subcortical dementia), neoplastic (e.g., olfactory groove meningioma), and traumatic (e.g., frontal lobe contusions).   – A A

akinetic apraxia

n. Type of apraxia characterized by the inability to move spontaneously.   – A A

▶ *See also* **APRAXIA**

alarm reaction

n. The first stage in the general adaptation to stress syndrome during which a person experiences a shock with dropping blood pressure and then physiological arousal with elevated serum levels of adrenaline, noradrenaline, and cortisol. In the general adaptation syndrome alarm stage is followed by the resistance stage and then the collapse stage.

albedo

n. The degree to which a surface reflects light, determined by the ratio of light falling on the surface to light reflected by the surface.

alcohol abuse

n. The use of alcohol in a manner that produces significant negative consequences for an individual or those around the individual. The use of alcohol to escape from situational or psychological problems, which leads to the syndrome commonly called alcoholism or alcohol dependence. Alcohol produces a strong addiction with tolerance and withdrawal that can be life threatening. Addiction usually marks the difference between alcohol abuse and alcoholism.

alcohol amnesic disorder

n. Usually known as Korsakoff's psychosis or Wernicke-Korsakoff syndrome, it is a disproportionate impairment in memory in comparison to other cognitive functions observed in some chronic alcohol abusers. Most prominent is anterograde amnesia for both verbal and nonverbal information. The sensitivity to interference is the principal characteristic of the memory impairment. Confabulations may also occur, although primarily in the acute stage of the disorder. Confabulation represents a tendency for patients to fill in gaps in memory when faced with questions they cannot answer. Declarative memory (factual knowledge) is significantly impaired, whereas procedural memory (motor learning) is preserved. Korsakoff's syndrome is directly linked to a deficiency of thiamine (vitamin B_1). It has also been described in the context of a number of other disorders that cause malnutrition or malabsorption, including persistent vomiting, hyperemesis gravidarum, intravenous feeding, gastrointestinal carcinoma, bowel obstruction, dialysis, and AIDS. Vulnerability to Korsakoff's syndrome is highly variable. Among alcoholics with extensive drinking histories and malnutrition, only a minority develop the syndrome. A genetic predisposition to impaired thiamine metabolism has been postulated in individuals with Korsakoff's syndrome.   – A A

alcohol dependence

n. Physical addiction to alcohol such that larger doses are needed to attain the same effects and withdrawal is experienced on reducing alcohol dosage. Long-term alcohol dependence includes brain damage, digestive system degeneration, deteriorating social and work functioning, and eventually deliria and death.

alcoholic

n. A person who has used alcohol excessively to the point of having a well-formed syndrome of pathology as a result of alcohol use. This includes both alcohol abuse and alcohol addiction and all the consequences that follow them.

alcoholic dementia

n. Dementia produced by excessive alcohol use. A chronic state of deliria marked by physical trembling, hallucinations, perceptual distortions, wildly fluctuating emotions, disordered thinking, and marked physical discomfort upon the withdrawal of alcohol from an alcohol addict.

alcoholic psychosis

n. Psychotic state produced by alcohol intoxication. This is usually a symptom of nervous system degeneration from prolonged alcohol abuse but can occur in new drinkers, usually at higher than usual doses of alcohol.

alcohol intoxication

n. The state of being drunk or having had one's normal control mechanisms noticeably affected by alcohol consumption. Symptoms usually include motor incoordination, faulty judgment, and maladaptive behavior. Legal definitions of alcohol intoxication are high enough that all the symptoms of intoxication are present at much lower doses than the legal level for presumed drunkenness.

alcoholism

n. The syndrome of predictable symptoms deriving from abuse of alcohol. These include addiction, digestive and mental deterioration, and loss of social and personal capacities. Alcoholism is often a fatal disease.

alcoholism, acute

n. Short-term abuse of alcohol, as in binge drinking or situational drunkenness that significantly interferes with an individual's capacity to function in life.

alcoholism, chronic

n. Long-term abuse of alcohol that significantly interferes with an individual's capacity to function in life. All the symptoms of alcoholism tend to appear in chronic alcoholism.

alcohol-related disorders

n. The set of disorders related to alcohol abuse defined by the DSM-IV-TR. These include

alcohol abuse, dependence, intoxication, and withdrawal

alcohol intoxication or withdrawal delirium

alcohol-induced persisting dementia

alcohol-induced persisting amnestic disorder

alcohol-induced psychotic disorder with delusions

alcohol-induced psychotic disorder with hallucinations

alcohol-induced mood disorder

alcohol-induced anxiety disorder

alcohol-induced sexual dysfunction

alcohol-induced sleep disorder

alcohol-related disorder not otherwise specified

alcohol withdrawal

n. The life threatening syndrome of physical and mental symptoms experienced by a person addicted to alcohol after the withdrawal of alcohol. Symptoms include physical trembling, tics and cramps, body aches and vomiting, hallucinations, perceptual distortions, wildly fluctuating emotions, and marked physical discomfort.

alcohol withdrawal delirium

n. A delirium marked by physical trembling, hallucinations, perceptual distortions, wildly fluctuating emotions, disordered thinking, and marked physical discomfort upon the withdrawal of alcohol from an alcohol addict. Also called delirium tremens.

aldehyde dehydrogenase

n. A family of enzymes that catalyze the oxygenation of aldehydes. Alcohol aldehyde dehydrogenase catalyzes the oxygenation of ethyl alcohol into acetaldehyde, which in turn is catalyzed by acetyl aldehyde dehydrogenase into acetic acid or vinegar. Acetyl aldehyde dehydrogenase's action is blocked by Antabuse (disulfram) leading to an accumulation of acetaldehyde, which sickens the person.

aldosterone

n. A mineralocorticoid produced in the adrenal gland and very active in the regulation of choline and in the balance between potassium and sodium by the kidneys.

alexia

n. Pure alexia is a form of acquired word blindness in which writing and spelling can be unaffected (i.e., alexia without agraphia). Single-letter recognition is usually intact, and comprehension and production of spoken language are normal, allowing patients to use an oral spelling strategy to recognise written words (e.g., *cap* = *C*, *A*, *P*). A striking feature of pure alexia is that patients are unable to read aloud words they have themselves just written. Patients appear to decode words as a sequence of isolated letters without any access to holistic word recognition processes that are used by the normal reader. Letter-by-letter reading appears to arise from a disconnection that prevents the parallel mapping of abstract letter identities onto word level representations so that access to word forms is sequential. Reading of words and non-words is slow, and reading time is a linear function of the number of letters in a letter string. Pure alexia often resolves rapidly after brain injury. Rehabilitation involves using intact reading mechanisms in the right hemisphere.   – BW

alexia/dyslexia

n. The terms *alexia* and *dyslexia* both denote the presence of a reading disorder that impairs production or comprehension of language. Dyslexia is a class of reading disorders resulting from brain damage or learning disability; alexia is a more specific deficit in word or letter reading resulting from brain damage. There are several types of dyslexia, each presenting with a different cause and etiology. At the highest level there exists the distinction between the acquired dyslexias and the developmental dyslexias. Four types of acquired dyslexias have been identified: pure alexia, surface dyslexia, phonological dyslexia, and deep dyslexia. Each of these acquired forms is caused by a particular type of cortical damage and has distinctive symptoms. Developmental dyslexia is a developmental learning disability that is characterized by specific difficulty in reading and spelling despite average or above-average intellectual ability. Children with developmental dyslexia are thought to have a core deficit in phonological coding or processing.   – NL

alexithymia

n. A disruption in both emotional and cognitive processes such that the person has trouble recognizing his or her own emotions and has a reduced emotional and fantasy life so that he or she seems concerned only with details of everyday life without a sense of direction or purpose. Alexithymia is often found in persons with long-standing drug addictions and those with psychosomatic disorders.

algorithm

n. A procedure for solving a problem, usually computational, consisting of a series of steps which will always produce a correct solution but which often require more effort than other, less certain methods for solving the same problem. Computer programs are the most common form of contemporary algorithms. The opposite of an algorithm is a heuristic, which is a rule of thumb for seeking a solution, which usually requires less effort than an algorithm but sometimes makes errors.

algorithmic-heuristic theory

n. A theory of learning in which the mental processes involved in problem solving are broken down into algorithmic, heuristic, and semialgorithmic and semiheuristic steps. Students are taught to discover the necessary steps in solving a problem by learning to break down a problem into its mental components, selecting an algorithmic or heuristic approach for each component, and then combining the steps to reach a solution.

alienation

n. **1.** A state of being or the experience of being separated from. In existential psychology it is used to describe a sense of being separated from one's own experience so that experience seems foreign, more like a play or television show than real. In social psychology it is often used to describe a process in which a person or thing is in a category separate from one inclusive self so that the person or thing can be treated with less consideration or respect. **2.** The process of separating one's self or another person from another person or group of people. **3.** Causing or inducing someone to turn away from or become hostile to another person or group of people. **4.** An archaic term for the process of psychotic separation from reality. Sociological social psychologists have used this concept heavily (e.g., Seeman's writings), drawing especially on Marx's idea of self-alienation, which occurs when the person finds no meaning in his/her work.

alienation, coefficient of ▶ *See* COEFFICIENT OF ALIENATION

alienist
n. An expert who testifies in court as to the mental competence of a party in a legal case. An old-fashioned term for a forensic physician, psychiatrist, or psychologist.

alimentary canal
n. The series of organs from mouth to anus which form a tube through which food passes in the process of digestion. It includes the mouth, pharynx, esophagus, stomach, small intestine, large intestine, and bowel. Also known as the digestive system and gastrointestinal tract.

allele
n. One of two or more possible forms of a gene which exist in a particular location on a chromosome and are responsible for a particular genotype or form of a single characteristic such as eye color in humans or petal color in many flowers.

allocentric
n. A personality pattern that is commonly found in collectivistic cultures. The pattern is found by examining data within culture; thus it is an individual differences variable. In such data allocentrism and idiocentrism are more or less unrelated to each other.

There are allocentrics and idiocentrics in all cultures, but there are more allocentrics in collectivist than in individualist cultures. Good mental health requires a fit between culture and personality. Thus, allocentrics are better adjusted if they live in a collectivist culture. If they live in an individualist culture, they are likely to seek to join groups, associations, unions, sects, clubs, and communes but may feel dissatisfied with their interpersonal relationships in such groups because these

relationships may not be sufficiently intimate and extensive.

Allocentrics tend to be unusually concerned with the actions of their in-group members, are high in affiliation and sociability, and are very sensitive to rejection.
— HTT

allocentrism
n. A personal attribute commonly found among allocentrics, especially in collectivist cultures.

Allocentrism and idiocentrism are more or less unrelated in collectivist cultures, but in individualist cultures they are negatively correlated. Those high on this attribute are high in collective efficacy (e.g., my group will do very well) and in conformity, sociability, and affiliation. They behave in traditional, group-oriented ways.

In one study allocentrism was correlated negatively with wellness and positively with anxiety and depression. However, this study was done in an individualist culture, and the fit between culture and personality is important in subjective well-being. During crises (e.g., unemployment, death in the family) allocentrics reported receiving more social support than did idiocentrics. Those high in allocentrism are high in subjective well-being when they are well integrated into groups, and they receive much social support when they need it.
— HTT

all-or-none law
n. **1.** In neurophysiology, the theory that the axon of any neuron propagates its impulse at full strength or does not propagate an impulse at all. Thus the strength of a neural input does not affect the strength of the next neuron's output though it may affect the frequency of impulses. **2.** In learning, the theory that associations are formed in a single trial. If an association is formed in a single trial, its strength may be increased by further trials but the association itself is an all-or-none situation.

alogia
n. Poverty of speech; an inability to generate spontaneous speech or varied or elaborate responses to questions. Patients with

alogia respond to open-ended questions (e.g., "Describe how your mood has been lately" or "Tell me about your childhood") with very limited responses (e.g., "OK" or "It was good"). Alogia is a common negative symptom of schizophrenia. These short responses are not thought to be motivated by a resistance to responding to open-ended questions (i.e., giving limited information as a way of preventing the interviewer from knowing more) but instead are thought to result from a lack of varied or spontaneous responses for whatever reason (e.g., being preoccupied with internal stimuli).　　　　　　　　– DGa

alpha blocking
n. The suppression of the alpha rhythm in an electroencephalogram (EEG) produced by a shift of attention from an unfocused one to focus on a particular stimulus.

alpha male
n. In animal behavior a designation for the individual male who is deemed at the top of a dominance hierarchy in a particular animal group.

alpha reliability coefficient
n. In psychometrics, an index of internal consistency among items in a scale. Mathematically, the average of all possible split-half reliability coefficients corrected for attenuation of a scale with more than two possible outcomes and commonly used with Likert type scales. It ranges from 0, no internal consistency, to 1, which indicates complete internal consistency, or no difference among the items in the way in which they are answered by test takers. Also called Cronbach's alpha and the alpha coefficient.

alpha rhythm
n. A high-amplitude electroencephalogram (EEG) wave of brain electric activity of 8–12 hertz which is often found in relaxed individuals whose eyes are closed. Also called an alpha wave.

alpha wave
n. A high-amplitude electroencephalogram (EEG) wave of brain electric activity of 8–12

hertz which is often found in relaxed individuals whose eyes are closed. Also called an alpha rhythm.

alprazolam
n. An antianxiety drug, triazolobenzodiazepine ($C_{17}H_{13}ClN_4$), sometimes marketed under the brand name *Xanax* which affects GABA receptor sites. It is used in anxiety disorders and occasionally for depression.

altered state of consciousness
n. Any change in consciousness out of the normal range. The term is usually used in conjunction with the effects of hallucinogenic or euphoriant drugs but also with altered states of mental function, as in a trance, depersonalization, peak or ecstatic experience, or psychosis.

alter ego
n. **1.** An alternate or identity for the self markedly different from one's usual sense of self, as in having a consistent idea of one's self as heroic or unbound by social convention which is not usually enacted in daily life. **2.** Another person who is very close to one and who serves as an alternate self.

alternate forms reliability
n In psychometrics, a method of ensuring the consistency of measurement of a scale by comparing two scales supposedly measuring the same thing in the same way. This method of ensuring reliability is seldom used because of the difficulty in creating two scales which measure the same characteristic.

alternating personality
n. **1.** Multiple personality disorder in which a person has two or more selves, each of which may be unaware of the others. **2.** Any one of the selves in an individual with multiple personality disorder.

alternative hypothesis
n. In statistics, the hypothesis that there is no difference between the means of different groups in an analysis of variance, implying that there is no relationship between levels of

the independent variable and the dependent variable. This is used as a dummy hypothesis so that when it can be statistically rejected, the null hypothesis that there is a difference between groups can be accepted and so demonstrate that it is not unreasonable to believe that there has been an effect produced by the independent variable on the dependent variable.

alternative medicine
n. Any treatment for illness, injury, or malaise which is not sanctioned by Western medicine and especially those that focus on health as a goal rather than the absence of illness, which is part of the traditional Western medical approach. Most traditional Asian and other approaches to healing arts fall under this umbrella term, including acupuncture, ayurvedic herbology, and the indigenous herbology of peoples around the world.

altricial
adj. Of or relating to those species of birds that are blind, without feathers, and completely dependent for survival on their parents for food and care when they hatch.

altruism
n. 1. Putting others' interests before one's own sometimes to the point of sacrificing one's own interests or life in the process. 2. In sociobiology, furthering the interests of those with whom one shares genetic relationship while sacrificing one's immediate interests for a longer-term genetic gain in assuring that one's genes continue in the gene pool of the next or future generations.

altruism, reciprocal
n. In sociobiology, the sharing of resources or efforts with another in the expectation that the other or others in general will share similarly with oneself in the future.

altruistic suicide
n. Taking action which results in one's own death for the benefit of others, as when a soldier takes on a suicide mission for the benefit

of society or an elderly Inuit adult whose physical degeneration puts his or her family in danger voluntarily leaves the group to face certain death alone so the family will not have to care for her or him. In Japan altruistic suicide has been common.

alveolar
1. adj. Of or relating to the alveolus, or hard ridge of the gums, containing the sockets for the upper teeth and the area just behind the front teeth. The alveolus is involved in making the sounds involved in speaking the alveolar consonants, which, in English, include d, l, n, t, s, and z. 2. n. In biology in general, any small pocket in tissue and particularly the small pockets in the lung which form the areolae for oxygen absorption.

Alzheimer's disease
n. A form of senile dementia characterized by progressive brain deterioration and the formation of neurological plaques and neurofibrillary tangles in the brain. It is a common form of senile dementia and can be diagnosed only after death by examination of brain tissue for plaques and neurofibrillary tangles. The first symptom is usually a reduction in the capacity to detect odors which often is unnoticed as there are many causes of reduced ability to smell. It is characterized by progressive loss of cognitive abilities and memory, and death results when brain impairment progresses to the state where physiological capacities are affected such as ability to swallow or perform other bodily maintenance activities. It is usually first detected in persons over age 65, and its incidence increases rapidly after that age. Accurate rates of occurrence are difficult to determine as postmortem examination of the brain is seldom done in elderly persons who die with dementia, and so it is easily confused with other forms of dementia such as multi-infarct dementia. It has been correlated with the presence of the ApoE4 allele on chromosome 19, but that is not a sole cause of the disorder.

amaurotic familial idiocy
n. A family of recessive genetic diseases in which brain function is impaired by a

gradual buildup of fat in brain tissues. Tay-Sachs syndrome and Batten's syndrome are the most commonly seen forms of this group of diseases.

ambiguity tolerance

n. The capacity to acknowledge or tolerate holding contradictory beliefs or uncertainty about perceptions, situations, or beliefs. A cognitive style or personality trait characteristic of people who are able to regulate their emotions and accurately perceive reality in the face of the inherent uncertainty of life. Individuals with low tolerance for ambiguity tend to be rigid; to distort reality by failing to perceive change in the environment; to oversimplify in thought; to long for clear-cut and simple answers in the face of complexity; to become angry with persons of different cultures, customs, and beliefs; and to cling tightly to politically conservative ideas.

ambiguous figure

n. Any of a class of images which have two or more possible interpretations and in the interpretation of which perception usually flips from one to the other interpretation. Examples include the old woman/young woman image of Boring, Necker cubes, the Mach illusion, the Schroeder staircase, and the reversible goblet.

ambisexual

adj. **1.** Having no sexual differentiation or having a mixture of the traits and characteristics believed to belong to both or all sexes. **2.** Capable of being aroused by all other persons, animals, or things regardless of sex, age, or social construal of their appropriateness as sexual partners or objects.

ambivalence

n. The experiencing of two strong but conflicting emotions or desires at the same time (for example, feeling both love and hatred for someone or feeling both the desire to do something and the strong desire not to do it as well). In psychoanalytic terms *ambivalence* refers to a common state of experiencing two conflicting emotions about someone

or something but being consciously aware of only one (for example, feeling both love and hatred for an attachment figure, such as one's mother, but only being consciously aware of feelings of love toward her). Usually this conscious awareness of only one side of one's experience results from a fear (also unconscious) of what it would mean to experience the negative side of ambivalence as well.   – DGa

ambivalent attachment

n. A style of attachment in which children are uncertain in their response to their mother, going back and forth between seeking and shunning her attention. Such mothers have been characterized as insensitive and less involved.

amenorrhea

n. The absence of menstruation usually due to a pathological condition or pregnancy.

American College Testing Program

n. (ACT) A test of academic learning used to predict academic performance widely used by college admission committees in the United States. It is the largest competitor of the Scholastic Aptitude test (SAT). The ACT has subtests in English Usage, Social Sciences, Mathematics, and Physical Sciences from which a composite score is calculated as a summary predictive index of future academic performance.

American Psychiatric Association (APA)

n. A professional organization of psychiatrists in the United States which is responsible for producing the DSM-IV-TR, which is used to define categories of mental disabilities and embody current research and understanding of pathology in general and specific pathological processes.

American Psychological Association

n. (APA) A professional organization of persons holding doctoral degrees in psychology which promotes the clinical practice of psychology (among the many disciplines of psychology), sets ethical guidelines for psychologists, and publishes numerous research journals.

American Psychological Foundation

n. A branch of the American Psychological Association which has created an endowment to promote research in the field of psychology.

American Psychological Society

n. (APS) The original name for the Association for Psychological Science, an organization of persons holding doctorates in psychology formed to promote the scientific study of psychology. APS was formed by a group of academic researchers who believed that the APA was too oriented to clinical practice and was not adequately representing their interests and point of view.

American Sign Language

n. American Sign Language (ASL) is a sign language with 100,000–500,000 primary users predominantly in the United States and parts of Canada and Guatemala. ASL is also used to varying degrees in parts of Asia and Africa. ASL developed in the American deaf community, with significant influence of French Sign Language (FSL) when the latter was introduced into the United States in the early 1800s. ASL and FSL share portions of their lexicons. However, they are not mutually intelligible. ASL is not related to English but has an entirely different grammar and lexicon. For example, ASL uses different signs to express the two senses of the English word *right* ("correct" and "not left"). Unlike in English, the canonical word order for ASL is subject-object-verb. Meanings that require multiple words in English (e.g., He shows me) can be conveyed in ASL by a single sign accompanied with simultaneous movements.   – EMF

Ames room

n. A room with a peephole at one end and constructed with trapezoidal rather than square features. This affects the human optical system's tendency to interpret narrowing lines as distance so that the room, whose dimensions shrink from the near end to the far end, looks like a square, deep room and objects in it seem to grow as they move from the near end to the far end.

amine

n. Any of a large group of chemicals formed by replacing a hydrogen atom in ammonia with one or more hydrocarbons. Amines include many that are biologically important such as the neurotransmitters norepinephrine, dopamine, serotonin, histamine, and tryptamine.

amino acid

n. A large group of chemical compounds containing both an amino group, NH_2, and a carboxyl group, COOH, about 20 of which form all the proteins and peptides which make up living tissue in all living things on Earth. Some amino acids such as glutamate, glycine, and tyrosine are synthesized in the body, and some, called essential amino acids, such as lysine, tryptophan, and phenylalanine, have to be gleaned from the environment, usually in the diet.

amitriptyline

n. Amitriptyline nitrate is one of the most commonly prescribed of the tricyclic antidepressants, which work primarily by blocking the reuptake of serotonin and other amine-based neurotransmitters.

Ammon's horn

n. Ammon's horn (also known as cornu ammonis) represents one division of the hippocampal formation with the dentate gyrus and the subiculum. It is a three-layered archicortical structure divided into four different fields, named CA1, CA2, CA3, and CA4. CA4 is also called hilus and indeed is considered part of the dentate gyrus. CA1–CA3 fields are frequently referred to as the hippocampus proper. Ammon's horns are situated in the medial temporal lobe at the level of the floor of the inferior horn of the lateral ventricles. The hippocampus proper is thought responsible for the acquisition of consciously accessible, declarative

memory. Damage in these structures is associated with a severe amnesia without confabulation and confusion. The left hippocampus seems more involved in semantic memory, whereas the right one seems more directly related to spatial memory.
— A A

▶ *See also* **MEMORY**

amnesia

n. Memory disorder. Different types of amnesia are distinguished. A major distinction in amnesia has been established between specific and nonspecific amnesia. Specific amnesia refers to amnesia for certain particular types of information (e.g., for verbal information), whereas the ability to memorize other types of information (e.g., spatial information) is well preserved. Nonspecific amnesia refers to a memory disorder for every type of information. Patients with amnesia may have difficulty in retaining new information (anterograde amnesia) and/or recalling previously stored information (retrograde amnesia). In general, specific amnesias are observed in cases of cortical damage, whereas nonspecific amnesias are more frequently found in cases of damage in the so-called brain memory system, in particular the mesial structures of the temporal lobe; for instance, damage in the hippocampus, mammillary bodies, and some thalamic nuclei is associated with significant amnesia. Amnesia due to damage in the mammillary bodies and some thalamic nuclei is also called diencephalic amnesia and may be associated with confabulation. Damage in the hippocampus is not associated with confabulation and represents a type of amnesia unrelated to other defects in cognition.
— A A

▶ *See also* **ALCOHOL AMNESIC DISORDER, ANTEROGRADE AMNESIA, MEMORY, RETROGRADE AMNESIA,** *and* **SOURCE AMNESIA**

amnesia, post-traumatic ▶ *See* **POST-TRAUMATIC AMNESIA**

amnesia, retrograde ▶ *See* **RETROGRADE AMNESIA**

amnesia, source ▶ *See* **SOURCE AMNESIA**

amniocentesis

n. A prenatal diagnostic tool, the amniocentesis allows for screening of genetic abnormalities. This procedure consists of a needle's being inserted into the abdomen wall of the pregnant woman to obtain a sample of amniotic fluid. An ultrasound is used in conjunction with this needle insertion to protect the developing fetus. Within the amniotic fluid are cells that can be grown in a laboratory dish and analyzed to determine genetic information. This procedure typically cannot occur until approximately 16 weeks of gestation and then can require an additional 3 weeks for growth and testing of cells.
— S R B

amok

n. An acute, violent frenzy usually preceded by a period of hostile brooding and paranoid ideation usually after an insult. The frenzy usually continues until exhaustion and is followed by amnesia for the period of the frenzy. *Amok* is a Malaysian word which has been adopted by Euro-American psychology for the syndrome, which was first described among Malaysian people but is also found in the Philippines, Papua New Guinea, Laos, Polynesia, and Puerto Rico and among the Navaho people of North America. It was originally believed to be a culture-specific syndrome, but that claim has been disputed by its discovery in a relatively wide area and questions over whether it is simply more of a focus in some cultures than others.

amorphognosia

n. An inability to recognize objects by touch associated with damage to the caudal portion of the first postcentral gyrus in the human brain.

amphetamine

n. A family of drugs including Benzedrine, Dexedrine, and Methedrine which act as strong central nervous system stimulants mimicking the effects of norepinephrine and dopamine. Amphetamines raise heart rate and blood pressure, suppress immune function and sleep, increase blood flow to skeletal muscles and away from the digestive tract and teeth, suppress appetite, and produce feelings of energy and well-being and, in high doses, euphoria. Prolonged use can result in anxiety, panic, acute paranoia, dental problems, and malnutrition. Amphetamines are widely and illegally used for staying awake and for the euphoria of high doses. Amphetamines are addicting in the traditional sense of producing tolerance and withdrawal. The withdrawal is due to an insufficiency of norepinephrine and dopamine in the brain, which results in a sense of depression, fatigue, and lack of motivation.

amphetamine effects

n. Short-term effects include sensations of alertness, well-being, sexual desire, euphoria, inability to keep still, talkativeness, and a jittery feeling, followed by fatigue, social withdrawal, and depression as the drug effects fade. Physically amphetamines produce raised heart rate and blood pressure, suppressed immune function and sleep, increased blood flow to skeletal muscles and away from the digestive tract and teeth, and suppressed appetite. Prolonged use can result in anxiety, panic, acute paranoia, dental problems, and malnutrition. Amphetamines are widely and illegally used for dieting, staying awake, and the euphoria of high doses. Amphetamines are addicting in the traditional sense of producing tolerance and withdrawal. The withdrawal is due to an insufficiency of norepinephrine and dopamine in the brain, which results in a sense of depression, fatigue, and lack of motivation.

amphetamine psychosis

n. An acute paranoid psychosis brought on by prolonged use of amphetamines, which normally disappears within a week or two of abstinence from amphetamine use.

amplification

n. Making larger in general. As examples, amplification of sound is making it louder while amplification of an idea is expanding on it sometimes without normal bounds of reasonability.

amplitude

n. **1.** Generally the size, amount, extent, or magnitude; it is frequently used in describing waves, as in sound. **2.** In describing waves the displacement from a zero point as in an ocean wave whose amplitude is 4 feet above and below the average level of the water. **3.** The maximal displacement of a periodic wave.

amygdala

n. Either of a pair of almond shaped neural centers located on the inside of each temporal lobe beside the hypothalamus and hippocampus and closely connected to the olfactory cortex, cingulate gyrus, and septum. The amygdalae are involved with the sense of smell, appetite, memory, physiological arousal, and negative emotions, particularly anger and fear. Several persons who have engaged in explosive violence have been found to have tumors or damage to one or both of the amygdalae. Electrical stimulation of the amygdala usually produces intense fear or panic.

amyloid plaque

n. A deposit of any one of several types of nonfunctional fibrous protein in an organ. Beta-amyloid protein (BAP) forms amyloid plaques in the brain, and especially in the frontal lobe, hippocampus, amygdala, and entorhinal cortex, which are characteristic of people over the age of 70 who have reduced brain function. Amyloid plaques in the brain are used as a diagnostic of Alzheimer's disease.

anabolism

n. The form of metabolism in which proteins are built up and energy is stored. It is the opposite of catabolism, in which proteins are broken down and energy released.

anaclitic object-choice

n. In psychoanalysis, the choice of a significant other who resembles one's mother or other caretaker from childhood and toward whom one tends to express dependency needs, as the love of mother or caretaker in infancy is related to the satisfaction of basic biological needs such as food, warmth, and protection.

anagram

n. **1.** A word or phrase whose letters can be rearranged into another word as in *slot* and *lots*. **2.** A type of verbal problem in which subjects are asked to form a word or words from a target word or given set of letters.

anal character

n. In psychoanalysis, a personality formed around the early or later part of the anal stage and retaining the characteristics of that period. An anal expulsive character is formed around pleasure in the expulsion of bowel movements and is marked by untidiness, generosity, easygoing attitude, and resistance to authority. An anal retentive character is marked by excessive cleanliness and need for order, overemphasis of rule following, stinginess, and petulance.

anal eroticism

n. Sexual excitement and pleasure connected with stimulation of the anus. In psychoanalysis it is believed that this results from fixation in the anal stage of development.

anal-expulsive phase

n. The first half of the anal stage, in which the child is focused on the pleasure of expelling feces. In the anal stage the focus of pleasure shifts from the mouth to the anus as the enervation of the anal region develops sufficiently for both muscular control and more accurate perception beginning before age 2 and usually ending after age 3.

analgesia

n. Relief from pain usually by painkilling drugs but sometimes through hypnosis, acupuncture, or other means.

analogical reasoning

n. A method of reasoning in which a decision about one thing or event is deduced by the similarity of that thing or event to another belonging to a known class of things or events.

analogies test

n. A measure of ability or achievement in which two terms are given and the subject has to infer their relationship. Then a new term

is given and the subject has to complete the analogy by finding a fourth term that has the same relationship to the third one as the second to the first. As an example, "A boat is to sailing as an airplane is to _____."

anal-retentive phase

n. The second half of the anal stage, in which the child is focused on the pleasure of controlling the expulsion of feces. In the anal stage the focus of pleasure shifts from the mouth to the anus as the enervation of the anal region develops sufficiently for both muscular control and more accurate perception beginning before age 2 and usually ending after age 3.

anal sadistic stage

n. Another name for the anal stage, which emphasizes the basically aggressive nature of anal control impulses.

anal stage

n. In psychoanalysis, the second stage of development, in which the focus of pleasure shifts from the mouth to the anus as the enervation of the anal region develops sufficiently for both muscular control and more accurate perception, beginning before age 2 and usually ending after age 3. In the early portion of this stage the child is focused on the pleasure of expelling feces and in the second part of the stage with controlling the expulsion of feces. Integrating parental demands for bowel control with the pleasure of expelling feces at appropriate times leads to the beginnings of the development of superego and the strengthening of ego.

anal triad

n. In psychoanalysis the three traits characteristic of anal retentive personalities: orderliness, obstinacy, and miserliness. Also known as the three Ps of pedantry, parsimony, and petulance.

analysis by synthesis

n. Any of a number of processes of information processing in which both bottom-up (data-driven) and top-down (concept-driven) processing are used in sequence in the interpretation of sensory information. The process begins with an initial analysis of sensory data according to its physical attributes and patterns, which are then compared along with contextual information with previously learned patterns, and creates an internal working model of the sensory input which is again compared with the sensory data. The process then either terminates with a match or attempts a new internal representation, and the process is repeated until a match is obtained. This process is usually used to describe speech recognition and language perception.

analysis of covariance
n. (ANCOVA) An analysis of the variance between groups defined by independent variables in which the variance of one or more other variables (covariates) has been removed by regression techniques.

analysis of variance
n. (ANOVA) A calculation of the ratios of within- to between-group differences in a dependent variable in two or more groups defined by independent variables. This is used to test hypotheses about differences among the groups with the object of being able to attribute any such differences to effects of the independent variable(s) on the dependent variable.

analyst
n. In psychology one who does any sort of psychoanalysis.

analytical psychology
n. A term coined by Carl Jung to differentiate his approach to psychology from that of Sigmund Freud. Jung's psychology takes a teleological perspective on psychology and seeks to describe inherited structures of mind (collective unconscious) and their fruition in the course of an individual's life rather than assuming mind has a few basic parts from which all later complexity evolves in a causal chain, as did Freud.

anankastic personality disorder
n. The anankastic personality disorder is a synonym for the obsessive-compulsive personality disorder (OCPD), and one of the 10 personality disorders described on Axis-II of the DSM-IV-TR, published by the American Psychiatric Association as their official diagnostic and descriptive nomenclature of mental disorders. The anankastic personality disorder or OCPD is a pattern of preoccupation with orderliness, perfectionism, and mental and interpersonal control starting by early adulthood and manifested in a variety of contexts affecting and impairing the person's familial, social, and/or professional functioning. Central to the notion of personality disorders (in general) is that they are inflexible, maladaptive, and persisting and cause significant functional impairment or subjective distress.

Symptoms (DSM-IV-TR) are (a) a preoccupation with rules, procedures, and schedules; (b) a drive for extreme perfectionism inhibiting progress and task completion; (c) an excessive preoccupation with work and productivity at the expense of leisure time without an obvious necessity to do so, as individuals always have the feeling that they have to work; (d) an inflexible moral and value system; (e) an inability to discard worthless objects without sentimental value; (f) an inability to delegate work because of fear that others will not do it exactly as it has to be done; (e) a miserly or stingy spending style, hoarding money and resources; and (f) a rigid thinking style. Individuals have to meet four or more of these symptoms in order to be diagnosed as anankastic or having OCPD.

The prevalence rate for anankastic personality disorder is estimated to be around 1% in community samples, and about 3% to 10% in individuals consulting mental health services. OCPD is diagnosed twice as often in males as in females.   – FDF

anaphora
n. The use of a pronoun to refer to something previously mentioned in the same text. As an example: "Mark Spitz won a gold medal and I am going to get one, too," in which *one* refers to a gold medal.

anaphylaxis
n. Heightened sensitivity to a substance resulting from previous exposure to the substance.

Symptoms of anaphylaxis include wheezing, tightness in the chest, difficulty in breathing, reddening of the face, and sometimes convulsions and cardiac arrest.

androgyny

n. The state of having both male and female characteristics to a much higher degree than is statistically normal. Male and female characteristics are much debated, as many once deemed biological have been found to be cultural or related more to sex role than to genetic sex.

androgyny scale

n. A scale which measures the relative degree of sexual or sex role differentiation. Androgyny can be thought of as a lack of differentiation or as the elevated presence of both maleness and femaleness.

anecdotal evidence

n. Reports by individuals on a topic without systematic observation or experimental control and so not a good basis for making generalizations but the usual basis for new lines of investigation.

anencephalus

n. The failure of the brain to develop, which, in humans, is usually due to a genetic defect or fetal poisoning.

anesthesia

n. Absence of sensation, usually as the result of anesthetic drugs, trauma, or a neural disorder. Anesthesia can be localized or throughout the body.

anesthesia, glove

n. The absence of sensation in the hand and lower wrist in an area such as would be covered by a glove. There is no simple physical cause for glove anesthesia, and it is usually considered a psychosomatic symptom.

angel dust

n. Colloquial or street name for phencyclidine (phencyclihexylpipiridine [PCP]), a drug which causes widespread depolarization of synapses which results in erratic nerve impulses in the brain. Subjective effects include a sense of depersonalization, analgesia, feelings of invulnerability, and sometimes euphoria.

anger

n. One of the six basic emotions, in which a situation is perceived as strongly negative and someone or something else is to blame for that negative state. Anger is almost always preceded by real or imagined frustration. Anger is usually accompanied, at least momentarily, by a facial expression in which the lips tighten, jaw muscles tense, the lips are slightly parted, eyes are narrowed, and the forehead is furrowed.

angina

n. Chest pain accompanied by a choking sensation. Angina pectoris is angina caused by insufficient blood supply to the heart and is a symptom of heart attacks. Tracheal angina is a disease of the pharynx, one of whose symptoms is choking with chest pain.

angst

n. German word for anxiety used in existential psychology to denote anxiety due to the uncertainty of the future and the necessity of choosing a course of action in a state of uncertainty.

angular gyrus

n. A visible bulge on the posterior parietal lobe close to the occipital and temporal lobes (parietal-temporal-occipital junction). It corresponds to the Brodmann's area 39. Located at the junction of the temporal, parietal, and occipital lobes, the angular gyrus is limited by the supramarginal gyrus of the parietal lobe, the posterior-superior temporal gyrus, the inferior parietal lobule, and the occipital lobe. Lesions in the left hemisphere angular gyrus can be associated with the so-called Gerstmann's syndrome (or angular gyrus syndrome), which includes acalculia, agraphia, right-left confusion, and finger agnosia. So-called semantic aphasia has also been described in cases of left angular gyrus pathology. Right hemisphere angular gyrus lesions can result in spatial disturbances, constructional defects, and hemispatial neglect. Angular gyrus is considered as a cortical area involved in cross-modal association among somatosensory (body-knowledge) information, auditory information, and visual information. Learning to read and to write is probably heavily dependent on this brain area. Developmentally, the angular gyrus is one of the last to mature functionally and anatomically, and those abilities related to the angular activity (such as reading, writing, and calculations) develop late.   – AA

anhedonia

n. Diminished ability to experience pleasure. Anhedonia is one of two essential symptoms of a major depressive episode in the DSM-IV-TR (the other essential symptom is depressed mood; to have a major depressive episode, the patient must have either depressed mood or anhedonia) and the International Statistical Classification of Diseases and Related Health Problems-10 (ICD-10). Anhedonia in depression is described as an experience of no longer enjoying things that used to give one pleasure (e.g., taking walks, favorite foods, spending time with friends). Therefore, in depressed individuals anhedonia is thought to be a "state" experience – that is, once the depression (and symptom of anhedonia) lifts, the individual should find things enjoyable again. In schizophrenia, anhedonia is a common "negative" symptom and is thought to be more "trait" oriented, or a set personality feature.   – DGa

anima

n. The inherent image of woman in the collective unconscious, which is a part of the makeup of all humans in Jung's analytical psychology.

animal aggressive behavior

n. Any form of threatening action or attack by one nonhuman on another. Subcategories of aggression include predation, maternal defensive behavior, territorial defense, dominance or status conflict, competition for sexual partners, defensive aggression against predators, instrumental aggression for other rewards, and fear-induced aggression.

animal communication

n. **1.** Communication between animals. **2.** A branch of ethology, sociobiology, and animal cognition also called zoosemiotics which studies methods animals use to transfer information between them. In the second half of the 20th century researchers began discovering that animals communicate in numerous ways not previously recognized, many of which are outside human sensory abilities. Attempts to define differences in human and animal communication have usually been frustrated as new aspects of communication among animals have been discovered which were previously believed to be exclusively human.

animal intelligence

n. **1.** The capacity of nonhuman organisms to modify their behavior to adapt better to their environment. **2.** The study of animals' intellectual capacities including problem solving, memory, and other aspects of cognition and communication.

animal models

n. The use of animals to investigate aspects of human function that are difficult to study in humans. Animal models are frequently used in medicine, in which animals can be subjected to diseases or other treatment contemporary ethics prevents scientists from using with humans. Animal models are also used when their functioning in some area is much simpler or easier to study than in humans; for example, aplasia, a kind of flatworm, is used in many neuronal studies because it has few and large neurons.

animal psychology

n. The study of the mental functioning of nonhuman animals.

animism

n. **1.** A usually derogatory term for a large number of belief systems in which things such as trees, mountains, rivers, or animals are considered to have spiritual aspects which are not considered to have any spiritual character from the Judeo-Christian-Islamic point of view traditional in Euro-American cultures. **2.** In anthropology, some anthropologists believe it is a religious point of view involving a large number of spiritual beings which is an outgrowth of earlier forms of religion in which there is a general spiritual essence which is the same in all things. **3.** In Piagetian theory, a form of preoperational thought in which inanimate objects are thought of as having humanlike characteristics.

animus

n. The inherent image of man or maleness in the collective unconscious, which is a part of the makeup of all humans in Jung's analytical psychology.

anion

n. A negatively charged ion which is usually part of a molecule separated from its positively charged component.

Anna O

n. The fictitious name assigned to Bertha Pappenheim, a patient of Sigmund Freud and Josef Breuer, whose case was used as an illustration in early formulations of psychoanalysis and published in a volume entitled *Studies in Hysteria*. Pappenheim, who was a social worker in her adult years, complained that Freud and Breuer had misrepresented her case.

anniversary reaction

n. A strong emotional reaction on or around the anniversary of an emotionally charged event such as the death of a loved one.

anomalous dichromacy

n. A partial form of color blindness caused by a defect in the cones of the retina in which only two of the primary colors can be seen – usually yellow and blue.

anomalous sentence

n. A sentence that is grammatically correct but has no semantic meaning. The most famous is "Colorless green ideas sleep furiously," written by Noam Chomsky to illustrate the difference between grammatical and semantic coherence.

anomalous trichromacy

n. A form of color blindness in which all three types of color-sensitive cones are present but one type of cone is less sensitive than are the others, resulting in an unbalanced perception of color usually in the red-green color system. Also called anomalopia.

anomic aphasia ▶ *See* ANOMIE

anomic suicide

n. Suicide that results from a sense of alienation from the social world and feelings of hopelessness usually due to rapid changes in the social world. It can be either acute or chronic and domestic (related to rapid changes in the life of an individual) or economic (related to rapid changes in society as a whole). So one person might feel alienated and hopeless because of the death of a spouse or similar personal change, while another might feel alienated and hopeless because of a societal event such as an unnecessary war or a stock market crash.

anomie

n. A term coined by the French sociologist Emile Durkheim to describe a state of alienation from society and a sense of hopelessness engendered by rapid social change and especially a change in values or beliefs.

anorexia nervosa

n. The first criterion for anorexia nervosa is the refusal to maintain body weight at or above a minimally normal weight for age and height. The weight limit is usually characterized as weighing less than 85% of normal body weight or having a body mass index equal to or less than 17.5. Some individuals develop anorexia nervosa during early adolescence. Rather than losing weight, they remain at the same weight while their height increases.

The second criterion is an intense fear of gaining weight or becoming fat, even though underweight. These individuals make conscious attempts to be underweight. They restrict their food intake to items that contain little or no fat. They often skip meals and exercise excessively to burn calories and to raise their sense of well-being. Although these individuals are underweight, they have an intense fear of becoming overweight. Most of these individuals have never been overweight; nor are they likely to be members of families with obesity. This fear of becoming fat typically intensifies as weight loss increases.

The third criterion involves the disturbance in the way in which one's body weight or shape is experienced, undue influence of body weight on self-evaluation, or denial of the seriousness of the current low body weight. These individuals view themselves or specific parts of their body as too big. Individuals with anorexia often perceive their size accurately; the problem arises with their judgment of the size they see. They often admit that they need to gain weight, but they do not think that their low weight is of concern and requires medical or psychiatric intervention. Common to individuals with anorexia nervosa are low self-esteem, depression, and anxiety. Depression and anorexia nervosa are highly comorbid.

In the first half of the 20th century, there were conflicting views of anorexia nervosa. Pierre Janet considered anorexia nervosa as a pure psychological disorder and categorized the disorder into two subtypes: obsessional and hysterical. Individuals of the obsessional type refused to eat because of a fear of becoming fat and of achieving psychosexual maturity. These individuals loathed their bodies and refused food in spite of intense hunger. The hysterical type was less common and involved total cessation of hunger.

In 1914, a landmark paper by Morris Simmonds described pituitary insufficiency as leading to severe weight loss in some patients. This view was widely accepted until 1930, when the writings of Berkman once again moved to the application of a psychogenic interpretation to anorexia nervosa. Berkman described the physiological disturbances as secondary to psychological disturbances.

Many of the developments in the past 30 years have been refinements of the principles of Hilde Bruch, Arthur Crisp, and Gerald Russell. Bruch proposed that self-starvation in anorexia nervosa is a struggle for autonomy, competence, control, and self-respect. Bruch set the groundwork for modern cognitive therapy through the emphasis on the patient's beliefs and assumptions in the conduct of psychotherapy. Crisp emphasized the importance of the developmental model, in which anorexia nervosa is rooted in the biological and psychological experiences accompanying achievement of an adult weight. According to this view, anorexia nervosa is associated with fears and tribulations of maturity. Russell emphasized the morbid fear of fatness as the underlying condition of anorexia nervosa. He suggested that in order to remove the self-perpetuating state of starvation, correction of the starvation state must take place first.

Anorexia nervosa is categorized into two subtypes: restricting type and binge-eating/purging type. The restricting type entails that during the current episode of anorexia nervosa, the person has not regularly engaged in binge-eating or purging behavior (i.e., self-induced vomiting or the misuse of laxatives, diuretics, or enemas). Individuals with anorexia nervosa rarely have complete suppression of appetite. These individuals exhibit a strong resistance to eating drives while eventually becoming preoccupied with food and eating rituals to the point of obsession. The binge-eating/purging type entails that during the current episode of anorexia nervosa, the person has regularly engaged in binge-eating or purging behavior.

Most cases of anorexia nervosa emerge during adolescence, although anorexia nervosa can occur in children. Onset is before 18 in half of the cases. Onset spikes at puberty and college. Of individuals with anorexia nervosa 0.1–1% are men and 99% are women. Roughly 50% of individuals will eventually have reasonably complete resolution of anorexia nervosa; 30% will have lingering features that will continue into adulthood. Ten percent of people will develop a chronic course of anorexia nervosa, and the remaining 10% will eventually die from the disease. Anorexia nervosa is the third most chronic medical condition in adolescents and has the highest mortality rate of any psychiatric condition. The usual causes of mortality are heart attack and suicide. Underweight purgers have the highest risk of death.

Treatment for anorexia nervosa has not been very successful. Weight gain can be achieved in many patients through a combination of supportive nursing care and behavioral techniques. Pharmacotherapy has little effect in the treatment of severely ill patients. In some acutely ill individuals, improvement in body mass and general psychosocial adjustment can be achieved through cognitive behavioral, psychoeducational, and family therapy techniques. Although treatment plans can be applied to more chronic, long-standing cases, treatment gains are less successful.

Fluoxetine improves the outcome and reduces relapse after weight restoration. Fluoxetine is associated with significant reduction in core eating disorder symptoms, such as depression, anxiety, and obsessions and compulsions. Selective serotonin reuptake inhibitors (SSRIs) are not successful when individuals with anorexia nervosa are malnourished and underweight.

Although the definition of recovery is not formalized, usually an individual with anorexia nervosa is considered recovered when he/she has a stable and healthy body weight for months or years and has not been malnourished or engaged in pathological eating behavior during the period of recovery. In women who have recovered from anorexia nervosa, obsessional behaviors persist, as do inflexible thinking, restraint in emotional expression, and a high degree of self- and impulse control. The women are socially introverted, overly compliant, and limited in social spontaneity and exhibit greater risk avoidance and harm avoidance. Furthermore, individuals who have recovered from anorexia nervosa still exhibit core eating disorder symptoms, such as ineffectiveness, a drive for thinness, and significant psychopathology related to eating habits. Eventually, 54% of individuals with anorexia nervosa will convert to bulimia nervosa.

The physical signs of anorexia nervosa are inanition, bradycardia, hypotension, orthostasis, brittle hair and nails, alopecia, lanugo, decreased body temperature, dry skin, peripheral edema, and carotenodermia. In postmenarcheal females, amenorrhea, the absence of at least three consecutive menstrual cycles, takes place. A woman who menstruates only while taking birth control pills is still considered to experience amenorrhea. While women who have anorexia nervosa produce little estrogen, men with anorexia nervosa produce little testosterone. The behaviors contributing to physical complications include restriction of calories (food and fluids), starvation, excessive exercise, and caloric replacement (refeeding). Calorie restriction and/or refeeding can lead to loss of cardiac muscle and congestive heart failure. Although refeeding may cause these illnesses, if refeeding is properly executed, then it may reverse the course of the cardiac problems. Anorexia nervosa also leads to refeeding pancreatitis and constipation. Moreover, individuals with anorexia nervosa have disturbances in the endocrine and metabolic systems. Individuals have delayed onset of puberty, growth retardation, increased risk of fracture/osteoporosis, vitamin deficiency, and infertility. Furthermore, individuals exhibit dehydration, refeeding hypophosphatemia, respiratory failure, anemia, bone marrow failure, enlarged brain ventricles (pseudoarophy), and impaired thermoregulation.

Risk factors for anorexia nervosa can be divided into individual risk factors, sociocultural risk factors, and family risk factors. Risk factors for anorexia nervosa may vary with age, social class, ethnicity, and gender. They also vary with comorbidity. In different individuals, different factors may be responsible for onset, maintenance, recovery, and relapse. The individual risk factors include genetics, weight concerns, body image dissatisfaction, and dieting. Early maturation increases the chance of anorexia nervosa. Internalization of the thin ideal, the belief that thinness equals success, is a risk factor for anorexia nervosa. Moreover, individuals with anorexia nervosa tend to express perfectionism, low self-esteem, inadequate coping skills, affective disregulation (depression and mood disorders), and impulsivity.

Family risk factors include parent's weight, especially if parent is overweight; eating disorders in the family; concerns with weight and shape in the family; problematic parenting (overprotectiveness, parental neglect, parental absence, and parental psychopathology); and family conflict. The sociocultural risk factors include thin beauty ideal for women, the importance of appearance to success in women, media influences, gender role conflict, teasing about weight and shape, eating disorders or weight concerns among friends, and physical or sexual abuse. Although the Latino culture prefers larger body sizes and has less concern about weight, Latina women show similar rates of eating disorders compared to Caucasians. African Americans are less likely to have anorexia nervosa than Caucasians.

Although there are numerous risk factors, there are also individual, family, and sociocultural protective factors. Individual protective factors include being assertive or self-directed, success in multiple roles, good coping skills, high self-esteem, genetic predisposition to be slender, knowledge about the dangers of dieting, and participating in sports. A close, but not overdependent or enmeshed relationship with parents and a family in which there is not an overemphasis on attractiveness or weight provide a family protective factor. Sociocultural factors also provide protection against anorexia nervosa. Social support and social acceptance of a broad range of body shapes and sizes provide protection. If the culture or ethnic background values larger body sizes, the individual is less likely to develop anorexia nervosa. This also applies to close relationships with friends and romantic partners who are relatively unconcerned with body size. Although some sports may increase the risk of an eating disorder, they largely protect against onset of an eating disorder.

– TJM

anorgasmia
n. An inability to reach orgasm despite appropriate sexual stimulation.

anosmia
n. A deficiency in the sense of smell. It may be total or for some limited sets of odors. Anosmia can be congenital or associated with any of a large group of disorders ranging from sinusitis to brain trauma and frontal lobe tumors.

ANS ▶ *See* **AUTONOMIC NERVOUS SYSTEM**

Antabuse
n. Trade name for disulfram, a drug which blocks the action of enzymes that catalyze the oxygenation of aldehydes. Alcohol aldehyde dehydrogenase catalyzes the oxygenation of ethyl alcohol into acetaldehyde, which in turn is catalyzed by acetyl aldehyde dehydrogenase into acetic acid or vinegar. Acetyl aldehyde dehydrogenase's action is blocked by Antabuse, leading to an accumulation of acetaldehyde which sickens the person.

antagonist
n. **1.** One who acts in opposition. **2.** A chemical that reduces or eliminates the action of another chemical or drug. **3.** The contraction of a muscle opposing the movement of an intended muscle so as to limit or modify the original movement.

antecedent
n. **1.** In general, anything that happens before some given event. **2.** In linguistics, the noun or noun phrase to which a later part of a sentence refers. **3.** In logical propositions of the "If A then B" form, the circumstances to which the "If" refers, as opposed to the consequent, to which the "then" portion of the proposition refers.

anterior
adj. Toward the front of the head or body, as the frontal lobe lies anterior to the parietal lobe.

anterior commissure
n. A large tract of neural fibers which links the foremost parts of the two temporal lobes of the cerebral cortex and the olfactory bulbs and lies in front of the central and posterior commissures.

anterograde
adj. Moving forward in space or time.

anterograde amnesia
n. Defect in acquiring new memories. It can be interpreted as a failure in transferring information to a long-term memory system.

It is generally associated with some degree of retrograde amnesia. Anterograde amnesia can be observed in diverse pathological conditions, such as traumatic head injury, Alzheimer's disease, and Korsakoff's syndrome, but some degree of anterograde amnesia can also be found during normal aging. Memories for events that occurred before the pathological condition (e.g., the head injury) can be spared, but the patient is partially or totally unable to acquire new memories for the events occurring after the pathological condition. Anterograde amnesia usually impairs semantic memory (memories mediated through a semantic system, such as verbal memory) and episodic memory (memory for events), but procedural memory (skills and habits) is usually relatively well preserved. Anterograde amnesia is observed in cases of damage of different structures of the so-called brain memory system, such as the hippocampus, the fornix, and the mammillary bodies. Anterograde amnesia can also be observed in cases of frontal lobe pathology – particularly damage of the basal areas – and also the dorsomedial nucleus of the thalamus.   – A A

▶ *See also* **AMNESIA**

anterograde degeneration

n. Degeneration after an injury that extends from the point of injury in the direction in which a nerve sends impulses. Anterograde degeneration following injury to a sensory nerve would extend from the damage along the nerve tract toward the brain while anterograde degeneration following injury to an afferent nerve would spread in the direction of the muscle or organ toward which the tract runs.

anthropocentrism

n. **1.** A point of view in which humans are given an unquestioned central role in considering other species. An example would be thinking our dogs have human characteristics and emotional reactions without attempting to understand them from an ecological or uniquely canine point of view. **2.** An exaggerated conception of the place of the human species in the natural world or in the universe.

anthropoid

1. *adj.* Resembling a human being or the human species as in the phrase "anthropoid apes." **2.** *n.* A member of a species which resembles humans such as a chimpanzee or an orangutan.

anthropomorphic thinking

n. Thought which uses comparisons to humans as a starting point or assumes other species are similar to humans.

anthropomorphism

n. **1.** The understanding of the mental processes or behavior of nonhuman animals in terms of human functioning with the assumption that such human functioning is well understood. Thus a cat which rubs against its owner's leg might be said to love its owner. **2.** The attribution of human characteristics to nonhuman animals, gods, geographical features, the weather, plants, inanimate objects, or other things.

antianxiety drug

n. Any of several types of drugs which have the effect of lowering anxiety level. Minor tranquilizers such as the benzodiazepines and some of the selective serotonin reuptake inhibitors (SSRIs) fall into this category.

antibody

n. A protein modified by beta lymphocytes in reaction to the presence of an antigen which renders the antigen harmless to the host organism.

anticipation method

n. **1.** A procedure in verbal learning experiments in which one item in a list serves as a cue to recall the next item in a list. **2.** Using an item to prompt for the next item.

anticonformity

n. The tendency to rebel against group pressure. In conformity studies a small percentage of subjects express erroneous opinions which are in the opposite direction from a group's expressed opinions. There is an assumption that the motivation of nonconformity is rebellion against group norms rather than the expression of genuine or preexisting personal points of view.

anticonvulsant

n. A drug or chemical such as Dilantin which has the effect of reducing or eliminating epileptic or other types of convulsions.

antidepressant

n. Any of several classes of drugs such as the benzodiazepines or the selective serotonin reuptake inhibitors (SSRIs) which have the effect of reducing or eliminating depression.

antidiuretic hormone

n. (ADH) Also known as vasopressin, antidiuretic hormone helps regulate the retention of water in the body and the blood pressure. It is synthesized in the hypothalamus and released by nerve cells in the pituitary gland. It has the effect of causing the body to produce less urine and so retain more water and of constricting capillaries, both of which raise blood pressure. ADH is also part of the hypothalamic-pituitary-adrenocortical system, which controls overall metabolism and arousal.

antiepileptic drugs

n. Drugs or chemicals such as Dilantin which have the effect of reducing or eliminating epileptic convulsions.

antigen

n. Any object or substance which causes an immune response in the body, which usually has the effect of rendering the antigen harmless. Viruses, bacteria, toxins, and malformed cells are commonly treated as antigens by the immune system.

antihistamine

n. Drug or other chemical that counteracts the effects of histamine at any of the three types of receptor sites. Those that block the H1 receptor are used as over-the-counter sleep aids and antiallergy drugs. H2 receptor

blockers are used to suppress gastric acid secretion in cases of heartburn or gastric reflux disease. No use has been found for H3 blockers.

anti-Mullerian hormone

n. (AMH) A hormone produced in the testes during gestation that prevents the Mullerian ducts from turning into female sexual organs. Also called Mullerian inhibiting hormone (MiH). Each testis produces AMH only for its own side of the body, and failure of one or both of the testes to produce AMH can result in the development of a rudimentary uterus and failure of the testes to descend during puberty.

antipsychotic drug

n. Any of numerous drugs used to treat schizophrenia, delusional disorder, mania, deliria, and other extreme thought disorders and behavioral bizarreness or agitation. This class of drugs includes drugs developed in the middle of the 20th century called typical antipsychotics, such as the phenothiazines, butyrophenones, and thioxanthenes. Newer antipsychotic drugs are called atypical antipsychotics; they include clozapine, which has negative effects on the immune system, and more recently olanzapine, risperidone, quetapine, ziprasidone, and aripiprazole.

antisocial behavior

n. Acts which are in marked contrast to those expected of a member of a society and which show disregard for or a desire to harm others. Antisocial behavior tends to be impulsive and violent and show a disregard for the consequences to the actor as well as the victim of the behavior. Antisocial behavior is highly correlated with the use of alcohol in most societies.

antisocial personality disorder

n. An enduring pattern of behavior and action which shows disregard for social norms and for the rights of others. It begins in childhood in persons classified as having oppositional and defiant disorder and is more common in males than in females. Childhood symptoms include lying, stealing, bullying, torturing or killing small animals, fire setting, truancy, vandalism, substance abuse, and sexual misconduct. In adults symptoms include fighting, beating others, failure to hold a job, failure to establish long-term relationships, repeated violations of the law, failure to function adequately as a parent, financial irresponsibility, frequent moves, habitual lying and manipulation of others, and extreme recklessness in driving. The original term for this sort of person was *moral imbecile*, later *psychopath*, then *sociopath*. In the original formulation of this disorder an absence of normal conscience and guilt was a central theme, but this has been eliminated in the most recent official formulations of the disorder. ICD 9 uses the term *dissocial personality disorder*.

anxiety

n. **1.** A fearful mood that has a vague or no specific focus and is accompanied by bodily arousal. **2.** In learning theory a secondary or conditioned drive which leads to an avoidance response. **3.** In Freudian theory it can be realistic fear of possible events, a conscious expression of unexpressed and usually conflicted energy, or moral qualms. **4.** In existential theory, anxiety is the emotional aspect of the constant state of uncertainty of human beings who have to choose courses of action in a world in which there are no inherent guidelines.

anxiety disorder

n. Any one of several mental disorders in which anxiety is the central feature, including panic disorder and agoraphobia, generalized anxiety disorder, phobias, obsessive-compulsive disorder, post-traumatic stress disorder, and anxiety disorders due to medical condition or drug abuse.

anxiety disorders of childhood or adolescence

n. Any one of several mental disorders during childhood in which anxiety is the central feature, including separation anxiety disorder, panic disorder and agoraphobia, generalized anxiety disorder, phobias, obsessive-compulsive disorder, post-traumatic stress disorder,

and anxiety disorders due to medical condition or drug abuse.

anxiety, free-floating

n. A vague and general sense of uneasiness not linked to any specific situation or object.

anxiolytic

n. Any of several types of drugs which have the effect of lowering anxiety level. Minor tranquilizers such as the benzodiazepines and some of the selective serotonin reuptake inhibitors (SSRIs) which are primarily used as antidepressants fall into this category.

apathy

n. Lack of normal responsiveness and interest in one's self, surroundings, and others.

Apgar score

n. An evaluation method for the health of newborn infants including skin color, heart rate, respiration, reflexes, and muscle tone, each of which is scored on a 0–2 scale with a maximal possible score of 10. Scores below 3 indicate severe distress, scores between 4 and 7 indicate moderate distress, and scores of 7+ are considered normal.

aphagia

n. An inability or lack of desire to eat or swallow. This can be due to damage to the glossopharyngeal or hypoglossal nerve, lesions in the lateral hypothalamic region, psychogenic problems, or senile dementia in its final stages.

aphasia

n. Aphasia is an acquired impairment to the language processing skills (production and comprehension) after brain damage. Aphasia follows damage to the brain resulting from traumatic brain injury, cerebrovascular accident (stroke), dementia, tumor, and infectious disease. Patterns of aphasia are divided according to fluency. The characteristic feature of Broca's aphasia is telegraphic speech, in which articles, conjunctions, prepositions, auxiliary verbs, and pronouns (function words) and morphological inflections (e.g., plurals, past tense) are omitted. However, nouns, verbs, adjectives, and adverbs (content words) may be retained. The characteristic feature of Wernicke's aphasia is preserved speech with empty content. This may vary from the insertion of a few incorrect or nonexistent words (neologisms) to a profuse outpouring of jargon or word salad. In fluent aphasia lesions are usually in brain regions that are posterior to the fissure of Rolando (the central sulcus). In nonfluent aphasia lesions are anterior to the fissure of Rolando.

– BW

aphasia, Broca's

n. Expressive impairment secondary to brain damage, typically in the left inferior frontal gyrus or convolution (Broca's area or Brodmann's area 44) and, in more severe cases, extending to the adjacent premotor and motor regions and underlying white matter. Symptoms may include a combination of various deficits, such as nonfluent, agrammatic oral expression; apraxia of speech (difficulty sequencing the sounds in a word); dysarthria (abnormal strength in speech musculature); poor repetition of words and phrases; and limited naming abilities (e.g., anomia and semantic paraphasias). Auditory comprehension is relatively spared, functional for everyday conversation but deficient for complex sentences (e.g., passive sentences: The apple was eaten by the girl). Writing errors may resemble oral production deficits. Reading comprehension may parallel auditory comprehension skills. Broca's aphasia may be confused with transcortical motor aphasia, as both patient groups exhibit similar symptoms. Yet, unlike in Broca's aphasia, word/phrase repetition is not impaired in transcortical motor aphasia.

– JGC

aphasia, Wernicke's ▶ *See* WERNICKE'S APHASIA

aphrodisiac

n. Generally mythical agent which stimulates sexual desire; no genuine aphrodisiac has been found. Most folk aphrodisiacs such as oysters, raw eggs, yohimbine, and rhinoceros horn have no measurable aphrodisiac power. Modern drugs such as Cialis and Viagra increase blood flow to the sexual organs, making sexual arousal more likely with stimulation, but do not affect sexual interest or arousal directly. Spanish fly causes irritation to the urinary lining, giving rise to desire to scratch, which can be mistaken for sexual desire. Alcohol lowers inhibitions to sexual activity but also makes sexual performance more difficult. The ergot alkaloids in nutmeg bring about sexual desire along with visual distortions but are also toxic and cause vomiting, and no systematic studies have been undertaken on these substances. Marijuana usually causes a greater focus on sensory input, which can enhance sexual experience. Empathogens such as Ecstasy bring about feelings of closeness but do not directly enhance sexual arousal.

apomorphine

n. A morphine derivative that has been used as an expectorant and an agent to induce vomiting.

apoplexy

n. An old-fashioned word for an acute loss of consciousness and paralysis due to brain hemorrhage, embolism, or thrombosis.

a posteriori

adj. Latin phrase literally meaning "from later" used to mean after the fact. Often used to describe observations or theories derived from observations as opposed to theories that predict future occurrences.

apparent motion

n. An illusion of motion, especially when two visual stimuli are displayed in rapid alternation close together. This phenomenon underlies the effects of neon signs with arrows that appear to move and movies and television which show a series of still pictures in rapid succession with each frame changing slightly so that there appears to be continuous motion. Also called apparent movement.

apparent movement

n. An illusion of motion, especially when two visual stimuli are displayed in rapid alternation close together. This phenomenon underlies the effects of neon signs with arrows that appear to move and movies and television which show a series of still pictures in rapid succession with each frame changing slightly so that there appears to be continuous motion. Also called apparent motion.

appeasement behavior

n. Any behavior such as cowering which prevents or terminates aggressive behavior of an organism of the same species. Also called submissive behavior.

apperception

n. **1.** A final clear phase of perception which includes recognition, identification, and comprehension of what has been perceived. **2.** The assimilation of a perception into the knowledge organization of the individual. **3.** The active process of focusing attention so as to select and structure experience.

apperceptive agnosia

n. A subtype of visual agnosia. During the 19th century Lissauer proposed a distinction between apperceptive and associative visual agnosia. This distinction remained somehow unnoticed until the second half of the 20th century, when it was integrated in the contemporary interpretations of visual agnosias. According to Lissauer, visual recognition supposes two different processes: **(1)** the process of perceptual recognition of the sensory impression and **(2)** the process of associating this perception with previously stored perceptual information. Apperceptive agnosia is characterized by a fundamental defect in visual perception, resulting in an inability to recognize differences between two similar objects and mentally reconstruct the visual shapes. Conversely, in associative agnosia the patient can recognize shapes but cannot interpret them. Patients with associative agnosia can match similar pictures and even copy them but cannot relate the shapes with the objects. It is supposed that apperceptive visual agnosia most often is observed in cases of right hemisphere lesions, whereas associative visual agnosia is associated with left hemisphere pathology.   – A A

▶ *See also* **AGNOSIA**

apperceptive mass

n. The body of existing knowledge which can be modified or increased through the process of apperception.

appetite

n. Physiological desire which may be directed toward different targets through learning. Most usually applied to the desire for food, it may also be used with other physiological needs such as for sex or water.

appetite disorders

n. A category of disorders, the central aspect of which is abnormal desire for food. A symptom of anorexia nervosa and depression is often a lack of appetite. Complete lack of desire for food is usually caused by neurological deficit. Hyperphagia, or excessive overeating, is a disorder in which appetite is much greater than the physical need for food and can result from using food for mood control or emotional avoidance or from numerous physiological pathologies.

appetitive behavior

n. A general term for behavior that is assumed to have the satisfaction of a physiological desire as its base motivation. Thus a lion hunting zebra is said to engage in appetitive behavior as it is inferred that the behaviors associated with hunting are motivated by need for food.

appetitive phase

n. The beginning phase in sexual behavior in which the organism seeks a partner and engages in courtship rituals, as opposed to the consummatory phase, in which the organism engages in copulatory or other behavior leading to orgasm.

applied psychology

n. The application of the theories and findings of psychology to practical problems in everyday life. Fields of applied psychology include clinical, educational, school, industrial/organizational, forensic/criminal, community, and health psychologies.

applied research

n. Utilization of the scientific method to solve practical problems or questions through the application of information. Applied research builds upon the knowledge gained through basic research in order to address real-world problems. For example, while a basic research question might be "What neurological processes are involved in the process of forgetting?" applied research goes one step further to ask, "How can our understanding of the neurological processes involved in the process of forgetting be used to enhance memory strategies in patients with Alzheimer's disease?" Basic and applied research are closely linked, with the primary difference being the immediate goal of the research process; basic research has the goal of discovery for the sake of knowledge while applied research targets discovery for the sake of practical application.   – BJM

appraisal

n. A cognitive evaluation of a situation or event relative to the needs of the organism. In cognitive theories of emotion, appraisal is a central event in determining emotional response. Primary appraisal is an evaluation of the situation or event itself, and secondary appraisal takes into account one's coping resources and efforts in the evaluation and emotional response.

apprehension span

n. The maximal number of units that can be perceived in a single sensory moment. It is usually measured by having subjects report the number of items they can identify after a single short exposure to an array of items.

approach-approach conflict

n. When there is more than one mutually exclusive course of action open to an organism all of which are associated with positive outcomes, the organism experiences conflict over the choice of goals. This conflict is strongest when the organism is at a point on the different approach gradients where the motivation to approach each goal is about the same.

approach gradient

n. The strength of the tendency to move toward a desired goal, which varies with distance to the goal. Thus being close to a goal leads to

greater tendency to move toward it while being far away from the goal leads to a lesser tendency to move toward it. The approach gradient tends to be less steep than the avoidance gradient so that positive goals motivate action at a greater distance from the goal but tend to be abandoned at closer distances if there is also an avoidance motive associated with the goal.

apraxia

n. Apraxia is the loss of the ability to produce purposeful, skilled movements as the result of brain pathology. This impairment in the production of learned (or skilled) movements is not caused by weakness, paralysis, lack of co-ordination, or sensory loss. Three subtypes of motor apraxia are described: (**1**) limb kinetic apraxia, (**2**) ideokinetic or ideomotor apraxia, and (**3**) ideational apraxia. Limb kinetic apraxia is a loss of the kinetic components of engrams resulting in coarse or unrefined movements. Ideokinetic or ideomotor apraxia is a loss of the voluntary ability to perform learned movements. Ideational apraxia is an impairment of ideational (conceptual) knowledge resulting in loss of the conceptual linkage between tools and their respective actions as well as the ability to sequence correctly produced movements. Ideomotor apraxia can be divided according to the body segment where apraxia is observed: face apraxia (ocular and oral apraxia), limb apraxia (upper limb apraxia and gait apraxia), and axial apraxia (body trunk apraxia). Sometimes a further distinction between motor apraxias (limb kinetic apraxia, ideokinetic or ideomotor apraxia, and ideational apraxia) and spatial apraxias, associated with an inability to manipulate objects (constructional apraxia and dressing apraxia), is introduced. Some authors, however, argue that so-called spatial apraxias should not be considered apraxias, but simply interpreted as visuoconstructive/visuospatial defects.   – AA

a priori

adj. Latin phrase literally meaning "from before" used to mean before the fact. Used to describe theories or beliefs about likely outcomes before an actual observation is made. An a priori argument is one based on opinion, theory, or deduction in the absence of actual knowledge.

aptitude

n. Potential capacity to perform an action, skill, or art which may or may not have been previously utilized. Aptitudes cannot be measured directly but only in terms of previously acquired abilities.

aptitude test

n. Any test of ability which is intended to predict future acquisition of performance, skill, or level of ability. The Scholastic Aptitude Test (SAT) is a good example of ability tests in general, which measure acquired capacity to perform with the intention of predicting future learning and performance.

aptitude treatment interaction

n. An interaction between treatment and aptitude such that persons with one set or level of abilities react differently to a treatment than do persons with different levels or sets of aptitude. Thus a person with a high aptitude for mathematics might find a lecture on six-dimensional space interesting while a person with low mathematical aptitude might find it tedious and not attend to it.

aqueduct of Sylvius

n. A passageway between the third and fourth ventricles of the brain filled with cerebrospinal fluid.

aqueous humor

n. The liquid which fills the eyeball and the space between the iris and the cornea in the eye.

arable land

n. the amount of land on which food can be grown that will allow for consumption and survival. A country may have a large total land size, but only part of it will be arable land. Arable land has been shown to be an important factor in influencing the creation of human cultures. Cultures in areas where arable land is scarce will be different than those in areas where arable land is abundant.

arachnoid membrane

n. The middle of the three membrane layers which surround the brain and spinal cord, which resembles a spider web.

arborization

n. **1.** The development of branching connections to other neurons in the dendrite of a neuron. **2.** The branching, treelike structure of a dendrite.

archetypal form

n. The image, pattern, or theme associated with an archetype in analytical psychology.

archetype

n. **1.** The structural components of the collective unconscious which are inherited and have developed through the consistent experiences of previous generations and seek expression in individual lives. Examples of archetypes include self, shadow, anima and animus, mandala, hero, god, sage, great mother, acolyte, the sun and moon, mother, father, son, daughter, and various animals. **2.** A perfect example of a category.

arcuate fasciculus

n. Neural pathway connecting the posterior part of the temporoparietal junction (Wernicke's area) with the posterior frontal cortex (Broca's area). Damage to the arcuate fasciculus can result in a particular type of language impairment (aphasia) known as conduction aphasia. In conduction aphasia, regardless of relatively well preserved auditory comprehension and speech production, significant difficulties in language repetition are observed.   – A A

   ▶ *See also* **CONDUCTION APHASIA**

arcuate nucleus

n. **1.** An arch-shaped area in the hypothalamus containing the cell bodies of neurons that produce hormones. **2.** Any of numerous small groups of neurons on the surface of a pyramidal area of the medulla oblongata which are extensions of pontine nuclei associated with facial sensations.

area postrema

n. A brain area at the top and back of the fourth ventricle with a high density of blood vessels in which the blood-brain barrier is more permeable than in most areas of the brain, allowing toxic substances to enter more easily. Because it also controls the vomiting reflex, it allows quicker vomiting after ingestion of toxins than would be possible otherwise.

arithmetic mean

n. The sum of a set of numbers divided by the number of numbers added. The most common meaning of the word *average*.

Army Alpha and Beta tests

n. Two screening devices developed by psychologists for the U.S. Army to classify the large number of recruits who entered the service for World War I. The Army Alpha test was a verbal test of intelligence, and the Army Beta test was a nonverbal test of intelligence used for illiterate and non-English-speaking individuals. These tests were the first intelligence tests given to large groups of individuals (over 1,700,000), as opposed to the commonly used individual administrations of intelligence tests. The findings from this large normative sample fueled a great deal of interest in intellectual testing. The design of these tests provided some of the foundation (along with the Stanford-Binet and Bellevue intelligence scales) for later intelligence tests including the Wechsler Adult Intelligence Scale.　　　　　　　　　　　　　　　　　　　　– DGA

arousal

n. A general term for bodily preparation to act usually involving the reticular activating system (RAS), increased heart and respiration rates, diversion of blood to the skeletal muscles and away from the internal organs, suppression of immune function, and increased alertness with a narrowed focus and a faster response time. *Arousal* is sometimes used in a more specific sense to denote higher levels of activity in a particular brain area such as in occipital arousal.

arteriosclerosis

n. Hardening of the arteries, usually resulting from fatty plaques on the inside of the arterial walls, that often leads to blockage that is called a stroke when it occurs in cerebral arteries.

articulation

n. Articulation in phonetics refers to the way the articulators of the vocal apparatus are configured in the production of sounds. The articulators include the lips, the tongue, the epiglottis, and the larynx, as well as the teeth, the alveolar ridge, the hard palate, the velum or soft palate, and the uvula. Sounds occurring in the world's natural languages can be described as having a place of articulation involving one or more of these articulators. For example, sounds produced with both lips (the consonants in *bib*) have bilabial place of articulation; sounds produced with the tip of the tongue touching the alveolar ridge (the consonants in *did*) have alveolar place of articulation. Manner of articulation is a different articulatory parameter to classify sounds, based on the way they are produced. By manner of articulation, consonants are classified into oral stops, nasal stops, affricates, fricatives, flaps, trills, and approximants. A broad distinction is also made between obstruent and sonorant sounds, produced, respectively, with major or minor obstruction to the airflow. Vowels belong to the class of sonorants, along with nasal stops, flaps, trills, and approximants, while stops, affricates, and fricatives are obstruents.　　　　　　– EMF

articulatory loop

n. The articulatory loop (also phonological loop) handles acoustic information in working memory. It is one of the three modules of a multicomponent model of working memory proposed to explain how information is temporarily maintained and manipulated. In the model, a central executive system is aided by the articulatory loop and by a sketchpad, which processes visuospatial information. The articulatory loop itself has two separable subcomponents: one is a phonological store, subject to a two-second decay unless the information is refreshed by the second subcomponent, an articulatory rehearsal system, or articulatory store. The phonological store serves to explain the phonological similarity effect, by which it is more difficult to recall a list of items when they sound similar (e.g., *B, T, C, D, G, P*) than when they sound different (e.g., *L, U, W, M, R, Q*). Recent evidence suggests that the articulatory loop plays a key role in language acquisition: representations of new words are maintained in the loop to optimize learning.   – EMF

articulatory store

n. The articulatory store, an articulatory rehearsal system, is a subcomponent of the articulatory loop (or phonological loop), the working memory module that manipulates acoustic information. The articulatory loop has a phonological store which is subject to a two-second decay, unless the information is refreshed by rehearsal in the articulatory store. The articulatory store accounts for the word length effect, according to which lists of longer items are harder to recall than lists of shorter items, because rehearsing longer items will take more time. The word length effect is eliminated with articulatory suppression (e.g., in experimental contexts in which participants repeat an irrelevant word, such as *the*, while performing a memory task), presumably because articulatory suppression prevents rehearsal from taking place in the articulatory store.   – EMF

artifact

n. **1.** An erroneous finding that may be due to random error, faulty instrumentation, faulty experimental design, or other human error. **2.** Any manufactured object, especially applied to historical or anthropological discoveries. **3.** In some types of manufacturing a prototype upon which others are modeled or standard of measurement.

artifact, cultural

n. A manufactured object of a particular culture which is used to infer cultural values and technology. Changes in cultural artifacts over time are used as clues to make inferences about cultural evolution.

artifact, methodological

n. A false finding in research due to problems in instrumentation or research design.

artifact, statistical

n. A false finding in research due to random variation in data. Most statistical procedures make the assumption that when an error has less than a 20%, 10%, or 1% chance of occurring, an error has not occurred, when in fact errors do occur in 20%, 10%, or 1% of cases, depending on the level of confidence selected in performing statistical tests.

artificial intelligence

n. (AI) A subdiscipline in cognitive psychology, computer science, psycholinguistics, and philosophy that attempts to simulate human intelligence and to consider the nature of intelligence. Intelligent programming either models behavior as in robotics and expert systems or attempts to model learning so that the computer alters its own programming to work better.

artificial language

n. Any language that has been intentionally created, usually for a specific purpose, as contrasted with natural languages, which develop among groups of people (and possibly other species) over time. Sign language, Esperanto, and computer programming systems are examples of artificial languages.

art therapy

n. A form of psychotherapy in which clients engage in artistic activities such as painting, modeling with clay, or basket making as a way of expressing and working with mental conflicts and blocks while avoiding usual intellectual and/or verbal defensiveness.

ascending reticular activating system

n. (ARAS) The nerve pathway from the reticular formation in the brainstem which connects with the thalamus and all parts of the cerebral cortex and is especially involved in arousal, including wakefulness, attention, and concentration.

Asch experiment

n. **1.** A set of experiments investigating conformity conducted under the direction of Solomon E. Asch (1907–1996). Typically subjects are seated in a group and asked to make an easy judgment in perception such as which of two lines is longer, on which people almost never make errors. Unknown to the subject, the other persons in the group were all confederates with instructions to make intentional errors part of the time and so place the subject in the position of disagreeing with a group of other people or making false reports of his or her perceptions. Asch found that most participants at least sometimes reported perceptions conforming to the false reports of the confederates when all the confederates made the same intentional errors but almost no one made errors if a single confederate gave a correct response. A small minority of participants reported perceptions distorted in a direction opposite to the group's reports, and a few subjects reported accurate perceptions unaffected by the group. In postexperimental interviews Asch and his colleagues found that among the participants who had conformed to the false group reports, some subjects said they actually believed their own false reports, some subjects said they went along with the group so as not to cause trouble or embarrassment in the group, and some participants said they doubted their own perceptions and believed the group must be right. Almost all participants reported feelings of stress when they disagreed with the group regardless of whether they conformed or not. **2.** An experiment using an experimental setup like Asch's in which participants are placed in a position of having to disagree with a group of others or make false reports about their perceptions.

asocial

1. *n.* Avoidance of participation or failure to participate in social interactions for any reason. **2.** *adj.* Lacking normal insight and sensitivity to others. **3.** *adj.* In biology, solitary in nature as in the asocial ants or wasps which live alone except for mating and laying eggs.

aspartate

n. The anion of aspartic acid ($C_4H_7NO_4$) is a nonessential amino acid which can act as an excitory neurotransmitter.

aspartic acid

n. Aspartic acid ($C_4H_7NO_4$) is a nonessential amino acid which can act as an excitory neurotransmitter.

Asperger's disorder

n. A pervasive developmental disorder in which the child has mild to moderate deficits in social perception, language skills, and social behavior. Other symptoms may include difficulty in dealing with environmental change and restricted, repetitive, and stereotyped behavior or interest patterns. In contrast to those who have autism, children with Asperger's disorder are normal in intelligence and language development and often can function normally except for social interactions.

assertiveness training

n. A program or method of counseling which intends to aid persons to express their desires and feelings openly, positively, and directly so that others will respond to them in more satisfying ways. Developed in the late 1940s, this sort of training was widely adopted by the women's movement in the 1970s in order to help women overcome the social inhibitions of the feminine role in a positive and productive way.

assessment center

n. An organization in which persons are observed and tested with the intention of predicting their future behavior for either organizational or research purposes. Assessment procedures can include paper and pencil tests, in-baskets, game and role playing, and individual and group exercises often simulating job tasks and environment. The idea of an assessment center was developed by Henry Murray first as a research tool and later for selection of agents for the Office of Strategic Services (OSS) during World War II.

assimilation

n. In acculturation psychology, the term *assimilation* refers to the pattern of cultural change which arises when a person engages with a new cultural group and potentially adopts its psychological characteristics, while simultaneously reducing the amount of contact with the cultural group of origin and relinquishing its characteristics. The terms *assimilation* and *acculturation* are sometimes used synonymously to reflect a cultural shift in psychological characteristics from the culture of origin to those of a new culture, although more recently there is a growing tendency to adopt the terminology proposed by John Berry, in which *acculturation* refers to the phenomenon of cultural change that occurs as a result of firsthand intercultural interaction, and *assimilation* refers to a specific pattern of acculturation in which a person adopts the characteristics of a new cultural group and gives up the characteristics of the original cultural group.

Some scholars, particularly those who study immigration patterns, retain the term *assimilation* to refer to the general phenomenon of participation in a new society. This participation can have different aspects, including economic, behavioral, and linguistic aspects. *Acculturation* is used specifically to refer to the adoption of cultural characteristics. The term *segmented assimilation* recognizes that immigrants can be received by different segments of the receiving society, including privileged middle-class or disadvantaged neighborhoods. Depending on the resources available to the immigrants and the dynamics of the receiving society, some will experience upward mobility into the middle-class, mainstream society, and others will experience downward mobility (or stay at the same level).   – KN

assimilation-contrast theory

n. A theory of attitude change and resistance to change in which it is assumed people have preformed categories which they use to evaluate incoming persuasive positions and into which they try to fit or assimilate new information. When we hear an opinion that falls near our zones of acceptance or rejection we tend to distort that information to make it fit into our existing belief. When we hear something that is highly different from our preexisting beliefs we simply reject it and may even move our opinions in the opposite direction. It is only when new information is close to our opinions but contrasting sufficiently that we cannot assimilate it that we change our attitudes and do so in small degrees.

assimilation effects

n. Assimilation refers to the tendency to interpret a new experience in a manner that is consistent with one's preexisting concepts and knowledge. It is distinguished from *accommodation*, or the modification of established concepts and knowledge to take into account unique features of a new experience. In social psychology, the term has been used more broadly to refer to the judgment of a stimulus as more similar to a standard of comparison than would be the case if the standard were not applied.

Both cognitive and motivational factors theoretically lead to assimilation, and several cognitive processes can underlie it. These factors and processes depend on the stage of cognitive activity at which the effect occurs and the nature of the standard that is applied. Several quite different theories have implications for the conditions in which assimilation can occur. The following summary is representative of the diversity of these theories and the phenomena they purport to explain.

Concept accessibility. If information can be interpreted in terms of more than one concept, its interpretation is likely to depend on the concept that comes to mind most quickly at the time the information is received. A person's decision to sky dive, for example, might be interpreted as either "adventurous" or "reckless." Similarly, covering up for a fellow student who cuts class to go swimming might be interpreted as either "kind" or "dishonest." Note that the concepts that might be applied in each case have different evaluative implications. Consequently, once the behavior is interpreted, judgments of its favorableness (and, perhaps, evaluations of the person who performed the behavior) are assimilated to the evaluative implications of the attribute concept that was used to interpret it.

More general bodies of knowledge may have analogous effects. For example, prior knowledge of an individual's beliefs and opinions can influence the interpretation of the person's statements and behavior. A person's expression of admiration for an American president whose policies favor big business at the expense of social and economic concerns might be viewed as a genuine expression of approval if the speaker is a conservative Republican but as sarcastic if the speaker is a liberal Democrat.

Confirmatory information seeking. People with an a priori expectation for what a person or object will be like may selectively seek and attend to information that is consistent with this expectation. Thus, people who expect a person to be extroverted might selectively attend to information about the person that confirms this expectation, while giving less weight to information that calls this expectation into question. Alternatively, individuals who expect a product to be of high or low quality on the basis of its appearance or brand name may give greater weight to attribute information that confirms this expectation than to information that disconfirms it.

Comparative judgment processes. People are likely to assign a higher value to a stimulus along a given attribute dimension if they have previously compared the stimulus to an arbitrarily high value than if they have compared it to an arbitrarily low value. (For example, they estimate the price of a car to be higher if they have previously considered whether the car would cost more or less than $50,000 than if they have considered whether it would cost more or less than $5,000.) In order to make these comparisons, people apparently think about attributes of a person or object that might conceivably have the value they are considering. Although they may reject this value as implausible, attributes that are called to mind in the course of doing so, whose implications are biased in the direction of the rejected, influence the estimate that participants report later.

Affect. People often use the affective reactions they are experiencing and attribute to a stimulus as a basis for judging this stimulus. However, they often cannot distinguish between their actual reactions to the stimulus and the feelings they are experiencing for other, objectively irrelevant reasons. Consequently, people are inclined to evaluate stimuli more favorably if they happen to be in a good mood at the time than if they happen to be in a bad mood.

Motivational factors. People who are motivated to maintain a favorable self-image may interpret information they receive in a way that confirms this image. Thus, for example, they may take personal responsibility for success and for events that reflect positively on them but may attribute events that potentially threaten their self-esteem to external factors. By the same token, people who find they have behaved in a way that is inconsistent with their previously formed beliefs or attitudes may experience cognitive dissonance and may reduce this dissonance by changing their beliefs or attitude to be consistent with the implications of the behavior. For example, people who have publicly advocated a position with which they disagree may later modify their attitude to be consistent with implications of the behavior.

A related theory of social psychology assumes that people are motivated to maintain beliefs that the world is just, and, therefore, that people both get what they deserve and deserve what they get. Thus, they may hold a person to be more responsible for an accident if the person is seriously injured than if he or she escaped without harm. Furthermore, they may believe not only that the defendant in a rape case will be punished but also that the victim was partly responsible for the incident's occurrence.

The examples summarized provide an indication of the wide range of phenomena that potentially fall under the heading of assimilation and of the diversity of theories that potentially account for them. Beliefs, attitudes, and judgments may be assimilated to concepts and knowledge that happen to be salient at the time the information is received, to expectations concerning the implications of the information, to previously formed beliefs and attitudes, to implications of the behavior one has manifested, and to the evaluative implications of the affect one happens to be experiencing. Some of these phenomena and the theories that account for them are more firmly established than others, and the conditions on their occurrence are subject to qualification. Nevertheless, assimilation phenomena clearly occupy a central role in social psychological theory and research.   – RSW

assimilator

n. A person who uses inductive reasoning to elaborate abstract concepts to encompass new experience, i.e., an experiential learning style. Assimilators are contrasted with accommodators, who focus on the environment and readily change their schema; convergers, who fit new information into old concepts; and divergers, who use a brainstorming approach to discover new ideas to fit experience.

association area

n. The parts of the cerebral cortex that are not devoted to either sensory or motor function and are believed to be involved in higher mental processes of associating information in new patterns. Also called association cortex.

association by contiguity

n. The theory that associations are formed primarily by contiguity in space and time. Also called law or principle of contiguity.

association cortex

n. Cortical areas that are neither primary motor nor primary sensory areas but are thought to be involved in higher processing of information. Association areas can be subdivided into the following categories: (1) The unimodal association cortex: cortical areas involved in processing one particular type of sensory information (visual association area, auditory association area, etc). They are located around the primary sensory area. Damage in these cortical areas results in inability to recognize and understand that specific type of sensory information (i.e., agnosia), as well as difficulties in recalling that form of information (specific

amnesias). (2) Polymodal association areas: they process information from different sensory systems and participate in cross-modal associations. A major polymodal association area is the parietal-temporal-occipital area, situated in the interface of these three lobes. A polymodal association area may also be referred to as a tertiary area. (3) Sometimes a further division is included, and the prefrontal association cortex is regarded as a supramodal area. The prefrontal cortex is involved not in processing specific forms of information, but rather in organizing, controlling, and planning cognition and behavior. Frequently, however, the prefrontal cortex is regarded together with the parietal-temporal-occipital area as the two tertiary cortical areas.   – AA

association, free

n. An activity in which a person says whatever comes to mind without hesitation or censorship. This was the main technique of psychoanalysis developed by Sigmund Freud.

associationism

n. Any of numerous theories which suppose that simple mental associations are the building blocks of all or almost all mental processes, with the most complex built up of numerous simpler associations. The theory was first suggested by Aristotle about 2,400 years ago and elaborated by English philosophers and more recently by such diverse schools of psychology as psychoanalysis and behaviorism and by some cognitive psychologists and psycholinguists.

association test

n. Another name for the word association test first developed by Carl Jung.

associative illusion

n. Any of a large number of visual illusions in which one part of the image is misperceived because of another part of the image.

associative interference

n. The interference of either learning or recalling an association due to another association which is incompatible in some way with the first association.

associative laws
n. Three principles which determine whether an association will be made or not, including the law of contiguity, the law of frequency, and the law of recency.

associative learning
n. A type of learning in which links are formed between two elements. These elements have been conceptualized as mental events; observable events, as in stimulus and response in learning theory; or theorized physical events, such as links in neural networks.

associative memory
n. Memory triggered by a cue. This is the basis for all forms of behaviorism and many approaches to verbal learning.

associative network
n. A network of processes or nodes and their links commonly used in information processing approaches to psychology.

associative strength
n. **1.** In behaviorism, the likelihood that a particular stimulus will be followed by a particular response. **2.** In cognitive psychology the strength of the activation of a particular node by the activation of another node.

assortative mating
n. Mating in which the partner is chosen on the basis that a particular trait is either the same (positive assortative mating) or different (negative assortative mating) from that of the one doing the choosing. Also called assortive mating.

astrology
n. Any of a large number of belief systems in which the alignment of planets and constellations relative to Earth is believed to influence persons and events on Earth. Most ancient societies had beliefs of this sort, which have persisted in the face of contrary evidence up to the present era as astrologers were consulted

to help make important decisions by such disparate individuals as Adolf Hitler and Nancy Reagan.

ataque de nervios
n. A syndrome of panicky outbursts in which the individual experiences a sense of heat or pressure in the chest and head and a sense of loss of control which leads to intermittent periods of weeping mixed with verbal or physical aggression, shaking, fainting, and occasional seizurelike behavior, all of which is followed by amnesia.

ataxia
n. Impairment in the ability to coordinate voluntary movements. Ataxia is usually the consequence of some type of cerebellar pathology. The cerebellum is involved in regulating the body's posture and the strength and direction of the movements. *Ataxia* is the general term used to refer to the movement disorder associated with cerebellar pathology. Motor difficulties in ataxia can have different manifestations: unsteady gait with tendency to fall to the sides (ataxic gait), difficulties in visually guiding the movements, impaired ability to perform the rapid alternating movements (dysdiadochokinesia), difficulties in the timing of the movements in which an act is not performed smoothly or accurately because of lack of harmonious association of its various components (dyssynergia), intention tremor, and dysarthria (speech articulation defect). Many ataxias are hereditary, for example, Friedreich's ataxia. Ataxia can also be acquired.   – AA

atherosclerosis
n. The most common form of arteriosclerosis, which involves fat deposits along the inner walls of veins and arteries which lead to stiffening of the blood vessels and partial blocking of blood flow in them. This condition is dangerous as it makes the blood vessel more likely both to break and to be blocked by small blood clots or other matter in the bloodstream. Such blockages deprive some tissue of blood circulation and thus oxygen

and nutrients. Such blockages occurring in the arteries leading to the heart are called heart attacks and in the brain are called strokes.

athetosis
n. A neuromuscular condition due to problems with cerebral blood flow or cerebral lesions in basal ganglia or the upper pyramidal tract which results in uncontrollable, slow writhing movement of the tongue, fingers, hands, toes, and legs.

athletic body type
n. In the Kretschmer body typology, a body characterized by muscular, broad-shouldered physique; individuals who have this body type are aggressive and energetic in character and somewhat prone to schizophrenia.

atmosphere effect
n. **1.** The tendency of a person to behave or perceive in one situation as he/she does in another in which the behavior may be more appropriate. Thus a Catholic may cross himself or herself when entering a civic building that has the atmosphere of a church, or a person may use hand gestures to communicate while speaking on the telephone. **2.** In person perception, the way possession of one trait colors the perception of other traits or acts.

atrophy
1. n. Wasting away or degeneration of a body part through disease, malnutrition, or lack of use. **2.** v. to waste away through disease, malnutrition, or lack of use.

atropine
n. Atropine ($C_{17}H_{23}NO_3$) is a muscarin antagonist derived from the belladonna plant and used to prevent heart stoppage under anesthesia and in eye surgery to dilate the pupil and stop the blinking reflex. In medieval Italy wide pupils were perceived as beautiful and so women in that era used belladonna extract containing atropine to widen their pupils so as to make themselves more attractive.

attachment behavior
n. **1.** In attachment theory, behavior infants use to gain control over proximity to a caregiver including smiling, cooing, crying, gesturing, and clinging. **2.** It is also used to describe the behavior of noninfants who are in the process of forming close emotional attachments and especially sexual ones.

attachment disorder
n. A disorder of social interaction in infancy and early childhood in which the child displays disturbed and developmentally inappropriate patterns of social relating in the presence of inadequate care by adults. Symptoms include inappropriate failure to initiate and respond in social interactions (inhibited type) or an indiscriminate overresponse to all social opportunities (disinhibited type). Also called reactive attachment disorder.

attachment style
n. The particular pattern of interaction with a caregiver developed by an infant or the carryover of such a pattern into more mature behavior. Three general styles of attachment have been identified: secure, in which the child seeks out and is comforted by contact with a caregiver; anxious-ambivalent, in which the child seeks contact with a caregiver but remains anxious and alternately clingy and hostile to the caregiver; and anxious-avoidant, in which the child is hostile to the caregiver and makes little attempt to make contact with him or her. Various researchers have described subtypes of these styles, and some researchers include a detached or disorganized pattern characteristic of traumatized children in which there is not a consistent pattern of attachment.

attachment theory
n. A theory which supposes that infants between about 1 year and 3 years of age have an instinct to form social attachments to one or more caregivers with whom the child attempts to maintain and control proximity and that this instinct has had marked survival advantages for the human species.

attention

n. Focusing the apparently limited capacities of consciousness on a particular set of stimuli more of whose features are noted and processed in more depth than is true of nonfocal stimuli. Attention has been a focus of research since the 1960s, and numerous models have been generated noting certain features of attention and then been found wanting. Important features of attention include limited capacity, focus, differential processing of focal and nonfocal stimuli, leaking of information from nonfocal stimuli into awareness, effect of expectations on attentional focus and perception, and cultural differences in attentional patterns.

attentional blink

n. A failure or decrement in ability to identify a target immediately after another target in a rapid series of visual stimuli usually attributed to the attention's being diverted to the first target.

attention capture

n. The reflexive allocation of a limited processing resource to an external stimulus, without the intent of the observer. Although attention restricts full processing to subsets of information from the outside world, attention capture provides a way for consistently important or potentially threatening aspects of the environment to become attended and provides a starting point for processing by highlighting salient stimuli. The stimulus could be an abrupt sound, your own name, an emotionally charged word, an unexpected touch, a strikingly unique object, a flashing light, or a sudden motion. These stimuli could trigger a reflexive shift of attention to an auditory location or frequency, a location on the body, a location or feature dimension in the visual world, or even a movement of the eyes, head, or body. Research on attention capture includes the types of stimuli that capture attention; the type of processing resources captured (e.g., awareness); the influence of context, top-down control, and individual differences; and applications to user interfaces and information displays.
— SF

attention deficit disorder

n. A psychological disorder in which a child is noted to fail to pay normal levels of attention to a greater level than other children of the same age.

attention deficit–hyperactivity disorder

n. A psychological disorder in which a child is noted to fail to pay normal levels of attention and acts impulsively to a greater level than other children of the same age.

attention span

n. **1.** The length of time an individual can focus attention on one thing or topic. **2.** The amount of information an individual can take in during a brief exposure to it.

attenuation

n. **1.** The weakening of or interference with a signal so it is more difficult to detect. **2.** In statistics, the reduction in size of a correlation due to an error in measurement.

attitude

n. Attitudes are evaluations of objects occurring in ongoing thoughts about the objects or stored in memory. Attitudes can be influenced by and can influence beliefs, affect, and behavior in relation to the attitude object. For example, people often infer attitudes toward an entity from their affective feelings in the presence of this object and beliefs about the object's attributes. For example, one might form a positive attitude toward a new type of computer on the basis of one's mood at the time or beliefs that the computer is fast and user-friendly. However, attitudes can be distinguished from affective feelings in that attitudes entail a cognitive evaluation. Attitudes are also distinct from beliefs in that beliefs can be verified or falsified with objective criteria. Attitudes can be measured with direct procedures requiring attitude report (explicit measures) or indirect ones tapping spontaneous associations that are difficult to control (implicit measures).   — HLi, DA

attitude-behavior consistency

n. Attitude-behavior consistency is the degree to which an attitude toward an object predicts behavior toward this object. For example, this consistency can be established by estimating an association (i.e., correlation) between people's attitudes toward organ donation and their legal agreement to organ donation at a particular point in time. There are several factors that influence attitude-behavior consistency. Specifically, attitude-behavior consistency increases along with more valid and reliable measurement of attitudes and behaviors, more knowledge about the attitude object, greater attitude stability and confidence, and less two-sided information about the object. In addition, having direct (vs. indirect) experience with the attitude object and expressing attitudes repeatedly increase attitude-behavior consistency by making attitudes easier to recall.   — HLi, DA

attitude change

n. An attitude is a general and relatively lasting evaluation an individual holds regarding another person, object, or idea. Attitudes can be positive, negative, or neutral and can range from moderate to quite extreme (e.g., slightly positive to very positive). *Attitude change* refers to any alteration in a person's overall evaluation of an attitude object, including shifts in valence, extremity, or the development of an attitude where none existed before.

According to the elaboration likelihood model and other contemporary dual-process theories of social judgment, attitude change can occur through two general types of processes: those that require low cognitive effort and those that require high cognitive effort. The degree of effort applied is determined by the individual's willingness and ability to think critically. In general, high-effort processes yield attitudes that last longer, are more resistant to change, and are better predictors of behavior than those changed through low-effort processes.   — MM

attitude measurement

n. Any procedure which assigns quantitative values to the degree of individuals' relatively enduring evaluative belief about a particular person, group, object, or idea. Likert scales are the most common form of attitude measures.

attitude object

n. An attitude object is any distinct object that is evaluated. It may be a concrete target, a person, an event, an abstract entity, a social group, the self, or any aspect of the world. For example, an abstract entity such as equal rights and a concrete target such as a consumer product can both be attitude objects. Changes in aspects of the objects have been shown to produce changes in the attitude itself. For example, a red strawberry is appealing, but a brown strawberry is not. Due to the learned association between the object and the attitude, exposure to the object can activate its stored, associated attitude automatically. The attitude about an object can also be linked to beliefs about the attributes of the product. Strong associations with favorable attributes make attitudes about the product favorable. Objects can be evaluated with or without intention.   — KCM, DA

attitude scale

n. A measurement instrument which assigns quantitative values to the degree of individuals' relatively enduring evaluative belief about a particular person, group, object, or idea. Likert scales are the most common form of attitude scales.

attraction

n. **1.** A feeling of being drawn to another person or thing, usually with a positive feeling toward the other. **2.** A person or thing or a characteristic of a person or thing that evokes a desire to approach in another person as in "The carnival holds an attraction for children." **3.** A tendency to move closer to another.

attractiveness

n. The state of or degree to which one possesses the qualities that lead others to want to approach him or her, often sexually.

attribute

n. A character, quality, or aspect of any phenomenon whether person, thing, event, or idea.

attribution

n. The ascription or proscription of a characteristic, quality, feature, reason, or emotion to something or someone. For example, the attribution of an emotion refers to an inference made about someone's or something's emotional state. The attribution of causality refers to the tendency to create causal explanations for events that occur.

attributional bias

n. The tendency to create causal explanations with predictable flaws in them. The most common is the tendency to create explanations in which one's own negative actions are due to environmental circumstances while others' negative actions are due to enduring personal characteristics.

attributional error, fundamental ▶ *See* FUNDAMENTAL ATTRIBUTION ERROR

attributional style

n. Attributional style relates to individual differences in the way one makes attributions or estimates about the causes of behavior. Some individuals have individual, personal preferences or biases in the types of attributions that they make. Much of the research on attributional (or explanatory) style is tied closely to the concept of locus of control. People are generally fairly moderate in terms of their locus of control, but some people tend toward emphasis on internal or external factors. Individuals who have a highly internal locus of control tend to explain events in terms of internal (person-related) causes, while individuals who have a highly external locus of control tend to explain things in terms of the environment or other factors out of the individual's control (e.g., fate). Some individuals adopt a negative attributional style in which they explain positive events in terms of external factors and negative events in terms of internal factors. Research has also shown that some individuals are predisposed to interpret ambiguous events as aggressive, an effect known as the hostile attribution bias.   – MP

attribution error

n. Any error in assigning causes to behavior or events and especially the tendency to believe one's own (negative) actions are due to situational factors while others' negative

actions are caused by enduring traits internal to them. Also called fundamental attribution error.

attribution of causality

n. The human tendency to create causal explanations for events in which two or more objects move in space in ways that appear, to humans, to be related. This tendency has been observed in infants as young as 4 months. There has been much debate in psychology about which perceptual events are seen as causal, whether this tendency is an innate part of the human mind, and whether causality exists outside the human mind.

attribution of emotion

n. A theory of emotion in which a person observes his or her own physiological arousal and creates an explanation for it in emotional terms using context as a guide.

attribution theory

n. Attribution theory is a major area of research in social psychology that has several variations and has changed substantially since it was first proposed in the 1940s. Attribution theory involves the way in which people explain behavior. There are two basic categories of attributions, internal (dispositional) causes and external (situational) causes. Situational attributions hold that the behavior occurred because of some external cause or factor operating with the situation. Dispositional attributions hold that the behavior occurred because of some internal cause such as a personal trait, motive, or attitude.

Research has also shown that our attribution processes differ, depending on whether we are trying to estimate the causes of others' behavior versus attributions about our own behavior, a discrepancy known as the actor-observer effect. For estimating the causes of others' behavior, people generally commit the fundamental attribution error: they tend to underestimate the importance of environmental (external) causes and overestimate the importance if individual (internal) causes. People's estimates about the causes of their own behavior are subject to what is known as the self-serving bias: their attributions about their own behavior vary, depending on which explanation is most favorable to them. Through their attributions, people generally tend to take credit for their successes and deny responsibility for their failures. When our own behavior is desirable or leads to a positive outcome, people tend to make dispositional (internal) attributions, whereas people are more prone to making situational (external) attributions for behavior that is less than desirable and/or results in a negative outcome. Many researchers believe that this self-serving bias is a defense mechanism designed to protect our self-esteem.

A special case of the fundamental attribution error occurs when we make internal attributions on the basis of negative stereotypes that we hold about an out-group. This is referred to as the ultimate attribution error. The ultimate attribution error relates closely to the group-serving bias, which is similar to the self-serving bias. Research on group-serving bias shows that, in general, in-group members are credited for successes while out-group members' successes are attributed to external factors (e.g., luck). In-group failures are attributed to external causes, while out-group failures are attributed to internal causes that are common to all group members (e.g., they are weak or stupid).   – MP

attrition
n. A lessening of quantity or amount, especially the lessening of the number of subjects in a study for unspecified reasons.

A-type personality ▶ *See* TYPE A PERSONALITY

atypical
adj. Different from normal in some important way.

atypical antipsychotic
n. Newer drugs used to treat schizophrenia, delusional disorder, mania, deliria, and other extreme thought disorders and behavioral bizarreness or agitation are called atypical antipsychotics; they include

clozapine, which has negative effects on the immune system, and more recently olanzapine, risperidone, quetapine, ziprasidone, and aripiprazole. These contrast with the older or typical antipsychotics developed in the middle of the 20th century called typical antipsychotics, such as the phenothiazines, butyrophenones, and thioxanthenes, which had more extreme side effects including extrapyramidal reactions.

atypical autism
n. A pervasive developmental disorder characterized by deficits in play, social interaction, and communication but with sociability that is higher than in autistic children in general.

audibility range
n. The range from about 20 Hz to about 20,000 Hz. However, the range of human speech, 250 Hz to 4,000 Hz, is heard much better than are extreme tones at either end of the spectrum.

audience design
n. Adaptation in speech or visual presentations so as to communicate with an audience with particular characteristics. Most people's speech patterns change when speaking with, for instance, a peer, a parent, and a child to one considered more appropriate for the person with whom they are talking.

audioanalgesia
n. A lessening of pain during loud sounds or a distraction from pain such as by music.

audiogenic seizure
n. A seizure induced by prolonged exposure to loud noises, especially in rodents and rabbits.

audiogram
n. A graphic record of a listener's threshold to pure tones plotted by the frequency of the tones and the loudness in decibels necessary for perception which is often plotted as a deviation from the norm for the combination of tone and loudness. Audiograms are the most basic and widely used measure of hearing function.

audiometer

n. A device for measuring sensitivity to sound across a large range of sound frequencies and intensities and which usually produces an audiogram.

audiometry

n. The science and technology of measurement of hearing acuity.

audition

n. The sense of hearing.

auditory

adj. Related to sound and hearing.

auditory acuity

n. The ability to detect and discriminate among sounds of different qualities.

auditory agnosia

n. Inability to recognize and understand auditory information in the absence of decreased auditory acuity for pure tones. Normal auditory perception supposes the ability to recognize and discriminate differences among sounds. Auditory perception for verbal information implies the ability to recognize functional language sounds (phonemes). Auditory agnosia is observed in cases of damage of temporal auditory association areas. The auditory association area in the left hemisphere corresponds to the Wernicke's area. Two major subtypes of auditory agnosia are described: verbal auditory agnosia (inability to recognize the functional language sounds, that is, the language phonemes; in its most extreme form, it is known as pure word deafness, but in Wernicke's aphasia some phoneme discrimination defects may be found) and nonverbal auditory agnosia (inability to recognize and understand nonverbal auditory information). — A A

▶ *See also* **AGNOSIA, AUDITORY PERCEPTION, WERNICKE'S APHASIA,** *and* **WORD DEAFNESS**

auditory aphasia

n. Inability to understand spoken language, with sparing written language understanding and language production. Because of the preserved ability to understand written language, it can be interpreted as an auditory processing defect (verbal auditory agnosia). It roughly corresponds to word deafness. — A A

▶ *See also* **WERNICKE'S APHASIA** *and* **WORD DEAFNESS**

auditory canal

n. There are two auditory canals: external and internal. The external auditory canal (or external acoustic meatus) is a slightly curved tube extending from the outer ear (pinna or auricle) to the tympanic membrane (eardrum). It is about 2.5 cm long and 0.7 cm in diameter. The internal auditory canal (or internal acoustic meatus) is an orifice near the posterior surface of the temporal lobe corresponding to its petrous portion. It is a rounded canal about 0.8 cm long and 0.4 cm in diameter. It transmits two different cranial nerves, the facial (VII cranial nerve) and the acoustic (VIII cranial nerve), and the internal auditory branch of the basilar artery. — A A

auditory cortex

n. Cortical area involved in the reception and processing of auditory information. Auditory information is projected to the cortex from the medial geniculate body of the thalamus through the so-called auditory radiation. The cortical area known as the transverse temporal gyrus of Heschl (Brodmann's area 41 and probably Brodmann's 42) is the specific cortical area where the auditory information arrives. This area is the primary auditory cortex. This primary auditory area contains a frequency map: different neurons respond best to particular frequencies. This frequency distinction is also found in the cochlea and the auditory pathway to the brain. It means the primary auditory cortex possesses a tonotopic organization. Around the primary auditory area is located the auditory association area (Brodmann's areas 22 and 52) involved in complex processing of auditory information (e.g., music, language). In the left hemisphere the auditory association area is known as Wernicke's area. Bilateral lesions of Heschl's gyri may result in central deafness. Lesions in the auditory association areas result in auditory agnosia.   – A A

▶ *See also* **AUDITORY AGNOSIA** *and* **AUDITORY PERCEPTION**

auditory discrimination

n. The capacity to perceive differences in sound based on tone, intensity, harmonics, and other qualities of sound.

auditory hallucination

n. Hearing something (e.g., voices, noises) that does not exist in the form of an external stimulus in the environment. Auditory hallucinations are the most common form of hallucinations in individuals with psychotic disorders such as schizophrenia. Recent neuroimaging research has indicated that schizophrenia patients who experience auditory hallucinations may be mistaking their own thoughts for external auditory stimuli. Specifically, individuals who are actively experiencing auditory hallucinations, such as voices, show increased activation in the speech production (Broca's) area of the brain, indicating that they may be hearing something that is being internally produced (i.e., their own thoughts). It has therefore been hypothesized that these individuals may have some difficulty or impairment in the area of the brain that differentiates internal versus external stimuli.   – DGa

auditory illusion

n. Any perception in the sense of hearing which is not in accord with the physical stimuli. As instances, a hoot from a hidden speaker will be perceived as being from a stuffed owl located some distance away from the speaker, or stereophonic sound systems can be used to create an illusion of movement by varying the loudness and timing of the sounds from the two speakers.

auditory localization

n. The process of locating the source of sounds and their movements from acoustic cues.

auditory masking

n. A reduction in the ability to detect or discriminate characteristics of one sound by the presence of another sound. This is often measured in the decibel increase necessary in the target sound to be heard in the presence of a masking sound as opposed to hearing the target in silence.

auditory meatus

n. The auditory canal.

auditory ossicles

n. Little bones of the middle ear, which are the three smallest bones in the human body. The ossicles are named hammer (or malleus), anvil (or incus), and stirrup (or stapes), because of the shape of the bones. The hammer is attached to the tympanic membrane, whereas the stirrup is located in the oval window of the cochlea. When the tympanic membrane vibrates, the ossicles transmit the vibration to the fluid of the cochlea. Auditory ossicles act as a lever, providing a mechanical advantage. There are two muscles attached to the ossicles (tensor tympani and stapendius); their function seems to be related to protecting the inner ear in cases of excessive loudness.   – A A

auditory perception

n. Process of recognizing, interpreting, and providing meaning to auditory information. Disturbances in auditory perception are known as auditory agnosia (inability to recognize and understand auditory information in the absence of decreased auditory acuity for pure tones). Auditory perception supposes the ability to recognize and discriminate differences among sounds. Auditory perception for verbal information implies the ability to recognize functional language sounds (phonemes) and may be disturbed in cases of word deafness and Wernicke's aphasia. Nonverbal auditory agnosia may be found in cases of damage in the auditory association areas of the right hemisphere. Auditory perception requires ability to distinguish the relevant auditory signal from the auditory background (figure-background discrimination), referred to in the auditory system as signal-to-noise discrimination. Sometimes the relevant auditory signal is incomplete, and an auditory closure may occur. When fragments of the auditory information are presented, the fragments can blend to be perceived something significant; this phenomenon is known as auditory blending.   — A A

▶ *See also* **AUDITORY AGNOSIA, WERNICKE'S APHASIA,** *and* **WORD DEAFNESS**

auditory receptor
n. Hair cells in the inner ear are of two different types: inner hair cells, which are the auditory receptors, and outer hair cells, contributing to "tuning" the cochlea, though they also have a supporting role. Hair cells are located between the so-called tectorial and basilar membranes in the chamber known as scala media of the cochlea. The movement of the liquid inside the scala media (endolymph) as a result of the action of the ossicles of the middle ear causes a bending of the stereocilia (hairs) attached to the tectorial membrane. A receptor potential is generated and eventually may result in an action potential. The auditory information will be transmitted to the brain by the VIII cranial nerve (vestibulocochlear or auditory nerve).
                                               — A A

auditory spectrum
n. The range of normal hearing, which runs from about 20 Hz to about 20,000 Hz. However, the range of human speech, 250 Hz to 4,000 Hz, is heard much better than are extreme tones at either end of the spectrum.

augmenting principle
n. In attribution theory, the idea that if a person acts in a particular way in the face of risks, costs, or constraints for doing so, then the motivation for doing so must be higher than the inhibition caused by the costs, risks, and constraints.

aura
n. **1.** A subjective sensation of discomfort that frequently precedes migraine headaches and epileptic seizures. **2.** A distinctive quality of atmosphere or ambience that seems to project from someone or something. **3.** A subtle halo of energy that some claim surrounds all living things.

aural
adj. Related to sound perception.

aural harmonic
n. A concordance of tone generated by the physical limitations of the auditory system.

authoritarian
1. *adj.* Of or relating to a system of centralized political or social power that limits individual autonomy in favor of centralization of decision making usually hierarchical in structure. **2.** *n.* An individual who acts in an authoritarian manner, usually with herself/himself at or near the top of the decision hierarchy.

authoritarian character
n. A personality pattern characterized by preoccupation with power, control, and status and desire for adherence to a strict and simplistic code of values and behavior: enacting deference to those higher in the social hierarchy, expecting abject deference from those lower in the hierarchy, and characterized by excessive and irrational hostility toward those who deviate from or are outside the perceived social hierarchy.

authoritarianism
n. **1.** A personality pattern characterized by preoccupation with power, control, and status and desire for adherence to a strict and simplistic code of values and behavior: enacting deference to those higher in the social hierarchy, expecting abject deference from those lower in the hierarchy, and characterized by excessive and irrational hostility toward those who deviate from or are outside the perceived social hierarchy. **2.** Any organizational system or system of political belief in which individuals are subjected to wide restrictions under a strictly hierarchical organization.

authoritarian parents
n. Parents who have a parenting style of imposing unquestioning obedience on a child, avoiding dialog and reasoning with the child, ignoring or belittling the child's point of view, and focusing on punishment rather than reward or modeling as a means of guiding the child's behavior.

authoritarian personalities

n. In an ordinary dictionary – not a fine one like this – you will see that *authoritarian* has two main meanings. First, it means believing in submitting to authority. Second, it means being dictatorial or tyrannical. So people who strongly believe in submitting to authority could be called authoritarians. And so could tyrants who insist that everyone obey them – which is the sort of thing you usually get from tyrants.

Psychology is hot on the trail of understanding these two kinds of authoritarians. The submitters are called authoritarian followers, and we know a lot about them because researchers have been studying them since the Second World War. The aspiring tyrants are called social dominators and we do not know very much about them yet. You may wonder why. After all, a number of authoritarian dictators strutted across the global stage during World War II. Why didn't social scientists study their lot too? Mainly because, oddly enough, they aren't seen as being the basic problem. There will always be people around who lust after absolute power, and it is not hard to figure out why they want it. But these wannabes amount to nothing in a democracy unless a huge wave of supporters lifts them to power. That is why researchers have concentrated on the followers.

So who's out there doing the wave, and why would anybody want to elect a dictator?

Authoritarian followers have the psychological characteristic known as right-wing authoritarianism. This personality trait consists of authoritarian submission, a high degree of submission to the established authorities in one's society; authoritarian aggression, aggression directed against various persons in the name of those authorities; and conventionalism, a strong adherence to the social conventions endorsed by those authorities.

Why do psychologists call authoritarian followers "right-wing" authoritarians? Are they all members of a conservative political party? No. *Right-wing* is used here in a psychological sense, meaning wanting to please established authority. One of the original meanings of the adjective *right* (*riht* in Old English) was

"lawful, proper, correct," which in those long-ago days meant doing what your local lord and the king wanted. Conversely, you could have left-wing authoritarians who submit to a revolutionary authority, as Maoists in Western countries did in the 1970s. But you'd end up pretty lonely if you tried to organize a Maoist get-together in London or Washington these days.

Right-wing authoritarians, however, abound. Scientifically, they are identified by their scores on a personality test called (naturally enough) the Right-Wing Authoritarianism (RWA) scale. Here is a sample item from this measure: "'Our country desperately needs a mighty leader who will do what has to be done to destroy the radical new ways and sinfulness that are ruining us.' Do you agree or disagree with this statement?" Can you see that someone who strongly agrees with it is showing authoritarian submission, authoritarian aggression, and conventionalism? The other items on the RWA scale also try to assess these three inclinations in various ways.

What has the RWA scale shown us about authoritarian followers? In North America, where this research has mainly been done, persons who get high RWA scale scores quite readily submit to the established authorities in their lives and trust them far more than most people do. They supported Richard Nixon to the bitter end during the Watergate crisis. High RWAs also believed George W. Bush when he said Iraq had weapons of mass destruction, and they supported the war in that country long after others had signed off. High RWAs also are relatively willing to let authorities run roughshod over civil liberties and constitutional guarantees of personal freedom. They seem to think that authorities are above the law. They also hold authorities relatively blameless when the latter unjustly attack someone.

Speaking of attacks, right-wing authoritarians show a chilling inclination, compared to most people, to help the government persecute any group it targets. Also, if asked to play the role of judge, they will sentence convicted defendants to longer prison terms than most people will – unless the defendant is an authority or has attacked someone the authoritarian follower would like to see attacked. High RWAs favor capital punishment. As well, they deliver stronger electric shocks in "punishment" learning experiments. In general they believe that a good thrashing "works." But they also admit they get personal pleasure from punishing others and seeing wrongdoers get "what's coming to them." Finally, right-wing authoritarians tend to be highly prejudiced against most racial groups, feminists, homosexuals, people with different language backgrounds, and those with different religious views. Speaking of religion, the authoritarian follower's family religion produces a lot of his/her conventionalism. High RWAs tend to be fundamentalists in whatever religion they belong to, and fundamentalist churches are not shy about insisting everyone follow their beliefs about what is right, wrong, and normal. Those who walk other paths are often considered immoral and repugnant. Right-wing authoritarians also absorb the beliefs and teachings of the nonreligious authorities in their lives. This was well illustrated by a study that found high RWA American students in the late 1980s strongly believed America was the "Good Guy" during the ongoing Cold War, while high RWA Russian students thought the opposite. The authoritarians in both countries thus accepted, more than most of their fellow citizens did, the version of world events that their leaders presented.

Authoritarian followers thus appear to be, indeed, submissive, aggressive, and conventional. Further research with the RWA scale has uncovered a lot more about them, such as that they have weak reasoning skills and are gullible when people tell them what they want to hear; they fall back on dogmatism and social support when challenged, since they have little else to back up their beliefs; they are profoundly ethnocentric, identifying with their narrow in-groups, to which they give strong loyalty and in which they expect great cohesiveness; they are zealous in their causes and given to proselytizing; and they tend to be political and economic conservatives. "Deeper down," they use a lot of double standards in their judgments and often behave hypocritically; they are fearful and self-righteous, defensive, and unaware of themselves. Deep, deep down inside they seem to harbor secret doubts about the things they say they believe in most. So the picture of authoritarian followers after all these years of research is far from flattering – unless you are a potential dictator. If you are, these narrow-minded, closed-minded, easily fooled, zealous bigots looking for a man on horseback are exactly the kind of people you're looking for. Who are the potential dictators? Most of all, they seem to be power-hungry individuals who live their lives according to the law of the jungle.

They believe either you dominate others or you will be dominated instead. Thus they score high on the Social Dominance Orientation scale, which is the main way of identifying them. High dominators purposely make others afraid of them, believe in vengeance and using power however they must to get their way, and will try to crush whoever opposes them. They also tend to be believe that right and wrong do not matter at all, that people are objects to be manipulated, and that deceit and treachery are justified if they get you to the top. Authoritarian leaders have some traits in common with authoritarian followers. They too are highly prejudiced and favor conservative political parties and economic philosophies. But most social dominators are not really religious, and their amorality would turn off most high RWAs. However, a nonreligious but skilled social dominator has little difficulty persuading authoritarian followers that he/she shares their beliefs, and some social dominators are in fact religious and seem to have an especially good chance of heading an authoritarian movement. Experiments have found that when social dominators become leaders of groups of right-wing authoritarians, this "lethal union" produces aggression and exploitation in laboratory settings – just as it does in the real world.

– BA

authoritative parents

n. Parents who have a collaborative approach to guiding their child which simultaneously encourages the child's autonomy and provides clear limits on the child's behavior, usually through a process of explaining and reasoning with the child. In achievement situations they set high levels of aspirations and at the same time provide support to meet them.

autism
n. A pervasive developmental disorder of early childhood characterized by impaired social learning and communication; restricted interests, activities, and learning; diminished imaginative thought; and stereotyped or repetitive nonfunctional movements or verbalizations. The usual age of onset is before age 3 and the symptoms can vary across an individual childhood and are usually associated with some intellectual retardation.

autistic
n., adj. Characterized by impaired social learning and communication, restricted interests, diminished imaginative thought, and stereotyped or repetitive nonfunctional movements or verbalizations.

autobiographical memory
n. A vivid form of episodic memory about one's personal past experiences often characterized by a sense of meaning, clarity of details, and a sense of certainty of accuracy, the latter of which has not been supported by research findings.

autochthonization
n. The process of making something indigenous to an individual or culture. In psychology the process involves selecting research and theoretical processes and variables that emanate from a culture, adequately represent that culture's point of view, and finally reflect upon the findings within the context of the culture.

autochthonous psychology
n. Psychology from the point of view of the internal processes of an individual or a culture, as opposed to the imposition of an extraneous psychology on a culture different from the one in which the psychology originated. There has been a recognition within the field of anthropology and cross-cultural psychology that analysis of a culture from the

point of view of another culture often misses or does not properly assess the importance of many aspects of human life and culture.

autocorrelation
n. The tendency of repeated measures of the same thing over time to correlate. As an example, the pain rating of a person with arthritis taken at noon of one day tends to be correlated with the pain rating at noon on other days.

autocratic leadership
n. Leadership that is self-centered, arrogant, overcontrolling, and not permitting of dissent.

autoerotic
adj. Of or relating to sexual stimulation of one's own body, or masturbation.

autoeroticism
n. **1.** Any form of sexual self-stimulation, whether masturbation, fantasy, or stimulation of body parts other than the genitals for sexual pleasure. **2.** Sexual desire for one's own body. **3.** In psychoanalysis, the infantile form of sexuality in which desires are gratified without an external object.

autogenic training
n. Relaxation training in which the individual learns to relax through imagining and focusing on a sense of heaviness and warmth in the limbs, the pulse, warmth in the abdomen and chest, and a coolness in the forehead. The goal is to reduce stress and learn to control stress so as to control anxiety and increase performance.

autohypnosis
n. Any self-induced trance or trancelike state in which the individual is very suggestible, including self-suggestion. Also called self-hypnosis.

autokinetic effect
n. This is a well-documented perceptual phenomenon. In a darkened room, or under other circumstances in which a visual point of reference is unavailable (such as looking at a single

star through a paper cylinder), a stationary light will appear to move. Psychologists attribute the apparent movement to some combination of involuntary eye movement and the necessity of visual reference points for perception of movement. The autokinetic effect has been used to demonstrate social influence: participants' estimates of the movement of the light will vary greatly, depending on estimates provided by prior participants. For example, if a participant observes the autokinetic effect and hears prior estimates of either (1) 1 foot or (2) 5 feet, the participants' estimate of the light's movement will generally be higher in condition 2 as compared to condition 1.
– MWP

automatic anxiety

n. In psychoanalysis, the fear of an infant upon experiencing its helplessness to care for its own needs or the re-experience of this anxiety by an older child in a situation in which he or she is helpless.

automaticity

n. The characteristic of requiring no conscious attention or effort in performing some act or task.

automatic process

n. Any mental process that occurs involuntarily and without conscious awareness or intervention.

automatic processing

n. Mental processing that occurs without consciousness or effort such as recognizing one's face in a mirror.

automatic thought

n. **1.** In cognitive therapy, habitual thoughts that occur so rapidly that they are barely conscious and that guide a person's mood, attentional focus, and actions, often without the person's realizing that they are doing so. Becoming conscious of these thoughts allows a person to change them to more accurate ones which are better guides to feeling, thinking, and acting. **2.** Thoughts that have been so well learned that they no longer take conscious effort or attention.

automatic writing

n. Writing that occurs without conscious effort or attention, as sometimes happens in a hypnotic or other trance. Hypnotherapists sometimes use it as a therapeutic technique for self-discovery.

autonomic

adj. Of or relating to the autonomic nervous system.

autonomic arousal disorder

n. A disorder characterized by persistent or frequently recurring episodes of inappropriate actions in systems usually controlled by the autonomic nervous system such as heart palpitations, nausea, excessive sweating, or hyperventilation.

autonomic nervous system

n. (ANS) Literally, the system of self-knowledge. ANS is a division of the body's neural systems which has the role of regulating involuntary activity of the glands, internal organs including the heart, and the smooth muscles of the vasculature. The ANS's multiple, well-coordinated effects are slow and widespread, operating through an extensive network of neurons.

The ANS is divided into two major divisions. The action of each division tends to be opposite the other division's in direction, moving toward physiological balance, or equilibrium. The sympathetic nervous system (SNS) tends toward catabolism, the expenditure of energy, whereas the parasympathetic system tends toward anabolism, the storage of energy. Central nervous system (CNS) activity monitors ANS activity, so that when one of the divisions of the ANS is actively stimulated, the other division is less active, thus encouraging clarity of response to autonomic stimulation.

There is also an enteric division of the ANS in the lining of the esophagus, stomach, and intestinal region, which controls the transport and digestion of food in the digestive tract.

The ANS was once considered to be self-regulating, and not subject to conscious cognitive influence. Extensive biofeedback studies have demonstrated, however, that several autonomic functions, such as blood pressure and brain wave activity, can be modified by the CNS through cognitive processes.

– vs

autonomous

adj. Free of outside control; independent and self-determined. Excessive focus on self-determination is a risk factor for depression.

autonomous work groups

n. Small task groups within a larger organization that have the capacity to set their own agenda and decide upon their own organization and procedures for accomplishing their assigned tasks.

autonomy

n. Freedom from outside control; having independence and self determination.

autonomy, functional

n. The tendency for ideas or habits to become independent of their origin. As an example, if one forms the habit of brushing one's teeth to escape parental reprimand as a child, then, by the time one is in middle age, brushing one's teeth is likely to be independent of parental evaluation and to have its own motivational force and place in the individual's intellectual organization.

autonomy versus shame and doubt

n. The possible outcomes of Erik Erikson's second, muscular-anal, stage of epigenetic development in which a child must learn to control herself/himself in ways which are both personally satisfying and socially acceptable. If he/she succeeds in general in these tasks, then he/she develops a sense of autonomy, or being able to choose one's course of action for one's self. On the other hand, if he/she fails, then he/she feels shamed and doubts her/his capacity to choose her/his own course of action and tends to fall back on rule governed behavior so as to forestall being shamed.

autopsy, psychological

n. A postmortem examination of the possible causes of a person's death and especially if suicide is an issue; it consists of examining evidence from a person's recent life such as notes, letters, e-mails, behavior patterns, and interviews of witnesses.

autoreceptor

n. A chemical messenger in the presynaptic membrane of a synapse that reacts to neurotransmitters and conveys information about the level of neurotransmitter in the synaptic cleft.

autoshaping

n. A method of establishing an operant response to a signal by automatically reinforcing the response when it occurs in the presence of or shortly after a signal. This process only works when establishing a connection between a naturally occurring behavior and a species-appropriate signal.

autosome

n. Any of the 22 pairs of chromosomes that are not sex chromosomes.

autostereotype

n. A stereotype about a group one belongs to which one includes in one's self-concept.

autotopagnosia

n. Inability to name, recognize, or point on command to parts of the body. Patients have significant difficulty in localizing and naming body parts, not only of their body, but also of the examiner's body, a doll's, or a representation of the human body. A discrepancy between the ability to point to and name external objects and body parts is observed. Rarely, this defect is found without any other aphasic manifestation.

Patients seem to understand the name of the body part, but they fail in finding where specific body parts are located. Sometimes, they present an approximate answer: that is, they look for the eyes in the head, not in the trunk. Occasionally, they fail in finding the body part but can point to it correctly if it is named by another person.

Different hypotheses have been proponed to explain this syndrome: (**1**) there is a language defect restricted to the conceptualization of the body parts, (**2**) there is an impairment in the spatial representation of the body, (3) considering that sometimes patients also have difficulties in pointing to and naming parts of objects, it has been suggested that there is a global defect in the perceptual integration of elements in a whole.

Autotopagnosia is usually correlated with left hemisphere lesions, particularly posterior parietal damage, but has been also observed in cases of extensive bilateral lesions. Autotopagnosia is frequently associated with signs of the Gerstmann syndrome, or angular gyrus syndrome (acalculia, agraphia, disorders in right-left orientation, and finger agnosia)   – A A

availability heuristic
n. An inferred mental strategy of judging the relative frequency of an event by the ease with which such an event can be called to mind. This strategy is often called a bias as it is easily biased by such features as the recency of exposure to one kind of event or emotional vividness of some events.

average deviation
n. The arithmetic mean of a set of deviations that is the sum of a set of deviations divided by the number of deviations. This statistic is seldom used as in many data sets it is near zero and so is minimally informative as to the distribution from which it arises. Statisticians prefer the standard deviation, which is the square root of the average of the squared deviations.

average error method
n. A method of measuring sensory threshold for differences in which a sensory signal is adjusted until it is perceived as the same as a standard. The difference between the signal and the standard is the error in adjustment, and threshold for differences is calculated as the median of errors in adjustment. Also known as the method of adjustment.

average evoked potential
n. The average amplitude of a number of evoked potentials from the same stimulus over time used in order to reduce the effect of noise in the measurement system.

average linkage between groups method
n. A method of cluster analysis in which the distance between clusters is defined as the average of the distance between all possible pairs of cases from each group.

average linkage within groups method
n. A method of cluster analysis which uses the least average distance within clusters as a criterion for assigning cases to a cluster; distance between clusters is defined as the average distance between all possible cases were the clusters to be combined.

averaging model
n. Any mathematical model which uses the average of past observations to predict future observation. Linear regression is a commonly used averaging model.

aversion
n. A turning away, repugnance, or dislike for something.

aversion conditioning
n. A form of classical conditioning used as behavior therapy in which an unpleasant stimulus is paired with the behavior one wishes to extinguish. Thus one might pair an electric shock with lighting a cigarette in order to reduce the likelihood of smoking.

aversion therapy
n. A form of classical conditioning used as behavior therapy in which an unpleasant stimulus is paired with the behavior one wishes to extinguish. Thus one might pair an electric shock with lighting a cigarette in order to reduce the likelihood of smoking.

aversive
adj. Tending to repel, disgust, or dissuade.

aversive behavior
n. Reactions to aversive stimuli, which are usually discussed as escape learning, avoidance learning, and punishment.

aversive conditioning
n. A general term which describes the process of learning to react to noxious stimuli. Escape

learning, avoidance learning, and punishment are the three major categories of aversive conditioning.

aversive control

n. A general term for situations in which aversive conditioning is the basis for observed behavior.

aversive stimulus

n. Any stimulus which is repellent, disgusting, painful, or otherwise noxious to the organism and which can be used to punish or to condition escape or avoidance behavior.

avoidance-avoidance conflict

n. The difficulty in deciding on a course of action in a situation in which the two possible choices are both associated with aversive stimuli. One of three kinds of decision making conflict in social cognition; the others are approach-approach and approach-avoidance conflicts.

avoidance conditioning

n. An operant conditioning technique involving the removal of a noxious stimulus (negative reinforcement) when a desired behavior is emitted which increases the likelihood of the behavior's being repeated in the future.

avoidance gradient

n. A graph of the variation of the strength of an aversive stimulus to motivate avoidance or escape behavior across distance. Avoidance gradients are generally steeper than approach gradients; thus aversive conditioning is more powerful when the noxious stimulus is close but approach gradients reach farther.

avoidant/insecure attachment

n. A pattern of attachment by an infant to a caregiver in which the infant does not feel comforted by the caregiver's presence, does not seek out contact with the caregiver in times of stress, and does not experience an increase in anxiety upon separation from the caregiver.

avoidant personality

n. A pervasive and persistent pattern of individual adjustment in which the individual avoids social contact though desiring it, is oversensitive to criticism and rejection, longs for uncritical acceptance, and has low self-esteem.

avoidant personality disorder

n. The avoidant personality disorder is one of the 10 personality disorders described on Axis-II of the DSM-IV-TR, published by the American Psychiatric Association as their official diagnostic and descriptive nomenclature of mental disorders. The avoidant personality disorder is characterized by a pervasive pattern of social inhibition, feelings of inadequacy, and hypersensitivity to negative evaluation, starting by early adulthood and manifested in a variety of contexts. Central to the notion of personality disorders (in general) is that they are inflexible, maladaptive, and persisting and cause significant functional impairment or subjective distress. The avoidant personality disorder seriously affects social and professional functioning.

Symptoms (DSM-IV-TR) are (a) avoidance of interpersonal activities due to fear of rejection and criticism; (b) unwillingness to get involved with people, except when certain of being liked and accepted, and as a result often being isolated; (c) preoccupation with criticism or rejection in social situations; (d) feelings of inadequacy in new social situations manifested in inhibitedness and social fear; (e) feelings of inferiority, of being personally unappealing, and of social isolation; and (f) reluctance to take personal risks or to engage in any new activities, fearing embarrassment. Individuals have to display four or more of these symptoms in order to be diagnosed as avoidant.

The prevalence rate for avoidant personality disorder is estimated to be less than 1% in community samples, and about 10% in individuals consulting mental health services. Avoidant personality disorder is diagnosed equally frequently in males and females.

— FDF

avolition

n. The inability or lack of desire to engage in goal-directed or motivated activities. Avolition is a common negative symptom in schizophrenia.   – DGa

awareness, learning without

n. Learning which takes place without the subject's conscious awareness of the matters which have been learned. This is a controversial field in which learning is inferred from behavior change of which the subject is unaware or which the subject is unable to explain. ▶ *See also* **IMPLICIT LEARNING**

axiom

n. An assertion which is taken as self-evidently true and which is not capable of being proved or disproved. A classical example is the Euclidean axiom that one and only one straight line can be drawn between any two points.

axon

n. The tubular part of a nerve cell which normally carries impulses away from the cell body.

axonal transport

n. The process of moving molecules along an axon back to the cell body or out from the cell body to the dendritic terminals. Also called axoplasmic flow.

axon hillock

n. The roughly conical bump on a nerve cell body from which the axon extends. Nerve impulses begin with a depolarization of the axon hillock, which, when it reaches a critical threshold, begins a wave of depolarization along the axon.

babble

n. Prespeech sound such as *mamama* or *dadada* made by infants beginning at about the age of 6 months which is mainly composed of sounds the infant hears that are included in the language(s) of its caregivers and generally lacks sounds that are not in the caregivers' language(s) but are in some other languages.

babbling

n. Babbling is one of the landmark developmental stages in first language acquisition. During the first 6 months of life, infants engage in prebabbling behavior, their vocalizations essentially consisting of coos and gurgles, perhaps including sounds (e.g., raspberries) that do not exist in natural languages. At approximately 6 months of age, vocalizations take on a more deliberate character as infants enter the babbling stage. Characteristic of early babbling is the production of multiple repetitions of reduplicated syllables, like [dada], uttered with sentence-like intonation. The segments are usually stop consonants plus the low central vowel, [a]. Advanced babblers produce sequences in which the consonants are more varied, such as [bada baga]. Babbling is a developmental stage that all infants go through, even infants acquiring a sign language, in which case the babbling is performed gesturally rather than vocally. Infants do not babble to communicate; rather, babbling marks a stage during which infants appear to be at play with the phonemic and prosodic building blocks of the language they are acquiring. At around 12 months of age, vocalizations begin to be used meaningfully as the infants' first words emerge and the transition from babbling to the one-word stage takes place.   – EMF

Babinski reflex

n. Also referred to as the plantar response, the Babinski reflex is a newborn reflex whereby the stimulation of the sole of the foot from heel to base of the toes (or vice versa) causes the newborn's toes to fan and curl. This reflex gives an indication of neurological functioning and should disappear within the first few months. If the Babinski reflex is seen in an older child or adult, it is taken as a sign of a problem with the central nervous system. — SRB

baby talk ▶ *See* MOTHERESE

back channel response
n. Any short utterance such as *uh-huh*, *yeah*, or *right* produced while the other person in a conversation is speaking which indicates attentiveness, does not interrupt the other person, and does not require acknowledgment by the other person. These typically account for one-fifth or more of all utterances in American English and differ greatly among languages and cultures. Linguistically or culturally inappropriate back channel responses or a lack of such responses contributes significantly to difficulties in cross-cultural communication.

back translation
n. A back translation is a translation, back into the original, of a text that had been previously translated into a language other than the original by translators independently of those who translated the original. Comparison of the back translation with the original version is informative regarding the degree of equivalence between texts in two languages. Back translation is sometimes used as a technique in discourse analysis, particularly in research on cross-cultural differences in discourse. It is also used as a technique to validate or improve upon an existing translation. — EMF

backward association
n. An association formed by presenting a neutral stimulus after an unconditioned stimulus. This seldom results in the formation of an association as the order of presentation prevents the neutral stimulus from having any signal value for the organism.

backward conditioning
n. A learning procedure in which a neutral stimulus is presented after an unconditioned stimulus. This seldom results in formation of an association as the order of presentation prevents the neutral stimulus from having any signal value for the organism.

backward masking
n. Backward masking is a form of masking in which the target (i.e., a to-be-identified item) temporally precedes that mask stimulus (an image, a tone, or a chemical). The mask can occur immediately after the target or after a delay. The difficulty in one's ability to perceive the target in this situation is referred to as the masking effect. This effect is influenced by the interval between the presentation of the mask and target, the location of the mask and target relative to each other (e.g., whether two images are superimposed or not), the intensity of the mask and target (e.g., the brightness of a letter), as well as other characteristics (e.g., direction of the line segments). All else being equal, masking is generally stronger as the interval between the presentation of the mask and that of the target is reduced.

An example of backward masking: in general, the participant is asked to look at the center of a computer screen and identify words that appear in that location. As the participant focuses on the screen, a word occurs (e.g., *bird*), followed either immediately or after a short delay (e.g., 0.1 second or 100 milliseconds) by a mask (e.g., &&&&). The presence of the ampersand pattern in the same location as the word makes it difficult for the participant to perceive two separate images; instead the two images become intermixed. The intermixing of the mask and target images makes identifying the word more difficult than if the mask had not occurred. This sequence of events is an example of backward masking in the visual domain. — DGr
▶ *See also* MASKING

balanced bilingual
n. A term used to describe an individual who has the same fluency in two languages, typically with native fluency and proficiency in both. Fluency and proficiency may be assessed using standardized measures for language aptitude and language ability. The balanced bilingual can typically function equally well in most situations in his or her two languages. Proficiency would be similar

in all skills including reading, writing, and speaking. This term also describes an individual who can communicate effectively and efficiently in two languages. Few bilinguals are equally competent in two languages in all areas of language processing.   – JA

▶ *See also* **BILINGUAL, BILINGUALISM**

balance theory

n. A theory in social cognition in which people are noted to create and be comfortable with cognitive systems which are internally consistent according to a triangular logic. In this logic if two sides of a relationship triangle are negative, the other must be positive, and if two sides are positive, the third must also be positive. Thus if A hates B and B hates C, then A will tend to like C – the enemies of my enemies are my friends. And if X likes Y and Y likes Z, then X will also tend to like Z – the friends of my friends are also my friends. The relationship also works for person–inanimate object relationships so that if Jeff likes modern art and Mulan likes Jeff, then Mulan will tend to like modern art. ▶ *See also* **COGNITIVE DISSONANCE**

bandwagon effect

n. In social psychology and political science, an accelerating tendency of more and more individuals to join in the behavior of some members of a group when they perceive the new behaviors will serve their interests.

barber's pole effect

n. The illusion that a cylinder with spiral markings, such as a barber's pole, appears to be moving up or down as it rotates in place.

Bard-Cannon theory ▶ *See* **CANNON-BARD THEORY**

Barnum effect

n. The tendency of people to believe vague and general predictions or comments about them are both true and unique. This has been used to explain the persistent popularity of astrology and the predictions of seers such as Nostradamus.

baroreceptor

n. Pressure-sensitive nerve cell in the heart and large arteries that sends impulses toward the hypothalamus when blood pressure drops, which sometimes results in a sensation of thirst and/or the release of angiotensisn II, which tends to raise blood pressure.

basal forebrain

n. The area at the bottom of the forebrain near the hypothalamus which includes the nucleus basalis, diagonal band, medial septum, and substantia innaminata, which produces acetylcholine and is important in the regulation of sleep and in brain plasticity and memory. Damage to this area often results in memory loss and confabulation in older persons.

basal ganglia

n. Three pairs of nuclei at the base of the cerebral cortex including the caudate nuclei, putamen, and globus pallidus with connections to the motor cortex and the brainstem which control voluntary movement and posture.

basal metabolic rate

n. The average minimal expenditure of energy of a body awake and at rest. It is measured after fasting a minimum of 12 hours in kilocalories of heat per square meter of skin.

baseline

n. The average of a variable over time before any experimental intervention; it is used to compare with averages after intervention so as to gauge the effect of the intervention.

base rate

n. The naturally occurring frequency or average of a variable in a population within a given period. This rate is often used to compare with a different period in which it is supposed some factor is affecting the rate of the variable.

basic emotions

n. The basic emotion theory claims that there is a core set of emotions, referred to as basic emotions, which evolved to aid in fundamental life tasks. According to this theory, the basic emotions are more likely to be found across cultures and in various species relative to other types of emotions. Paul Ekman suggests nine characteristics that distinguish basic emotions from other affective phenomena: distinctive universal signals; distinctive physiology; distinctive universals in antecedent events; distinctive developmental appearance; distinctive thoughts, memories, and images; distinctive subjective experience; automatic appraisal; presence in other primates; quick onset, brief duration, and unbidden occurrence. According to research findings, the well-established basic emotions are anger, disgust, enjoyment, fear, sadness, and surprise.   – LMB

basic level category

n. A grouping in a natural language system at the level of abstraction at which category members share the most similarity within the category and are the most distinct from other available categories. Using a word at the basic level conveys more information to a native speaker of the language than would a word for a category at a higher or lower level of abstraction. Thus the word *bird* conveys more information about category members than would a more general word such as *animal* while a more particular word such as *robin* indicates fewer differences from other available categories such as *blue jay* or *parakeet*. Languages tend to use shorter words for the basic level than other levels of categories, and they are more easily learned and more rapidly recognized than are words for other levels of abstraction. As languages increase the number of words they contain, they tend first to develop words for categories at the basic level of abstraction, then at higher or lower levels of abstraction.

basic mistrust

n. Failure to establish a belief in the possibility of satisfying relationships in the first, oral-sensory, of Erik Erikson's eight epigenetic stages of the growth of the self. Basic mistrust leads to social withdrawal and despair. Mistrust-trust is not an all-or-none phenomenon, and infants with complete mistrust tend to die or lack contact with reality while those

with predominant mistrust with a little admixture of trust tend to be shy, hypersensitive to rejection, and suspicious. Infants develop a mistrust of the world when there is a failure of their efforts to interact with the world to produce significant need satisfaction, as when they are severely neglected.

basic needs

n. In Maslow's hierarchy of needs the basic needs are physiological ones such as needs for oxygen, heat, food, water, and bodily safety.

basic research

n. Utilization of the scientific method to discover knowledge for the pure advancement of understanding with no immediate goals concerning the practical application of information. The driving goal behind basic research is knowledge for the sake of knowledge. Basic research is fundamental in the development and advancement of theories. For example, a basic research question might be "Which neurological processes are involved in the process of forgetting?" While knowledge gained through basic research may provide the foundation for practical, applied investigations, the purpose of basic research is simple discovery.   – BJM

basic trust

n. A belief in the possibility of need satisfying relationships attained during the first, oral-sensory, stage in Erik Erikson's epigenetic growth of the self. Trust leads to hope that needs can be met even if temporarily frustrated and so gives emotional strength to the ego's plans for the future.

basic trust versus basic mistrust

n. The first of Erik Erikson's eight stages of psychosocial development, this stage, which occurs in the first year of life, sets the foundation of human growth and development. Newborns and infants by their nature are solely dependent upon the adults around them to care for their every need. If the responses infants experience involve consistent, nurturing meeting of their needs, they will learn to develop a sense of trust and security. When needs are not consistently met, infants will learn a sense of mistrust. Erikson does not speak in all-or-nothing terms; in fact, he suggests that the ideal is a proper equilibrium between trust and mistrust, which will allow for the development of hope. Ultimately Erikson saw hope as an ego strength that consists of openness to experiences in combination with caution toward danger. 　 – SRB

basilar membrane

n. The fibrous membrane on the organ of Corti in the inner ear, which vibrates with changes in air pressure waves, stimulating the hair cells inside the organ of Corti, which send impulses toward the auditory cortex. Different sound frequencies cause the membrane to swell at different points along its approximate 34-mm length, and the points of maximal swelling determine the pitch of the sound heard.

basking in reflected glory

n. The universal human tendency to feel good when one can associate one's self with persons or groups with high prestige.

battered child

n. A child who has been physically abused, usually in a serious or prolonged manner.

battered child syndrome

n. A constellation of physical and behavioral symptoms characteristic of children who have been physically abused. Physical symptoms include bruises, cuts, burns, bone fractures, and internal injuries. Behavioral symptoms include social withdrawal, fearfulness, anxiety, emotional flatness, inability to concentrate, constipation or encopresis, and lack of appetite.

battered wife syndrome

n. A theoretical term for a large constellation of nonspecific mental and behavioral symptoms associated with prolonged abuse by a spouse. Symptoms include a pervasive sense of helplessness, low self-esteem, blaming self for the abuse, belief in the omniscience and omnipresence of the abuser, headaches, generalized anxiety, difficulty in concentrating, insomnia, hypervigilance, and exaggerated startle response. Battered wife syndrome has not been included in the DSM-IV-TR as its symptoms are too varied and unpredictable to be diagnosable in a consistent manner. The diagnosis of post-traumatic stress disorder is most often given to women who suffer psychopathology after having been battered.

Bayesian inference

n. Statistical inference based on Bayes' theorem which uses observation to estimate probabilities of related conditional events.

Bayes' theorem

n. In statistics, a formal expression of the probability that one event will occur, given that another event occurs when the usual probabilities of the events are known. In written form, the probability of any event A given the occurrence of another event B, $P(A/B)$, is given by the formula

$$P(A/B) = \frac{P(B/A)\,P(A)}{P(B)}$$

where $P(A)$ is the prior probability of event A, $P(B)$ is the prior probability of event B, and $P(B/A)$ is the prior probability of event B given the occurrence of event A.

Bayley Scales of Infant Development

n. A widely used set of scales to measure child development from birth to $3\frac{1}{2}$ years of age with mental, motor, and behavioral scales. The mental scales combine tests of memory, perception, and learning. The motor scale measures gross and fine motor movements such as crawling, sitting, grasping, and manipulation of objects. The behavioral scales measure attention and arousal, orientation and engagement, emotional engagement, and quality of movements.

Beck Depression Inventory

n. (BDI II) A self-report inventory for persons over the age of 13 years consisting of 21 multiple-choice items reflecting the severity of cognitive and somatic symptoms of depression described in the DSM-IV-TR and in Aaron Beck's books on depression. The BDI II is one of the most widely used measures of depression in the world, having been translated into several languages and used in many countries with the popularity of Beck's theories of the cognitive nature of depression.

bedwetting

n. The discharge of urine during sleep. Bedwetting normally occurs until a child's bladder grows enough to be able to hold the urine produced during the hours of sleep, normally by 3 to 5 years of age. Bedwetting after the age of 5 is usually due either to a physical problem with the urinary system or to a failure to attend to sensory signals that the bladder is full during sleep.

behavior

n. All the activities that living organisms exhibit. Some research strategies limit the definition of behavior to those fitting a priori categories which may be more or less well defined.

behavioral

adj. Of or relating to the activities of an organism, most commonly used to describe the gross behavior of animals such as rats, pigeons, and human beings.

behavioral assessment

n. A research methodology designed to examine a target behavior critically with consideration of the environmental antecedents and consequences that serve to produce and maintain the behavior. While assessment is often based on direct observation of a target behavior, researchers may also integrate interviews, rating scales, or environmental manipulations to gain a comprehensive understanding of the specified behavior. Evolving from work in applied behavior analysis, functional behavior assessments are often used in educational settings to gain a better understanding of the cause of a student's problematic behavior so that effective interventions can be introduced to elicit behavioral change. When conducting behavioral assessments, researchers must be cautious about the accuracy of true scores versus observed scores: in essence, concerns over potential human error or bias in the monitoring and recording of behavioral data.   – BJM

behavioral contagion

n. A quick copying of behavior of a few individuals by those nearby which spreads as a wave among a group often with little conscious reflection by the copiers. This usually occurs when a new behavior is performed by high-status individuals and is seen as immediately responsive to unmet needs of individuals in the group.

behavioral contrast

n. **1.** A pattern of response to reward such that if an organism is given a small reward for a particular response, if the reward is subsequently increased, the rate or intensity of the response is increased to a greater level than if the greater reward is given from the start. Or it can be a lessened rate or intensity of response after reward for a response is lessened. **2.** In clinical practice, an increase of a behavior in a nontreatment setting as it decreases in the treatment setting. Thus if a treatment works at school, it may lead to an increase in the response at home.

behavioral ecology

n. The study of the relationships between environment and the behavior of the organisms within it within the general framework of evolution. Thus it includes studies of the ways individuals and groups adapt their behavior with changes of environment as well as uses of environmental resources.

behavioral endocrinology

n. The interdisciplinary study of relationships among overt behavior, the production and excretion of hormones by the endocrine glands, and the functioning of nerves in the endocrine glands.

behavioral inhibition

n. The restraint of tendencies to act along with environmental monitoring. As a temperament, this refers to individuals who are timid, shy, withdrawing, and fearful; who tend to experience negative emotions at a higher rate than normal; and who do not explore the world around them actively.

behavioral intervention

n. An alteration of the contingencies of reinforcement so as to bring about a desired alteration in behavior.

behaviorally anchored rating scales

n. A behavior-based rating of job performance in which it is behaviorally described systematically from behavior consistent with lower levels of job performance to behavior consistent with high levels of job performance. The rater compares the individual's behaviors with the descriptions of different levels of job performance and selects the one that best describes his or her performance.

behavioral medicine

n. A multidisciplinary field including physicians, nurses, social workers, psychologists, counselors, dieticians, and others who examine the relationships between behavior and health outcomes and work to integrate the biological, social, and psychological dimensions of health care.

behavioral modeling

n. **1.** A therapeutic approach in which desired behavior is modeled for a client who learns vicariously to use the behavior in his/her own life. **2.** A teaching technique in which adults model appropriate behavior for children, who learn by imitation.

behavioral science

n. Any of the social sciences that attempt to study and understand behavior.

behavioral toxicology

n. The study of the behavioral changes brought about by exposure to toxic substances. The field has been growing in importance as evidence that subtoxic levels of many substances bring about significant changes in behavior. Lead is the best example as low levels of lead have been found to be related to impulsivity and aggression in children and particularly in boys, as well to lowered reading and math scores and lower overall IQ scores for both boys and girls.

behavior analysis

n. The observation and modification of behavior through environmental manipulation so as to produce more socially adaptive behavior. Behavior analysis is usually an application of learning techniques to improving the social behavior of autistic or similarly handicapped persons.

behavior contract

n. A behavior modification option whereby a student makes a formal written agreement with the therapist, educator, parent, or another interested party to attempt to reach a particular goal related to a specific target behavior. Usually the contract is created with the help of the child, and the goal, the possible reinforcers, and the criteria for reinforcement are all mutually agreed upon. The contract should include a clear definition of the target behavior, as well as the positive consequences of meeting that goal and/or the negative consequences of failure to emit the target behavior. The contract should be clear about what adult and child are expected to do, and it should include a plan for maintaining the desired behavior. The contract is written, and both the adult and the child sign the contract. The idea is that this formal document will help motivate the child to change, as he/she has officially signed a commitment to reaching this particular goal.   – EF

behavior contrast

n. **1.** A pattern of response to reward such that if an organism is given a small reward for a particular response, if the reward is subsequently increased, the rate or intensity of the response is increased to a greater level than if the greater reward is given from the start. Or a lessened rate or intensity of response may occur after reward for a response is lessened. **2.** In clinical practice, an increase of a behavior in a nontreatment setting as it decreases in the treatment setting. Thus if a treatment works at school, it may lead to an increase in the response at home.

behavior control

n. **1.** A field of study and practice within child psychology that examines maladaptive child behavior and its relationships with adult behavior. **2.** Learning approaches to modification of one's own behavior.

behavior genetics

n. The study of the heredity of behavior patterns in humans and other animals using a multidisciplinary approach which includes ethology, molecular biology, and modern genetics among other disciplines.

behaviorism

n. An approach to psychology which limits itself to a description of relationships between observable environmental events and ensuing observable behavior of organisms in the environment. Typically behaviorism rejects subjective experience as a proper topic of study and resists explanations of observable acts in terms of inferred but unobservable mental processes.

behaviorist

n. A person who adopts a learning approach to social and psychological problems limiting himself or herself to a description of easily observable behavior and environmental circumstances and the links between them.

behavioristic

adj. Of or like a behavioral approach.

behavior modification

n. Application of operant conditioning principles to individual cases. This has been applied primarily in schools in the United States with students described as having behavioral problems, developmental delays, and autism.

behavior setting

n. In ecological psychology, the interaction of social, physical, and ecological situations with behavior.

behavior therapy

n. The use of classical and operant conditioning principles to bring about therapeutic change. Techniques of behavior therapy include systematic desensitization, flooding, biofeedback, aversion therapy, shaping, and token economies. Behavior therapy has been particularly successful in treating phobias.

beliefs

n. A belief is a proposition that is regarded as true. A belief may be factually correct ("The world is round") or incorrect ("The Earth is the center of the universe"). Two main distinctions are made regarding beliefs: dispositional versus occurrent beliefs and implicit versus explicit ones. Dispositional beliefs refer to beliefs about an enduring property that remains unchanged across time and situations (e.g., "Birds of feather flock together"), whereas occurrent beliefs refer to beliefs about a temporary state of being (e.g., "I believe she was upset"). Explicit beliefs refer to those for which the mind has a coherent mental representation, whereas implicit beliefs are those that are not coherently represented in the mind and may be difficult to communicate.   – EWMA, CYC

▶ *See also* **IMPLICIT THEORIES** *and* **LAY THEORIES**

belladonna

n. Atropine or hyoscyamine, both of which are derived from deadly nightshade plant. They were used in medieval times as a beauty aid as one of their effects is to enlarge the pupils of the eyes, a feature which was considered particularly attractive in medieval Italy. *Bella donna* is Italian for "beautiful woman."

bell curve

n. The graphical representation of a normal distribution which appears as a unimodal (single-peak), symmetrical curve that resembles a bell. In a bell curve, the majority of scores are in the middle of the distribution and fewer scores near the ends of the distribution (however, the tails of the distribution are infinite and the base of the bell is never complete); this pattern is responsible for producing the familiar bell shape. While the area under a bell curve is always constant (equal to 1), the height and spread of the curve vary as a mathematical function of the mean and standard deviation. The mean provides the midpoint for the peak of the curve and the standard deviation tells how tightly the data is clustered around the mean. When the standard deviation is small, the bell-shaped curve is steep; when the standard deviation is large, the bell curve is relatively flat. The x-axis of the bell curve is the horizontal dimension; the x-axis pertains to the value in question. The y-axis is the vertical dimension and accounts for the number of data points for each value on the *x*-axis.   – BJM

Bellevue-Wechsler scales ▶ *See* **WECHSLER-BELLEVUE SCALES**

Bell-Magendie law
n. The observation that motor neurons have their roots in the ventral or front side of the spinal column while sensory neurons have their roots in the dorsal or back side of the spinal column.

Bell's palsy
n. Paralysis due to problems with one of the seventh pair of cranial (facial) nerves, which control muscle movement in the face. Usual symptoms include partial or total paralysis of one side of the face, an inability to close the eye or mouth, distorted facial expressions, and partial loss of the sense of taste. Bell's palsy is usually due to viral infection which causes swelling which compresses the nerve, and recovery is usually spontaneous but takes several months. It commonly affects only one side of the face.

Bem Sex Role Inventory
n. (BSRI) A measure of masculine and feminine sex roles which adopts the point of view that sex roles are two independent positive social coping strategies. Because they are independent an individual can be above average on both, above average on only one, or below average on both. Persons who are above average on both are designated androgynous, those high on only one are designated masculine or feminine as appropriate, and those below average on both are designated as undifferentiated.

Bender Gestalt Test
n. A test in which subjects copy nine line drawings as accurately as possible onto a blank sheet of paper. The test is used as a screening instrument for brain damage in adults and for developmental problems in children. Also called the Bender Visual-Motor Gestalt Test.

benefit-cost analysis
n. A theoretical viewpoint which considers relationships between the expenditure of time, energy, or resources of the organism and the gains to the organism of things, relationships, and situations which are deemed beneficial to the organism. This analysis is often used in economic approaches, in which costs and benefits are expressed monetarily. In behavioral ecology the analysis is most often expressed in relative survival rates or biological energy units. Also called cost-benefit analysis.

benzodiazepine
n. A family of addictive central nervous system depressants drugs which are used to treat anxiety, sleeping problems, and seizure disorders and to relieve symptoms of alcohol withdrawal. They are frequently prescribed to depressed individuals because the overdose potential is low as it takes more than a thousand normal doses to be fatal to an average adult. This group includes chlordiazapoxide, alprazolam, bromazepam, clonazepam, clorazepate, diazepam (Valium), estazolam, flurazepam, loraeapam, midazolam, oxazepam, quazepam, temazepam, and triazolam.

bereavement
n. **1.** The state of having a loved one die. **2.** The emotional reaction to the death of a loved one, which commonly includes grief, sadness, anger, a sense of loss, and guilt, whose occurrence, though, is often unpredictable in timing and sequence.

Bernoulli trial
n. In probability, the outcome of an experiment with two possible outcomes and a known probability for each outcome such as flipping a coin.

Bernreuter Personality Inventory
n. A forerunner of modern personality inventories published in 1931, which was one of the first to use true-false items and report multiple outcomes, including neurotic tendency, self-sufficiency, introversion-extroversion, dominance-submission, sociability, and confidence.

bestiality
n. The practice of humans' having sex with nonhuman animals. This often is considered a deviation although it is considered normal

behavior for young men in some cultures and subcultures. Also called zooerasty.

beta

n. (β) **1.** In statistics the symbol for failing to reject the null hypothesis when the null hypothesis is false (type II error). **2.** A variable weight in a regression analysis.

beta-blocker

n. A drug which blocks beta-adrenergic receptors, which are found in the central nervous system, the sympathetic nervous system, the heart, and other organs. Beta-adrenergic receptors are a type of adrenaline- (epinephrine-) sensitive receptor sites. Treatment with a beta-blocker decreases the rate and force of heart muscle contraction and decreases sympathetic nervous system activity. The former action is useful to treat tachycardia (rapid heart rate) and/or high blood pressure, arrhythmias, and angina. The latter action of a beta-blocker is useful in treating people with excessive startle responses or with stage fright. The prototypic beta-blocker is propranolol, though many other beta-blockers are available for specific uses.   – vs

beta-coefficient

n. A multiplicative constant in a regression equation which reflects the relative contribution of a variable to the prediction, given the other variables in the equation. Also called beta weight.

beta lymphocyte

n. A form of white blood cell formed in lymph tissues which creates antibodies upon contacting an antigen anywhere in the body. An accumulation of beta lymphocytes at a site of infection is called pus.

beta wave

n. A pattern of electrical activity in the brain characteristic of normal, awake alertness as measured by an electroencephalograph, normally between 12 and 40 Hz.

between-groups variance

n. In analysis of variance (ANOVA), the portion of the total variance in a dependent variable that is attributable to differences between groups, which is compared to within-group means so as to determine whether it is likely the groups are drawn from the same population.

between-subjects design

n. In research design, an experiment in which different groups of subjects are treated differently and their scores on a dependent variable(s) are measured so as to assess the effects of the difference(s) in treatment on the dependent variable.

bicultural identity

n. Bicultural identity is the condition of identifying with (i.e., having strong attachment and loyalty to) two different cultures. Bicultural identity is one component (perhaps the most important) of the more complex and multidimensional notion of biculturalism. Note that an individual who has been exposed to and learned two cultures is a bicultural person, but only if this individual expresses attachment and loyalty to the two cultures can we say that the individual has a bicultural identity.

Bicultural identities, like other types of dual or hybrid identities where different roles and self-concepts intersect (e.g., identifying oneself as a "working mother" or "gay"), are complex and multifaceted. For instance, bicultural individuals often talk about their dual cultural heritage in complicated ways, including mostly positive terms but often also expressing some negative feelings. Biculturalism can be associated with feelings of pride, uniqueness, and a rich sense of community and history, while also bringing to mind identity confusion, dual expectations, and value clashes. Further, there is not just one way of being bicultural. Regardless of their level of attachment to each culture (e.g., moderate or high), bicultural individuals differ in the degree to which they see their cultural identities as compatible and integrated versus oppositional and difficult to integrate. These differences can be described under the rubric of what psychologists call *bicultural identity integration* (BII). Individuals high on BII tend to see themselves as part of a "hyphenated culture" (or even part of a combined, "third" emerging culture) and find it easy to integrate both cultures in their everyday lives. Biculturals low on BII, on the other hand, report difficulty in incorporating both cultures into a cohesive sense of identity and are particularly sensitive to explicit or implicit differences and clashes of the two cultural orientations.

More recently psychologists have discovered that variations in BII do not define a uniform phenomenon, as previously thought, but instead encompass two separate independent constructs: perceptions of overlap (vs. distance) and perceptions of harmony (vs. conflict) between one's two cultural identities or orientations. Work on this topic also has shown that these two psychological identity dimensions have distinct personality, acculturation, and sociodemographic antecedents. – VB-M

biculturalism

n. Biculturalism is the condition of having or endorsing two cultures. Although the term *biculturalism* or *bicultural* is typically used to describe individuals (e.g. a bicultural child), it can also be used to describe nations (e.g., bicultural Canada, where anglophone and francophone cultures coexist) and institutions and policies (e.g., bicultural or bilingual education). Although the term is recent, the concept of biculturalism goes back to the origins of modern Canada (1774, when the British authorities allowed French Canadians full use of their language, system of civil law, and freedom to practice their Roman Catholic faith). Biculturalism should not be confused with bilingualism (having fluency in two languages), although these terms are conceptually related since often (but not always) bicultural individuals and institutions are also fluent in two languages.

Biculturalism is a very prevalent societal phenomenon. The cultural contact and mixing resulting from phenomena such as migration, colonization, economic globalization, multicultural policies, travel, and media exposure explain why more and more individuals describe themselves as bicultural or multicultural. In fact, in the United States,

for instance, one of every four individuals has lived in another country before moving to the United States, has internalized values and behaviors representative of both the culture of origin (e.g., Chinese, Mexican) and the receiving U.S. host culture and thus can be described as bicultural. The prevalence of biculturalism is also large in countries such as Canada, Australia, the Netherlands, and Singapore. These impressive statistics do not include ethnic and cultural minorities who are descendants of immigrants, for whom identification and involvement with their ethnic cultures in addition to mainstream culture are also the norm. In sum, biculturalism is a prevalent phenomenon typically found in nations where migration is strong (e.g., Canada, Australia, Western Europe) or where there is a history of colonization (e.g., Hong Kong).

Biculturalism has received growing attention in psychology, particularly in the subfields of cultural, cross-cultural, social, and ethnic minority psychology, where this topic is studied at the individual (e.g., second-culture learning) and group levels (e.g., how different cultural groups interact in bicultural or monocultural societies). Early sociological views prevalent during the first half of the 20th century described biculturals as marginal people with a divided self; underlying this view was the assumption that individuals should have a single cultural identity and that involvement with more than one culture is psychologically undesirable and leads to identity confusion. Recent empirical psychological research on biculturalism, however, shows that biculturalism not only is rarely unhealthy or undesirable, but seems to have positive cognitive and social consequences for the individual (e.g., increase in metacognitive abilities, wider behavioral repertoires). Further, invalidating the notion that learning a new culture is an "all-or-none" process whereby moving toward a new culture invariably implies moving away from the native culture, current research on this topic shows that biculturals can retain and "use" their two cultures through a process known as cultural frame-switching. Specifically, biculturals have the ability to switch between different culturally based cognitive frames of reference or behavioral repertoires in response to (explicit or implicit) cultural cues in the situation (e.g., language being spoken, ethnicity of people present, role expectations) which signal which behavior or frame of reference is appropriate.

Finally, it is important to acknowledge that biculturalism, according to a widely accepted framework, is only one of the four possible outcomes of situations of cultural contact or acculturation. In these situations, individuals and societies have to deal with two central issues: (1) the extent to which they are motivated to retain (in the case of immigrants) or allow (in the case of nations) involvement with the ethnic or minority culture (e.g., Mexican culture in the case of Mexican-American immigrants or native African cultures in the case of South Africa) and (2) the extent to which they are motivated to learn (in the case of immigrants) or require involvement with the mainstream, dominant culture (e.g., largely Anglo-based U.S. or Afrikaner culture). The negotiation of these two central issues results in four distinct acculturation positions: assimilation (identification with or support for the dominant culture only), biculturalism/integration (identification with and support for both cultures), separation (identification with or support for the ethnic culture only), or marginalization/diffusion (low identification with or support for any of the cultures). Empirical psychological work on the four acculturation attitudes or strategies reveals that, at least at the individual level, the most common strategy used by immigrant and cultural minorities is integration or biculturalism, followed by separation, assimilation, and diffusion. Further, individuals who use the integration strategy have the best psychological and sociocultural adaptation outcomes, while those with a diffuse strategy have the worst.   – VB-M

▶ *See also* ACCULTURATION, BICULTURAL IDENTITY, *and* MULTICULTURALISM

big five personality traits

n. The five factor model (FFM) of personality traits, popularly called the "big five," refers to an organization of individual differences into five broad factors or traits that subsume most specific personality traits. The term was first applied to dimensions discovered in analyses of trait terms in laypeople's vocabularies; the same factors were subsequently discovered in psychological questionnaires. The FFM has become the dominant model of trait structure and the object of extensive research, which has established that all five factors can be consensually validated by different observers, have a strong genetic basis, are stable in adults, and are found around the world. The FFM factors and the traits that define them have been shown to be important in understanding and predicting a wide variety of outcomes, such as vocational interests, health risk factors, political ideology, job performance, and mental disorders.   – RRM

bilabial

n. Sounds articulated with both lips are bilabial. English has three bilabial sounds in its phonemic inventory: [p b m], the consonants in the words *Bob*, *pop*, and *mom*, respectively. Round vowels, like [u] in *boot*, also involve the lips in their articulation. The lower lip is used to articulate labiodental fricatives like [f v] – the two consonants in the word *five* – and the labiodental nasal [K], occurring at the end of the first syllable in the word *symphony*. The upper lip, however, is never used without the lower lip to articulate sounds in natural languages.   – EMF

bilateral transfer

n. Improvement of a skill on one side of the body when the other side of the body receives training in the skill. If, in learning to eat with chopsticks in the right hand, the capacity to eat with chopsticks in the left hand improves, then bilateral transference is said to occur. This has been used as a basis for inferring a generalized motor program.

bilingual

n. A bilingual is any individual with communication skills in two languages. Those skills may represent the written, spoken, or auditory domains with any degree of fluency or proficiency in each language. For example, a bilingual individual may have listening comprehension in one language and both spoken and written comprehension in a second. Fluency and proficiency may be assessed using standardized measures for language ability. A narrow view of this term would include only individuals who have native-like fluency in each of their two languages. In contrast, the most inclusive definition may include an individual who has spoken skills in a language other than the native language. Typically, bilinguals are dominant in one of their languages. An individual who is able to understand utterances in a language but has no productive competence in that language and is fluent in his/her native language is referred to as a receptive or passive bilingual. – JA

▶ *See also* **BALANCED BILINGUAL** *and* **BILINGUALISM**

bilingualism

n. This term describes the ability to function in two or more languages in everyday life. Each language may be used in different circumstances and for different purposes. Degree of proficiency may vary in each language. Proficiency may be assessed using standardized measures for language aptitude and language ability. Simultaneous or compound bilinguals are individuals who have learned their languages at the same time, prior to age 3. These individuals may also be referred to as early bilinguals. Coordinate bilingualism occurs when one language was learned in a separate location and at a later time than the first or native language. These individuals are also referred to as late bilinguals. Overall, individuals may not possess equal fluency in both languages but can communicate and are competent in two or more languages. This term also describes individuals who have learned one or more foreign languages while still retaining their native language. – JA

▶ *See also* **BALANCED BILINGUAL** *and* **BILINGUAL**

bimodal distribution

n. A statistical distribution of data in which there are two distinct peaks or modes (as contrasted to the unimodal, or single-peak, distribution depicted by a bell curve). A bimodal distribution may indicate that there are actually two different samples or distributions being summed together. For example, many gender studies produce a bimodal distribution. When information (i.e., attitudes, opinions, traits, values) from males and females is averaged together, it generally produces a normal distribution, but when the data from males and females is considered separately, there are often two different means with their own standard deviations. These different means produce the two peaks, or modes, characteristic of a bimodal distribution. Bimodal distributions may be used to demonstrate how deceptive simple descriptive or summary statistics can be, or may be an impetus to further investigation and improved exploratory modeling of a target phenomenon. – BJM

binaural

adj. Of or relating to hearing with both ears at the same time, as opposed to monaural hearing with only one ear.

binaural time difference

n. The difference in time between the arrival of a sound pressure wave at one eardrum as opposed to the other eardrum, which is a cue used in locating sound sources and separating sounds. Also called phase delay.

binding

n. **1.** Attachment of a neurotransmitter to a receptor site on a dendrite. **2.** In psychoanalysis, a restriction in the flow or expression of energy, usually due to the ego delaying expression of an id impulse.

binge eating

n. As defined by the current edition of the DSM-IV-TR, an episode of binge eating is characterized by **(1)** eating, in a discrete period of time, an amount of food that is definitely larger than most people would eat during a similar period and under similar circumstances and **(2)** a sense of lack of control over eating during the episode.

Some studies suggest that occasional binge episodes are common in the general population. It is only when these episodes occur frequently or are accompanied by distress or inappropriate compensatory methods such as vomiting or excessive exercising that they would be considered to be a symptom of a psychological disorder. Binge eating is most identified with the eating disorders, particularly bulimia nervosa and binge-eating disorder, but it can also occur in anorexia nervosa.

Frequent binge episodes can also lead to weight gain, although most obese individuals do not meet the criteria for a diagnosis of an eating disorder.   – DAA

binge-eating disorder

n. Binge-eating disorder is characterized by recurrent episodes of binge eating in the absence of regular use of inappropriate compensatory behaviors that are characteristic of bulimia nervosa and does not occur exclusively during the course of anorexia nervosa or bulimia nervosa. To be characterized as having a binge-eating disorder, the individual must exhibit behaviors of binge eating at least 2 days a week for 6 months. An episode of binge eating is characterized by the following:

eating in a discrete period of time (e.g., within any 2-hour period) an amount of food that is definitely larger than most people would eat during a similar period under similar circumstances

a sense of lack of control over eating during the episode (e.g., a feeling that one cannot stop eating or control what or how much one is eating)

The end of a binge is difficult to establish in the absence of discrete compensatory behaviors such as vomiting. Therefore, the binge-eating episodes are associated with three (or more) of the following:

eating much more rapidly than normal

eating until feeling uncomfortably full

eating large amounts of food when not feeling physically hungry

eating alone because of embarrassment about how much one is eating

feeling disgusted with oneself, depressed, or very guilty after overeating

There is a marked distress among individuals with binge-eating disorder due to the loss of control one exhibits and the implications of a binge for one's weight and medical health. Approximately one-third of obese patients seeking treatment meet the criteria of a binge-eating disorder and 10–20% of individuals with binge-eating disorder are obese.

The physical complications due to binge-eating disorder include hypertension, congestive heart failure, gastric dilation/rupture (from binges), gallstones, inflammation of the liver (liver failure), decreased fertility, osteoarthritis, type II diabetes, gout, and sleep apnea. Individuals who have binge-eating disorder are also at an increased risk of cancer and death due to complications of obesity.

Therapies for binge-eating disorder include cognitive-behavioral therapy, interpersonal psychotherapy, and antidepressant treatment. However, combination treatment of antidepressants plus cognitive-behavioral therapy does not yield a greater reduction in binge eating compared to cognitive-behavioral therapy or weight loss therapy alone. Interpersonal psychotherapy applied in a group setting is also as effective as cognitive-behavioral therapy for individuals with binge-eating disorder. Exercise and a good nutrition plan are also advised during treatment.
                                        – TJM

binocular

adj. Of or relating to the simultaneous use of two eyes in seeing.

binocular cue

n. A difference in the pattern of light striking each of the retinas (retinal disparity) or the pattern of muscular tension required to focus each eye on the same object (convergence), both of which are used to make inferences of depth in a perceptual scene.

binocular disparity

n. The differences in the retinal images between the two eyes in viewing a three-dimensional scene, which allow an estimate of the depth of different parts of the scene. The difference in retinal images in the two eyes is called parallax and increases as an object nears the eye so that the image of near objects has greater disparity while distant objects have less disparity in the images cast on the two retinas.

binocular fusion
n. The union of the slightly different views of each eye into a single image in the mind.

binocular perception
n. Any visual image using the combined information of both eyes.

binocular rivalry
n. A state in which the two eyes are unable to fuse what they see into a single perception; the view from each eye tends to predominate for a short time and then that of the other eye with vision that seems fuzzy much of the time.

binocular vision
n. A form of three-dimensional perceiving made possible by depth cues when using both eyes and fusing the images which is normal for human beings.

binomial
1. *adj.* Having two separate possible outcomes.
2. *n.* Any collection containing two distinct kinds of things.

binomial test
n. A probability test to see whether a sample in which each member has two possible outcomes results from a binomial distribution of known probabilities.

bioacoustics
n. The field of study whose object is communication through sound by living organisms. The field includes study of mechanisms of sound production and reception, physical characteristics of such signals, and their interaction with other forms of behavior.

bioengineering
n. The practical science of creating artificial replacements for damaged body parts. This includes artificial limbs and joints, kidney dialysis machines, and electronic substitutes for sensory and mental functions.

biofeedback
n. A procedure involving measuring biological processes and converting the information to a form discernible by humans so as to provide conscious, external information on biological functioning, often with the goal of learning to alter and control some of the processes measured.

biofeedback therapy
n. Using biofeedback techniques to solve medical and psychological problems. Biofeedback has been found helpful in dealing with hypertension, migraines, stress disorders, and chronic pain.

biogenic
adj. Produced by naturally occurring processes in living organisms, of biological origin.

biogenic amine
n. Any of a large family of chemicals with an amine group created within organisms including the neurotransmitters, dopamine, epinephrine, and norepinephrine. Amines are nitrogen atoms bonded to three other atoms no more than two of which are hydrogen. Ammonia, NH_3, is broken down by the replacement of a hydrogen atom to become an amine.

biological clock
n. An inferred mechanism of mind which explains the capacity of organisms to follow predictable cycles in their lives, sometimes without external time cues. Mechanisms governing daily cycles of sleep and wakening are the best known biological clocks.

biological essentialism
n. In sexuality studies, the idea that sexual characteristics and behavior are determined by genetics and little influenced by ecological, social, and cultural environments.

biological psychology
n. The science that studies the areas of overlap between biology and psychology and the interactions of mind and body.

biological rhythm
n. Any predictable pattern in an organism's functioning over time. Rhythms are noted in areas such as breathing, sleeping, eating,

arousal level, sexual activity, menstruation, and mood. Daily, or circadian, rhythms are the best studied but biological rhythms occur in both short- and long-duration activities.

biomedical model
n. A level of explanation in psychology which describes mood, personality, and behavior through their biological or medical origins. Reliance on this model alone would describe genetics, neural structure, and neurochemistry, as well as the effects of drugs on the body. Strict reliance on this model would not involve psychological analyses of the causes of variant moods and behaviors. However, most psychologists today interweave biological/medical analysis with a psychological model. For example, in the biomedical model, the root cause of depression might be explained as an error in circadian rhythms affecting a biological clock, in particular the balance of slow-wave sleep, which can be reset through appropriate pharmacological intervention. By contrast, a psychotherapist might look for an individual's predisposition to depression caused by childhood loss or trauma or by particular patterns of thinking, as well as the physiological roots of the problem.   – vs

biopsychology
n. The science that studies the areas of overlap between biology and psychology and the interactions of mind and body.

biopsychosocial model
n. A view of development as a complex inter-action of biological, psychological, and social processes. Biological processes incorporate the changes within the body that alter the body's structure and function, which are asso-ciated with the passage of time. Psychological processes involve cognition, personality, and emotion. Social processes reflect the environ-ment or context, and they include indicators that reflect the individual's position in the social structure or hierarchy.   – TJM

biorhythm
n. Any predictable pattern in an organism's functioning over time. Rhythms are noted in areas such as breathing, sleeping, eating,

arousal level, sexual activity, menstruation, and mood. Daily or circadian rhythms are the best studied but biological rhythms occur in both short- and long-duration activities.

bipolar affective disorder
n. A family of psychopathologies character-ized by wide swings in emotional state or mood. Bipolar I disorder is characterized by manic episodes alternating with either depressed periods or periods of relative normality. Bipolar II disorder is character-ized by recurrent major depressive episodes interspersed with periods of hypomania. Cyclothymic disorder is characterized by chronic fluctuation of hypomania and de-pressive episodes.

bipolar cell
n. A cell located in back of the retina with only one dendrite branch and one axon, which connect light receptor cells to amacrine, horizontal, and ganglion cells. Bipolar cells modulate the activation of ganglion cells by depolarizing and hyperpolarizing in reaction to patterns of light striking receptor cells, thus making vision more accurate.

bipolar disorder, rapidly cycling
n. Bipolar I disorder or bipolar II disorder in which there are more than four episodes of depression to mania or hypomania in a year. In a few persons these swings can occur in a few hours' time.

bipolar disorders
n. A family of disorders characterized by swings from depression to mania or hypoma-nia including bipolar I disorder, bipolar II disorder, bipolar disorder not otherwise specified, and cyclothymic disorder.

bipolar I disorder
n. A psychopathology characterized by at least one manic episode with or without depressive periods and psychotic features. This disorder is widely known as manic-depression.

bipolar II disorder
n. A psychopathology characterized by depres-sive episodes alternating with hypomanic

episodes which may or may not have psychotic features. This disorder is widely known as manic-depression.

birth order

n. The ordinal position of a child in a family with more than one child. Birth order is a secondary variable relating to many others which have been found to have influence on family dynamics and the differing experience of each child in a family that affect personality, academic achievement, sexual orientation, and hormonal levels. Numerous theorists have supposed birth order is an important variable in personality development, but empirical studies have found it to be a weak predictor whose affects are mediated through other variables.

birth order and personality

n. The supposition that ordinal position in a family has an influence on personality. Numerous theorists have supposed birth order is an important variable in personality development, but empirical studies have found it to be a weak predictor whose effects are mediated through other variables.

biserial correlation

n. A measure of relationship between a continuous variable and a dichotomous one.

bisexual

adj. **1.** Having the characteristic of being aroused by or engaging in sexual activities with both men and women. Most people are at least somewhat aroused by both sexes at some times; most people at most times have a preference for one sex over the other, although this characteristic sometimes changes over the life span. Some cultures accept and assume the bisexuality of their members while others repress and attempt to deny bisexuality. **2.** Having both male and female genitalia.

bivariate

adj. Of or relating to two variables or characteristics.

bivariate association

n. The relationship between two variables ignoring the effects of any other variables.

bivariate statistic

n. Any statistic which describes the relationship between two variables, especially correlations.

Blacky pictures

n. A set of 12 cartoon pictures depicting a dog called Blacky in human-like situations used as a Thematic Apperception Test (TAT)–like test for children. The child subject is asked to make up a story about each picture, and the responses are scored on a variety of dimensions.

blaming the victim

n. The tendency of people to find fault with the weaker party in a dispute even or especially if the weaker party would not normally be held to have moral guilt for the occurrence. This has been widely noted in cases of rape, racial conflicts, and international aggression.

blindness

n. A lack of visual perception which can be partial or total. Legal blindness is defined as visual sharpness at 20 feet worse than a normally sighted person would have at 400 feet or having a visual field less than 20 degrees. In some forms of blindness a person is able to detect the presence or absence of light but not perceive objects in space.

blindness, cortical

n. Loss of vision, associated with anatomically and structurally intact eyes and intact anterior visual pathways. It is due to the bilateral lack of cortical functioning of the primary visual cortex in the occipital lobes. Pupil response to light is preserved. Cortical blindness can be associated with visual hallucinations and preserved ability to perceive moving objects (Riddoch phenomenon). Sometimes, patients deny the blindness (Anton syndrome).   – A A

blindness, functional

n. Loss or deterioration of visual perception without any apparent physical problem in the physiology of the visual system. This is commonly related to somatization disorder and was once called hysterical blindness. Also called psychogenic blindness.

blindness, psychogenic
n. Loss or deterioration of visual perception without any apparent physical problem in the physiology of the visual system. This is commonly related to somatization disorder and was once called hysterical blindness. Also called functional blindness.

blindsight
n. The capacity of some fully or partially blind individuals to detect and react to visual stimuli in their area of blindness without conscious awareness of perception. Blindsight has been demonstrated primarily among persons with damage to the visual cortex, and it is theorized that connections between the optic nerve and the midbrain provide nonconscious forms of visual information processing.

blind spot
n. **1.** In vision the portion of the retina which has no light receptors where the optic nerve and optic blood vessels exit the eyeball, creating an area in the visual field in which nothing can be seen by the eye. The area of a blind spot is normally covered by light receptors in the other eye, and so people do not usually notice they have a blind spot. **2.** A limited area in which an individual lacks knowledge, insight, or awareness.

blink reflex
n. An involuntary, rapid closing of the eye in response to rapid change in the visual field or eye sensations such as a puff of air or irritation to the cornea.

block design
n. A research design in which subject variables are treated as independent variables by assigning subjects to blocks based on the subject variables. Homogeneity within blocks increases the statistical power of the design.

block design test
n. **1.** An intelligence subtest on the Wechsler intelligence scales in which subjects have to copy patterns formed using blocks with one

of two colors. **2.** Any other test using multicolored block patterns to test for ability.

block diagram
n. A bar graph, histogram, or flowchart using blocked areas to designate frequency or amount.

blocking
n. **1.** In classical conditioning the prevention or reduction in the strength of an association between a stimulus and response by the prior presentation of another stimulus. Thus if a dog hears a tone and then a buzzer of equal sensory salience shortly before being fed, at each meal the dog will quickly begin to salivate when it hears the tone alone but will not do so or will do so less if it hears the buzzer alone. **2.** An inferred process causing a sudden interruption in speech, thought, or other activities without conscious cause.

blood alcohol concentration
n. The proportion of alcohol as a percentage of total blood fluid. In most of the United States a concentration of either 0.8% or 1.0% is considered prima facie evidence of intoxication.

blood alcohol level
n. The proportion of alcohol as a percentage of total blood fluid. In most of the United States a concentration of either 0.8% or 1.0% is considered prima facie evidence of intoxication.

blood-brain barrier
n. A semipermeable membrane lining capillaries which supply blood to the brain which blocks most antigens and large molecules, including many drugs, from entering the brain and thus protects the brain. Lipid- (fat-) soluble chemicals usually cross the barrier more easily than do water-soluble molecules.

blunted affect
n. A dulling or absence of normal affective expression and experience which is a common symptom of bereavement, trauma, schizophrenia, and other disturbances.

body dysmorphic disorder

n. A psychological disorder in which a person is excessively preoccupied with an imaginary or minor bodily defect in appearance which is imagined to be dangerous, life-threatening, or severely disfiguring despite medical and other reassurances to the contrary.

body image

n. A person's mental representation of his or her own body and its function, attractiveness, and worth based upon self observation and the reaction of others to one's self.

body language

n. The conveyance of information by bodily postures, movements, and facial expressions. Also called kinesics and nonverbal communication.

Bogardus social distance scale

n. A Guttmann-type scale in which persons are asked whether they would be willing to participate in a ranked range of social activities from marrying to allowing into the country with unspecified members of a named group of people. Social distance is assumed to be a measure of prejudice.

bogus pipeline

n. In bogus pipeline studies, social psychologists deceive participants by (falsely) making them believe they are strapped to a lie-detector machine. The machines are elaborate, but fake devices that participants are told can measure their feelings. The bogus pipeline paradigm has been used to avoid effects of social desirability (presenting oneself in a manner that seems favorable), a major problem with self-report data. Findings from bogus pipeline studies show that social desirability may dramatically skew responses on a host of sensitive issues. Researchers have demonstrated much higher affirmative response rates among bogus pipeline participants when compared to participants who are not strapped to an ostensibly lie-detecting machine, on issues such as drug and alcohol use, oral sex, and smoking. Bogus pipeline studies suggest that research participants are less than truthful under most circumstances, especially when asked about sensitive issues. These data have been invoked by researchers who argue that self-report measures, which are among the most common type of data collected by psychologists, are inherently flawed and should be carefully scrutinized and interpreted with extreme caution.   – MWP

bonding

n. The process of creating and strengthening close personal relationships, especially between infants and their caregivers.

bone conduction

n. In hearing, the transmission of sound through the bones of the skull to the middle ear and inner ear.

Bonferroni correction

n. In statistics a correction in making statistical inferences which takes into account the number of inferences made by increasing the criterion for rejection of the null hypothesis in proportion with the number of inferences made. Thus, if 10 inferences are made in a study, the criterion will be increased 10 times so that if a .05 criterion were originally intended, it would be increased to .005.

boomerang effect

n. **1.** In social psychology, an attitude change in the opposite direction of that desired in communicating a persuasive message. **2.** In general, any effect that is the opposite of that which was intended to be the result of an action.

bootstrap

n. **1.** Any procedure for creating a criterion or process using some sample of the data to be measured in creating the criterion or using the process to create the process. **2.** In psychology, the substitution of a statistical model of a judge's decisions, which often proves more accurate than the judge's. **3.** In programming, writing a compiler for a programming language using the language itself. **4.** In linguistics, the idea that children use syntactic information to help learn the meaning of words. **5.** In statistics, using a sample to estimate population parameters which are then used to analyze the sample.

bootstrapping

n. **1.** The process of engaging in a bootstrap operation which is creating a criterion or process using some sample of the data to be measured in creating the criterion or using the process to create the process. **2.** In psychology, the substitution of a statistical model of a judge's decisions, which often proves more accurate than the judge's. **3.** In programming, writing a compiler for a programming language using the language itself. **4.** In linguistics, the idea that children use syntactic information to help learn the meaning of words. **5.** In statistics, using a sample to estimate population parameters which are then used to analyze the sample. **6.** In programming, using simple procedures with a computer to have the computer build more complex procedures.

borderline

1. *adj.* Difficult to categorize as a result of having characteristics, affordances, or aspects of more than one category. **2.** *n.* A person with borderline personality disorder.

borderline intelligence

n. Having an IQ in a range between that considered normal and that considered significantly abnormal. The usual threshold between the two is an IQ of 70–75, and different theorists would describe different limits to the borderline area.

borderline personality disorder

n. A persistent and pervasive pattern of personal adjustment characterized by instability in interpersonal relationships, self-image, and affect. Persons with this disorder usually spend a great deal of time brooding over real and imagined wrongs, being fearful of desertion, feeling empty, and thinking about suicide. They also tend to act impulsively, have inappropriate outbursts of anger, and show transient paranoia and dissociative thinking.

bottom-up processing

n. Any process of analysis which begins with data and seeks pattern or meaning: inductive reasoning. The opposite of deductive reasoning, or top-down processing, which imposes preexisting categories on data.

bounded rationality

n. The idea that humans are predictably rational in their decision making given their limited knowledge, the costs of human information processing, and the complex nature of real life, in which all decisions are made in conditions of numerous interacting variables, many of which are unknown to the decision maker.

box plot

n. A data display which shows a line anchored by the extreme scores and a box in the middle with lines at the 25th percentile, the median, and the 75th percentile, frequently used in exploratory data analysis.

bradykinesia

n. Abnormally slow bodily movement along with fewer than normal spontaneous movements.

Braille

n. A system of writing using patterns of small bumps read with the fingers which was created for use by blind persons or communication with blind persons. The patterns of small bumps comprise 64 possible patterns of bumps in two columns of three with the pattern of presence and absence of bumps indicating letters, numbers, punctuation, and scientific and musical notation.

brain laterality

n. Usually understood as hemispheric specialization.   – AA

▶ *See also* **HEMISPHERIC SPECIALIZATION**

brain lesion

n. Any damage of a portion of the brain leading to cell death or cessation of neuronal function regardless of cause, which can include injury, disease, poison, stroke, cancer, and inflammation.

brainstem

n. The enlarged area at the top of the spinal column that connects the spinal cord with the cerebrum and is composed of the midbrain, pons, cerebellum, and medulla oblongata.

brainstorming
n. A technique for promoting creativity and problem solving through the spontaneous generation of a list of potential ideas or solutions in response to a problem, challenge, or stimulus. While brainstorming can be completed alone or as a group, it is often promoted as a group activity that facilitates the creative generation of novel ideas via the encouragement of group members to build and expand on the ideas generated by others. The goal of effective brainstorming is to generate a wide range of potential ideas or solutions with no evaluation, restrictions, or criticism; as such, brainstorming may produce a number of unique, novel, and/or radical approaches. Brainstorming should be time-limited and remain focused on a single problem or stimulus. The purpose of brainstorming is idea generation, as opposed to idea development, selection, or evaluation.   – BJM

brainwashing
n. A process of attempting drastic change in attitudes and beliefs through prolonged coercive tactics such as sensory and sleep deprivation, starvation, physical torture, social pressure, and intense interrogation and verbal manipulation. Also known as thought reform. Brainwashing was first described during the treatment of POWs during the Korean War and widely practiced in China during the Cultural Revolution and has continued up to the present day in U.S. and other countries' treatment of suspected terrorists.

brain waves
n. Rhythmic patterns in the gross electrical activity of the brain as measured by an electroencephalograph.

Brazelton Scale
n. A neonatal scale of development which assesses neurological and behavioral development from birth to 2 months of age. The scale consists of 14 neurological items and 26 behavioral items. Also called the neonatal behavioral assessment scale (NBAS).

breathing-related sleep disorder
n. Chronic sleep disruption caused by breathing difficulties such as sleep apnea and central alveolar hypoventilation, which leads to daytime sleepiness.

bregma
n. The Y-shaped junction on the top of the skull between the frontal bone and the two parietal bones.

brief psychotherapy
n. Any of numerous approaches to psychotherapy which generally require 10 to 20 sessions or fewer for completion.

brief psychotic disorder
n. A mental disorder characterized by the sudden onset of delusions, hallucinations, disorganized speech, or grossly disorganized catatonic behavior that persists for at least a day but usually less than 1 month. Individuals who have this disorder usually experience extreme emotional distress and mental confusion.

brightness
n. The perceived intensity of light, which depends on objective intensity, wavelength, the state of adaptation of the eye, and any intervening stimuli.

brightness constancy
n. A tendency in humans to perceive familiar objects to have the same brightness regardless of changes in the actual intensity of the light they are reflecting under different lighting conditions.

brightness contrast
n. Differences in perceived brightness when a stimulus is presented against backgrounds of contrasting brightness. Thus a gray disk will seem brighter when seen against a black background than when seen against a white background.

Briquet's syndrome
n. An archaic name for somatization disorder.

Broca's aphasia
n. Broca's area, named after the French surgeon and anthropologist Pierre Paul Broca

(1861), who first described nonfluent speech, secondary to frontal lobe damage, later identified as Broca's aphasia. Also known as Brodmann's area 44, this area is located in the left inferior frontal convolution or gyrus. Though Broca limited his patients' cortical lesion to the left inferior frontal gyrus, technological advances (e.g., computed axial tomography) have shown that while mild Broca's aphasia is confined to Broca's area, more severe cases of this impairment extend beyond Broca's area, including the adjacent premotor and motor regions and underlying white matter. Broca's area is anterior to the section of the precentral gyrus, or primary motor strip, which controls jaw, lip, tongue, and vocal cord movements. Because of this proximity to such important sites of oromotor control, lesions in Broca's area tend to result in Broca's aphasia as well as right-sided muscular deficits in the speech areas indicated.   – JGC

▶ *See also* **APHASIA, BROCA'S**

Brodmann's area

n. Any of about 200 areas of the cerebral cortex whose cell structure and density are different from those of the surrounding areas.

Bruce effect

n. In rodents, the miscarriage of a pregnancy within the first few days after fertilization caused when pheromones from a strange male rat's urine inhibit the female's secretion of prolactin, which is necessary for implantation of an embryo in the wall of the uterus.

Brunswik faces

n. Simplified or schematic line drawings of faces in which parameters such as eye separation and height, mouth width and height, and nose length can be varied for use in studies of discrimination and categorization.

Brunswik ratio

n. An index of perceptual constancy given by the ratio $(R-S)/(O-S)$, where R is perceived magnitude or intensity of the stimulus, S is the magnitude or intensity of the stimulus

at the sense organ, and O is the objective magnitude or intensity of the stimulus.

bruxism

n. Habitual grinding of the teeth and especially during sleep.

B-type personality ▶ *See* **TYPE B PERSONALITY**

buccal

adj. Of or relating to the cheeks or the cavity of the mouth.

buffer store

n. A temporary memory or store of information for short periods, as in the working memory in the human mind or a temporary store of data waiting to be sent to a device in a computer.

bulimia nervosa

n. Bulimia nervosa, first described as a variant of anorexia nervosa, was identified in 1979 but probably commenced between the 1940s and 1960s. Bulimia, simply meaning "overeating," has been recognized since antiquity. This is, however, not relevant to the origins of bulimia nervosa. In 1979, Gerald Russell revealed three sets of disturbances in his patients: (**1**) intractable urges to overeat, (**2**) avoidance of fattening effects of food by vomiting and/or abusing purgatives, and (**3**) a morbid fear of becoming fat. Russell also concluded that there had often been a previous episode of anorexia nervosa.

When DSM-III was published, it included the term *bulimia*, but it differed from bulimia nervosa. Specific psychological disturbances, such as the patient's fear of fatness, were not given enough emphasis. Also, the diagnosis excluded patients in whom the bulimic episodes were attributable to anorexia nervosa. Bulimia nervosa, as it is considered today, was mostly unknown until the 1970s. After the 1970s, the disorder became relatively common.

Bulimia nervosa exhibits recurrent episodes of binge eating. An episode of binge eating is characterized by the following:

eating in a discrete period of time (e.g., within any 2-hour period) an amount of food that is definitely larger than most people would eat during a similar period under similar circumstances

- a sense of lack of control over eating during the episode (e.g., a feeling that one cannot stop eating or control what or how much one is eating)

The most prominent behavioral characteristic of bulimia nervosa is the frequent incidence of binge-eating episodes. Individuals with bulimia nervosa consume a variety of foods during a binge. The most typical is the consumption of desserts and snack foods. Individuals also consume large amounts of liquids to assist in vomiting. Bulimia nervosa involves recurrent inappropriate compensatory behavior in order to prevent weight gain, such as self-induced vomiting; misuse of laxatives, diuretics, enemas, or other medications; fasting; or excessive exercise. Individuals engage in purging behaviors to avoid weight gain. An individual is over-concerned with body shape and weight and bases his or her self-esteem on these aspects of appearance. The person feels under pressure to diet and to lose weight, and when he or she does not lose weight or gains weight, he/she reports feeling distressed. Many individuals with bulimia nervosa eventually induce vomiting not only after large binges but also after the consumption of any meal, whether large or small. The key features of bulimia nervosa are binge eating (large amounts of food and perceived loss of control), purging behavior, intensive exercise, hoarding and/or stealing food, going to the restroom/shower after meals, and shame and fear of gaining weight.

To be diagnosed with bulimia nervosa, both the bingeing and purging behaviors need to occur on average at least twice a week for 3 months. Bulimia nervosa usually emerges after a period of dieting. The disturbance does not occur exclusively during episodes of anorexia nervosa. That is, if an individual meets the criteria for both anorexia nervosa and bulimia nervosa, he/she is given the diagnosis of anorexia nervosa, binge-eating/purging type.

Bulimia nervosa has two subtypes: purging type and nonpurging type. The characteristic of the purging type is that during the current episode of bulimia nervosa, the person has regularly engaged in self-induced vomiting or the misuse of laxatives, diuretics, or enemas. The nonpurging type involves that the individual during the current episode of bulimia nervosa has used other inappropriate compensatory behaviors, such as fasting or excessive exercise, but has not regularly engaged in self-induced vomiting or the misuse of laxatives, diuretics, or enemas. Individuals with the purging type of bulimia nervosa usually have lower body weights, more symptoms of depression, and greater concern with body shape and weight than the individuals with nonpurging type. They are also more likely to exhibit fluid and electrolyte disturbances. The purging type are more likely to be multi-impulsive in that they are far more likely to have histories of substance abuse, shoplifting, and self-injurious behaviors.

Bulimia nervosa is prevalent in 1–3% of the population, and 25–30% of bulimic women have a history of anorexia nervosa. Bulimia nervosa affects 0.1–0.7% of males and 1.1%–3.5% of females. Of people with bulimia nervosa, 10% are males. Furthermore, borderline personality disorder and bulimia nervosa are highly comorbid. There are several behaviors exhibited in bulimia nervosa that contribute to physical complications; vomiting results in gland enlargement and dental erosion; diuretic, sauna, and diet pill abuse can lead to brain hemorrhages, seizures, and irregular heartbeat; enema and laxative abuse leads to the dysfunction of the colon; thyroid hormone abuse can lead to both hyperthyroidism and death; abuse of ipecac, which has a very long half-life, can lead to its accumulation in the heart muscles and bones.

The medical complications that can result from bulimia nervosa are cardiac arrhythmias, sudden cardiac death, changes in blood pressure, gland enlargement, tears in the esophagus and bleeding/rupture, gastric dilation/rupture, loss of colonic function (may require colonic resection), osteoporosis, infertility, subcutaneous emphysema, aspiration pneumonitis, hypokalemic "contraction" metabolic alkalosis, dental enamel erosion, abnormal cytokine levels, and Russell's sign. Russell's sign is a prominent indicator of bulimia nervosa in which abrasions and scars occur on the back of the hands as a result of manual attempts to induce vomiting.

Bulimia nervosa is found to be familial in twin studies. Bulimia nervosa has a relatively stereotypical clinical presentation, sex distribution, and age of onset, which support the possibility of some biological vulnerability. There are moderate to substantial effects due to genetic factors. Chromosome 10 provides a significant linkage to bulimia nervosa while chromosome 14 provides a suggestive linkage. There are also increased rates of both anorexia nervosa and bulimia nervosa in relatives of individuals with bulimia nervosa. Bulimia nervosa, however, varies in presentation, but of the core features, frequency of vomiting has been shown to be reliable and heritable. Individual environmental factors provide moderate effects while shared environmental effects appear less important.

The most effective treatment for bulimia nervosa is cognitive-behavioral therapy (CBT). CBT focuses on challenging the patient's thinking and beliefs about food and weight, changing eating behaviors, and developing problem-solving skills. CBT improves certain core symptoms such as body dissatisfaction, pursuit of thinness, and perfectionism. CBT is more effective than antidepressants. The benefits of antidepressants may diminish over time in a significant proportion of individuals who respond initially. Antidepressants also suppress bulimia nervosa symptoms in nondepressed individuals. While 30–70% of outpatients recover from bulimia nervosa, only 13–40% of inpatients recover, because inpatients have more severe cases of bulimia nervosa. After onset, disturbed eating behavior continues over the course of several years in a high percentage of clinic cases. After remission, approximately 30% of women experience relapse into bulimia nervosa symptoms.

Although the definition of recovery has not been formalized, individuals who have abstained from binge eating and purging for months or years are classified as recovered. Individuals who have recovered from bulimia nervosa continue to be overly concerned with body shape and weight, to engage in abnormal eating behaviors, and to experience dysphoric mood. Individuals tend to have greater than normal perfectionism, and their obsessional target symptoms are the need for symmetry and ordering/arranging. Pathological eating behavior and malnutrition tend to exaggerate these symptoms; however, these symptoms continue at a less intense level after recovery.   – TJM

bundle hypothesis
n. A derisive term used to ridicule points of view in psychology that perception is no more than the sum of individual sensory bits bundled together.

Bunsen-Roscoe law
n. The observation that the reaction of any photoreactive chemical or pigment is a function of the intensity and duration of the light to which it is exposed at least within certain ranges. This has been used in developing films and is true of biological physical systems in the brief periods after a flash of light and before adaptation takes place. Also known as Bloch's law.

burnout
n. A state of physical, emotional, and mental exhaustion following prolonged effort and stress along with a generally negative attitude and lowered motivation and performance, particularly used in describing exhaustion with job and career.

buspirone
n. An anxiolytic drug (buspirone hydrochloride, Buspar) which lessens anxiety without producing sedation, dependence, or behavioral disinhibition which is characteristic of central nervous system (CNS) depressants such as the benzodiazepines. Its physiological action is not fully understood, although it has

been shown to react with dopamine and serotonin receptor sites.

butyrophenone

n. A type of older antipsychotic drug including haloperidol used primarily in cases of schizophrenia, bipolar disorder with psychotic features, and extreme agitation. This class of drugs has high rates of extrapyramidal symptoms, tardive dyskinesia, and neuroleptic malignant syndrome.

bystander effect

n. The bystander effect is a well-established social psychological phenomenon whereby an individual is slower and less likely to respond to a person in distress if others are present. Research into this phenomenon was a result of a highly publicized case in which a woman (Catherine "Kitty" Genovese) was brutally attacked while 38 of her neighbors watched. Kitty's death triggered hundreds of investigations into how so many people could stand by and do nothing to help the victim. The bystander effect has been found in laboratory settings and in real-life emergency and non-emergency situations.

Researchers suggest that social influence, evaluation apprehension, and diffusion of responsibility can help explain the bystander effect. Additionally, individuals are less likely to engage in the bystander effect when they feel good, feel guilty, know how to provide assistance, perceive the victim as needing and deserving help, observe others helping, and/or know the victim.   – LMB

bystander involvement

n. A tendency for people not to offer to help strangers when others are present, which has been attributed to a diffusion of responsibility and deference of judgment about the necessity of help to others who are not acting.

byte

n. The most common unit of information processing capacity, equal to eight consecutive bits or switches or 0 or 1 values and which is the computer equivalent of a word.

C

caffeine-induced disorders

n. A family of disorders caused by caffeine use, including caffeine intoxication, caffeine-induced anxiety disorder, caffeine-induced sleep disorder, and caffeine-related disorder not otherwise specified (NOS), all of which are related to caffeine's stimulating effect on the central nervous system.

caffeine withdrawal

n. A syndrome subsequent to the cessation of caffeine use after addiction has occurred, which usually persists for less than a week. Symptoms include headache, fatigue, sleep disturbance, lethargy, difficulty in focusing, low motivation, and achy, flulike symptoms.

calcium (channel) blocker

n. A family of drugs which work by partially blocking voltage-sensitive calcium channels which are present in electrically excitable cells including muscle, nerve, glial, and blood vessel cells. There are three types of calcium blockers: T types work most in the heart and blood vessels and are used to treat hypertension and arrhythmia; their use results in lower levels of calcium in the walls of blood vessels and in the muscles of the heart, which makes it more difficult for them to be excited and so leads to dilation in blood vessels and lowered output of each heartbeat, both of which lower blood pressure, as well as to a slower and more rhythmic pulse. N type calcium channel blockers have a greater affinity for nerve cells and are used as analgesics, while L type calcium channel blockers are used as antiepileptics.

calcium channel

n. An area of a cell wall that has greater permeability for calcium ions than most parts of the cell wall due to variations in the electro-chemical configuration of the proteins in the cell wall.

California Psychological Inventory

n. (CPI) A self-report personality inventory scaled for folk concepts of personality and used to predict future social, educational, and vocational behavior and achievement. The CPI has 20 measures of positive attributes for categories of (a) interpersonal dispositions such as self-assurance and independence, (b) prosocial values and social compliance, (c) achievement potentials, and (d) role-enactment characteristics. In addition, three higher-order vector scales define four ways of living or lifestyles. The CPI has been widely used in cross-cultural research, training for leadership, and personnel psychology.

cannabis

n. Three related plant species (*Cannabis indica*, *C. ruderalis*, and *C. sativa*), all of whose leaves and flowers contain intoxicating cannabinoid chemicals and especially delta 9 tetrahydrocannabinol (THC), which produce mild euphoria, relaxation, and increased appetite and attention to sensory stimuli and inhibit memory when smoked or ingested. Some persons experience increased anxiety when using cannabis, and hallucinations and other sensory distortions occur at high dose levels. Cannabis is not generally considered addictive. Commonly called marijuana or hemp, it is grown in many areas of the world for its fiber, which makes strong rope and woven products.

Cannon-Bard theory

n. A theory of emotion in which it is supposed that a situation is first evaluated in the thalamus and then simultaneously in the cerebral cortex, where ideas and feelings of emotion occur, and the hypothalamus, where physiological reactions such as flight-fight arousal occur. This theory was in reaction to the James-Lange theory, which suggested that emotion was the perception of reaction to situations.

Capgras syndrome

n. The delusion that others, usually close relatives or friends, have been replaced by identical looking imposters, exact doubles. Patients presenting this delusion claim that although the imposter may look exactly the same as the real person, they know well they are not the same. The imposter is usually a significant person for the patient and may be the husband or wife or somebody else in a particularly significant relationship to the patient. Capgras syndrome may be associated with other disorders or conditions and can be interpreted as a particular subtype of a delusional misidentification syndrome. Capgras syndrome has not only been reported in specific psychiatric conditions, usually paranoid schizophrenia and other psychotic disorders, but also been associated with a neurological pathology, such as a temporal lobe abnormality.   – A A

cardiovascular

adj. Of or relating to the heart and blood vessels and the circulation of blood throughout the body.

carpentered world

n. The visual environment of urban dwellers, which is largely a constructed rather than a natural environment and was supposed to have more straight lines and right angles than natural environments, resulting in differences between rural and urban dwellers in visual perception. Little evidence has supported this theory in terms of either differences in perception or the greater preponderance of straight lines and right angles in urban environments.

Cartesian

adj. Of or relating to the ideas or person of the French philosopher Rene Descartes (1596–1642), who is best known for suggesting that there are two basic substances in the universe, usually called mind and body (a philosophy called dualism), and for applying linear algebra to geometry.

Cartesian dualism

n. The idea proposed by the French philosopher Rene Descartes that there are two kinds of things in the world: mind (*res cogitans*), which has no extension or presence in space, and body (*res extensa*), which does have presence and extension in space. He also supposed the two both interact and are independent of one another.

case study

n. A thorough observation or analysis of one or a few participations. Case studies can be used as a basis for further research or be employed in situations where a large number of participants are not available. Case studies can also be used in psychological research for clinical applications, such as to investigate the success of different treatments of a disorder. – SRB

castration anxiety

n. **1.** In psychoanalysis, little boys fear that their father wants to castrate them, a projection onto the father of the son's desire to castrate the father so as to render him impotent in a competition for the mother's love so that the son can become the mother's lover. **2.** In Henry Murray's psychology, it was literally a fear of castration due to parental suppression of childhood masturbation.

castration complex

n. **1.** In psychoanalysis, a whole constellation of fears and projections of young children centered on being deprived of a penis in boys and of already having been deprived of a penis in girls. **2.** In Henry Murray's psychology, an invariant motivation to protect one's self from castration which leads to being overdramatic, attention seeking, and hysterical and arose as a reaction to suppression of childhood masturbation by the parents and particularly by the father.

catalepsy

n. A state of rigid immobility that may be maintained over many hours, usually by persons suffering from catatonic schizophrenia.

cataplexy

n. **1.** A sudden loss of muscle tone and control, sometimes localized and sometimes in the entire body, which leads to physical collapse and is usually preceded by an extreme emotional situation to which cataplexy is believed to be a response. **2.** A defense against predation in some animals consisting of complete immobility without muscle tone which makes the animal appear to be dead.

catastrophe theory

n. A field of mathematics that formally describes processes in which small and gradual changes in parameter are associated with large and abrupt changes in another parameter such as when a pathway leads over the edge of a cliff. Many attempts have been made to apply this to psychological and social phenomena, such as a person's having a nervous breakdown and herd animals' changing direction.

catatonia

n. Marked abnormality of muscle tone, posture, or behavior often observed in catatonic schizophrenics in which the subject may adopt immobile postures for hours, engage in repetitive nonutilitarian motions, remain mute, or stay in odd postures for long periods.

catatonic rigidity

n. A state of rigid immobility that may be maintained over many hours, usually by persons suffering from catatonic schizophrenia.

catatonic schizophrenia

n. A rare form of schizophrenia in which there are rigid immobility or marked abnormality of posture or movement in repeated patterns, mutism, echolalia, as well as disturbance in thought, affect, and responsiveness generally characteristic of schizophrenia.

catatonic stupor

n. An immobile and unresponsive state such as is characteristic of catatonic schizophrenics.

catch trial

n. A trial in a series of trials in which the independent variable is not presented and the subject's response is recorded. Catch trials are often used in psychophysical studies to determine the baseline response level of a subject or to determine bias toward responding positively.

catecholamine hypothesis
n. The theory that the variations in the levels of catecholamine neurotransmitters, dopamine, epinephrine, and norepinephrine, are responsible for depression and mania, depending on whether there was too little or too much neurotransmitter in the brain.

categorical perception
n. The perception of a thing as distinctly of one kind or type, despite ambiguity in the stimulus characteristics which might lead to a different categorical judgment. Thus when we see a person, we see him or her as male or female, although some males look like females and some females look like males in the conditions in which they are being seen.

categorical scale
n. A measurement scale that divides responses into category labels with no numerical meaning. Also called discrete or symbolic scales, categorical scales are typically used for data labeling. If categorical scales have no explicit ordering on the category labels, they are nominal scales (e.g., gender). If categorical scales have an inherent ordering of labels, then they are ordinal scales (e.g., rank). The data from categorical scales can be analyzed via nonparametric measures. – BJM

categorical variable
n. A nonquantitative variable with a limited number of subtypes, levels, or values. Also called nominal variables, categorical variables are used to identify the various subtypes or categories within the domain of the categorical variable. For example, within the domain of the variable "gender," there are typically two categories: male and female. While numerical values may be assigned to the values of categorical variables, these numbers are simply used for labeling purposes and have no ordinal, mathematical meaning. – BJM

categorization
n. The mental process of sorting things into types depending on some criterion or criteria.

In natural categories of objects, events, and experiences we use many sensory aspects, usually those most salient either sensorily or in terms of their utility to us.

category size effect
n. A difference in time taken to make category decisions depending on category size. Decisions about membership in large categories take longer than those about membership in smaller categories, so, for instance, it takes longer to decide whether robins are stones than whether rubies are stones, as gems is a subset of the larger category of stones.

catharsis
n. **1.** The release of strong, pent-up tension or emotion in an outburst of expression. **2.** In psychoanalysis, the release of suppressed libido often associated with recalling repressed traumatic events of the past.

cathexis
n. In psychoanalysis, the process of directing the energy of one's desires toward a particular source of satisfaction. Thus a child usually cathects her/his mother as she usually is the one he/she wants when desires arise.

CAT scan ▶ *See* **COMPUTED (AXIAL) TOMOGRAPHY**

caudate nucleus
n. One of a pair of nuclei in the basal ganglia which have a tail-like shape and are involved in inhibitory control of movement.

causal attribution or casual inference
n. Causal attribution refers to the process through which laypeople try to understand the underlying cause of a behavior. Through this process, individuals use their perceptions about the self, others, and the world to make sense of social interactions, other people's behaviors, and behaviors of their own. The two most studied explanations of behaviors are dispositional attributions and situational attributions. Dispositional attribution relates to the use of factors that lie within the individual (i.e., actor), such as personality traits,

to explain the cause of a behavior. This type of attribution is also referred to as an internal attribution. In contrast, situational attribution refers to the use of factors that are external to the individual, such as situational constraints and group influence that would have influenced the actors' behavior, to explain the cause of a behavior. This type of attribution is also referred to as an external attribution.

— EWMA, CYC

causality
n. 1. The philosophical belief that all events and states are the result of forces acting on previous events and states. Causality was once assumed to be a basic tenet of scientific inquiry, but this idea was called into question by quantum physics and psychology in the middle 1900s, and its place in the philosophy of science is now uncertain. 2. A tendency of the human mind to perceive events in a way so as to believe that all events and states are the result of forces acting on previous events and states.

causal reasoning
n. Human thoughts which seek to delineate a set of causal relations between things and events.

causal variable
n. A variable whose relationship to another is inferred to be causal in nature. Thus the blood alcohol level is held to be a causal variable in relation to a temporary lack of motor coordination.

causation
n. 1. The necessary and sufficient conditions to predict that a particular event or outcome will occur. 2. In research design, the inference that X causes Y as all other possible causes have been found to be unlikely.

ceiling effect
n. The inability of a measure or test to show valid differences above a certain point due to the easiness of the items or lack of sufficient number of items.

cell
n. In biology, one of the basic structures of most living organisms comprising a cell membrane delimiting its extent, a nucleus containing genetic and regulatory mechanisms and cytoplasm, all other constituents of the cell floating in a water solution. 2. In research design, the combination of two or more independent variables each at a particular level. As an example, a study of perception of emotion might have ethnicity and gender of subjects as independent variables, in which case Asian women might be one cell in the design.

cell body
n. The central portion of a nerve cell not including the axon or the dendrites, which includes the nucleus and most of the cell's maintenance structures. Also called soma.

censorship
n. 1. The practice of limiting publication or dissemination of materials that are not within the limits set by the censor. 2. In psychoanalysis, the preconscious function that prevents materials disturbing to the functioning of the ego from reaching consciousness.

centile
n. A percentile, or one one-hundredth of a total.

central deafness
n. Loss or impairment of hearing caused by pathology in the central nervous system. Central deafness can result from different types of retrocochlear lesions. It is generally accepted that central deafness is extremely rare. Both Heschl's gyri (primary auditory cortex) are involved in the majority of the cases, but central deafness has also been reported in cases of bilateral damage at the level of the inferior colliculi of the midbrain, the internal capsule, and the insula. When the damage is cortical, the term *cortical deafness* is used. Pure word deafness (inability to understand spoken language associated with normal written language understanding) may be regarded as a subtype of central deafness.

— AA

▶ *See also* **CONDUCTIVE DEAFNESS** *and* **WORD DEAFNESS**

central fissure

n. Fold in the cortex separating the frontal and parietal lobes. It is also referred to as the Rolandic fissure, fissure of Rolando, or central sulcus. It is located in front of the primary motor area (Brodmann's area 4) and behind the primary somatosensory area (Brodmann's areas 3, 1, and 2).   – A A

central limit theorem

n. An important mathematical theorem in applied statistics which states that the distribution of the averages (or other linear combinations) of repeated sampling from a random distribution will be normal regardless of the shape of the original population's distribution as the number of samples grows large.

central nervous system

n. (CNS) The spinal cord and brain of a vertebrate organism, contrasting with the peripheral nervous system, which is composed of the sensory and motor neurons throughout the rest of the body.

central tendency

n. The middle of any distribution of measures, usually using the mean, the median, or the mode as a description.

central tendency measures

n. Any measure of central tendency in a distribution of measurements, the most common of which are mean, median, and mode.

central trait

n. Any of a small number of common traits which best describe an individual within her/his culture.

central vision

n. Perception in the center of the visual field. In humans this area is more acute than peripheral vision because of the high density of receptors in the macula and particularly in the fovea, the portion of the retina upon which light from the center of the visual fields falls.

centration

n. A tendency to attend to only one aspect of a problem ignoring other, potentially

useful aspects in Piaget's theory of intellectual development.

centroid

n. **1.** A point of convergence in a multidimensional space of all hyperplanes which divides all the dimensions into equal moments. **2.** In physical objects the center of mass.

cephalocaudal

adj. Moving from the head toward the tail.

cephalocaudal development

n. The head-to-tail progression of sensory acuity and motor development in human infants such that motor coordination and sensory acuity first develop around the head and then move toward the tail (base of the spinal column) and later the legs and feet.

cerebellum

n. A large bump at the back of the spinal cord immediately below the occipital lobe which is involved in temporal integration of sensory and motor functions in fine muscle movement; gross muscle coordination, including balance and posture; and language and music perception.

cerebral aqueduct

n. A small space between the third and fourth ventricles which allows cerebrospinal fluid to drain into the fourth ventricle. Blockage of this aqueduct is usual in the hydrocephalus in infancy.

cerebral cortex

n. The large, exterior mass of gray matter about 2–4 mm thick that is divided into two halves and that covers most of the upper portion of the brain, including the frontal, parietal, temporal, and occipital lobes. The cerebral cortex is involved in sensory, motor, memory, thought, and judgment functions of the brain. The cerebral cortex is folded so that it has a much greater surface area than would be the case were it uniform, and the folds demarcate different functional areas.

cerebral dominance

n. Sometimes used as synonymous with hemisphere specialization or brain asymmetry.

The term *cerebral dominance* emphasizes that there is a specialization (dominance) for some cognitive function, usually language. Sometimes in the past it was usual to refer to a dominant or major hemisphere (generally the left) and a nondominant or minor hemisphere (generally the right). Cerebral dominance is a term that has been progressively disappearing and is used less and less in the scientific literature.   – AA

▶ *See also* **HEMISPHERIC SPECIALIZATION**

cerebral hemisphere

n. One of the two halves of brain separated by the longitudinal or interhemispheric fissure. They are relatively symmetrical. In the convexity of the cerebral hemispheres four lobes are distinguished: frontal, parietal, temporal, and occipital. Two major landmarks are observed: the central (or Rolandic) fissure, separating the frontal and parietal lobes, and the lateral (or Sylvian), separating the temporal lobe from the parietal and the frontal. Parietal and occipital lobes are separated by the parietal-occipital sulcus; there is no evident landmark separating the temporal and occipital lobes. Sometimes, the insula (deep in the lateral fissure) is regarded as a fifth cortical lobe. Both cerebral hemispheres are interconnected mainly by the corpus callosum, as well as by some other smaller commissures: the anterior commissure, posterior commissure, and hippocampal commissure. The outer layer of the cerebral hemispheres corresponds to the cerebral cortex, composed of six layers of neurons (gray matter); internally, they are mainly composed of incoming and outgoing fibers from gray matter (white matter). Cerebral hemispheres are covered by three membranes known as meninges (the dura, arachnoid, and pia).   – AA

▶ *See also* **CEREBRAL DOMINANCE** *and* **HEMISPHERIC SPECIALIZATION**

cerebral palsy

n. (CP) A lack of coordination, including spasticity, awkward movements, paralysis, difficulty in walking, and speech problems, resulting from damage to the brain during gestation or the first 5 years of life. Spastic CP results from damage to the motor cortex, corticospinal tract, or pyramidal tract. Dyskinetic CP results from damage to the basal ganglia, ataxic CP from damage to the cerebellum, and mixed CP from damage to multiple sites.

cerebrospinal

adj. Of or relating to the brain and spinal cord.

cerebrospinal fluid

n. The nearly pure saline solution that bathes the brain and spinal cord and acts as a cushion to them in the event of trauma. In addition to salt, the cerebrospinal fluid contains microglial cells, which are a part of the immune system which disposes of unconnected cells and other debris.

cerebrovascular

adj. Of or relating to the blood vessels in the brain.

cerebrovascular accident

n. The breaking or blockage of a blood vessel in the brain which results in an interruption of the supply of oxygen and nutrients to the brain, temporarily or permanently interrupting brain function. Also called a stroke.

cerebrum

n. The largest part of the human brain, lying above the cerebellum and surrounding the midbrain and consisting of four main pairs of lobes on either side of the central fissure and the corpus callosum and commissures connecting them. Also called the telencephalon.

cerveau isolé

n. A surgical operation for research purposes in which the brainstem is severed between the diencephalon and hindbrain or between the inferior and superior colliculi. This usually results in a permanent sleep-like state.

chained reinforcement schedule

n. A compounded schedule of reinforcement in which a subject must complete one or more reinforcement schedules, receive a signal, and then complete more reinforcement schedules before being reinforced. These types of schedules were used to study and to attempt to explain complex learning.

change blindness

n. An inability to detect changes in visual scenes when the person sees one scene first and then the same scene with one or more aspects altered.

change-of-standard effect

n. The change-of-standard effect refers to the way memory is distorted when a past judgment about some stimulus property is used in the present to recall that property without taking into account that the standard currently being used to decode the meaning of that earlier judgment is different from the standard originally used to encode the judgment. With rare exception, judgments involving trait-related constructs, such as friendly, intelligent, tall, and attractive, are comparative judgments that require some standard of comparison. For example, to judge that "Tom is friendly" is to judge that Tom is more friendly than some standard of friendliness one has in mind, such as the friendliness of your friends or the friendliness of people in general (the "average" person).

It is necessary to use standards not only to encode comparative judgments, but also to decode the meaning of those judgments. When trait-related judgments are decoded or comprehended, the position of the target along the dimension of judgment is interpreted as being away from the standard in the direction of the region anchored by the judgment. For example, the judgment, "Bob is short" means that Bob's position along the height dimension is away from the standard in the direction of the short region of the height dimension. But what height is actually inferred depends on what standard is used. Imagine that you attend a party where most of the guests are college volleyball players, and someone mentions that Bob, whom you have not met, is "short." Your inference about Bob's actual height will vary, depending on whether you use the immediate context of volleyball players as the standard for decoding the judgment or use people in general as the standard.

Some standard, therefore, must be used both to encode and to decode trait-related judgments. However, there is no assurance that the standard used to encode the judgment will be the same as the standard used to decode the judgment. This is true whether the encoder and the decoder are the same person or two different people. The change-of-standard effect concerns the case where the encoder and decoder are the same person at two different points in time – a person attempting to decode the referential meaning of an earlier judgment that he or she made. A common example of standards changing from the time of encoding to the time of decoding is when the standard individuals use to encode a target person's trait is determined by the context of other people with the target person at the time (e.g., the other volleyball players at the party), but the standard they use to decode the trait judgment is people in general. In the example of Bob, this could produce a memory of Bob as being shorter than average when he is actually only shorter than taller-than-average volleyball players. The change-of-standard effect can also occur because a standard itself can change over time, such as what one believes is "average." A version of this is using oneself as the standard, the reason adults often inaccurately remember the house they lived in briefly as a young child as being huge (it was huge compared to their size at the time). Finally, research has shown that the change-of-standard effect is robust and difficult to debias – the memory distortion occurs even when individuals are reminded of the different standard they used to make their initial judgment from the standard they are currently using to decode that judgment.   – ETH

character

n. The whole of the mental processes and behavioral aspects of a person which differentiate him or her from other persons and particularly the prospects and aspects which are consistent over time.

character disorder

n. A pervasive and enduring pattern of dynamic psychophysical processes, subjective experience, perceptual distortion, and behavior which is markedly maladaptive within a culture. These patterns tend to develop before adulthood, persist in the face of punishment, and lead to personal unhappiness and interpersonal difficulties. Also called personality disorder.

charisma
n. The capacity to gain the attention of and positively influence other people.

chemoreceptor
n. A sensory nerve surface on the taste buds of the tongue or in the nasal epithelium capable of reacting with particular molecules in the environment so as to develop a sensation of taste or smell.

chemotherapy
n. The process of treating cancer with chemicals which are more toxic to cancer cells than to normal tissues.

child abuse
n. Any form of mental, physical, or sexual behavior toward a child which is detrimental to the child and well beyond that normally associated with caregiver behavior within a culture.

childhood disintegrative disorder
n. An insidious and marked deterioration in language, social skills, bowel or bladder control, play, and motor skills in a child with more than 2 years of normal development that is associated with profound mental retardation and is likely to be due to neurological damage.

childhood schizophrenia
n. Schizophrenia beginning in childhood instead of the normal course in which schizophrenia appears during late adolescence or early adulthood. In earlier times *childhood schizophrenia* was a broader term which included autism and other pervasive developmental disorders.

child neglect
n. A failure to provide a dependent child with the sustenance, protection, attention, stimulation, or affection that the child needs for normal development.

child psychology
n. The branch of psychology devoted to the study of children and their development.

Children's Apperception Test
n. A version of the Thematic Apperception Test, which was developed for use with children using drawings of animals in humanlike relationship settings. The test is usually interpreted intuitively by a psychologist in accord with her/his theoretical orientation.

chimeric face
n. A composite face formed by photographically joining the left side of one person's face to the right side of another person's face for use in studies of differences in the functioning of the two brain hemispheres.

chi-square distribution
n. Any distribution of the summed squares of the deviates of a normally distributed variable or a probability distribution theoretically derived from the summed squares of a normal distribution. Chi-square distributions are used to assess the probability that a chi-square statistic computed from a data sample is likely to be drawn from a randomly distributed population.

chi-square test
n. A statistical test in which the sum of the squared deviations of observed frequencies minus theoretically expected frequencies is compared to that expected in a chi-square distribution which tests whether or not the observed and expected frequencies are likely to be drawn from the same population.

chlordiazepoxide
n. The first benzodiazepine marketed (1957) as an anxiolytic drug, under the brand name Librium, and still widely used to alleviate the symptoms of alcohol withdrawal. It is an addictive central nervous system depressant drug which is sometimes prescribed to depressed individuals because the overdose

potential is low, as it takes more than a thousand normal doses to be fatal to an average adult.

chlorpromazine
n. An antipsychotic drug of the phenothiazine family which works by blocking dopamine receptors and has marked side effects, including tardive dyskinesia, extrapyramidal reactions, neuromuscular rigidity, cognitive slowing, and sedation. Its use has been largely supplanted by newer drugs which are more effective and have fewer side effects.

choice reaction time
n. The time a subject takes to make a response after presentation of a stimulus in a task requiring the subject to make different responses depending on the characteristics of the stimulus. This has been a very widely used dependent variable in cognitive psychology.

choice shift
n. Any shift in choice made by an individual in the presence of others versus when alone, including the risky shift, cautious shift, and group polarization phenomena.

cholecystokinin
n. (CCK) A peptide hormone found in both the duodenum and the brain which acts as a neurotransmitter at a limited set of receptors and is believed to have a role in controlling appetite.

choline
n. An amine synthesized from lecithin and a precursor to acetylcholine and numerous methyl groups used in other processes of metabolism. Besides acting as a precursor to acetylcholine, choline is necessary for the structural integrity of cell walls and in signaling in cell membranes.

cholinergic
adj. Of or relating to choline or the choline-derived neurotransmitters.

chorea
n. Rapid, involuntary, and purposeless jerky movements of the arms, legs, and facial muscles characteristic of Huntington's disease. When chorea becomes extreme and the whole body begins to thrash, it is referred to as ballism. Huntington's chorea is caused by excessive levels of dopamine in motor areas of the brain, and its symptoms are alleviated with antidopaminergic drugs.

chromatic color
n. Colors that have the visual characteristics of hue and saturation, which are all colors except black, white, and gray.

chromatic vision
n. The perception of color along with light intensities which is characteristic of normal human vision without color blindness.

chromosomal anomaly
n. Any change in the normal number or structure of chromosomes which is usually detected when it results in physical or mental abnormalities.

chromosome
n. A roughly rod shaped structure in the nucleus of cells containing deoxyribonucleic acid (DNA) which is the genetic blueprint for cell function and body growth. Humans have 23 pairs of chromosomes, which contain more than 33,000 individual genes, each of which is involved with the formation of a particular set of proteins within cells. Each individual in sexually reproducing organisms receives half of its chromosomes, one of each pair, from each of its parents.

chromosome disorder
n. Any disorder caused by abnormality in the number or structure of the chromosomes. About 7–8% of all pregnancies are spontaneously aborted as a result of chromosome disorders in the developing fetus. Down syndrome, a form of mental retardation, is caused by abnormalities in chromosome 21; Turner's syndrome is caused by a partial or missing X, or female, chromosome; and some people inherit two Y, or male, sex chromosomes and are likely to have hypermasculine characteristics.

chronic brain disorder

n. Any long-lasting disorder due to problems with brain function or formation, often resulting from brain trauma. These include Down syndrome, Huntington's chorea, stroke, most forms of epilepsy, and mad cow disease.

chronic fatigue syndrome

n. A controversial disorder first described in 1988 in which a person suffers from fatigue for 6 months or more which is not alleviated by sleep and has impaired recent memory and concentration, sore throat, muscle and joint pain, and swelling and headaches. There is no known cause of chronic fatigue syndrome, although some hypothesize that it is the result of viral infection. There has been much debate as to whether this syndrome has physical or mental causes, and in recent years most physicians have moved to a belief that there are unknown physical causes.

chronic pain

n. Any pain which persists for long periods. It is usually due to nerve or organ damage which does not heal and can be treated with some success with psychological interventions.

chronic undifferentiated schizophrenia

n. A form of schizophrenia in which there are at least two of the following symptoms: delusions, hallucinations, disorganized speech, disorganized or catatonic behavior, or affective flattening, alogia, or avolition, without prominent symptoms of paranoid, disorganized, or catatonic schizophrenia.

chronological age

n. The amount of time which has elapsed since the birth of an individual.

chunk

n. A mental unit of which about seven can be held in short-term memory. All information can be organized in various ways, and so the amount of information in any mental process depends on its organization. As an example, people frequently remember well known area codes as a single chunk despite their having three digits, while most digits are remembered as a chunk.

chunking

n. The process of organizing information into a unit with a single mental representation. The human mind can deal with about seven chunks at a time, and so good communication requires information to be organized in ways so that seven or fewer than seven chunks or organized units need to be considered at any one time.

cilia

n. Plural of *cilium.* **1.** An eyelash. **2.** A hairlike projection from a cell body as in the hair cells of the inner ear or the movement-generating cilia of some microbes.

cingulate gyrus

n. Prominent gyrus in the mesial part of the brain, limited above by the cingulate sulcus and below by the corpus callosum. It receives input from the somatosensory cortex (parietal lobe) and the anterior nucleus of the thalamus. It projects to the entorhinal cortex. The cingulate gyrus is included in the so-called limbic system (emotional system of the brain, involved in emotion but also in memory and learning). It is thought that it participates in coordinating emotional responses according to the sensory input, modulating emotional responses to pain, responding to environmental stimuli, and regulating mood, and in memory and learning.   – A A

circadian rhythm

n. Any daily or near-daily pattern in physiological change or overt behavior; the sleep-wake cycle is the best example.

circadian rhythm sleep disorder

n. A sleep disorder caused by a mismatch between a person's circadian rhythm and the demands of the world around her/him resulting in the person's feeling sleepy when he/she should be awake and feeling energetic when he/she should be sleeping. In the delayed sleep-phase type the person's circadian rhythm is longer than 24 hours so he/she has difficulty falling asleep and waking up as early as required. In the jet-lag type a person's circadian rhythm is appropriate for a different time zone, causing him or her to want to be awake and asleep at inappropriate local times. In the shift-work type repeated changes in work shift result in a mismatch between sleep/work schedule and bodily clock; this is usually worse when change in work schedule moves from later to earlier, as opposed to earlier to later. Most people cope better with waking and sleeping at later times than they do at earlier times.

circular reasoning

n. A fallacious type of reasoning in which the conclusion of an argument is already contained in the assumptions at the start of the argument. As an example one might say, "Rich people are naturally conservative and you can tell because they are more likely to be Republicans than Democrats."

circumplex model of emotion

n. A model of emotion in which emotions are arranged in a circle such that near emotions are similar, emotions across the circle are nearly opposite, and emotions close to right angles are largely unrelated. Such models are appealing for their visual symmetry but have little predictive power when compared with other models.

circumvallate papilla

n. Seven to 11 small ridges at the back of the tongue separated by trenches which are lined with taste buds, most of which are sensitive to bitter tastes.

clairvoyance

n. The capacity to perceive the past, the future, distant things, or events or things not seen with normal vision.

clang association

n. The mimicking of a given sound, or perseveration on particular sounds that rhyme. For example, a clang association to the word *hop* would be "bop, sop, top, sop, sop, top, rop." A clang association is a disorganized symptom in schizophrenia.   – DGa

classical conditioning

n. The learning theories of Ivan Pavlov, in which only observable events such as stimulus conditions and change in responses are used to define and explore learning. In the basic process of classical conditioning, a new or conditioned response (CR) replaces or appears in addition to an unconditioned response (UCR) when a conditioned stimulus (CS) is paired with an unconditioned stimulus (UCS) that is usually followed by the unconditioned response. In the classic experiment, it was observed that when a bell was rung shortly before dogs were fed, the dogs soon began to salivate upon hearing the bell whether food was subsequently presented or not. So the UCR of salivating to UCS, food, had a CR of salivation to the bell added after pairing of the CS, bell, with the UCS, food.

classical psychoanalysis

n. The psychoanalysis of Sigmund Freud in which the therapeutic process occurs through a patient's saying whatever enters her/his mind without censorship (free association), which is interpreted by the therapist to the patient, who overcomes resistance to conscious acknowledgment of the interpretation using the energy of the emotional attachment (cathexis) he/she has transferred to the therapist; thus the patient becomes able to form new patterns of association which lead to better functioning.

classic test theory

n. Theory of testing in which each test score is supposed to be the sum of random error and true measurement. As random error is normally distributed, it allows computation of the reliability of scores either through repeated testing as in test-retest reliability or through examination of internal consistency of items as through part-whole correlations or more recently factor analysis. Later versions of test theory considered test scores to be the sum of truth, random error, and bias (consistent error), thereby facilitating calculations of validity.

class interval

n. The range of scores which are included within a particular bin or group in a frequency table or histogram with a defined upper and lower limit and usually described by its midpoint. Thus a histogram of age distribution might have one bin for those from birth to age 10, and another for every 10 years of age.

class limits
n. The defined boundaries of a class interval.

Clever Hans
n. The name of a horse famous in the early 1900s for being able to give the correct answer to any question its owner asked of it by tapping its hooves on the ground. It was eventually found that Clever Hans could only answer questions to which his owner knew the answer and only when he could see his owner, and it was supposed that the owner was unconsciously giving Hans cues and rewards when he tapped his feet appropriately to answer questions. This story has been used ever since that time as an example of reaching false conclusions by overlooking important variables in research.

client-centered therapy
n. The therapy developed by Carl Rogers which assumes that each person lives in a reality of his or her own, has inherent drive to actualize his/her own unique potential, and will do so unless prevented by need for the positive regard of significant other people. Conditional regard from important other persons leads an individual to have and to act on false beliefs about himself or herself in a process which leads to anxiety and poor choices in life. This nondirective therapy consists of the therapist's helping the client verbally explore the issues that the client selects by acknowledging that the therapist understands what the client is expressing and does not condemn the client for the experience. This leads the client to acknowledge the parts of himself/herself he or she has been ignoring or denying and thus gain better information with which to make choices in life as well as to a lessened tendency to ignore parts of his or her experience in the future.

clinical data combination
n. The integration of multiple measures of functioning into a decision or classification of a subject. This can be done mechanically by a statistical procedure derived from previous data or intuitively by a clinician or team of clinicians. Mechanical/statistical procedures are more likely to give correct results as long as they have an adequate base of information for comparison.

clinical psychologist
n. An individual with a doctorate in psychology who performs psychological testing, assessments, therapy, consultations, or other psychological tasks in applications to individuals or groups with mental disorders.

clinical psychology
n. The branch of psychology that attempts to apply the results of psychological science to the treatment of mental disorders or to research the treatment of mental disorders.

clinical trial
n. A research study on groups of people or animals in which the effects of a treatment are assessed, usually with a view of comparing the effectiveness of different possible treatments.

clinical versus statistical prediction
n. A comparison of the accuracy of clinicians' intuitions about patients' future behavior versus those made by mechanical statistical programs. Mechanical/statistical procedures are more likely to give correct results as long as they have an adequate base of information for comparison.

clitoris
n. A small body of highly enervated erectile tissue whose outer portion is inside the labial folds and anterior to the vaginal opening. It extends 3–4 inches into the labial tissue with two branches or drure, each of which contains a corpus cavernosum, as does the shaft of the penis, and includes the bulbs of the vestibule. The clitoris arises from the same embryonic tissue as the penis does in males and has analogous parts: the clitoral hood is analogous to the penal foreskin, the clitoral glans

to the penal meatus, and both clitoris and penis have corpus cavernosum. The clitoris is the center of sexual stimulation and pleasure in the human female.

closed-mindedness

n. Closed-mindedness is an unwillingness to entertain seriously the validity of conceptions that deviate from one's own. Closed-mindedness is often described in terms of its manifestations, which include a tendency to leap to conclusions while ignoring relevant information and to stick to one's beliefs even if reality proves to have little or no justification for such beliefs. As a result of these tendencies, closed-mindedness is often associated with black-and-white thinking and ideological extremism. Closed-mindedness refers to a motivational propensity rather than a lack of ability to consider alternative views. For instance, while a lack of intelligence may cause an individual to overlook new information, closed-mindedness typically involves the lack of willingness to do so, or the active willingness to avoid any ideas or conceptions that might threaten the integrity of one's existing knowledge system. Moreover, closed-mindedness can be considered a trait inherent to a particular person, but it may also be evoked by particular situations.

The concept of closed-mindedness has been central in a variety of prominent traditions in psychology. Psychodynamic perspectives have considered closed-mindedness a psychological defense mechanism consisting of a basic mistrust in the world that originates in frustration of the search for oral gratification during early childhood. Lack of such frustration is assumed to create openness to new experiences, a tendency considered to be adaptive in dealing with the outside world. The social excesses that may originate from closed-mindedness have figured prominently in Adorno and Frenkel-Brunswik's treatment of the authoritarian personality. Their central term, *intolerance of ambiguity*, a term highlighting the motivational facets of closed-mindedness, is argued to give rise to a type of personality that is especially likely to follow leadership and rules of any kind slavishly.

While the authoritarian personality as a psychological construct was specifically developed to describe and explain the rise of fascist ideology, subsequent theorizing has deemphasized the relation between closed-mindedness and ideological content. In the early 1960s, Rokeach was especially influential in stressing that closed-mindedness, as captured by him under the label of *dogmatism*, is to be understood as a process rather than a content. Irrespective of the ideology one may hold, the closed as opposed to the open mind manifests itself through the aversion to anything that deviates from this ideology.

This process-based, content-free analysis of closed-mindedness dominates the recent history and contemporary thinking on the phenomenon. Closed-mindedness is also taken out of the realm of the pathological. While it may be the result of a traumatic experience, closed-mindedness is now considered by many a natural response to a social world characterized by an informational load that would be impossible to deal with using piecemeal processing alone. It may not be – just – personal uncertainties that give rise to closed-mindedness; situations may also necessitate an information processing strategy whereby reliance on existing knowledge is preferred to new information. Furthermore, to the extent it can be considered a normal, adaptive response to complex environments, closed-mindedness should encompass a broad range of implications, not only related to one's belief system, or how one treats different-minded others, but also to basic information processing strategies.

Over the past decades, research on the need for nonspecific closure by Arie Kruglanski and colleagues has indeed unveiled such a wide range of implications of closed-mindedness for the processing of (social) information. The need for closure refers to the desire for immediate and definite knowledge and the aversion to the uncertainties associated with the lack thereof. Given the conceptual overlap of the need for closure and closed-mindedness, the research program on the need for closure provides important insights for the understanding of closed-mindedness. Consistently with the modern view of closed-mindedness, the need for closure is considered both a personality characteristic and a state that can be induced in a particular situation. A number of factors may help to induce the need for closure. In an experimental setting, a state of closed-mindedness is often created by having participants perform particular tasks under heightened time pressure while performing cognitively demanding tasks or while being exposed to aversive ambient noise.

At the heart of the need for closure research program lies the notion that the way ordinary people come to believe particular things is essentially the same as the way scientists arrive at their insights. Like scientists, laypeople begin to believe by observing, developing expectancies about a particular domain, and subsequently testing and evaluating the validity of these expectancies. These processes of hypothesis generation and hypothesis validation are of relevance to demarcate the workings of the closed versus the open mind.

Within this framework, closed-mindedness is to be understood as a tendency to use relatively few observations to form particular hypotheses and to consider relatively few pieces of evidence to accept the hypotheses. Closed-mindedness thus manifests itself in very basic psychological operations, as well as more complex forms of social behavior and thought. On a basic level, closed-mindedness restricts the extent to which information is deemed useful to form a particular judgment. It further limits the number of hypotheses that an individual is willing to generate while making a particular judgment. Research has also revealed that closed-minded individuals tend to have greater confidence in the hypotheses they do form than their open-minded counterparts. Furthermore, closed-mindedness has been found to encompass information search strategies that confirm existing categorizations rather than enable further crystallization of stimulus information, thus showing that closed-mindedness not only affects the amount of information processing, but also the type of information that is processed.

Closed-mindedness is also associated with the tendency to base a judgment on early cues. Closed-minded individuals are thus especially likely to base impressions of a target on information presented early versus late in a sequence, a phenomenon called the primacy effect. The use of early cues is also reflected in their greater likelihood to exhibit anchoring effects, whereby information that is presented just prior to a particular judgment comes to play a particularly influential role in that judgment. In the domain of social perception and communication, closed-mindedness encompasses a variety of implications. Their greater reliance on existing knowledge makes closed-minded individuals especially likely to base interpersonal judgments on stereotypes. More generally, closed-mindedness has been found to reduce the ability to empathize with interaction partners and to tune one's communications and adaptations to intended audiences, thus reducing effective communication and interaction.

On a group level, the motivational nature of closed-mindedness implies the utility of membership of groups that share a similar reality with the closed-minded individual. As a result, the group dynamics among the closed-minded is characterized by a cluster of features that serve to reduce uncertainty and maintain a simple, stable shared reality. Research has identified a number of these features, including pressures to opinion uniformity among group members, endorsement of an autocratic leadership and decision-making structure, intolerance of diversity in group composition (that betokens the potentiality for dissent), rejection of opinion deviates and extolment of conformists, in-group favoritism and out-group derogation, attraction to groups (both in- and out-groups) possessing strongly shared realities, conservatism and adherence to the group's norms, and loyalty to one's in-group qualified by the degree to which it constitutes a "good" shared reality provider.

The research showing these relations between closed-mindedness and group dynamics has often induced the state of mind by using techniques such as imposing time pressure or having participants perform particularly cognitively demanding tasks. Hence, also with regard to group dynamics, the concept of closed-mindedness has been studied in mundane and content-free ways. Nonetheless, despite the ease with which experimental techniques can be employed to induce closed-mindedness, its often adaptive function in particular contexts, and its frequent manifestations in everyday life, the concept continues to have a pejorative connotation. A recent publication arguing that there might be a relation between political conservatism and closed-mindedness has given rise to considerable controversy both inside and outside academia. The controversy again centered on the alleged suggestion that political conservatism in the light of its relation with the need for closure could be considered a pathological tendency, thus raising issues reminiscent of Adorno's work on the authoritarian personality. Nonetheless, it should be stressed that the contemporary analysis of closed-mindedness suggests that it can be adaptive in dealing with particular situations. For example, closed-mindedness may be associated with generally valued characteristics such as personal commitment and unwavering loyalty. As such, the contemporary concept of closed-mindedness does not encompass any guidance for demarcating the normal from the pathological.   – MD, AK

closed question
n. A question which must be answered by selecting from a limited set of responses such as true/false or multiple-choice items on an exam or a question like "Did you turn left or right?" Closed questions control the responses of a partner in conversation and limit his/her ability to express his/her ideas while open-ended questions such as "What do you think about X?" generally share control of the conversation and lead to greater exchange of information and greater openness and satisfaction with the conversation of the responder.

close relationships
n. Close relationships refer to a bond between two individuals that is characterized by one of the following: feelings of interdependence, emotional attachment, and fulfillment of psychological needs. Examples include parent-child relationships, romantic relationships, and companionship/friendship.   – EWMA, CYC

closure, law of
n. One of the laws of Gestalt perception, which suggests that people tend to perceive objects with missing parts as complete although they can discern the missing parts if they focus on them and to perceive asymmetric objects as symmetric. Thus this figure < > is likely to be perceived as a diamond or tilted square shape even though it is really two separate angles.

clozapine
n. An atypical (recent) antipsychotic medication of the dibenzodiazepine family first introduced to the U.S. market in 1990. It has effects at both the dopaminergic and serotonergic receptor sites. It is an effective antipsychotic agent but suppresses immune function (agranulocytosis) in a significant minority of patients, and so its use is usually limited to patients who have not responded to other drugs.

Cloze procedure
n. The Cloze procedure is an examination or experimentation technique that requires students or participants to fill in blanks with a missing word (e.g., Bobby and Suzy take the _____ home from school together every day). This procedure is often used to assess the student's or participant's comprehension ability, vocabulary ability, or general knowledge. Performance on Cloze tasks is highly correlated with performance on standardized measures of comprehension ability. In addition to testing, this task is used in experimental research to determine properties of a sentence or text such as its predictability, readability, and coherence.   – NL

cluster analysis
n. Any of several statistical procedures in which a vector space is created using the variables in a study and the individual cases are grouped by closeness to each other and distance from other cases in the vector space.

clustering
n. **1.** The tendency of people to group together items in memory on the basis of subjective

dimensions of similarity regardless of the order in which they are presented. **2.** The tendency of cases to be close to some other cases and far from other cases in a multidimensional vector space. **3.** In industrial psychology, an interview process of noting key ideas and then grouping them together as the interview progresses. The clusters can then be used to create taxonomies, menus, or task lists.

cluster sample
n. A sampling procedure in which a population is divided into clusters, a sample of clusters is selected, and a sample is drawn from the selected clusters and used to estimate population characteristics. This procedure is usually cheaper and more practical than a random sample would be, but error is introduced in creating and selecting the clusters and so the sample is likely to be less accurate than a true random sample.

coalition formation
n. The process of forming temporary alliances among group members in order to control group processes and outcomes. These groups are formed by most social animals and occasionally occur cross-species and tend to be short-lived as interests and situations change.

cochlea
n. A hollow snail-shaped bone in the inner ear. It receives pressure from the middle ear via the oval window, pressure which travels through the diminishing winding tube of the cochlea to the organ of Corti, within which hair cells transmute pressure waves into impulses in the auditory nerve which we experience as sound.

cocktail party phenomenon
n. The observation that humans will notice background sounds which have importance to them while focusing on a different source of sound. Thus, a person who is carrying on a conversation with one person in a crowded cocktail party and is not attending to other people's conversation will nonetheless hear his or her own name or some other personally important thing if it comes up in one of the other conversations. This is used as evidence that we at least partially process information to which we are not attending or of which we are not conscious.

code frame switching
n. The process by which bilinguals switch between one cultural meaning system and another when switching languages. It is also known as cultural frame switching.

codependency
n. **1.** A pathological form of relationship in which two persons are mutually controlling, one by engaging in addictive behaviors and the other by sequentially attacking and supporting the addicted person, enabling him or her to maintain the addiction at the price of emotional devastation. Thus, a codependent person in a relationship with an alcoholic may lie to his/her boss and buy him/her alcohol when the alcoholic is unable to do so and at the same time demean the alcoholic either overtly or covertly. **2.** The state of being mutually dependent in a relationship.

coding
n. **1.** The conversion of information into an altered form either for ease of processing or for secrecy. **2.** The organization of information into forms and categories usable in an analytic process.

coefficient alpha
n. An index of the internal consistency of a set of items which can have more than two possible responses which is the average of all possible split-half correlation coefficients corrected for attenuation. Coefficient alpha is a derivative of Kuder-Richardson formula 20 (KR20), which performs the same function for tests in which only one of two answers is possible for each item. Coefficient alpha is strongly related to the length of the scale so that scales with a length greater than 100 items always approach 1.00, or perfect consistency. Also called Cronbach's alpha.

coefficient of alienation
n. (*k*) An index of the variance between two variables not explained by their covariance. It is given by the formula $1 - r^2$, where *r* is

the Pearson product-moment correlation between two variables. Also called the residual and the coefficient of nondetermination.

coefficient of concordance

n. (W) An index of the degree to which rankings by independent judges agree with each other.

coefficient of correlation

n. A numerical index of shared relationship between two variables. The product-moment correlation is the most widely used correlation coefficient, measures linear relationship, and is appropriate for use with ratio variables and used with interval data. It shows relationship on a scale where 0 is no relationship, +1 is a perfect positive relationship, and −1 is a perfect negative relationship. Kendall's tau is often used with ordinal variables, and Spearman's rho is often used with rank order correlations.

coefficient of determination

n. The coefficient of determination, a statistical term used by psychologists, is the percentage of variance accounted for in a variable of interest, also known as the criterion variable. The coefficient of determination represents the percentage of explained variance in proportion to the total amount of variance in the criterion variable. This is the percentage of total variation in the criterion variable that can be predicted by knowing the value of the other variable or variables in the equation. Also known as "r squared," the coefficient of determination is computed by squaring the simple correlation between two variables (r) or by squaring the multiple correlation (R) from a regression analysis of a criterion (dependent) variable onto more than one independent variable. Because the coefficient of determination is a squared version of the correlation coefficient, and because correlation coefficients range in value from −1 to +1, the coefficient of determination ranges in value from 0 (0%) to 1 (100%).　　– MWP

coefficient of reliability

n. A numeric index which reflects the stability of a test score or the relative proportion of true score and random error within a test score. The most important coefficient of reliability is a test-retest correlation coefficient, which estimates the temporary stability of a test. Kuder-Richardson 20, coefficient alpha, and split-half reliability coefficients are all measures of the internal consistency of a test, which is important when unidimensionality is an issue or when the dimension being measured is not expected to have temporal stability, as in a mood scale. The alternate forms reliability correlation coefficient is rarely used as it is difficult to ensure alternate forms are actually equivalent. ▶ See also **RELIABILITY COEFFICIENT**

coefficient of validity

n. An index of the degree to which a test measures what it is intended to measure, as opposed to extraneous variables and random error. A test-criterion correlation coefficient is the most commonly used and important of these. In cases in which a theoretical single dimension is being measured, coefficient alpha can be used as a measure of validity.

cofigurative culture

n. A culture in which change occurs rapidly. Both adults and peers socialize young people. Young people may have to turn to one another for advice and information in this type of culture.

cognition

n. **1.** A general term for all forms of mental processes including conscious ones such as perception, thought, and memory, as well as nonconscious processes such as grammatical construction, parsing of sensory data into percepts, and the neural control of physiological processes. **2.** A particular thought.

cognitive ability

n. The aptitude for or skill at performing mental tasks such as memory, perception, judgment, decision making, comprehension, attention, reasoning of various kinds, intuition, language, and mathematics. This phrase has become a substitute for the older term *intelligence* and is usually used in an educational setting.

cognitive aging

n. Normal changes in the thought processes of adults as they grow older, which include slowed reaction time, more positive affect and greater ability to regulate emotion, less ability to remember recent events, greater semantic memory, and better judgment in complex tasks.

cognitive behavior therapy

n. (CBT) A form of psychotherapy that attempts to meld the techniques of cognitive therapy with behavioral therapy. It includes a belief that thoughts, emotions, and behavior are aspects of a single system in which changing any one affects the others. CBT borrows the techniques of identifying and changing problematic thoughts from cognitive therapy and behavioral change techniques from behavior therapy.

cognitive busyness

n. The degree to which the mind's capacity for processing information is taken up with a task or tasks which limit or interfere with its ability to accomplish other tasks. Thus if a person is working on a problem, his or her mental busyness level is higher than if he/she were simply sitting and watching a blank screen.

cognitive development

n. The appearance, expansion, and alteration of mental processes from birth until death including sensory and motor perception and control, all types of memory, consciousness, attention, analyzing, solving problems, emotional experience and regulation, counterfactuals, and conscious thought.

cognitive dissonance

n. A state of being made anxious by the incompatibility of two or more ideas, experiences, or perceptions within one's belief structure. This usually occurs when a person is forced by circumstances into the acknowledgment of an inconsistency that has some importance to the individual, who is then motivated to resolve the dissonance. This can be done by reducing the importance of the perceived contradiction in one's understanding of things; altering one's perception of one or both ideas, experiences, or perceptions; or elaborating justifications for the contradiction.

cognitive dissonance theory

n. The theory that people have a positive need to maintain consistency in their mental maps of themselves and the world. When experience or reasoning leads a person to realize there is a contradiction in his/her mental system, he or she experiences discomfort and is motivated to reduce or eliminate the contradiction by reducing the importance of the perceived contradiction in his/her understanding of things, altering his/her perception of one or both ideas or experiences, or elaborating justifications for the contradiction.

cognitive heuristic

n. **1.** A mental strategy or rule of thumb for solving a problem that is relatively efficient in terms of processing time and usually finds a good solution but does not always find the best solution, as opposed to an algorithm, which involves an exhaustive search for solutions and guarantees the best outcome. **2.** In industrial psychology it is a process of testing an idea or product by using independent testers following standard protocols but not actual use testing of the idea or product. **3.** A working model of a problem used to test aspects of it while ignoring other aspects. ▶ *See also* **AVAILABILITY HEURISTIC, REPRESENTATIVENESS HEURISTIC,** *and* **SIMULATION HEURISTIC**

cognitive interview

n. A structured interview for witnesses designed to improve information recall and to reduce cognitive distortions in testimony, which has been found to increase the amount of information recalled without introducing distortions into it. The process includes asking witnesses to recall by reinstating the context, prompting not to hold back any detail no matter how inconsequential it may seem, altering the sequence of recollection, asking witnesses to say what other witnesses could and could not see, and then finally prompting for details.

cognitive map

n. A mental representation of an environment or locale that is mentally scannable for distance, location, and other relationships of importance to the individual. The term was coined by Edward Tolman to describe the relative ease rats had in finding a new route to a reward site after their usual route was blocked.

cognitive miser

n. One of several competing theories among contemporary (early 21st-century) social cognitive perspectives about human thought processes in the social world. According to the cognitive miser perspective, which is supported by a wealth of research, humans are inherently frugal with cognitive resources because we have only a limited amount of mental resources to deal with our complex social environment. Therefore, we develop heuristics, or "mental shortcuts," to make our cognitive processes more efficient. By using such mechanisms as schemas and stereotypes, we simplify our cognitive processing of social situations. Rather than taking a thorough, data-driven, labor-intensive, slower approach to understanding social situations, we tend to employ these mental shortcuts in order to conserve cognitive energy.
                                              – MWP

cognitive neuroscience

n. The study of how mental processes occur in the central nervous system, focusing on relationships between mental functions and the physiological functioning of neurons, which is an integration of the fields of neuroscience and cognitive psychology. It has been very successful in exploring the causes of functional impairments and finding routes to remediation.

cognitive psychology

n. This term describes a subdiscipline of psychology that examines mental processes involved in perception (both visual and auditory), reasoning and problem solving, language processing, memory, and the processing of various types of information. This field developed from the earlier Gestalt school of psychology pioneered by Max Wertheimer; the work of Jean Piaget, who examined cognitive development in children; and the writings of Noam Chomsky, who initiated the movement toward the study of language in terms of mental processes. Cognitive psychologists seek to understand the mental representations and structures that lead individuals to comprehend, define, and develop knowledge. In the area of memory, researchers seek to understand how information is encoded, stored, and retrieved in the mind. Two main aims in cognitive psychology are, first, to provide a theoretical description of the mind (mental structures or abstract representations, and processes) and, second, to provide experimental and quantitative evidence regarding mental functioning.   – JA

cognitive response analysis

n. An investigation of the mental rehearsals a person engages in while evaluating a piece of persuasive information, with the supposition that the more positive mental rehearsals a person engages in with regard to a particular piece of persuasive communication the more likely it will be that those rehearsals will become part of the person's repertoire of responses and so the more effect the persuasive communication will have on the person.

cognitive restructuring

n. A technique of examining one's beliefs as embodied in automatic thoughts and substituting more accurate beliefs for those found to be distorted or inaccurate. This technique was developed in cognitive therapy and has been applied in other settings.

cognitive schema

n. A mental representation of some aspect of past experience or some part of one's general knowledge. Schemas are a basic unit of analysis in some areas of cognitive psychology. It is supposed by cognitive psychologists that schemas are constantly being created, modified, and imposed on perceptions, situations, understanding, and processes. In cognitive therapy there is an attempt to change maladaptive cognitive schemas.

cognitive science
n. The interdisciplinary science of mind which includes and attempts to integrate approaches from psychology, linguistics, philosophy, anthropology, computer science, and physiology.

cognitive style
n. A characteristic mode of processing information including perceiving, conscious reasoning, remembering, solving problems, and understanding the world in general. Numerous typologies of mind have been suggested, first by Carl Jung in 1923 and continuing to contemporary ideas such as field dependence/independence, cognitive complexity/simplicity, leveling/sharpening, reflectivity/impulsivity, tolerance/intolerance of ambiguity, and abstract/concrete thinking.

cognitive theories of emotion
n. Any of a number of theories of emotion in which conscious thought, self-perceptions, self-relevant appraisals, or some other information processing beyond simple perception and physiological arousal plays a central role.

cognitive therapy
n. (CT) A form of psychotherapy that attempts to alter the content of irrational or distorted automatic and conscious thoughts so as to bring about positive change in the individual. It includes a belief that thoughts, emotions, and behavior are aspects of a single system in which changing any one affects the others. The therapist takes an active role in helping the client notice, evaluate, and revise his or her thinking to more realistic and so more useful patterns.

cognitive tuning
n. The theory that emotion and bodily sensations are used to adjust or select cognitive processes appropriate for a situation. Thus a person might select a heuristic approach in a relaxed, cheerful situation and a more thorough analytical one in a tense, fearful situation.

cohesion
n. The tendency of group members to form affective bonds both to the group as a whole and to individual members of the group which would not be predicted by an analysis of the dyadic interactions of the individual and individual group members, as well as group members' tendency to agree and to act in concert.

coitus
n. Sexual intercourse, usually involving the insertion of the penis in the vagina coupled with rhythmic movements until ejaculation is achieved. It can also include insertion of the penis into other parts of the body such as between the thighs or breasts of a partner.

coitus interruptus
n. Sexual intercourse in which the penis is removed from the vagina before ejaculation and ejaculation usually occurs but outside the vagina, which is often used to attempt to prevent pregnancy. This is a very ineffective birth control method as semen usually seeps out of the end of the penis long before ejaculation occurs.

cold pressor pain
n. Pain resulting from immersion of a limb or part of a limb in iced water for the purpose of testing sensory nerve function.

collective action
n. The pursuit of some goal or goals by more than one person in an at least partially coordinated way. In sociology and political science it is the study of the processes of social and political movements, including the situations in which they occur and their persistence, success or failure, and dissolution. In economics it is the provision of public goods through collaboration and the effect of external variables on this process.

collective control
n. A type of control in which one attempts to control the environment as a member of a group, and the group serves as the agent of control.

collective self
n. The part of the self or self-concept that is shared by all the members of each group to

which the person belongs or believes he or she belongs and is distinguished from the private and public selves. Also called the social self.

collective threat
n. The fear that an in-group member's behavior can reinforce negative stereotypes about one's group.

collective unconscious
n. In Jungian psychology, the totality of the inherited structure of the mind formed over the course of evolution of prehuman and human ancestors which have left traces of often-repeated experiences in the form of archetypes or structural components which can also be considered as inherited potentialities. The collective unconscious determines our capacities to perceive and has predetermined categories into which experiences are fit, behavioral patterns and tendencies to respond, and an impulse to develop all of the inherited capacities of the individual, which is the full realization of the individual. This is distinguished from the personal unconscious, which contains repressed, suppressed, weak, and forgotten memories, as well as individually created organizations of perception and understanding. Also called the transpersonal unconsciousness.

collectivism
n. A cultural pattern found in cultures that tend to be simple and traditional and have many rules and norms that are imposed tightly. This cultural pattern is determined by examining data across cultures. In such data collectivism is the opposite of individualism. Individuals in collectivist cultures define themselves as members of groups, give priority to group goals, behave mostly according to group norms, and do not leave their groups even when they are dissatisfied with them.

High levels of collectivism are found in rural, homogeneous, isolated cultures with much traditional shared ideology and distinct customs and where there is punishment for not doing what the in-group expects. Self-sacrifice for the sake of the in-group is frequent.

This cultural pattern is especially likely when the population density is high, among older members of a culture, among the lower social classes, among those who are religious, and among those who have experienced a common fate.   – HTΓ

▶ *See also* **INDIVIDUALISM**

colliculus
n. The word *colliculus* (plural *colliculi*) refers to a small elevation (hill) above the surrounding parts of a structure. In the midbrain four elevations known as colliculi are found: two superior colliculi and two inferior colliculi. Superior and inferior colliculi are collectively known as corpora quadrigemina. Superior colliculi are related to visual information and inferior colliculi to auditory information. In humans superior colliculi participate in controlling the eye movements. The inferior colliculi are the principal midbrain nucleus of the auditory pathway.   – AA

color adaptation
n. A decrease in sensitivity to a particular color after prolonged stimulation with that color. This occurs as the retinal neurons attuned to that color have been stimulated beyond their capacity to replace the photoreactive chemicals in the cell. Also called chromatic adaptation.

color blindness
n. The inability to perceive a normal range of colors, which may be total or partial. In total color blindness an individual perceives only black, white, and shades of gray. In partial color blindness an individual can lack the capacity to distinguish red, blue, or green colors, depending on which type of photoreceptors are absent form her/his eyes. Most color blindness is inherited and is sex linked but it may also be caused by trauma or disease. Inability to distinguish between red and green is the most common form of color blindness.

color constancy
n. The tendency of humans to perceive that the color of an object remains constant despite

the fact that the colors of the light reflecting from the object and striking the retina will vary with angle, illumination, movement, and other variables. Thus when we see a red ball, we perceive it as being the same color all over, although the actual light reflected from it will vary over its surface.

color mixing

1. *v.* Producing a new color by mixing two or more other colors, as in mixing paint colors for a house. **2.** *n.* The process of color mixing.

colors, primary

n. Red, blue, and yellow or green, which can be mixed to obtain white. From the point of view of the human visual system, all four colors are primary as they correspond to the wavelengths of particular visual receptors.

color vision

n. The ability to distinguish among lights of various wavelengths.

color vision, theories of

n. Any of several explanations of the ability to distinguish among lights of various wavelengths and the existence of primary colors, complementary colors, and afterimages; the laws of color mixing; and different kinds of color blindness. These include the Young-Helmholtz, Hering, Ladd-Franklin, Granit, trichromatic, and opponent process theories.

coma

n. An abnormal state of unconsciousness marked by complete or nearly complete unresponsiveness to stimuli including the absence of normal reflexes. Physical or chemical brain trauma, interruption of blood flow or oxygen to the brain, diabetes, hydroencephalitis, and brain tumors are the most common causes.

commissure

n. Site where two elements are joined. In anatomy it is used to refer to the nerve pathways crossing from one side to the other in the brain (and also the spinal cord) as well as to the site or point where two parts join, for example, in the lips. The brain commisures are the corpus callosum, the anterior commissure, and the posterior commissure. The corpus callosum (the largest white matter structure in the human brain) is situated ventral to the cortex, connects the right and left hemispheres, and contains about 250 million axons. The anterior commissure is a neural pathway connecting the cerebral hemispheres across the middle line, at the level of the fornix. The posterior commissure crosses the midline at the upper end of the cerebral aqueduct.   – AA

▶ *See also* **CORPUS CALLOSUM**

commissurotomy

n. Incision of a body commissure. Commissurotomy of the corpus callosum (callosotomy) results in the so-called split-brain syndrome (the right and left hemispheres become disconnected one from the other). Callosotomy was used for treating some refractory types of epilepsy, but also to treat certain psychiatric disorders.   – AA

commitment

n. **1.** Confinement to a mental institution usually without the consent of the person involved. In most states, involuntary commitment is possible only if a person presents a clear danger to herself/himself or to others. **2.** A cognitive or emotional state of intention to follow a course of action regardless of obstacles. **3.** Financial investment in an enterprise or some other business matter. **4.** Investment of material or psychological resources in a person, group, idea, or activity such that withdrawal entails costs and therefore the investment is maintained.

common fate

n. A Gestalt principle that notes that objects that move in unison tend to be grouped together in perception. Also called the factor of uniform density.

common in-group identity model

n. A theoretical model of group interventions designed to reduce prejudice against an out-group by bringing about a recategorization to include the out-group in the in-group.

commons dilemma

n. The commons dilemma, also known as the tragedy of the commons, refers to the conflict of serving the interests of the self or the interests of the common good. If every individual chooses to serve the interests of the self over those of the common good, the outcome will be detrimental to everyone. Therefore, the optimal solution to this dilemma is for everyone to sacrifice some individual interest for the sake of benefiting everyone.   – EWMA, CYC

▶ *See also* **PRISONER'S DILEMMA**

communality

n. The proportion of the total variance of a variable that is accounted for by the factors making up the variable in a factor analysis. The sum of the squared factor loadings of the variable for all factors in the factor analysis, which can range from 0 to 1.

communication

n. **1.** The transference of understanding from one individual to another or the transfer of data from one source to another in any of a very large number of natural and artificial ways. **2.** The message or actual data being transferred in an act of communication.

communication accommodation theory

n. Communication accommodation theory (CAT) was formulated in the early 1970s and has been refined and elaborated many times since. It is concerned with how and why people reduce and magnify communicative differences among themselves – as well as the social consequences of so doing. Major accommodation strategies include converging toward, or diverging away from, another. These can be achieved by a host of verbal and nonverbal means: via language choice, modifying one's accent or speech rate, changing patterns of smiling, pitch, and gestures, and others. Generally, people converge toward those whom they like or respect or those who have power, while they diverge to underscore the importance of their social identities to others. Importantly, CAT claims people will accommodate to where they believe others to be rather than to where they objectively are.

CAT is regarded as a major theory in the social psychology of language and communication, its propositions receiving much empirical support across an array of cultures and languages. The theory, invoked within many disciplines, has also led to a range of satellite theories, including the intergroup model of bilingualism.   – HG

communication disorder

n. Any of a family of disorders in which a person's capacity for speech and language performance is impaired including expressive language disorder, mixed receptive-expressive language disorder, phonological disorder, stuttering, and communication disorder not otherwise specified (NOS).

communication game theory

n. The application of multipart decision theory to communications in which parties have different interests and have more than one possible strategy or action they can take and whose outcome depends on the actions of the other party(ies). Different communication strategies are analyzed; possible outcomes are delineated on the basis of either logic, previous experience, or both; strategies are adopted; and their outcome is tested.

community psychology

n. A branch of applied psychology that focuses on person-environment interactions usually at the level of the community and is aimed at improving the general quality of life within a community.

comorbidity

n. **1.** The simultaneous presence of more than one disease or disorder in the same person. **2.** The increased likelihood of death due to the presence of additional diseases or disorders along with one considered the primary disease or disorder.

companionate love

n. Love in which there are intimacy and commitment but no passion in Robert J. Sternberg's triangular theory of love.

comparable forms

n. Alternative forms of a test which have similar content but whose psychometric qualities have not been demonstrated.

comparative psychologist

n. A person holding a doctoral degree in psychology whose area of research is the psychological similarities between species of animals. Such studies are often made both to understand a particular species as well as to provide a comparison for humans or some other group of animals.

comparative psychology

n. The branch of psychology concerned with the similarities and differences in the minds of different species of animals including the human species. Ethology, sociobiology, psychobiology, and behavioral genetics are closely related fields.

compatibility principle

n. In control systems, the idea that information displays work best when a control for a variable is placed close to the information display for that variable or the data and control efforts together create an emergent display that combines variable level with control effort. Also called proximity compatibility principle.

compensation

n. **1.** In Adlerian psychology, the development of one area of competence to make up for perceived lack of competence in another area, which can be healthy in the case of real limitation or misdirected in the case of an inferiority complex. **2.** In Piagetian psychology, the intellectual ability to understand that for any operation there exists an operation that reverses that operation; thus if the height of an object is increased, its depth or width can be decreased to make size remain constant. **3.** In psychoanalytic psychology, the adoption of one behavior when another is unsuccessful.

compensation principle

n. An economic theory concerning changes in an economic system in which it is held that total economic benefit to a society from economic change is maximized when those who directly benefit from the economic change compensate those who are harmed by the economic change.

competence

n. A term in psychology that can be understood as both an objective outcome and a subjective or phenomenological experience. In either sense, developing competence can be defined as the ongoing process of acquiring and consolidating a set of skills needed for performance in one or more life domains; it is, in its most basic form, learning. Researchers often study competence in the domains of sport, industry, academics, and the arts. However, competence is relevant to a much wider array of domains and activities, particularly with regard to development, for example, learning to ride a bike or tie one's shoes, becoming toilet trained, or learning to self-regulate more generally. All of these activities and more fall under the auspices of competence.

In particular, psychological research on competence has been focused on the intrinsically motivating properties of this phenomenological experience. That is, researchers, such as Robert White, have found that the experience of feeling competent or effective is a rewarding one in its own right. People seem to have a natural inclination to seek out new challenges for the sake of experiencing a sense of competence – even when there are no extrinsic rewards (such as cash or prizes) to be earned or won. A prototypic illustration of how the feeling of competence can be intrinsically rewarding can be observed in children at play. When a small child works diligently at creating a castle made of sand, typically his or her only reward is the sense of satisfaction this activity brings in that moment. Many adults labor every week to complete a crossword puzzle, even when the completed puzzle is unlikely ever to be seen by another person's eyes. Again, the motivation for this action can be understood as resulting from the intrinsic satisfaction derived from developing and exercising a set of skills: that is, from developing and experiencing competence.

On the basis of years of research conducted on both animals and humans, researchers posit that this feeling of competence represents a basic and universal psychological need. As such, the experience of competence is necessary for optimal health and well-being, and when this experience is thwarted, ill-being results. For example, the learned-helplessness model of depression can be understood as characterizing the condition of clinical depression as resulting from a chronic lack of perceived competence, which has become generalized across domains. The need for competence is understood to be inborn or innate and thus is present in all people from the earliest stages of development onward, from all different cultures and corners of the globe. The natural inclination we have to seek out the experience of competence is understood to be adaptive in the sense that it promotes both physical and mental development.

Importantly, researchers have noted that competence-relevant behavior is not only motivated by the positive, appetitive possibility of competence but also by the negative, aversive possibility of incompetence. Although the need for competence may initially be a thoroughly appetitive motivational source that orients infants toward competence, a variety of factors, including temperament and socialization, can rechannel this naturally appetitive form of motivation toward the avoidance of incompetence (e.g., fear of failure). While potentially a powerfully motivating force, focusing on the avoidance of incompetence is understood to be a nonoptimal form of self-regulation, primarily serving a self-protective function. As such, these aversive forms of motivation often do a poor job of satisfying the underlying positively focused need for competence, which is required for continued growth and development. For instance, avoidance goals, specifically performance-avoidance goals, have been associated with various forms of self-handicapping, such as withholding effort or commitment to properly preparing, strategies that are ultimately self-destructive. Over the long term, research suggests that pursuing avoidance goals in general leads to a decrease in life satisfaction and physical health.

The experience of competence is understood to be intrinsically rewarding and is characterized by emotions such as joy, pride, and happiness. By contrast, negative competence-related outcomes or failure are characterized by emotions such as sadness, shame, and anxiety. Researchers have demonstrated that the precise nature of affective experience following positive or negative outcomes can vary as a function of approach and avoidance motivation. When people are appetitively focused on gaining competence, positive outcomes lead to joy and pride, whereas negative outcomes produce sadness and disappointment. By contrast, when people are aversively focused on avoiding incompetence, positive outcomes tend to result in relief, whereas negative outcomes result in shame and distress. To the extent that joy and pride are considered more desirable outcomes than relief, these findings provide further support for encouraging individuals to focus on approaching competence as opposed to avoiding incompetence.

In sum, competence is integral to physical and psychological functioning, and the pursuit of competence is a pervasive feature of daily life for human beings of all ages and races, regardless of gender. Competence strivings have many different forms, and one's successes and failures in these strivings have important implications for one's overall health and well-being.   – ACM, AJE

competition

n. The pursuit of the same resources or goal by two or more entities in which the success of one lessens or negates the possibility of the success of the other. It can be an artificial competition as in a game or sport or a natural one as when two squirrels gather acorns under the same tree.

complementary colors

n. Any pair of colors that produce white or gray when mixed in the correct proportion: colors on the opposite sides of the color circle such as blue and yellow or red and green.

complex reaction time

n. The amount of time a subject takes in a multiple-choice experiment to indicate his or her choice after the presentation of a stimulus.

compliance

n. Obedience to the commands, requests, suggestions, or desires of another. In medicine it is following a doctor's orders, in psychology it is following the experimental protocol, in social situations it can be going along with other members of a group regardless of one's own desires.

componential intelligence

n. A theory of intelligence in which capacity to perform tasks is analyzed into three component parts, including metacomponents used to plan, monitor, and evaluate problem solving; performance components, which are mental tools used to solve problems; and knowledge acquisition components, which are used to learn how to solve problems or make decisions.

compound reaction time

n. The amount of time a subject takes in a multiple-choice experiment to indicate his or her choice after the presentation of a stimulus. Also called complex reaction time and choice reaction time.

compulsion

n. **1.** The experience of a subjectively irresistible impulse to a course of action usually against the conscious wishes of the self. **2.** A course of action toward which an individual feels an irresistible impulse such as repetitive hand washing, unnecessary counting of objects, or praying. **3.** The mental mechanism underlying compulsive behavior.

compulsive personality

n. **1.** An enduring and pervasive pattern of personal adjustment characterized by the experience of a subjectively irresistible impulse to a course of action usually against the conscious wishes of the self, usually co-occurring with mental rigidity, perfectionism, excessive attention to detail, cleanliness, obsession with order and performing one's duties, inhibition, guilt, lack of humor, bodily tension, and anal sexuality.

computed (axial) tomography

n. (CT or CAT scan*)* A process of generating a three-dimensional set of images of a person's or object's internal structure by using a series of axial X rays, whose images are then connected or filled in using imaging software so as to present computer images that appear whole to the viewer. It is very useful in diagnostic imaging, where it is difficult for a person mentally to fill in between numerous single X-ray images to understand the three-dimensional situation.

computer assisted instruction

n. Any of numerous forms of instruction in which computers are used in addition to more traditional teaching methods to aid the learning of students. Usually individual drill or problem solving geared to a student's past performance is used to adjust instruction to an individual student's level of ability. It is also used to present instruction in different formats such as simulations or games.

concept

n. The mental representation of a thing or class of things so that an individual can decide whether a specific stimulus is an instance of that object or class of objects and act on the basis of that judgment. Concepts can be inferred from consistencies in the actions of an organism without verbal expression of the concept, as when animals learn to respond to compound reward schedules or when preverbal infants react differently to stimuli in and outside of abstract conceptual classes.

concept acquisition

n. The process of learning or acquiring a concept, which can be inductive, as by discriminating among particular instances, some of which are examples of the concept and some of which are not, or deductively, as by another person's verbalization of the construct.

concept formation

n. The process of learning or acquiring a concept from particular instances, some of which are examples of the concept and some of which are not.

concept formation and learning

n. In education, concept formation in which a concept can be applied to new situations and related to other concepts is differentiated from simple rote learning, in which a response is given to a single stimulus or a few stimuli but does not become an integrated part of the individual's general knowledge.

concept learning

n. The process of acquiring concepts in which the individual forms a list of attributes or a prototype or best example of a category in which the attributes related to the category are embodied and to which future possible instances are compared.

conceptual perspective taking

n. Adopting the perspective of another person or other living thing through a process of imagining what the other point of view must be.

concrete operational stage

n. In Piagetian theory, a stage of intellectual development in which children can think logically about specific objects, which requires them to let go of their perceptually centered point of view. This usually occurs between 7 and 11 years of age and is the third stage in Piaget's stages of intellectual development.

concrete operations

n. Logical thought about specific objects or situations, which involves letting go of (decentering) one's perceptually centered viewpoint and thinking in somewhat abstract terms.

concurrent schedules

n. The simultaneous presence of two independent schedules by which a subject can achieve reinforcement, usually with different responses.

concurrent validity

n. The extent to which two nearly simultaneous measures of the same thing discover similar results. Thus if two tests of the same thing given at about the same time to the same group of people show the individuals scoring at about the same relative levels, then the two tests are said to have concurrent validity.

conditional positive regard

n. In Rogerian psychology, a relationship in which a person is deemed worthy and good by one person only when he or she acts, thinks, believes, or feels in ways preferred by that person. Such an approach, particularly by parents, is believed to inhibit psychological growth and personal adjustment in the person subjected to it.

conditional probability

n. The probability that one thing will occur given that another thing has already occurred.

conditioned aversion

n. A learned preference to avoid or escape from a stimulus or situation that has no intrinsically negative characteristics as a rat can learn to avoid or escape the left side of a box if that side has an electrically charged floor which shocks the rat's feet.

conditioned avoidance

n. A learned avoidance of a stimulus or situation that has no intrinsically negative characteristics as a rat can learn to avoid the left side of a box if that side has an electrically charged floor which shocks the rat's feet.

conditioned emotional response

n. An emotional response to a stimulus that has been learned through pairing with another stimulus to which the emotional response already occurs. As an instance, a fuzzy white stuffed rabbit might be paired with a sudden very loud sound for an infant, and soon the infant will react with fear to the fuzzy stuffed rabbit as it originally did to the sudden very loud sound.

conditioned escape

n. A learned preference to escape from a stimulus or situation that has no intrinsically negative characteristics as a rat can learn to escape the left side of a box if that side has an electrically charged floor which shocks the rat's feet.

conditioned food aversion
n. Food that has been paired with digestive distress or other negative stimuli will tend to be avoided by the organism in the future. When the aversive stimulus is digestive distress, this is an instance of one form of trial learning which is a special case, in which learning curves do not follow normal, gradual patterns of acquisition and extinction but are acquired in a single trial and have marked resistance to extinction. This contradicts the supposition in much of behaviorism that stimuli and responses are essentially equal.

conditioned inhibition
n. The lessening of a conditioned response either during learning trials or during an extinction phase when a stimulus not associated with a conditioned response is presented simultaneously with the conditioned stimulus.

conditioned reflex
n. A reflex action to a stimulus which originally did not result in the response after a learning period in which the stimulus is paired with another stimulus which does produce the response. Also called a conditioned response.

conditioned reinforcer
n. A stimulus which was originally neutral but has been paired with an unconditioned reinforcer and to which the subject has come to react in a manner similar to the reaction to the unconditioned reinforcer. Thus, when a particular voice is coupled with feeding a hungry animal, the animal will soon begin to seek and be rewarded by the sound of the voice alone.

conditioned response
n. A response in the presence of a stimulus which did not originally evoke the response but which has been paired with an unconditioned stimulus until the stimulus provokes a response similar to the one originally evoked by the unconditioned stimulus. Thus if a dog hears a bell immediately before being fed, it will come to salivate when it hears the bell without being fed; the salivation to the bell will be the conditioned response.

conditioned stimulus
n. A stimulus which does not initially provoke a response but begins to do so after repeated pairing with a stimulus which does provoke a response. Thus if a dog hears a bell immediately before being fed, it will start to salivate when it hears the bell without being fed; the bell will be the conditioned stimulus.

conditioned suppression
n. The reduction in the rate of operant responding produced by the presence of a stimulus previously associated with punishment. Thus a rat which has been conditioned to press a bar for food and is given a shock when it hears a tone will press the bar less when it hears the tone than when it does not hear the tone.

conditioned taste aversion
n. A taste which was originally either positive or neutral will come to be avoided if it is paired with digestive distress or other noxious stimuli subsequent to eating.

conditioning
n. The process of learning analyzed from a behavioristic point of view, usually described as the increase or decrease of particular actions after their pairing with particular stimuli.

conditioning by successive approximations
n. A process of shaping behavior by breaking a desired behavior into a series of steps back to present behavior and then rewarding each successive step toward the desired behavior only once so that a further step has to be taken to be rewarded the next time. This procedure is followed until the desired response is obtained.

conditioning, excitatory
n. Another name for classical conditioning in which the pairing of an unconditioned stimulus (US) with a conditioned stimulus (CS) leads to the establishment of a conditioned response (CR). As an example, if a dog normally salivates when it is presented with food

(US) and a bell (CS) is rung before the food is presented several times in a row, the dog will soon begin drooling (CR) when it hears the bell rung without the presentation of food.

conditioning, inhibitory

n. In classical conditioning when the unconditioned stimulus is paired with another stimulus less often than the unconditioned stimulus is presented without the other stimulus, the other stimulus becomes a conditioned stimulus, which makes it less likely the conditioned stimulus will occur.

conduct disorder

n. A disorder of childhood characterized by frequent violation of the basic rights of others and the flouting of social norms and rules. This includes threatening others, harming other people or animals, damaging property, frequently lying, stealing, and breaking rules at school, in the home, and in society in general.

conduction aphasia

n. Aphasia characterized by relatively good spontaneous language, good comprehension, and poor repetition with a significant number of phonological paraphasias (words incorrect from the point of view of the phonological composition). Three basic and five secondary characteristics are usually included in the definition of conduction aphasia. The three basic characteristics are (**1**) fluent but paraphasic conversational language, (**2**) near-normal language comprehension, (**3**) significant difficulties in language repetition. Conduction aphasia very often also includes (secondary characteristics) (**1**) defective naming with significant number of phonological paraphasias; (**2**) reading difficulties (reading aloud is defective, whereas reading understanding may be near normal); (**3**) writing defects, ranging from mild spelling errors to severe agraphia; (**4**) ideomotor apraxia; and (**5**) neurological abnormalities, including loss of cortical sensitivity and some degree of right hemiparesis. Language repetition defects in conduction aphasia have been explained in two different ways: (**1**) as a disconnection between Wernicke's and Broca's areas and (**2**) as

a segmentary ideomotor apraxia, specifically a verbal apraxia. The first explanation was proposed by Wernicke when this aphasia syndrome was initially described. The second explanation was first proposed by Luria.

     – AA

conductive deafness

n. Disruption of conduction of sound vibrations through the outer and middle ear. Because of this disruption the ossicles of the middle ear cannot pass along the sound vibrations to the cochlea, resulting in deafness. If the abnormality is located in the inner ear, the nerve pathways of the auditory information to the brain, or the brain areas receiving the auditory information (primary auditory areas in the temporal lobes), the term *sensorineural deafness* is used. Different abnormal conditions can cause conductive deafness, including otitis media, foreign bodies or impacted wax in the external auditory canal, otosclerosis (spongy bone formation that results in fixation of the stapes, the last of the three middle ear ossicles), and perforation or rupture of the tympanic membrane.   – AA

▶ *See also* **CENTRAL DEAFNESS**

cone

n. A cone-shaped retinal light receptor cell primarily located in the fovea of the human eye which differentially reacts to brightness in general or to specific wavelengths of colored light, which is the basis for color perception. Cones have higher thresholds for reaction than do rods, which predominate in the periphery of the retina, and so the central area of human vision is less accurate under very dim lighting conditions.

confabulation

n. False statements made by persons who have memory lapses so as to fill in conversations when they are unable to recall accurate information. The statements are usually believed by the person who makes them. Confabulation is characteristic of Korsakoff's syndrome and senile dementia and occasionally appears in children and adults who are pressured for information they lack but believe they should know, as when they are witnesses in court.

confederate

n. Confederates are pretend research participants, who are actually accomplices of the researchers. The actual participants are unaware (until after the session is over) that the confederates are not bona fide participants. Research with confederates is common in social psychology when researchers wish to simulate a particular type of social situation to examine how participants will react. For example, researchers studying conformity have often employed confederates in their research. − MWP

confidence interval

n. The range of values in which a population parameter is likely to fall when estimated from a sample statistic. Usually the probability of the confidence interval is defined prior to calculation of the sample statistics; 5% and 10% are the most conventionally used ranges.

confidence limit

n. The upper and lower ends of a confidence interval or range of values in which a population parameter is likely to fall when estimated from a sample statistic.

confidentiality

n. A principle of law and professional research ethics in which researchers and professional practitioners are required to limit disclosure of information they have acquired in the practice of their profession, including the name of their clients or subjects and all other data that has been collected about the clients or subjects without their informed consent.

configurative culture

n. A culture in which one's contemporaries instead of one's elders are the cultural icons one learns from and upon whom one models one's self. As an example, it has been argued that U.S. culture became a configurative culture in the 1960s and then returned to a postfigurative culture in the 1980s in which the elder generation is the one to whom young persons turn for lore and models.

confirmation bias

n. The observation that individuals selectively seek out and attend to information which agrees with their beliefs or presuppositions while failing to seek and tending to ignore or discount information which does not agree with them.

confirmatory factor analysis

n. A procedure used in factor analysis to show that a group of variables possesses a predicted factor structure.

conflict, approach-approach

n. Conflict in which we are forced to decide between two desirable alternatives, for example, choosing between two delicious desserts. − SRB

conflict, approach-avoidance

n. Conflict in which we are attracted to the positive features of the alternative but are repelled by the negative features. For example, you want to go to the movies tonight, but that decision means you are not able to study for an upcoming exam. In this situation, there often is a wavering between the choices, and not until one desire outweighs the other will the conflict be resolved. − SRB

conflict, avoidance-avoidance

n. Conflict in which we are forced to decide between two undesirable alternatives. For example, you can suffer a toothache or go to the dentist (assuming you are avoidant of dentists). − SRB

conflict, double approach-avoidance

n. The inner experience of indecision and anxiety when confronted with choice between two options, both of which have desirable and undesirable results.

conformity

n. The tendency to make one's attitudes, actions, opinions, and perceptions match those of another person, group of people, or belief system. Conformity may be mere compliance, in which an individual acts in accord with a group without accepting the attitudes of the group, or conversion, in which the person

127

adopts the beliefs as well as going along or, in extreme cases, when the individual abandons personal point of view in favor of groupthink.

confound(s)

n. In experimental design, an uncontrolled variable(s) which affects the results of an experiment, rendering interpretation of the results ambiguous and so problematic.

confounding

n. The process of an uncontrolled variable's affecting the results of an experiment such that no clear interpretation of the results can be made.

congruent validity

n. Congruent validity is the relationship between a measure and a known valid and reliable measure of the same construct. A measure that has a strong, positive correlation with a previously validated test has high congruent validity with that test. Congruent validity emphasizes intertest correlations and emphasizes the logical coherence between new and known measures.   – BJM

congruity theory

n. A theory of attitude change in which cognitive simplicity or balance is sought such that if there is an inconsistency between evaluation of a person and his or her persuasive communication, then the listener will tend to revise both evaluations until the inconsistency disappears.

conjunctive fallacy

n. A tendency to believe that the occurrence of two or more events is more likely than the occurrence of either event alone. This occurs when the predictor uses cognitive coherence as the basis for making the judgment as when a story is made more coherent by the presence of both events than by either alone.

conjunctive schedule

n. A kind of intermittent reinforcement schedule in which two or more separate schedules must both or all be satisfied before behavior is rewarded.

connectionism

n. **1.** A theory of learning in which neural connections between stimuli and responses are the basis of learning. **2.** In cognitive psychology, an approach to learning and memory in which knowledge is encoded as connections between multiple nodes rather than in a single location or memory entity. This suggests that knowledge is distributed rather than local and is defined by a net of activation that has a particular spread. It includes artificial intelligence programs that use spreading nets of activation to model neural networks.

conscientiousness

n. Conscientiousnes is one of the dimensions of the five factor model. It contrasts individuals who are methodical, persevering, and goal-oriented with those who are disorderly, careless, and unambitious. It has proactive and inhibitive aspects. Proactive traits stress the hard-working and sustained pursuit of goals, a high need for achievement. Inhibitive traits show a self-disciplined control of impulses and the environment; conscientiousness people are guided by a strong sense of duty and a need for order. Considered as an aspect of character, conscientiousness is associated with a strong will, scrupulousness, and responsibility. However, conscientiousness is not merely an evaluation; it is a consensually validated trait that is in large part heritable.   – RRM

consciousness

n. The phenomenon of personal, subjective experience. The experience is sensory, remembered, or imagined in nature and interacts with environment and physiological states so as to produce changes in the state or aspects of subjective experience.

consensual validity

n. Consensual validity is agreement between at least two observers on the existence or quantity of some thing or characteristic. Agreement among observers is one of the fundamental tests of the reality of a phenomenon. In dealing with abstract psychological characteristics, consensual validity is a matter of degree. When judgments are made about a series of individuals by two or more judges, it is possible to quantify consensual validity as cross-observer agreement expressed by an intraclass correlation. In studies of personality traits, these correlations suggest that there is moderate, but far from perfect agreement. Consensual validity of any degree is not definitive proof of reality, because observers can agree without being correct; it is thus an important but not sufficient condition for accepting the scientific reality of an object or characteristic.   – RRM

conservation

n. In Piagetian psychology, the understanding that physical quantity is not the same as an individual perceptive dimension so that one dimension can be altered and the quantity remain the same as long as there are compensatory changes in the other dimensions. As an example, a tall thin bucket of sand can hold the same amount of sand if it is squashed in such a way that the enlargement of the horizontal dimension matches the decrease in the vertical one.

conservatism

n. An attitude set characterized by simplicity and rigidity of thought, a positive characterization of the past or the status quo, and discomfort with change.

consistency theory

n. Any of a set of theories of social cognition which suggest that people have a strong desire to maintain cognitive consistency, which partially determines beliefs, perceptions, and choices of actions.

consolidation

n. The formation of a permanent memory selected from among many short-term memory traces or impressions, often believed to be biological in nature.

constant stimuli method

n. A psychophysical procedure for determining both difference and absolute thresholds. In difference thresholds a randomly ordered set of stimuli are presented and are compared to a standard stimulus, with the threshold calculated as the smallest difference that can be detected 50% of the time. In determining absolute thresholds, weak stimuli are presented in random order and the threshold is the intensity level whose presence can be detected 50% of the time.

construal level theory

n. (CLT) Construal level theory is an account of how psychological distance influences individuals' thoughts and behavior developed by Nira Liberman and Yaacov Trope. According to CLT, objects/events are psychologically proximal in the following ways: (1) when there is no social distance from an object/event (i.e., people represent in their mind information about an object/event that they have personally interacted with and experienced, as opposed to information about an object/event that someone else has interacted with and experienced), (2) when there is no temporal distance from an object/event (i.e., people represent in their mind information about an object/event that they are currently interacting with and experiencing, as opposed to an object/event that they have already interacted with and experienced in the past or an object/event that they will interact with and experience in the future, (3) when there is no spatial distance from an object/event (i.e., people represent in their mind information about an object/event that is physically close to them, as opposed to an object/event that is physically far from them), and (4) when there is no suppositional distance from an object/event (i.e., people represent in their mind information about an object/event that is real and certainly exists, as opposed to an object/event that is hypothetical and may not exist).

Psychologically proximal objects/events are directly experienced. As people's experience with an object/event become less direct, as they become more distant from an object/event, people can still represent in their mind information about an object/event. That is, people can still form a mental representation or construal of a psychologically distant object/event. CLT asserts that people construe objects/events differently, depending on their psychological distance from them. From a distant perspective, people purportedly form high-level, more abstract construals of objects/events. A high-level construal captures the perceived essence, gist, or summary of the given information about an object/event. The cognitive process that leads to the formation of a high-level construal is one that entails extracting the defining aspects of an object/event. From a proximal perspective, people purportedly form low-level, more concrete construals of objects/events. A low-level construal captures the secondary and nondefining aspects of an object/event. An aspect is defining for an object/event if its omission or alteration changes the meaning of the object/event for the perceiver. In this sense, the content of a construal is idiosyncratic, because the meaning of an object/event can vary from one person to another.

CLT assumes that the association between psychological distance and level of construal evolves as a result of differences in what people typically know about proximal and distant experiences. Information about secondary or nondefining aspects of events, including the context in which they will occur, typically becomes more available and reliable as people become psychologically closer and have more direct experience with objects/events. As a result, primary and defining information about objects/events often receives the most attention when people are psychologically far from experiencing them. The many secondary and nondefining aspects of objects/events are considered only as people become closer to experiencing them. For example, when people are planning a vacation, they typically resolve issues regarding their destination and mode of travel (primary concerns) long before the vacation is set to occur, whereas issues regarding meals and clothing (secondary concerns) are not resolved until they are actually on vacation.

CLT assumes that the association between psychological distance and level of construal is overgeneralized, causing people to continue to form high-level construals for psychologically distant objects/events and low-level construals for psychologically near objects/events, even when information about the secondary aspects is reliable. So, even in situations in which information about the secondary and primary aspects of an object/event is known to be reliable, individuals with a psychologically distant perspective will still construe information about the object/event in a more abstract fashion, focusing more on the primary or defining aspects of the object/event. For example, as attending a U2 concert gets closer in time, low-level, secondary features such as "the quality of the food served at the concession stands" are likely to become more prominent relative to more central features of the concert such as "the quality of the opening act."

Because CLT assumes that a generalized association exists between level of construal and psychological distance, objects/events that are construed in higher-level terms are thought to be perceived as more psychologically distant, and objects/events that are construed in lower-level terms are thought to be perceived as more psychologically proximal. For example, as a homework assignment is construed in lower-level, more concrete terms, individuals are likely to experience the deadline for the assignment as closer time.

Research continues to explore the relationship between psychological distance and level of construal and its impact on judgments, evaluations, and behavior.   – MDH, YT

constructive memory

n. **1.** Memory for events which substitutes general knowledge or details from other memories for details in the memory for a particular event. **2.** The storage and reproduction of memories in forms consistent with previous knowledge and mental schema.

constructivism

n. **1.** A point of view that holds that perception is an active construction of perceptual wholes from fragmentary data points rather than passive compilations of sensory data. **2.** A cognitive point of view that mental processes are themselves constructed by the mind in interaction with the environment and are then applied to understanding new information and recalling the past. **3.** A sociological point of view that holds that all of experience and understanding is a shared, social construction.

construct validity

n. The degree to which a test embodies a theory or abstract idea. This is evaluated by comparison of the test to the theory and is usually nonempirical. Some theorists suppose that unidimensionality in a factor analysis of a set of items whose content is all on the same topic is a form of construct validity.

consumer psychology

n. Consumer psychology concerns all aspects of human behavior pertaining to consumption (obtaining, consuming, and disposing of products and services) and the operations of the consumer market. Research in consumer psychology covers at least four broad topic areas: (1) perception and experience of products and services; (2) representation and processing of market information (e.g., branding and pricing information in advertisements); (3) processes and consequences of preference, choice, and decision, in both individual and group settings; and (4) social interactions in consumption environment (e.g., consumer-salespeople interactions). Studies usually intersect topic areas with psychological variables, such as personality and individual differences (e.g., gender and cohort effects), cultural influences, emotion and motivation, nonconscious and automatic factors, and interpersonal and group dynamics.
         – SYYC, CYC

consummate love

n. A combination of erotic passion, emotional commitment, and communicative intimacy in Robert J. Sternberg's triangular theory of love.

contact hypothesis

n. A theory that increased contact with another group of people will reduce prejudice toward that group. Research findings have suggested this is the case only when the contact has several positive attributes, including equal status, cooperation, lack of competition, and an inclusive system of person perception.

contagion, behavioral/social

n. The rapid spread of ideas, attitudes, and behaviors through crowds of people and other animals.

contamination (statistical)

n. 1. The process of allowing one's point of view to influence research design or clinical judgment so as to make research a process of self-fulfilling prophecy. 2. In projective testing the mixing together of two or more perceptions of the same area of the test image.

content analysis

n. A research methodology relying on the analysis of textual information to identify its properties systematically. In a content analysis, researchers code, or break down, text into manageable categories to determine the presence of specific words or concepts within a target text or set of texts. The information obtained through this analysis is then analyzed and quantified to determine frequency, meaning, and relationship of information. Typically, the categorization and interpretation of information are guided by a theoretical framework which serves to organize and structure the final data interpretation. Data obtained through a content analysis can be used to make inferences about a range of targets (i.e., the meaning of the text, authors, audience, culture, zeitgeist, etc.). There are a number of approaches to content analysis; most commonly, content analysis is driven by either a quantitative (conceptual) or qualitative (relational) approach. In a quantitative or conceptual content analysis, preset categories are based on a guiding theoretical framework; then, data is examined as a function of the frequency by which texts, themes, or concepts appear in each category. In qualitative or relational content analysis, data is typically examined to determine emerging themes or trends in the text, often without a preexisting framework or set of guiding categories. In a qualitative analysis, there is less emphasis on the frequency of occurrence; rather, the focus is on the meaning and significance of emergent themes.
         – BJM

content, latent and manifest

n. In Freudian interpretation of dreams, the dream is a construction in which an unconscious (latent) content is masked by a morally acceptable (manifest) content through the substitution of associated images. Thus an image of desiring to have sex with one's father might (latent content) be masked by an image of desiring to have sex with one's spouse, who has some characteristics that remind one of one's father (manifest content).

content validity

n. Content validity is the extent to which test items match or align with the target topic, performance, or content domain. Content validity relies on the ability of test items to measure the full content domain implied by the construct label, a task that can be particularly challenging when determining the criteria necessary to represent the full domain of abstract psychological constructs. For example, if one were developing a measure of self-esteem, content validity would focus on the extent to which test items effectively measure all aspects relevant to self-esteem. Generally, content validity is established via expert analysis relevant to the target construct. For example, the content validity of a subject test on the Scholastic Aptitude Test (SAT) may be established by a committee of teachers who can provide expert analysis of the relevance of the items to measure all relevant subject factors.   – BJM

context effect

n. Any influence of the physical, emotional, or social environment on an organism's response to a particular thing or event.

contextual intelligence

n. In the triarchic theory of intelligence, the capacity to make one's self fit better with the environment through the processes of adapting one's self to the environment, changing the environment to suit one's self better, and selecting the best environment for one's self. It could also be called street smarts.

contiguity theory

n. The supposition that all learning derives from closeness of association in time and space, that the last response to occur in a stimulus setting was learned, and that change occurs in an increasingly complex chaining of responses. This theory, developed by E. R. Guthrie, is no longer actively researched or applied in the field of psychology.

contingency

n. A relationship between two events or variables such that one affects or is associated with different probabilities of the other.

contingency coefficient

n. In statistics, a measure of association between two categorical variables based on the chi-squared statistic and ranges from 0, no association, to 1, perfect association; it is equal to

$$\sqrt{\frac{ChiSquare}{ChiSquare - N}}$$

where *N* equals the number of observations.

contingency management

n. A technique in behavior therapy in which the therapist and family members ignore behavior symptomatic of a client's disorder and actively reward behavior incompatible with the disorder.

contingency table

n. A cross-tabulation of two variables showing the frequencies of all interstices.

continuity

n. The observation that lines that appear to move in the same direction tend to be grouped together perceptually. Thus the two lines in > are seen as one wedge while Ø is seen as a circle with a line through it. Also called the principle of good continuation.

continuous reinforcement

n. A schedule of reinforcement in which each adequate response is rewarded.

continuous variable

n. A variable for which any value within the limits of the variable range is possible; as such, it is always possible to break down a continuous variable into an infinite number of smaller parts. For example, time is a continuous variable as the time required to complete a task can be differentiated via an infinite breakdown from hours to minutes to seconds to milliseconds, and so on. While it can be theoretically argued that no measured variable is truly continuous, variables that can be measured with considerable precision are typically considered continuous variables. Variables that are not continuous are called discrete variables.   – BJM

continuum
n. **1.** Any gradually changing sequence or dimension in which adjacent points are nearly indistinguishable but the extreme points are obviously different. **2.** In mathematics, any continuous variable. **3.** In psychology, any dimension that can be reasonably presented as two end points with an undetermined number of intermediate points.

contralateral
adj. Of or pertaining to the opposite side, as when the right motor cortex controls movement in the contralateral (left) side of the body.

contrast effect
n. The perceptual intensification of a stimulus when it is presented in juxtaposition with a very different one. Thus a gray patch will appear lighter on a black background and darker on a white one.

control
n. **1.** In psychology, the regulation of all extraneous variables in an experiment so that changes in the dependent variable can be attributed to changes in the independent variables. **2.** A capacity to regulate events or behavior. **3.** Any mechanism that governs the functioning of a mechanistic system.

control group
n. In research design a group of subjects not given any of the experimental treatments used as contrast to infer the presence or size of the effect of the independent variable(s) on the dependent variable.

control, statistical
n. Any statistical technique for removing unwanted variance from a mathematical model used when experimental design does not eliminate variables which are not of interest to the researcher.

control variable
n. A variable held constant across different conditions of an experiment so as to negate any possible interference in making inferences about the relationship between independent and dependent variables in the experiment.

convenience sample
n. The most commonly used type of sample in all areas of psychology, which is composed of subjects who are easy to obtain rather than subjects who are representative of the population about which the sample will be used to make inferences. The most frequently used sample of convenience is students in introductory psychology classes.

conventional morality
n. In Kohlberg's theory of moral development, this is the second level of moral reasoning, characterized by an awareness and focus on societal laws, norms, and rules. Two stages comprise this level of moral reasoning. In stage 3, good-boy-good-girl orientation, individuals judge behaviors on the basis of how closely actions conform to accepted norms of behavior, and what is considered appropriate or is approved of by others. In stage 4, authority orientation, individuals judge actions on the basis of their adherence to authority and rules, and insofar as they maintain the social order or fulfill obligations. In this stage, there is respect for rules, authority, and the social order not because of any underlying principles or the benefits that can be reaped but because of unquestioning respect for authority. Youth in the early to mid-adolescent years are typically categorized in this level of moral reasoning.   – MRTG

convergence
n. **1.** Any process of coming together. **2.** Ocular convergence is the inward rotation of the eyes to focus on a light source so that the image falls on the fovea, which puts the image into sharpest focus possible and provides the muscular tension required to serve as a depth

cue. **3.** In physiology the coming together of one or more structures, as in the convergence of a neural pathway on a neural center.

convergent thinking
n. Deductive problem solving or thought processes in general that depend on the application of previous knowledge to the present situation.

convergent validity
n. The degree to which a test is correlated with other measures of the same thing.

conversation analysis
n. A linguistic approach which studies the orderliness, structure, and sequential patterns in talk in interaction including such topics as turn taking, sequence organization, and repair of misunderstandings.

conversion disorder
n. A disorder in which there is functional impairment of sensory or voluntary motor functions suggesting a medical condition which is judged to be due to psychological factors but not intentional malingering because of the absence of medical problems and the presence of alterations in the symptoms with psychological fluctuations.

convolution
n. A folding or twisting, as in the folds of the brain or a complicated story.

convulsive disorders
n. Any disorder such as epilepsy or uncontrolled type I diabetes that is characterized by recurrent convulsions.

convulsive shock therapy
n. The intentional induction of convulsions through sending low-voltage electrical current through the head or administering insulin or other drugs to treat severe depression. Also called electroconvulsive shock treatment (ECT).

Coolidge effect
n. Increased sexual desire, decreased latency between sexual acts, and increased instances of sexual intercourse when multiple sexual partners are present. This is attributed to former President Calvin Coolidge in an urban legend which asserts that on a visit to a chicken farm, Coolidge's wife remarked on the high frequency with which a rooster mated and President Coolidge asked an aide to point out to his wife that the rooster was having sex with a different hen each time.

cooperation
n. The process of working together toward a common goal.

Coopersmith Self-Esteem inventories
n. A set of three tests measuring self-esteem, two of which are designed for children and one for adults.

coping
n. A process of managing in difficult circumstances which includes developing strategies to deal with both internal and external stress and to expend effort in the most useful ways while postponing some tasks in order to accomplish the most pressing first.

coprolalia
n. Uncontrollable and inappropriate use of profanity and particularly expressions referring to feces which is sometimes observed in Tourette's Disorder.

cornea
n. The transparent outer covering of the eye, composed of five fibrous layers, which accomplish about two-thirds of the light refraction which focuses light on the retina.

corporate culture
n. The system of assumptions, beliefs, norms, procedures, and rituals shared by the employees of a corporation which interact with its formal organization.

corpus callosum
n. The largest brain commissure in mammalians. It is a thick band of fibers composed of about 200–250 million axons (white matter) connecting the right and left hemispheres.

The corpus callosum allows integrated activity of both hemispheres. The corpus callosum is divided into three different portions: the genu (or knee) connects the frontal lobes, the body mainly connects the parietal lobes, and the splenium mainly connects the occipital lobes. In the so-called agenesis of the corpus callosum there is a complete or partial absence of the corpus callosum. It is an unusual congenital disorder due to an abnormality in the brain development. People with agenesis of the corpus callosum may have visual defects, poor motor coordination, speech and language development delay, and some mental retardation.   – AA

▶ *See also* **COMMISSURE**

correction for attenuation
n. In testing, a method for estimating the true correlation between scores on two measures by removing the random error associated with each measure using the reliability coefficients of each scale along with their observed intercorrelation in the formula

$$r_{XY} = \frac{observed\, r_{XY}}{\sqrt{r_{XX} * r_{YY}}}$$

correction for guessing
n. Any of several formulas which use the proportion of incorrect answers along with the number of possible wrong choices per item on a multiple-choice test in order to correct for or penalize guessing.

correlation
n. **1.** The degree of relationship between two or more variables. **2.** A mathematical index of association between two or more variables.

correlational method
n. A research approach in which two or more variables are measured, usually in naturalistic settings, and the covariance of the variables is examined to find relationships between or among them. This approach lacks the control of extraneous variables present in good experimental research, and so causal inferences are seldom properly made from correlational studies. This approach is often used when experiment is impossible, ecological

validity is a primary concern, or ethical limitations prevent experimental research.

correlational statistics
n. Any of a family of statistics that describe the relationship between two or more variables.

correlational study
n. A study of the relationships between two or more variables, usually using correlational statistics to describe the relationship.

correlation, biserial
n. A measure of linear relationship between a continuous variable and a dichotomous one.

correlation coefficient
n. A mathematical index of association between two or more variables and usually a linear index scaled so that 0 indicates no relationship, +1 indicates a perfect positive relationship, and −1 indicates a perfect inverse relationship.

correlation, curvilinear
n. The degree of relationship between two variables which is not mathematically linear.

correlation matrix
n. A square matrix whose margins are identical lists of variables, which presents the correlations between each pair of variables in the cell which is the intersection of the row and column of a pair of variables. The left-to-right diagonal of such a matrix represents the correlation of a variable with itself, which would be 1, but is often filled with a reliability correlation of the variable involved.

correlation, multiple
n. The degree of relationship between one variable and two or more other variables, usually measured with a linear equation and indicated by the symbol *R*.

correlation, negative
n. The degree of inverse relationship between two variables, usually indicated by a minus sign with a correlation coefficient.

correlation, nonlinear
n. The degree of relationship between two variables which is not mathematically linear.

correlation, part
n. The correlation between two variables with a third variable removed from only one of the variables. Also called a semipartial correlation.

correlation, partial
n. A correlation between two variables with the statistical effects of one or more other variables removed from the relationship.

correlation, Pearson product-movement
n. The most commonly used correlation coefficient, which measures the degree of linear relationship between two continuous variables scaled so that 0 indicates no relationship and +1 indicates a perfect positive relationship while −1 indicates a perfect inverse relationship.

correlation, perfect
n. A relationship between two variables such that one variable perfectly predicts the other and usually indicated by a correlation coefficient of +1 or −1.

correlation, phi
n. A linear measurement of the degree of relationship between two dichotomous and randomly distributed variables which equals the product-moment correlation if the variables are coded using 0 and 1 for the dichotomous values.

correlation, point-biserial
n. A linear measure of relationship between a continuous variable and a dichotomous one.

correlation, positive
n. An index of the degree of relationship between two variables in which an increase in one predicts an increase in the other and a decrease in one predicts a decrease in the other.

correlation, product-moment
n. The most commonly used correlation coefficient, which measures the degree of linear relationship between two continuous variables scaled so that 0 indicates no relationship and +1

indicates a perfect positive relationship while −1 indicates a perfect inverse relationship.

correlation, rank difference
n. An index of the degree of relationship between two variables that consist of rank orderings.

correlation, rank order
n. An index of the degree of relationship between two variables that consist of rank orderings.

correlation ratio
n. In statistics, a mathematical index which provides a measure of nonlinear relationship between two variables often called eta.

correlation, semipartial
n. The correlation between two variables with a third variable removed from only one of the variables. Also called a part correlation.

correlation, Spearman rank-order
n. An index of the degree of relationship between two variables that consist of rank orderings.

correlation, split-half
n. The product-moment correlation between paired scores for a group of subjects on each half of a test, which was often used to estimate the internal consistency reliability of the test. This statistic underestimates true internal consistency because of attenuation and includes random error because of differences in the many possible ways of splitting a test in half. Its use has largely been supplanted by use of Kuder-Richardson formula 20 and Cronbach's alpha coefficient.

correlation, spurious
n. An observed correlation that occurs by chance in a sample of scores when there is actually no correlation between the population of scores on the two variables involved.

correlation, tetrachoric
n. A product-moment correlation calculated using the column and row totals in a 2×2 contingency table which estimates the value

of a correlation of the two variables were they continuous.

correspondence bias ▶ *See* **FUNDAMENTAL ATTRIBUTION ERROR**

correspondence inference
n. Correspondence inference refers to the judgment of the extent to which one's behavior provides an accurate indication of an individual's enduring dispositions. Three important criteria have been proposed to determine whether the behavior reflects a person's disposition: (a) Choice – did the individual choose to act in this way? (b) Expectedness – was this behavior typical of the individual or typical for a person in that particular role? (c) Consequence – how positive is the outcome? Perceivers tend to make correspondence inferences when the behavior reflects an enduring element of the individual if the act is engaged in because of a personal choice, is unexpected, and does not lead to highly positive outcomes.   – EWMA, CYC
   ▶ *See also* **DISPOSITIONAL INFERENCES**

cortex, motor ▶ *See* **MOTOR CORTEX**

cortex, sensory ▶ *See* **SENSORY CORTEX**

corticosteroid
n. Any of a family of hormones produced in the adrenal gland and synthetic drugs with similar physiological effects. These include glucocorticoids such as cortisol, which are necessary for the metabolism of carbohydrates, and the mineralocorticoids, which are involved in electrolyte balance.

corticosterone
n. A hormone produced in the adrenal gland which is secreted under stress or after traumatic injury which has the effect of shifting the body from carbohydrate to fat metabolism and has a role in regulating blood pressure, suppressing immune function, and limiting inflammation.

cortisol
n. A glucocorticosteroid hormone released from the adrenal cortex. Cortisol enhances sugar metabolism, thus contributing to increased energy levels. Cortisol also suppresses the immune system via a decrease in lymphocytes, which slows the formation of antibodies. Cortisol also directly affects neurons within the central nervous system, in particular cells in the hypothalamus associated with flight-or-fight responses and cells in the hippocampus associated with the consolidation of memory. Cortisol is known as the "healer-killer": low or acute levels of cortisol are useful in healing and in necessary response to stress; high or chronic levels lead to neural and tissue damage and decreased immune function. The secretion of cortisol increases in response to both positive and negative stressors, emotional and physical anxiety, and trauma. Cortisol levels may be measured noninvasively by careful analysis of saliva.   – VS

counseling
n. The process of helping people make adjustments in normal developmental processes across the life span, including educational, vocational, and marital adjustment and planning; family dynamics; aging; and rehabilitation after disability.

counseling psychologist
n. A person holding a doctoral degree in psychology or in counseling who specializes in helping people in the normal developmental processes across the life span including educational, vocational, and marital adjustment and planning; family dynamics; aging; and rehabilitation after disability.

counseling psychology
n. The branch of psychology that deals with studying and assisting people in normal developmental processes across the life span including educational, vocational, and marital adjustment and planning; family dynamics; aging; and rehabilitation after disability.

counterbalancing
n. In research design, a method of controlling nuisance variables such as practice effects, fatigue, and habituation by arranging experimental procedures in a way that such effects

are evenly divided across different levels of the independent variable(s).

counterconditioning

n. A learning procedure in which an organism that has been conditioned to respond in a particular way to a stimulus is conditioned to respond to the stimulus in a way that is incompatible with the original conditioned response.

counterfactual

n. Any statement contrary to fact. In linguistics, counterfactuals are often used as conditional clauses as in "If Al Qaeda had not attacked the World Trade Center, George Bush would not have won reelection." Used also in decision making, studies of mental simulations.

counterfactual reasoning

n. Counterfactual reasoning consists of mental constructions of alternatives to facts or events. These thoughts of "what might have been" are associated with a variety of emotional, cognitive, and behavioral consequences.

Explanation. Counterfactual means literally "contrary to facts or actual events." Counterfactual reasoning involves thoughts of "what might have been": how things might have turned out differently, had some aspect of the past been different. Counterfactuals are generally phrased as conditional propositions: IF some event in the past had been different, THEN the present would be altered in some way (e.g., "If I had done better on my SATs, then I might have gotten into a better college"; "If I hadn't ordered the ceviche, I wouldn't have gotten food poisoning"). Counterfactual reasoning, in the context of everyday cognition, is generally focused on personal goals and desires, identifying means by which individuals might have attained some desired end (in the examples, through better test performance or different entree selection). For this reason, counterfactual reasoning is highly functional in that it may provide a road map for similar desirable ends which may be realized in the future.

Development and details

Typology. Counterfactual thoughts are commonly classified along two main dimensions: direction and structure. *Counterfactual direction* refers to whether the imagined outcome is better or worse than the actual state of affairs. Imagined outcomes that are better than reality are termed *upward counterfactuals* (e.g., "If I had been on time to the interview, I might have gotten that great job"). In contrast, counterfactual outcomes worse than the actual state of affairs are called *downward counterfactuals* (e.g., "If I had taken the interstate, I would have been caught in that terrible traffic jam"). *Counterfactual structure* is independent of counterfactual direction and refers to the phrasing of the counterfactual thought. Counterfactuals that add an event or action which did not occur (e.g. someone who did not attend college who thinks, "If I had gone to college") are termed *additive counterfactuals*; counterfactual thoughts which "undo" an event or action which did occur (e.g., a philandering spouse's thinking, "If only I hadn't cheated") are termed *subtractive counterfactuals*.

Antecedents and functions. Counterfactual reasoning has been theorized to operate according to a two-stage model. The first stage, *counterfactual activation*, refers to whether or not a counterfactual thought has been generated. The second stage, *counterfactual content*, refers to the specific nature of the counterfactual generated, for example, which aspects of reality have been altered or mutated.

A number of antecedents for activation have been identified, the most notable of which is recognition of a problem. When something undesirable occurs, thoughts of how it could have been avoided or of how a better outcome might have been attained spring very naturally to mind. In addition to negative affect, antecedents of counterfactual activation include event abnormality and counterfactual closeness. People tend to generate counterfactuals more frequently after abnormal events than after typical events because abnormal events violate expectancies and thus attract attention (per the old axiom that "Man bites dog" is news, while the converse is not.) *Counterfactual closeness* refers to the ease with which the counterfactual outcome might have been obtained: missing a flight by 5 minutes is more likely to activate counterfactual reasoning than is missing the flight by 50 minutes, because the counterfactual antecedent is more salient in the former than the latter case.

In general, counterfactual reasoning is a valuable way by which individuals may identify potential future improvements. Negative affect identifies an outcome as problematic; through counterfactual reasoning, a potential path to avoiding this problem in the future is identified. This perspective helps to explain the role of two frequently studied determinants of the content of counterfactual thoughts, normality and controllability. An aspect of a past event which deviates from the usual state of affairs will be easy to alter in the future: for example, a student who usually gets plenty of rest before exams but pulls an all-nighter and then performs badly on an exam the next day would be well advised to return to his or her original sleep schedule. Counterfactual reasoning will thus tend to focus on ways to restore normality after a negative event. Similarly, aspects of events under direct control of an individual suggest a clear pathway by which the individual might alter the outcome of a similar event in the future. A dishwasher who drops and breaks a soapy, wet dish would be less likely to break a dish in the future if he thought, "If only I had worn rubber gloves" or "If only I had dried the dish" than if he thought, "If only porcelain weren't breakable" or "If only there were no gravity." Thus, the content of counterfactual thinking in everyday life tends to center on the controllable aspects of events.

Consequences. Counterfactual reasoning has both affective and cognitive consequences. Counterfactual thoughts have the potential to change the nature of the emotional reaction to an event. Through a contrast effect, upward counterfactuals lead individuals to feel bad about the actual state of affairs, relative to the positive outcome they missed, and downward counterfactuals lead to positive affect about an outcome, given the worse state of affairs imagined in the counterfactual thought. In certain circumstances, however, individuals may experience affective assimilation effects, in which an upward counterfactual leads to positive affect, and a downward counterfactual to negative affect. Such assimilation effects will tend to occur if a counterfactual is generated during the course of an ongoing event; for example, if a team is down by one point at halftime, the thought "If only we'd made that shot at the buzzer, we'd be ahead" is more likely to elicit positive affect (unlike the same thought generated at the end of the game). However, most counterfactual thinking seems to involve negative emotions, and the word *regret* is used by many researchers to describe dissatisfaction stemming from an upward, self-focused counterfactual thought.

Counterfactual reasoning influences judgment in a variety of ways. For example, the misfortune of a victim may be seen as more poignant to the extent that it was nearly avoided, thus influencing the sort of compensation recommended for the victim. Counterfactual reasoning is closely tied to causal reasoning. Causation implies a relation between two variables in which one produces change in the other. A counterfactual condition nearly always implies a causal relation. That is, by identifying an antecedent-consequent pair that diverges from a factual antecedent-consequent pair, counterfactual bears a strong resemblance to J. S. Mill's method of difference for determining causation. For instance, the counterfactual statement "If we had watered the plant, it wouldn't have died" implies that the cause of the plant's death was a lack of water. Behaviorally, counterfactual reasoning is associated with the formation of behavioral intentions. By identifying the cause of a negative outcome, counterfactual reasoning implies a means to avoid that outcome in the future and leads to the formation of behavioral intentions to make the identified changes in behavior.

Conclusion. Counterfactual thinking, "what if" thoughts of alternatives to past events, is a common aspect of daily mental life commonly elicited by negative affect. Counterfactual reasoning has influences on cognitive processes including causal reasoning and social judgment, as well as on emotion and behavioral intentions. — AS, NR

countertransference

n. There are two meanings of the term. In the classical psychoanalytic sense, countertransference refers simply to the therapist's transference toward the patient. That is, countertransference is the therapist's unconscious feelings toward one person (usually an attachment figure) redirected or transferred to the patient, thereby biasing the view of the therapist toward the patient (e.g., a therapist may unconsciously feel that her patient reminds the therapist of her father and consequently interact with the patient in ways that are not about the patient). Recently, countertransference has come to refer to the emotions, thoughts, and behaviors that a patient elicits in a therapist through the patient's behavior that is not due to the therapist's past. Different patients elicit different reactions in therapists, and this information is useful (e.g., a patient who is very sensitive to rejection elicits very different reactions than a patient who is always hostile and argumentative).   – DGa

couples therapy

n. Psychotherapy in which both parties in a committed relationship are treated together and dealing with issues both of individual disorders in one or both of the partners and their difficulties in relating to one another and dealing with the demands made by the rest of their world.

courtship rituals

n. Species- and/or culture-specific patterns of behavior engaged in as a preliminary to mating including sexual display, wooing, mate selection, establishing a social hierarchy and/or territory, home building, and synchronizing hormonal levels.

covariance

n. A mathematical index of the degree of relatedness between two variables, most usually the average of the product of the deviations of each variable from its mean.

covariate

n. A variable whose variance is statistically removed from an analysis of variance so as to show the relationship between independent and dependent variables more specifically.

covariation

n. The correlation of changes in any thing or process with those in another thing or process.

coverbal behavior

n. (CVB) Nonverbal gestures, postures, movements, and expressions that occur during speech and modify the meaning of the speech. These behaviors differ markedly across cultures and subcultures such that the same gesture, expression, or movement can mean exactly the opposite in one culture or subculture of what it means in another culture or subculture.

covert conditioning

n. A process of learning new behavior by imagining one's self performing the new behavior and then imagining rewarding one's self for performing the new behavior. There is an underlying assumption of a correlation in imaginary and overt behaviors such that altering one will alter the other.

covert extinction

n. A process of behavior change in which a person imagines performing an unwanted behavior and failing to be rewarded for it. There is an underlying assumption of a correlation in imaginary and overt behaviors such that altering one will alter the other.

covert reinforcement

n. A process in behavior change in which a person imagines receiving reinforcement or reward after performing a desired behavior. There is an underlying assumption of a correlation in imaginary and overt behaviors such that altering one will alter the other.

cranial nerve

n. Any of 12 pairs of nerves that exit the cranium above the level of the spinal cord including the olfactory, optic, oculomotor, trochlear, trigeminal, abducens, facial, vestibulocochlear (auditory), glossopharyngeal, vagus, accessory, and hypoglossal nerves.

cranium

n. The skull minus the mandible, or jawbone, which encloses the brain in adults. In children the cranium is composed of eight bones which weld together over time.

creationism

n. A neo-religious belief system which rejects almost all biological and geological evidence as to the development of the Earth and its inhabitants while purporting to be a scientific theory. It is based on a literal interpretation of some parts of the King James version of the Christian Bible.

creative intelligence

n. The mental capacity to fabricate new and better ideas and ways of doing things and juxtapose concepts, as well as to perceive and think with greater freedom and less restriction by past experience and learned ideas than is normally the case. Along with analytical and practical capacities this is part of the triarchic theory of intelligence.

creativity

n. The capacity to produce new art, ideas, techniques, or other products which are useful, aesthetically appealing, meaningful, and correct within a particular field.

credibility

n. In persuasion, an important factor is the credibility of the source of a message. Trustworthiness and expertise are associated with a source's credibility, such that trustworthy (i.e., honest) and expert (i.e., knowledgeable) sources are seen as credible. Source credibility can play multiple roles in persuasion. When people are not thinking carefully, credibility information can act as a shortcut or simple cue to make quick judgments (e.g., "experts are right"). When individuals' level of thought is not constrained, credibility information can affect the amount of thought people devote to the message. When thinking is high, credibility information can be used as an argument or bias processing of the message (i.e., causing people to search for thoughts consistent with the source's position). If thinking is high and credibility information follows the message, it can affect the amount of confidence people have in their thoughts about the message.   – KD

cretinism

n. A syndrome of retarded physical and mental development which can be due to congenital hypothyroidism and treated with thyroxine or due to iodine deficiency in the diet. Symptoms include pallor, short limb bones, delayed sexual maturity and infertility, lack of muscle mass and coordination, and mental retardation.

crib, air

n. A soundproof cabinet with a large window, air conditioning, and a moving sheet to remove waste, built as an ideal crib by B. F. Skinner to teach babies not to cry for attention while having their physical needs met.

criterion-referenced test

n. A test that has a predetermined passing score which reflects a proficiency standard. An example is a typing test with a passing mark of 40 words per minute without errors.

criterion validity

n. In testing, the assurance that a test measures the dimension it is intended to measure by correlation with nontest criteria of the same dimension.

criterion variable

n. A dependent variable or one that is predicted in regression, canonical correlation, and discriminant function analysis.

critical flicker frequency

n. The rate of flicker or variation in a visual stimulus at which the flicker disappears from perception and the stimulus is seen as constant. The rate varies among individuals and with characteristics such as brightness and size but is usually around 30 cycles per second. In the United States, television images are shown at a flicker rate of 30 per second, but each image is shown twice to increase the functional flicker rate to 60, which is well above the threshold.

critical period

n. A critical period is a window of time in an organism's life cycle during which the organism exhibits heightened sensitivity to environmental stimuli, which in turn trigger some aspect of development. For example, graylag goslings develop filial imprinting during the first 36 hours of life, becoming irreversibly bonded to the first moving object they encounter. In language acquisition, the critical period hypothesis has been the subject of extensive and inconclusive study. It is unclear whether lack of early exposure to a first language results in failure to acquire a normal system, though case studies of feral children and congenitally deaf adults strongly suggest that this is the case. Studies examining second-language learners consistently report age effects: older learners do not come as close to native-like attainment of the second-language grammar as do younger learners. However, the reported age effects are not always consistent with details of the predictions of a hypothesized critical period for second-language acquisition, particularly because studies have not consistently found evidence of a sharp turning point (e.g., at the onset of adolescence) in levels of ultimate attainment. Instead, the evidence points to a gradual decline that persists well beyond adolescence and through adulthood.   – EMF

critical ratio

n. The ratio of the difference between two statistics to the standard error of the difference.

critical region

n. The area of a frequency distribution of statistics beyond the minimum that will lead to rejection of the null hypothesis.

critical thinking

n. A problem solving strategy in which possible solutions are continually tested to guide work toward a solution.

Cronbach's alpha

n. Cronbach's alpha is a gauge of the degree of reliability for multiple measures of a single construct. Similarly to the average correlation among items, Cronbach's alpha is used by researchers to determine the degree to which measures are accomplishing their objective, or the degree to which the measures hang together from a statistical standpoint. Cronbach's alpha is an indication of internal consistency, the degree to which items are measuring the same thing. Cronbach's alpha generally ranges from 0 to 1 but can occasionally yield values below 0 because of the way in which it is computed. Values closer to 1 indicate higher interitem consistency. There is no specific statistical test of significance for Cronbach's alpha. Instead, researchers make subjective interpretations of the value of Cronbach's alpha.   – MWP

cross-cultural counseling

n. A process of counseling which takes into account the diversity of clients including their different cultures, ethnicities, spiritualities, sexualities, classes, economic situations, group histories, and social position relative to the dominant culture and that of the therapist and attempts to account for the cultural point of view of the therapist in such a way as to allow a meeting of minds to occur.

cross-cultural method

n. A research approach in which the cultural group of the individual is considered as a variable and is often used in comparing the behavior of persons in different cultural groups as a researcher might compare child rearing practices in Japan and the United States. Such research has problems in equating behavior in different groups due to differences in language, social meanings of behavior, sampling, response biases, and theoretical viewpoint, as well as problems associated with linking particular findings with particular aspects of differences in cultural practice.

cross-cultural psychological assessment

n. Performing psychological evaluations of persons in a way so as to ensure that the procedures are appropriate for the subject's culture and that the cultural perspective of the subject being assessed is given weight in the interpretation of the results.

cross-cultural psychology

n. Cross-cultural psychology is the systematic study of how cultural contexts differ and how these differences relate to human development, behavior, and cognitive and emotional processes. Psychologists have often assumed that the processes they identify are basic to being human. Cross-cultural psychology seeks to identify processes that are universal across humankind and those that vary across cultural contexts. In addition, cross-cultural psychology aims to explore relationships between (individual-level) psychological variables and (culture-level) sociocultural, ecological, and biological variables. Researchers do both in-depth studies of particular cultural groups and comparative studies across diverse groups, frequently including national or ethnic groups. Applied fields that the cross-cultural perspective has particularly enriched include immigration, intergroup relations, culturally appropriate psychotherapy, education, and industrial/organizational psychology. A special challenge for the field is to develop methods that cope with the problems of equivalence in the meaning of experiments, surveys, personality questionnaires, and so on, in comparative studies.

cross-cultural research

n. Any research that involves the comparison of two or more cultures on some psychological variable of interest. It is the dominant methodological paradigm in cultural and cross-cultural psychology.

cross-cultural sample

n. A sample of subjects from more than one culture in which culture is usually an independent variable.

cross-cultural studies

n. Any research that examines similarities or differences of individuals from two or more cultures.

cross-cultural survey

n. Any investigation which compares the distribution of attitudes, opinions, mental diseases, or other personal characteristics in more than one society or social group.

cross-cultural training programs

n. Used in a variety of academic and business settings, cross-cultural training programs seek to increase understanding, communication, and intercultural competency of individuals and groups from different cultures. Such programs either emphasize general awareness of another culture or address the specific needs of a client group. Cross-cultural training may include presentation and discussion of specific country or cultural values, morals, ethics, communication styles, and etiquette; language instruction; assessment and reduction of relocation stressors or culture shock; or the improvement of interpersonal/business relations. These topics are generally addressed through the use of multimedia presentations, case studies, culture-assimilator exercises, or role-playing scenarios.
— JW, DM

cross-cutting group membership

n. Any situation in which a member or members of one group belong to a second group whose membership overlaps with membership in a different first group. For example, registered Democrats may belong to a country club whose membership includes registered Republicans. Such cross-cutting membership has been found to reduce the predictive power of initial group membership in social and psychological behavior.

cross-dressing

n. The practice of dressing in the clothes usually worn by members of the opposite sex within one's own culture. Also called transvestitism.

cross-language priming

n. This term is used to refer to the advantage in processing a stimulus in one language that is immediately preceded by a related stimulus in a different language. It is said that the first stimulus "primes" the second and provides for ease of accessing and processing the second stimulus, as compared to a situation where the two stimuli are unrelated. For example, the word *perro* (the Spanish translation of the English word *dog*) may be responded to more quickly when preceded by the word *cat* versus the word *box*. It is said that the word *cat* activates related words including those known by an individual in another language, and when one of those words appears, the individual is ready to respond. Thus, his or her reaction time to respond to the target word, *perro*, is sped in the related condition. This finding is typically explained through the theory of spreading activation.   – JA

▶ *See also* **SPREADING ACTIVATION**

cross-sectional method
n. A research method in which different age groups are sampled for comparison. This sometimes provides results which are different from results of longitudinal samples measuring the same variables for comparison.

cross-sectional research
n. Research using cross-sectional samples, usually for the purpose of exploring age related differences.

cross-sectional study
n. A study using a varied age sample and using age as an independent variable.

cross-tabulation
n. A tabular method of presenting data, usually with one variable on one axis and another variable on the other axis in order to show co-variation of the two variables.

cross-tolerance
n. The diminishing of the effects of one drug when the body has adapted to the continued presence of a similar drug, reducing its effectiveness as well. This is often the case with central nervous system depressants such as alcohol, barbiturates, and the benzodiazepines.

cross-validation
n. A statistical technique that splits a sample of data into two or more subsamples in order to provide separate data sets for initial and validation analyses. The theory of cross-validation was developed in response to concerns about testing hypotheses suggested by the data. Cross-validation helps guard against type I error by performing initial analysis on one

subset of data while reserving remaining samples for follow-up analysis. Cross-validation techniques are particularly valuable when additional samples are too expensive or dangerous to obtain, or when it is impossible to collect further samples. Cross-validation can be conducted via holdout (also called split-sample method), K-fold, or leave-one-out methodologies.   – BJM

crowding
n. The concentration of organisms into a higher than normal density which often results in stress and other changes in behavior which vary from one species to another and may include reduced reproduction, increased aggression, and higher mortality.

crucial experiment
n. An experiment which provides data which demonstrate the superiority of one theory over another competing theory.

cryptesthesia
n. A mode of perception beyond the normal senses as in extrasensory perception (ESP), clairvoyance, or telepathy. Also spelled *cryptaesthesia*.

crystallized intelligence
n. Set of knowledge or skills that are developed within the context of experience or education. This form of intelligence is thought to increase throughout the life span but be limited to cultural exposure.   – SRB

CT scan ▶ *See* **COMPUTED (AXIAL) TOMOGRAPHY**

cue
n. Any sensory stimulus that serves as a signal to guide memory, thought, or behavior.

cultural affordances
n. **1.** The perceptual, cognitive, and behavioral possibilities created or fostered by the customs, beliefs, attitudes, knowledge, art, technology, and language of a particular culture. **2.** The particular potential uses that culture makes obvious or possible for its members in perceiving the environment.

cultural anthropology

n. The focus within the field of anthropology that examines the customs, beliefs, attitudes, knowledge, art, technology, and language, and the development, change, and interactions of these with the environment. It is contrasted with physical anthropology, which studies the physical artifacts of cultures.

cultural artifact

n. Any physical evidence of a culture or the persons who are or were part of it and the particular form and function of the object within that culture.

cultural assimilation

n. The processes through which members of one social group become integrated into another group. Most often this refers to adaptation to a new society by members of a minority group who immigrate. It often involves acquiring values, beliefs, ideas, behaviors, and ideas about self that enable newcomers to fit in with the majority culture. Majorities may encourage or discourage assimilation and minorities may seek it or reject it. Assimilation may occur more or less often on some dimensions (e.g., behaviors) than others (e.g., values). Assimilation is often accompanied by stress and is psychologically difficult for some immigrants.

cultural attribution fallacy

n. The ecological fallacy applied to cross-cultural research involving quasi-experimental designs, in which cross-cultural differences are produced, but the design of the study allows for no empirically justified interpretation of the source of the differences, and researchers nevertheless interpret the differences as cultural.

cultural bias in testing

n. Cultural bias in testing refers to score variance attributable to ethnicity, race, religion, language, or social class rather than the target construct. Such variance may cause lower scores of individuals with these cultural or racial attributes and can have detrimental effects, particularly in school settings and aptitude assessment. Interest in the identification, quantification, and removal of cultural

bias in standardized measures continues to increase.   – JW, DM

cultural code frame switching ▶ *See* CODE FRAME SWITCHING

cultural determinism

n. The theory that culture determines the personalities, perceptions, beliefs, and understanding of individuals within the culture.

cultural difference

n. Any difference between identifiable groups of people in their customs, beliefs, attitudes, knowledge, personality, norms, behavior, art, and language, and the development, change, and interactions of these with the environment.

cultural display rules ▶ *See* DISPLAY RULES

cultural frame switching ▶ *See* CODE FRAME SWITCHING

cultural identity

n. An individual's psychological membership in a distinct culture.

cultural norms

n. The set of rules, values, and standards that determine appropriate behavior within a given cultural group and the rewards and sanctions which are applied when the norms are obeyed or violated.

cultural pluralism

n. **1.** The existence and acceptance of more than one culture within a country, locale, or society in which each culture has an identity and norms. **2.** The positive valuation of multiculturalism within a society.

cultural psychiatry

n. An interdisciplinary approach to mental disorders that focuses on cultural differences in the definition, etiology, course, and treatment of the disorders.

cultural psychology

n. An interdisciplinary movement which regards culture as central in any conception of human beings so that individual behavior and culture are seen as inseparable components of the same phenomenon with mind being a co-construction of the individual and the culture. It tends to focus on everyday life events conceptualized as mediated action in context and assumes that individuals are active agents in their own cognitive development but make choices in settings only partially chosen.

cultural reaffirmation effect
n. The amplified endorsement of home cultural values by bicultural individuals.

cultural relativism
n. A point of view which suggests that human phenomena can only be correctly understood within the cultural framework in which they occur and cannot be accurately understood by the standards of another culture. Thus, no psychological approach is anything other than a cultural production with all the affordances, constraints, norms, and attitudes of the culture which produced it, which are not fully applicable to other cultures.

cultural response sets
n. In testing, the tendency of persons from different cultures to respond to items in systematic ways unrelated to the content of the items.

cultural transmission
n. The passing on of values, opinions, beliefs, attitudes, knowledge, and norms that characterize a culture from one generation to the next, or from one group of people to another.

cultural worldview
n. The point of view created by the customs, beliefs, attitudes, knowledge, art, technology, and language of a particular culture. It is a way of understanding the world, other people, and oneself. It is often the unconscious theory of the mind and the world that people have and operate with. Worldviews are constructed as part of the enculturation process, and are an important part of our cultural backgrounds.

culture
n. Three anthropologists defined culture as follows: Culture is to society what memory is to individuals (Kluckhohn). Culture is the human-made part of the environment (Herskovits). Culture is shared understandings made manifest in act and artifact (Redfield). Most recent thinking is especially supportive of Redfield's definition. In contemporary psychology, culture refers to a network of loosely interconnected knowledge items produced, reproduced, and updated by a collection of interdependent individuals. An item in the network may refer to a certain declarative knowledge (know what: e.g., beliefs about the relationship between the self and the society, social norms) or a certain procedural knowledge (know how: e.g., thinking styles). Culture is developed and reproduced to address complex coordination problems in the society and to meet individuals' psychological needs (such as the needs for meanings of life, social belongingness, and epistemic certainty). Culture is encoded in social institutions (e.g., the legal institutions), is transmitted across space and generations through various external media, and evolves in response to the changing social ecology.
                                                            – CYC

culture affiliation hypothesis
n. The hypothesis that immigrant bilinguals who speak different languages in their home and adopted countries will mentally associate themselves with the culture whose language they are using at a particular time. This causes them to respond differently according to which language they are using at a particular time.

culture-assimilator training
n. A procedure in which trainees are presented with a series of short scenarios describing cross-cultural interactions in which some difficulty has arisen. Each scenario is accompanied by four possible explanations of why the problem arose. Trainees increase their cross-cultural understanding by choosing among the explanations and reading why their choices are right or wrong.   – PS

culture-bound disorder

n. Any locality-specific pattern of maladjustment and troubling experience which may or may not fit within an official manual of disorders. Such disorders include amok, *ataque de nervios, bilis y colera, boufeé delirante,* brain fag, *dhat,* falling out, ghost sickness, *hwa-byung, koro, latah, locura,* evil eye, *nervios, pibloktoq, chi-gong* psychosis, rootwork, *sangue dormido, shenjing shuairuo, shenkui, shin-byungsusto,* trances, *taijin kyofusho,* and *zar.*

culture-fair test

n. A theoretical instrument which would measure all cultural groups equally well. In fact, such an instrument has not been developed; nor is one likely to be developed, because of the profound impact of culture on perception, cognition, and motivation for test taking.

culture-free test

n. In theory, a test which is equally valid for use with individuals in all cultures. In practice, no such psychological test has been devised as cultural effects are so profound as to make such a test unlikely.

culture-level analysis

n. An analysis in which a culture or nation group is treated as an individual or single case.

culture of honor

n. Cultures of honor are characterized by values and behavioral norms emphasizing the centrality of status and reputation. For males, this means demonstrating toughness and the willingness to use aggression if one's reputation is challenged or to avenge a perceived insult. For females, codes of honor often focus on avoiding behaviors that could cause shame or dishonor for oneself or one's family. This often means placing a strong emphasis on female modesty and moral (particularly sexual) purity. Cultures of honor often have elaborate informal rules about politeness, codes of conduct, and proper rules for redressing grievances. These cultures also tend to be characterized by extreme sensitivity to insult; consequently, rates of violence tend to be relatively high in honor cultures. Scholars have recorded detailed ethnographies of honor cultures in the Mediterranean, the Middle East, Latin and South America, and the American South. In addition, certain subcultures such as the military, the mafia, and those in the inner cities emphasize honor or related constructs.
— JAV

culture shock

n. A pervasive sense of disorientation, tension, and anxiety experienced by persons who suddenly find themselves in an alien culture.

cumulative frequency distribution

n. A graphical presentation of a data set that presents frequency on the *y*-axis and the value or interval of the variable on the *x*-axis. A normal curve is an example of a frequency distribution.

cumulative record

n. A learning curve created by a steadily moving roll of paper on which a pen moves up a fixed amount for every new response and thus keeps a running record of how many responses an organism makes in a given time interval.

cumulative recorder

n. An instrument which creates a learning curve by steadily moving a roll of paper on which a pen moves up a fixed amount for every new response and thus keeps a running record of how many responses an organism makes in a given time interval.

cuneate nucleus

n. Either of two somatosensory relay stations where the right and left fasciculus cuneatus end in the medulla oblongata.

cupula

n. Any of three dome-shaped gelatinous masses within each of the three semicircular canals of the ear which are part of our sense of balance and movement. The cupulae are pressured by movements of the liquid inside the semicircular canals and in turn press on the crista, which activates hair cells within the crista which give rise to nerve impulses toward the neural centers of balance and movement.

curare
n. Any of several plant extracts that act as neurotoxins by blocking the actions of acetylcholine at the synapse, resulting in paralysis and death due to asphyxiation when breathing ceases as a result of paralysis. It is used to poison arrows and spears by indigenous people in the areas where curare containing plants grow.

curvilinear correlation
n. An index of the degree of relationship between two variables which is not mathematically linear.

curvilinear regression ▶ *See* REGRESSION, CURVILINEAR

curvilinear relationship
n. A relationship between two variables which does not produce a straight line when graphed.

customs
n. Shared behavioral habits and methods for accomplishing tasks. They are an important part of any cultural group.

cutaneous sense
n. Any of the senses having receptors located in the skin, such as pressure, texture, vibration, temperature, and pain.

CVC trigram
n. A string of three letters composed of a consonant, vowel, and consonant (CVC) in that order such as *zib*, *dog*, or *mun*, which may or may not constitute a word in English or other language. CVCs have often been used as stimuli in memory and forced-choice tasks in cognitive psychology.

cybernetics
n. The study of self-regulating control processes in both machine and biological systems. These systems usually develop for a purpose and have a starting and stopping mechanism and a system for gathering feedback relative to the purpose of the system.

cyclic AMP
n. Cyclic adenosine monophosphate (AMP) is a metabolite of adenosine triphosphate which is created in the mitochondria of all cells and serves as a second messenger in changing the electric potential of nerve cell membranes during a nerve impulse.

cyclic GMP
n. Cyclic guanosine monophosphate (GMP) is a compound found in retinal rods and cones which regulates the sodium channels in those cells, increasing and decreasing the likelihood of action potentials depending on the state of its ring structure, which can be altered by light. It is also found in smooth muscle cells and facilitates the engorgement of the penis and the clitoris during sexual excitement.

cyclic guanosine monophosphate ▶ *See* CYCLIC GMP

Cyclopean eye
n. **1.** A hypothetical brain structure which brings together the information of both eyes in an integrated picture. **2.** A working model of visual perception used in descriptions of space.

cyclophoria
n. Abnormal rotation of the eye when not focused on an object due to weakness in the oblique eye muscles.

cycloplegia
n. Paralysis of the ciliary eye muscles which control the shape of the lens, which makes it impossible to focus clearly on an object. This is a common effect of anticholinergic drugs.

cyclothymia
n. A mental disorder in which there is a chronic fluctuation between hypomania and depression which usually begins in late adolescence and develops into bipolar disorder in about one-third of cases. Also called cyclothymic disorder.

cyclothymic disorder

n. A mental disorder in which there is a chronic fluctuation between hypomania and depression which usually begins in late adolescence and develops into bipolar disorder in about one-third of cases. Also called cyclothymia.

cytology

n. The study of the development, function, and structure of biological cells.

cytoplasm

n. The matter inside a biological cell excluding the nucleus.

cytosine

n. A base which is one of the basic building blocks of DNA and RNA, usually designated by the letter *C* in descriptions of DNA, which has an affinity for guanine.

cytotoxic

adj. Poisonous to biological cells.

daily process methods ▶ *See* **DIARY METHODS**

daltonism

n. The inability to distinguish between red and green usually due to a recessive genetic defect on the X chromosome which causes the absence of the forms of cones in the retina which make the red-green distinction. It occurs about 20 times as often in men as women (8% vs. 0.4%) as women have two X chromosomes while men have only one, and the probability that both X chromosomes will be defective is about one-twentieth the probability that only one will be defective. Also called red-green color blindness.

dance therapy

n. A form of psychotherapy in which any kind of dance is used as a way to bring people into the present moment of awareness, break down social isolation, interrupt fantasies or delusions, and disturb the daily patterns of withdrawal and negative thinking associated with most forms of psychopathology.

dark adaptation

n. An increased sensitivity to light caused by the expansion of the pupils and the replacement of rhodopsin, the photosensitive pigment in the retinal rods, which is normally depleted by continuous exposure to light.

Dark adaptation depends on previous level of exposure to light but is usually complete in about 20–30 minutes in complete dark.

dark light

n. The sensation of dim light produced by random electrical activity (impulses) in the retinal cells in the absence of any light.

Darwinian fitness

n. The relative level of success of different genotypes in surviving, reproducing, and caring for their offspring until they reach maturity over the course of a lifetime.

Darwinism

n. Evolution by means of natural selection as described by Charles Darwin. Genetic discoveries and ethological observation have made modern evolutionary theory markedly more complex and specific over the century and a half since Darwin first proposed his theory without altering his basic ideas very much.

data

n. Any information acquired through the senses, in the course of research, or in any other manner.

data-driven processing

n. Any process of data analysis that is derived from patterns in the data rather than imposed from preexisting rules or structures. Also called bottom-up processing.

daydream

n. A fantasy or dreamlike thought pattern that occurs while a person is awake and markedly removes attention from present surroundings.

deafness, functional

n. A hearing loss that has no known physical mechanism.

deafness, nerve

n. Hearing loss caused by damage to or deterioration of the inner ear or any part of the auditory nerve tract. The most common causes are breaking and death of hair cells within the cochlea by exposure to loud noises, overexposure to drugs such as aspirin and quinine, mumps, rubella, and tumors. Also called sensorineural deafness.

death anxiety

n. Generally defined, death anxiety is fear of death; it is often concerned with one's own death but can include a more generalized fear. Researchers Conte, Bakur-Weiner, and Putchik have developed a useful tool for assessing death anxiety (the Death Anxiety Questionnaire) and explaining the concept in greater depth. Through their and others' research, death anxiety can be separated into four different factors: fear of the unknown, fear of suffering, fear of loneliness, and fear of personal extinction.   – SRB

death instinct

n. An individual's fundamental need to die. This concept, also called Thanatos, was developed by Sigmund Freud. The death instinct represents the wish to relinquish the hardships of living and return to the calm and stillness of death. In the human mind, the death instinct coexists with the life instinct, or Eros. Freud posited that humans live according to the pleasure principle, maximizing experiences that produce pleasure and minimizing those that are unpleasant. Freud also noted, however, that humans tended to enact aggressive and self-destructive events. He saw this

as a need and labeled it the death instinct. According to Freud's view of the death instinct, all living beings have a fundamental yearning to return to a preorganic state. This need is one component of the individual's id, or the part of the mind that houses primitive desires.   – TJM

death wish

n. An individual's specific desire to return to a preorganic state. A part of the more comprehensive *death instinct* proposed by Sigmund Freud, this is most closely associated with the part of the mind that houses primitive desires, the id. From a Freudian perspective, self-destructive behaviors are associated with a strong id, and therefore with the desire to die.   – TJM

debriefing

n. **1.** The process of discussing their participation with research participants in order to assure they were not harmed or to ameliorate any harm done them as well as to offer a more complete explanation of experimental procedures than was given before participation. **2.** The process of giving participants in a task, research project, or process group an opportunity to discuss their experience. **3.** A meeting held to debrief.

decategorization

n. **1.** Any process in which something is removed from a category. **2.** In social psychology, the process of emphasizing individual uniqueness as a way of breaking down group categorization of individuals. **3.** In political funding, the process of reducing central control over funding for social services so local governments can develop programs that cross bureaucratic boundaries.

decathexis

n. The process of removing emotional investment from an object.

decay theory

n. A memory theory in which short-lived traces of sensory experiences are created in the brain but automatically decay unless rehearsed or recoded.

decentering

n. The process of taking another point of view which can be either the point of view of another person or an abstract point of view in which the self is viewed as an object.

deception

n. Misleading another through lies, withholding of information, or actions intended to convey a false impression usually for the purpose of individual gain at the expense of another. Deception occurs in animals other than humans and follows the same basic form except without human language.

decerebrate rigidity

n. A rigidity of the body which occurs when the cerebrum is disconnected from the rest of the brain and body and is characterized by muscular rigidity and particularly of the limbs.

decibel

n. (dB) A logarithmic unit in a scale of loudness or sound pressure level (SPL) equal to one-tenth of a bel, which is a 10-fold increase in sound pressure level. Because it is logarithmic, the dB scale is not additive in a linear fashion. The scale has been arbitrarily set at 0 for a 20-micropascal sound pressure level at 1-kHz tone, which is about the normal human threshold for hearing, so positive and negative values for dB are possible.

decision making

n. The process of choosing between two or more alternatives which involves numerous cognitive processes including perception, memory, valuation, and critical judgment. Numerous approaches have been pursued in the study of decision making including mental heuristics, statistical modeling, and experimental modeling of simple choices.

decision theory

n. A family of theories which attempt to describe and explain how humans and other organisms and group entities make decisions often with the intent of discovering optimal ways of arriving at decisions under different circumstances.

declarative knowledge

n. Knowledge that can be recalled or expressed verbally, in contrast to implicit knowledge, which can be used but is difficult to express. Ability to say one's name is an example of declarative knowledge while being able to use chopsticks is implicit knowledge.

declarative memory

n. Knowledge that can recalled and expressed verbally in contrast to implicit memory such as how to ride a bicycle, which can be used but is difficult to express.

decoding

n. Decoding is the process of converting a word's printed (*orthographic*) information (i.e., the letters) into the corresponding sounds (*phonology*); colloquially known as "sounding out." Decoding is a necessary step in learning to read words. This process is more difficult in deep orthographies such as English where mappings between orthography and phonology are not always one to one (for example, the word *island*), compared with shallow orthographies such as Finnish, where each letter always has the same pronunciation. Decoding is a particularly difficult skill to master for children with reading disability or developmental dyslexia. This difficulty is most likely due to a core phonological coding or processing deficit. – NL

decoding rules

n. rules that govern the interpretation and perception of emotion. These are learned, culturally based rules that shape how people of each culture view and interpret the emotional expressions of others.

deconstruction

n. A from of critical analysis of texts focusing on the relative coherence or clarity and internal consistency of a text which makes the assumption that there is no absolute reference nor proof of truth.

decortication

n. The surgical removal of the cortex of the brain while leaving the rest of the brain intact.

deduction

n. **1.** A conclusion reached through a logical process of application of general principles to a particular instance. **2.** A monetary subtraction for a particular category of tax, benefit, or some other reason.

deductive reasoning

n. Logical analysis through a process of the application of general principles to particular cases. Also called top-down processing.

deep dyslexia

n. A form of acquired dyslexia in which people have difficulty reading nonword letter strings, make semantic errors (such as substituting *king* for *president*), have difficulty in reading abstract rather than concrete words, and have problems with function words such as *the, and, or.*

deep structure

n. Deep structure is the underlying hierarchical structure for a sentence generated by phrase structure rules. It is a level of representation proposed in early versions of *generative grammar*, set up to account for the fact that sentences with different surface forms are nonetheless syntactically related. For example, in the sentences *The cop arrested the thug* and *The thug was arrested by the cop*, the main verb of the sentence, *arrest*, has the same agent, *cop*, and the same patient, *thug*, even though these two nouns occupy different structural positions. The phrase structure rules that generate deep structure are rules that expand sentence constituents. For example, a sentence (S) has two obligatory major constituents: a subject noun phrase (NP) and a predicate verb phrase. The rule generating this structure might be formulated as $S \rightarrow NP\ VP$.   – EMF

defense mechanism

n. In psychoanalysis, any of a number of strategies the ego employs to prevent the energy of an unfulfilled desire from disrupting its plans. It usually involves repression of the desire and a redirection of the energy. In reaction formation the energy is directed into proclaiming and acting as if one's self wish were the opposite of the desire. In sublimation the energy is directed into work or other activity having no obvious resemblance to the original desire or its object. In repression the desire and its object are simply pushed into the unconscious and expression of the energy is delayed. In displacement the energy is redirected to an object acceptable to the ego's plans.

defense, perceptual

n. The misperception or ignoring of a stimulus that would be threatening to a person. Thus a person seeing a close-up picture of a penis might imagine it to be a mushroom.

defensive attribution

n. A bias in estimating the probability of a threatening event so as to minimize the perceived threat to one's self and so escape anxiety about the event. Thus a sailor may attribute a boat's sinking to the captain's error rather than an unpredictable chance combination of weather events, as it makes it more likely he or she can control the occurrence of the event by not drinking and thus lessen anxiety.

degrees of freedom

n. (df) The number of elements that can vary in a statistical calculation or the number of scores minus the number of restrictions.

dehumanization

n. The process of reducing human beings to something less than human, which can be a mental exercise in recategorization or a set of actions that has significant negative effects on a person or a group of people.

dehumanization of the victim

n. A mental process whereby a person who harms someone reduces the value of the victim in his or her own mind so as to escape the guilt the action would normally elicit. This is done by suggesting the person lacks some aspect of humanity, as in "They don't have feelings like we do"; deserves to be harmed, as in "Terrorists have no rights"; or are not really human, as in "They are subhumans."

deindividuation

n. The process of losing one's sense of individual agency, which results in altered perceptual and conceptual states including the absence of some normal behavioral restraints with the result that he or she often engages in actions he/she would not ordinarily do. This sometimes happens as a contagious process in groups or with individuals who experience very high levels of stress.

déjà vu

n. The uncanny sense that one has already been through the same experience before or seen the same scene before.

de la Tourette's syndrome

n. A tic disorder characterized by a combination of facial tics and vocal tics which may be yelps, grunts, snarls, words, or obscenities. Also called Tourette's disorder.

delay conditioning

n. A form of classical conditioning in which the duration of the conditioned stimulus is gradually extended until there is a considerable time lapse between the beginning of the conditioned stimulus and the unconditioned stimulus. Pavlov found that eventually the organism delays the conditioned response until near the end of the prolonged conditioned stimulus.

delayed auditory feedback

n. An experimental procedure in which a speaker hears his or her own speech through headphones after a short time delay. It has been used to help persons who stutter and have some other speech problems but can also induce speech problems in normal speakers.

delayed conditioning

n. A form of classical conditioning in which the duration of the conditioned stimulus is gradually extended until there is a considerable time lapse between the beginning of the stimulus and the unconditioned stimulus. Pavlov found that eventually the organism delays the conditioned response until near the end of the prolonged conditioned stimulus.

delayed gratification

n. The process of restraining impulses to act for immediate reward in order to carry out plans for greater reward in the future. Thus a person may resist grabbing a hamburger and fries to eat on the way home and instead wait and eat a healthy meal with balanced nutrition to enjoy better health and receive more social approval in the future.

delayed matching to sample

n. An experimental procedure in which a subject is presented with a sample stimulus and then after a time delay has to choose which one of two or more stimuli matches the original one.

delayed reinforcement (procedure)

n. An operant conditioning procedure in which reward is delayed for some period after a response is made. This tends to retard the acquisition of a response and its extinction after reinforcement ceases.

delayed sleep-onset insomnia

n. A form of sleep disorder characterized by inability to fall asleep and subsequent sleepiness on the following day.

delirium

n. A short period of disturbed perception and thought which often mimics psychosis. Symptoms can include hallucinations, delusions, paranoia, perceptual distortion, loss of bodily control, twitching, and inability to concentrate. There are numerous causes of delirium including but not limited to alcohol and drug intoxication or withdrawal, poisoning, brain tumors, and head trauma.

delirium tremens

n. (DTs) The delirium characteristic of alcohol withdrawal, which can be life threatening if untreated.

delta wave

n. A high-amplitude, low-frequency wave (1–3 Hz) of electrical activity in the brain measured by electroencephalography which is characteristic of deep, dreamless sleep.

delusion

n. A fixed false belief. Delusions are beliefs that are held with absolute certainty in spite of any evidence to the contrary. Delusions can be nonbizarre (e.g., believing the CIA or FBI is following you) or bizarre (e.g., believing that aliens are harvesting your organs while you sleep). In both cases the individual is not at all open to alternate explanations, no matter how compelling they may be (e.g., confirmation from the authorities that they are not keeping a file on you; a CT or MRI scan indicating all organs are intact and functioning well). Delusions are most commonly found in individuals with psychotic disorders such as schizophrenia but can also occur in severe cases of bipolar disorder, major depressive disorder, and stimulant abuse and dependence.   – DGa

delusion, nihilistic

n. A belief that one's body or mind or the external world has ceased to exist.

delusion of grandeur

n. A fixed false belief where the individual believes that he or she is an important figure in some way. For example, the individual may believe he or she is Jesus or the Buddha or may believe that he or she is an important world figure, such as the president of the United States. As with all delusions, there is no amount of conflicting evidence that will diminish the individual's false belief.   – DGa

delusion of persecution

n. A fixed false belief where the individual believes that he or she is in some way being singled out and is the subject of maltreatment or harassment. These beliefs can be nonbizarre (e.g., believing that the authorities are surveying your every move and intentionally making life more difficult for you) or bizarre (e.g., believing that insects are conspiring to attack you at every turn). As with all delusions, there is no amount of conflicting evidence that will diminish the individual's false belief.   – DGa

delusion of reference

n. A fixed false belief where the individual believes that he or she is in some way the object of special attention. For example, someone with a delusion of reference might believe the evening news anchor is speaking directly to him or her or that specific world events have been contrived as a sort of message to him or her. As with all delusions, there is no amount of conflicting evidence that will diminish the individual's false belief.   – DGa

demand characteristics

n. Demand characteristics are aspects of a research study that cue participants to the objectives or desires of the researcher. These effects can be either conscious or unconscious; participants may not realize that demand characteristics have affected their behavior. Demand characteristics may include aspects of the stimulus materials or other elements of the environment, or subtle cues given off by the researcher, including verbal and nonverbal behavior. Research has shown that demand characteristics can have powerful effects on research participants, and that researchers are not very skilled at reducing demand characteristics that are present in their behavior. One common remedy to the problem of demand characteristics in terms of experimenter behavior is the double-blind study, in which both participants and experimenter are unaware of the researchers' objectives and/or the particular experimental condition.   – MWP

dementia

n. A clinical syndrome characterized by deterioration in intellectual ability sufficient to interfere with usual social or occupational functioning. The syndrome of dementia involves persistent impairment in two or more of the following domains of psychological functioning: memory, language, visuospatial skills, judgment or abstract thinking, and emotion or personality. More specifically, dementias are associated with short- and long-term memory impairment, difficulties in producing and understanding speech, difficulties in maneuvering through space and in conceiving of spatial orientation, lapses in judgment, and personality changes.

Dementia is associated with more than 70 different causes of brain dysfunction with Alzheimer's disease and vascular dementia the most common forms. Until the 1980s, dementia was considered a ubiquitous condition of global intellectual impairment. Since that time researchers have been able to delineate distinct patterns or preserved and impaired cognitive abilities associated with different dementing illnesses.   – TJM

dementia, AIDS

n. A pervasive general deterioration of mental functioning caused by cortical atrophy due to AIDS which includes cognitive impairment, loss of motor skills, and failure to perform normal daily actions such as washing and using a toilet.

dementia praecox

n. An archaic term for schizophrenia.

demography

n. The study of populations with regard to geographic distribution and characteristics such as ethnicity, age, sex, genetic markers, and susceptibility to disease.

dendrite

n. The branching portion of a neuron which extends from the cell body to synapses with the axons of other neurons or to sensory transducers.

denial

n. A primitive defense mechanism where the individual wards off unwanted emotions and experiences by not noticing or remembering experiences which are quite salient to others. In psychoanalytic terms this defense mechanism is an unconscious maneuver to avoid conflict. For example, Jane has had a difficult childhood filled with physical abuse and neglect. As an adult she is very attracted to Steve and feels "protected" by his rough exterior. Though she is around him when his behavior is controlling, hostile, and rude to others, she unconsciously does not allow herself to experience or remember these aspects of his behavior because of the unconscious conflict it stirs up in her. Though her friends may point out these experiences that they clearly observe and remember, because of her use of denial, Jane will be unable to remember or see what they are describing.   – DGa

dentate gyrus

n. A crescent-shaped strip of gray matter running from the hippocampus to the entorhinal formation.

deoxyribonucleic acid

n. (DNA) A nucleic acid which forms long chains containing the genetic information of all cellular organisms. Human DNA is composed of about 32,000 genes made up of differing combinations of four bases, adenine, thymine, guanine, and cytosine, whose combinations and spacing serve as templates for creating the different proteins of which the body is composed. It is inherited from each parent in the form of a long strand which entwines with the DNA strand from the other parent to form a double helix.

dependence, physiological

n. In physiology, dependence is a state in which the body has adjusted its metabolic processes to accommodate the continued presence of the drug so that increased doses of the drug are needed to achieve the same effect and withdrawal symptoms occur if the drug is withdrawn.

dependence, psychological

n. **1.** The habitual use of a drug to cope with daily life so that without the drug the person suffers high levels of anxiety and engages in uncoordinated and unsatisfactory attempts to find satisfaction in life. **2.** Emotional dependence is a state of real or imagined need for the support and assistance of others to cope with daily life.

dependent personality disorder

n. A pervasive and enduring pattern of adjustment which is characterized by an unrealistic desire to be taken care of by others, submissiveness and clinging to others, and preoccupation with fears of abandonment. Persons with this disorder attempt to induce others to take responsibility for them, to make their decisions for them, and to reassure and nurture them constantly. They are usually uncomfortable alone and seldom take initiative to improve their own lives other than by finding someone to take charge of their lives, toward whom they feel both all-encompassing love and bitter resentment.

dependent variable

n. The outcome factor or variable of interest in an experiment that is compared to determine whether differences exist between experimental conditions as a result of manipulation or treatment conditions. Within basic experimental design, changes in the dependent variable are measured to examine the relative impact of another variable (the independent variable). For example, in an experiment to examine the impact of alcohol consumption on memory, the researcher will vary the amount of alcohol consumed (independent variable) to examine changes in memory (dependent variable). The dependent variable is measured and compared in order to draw conclusions about the relative impact of the independent variable.   – BJM

depersonalization

n. A state of mind in which a person's experiences seem strange, unreal, and foreign to him or her so that he or she feels as if he/she is watching life rather than living it. Most people feel this way on occasion, and it is characteristic of persons who have been avoiding difficult choices in life and those who suffer from depression, hypochondriasis, dissociative states, temporal lobe epilepsy, and early stages of schizophrenia.

depersonalization disorder

n. A disorder characterized by a prolonged state of mind in which a person's experiences seem strange, unreal, and foreign to him or her so that he or she feels as if he/she is watching life rather than living it.

depolarization

n. A reduction in the normal difference in electrovalence inside and outside a cell wall and especially in neurons. Normally the inside of a neural cell wall is negatively charged while the outside is positively charged, and depolarization occurs when sodium and potassium ions exchange places outside and inside the cell wall in a wavelike pattern which constitutes a nerve impulse.

depression

n. A state of mind characterized by negative mood, low energy, loss of interest in usual activities, pessimism, unrealistically negative thoughts about self and the future, and social withdrawal. Short states of depression are normal after personal losses of various sorts and are considered disorders only when they persist for long periods or significantly interfere with daily functioning as in the various depressive disorders.

depression, endogenous

n. Depression which arises from internal causes rather than as a reaction to external circumstances.

depressive disorders

n. A family of disorders, all of which involve a state of mind characterized by negative mood, loss of interest in usual activities, low energy, pessimism, unrealistically negative thoughts about self and the future, social withdrawal, and sometimes sleep and appetite disturbances. These disorders include major depressive disorder, dysthymic disorder, and depressive disorder not otherwise specified (NOS).

depressive episode

n. A period of time in which a person experiences persistent negative mood, low energy, pessimism, unrealistically negative thoughts about self and the future, and social withdrawal. Sleep and appetite disturbances may also be present.

depressive episode, major

n. A period of negative mood, low energy, loss of interest in usual activities, pessimism, unrealistically negative thoughts about self and the future, and social withdrawal which interferes with daily life and persists for at least 2 weeks. Psychomotor agitation or retardation, sleep and appetite disturbance, and difficulty in concentrating are common as well.

depth of processing

n. The degree to which a stimulus is processed at different levels of mind which affects the likelihood of its being remembered. Thus a stimulus like *bird* may be seen as a pattern of light and dark, a string of letters, a word, a word with a rich set of connections, and something meaningful related to our self. The more of these levels or types of processing which occur the more likely is the memory of seeing the stimulus to be remembered.

depth-of-processing hypothesis
n. The hypothesis that memory is dependent on the degree of thoroughness with which an experience is processed.

depth perception
n. The capacity to make accurate judgments of depth from sensory clues. Visual cues such as parallax, perspective, visual accommodation, convergence, and retinal disparity are those mainly used, but auditory and tactile clues are sometimes important as well.

descriptive norm
n. **1.** An average or usual range of values for a variable used as a standard for comparison as in the arithmetic mean or median of a group of test scores. **2.** Consensual standards within a given social group in a particular situation concerning appropriate behavior, evaluation, and cognitive processes.

descriptive research
n. Empirical research which seeks to describe, categorize, and count usually in naturalistic settings rather than to control situations to test specific hypotheses.

descriptive statistics
n. Any numerical index used to describe an aspect of a data set including statistics such as the range, interquartile range, mean, median, mode, and standard deviation.

desensitization
n. The process of lessening physical or emotional reactivity to a stimulus which may be through repeated exposure, antithetical response learning, psychological insight, or any other means.

desensitization procedure
n. A procedure to produce a lessened emotional and physical reactivity to a stimulus

such as reducing phobic reactions. Such procedures most commonly involve learning relaxation techniques, graded systematic exposure, and acquisition of a competing response (relaxation) in the presence of the anxiety-producing object.

design, experimental
n. A research strategy in which an experimenter systematically varies one or more *independent variables* while measuring one or more *dependent variables*, thus creating two or more distinct *treatment conditions*. There are two broad types of experimental designs:
- in the between-subjects or randomized groups design, different participants are randomly assigned to the different treatment conditions. For example, one group of depressed participants receives a drug and a separate group of participants receives a placebo pill instead of the drug (control group).
- in the within-subjects or repeated measures design, participants' behavior is measured across all treatment conditions. For example, each participant rates both neutral and smiling faces on physical attractiveness.

One alternative to the repeated measures design is the matched-subjects design. In this design, different groups of participants are matched on some variable believed to be relevant to the results of the study (e.g., intelligence).   – KDM

design, factorial
n. An experimental design in which two or more independent variables are simultaneously and systematically varied so as to compare their individual and compounded influences on a dependent variable.

determinism
n. A philosophical point of view which supposes that there are specific causes to all events such that if all variables could be specified, both the past and the future could be known. This is the position of logical positivism in science, which was the dominant point of view in 16th- through 19th-century science but was supplanted by relativistic views in the

early 20th century. In psychology, this point of view included psychoanalysis, behaviorism, and some physiological approaches.

detoxification

n. The process of removing poisonous substances from a person. The substance is usually a drug such as alcohol which has altered the body's physiological balances such that there is a period of marked discomfort and physiological danger in the early stages. Other sorts of detoxification may include vomiting, gastric lavage, dialysis, or other forms of removing the toxins from the body.

developmental age

n. The score of an individual on a test of development compared to the average scores on the test by persons at each age level. Thus a person who is 4 years old and whose scores match the average scores for children who are 5.1 years old would have a developmental age of 5.1.

developmental coordination disorder

n. A marked impairment in the development of motor coordination that interferes with academic or daily life and is not due to a general medical condition.

developmental disorder, pervasive

n. A family of developmental disorders characterized by profound impairment in several areas of development including social interaction, communication, and the presence of stereotyped behaviors, interests, and activities. These disorders include autistic disorder, Rett's disorder, childhood disintegrative disorder, Asperger's disorder, and pervasive developmental disorder not otherwise specified (NOS).

developmental milestone

n. Any particular act or ability in physical or mental development that is obvious and predictable so that children all over the world develop it at about the same time and it can be used for comparison purposes to measure development. Cooing, babbling, saying a recognizable word, taking a step without support are all examples of milestones.

developmental norm(s)

n. The average levels of developments associated with children at a particular age.

developmental psychologist

n. A person holding a doctoral degree in developmental psychology or a closely related degree who specializes in conducting research on the development of children or who practices in clinically treating children.

developmental psychology

n. A subfield of psychology that draws upon the knowledge base and expertise of many different disciplines (e.g., psychology, sociology, biology, chemistry, genetics, anthropology, and economics) to help explain how and why people stay the same and how and why people change as they develop throughout the life span. Within the field of developmental psychology there are subfields that focus on specific aspects (e.g., social/emotional development, language development, physical development, cognitive development) and diverse age ranges (i.e., prenatal development, infancy, early childhood, school age, adolescence, young adulthood, middle age, and older adulthood). Thus, the theories and research that constitute this field are from many and diverse individuals, who have varied interests but have the common goal of understanding human development.   – SRB

deviance

n. Acting or being different from the norm in some measurable way.

deviation, average

n. The sum of all deviations from the mean divided by the number of the deviations included in the sum. This number is seldom used as it often has a value near 0 as the positive and negative deviations cancel each other out. So the standard deviation, or an average of absolute deviations, is usually used instead.

deviation IQ

n. An intelligence quotient (IQ) calculated using comparisons to the mean and standard deviations of scores on the test for children of a child's age with the average score arbitrarily set at 100 and a standard deviation adding or subtracting 15 (or 16) points, depending on the test, so that a child who scored one standard deviation above the norm would have a deviation IQ of 115 while a child who was one standard deviation below average would have a deviation IQ of 85.

deviation score

n. The difference between an observed score and the mean of scores, calculated by subtracting the mean score from the observed score. Thus deviation scores can have both negative and positive values.

deviation, standard

n. The square root of the average of the squared differences from the mean of a set of numbers.

diagnosis

n. The categorization of a person's symptoms into one or more than one of an official set of disease and disorder categories based on an exploration of the symptoms a person exhibits using known patterns of symptoms as a basis for further exploration of possible symptoms.

diagnosis, differential

n. The process of deciding among different possible categories of disorders for assignment to the set of symptoms of an individual using an official set of categories for classification.

Diagnostic and Statistical Manual of Mental Disorders

n. (DSM, DSM-IV-TR) A publication of the American Psychiatric Association containing lists of mental disorders, their symptoms, criteria for diagnosis, and demographic information about the disorders that is used as a professional guide to diagnosis of mental disorders in the United States.

diagnostic interview

n. A structured conversation between a professional and a client in which the object is to reach a diagnosis of the problems of the client and form an initial treatment plan by exploring the symptoms, history, and current situation of the client.

diagnosticity

n. The quality of predicting something else. Thus the presence of hallucinations predicts the presence of schizophrenia but does not do so perfectly as there are other reasons for hallucinations such as LSD intoxication.

dialect

n. A variety of a language that is used by a certain subgroup within the group that uses the language as a whole. Thus there is usually an adolescent dialect in the United States as there are dialects used by people in different geographical and ethnic groups within the country. Nonhuman animal languages have dialects just as do human languages.

dialectical reasoning

n. A form of thinking in which it is assumed that there are contrary points of view on all topics and that through the rational examination of alternative points of view a synthesis of ideas which is closer to the truth than any of the contrary points of view results. It also assumes that each new synthesis implies an opposing point of view and through continuing an examination of this new set of conflicts a spiral of thinking occurs which approaches more and more closely to the truth.

diary methods

n. Diary methods refer to a collection of procedures used in the psychological sciences in which people complete brief surveys about their experiences over time in daily life. Researchers use diary methods (a) to minimize memory biases by capturing experiences close to their actual occurrence, (b) to maximize ecological validity by testing hypotheses in real-world contexts, and (c) to examine dynamic changes in phenomena over time and situations. Diary studies typically last from a week to a month, with as few as one nightly report to as many as 10 reports per day. Surveys can be implemented using paper booklets, cell phones, Internet Web sites, and personal digital assistants (PDAs). When people complete surveys in response to a semirandom signal via pager, alarm watch, or PDA, this procedure is also called experience sampling. Diary methods are used in social, personality, clinical, and health psychology, and in the medical sciences under the name *ecological momentary assessment.*

— TSC, HTr

diathesis-stress hypothesis

n. A hypothesis about the cause of certain disorders that argues that specific genetic factors predispose an individual to a certain disorder, but that sufficient environmental stress factors must be triggered in order for the potential risk to manifest itself. For example, research indicates that genes influence the risk for schizophrenia, creating a diathesis. However, in some identical twins only one twin develops schizophrenia and the other does not. Because identical twins possess identical genes, some nongenetic factor, or stress, must play a role in the development of the disease.   — TJM

diazepam

n. A member of the benzodiazepine family of drugs which is a central nervous system depressant and is used as an anxiolytic, in alleviating the symptoms of alcohol withdrawal, as a muscle relaxant, and as an anticonvulsant. It has a long half-life and is sold under the brand name Valium.

dichotic

adj. Of or relating to a difference in sound reaching the left and right ears, as in a dichotic listening task, in which a person consciously attends to a conversation in one ear while another conversation or other sounds are played in the other ear.

dichotomous variable

n. The simplest type of categorical variable in which there are only two possible values or levels (e.g., true or false, male or female). Dichotomous variables are considered discrete, qualitative variables as they provide categorical classification with no quantitative relationship between the levels of the variables. When coding dichotomous variables, one can use any coding system that specifies two different values. If a 1/0 system is used, it is referred to as dummy coding; if a 1/−1 system is used, it is called effect coding. Dichotomous variables are most useful for examining broad comparisons.   — BJM

diencephalon

n. The bottom or central part of the forebrain including the thalamus, basal ganglia, hypothalamus, and epithalamus, which link the midbrain and the cerebral cortex.

difference limen

n. The smallest difference in perceptual intensity that can be discriminated, usually using 75% accuracy as the standard. Also called the difference threshold or the just noticeable difference (JND).

difference threshold

n. The smallest difference in perceptual intensity that can be discriminated, usually using 75% accuracy as the standard. Also called the difference limen or the just noticeable difference (JND).

differential conditioning

n. The presentation of two or more discriminable stimuli in different orders with different schedules of reinforcement which results in different responses of the organism to the two stimuli approximately in accord with what would be expected were each stimulus presented alone.

differential item functioning

n. The differences in validity of an individual test item for different groups of people, which cause the item to be biased in its predictions.

differential psychology

n. The branch of psychology that studies differences in mental functioning between individuals, groups, and species and seeks to explain the observed differences.

differential reinforcement

n. The establishment of different schedules of reinforcement for different behaviors so as to increase some behaviors and decrease other behaviors.

differential reinforcement of appropriate behavior

n. The establishment of different schedules of reinforcement for different behaviors so as to increase appropriate behaviors and decrease inappropriate behaviors.

differential reinforcement of high response rates

n. The establishment of schedules of reinforcement that depend on rapid response after onset of the signal stimulus.

differential reinforcement of low response rates

n. The establishment of a schedule of reinforcement in which the time lag between signal and behavior is beyond a preset threshold.

differential reinforcement of other responses

n. The establishment of different schedules of reinforcement for different behaviors so as to decrease the target behavior and increase the rate of alternative behaviors.

differential validity

n. The capacity of a test battery to predict differences in performance on two or more criterion behaviors.

difficult temperament

n. A type of temperament that is characterized by an intense, irregular, withdrawing style that is generally marked by negative moods.

diffusion of responsibility

n. A state in which an individual perceives her/his own responsibility as less than usual because it is shared by a group of people. This is the hypothesized cause of the bystander effect, in which bystanders' likelihood of acting to help after witnessing an accident, crime, or other incident depends on the number of other people who are also witnesses or believed to be witnesses to the same incident.

digit span test

n. A test of short-term memory in which a person is asked to recall random strings of digits; it is part of many tests of intelligence or mental functioning including the Wechsler Adult Intelligence Scale (WAIS). The test often includes the task of repeating the digit string backward as well as forward. Forward digit span in normal adults from industrialized societies averages seven plus or minus two.

digit-symbol test

n. A subtest included in the Wechsler Adult Intelligence Scale (WAIS) in which a person has to transcribe a set of symbols into digits using a key supplied by the test. It is considered a measure of fluid intelligence, and scores tend to decrease with age.

dilemma, prisoner's

n. A game in which each player is forced to choose between an option which gives her/him high reward and no reward or loss to the other player and an option that gives both parties lesser rewards. It received its name from the police tactic of separating a pair of suspected criminals and offering to set one of them free if he or she testifies against the other.

direct control

n. A type of control in which the self acts as an agent, and individuals feel themselves to be more self-efficacious when their agency is made explicit, leading to greater feelings of autonomy and efficacy. Direct control may be the preferred mode of behavior in cultural contexts that promote independence or autonomy, such as in the United States.

directed forgetting

n. Forgetting that occurs after having been instructed to forget something. It is used to contrast with attempts to remember in studies of memory.

directional test

n. A statistical test whose criterion for rejection of the null hypothesis is that the observed statistic lies in one tail of the probability distribution for the test statistic. Also called a one-tailed test.

direct speech acts

n. Utterances in which the meaning is contained in the structure of the utterance as in "There is a woman in your bed" or "May I have a glass of water?" as opposed to indirect speech acts in which meaning is implied such as "Did you know there was a woman in your bed?" or "It has been a long time since I have had a drink."

discontinuity theory

n. A point of view originating in Gestalt psychology that processes of learning and problem solving occur not smoothly with an accumulation of data but in moments of sudden realization of a perceptual, procedural, or conceptual whole.

discontinuous variable

n. A variable which for certain values or between certain values of the variable does not vary continuously as the variable increases. The discontinuity may consist of an abrupt change in the value of the function, or an abrupt change in its law of variation, or the variable may not exist or may become imaginary within some ranges, such as the number of professional football teams which have won more than 200 games in one season.

discounting principle

n. **1.** In attribution theory, the idea that the contribution of a particular cause to a particular result should be given less weight if other possible causes are also present. **2.** The idea that unexpected or unusual information carries more weight than what is expected.

discourse

n. A discourse (also *text*) is a series of connected sentences that have internal organization and are linked with cohesion devices. Discourse may be oral or written; different types of discourses include communication contexts such as conversations, lectures, interviews, letters, poems, and novels. Discourse processing involves not only extracting meaning from individual sentences or utterances, but also making connections between those sentences or utterances, by relying on cues that transcend individual sentences. One way to find such connections is through the identification of the referents for anaphors in a text – for example, the nouns to which pronouns in a discourse might refer. Inferences also play a key role in discourse processing. For example, in a conversation about picnic supplies, the mention of a *container* may lead to a different inference about the nature of the container than in a conversation about transatlantic relocation services.   – EMF

discourse analysis

n. Discourse analysis is the study of the principles underlying the organization of discourse, a unit of language spanning beyond individual sentences. Discourse analysts are predominantly concerned with analyzing language that occurs naturally, rather than language elicited artificially. Methodologically, discourse analysis relies heavily on the transcription of recorded speech and therefore demands careful consideration regarding the way such recordings are to be obtained. Discourse analysis can also be performed on corpora from written sources, including newspapers as well as Internet chat rooms and other such electronic forms of communication. Research on discourse analysis has important applications in areas such as language instruction and human-machine interaction.
    – EMF

discrete variable

n. A variable that may take on only one of a number of possible values; as such, discrete variables cannot represent all possible values within the limits of the variable range. For example, if one is responding on a rating scale in which he/she must select 1, 2, 3, 4, or 5, these are the only response values possible; the variable cannot be anything but one of these numbers (it cannot have the value of 3.5

or any other variation of the number choices). In contrast, variables that can take on any value within the range are called continuous variables. – BJM

discriminability

n. The quality of being discernible from something else by an observer.

discriminant function analysis

n. A branch of statistics that uses multiple variables to classify individuals or groups into classes with the least possible error.

discriminant validity

n. Discriminant validity, a type of construct validity, is the extent to which a measure can effectively differentiate among various theoretical constructs. In essence, measures of different constructs should not be so highly correlated that they appear to measure the same thing. Discriminant validity is determined by examining the correlation of a measure across various indicators. For example, a measure of clinical depression would want to show that it could effectively differentiate between depression and anxiety. Low correlations provide evidence for discriminant validity. – BJM

discrimination

n. **1.** The capacity to distinguish among different stimuli. **2.** Differential treatment of different racial, ethnic, age, sex, or other groups. **3.** The ability to perceive and respond differently to different stimuli.

discrimination learning

n. A form of conditioning in which the organism must make a correct discrimination among stimuli in order to form an association.

discriminative response

n. In conditioning, a response that is made to one stimulus but not to another, usually similar one.

discriminative stimulus

n. In operant conditioning, a stimulus which signals a change in the probability of

reinforcement after having established an operant response.

disinhibition

n. **1.** A lessening of the normal level of control over actions often due to the presence of alcohol or other intoxicating drugs. **2.** In conditioning, the recurrence of responding which had previously become extinct in the presence of new stimulus conditions.

disjunctive concept

n. A formal concept based on a set of attributes not all of which need to be present in all instances. As an instance, schizophrenia has five characteristic symptoms, but only two (or more) are required for a diagnosis of schizophrenia.

disorientation

n. An impaired capacity to perceive one's place in time, space, or situation. Long-term disorientation can be caused by organic neurological disorders. Short-term disorientation has many possible causes, including fatigue, intoxication, stress, and trauma.

disparity, retinal

n. The small differences between the images cast on the right and left retinas, which is used as a depth cue and covered up by our tendency to fuse the two images into one in conscious perception. Also called binocular disparity.

dispersion

n. The degree of scatter among a number of data points. Also called spread or deviation.

displacement

n. A defense mechanism whereby unwanted emotions are redirected to a "safer" recipient. For example, Erica may be very angry with her boss after being mistreated for several days. Instead of directing this anger at her boss (because there may be negative repercussions), she takes out her frustration on her partner. Unconsciously the anger is given a less dangerous outlet. As with most defense mechanisms, this process is unconscious; the individual has no idea that the emotion is being redirected. In the given example, Erica only experiences anger at her partner; she is unaware that her expression of frustration is meant for her boss.   – DGa

display

n. **1.** In ethology, a species-specific stereotyped set of postures and movements used to convey information usually intended to establish place in social hierarchy, serve as a warning, or entice a partner to mating. **2.** Any presentation of stimuli to the senses and particularly to vision.

display rules

n. **1.** In humans the social mores governing the display of emotion depending on social circumstances, which are learned and vary considerably from culture to culture. **2.** The rules governing any organism in making displays.

dispositional attribution

Definition. *n.* When trying to explain a person's behavior (what is referred to in psychology as making an attribution for the person's behavior), a dispositional attribution is made when it is assumed that the person has behaved in such a way because of enduring personality characteristics. In other words, the behavior is the result of the person's disposition or personality.

Explanation. Dispositional attributions are a special case of internal attributions, and the two concepts are often confused. An internal attribution is made when it is judged that a particular behavior was performed because of some factor internal to the person. These internal factors include personality, thoughts, beliefs, attitudes, or basically anything else internal to the person that influences him or her to behave that way. For example, if a person does poorly on a test, an internal attribution would be "That person did poorly on the test because he did not study." The person did not study, so the factor influencing the behavior was internal to the person, but the person may not have studied because he was tired and not feeling well. A dispositional attribution is a special case of an internal attribution because it is made about

behaviors that are performed specifically because the person is predisposed to behaving that way. In the example, a dispositional attribution would be "The person did poorly on the test because he did not study for it. He is lazy and never studies for tests!" When people make dispositional attributions, they are not surprised the person behaved in that fashion because the person regularly behaves that way. It may be helpful to note that all dispositional attributions are internal attributions, but not all internal attributions are dispositional attributions.

Development and details. Making attributions about other people's behaviors influences the way we think about and behave toward those people. If a dispositional attribution is made about a negative behavior, people are more likely to have a bad overall impression of the person who engaged in the behavior. Others are also not likely to expect the person to change the behavior. In the example, the student would be judged as lazy and unmotivated. If people have an overall negative impression of a person due to what they believe are the person's enduring personality characteristics, the people making the attribution are more likely to treat the person in a negative fashion. The consequences of such actions could be substantial. For example, if a boss attributes her employee's poor performance to laziness, the boss could decide to fire the employee because she does not believe that the employee can become more motivated. If juries make dispositional attributions about criminal trial defendants, the defendant may be sent to prison for a long time because the jurors are concerned that the person will behave that same way again.   – VKP

dispositional inferences, correspondence bias

n. Dispositional inference refers to the process by which the perceiver infers a correspondent trait from the target's behaviors. By making such an inference, the perceiver assumes that the individual's behavior is truly reflective of his/her enduring dispositions, that these traits do not change across time and situations, and that situational constraints are unlikely to have influenced the target's behavior. When the perceiver makes correspondent dispositional inferences from a limited sample of behaviors and ignores situational constraints on the behaviors, the perceiver commits the correspondence bias.   – EWMA, CYC

▶ *See also* **THEORIES OF BEHAVIORAL CAUSALITY**

dispositions
n. Recurrent intentions to think, feel, act, or react in a particular way which is unique to the individual. Dispositions contrast with common traits, which are dimensions of a characteristic shared by members of a culture which differ significantly among members of the culture and are useful in distinguishing the individuals in the culture from one another.

dissociative amnesia
n. A disorder characterized by inability to remember important personal information often of a stressful or traumatic nature.

dissociative disorders
n. A family of disorders all of which are characterized by a mental disconnection in memory, identity, or perception. This includes dissociative amnesia, dissociative fugue, dissociative identity disorder, depersonalization disorder, and dissociative disorder not otherwise specified (NOS).

dissociative fugue
n. A disorder characterized by sudden unplanned flight from one's usual circumstances coupled with partial or complete amnesia for one's personal history and uncertainty as to personal identity.

dissociative identity disorder
n. A disorder characterized by the presence of two or more distinct personalities or identities in the same person, who recurrently exchange control of the person and who may have only some knowledge about each other and the history of the person involved.

dissociative trance disorder
n. A research disorder not yet granted official status as a disorder in DSM-IV-TR characterized by an involuntary trance state not considered normal with the person's culture which causes significant distress and disorder within the person's life.

dissonance reduction
n. A process of reducing the anxiety caused by the incompatibility of two or more ideas, experiences, or perceptions within one's belief structure. This can be done by reducing the importance of the perceived contradiction in one's understanding of things; altering one's perception of one or both ideas, experiences, or perceptions; or elaborating justifications for the contradiction.

dissonance theory
n. The theory that people have a positive need to maintain consistency in their mental maps of themselves and the world. When experience or reasoning leads a person to realize there is a contradiction in his/her mental system, he or she experiences discomfort and is motivated to reduce or eliminate the contradiction by reducing the importance of the perceived contradiction in his/her understanding of things, altering his/her perception of one or both ideas or experiences, or elaborating justifications for the contradiction.

distal defense
n. Distal defense is a strategy used to defend against a psychological threat that does not appear to be logically or semantically related to the threat. The concept of psychological defense was popularized by Sigmund Freud. Psychological defenses are strategies to minimize the amount of negative affect that a particular thought might arouse in an individual.

The concept of distal defense is part of a dual-defense model developed to account for findings from research designed to assess terror management theory. The theory posits that because humans are aware of their own mortality, they have a deep-seated unconscious fear of death, which is controlled by continual psychological defenses. These defenses serve to sustain the belief that the individual is an enduringly significant contributor to a meaningful universe. This belief allows people to deny they are just material creatures fated only to obliteration upon death and thereby minimize their potential death-related anxiety. The primary hypothesis derived from the theory is that reminding people of their own death (known as a mortality salience induction) will lead them to bolster faith in the worldview by which they view life as meaningful and faith in their self-worth within the context of that worldview.

Mortality salience inductions have been found to lead to a sequence of two types of defenses. The first type of defense, known as proximal defense, occurs immediately after mortality is made salient and is directed toward denying that death is a problem and removing death-related thoughts from consciousness. Study participants are generally very quick to remove these thoughts from focal attention, a phenomenon known as thought suppression. However, after participants have successfully distracted themselves from death-related thoughts, the thoughts remain close to consciousness or high in accessibility. It is when death-related thought is not in focal consciousness but is high in accessibility that distal defenses occur. These distal defenses bear no logical relationship to the problem of death, but they serve terror management by strengthening individuals' faith in their worldview or in their self-worth. For example, after a mortality salience induction and a distraction task, American participants become more favorable toward a pro-American essay and more unfavorable toward an anti-American essay. Once these defenses are engaged, the potential for death-related anxiety is reduced and the heightened death thought accessibility is reduced to the level where it was prior to the mortality salience induction.

This dual-defense model developed from terror management research may also be applicable to defenses against other threats. For example, poor performance on an exam could threaten a student's self-esteem.

A common proximal defense against this threat is to blame the teacher or the poor construction of the exam. But another defensive response to such a threat, known as compensation, is to exaggerate one's abilities in another self-esteem relevant domain, such as athletic prowess. Compensation can be viewed as a distal defense because it is not logically or semantically related to the original threat, poor performance on the exam.

— JG

distal stimulus
n. The actual object or source of sensory stimulation from which light is reflected, sound or odor emanates, and so forth.

distance receptor
n. Any of several types of sensory neurons that can receive information from a distance such as rods and cones and odor receptors.

distractor
n. A stimulus or task that has nothing to do with the task or activity of interest, which serves as an element of increased difficulty in memory and perception studies.

distributed practice
n. A learning procedure in which practice is spread over time with nonpractice intervals between practice periods rather than in massed practice where all attempts to learn happen consecutively. Distributed learning has been found to be significantly more efficient than massed practice.

distribution
n. The values a variable may take and their dispersal.

distribution, binomial
n. The distribution of the number of one of two outcomes in repeated trials of a task which has only two possible outcomes with fixed possibilities. Also called a Bernoulli distribution.

distribution, chi-square
n. Any distribution of the summed squares of the deviates of a normally distributed

variable or a probability distribution theoretically derived from the summed squares of a normal distribution. Chi-square distributions are used to assess the likelihood a chi-square statistic computed from a data sample is drawn from a randomly distributed population.

distribution, cumulative frequency
n. A graphical presentation of a data set that presents frequency on the *y*-axis and the value or interval of the variable on the *x*-axis. A normal curve is an example of a frequency distribution.

distribution, F
n. A graphic representation of the frequency distribution of the F statistic with a given number of degrees of freedom.

distribution-free
adj. Making no assumptions about the distribution of a population.

distribution-free test
n. Any inferential statistic which makes no assumptions about the distribution of the population from which the sample is drawn.

distribution, frequency
n. A graphic representation of relationship between the value of a variable and the frequency with which it occurs.

distribution, grouped frequency
n. A graphic representation of relationship between the value of a variable grouped into ranges and the frequency with which it occurs.

distribution, normal ▶ *See* **NORMAL DISTRIBUTION**

distribution, probability
n. A graphic representation of relationship between the value of a variable and the frequency with which it occurs.

distribution, sampling
n. Any distribution that results from taking samples from a population.

distributive justice
n. **1.** Justice relative to the distribution of goods and services within a society such that each member receives what is right or just for her/him. **2.** In Piagetian psychology, the point of view that rules can be changed and rewards and punishments meted out while taking situational factors into account to arrive at equity and equality.

diurnal
adj. **1.** Of or relating to a period of approximately 24 hours or the course of 1 day. **2.** Active or occurring during the daylight hours, as opposed to nocturnal.

divergent thinking
n. A form of imaginative thought in which numerous possible solutions to a problem are generated and then evaluated. It is often linked to creativity.

dizygotic
adj. Arising from or relating to two separate embryos.

dizygotic twins
n. Two children sharing a gestation period within the same womb and conceived by two separate unions of sperm and ova.

DNA
n. Deoxyribonucleic acid, a nucleic acid which forms long chains containing the genetic information of all cellular organisms. Human DNA is composed of about 32,000 genes made up of differing combinations of four bases, adenine, thymine, guanine, and cytosine, whose combinations and spacing serve as templates for creating the different proteins of which the body is composed. It is inherited from each parent in the form of a long strand which entwines with the DNA strand from the other parent to form a double helix.

domain-specific
adj. Of or relating to something that applies only in a specific and delimited environment.

dominance, hemispheric

n. The relative importance of one cerebral hemisphere in the performance of a specific task. Thus, for most right-handed men, the left hemisphere is dominant in most language tasks. Also called hemispheric lateralization.

dominance hierarchy

n. A relatively stable rank ordering of prestige, authority, and access to goods or services within the social organization of any higher animal species. Also called pecking order.

dominant gene

n. A gene whose expression takes precedence over another gene in the same cell or organism which governs the same processes. Thus the gene(s) for brown eyes is expressed and that for blue eyes is not when both occur in the cells of the same organism.

dominant trait

n. A trait whose genes take precedence in expression over the genes of another trait in the same cell or organism which govern the same processes. Thus the gene(s) for brown eyes is expressed and that for blue eyes is not when both occur in the cells of the same organism.

door-in-the-face technique

Definition. *n.* The door-in-the-face (DITF) technique is used to elicit a desired behavior via a two-step process. First, a requester asks an individual to help with a very large request, to which almost no one agrees. After a refusal to gain agreement for the first task, the requester asks the individual to aid with a second, smaller request, which frequently is related to the first. The requester's original goal was always to garner agreement to this second request; therefore, failing to gain agreement to the first appeal was simply a means to an end. Having refused to agree to help with the first task makes it more likely that someone will agree to help with the second request, compared to a situation in which that person had not been asked to help in the first place.

Examples. The DITF technique is applied in a variety of settings, including gaining volunteer assistance. For example, a common application of the DITF technique is first to ask individuals to volunteer an excessive number of unpaid work hours in support of some cause (e.g., 2 hours a week for 2 years: an excessively difficult task), then to follow that request with a plea to volunteer a more reasonable amount of time in support of the same cause (e.g., 2 hours total: a less costly request). After failing to agree to volunteer a large number of hours in support of a particular cause, individuals are more likely to agree to donate at least a few hours to that cause than if they had not originally been asked to help. Other applications of the DITF technique have been in sales settings (e.g., clothing salespeople typically aim to sell big-ticket items first, such as a complete suit, then smaller items such as ties) and negotiations settings (e.g., job candidates may first request an extremely large salary they do not expect to receive, followed by a smaller, more reasonable salary request).

Explanation. Several theories explain why the DITF technique increases agreement with requests. One is reciprocity, which states that people feel inclined to help those who have previously helped them. According to this explanation, when an individual fails to help with the initial task and the requester follows with a request to help with a less difficult task, the individual being asked feels as though the requester has done him or her a favor that must be repaid. In other words, the individual feels the need to reciprocate the requester's making an easier request by agreeing to help with the second task.

Another common explanation for the effectiveness of the DITF technique in eliciting desired behaviors is contrast theory. According to contrast theory, after one has been asked to perform an extremely large task, subsequent smaller requests seem even smaller than they would than if they had not been preceded by the large request. People may agree to help with the second, less costly request because in the context of following the first request, it does not seem a taxing request; certainly, it seems less taxing than if no initial request had been made.

Finally, self-presentation theory may explain why the DITF technique is effective in eliciting desired behaviors. In essence, the self-perception explanation states that individuals feel bad after refusing to help initially, so they agree with the follow-up request to feel better about their previous refusal to help.   — AEC, LAB

dopamine
n. ($C_8H_{11}NO_2$) A catecholamine neurotransmitter and hormone that is important in controlling motor coordination, the pleasure pathway, and numerous mental disorders. Dopamine is metabolized into epinephrine and norepinephrine in the adrenal medulla. A lack of dopaminergic cells in the substantia nigra is associated with the development of Parkinson's disease, and many antipsychotic medications seem to work by blocking dopamine receptors.

dopamine hypothesis
n. The theory that overactivity in dopaminergic systems is the cause of schizophrenia; that is why drugs that partially block dopamine receptors often help alleviate the symptoms of schizophrenia.

dopamine hypothesis of schizophrenia
n. The theory that overactivity in dopaminergic systems is the cause of schizophrenia; that is why drugs that partially block dopamine receptors often help alleviate the symptoms of schizophrenia.

dopamine-serotonin interaction hypothesis
n. The theory that dopaminergic pathways are primarily involved in the positive symptoms of schizophrenia while serotonergic pathways are primarily involved in the negative symptoms. This is supported by findings that drugs which reduce both dopamine and serotonin activity are better at relieving both positive and negative symptoms of schizophrenia and are also associated with more normal electroencephalographic patterns in the brain than are dopaminergic drugs alone.

dorsal
adj. Toward the spine or the back of an organism with a spinal column and toward the top of the brain.

dorsal root
n. Any of the many short pathways into which sensory nerve fibers divide near their point of attachment to the back (dorsal) of the spinal column. Also called sensory root and posterior root.

double-blind
adj. Of or relating to an experimental design in which both researcher and subject are ignorant of the particular experimental conditions to which the subject is assigned. The purpose of the double-blind is to prevent the expectations of both the researcher and the subject from affecting the outcome of a study.

double-blind design
n. An experimental design in which both researcher and subject are ignorant of which experimental conditions a particular subject is given until after the experiment ends. The purpose of the double-blind is to prevent the expectations of both the researcher and the subject from affecting the outcome of a study.

double-blind study
n. A study with an experimental design in which both researcher and subject are ignorant of which experimental conditions a particular subject is given until the experiment ends. The purpose of the double blind is to prevent the expectations of both the researcher and the subject from affecting the outcome of a study.

double-blind technique
n. An experimental technique in which both researcher and subject are ignorant of the particular experimental conditions to which the subject is assigned. The purpose of the double-blind is to prevent the expectations of both the researcher and the subject from affecting the outcome of a study.

double vision

n. A failure of visual convergence so that a person sees different images with the two eyes which correspond to the retinal images. This is usually due to strabismus or occipital lobe damage if chronic but often occurs in cases of extreme intoxication and fatigue.

Down syndrome

n. A congenital condition characterized by mild to severe mental retardation, pleasant disposition, a flat face, stubby fingers and toes, epicanthic folds in the eyes among non-Asians, tongue fissures, and unusual patterns of skinfolds on the palms of the hands and soles of the feet. It is caused by the presence of an extra chromosome 21 or, in rare cases, by an extra copy of chromosome 22 and is associated with an early onset of Alzheimer's disease.

downward social comparison

n. A tendency of people to compare themselves to others who are worse off than they are as a way of making themselves feel better about themselves or their situation.

d prime

n. (d') In signal detection theory, a measure of signal detection (or perception) independent of response bias, which is derived from a receiver operating characteristic curve (ROC) in which it is the difference in standard deviation units between the means of the noise and the signal plus noise distributions.

Draw-a-Person test

n. A projective test in which the subject is asked to draw a person on a blank sheet of paper and then is asked to draw a person of the opposite sex (to the first drawing) on another blank sheet of paper. The subject is then asked to indicate the age, educational level, fears, and ambitions of the people portrayed in each of the drawings. The drawings are variously interpreted but often with the supposition that acceptable impulses are projected onto the same-sex drawing and unacceptable impulses onto the opposite-sex drawing.

dream

The word *dream* has four interrelated meanings that follow one from the other. First, a dream is a form of thinking during sleep that occurs when (a) there is a certain, as yet undetermined, minimal level of brain activation; (b) external stimuli are blocked from central processing at sensory gates; and (c) the "self-system" is shut down. Second, a dream is something people "experience" as an ongoing narrative because the thought patterns simulate waking reality. Third, a dream is what people remember in the morning, so it is a "memory" of the dreaming experience. Finally, a dream is the spoken or written "report" to researchers based on the memory of the dreaming experience.   – GWD

dream interpretation

n. **1.** The act or any of numerous processes of inferring meaning from the content of dreams. **2.** The meanings inferred during a process of dream interpretation. Also called dream analysis.

dreamwork

n. In psychoanalysis the process of constructing a dream, which involves imagining the satisfaction of a wish or wishes in a form acceptable to the ego and superego, which causes the actual (manifest) dream to differ from the basic (latent) wish or wishes in the dream.

drive

n. **1.** An inferred process of motivation which energizes a person and directs him or her toward a goal or goals. **2.** In psychoanalysis, the biological energy which underlies a motivation.

drive reduction hypothesis

n. **1.** In some learning theories the idea that all motivated behavior is directed toward the reduction in one or more drives. **2.** In psychoanalysis, the idea that all pleasure results from the reduction in a biological drive.

drive-reduction theory

n. Drive-reduction theory, also known as drive theory, is a perspective on human motivation as the process by which we are moved to action and guided in our actions. According to drive-reduction theory, we are motivated to behave in ways that help to fulfill our needs. In a very basic sense, motivation results from our physiological needs. Needs are the most basic requirements for human survival. Our biological needs are driven in part by homeostasis, our natural tendency to seek inner balance. When we are out of balance, a condition psychologists refer to as being in a state of need, we are motivated to do something to restore balance. This motivation to restore balance (homeostasis) is referred to as a drive. Drives are internal states of arousal that lead us to engage in need-reduction behaviors. Needs are considered to be physiological deficits, and drives are psychological desires to satisfy needs and return to a state of balance, or homeostasis.

Drive-reduction theory is more about what motivates us to act, and less about exactly how we act. People may respond in different ways to needs, but we generally repeat behaviors that have the effect of reducing our needs and restoring us to homeostatic balance.

Thirst is a drive that arises when the body requires water. When the fluid inside or outside the cells in the body is low, homeostasis is disrupted and we become thirsty. Thirst is the psychological manifestation of our body's need for water, which is triggered by the hypothalamus. What do we do when we are thirsty? We drink fluid, and the fluids that we drink are generally composed mostly of water. At some point, our body tells us that we are all set; that we no longer require water. At that point, we have returned to a state of homeostasis and our thirst ends. So, we have traveled from a state of homeostatic balance, to a state of physiological need for water, which results in a psychological drive (called thirst) to satisfy that need for water, which leads to the need-reducing behavior of drinking fluid, which addresses the need and restores us to homeostasis.   – MWP

drive strength

n. The motivating power of an inferred motivational drive, which can be operationally defined as length of a deprivation period.

DRL

n. Differential reinforcement of low rate of responding.

DRO

n. Differential reinforcement of other behaviors besides the target behavior.

drug abuse

n. The use of a drug in a manner so as to cause recurrent adverse consequences to the person using the drug or those around him or her through the person's behavior while intoxicated.

drug addiction

n. A state in which a person is both physiologically and psychologically dependent on a drug. Thus the person's metabolism has shifted to deal with the chronic presence of a drug, manifested by need for increased doses of the drug to obtain the same effects and physiological disequilibrium upon withdrawal of the drug, which may produce unpleasant and/or life-threatening symptoms. In addition the person does not know how to cope with daily life without the drug and has habitual patterns associated with drug use which are resistant to change.

drug tolerance

n. A state in which an organism's metabolism has shifted to deal with the chronic presence of a drug, manifested by need for increased doses of the drug to obtain the same effects and physiological disequilibrium upon withdrawal of the drug, which may produce unpleasant and/or life-threatening symptoms.

DSM-IV-TR

n. The revised fourth edition of a publication of the American Psychiatric Association containing lists of mental disorders, their symptoms, criteria for diagnosis, and demographic information about the disorders that is used as a professional guide to diagnosis of mental disorders in the United States.

dual-code theory

n. **1.** The hypothesis that linguistic information is coded in both visual and linguistic formats in memory. **2.** A theory of imagery in which there are separate and interacting systems coding images and linguistic information in all visual images. **3.** The hypothesis that bilingual people have distinct stores of information associated with each language.

dualism

n. The belief proposed by the French philosopher Rene Descartes that there are two kinds of things in the world, mind (*res cogitans*), which has no extension or presence in space, and body (*res extensa*) which does have presence and extension in space, and that the two both interact with and are independent of one another.

dual personality

n. A disorder characterized by the presence of two distinct personalities or identities in the same person who recurrently exchange control of the person and who may have only some knowledge of each other and the history of the person involved.

Duchenne smile

n. An authentic smile characterized by symmetrical upturns of the corners of both sides of the mouth and symmetrical tensing of the orbicularis oculi muscles, causing crinkling at the corners of the eyes, which is recognized as an expression of happiness in all cultures. These smiles are contrasted with posed, social, or phony smiles, in which there are less involvement of the eyes and often an asymmetrical or exaggerated upturn of the corners of the mouth.

Duncan's multiple range test

n. A post hoc multiple comparison procedure in which several means are ranked from lowest to highest, and then the number of steps that two means are apart is used to compute a range statistic for each comparison, which is used to determine which of several means differs significantly while controlling type I error.

duping delight

n. A term coined by Paul Ekman, it refers to the enjoyment that some people feel when they believe they are successfully lying to someone, especially to someone who is regarded as being good at detecting lies.

dynamic social impact theory

n. The hypothesis that in pluralistic settings groups of like-minded people tend to group together in areas of physical and communication space, and to develop patterns of consensus in attitudes, values, practices, identities and meanings which come to constitute subcultures.

dyskinesia

n. Difficulty or distortion in performing voluntary movements, as in tic, ballism, chorea, spasm, or myoclonus.

dyskinesia, tardive

n. A form of difficulty and distortion in voluntary movements characterized by tremor and rhythmic movements of the face, tongue, jaw, arms, or legs. It is often caused by the use of typical antipsychotic medication and is insidious with no known treatment.

dyslexia

n. A difficulty or inability to read, spell, and write independent of general intelligence and thought to be neurological in origin.

dysphoria

n. A mood characterized by sadness, dissatisfaction, and sometimes motor agitation.

dysphoric mood

n. A state characterized by sadness, dissatisfaction, and sometimes motor agitation.

dysthymic disorder

n. A mental disorder characterized by chronic mild depression including sleep and appetite disturbance, low energy, poor self-image, difficulty in concentration and decision making, feelings of hopelessness, and irrational beliefs concerning one's capacity to make positive changes in life.

dystrophy
n. **1.** Any abnormality or degenerative disorder arising from lack of adequate nutrition. **2.** Any of many disorders involving weakening and wasting away of muscle tissue.

E

ear
n. The auditory sense organ which includes the exterior ear, or pinna, and a canal leading to the middle ear, which transduces sound to the inner ear, which contains the receptors, which are the beginning of the auditory nerve tract.

eardrum
n. A thin membrane which separates the ear canal from the middle ear and transforms variations in air pressure wave into mechanical vibrations which reach the ossicles of the middle ear, the first of which attaches to the inner surface of the eardrum. Also called the tympanic membrane.

easy temperament
n. A type of temperament that is defined by a very regular, adaptable, mildly intense style of behavior that is positive and responsive.

eating disorders
n. The eating disorders are psychological disorders that center around issues of eating behavior as well as body weight and shape. The DSM-IV-TR currently recognizes the disorders anorexia nervosa and bulimia nervosa and is considering the diagnosis of binge-eating disorder. Distinctions between the disorders are largely related to the individual's weight status, presence or absence of binge eating, and presence or absence of compensatory mechanisms such as vomiting or excessive exercise.

The eating disorders are thought to mainly affect females, with onset usually in the teens or 20s. The exact causes are unknown, but genetic, biological, psychological, and cultural factors are all thought to play roles in their development. Eating disorders can have serious health consequences, and anorexia nervosa is thought to have the highest mortality rate of any psychological disorder. The eating disorders tend to run a chronic course if left untreated. There are widely recognized treatments for both bulimia nervosa and binge-eating disorder, and promising treatments have been developed for anorexia nervosa.

     – DAA

Ebbinghaus curve
n. A negatively accelerated curve of forgetting over time since learning, usually of nonsense syllables. This curve demonstrates that there is a very rapid reduction in memory beginning in the first few minutes after learning, which quickly slows, showing a small amount of memory over long periods.

echolalia
n. A speech pattern in which a person echoes what is said to him or her. It is an occasional symptom of autism, catatonic schizophrenia, Tourette's disorder, latah, and several forms of neural degeneration including Alzheimer's disease.

eclectic approach
n. Any approach which does not adhere to one approach but includes diverse conceptual schemes or techniques whenever practical in attempting to reach a solution or select a best course of action regardless of the origin of the scheme or technique.

eclectic psychotherapy

n. Any approach to psychotherapy which does not adhere to one approach but includes and blends diverse conceptual schemes and techniques whenever useful regardless of the origin of the scheme or technique.

eclectic therapy

n. Any approach to therapy which does not adhere to one approach but includes and blends diverse conceptual schemes and techniques whenever useful regardless of the origin of the scheme or technique.

ecological fallacy

n. The inference that what is true of group members in general is true of a particular individual who is a member of that group or the inference that what is true in general is true of a particular case.

ecological-level analysis

n. An analysis conducted using group means for data which reduces the actual variability in the data and frequently produces results that may be true of groups but are not true of individuals in the real world. This is an analytic technique often used in cross-cultural studies, in which cases are countries or cultures and the data are country- or culture-level data.

ecological momentary assessment ▶ *See* DIARY METHODS

ecological niche

n. **1.** The functional role of a species within a biological environment. **2.** The geographical area inhabited by a species.

ecological psychology

n. The branch of psychology that attempts to understand mental and behavioral functioning within and in interaction with its context. Research tends to focus on the effects of physical setting and social and cultural beliefs about the setting on the minds and behavior of individuals in the setting.

ecological validity

n. **1.** The accuracy with which research findings correspond to the world in general. The conditions under which research are conducted are usually those convenient for the researcher, which often influences the results in such a way as to make the research biased and unrepresentative of the world in general. **2.** The degree of agreement between perception of an object and the way the object actually is.

ecology

n. The study of biological environments using a system level analysis which seeks to understand the interactions in functioning of all the different individuals, species, and their social behavior, and their physical environment.

ecology, behavioral

n. The study of the interactions between an environment and the behavior of organisms within that environment as well as how behavior changes from one environment to another. Such studies are usually carried on within an evolutionary framework, seeking to understand the adaptations in behavior the environment imposes on an organism and how that behavior affects the environment and other organisms within it.

ecosystem

n. Any environment and the interactions between the physical characteristics of the environment and the dynamics of balance and change among the living things in the environment. It includes the understanding that change in the behavior of any one individual or species affects the whole of the system, that the behavior is a reaction to the whole system, and so behavior can only be understood within the framework of the whole system.

ECT

n. Electroconvulsive therapy: the intentional induction of convulsions through sending low-voltage electrical current through the head, which is used to treat severe depression and occasionally other disorders. Also called electroconvulsive shock treatment or electroconvulsive shock therapy.

edge detector

n. **1.** The name given to the set of neurons in the visual system which react maximally to low-spatial-frequency stimuli which appear to the eye as fuzzy edges. **2.** Components of hypothetical models of vision or computer systems which react to rapid changes in light-dark patterns.

educational mainstreaming

n. The practice of placing students who are markedly above or below average in academic performance in the same classrooms with students who are in the average range in academic achievement.

educational psychology

n. The branch of applied psychology that studies the mental processes involved in formal education including both learning and adjustment of individuals within the educational system. It includes attempts to apply theory both in individual cases and to groups and school systems as a whole.

Edwards Personal Preference Schedule

n. A forced-choice self-report personality inventory in which takers are required to select which of each of 225 paired choices they prefer. The choices consist of pairings of examples of fifteen of Edward Murray's basic needs. The relative preferences of needs to one another are then computed, as are norms for preferences on each of the needs, so both ipsative and normative data are provided for feedback. The test also includes a consistency scale in which responses on identical items are compared with one another.

EEG

n. The EEG (or electroencephalogram) is the graph of an electrical signal produced by large groups of neurons in the brain that can be picked up by scalp electrodes. Scalp EEG recordings are frequently used in psychological or neuroscience experimentation because the process is noninvasive. Participants wear an electrode cap that records the underlying voltage fluctuations in the brain with little or no discomfort to the participant.

The EEG has very high temporal resolution and is capable of detecting millisecond-level changes in electrical activity in the brain. Most important to experimental research are ERPs (event-related potentials), which are portions of the EEG that are time locked to a stimulus onset. ERP recordings consist of a series of positive and negative peaks, whose amplitude and latency are informative about cognitive processes. The peaks of an ERP are labeled by their polarity (negative [N] or positive [P]) and their typical latency in milliseconds (e.g., P300).   – NL

effect, empirical law of

n. The statement that rewarded behavior tends to be repeated. It is also called the weak law of effect, as it does not include the original supposition that punished behavior tends to disappear.

effect, law of

n. The statement that rewarded behavior tends to be repeated while behavior that is punished tends to disappear.

effector

n. **1.** Any biological part or system such as a muscle or organ that produces a particular effect. **2.** A motor nerve that causes muscle movement and hormonal secretion. **3.** The part of the body that accomplishes a particular movement or task.

effect size

n. The magnitude of an experimental result usually expressed in standard deviation units. It differs from statistical significance in that statistical significance is dependent on variability so that, in homogeneous groups, very small differences can reach statistical significance, while in heterogeneous groups much larger differences can lack statistical significance.

efferent

adj. Of or relating to neurons whose impulses travel away from the brain or spinal cord toward the rest of the body. These are the complements of afferent neurons, which convey impulses along parallel pathways toward the spinal cord and brain.

efferent nerves

n. Groups of neurons whose impulses travel away from the brain or spinal cord toward the rest of the body. These are the complements of afferent nerves, which convey impulses along parallel pathways toward the spinal cord and brain.

efficacy

n. **1.** The capacity to succeed at tasks. **2.** A personal sense of power to deal with life's difficulties. **3.** In pharmacology, the medical utility of particular drugs at different doses.

ego

n. **1.** The conscious sense of personal identity for many theorists, including Jung and Murray. Jung differentiated between the ego and the self, which was an archetype of unity which lay between the conscious and unconsciousness. **2.** In psychoanalysis, the executive function of the personality, which includes the self and makes decisions about actual behavior and mediates the desires of the id, the moral restraints of the superego, and the constraints and opportunities of reality using rational thought to make plans and carry them out. **3.** The sense of self-worth.

egocentric

adj. Being self-centered, preoccupied with one's own concerns to the exclusion of noticing or caring about others.

egocentrism

n. **1.** The state of being self-centered, preoccupied with one's own concerns to the exclusion of noticing or caring about others. **2.** In Piagetian psychology, an early stage in cognitive development in which the child is unable to understand that another person would have a different point of view than his or hers.

ego development

n. A comprehensive theory of individual differences and human maturation proposed by Jane Loevinger that includes three components: impulse control, cognitive complexity, and interpersonal autonomy. Loevinger's model of ego development derives from cognitive-developmental theory and tracks changes in emotions, thinking, and behavior through eight invariant, sequential stages. The primary method for the assessment of these eight stages, or ego levels, is the Washington University Sentence Completion Test (WUSCT). The first stage of ego development is preverbal and consists of the infant's constructing a stable world made of objects and self. The first measurable stage is the impulsive stage, which is evident mainly in young children. The impulsive stage is characterized by low impulse control, dependency on others to meet physical needs, and egocentric and dichotomous thinking. The self-protective stage transforms this lack of impulse control into an ability to delay gratification, to recognize opportunities for gain, and to avoid trouble by manipulation and redirecting blame. The conformist stage usually corresponds to grade school ages, and, at this stage, rules and social norms are adhered to in order to obtain approval from peers and belong to the group. The rigidity of the earlier stages loosens, and the person in the self-aware stage recognizes the importance of inner life and feelings. The self-aware person understands that there are exceptions to the rules and that it is acceptable also to be different from others. This enhanced awareness of inner life develops further in the conscientious stage, in which greater awareness of personal motives is achieved. The conscientious person is preoccupied with self-improvement and develops a heightened sense of responsibility for the well-being of others. Normative studies of WUSCT scores show that few adults progress beyond the conscientious stage and some do not progress beyond the conformist stage. The person at the individualistic stage is better able to differentiate between external appearances and the more important inner self. Individuality is accepted and respected and there is a greater tolerance for ambiguity. For those very few adults who reach the autonomous stage (E8), autonomy of the self is fully recognized as well as the capacity to grant autonomy to others. The autonomous person is no longer fearful or disdainful of the complexities of people and situations, and self-fulfillment is achieved by becoming involved in a broad diversity of relationships and activities. – JK

ego ideal
n. **1.** In psychoanalysis the part of the super-ego which was the ideal self derived from parental ideals adopted by the individual and which serves as a comparison for the actual ego. **2.** In Murray's personology, the conscious ideals with which a person compares himself/herself and ambitions toward which he/she strives which are separate from the largely unconscious superego.

ego identity
n. **1.** A comprehensive view of the self including one's place in the universe, cultural and social roles including sexual roles, standing in the social hierarchy, ideals, and the meaning of life, which is the outcome of the fifth stage of epigenetic development in Erikson's development cycle. **2.** In psychoanalysis, a part of the superego which is a combination of infantile narcissism and ideals borrowed from the parents, which constitutes the superego's goal for the ego.

ego integrity
n. A recommitment to the order and meaning of one's life as it has been led, including all the failures and in the face of approaching death, which requires some detachment coupled with active caring for others. This is the successful resolution in Erik Erikson's eighth stage of development after age 60 whose opposite is despair and pretense.

ego integrity versus despair
n. The task in Erik Erikson's eighth stage of epigenetic development in which a person over the age of about 60 must recommit to the order and meaning of his/her life as it has been led including all the failures and in the face of approaching death, which requires some detachment coupled with active caring for others. Failure to attain this wisdom of ego integrity results in despair, in which the person is preoccupied by the fear of death and regret for the limitations and failures of his/her life.

ego involvement
n. **1.** A state of having committed one's self to something. **2.** The degree to which something is important to one's self-esteem.

egoistic suicide
n. Suicide that occurs when social integration within a society is high but the individual feels himself/herself not to be a part of that order often because of his/her own sense of failure to live up to social and personal expectations. This is opposed to anomic suicide, in which the person feels meaningless because of a lack of coherent social structure; altruistic suicide, in which the person is killing himself/herself for the higher good of society; and fatalistic suicide, in which the individual feels overwhelmed and hopeless because of the rigid structures of society and kills himself/herself to escape from it.

ego strength
n. In psychoanalysis, the capacity of the ego to make and carry out plans without disruption from external frustration, id impulses, or moral inhibitions.

eidetic image
n. A mental image of a visual scene that is maintained in near entirety for long periods so that a person can mentally scan the image to find details not brought to consciousness before.

eigenvalue
n. In statistics, a numeric index of the relative contribution of one independent variable to the variance of a factor or dependent variable.

elaborative rehearsal
n. A term that is used to identify a method of facilitating the transfer of information from brief storage in short-term memory into permanent long-term memory. Specifically, this method requires people to associate new information with information that is already in long-term memory. Making these associations requires effortful thought, which allows for the creation of strong, durable memories in contrast to rote memorization. This type of

rehearsal also creates a great variety of cues that one can use to retrieve a memory at a later time. An example of elaborative rehearsal is the examination of the actual meanings of the words in a word list rather than reliance solely on the rehearsal of the sound or spelling of the words.

Aside from formulating associations, there are additional techniques that are used for elaborative rehearsal. These include the creation of mnemonic devices, such as forming acronyms that make it easier to transfer information into long-term memory, which in turn, creates strong and durable memories that are easy to retrieve. Moreover, one can organize new information by incorporating it in a related group of concepts or into a story based upon prior knowledge that is stored in long-term memory.   – JLG

Electra complex

n. In psychoanalysis, the process that girls go through in middle childhood in which they first become focused on pleasant feelings in the clitoris. They want to have sex with their mother and are jealous of their father because he is their mother's lover. The little girl then becomes envious of the father's possession of a penis and feels she has been castrated by her father and blames her mother for not protecting her from this. Eventually the tension of the little girl's hatred and envy of the father and anger toward the mother becomes too great, and she enters latency by repressing all her sexual feeling and all direct expression of sexuality in favor of directing that energy into becoming a woman like her idealized idea of her mother. This is done so that she will be able to grow up and be like her mother and attract and marry a man like her father, because doing so will give her possession of the power of his penis, which will lead to emotional connection with the mother by becoming a mother herself.

electrical brain stimulation

n. Application of very weak electrical current to localized areas of the brain. This has been used as a tool so that the function of different brain areas can be mapped by observing the effect of the stimulation on different areas of the brain.

electric shock therapy

n. (ECT) The intentional induction of convulsions through sending low-voltage electrical current through the head, which is used to treat severe depression and occasionally other disorders. Also called electroconvulsive shock treatment.

electroconvulsive shock therapy

n. (ECT) The intentional induction of convulsions through sending low-voltage electrical current through the head, which is used to treat severe depression and occasionally other disorders. Also called electroconvulsive shock treatment.

electroencephalogram

n. (EEG) A graph made by recording the electrical current passing through different portions of the brain over time by means of a set of electrodes attached to the skin of the head in a standard pattern.

electroencephalography

n. The process of making graphs of the electrical current passing through different portions of the brain over time by means of a set of electrodes attached to the skin of the head in a standard pattern.

electromagnetic spectrum

n. The range of electromagnetic waves from the very short gamma rays to the very long waves used by radio. The names for the different wavelengths in order from shortest to longest are gamma rays, X-rays, ultraviolet rays, visible light, infrared light, microwaves, and radio waves.

electromyogram

n. (EMG) A graphic representation of the electrical activity of a muscle or group of muscles over time recorded by electrodes attached to the skin over the muscles.

elevated mood

n. An emotional tone characterized by positiveness, as in happiness, cheerfulness, well-being, elation, and gaiety.

elicit

v. To bring forth, as a stimulus of a particular kind brings forth a response of a particular kind.

embeddedness

n. A cultural value that refers to the degree to which individuals in a group value their in-groups, see themselves as integral and fundamental parts of their in-groups, and consider themselves as fundamentally interrelated with others in their in-group.

emblem

n. **1.** A gesture that takes the place of a verbal expression and is understood by most of the members of a particular culture or subculture. **2.** A physical object, symbol, or representation of something else which conveys a meaning within a particular culture or subculture.

embryo

n. **1.** A fertilized egg after the zygote has split up until it is born. **2.** In humans, the stage of development of a fertilized egg from the cleaving of the zygote until about 8 weeks, when the major organs develop and it begins to be called a fetus.

EMG

n. A graphic representation of the electrical activity of a muscles or group of muscles over time recorded by electrodes attached to the skin over the muscles.

emic

1. *adj.* Of or relating to an approach to studying or understanding human functioning from within the perspective of the culture being examined. Thus all published psychology studies by U.S. researchers using subjects from the United States and whose results are interpreted using mainstream psychological theories could be regarded as emic studies, as could the narrative description of an Australian Tiwi (bushman) of his understanding of the creation of the universe. **2.** *n.* A culture-specific psychological process or construct, that is, one that is valid or applicable in only one culture.

emit

v. To send forth, as a decaying radioactive element may emit a particle of radiation or an organism may be said to emit a behavior.

emitted behavior

n. A spontaneous, voluntary behavior that occurs without external motivation; contrasted with elicited behaviors, which are evoked by a stimulus. When an emitted behavior is strengthened or weakened by the events that follow the response, it is called operant or respondent behavior.   – BJM

emotion

n. A transient, neurophysiological response to a stimulus that excites a coordinated system of bodily and mental responses that inform us about our relationship to the stimulus and prepare us to deal with it in some way.

emotional intelligence

n. Emotional intelligence (EI) was formally defined by Peter Salovey and Jack Mayer in 1990 as a member of an emerging group of mental abilities alongside social and practical intelligence. EI refers to the processes involved in perceiving, using, understanding, and managing emotions to solve emotion-laden problems and to regulate behavior. Perceiving emotion refers to the ability to identify emotions in oneself and others, as well as in other stimuli, including voices, stories, music, and works of art. Using emotion refers to the ability to harness feelings to assist in certain cognitive activities such as problem solving, decision making, creative thinking, and interpersonal communication. Understanding emotions involves knowledge of both emotion-related terms and the manner in which emotions combine, progress, and transition from one to the other. Managing emotions includes the ability to employ strategies that alter feelings, and the assessment of the effectiveness of these regulation strategies.

The public and academia were mostly unaware of EI until 1995, when Daniel Goleman, psychologist and science writer for the *New York Times*, popularized the construct in his book *Emotional Intelligence: Why It Can Matter More Than IQ.* Emotional intelligence quickly captured the attention of the media, general public, educators, and researchers. Goleman, however, made extraordinary and difficult-to-substantiate claims about the importance of EI. The definition of EI in the book was not confined to the abilities described in Salovey and Mayer's original ability model of EI; it now encompassed a broad array of personal attributes, including self-confidence, optimism, and self-motivation, among other desirable personality attributes.

Research on EI is only in its incipient stages: the theory was published just 15 years ago, and performance measures of the construct have been used in scientific investigations for only about 4 years. The theory of EI will certainly be expanded upon in the coming years, and new tasks to measure different aspects of EI also are under way. There is much to be learned about EI theory and measurement, and its application at home, school, and the workplace.   – MAB

emotional stability
n. The predictability and evenness of affect and the general absence of sharp or unpredictable variations. In general the absence of extremes of emotion characteristic of mental disturbances and a high level of reactivity to events.

Emotional Stroop Test
n. An experimental procedure in which subjects are required to report the color in which words are printed as rapidly as possible, and the time it takes to report emotion-laden versus emotionally neutral words is compared. It has been used to explore the interactions between emotional and cognitive variables.

emotion, theory of
n. Any of a number of explanations for the phenomena of emotion, including but not limited to the James-Lange theory, the arousal theory, the two-factor theory, and Lazarus's appraisal theory.

emotive imagery
n. A technique used in behavioral therapy in which a subject first relaxes and then imagines emotion-arousing scenes while continuing to relax. The idea is that relaxation is a response incompatible with fear and anxiety, with which the subject usually responds to the imagined situations, and that the subject will learn to respond with relaxation rather than fear and anxiety when confronted with the emotion-laden situations in real life.

empathy
n. **1.** The capacity to understand the point of view of another person so that one vicariously shares the other person's feelings, perceptions, and thoughts. **2.** The process of experiencing another's thoughts, feelings, and perceptions. **3.** An unverbalized and covert mode of communication between two people who share an interpersonal attunement.

empirical
adj. **1.** Based on experience or observation rather than speculation, theory, or authority. **2.** Inductive as opposed to deductive approaches to analyzing data. **3.** Of or relating to philosophical empiricism.

empirical law
n. A summary principle or general statement of the relationship between variables based on observations often including experimental findings.

empiricism
n. An approach to knowledge and understanding that supposes that all facts arise from experience or require the validation of experience and that all theories must be judged on the basis of systematic observation and experimentation. The opposite of idealism.

encephalitis
n. An inflammation of the brain usually caused by viral infection. External symptoms range from headache and neck pain to nausea, fever, vomiting, confusion, sleepiness, convulsions, coma, and occasionally to death.

encephalogram
n. An X-ray image of the brain often using air or dye to replace the cerebrospinal fluid so as to get better pictures of the ventricles.

encephalon
n. The brain.

encoding
n. **1.** A theoretical process in which sensory data are converted into a form in which the mind can process and store them. **2.** In data processing, the process of converting information into a form which the computer is capable of processing. **3.** The process of putting information into a form uninterpretable by anyone who does not know the key to the code.

encoding specificity
n. The idea that human memory performs best when the conditions of remembering are the same as the conditions at the time when the memory was formed. The supposition is that any memory has many associations, and the more of these associations there are at the time of recall, the more likely it is that the information will be recalled. As an example, it has been found that students given a final exam in the same room in which they had a class get better scores on a test than students from the same class who take the test in a different room.

encopresis
n. A disorder of childhood in which the child repeatedly defecates in inappropriate places, whether voluntarily or involuntarily, after the age of 4. It is usually involuntary and is associated with poor toilet training and stress.

enculturation
n. The process of nonconscious learning and adopting the language, worldview, values, manners, skills, and behavioral patterns of a culture by incorporation in that culture. This usually occurs over the course of childhood but may occur later in life if the person moves from one culture to another.

endocrinology
n. The study of the anatomy, biochemistry, physiology, function, and pathology of the endocrine glands.

endogenous
adj. Arising within the body as a result of normal processes.

endogenous depression
n. A state of mind characterized by negative mood, low energy, loss of interest in usual activities, pessimism, unrealistically negative thoughts about self and the future, and social withdrawal, which arises as a result of internal processes rather than as a result of external circumstances.

endogenous opiate
n. Any substance produced by the body which has painkilling and euphoric effects similar to those of morphine or heroin. These include the enkephalins, beta-endorphins, dynorphins, orphanin, and two kinds of endomorphins, all of which bind to the same receptors as do morphine and similar drugs and block pain.

endorphin
n. A family of substances produced in the brain which bind to the same receptors as do morphine and similar drugs and block pain.

endorphins/enkephalins
n. Any substance produced by the body which has painkilling and euphoric effects similar to those of morphine or heroin. These include the enkephalins and beta-endorphins, which bind to the same receptors as do morphine and similar drugs.

end plate
n. A small circular region of muscle membrane that faces the terminus of a motor neuron and is receptive to electrochemical stimulation by the neuron, which can lead to tensing of the muscle.

enuresis
n. Repeated involuntary urination in inappropriate places after the age at which voluntary bladder control is expected within the culture. It may occur during the day (diurnal) or at night (nocturnal or bedwetting). Nocturnal enuresis is related to the growth of the bladder to a size which is large enough to hold the urine throughout the night and which is quite variable, so that some children can hold their urine through the night as

early as 2 years while others cannot do so until they are 5 or even 6 years old. It is also related to poor toilet training and stress.

environmental psychology

n. The branch of psychology devoted to the study of the interactions between the physical aspects of the environment and the functioning of the mind. It is often concerned with such issues as environmental stressors; house, office, and building design; ergonomics; architecture and city planning; and their relationships with natural aspects of the environment.

environmental stress

n. A prolonged state of psychological and physiological arousal leading to negative effects on mood, cognitive capacity, immune function, and physical health caused by environmental factors.

enzyme

n. Any of a large number of proteins produced in the body that act as biological catalysts that speed up biochemical reactions without themselves being changed by the reactions. Most enzymes are involved in digestive processes and help the body to break food down into chemicals it can use.

epidemiology

n. The study of the frequency and location of diseases and disorders. Such studies usually attempt to correlate location, age, sex, heredity, environment, nutrition, and ethnicity with the occurrence of disease.

epidermis

n. **1.** The outer layer of skin of vertebrate animals, which contains some of the touch and pain receptors but no blood vessels. Also called the epithelial layer. **2.** The outermost layer of skin of nonvertebrate animals, leaves, and new growth in plants.

epigenesis

n. **1.** The theory that the genetic or inherent characteristics of an organism interact with the environment so that the actual characteristics of an individual are a product of both

heredity and environment. **2.** In genetics, the appearance of a heritable change in gene function that is not the result of a change in the DNA. **3.** In developmental psychology, the point of view that as the organism grows, it interacts with the environment with different goals.

epilepsy

n. A family of chronic brain disorders characterized by uncontrolled electrical activity in the brain, some of which produce seizures, clouding of consciousness, unconsciousness, and various sensory and cognitive malfunctions depending on which parts of the brain are involved. Brain trauma is the most common known cause of epilepsy, but in many cases the cause is unknown.

epilepsy, major

n. A form of epilepsy involving seizures which are characterized by full body convulsions, loss of consciousness, and loss of bodily control over bladder and bowels. These are often preceded by a mental aura in which the person knows he or she is about to have a seizure. Also called grand mal epilepsy.

epilepsy, minor

n. A form of epilepsy in which there are no gross motor seizures. Sometimes there are momentary lapses of consciousness or minor sensory or motor dysfunction, and sometimes there are no visible exterior symptoms. Also called petit mal epilepsy.

epinephrine

n. A hormone ($C_9H_{13}NO_3$) and neurotransmitter created in the adrenal glands which acts primarily as an arousal agent. Epinephrine causes an increase in heart rate and heart stroke volume, dilates the pupils, increases blood sugar levels, reduces blood flow to the skin and digestive tract, increases blood flow to the muscles, and suppresses immune function. It is used to stimulate the heart in cases of cardiac arrest and sometimes in cardiac arrhythmias. Epinephrine is one of the main neurotransmitters in the flight-or-fight response and in activating the reticular activating system (RAS). Its action is mimicked by amphetamines, caffeine, and Ritalin. Also called adrenaline.

epiphenomenon
n. A phenomenon that accompanies or is a by-product of a process that has no effect on the process itself and is believed to have no interesting effects on anything.

episodic memory
n. Any recollection of the experience of a specific event or occurrence. Theoretically, episodic memory is distinguished from semantic memory, but in experimental practice the two overlap significantly.

epistemic
adj. Of or relating to knowledge or the acquisition of knowledge.

epistemology
n. The branch of philosophy that is concerned with the origins, nature, limits, and methods of human knowledge. This is a very important question in any science, which must have an acceptably logical set of reasons for its methods in order to be acceptable as a science.

epoche
n. **1.** A moment in which all belief is suspended, which is important for critical analysis in science. **2.** The suspension of preconceptions, interpretations, and explainability as preconditions for the experience and description of uninterrupted sense experience and ideas. Also called bracketing.

EQ
n. **1.** The educational quotient or educational age divided by chronological age times 100. **2.** The emotional intelligence quotient, which is an index of emotional intelligence.

equipotentiality
n. **1.** The archaic theory that different areas of the cerebral cortex are equally involved in performing different functions and can take over those functions if one part is damaged. This is now known not to be generally true as many parts of the cortex are specific in function but may be true of some limited areas of the

cortex. **2.** The state of having equal potential, as identical twins at birth may be considered to have equal intellectual potential.

equity theory
n. A theory of social justice in which people consider as fair outcomes those in which they receive the same ratio of benefit to investment that the others to whom they compare themselves receive. Investments and benefits can be of many kinds, including time, affection, and money among many others. Inequity is said to be experienced as uncomfortable even when it is in one's favor and to motivate attempts to create a more equitable system.

equivalence
n. A similarity of two or more things such that one may replace another without altering a situation. Thus five $1 bills are equivalent to one $5 bill. In cross-cultural studies, it refers to the state when measures of a psychological construct mean the same thing in the cultures being tested and are measured equally well in all the cultures being tested. It is a necessary condition for data obtained from two or more cultures to be comparable to each other.

erectile dysfunction/disorder
n. The persistent or recurrent inability to maintain an adequate penile erection for the completion of sexual activity which normally causes significant frustration, personal distress, and interpersonal difficulties.

ergonomics
n. The applied science of human motion and work which uses knowledge of physiology, biomechanics, and industrial technology and equipment design to reduce strain and to improve performance and well-being of persons in the workplace.

Eriksonian developmental stages
n. The eight ages of man or epigenetic stages in the development of self described by Erik Erikson: **(1)** The oral-sensory stage, in which the infant must make sense of the world and decide the degree to which it is sufficiently predictable so as to sustain continuing social

183

relationships, which is called *basic trust*. **(2)** The anal-muscular stage, in which the young child learns to control its body and decides on the degree to which he/she has the capacity to exercise control over the self rather than relying on external controls, which is called *autonomy*. **(3)** The locomotor-genital stage, in which the child learns to control its abundant energy and channel it into socially defined roles and decides the degree to which her/his energy can be used in socially approved ways, which is called *purpose*. **(4)** The latency stage, in which the child applies her/his energy and abilities to learning the skills, tasks, and roles which the culture deems appropriate for her/him and decides the degree to which he/she can succeed within the culture, which is called *industry*. **(5)** The puberty and adolescence stage, in which the teen begins to think for himself/herself using a larger social frame of reference and begins switching the identification of self from a relatively narrow one of family and the short term to society as a whole and lifelong goals, often undergoing a crisis in self-understanding whose resolution is called identity, which is a commitment to sexual, group, economic, and moral roles. **(6)** The young adult stage, in which the individual seeks a sexual/procreational partner and establishes a long-term emotional, social, and economic partnership with him/her for the purpose of creating a family, whose completion is called *intimacy*. **(7)** The stage of adulthood in which the individual applies his/her skills and creative abilities to the tasks of supporting himself/herself and family through accomplishing work in a varied set of roles which both sustain and change the culture as a whole, whose accomplishment is called *generativity*. **(8)** The stage of maturity in which the self must accept the limitations of one human lifetime with a psychohistorical perspective and accept death while maintaining interest and commitment to life, whose achievement is called ego *integrity*.

erogenous zone
n. Any portion of the body capable of arousing or increasing sexual excitement when stimulated. Aside from the genitals and nipples, these zones are greatly variable among people as the whole epidermis has receptors whose stimulation can be pleasurable and their association with sexuality is probably learned.

error, measurement
n. The difference between a measurement and the true magnitude of the variable being measured, which is usually assumed to be the sum of bias and random error in the measurement.

errors (types I and II)
n. In using inferential statistics error it is possible to make an error by rejecting the null hypothesis when it is true; the false positive result is called a type I error. It is possible to make an error by failing to reject the null hypothesis when it is false; this is called a type II error. Type I error is associated with random error and setting a criterion statistic too low, while type II error is associated with a lack of statistical power in a research design.

error, sampling
n. **1.** The variation in a measurement used to estimate a population parameter that is due to a sample that is not representative of the population. **2.** The error due to random variation between samples of a population. **3.** The extent to which a sample is not representative of a population.

error variance
n. The proportion of variance in a dependent variable that is independent of the independent variables. Theoretically it can have two components, random error and bias. Also called the residual.

escape-avoidance learning
n. A form of operant conditioning in which an organism learns to move away from an aversive stimulus, eventually avoiding it altogether. Thus if a person is given a shock on the seat after a bell rings, he or she soon learns to leave the seat when the bell rings and soon will not sit in the same seat at all.

escape conditioning

n. A form of operant conditioning in which an organism learns to move away from an aversive stimulus. Thus if a person is given a shock on the seat after a bell rings, he or she soon learns to leave the seat when the bell rings.

escape learning

n. A form of operant conditioning in which an organism learns to move away from an aversive stimulus. Thus if a person is given a shock on the seat after a bell rings, he or she soon learns to leave the seat when the bell rings.

Escher figure

n. Any of numerous drawings by M. C. Escher or mimicking his style of drawing in which tricks of perspective are used to construct drawings of buildings which cannot exist in three dimensions.

ESP

n. Any capacity to know without using any of the five senses such as in clairvoyance, precognition, and telepathy.

ESP cards

n. A set of 25 cards on the face of which is printed a circle, cross, square, star, or wavy lines, used for research in the area of extrasensory perception. Also called Zener cards.

eta squared

n. A calculation of the proportion of the variance accounted for by the relationship between independent and dependent variables in independent group *t* tests and analyses of variance.

Ethical Principles of Psychologists and Code of Conduct

n. A document adopted by the American Psychological Association delineating the professional code of ethics and expected behavior for psychologists in the performance of their duties as psychologists.

ethical treatment of animals

n. An area of ethics which deals with the care and treatment of animals especially in research settings, in which there is presently a great deal of disagreement.

ethics

n. **1.** The principles which define morally acceptable conduct, often within a particular group or profession. **2.** The field of study within philosophy which debates the nature and content of moral judgments.

ethics of psychological research

n. The principles which define morally acceptable conduct within the field of psychological research. These are spelled out in various professional and legal codes.

ethnic group

n. Any large social group that shares a common ethnic identity created by history, culture, and sometimes language and religion as well.

ethnic identity

n. An individual person's belief in his or her being a part of one or more ethnic groups.

ethnicity

n. Ethnicity refers to an ethnic quality or affiliation with a particular group usually based on a presumed common ancestry. Members of an ethnic group often share common cultural, behavioral, linguistic, or religious practices, and they often constitute an identifiable sociological group within a larger nation-state. Members of an ethnic group also share genetic similarities and physical features due to endogamy (mating or marriage within the same ethnic group), which is reinforced by cultural familiarity, societal pressure, and propinquity. The word is derived from the Greek word *ethnos*, which means "people of a nation or a tribe."

Within and outside psychology, the term *ethnicity* has often been used interchangeably with the terms *culture* and *race*. In many cases, *ethnicity* is used to refer to broad groups (e.g., people of European, African, or Asian descent) because the concept of race is fraught with controversy. Race has generally been defined with respect to physical characteristics (e.g., skin color, hair type, facial features) with presumed biological bases for the observed differences that extend to the groups' behavioral characteristics, but the classifications of people into races have been criticized as arbitrary social constructions. In other cases, ethnicity is used in references to cultural characteristics of a particular group, such as the norms, values, attitudes, behavior, and meaning systems that are shared by an identifiable segment of a population. Finally, ethnicity is discussed with focus on the experiences of non-White minority populations, such as minority status, discrimination, and racism.

Although there is no standard definition of ethnicity, scholars agree that ethnicity must be considered as a multidimensional and dynamic construct rather than as a static categorical variable. Psychological research on ethnicity has encompassed multiple related constructs. One aspect of ethnicity that has received much scholarly attention is ethnic identity, an aspect of one's identity associated with ethnic group membership. Research has shown that ethnic identity constitutes a more salient source of identity for individuals from ethnic minority groups, that strength and importance of ethnic identity can vary over time and context, and that it has implications for mental health and well-being of ethnic minority individuals. Different questionnaires have been developed in efforts to assess the levels of various dimensions of ethnic identity. Another aspect of scholarly work on ethnicity has examined psychological variables that may be culturally based. For example, psychosocial experiences of contemporary African Americans may be understood as reflecting the continued influences of African cultural dimensions such as collective survival, oral expressions, and spirituality. Finally, social and organizational psychology research has examined interethnic relations and the effects of interethnic contacts on individual and group outcomes.   – sok

ethnic minorities

n. Ethnic minorities are ethnic groups or members of ethnic groups in a given society who constitute a sociological minority. Although they may not necessarily constitute a numerical minority, ethnic minorities are often disadvantaged with respect to the dominant majority group in terms of social status, political power, wealth, or access to social capital. In the contemporary United States, the main groups of ethnic minorities are African Americans, Hispanics, Asian Americans, American Indians and Alaskan Natives, and Native Hawaiian and other Pacific Islanders. Ukrainians in Poland, Hungarians in Romania, Muslim Turks in Bulgaria, and Roma (Gypsies) in several European countries are other ethnic minorities.   – sok

ethnocentrism

n. Ethnocentrism is the nearly universal tendency to view the world and to judge others primarily from the perspective of one's own in-group culture. Ethnocentrism often entails the overt or covert belief that one's in-group is the most important group and that its culture is superior to those of other groups. This bias toward viewing the characteristics of one's in-group as the golden standard is often accompanied by derogation of characteristics associated with out-groups. Ethnocentric behaviors entail cooperation among in-group members and lack of cooperation with or hostility toward members of out-groups. The group boundaries are typically drawn along readily identifiable features such as language, religion, or physical features that are socially meaningful. The particular markers of the group distinction may vary over time and are shaped by culture.

Although ethnocentrism, or in-group favoritism, of any particular ethnic or cultural group likely involves a complex set of historical and contextual factors, laboratory studies have shown that ethnocentric behaviors can be elicited with even the most arbitrary and trivial group distinctions and that such behaviors can occur in the absence of reciprocity or any opportunities for gains in the interest of the self or of the in-group (such as in classic minimal group paradigms in experimental social psychology). In fact, social cognition studies have indicated that categorization and discrimination of group memberships can occur at a rapid and pre-conscious level. This led some scholars to conceptualize ethnocentric bias as an inevitable perceptual consequence of social categorization. On the other hand, there is also evidence that social status of the in-group can influence the extent to which group members show ethnocentric bias, with some studies showing that higher-status groups demonstrated more ethnocentrism and other studies showing that lower-status groups show more ethnocentrism. Meta-analytic evidence suggests that in-group bias is higher for high-status groups in artificial group settings but higher for low-status groups in realistic group settings.

Various theories for origins of ethnocentrism have been offered. Social identity theory argues that groups are motivated to achieve positive group distinctiveness, which in turn serves to protect and enhance a favorable social identity for group members. Social identity theory proposes that the strength of individual identification with the group is generally associated with the degree of in-group favoritism. Realistic group conflict theory argues that ethnocentrism arises out of real or perceived threat to an in-group's interest and is motivated by psychological need for power, control, and enhanced collective self-esteem of the group. Genetic similarity theory asserts that the level of conflict among organisms is a direct inverse function of the proportion of shared genes; thus ethnocentrism is likely to occur between groups that are genetically dissimilar to each other. Recent evidence points to a complex set of factors that appear to determine the motivation for ethnocentrism and suggests that in-group bias cannot be understood apart from the social context in which it is expressed. Specifically, ethnocentric bias may serve multiple functions, including achievement of instrumental goals (such as promotion of change in social status of groups) or expressive function (such as promotion of positive group identity), and the strength and the expression of in-group bias may depend on not only the hierarchical status of the in-group but also the perceived stability of the group status.

The concept of ethnocentrism has been applied to research in marketing, consumer behavior, and organizational behavior as well as in analyses of ethnic conflicts. Finally, in the context of the multicultural psychology movement in the United States and critical psychology movement primarily in Europe, psychology as a discipline has been criticized as being ethnocentric in its Western bias with respect to the field's epistemology, theories, and methods.   – sok

ethnography

n. **1.** A holistic and systematic description of a society and its dynamics usually written by an anthropologist living within the culture. **2.** The branch of anthropology that scientifically studies individual human cultures or societies.

ethnopedagogy

n. The scientific study of folk methods of teaching children, including traditions, customs, sayings, and games.

ethology

n. The scientific study of animal behavior in natural settings within an evolutionary framework. The focus of ethology is usually on species-specific behavior patterns and their interaction with the environment. The field overlaps with comparative psychology.

ethos

n. The particular guiding beliefs, sentiments, values, morals, and spirit of a person, group, culture, era, or social, intellectual, or artistic movement.

etic

1. *adj.* Of or relating to the application of an outside cultural perspective to the study and understanding of human functioning within a particular culture. **2.** *n.* A psychological process or construct that is applicable across all cultures, that is a universal.

etiology

n. The causes and course of development of a disease or disorder. Also spelled *aetiology.*

eugenics

n. A pseudoscientific social and political philosophy which seeks to eradicate genetic defects and improve the genetic makeup of populations in general through selective breeding. Positive eugenics seeks to increase the number of children of those who are considered genetically superior, and negative eugenics seeks to reduce the number of those who are considered to have genetic defects. The eugenics movement was popular in Germany before and during the Nazi era and in Britain and the United States through much of the 20th century, leading to the forced sterilization of retarded, mentally ill, and homosexual individuals.

euphoria

n. A state of elevated well-being and elation.

eustachian tube

n. A small tube extending from the middle ear to the pharynx which serves to equalize the air pressure on the two sides of the eardrum.

euthymia

n. A prolonged mood of well-being and tranquility.

event-related brain potential

n. (ERP) Neurons produce extremely small changes in their surrounding electrical fields as they are activated. When many neurons act in synchrony, their electrical fields combine to produce positive or negative changes in the electrical field. Event-related brain potentials (ERPs) represent changes in these electrical fields recorded at the scalp in response to specific events. ERP waveforms are described in terms of the latency (time from stimulus onset) and polarity (positive or negative) of peaks in the waveform, called components. For example, if a list of words is visually presented for a person to remember, a negative peak 100 ms after each word (N100) and a positive peak 300 ms after each word (P300) are produced. Early components (typically less than 200 ms) reflect automatic responses to stimuli, such as detection of a visually presented word. Later components (typically 200 ms or later) reflect higher-order processes, such as trying to remember words.

– GER, FD

everyday cognition

n. An area of study that examines cognitive skills and abilities that are used in everyday functioning that appear to develop without formal education, but from performing daily tasks of living and working.

evoked potential

n. (EP) An increase in electrical activity in a portion of the brain or other neural tissue brought forth by a specific stimulus. Thus a bright flash of light will reliably evoke an increase in the amplitude of the electrical potential recorded by an electroencephalogram (EEG) electrode positioned near the visual cortex.

evolution

n. **1.** The process of gradual change over time of one thing or group into another thing or group most often used to describe biological evolution of species. **2.** The process of change through natural selection that has occurred among plants and animals on the Earth over, approximately, the last billion years.

evolutionary psychology

n. Evolutionary psychologists propose that the human mind consists predominantly of highly specialized mechanisms designed to solve specific problems. The specific problems that the human mind is designed to solve are those that repeatedly confronted our ancestors over evolutionary time.

The ancestral environment that humans evolved in is termed the *environment of evolutionary adaptedness* (EEA). This environment consists of a set of problems that must be solved if the animal is to avoid extinction. For example, over evolutionary time, humans and their primate ancestors had to be able find mates and raise children, and they had to form alliances with others. They had to be able to find food, and they had to avoid dangerous predators and poisonous plants and animals. The problems that humans faced during their evolution were quite different from the problems faced by other living organisms. For example, an ocean-dwelling mammal such as a whale must solve a wide range of problems stemming from its need to adapt to living in the ocean, and parasites must often adapt to the internal environment of a variety of hosts.

For humans, the EEA is considered to be the Pleistocene geological era, which spanned a period from 1.8 million years ago to 12,000 years ago. During this period, humans lived as hunter-gatherers, so it is expected that human psychological adaptations are adapted to life during this period. Because human culture has changed so dramatically, there may be mismatches between psychological adaptations and the modern world. An example is that food was relatively scarce and unpredictable in the EEA compared to the modern world of readily available high-calorie, high-fat food. The result is that modern humans are prone to obesity because our psychological mechanisms are geared to an environment of scarcity that no longer obtains in many parts of the world.

Evolutionary psychologists emphasize that all of these problems presented themselves repeatedly over evolutionary time so that there would be sufficient opportunity for natural selection to design mechanisms that would solve the problems. According to evolutionary psychology, these problems were solved by evolving a set of specialized psychological mechanisms designed to deal with these specific problems. These mechanisms are adaptations – mechanisms designed by natural selection to solve a particular problem. For example, on the basis of a large body of theory and data, evolutionary psychologists argue that humans evolved mechanisms that allow them to choose mates in an adaptive manner: women are attracted to men willing and able to invest in their children, and men are attracted to youthful, physically attractive women because these traits are signs of fertility.

When the environment presents long-standing problems and recurrent cues relevant to solving them, the best solution is to evolve domain-specific mechanisms, or modules, specialized to handle specific inputs and generate particular solutions. Modules are designed to solve problems in specific domains by mapping characteristic inputs onto characteristic outputs. For example, the human visual system contains specialized cells that are designed to respond to particular types of sensory input (horizontal lines, vertical lines, motion), and there are specific pathways in the brain that are specialized to transmit visual information. These pathways are specific to the visual system and are unresponsive to other stimulation, such as sound. Modules are therefore domain specific. That is, each module processes information peculiar to its own area of "expertise," so that, for example, verbal and spatial information are processed with different mechanisms.

The operation of modules is mandatory (i.e., they are automatically triggered in the presence of appropriate environmental stimulation), fast, and unconscious. For example, when we look around the room, our brains are automatically carrying out millions of operations that allow us to see the objects in the room. The calculations are done very rapidly, and we are unaware of them. Modules operate in parallel, processing massive amounts of information in a variety of relatively independent circuits at the same time. For example, when we converse with people in garden-variety social contexts, we unconsciously process their facial expressions, age- and gender-related cues, vocal intonation, posture, psychological traits, and language.

Research in evolutionary psychology has been influenced by several theories compatible with general evolutionary theory. The most important of these theories are parental investment theory, inclusive fitness theory, parent-offspring conflict theory, and the theory of senescence.

Inclusive fitness theory emphasizes that genes are selected for their beneficial effects not only on the reproductive success of individuals but also on their relatives. This occurs because relatives share genes depending on how closely related they are (e.g., full siblings share half of their segregating genes). This theory predicts that psychological mechanisms sensitive to kinship will favor helping relatives over nonrelatives and more closely related kin over more distantly related kin.

Parent-offspring conflict theory is based on the hypothesis that differing degrees of genetic relatedness within families produce conflicts of interest. For example, parents and children are expected to differ on the ideal amount of investment parents provide children: parents share half of their segregating genes with each of their children, but it is in each child's interest to favor itself over its siblings. This theory predicts that parents will encourage children to be more cooperative than is in the children's interest. And it predicts conflicts of interest over time of weaning, with parents more inclined to invest in new children and children seeking more investment in themselves.

Senescence theory proposes that genes that promote reproductive success early in life will be retained even if they shorten the life span. This follows from the fact that offspring produced relatively early in life have a greater effect on an individual's reproductive success than offspring produced later in life. These effects are especially pronounced in males because sexual competition is expected to be higher for males than females. Senescence theory therefore predicts that males will have shorter life spans than females on average.

Although mapping modular mechanisms and exploring the predictions resulting from evolutionary theory characterize the great bulk of research in evolutionary psychology, there has been increasing interest in the evolution and function of domain general mechanisms, especially among evolutionary psychologists interested in human development. An important set of domain general mechanisms comprises general intelligence, particularly working memory and attentional control. Unlike the unconscious workings of the modular mechanisms described earlier, general intelligence involves explicitly conscious, effortful problem solving. Whereas the modules are relatively independent processors operating in parallel, the explicit mechanisms of general intelligence operate on very limited bits of information in a sequential manner. And whereas the modules are domain specific, general intelligence is domain general: it operates on a wide range of input, including verbal and spatial information.

Because general intelligence is fundamentally concerned with coping with environmental novelty, there are three types of hypotheses regarding the main factor driving the increase in human intelligence: climatic variation, ecological pressure, and social competition. The climatic variation hypothesis proposes that human intelligence was mainly beneficial in decoupling humans from dependence on any particular ecology defined by a constant climate or other invariant features. According to this hypothesis, general intelligence allowed humans to adapt to rapidly changing climates of the Pleistocene and greatly increased their range of settlement. The foraging hypothesis highlights the advantages to be gained from better methods for extracting resources from the environment (e.g., managed foraging) and in enlarging the range of human settlement and supporting larger populations. The foraging hypothesis is supported by data indicating that humans evolved as superpredators and manufacturers of highly complex tools by around 50,000 years ago, resulting in a wave of mass extinctions of large animals. These changes coincide with not only a larger brain but a smaller gastrointestinal tract and higher metabolism dependent on high-quality food made possible by these improved foraging techniques. The social competition hypothesis proposes that after humans achieved ecological dominance, intelligence evolved because it was beneficial for between-group and within-group competition among humans. This hypothesis emphasizes that cognitively, socially, and behaviorally sophisticated individuals are able to outmaneuver and manipulate other individuals to gain control of resources in the local ecology and to gain control of the behavior of other people. This hypothesis is supported by correlations between brain size and group size, especially where there are complex social relationships within groups.

– KM

▶ *See also* **PARENTAL INVESTMENT THEORY**

evolutionary theory

n. Any theory which describes and accounts for the gradual change of one species into other species across many generations. Most, but not all, modern theories of evolution include some form of natural selection as the most important mechanism of change.

excitatory conditioning

n. Another name for classical conditioning in which the pairing of an unconditioned stimulus (US) with a conditioned stimulus (CS) leads to the establishment of a conditioned response (CR). As an example, if a dog normally salivates when it is presented with food (US) and a bell (CS) is rung before the food is presented several times in a row, the dog will soon begin drooling (CR) when it hears the bell rung without the presentation of food.

excitatory postsynaptic potential

n. A wave of depolarization in a dendrite which increases the likelihood of a neural impulse which has been caused by the release of neurotransmitters into the synaptic cleft after a depolarization potential in the presynaptic axon.

excitatory potential

n. A neural depolarization which changes the electrical configuration of a cell membrane, making it more likely that a nerve impulse will occur by means of a wave of depolarization sweeping down the axon to the synapse.

executive functions

n. Complex forms of cognition and behavior, including but limited to (1) controlling cognition (metacognition), (2) programming behavior, (3) inhibiting immediate responses, (4) abstracting, (5) problem solving, (6) verbal regulation of behavior, (7) reorienting behavior according to the behavioral consequences, (8) subjecting behavior to learned social norms, (9) delaying reinforcement, (10) temporality of behavior, (10) personality integrity, (11) prospection of behavior, (12) morality, and (13) self-awareness. Executive functioning can be regarded as complex processing requiring the coordination of several subprocesses to achieve a particular goal (i.e., goal-directed activity). Intact frontal processes, although not synonymous with executive functioning, are integral to its function. Although attempts to correlate executive functioning with the activity of specific discrete frontal areas have been inconclusive, the emerging view is that executive function is mediated by dynamic and flexible networks basically depending on the prefrontal brain areas. Neuroimaging results have also implicated posterior, cortical, and subcortical regions in executive functioning.

– A A

▶ *See also* **PREFRONTAL CORTEX**

exemplar theory

n. A theory that mental categorization uses remembered examples of a category with which new impressions are compared in order to determine membership in the category. This theory contrasts with prototype- and feature-based theories of mental categorization.

exhaustion stage

n. The final stage in the general adaptation syndrome (GAS), in which prolonged stress finally leads to physical and emotional breakdown, characterized by sleep disturbance, irritability, inability to concentrate, restlessness, trembling, chronic fatigue, low startle threshold, anxiety, depression, and crying fits.

exhibitionism

n. **1.** A disorder characterized by intense sexual arousal by fantasies of or actual exposure of one's genitals to strangers. **2.** An unusually strong tendency to make oneself the center of attention in any social group.

existential anxiety

n. Anxiety is a feeling of nervousness, jitteriness, or dread that is generally a consequence of anticipating a perceived future threat. The adjective *existential* denotes pertaining to the basic inescapable realities of the human condition. Hence, existential anxiety is anxiety regarding one or more of these realities.

Research in psychology has recently directed a large amount of attention to the nature and consequences of existential anxiety, leading to the emergence of a subfield labeled *experimental existential psychology*. This subfield has focused on the big five sources of existential anxiety: death, meaninglessness, identity uncertainty, isolation, and freedom.

The knowledge that one will inevitably die conflicts with the human desire for continued life and all it has to offer. A variety of self-report instruments have been developed to measure death anxiety. Terror management theory proposes that the potential for anxiety engendered by this awareness of one's mortality is managed by embracing a culturally based conception of reality, or cultural worldview, which allows individuals to believe they are eternally significant members of a meaningful universe, rather than material animals fated only to obliteration upon death. A large body of experimental research has supported the theory by showing that reminders of mortality lead individuals to bolster faith in their cultural worldview and the belief that they are enduringly significant contributors to the world. Reminders of mortality also seem to increase the appeal of ideologies and leaders who promote the righteousness of the in-group and the quest for a heroic triumph over out-groups designated as evil.

Given that we will all die, that our understanding of the universe is limited, and that cultures around the world have very different ideas about the nature and purposes of human existence, how can we sustain meaning in our own lives, and in life in general? Meaning is generally provided for people over the course of socialization by parents, teachers, mass media, and religious, social, and political institutions. However, knowledge of alternative views of life's meanings and specific unexpected life events often challenge our beliefs about what is meaningful, and when they do, anxiety is likely to result. People are often motivated to reduce this anxiety by either affirming the validity of their own meaning systems or seeking new meaning systems, as happens when people convert to a new religion or cult.

We all want to have a clear identity, to know who we are. In addition to providing a meaningful conception of the world, cultures provide us with names, roles, and group identities that help give us that identity. Erik Erikson posited that for most people adolescence is a key time for developing a clear sense of identity. However, because most if not all of our beliefs about ourselves originate with other people, and we may fall short of the expectations associated with our desired identity, at different times in life we may feel uncertain about aspects of our identity. This personal uncertainty can arouse considerable anxiety. To attempt to reduce this anxiety, people often cling more tightly and rigidly to their cherished beliefs about themselves. But they may also seek new group affiliations, relationships, and career paths to establish a sense of who they are more firmly.

On the basis of our mammalian ancestry and inclination toward group living, many theorists have posited that we humans have a need for affiliation and intimacy, to belong, to attach to or connect with our fellow humans. However, we all have interior subjective experiences that can never be shared with another. We can touch another's skin, and we can try to communicate our inner experience through words, facial expressions, and body language, but we can never fully, accurately know another's conscious experience and no one can ever know ours. Thus, no matter what we do, there is always a gap between us and others, and this realization can arouse feelings of loneliness and isolation that generate anxiety. Research suggests that people try to cope with these feelings by seeking intimacy in their close relationships and by sustaining interpersonal affiliations and group identities that help them conceive of themselves as part of a larger whole rather than as an isolated organism. One effective way to feel less isolated is to develop a relationship with someone who seems to have a similar subjective experience of reality to ours, a process known as I-sharing.

We usually think of freedom as a good thing, but Otto Rank, Eric Fromm, and other theorists have noted that freedom may offer people so many potential choices that they can become mired in uncertainty and indecision.

Furthermore, freedom entails a great burden of responsibility for one's own actions, and potential guilt, shame, and regret. Therefore people often experience anxiety regarding their freedoms. As a consequence, they often rely on close others, leaders, and social institutions to make decisions for them, thereby sacrificing their freedom to reduce their uncertainty, anxieties, and potential for guilt, shame, and regret.

The existential anxiety aroused by these five existential concerns can fuel personal growth or can contribute to maladaptive defenses and mental health problems. Existential psychotherapy, an approach summarized by Irvin Yalom, is focused on helping people whose problems seem to stem from existential anxiety. Yalom proposed that these existential concerns generate anxiety when people have inadequate ways to address them; this anxiety, in turn, may contribute to additional maladaptive coping strategies or defenses. Existential psychotherapy focuses on helping individuals let go of these maladaptive defenses and construct more beneficial modes of addressing their existential concerns, modes that contribute to rather than hinder effective functioning and life satisfaction.   – JG

existentialism
n. A philosophical and literary point of view which takes the phenomena of existence as its subject without any reference to ideas, principles, or mechanisms outside experience. It was primarily a 20th-century movement exemplified by the works of Martin Heidegger and Jean Paul Sartre. The central concept of existentialism is Dasein, or a sense of being there in one's experience, including the lack of choice over many aspects of the situation and the necessity to choose one's course of action.

existential psychology
n. A general approach to psychology that employs an examination of the phenomena of experience as its materials without reference to anything outside experience. Thus there is no theory in which inferred mental processes produce experience, simply an examination of experience itself. It notes that in experience there is a sense of choice and anxiety over choosing, that some choices have a sense of moving one toward a felt but undefined goal while others do not, and our experience of meaning in life is dependent on making choices which seem fraught with meaning despite the anxiety they involve.

existential psychotherapy
n. Any of numerous therapies which focus on the immediate experience of the individual as the process of change without reference to general ideas about motivation, desirability, or specific aim other than authentic presence in the moment and acknowledgment of responsibility for choice in the moment.

existential therapy
n. Any of numerous therapies which focus on the immediate experience of the individual as the process of change without reference to general ideas about motivation, desirability, or specific aim other than authentic presence in the moment and acknowledgment of responsibility for choice in the moment.

exogenous
adj. Originating outside the person.

exogenous depression
n. A depression which occurs primarily as a reaction to a person's circumstances rather than problems in internal adjustment. Also called a situational depression.

expectancy
n. 1. The mental set of beliefs about the immediate future that predisposes an individual to perceive and conceive in particular ways. 2. In probability and statistics, the relative likelihood of various occurrences given by the frequency of their occurrence in previous experience. 3. The increased attentional level and muscular tension in situations in which previous conditioning has led to a known stimulus-reward relationship. 4. In motivational psychology, the likelihood that one's actions will receive a reward of a particular magnitude.

expectancy effect

n. **1.** The observer expectancy effect is the misperception of events in the direction of what is expected. **2.** The subject expectancy effect is the effect one person's expectations have on another's behavior.

expectancy theory

n. **1.** In motivation, a theory that attitude is weighed by the value of a possible outcome multiplied by its likelihood of occurrence. **2.** In cognitive psychology, the idea that learning is the development of dispositions to act in the presence of a particular kind of stimulus as though it were a signal for other stimuli whose occurrence is contingent on one's actions.

expectancy-value theory

n. Human beings have a natural tendency to react with some degree of positive or negative affect to any object or concept of psychological significance. We like or dislike certain people, support or oppose various policies, regard some activities as pleasant and others as unpleasant, have favorable views of certain institutions but unfavorable views of others, and so forth. Expectancy-value (EV) theory is, first and foremost, concerned with the origins and structure of these social attitudes. According to EV theory, the overall evaluation or attitude toward a psychological object is a function of the information or beliefs we have about the object in question. In the course of our daily lives our experiences lead us to acquire many different beliefs about various objects, actions, and events. These beliefs may be formed as a result of direct observation; they may be acquired indirectly by accepting information from other people or from printed and electronic media; or they may be self-generated through inference processes. Each belief associates the attitude object with an attribute. For example, we may come to believe that genetically modified food (the object) increases agricultural yields, contaminates the environment, and causes birth defects (the attributes). Because the attributes that become associated with the object are already valued positively or negatively, we simultaneously and automatically acquire an attitude toward

the object. Specifically, the subjective value of each attribute contributes to the attitude in direct proportion to the strength of the belief, that is, to the subjective probability that the object has the attribute in question. The way in which beliefs about an object combine to produce an overall attitude is shown in the following:

$$A; \sum b_i e_i.$$

It can be seen that the strength of each belief (*b*) is multiplied by the evaluation of the associated attribute (*e*), and the resulting products are summed over all beliefs about the object. According to the expectancy-value model, a person's attitude (*A*) is directly proportional to this summative belief index. In this fashion, we learn to like objects we associate with largely desirable characteristics and to form unfavorable attitudes toward objects we associate with mainly undesirable characteristics.

Of course, individuals are not expected actually to perform the mental calculations specified in the equation. The EV model is taken not as an accurate description of the way in which attitudes are formed, but rather it is assumed that the attitude formation process can be modeled as if individuals were performing the stipulated calculations. It is also important to realize that people can form many beliefs about any psychological object, but that only a relatively small number – perhaps 6 to 10 – are readily available in memory at any given moment. It is these readily accessible beliefs that are assumed to be the prevailing determinants of a person's attitude.

To acquire a good understanding of the factors that serve as the basis for existing attitudes, accessible beliefs about the attitude object are elicited in a free-response format. Individuals are asked to list any positive and any negative aspects of the object that come readily to mind. In most applications of the EV model, the most frequently listed responses are selected to construct a list of modal accessible beliefs, that is, beliefs that are common in the population of interest. Once a list of accessible attributes has been constructed, a new sample of participants are asked to rate the likelihood and the valence associated with each attribute. That is, they are asked to rate how likely it is that the object has the attribute (belief strength) and to rate the attribute on an evaluative scale (attribute evaluation). These two ratings are multiplied, and the products are summed in accordance with the preceding equation. In addition, as a direct measure of attitude, participants are also asked to rate the attitude object itself on an evaluative scale. In accordance with EV theory, empirical research has demonstrated strong correlations between this direct attitude measure and the summed belief × evaluation index.

In short, in EV theory it is assumed that our beliefs form the informational foundation for our attitudes. Although often quite accurate, beliefs can be biased by a variety of cognitive and motivational processes. They may be irrational, be based on invalid or selective information, be self-serving, or otherwise fail to correspond to reality. However, no matter how they were formed or how accurate they are, beliefs represent the information we have about the world in which we live, and they form the cognitive foundation for our attitudes toward aspects of that world.

However, expectancy-value theory can be used not only to account for the formation and structure of attitudes but also to help explain behavioral decisions. People form attitudes not only toward physical objects, institutions, social groups, events, and policies but also toward behaviors. Thus, we may hold favorable or unfavorable attitudes toward eating genetically modified food, drinking alcohol, exercising, participating in a demonstration, and so forth. When the object of the attitude is a behavior, the relevant beliefs that determine the attitude are readily accessible beliefs about the consequences of the behavior. These behavioral beliefs are again elicited in a free-response format, a list of modal behavioral outcomes is constructed, and participants are asked to rate the likelihood that the behavior will produce each outcome and to rate the valence of each outcome on an evaluative scale. Belief strength and outcome evaluation ratings are multiplied and the products are summed to produce the expectancy-value composite, which is again found to correlate well with a direct measure of attitude toward the behavior.

The EV model of attitude toward a behavior is a central factor in the theory of planned behavior (TPB), a popular model for the prediction of human social behavior. The theory has been used successfully in attempts to provide a better understanding of such diverse behaviors as exercising, donating blood, adhering to a low-fat diet, using condoms for AIDS prevention, using illegal drugs, wearing a safety helmet, and choosing a career, among many others.

Briefly, according to the TPB, human action is influenced by three major factors: a favorable or unfavorable evaluation of the behavior (attitude toward the behavior), perceived social pressure to perform or not perform the behavior (subjective norm), and self-efficacy in relation to the behavior (perceived behavioral control). In combination, attitude toward the behavior, subjective norm, and perception of behavioral control lead to the formation of a behavioral intention. As a general rule, the more favorable the attitude and subjective norm, and the greater the perceived behavioral control, the stronger should be the person's intention to perform the behavior in question. Finally, given a sufficient degree of actual control over the behavior, people are expected to carry out their intentions when the opportunity arises.

The three major determinants in the theory of planned behavior – attitudes toward the behavior, subjective norms, and perceptions of behavioral control – are traced to corresponding sets of accessible behavior-related beliefs. As noted, attitude toward the behavior is assumed to be determined by beliefs about the behavior's outcomes, each belief weighted by the subjective value of the outcome in question. A similar logic applies to the relation between normative beliefs and subjective norm, and the relation between control beliefs and perceived behavioral control. Normative beliefs are the perceived behavioral expectations of such important referent individuals or groups as the person's family, friends, and coworkers. These normative beliefs – in combination with the person's motivation to comply with the different referents – determine the prevailing subjective norm regarding the behavior. Finally, control beliefs are related to the perceived presence of factors that can facilitate or impede performance of the behavior. The perceived power of each control factor to impede or facilitate behavioral performance contributes to perceived control over the behavior in direct proportion to the person's subjective probability that the control factor is present.

We have seen that expectancy-value theory accounts for attitudes toward performance of a given behavior by directing attention to the behavior's perceived consequences. In addition, the theory has been extended to account for subjective norms and perceptions of behavioral control. As in the case of attitudes, formation of these factors is traced to readily accessible beliefs: normative beliefs in the case of subjective norms and control beliefs in the case of perceived behavioral control. As a result, the theory has done much to further our understanding of the factors that determine human social behavior.   – I A

Experiences in Close Relationship Scale
n. An online scale which measures two dimensions of adult attachment security versus insecurity with the availability and responsiveness of one's partner and discomfort with intimacy versus security in depending on others. The original version of the scale was developed through a factor analysis of items believed to be related to adult attachment and the revised version through an item analysis of responses to the scale.

experiment
n. An arrangement of conditions and procedures which allows observations of the relationships between the controlled circumstances (independent variables) and the uncontrolled outcomes (dependent variables) with an intent to make inferences about causal relationships between the independent and dependent variables.

experimental analysis of behavior
n. An approach to experimental psychology that adopts observable behavior and antecedent conditions as the only proper variables in a psychological experiment.

experimental condition
n. One of two or more sets of controlled circumstances in which a dependent variable is measured in the course of an experiment.

experimental control
n. The regulation of all extraneous variables in an experiment so that changes in the dependent variable can be attributed to changes in the independent variables.

experimental design
n. A plan for the procedures to be followed in an experiment including all of the controls and methods for measuring variables.

experimental error
n. A combination of random error and error introduced by faulty experimental design.

experimental extinction
n. **1.** The gradual disappearance of a conditioned response when the conditioned stimulus is repeatedly presented without being followed by the unconditioned stimulus. **2.** The gradual disappearance of an operant response after it is no longer reinforced.

experimental group
n. In an experiment, any group of subjects who receive the same set of experimental treatments, as opposed to other groups who receive different sets of treatments and the control group, who receive no experimental treatment.

experimental hypothesis
n. A specific prediction or explanation of the relationship between target phenomena that is based upon theory, observation, or past research. For example, an experimenter may propose the hypothesis that "children who receive verbal praise for cleaning their own room will demonstrate increased self-efficacy compared to children who receive an

allowance for the same behaviors." Hypotheses must be testable and falsifiable; that is, hypotheses must have the possibility of being proven true or false under specific conditions. Research may then be designed to test the accuracy of a hypothesis under specific experimental conditions. – BJM

experimentally induced false memory
n. Inaccurate reports of recollection induced in subjects through various types of suggestion including discussing aspects of events that did not occur and asking questions in a leading way.

experimental manipulation
n. Any control by the experimenter of an independent variable across whose different conditions the dependent variable is measured.

experimental methods
n. A system of procedures and materials used systematically to investigate the relationships between controlled (independent) variables and uncontrolled (dependent) ones.

experimental neurosis
n. Anxious behavior and disorganized behavior brought about by subjecting an animal to punishment or the withdrawal of food which it is unable to control.

experimental psychology
n. The branch of psychology which uses controlled circumstances, often in a laboratory, to develop quantitative theories of mental or physical behavior.

experimenter bias
n. Systematic errors by a researcher in observation, record keeping, interpretation, or computation, usually led by the researcher's expectations.

experimenter effect
n. Bias entering into an experiment either through the experimenter's expectancies or other characteristics or behavior affecting the way subjects respond to experimental conditions or systematic errors by a researcher in observation, record keeping, interpretation, or computation, usually led by the researcher's expectations.

experimenter expectancy effect
n. Systematic errors by a researcher in observation, record keeping, interpretation, or computation, usually led by the researcher's expectations.

expert system
n. A problem solving computer program which uses a database of information and a procedure for decision making. These programs may be modeled on the thinking of human experts in the field or statistical models of optimal decision making including a cost/benefit analysis of different outcomes.

explanatory style
n. **1.** The individual style with which a person understands and explains events in general and his/her own and others' behavior. **2.** Dimensions of explanatory style include internal versus external locus of control, stable versus unstable attribution, and global versus particular focus of attribution.

explicit memory
n. Aspects of memory that can be recalled at will from both episodic and semantic memory, as opposed to implicit memory for such things as how to ride a bicycle or speak one's native language.

explicit prejudice
n. Prejudice that is verbalized and thus made public.

exploratory behavior
n. In ethology, interactions with the world with no obvious goal other than its exploration.

exploratory data analysis
n. Analysis of data with the intent of discovering patterns for further investigation.

exploratory factor analysis
n. A set of analytic techniques applied to a correlation or covariance matrix seeking

to discover its internal structure of relatedness. Vectors called factors are selected, pass through the densest areas in multidimensional space, and are then rotated, usually to select the ones which collectively account for the most covariance and are most uncorrelated with one another.

exploratory research

n. Studies of a field which seek to discover interesting patterns and facts but without preformed hypotheses.

explosive disorder

n. A disorder characterized by discrete episodes of impulsive aggressiveness which results in serious assaultive acts or destruction of property. This can be either a single episode or a recurrent disorder. Also called intermittent explosive disorder and isolated explosive disorder.

exposure therapy

n. A procedure in behavior therapy in which an individual is confronted with the thing he or she fears most either in imagination or in real life under safe circumstances. Eventually the person becomes habituated to it and the initial fear responses gradually diminish and disappear. Also called flooding.

expressive aphasia

n. Inability or seriously diminished capacity to speak, write, or use gestures to communicate, usually associated with injury to Broca's area in the lower part of the left frontal lobe.

expressive behavior

n. Any action of an organism which communicates information to another and particularly information about the emotions, desires, or intents of the expresser.

expressive language disorder ▶ See MOTOR APHASIA

expressivity

n. In genetics the degree to which a gene is likely to be expressed in the phenotype or actual body of the individual.

external attribution

Definition. n. When trying to explain a person's behavior (what is referred to in psychology as making an attribution for the person's behavior), an external attribution is made when it is assumed that the cause of an event is some factor outside (or external to) the person being observed. In other words, an external attribution suggests that the individual is not personally responsible for the behavior or its outcome.

Explanation. Attribution theory states that people have a desire to explain events in the world around them. Making external attributions indicates that the reason an event happened is due to factors purely outside the person (e.g., luck) rather than factors internal to the person (e.g., personality, ability, effort exerted). External factors are outside a person's control. People tend to make an external attribution when negative events happen to them or their friends or when positive events happen to their competitors. People tend not to take the blame for their own negative circumstances, and they tend to downplay their competitors' credit for their successes. For example, when students score poorly on a test, they tend to make external attributions by deciding that the poor performance was due to their being unlucky that day, the teacher's not being good at explaining the material, or the teacher's being bad at writing tests. Students in such circumstances can use many explanations rather than taking responsibility for the outcome themselves (rather than acknowledging that the failure may have been their own fault because they did not study enough or they are not as bright in the content area as some of the other students). However, when student competitors do well, the other students frequently assume that their competitors succeed because the teacher grades unfairly or that they are just lucky.

People may use external attributions to preserve their own self-esteem. Making external attributions for failures allows people still to feel good about themselves despite the failure. Similarly, attributing other people's successes to something other than their ability makes their accomplishments less threatening to the individual's self-esteem. Making external attributions also influences the way people react to similar events in the future. For example, if students think their grades are due to factors outside their control, they are not likely to change their behavior to improve their grades (e.g., studying harder next time).   — VKP, LAB

externalization
n. **1.** In psychoanalysis a defense mechanism in which aspects of the unconscious are attributed to the outer world. **2.** The process of learning to distinguish between bodily self and external world in childhood. **3.** A process by which a drive is aroused by an external stimulus as the smell of a bakery may make us hungry. **4.** The belief that some of one's actions are attributable to aspects of the outer world and one is not personally in control of nor responsible for them. **5.** In cognitive science, the process of putting one's thoughts out into the world through signs, behavior, and material artifacts.

external locus of control
n. External locus of control refers to the degree to which individuals expect that a reinforcement or an outcome of their behavior depends on causes external to the individual, or is a function of chance or luck, or even is simply unpredictable. The original internal-external scale developed by Rotter in 1966 proposed considering external and internal locus of control on a continuous bipolar scale. However, other authors proposed considering external and internal locus of control as two independent dimensions, and some even suggested distinguishing different externality dimensions, as chance or powerful others. External locus of control is affected by several demographic variables and is negatively related to academic achievement. No relation has been observed between locus of control and intelligence. Several clinical populations seem to have higher external locus of control, such as depressive patients, and this level seems to be negatively associated with the outcomes of treatments.   — JR

external rectus
n. The eye muscle on the outside midline of the eye that rotates the eye away from the nose. Also called lateral rectus.

external validity ▶ *See* **VALIDITY, EXTERNAL**

exteroceptor
n. Any sensory receptor that takes in information from the external world as in the skin or mucus membranes.

extinction
n. **1.** The gradual disappearance of a conditioned response when the conditioned stimulus is repeatedly presented without being followed by the unconditioned stimulus. **2.** The gradual disappearance of an operant response after it is no longer reinforced. **3.** In biology, the complete disappearance of a species.

extinction, latent
n. **1.** In operant conditioning, extinction that occurs in the absence of a response as in placing a rat in an empty goal box at the end of a maze. **2.** In biology, an environmental state in which the extinction of a species is imminent and irremediable but has not yet occurred.

extinction trial
n. An instance of presenting an organism with a stimulus previously paired with either an unconditioned stimulus or a reinforcement and then not having the unconditioned stimulus or reinforcement.

extinguish
v. To carry out an extinction procedure so that an established behavior disappears.

extracellular thirst
n. Thirst caused by a loss of extracellular liquid as through bleeding or vomiting. Also called hypovolemic thirst.

extraocular muscle
n. Any of the rectus or either of the oblique muscles which control rotation of the eye within its socket.

extrapyramidal

adj. Of or relating to the extrapyramidal nerve tract, which includes the motor cortex, basal ganglia, corticospinal tract, and motor neurons.

extrapyramidal motor system

n. The neural system which controls voluntary motion, consisting of the motor cortex, basal ganglia, corticospinal tract, and motor neurons.

extrapyramidal syndrome

n. Symptoms arising as a result of injury to the extrapyramidal system or the effect of antipsychotic drugs on it, which is characterized by tremors; rhythmic movements of the face, tongue, jaw, arms, or legs; drooling; and lack of normal facial expressions.

extrasensory perception

n. (ESP) Any capacity to know without using any of the five senses such as in clairvoyance, precognition, and telepathy.

extrastriate cortex

n. Region of the occipital lobe beside the primary visual area (V1, striate cortex, located in the calcarine fissure in the occipital lobe). It corresponds to the Brodmann's areas 17 and 19, whereas the striate cortex corresponds to the Brodmann's area 17. In primates, the extrastriate cortex is subdivided into four areas, known as V2 (coding simple visual properties such as orientation, spatial frequency, and color), V3 (motion and localization), V4 (orientation, spatial frequency, and color of objects of some complexity), and V5 (complex visual motion stimuli).   – A A

▶ *See also* **PRIMARY VISUAL AREA** *and* **STRIATE CORTEX**

extreme response bias

n. The tendency to use the ends of a scale regardless of item content.

extrinsic eye muscle

n. The muscles that move the eye within its socket including the rectus and oblique muscles.

extrinsic motivation

n. A drive or desire to do something due to the effects that it will have rather than for the intrinsic pleasure of doing it.

extroversion

n. Extroversion/introversion (or extroversion), one of the dimensions of the five factor model, contrasts active, sociable, and cheerful extroverts with reserved, solitary, and somber introverts. Extroversion is the most easily inferred of the five factors, often apparent from seeing a photograph or hearing a spoken sentence or two. Extroverts are cheerful and friendly, but introverts are not depressed and hostile; introverts simply lack positive feelings and prefer to be alone. Extroverts prefer enterprising vocations and have higher lifetime earnings than introverts. There is a growing body of evidence that Europeans and their descendants are, on average, higher in extroversion than Asians and Africans.
– R R M

extrovert

n. Extroverts (extraverts) are individuals who are high in terms of outward focus. Extroverts are at one end of an introversion-extroversion continuum on which most people fall somewhere in the middle range. Extroverts tend to be outspoken, outgoing, and optimistic. Extroverts tend to have limited interest in solitude, introspection, and quiet pastimes. There is research evidence that extroversion stems, at least in part, from differences in the basic stimulation level of the ascending reticular activation system (ARAS) in the brainstem, commonly referred to as the attention center of the brain. Extroverts have inherently lower levels of stimulation in the ARAS and therefore require more activity in order to stimulate the attention center of the brain. Introverts, on the other hand, are already sufficiently stimulated and therefore require far less outward stimulation. Stimulant drugs such as Ritalin commonly used for treatment of attention disorders operate on this principle; by stimulating the attention center of the brain, the individual becomes less motivated to seek outward stimulation.   – M W P

eye dominance

n. A preference for using one eye over the other.

eye-movement desensitization and reprocessing

n. (EMDR) A therapeutic technique in which a person recalls traumatic events while concentrating on a moving image such as a therapist's finger, which is supposed to disrupt the motor memories of watching the traumatic event.

eye-voice span

n. In reading aloud the distance between the word being spoken and the word on which the eye is focused at a particular moment.

eyewitness testimony

n. Eyewitness testimony is the information that an individual can provide about a crime. This includes information about the perpetrator(s) as well as information about the crime and crime scene. Research has shown that factors present during the crime can influence the accuracy of an eyewitness's memory. These include duration of the event, lighting, presence of a weapon, race of the perpetrator, violence level of the event, use of disguises, and the distinctiveness of the perpetrator's physical appearance. The eyewitness's level of stress, age, biases, and expectations can also influence accuracy. When reporting the event, other factors can play a role such as the length of time between the event and questioning, the wording of the questioning, the interview technique, the use of hypnosis, the use of imagery, the construction of the lineup, the use of a mug shot search, and the presence of leading questions, suggestive comments, and misleading information.   – LMB

Eysenck Personality Inventory

n. (EPI) A self-report personality test measuring introversion-extroversion and neuroticism written by Hans Eysenck, which was later expanded into the Eysenck Personality Questionnaire.

Eysenck Personality Questionnaire

n. (EPQ and EPQ-R) A self-report personality test measuring introversion-extroversion, neuroticism, and psychoticism written by Hans Eysenck. The fourth scale, measuring social desirability, is increasingly claimed to indicate conformity as a personality trait rather than response style.

F

face (concept of)

n. The public image of one's self and especially social perceptions of one's moral character and prestige, which leads one to avoid being seen to act in ways the culture perceives as lacking good moral character. The concept of face has additional significance in many East Asian cultures.

face recognition

n. The capacity to recognize an individual by perceiving her/his face linked to the fusiform area of the visual cortex.

face validity

n. In testing, face validity refers to the degree to which the test resembles the variable being measured. Sometimes used to denote the degree to which a test includes all aspects of the variable which the test intends to measure.

facial nerve

n. Either of the seventh pair of cranial nerves, which control most of the muscles of the face, the platysmal muscle of the neck, and the sublingual glands and receive sensory input from the front two-thirds of the tongue and some skin areas of the external ear.

facilitated communication

n. **1.** A controversial technique in which facilitators help a person whose disabilities prevent him or her from communicating unaided to use a keyboard, picture board, or voice synthesizer in order to communicate. It is unclear how much of such communication is that of the disabled person and how much is the imagination of the facilitator. **2.** Communication that is enhanced technologically such as the artificial speech device used by the famed physicist Stephen Hawking.

factitious disorder
n. The intentional imitation or cause of the symptoms of a physical or mental disorder by the person who appears afflicted, usually motivated by external incentives and the adoption of a role as a sick person.

factor
n. **1.** In experimental design, any variable that may affect or cause a result. **2.** In factor analysis, a vector representing a portion of the communality of a correlation or variance matrix. **3.** In algebra, one of several quantities whose product is a term in an equation.

factor analysis
n. Any of a set of analytic techniques applied to a group of observed variables seeking to discover a smaller set of artificial variables which capture or explain the relatedness of the observed variables. Artificial variables, called factors, are selected; they pass through the densest areas in the multidimensional space created by all the variables and are then rotated, usually to select the ones which collectively account for the most linear covariance, and are most uncorrelated with one another. Some of these procedures can also be used to test whether an a priori factor structure is the best fit.

factor, fixed
n. A quasi-independent variable whose values are determined by external circumstances. Thus biological sex is usually measured as a set of two possible values, female and male.

factorial analysis of variance
n. An analysis of variance which compares the between-groups differences in the dependent variable associated with different levels in each independent variable and all combinations of the levels of the independent variables in an experimental design in which two or more independent variables are simultaneously and systematically varied so as to compare their individual and compounded influences on a dependent variable.

factorial design
n. An experimental design in which two or more independent variables are simultaneously and systematically varied so as to compare their individual and compounded influences on a dependent variable.

factorial invariance
n. The degree to which the results of a factor analysis remain unchanged when the analysis is repeated, including data from different subjects or including new variables.

factor loading
n. A numerical index reflecting the degree of relatedness between observed variables and a factor or artificial variable created in a factor analysis.

factor matrix
n. A tabular presentation of the factor loadings or intercorrelations which emerge from a factor analysis.

factor rotation
n. In factor analysis, the shifting of factors to a new configuration which satisfies an a priori criterion such as maximal independence of the factors.

factor structure
n. The set of relationships of the factors derived in a factor analysis.

faculty psychology
n. An archaic approach to psychology in which the functions of mind are divided into specialized abilities which can be improved

with practice. These faculties included will, reason, perception, instinct, and memory.

failure to thrive

n. A general decline in weight, responsiveness, and development in a child under 2 years of age associated with a lack of growth hormone. It is associated with emotional and physical neglect by the caretakers and has been found to be prevalent in highly overcrowded orphanages.

false alarm

n. In signal detection theory, the prediction of the presence of a stimulus when the stimulus is absent.

false consensus effect

n. False consensus effect is people's overestimation of the extent to which others are similar to them, in terms of attitudes, behaviors, and attributes. This effect is accentuated when the actual percentage of individuals who share the similarity is low, and attenuated when the estimation is made for an out-group. This effect may happen because people are motivated to perceive others as sharing their opinions, beliefs, or attributes. It may also result from biased recall of instances of others' opinions that are similar to one's opinions.

— EWMA, CYC

▶ *See also* **AVAILABILITY HEURISTIC** *and* **SELF-SERVING BIASES**

false memory

n. A distorted or fabricated memory sometimes produced in situations in which demands are made to remember events or details of events not actually experienced, as in cases in which clients are expected by therapists to remember incidents of childhood sexual abuse and witnesses are led or pressured by the police or an attorney to produce evidence.

false memory syndrome

n. The distorted or fabricated memory of having been sexually or physically abused during childhood, which some theorists claim occurs when psychotherapy patients are expected by therapists to remember incidents of childhood abuse.

false negative

n. In signal detection theory, a report of no signal when a signal is actually present.

false positive

n. A positive result on a test when the condition or situation is actually not present. In medical tests, a false positive might report the presence of a disease or pathogen when none is actually present.

false uniqueness effect

n. The observation that most people falsely believe themselves to have abilities, positive characteristics, or a combination of them that others do not possess.

falsifiable

adj. Having the capacity to be proved wrong. All scientific theories must be falsifiable or they cannot be tested.

family resemblance

n. In the study of categorization, the idea that category members are recognizable through a varied set of attributes, no one of which is necessary for inclusion in the category but all members share some attributes with some other members.

family therapy

n. Any form of psychotherapy that takes the family as the unit of therapy and focuses on patterns of communication and relationship within the family as targets for therapeutic change. Family therapy originated in the work of Alfred Adler and has since been taken up from numerous theoretical viewpoints such as object relations and nondirective therapy and has numerous techniques and points of focus. The single commonality is the treatment of the family as a whole at least part of the time.

F distribution

n. A graphic representation of the frequency distribution of the F statistic or ratio of the between-groups variance divided by within-groups variance with a given number of degrees of freedom.

fear of success

n. Anxiety connected with accomplishment or being seen as a success by other people, which may lead to avoidance of accomplishment or success. This was originally believed to be particularly characteristic of women who believed there was a conflict between success and femininity but has been found to be equally prevalent in men and women.

feature detection theory

n. **1.** In perception, the idea that the visual and perhaps other sensory systems have individual detectors for particular sorts of features, and perception is a process of adding the features together into perceptual wholes. **2.** In categorization, the idea that categorization of objects occurs through the breaking down of the objects into smaller units, which are compared with lists of criteria for each possible category of objects.

feature detector

n. A hypothetical neural structure that responds to stimulation from a particular kind of feature in the external world. Thus the visual system is supposed to have bar and edge detectors and a system for recognizing facial features, while the auditory system is supposed to have detectors for particular aspects of speech sounds such as voice onset time.

Fechner's law

n. The idea that the perceived intensity of a sensation increases as the log of the physical intensity of the stimulus multiplied by a constant for each sense. This implies that perception changes linearly as the stimulus changes geometrically: perceptual intensity = $k_s$log physical intensity. The constant was supposed to be different for different senses. This was an improvement on Weber's law, which had supposed that increases in sensation increased linearly with stimulus intensity, and has been largely replaced by the power law, which suggests that perceived

intensity is a power function of the physical intensity of the stimulus. Gustav Fechner was a philosopher who was pondering the mind-body problem in philosophy and believed he had discovered a proof of the existence of God by discovering a mathematical relationship between mind (perception) and body (physical stimulus).

Fechner's paradox

n. An increase in the apparent brightness of an object when looking at it with one eye after having stared at it with both eyes for a few seconds.

feedback loop

n. In cybernetic theory, the communication between a sensor and an on-off switch which controls a mechanism which affects whatever the sensor measures. As an example, a thermostat has a thermometer which feeds back temperature to the on-off switch, which turns a furnace on or off, thus raising the temperature or allowing it to cool, depending on whether the thermometer is above or below a preset limit.

female orgasmic disorder

n. A recurrent delay in or inability to reach orgasm after becoming sexually excited. Women vary widely in the type and amount of stimulation required to reach orgasm, and this diagnosis is made only if there is an inability to reach orgasm with adequate stimulation or the time and effort required to reach orgasm are beyond the normal range and cause distress to the woman or relationship difficulties for her. This diagnosis is not made if the problem is a lack of stimulation appropriate for the individual woman. This disorder is correlated with a repressive sexual upbringing.

female sexual arousal disorder

n. A persistent or recurrent inability to attain and maintain sufficient swelling and lubrication of the vulva to allow desired sexual activity. This diagnosis is not made if this inability is due to a medical condition such as menopause, estrogen deficiency, vaginal atrophy, diabetes mellitus, or radiation poisoning.

This disorder is usually related both to difficulties in becoming sexually aroused and to repressive sexual upbringing.

femininity
n. The state of embodying or displaying the characteristic appearance, traits, and behavior patterns deemed appropriate for a female within a given culture. Cross-culturally femininity includes having hips wider than the waist and a family focus including concern with child care and emotional connecting, while other dimensions such as economic activity seem more culture specific.

feral child
n. A child who is supposed to have been raised by wild animals or otherwise raised largely in isolation from human contact and control, such as the wild boy of Aveyron and Kaspar Hauser in Germany.

fertilization
n. The process of union of an ovum and a sperm cell which produces a zygote. This occurs in the fallopian tubes in human females and can occur inside or outside the body in other species. In salmon, for instance, eggs are laid in the gravel of a river bottom and then fertilized by a sperm from a cloud of semen ejected by a male salmon over the eggs.

fetal alcohol syndrome
n. (FAS) A highly variable syndrome of low birth weight, retarded growth, abnormalities in the cranium and facial bones, and neurological difficulties, which may result in behavioral difficulties and retardation associated with alcohol consumption during pregnancy. In general, the more alcohol and the earlier in pregnancy it is consumed the greater the likelihood of these symptoms.

fetish
n. 1. An object toward which an individual feels strong sexual arousal which is not usual within the person's culture. 2. A manufactured object believed to have power over other people, often containing the blood, hair, or other body part of the person being controlled. 3. In economics, the definition of social relations through the exchange values placed on different commodities, which are often very different from their use values. Thus ownership of a status symbol like a BMW is given a value larger than its utility, which is a primitive form of religious belief since it is irrational from a utilitarian point of view.

field dependence-independence
n. A dimension of cognitive style in which a person is placed on a continuum of using external or internal cues in perception and categorization. This is most commonly tested using a rod and frame device in which a frame is tilted and the degree to which this tilting affects the person's ability to judge vertical and horizontal orientation is measured.

field experiment
n. An arrangement of conditions and procedures which allows observations of the relationships between the controlled circumstances (independent variables) and the uncontrolled outcomes (dependent variables) with an intent to make inferences about causal relationships between the independent and dependent variables, which is carried out in a field setting instead of in a laboratory.

field research
n. A research methodology that requires observation of target phenomena in a natural setting (in contrast to laboratory research, which occurs in an artificial environment). Field research may vary in the degree to which the researcher observes or participates in the target setting.   – BJM

field theory
n. In psychology, a system of thought in which phenomena are explained in terms of the interrelationships between individuals and their mental situation, including the environmental, social, cognitive, and emotional elements.

figure-ground
n. A pair of terms used to describe the aspect of perception in which part of the perceptual field stands out distinctly while the rest

is perceived as somewhat vague and homo-geneous. In visual perception, the figure is seen in front of the ground, and the border between figure and ground is seen as part of the figure, although it is physically neither figure nor ground. The figure-ground orga-nization is an emergent property of the rela-tionship between the perceptual system and the stimulus, as can be seen from the capac-ity to change focus so that different parts of a perceptual field can be perceived as figure as well as the fact that some parts of a stimulus are easier to focus on than are others.

figure-ground organization
n. The aspect of perception in which part of the perceptual field stands out distinctly while the rest is perceived as somewhat vague and homogeneous. In visual perception, the figure is seen in front of the ground, and the border between figure and ground is seen as part of the figure, although it is physically neither figure nor ground. The figure-ground organization is an emergent property of the relationship between the perceptual system and the stimulus, as can be seen from the capacity to change focus so that different parts of a perceptual field can be perceived as figure as well as the fact that some parts of a stimulus are easier to focus on than are others.

figure-ground reversal
n. The capacity of the human sensory system to change focus within a perceptual field so that first one part or object and then another seems to stand out distinctly against the rest of the field, which seems homogeneous and less important. Thus if we are looking at a farm, we first might notice the barn, which stands out, and then switch focus so that we are seeing a cow clearly, in which case the barn seems less distinct and perceptually important.

figure, impossible
n. A two-dimensional picture or drawing which uses visual cues to suggest an object with mutually exclusive characteristics so that it could not exist in three-dimensional space.

file drawer problem
n. In psychology as well as most sciences, the fact that most studies are not published (exist-ing only in someone's file drawer) and so are unavailable for review, leading to much dupli-cation of effort and uncertainty as to the mean-ing of meta-analyses which use average effect size as a method for judging fields of study.

filial piety
n. Love and respect for one's parents and ancestors; the code of behavior which derives from it was considered the first virtue in Chinese culture and remains important in most Asian societies. It includes both an inner personal state and external behavior, includ-ing caring for parents, being obedient and courteous to them, producing a male heir, concealing parents' mistakes, mourning their sickness and death, and making sacrifices to their spirits after they die.

filled pause
n. A hesitation in speech which is filled by a meaningless sound or word sound, such as *um* or *er* or *like*, as in the sentence "I er went out with her for um awhile because she was like good-looking."

filter theory
n. **1.** A description of mate selection in which possible mates are ruled out in a stepwise fash-ion until only one is left. **2.** An early information processing model of attention which suggested that unattended channels of information were stopped by a cognitive filter allowing focus on a single channel, which was quickly shown to be unworkable and has been supplanted by numerous other models such as the leaky switch and various attenuation models.

finger spelling
n. The process of spelling out words using the hands to make the shape of letters, which is used in sign language to convey meanings or spell names for which there are no standard signs. Also called dactylology.

Fisher's exact test
n. A test of the significance of relationship between two categorical variables which

makes no assumptions about the population distribution and is appropriate for small samples for which a chi-square test would be inappropriate.

Fisher's *r* to *z* transformation

n. A mathematical transformation of the product-moment correlation into a *z* score which is normally distributed, making interpretation easier in some cases and also allowing testing for the significance of a difference between two correlation coefficients.

fissure

n. **1.** In physiology, the deep grooves in the brain which markedly increase its surface area and so proportion of gray matter. Also called a sulcus. **2.** Any other cleft, crack, groove, or indentation in tissue.

fit, goodness of

n. An index of the degree to which a theoretical or mathematical projection of a variable fits actual data.

five factor model ▶ *See* BIG FIVE PERSONALITY TRAITS

fixation

n. **1.** In visual perception, the process of becoming focused on a particular thing or the thing on which vision is focused. **2.** An abnormal preoccupation with a particular idea, desire, or object of desire. **3.** In psychoanalysis, a continuation of an early mode of satisfaction in later life, as in the persistence of oral or anal satisfactions in adult life.

fixed-action pattern

n. A species-specific behavioral sequence that is exhibited by all members of a species (unless sex linked) and markedly resistant to change. It is thought to be genetically determined and part of the organism's advantages that have allowed it to succeed in a particular ecological niche.

fixed effects model

n. A statistical model that stipulates that the units under analysis (people in a trial or study in a meta-analysis) constitute the entire population so that only within-study variation is taken to influence the uncertainty of results as reflected in the confidence interval of a meta-analysis. Variation between estimates of effect from each study (heterogeneity) does not affect the confidence interval in a fixed effects model.

fixed-interval schedule

n. In operant conditioning, a schedule of reinforcement in which a target behavior is reinforced the first time it is emitted after a predetermined time interval. If the time periods in a fixed-interval schedule are more than a few seconds, organisms tend to develop a pattern of responding in which there are few or no responses at the start of the interval and more toward the end of the interval. This type of schedule leads to behaviors that are more resistant to extinction than are those conditioned through continuous reinforcement.

fixedness, functional

n. The state of having a particular mind-set which does not include all aspects of the situation and so limits possible strategies in problem solving.

fixed-ratio schedule

n. In operant conditioning, a reinforcement pattern in which the target behavior is reinforced only a predetermined proportion of the time. Thus a behavior may be reinforced every 10th time it is emitted. This type of schedule leads to behaviors that are more resistant to extinction than are those conditioned through continuous reinforcement.

flashback

n. **1.** A short period of reliving the state of intoxication previously experienced under the influence of a hallucinogen, usually LSD and usually quite pleasant. **2.** A short period of reliving a traumatic incident, as is common in soldiers returning from combat and in persons who have had car accidents or similar experiences out of the normal course of events. **3.** A literary device in which the story line reverts to an earlier period of the narrative.

flashbulb memory

n. A vivid episodic memory of an emotionally significant event in which the person subjectively believes he or she remembers an unusual number of minor details with clarity although research suggests the clarity is illusory and the details are often supplied by semantic memory.

flavor

n. The perceptual quality of food or drink, which is a combination of taste, smell, texture, temperature, sound, color, and pain.

flight-or-fight response

n. A term for the stress response identified by Walter Cannon in 1939. In response to a threat or challenge, this reaction prepares an organism to respond efficiently and effectively by mobilizing mental and physical abilities. The hallmark of the response is considered to be sympathetic nervous system arousal; it increases heart rate, blood pressure, and respiration in order to allow more oxygen to reach the brain and muscles.   – TJM

flooding

n. A procedure in behavior therapy in which an individual is confronted with the thing he or she fears most, either in imagination or in real life under safe circumstances. Eventually the person becomes habituated to it, and the initial fear responses gradually diminish and disappear. Also called exposure therapy.

floor effect

n. In measurement and statistics, a lower limit of a variable which skews the distribution of scores. Thus a test with a floor effect is too difficult for the sample on which it is being used, as many scores accumulate at the bottom end of the range of scores and make impossible a discrimination among the low scorers on the characteristic being measured.

fluid intelligence

n. The ability to adapt to new knowledge or information and think in flexible ways. Fluid intelligence also includes the ability to understand and make conceptual relations. Often tested on intelligence tests, fluid intelligence includes examination of inductive reasoning and complex problem solving skills. Research suggests a decline in fluid intelligence throughout adulthood.   – SRB

fluphenazine

n. An antipsychotic drug of the phenothiozine group of drugs which is soluble in oil and often given by means of injection, allowing long periods between doses. It tends to produce marked extrapyramidal and neuromuscular side effects colloquially known as the Prolixin stomp. Also called Prolixin.

Flynn effect

n. The Flynn effect is the continued rise in intelligence test scores from generation to generation that has been universally detected across all measured populations. Named for its discoverer, James R. Flynn, the Flynn effect shows an average increase in intelligence test scores of approximately 3 points per decade, although the rate of increase varies somewhat from country to country. In addition, there is some evidence that the rate of increase is accelerating. While the Flynn effect appears regardless of the specific intelligence test examined, the greatest gains in intelligence occur on tests targeting fluid intelligence rather than crystallized intelligence. Because intelligence test norms are restandardized periodically to maintain the average score of 100, the Flynn effect was not detected until cross-generational comparisons of scores were conducted. On the surface, the Flynn effect seems to provide evidence that each generation is progressively more intelligent than previous populations, but Flynn does not support this explanation. Rather, he proposes that societal advances in the promotion of abstract thinking, combined with the emphasis of this skill in traditional intelligence tests, are responsible for the apparent increase in intelligence. In addition, other theorists have hypothesized that the gains in intelligence may be attributed to increased education, enhanced nutrition, adaptation to time-limited testing, and the trend toward smaller families. Despite the clear, consistent trends identified by the Flynn effect, there is still considerable controversy in explaining the roots of this phenomenon.   – BJM

fMRI

n. The use of an MRI to detect which brain areas are active while performing different tasks by detecting the increased blood flow to the activated areas. ▶ *See also* **FUNCTIONAL MAGNETIC RESONANCE IMAGING**

folie à deux

n. A delusion shared by two individuals. The individuals involved usually share a close relationship either by kinship or romance.

folk psychology

n. **1.** The common beliefs of persons in any culture about the workings of the mind and their interaction with behavior. **2.** An older name for cultural psychology, which is the field of study that examines the study of psychology within different cultures. **3.** The study of cultural products as a means of understanding the workings of the minds of individuals within the culture.

follicle-stimulating hormone

n. (FSH) A hormone produced in the pituitary gland that migrates to the gonads. It stimulates the development of the Graafian follicles in the ovaries, which are the egg-producing cells there, and it stimulates the Sertoli cells in the testes to produce sperm.

foot-candle

n. A unit of measure of the intensity of light, now largely replaced by the lux, so that 1 foot-candle = 10.76 lux.

foot-in-the-door phenomenon

n. A manipulative technique for gaining compliance in which a small and socially common request is made and when compliance is gained, a large and uncommon request, which is made harder to refuse after agreeing to the initial request, follows.

foot-in-the-door technique

n. The foot-in-the-door (FITD) technique is used to elicit a desired behavior via a two-step process. First, a requester asks an individual to help with a very small request, to which almost everyone agrees. Upon gaining agreement with the first task, the requester asks the individual

to aid with a second, larger request, which is frequently related to the first. The requester's original goal was always to garner agreement with this second request; therefore, gaining agreement with the first appeal was simply a means to an end. Having already agreed to help with the first task makes it more likely that someone will agree to help with the second request, compared to a situation in which that person had not helped in the first place.

The FITD technique is applied in a variety of settings, including charity fund-raising. For example, a common application of this technique is first to ask individuals to sign a petition in support of some cause (a seemingly harmless task), then to follow that request with a plea for monetary donations for the same cause (a more costly request). After agreeing to sign the petition in support of a particular cause, individuals are more likely to agree to donate money to that cause than if they had not originally signed the petition. Other applications of the FITD technique have been in sales settings (e.g., testimonial contests simply asking potential customers to describe why they like a particular brand increases the likelihood they will purchase that brand in the future) and health settings (e.g., first asking individuals to quit cigarette smoking for a short period increases the likelihood they will later give up cigarette smoking for a longer period).

Several theories explain why the FITD technique increases agreement with requests. One is self-perception theory, which states that people can infer their attitudes from their behavior. Having agreed to sign a petition for a cause, an individual can infer that he or she supports the cause. Thus, when asked to donate money for the same cause, the individual is likely to act in accordance with the inferred attitude that the cause is worth supporting by donating money.

Another common explanation for the effectiveness of the FITD technique in eliciting desired behaviors is consistency theory. According to consistency theory, after agreeing to help with an initial request in support of some cause, individuals would appear to be inconsistent to the requester if they did not agree to help with the target request. Such inconsistency creates an unpleasant

feeling. People may agree to help with the second, costly request to avoid the feeling resulting from behaving inconsistently.
                                        – AEC, LAB

foramen magnum

n. The large opening at the bottom of the skull through which the spinal cord and vertebral arteries pass.

forced-choice

n. A task format in which a subject must choose one of a preset number of choices such as true-false, present-absent, or a, b, c, or d.

forebrain

n. The front part of the brain, including the cerebral hemispheres, thalamus, hypothalamus, basal ganglia, and hippocampus, which develops from the anterior portion of the neural tube during gestation.

foreign language effect

n. A temporary decline in the thinking ability of people who are using a foreign language in which they are less proficient than in their native tongue.

foreign language processing difficulties

n. Problems associated with learning in a foreign language, such as taking more time to respond and experiencing cognitive difficulties while processing information.

forensic psychology

n. The branch of psychology that applies the theories, techniques, and findings of psychology to legal proceedings including psychological assessment; it includes diagnosis, expert testimony, treatment of those labeled as criminal or criminally insane, research on legal issues, and the analysis of the effect of laws on individuals and groups.

forgetting

n. The process of losing information from memory.

formal operations stage

n. In Piagetian psychology, the last stage in the intellectual development, characterized by logical and systematic thinking including abstract ideas. It includes hypothetico-deductive reasoning, scientific-inductive reasoning, and reflective abstraction.

form constancy

n. The tendency of humans to perceive that the shape of an object remains constant despite the fact that the light reflecting from the object and striking the retina will vary with angle, illumination, movement, and other variables. Thus, when we see a square, we perceive it as remaining square even if we move so that it begins to look like a diamond or trapezoid when seen at an angle. Also called shape constancy.

fornix

n. **1.** In psychology, the arching neural tract between the hippocampus and the mammillary bodies of the hypothalamus. **2.** In biology, any bodily structure resembling an arch.

forward masking

n. Forward masking is a form of masking in which the mask (an image, a tone, or a chemical) temporally precedes a target (i.e., a to-be-identified item). The target can occur immediately after the mask or after some delay. The difficulty in one's ability to perceive the target in this situation is referred to as the masking effect. This effect is influenced by the interval between the presentation of the mask and the target, the location of the mask and target relative to each other (e.g., whether two images are superimposed or not), the intensity of the mask and target (e.g., the brightness of a letter), as well as other characteristics (e.g., direction of the line segments). All else being equal, masking is generally stronger as the interval between the presentation of the mask and that of the target is reduced.   – DGr
  ▶ *See also* **MASKING**

fourfold-point correlation

n. A linear index of the degree of relationship between two dichotomous and randomly distributed variables which equals the product-moment correlation if the variables are coded using 0 and 1 for the dichotomous values. Also called the phi coefficient.

Fourier analysis

n. A mathematical process in which any extended pattern of variability can be reduced to a series of sine waves which add up to the original pattern. It is particularly important in the study of hearing and vision, as our sensory systems accomplish the same tasks as a Fourier analysis in forming percepts from the raw data of air pressure variations and light patterns.

fovea

n. A small depression in the retina of the eye in which light receptor cells (cones and some rods) are most densely packed and onto which the center of the visual field is projected and most clearly focused. Also called fovea centralis.

fragile X chromosome syndrome

n. A genetic defect in which the long arm of the X chromosome often breaks off, leading to mental retardation. This syndrome is more common in males and is the second leading cause of mental retardation among males and often accompanied by attention deficit–hyperactivity syndrome or autism. Although there are no definitive physical characteristics for the syndrome, it is associated with large testes, large ears, long face, and malocclusion of the teeth. Also called the Martin-Bell syndrome.

framing

n. The process of constructing the mental set or context within which experience and thought occur, which tends to constrain thinking within the mental set and thus influences and limits perception and judgment.

framing effect

n. The limiting and directing effects of adopting a particular mental set.

fraternal twins

n. Two children who develop from different zygotes, share their mother's womb during gestation, and are born at nearly the same time.

F ratio

n. In an analysis of variance, a ratio of the between-groups variance divided by the within-groups variance in a comparison.

free association

n. The process of verbalizing whatever enters the mind without censorship or conscious selection no matter how embarrassing, immoral, illogical, or silly it may seem to the person doing the free associating. It is used in psychoanalytic therapy to preclude the second censorship between the preconscious and conscious and so better allow the therapist to discover patterns within the mind of the client.

free-floating anxiety

n. Vague and chronic fear without object or apparent cause. This is a usual symptom of generalized anxiety disorder but is not sufficient for such a diagnosis.

free nerve ending

n. The branched ending of the axon of a neuron located primarily in the skin, which is believed to be a pain or temperature receptor.

free operant

n. Any response that may be emitted at any time in a particular situation before any schedules of reinforcement have been applied to the behavior.

free recall

n. A memory task in which people are asked to remember particular information in any order with minimal cuing. In remembering lists, it is usual for the first and last items to be recalled best, with accuracy diminishing toward the middle of the list from both ends.

free response

n. Any behavior that may be emitted at any time in a particular situation before any schedules of reinforcement have been applied to the behavior.

free will

n. The idea or belief that individual people have volition and the capacity to choose their own courses of action without being fully determined by internal or external forces.

frequency

n. 1. The number of regularly periodic waveforms that occur in a given amount of time. A normal human auditory system can hear air pressure waves with frequencies between about 20 and 20,000 cycles per second. 2. The number of observations of a particular kind in a data set. In a class of 20 persons the frequency of A grades might be 4.

frequency distribution

n. A graphic representation of the number of occurrences at each level of a variable, usually arranged from lowest to highest.

frequency polygon

n. A graphic representation of the number of occurrences at each level of a variable, usually arranged from lowest to highest with the high point of each category connected with a line.

frequency theory

n. A theory of pitch perception in which it is supposed that the ear converts air pressure waves into nerve impulses by sending one impulse for each cycle of the air pressure wave. The neural system has a maximal firing rate of about 500 cycles per second, and so this may occur at low frequencies but cannot account for high-frequency hearing, which normally extends up to 18,000–20,000 cycles per second.

Freudian

adj. Of or relating to Sigmund Freud, his theories, or his works.

frigidity

n. For a woman, the state of lacking sexual desire or being unable to reach orgasm. This is a nonclinical term with somewhat vague boundaries and has been applied to women with a wide variety of sexual preferences or problems.

frontal lobe

n. The part of the cerebral cortex in front of the central sulcus which is involved in executive functions and motor control.

frontal lobe syndrome

n. Usually used as synonymous with dysexecutive syndrome. It is also referred to as prefrontal syndrome.   – A A
▶ See also EXECUTIVE FUNCTIONS and PREFRONTAL CORTEX

frontal lobotomy

n. A surgical procedure in which the connections between the frontal lobe and the rest of the brain are cut or in which part or all of the frontal lobe is removed. This surgical procedure was used in attempts to cure depression, schizophrenia, epilepsy, anxiety, aggressiveness, and pain but was discontinued in the 1950s after it was generally accepted that it produced a kind of generalized apathy and lack of self-direction. Also called a frontal leucotomy.

frontal section

n. A vertical cross section through the brain that divides the front or anterior portion from the back or posterior portion. Also called coronal section.

front horizontal foreshortening theory

n. The idea that in viewing drawings, pictures, or other two-dimensional representations of things, we interpret vertical lines as horizontal lines extending into the distance.

frotteurism

n. A sexual behavior in which sexual arousal is achieved through touching or rubbing up against a nonconsenting person, often accompanied by sexual or romantic fantasy. This is primarily an activity associated with sexually frustrated young men between the ages of 15 and 25.

frozen noise

n. A recorded sample of white noise that is played over and over again in experiments in which it is desirable to avoid the inherent variation of white noise and to ensure each experimental condition hears the same background noise.

frustration

n. 1. The blocking of or preventing the success of attempts to obtain something desirable.

2. The emotional reaction to the blocking of attempts to obtain something desirable.

frustration-aggression hypothesis

n. The idea that all aggression has as its motivation some form of frustration and that all frustration produces aggression in either overt or covert form.

F scale

n. On the Minnesota Multiphasic Personality Inventory (MMPI), a scale composed of items which are answered in the scored direction by less than 5% and often less than 1% of the population used to detect randomly answered test protocols.

F statistic

n. In an analysis of variance, a ratio of the between-groups variance divided by the within-groups variance in a comparison.

F test

n. In an analysis of variance, the ratio of the between-groups variance divided by the within-groups variance in a comparison to a critical value.

fugue

n. A disorder characterized by sudden unplanned flight from one's usual circumstances, coupled with partial or complete amnesia for one's personal history and uncertainty as to personal identity. Also called dissociative fugue disorder.

Fullerton-Cattell law

n. The idea that the minimal amount of change in stimulus intensity needed to be detectable by humans is proportional to the square root of the intensity. In equation form this is

$$\Delta I \approx k\sqrt{I}.$$

functional

adj. **1.** Of or relating to utility rather than structure. **2.** In psychological and medical disorders, of or relating to changes in behavior or action without apparent physical or neurological changes.

functional analysis

n. **1.** An analysis of a complex system to determine the functions of the varied aspects of the system and their interrelation in action. **2.** In operant conditioning, an analysis of the schedules of reinforcement that maintain a behavior or pattern of behaviors.

functional analysis of behavior

n. An analysis of an individual's behaviors and the schedules of reinforcement that maintain behaviors or patterns of behavior.

functional autonomy

n. The tendency for motives and ideas to become independent of the circumstances in which they were first acquired. Thus a person may begin playing the piano because his or her mother makes him or her do it but continue to do so because it has become pleasurable in and of itself. Similarly ideas such as democracy may originally be values because they are presented with approval by authority figures but later be valued for other reasons.

functional fixedness

n. A mental block against using an object in a new way that is required to solve a problem. The state of having acquired a mind-set about the utility of an object and being unable to think outside that mind-set.

functionalism

n. A general point of view in psychology that analyzes mental and behavioral phenomena in terms of actively adapting the organism to its environment within an evolutionary framework. This was particularly applied to education, which was understood as having functional value in the life of the student and the society. Also called functional psychology.

functional magnetic resonance imaging

n. (fMRI) The use of an MRI to detect which brain areas are active while performing different tasks by detecting the increased blood flow to the activated areas.

functional MRI ▶ *See* FUNCTIONAL MAG-
NETIC RESONANCE IMAGING

functional psychology

n. A general point of view in psychology
that analyzes mental and behavioral phenomena in terms of actively adapting the
organism to its environment within an evolutionary framework. This was particularly
applied to education, which was understood as
having functional value in the life of the student
and the society. Also called functionalism.

function type

n. Any of the personality types identified by
Carl Jung, including the rational types, thinking and feeling, and the irrational types, sensing and intuiting, as well as extroverts and
introverts.

function word

n. Function words are words that serve a
grammatical function inside a sentence. In
contrast to content words (e.g., nouns, verbs,
and adjectives), which carry meaning and
which make up an infinite class, function
words do not carry meaning but serve to
perform grammatical functions and always
make up a finite class in any given language. In
English, the class of function words includes
prepositions (*in, at, on, . . .*), modal and auxiliary verbs (*can, may, have*), conjunctions (*and,
or, . . .*), pronouns (*I, you, she, . . .*), determiners
(*the, a, . . .*). The grammatical functions such
words perform include providing information on person, number, gender, tense, mood,
aspect, and so forth.   – EMF

fundamental attribution error

n. Fundamental attribution error is the tendency to make dispositional attributions

when explaining other people's behaviors,
even when there is an obvious situational
explanation for the behaviors. For example,
the perceiver may attribute a student's good
performance in a statistics class to his or
her quantitative ability (a dispositional attribution) even when the class is known to
be easy (situational explanation). The term
suggests that individuals spontaneously use
dispositional explanations to understand behavior. This may happen because the actor
is the most salient aspect of the perceptual
field, and the stimulus that engulfs the field
is likely to be viewed as having causal power.
                                    – EWMA, CYC

▶ *See also* DISPOSITIONAL INFERENCE,
LAY DISPOSITIONAL THEORY, *and* LAY DIS-
POSITIONISM

fundamental color

n. Red, blue, and yellow or green, which can
be mixed to obtain white. From the point
of view of the human visual system, all four
colors are primary as they correspond to the
wavelengths of particular visual receptors.
Also called primary colors.

fuzzy logic

n. A branch of mathematics in which items
have probabilities of being included in any set
rather than clearly defined membership. Thus
some items have higher probabilities of being
included in a set than others, and items may
have nonzero probabilities of being included in
two sets that would be mutually exclusive were
they defined by either-or rules. This theoretical approach has been widely used in computer
science, where it finds applications in control and expert systems. It has also been used
to model the prototype approach to human
categorization.

GABA

n. Gamma-amino butyric acid, a common inhibitory neurotransmitter in the human central nervous system. When released in the synaptic cleft, GABA tends to inhibit the axon from creating action potentials and thus sending a message to other neurons.

GABA receptor complex

n. The structure in some neurons that has three types of receptor sites, to one of which GABA binds; another binds sedative and hypnotic drugs such as the barbiturates and is blocked by convulsive drugs; the third binds benzodiazepines. This complex is generally inhibitory in its effect on the neuron and on neurons farther away in the pathway to which the neuron is attached, while convulsant drugs promote stimulation in the same neurons and pathways.

Gage, Phineas

n. A man injured in a mining accident when an explosion shot a steel rod over 3 feet long and over 1 inch in diameter through his head, from below his left cheek out through the top behind his left eye, destroying the left prefrontal cortex. He survived but with a markedly altered personality. The case is important because it linked the forebrain to higher mental functions and showed it was not necessary for basic life support functions.

Galton whistle

n. A crude variable pitch whistle invented by Francis Galton used to determine the upper frequency limits of auditory perception in animals and humans. It was the first to show that dogs and other animals can hear pitches beyond the human range of hearing.

galvanic skin response

n. (GSR) A change in the level or degree to which the skin conducts electricity, which tends to decrease when subcutaneous muscles relax and to increase when those muscles tense and is used as a crude estimate of general bodily tension. This has been used in crude and usually inaccurate attempts to create a lie detector.

gambler's fallacy

n. An erroneous belief that random events such as occur in honest games of chance are self-correcting processes so that a run of bad luck will correct itself with an equal run of good luck. In actuality a chance process is not affected by prior occurrences so that after tossing a coin and getting 10 heads in a row, the occurrence of a tail on the next toss remains the same as if any other result had occurred in the previous 10 tosses.

gambling, pathological

n. Persistent and recurrent gambling that disrupts personal, family, and vocational functioning. Individuals with this disorder are often preoccupied with gambling, ruminating over losses and planning their next gambling episode and scheming to get money with which to gamble. *See also* pathological gambling

gamete

n. Either the ovum or the sperm, which must unite to form a zygote in the process of sexual reproduction. Each gamete has half the number of chromosomes that is present in the rest of the cells in the body, and these join to form the chromosomes in all the cells in the new body excepting the new gametes, which will have half of the chromosomes from each of the parent gametes.

game theory

n. A mathematical approach to describing how people make constrained choices with the intention of understanding human conflict. Experimental games are usually set up so that there is a possibility of both competition and cooperation, and game theory examines the circumstances and personal characteristics associated with the choices made.

gamma-amino butyric acid

n. (GABA) A common inhibitory neurotransmitter in the human central nervous system. When released in the synaptic cleft, GABA tends to inhibit the axon from creating action potentials and thus sending a message to other neurons.

gamma motor neuron

n. A kind of motor neuron in the gamma tract of the spine which controls the sensitivity of muscle spindles.

ganglion

n. A collection of neuronal cell bodies outside the central nervous system except for the basal ganglia. Many organisms do not have a central nervous system and instead have one or more ganglia distributed through their bodies.

ganglion cell

n. **1.** Any neuron making up the retinal layer closest to the front of the eye, which receives inputs from bipolar and amacrine cells. There are several types of retinal ganglion cells. On or off ganglion cells respond oppositely to a spot of light and are inhibited by a ring of light around the spot in a particular area of the retina. There are also large ganglion cells, which form the front layer of ganglions and are simply additive in their reactions to inputs from all three types of cones, in contrast with small ganglion cells, which are differentially activated by different types of cones. **2.** Any neuron whose cell body is located within a ganglion.

Ganzfeld

n. An undifferentiated visual field characterized by dim white light in which a person looking into such a field is eventually unable to make visual distinctions; it is also called snow blindness. This can be produced experimentally by having people look into translucent white plastic hemispheres through which dim light is shining.

Garcia effect

n. One-trial learning in which an animal learns to avoid a food after it has been sickened and especially if it has regurgitated after having eaten that food, whereas other stimuli such as buzzers and flashing lights do not produce such one-trial learning. This was important in showing that not all learning is equivalent, as had been supposed by behavioral theorists. Garcia's ideas were so controversial he was not awarded his doctorate until 17 years after he left graduate school and his ideas had gained wide acceptance.

gate-control theory

n. A theory of pain in which it is supposed that there are neural gates in the spinal cord which regulate the amount of pain information flowing up the spinal cord to the brain and thus modulate pain perception. The gate consist of large sensory nerve fibers not directly connected in pain transmission, whose firing inhibits the small pain fibers from firing.

gating

n. The exclusion from conscious experience of some sensory information while attention is focused on either other sensory information or internal processes such as thoughts or images.

gaze aversion

n. Active avoidance of eye contact with another person. This is characteristic of normal people in moments of embarrassment or when feeling submissive or wishing to avoid direct communication in most Western cultures and is normal behavior in many non-Western cultures. It is also typical of autistic individuals all or most of the time in all cultures.

gender

n. **1.** The condition of being female, male, neuter, or androgynous. In recent times there has been a differentiation between sex and gender in describing human beings and to a lesser extent other animals such that *sex* refers to the biological aspects of femaleness and maleness while *gender* refers to the cultural, social, and psychological aspects of being defined as female or male. **2.** The categories into which nouns are divided and marked as having gender in some languages such as French and Spanish. Thus *house* is feminine (*la maison*) and *cat* (*le chat*) is masculine in French.

gender difference

n. Any usual or statistically significant variance of a trait or other characteristic between those who identify as men and those who identify as women within a particular culture. These frequently include differences in available social roles, careers, economic motivation and style of achievement, communication styles, person versus task orientation, aesthetic sensitivity, and sexual motivation.

gender dysphoria

n. The psychological state of discomfort or dissatisfaction with the individual's social assignment as either male or female, usually made on the basis of the genitalia. The person does not experience a tolerable unity of personal gender identity, anatomical sexual characteristics, and the social expression of a corresponding gender role. There are multiple contributing factors and social manifestations. Some individuals may seek to alter physical aspects of their bodies associated with being male, female, or in-between. Other individuals may seek to alter the way they participate in male or female or transgendered social roles, or their internalized conceptualizations of their gender.   — GKL

gender identity

n. Gender identity is the identification of oneself as female or male; that means that gender identity is a cognitive process distinct from gender role behaviors. Gender identity development begins during early childhood. To develop gender identity, a child must gain some knowledge of categories of gender, what distinguishes the two sexes, what labels apply to each, and how she or he fits into one (and not the other) category. During the development of gender identity, children experience some confusion and make mistakes in their classifications, which may continue until about age 8 years.   — LB

gender identity disorder

n. Gender identity disorder (GID) is a problem in accepting the gender identity that matches an individual's biological sex. Symptoms of GID appear during childhood and include a combination of cross-sex behaviors, toy preferences, and activity preferences, combined with cross-dressing and choice of other-sex rather than same-sex friends. The most revealing symptom of GID is a child's stated and repeated desire to be the other sex. The DSM-IV-TR recognizes GID as a mental disorder among children but includes no equivalent diagnosis for adults. Boys are more often diagnosed with GID than girls, and as adults individuals with GID often seek sexual reassignment surgery.   — LB

gender role

n. A gender role is a learned set of behaviors associated with women or men. These behaviors are so strongly associated with each sex that the set of behaviors comes to define masculinity and femininity in any given culture. The underlying basis for gender roles is biological sex differences, but most authorities agree that gender role behaviors are learned. Children receive messages about gender role behaviors through rewards for performing some behaviors and punishments for other behaviors. Children also learn gender roles through the processes of observing other people. By observing and modeling others who are attractive or similar to them, children learn a wide variety of gender-related behaviors. Gender roles exist in all cultures, but the specific behaviors that are associated with the female or male gender role vary across cultures, making gender roles universal yet specific to each culture.   — LB

gender role ideology

n. Gender role ideology is the conception of what gender roles should be, which may vary from gender role behaviors. Gender role ideology varies along a dimension that ranges from *traditional* to *egalitarian*. Those with traditional gender role ideology believe that men and women have different natures and abilities and thus should have different appearances and behaviors. Both women and men may hold traditional gender ideology, but men are more likely to do so than women. Those with an egalitarian gender role ideology believe that men and women should be treated equally. People with this ideology may hold varying beliefs about the underlying natures of women and men, but they believe that neither women nor men should be discriminated for or against on the basis of their sex. Both women and men may hold egalitarian gender ideology, but women are more likely to do so than men.   – LB

gender schema (theory)

n. The idea that children learn what it means to be male and female from the culture in which they are raised; it is stored in the mind as mental models and these mental models condition expectations of self and others so that the individual's behavior and understanding are controlled to fit into cultural expectations of men and women within the culture.

gender stereotype

n. The beliefs about differences between men and women and differences in what is appropriate for each that are generally held within a culture. Some cultures hold these beliefs more rigidly than others and tend to be punitive toward those who do not conform to the stereotypes while other cultures are neither rigid nor punitive toward nonconformists.

gender-typing

n. The process of forming or applying expectations about differences in behavior between men and women.

gene

n. A basic unit of heredity, which is composed of a promoter region which controls the action of a gene and a coding sequence which can act as a template to form RNA, which in turn serves as a template to produce proteins, which are the building blocks of the body. Genes control the form of the body by controlling which proteins are produced and where and when and how many are produced. The proteins from some genes determine some bodily characteristics, but more often a combination of genes control the characteristics of the body in interaction with the environment.

gene expression

n. **1.** The production of proteins through the creation of RNA by a gene. **2.** The appearance of the characteristics associated with a gene in the phenotype or actual organism. Many genes are not expressed or only partially expressed because of the presence of a more dominant gene controlling the same feature or lack of environmental opportunity for the expression of a gene.

gene frequency

n. The frequency of a particular version of a gene or allele in a population relative to the frequency of other versions or alleles.

gene pool

n. The total number of genes and their variations present in an interbreeding population of a species at a given time.

general ability ▶ *See* **GENERAL INTELLIGENCE**

general adaptation syndrome

n. (GAS) A description of response to chronic stress in three stages: alarm, resistance, and exhaustion. In the first stage of response to stress, the body first goes into shock, in which body temperature, blood pressure, tissue water level, and muscle tone drop, and then into arousal or countershock, in which there is arousal of the sympathetic nervous system into its flight-or-fight stance. The second stage is becoming subjectively accustomed to the elevated blood pressure and hormone levels and decreased digestive and immune function characteristic of sympathetic arousal. These changes can lead to organ damage if arousal continues chronically. In the exhaustion stage there is a breakdown of function characterized by sleep disturbance, restlessness, irritability, anxiety, crying fits, depression, loss of concentration, becoming easily startled, disturbed coordination, and tremor. The probability of illness is significantly raised after prolonged stress.

general intelligence

n. (g) A theoretical construct that assumes there is a generalized mental ability underlying the various skills and abilities measured by traditional intelligence tests. Based on factor analysis, the general intelligence (g) factor gains support from the positive correlations typically found on the subtest scores of intelligence tests. These positive correlations are then attributed to the existence of a larger factor, general intelligence, which is primarily responsible for all subtest abilities. Despite a large body of evidence supporting biological and social correlates of the general intelligence factor, the existence of the g factor is quite controversial. Opponents of the g factor challenge the existence of a unitary intelligence and criticize the role of traditional intelligence testing in measuring cognitive potential.   – BJM

general intelligence factor ▶ *See* **GENERAL INTELLIGENCE**

generalization
n. **1.** A statement of widely applicable principle which is held to be true in all or at least most circumstances. **2.** The process of applying an idea or practice derived from specific cases to all cases in general. **3.** In learning, the appearance of a response to stimuli or situations different from but resembling those in the original conditioning situation.

generalization gradient
n. A graphic representation of the decline in the magnitude of response by an organism to stimuli as they vary from the conditioned stimulus. Thus if a dog is conditioned to salivate when it hears a bell ring, then the dog will salivate to another bell but less than it will to the original bell. The reduction in salivation depends on how similar the new bell is to the original bell.

generalization, response
n. The observation that when a response is reinforced, it increases the likelihood of similar responses to a degree related to their similarity to the conditioned response.

generalization, stimulus
n. The observation that when a stimulus produces a response, similar stimuli will also produce the same response although with lower frequency or intensity than will the original stimulus.

generalized anxiety disorder
n. A disorder characterized by excessive anxiety and worry more days than not for at least 6 months. During this period the individual tends to feel restless, keyed up, and on edge and is easily fatigued, has difficulty in concentrating and has a tendency for the mind to go blank, is irritable, and experiences muscle tension and sleep disturbance.

generalized habit strength
n. The strength of a habit in a particular situation. This depends on the similarity of the present situation to the situation(s) in which the habit was originally conditioned as well as the habit strength in the original situation.

general psychology
n. **1.** The study of basic principles of human mental functioning and behavioral control. **2.** A name for an introductory or survey course in psychology, which usually includes a section on each major field within psychology including research methods and statistics, personality, social psychology, biological psychology, human development, learning, sensation and perception, cognition, measurement, abnormal and clinical psychology, and motivation.

generational gap
n. Generational differences due to life-cycle changes associated with aging or to historical and socialization experiences between birth cohorts have been around since antiquity, but it was not until the 1960s that the term *generational gap* became prominent. Rock music, long hair, marijuana, premarital sex, and student protests against the Vietnam War that were popular among baby boomers (born between 1946 and 1964) alarmed the "silent generation" (born between 1929 and 1945). Later, boomers were at odds with their juniors (Generation X), who thought boomers had "sold out" their youthful ideals of the 1960s. The next upcoming birth cohort, Generation Y (born between 1978

and 1994), is marked by its computer savvy, adept access to digital information, and self-absorption in the cyber culture. As these computer-mediated activities and life-style habits are often segregated from their elders, feelings of mystery mixed with suspicion among the latter may lead to another generation gap.   – SHN

generation effect

n. The observation that memory for items in memory studies is better if the subjects help to generate the items. Thus if part of the learning includes a task such as saying what the opposite of *high* is, then the word *low* will be better remembered than if the word *low* was simply read or repeated in the learning period. ▶ *See also* **DEPTH OF PROCESSING**

generative grammar

n. A description of language in terms of a finite set of explicit rules capable of generating the unlimited set of grammatical utterances of human beings in a language without error or addition. Also called psycholinguistics.

generativity versus stagnation

n. In Erik Erikson's epigenetic cycle of development, the possible outcomes of development in middle adulthood when the individual is the generator of the culture. In this period of life one has the fullest capacity to use her/his creative potential and to do so must find multiple roles in society to allow these developments in ways that both fulfill the individual and contribute to society. A failure to do this results in both a sense of futility and a sense of personal failure, which often leads to defensiveness about self and a projection of blame for the futility and failure onto others. As one ages and recognizes that the end of life approaches, there is a growing sense of urgency to do it now, which can create a crisis in the middle of life.

generator potential

n. A change in the electric potential across the membrane of a sensory receptor resulting from a sensory stimulus, which tends to change the likelihood of an action potential in an associated sensory neuron in either a positive or a negative direction. Also known as a receptor potential.

genetic counseling

n. The interactive process of providing personal information to individuals, couples, or, occasionally, families about genetic testing and reproductive risks associated with the results of genetic tests, as well as dealing with the psychological effects such information may have on the individuals involved. This can include providing information about genetic defects and their probabilities and likely effects, options for monitoring during pregnancy and terminating pregnancy, as well as referral to psychotherapists or other medical practitioners.

genetic dominance

n. The degree to which one gene's expression takes precedence over another gene in the same cell or organism which governs the same processes. Thus the gene(s) for brown eyes is dominant over the gene for blue eyes when both occur in the cells of the same organism.

genetic dominance and recessiveness

n. The relative likelihood that one versus another form (or allele) of a gene will find expression in the body of the individual who has both genes. Thus the gene(s) for brown eyes exercises dominance over the gene for blue eyes, which is recessive, when both occur in the cells of the same organism.

genetic drift

n. Change in the relative frequencies of genes in a population across generations due to mutation rather than natural selection.

genetic epistemology

n. The psychology of Jean Piaget, which focuses on the development of understanding in the child. It involves the ideas that knowledge becomes more organized and adaptive as a child grows and that this is dependent on the active construction of mental facilities by the child in attempting to deal with the demands of a complex and changing environment.

genetic fitness

n. The degree to which an organism is adapted to its environment so that it can survive and produce viable offspring and, in some cases, rear offspring to reproductive age so that its genes and alleles are passed on to a new generation. Relative genetic fitness is the likelihood that one's particular complement of gene forms (alleles) versus another's increases or decreases in the next generation.

genetic psychology

n. **1.** The study of genetic and early environmental influences on the development of the child. **2.** An archaic term for developmental psychology.

genetics

n. The interdisciplinary study of genes, heredity, and variability among species. It includes the specialty areas of classical genetics, behavioral genetics, clinical genetics, molecular genetics, population geneticsm, and genomics.

genital stage

n. In psychoanalytic theory, the adult stage in mental and physical development from puberty onward. It is characterized by the emergence of mature genital focus, overt sexuality, and the inclusion of sexuality in the self-concept.

genotype

n. **1.** The genetic makeup of an individual. This is opposed to the phenotype, which is the actual body of an individual, which is influenced both by genetics and interaction with the environment so that two individuals with the same genotype will have differences due to both the uterine and postuterine environments. Thus some people who have had their pet cats cloned have been surprised to find they do not have the same color fur nor the same disposition as their original pets had. **2.** The particular variant of a gene possessed by an individual.

Gestalt

n. A perceptual whole that is more than the sum of its parts and cannot be completely described in terms of its parts.

Gestalt laws of organization

n. A set of observations about the interrelation between aspects of the physical world and the formation of perceptual wholes by humans. These include the laws of grouping, closure, common fate, continuity, proximity, similarity, and symmetry.

Gestalt psychology

n. A school of thought in psychology that focused on perception and emphasized the organization of experience into wholes that were more than the sums of their parts. It developed the Gestalt laws of perceptual organization and applied them to other areas of psychology. It also was the first modern point of view that emphasized creative insight in problem solving.

Gestaltqualität

n. A perceptual attribute or quality that emerges from the organization of sensory elements but is not reducible to the sum of those elements. A melody is a good example of this. The melody is not in the notes as the melody's key can be changed so none of the notes are the same, and the original notes can be rearranged so as to form a different melody.

Gestalt therapy

n. An approach to psychotherapy that combined the ideas of Gestalt formation with an existential framework. In Gestalt therapy the therapist feeds back observations about a client's behavior in the present moment, asks the client about his or her experience in the present moment, and has him/her engage in activities mimicking the experienced ideas, emotions, or conflicts. These systematically frustrate the client's avoidance of present experience until he/she experiences a Gestalt or completion of the avoidance and enters the experience of the here and now.

gestural language

n. **1.** A complete language independent of spoken language such as American Sign Language. **2.** Communication via body movements understood by other members of a species in nonhuman animals. **3.** A nonverbal form of communication based on culturally meaningful gestures which can accompany, modify, and amplify a spoken language or be used in place of the spoken language.

g factor
n. The hypothesized portion of ability in any specific task that is associated or correlated with most or all other intellectual tasks. Following the theories of Francis Galton, Robert Spearman hypothesized that the ability to accomplish all tasks is composed of task-specific abilities, which he designated as *s*, plus a general ability, which he designated *g* for "general ability."

ghost in the machine
n. A phrase coined by Arthur Koestler to note the problem of the interrelation of the mind and body in a Cartesian system in which they are believed to be separate.

Gilles de la Tourette's syndrome
n. A tic disorder characterized by a combination of facial tics and vocal tics, which may be yelps, grunts, snarls, words, or obscenities. Also called Tourette's disorder.

gland
n. Any organ whose function includes the secretion of a substance needed by the body. Glands which excrete substances on the outside of the body such as sweat and tear glands are categorized as exocrine glands, while glands which secrete substances within the body are called endocrine glands, for example, the liver and adrenal gland.

glaucoma
n. A disorder usually characterized by a buildup of pressure in the fluid (aqueous humor) inside the eye, which kills ganglion cells in the retinal nerve, causing loss of vision, and can cause total blindness if untreated. It is often caused by a blockage of the trabecular meshwork or Schlemm's canal, which carry fluid away from the eye into the circulatory system. It may also be caused by lessened blood flow to the retinal nerve ganglia. Glaucoma sometimes occurs in the absence of elevated interocular pressure, and its cause is not well understood. In acute glaucoma the blockage is caused by the pupil's dilating in a way which causes the iris to fold against the cornea and block the exit of the aqueous humor. This can cause blindness in a few days if not treated with eye drops which cause the pupil to constrict.

glia
n. Any tissue made up of glial cells, which are nonneural cells within the nervous system which provide structural support, nutrition, or other assistance to nerve cells. Two types of glial cells, oligodendrocites and Schwann cells, form the myelin sheath which surrounds nerve tracts and increases the speed of impulse transmission. Other types of glial cells include astrocytes, which are star-shaped cells which outnumber neural cells by 10 to 1 in the brain; microglia, which provide immune function in the brain; and ependymal cells, which line the walls of the ventricles within the brain.

glial
adj. Of or relating to glia cells.

global amnesia
n. Severe or total anterograde amnesia which includes both verbal and nonverbal information and regardless of the modality in which information is presented. It is often accompanied by some retrograde amnesia, but short-term memory and perceptual-motor skills are usually left intact. It is usually caused by severe trauma to the temporal lobe or diencephalon.

globus pallidus
n. Either of a pair of pale yellow dome-shaped structures which are part of the basal ganglia and serve an output function for the basal ganglia with nerve fibers which reach to the thalamus influencing posture, muscle tone, eating, and drinking.

glottal
adj. Sounds with place of articulation at the glottis are called *glottal*. English has a glottal fricative, [h], that is restricted to syllable-initial position, occurring in words like *house* and *ahoy*. This sound is made with the

glottis in a state of aspiration: the airflow is constricted and therefore turbulent, by narrowing but not closing the vocal cords, as it passes through the glottis. English also has a glottal stop, [|], in its phonetic inventory. This sound is produced by stopping the airflow completely by closing the glottis and releasing the airflow audibly. In English, vowel-initial words are frequently preceded by a glottal stop; the interjection *uh-oh!* contains two glottal stops; in some dialectal variants of English, words like *kitten*, *cotton*, and *Manhattan* are produced with a glottal stop in place of the intervocalic /t/.   – EMF

glottis

n. The glottis is the space between the vocal cords. The glottis is open during normal breathing, and closed during phonation, in the production of speech. While whispering, and in the production of [h], the first consonant in the word *house*, the glottis is in a state of aspiration: the vocal cords are tense, causing turbulence at the glottis as air is forced through. In the production of a glottal stop, [|] – as in the interjection *uh-oh!* – the glottis is closed and subsequently opened with the built-up pressure causing an audible release.
                                              – EMF

glucostatic theory

n. A homeostatic approach to hunger that supposes that eating is governed by the brain, which monitors the difference in levels of glucose between the arteries and veins as an indicator of the rate of glucose metabolism rather than monitoring total blood levels of glucose.

glutamic acid

n. $C_5H_9NO_4$, a nonessential amino acid that is a precursor to GABA, which is a major inhibitory neurotransmitter in the brain, is involved in the citric acid cycle of metabolism, and acts as a neurotransmitter in the dorsal horns of the spinal cord and in the cerebellum.

glycine

n. $C_2H_5NO_2$, an amino acid that serves as one of the two major inhibitory neurotransmitters in the central nervous system and particularly in alpha motor neurons in the spinal cord.

goal-directed behavior

n. Behavior aimed at the attainment of a particular desired end. Goal-directed behavior may be initiated as a result of external stimulation or as a result of mental planning. Goals may operate automatically or be controlled by effortful mental activity. Goal-directed behavior is typically analyzed in terms of the goals, the interrelationships among various active goals, and the means to attain the goal. To a certain degree, all normal human cognitive and overt actions can be considered goal directed.   – MD, AK

Goldstein-Scheerer tests of Concrete and Abstract Thinking

n. A set of tests requiring abstract thinking and category formation intended to detect neurological deficits. They include tasks such as copying colored designs, reproducing designs from memory by arranging sticks, and sorting items into categories using multiple criteria.

Golgi apparatus

n. An irregular stack of membrane bound sacs which process and store proteins and lipids within the cytoplasm of eukaryotic cells.

Golgi tendon organ

n. A sensory receptor in muscles near tendons which sends nerve impulses to the central nervous system when the muscle contracts and inhibitory impulses toward the motor neurons of the muscle when tension is too high.

good continuation

n. The observation that lines that appear to move in the same direction tend to be grouped together perceptually. Thus the two lines in > are seen as one wedge, while Ø is seen as a circle with a line through it. Also called the principle continuation.

Goodenough Draw-a-Man test

n. A test of a child's intellectual ability based on his or her ability to draw a man accurately and completely, which was developed by Florence Goodenough in 1926 and revised and expanded by Harris in 1963 into the Goodenough-Harris Drawing test.

good Gestalt

n. The quality of forming a clear, complete, and stable perceptual figure or whole with simplicity, regularity, and symmetry.

goodness of fit

n. **1.** This refers to how well a statistical model fits a set of observations. The chi-square test statistic is used to see whether the observed proportions in two or more categories differ significantly from a priori, or theoretically expected, proportions. In other words, it looks for a discrepancy between observed values and the expected values. This test can be used in statistical hypothesis testing, as when one tries to see whether two samples are drawn from the same population, or when one tests for the normality of residuals. It is also used to see whether outcome frequencies follow a specified distribution. **2.** The goodness of fit model takes into account the interactionist belief that an individual is a product of physical and environmental factors. The belief is that children of certain temperaments (a biologically based factor) may be at risk for future pathology. However, having a difficult temperament does not predict a negative outcome. Parental attitudes and practices, dynamics of the family system, early life experience, and stressors in the community combine with biological factors to influence the child. If the goodness of fit exists between the child's biology and his/her environment, then there will be a positive result. This result cannot be identified by any one characteristic, as it is not a sum of factors, but the way they interact with one another.   − EF

graded potential

n. A nerve potential that varies in amplitude according to the degree of stimulation and does not produce a conventional all-or-nothing wave of depolarization of the axonic membrane but is conducted passively as a nerve signal, declining with time and distance from its origin. Retinal receptor cells show only graded potentials, whereas some other neurons with short axons show graded potentials to some limit and then generate a typical action potential.

gradient of texture

n. The progressively smaller appearance of the same texture as it moves away from the perceiver.

Graduate Record Examinations

n. (GREs) Any of several tests designed to predict potential for success in graduate school. The GRE is a general aptitude test currently consisting of two essay tests and numerous multiple-choice items which produce scores on critical thinking, analytical writing, verbal reasoning, and quantitative reasoning. There are also eight multiple-choice subject examinations in the areas of biochemistry, biology, chemistry, computer science, literature in English, mathematics, physics, and psychology.

Graduate Study in Psychology

n. A book published by the American Psychology Association which lists information about accredited graduate training programs in psychology in the United States and Canada. It does not contain any information about the numerous schools approved by states or other agencies but not regionally accredited nor about schools outside the United States excepting Canada. The information about the schools in the book includes the number of applications and number of individuals accepted in each program, dates for applications and admission, types of information required for an application, tuition costs, internships and scholarships, graduate employment information, and the orientation and emphasis of departments and programs.

grammar

n. All natural languages are principled systems, and the principles governing use for a given language are collectively referred to as that language's *grammar.* The components of a grammar include a *phonology* to specify sound structures, a *morphology* to account for word formation, a *syntax* to generate phrases and sentences, and a *semantics* to derive meaning. Each of these components consists of a finite number of formal principles, which, paired with the set of lexical entries represented in the lexicon (vocabulary store), generate the infinite set of possible sentences in that language. The form and operation of grammatical principles are understood as being universal and part of the genetic endowment of humans.   – EMF

grammar, generative

n. A generative grammar (also *transformational grammar, transformational generative grammar*) is a grammar formulated in the tradition developed by Noam Chomsky beginning in the 1950s. This tradition assumes that the grammars of natural languages are subsumed under the principles of *universal grammar*, which have language-specific settings to account for the cross-linguistic variation in the world's languages. Such formal principles represent the linguistic competence` – knowledge of language – that speakers have about their language, which is put to use through performance mechanisms. The earliest generative grammars included rules of two types: phrase structure rules to generate *deep structure* and transformations to convert deep structures into surface representations. Transformations account for the relationship between active and passive sentences like *The cop arrested the thug* and *The thug was arrested by the cop*, which share underlying deep structure but differ in their surface structure: a transformation has been applied to generate the surface form of the passive. The notion of transformation remains a central component of most theories of grammar formulated in the Chomskyan framework; rule types and levels of representation have evolved dramatically, though.   – EMF

grammar, transformational ▶ *See* GRAMMAR, GENERATIVE

grammar, universal

n. A theoretical human grammar that is supposed to underlie all the structures of all natural languages and to have the capacity to be developed into an unlimited number of new languages, all of which would share basic structures with all natural languages.

grandiose ideas

n. Thoughts which are unrealistically grand, self-important, and nearly impossible to bring into reality.

grandiose self

n. Thoughts which portray the self in an unrealistically grand, important, and nearly omnipotent way.

grand mal

n. A form of epilepsy which involves the motor cortex and so produces tonic-clonic convulsions as part of the seizure process. Also called tonic-clonic.

graphic rating scale

n. Any rating scale in which a response is made by marking a position on a line such as those anchored by "disagree strongly" at one end and "agree strongly" at the other end.

graphology

n. The study of the physical characteristics of handwriting, either with a view to discriminating among different individuals' writing, as is used in expert testimony in court, or as a means of inferring individual characteristics, which has not had much empirical success.

graphorrhea

n. Excessive, uncontrolled, and incoherent writing such as in lists or memoirs. This is a frequent symptom of mania or hypomania.

grasp reflex

n. An involuntary reflex in which the fingers close around an object that touches or strokes the palm of the hand, which is present in newborn infants. The reflex quickly disappears in human infants, and its reappearance or maintenance is often a symptom of neurological disorder.

gratification

n. **1.** The pleasure of having one's desire fulfilled. **2.** The object which fulfills one's desire.

gray matter

n. The parts of the brain and spinal cord in which cell bodies and unmyelinated nerve fibers, which are gray in color and contrast with the shiny yellow-white myelin sheaths of neuronal fibers, predominate.

great divide theories

n. **1.** The assertion that individuals in oral and literate societies differ profoundly and particularly in the way they think or experience the world. This has not been shown to be the case in general. Although there is significant cultural variation, no consistent cognitive or perceptual differences have been found between individuals from cultures with and without written languages. **2.** Any binary account or explanation of a phenomenon.

greenspoon effect

n. The modification of speech without the speaker's awareness through nonverbal reinforcement by the listener or listeners.

Gricean maxims

n. A set of four conversational guides for maximizing the efficiency of conversation proposed by the philosopher Paul Gricel: **(1)** The maxim of quality or truth, which suggests that one should not say what one knows to be false or for which one lacks the evidence of its truth. **(2)** The maxim of quantity of information, which suggests that the amount of information should be as much as required for a conversation but not more than is required. **(3)** The maxim of relation or relevance, which suggests what is said should pertain to the conversation rather than be a distraction from its topic. **(4)** The maxim of manner or clarity, which suggests the speaker should avoid ambiguity, be orderly in presentation of information, be brief, and avoid saying things in difficult-to-understand manners (eschew obfuscation). These maxims have been widely used in analysis of natural language and in computer models of language.

grief

n. The emotion experienced after a great loss, as in the death of a close relative. A feeling of distress and intense sorrow.

grooming

n. **1.** Caring for the appearance of one's body and clothing. **2.** In animal behavior, the act of picking lice or other small objects out of the fur of another of one's species, which serves to strengthen social bonds as well as maintain hygiene.

group behavior

n. The actions of a group as a whole or the actions of an individual in a group and especially as they differ from similar actions when alone.

group cohesivieness

n. A social group possesses a high level of group cohesiveness when its members share common goals and are willing to coordinate their efforts to achieve the group goals. Members of high (vs. low) cohesive groups are more likely (a) to have a salient collective identity (use group memberships to define the self), (b) to be cooperative with each other, and (c) to remain loyal to the group. A group that is perceived to be cohesive is likely to be perceived as an entity rather than a collection of individuals.   – CYC

group consciousness

n. **1.** The collective awareness or experience of a group. **2.** The place or importance of group membership in the self-image and experience of members of the group.

group contagion

n. The rapid spread of ideas, attitudes, and behaviors through crowds of people or other animals.

group difference

n. Any change in the average of a variable between experimental groups or any other characteristic difference between naturally occurring groups.

group dynamics

n. **1.** The ongoing processes and changes that go on in functioning groups, including affiliation, cohesiveness, consciousness, communication patterns, conflict and conflict management, decision making, leadership, norms, and conformity. **2.** The scientific study of group processes.

grouped frequency distribution

n. A graphic representation of the number of occurrences in specified ranges of variables, usually arranged from lowest to highest.

grouping

n. The formation of a group from individual components. In perception, this usually involves Gestalt formation. In research design, it involves assigning subjects to experimental conditions. In everyday life, it is the placement of things, such as furniture, in a group or noticing that some things appear together.

grouping error

n. An experimental error caused by the manner in which the data were combined or grouped. In most statistical procedures there are assumptions that data in a group or range have an average near the median of the range and a normal distribution. If these assumptions are not met, distortion is introduced into the data. Thus, if we have two groups of children, one of which includes children from 1 to 5 years of age and one which includes children from 6 to 19 years of age, we would expect different results if one experiment had groups with nothing but 5- and 6-year-olds in it and in another experiment the groups had nothing but 1- and 10-year-olds in it.

group polarization

n. Group-produced enhancement of members' preexisting tendencies; a strengthening of the members' average tendency, not a split within the group.

group psychotherapy

n. Any of numerous processes of psychotherapy done in a group setting. Most approaches use the group to provide emotional support and alternative points of view for the members in dealing with psychological disorders.

group test

n. A psychometric evaluation that may be administered by a single examiner to more than one person simultaneously (in contrast to an individual test, which must be conducted in a one-on-one setting between the test taker and the test administrator). Typically, in a group test, the test administrator provides directions and imposes time limits while the test taker records his/her own responses. The objective nature of most group tests translates into more efficient and reliable scoring with less training and skill required of the test administrator. These factors, combined with the ability to test many people at one time, make group tests extremely efficient. The drawback to group tests is the lack of individualized information that can be obtained unique to each test taker. Group testing offers no safeguards to ensure that individual test takers are motivated and performing at the optimal level. As such, low scores on group tests can be difficult to interpret as there is no information to ensure that scores obtained from a group setting are not attributable to nonability factors such as motivation, cooperation, or emotional state.   – BJM

group therapy

n. Any of numerous processes of psychotherapy done in a group setting. Most approaches use the group to provide emotional support and alternative points of view for the members in dealing with psychological disorders.

groupthink

n. A collective pattern of conformity, defensive avoidance of nonconforming ideas, self-congratulation, demonizing of out-group members, and belief in the group's moral and intellectual superiority to other groups which is characteristic of some organizations. The causes of groupthink are believed to include high cohesion, isolation, rigid belief systems, poor leadership, and stress.

growth hormone

n. (GH) A chemical released by the anterior pituitary gland which promotes the synthesis of proteins essential to the growth of muscles, long limb bones, and other body tissues. In humans excessive secretion of growth hormone leads to gigantism in children and acromegaly in adults and is usually caused by a benign tumor on the pituitary gland. Also called somatotrophin.

GSR

n. Galvanic skin response is a change in the ease with which the skin conducts electricity, which tends to decrease when subcutaneous muscles relax and increase when those muscles tense. It is a crude indicator of general bodily tension and has been used in inaccurate attempts to create a lie detector.

guanine

n. On of the four basic chemicals which form all DNA and RNA.

gustation

n. The sense of taste. Perceptions of taste are composed of the sensation from receptors for sweet, sour, bitter, and salt combined with odor, texture, and pain.

Guttman scale

n. An attitude scale which has its items arranged in a hierarchy so that agreement with any item implies agreement with all items below it on the list. Guttman Scales are constructed through scalogram analysis, in which a pool of potential items are administered to a group, who mark the items with which they agree. Items are then selected which can be formed into the hierarchy Guttman Scales require.

gyrus

n. A ridge or raised portion of the brain; a convoluted surface, as opposed to a sulcus, which is an indentation or crevice in the brain's surface.

H

habit

n. **1.** A default pattern of behavior that is usually repeated without conscious decision making in appropriate circumstances. **2.** A conditioned response.

habitat

n. The environment in which an organism, a species, or an identifiable group of people live. In ecology, it includes the physical environment, food sources, and other organisms that share the environment.

habit reversal

n. A kind of conditioning in which an organism is reinforced for making one of two possible choices, and, after this behavior has been well established, the reinforcement is reversed and the other choice is reinforced until the organism reliably makes the second choice. Also called reversal learning.

habit strength

n. The strength between a stimulus and response measured by the number or amount of reinforcement, rapidity of response, and response-reinforcement interval.

habituation

n. **1.** The weakening in response to a sensory stimulus when it is repeated many times or in a prolonged way. **2.** The process through which something becomes normal or expected.

habituation, drug

n. **1.** A dependence on a drug in which the person feels pleasure or release from tension in using the substance and fears being without the drug. **2.** The process of altering metabolism to accommodate the continuing presence of a drug in the body so that the person needs increasing doses to reach a given level of reaction (tolerance) and unpleasant and sometimes dangerous consequences when the substance is withdrawn.

hair cell

n. **1.** A long, slender, hairlike cell in the in organ of Corti in the inner ear, which transduces pressure waves into electrical impulses in the auditory nerve. **2.** A long, slender, hairlike cell in the ampullae of the semicircular canals, which transduces pressure into electrical impulses sent through the afferent vestibular nerve to the vestibular nucleus and the cerebellum.

Haldol

n. The brand name for haloperidol, a high-potency, relatively long-lasting antipsychotic drug in the butyrophenone family of drugs developed in the late 1950s. It frequently causes pronounced side effects including tardive dyskinesia and extrapyramidal effects which sometimes become endogenous if the drug is used for long periods. It does not have the anticholinergic effects and negative cardiovascular effects of phenothiozines. Its use has been sharply curtailed since the development of atypical antipsychotic drugs, which have fewer side effects.

halfway house

n. A transitional living institution for persons moving from an institutional setting, such as a prison, drug treatment center, or mental hospital, back into the community. These situations are usually relatively small and provide assistance in making transitions such as counseling and job placement.

hallucination

n. A sensory perception in the absence of any external stimulus. Hallucinations can be auditory, visual, tactile, olfactory, or gustatory; auditory hallucinations are by far the most common. Hallucinations are most commonly seen in the psychotic disorders, specifically schizophrenia, although they can be found in severe cases of bipolar disorder, major depressive disorder, substance abuse and dependence (including alcohol and stimulant abuse and dependence), and occasionally borderline personality disorder.   – DGa

hallucinogen

n. Any drug which causes perception in the absence of the things perceived. Typically they also produce dreamlike alterations in thinking, mood, and perception. Most hallucinogens work by stimulating serotonin or catecholamine receptors. LSD (lysergic acid diethylamide), psilocybin, and dimethyltriptamine and diethyltriptamine (DMT, DET) primarily stimulate serotonin receptors, while mescaline, 3,4-methylenedioxyamphetamine (MDA), dimethoxymethylamphetamine (DOM), and 3,4-methylenedioxymethamphetamine (MMDA) work primarily via the catecholamine receptors. Hallucinogens have shown some promise in psychotherapy, but their use in the United States has been banned. Also called psychedelic drugs.

hallucinogenic drug

n. Any drug which causes perception in the absence of the things perceived. Typically they also produce dreamlike alterations

in thinking, mood, and perception. Most hallucinogens work by stimulating serotonin or catecholamine receptors. LSD (lysergic acid diethylamide), psilocybin, and dimethyltriptamine and diethyltriptamine (DMT, DET) primarily stimulate serotonin receptors while mescaline, 3,4-methylenedioxyamphetamine (MDA), dimethoxymethylamphetamine (DOM), and 3,4-methylenedioxymethaphetamine (MMDA) work primarily via the catecholamine receptors. Hallucinogens have shown some promise in psychotherapy, but their use in the United States has been banned. Also called psychedelic drugs.

halo effect

n. Research on person perception demonstrates that we form initial impressions of others very quickly. Research has shown that once we form an initial positive impression of a person, we tend to have a bias in our subsequent perceptions of that individual such that we pay attention to behavior confirming our positive impressions, and we discount or ignore information that is inconsistent with our positive impression. This impression-confirmation bias is known as the halo effect. Researchers have also demonstrated a parallel bias for confirming initially negative impressions, which is sometimes referred to as the horns effect.   – MWP

haloperidol ▶ *See* HALDOL

handedness

n. A preference to use one hand versus the other for most tasks with the preferred hand showing greater dexterity in a variety of tasks. This corresponds with a greater activity in the motor cortex on the opposite side of the brain.

Hans, Little

n. The name assigned to a little boy in a published case history in which Sigmund Freud traced a phobia for horses back to the boy's castration anxiety. This was caused by anxiety over masturbation, hatred and envy of his father, and sexual desire for his mother and the guilt these entailed, all of which were projected onto horses.

hardiness

n. **1.** In psychology, the ability to adapt to sudden or unexpected changes and stress as well as to maintain a sense of personal control, emotional commitment, and high activity level in daily life. **2.** In gardening, the ability to withstand disease and a wide variety of conditions of temperature, soil, moisture, and sunlight.

harmonic mean

n. An average calculated by taking the reciprocal of the arithmetic mean of the reciprocals of a group of numbers. Thus the harmonic mean of 1, 2, and 3 is equal to

$$\frac{1}{1}+\frac{1}{2}+\frac{1}{3}=\frac{1.8333}{3}=.6111, \frac{1}{.6111}=1.636$$

hate ▶ *See* HATRED

hatred

n. An attitude or disposition that includes intense feelings of dislike, animosity, hostility, and aversion toward a person, group, or object. Although many individuals believe that hatred is an emotion, it is better considered an attitude or disposition, because it is long-lasting and not temporary or transient, as fleeting emotions are. Hatred is considered to play a central role in many theories of aggression, including those involving terrorist groups and other ideologically motivated groups. Hatred may result from the combination of repeated experiences of anger and disgust toward the hated object.

Hawthorne effect

n. The effect on people's behavior of knowing they are being observed or studied. The name *Hawthorne* is taken from the Hawthorne plant of the Western Electric Company, in which it was noted that productivity rose as soon as workers knew they were being observed by a research team. A set of seven studies of this plant are sometimes considered the birth of the human relations approach to management.

health psychology

n. Health psychology is a field of psychology that focuses on health, illness, and health care. Health psychologists use psychological theory and research to understand and promote health and to prevent and treat illness. Health psychologists recognize that health and illness are influenced by many factors, such as behavioral, cognitive, emotional, social, environmental, and biological factors. Knowledge from health psychology can be used to help individuals of all ages develop and maintain healthy habits, reduce stress, and cope with illness. On a broader scale, knowledge from health psychology can be used to improve health care delivery and policy.   – SD-B

hearing

n. The auditory sense in which knowledge of the environment is inferred from changes in the air pressure level at the ears. The human capacity to detect sound is generally between the wavelengths from about 15–20 cycles per second up to about 20,000 cycles per second. Some animals such as bats can hear much higher frequencies, and others, such as whales, can hear lower frequencies. Also called audition.

hebephrenic schizophrenia

n. An archaic term for disorganized schizophrenia, which is characterized by disorganized speech and behavior and by inappropriate affect. The speech of individuals with this disorder is often incoherent and accompanied by laughter or silly gestures unrelated to the content of the speech. Individuals with this disorder are unable to perform daily self-care or follow a course of action. The onset of this disorder is usually in adolescence and the course is insidious, usually without periods of remission.

hedonic tone

n. The degree of pleasantness or unpleasantness of an experience.

hedonism

n. The belief or theory that pleasure is intrinsically good and the natural object of all human activity, which has been a central point of debate in both philosophy and psychology. It is often qualified with short-term versus long-term pleasures, the necessity of enduring discomfort to obtain greater pleasure, and group versus individual needs and motivations.

helping behaviors

n. Helping behaviors are those actions that individuals engage in that are intended to aid another. The term *helping behaviors* covers a wide range of actions, from sharing to volunteerism and philanthropy. There are several different forms of helping, and there can be different motives for helping. One type of helping that has attracted much attention is altruism. *Altruism* refers to helping behaviors whose primary intent is to benefit another person. These behaviors often entail a risk or high cost to the helper (such as pulling a person out of a burning building). Altruistic acts are usually motivated by strongly internalized principles or by compassion. However, there are other forms of helping that may be motivated by social norms or conventions (such as opening the door for someone) or may be motivated by trying to gain another person's approval (such as when a student tries to impress a teacher by helping). Thus, some helping behaviors are selflessly motivated and others may be egotistically motivated. The study of helping behaviors has been of great interest to many scholars because of the important social (including health and education), political, and economic implications.

Topics of interest in the study of helping behaviors include age and gender differences, biological (e.g., temperament, genes) origins, situational (e.g., mood, bystanders, characteristics of victim) influences, socialization (e.g., parents, peers, media) mechanisms, and cultural group differences. There is considerable evidence of age and gender differences in helping behaviors. Helping behaviors such as sharing and cooperation begin to emerge around 2–3 years of age and continue to be shaped throughout childhood. Generally, the occurrence of helping behaviors will increase with age into adulthood, although some evidence suggests that there might be a small decrease in helping behaviors during early adolescence. Age-related changes may be due to corresponding changes in cognitive

and emotional skills and changes in social context. The research on gender differences is more mixed. Generally, studies of self-report helping behaviors find gender differences favoring women, while observational studies sometimes report (smaller) gender differences and at other times report none. Studies of helping behaviors in younger children sometimes report gender differences favoring girls, while others report no gender differences. In studies of stranger helping behaviors, men have been found to help more often than women. However, these findings may be influenced by certain design characteristics of the study. For example, these gender differences are greatest when a helping situation has a high degree of danger.

There is also evidence that helping behaviors can be influenced by an individual's temperament or personality. *Temperament* describes children's personal characteristics of how they interpret external stimuli and how they respond to these stimuli. For example, children's ability to regulate the emotions evoked by a situation may affect their ability to provide help. Children with a more easygoing, compliant temperament may be more willing to provide help when asked. On the other hand, children with a more difficult temperament may more often feel disinclined to offer assistance. Similarly to temperament, adult personality characteristics are also related to helping behaviors. People high in agreeableness and conscientiousness tend to engage in more helping behaviors.

Although more enduring characteristics of temperament and personality may influence helping behaviors, the situational demands have also garnered a lot of attention. For example, sparked by the case of Kitty Genovese (when onlookers who witnessed a fatal attack on Kitty failed to intervene or call the police), many studies have examined the circumstances that influence whether a bystander will intervene to help an anonymous other. Such studies have found that the number of bystanders present influences whether helping occurs and how fast the response is. It is now referred to as the *diffusion of responsibility* that when more people are present, the less likely it is that any one of them will offer help. Other situational aspects that influence the occurrence or speed of helping behaviors include the characteristics of the victim, such as age, gender, race/ethnicity, and perceived attractiveness.

A variety of socialization forces, such as parents, peers, and the media, have also been linked to helping behaviors. Various aspects of parent-child interactions and socialization contexts can foster the internalization of values, which, in turn, might promote or diminish helping behaviors. Parents can model helping behaviors, as well as communicate beliefs or values concerning helping behaviors. Despite the heavy focus on the negative influence of peer pressure, peers can also act as positive models and provide a social context that fosters helping behaviors. Since the peer-peer relationship is more similar in power structure than adult-child relationships, peers offer a unique opportunity to negotiate the give-and-take nature of relationships, including the exchange of helping behaviors. Similarly to the predominant focus on the negative influence of peers, the influence of the media has been cast almost solely in a negative light. However, research also indicates that children who watched media with positive role models engaging in helping behaviors were more likely to engage in future helping behaviors. These children were also more likely to select prosocial media content over the course of development, perhaps creating a positive cycle of reinforcing helping behaviors.

Finally, there are many cross-cultural differences in helping behaviors. Differences in parenting socialization and the expectations placed on children can influence helping behaviors. For example, in cultures where children are typically assigned caretaking roles of younger siblings or other family members, these children often exhibit greater amounts of helping behaviors, particularly within the extended family group. Other research on cross-cultural differences in helping behaviors has focused on the individualistic/collectivistic orientation of societies. Collectivistic societies (where there is an emphasis on group needs and outcomes) tend to have higher rates of helping behaviors than individualistic societies (where the emphasis is more on individual concerns and needs). Despite strong and intriguing evidence for the existence of cross-cultural differences in helping behaviors, more research is needed in this area to understand better the roles of the individual, family, and society in fostering or inhibiting helping behaviors.   – GC, RH

▶ *See also* **PROSOCIAL BEHAVIORS**

hemisphere
n. **1.** Half of a sphere or solid circular shape. **2.** Either half of the cerebrum.

hemispherectomy
n. The surgical removal of one side of the cerebral cortex.

hemispheric specialization
n. Asymmetric representation of higher-level functions in the cerebral hemispheres. Cerebral specialization (or simply, brain asymmetry) means that the brain organization of higher-level functions is not duplicated in both the right and the left hemispheres but is associated with the activity of only one cerebral hemisphere. In general, the left hemisphere is specialized in linguistic processes and has a more analytic way of processing information. Disturbances in both oral and written language (aphasia, alexia, and agraphia), arithmetical ability impairments (acalculia), semantic amnesia, and inability to perform some previously learned movements (apraxia) are found in cases of left hemisphere pathology in the majority of the people. The right hemisphere is specialized in visuoperceptual and visuoconstructive abilities and has a more holistic way of processing the information. Disturbances in spatial orientation (spatial agnosia and spatial amnesia), recognition of faces and places impairments (prosopagnosia and topographic agnosia), episodic amnesia, and difficulties in the auditory recognition of nonverbal information including music (nonverbal auditory agnosia and amusia) are found in cases of right hemisphere pathology in the majority of the people.   – AA

▶ *See also* **CEREBRAL DOMINANCE**

hereditarianism

n. The belief that most or all individual differences in behavior or ability are due to genetic differences. This is one extreme point of view within the nature versus nurture conflict within psychology.

heredity

n. **1.** The transmission of characteristics from parents to their children via the process of DNA or gene transmission. **2.** The characteristics inherited from one's parents.

Hering theory of color vision

n. The theory that there are three sorts of color receptors in the human eye, one sensitive to black and white, one to red and green, and one to blue and yellow. Included in the theory is that there is a chemical substance within each pair of cell types broken down by one color of the pair and built up by the other. Color blindness was thought to be due to the absence of one or more of these receptors.

heritability ratio

n. The proportion of the total phenotypic variation of a population contributed by genetic factors. This is calculated in a broad sense as the variance due to genetic variability divided by the total phenotypic variability of the population. It is calculated in a narrow sense by the genetic variance due to additive genes divided by the total phenotypic variation.

hermaphrodite

n. Any plant or animal having the reproductive organs of both sexes. In humans it is usually the case that a hermaphroditic person has some parts of the reproductive organs of both sexes and is incapable of reproduction. Many plants have both sets of organs in slightly different locations. Some animals, such as geckos, can alternate between playing male and female roles in reproduction.

hermeneutics

n. **1.** In psychology, the interpretation of behavior, speech, and writing in terms of meaning and intention. **2.** The study of interpretation, especially of texts and scriptures. **3.** In existentialism, the meaning of life.

heterogeneity of variance

n. The situation in which the variance in different experimental conditions is significantly different. Also called heteroscedasticity.

heteroscedasticity

n. The situation in which the variance in different experimental conditions is significantly different. Also called heterogeneity of variance.

heterosexual

1. *adj.* Of or relating to the state of being sexually attracted to or engaging in sexual behavior with members of the opposite sex. **2.** *n.* A person who is attracted to or engages in sex with members of the opposite sex.

heterosis

n. The increased vigor or increase in favorable characteristics in the offspring of parents with differing genetic makeup. Also called hybrid vigor.

heterostereotype

n. Generalized beliefs about the characteristics of one group of people held by another group of people.

heterozygote

n. The state of possessing two different forms of a particular gene, one inherited from the mother and the other from the father.

heterozygous

adj. Of or relating to the possession of two different forms of the same gene, one inherited from the mother and one from the father.

heuristic

n. A rule of thumb for making decisions of a particular kind which usually works but does not guarantee a correct solution. This contrasts with an algorithm, in which there is an exhaustive comparison of all possible options. *See also* availability heuristic, representativeness heuristic, *and* simulation heuristic

heuristic, cognitive

n. A rule of thumb for making decisions of a particular kind which usually works but does not guarantee a correct solution. This contrasts with an algorithm, in which there is an exhaustive comparison of all possible options. *See also* availability heuristic, representativeness heuristic, *and* simulation heuristic

hidden figure

n. A figure embedded within a larger figure which makes it difficult to see. Also called embedded figure.

hidden observer

n. A phenomenon in which highly susceptible individuals who are asked to block out certain stimuli can do so in a way so that they are not conscious of the stimuli but can unconsciously signal their presence via hand signals. Thus it is as if the person had two observers, one of which is hidden from the person's consciousness.

hierarchical linear modeling

n. A statistical technique in which a model of data is created with multiple levels of analysis in which variables are nested within each other and analyzed in a hierarchy of inclusiveness. Thus an analysis might look at students and include variables for classroom, school, school system, and geographical area, and the data would be analyzed at each of those levels, which form a hierarchy of inclusiveness or generality.

hierarchy of needs

n. An ordering of human needs according to their relative importance to human beings suggested by Abraham Maslow. In this hierarchy physical needs such as oxygen, warmth, water, and food are most important. Second are needs for safety. Third are needs for social connection. Fourth are needs for self- and social esteem. Fifth and last is a set of growth needs, which vary unpredictably from one individual to the next and frequently include beauty, harmony, knowledge, and order. When one level of needs is satisfied, the next level begins to have the same urgency, as do lower needs when they are unsatisfied. So

when the lower four levels of needs are satisfied, the growth needs can be just as compelling as are the needs for food or shelter when they are not fulfilled.

high-context cultures

n. Cultures that promote communication in which many messages are conveyed indirectly in context rather than directly in verbal language.

higher mental processes

n. Complex psychological abilities mediated by the cerebral cortex, particularly the prefrontal cortex, involved in complex cognition, such as reasoning, problem solving, thinking, decision making, and self-awareness. They are implicitly contrasted with "lower mental functions," such as sensations. Different names have been used throughout history to refer to these complex psychological functions: *higher mental functions, higher psychological functions, higher psychological processes, complex cognition,* and the like. These abilities roughly correspond to contemporary executive functions. Two different dimensions have been emphasized in higher mental processes: (**1**) the biological/neurological dimension: higher mental processes depend upon a certain level of brain evolution, in particular, the enlargement of the frontal lobes; they appear in the child correlated with the brain maturation, in particular, the maturation of the frontal lobes. (**2**) Some researchers, especially Vygotsky, have emphasized the social/cultural dimension of the higher mental processes. Vygotsky emphasized that an intrinsic factor in the organization of higher forms of cognition (higher mental processes) is the engagement of external elements (e.g., representing spoken language in writing, representing the environmental space in a map, using external devices in arithmetical operations). According to Vygotsky, higher mental processes are social in origin and complex and hierarchical in their structure.   – AA

▶ *See also* **EXECUTIVE FUNCTIONS**

higher-order conditioning

n. A learning procedure in which the conditioned stimulus from one set of trials is used as the unconditioned stimulus for a second set of trials in which a neutral stimulus becomes a conditioned stimulus. If a bell has been paired with food so that it produces drooling, then a flashing light or other stimulus can be paired with the bell and can be made to produce drooling with food never paired with the light.

hindbrain

n. The part of the brain toward the bottom and back of the skull including the pons, cerebellum, and medulla oblongata, which develop from three bulges on the posterior end of the embryonic brain. These areas are important in regulating motor activity, balance, posture, sleep, and bodily functions such as heartbeat and respiration.

hindsight bias

n. The tendency to perceive events that have already occurred as much more easily predictable than they appeared before their occurrence. Thus in looking back on historical events they seem to have been nearly inevitable while the future seems uncertain.

hippocampal formation

n. A portion of the limbic cortex located in the temporal lobe of the forebrain. This formation includes the dentate gyrus, longitudinal striae, as well as the hippocampus itself. Stimulation of the hippocampal formation can produce lasting synaptic changes called long-term potentiation. These changes, which can be produced in many regions of the hippocampal formation, are associated with learning and the development of memory.   – vs

hippocampus

n. Part of the limbic system, a neural structure located in the medial-temporal lobe adjacent to the cerebral cortex, at the level of the lateral ventricle. The interior of the hippocampus is composed of gray matter (cell bodies), which is covered by white matter (nerve fiber pathways). The hippocampus plays an important role in declarative (cognitive) long-term memory consolidation, spatial memory, and emotional memory. Neural input to the hippocampus travels via pathways originating in cortical association areas which have processed information from all sensory modalities. Stimulation of this region increases the magnitude of excitatory postsynaptic potentials in postsynaptic neurons. This action is known as long-term potentiation, considered a possible neural template of memory formation. Lesions in the hippocampus and surrounding area may produce severe anterograde amnesia, which prevents the consolidation of new memories.

One of the causes of memory losses occurring in aging is degeneration of the hippocampus, possibly resulting from decreased blood circulation in this region. In the hippocampus, the problem of decreased circulation is heightened by the presence of stress hormones, particularly cortisol, to which the hippocampus is especially sensitive.   – vs

Hiskey-Nebraska Test of Learning Aptitude

n. A nonverbal test of intelligence developed for use with deaf children which yields a learning quotient (LQ) and correlates highly with performance scores on the Wechsler Intelligence Scale for Children (WISC-R). The test has relatively low test-retest correlations and scores are not normally distributed, being skewed toward both extremities.

histamine

n. ($C_5H_9N_3$) A chemical synthesized from the amino acid histidine and present in most body tissues which has four major receptor sites in the body. The first type of receptors (H1) occur in smooth muscles and the endothelium, where they cause vasodilation, smooth muscle contraction, swelling, rhinitis, pain, and itching. The second type of receptors (H2) are in the parietal lobe of the brain, where they are associated with the release of gastric acid. The third (H3) type of receptors are located throughout the brain and are associated with lowering the levels of acetylcholine, norepinephrine, and serotonin. The activity of the fourth (H4) sites, located in the thymus, small intestine, spleen, and colon, is not understood.

histogram

n. A graphical display of a frequency table in which the unit intervals are mapped on the x-axis and the number of scores in each interval is represented on the y-axis. The purpose of a histogram is to show what proportion of data falls into each interval; all intervals are disjointed, nonoverlapping, adjacent categories (also called bins). The width and number of bins will influence the shape and interpretation of a histogram.   – BJM

histrionic personality disorder

n. A pervasive and persistent pattern of adjustment characterized by excessive emotion expression and attention seeking. Persons with this disorder need to be the center of attention; if they are not, they feel uncomfortable and draw attention to themselves in a variety of ways, including flirtatiousness, seductiveness, exaggerated and shallow expressions of emotion, and vague speech. They tend to have shallow relationships, which they believe to be deep, and to be easily influenced by others.

hit

n. A correct prediction of the presence of a signal in a signal detection task. 2. In computer science, an instance of a Web site's being opened by someone, which is used as a measure of the success of the site.

holophrase

n. A single-word utterance that is interpreted as a whole sentence, especially in the speech of infants or other persons lacking language fluency. Thus a child's uttering the word *cookie* is likely to be interpreted by a parent as "I want a cookie" or "Give me a cookie."

homeostasis

n. The self-regulation of an equilibrium in any physiological, biological, social, psychological, or ecological system. This involves monitoring some aspects of the system and taking action to modulate them whenever any aspect moves away from a desirable range.

hominid

1. n. Any modern human or his or her extinct ancestors included in the biological family Hominidae. 2. adj. Of or relating to human or humanlike beings.

homogeneity

n. 1. The state of being equally distributed, especially as applied to different conditions of an experiment or distribution of a variable in different ranges of the variable. 2. In Piagetian psychology, the assumption that mental processes are similar across different tasks and situations.

homogeneity of variance

n. The state of being in which different groups or cells in an experiment have equal average distances from the mean.

homographs

n. Homographs are two unique entries in a language's lexicon with identical spelling in the writing system. Homographs need not be homophonous, that is, have identical pronunciation. For example, the pronunciation of *dove* (a noun used to identify a certain type of bird) differs from that of *dove* (the simple past form of the verb *dive*). However, homographs frequently are homophones, as *bear* (a noun referring to a type of omnivorous mammal) and *bear* (a verb meaning to carry or put up with something).   – EMF

homoscedasticity

n. Equal scatter or variability about a mean or a regression line.

homosexual

1. adj. Of or relating to being sexually excited by or engaging in sexual relations with a person of the same sex. 2. n. An individual who feels attracted to or engages in sexual activities with another person of the same sex.

homosexuality

n. Sexual attraction to or sexual activities between members of the same sex. It is currently more often applied to men than women.

homozygote

n. An organism that has the same form (allele) of a particular gene in both locations on the DNA strand.

homozygous

adj. Characterized by having the same form (allele) of a particular gene in both locations on the DNA strand.

homunculus

n. **1.** A theoretical tiny man inside the brain that perceives or makes decisions, or an explanation in terms of the thing itself. **2.** A distorted drawing of a human that portrays the distribution of sensory neurons in the body by the size of the body parts.

honestly significant difference test

n. A post hoc testing procedure that allows for all possible comparisons while maintaining a prescribed significance level. This statistic is computed using the following formula:

$$\text{HSD} = \frac{larger\ mean - smaller\ mean}{\sqrt{\dfrac{mean\ square\ error}{harmonic\ mean}}}$$

Also known as Tukey's honestly significant difference test.

honorific speech

n. Speech styles in certain languages that denote status differences among interactants.

horizontal-vertical illusion

n. A visual illusion in which a vertical line and a horizontal line of the same length form a T, which causes the vertical line to appear longer than the horizontal line.

hospice

n. **1.** A nursing home for the care of the terminally ill with short life expectancies emphasizing comfort, pain relief, and psychological well-being. **2.** A form of nursing care designed for the terminally ill with short life expectancies emphasizing comfort, pain relief, and psychological well-being.

hot spot ▶ *See* NONVERBAL HOT SPOT

house-tree-person technique

n. A projective test in which a subject is asked to draw a house, a tree, and a person and then is asked questions about the drawings. The details of the drawings and answers to the questions are then interpreted quantitatively and can be used to estimate intelligence or detect brain damage and interpreted intuitively by the tester to infer personality and psychological state. The test has questionable reliability and validity.

house-tree-person test

n. A projective test in which a subject is asked to draw a house, a tree, and a person and then is asked questions about the drawings. The details of the drawings and answers to the questions are then interpreted quantitatively and can be used to estimate intelligence or detect brain damage and interpreted intuitively by the tester to infer personality and psychological state. The test has questionable reliability and validity.

Hullian learning theory

n. A form of learning theory formulated by Clark Hull (1884–1952) in which all behavior and learning are initiated by needs and directed toward the reduction of those needs. In the theory, habits are formed by the reinforcement of random behaviors, and there are mathematical relationships among numerous variables, including habit strength, reinforcement, stimulus generalization, extinction, and delay in responding. The theory is largely ignored in recent decades because of its failure to predict behavior accurately.

human factors

n. **1.** The impact of human capacities, needs, and limitations on the functioning of a system. **2.** The study of the design of systems which accommodate human needs and optimize them for use by human beings. Also called ergonomics.

human factors psychology

n. The branch of psychology which works on ergonomic problems, such as designing instrument display panels, in which visual salience of each display is matched by the importance of the monitoring of the information by the human operator.

human intelligence

n. The human capacity to obtain information from the environment, store it, analyze it, and use it to adapt to the environment. There are many specific forms of intelligence, applicable in some situations and tasks but not in others.

humanistic approach

n. Any approach to any discipline in which the positive valuation of individual human beings takes a central part.

humanistic psychology

n. A school of psychology which emphasizes the inherent and basic goodness of human beings, assumes that they have an inherent tendency to actualize unique potentials, and focuses on psychological health and growth. It includes an emphasis on individual choice, creativity, and experience versus theory. It derives from phenomenology and existentialism and is most prominently represented in the works of Gordon Allport, Abraham Maslow, and Carl Rogers.

human nature

n. The innate characteristics of human beings, which have been very differently defined by different theorists, including some who deny the existence of human nature.

hunger

n. A desire for food, or more generally, a desire for anything.

Huntington's chorea ▶ *See* HUNTINGTON'S DISEASE

Huntington's disease

n. A progressive neurodegenerative disease typified by the slow and steady development of involuntary muscle movements in the hands, feet, face, and trunk. Involuntary motor responses may include rapid, jerky movements, called chorea. Huntington's disease is also characterized by dementia, or a progressive deterioration of cognitive and memory functioning. Dementia in Huntington's disease is typically associated with disorientation, confusion, personality and behavior changes, memory impairment, and agitation.

Huntington's disease is an inherited disease that is caused by a mutated gene. It is often diagnosed by blood test. Symptoms generally appear in midlife. Among younger people, symptoms tend to be more severe and progress more quickly. It is rare for this disease to be seen in children.

The disease has a gradual progression, with increasingly prominent symptoms in later stages associated with more widespread neuron damage. Most cell loss occurs in the caudate nucleus and putamen, with some damage in the globus pallidus. The earliest signs of Huntington's disease may include changes in personality and cognitive abilities. Early physical symptoms such as mild balance problems, clumsiness, and involuntary facial movements may also be seen. Later in the disease, prominent involuntary movements throughout the body, acute balance and coordination problems, broken or slurred speech, and a wide gait may be present. Finally, ability to perform basic functions such as swallowing, eating, speaking, and walking tends to decline with time. Because of the slow decline of functioning, individuals with Huntington's disease may become depressed and can be at risk for suicide.

Currently, although medications may assist with some involuntary movements and behaviors, there is no cure for Huntington's disease. After the onset of Huntington's disease, symptoms persist until death. Death typically occurs as the result of complications such as infections or injuries between 10 and 30 years after symptoms first appear.   – TJM

hybrid

n. The offspring of the cross-breeding of genetically dissimilar plants or animals.

hybrid vigor

n. The increased vigor or increase in favorable characteristics in the offspring of parents with differing genetic makeup. Also called heterosis.

hydrocephalus

n. A disorder characterized by excess liquid inside the skull which increases intracranial pressure and can lead to brain damage, enlargement of the head, and death. External symptoms range from headache and neck pain and nausea, to fever, vomiting, confusion, sleepiness, convulsions, coma, and occasionally death.

hyperactive child
n. A child with attention deficit–hyperactivity disorder.

hyperactive child syndrome
n. An archaic name for attention deficit–hyperactivity disorder, predominantly hyperactive-impulsive type, which is characterized by chronic fidgeting, squirming, inability to sit still, inability to remain quiet for more than a few moments, excessive motor activity, difficulty in turn taking, and verbal interrupting, which impair learning and social integration.

hyperactivity
n. Excessive motor activity, including fidgeting, squirming, inability to sit still, inability to remain quiet for more than a few moments, difficulty in turn taking, and verbal interrupting, which impair learning and social integration. Also known as hyperkinesis.

hyperkinesis
n. Excessive motor activity, including fidgeting, squirming, inability to sit still, inability to remain quiet for more than a few moments, difficulty in turn taking, and verbal interrupting, which impair learning and social integration. Also known as hyperactivity.

hyperphagia
n. A pathological tendency to overeat which can be caused by psychological disturbance, metabolic disorder, or damage to the amygdala, temporal lobe, or ventromedial nucleus of the hypothalamus.

hyperpolarization
n. An increase in the membrane potential in a cell, especially a neuron, in which the electrical charge on the inside of the membrane becomes more negative relative to the outside of the membrane. This results in an inhibition of neural potentials.

hypersomnia
n. A disorder characterized by prolonged, excessive sleepiness during normal waking hours causing significant distress and dysfunction in the person's life.

hypertension
n. High blood pressure, a standard for which is arbitrarily set at 140/90 mm of mercury when measured by a standard sphygmomanometer (blood pressure cuff).

hyperthymia
n. Excessive emotional response; this often occurs during episodes of mania or hypomania.

hyperthyroidism
n. Overproduction of thyroxin or triiodothyronine. This tends to lead to elevated metabolism and can lead to weight loss, hyperactivity, confusion, and paranoia.

hypertonic
adj. Of or relating to excessive muscle tension.

hypertrophy
n. An abnormal enlargement of an organ or tissue area due to the increase in the size of its cells rather than an increase in the number of cells in the organ.

hypertropia
n. A misalignment of the eyes making binocular fixation and vision impossible. An individual with hypertropia may have double vision, or the brain may block out the vision of one eye so the person has monocular vision, making depth perception less accurate. Also called strabismus.

hypnagogic image
n. A vivid dreamlike image perceived by a person in a state between waking and sleeping in which he or she is unable to move. Also called a hypnopompic image.

hypnoanalysis
n. A brief form of psychoanalysis aided by hypnosis which is used to uncover memories

especially of infancy and childhood which are believed to be the source of current emotional problems. This is a controversial technique within psychoanalysis in part because of recent research that suggests that hypnotically aided memories are often false.

hypnogenic
adj. Sleep or hypnosis inducing.

hypnopompic image
n. A vivid dreamlike image perceived by a person in a state between waking and sleeping in which he or she is unable to move. Also called hypnogogic image.

hypnosis
n. **1.** The process of inducing a state of hypersuggestibility in another person in which his or her experience, memory, and behavior are influenced by suggestion to a greater degree than in normal states. **2.** The state of hypersuggestibility.

hypnosis as a research tool
n. The use of suggestive trances to investigate psychological and other variables including hypnosis itself. Subjects in suggestive trances often experience changes in perception, memory, thoughts, feelings, and behavior which may persist after the trance ends and have been found to be related to many non-trance behaviors. For example, it has been found that people in a hypnotic trance are more likely to report information from memory which may be either true or false than are people who have not been hypnotized; thus testimony from people who have been hypnotized is often inadmissible as evidence in courts in the United States and some other countries.

hypnotherapy
n. Any form of psychotherapy that uses hypnosis (induced hypersuggestibility) as a technique. It is frequently used to recover repressed memories and to make behavioral suggestions intended to reduce symptoms or undesirable habits such as smoking or overeating.

hypnotic
adj. Of or relating to hypnosis.

hypnotic age regression
n. A technique in hypnotherapy in which the therapist suggests to the client that he or she is becoming younger, intended to help him/her recover memories form an earlier period in life.

hypnotic analgesia
n. A reduction in pain caused by suggestions made during a period of induced hypersuggestibility.

hypnotic susceptibility
n. The ease with which or degree to which an individual can be induced to enter a state of hypersuggestibility.

hypnotizability
n. The ease with which or degree to which an individual can be induced to enter a state of hypersuggestibility.

hypoactive sexual desire disorder
n. A psychological disorder characterized by the absence of or a deficiency in sexual fantasy and desire, resulting in significant personal distress or interpersonal difficulty.

hypochondriasis
n. A psychological disorder which is characterized by chronic, irrational preoccupation with fears that one has a serious illness, misinterpretation of bodily symptoms, and mistrust of medical opinions and advice, which cause significant distress or impairment of functioning.

hypochondriasis scale
n. The first clinical scale on the Minnesota Multiphasic Personality Inventory, which was constructed by selecting items answered differently by patients diagnosed as hypochondriac and visitors in the waiting room of a state hospital. Persons with actual physical illness tend to receive moderately high scores on the scale (55–65) while persons receiving higher scores tend to be hypochondriacal, pessimistic, sour

on life, and manipulative and to have long-standing inadequacies in their adjustment to life. Low scorers (below 45) tend to be alert, spontaneous, and intelligent.

hypoergastia
n. An archaic term for depression and particularly the depression in bipolar disorder.

hypogeusia
n. Partial disturbance in taste recognition, particularly on tasting sweet, sour, bitter, or salty. When there is a complete disturbance in taste recognition, the term *ageusia* is used.

– A A

▶ *See also* **AGEUSIA**

hypoglossal nerve
n. Either of the 12th pair of cranial nerves, which runs from the tongue, lower jaw, front part of the neck, and upper chest to the medulla oblongata in the brain just below the fourth ventricle.

hypokinesis
n. Abnormally slowed or diminished bodily movement. Also called psychomotor retardation.

hypolexian
n. A person who has inability to read, spell, and write or difficulty in doing so that is independent of general intelligence and thought to be neurological in origin. Also called dyslexian.

hypologia
n. Poverty of speech.

hypomania
n. A state of abnormally elevated, expansive, or irritable mood, usually accompanied by grandiosity, decreased sleep, rapid or pressured speech, a flight of ideas, distractibility, high level of motor behavior often goal directed, psychomotor agitation, and abnormally high level of involvement in pleasurable activities that have negative consequences such as a sexual binge or wild spending or investing of money.

hypomnesia
n. Significant memory loss that does not reach the level of amnesia.

hypophoria
n. A form of strabismus in which the eye tends to deviate downward, making binocular fixation and vision impossible. In hypophoria either there may be double vision or the brain blocks out the vision of one eye so the person has monocular vision, making depth perception less accurate.

hypophrenia
n. Mental retardation.

hypophysis
n. The pituitary gland. Also called hypophysis cerebri.

hyposmia
n. A reduced sensitivity to odor which may be general or limited to certain odors. This can be caused by irritation of the nasal passages, nasal polyps, or head trauma.

hyposthenia
n. A general weakening or lack of strength, often caused by severe infections or trauma.

hypothalamic-hypophyseal portal system
n. A system of blood vessels connecting capillaries of the hypothalamus and the anterior pituitary (hypophysis) through which hormones travel from the hypothalamus to the pituitary. This system is important in stress reactions as it carries corticotropin-releasing hormone from the hypothalamus to the pituitary, while increasing the release of adrenocorticotropic hormone in the pituitary and bringing about the increased production and release of cortisol and other hormones associated with stress. Also called hypothalamic-pituitary portal system.

hypothalamic syndromes
n. Any of several patterns of reaction to damage to the hypothalamus by tumors, abnormal growth, or head trauma, which can

include insomnia, amnesia, gross obesity, and disturbance of autonomic function.

hypothalamus

n. (HT) A diencephalic brain structure at the level of the third ventricle and underneath the thalamus. The neurosecretory portion of the hypothalamus is embryologically derived from the same blood-rich tissue as that of the soft upper palate of the mouth, which is located just beneath the HT. There are numerous neural nuclei and fiber tracts within the HT, to organize fight, flight, feeding, temperature, and sexuality, as well as the autonomic nervous system, in the role of the HT as a homeostatic regulator of somatic survival functions.

The HT is connected via a neuroendocrine stalk to the pituitary gland, which regulates the endocrine system through both neural and hormonal secretary pathways. The HT is part of the hypothalamic pituitary adrenal axis (HTPA), a pivotal feedback loop in the body's response to stress.   – vs

hypothesis

n. A tentative explanation for some phenomenon or a statement about the relationship between variables in specified conditions which is subject to empirical verification and logical criticism.

hypothesis, null

n. The hypothesis that any results subjected to a statistical test will be due to chance processes.

hypothesis testing

n. **1.** The general method of science, in which a theory is formulated and subjected to empirical verification. **2.** A statistical process in which a test is used to accept or reject the idea that a result is due to chance processes based on the probability of the outcome were it generated by a chance process.

hypothetical construct

n. An explanation for observed phenomena that goes beyond the observed data and makes predictions about future observations.

hypothetico-deductive method

n. The scientific method in which an explanatory theory is formulated on the basis of observations and the accuracy of theoretical predictions is then empirically tested such that the greater the accuracy of the predictions the more credence a theory is given.

hypothymia

n. Diminished emotional response, as is often found in depressed individuals.

hypothyroidism

n. An underproduction of thyroxin and/or triiodothyronine by the thyroid gland, which results in lowered metabolism, tiredness, and lethargy. It can lead to weight gain, constipation, and, in severe cases, to mental retardation, coma, and death.

hypotonic

adj. Of or relating to muscle relaxation.

hypovolemic thirst

n. Thirst caused by a loss of extracellular liquid as through bleeding or vomiting. Also called extracellular thirst.

hypoxyphilia

n. Sexual arousal resulting from being strangled or otherwise deprived of oxygen.

hysteria

n. Emotional outbursts, suggestibility, and conversion symptoms which once were considered a disorder but are now considered symptoms of other disorders, including conversion disorder, dissociative disorder, histrionic personality disorder, or another disorder.

hysteria scale

n. The third clinical scale on the Minnesota Multiphasic Personality Inventory (MMPI), which was originally constructed by selecting items answered differently by patients diagnosed as hysterical and visitors to a state hospital. High scorers on the scale are likely to be self-centered, immature, demanding, manipulative and to have emotional outbursts and conversion symptoms. Low scorers on the scale tend to be unadventurous, socially isolated, conforming and to have narrow interests and see life in negative terms.

hysterical

adj. Characterized by excessive emotion, emotional outbursts, suggestibility, and conversion symptoms.

hysterical blindness

n. Loss or deterioration of visual perception without any apparent physical problem in the physiology of the visual system. This is commonly related to somatization disorder and is also called functional blindness.

hysterical paralysis

n. The loss of function of voluntary muscles without any apparent physical cause, which is attributed to psychological causes. It is a common symptom in conversion disorder.

hysterical personality

n. An enduring pattern of personal adjustment characterized by emotional outbursts, suggestibility, and conversion symptoms. This is not currently an official diagnosis but a frequently observed symptom pattern in persons now diagnosed as having conversion disorder.

I

1. *pron.* The nominative pronoun referring to one's self. **2.** *n.* In William James's psychology, the aspect of self which knows the self or is aware of me.

ibogaine

n. A hallucinogenic drug found in the root of *Tabernanthe iboga*, an African forest plant. It is an extremely potent hallucinogen whose mechanism of action is unknown and whose effects may last as long as 3 days. It has been used in religious ceremonies for many generations by the indigenous people, especially among the Bouiti.

ICD

n. Abbreviation for the *International Classification of Diseases*, which is an official taxonomy of diseases compiled and published by the World Health Organization and is currently in its ninth revision.

icicle plot

n. In statistics, a graphical representation of the results of a cluster analysis in successive steps which are represented in columns while individual cases are represented in the rows with those in the same cluster joined by a vertical line. Also called a horizontal icicle plot.

iconic memory

n. **1.** In cognitive psychology, a hypothesized very brief memory store for visual information which contains all or nearly all of the information taken in a single glance or moment of perception which lasts less than a second. This contrasts with short-term memory, which can last up to 30 seconds and has a capacity limit of about seven items. Also called very short term memory. **2.** The memory of an image in the mind.

iconic representation

n. In cognitive psychology, the storage of information as a virtual image in the mind.

iconic store

n. In cognitive psychology, a hypothesized very brief memory store for visual information which contains all or nearly all of the information taken in in a single glance or moment of perception which lasts less than a second. This contrasts with short-term memory, which can last up to 30 seconds and has a capacity limit of about seven items. Also called very short term memory and iconic memory.

id

n. The basic inherited motivations of the organism. In Freud's psychoanalytic theory, the id is primitive, impulsive, and pleasure seeking and needs guidance by the rational ego and the moral superego in order to function in the world. In later versions of Freudian theory, the id has only two instincts, Eros, or pleasure, and Thanatos, or death and aggressiveness. In other theories, such as Henry Murray's, the id is much more diverse and includes prosocial as well as selfish instincts.

idealism

n. **1.** In philosophy, any approach in which either some universal or mental idea is more basic or real than an individual object. Thus, a book is an example of ideal bookness and is a book to the degree it is an embodiment of the ideal book. **2.** A deep commitment to acting out a moral, political, or religious belief or belief system.

idealized self

n. **1.** A conception of the way one would like to be, as contrasted with the way one believes oneself to be, which may serve as a goal to improve oneself. **2.** A neurotically enhanced view of oneself in which one believes he/she has achieved his or her ideal.

ideal observer

n. A theoretical observer in signal detection theory who has complete knowledge and responds without bias. The ideal observer is used as a contrast for actual human observers in order to note discrepancies that point to the characteristics of human observation.

ideal self-guide

n. Self-guides are self-directive standards. These self-directive standards are a major source of people's emotions and motivation. They both directly prompt action as desired end states (i.e., goals to be attained) and, through their use in self-evaluation (i.e., standards to be met), arouse emotions that are themselves motivating. Ideal self-guides represent a person's hopes, wishes, and aspirations.

Ideal self-guides vary in strength. There are different modes of socialization that produce strong ideal self-guides. Strong ideal self-guides are produced by interactions with significant others that involve bolstering and

supportiveness, as well as love withdrawal for failure to meet an ideal self-guide. When self-guides are strong from socialization, they have high chronic accessibility. They predominate in self-regulation for years. Success and failure in meeting strong ideal self-guides arouse different emotions. When people's representation of what they are currently like, that is, their actual-self representation, is congruent with or matches one of their ideal self-guides, they experience cheerfulness-related emotions, such as feeling happy or joyful. When strong ideal self-guides predominate, people have a promotion focus on accomplishment and advancement. They prefer to use eager strategic means to make decisions and perform tasks. They appraise the world and remember past events in terms of the presence of positive outcomes (gains) and the absence of positive outcomes (nongains).

– ETH

ideas of reference

n. A belief that random events or actions are meaningfully related to oneself or caused by others' plots against oneself. These are a typical symptom of paranoia.

identical twins

n. Two children born as the result of a splitting of a single zygote in the mother's womb, who, consequently, have the same genes. This contrasts to fraternal twins, who are born of two zygotes fertilized at the same time and share gestation. Also called monozygotic twins.

identity

n. Identity is a catchall-phrase used throughout the social sciences to refer to the way individuals understand themselves and are recognized by others. Because different disciplines use the term in different ways, it is impossible to offer a single definition that fits all uses. Psychologists differentiate among three types of identities: personal identity, collective identity, and relational identity. *Personal identity* refers to people's beliefs about the qualities and attributes that distinguish them from others. For example, a person might think of himself/herself as outgoing, talented, or loyal. For most people, these qualities are more often positive than negative (e.g., most people believe they have a good sense of humor, not a bad one).

Collective identities comprise various social categories, such as our occupation, religion, or cultural heritage. A person might think of herself as an accountant, as Catholic, or as being from Boston. Instead of distinguishing us from others, collective identities highlight our connectedness with those who share similar characteristics. Some of these identities are of universal importance. For example, virtually all individuals develop a gender identity, racial identity, and ethnic identity, as they come to understand what it means to be a particular type of socially defined person.

Relational identities refer to individuals who are part of our extended self-concept (e.g., my children, my wife), as well as the qualities we display when we interact with other people. For example, a person might regard himself as "playful with his children," or "tender with his spouse."

Different situations and circumstances activate personal, collective, and relational identities. One factor that influences identity salience is distinctiveness. In general, individuals think of themselves in ways that distinguish them from their immediate social surroundings. To illustrate, an American is more likely to be thinking of her national identity when she visits a foreign land than when she is in her home country. Personal identities are most accessible when we are alone or interacting with other people who are demographically similar to us, whereas relational identities tend to be activated when we are interacting with relationship partners or simply thinking about them. Even unconscious reminders can activate relational identities. You might, for example, catch a glimpse of someone who reminds you of your mother and, without knowing why, find you are thinking of yourself in terms of your relationship with her.

Identity salience also differs across cultures. Some countries, such as the United States and the countries of Western Europe, value individualism and self-reliance. These values lead people to place more importance on their personal identities than their social or relational identities. This pattern is less apparent in countries that emphasize cooperation and interdependence, such as the countries of East Asia or South America. Rather than thinking of themselves in terms that distinguish them from others, citizens of these countries highlight qualities that signal their group identities and relationships with others.

Gender differences show a different pattern. Men are more likely than women to define themselves in terms of their collective identities, but women are more likely than men to define themselves in terms of their relational identities. Socialization practices underlie these tendencies, as women are generally taught to be more attentive to the needs of other people.

For most people, identity begins to form during adolescence. Younger children have autobiographical memories and possess a self-concept, but they do not integrate these various aspects of self into a coherent identity until they face a period in development Erik Erikson called the "adolescent identity crisis." The crisis arises because many of the physical, cognitive, and emotional changes that accompany adolescence are abrupt, and this discontinuity can create instability and confusion. Adolescents must also cope with increased societal expectations, new ways of relating to their peers, and changes in the relationships they have forged with their primary caregivers. To reconcile these changes, adolescents must find a way to establish continuity between their prepubertal self and the person they have become and do so in ways that are recognized and accepted by other members of society.

Erikson believed the adolescent identity crisis was resolved when adolescents make three decisions (or identity commitments). First, they must choose a profession or settle on a career path. Second, they must establish a general worldview that includes their attitude toward religion and politics. Finally, they must define their sexual orientation and adopt age-appropriate sex-role behavior. In years past, these commitments were relatively easy to make. Prior to the industrial revolution, most adolescents worked on the family farm or served an apprenticeship that prepared them to work in the family business. They also tended to adopt their parents' religious and political beliefs and frequently allowed their parents to determine whom and when they married. This is much less true today. At least in contemporary Western societies, adolescents are free to choose their occupation, ideology, and marriage partners. Although this freedom has numerous advantages, it is not without costs. Today, adolescents must decide who they are and what they will be. In short, they must create an identity for themselves, leading to the crisis Erikson discussed.

Adolescents differ with regard to their progress in the process of making their identity commitments. Those who have successfully weathered an identity crisis and have made the occupational, ideological, and sexual commitments Erikson described are said to be identity achieved. Those who are actively working toward resolving their crisis but have yet to do so successfully are said to be in an identity moratorium. Individuals who are mired in an identity crisis and are not making any noticeable progress toward resolving it are classified as identity diffused. Finally, individuals who have made commitments in the absence of any crisis are labeled identity foreclosed. Usually, these individuals have uncritically accepted their parents' commitments, rather than struggling to forge their own identity.

identity crisis
n. A state of uncertainty about one's role, purpose, and meaning in life which is typical of adolescence and tends to resolve in late adolescence or early adulthood as the individual gains a sense of place and purpose in the larger society and gains a sense of commitment to social and sexual roles. In some individuals the crisis continues throughout adulthood, preventing them from settling into identification with particular adult social roles.

identity denial
n. A situation in when an individual is not recognized as a member of a group with which he or she identifies.

identity diffusion
n. A state of uncertainty about one's role, purpose, and meaning in life typical of adolescence, which, in some individuals, continues throughout adulthood, preventing them from settling into identification with particular adult social roles.

identity disorder
n. **1.** A disorder characterized by the presence of two or more distinct personalities or identities in the same person who recurrently exchange control of the person and who may have only some knowledge of each other and the history of the person involved. **2.** A disorder characterized by a strong and persistent sense that one is or should be the other gender and discomfort with one's socially assigned gender, which generates significant distress and impairment in the person's life.

identity formation
n. The process of forming a stable sense of self, including commitment to social and sexual roles and beliefs about the purpose and meaning of life. This usually takes place primarily in late adolescence.

identity theory
n. A form of materialism in which it is assumed that mental states are caused by and identical with physical states and activities of the central nervous system.

identity versus role confusion
n. Erik Erikson's fifth of eight stages of psychosocial development, which occurs during the teenage years or adolescent period. During this stage, according to Erikson, adolescents are in search of who they are and what they believe. In their efforts to do so, it is not uncommon for adolescents to "try out" multiple roles or experiment with many different identities or belief systems. During this process, some teenagers may become confused and experience what Erikson labeled an identity crisis (which is a result of or leads to role confusion), whereby they cannot decide upon who they are or what they believe. Successful resolution of this stage of development involves the adolescent's developing a

cohesive sense of self in a multidimensional identity. The ego strength Erikson believes results from this resolution is a sense of loyalty to self and others.   – SRB

idiocentric

n. Idiocentrics are independent of groups (such as family, race, religion, tribe, social class) and tend to do "their own thing." If there is a conflict between their personal goals and the goals of their group, they tend to use their own goals. They act more according to what they like to do than according to what they should do. If they are dissatisfied in a situation, they just leave it.

Idiocentrics have many friends, but their relationships with their friends are rarely intimate. The cocktail party is prototypic of their relationships with others. They enter and leave new groups with ease. They are logical, make eye contact easily, and have strong opinions. They feel unique and tend to have a very good opinion of themselves.   – HTr

▶ *See also* **INDIVIDUALISM**

idiocentrism

n. A personality attribute commonly found in individualist cultures, which contrasts with allocentrism, which is commonly found in collectivist cultures. Idiocentrism and allocentrism are unrelated in collectivist cultures, but in individualist cultures these personality dispositions are negatively correlated.

Those high in idiocentrism are high in personal efficacy. They feel unique and are independent of in-groups; they do not share their successes and failures with such groups. They tend to be high in hedonism and see a large distance between themselves and their in-group. They do what they like to do more than what they should do. If they are dissatisfied with their social situation, they leave it.

Those with this personality have many friends, but their relationships with their friends are rarely intimate. The cocktail party is prototypic of their relationships with others. They feel unique and tend to have a very good opinion of themselves.   – HTr

▶ *See also* **ALLOCENTRISM, COLLECTIVISM,** *and* **INDIVIDUALISM**

idiographic

adj. Of or relating to psychological approaches in which the individual is the unit of analysis as opposed to understanding people in general, which is called a *nomothetic* approach. This approach is embodied in the theories of Gordon Allport, who differentiated between individual dispositions and common traits, and the work of Henry Murray, who described the study of individuals as personology. Idiographic psychology focuses on the uniqueness of the individual, as opposed to the characteristics shared by some other people or all other people. Also spelled *ideographic.*

idiographic-nomothetic psychology

n. Idiographic-nomothetic psychology can be thought of as divergent metatheoretical approaches to thinking about behavior and as assessment techniques that can be used to study behavior. At a metatheoretic level, idiographic perspectives view behavior as a function of a constellation of affects, cognitions, and environments that are unique to a particular individual. Idiographic approaches consequently utilize assessment techniques that are designed to access and preserve the unique qualities of the individual and that make that individual distinct from other persons. In contrast, nomothetic perspectives view behavior in terms of general processes that can be used to describe or class the behavior of large groups of persons. Assessment techniques are therefore geared toward describing and classing the behavior of relatively homogeneous groups of persons and describing the ways these large homogeneous classes of persons differ from other homogeneous classes. Though these terms can be traced to Kantian philosophy, the nomothetic-idiographic distinction in psychology has its roots in Gordon Allport's early (1930s) conceptualizations of personality. Both terms are used in contemporary personality and clinical psychology.   – WGS

idiot savant

n. A mentally retarded or autistic person who has one area in which his or her abilities far surpass those of normal individuals. Typical areas of talent among idiot savants are calculation, calendar calculations, memory, and music.

IE Scale

n. **1.** The Introversion-Extroversion Scale on the Myers-Briggs Type Indicator, which attempts to embody Carl Jung's theory that people differ in their basic attitude toward life, some finding meaning and purpose in the internal world of feelings and ideas and some in the external world of people and things. **2.** Any scale with introversion and extroversion as polar opposites such as the Eysenck Personality Inventory, which measures introversion and extroversion as dimensions of the reactivity of the individual to the environment, or the NEO Personality Inventory, which measures them as dimensions of behavioral activity and expressivity and social involvement. ▶ *See also* **INTROVERSION-EXTROVERSION**

illocutionary act

n. **1.** The act that is inherent in making a statement, as opposed to the statement itself or the effect the statement has on others. Thus saying "It looks like rain" could be a warning, an order to prepare for rain, a statement of fact, or a request for information; the warning, order, statement, or request is the illocutionary act.

illusion

n. **1.** A perception of sensory information that is not inherent in the stimulus itself. **2.** Any stimulus that generally leads people to have false perceptions of sensory information. Thus in the figure ⊥ the vertical line appears to be longer than the horizontal line, although both are the same length. **3.** A false belief or memory.

illusion of control

n. The illusion of control is an expectancy of personal success probability that is inappropriately higher than the objective probability would warrant. It is a phenomenon that is taken from the observer's perspective. From the actor's perspective it is not an illusion but rather a belief in the possibility of outcome control. The illusion of control is instigated

in chance situations that superficially mimic skill or controllable situations. Thus, when factors such as choice, competition, familiarity, active involvement (practice), and passive involvement (thinking), which may increase control in skill-determined situations, are introduced into chance-determined tasks (such as lotteries, coin flipping, horse racing), we behave as if we can exert control over the outcome. If we believe that events are either controllable or uncontrollable, it is an illusion. If we believe events are either controllable or indeterminate, it may not be an illusion.
— EL

illusory correlation

n. Illusory correlation is the tendency to attribute an association erroneously between two statistically independent variables. People tend to perceive an illusory correlation between two infrequently encountered stimuli that seem to go together (e.g., old age and wisdom). Illusory correlation has been used to explain the perpetuation of minority stereotypes. For example, although mental patients and nonpatients may be equally likely to display physical violence, because mental patients are a minority in the population and violent behaviors are infrequent, people may misperceive an association between mental illness and physical violence.   — YHK, CYC

illustrators

n. Nonverbal behavior – especially gestures but also facial expressions – that serve to illustrate or exemplify speech content or amplify it. Some people, for instance, raise their brows when their voice pitch becomes higher or lower their brows when their pitch becomes lower.

imageless thought

n. Any thinking that occurs without an internal sense of perception of the object(s) of thought.

imagery

n. **1.** The process of creating internal experiences of sensory and particularly of visual perception. **2.** The content of creative writing likely to or intended to evoke internal perceptions.

imipramine

n. A tricyclic antidepressant which blocks the reuptake of the neurotransmitters norepinephrine and serotonin.

immediate memory

n. A hypothesized information store which is used as a work space for short-term storage of information in use, such as telephone numbers or the current focus of attention. Typically this storage lasts less than a minute and is a commonly measured component of intelligence tests. Also called short-term memory.

immune system

n. The substances, processes, and structures within the body that respond to antigens such as virus, bacteria, very small pieces of foreign substances, and aberrant cells. The chief organs of the immune system are the bone marrow, which produces lymphocytes, which are the chief circulating agents of immunity; and the spleen and lymph tissues, which absorb antigens and dead cells.

immunoglobulin

n. Any of a group of proteins synthesized by plasma cells derived from beta lymphocytes which act as antibodies in immune response. They are Y-shaped proteins with a binding area at each tip of the top of the Y shape which attaches to a specific antigen and either prevents its function or identifies it for attack by other parts of the immune system.

Implicit Association Test

n. The Implicit Association Test (IAT) is an indirect measure of thought and feeling. It measures speed and accuracy in the act of associating a concept (e.g., elderly) to an attribute (e.g., slow) to infer the strength of association between the two. From such measurement it predicts the presence of unconscious social cognition – thoughts and feelings that are not necessarily accessible to conscious awareness or control. The application of IAT methodology is broad, from marketing to clinical psychology. Its most extensive application has been in the domain of discrimination, with its signature result being the presence of bias toward social groups when no or minimal bias is expressed on measures of self-report. The IAT can produce effects that are relatively large, show dissociations from conscious cognition, be visible in children as young as age 5, predict consequential behavior, and show underlying social cognition to be highly malleable. See https://implicit.harvard.edu and http://projectimplicit.net/ to find more information and to sample an IAT yourself.

– DRC, MRB

implicit attitude

n. Unlike explicit attitudes, implicit attitudes are evaluations of an object that exist outside conscious awareness or conscious control. Implicit attitudes can be automatically activated without requiring the motivation and capacity to express them. The consistency between implicit and explicit attitudes depends in part on the nature of the attitude. Consistency is greater when the attitude is not controversial or subjected to social desirability concerns, whereas self-presentational concerns create dissociations. One of the most popular measures of implicit attitudes is the Implicit Association Test (IAT).   – HLi, DA

implicit communication

n. **1.** The transfer of information through culturally defined selection of environments or conditions such as holding a meeting in a tavern as opposed to a lecture hall. **2.** In computer science, the reaction of a system to environmental data rather than to command signals. **3.** In evolutionary studies, the structures and behaviors which communicate with other members of a species.

implicit learning

n. Learning from the environment rather than from what is being taught. Thus a child of highly punitive parents might learn that might makes right instead of whatever particular rules the parents are trying to teach the child.

implicit memory

n. Implicit memory, also known as indirect memory, is an unintentional and often unaware manifestation of retention of previously acquired information (e.g., words, pictures, or ideas). This is in contrast to explicit memory, which refers to the conscious recollection of prior episodes (i.e., what people commonly regard as "memory"). When taking an implicit memory test, people perform a perceptual or cognitive task apparently unrelated to the study phase, such as deciding whether or not a word is correctly spelled. They do not need to recollect the prior study episodes, and supposedly they do not realize that their memories are being assessed. Repetition priming, a measure of implicit memory, is manifested by a facilitation in processing speed for studied items (faster response or reaction time), processing accuracy for those items (better response accuracy), or response bias (a bias to choose or detect the studied item, relative to unstudied or "new" items). – CST

implicit personality theory

n. Implicit personality theory (IPT) refers to laypersons' co-occurrence expectancies for traits and behaviors. Persons expect, for example, that gregarious persons are talkative as well. Such assumptions tend to be shared by people. Thus the meaning of IPT is much more specific than the meaning of "implicit theories," which refer to lay theories concerning a wide range of phenomena.

The *structure* of IPT has been studied using two approaches, one direct and the other indirect. The direct approach involves letting judges estimate conditional likelihoods that persons with attribute A will have attribute B as well, for instance, that a gregarious person will also be talkative. The indirect approach relies on ratings by strangers that are based on minimal information. Strangers tend to disagree concerning the attributes of a particular person (what goes with *whom*), whereas within-judge correlations between ratings of different attributes (what goes with *what*) are similar across judges, reflecting their shared assumptions on attribute co-occurrences. For example, observers whose only information on Alice's personality is a photograph of her are likely to disagree on her nervousness. Nevertheless, judges who perceive Alice as nervous are likely to perceive her as anxious as well.

Direct and indirect approaches to IPT have yielded similar findings concerning its structure, and this structure resembles the structure of ratings by knowledgeable informants to some extent. But there are differences as well: ratings by strangers are more highly correlated than self-reports and ratings by close acquaintances, implying that the more judges know about a person, the more complex is their description of that person's personality. Moreover, IPT does not reflect asymmetries in conditional likelihoods that result from different base rates. For instance, because friendliness is more widespread than homosexuality, it is more likely that a homosexual person will also be friendly, compared to that a friendly person will also be homosexual. But judges estimate these two conditional likelihoods as by and large the same.

Experiments on person memory show that IPT operates as a schema: If research participants do not remember all information on fictitious characters, their recall tends to be biased in IPT-consistent ways. Thus, as far as information about personality cannot be recalled, it seems that persons rely on their IPT to fill the gaps. A related phenomenon is *illusory correlations*, that is, that persons sometimes report correlations that do not exist. One source of illusory correlations seems to be associative relationships, another shared distinctiveness: the co-occurrence of two rare events tends to be overestimated because rare events attract more attention and are therefore more accessible in the mental networks of their observers. This might explain why stereotyping is particularly strong for members of minority groups.

From experimental findings that co-occurrences *may* be misperceived, it has been concluded that the correlations among ratings of personality *are* fundamentally flawed, and that they reflect the structure of IPT but not the structure of personality. This, however, is contentious: Proponents of the view that IPT is illusory argue that it reflects the associative relationships among personality attributes that are unrelated to their actual co-occurrences, and that IPT therefore systematically distorts the correlations among ratings of personality. By contrast, proponents of the view that IPT is accurate argue that it reflects the accurately perceived co-occurrences among traits and behaviors and therefore does not contribute to biased correlations among ratings of personality. The issue is important because correlations among ratings of personality are a major data source in various fields of psychology. But it seems that the controversy on the illusory versus veridical nature of IPT has been misconceived as that actual co-occurrences among personality attributes partly reflect their meaning relations: There is evidence that similar traits refer to overlapping sets of indicators; for example, that nervousness is correlated with anxiety partly reflects that many indicators of nervousness (unpleasant affect, physiological arousal) are indicators of anxiety as well.   – PB

implicit prejudice

n. Prejudicial attitudes, values, or beliefs that are unspoken and perhaps even outside conscious awareness.

implicit social comparison

n. An unconscious evaluation of other people according to culturally defined standards that underlies social interaction.

implosive therapy

n. A procedure in behavior therapy in which an individual is confronted with the thing he/ she fears most either in imagination or in real life under safe circumstances. Eventually he/ she becomes habituated to it and the initial fear responses gradually diminish and disappear. Also called exposure therapy, flooding, or implosion therapy.

impossible figure

n. A two-dimensional picture or drawing which uses visual cues to suggest an object with mutually exclusive characteristics so that it could not exist in three-dimensional space.

impotence

n. **1.** The persistent or recurrent inability to maintain an adequate penile erection for the completion of sexual activity, which causes significant frustration and personal distress

and interpersonal difficulties. Also called male erectile disorder. **2.** The reality or sense of being powerless or helpless.

impression formation

n. The rapid process of creating an understanding of a situation, object, person, or group of persons on the basis of a large number of diverse characteristics. The creation of understanding of other individuals has been a focus of research in psychology related to areas such as prejudice, stereotyping, categorization, and emotion.

impression management

n. The process of attempting to control other people's attitudes or beliefs or perceptions of one's self or others. This is usually done through fitting behavior to a desired image, attempting to frame discussions in ways favorable to one's position, and controlling information availability so that only what is in one's favor is available to others.

imprinting

n. In ethology, the process of learning to respond instinctively to a particular stimulus during a critical period of learning. Thus baby greylag geese will follow the first large moving thing they see after hatching, which is usually their mother but may be any large moving object, including a scientist studying imprinting.

impulse-control disorders

n. Any of a group of disorders that involve inability to control an impulse to act in a way that is harmful to the person or to others. The impulse to act is experienced as a pressure to act accompanied by anxiety and then a sense of pleasure and relief when acting on the impulse. This group includes intermittent explosive disorder, kleptomania, pyromania, pathological gambling, trichotillomania, and the symptoms of other disorders such as obsessive-compulsive disorder; any addictive disorder, such as alcoholism or nicotine addiction; paraphilias; antisocial personality disorder, conduct disorder, some forms of schizophrenia, and some mood disorders.

impulsivity

n. A characteristic or trait in which the individual tends to act quickly on motives as they arise with little reflection as to the consequences of his or her actions or their effect on others or on plans for satisfying other motives.

inbreeding

n. The mating of closely related couples or groups. This is associated with an increase in genetic abnormalities and lessening of capacity to cope with change in real world populations and with the maintenance of certain preferred traits in laboratory populations.

incentive motivation

n. **1.** Impulse to act which results from external rewards for an act rather than inherent consequences of the act itself. **2.** The expectation of reward or other inducement to behave in particular ways within a stimulus environment.

incest

n. Sexual interaction between close blood relatives that is prohibited by a culture and may or may not also be illegal. The definition of incest is variable among cultures and among groups within cultures so that parent-child or sibling sexual relations are almost always banned but were allowed among, for instance, Egyptian royalty in some periods of history in order to preserve and concentrate the royal bloodline. Sexual activity among other close relatives such as first cousins, aunts, uncles, and grandparents is also usually forbidden within a culture, but in some cultures adolescents are introduced to sex by relatives of the parental or grandparental generation, and some sex acts, such as swallowing semen, are considered not sexual acts but a transmission of power from one generation to the next.

incest taboo

n. A name for the observation that all cultures have some rules against particular relatives' having sexual relations with one another.

incidental learning

n. Learning that occurs while the organism is focused on some other activity. Also called latent learning.

inclusive fitness

n. The degree to which the next generation includes the genes not only of an individual but of a close relative of an individual. Thus an individual organism that acts to secure the survival of a sibling, cousin, or other relative will increase the likelihood that some percentage of its own genes will survive. This is the basis for the idea of biological altruism.

incremental validity ▶ *See* VALIDITY, INCREMENTAL

incubation

n. **1.** The period or process of keeping eggs within the environmental conditions which allow the development and hatching of live organisms. **2.** The period or process of growing a culture of microorganisms. **3.** The period or process of keeping a premature or other at-risk infant alive until sufficient growth occurs to allow the infant to survive without continuous intervention. **4.** The period in which an idea or problem is processed without attention. **5.** The period between initial infection and the appearance of symptoms in a disease.

independent samples t test

n. A statistical procedure in which the ratio of variance within two different groups of subjects is compared with the between-group variance so as to determine the likelihood that the two groups are from the same population. The formula for groups 1 and 2 is

$$t = \frac{Mean1 - Mean2}{\sqrt{\frac{(N1-1) \times Variance1 + (N2-1) \times Variance2}{N1+N2-2} \times \left(\frac{1}{N1} + \frac{1}{N2}\right)}}$$

where N = number of scores in a group.

independent self-construal

n. A self-image in which oneself as an individual with unique dispositions and history is emphasized, as opposed to an interdependent self-image, in which one's relationships with others are emphasized. This is often considered one of the chief cultural differences between people from Asian and European-American cultures, although this difference is quite variable among cultures from each of the continents.

independent variable

n. A variable controlled or manipulated by an experimenter in order to observe the effect of the control or manipulation on one or more outcome or dependent variables. Quasi-independent variables are those such as sex or age that are treated as independent but are not under the control of the experimenter.

indigenous emotions

n. **1.** Categories of emotion that are specific to a particular culture and have no exact cultural or language equivalents. As an example, *amae* in Japanese is the emotion of relatedness between two people, *Schadenfreude* in Germany is the joy experienced from the pain or frustration of one's enemies, and *semteende* is the experience of being in a shameful social situation regardless of personal experience among the African group the Fulani. **2.** In constructionist approaches to emotion, culturally shared scripts of reactions to situations.

indigenous healing

n. The methods and process of regaining health particular to a particular culture. Theories of illness and health vary markedly among cultures.

indigenous healing system

n. Any healing system within a particular culture such as acupuncture and the ayurvedic system of India. These systems often include holistic, social, and spiritual dimensions which have been lacking in Euro-American tradition and have often been found beneficial in psychological disorders and promotion of immune function and as adjuncts to Western medicine in treating indigenous people.

indigenous personalities

n. Enduring and pervading patterns of individual adjustment showing meaningful differences among individuals within a culture. Conceptions of personality are more or less generalizable to other cultures so that a common trait in one culture may or may not have meaning to members of another culture.

indigenous psychology

n. Indigenous psychology is a scientific approach that seeks to describe and explain culturally relevant psychological phenomena using theories, concepts, and methods that reflect local cultural contexts and perspectives. Indigenous psychology can also refer to the knowledge base or content that results from this approach. Indigenous psychologies are rooted in the specific ecological, historical, sociocultural, and language contexts of a given culture and reflect the experiences, perspectives, and premises of its members. The indigenous perspective is typically contrasted with an alternative approach to cross-cultural research, in which theories, concepts, and methods developed in other (typically Western) cultures are transported and applied in cultural contexts for which they may be less relevant. Thus, in indigenous psychology, the culture of interest is the *source* of psychological concepts, methods, and knowledge, rather than the *target* of concepts, methods, and knowledge developed in other cultures.   – ATC

indirect control

n. A type of control in which one's agency is hidden or downplayed; people pretend they are not acting as an agent even though they are doing so in reality.

indirect speech act

n. Any speech act whose meaning does not appear explicitly in the verbal content of an utterance. Thus the meaning of the sentence "Apple pie tastes good" may be a request or command to the hearer to make an apple pie.

individual differences

n. Measurable variance on any dimension among persons or organisms in a group.

individualism

n. A cultural pattern found in cultures that tend to be complex, modern, and tolerant of deviations from cultural norms. It is found by examining data across cultures and is the opposite of collectivism.

This cultural pattern is especially likely to occur among affluent individuals, both across cultures and within culture. It is also very likely to be present among the more educated, widely traveled members of a culture; among those who have been exposed to highly heterogeneous, diverse cultures; among those raised in small families, in situations where there is fast social change, and in an open frontier. Exposure to Hollywood-made media increases individualism, because in such media the emphasis is on pleasure and fun, and rarely on doing one's duty.

People in such cultures tend to think of themselves as independent of their group. They give priority to their personal goals and do what they like to do rather than what they must do.   – HTr

▶ *See also* **COLLECTIVISM**

individual-level analysis

n. Any statistical or other procedure which uses single persons as a variable, as opposed to analyses that group people by culture, country, geographical area, age, socioeconomic status, or any other form of grouping.

individual psychology

n. Individual psychology was developed in the early 1900s by Alfred Adler, who believed that human behavior was holistic, goal driven, and socially oriented. Through interactions with family and immediate social surroundings, individuals develop a "private logic" or subjective view of life that organizes their thoughts about the world and their place in it and that influences their choice of social groups. Personality and behavior are thought to be crystallized in early childhood and to be stable throughout life. Although there is an absence of empirical work to support its core tenets, some contemporary clinical and counseling perspectives employ a distinctively Adlerian (individual psychology) perspective in treating psychological disorders, and individual psychology continues to be written about in the absence of empirical data in some segments of the field; for example, there is a journal explicitly devoted to individual

psychology. At present, individual psychology may be best relegated to the historical canon of theories in personality, though the spirit of Adler's theories can be found in many contemporary perspectives in social and personality psychology (e.g., self-handicapping).

     – WGS

individuation

n. **1.** In Jungian theory, the process of self-realization that accelerates in middle age in which a person attempts to develop and bring to consciousness the unfulfilled aspects of the collective unconscious, unify polarities and conflicts, and develop a unified self, including the appearance and realization of wisdom. **2.** In Mahler's object-relations theory, the period between the 18th and 36th months of life in which children begin to function independently of their mother. **3.** Any process of becoming an autonomous, individual personality.

induced psychotic disorder

n. A delusion shared by two individuals. The individuals involved usually share a close relationship either by kinship or romance. Also called folie à deux and shared psychotic disorder.

induction

n. **1.** A form of logical reasoning in which general principles are inferred from multiple observations. **2.** In classical conditioning, increasing the magnitude of a response to a conditioned stimulus brought about by presenting an inhibitory stimulus immediately before presenting the stimulus. **3.** Any act or process of bringing about a change, as of inducting a person into the military, putting someone into a hypnotic state, or producing an electrical current in a wire.

inductive reasoning

n. Logical inference using many instances to formulate a general rule.

industrial/organizational psychology

n. The branch of psychology that studies humans in the workplace and attempts to apply general psychological principles to workplaces to improve productivity and to improve working circumstances for those employed. I/O psychology stresses the study of motivation, group processes and organizational effectiveness, personnel selection, training, employee evaluation, and leadership.

industrial psychology
n. The branch of psychology that studies humans in the workplace and attempts to apply general psychological principles to workplaces to improve productivity and to improve working circumstances for those employed. Industrial/organizational (I/O) psychology stresses the study of motivation, group processes and organizational effectiveness, personnel selection, training, employee evaluation, and leadership.

industry versus inferiority
n. Erik Erikson's fourth of eight stages of psychosocial development, which occurs during childhood. In this stage Erikson believed the child develops a sense of accomplishment through task completion (in particular, he focused on academic task completion). If children can successfully complete assignments and chores, they then feel a sense of accomplishment and industry with the resulting ego strength of competence. However, if children are not able to complete or master tasks successfully, they are likely to develop a sense of inferiority and shame about their lack of ability.   – SRB

infantile amnesia
n. A name for the observation that most people have episodic memory that goes back to some point in childhood and then stops so that little or nothing before that point is remembered. This point varies between about 2 and 5 years of age.

infantile autism
n. A disorder of early childhood characterized by impaired social learning and communication, restricted interests, diminished imaginative thought, and stereotyped or repetitive nonfunctional movements or verbalizations. Also called autistic disorder.

infantilism
n. Behavior, thought, or physical characteristics of infants in older children or adults.

inference
n. **1.** Any mental process which considers information and draws conclusions which are not in evidence. **2.** In statistics, using a statistical procedure to make a conclusion about a population from a sample drawn from the population.

inferential statistics
n. The branch of statistics concerned with using samples to draw conclusions about populations by means of hypothesis testing.

inferior colliculus
n. Either of a pair of bumps on the midbrain lying behind the superior colliculi, which are the most important part of the auditory pathway in the midbrain.

inferiority complex
n. **1.** In Adlerian psychology, a combination of an erroneous belief of an individual that he/she is unable to cope with some aspect of life because of a real or imagined physical or psychological deficiency, feelings of depression, and a cessation of coping efforts in that area. **2.** A general term for a personal sense of inferiority.

inferior temporal cortex
n. Temporal area situated below the middle temporal gyrus. It is also referred to as the inferior temporal gyrus. It partially corresponds to the Brodmann's areas 20 and 37. It can be considered as a visual association area involved in the processing of visual shapes.
                                                            – AA

information processing
n. (IP) **1.** A cognitive approach to psychology in which processes of the central nervous system are modeled using computer programming concepts. This area includes study of sensation and perception, attention, learning, memory, decision making, and response mechanisms. **2.** The acquisition, storage, and manipulation of data by computers.

information processing (unconscious)

n. **1.** A cognitive approach to psychology in which processes of the central nervous system outside awareness are modeled using computer programming concepts, which includes the vast majority of such processes although the term is usually applied only to the processing of data which is potentially conscious. This area includes study of sensation and perception, attention, learning, memory, decision making, and response mechanisms.

information theory

n. A theory of communication in which knowledge is broken down into bits, which are encoded, stored, transmitted by the sender, and then decoded by the receiver of the communication.

informed consent

n. Voluntary agreement to participate, such as in a medical procedure or psychology experiment, after having been informed in a manner consistent with the person's capacity to understand of the risks, benefits, purpose, and alternatives to participation.

infundibulum

n. **1.** The funnel-shaped stalk of the pituitary which connects to the hypothalamus, carrying fibers responsible for introducing oxytocin and antidiuretic hormone into the blood. **2.** Any funnel-shaped cavity or organ in the body.

in-group

n. **1.** Any group to which one belongs, which contrasts with other groups toward whom one tends to feel superior or competitive. **2.** Any group with intense bonds among all members.

in-group advantage

n. Refers to any psychological process in which members of an in-group perform better than members of out-groups. In recent psychological research, it refers to the hypothesis that the ability of individuals of a certain culture to recognize emotions of others of the same culture is relatively better than the ability of those from a different culture.

in-group bias

n. The tendency to perceive members and things associated with groups to which one belongs in more positive ways than is true of persons outside one's groups. This tendency increases in situations of intergroup contact and especially conflict. Also called ethnocentrism.

inherited trait

n. Any characteristic of the individual which is controlled or significantly affected by genetics or which has been shown or assumed to have demonstrable familial patterns independent of environmental conditioning.

inhibition

n. **1.** The act of restraining, stopping, repressing, decreasing, or preventing a process, idea, impulse, or action. **2.** Any process that accomplishes the restraining, stopping, repressing, decreasing, or preventing of a process, idea, impulse, or action. **3.** In conditioning, the blocking or delay of a response to a stimulus with counterconditioning.

inhibition of delay

n. In delay conditioning, the reduced magnitude of the conditioned response during the early part of the stimulus period. Thus if a dog is fed after the end of a 2-minute tone and begins to salivate to the tone, it will salivate more during the second minute of the tone than during the first minute.

inhibition of return

n. Inhibition of return (IOR) is the second of two effects generally observed in a cue-response paradigm. In the cue-response paradigm, a cuing stimulus (a luminance change) is presented at a random location within a participant's gaze followed by a delay (either long or short) and finally a target (e.g., a letter). The participant's task is to indicate that the target has appeared or identify it in the presence of distractors. IOR is measured either as an increase in the amount of time necessary to detect a target or as a reduction in the accuracy with which a target is identified when that target is presented in a previously attended location after a delay of about a third of a second. This decrement in processing replaces the enhancement (faster or more accurate responding) in processing that typically occurs at attended locations prior to a third of a second.   – DGa

inhibition, proactive
n. Interference in new conditioning caused by previous learning of similar material. Thus memorizing a list of words may be made more difficult by already having memorized a similar list of words. Also called proactive interference.

inhibition, retroactive
n. Interference in recalling old material or performing learned patterns of behavior caused by learning new and similar material or behavior patterns.

inhibitory conditioning
n. In classical conditioning, when the unconditioned stimulus is paired with another stimulus less often than the unconditioned stimulus is presented without the other stimulus, the other stimulus becomes a conditioned stimulus, which makes the conditioned stimulus less likely to occur.

inhibitory postsynaptic potential
n. A hyperpolarizing potential in a postsynaptic neuron which decreases the likelihood that an action potential will be sent along the axonic fiber to the next set of synapses in the nerve.

initial values law
n. In physiology, the idea that the existing level of a physiological system or variable will have an effect on the response produced by any input to the system. Thus if a person has just finished jogging and his or her heart is beating rapidly and he/she is then scared by a falling meteor, his/her pulse rate will increase less than if he/she had been resting on a park bench and had a low pulse rate before the meteor scared him/her.

initiative versus guilt
n. This is the third stage in Erikson's theory of psychosocial development. Here, the child is about 4 or 5 years old and is trying to resolve the conflict of initiative versus guilt. The child is now able to take initiative in the form of undertaking, planning, and working on a task and does so simply for the sake of being active. The end result is not important; it is the "doing" that interests the child. On the opposite end of the conflict is the feeling of guilt. For the child to pass through this stage without feeling residual guilt, parents must provide opportunity for the child to engage in motor activities and imaginative play. Parents should not make the child feel that his/her actions are silly or stupid, and they should answer questions that the child asks. If parents fail to meet these needs of the child, he/she may develop a sense of guilt over self-initiated activities that may persist later in life.   – EF

injury feigning
n. The act of pretending to be injured when one is not, in fact, injured. This strategy is often used by birds wishing to lure a potential predator in a direction away from their nests and eggs or babies.

inkblot test
n. Any test in which the subject is presented with inkblots and asked "What might this be?" The best known such test, developed by Hermann Rorschach, includes 10 inkblots, some in black, white, and gray and some in color. Responses are scored for form, color, movement, detail, thematic content, and whether the whole figure is included, whether it is a popular response, and whether humans are present. The test is used to make inferences about the personality of the test subject. It has been found markedly lacking in reliability, and so its use is declining. Another inkblot test, constructed by Wayne Holtzman, uses 30 inkblots and can be reliably scored, but its use has never grown widespread despite its psychometric advantage over the Rorschach test.

innate
adj. 1. Present at birth due to inherent or genetic factors. 2. In philosophy, a characteristic of some ideas such that they are known

through reason without the necessity of being confirmed by experience.

innate releasing mechanism
n. In ethology, a control mechanism which initiates a complex sequence of behavior only when the organism encounters an appropriate circumstance for it. Thus a female cat engages in lordosis, or sexual posturing, only when it is in estrus and is in the presence of a potential sexual partner.

inner ear
n. Third division of the ear (external or outer ear, middle ear, and inner or internal ear). The inner ear is really composed by two different organs: the cochlea (audition) and the vestibular organ or labyrinth, including the semicircular canals and the vestibule (balance). The cochlea includes the organ of Corti, containing the auditory receptors. The inner ear transmits information to the brain by cranial nerve VIII (vestibulocochlear or auditory nerve), which has two different branches: a cochlear branch (hearing information) and a vestibular branch (semicircular canals and the vestibule).   – AA

insanity
n. A legal term usually denoting an incapacity to appreciate the illegality of an act or inability not to act illegally if the person does appreciate their action's illegality. The definition differs from one governmental entity to another and is connected with judicial ideas of responsibility.

insight
n. **1.** A clear and deep understanding of anything. **2.** The sudden appearance of a solution to a problem. **3.** A realization of some aspect or relationship in one's own internal organization. **4.** The capacity to understand one's own or others' mind and behavior.

insight learning
n. Learning that occurs by means of a sudden reorganization of mental elements so as to make a solution obvious. Such learning usually takes place after extended periods of experimenting with solutions and incubation.

insomnia
n. A disorder of sleep characterized by an inability to fall asleep or to remain asleep, resulting in fatigue sufficient to cause personal distress and interfere with daily functioning.

insomnia, delayed sleep-onset
n. A disorder of sleep characterized by an inability to fall asleep, resulting in fatigue sufficient to cause personal distress and interfere with daily functioning.

instinct
n. **1.** In ethology, a specieswide and species-specific complex pattern of behavior of obvious survival value in the environment of evolutionary adaptedness, which appears in altered or muted form even when normal opportunities for its expression are absent. **2.** In later psychoanalytic theory, Eros, or sexuality, and Thanatos, the death wish. **3.** Any motivation or behavior pattern that is considered innate.

institutional discrimination
n. Discrimination that occurs on the level of a large group, society, organization, or institution.

instrumental behavior
n. **1.** In operant conditioning, behavior that is learned and elicited through reinforcement. **2.** Any behavior which has the control of others' behavior as its goal. Thus a boss may encourage a subordinate in order to induce her/him to work harder, or a wolf may cringe and act helpless in order to escape the aggression of a superior in the pack. **3.** Any actions performed in order to obtain a reward.

instrumental conditioning
n. A process of learning in which a behavior is learned by means of reward of that behavior or successive approximations of that behavior.

insulin
n. A hormone synthesized in the pancreas which controls blood sugar level by making it easier for sugar molecules to pass through cell

membranes. Chronically insufficient insulin level is called *diabetes*; it results in excretion of sugar in the urine. High elevations of insulin level cause low blood sugar level (hypoglycemia) and can cause fatigue, coma, convulsions, and death.

insulin shock therapy
n. (IST) The intentional production of insulin coma and convulsions, which was sometimes used to treat schizophrenia and drug addiction before about 1960. The treatment has never been shown to have any positive effect.

integration
n. Within the psychological study of acculturation, and particularly the work of John Berry, integration refers to a pattern of cultural change in which an individual engages with a new cultural group and adopts its characteristics while maintaining a strong connection to the original cultural group. This involvement can take place on many levels. For instance, one can maintain interpersonal and/or mediated contact with the original cultural group; continue to observe behavioral traditions, such as food or clothing preferences; and preserve some degree of identification with that group. At the same time, the individual might seek contact with a new cultural group with the intention of adopting at least some of that group's cultural characteristics and perhaps eventually begin to identify with that cultural group. It is important to recognize, though, that not all aspects of a person's life will necessarily evidence integration. People may readily interact with members of another cultural group and acquire new behavioral characteristics, but they may not adopt new cultural values or identities. Thus, any description of a person as "integrated" needs to specify on which dimension this claim is made.

There are two common approaches to assessing a person's level of integration. First, a researcher may utilize instruments specifically developed to assess the construct of integration, whereby participants indicate their agreement with statements such as "I have good friends from Culture X and Culture Y." This approach has been criticized as having a variety of psychometric problems, not the least

of which is that participants may base their response on different aspects of the statement. Second, a researcher may ask participants to indicate their degree of cultural involvement in the cultural group of origin and then independently indicate their degree of involvement in the other relevant cultural group. Participants who claim that they are strongly involved in both groups are termed *integrated*.

These approaches to measuring integration reflect a theoretical assumption of the bicultural individual as somehow the additive sum of two or more cultures. Other formulations of biculturality have been offered. For instance, aspects of each culture may be selected and recombined into a cultural hybrid, a new form that is different from the sum of its parts (e.g., aspects of Cree and French cultures being reshaped into Métis). Young Kim has argued from a similar perspective that, through a process of stress, adaptation, and growth that takes place over time, a person exposed to a new culture will develop an "intercultural identity." Such a person is no longer rigidly bound by membership to any one particular culture but instead develops a broader perspective on culture and the human condition. In this case, the new form is greater than the sum of the parts. Still others retain the notion of cultural duality, arguing that the bicultural person does not engage both cultures simultaneously but rather shifts between cultural frames of reference in response to cues and negotiations with the social world. Still other formulations are possible, all potentially valid descriptions of different people in different circumstances. Some evidence suggests, for instance, that people who acquire a second culture early in life may have a different bicultural experience than those who acquire it later. As theoretical work on integration and biculturality grows, it is likely that these new conceptualizations will inform alternative approaches to measurement.   – KN

intelligence
n. A set of abilities to adapt better to the environment through experience. The nature of these abilities is much debated in psychology. Most intelligence tests include verbal abilities,

quantitative reasoning, memory capacity, and problem solving. Sternberg's theory supposes that there are three kinds of intelligence: analytical intelligence, which helps one do well with academic issues; a creative aspect, which is related to dealing with novelty and inductive reasoning; and a practical aspect, which is related to adapting to the demands of everyday life.

intelligence, crystallized
n. The form of intelligence associated with previously learned material such as deductive reasoning, vocabulary, general knowledge, reading comprehension, and solving analogies. It increases slowly throughout adulthood until the onset of physical decline in elderly people and is associated most closely with the hippocampus.

intelligence, fluid
n. The form of intelligence associated with learning new material, inductive reasoning, pattern detection, abstract reasoning, quantitative reasoning, and problem solving. It tends to peak at around age 25 and slowly decline thereafter. It is associated with the prefrontal and cingulate cortexes.

intelligence quotient
n. Originally it was the mental age as defined by a test divided by chronological age multiplied by one hundred. This form has been replaced by the deviation intelligence quotient, which is defined by one's place in a standardized curve of scores on an intelligence test which has a median of 100 and a standard deviation of either 15 or 16, depending on the test.

intelligence test
n. Any test that claims to measure general abilities or capacity to learn. The best known intelligence tests are the Wechsler scales of intelligence and the Stanford-Binet intelligence test. Both are individually administered tests which measure a variety of skills and make inferences about likely educational achievement and capacities to learn. Many shorter intelligence tests exist, many of which may be administered in groups. A limitation of all intelligence tests has

been the problem of separating exposure to different learning conditions, including different cultures and languages, from innate ability. Attempts to develop culture-fair or culture-free tests such as the Raven Progressive Matrices test have been only marginally successful.

intentionality
n. **1.** A characteristic of a person's actions involving motivation in the form of goals, desires or impulses, selection of means to fulfill those motivations, and a conscious desire for a future state. **2.** The property of mental experiences that they must have an object. Thus one cannot hear without hearing a sound, believe without a statement of or proposition of belief, or experience an emotion without a situation about which to feel the emotion.

interaction
n. **1.** A relationship of limited duration in which each party has an effect on the other. **2.** In statistics, the situation in which the relationship between an independent variable and a dependent variable is altered by changes in one or more other independent variables.

interaction effect
n. In statistics, the situation in which the relationship between an independent variable and a dependent variable is altered by changes in one or more other independent variables.

intercorrelation
n. The degree of relationship between all possible pairings of variables in a list.

intercultural adaptation
n. The process of adapting one's behavior when interacting with people in a culture different from that in which one was raised. This includes learning to take the perspective of the others in different social situations accurately as well as learning cultural rules, behaviors, and linguistic forms and adapting one's behavior to fit the situation. ▶ *See also* **INTER-CULTURAL ADJUSTMENT, INTERCULTURAL**

COMMUNICATION, INTERCULTURAL COM-
MUNICATION COMPETENCE, *and* INTER-
CULTURAL SENSITIVITY

intercultural adjustment

n. The degree to which a person has become comfortable when interacting with people in a culture different from that in which he/she was raised, which includes learning to take the perspective of the others in different social situations accurately as well as learning cultural rules, behaviors, and linguistic forms. ▶ *See also* INTERCULTURAL ADAPTATION, INTERCULTURAL COMMU-NICATION, INTERCULTURAL COMMUNICA-TION COMPETENCE, *and* INTERCULTURAL SENSITIVITY

intercultural communication

n. The process of accurately conveying human information between two or more persons with different cultural backgrounds which typically differ in not only in language but in pragmatics and the nonverbal parts of communication. ▶ *See also* INTERCUL-TURAL ADAPTATION, INTERCULTURAL ADJUSTMENT, INTERCULTURAL COMMUNI-CATION COMPETENCE, *and* INTERCULTURAL SENSITIVITY

intercultural communication competence

n. The ability to and effectively exchange information with a person or persons of another culture accurately, including not only language skills but metalanguage skills such as pragmatics and nonverbal communi-cation. ▶ *See also* INTERCULTURAL ADAP-TATION, INTERCULTURAL ADJUSTMENT, INTERCULTURAL COMMUNICATION, *and* INTERCULTURAL SENSITIVITY

intercultural sensitivity

n. The capacity to take the perspective of per-sons from other cultures so as to understand how they perceive, act, and communicate in different situations. ▶ *See also* INTERCUL-TURAL ADAPTATION, INTERCULTURAL ADJUSTMENT, INTERCULTURAL COMMUNI-CATION, *and* INTERCULTURAL COMMUNICA-TION COMPETENCE

interdependent self-construal

n. A self-image in which one's relationships with others define the self. This is opposed to an independent self-image, in which the indi-vidual with unique dispositions and history is emphasized. This is often considered one of the chief cultural differences between people from Asian and European-American cultures, although this difference is quite variable among cultures of each of the continents.

interference

n. **1.** The reduction in learning or remember-ing caused by the learning or remembering of other information. **2.** The interaction of two or more waves such that a new additive wave pattern is created. **3.** Noise which makes signal detection more difficult.

intermittent reinforcement

n. Rewards which do not appear for every occurrence of a behavior that is rewarded. There are many ways of creating intermittent reinforcement schedules, the most common of which are ratio and interval schedules. In ratio schedules a reward is issued after a cer-tain number of responses, and in interval schedules a reward is given at the end of a period in which an appropriate response has occurred.

intermittent schedule

n. An agenda of reinforcements in which not every occurrence of a target behavior is rewarded. There are many ways of creating intermittent reinforcement schedules, the most common of which are ratio and inter-val schedules. In ratio schedules a reward is issued after a certain number of responses, and in interval schedules a reward is given at the end of a period in which an appropriate response has occurred.

internal attribution

Definition. n. When trying to explain a per-son's behavior (what is referred to in psychol-ogy as making an attribution for the person's behavior), an internal attribution is made when it is assumed that the cause of an event is due to a factor within (or internal to) a per-son. Internal factors are such characteristics as a person's intelligence, abilities, values, or personality. When an internal attribution is made about another person's behavior, that person is considered to be responsible for the event because it was caused by an internal factor.

Explanation. Attribution theory states that people have a desire to explain events in the world around them. Making internal attributions assumes that an event is due purely to factors inside the person (e.g., personality, ability, effort) rather than factors outside the person (e.g., luck). Internal factors are within a person's control. Therefore, when internal attributions are made about people's behaviors, it is assumed that the people are responsible for their own outcomes. People tend to make an internal attribution when a positive event happens to them or when negative events happen to their competition. People tend to take credit for their own successes, but they tend to hold their competitors at fault for their failures. For example, when students score well on tests, they tend to make internal attributions by thinking the excellent performance resulted from their being very intelligent or very hard-working. They tend not to attribute the good performance to luck but believe that they deserve the grade. On the other hand, when student competitors do poorly on a test, students frequently assume that the bad grade was deserved because the competitor is not smart or is unmotivated.

People are also more likely to make an internal attribution when a good friend or someone they like succeeds, when the performer of the behavior succeeds at something from which they can benefit, and when a person who is known to be motivated to achieve the goal succeeds. One explanation for using internal attributions is the preservation of a perception of control over the world. When people are thought to be directly responsible for their outcomes, they can change their behavior in order to change the outcome. Making internal attributions affects the way people react to similar events in the future. Students who believe that their good grade was due to their motivation (studying hard) are more likely to study hard in the future.
— VKP, LAB

internal consistency

n. The degree to which responses to different items in a test or scale are correlated with each other. This is usually measured using Kuder-Richardson formula 20 or Cronbach's alpha coefficient. Also called internal reliability.

internal ear

n. Another name for the inner ear, usually including the middle ear.

internal-external scale

n. A 29-item forced-choice scale designed to measure the degree to which a person believes he/she has control over his/her life, versus the belief that forces outside him/her control life.

internalization

n. **1.** The process of taking ideas, behavior patterns, beliefs, and attitudes of other people and making them part of the self. **2.** In object-relations theory, the process of taking an object relationship into the mind which reproduces the external relationship as an internal process of mind.

internal locus of control

n. Internal locus of control is the degree to which individuals expect that a reinforcement or an outcome of their behavior depends on an internal cause such as their own behavior or personal characteristics. The original internal-external scale, developed by Rotter in 1966, proposed to consider internal and external locus of control on a continuous bipolar scale. However, other authors proposed to consider internal and external locus of control as two independent dimensions. Internal locus of control is affected by several demographic variables, such as gender, age, or socioeconomic status. Several studies have shown a positive relation between internal locus of control and academic achievement, but no relation has been observed between locus of control and intelligence. Relations to wealth and education were also found at the level of countries: wealthier and more educated countries showed more internal locus of control. Several clinical populations seem to have lower internal locus of control, such as alcoholics or people suffering from anxiety or depression, and internality seems to be positively associated with the outcomes of treatments.   – JR

internal reliability

n. The degree to which responses to different items in a test or scale are correlated with each other. This is usually measured using Kuder-Richardson formula 20 or Cronbach's alpha coefficient. Also called internal consistency.

internal validity ▶ *See* **VALIDITY, INTERNAL**

International Classification of Diseases

n. An official taxonomy of diseases compiled and published by the World Health Organization, which is in its ninth revision.

interneuron

n. Any neuron that connects other neurons, rather than being a sensory or effector neuron.

interoception

n. The process of perceiving the internal states of the body through bodily sense receptors.

interoceptor

n. Any sensory receptor within the body which transmits information about the body, such as blood pressure or temperature, to the central nervous system. These do not include proprioceptors, which sense bodily position for the maintenance of balance.

interpersonal attraction

n. The sense of liking and wanting to be close to another person. This may be based on a number of factors, including sexual desire, shared interests, perceived competence, social status, willingness to help, or desire for company.

interpersonal communication

n. The transfer of information between people, especially of a personal nature. This includes nonverbal communication such as voice characteristics, facial expressions, gestures, gaze direction, bodily movements, proxemics, and posture.

interquartile range

n. The range in a distribution of scores between the 25th and 75th percentiles.

interrater reliability

n. The level of a test's measurement error attributed to differences in the ratings, scores, or observations provided by different evaluators of the same event or phenomenon. When using people to evaluate or observe an event, there may be differences between true scores and recorded scores due to human error and/or perception; as such, interrater reliability (also called interscorer or interobserver reliability) is used to examine the extent to which different observers give consistent estimates, evaluations, or ratings of the same phenomenon. While there are various ways of calculating interrater reliability (such as percentage of agreement between raters or use of z score estimates of agreement), the most appropriate method for calculating interrater reliability is application of the kappa statistic, which reports interrater reliability as a proportion of complete agreement, taking into consideration corrections for chance agreement. Interrater reliability based on the kappa statistic ranges from 1 (perfect agreement) to –1 (less agreement than predicted by chance); kappa scores above 0.40 are generally considered satisfactory.   – BJM

intersexuality

n. The state of possessing some characteristics of both sexes such as sex organs, sexual behaviors, and especially secondary sex characteristics, such as facial hair and breast enlargement.

interstimulus interval

n. The amount of time that elapses between the end of one stimulus and the beginning of the next stimulus.

interstitial-cell-stimulating hormone

n. A hormone secreted by the pituitary gland that stimulates the growth of Graafian follicles in the ovary and causes the emission of an ovum in women. In men it stimulates the interstitial cells of the testis to secrete androgenic hormones. Also called luteinizing hormone.

interval reinforcement

n. In operant conditioning, a schedule of rewards in which a reward is given at the end of each fixed period in which a target behavior has occurred.

interval scale

n. A quantitative scale with magnitude and equal intervals but lacking an absolute zero. The lack of an absolute zero allows interval data to be added or subtracted to compare differences at any point on the scale, but values cannot be multiplied or divided to create meaningful ratios. The Fahrenheit scale is an example of an interval scale as a 10-degree difference at any point on the scale indicates a consistent variance in temperature (equal intervals), but there is no such thing as no temperature (absolute zero). Appropriate calculations of interval data include mean, median, mode, range, and standard deviation.   — BJM

intervening variable

n. A theoretical variable which affects the relationship between independent and dependent variables, which is inferred from the observed relationships of independent and dependent variables. Thus the intervening variable habit strength may be inferred from the relationship between stimulus and response frequency, and the intervening variable ego strength may be inferred from the relationship between attachment style and impulse control in kindergarten.

intimacy versus isolation

n. Erik Erikson's sixth of eight stages of psychosocial development, intimacy versus isolation, occurs during young adulthood. During this stage, young adults are seeking deeper and more meaningful connections with others. Erikson did note that successful intimacy is dependent upon successful resolution of the previous stage, identity versus role confusion. Should a person not resolve and define his/her identity and beliefs, then he/she will have a more challenging time committing to another person in consequential relationships. Erikson defines the goal for this stage as consisting of finding camaraderie with similar others and developing a love relationship. Should these companionships occur, the resulting ego strength is a sense of love; however, should a person not make these significant relationships, then he/she will likely become a loner or be involved in shallow relationships.   — SRB

intimate partner violence

n. The term *intimate partner violence* (IPV) has superseded the term *domestic violence* because it more accurately characterizes the variety of important dyadic relationships in which violence can occur. These relationships include, but are not limited to, violence between spouses, cohabiters, divorced couples, and individuals in a variety of dating relationships. IPV is inclusive of same-sex as well as heterosexual intimate relationships. There is general agreement that the act has to have been conducted with the intention to harm the recipient physically or psychologically in order to be considered IPV. However, debate ensues about the degree to which acts of psychological aggression, verbal abuse, or stalking and/or behaviors used to control, dominate, or isolate an intimate partner should also be subsumed under the term *intimate partner violence.* Controversy has also centered on whether acts of sexual violence, including rape, should be integrated into the definition of intimate partner violence. Some have argued that victim fear is an important component of IPV; however, including this requirement tends to reduce the number of men who can be considered victims of IPV. Proponents of battered women have strongly argued the need to assess the context in which the violence occurs, rather than the perpetration of the behavior alone, as some studies have shown relatively few gender differences in the rates of engaging in violent acts in intimate relationships. In light of these controversies it is not surprising that prevalence rates of IPV vary substantially with the definition being utilized and differ considerably even among national surveys. Reported rates of IPV also differ among individuals from different racial and ethnic backgrounds. Nonetheless, there is consensus that IPV is pervasive in U.S. society, that it is an ongoing public health concern, and that victims of IPV are at risk for physical injury, post-traumatic stress disorder, depression, and other negative consequences such as reduced workplace productivity.   — JL-R, KLD

intonation

n. The intonation of an utterance is its tune or melody. Along with phrasing or rhythm, intonation is part of the suprasegmental phenomena that are collectively referred to as *prosody*. Pitch movements signaling sentence-internal prosodic events reveal the intonational structure of an utterance. In English, intonation is the primary means for distinguishing between declaratives (*The people are revolting*) and interrogatives (*The people are revolting?*), the latter produced with rising intonation at the end, compared to falling intonation for the former. Within a sentence, intonational phrase boundaries are signaled by pitch movements, as well as by durational cues (pausing and/or lengthening of the phrase-final element). For example, in English, restrictive (*The students who live far away always arrive late*) and non-restrictive relative clauses (*The students, who live far away, always arrive late*) have different intonational contours. English also uses intonation to signal pitch-accented elements in sentences. In *Alice ate the pickle*, for instance, the pitch movements associated with the word *Alice* will differ, depending on whether the sentence answers *Did Bernard eat the pickle?* or *Did Alice eat the olives?*   — EMF

intoxication

n. Transient alterations in mental and physiological functioning due to the presence of alcohol, other drugs, or chemicals. The particular form of function alteration depends on the nature of the intoxicant. Typical intoxicants include depressants such as alcohol, painkillers, sleeping pills, and anxiolytic drugs; stimulants such as amphetamines, cocaine, and caffeine; and hallucinogens such as LSD, marijuana, ecstasy, MDA, mescaline, and psilocybin.

intracellular fluid

n. The saline solution which fills the interior of most cells.

intraception

n. The capacity to attend to and enjoy one's subjective reactions and experience including imaginative and aesthetic aspects.

intrapersonal

adj. Of or relating to events, processes, or relationships within the individual person including self-image, ideals, attitudes, self-esteem, and self-regulation.

intrapsychic

adj. Of or relating to events or processes within the mind, including ideas, emotions, impulses, and conflicts.

intrinsic motivation

n. The desire or impulse to engage in an activity for the satisfaction and fulfillment that derive from the activity itself rather than for external rewards.

introjection

n. **1.** In traditional psychoanalysis, the process of incorporating morals, ideas, attitudes, beliefs, behavior patterns, or some other aspect of another person into her/his self. **2.** In object-relations theory, the internalization of a mental representation of an external object into the self, where it has influence on thought and behavior.

introspection

n. The process of examining one's own experience or mental processes. This has been both an experimental technique and a therapeutic method in modern psychology.

introspectionism

n. The theory that introspection must be the primary experimental technique in psychology, which was a major tenet of a school of psychology called structuralism in the late 1800s. Modern psychology uses introspection as one of many approaches to gathering data.

introversion

n. **1.** A basic attitude toward life in which the individual finds meaning and a sense of direction in the inner world of thoughts and feelings. **2.** A pattern of reaction to external simulation in which the nervous system is highly reactive to stimuli, and so the individual tends to reduce the amount of stimulation so as to maintain a mental equilibrium.

introversion-extroversion

n. **1.** A dimension of personality in which people who are shy, withdrawing, and tending to experience negative emotions are on one end, and active, socially engaging people who tend to experience more positive emotions are on the other end of the spectrum. **2.** A dimension of a basic attitude toward life in which the individual finds meaning and a sense of direction in the inner world of thoughts and feelings, on one end of the spectrum, or an attitude in which the meaning and direction in life are discovered in the external world of things and actions. **3.** A dimension of the excitability of the nervous system in which persons who react strongly to stimuli are at one end and those who are relatively unreactive are on the other end. Since stimuli affect introverted persons more, they seek to reduce stimulation level, while extroverted persons are less affected and seek more stimulation, so both maintain an inner level of stimulation at about the same level.

intuition

n. **1.** An understanding derived neither from conscious reasoning nor in any obvious way from perception that is accurate, as in the linguistic notion of linguistic competence, in which native speakers are able to use correct grammar but often are unable to say what rules are involved in doing so, why it is grammatically correct, or how they arrived at that particular structure of speech. **2.** The capacity to understand in a holistic way without using conscious reasoning and going beyond obvious perceptual characteristics.

intuitive type

n. In Jungian psychology, the sort of person who emphasizes understanding in a holistic, instinctive way rather than focusing on the concrete details of experience and who tends to use sensory data subconsciously rather than in conscious reasoning and to focus on future possibilities more than the present moment.

invariable hue

n. Any color whose perception is not easily affected by changes in level of illumination, that is, a primary color.

inventory

n. **1.** Any list of items intended to be exhaustive of a domain. **2.** In psychometrics, a questionnaire or checklist, usually in self-report format, which attempts to measure intelligence, ability, personality, values, attitudes, preferences, or psychopathology.

inverted Oedipus complex

n. A reversal of the normal Oedipus situation so that a little boy desires the father and is jealous of and hates the mother. Or a situation in which a little girl comes to desire her mother's power and so wants to seduce her while resenting the father. This inversion usually results in a homosexual pattern of sexual adjustment.

in vitro

adj. Literally, "in glass," usually referring to a biological event occurring in the glass of a test tube or other laboratory glass vessel.

in vivo

adj. Literally, "in life," usually referring to the usual biological situation in which biological events occur.

in vivo desensitization

n. A technique of behavioral therapy in which the client is intentionally exposed to anxiety evoking situations, usually after relaxation training and with the goal of reducing the anxiety associated with the situations. Also called in vivo exposure therapy or desensitization.

involutional depression

n. An archaic term for a major depression occurring in middle age – during menopause for women – in which the individual feels anxiety, futility, and guilt for failing to have met his or her own or others' expectations in life.

I/O

n. Abbreviation of *industrial/organizational*, as in industrial/organizational psychology, the branch of psychology that studies humans in the workplace and attempts to apply general psychological principles to workplaces to improve productivity and to improve working circumstances for those employed. I/O psychology stresses the study of motivation, group processes and organizational effectiveness, personnel selection, training, employee evaluation, and leadership.

ion

n. A charged particle that is often attached to an ion of an equal and opposite charge to form a molecule. Cations have positive charges and anions have negative charges. When a molecule splits to form ions, part of the molecule retains one or more extra electrons, giving it a negative charge and causing it to become an anion, while the other part surrenders one or more electrons and so becomes a positively charged cation.

ipsative

adj. Of or referring to the self. In personology, for example, ipsative studies compare the relative strength of different motivations within the person without reference to other persons. In ipsative testing the elements of a test are arranged so a person is forced to choose between them, and raising one score necessarily lowers another score, as in the Edwards Personal Preference Survey.

ipsative scaling

n. A means of measuring scale values that utilizes an individual's own self-report responses and characteristics as the basis for comparison. Ipsative scales are often used in personality and interest inventories. Assessment questions utilizing ipsative scaling use forced-choice items and require test takers to select between provided alternatives or rank preferences and feelings. For example, the question "Would you rather read a book or watch a movie?" utilizes ipsative scaling, as it requires respondents to select between two alternatives. Ipsative scores are not an absolute measure as they only provide information about relative preferences or interests. Selecting one forced-choice option over another indicates nothing about overall preferences, interests,

or traits; rather, it provides a relative measure of the target of interest. In contrast to normative scaling (which can compare scores across individuals), ipsative scaling is only valid for intrapersonal analysis.   – BJM

ipsilateral

adj. Of or relating to the same side of a body or a geometric figure.

IQ

n. Intelligence quotient. This was originally calculated as the mental age derived from a score on a test divided by the chronological age multiplied by 100. In recent decades, a deviation IQ has become the norm. In this form of IQ, scores on an intelligence test within each age range are standardized to have a median of 100 and a standard deviation of either 15 or 16, which is used as the IQ.

IQ test

n. Any test of intellectual ability whose scores are reported as an intelligence quotient.

iris

n. A muscular disk around the center of the eye which expands and contracts to allow more or less light into the eye. The stroma of the iris contains pigment, which gives eyes their observable color, although the back of all irises is black, regardless of outer color of the eye.

irradiation

n. The process of being bombarded with electromagnetic particles. This usually refers to high-energy particles characteristic of radioactive decay such as is used in radiation therapy and are released in atomic explosions. Radiation from space includes a wide array of wave frequencies and energies such as visible light, ultraviolet light, radio waves, and gamma rays. Gamma rays are very high-energy rays which can pass all the way through the Earth so that some form of radiation is always striking both the Earth and our bodies and occasionally causing changes in our genes.

irrational type

n. One of Carl Jung's basic types of people, which includes both intuitive and sensing types and excludes judging and perceiving types. The use of the term *irrational* here means taking in information rather than reaching a conclusion about it.

irreversibility

n. The idea that physical and temporal occurrences are not reversible. This derives from the second law of thermodynamics, which suggests that all systems move toward maximal entropy. It is also a distinction between computational and mental systems as computational systems are reversible while minds and biological systems are irreversible.

irritable bowel syndrome

n. (IBS) A functional disorder of the colon characterized by pain and bloating sensations and often by constipation or diarrhea or an alternation of the two. There is no known cause for it, but it is correlated with anxiety and stress. Also called mucus colitis.

IRT ▶ *See* **ITEM RESPONSE THEORY**

ischemia or ischaemia

n. Insufficient blood supply to an organ or tissue due to abnormalities in the blood vessels irrigating it. It can be due to different conditions such as atherosclerosis (obstruction of arteries consequent to lipid-laden plaques), hypotension (low blood pressure), thromboembolism (clots or foreign elements moving in the artery system), and compression of the artery vessels due to an increase in the surrounding pressure. Some organs are particularly sensitive to the insufficient blood supply, such as the brain and the heart. Cell death (infarct or necrosis) will occur after some time. A transient ischemic attack is a temporary disturbance of brain functions caused by an ischemia but recovering in usually less than 24 hours.   – A A

island of Reil

n. Cortical area in the brain deep in the lateral (Sylvian) fissure, overlying the extreme capsule and lateral to the lenticular nucleus. It is also known as insular cortex, insular lobe, or simply, insula (*island*). From the cytoarchitectonic point of view, it is heterogeneous: agranular in

the anterior part and granular in the posterior region. It receives information from the ventral medial nucleus of the thalamus, the ventral posterior inferior nucleus of the thalamus, and the central nucleus of the amygdala. Reciprocal connections exist between the primary somatosensory cortex and the insula. It has been proposed that the insula is involved in emotional reactions to sensory information, visceral-autonomic functions, and pain. To a significant extent, the anterior insula has limbic functions, whereas the posterior insula may be more involved in auditory and somesthetic information processing. The left insula may be directly involved in language processing, the posterior portion in phoneme recognition, and the anterior part in the organization of sequences of movements in speech; damage in the anterior insula has been related to apraxia of speech.   – A A

isocortex

n. The six cell layers which cover most of the visible brain; it is the most recently evolved part of human and mammalian brains. Also called neocortex.

isolation

n. **1.** The state of being alone. **2.** In psychoanalysis, the process of preventing disruptive thoughts or memories from becoming associated with other thoughts or ideas and so making their recollection to consciousness less likely. **3.** In biology, the separation of populations preventing cross-breeding.

isolation effect

n. **1.** In psychoanalysis, the process of detaching the emotional component from a memory and particularly traumatic memories, leaving the experience of the memory bland and flat. This is an essential component of obsessions and compulsions in psychoanalysis. **2.** In learning, the observation that in learning a list, if one of the items is perceptually different, then it will be more easily learned and recalled. Also called the Von Restorff effect.

isolation of affect

n. A defense mechanism whereby the individual wards off unwanted emotion by separating it from his or her conscious experience. For example, a person may consistently compartmentalize his or her emotional experiences away from other mental processes as a way of not being overwhelmed by them. From a psychoanalytic perspective, the emotion has not been eliminated but instead has only moved out of conscious awareness, likely to reemerge in other areas (e.g., in behavior, dreams, slips of the tongue). As with most defense mechanisms, this process is unconscious; the individual has no idea that the emotion is being distanced from his or her experience. Of course, in the long term the use of isolation of affect is detrimental to interpersonal relations because (among other things) it keeps the individual at a distance from his or her real emotional experiences, probably distancing him or her from others.   – DGa

isomorphism
n. **1.** A perfect correspondence or match among all the parts of two or more physical bodies, mathematical or logical statements, or problems or grammatical forms. **2.** In Gestalt psychology, the assumption that for every perception there is an analogous neurophysiological representation of the perception. **3.** In psycholinguistics, the relationship between one linguistic form and another, as in a printed word and its spoken form.

isophonic contour
n. An equal-loudness contour in which the set of coincidences among different aspects of sound are perceived as identical. As an instance, pitch and loudness interact so that higher pitches tend to sound louder, so an isophonic contour of pitch and loudness would be the set of points at which different combinations of pitch and the amplitude of the air pressure wave would be perceived as equal.

isotonic
adj. **1.** Of or relating to two or more muscles which are equally tense at a given moment. **2.** Of or relating to two or more chemical solutions which have equal concentrations and so equal osmotic pressures.

item analysis
n. A process of evaluating the psychometric characteristics of a set of items, usually in order to select items for inclusion in a scale but also used to evaluate items on existing tests or scales. Typical methods of item analysis are internal consistency in attitude scales and correlation with external criteria in personality or ability scales.

item bias
n. In psychometrics, consistent error in measurement by an item in a scale. All scales contain some item bias in that items differently correlate with the reality which a scale is attempting to measure.

item difficulty
n. The proportion of the population which responds correctly to an item.

item discrimination index
n. A numerical measure of the degree to which persons who are high and low on a characteristic being measured respond differently to an item.

item reliability
n. The degree to which people give the same response to an item when they answer at different times.

item response curve
n. A graphical representation of an item response function in item response theory which is a mathematical model of the relationship between the latent traits an item is measuring and characteristics of the item itself.

item response theory
n. An area of psychometrics that creates mathematical models of people's responses to items as a way of constructing tests and interpreting their results. It assumes that responses to items are a function of one or more aspects of the characteristics being measured and one or more characteristics of the item. The relationships of these variables to a particular response to the item are given by an item response function and their values inferred from the responses actual people give to the item.

item validity

n. The degree to which an item measures what it is intended to measure. This is measured in attitude scales by the degree to which responses to the item correlate with responses to all the items in the pool of items. In personality and ability tests, it is usually measured by the degree to which responses to the item correlate with external criteria of the construct being measured.

J

Jacksonian epilepsy

n. A form of seizure disorder characterized by focal motor seizures with unilateral clonic movements that start in one group of muscles and spread systematically to adjacent groups, reflecting the spread of the seizure activity through the contralateral motor cortex.

Jacksonian motor epilepsy

n. A form of epilepsy that starts with a focal seizure in one part of the brain, usually involving the twitching of a finger or toe or the corner of the mouth, and then spreads throughout the motor cortex until the whole body enters a seizure, which ends with unconsciousness.

Jacksonian sensory epilepsy

n. A form focal of epilepsy accompanied by localized parasthenias such as burning, tingling, or numbness.

Jackson's principle

n. The theory that degeneration of mental functions through mental disorder or neurological impairment recapitulates ontogeny in the sense that the more recently evolved a mental function or structure is, the more quickly it will disappear as a disease progresses. Also called Jackson's law.

Jacobson's organ

n. A set of specialized sensors in the nose that in nonhuman mammals respond to sex pheromones and play a significant role in sexual physiology, arousal, and behavior. In humans the function of the receptors is not well understood. Also called the vomeronal nasal system and vomeronasal system.

Jacobson's progressive relaxation

n. A method of relaxation in which the subject is instructed to go through the body, focusing on one body area at a time and contracting and then relaxing the muscles in that area. Sometimes the procedure is used just to focus and relax without first tensing the muscle groups. This method is widely used in behavior modification, to reduce blood pressure and anxiety. Also called progressive relaxation and systematic relaxation.

James-Lange theory of emotions

n. The idea that emotions are perceptions of bodily states which are evoked by perception of exciting situations in the environment. Thus feelings cause emotions rather than emotions' causing feelings.

jargon

n. **1.** The specialized language and words associated with particular activities or professions. **2.** The type of childhood babbling which has the intonations and cadence of adult speech but contains no words. **3.** Meaningless speech intended to occupy the listener without actually communicating.

jargon aphasia

n. It is not a specific subtype of aphasia, but a term used to describe the characteristics of the language that sometimes is observed in fluent (Wernicke's) aphasias. In jargon aphasia patients' speech is abundant and easily produced, phonemes are recognizable, grammatical elements are used (and even overused), but speech contains abundant substitutions corresponding to neologisms (unrecognizable words) and paraphasias (words that are incorrect in their phonological composition – phonological paraphasias; or in their selection – verbal paraphasias), up to the point that language is completely incomprehensible to the listener. Jargon aphasia (or jargonaphasia) can be regarded as an extreme version of fluent aphasia found in usually extended left temporal or temporal-parietal lesions. Three subtypes of jargon can be distinguished, depending on the dominant substitutions: neologistic jargon, phonemic jargon, and semantic jargon, even though it is frequent to find a combination of all of them.   – AA

jealousy
n. The emotion experienced by a person who desires what another person possesses. Envy. This term is most commonly used in cases of romantic jealousy when one person wants to supplant another in a relationship.

jigsaw classroom
n. An educational technique in which students are divided into work groups who are assigned a general topic. Each member of the group is assigned a different aspect of the topic, and students with the same aspects leave their groups to work together to learn the aspect and then return to their work groups and teach their fellow group members what they learned outside the group. Also called the jigsaw method.

jnd ▶ *See* JUST NOTICEABLE DIFFERENCE

job satisfaction
n. The degree to which a worker is content with his or her job, including his/her attitudes toward the work itself, the social situation at work, pay, supervision, possibility of advancement, recognition, and status.

Jocasta complex
n. An erotic or unnaturally close emotional attachment between a mother and her son.

John Henry effect
n. A concept related to experimental validity; the term describes the phenomenon of special effort put forth by the control group in a research study. In an experiment in which the assignment of experimental and control conditions is made public and the control group will be at a disadvantage if a treatment is successful, the control group may be motivated to reduce any expected differences. Just as John Henry, the steel drivin' man, put forth extra effort in his desire to outperform a steam drill, under some conditions control group members may do likewise. For example, a company may wish to test the efficiency of automating production. If the employees perceive their jobs to be threatened if the test for efficiency shows the automated process to be superior to human performance, they may work at peak efficiency during the comparison period so as to minimize any overall differences in performance.   – TJM

Jost's law
n. The idea that the older of two associations of equal strength will be strengthened more easily and will be more resistant to decay.

judgment
n. **1.** The process of or capacity for considering evidence and forming an opinion. **2.** In psychophysics, a decision as to the presence or absence of a stimulus or the relative magnitude of stimuli.

Julesz stereogram
n. A set of two seemingly random dot patterns which contain a subset of dots that are slightly shifted to the other dots, so that when the two patterns are viewed simultaneously but separately by the two eyes, the shift produces retinal disparity, which makes the shifted dots seem to float above the background of unshifted dots.

jumping stand
n. A small raised stand on which a rat or other small animal was placed and trained to jump toward one of two doors, which were labeled with stimuli between which the rat was being trained to discriminate. If the rat made the correct choice, the door opened and the rat found food behind it. If the rat made the wrong choice, the door would be locked and the rat would fall, usually into a net below but sometimes into iced water or something else.

Jungian
adj. Of or relating to Carl Jung or his ideas, which are usually called analytical psychology.

Jungian analysis

n. In general, a form of psychoanalysis based on the work of Carl Jung which took into account the cultural history of the person and his or her family and various mental symbols associated with them. Jung noted that his therapeutic technique was to be one human being with another and that he used whatever form of therapy seemed to suit the relationship between a particular client and him.

jury decision making

n. **1.** A field of study within social and cognitive psychology which examines how psychological and demographic variables and interpersonal processes affect the decisions juries make. **2.** A field within forensic psychology which predicts jury decision making and is used by attorneys in selecting members of juries.

just noticeable difference

n. The smallest change in any dimension of a stimulus that can be reliably detected by an observer, usually using a 75% accuracy criterion. Also called a difference threshold and a difference limen.

just world hypothesis

n. The observation that most people in Western cultures believe or make judgments suggesting that they believe that there is a power at work in the world creating justice so that if a person commits an evil act, he/she is ultimately punished, and if he/she does good things, he/she is eventually rewarded. It is embodied in phrases like "What goes around, comes around." This has been used to explain other phenomena such as blaming the victim, in which it is supposed that if something bad happens to a person, he/she must have done something to deserve it. Also called the just world phenomenon.

juvenile delinquency

n. Illegal behavior by a person under the age of 18. Some of this behavior would not be illegal if the person were over 18, such as consuming alcoholic beverages and not attending school, and some would be illegal for anyone regardless of age, such as murder, rape, and arson.

K

kainic acid

n. A neurotoxic amino acid found in some species of red algae and the seaweed *Digenea simplex*, which potentiates the neurotransmitter glutamate and destroys postsynaptic cells with glutamate receptors. It is sometimes used in research to destroy small areas of the brain.

kakosmia

n. The hallucination of an unpleasant smell such as feces or something similarly repulsive. Also called cacosmia.

Kallikak

n. The pseudonym for a family used as an example of the hereditary transmission of feeblemindedness in the early 20th century.

The book describing this family became very popular and was used in the political movement called eugenics, which prescribed selective breeding in human society to reduce the incidence of moral depravity and feeblemindedness. It has since been used in psychology as an example of biased and improbable research demonstrating the need for improved research methodology and scientific disinterestedness.

Kanner's syndrome

n. A disorder of childhood characterized by impaired social learning and communication, restricted interests, diminished imaginative thought, and stereotyped or repetitive nonfunctional movements or verbalizations. Also known as autistic disorder.

kappa statistic

n. A numerical index of agreement between two raters classifying the same items, which ranges between 0 (no agreement) and 1 (perfect agreement) and takes chance agreement into account.

$$kappa = \frac{Percent\ Observed\ Agreement - Probability\ of\ Agreement\ by Chance}{1 - Probability\ of\ Agreement\ by Chance}$$

karyotype

1. *n.* A systematic array of the chromosomes of a single cell, including their number, structural features, appearance, and abnormalities. **2.** *v.* To create a karyotype for a cell.

Kaspar Hauser experiment

n. An experiment in which an animal is reared in isolation from other members of its species in order to attempt to determine which of its behaviors are innate and which are learned.

katasexualism

n. A sexual preference for dead people or people with characteristics like animals' or enjoyment of sex with people who dress up as animals.

K complex

n. A pattern of scalp electrophysiology recorded by an electroencephalograph with brief, high-amplitude spikes or spindles characteristic of the early stages of sleep.

Kendall coefficient of concordance

n. (*W*) An index of the degree to which rankings by several independent judges agree with each other.

Kendall correlation coefficient ▶ *See* KENDALL'S TAU

Kendall's tau

n. A measure of association between two pairs of rankings such that no association = 0 and perfect association = 1 using the formula

$$Tau = \frac{4p}{n(n-1)} - 1$$

where n = the number of pairs and p = the sum of the rankings greater than a particular ranking to the right of the ranking, when one variable is ordered by the other variable.

kinesics

n. The study of facial expressions, nonverbal aspects of voice, gestures, gaze, visual attention, and other body movements in communication. Voice kinesics include pitch, tone, cadence, pauses, intonation, and silence. Gestural kinesics include emblems like waving to say good-bye, illustrators such as using the hands to show size, adaptors which help cope with emotion such as putting one's hands in front of the face when embarrassed, and regulators that help turn taking in speech such as holding the hand palm outward to stop someone else from speaking. Kinesics vary widely from culture to culture so that a single gesture can have opposite or unrelated meanings in different cultures. Also called nonverbal communication.

kinetic depth effect

n. A visual phenomenon in which a moving shadow of a three-dimensional figure appears to move forward and backward from the flat surface on which it is cast as the object casting the shadow is rotated on an axis. The illusion disappears if the object is rotated while not moving or the rotation is in a plane perpendicular to the surface on which the shadow is cast.

kin selection

n. A form of natural selection whereby altruism shown by individuals toward closely related individuals increases their own fitness by helping relatives propagate shared genes.

kinship

n. Relatedness which may be by birth, genetics, marriage, or adoption, which varies considerably among cultures. As an example, in some cultures relationship is defined, in part, by the time of year one is born, in some polyandrous societies a child may have more than one father, and in other societies the order of plural marriages affects kinship.

kinship term

n. Any word which denotes relatedness in extended families. Languages and cultures vary considerably in such terminology. In the Japanese language, for example, there are different words for older and younger brothers and sisters. And in some languages and cultures there are religious or adopted kinships such as godfather in many Catholic cultures.

kleptomania

n. A psychological disorder characterized by compulsive stealing in which the person feels a pressure to steal and a combination of relief and pleasure during and immediately after the theft. The stealing is often of objects not needed or sometimes even not wanted.

Klinefelter's syndrome

n. A genetic disorder of males characterized by the presence of an extra X, or female sex, chromosome in all the cells of the body. Such males usually have very small testes, do not produce sperm, have enlarged breasts, and produce follicle-stimulating hormone. Behavioral problems are common among boys with this disorder, and it is not known whether they are due to the genetic abnormality or the difficulty in social adjustment caused by being physically different from other boys. Also called XXY syndrome.

Kluver-Bucy syndrome

n. A disorder caused by damage to both medial temporal lobes in which there are increased and indiscriminate sexuality; a tendency to want to examine all objects by touch or by placing them in the mouth; visual agnosia, or inability to recognize objects by sight; flattened affective responses; memory loss; and deficient attention. It can be caused by herpes simplex encephalitis or trauma to both sides of the head.

knee-jerk reflex

n. A reflexive action in which the leg jerks up when the flexed knee is tapped just below the kneecap. This reflex is commonly used as a quick test of the functioning of the nervous system.

knowledge

n. Any internal information, understanding, or capacity to accomplish tasks which has been learned. It is sometimes divided into declarative knowledge (knowing some fact like that water is wet), procedural knowledge (knowing how to do something like ride a bicycle), and acquaintanceship knowledge (recognizing your mother's face).

knowledge, declarative

n. Any learned information about the world which can be stated overtly such as "The sky is blue" or "4 divided by 2 is 2."

knowledge, procedural

n. Any learned ability to do something such as ride a bicycle or reach out and pick something up in a coordinated manner.

Kolmogorov-Smirnov test

n. A nonparametric test of the degree of fit between a sample and a theoretical population or a test of whether two samples have been drawn from the same population. Also called the K-S test.

koro

n. A mental disorder found only in some Southeast Asian and south Chinese cultures, which is characterized by sudden intense fear of the penis in men or belief that the nipples and vulva in women are shrinking and will disappear into the body, causing death. It is much more common among males than among females. Also called *shook yang, shook yong, suo yang, jinjinia bemar,* and *rok-joo.*

Korsakoff's psychosis

n. Korsakoff's psychosis is an organic disorder believed to be a subdivision of Wernicke-Korsakoff syndrome, resulting in short-term memory loss, hallucinations, delusions, and disorientation due to a thiamine deficiency. Persons may also experience anxiety, insomnia, and depression and may confabulate stories. Persons experiencing the symptoms of Korsakoff's psychosis are also likely to experience the confusion, vision abnormalities, and loss of voluntary muscle movements found in Wernicke's syndrome. Similarly to that for

Wernicke's and Korsakoff's syndrome, the recommended treatment involves administration of thiamine, but once the disorder has progressed from Wernicke's syndrome to Korsakoff's psychosis, the likelihood of recovery is reduced.

Although sometimes the term is used interchangeably with *Korsakoff's syndrome*, some researchers advocate that *Korsakoff's psychosis* is perhaps more accurately viewed as a variation of the memory loss demonstrated by persons with Korsakoff's syndrome. It is also important to differentiate the chronicity of Korsakoff's psychosis from a more acute psychosis induced after periodic consumption of alcohol.   – TJM

▶ *See also* **KORSAKOFF'S SYNDROME**

Korsakoff's syndrome – a subdivision of Wernicke-Korsakoff syndrome

n. Korsakoff's syndrome is characterized by a significant retrograde memory deficit in individuals who are not otherwise cognitively impaired. Wernicke's syndrome is marked by confusion, abnormal eye movements, and inability to control muscle movement. When significant memory loss accompanies this symptom triad, the term *Wernicke-Korsakoff syndrome* is often applied.

There is some debate among experts regarding the precise relationship between these two disorders. The pair can be conceptualized as either separate syndromes or as one disorder with varying levels. In the latter case, Wernicke's syndrome (also known as Wernicke's encephalopathy) is recognized as the more acute phenomenon, while Korsakoff's syndrome is more chronic. In fact, some researchers have described a temporal relationship between the two disorders, with an experience of untreated symptoms of Wernicke's syndrome leading to a subsequent diagnosis of the more severe memory loss indicative of Korsakoff's syndrome.

Korsakoff's syndrome reflects a nutritional depletion, usually a thiamine (vitamin essential for neural function and the proper metabolization of carbohydrates) deficiency. This lack of essential nutrients is most often caused by the poor diet adopted by persons with severe alcoholism. In the later stages of alcoholism, persons may become ill, reducing their ability to eat and creating a situation in which the majority of caloric intake results from alcohol consumption. However, because nutrition depletion can be caused by other factors, Korsakoff's syndrome can develop in the absence of alcohol. One should also be aware that Korsakoff's syndrome is not the only disorder that can result in memory loss. Many other disorders such as herpes encephalitis, severe hypoxia, and traumatic brain injury may also result in memory impairment, but these disorders are not typically associated with the nutritional depletion evident in cases of Korsakoff's syndrome.

The memory loss apparent in cases of Korsakoff's syndrome has also been linked to specific neuropathological changes, such as neuronal loss and microhemorrhages in particular areas of the brain. These distinct patterns of atrophy may serve to explain why some persons who experience symptoms of Wernicke's syndrome may later experience the amnesiac symptoms of Korsakoff's syndrome.

Some researchers disagree about the amount of recovery that is possible after diagnosis with Korsakoff's syndrome. In fact, it is extremely unlikely for a person who has reached the level of memory loss indicative of Korsakoff's syndrome ever to recover fully. However, some researchers advocate that with proper thiamine treatment and abstinence from future alcoholic intake, some degree of recovery is possible, as long as the individual's extent of brain atrophy is minimal.   – TJM

▶ *See also* **KORSAKOFF'S PSYCHOSIS** *and* **NONALCOHOLIC KORSAKOFF'S PSYCHOSIS**

Korte's laws

n. A description of the parameters affecting the illusion of apparent motion, including illumination level, separation of figures, exposure time, and interexposure interval.

K-R formulas

n. A series of statistical formulas developed by G. W. Kuder and M. W. Richardson concerning test stability. The most important of these is Kuder-Richardson formula 20. ▶ *See also* **KUDER-RICHARDSON COEFFICIENT**

Kruskal-Wallis test

n. A nonparametric test of whether three or more samples are drawn from the same population.

Kuder Preference Record

n. An occupational interest survey developed in 1939 which measured relative interest in 10 occupational areas: art, clerical, computational, literary, mechanical, music, outdoor, persuasive, science and social service. The test was upgraded several times and the latest version is called the Kuder Occupational Interest Survey.

Kuder-Richardson coefficient

n. This is Kuder-Richardson formula 20, which is a widely used measure of internal consistency of tests in which only two responses are possible (correct-incorrect or true-false, for example). KR20 is equal to the average of all possible split-half correlations corrected for attenuation.

$$KR20 = \left(\frac{n}{n-1}\right) \times \left(\frac{Variance - \sum pq}{Variance}\right)$$

where *Variance* = variance of total scores on the test.

kurtosis

n. A measure of the degree to which a probability distribution peaks around its mean. A distribution that is more peaked than a normal curve is called leptokurtic, one that is equally peaked is called mesokurtic, and one that is less peaked than a normal curve is called platykurtic.

kuru

n. A fatal prion disease of the central nervous system whose symptoms include ataxia, difficulty in balance and walking, squint, and tremors. It was prevalent among women and children in the Fore people in the highlands of New Guinea during the times they practiced cannibalism. It is caused by eating the brains of infected persons, a practice which was largely limited to women and children as the men ate the muscles of bodies and left the rest for women and children.

kymograph

n. **1.** An instrument for recording changes in psychological or physiological variables by means of a pen tracing a record on paper on a slowly revolving drum. These are seldom used in places where computers are now available for data recording. **2.** The paper record produced by a kymograph.

L

labeling theory

n. In sociology, the idea that when a label is attached to a person within a social group, the individual begins to behave according to her/his label, thus enacting a self-fulfilling prophecy. Thus labeling a schoolage boy as bad and the social reaction of the boy himself and those of the people around him to that label may lead him actually to become bad or at least be worse than he would have been otherwise. Also called societal reaction theory.

la belle indifference

n. A French phrase meaning "beautiful indifference," which was used by the French sociologist Emile Durkheim to describe the point of view of people who have already decided to commit suicide and so are not much affected or bothered by things around them.

labile personality

n. A pattern of extreme changeability in a person's emotions and adjustment to the world so that he/she has extreme mood swings and an unstable sense of who he/she is and is likely to act impulsively and then experience deep regret, depression, and despair. Also called cyclothymic and borderline personality disorders.

labyrinth

n. **1.** In anatomy, the network of intercon-necting system of cavities and canals within the temporal portion of the skull that is the inner ear. **2.** In general, any mazelike struc-ture or network of interconnecting tunnels and chambers.

Ladd-Franklin theory

n. An archaic theory of light perception in which it was supposed that there were differ-ent photoreceptive chemicals in the eye stim-ulated by red, green, and blue light, which in turn stimulated the retina to create color in vision.

lambda statistic

n. A measure of association between a cate-gorical dependent variable (DV) and an inde-pendent variable (IV) treated as categorical which gives the percentage reduction in error in using the independent variable to predict the dependent variable.

$$\lambda = \frac{(SumFi - Fd)}{total - Fd}$$

where *Fi* = the largest cell frequency within each category of the IV, *Fd* = largest marginal value of DV, and *total* = total number of obser-vations of the DV. Also called Goodman-Kruskal lambda.

language

n. Language is the implicit system that links an external linguistic signal, acoustic or writ-ten, and the message carried by that signal. Central to knowledge of language is *linguis-tic competence*, knowledge of the principles for combining sounds (*phonology*), morphemes (*morphology*), and words (*syntax*); the prin-ciples for determining meaning (*semantics*); and the vocabulary repository (the *lexicon*). In addition, *communicative competence* consists of principles that dictate felicitous language use (pragmatics), guiding speakers in their choice of expressions to perform speech acts. Knowledge of language is encoded and decoded into signals – sentences uttered, writ-ten, or signed – by means of performance mechanisms that enable the production and perception of sentences.   – EMF

language acquisition device

n. The language acquisition device (LAD), or language acquisition system (LAS), is the mental mechanism that guides language acquisition. The LAD takes as input environ-mental stimuli in the form of language heard by the learner, which may or may not have been directed at the learner. As this input is processed, internal mechanisms trigger the growth of a language-specific *grammar* and lexicon. The components of the LAD include the learner's knowledge of *universal gram-mar* and a handful of principles of language acquisition, both of which bias the learner to make certain types of assumptions and not others about the system being learned. One principle of language acquisition is the *whole object assumption*, by which a new word is ini-tially taken to refer to the whole object it is associated with, rather than to one of its parts, or its shape, color, and so forth. The LAD is a species-specific system hypothesized to be in place at birth. It is under debate whether the LAD's properties or operational functions remain intact from birth on or whether it is subject to critical period effects.   – EMF

language development

n. The acquisition of phonology, morphology, lexicon, syntax, semantics, and pragmatics of a language. Passive exposure to sounds and language begins before birth, while the baby is still *in utero*. Immediately after birth, infants become exposed to language more directly, as caregivers begin to interact with them and as they hear language sounds or see signing. From very early on, babies learn to detect reg-ularities in patterns of the language to which they are exposed. While healthy human infants are born with the ability to perceive and produce the sounds of all languages, over the course of the first year of life their linguis-tic system becomes fine-tuned to the struc-ture of the language around them, laying the foundation for native-language learning.

Infants begin to engage in communica-tion early on, initially by crying as they learn to express their needs. Language produc-tion develops with babies beginning to coo and then, by the age of 6 months, to babble. In the second half of the first year, the babble turns into nonsense speech that often has the rhythm and sound of language but does not include real words. On average, children are able to produce one or two words by their first birthday, although some children may take a little longer to utter their first word, while children with precocious language abilities often have larger vocabularies at that age. Through their first years of life, children are able to understand more words than they can produce. By 18 months, the average toddler can say 8 to 10 words. By their second birthday, children start putting two or more words together to form simple sentences, such as "more cookie" or "no milk." Researchers who study language development look at children's *mean length of utterance* to measure how many meaningful units of language a child can string together.

Children's vocabularies grow rapidly between the second and fifth birthdays, as their brains develop and mature and as they continue to explore their environment. By the time children enter kindergarten, they can already produce declarative, interrogative, exclamatory, and imperative sentences, and many can recognize some letters of the alphabet. Between the ages of 5 and 8, children typically acquire written language and learn to read and write. Language development continues through school age, with children continuously acquiring new words, learning to form increasingly complex sentences, and becoming experts at pragmatic aspects of language use.

Adults continue to hone their language skills throughout the life span, and many go on to learn second, third, or more languages. It is estimated that the majority of the world population is bilingual, trilingual, or multilingual, with individuals successfully acquiring more than one spoken and/or signed language to communicate. Although it is possible to acquire another language at any age, acquisition of a language later in life frequently results in accented speech and in difficulty distinguishing certain sounds, because the articulation and phonological systems are already fully developed and less malleable by new input. Some believe that children who have not been exposed to language prior to reaching puberty will fail to learn language, but the existence of such a critical period is difficult to test empirically since depriving a child of language input is unethical (and the documented cases of feral and isolated children are confounded by other factors).

In general, it is well accepted that language development is shaped by both innate and experiential influences, although the extent to which nature and nurture each contribute to language acquisition remains heatedly debated. On the one hand, language abilities seem to develop best in environments that are stimulating, rich in linguistic input, and full of opportunities to interact with other language users. On the other hand, environmental variables alone cannot account for many of the individual differences, nor for many of the universals observed in language development. One way to study the nativist and interactionist accounts of human language development is by studying the ability of other species to acquire language; research in this area is ongoing. Another way to gain insight into language development is by studying language change as a result of language interaction, for instance, in creole and pidgin languages and in dialects.

Healthy individuals do not normally lose language abilities later in life. However, when associated with medical conditions such as aphasia or dementia, aging can result in loss of language abilities and in difficulty communicating. Intervention approaches developed for remediation of speech and language problems are provided by trained speech-language pathologists and are aimed at individuals with medical conditions, as well as at children acquiring language outside the normal language-development spectrum. Other professionals who study language development include psychologists, linguists, psycholinguists, educators, and communication sciences specialists. – VM

language in great apes

n. **1.** The various abilities of bonobos, chimpanzees, gorillas, and orangutans to learn humanlike language in the forms of artificial sign languages and keyboards with symbols and to respond to human language. **2.** The communication systems among members of each species of the great apes.

Lashley jumping stand
n. A small raised stand on which a rat or other small animal was placed and trained to jump toward one of two doors, which were labeled with stimuli between which the rat was being trained to discriminate. If the rat made the correct choice, the door opened and the rat found food behind it. If the rat made the wrong choice, the door would be locked and the rat would fall, usually into a net below but sometimes into iced water or something else.

latah syndrome
n. A disorder characterized by hypersensitivity to sudden fright, often accompanied by command obedience, dissociation or trance, echolalia, or echopraxia. This is most common in middle-aged women in Malaysia and Indonesia but has been found throughout the world. Also called *amurakh, baah-ji, bah tschi, bah-tsi, ikota, imu, irkunii, mali-mali, menkeiti, myracgit, olan*, and *silok*.

latency
n. **1.** A characteristic or period of being present and unseen or unacted but capable of becoming active or visible.

latency period
n. **1.** In psychoanalysis, the period of middle childhood during which overt sexuality is latent. During this period sexuality is repressed and its energy is directed into becoming the child's ideal of a man or a woman. **2.** In Erikson's epigenetic cycle, the period of middle childhood, during which a child attempts to master the tasks her/his culture requires of an adult. In doing this he/she develops a sense of industry and a belief in his/her own competence.

latency, response
n. The time delay between a stimulus and a response.

latent content
n. In Sigmund Freud's theory of dreams, the unconscious motivation for a dream, whose energy is converted via the dreamwork into the manifest content of which the person is aware during the dream.

latent extinction
n. **1.** In operant conditioning, extinction that occurs in the absence of a response, as in placing a rat in an empty goal box at the end of a maze. **2.** In biology, an environmental state in which the extinction of a species is imminent and irremediable but has not yet occurred.

latent inhibition
n. **1.** In conditioning, previous exposure to a potential conditioned stimulus without its being paired with the unconditioned stimulus, which makes acquisition of the conditioned response more difficult. **2.** The capacity to reduce or shut out part of the stream of sensory information. Low levels of this ability are supposed to be related to psychosis and creativity, depending on the individual's capacity to manage the high information load.

latent learning
n. Learning that occurs through mere exposure without conscious intention, effort, or reinforcement and is not observable until elicited by an appropriate situation. Also called incidental learning and learning without awareness.

latent variable
n. **1.** A theoretical construct inferred to underlie observed results. **2.** A variable created through the process of factor analysis to represent a pattern of interrelation among observed variables.

lateral dominance
n. Preference in using one side of the body. Also referred to as lateral preference or simply laterality. It applies to both motor activity and sensory reception. Although the majority of the people prefer using the right hand in skilled movements (right-handedness), about 2–14% of humans have a preference for using the left hand (left-handedness) in skilled motor activities. This percentage, however, is variable in different cultural

groups. There is also a preference in using the foot, but the percentage of right-footedness is slightly smaller. From birth some lateral preference is observed, but laterality is only fully established around the age of 4–5 years. Lateral dominance is relative, and many people prefer to use the right hand in some motor activities and the left hand in other motor activities (mixed handedness). Sometimes the dominant hand and the dominant foot (or eye or ear) are on opposite sides of the body (crossed dominance). There is a significant but not perfect association between lateral preference and hemisphere specialization. For about 99% of right-handers and 70% of left-handers the language is lateralized to the left hemisphere.   – A A

▶ *See also* **CEREBRAL DOMINANCE**

lateral dorsal nucleus

n. **1.** The lateral dorsal nucleus of the geniculate nucleus is a relay center in the main visual pathway connecting retinal ganglia to the visual cortex. **2.** The lateral dorsal nucleus of the thalamus connects the hippocampus and mammillary bodies with the cingulate cortex and is thought to be involved in emotion and memory formation.

lateral eye movement

n. A movement of the gaze to the left or right. This is associated with hemispheric dominance so that the eyes tend to move left when processing spatial information and to the right when answering a verbal question.

lateral fissure

n. Fold in the cortex separating the temporal lobe from the parietal and frontal lobes. It is also referred to as the Sylvian fissure, fissure of Sylvius, or lateral sulcus. In the left hemisphere it represents the core of the so-called brain language area; it means that damage involving the left lateral fissure results in language disturbances (aphasia). Deep in the lateral fissure is situated the insula. Below the lateral fissure in its posterior portion in the left hemisphere is located the Wernicke's area, a crucial area in language understanding.   – A A

lateral hypothalamic syndrome

n. **1.** A pattern of symptoms including failure or inability to eat or drink characteristic of lesions to the lateral hypothalamus. **2.** A four-stage pattern of recovery from damage to the lateral hypothalamus in which the first stage is nearly complete failure or inability to eat or drink, which often results in death unless the animal is force fed. The second stage is a continued failure to drink and poor appetite, eating only wet, palatable food. In the third stage the animal will eat soggy food but continues to avoid drinking. In the fourth stage the animal establishes new eating and drinking habits but continues to eat and drink at a lower rate than before the damage to the brain.

lateral hypothalamus

n. The portion of the thalamus away from the center on each side of the brain that is believed to regulate appetite and appetitive behavior.

lateral rectus

n. The eye muscle on the outside midline of the eye that rotates the eye away from the nose. Also called external rectus.

Latin square

n. A within-subjects research design in which a square array of letters representing treatments occurs once in every row and every column so that each subject receives each treatment, but different groups receive them in different orders in an attempt to neutralize any order effects.

law of effect

n. The statement that rewarded behavior tends to be repeated while behavior that is punished tends to disappear.

law of exercise

n. The theory that the repetition of an act makes it more fluid, easier to perform, less prone to errors, and more likely to be repeated in the same situation in the future. Defining the same situation in a meaningful way has made this law of minimal utility in predicting behavior.

law of parsimony

n. A scientific principle that places preference on the least complex explanation for an observation, theory, or phenomenon. Often referred to as the simplicity rule, the law of parsimony is based upon Ockham's razor, which states that entities should not be multiplied needlessly. As such, when there are two or more competing theories that make the same prediction, the simplest explanation is preferred.　　　　　　　　　　　– BJM

lay theories of behavioral causality

n. Lay theories of behavioral causality refer to the naïve theories laypeople develop and use to explain social events. One widely studied lay causal theory is lay dispositionism, which refers to the use of stable personality traits as the unit of analysis in social perception. People who subscribe to lay dispositionism tend to view behavior as reflecting its corresponding disposition, believe that knowledge of a person's trait is predictive of the person's trait-relevant behavior in a particular situation, and expect behavior to be consistent across situations. In contrast, people subscribing to lay situationism tend to view situational forces as the primary determinants of behaviors and expect low levels of cross-situational consistency in behaviors. Other lay causal theories include lay group theory (the belief that the group has strong influence on an individual's behavior) and lay interactionism (the belief that traits and situations jointly determine a person's behavior).　　– CYC

leadership

n. Definitions of leadership have changed over the decades. In the 1930s to 1950s, researchers defined leadership in terms of the leader's qualities and traits. According to Bogardus, these trait conceptions considered leadership as "personality in action." Further, Weber suggested that the leader's heroic and inspirational personality was one source of legitimacy. Stogdill reconceptualized leadership, not as a property of an individual, but as a relationship between people in a social situation. Consistently with this situational approach, Pfeffer suggested that leaders emerge as a consequence of timing and circumstance regardless of their individual characteristics. Additionally, Pfeffer redefined the leader's role by suggesting that leaders do not directly affect material outcomes; instead, they manage symbols by constructing and maintaining attitudes, beliefs, and emotions. Contemporary definitions of leadership adopt an interactional approach that captures the characteristics of both the leader and the situation, thus suggesting that the specific qualities, characteristics, and skills vital for successful leadership are largely determined by the demands of the social situation.　　　　　　　　　　　　　– JS, TM

leadership styles

n. Leadership styles are the actual or perceived patterns of behavior (e.g., words and actions) that leaders engage in to influence others. Leaders have a variety of options in terms of style. In terms of their power, Lewin, Lippitt, and White suggested that leaders could be (1) autocratic or authoritarian – making decisions unilaterally; (2) democratic – sharing power with the group by encouraging participative decision making; or (3) laissez-faire – abstaining from exercising power, thereby keeping leadership activity to a minimum. In terms of their goals, Blake and Mouton suggested that leaders could emphasize tasks (concern for production and job requirements) versus relationships (concern for people and interpersonal relationships). Finally, in terms of the strategies they employ to influence and motivate followers, Bass contrasts transactional styles that use extrinsic motivation (i.e., rewards or punishments to motivate performance) with transformational styles that emphasize intrinsic motivation (i.e., inspirational motives, ideals, and values). The success of these styles hinges upon the interaction between individual and situational variables.　　　　　　　– JS, TM

learned flavor aversion

n. An avoidance of a flavor usually associated in the past with illness. The learning of food aversion often occurs in a single trial even if several hours elapse between eating and becoming sick. These flavor aversions are extremely resistant to extinction as many animals will never again eat anything with the flavor to which they have learned to be avoidant; some rats have starved to death rather than eat food which had made them sick in the past. In one-trial learning, an animal learns to avoid a food after it has been sickened and especially if it has regurgitated after having eaten that food, whereas other stimuli such as buzzers and flashing lights do not produce such one-trial learning. This was important in showing that not all learning was equivalent, as had been supposed by behavioral theorists. Also called the Garcia effect.

learned food/flavor/taste aversion
n. One-trial learning in which an animal learns to avoid a food after it has been sickened and especially if it has regurgitated after having eaten that food. Other stimuli such as sound and lights do not produce such one-trial learning. This was important in showing that not all learning was equivalent, as had been supposed by behavioral theorists. These flavor aversions are extremely resistant to extinction as many animals will never again eat anything with the flavor to which they have learned to be avoidant; some rats have starved to death rather than eat food which had made them sick in the past.

learned helplessness
n. A mental state in which exposure to inescapable shock or other aversive stimuli has produced a lack of effort and motivation so that the animal fails to learn new responses even when they are available. In humans learned helplessness is associated with depression.

learning
n. **1.** The act or process of acquiring new information, behavior, or skill, which lasts for a considerable period. **2.** In learning theory, the acquisition of any new stimulus-response pattern.

learning, associative
n. Any theory of learning in which it is assumed that learning occurs through the forming of associations among individual elements. These have included Sigmund Freud's ideas about mental associations, stimulus and response approaches, neural networks, and mental representations of sensory events.

learning curve
n. Any graphic display of the change in behavior of an organism that alters its behavior in a situation in which it has the opportunity to acquire new knowledge, behavior, or skill. Performance is usually plotted along the vertical axis and time or trials along the horizontal axis.

learning disability
n. Any difficulty in learning in a specific area of information or performance that is not associated with general intelligence. These may be due to perceptual problems or neurological disorders, but the cause of many learning disabilities is unknown.

learning, implicit
n. Any form of learning that occurs through mere exposure without conscious intention, effort, or reinforcement and is not observable until elicited by a task requiring the information. Also called incidental or latent learning.

learning, latent
n. Any form of learning that occurs through mere exposure without conscious intention, effort, or reinforcement and is not observable until elicited by an appropriate situation. Also called incidental or implicit learning.

learning, motor
n. Any increase in coordination or skill in any bodily motion or complex task, which usually comes about through integration of sensory and proprioceptive information over the course of practice. Motor learning through imagery and mental practice has been noted, but it usually is accompanied by small mimicry of muscle movement involved in the actual skill.

learning, observational
n. Any form of learning that occurs through observation without practice and is not observable until elicited by an appropriate task situation. Thus children frequently learn

by watching their parents but without actually practicing the observed behaviors.

learning, one-trial
n. **1.** Any form of learning which occurs in a single trial, such as the connection between taste and illness or some learning of words. **2.** The learning theory of Edwin Guthrie, who believed all learning occurred in a single trial.

learning, paired associates
n. An experimental procedure in which subjects are required to learn pairs of items, usually so that they can recall one at a later time when the other is used as a cue.

learning, selective
n. **1.** Any form of learning in which some of the available information is learned while other is not or some possible effective choices are learned while others are not. **2.** An experimental paradigm in which some stimuli are made salient to reward and others are not or some behaviors reinforced while others are not.

learning set
n. A form of discrimination learning in which subjects must learn a general rule in order to be successful. As an example, in a rat maze problem the rat may have to learn that red crosses and blue circles are rewarded and no other combination is rewarded. Acquiring the learning set allows faster and more accurate discriminations in the future. Also called learning to learn.

learning, S-R
n. An abbreviation for *stimulus-response learning*, in which an organism learns to respond with a particular response to a particular stimulus, as in classical conditioning.

learning, S-S
n. Any form of learning in which one stimulus is associated with another stimulus.

learning, state-dependent
n. Any relatively permanent alteration in mind or behavior that occurs as a reaction to experience in a certain mental or physical state and is then repeated only when in the same or similar state. Thus memories or knowledge acquired while drunk are often remembered when drunk and not when sober or are remembered more easily and more clearly when drunk than sober.

learning theories
n. **1.** In psychology, any of the theories of the relatively permanent acquisition of information, behaviors, or skills, which range from classical conditioning to contemporary cognitive and educational psychology. **2.** Any of the many behaviorist points of view in which there has been an attempt to reduce all learning to relationships between stimulus conditions and observable responses.

learning theory, mathematical
n. Any of the behaviorist points of view in which there has been an attempt to describe all learning as mathematical relationships between stimulus conditions and observable responses.

learning to learn
n. A form of discrimination learning in which subjects must learn a general approach to problems in order to be successful. As an example, in a rat maze problem the rat may have to learn that red crosses and blue circles are rewarded and no other combination is rewarded. Acquiring the learning set allows faster and more accurate discriminations in the future. Also called learning set.

learning without awareness
n. Any form of learning that occurs through mere exposure without conscious intention, effort, or reinforcement and is not observable until elicited by an appropriate situation. Also called incidental or latent learning.

least-effort principle
n. The observation that organisms will usually try to accomplish a task in a manner requiring the least amount of time and energy or in which they will meet with the least resistance. Also called cognitive economy.

least-significant difference test

n. In an experimental design, the computation of all possible pairwise comparisons using a t or F statistic with a pooled error term. This approach minimizes type II error but increases the probability of type I error.

least-squares method

n. A technique for estimating the values or the graph of an unknown variable from a number of observations by means of calculating values for the graph which create the minimal sum of the squared deviations of the observed values from the predicted value or graph of expected values.

lemma

n. In psycholinguistics, a lemma is a level of representation of a word between the semantic (meaning) and phonological (sound) levels of processing. Lemmas are abstract in that they contain no information about the sound of the word but are uniquely syntactically and semantically specified. The term derives from linguistics, where it refers to the standard form of a word chosen to represent all its possible variants.

The idea of a lemma is most used in speech production, in the context of a two-stage model of lexical retrieval. Semantic specifications are used to retrieve lemmas, which in turn are used to access phonological forms (sometimes called lexemes), although the process of phonological retrieval might itself be a multistage one. Specifying the lemma is called lexical selection, and specifying the phonological form is called phonological encoding. There is considerable evidence to support the two-stage model, with data from speech errors (where we find whole word substitutions related to the target by meaning or sound), the existence of semantic and phonological types of anomia (word-finding difficulties in aphasia), picture-naming studies, and brain imaging. When we are in a tip-of-the-tongue state for a word, we have retrieved the lemma but have not been able to retrieve its associated phonological form (although we might be able to retrieve some of it, such as the first sound of the word). The best evidence for the existence of lemmas is from studies that show that people in tip-of-the-tongue states or with anomia can retrieve gender information about nouns (in those languages that mark gender). Needless to say, there is some dissent as to whether lemmas are really necessary, and there are alternative interpretations of the data.

There have been two large but related debates about how we retrieve and use lemmas in speech production. The first is whether lexicalization (lexical retrieval in speech production) is a discrete or cascading process: that is, do we specify just one lemma before we can start retrieving phonological forms, or are a number of candidate lemmas (related semantically) still active simultaneously while we start to retrieve phonological forms? The second issue is whether or not there is feedback between levels: can the sound of a word affect lemma selection, and in turn can this influence which meaning representations are active? The main evidence, from primed picture-naming studies, is equivocal, and modeling in any case shows that cascading interactive models of lexical retrieval can reproduce any pattern of priming data.

Lemmas can be thought of as corresponding to the hidden level of units in a connectionist model of lexicalization.   – TH

lens

n. **1.** Any mechanism which refracts the light which passes through it in a symmetrical way. Convex lenses concentrate the light while concave lenses scatter the light **2.** The transparent, convex structure in the front of the eye which focuses light on the retina and the fovea in particular, thus improving the clarity of vision. The lens in the human eye is stretched by the muscles of the eye to allow focus on objects of varying distance, further improving visual clarity.

lens model analysis

n. A data analytic technique to examine human judgments, which is based on assumptions concerning an interactive process between a judge and the environment or ecology in which he or she is operating. The judgment ecology provides cues related to the event or object being judged. Different cues are better predictors of the event or object than others, and a lens model analysis isolates those cues in the environment that are the best in making judgments about the event or object.

leptin

n. A protein secreted by fat cells which is believed to be a messenger chemical that communicates level of fat to the brain and is used in the regulation of appetite and eating. Rats deficient in leptin rapidly become obese.

lesbian

n. A woman who is attracted to or engages in sexual activity with women rather than with men. Also called Sapphist and female homosexual.

lesion

n. Any damage or structural alteration to a limited area of any organ brought about by disease, toxin, trauma, or surgery.

level of measurement

n. The form and accuracy of observations. Observations can be recorded in nominal, ordinal, interval, and ratio scales so that a different set of operations can be performed on each. Thus taking the average of names or the standard deviation of ranks is not meaningful but is often essential for understanding interval or ratio data. Similarly the precision with which a set of categories fits the data or the accuracy with which an instrument measures a ratio variable also affects the usefulness of the data.

levels of processing

n. In information processing paradigms, the idea that that there are an ordered series or layers of analysis and that most information is processed only at the first layers, and at each layer there is a loss or screening out of information so that some information is processed more thoroughly or deeply than other information. The level of processing of any particular piece of information, then, is how many layers of processing it has gone through. Some paradigms assume the first process is an

encoding of data which loses or discards most data, the second level is a storage or memory of data which also loses some data, and the third level entails some further specific processing which includes an elaboration of the data through interconnection with existing data stores.

lexical decision task

n. In the lexical decision task participants decide, as quickly and accurately as possible, whether a string of letters is, or is not, a properly spelled word, and reaction times and accuracy at making these responses are recorded. By understanding the factors that speed or slow lexical decision responses, psychologists are able to develop and test theories related to lexical memory (the mental store of words) and semantic memory (the mental store of word meaning and general world knowledge). This task originated out of research into mental chronometry (the study of human information processing and its time course) and has become the most widely used experimental technique for studying word recognition processes. This task has been used to assess how various factors affect word recognition, including word frequency, word length, orthographic neighborhood density, stimulus degradation, number of syllables, number of morphemes, part of speech, and relatedness, to name just a few.   – TK

lexicon

n. All the words in a language or all the words an individual is able to use. The size of an individual's lexicon depends on the way it is tested. Most people can use more words than they can define and recognize the meaning of words in other people's speech that they do not use in their own speech.

libido

n. **1.** In psychoanalysis, the basic biological energy of the person (Eros) directed toward love, sex, and procreation, as contrasted with Thanatos, or the energy directed toward destruction and death. **2.** In analytic psychology, the basic life force or energy of the person, which includes sexuality but is not considered inherently sexual.

lie detection

n. Meta-analysis of hundreds of studies has found that people can detect when others are lying at a rate only slightly better than chance. In addition, there is no significant correlation between people's confidence in their judgments and their actual accuracy. Use of the polygraph – a device that monitors heart rate, breathing, skin moisture, and blood pressure to track the physiological arousal presumably associated with lying – produces somewhat higher rates of accuracy. Development of an infallible method of detecting lies would have enormous practical implications, especially for the legal system. Unfortunately, it may never be possible to detect lies reliably. Although measures of physiological changes continue to improve and to become more precise (brain scans are the latest advance that has been applied to the study of lie detection), there appears to be no unique physiological signal or pattern of behaviors that consistently reveals whether or not someone is lying.   – MC

lie scale

n. **1.** A scale on the Minnesota Multiphasic Personality Inventory consisting of 15 items which describe the test taker in an unrealistically perfectionistic and idealized manner which is used to detect dishonest responding to the test. **2.** Any scale used to detect lying or unrealistically positive responses (socially desirable responding) to any test with such a scale.

life-span development

n. **1.** The predictable, multidimensional changes an individual goes through over the course of growth from an infant, through childhood, adolescence, and across the adult years to senescence and death. **2.** The study of psychological development across the whole life span with an emphasis on adult change.

light adaptation

n. The process of becoming accustomed to ambient light levels so as to maximize perception at that level of illumination. This normally includes controlling the amount of light entering the pupil by widening when light level is low and narrowing the opening when there are higher light levels, depletion of light-receptive chemicals in the retinal rods and cones, and processes of reciprocal inhibition in the retinal nerve cells. In very low levels of illumination it also includes using edges of the retina rather than the center as the edges contain mostly rods, which are more light sensitive than are the cones, which are concentrated in the center of the eye.

likelihood ratio

n. **1.** In statistics, the ratio of the likelihood that some fact is true if a condition is true divided by the probability of the act's being true if the condition is not present. Thus one might calculate the ratio between the probability of a person's having a cough if the person has flu and divide it by the probability of a person's having a cough who does not have flu. **2.** In signal detection theory, it is the ratio of the likelihood that a response is due to a signal plus background noise divided by the probability that a response is due only to background noise at a particular cutoff criterion level.

Likert scale

n. Psychometric scale utilizing an item format that requires respondents to indicate their level of agreement with a list of statements. Often used in questionnaires, attitude measures, and personality tests, Likert scales provide a measure of the degree to which individuals endorse various ideas, positions, and attitudes. Likert scales can be created either to allow for a neutral answer or to force respondents to make a positive or negative response. For example, respondents may be asked to indicate their level of agreement with the statement "I am confident in novel situations." Using a traditional 5-point Likert scale, respondents may be asked to respond as "strongly agree," "somewhat agree," "neither agree nor disagree," "somewhat disagree," or "strongly disagree." The middle point allows for a neutral response to this statement. In contrast, if researchers want to create a forced-choice measure, a 6-point Likert scale can be utilized that requires respondents to select from "strongly agree," "moderately agree," "mildly agree," "mildly disagree," "moderately disagree," or "strongly disagree." Likert scales provide ordinal data that allows for the comparison of the relative endorsement of various attitudes but does not allow for more complex quantitative calculations that require equal intervals or an absolute zero. Likert scales may be subjected to factor analysis to determine statistical clustering of related items, attitudes, and values.   – BJM

limbic system
n. A ring-shaped area of the brain around the brainstem involved in emotion, memory, learning, and autonomic control of the body. There is no widely accepted definition of the boundaries of the limbic system, but definitions usually include the hippocampus, cingulate gyrus, fornicate gyrus, amygdala, hypothalamus, mammillary bodies, nucleus accumbens, orbitofrontal cortex, parahippocampal gyrus, and septum.

limen
n. **1.** A threshold or the magnitude of a stimulus or the change in a stimulus that will be detected 50% of the time. **2.** The lowest intensity of a stimulus that evokes a response in a subject.

limits, method of
n. In psychophysics, a technique for discovering the threshold for a particular stimulus by presenting a stimulus and lowering it or raising it in small steps until there is a change in response by the test subject as to the presence of the stimulus.

linear perspective
n. A cue used to perceive depth in which the size of an image on the retina is used to judge its distance. So the same thing seen close up casts a large image on our retina and a smaller one when far away, and we use the difference in size to estimate depth or distance. An instance of this most have experienced occurs when railroad tracks run away from us and the near tracks look larger than the far tracks and we perceive depth instead of that the track shrinks as it goes away from us.

linear regression
n. A form of statistical modeling in which a set of observations are used to create a line which is used to predict future values of the variable. The line created is the one which causes the lowest sum of squared distances from the line of all possible lines for the data set.

linguistic determinism
n. The idea that the ways people perceive the world and think are controlled by the language that they have learned. Thus it was believed by some early in the 20th century that monolingual Hopi speakers who have only one word for flying things could not distinguish among birds, bats, and butterflies. Subsequent research has not confirmed this strong version of the hypothesis, but the notion that language has some guiding effect on thought persists. *See also* linguistic relativity

linguistic relativity
n. The linguistic relativity hypothesis consists of a set of ideas proposed by Edward Sapir and Benjamin Whorf and has also been referred to as the *Whorfian hypothesis* or the *Sapir-Whorf hypothesis.* According to Whorf, there is no inherent structure in people's experiences; perceptual order emerges when people organize their experiences with mental categories, and language is the major cognitive tool people use to categorize their experiences. As a language evolves, it develops a coherent internal logic, which embodies a metaphysics or naïve conception of reality. As such, the internal logic of a language stands in isomorphic relation to that of its associated culture. *Linguistic determinism* is a stronger form of the linguistic relativity hypothesis. It states that markedly different languages evoke in the mind of speakers different mental representations of similar linguistic referents and that language constrains the development of nonlinguistic cultural norms. Little support has been found for linguistic determinism.
– CYC

▶ *See also* **LINGUISTIC DETERMINISM, SAPIR-WHORF HYPOTHESIS,** *and* **WHORFIAN HYPOTHESIS**

linguistics

n. The study of language whose major branches include phonetics, phonology, semantics, syntax, and pragmatics. In recent years the discipline has entered into inter-disciplinary studies with anthropology, psychology, sociology, philosophy, and computer science to create the field of psycholinguistics within cognitive science.

linguistic universals

n. Linguistic universals are facts that are true for all natural languages. Such universal properties are robust and are not necessarily driven by genetic relationships between languages. All languages build words by using consonants and vowels, and all languages have nouns and verbs which combine in sentences to form subjects and predicates. Such facts applicable to all languages are examples of *absolute universals*. Linguists have also studied *implicational universals*, tendencies that occur in many languages such that they could not plausibly be driven by chance. If a language has a three-vowel system, the three vowels are very likely to be /i a u/. If a language has subject-object-verb as its canonical word order, it is highly likely that it uses postpositions, rather than prepositions. Highly inflected languages, like Spanish, tend to have relatively free word order, while languages with more limited functional morphology, like English, tend to have rigid word order requirements.   – EMF

linkage

n. In genetics, the occurrence of two or more genes on the same chromosome, which makes it more likely they will stay together in the next generation. When sex cells divide in half to form ova and sperm, there is a period called crossing over in which the inherited chromosomes from the father and mother split up and some cross over to form new genetic strands so that each sex cell has a somewhat random half of the genes from each parent. If genes are on the same chromosome, the chance they will be in the same half in the sex cells and so be passed on together to the new generation increases.

lipid

n. Any of a number of fatty acids and waxes which form one of the major building blocks of living cells which are soluble in alcohol but not in water. This makes them usable in the construction of cell walls and linings as they will not be dissolved by the liquid around them.

lithium

n. A very light malleable silvery alkali metal. In the form of lithium carbonate it is used as a mood stabilizer for persons with bipolar disorder. Use of lithium as a mood stabilizer is dangerous as the fatal dose is only two or three times the therapeutic dose, and so close monitoring of blood levels of lithium is necessary in its clinical use.

Little Hans

n. The name assigned to a little boy in a published case history in which Sigmund Freud traced a phobia for horses back to the boy's castration anxiety. This was caused by anxiety over masturbation, hatred and envy of his father, and sexual desire for his mother and the guilt these entailed, all of which was projected onto horses.

Lloyd Morgan's canon

n. The idea that we should interpret animal behavior as a function of the lowest possible level of mental organization instead of thinking about it in terms of human thinking, which leads to anthropomorphizing, or perceiving animals from a human-centered perspective. This idea appeared in C. Lloyd Morgan's textbook *Comparative Psychology* (1894), in which he wrote, "In no case may we interpret an action as the outcome of the exercise of higher psychical faculty, if it can be interpreted as the exercise of one which stands lower in the psychological scale."

lobotomy

n. **1.** A surgical procedure in which the connections between the frontal lobe and the rest of the brain are cut or in which part or all of the frontal lobe is removed. This surgical procedure was used in attempts to cure depression, schizophrenia, epilepsy, anxiety, aggressiveness, and pain but was discontinued in the 1950s after it was generally accepted that it produced a kind of generalized apathy and lack of self-direction. Also called a frontal leucotomy and prefrontal lobotomy. **2.** A surgical procedure which severs the connections between any lobe of the brain and the rest of the brain.

lobotomy, prefrontal

n. A surgical procedure in which the connections between the frontal lobe and the rest of the brain are cut or in which part or all of the frontal lobe is removed. This surgical procedure was used in attempts to cure depression, schizophrenia, epilepsy, anxiety, aggressiveness, and pain but was discontinued in the 1950s after it was generally accepted that it produced a kind of generalized apathy and lack of self-direction. Also called a frontal leucotomy and lobotomy.

localization of function

n. The assumption that certain brain areas are responsible for particular kinds of mental functions such as experiences, memories, or movements.

loci, method of

n. A memory technique in which items to be remembered are associated with particular places or parts of places. Thus, to help remember material for a test a student might associate one end of the blackboard with one part of the material, the middle of the blackboard with another part, and the other end of the blackboard with other material.

lock-and-key theory

n. The theory that odors are detected when molecules have a particular electrochemical shape that fits into the electrochemical shapes on nasal receptors as a key fits into a lock.

locomotor ataxia

n. A progressive difficulty in walking due to the degeneration of the dorsal columns in the spinal cord which leads to muscle atrophy and gradual loss of deep tendon reflexes as well as loss of sensory information. It is caused by syphilis.

locus

n. The Greek word for "place," *locus* denotes the position of an anatomical structure, tumor, lesion, or other injury, as well as the position of a gene on a chromosome.

locus of control

n. A phrase coined by Julian Rotter that refers to a person's perception of how much or how little control he/she has over life. Rotter discusses two variations of locus of control: internal and external (which can be measured using Rotter's I/E Scale). Individuals who have an internal locus of control believe that they personally are in control of their own destiny. It is through their own efforts that they succeed or fail on a given task. Individuals with an external locus of control believe they are at the mercy of external factors such as luck or fate. They do not believe their efforts will lead to a change in their environment. Locus of control is believed be caused by past experiences individuals have with success and failure, other people's responses to those events, and cultural factors. These affecting factors influence individuals' expectancies for control over and outcomes of future occurrences.   – SRB

logagnosia

n. An inability to understand words in either spoken or written form. Also called Wernicke's aphasia and receptive aphasia.

logic

n. **1.** Any mode of analysis that follows an acceptable mode of making inferences from given data. **2.** The branch of philosophy and mathematics that is concerned with forms of inference that lead to valid conclusions from accepted premises. **3.** The creation of symbolic languages with rules for deduction and inference specified as part of the symbol system, often called symbolic logic.

logical positivism

n. An archaic philosophy in which spirituality and ethics are rejected as meaningless and the assumption is made that the only meaningful statements that can be made are simple propositions which can be immediately verified by observation. It was an important point of view in late 19th- and early 20th-century psychology in points of view such as behaviorism.

logic, formal
n. Logic based on a formally defined system rather than logic based on meanings.

logic, symbolic
n. A system of symbols with formally defined meanings used to analyze the logic of statements or arguments while avoiding the ambiguities present in natural languages.

log-linear analysis
n. In statistics, a method of analyzing frequency data in a cross-tabulation by modeling the logarithm of the frequency in a cell as a main effect and interaction effects. It can be used in analyzing the effects of more than one independent variable on the dependent variable and in estimating interaction as well as main effects.

logogen
n. A theoretical unit of long-term memory corresponding to a word, digit, or other unit of language. It is supposed to be activated by stimuli that are related to it. So the word *pear* will be fully activated by seeing the word *pear* and will be partially activated by seeing the letter *p* or the word *pair*. When sufficiently activated, the logogen then outputs its unit into memory as a recognition or a recollection or in speech.

logograph
n. Any written system in which a symbol represents a complete word, idea, or morpheme. Thus the Chinese written language and Japanese Kanji are logographic while contemporary English usage has only a few symbols, such as $, %, and +, which are logographic. Also called logogram.

logotherapy
n. A form of psychotherapy which focuses on the individual's coming to an understanding of the personal meaning of his or her experience in the world, the world itself, and his/

her need and capacity to interact with the world and other people in meaningful ways. It attempts to restore or develop a sense of meaning through activities which foster creative activities and experiences of art, culture, nature, and relationships with other people and encourages self-acceptance and appreciation of one's place in the world. It often explores one's attitudes to work, love, and life as a technique for discovery of and critical analysis of meaning.

longitudinal fissure
n. A deep crevice, running from front to back, between the two halves of the cerebral cortex with the corpus callosum, which connects the two hemispheres, at the bottom. Also called the interhemispheric fissure, principal sulcus, and longitudinal sulcus.

longitudinal method
n. The experimental process of measuring a variable or variables more than once with the same subjects with time delays between the measurements so as to perceive changes in the variables related to the passage of time.

longitudinal study
n. Any study which repeats measurements of the same variables with the same subjects spread across time, usually for the purpose of seeing the effect of development on the variables or their relationships.

long-term memory
n. (LTM) A hypothesized information store in the mind with unlimited capacity, consisting of a portion of the information originally in short-term memory that had been transferred for permanent storage. Whether information was ever lost from long-term memory was a debated topic.

long-term potentiation
n. An increased ease of synaptic transmission following brief repeated stimulation of a cell or cells that triggers stimulation of succeeding cells which can last for up to a month. This is believed to be a process which underlies memory in the hippocampus.

long- versus short-term orientation

n. A continuum of the time frame for thinking and planning, which describes a culture's time horizon, or the relative importance of the future versus the past and present. Long-term-oriented societies value thrift, status hierarchy, shame, and perseverance more highly. In short-term-oriented cultures, respect for tradition, protecting one's face, personal steadiness and stability, and reciprocation of gifts and favors are valued more. East Asian nations such as China and Japan tend to score toward the long-term end and developing countries such as Pakistan and Nigeria toward the short-term orientation. People in the United States and Western European nations tend to be low but not among the lowest. Within the United States different subcultures tend to score differently, with urban ghetto dwellers and some rural poor groups scoring toward the short-term end of the dimension and upper-middle-class individuals toward the long-term end of the dimension.

looking-glass self

n. The sense of self or identity derived from the communicated impressions, reactions, and opinions of other people to one's self which continues to change over the course of one's life.

loosening of associations

n. A symptom of mental disturbance in which mental associations become tangential, thought does not follow a coherent line of reasoning and is difficult to follow, and speech seems fragmented and incoherent. Also called cognitive derailment.

lorazepam

n. An addictive central nervous system depressant which is the drug of choice for relief of the symptoms of alcohol withdrawal as it has little effect on the liver, unlike other benzodiazapines. It is also used to treat anxiety, sleeping problems, and seizure disorders. It is frequently prescribed to depressed and suicidal individuals because the overdose potential is low. Also called Ativan.

lost-letter technique

n. A procedure for measuring attitudes in a geographical area in which two equal sets of letters are stamped and addressed to groups likely to have opposing views on the attitude being measured and are randomly scattered through an area. The number which are ultimately delivered is taken as an indication of a favorable attitude toward the attitude supported by the group to whom the letter was addressed as it is assumed people will be more likely to mail letters to groups of whom they approve than to organizations of whom they do not approve. Also called the lost-letter procedure.

loudness

n. The experienced intensity of sound, usually measured in phons, which roughly corresponds to its pressure level, measured in decibels; it is also affected by tone, expectedness, spectrum, and duration. It is sometimes called volume.

love

n. **1.** A state of being in which a person is preoccupied with, is unrealistically positive about, is intensely sensitive toward, and has intense feelings of tenderness, warmth, affection and lust toward another person. **2.** A sense of connection with and feelings of warmth and concern for another person, animal, plant, or thing. **3.** Warm but disinterested concern for the well-being of another.

love, companionate

n. A love relationship characterized by high levels of intimacy and commitment but lacking passion.

love, romantic

n. A love relationship characterized by high levels of passion and commitment but lacking intimacy.

love scale

n. Any of a large number of measures intended to gauge one person's feelings of connection, commitment, warmth, passion, intimacy, sexual attraction, or desire to be with another person.

lowball technique

n. A persuasive technique in which a seller offers an unrealistically low price for a desired item in order to obtain agreement and then increases the price after agreement is reached by adding unannounced fees or claiming there was a mistake in the original price. Compliance and selling price are higher with this technique than when an honest negotiation strategy is used.

low-context cultures

n. Cultures that promote direct communication in which messages are conveyed primarily and directly in verbal languages and the effects of context are minimized.

LSD (d iso lysergic acid diethylamide)

n. A powerful psychedelic drug that works primarily by neutralizing a serotonin antagonist. Created in 1938, LSD became widely known in the 1960s, when it was a central part of the hippie movement in the United States and Europe. The effects begin with a pregnant sense that something is about to happen, which is replaced after about half an hour by wild sensory distortion characterized by brilliant hallucinations and trans-sense experiences so that one may see odor or feel images. This period lasts up to 3 hours and is replaced by a period of seemingly heightened lucidity which can last up to 8 or 9 hours. Many people who have taken LSD experience flashbacks, which are periods lasting from a few seconds to a few minutes in which the symptoms of LSD intoxication return and which most people find both enjoyable and surprising. Some people who take LSD have what are called "bummers" or "bad trips," in which the experience is overwhelmingly frightening or sad; most report that deep insights accompany the fear or sadness. LSD has shown promise in psychotherapy, but its use was discontinued without being thoroughly studied when the drug was made illegal in the 1960s.

lucid dream

n. A dream in which the person is conscious of dreaming and has some sense of control over events in the dream.

lumen

n. A unit of subjective light intensity or the illumination equal to the flux of 1 candela of luminous intensity into a solid angle of 1 steradian. This is a scientific standard of the intensity of light that the eye actually perceives in a given unit of visual space. It differs from measures of radiant light, which are not adjusted to the perceptive capacities of the human eye but measure total illumination within a given visual space which could be very bright but unseen by a human eye if the wavelength of light were outside that seen by humans.

luminance

n. The amount of light adjusted for human sensitivity emitted or reflected by a surface, usually measured in candelas per square meter.

luminosity

n. The perception of brightness, which is influenced by the total radiance, sensitivity of the eye to the wavelengths of the light, the eye's adaptation level, and background luminosity.

luminosity coefficient

n. A mathematical index of the visibility of light of a particular wavelength. The coefficient is set at 1 for a wavelength of 555 nanometers, which is the wavelength around which most humans have peak sensitivity.

luminosity curve

n. A graph showing the intensity of light that is necessary at each wavelength in the visible spectrum for the different wavelengths to appear equally bright. A different curve is required for high and low levels of total illumination as different rods and cones have different sensitivities to and adaptation curves for brightness.

luminous flux

n. The rate at which light emitted from or reflected from a source is visible to humans. This differs from radiant flux, which is the total amount of light emitted or reflected not adjusted for the sensitivity of the eye to different wavelengths of light.

luminous intensity

n. The amount of perceived light or luminous flux emitted or reflected per unit of visible space (solid angle) in a given direction, usually measured in candelas.

Luria-Nebraska Neuropsychological Battery

n. (LNNB) A set of tests designed to diagnose general and specific brain dysfunction and to localize the dysfunction to particular brain areas. Its two forms have 269 and 279 items, which are scored on 11 clinical scales, including motor function, tactile function, visual function, rhythm, receptive speech, expressive speech, writing, reading, arithmetic, memory, and intellectual processes, with a scale for intermediate-term memory added in the second version. A pathognomonic scale and scales for right hemisphere function and left hemisphere function can also be calculated. It is intended for persons over the age of 15 and is among the most widely used neuropsychological tests.

luteotrophic hormone

n. A hormone secreted by the pituitary gland that stimulates the mammary glands to produce and secrete milk and the corpus luteum to secrete progesterone, which has a contraceptive effect, making pregnancy while nursing unlikely. Also called prolactin.

lux

n. A unit of perceived illumination equal to 1 lumen per square meter.

lymph

n. A pale yellow saline fluid resembling blood plasma and white blood cells (leukocytes) that is collected from body tissues and transported through the lymphatic capillaries before flowing passively into the bloodstream through a tube called the thoracic duct.

lymphocyte

n. Any of several types of white blood cells that form part of the immune system that are produced in bone marrow and found in lymph. Also called leukocyte.

lysergic acid diethylamide (d iso) ▶ *see* LSD (**D ISO LYSERGIC ACID DIETHYLAMIDE**)

M

Mach band

n. An illusion that appears when the edges of a light gray and a dark gray patch are placed together such that on the dark gray patch there appears to be a strip of even darker gray along the edge, and along the lighter gray patch there appears to be an even lighter gray strip along the edge so that the contrast between the two is heightened.

Machiavellianism

n. A character trait or social strategy of manipulativeness in which the person regards others impersonally and as means to his or her own personal ends without regard for their welfare, a course that typically allows the person to lie, cheat, and steal if it serves his/her goals.

machismo

n. The prominent exhibition of the male sex role including being a provider, as well as being unemotional, strong, enduring, authoritative, active, dominant, critical, and aggressive. The word is from Spanish-speaking cultures in which there are strong social expectations for machismo among men but also varied levels of liking for it.

macrocephaly

n. Enlargement of the head, usually due to a congenital defect that increases growth of tissues that support the brain. It can also be caused by hydrocephalus, which is abnormal accumulation of water in the cranium. Both can result in mental retardation.

mad cow disease

n. A fatal disease of the central nervous system in cows caused by defective proteins called prions which cause infected nerve cells to replicate the prion instead of the proteins usually manufactured within the nerve cell. These proteins cause the death of the cells and create spongy holes in the brain where cells have died. The disease has an incubation period of more than a year and usually occurs when the tissue of the nervous system is eaten by another animal. The disease became widespread in Great Britain during a period in which it was common to grind up the brains of cows in manufacturing cattle feed. The few human cases are variants of Kreutsfeldt-Jakob disease caused by eating diseased beef as prions are found in the bone marrow, blood, spleen, and lymph nodes, as well as in the central nervous system although at much reduced levels. Also called bovine spongiform encephalopathy and, in humans, variant Kreutsfeldt-Jakob disease (v-KJD).

magazine training

n. A process of familiarizing an animal in operant conditioning experiments with a machine called a magazine feeder that delivers food to a hopper where the animal can eat it. This is done with the supposition that familiarity will lead the experimental results to be uninfluenced by the operation of the machine.

magical number seven

n. "The Magical Number Seven" is the title of the cognitive psychologist George A. Miller's influential paper, which estimated the amount of information which can be held in short-term memory (a memory that lasts less than 30 seconds). He estimated that most humans' short-term memory can hold between five and nine pieces of information. These can be individual letters (e.g., *R, G, W, H, D, Y, Q, C, I*) or "chucks" (e.g., *CIA, FBI, CSI, NSA*). Chucking information into meaningful units can greatly increase the number of letters remembered, but still only five to nine chucks is typically remembered. Hence, the "magic number seven" is a durable estimate of the number of meaningful pieces of information that can be maintained within short-term memory.   – DGr

magical thinking

n. The belief that one's thoughts can influence the world and others around oneself. This is usual in children before the age of 5 or 6 but is replaced by logical thought after that except in some cases of wishful thinking.

magnetic resonance imaging

n. (MRI) Use of a medical device for creating three-dimensional images of the body by measuring the reactivity of the hydrogen atoms in tissues to intense magnetic fields. The MRI is more accurate than computed tomography (CT) scanning and shows more tissue differences than do X-ray images.

magnitude estimation

n. A psychophysical method for measuring the perceived intensity of a stimulus in which a subject uses numbers to indicate his/her judgment about the intensity of a stimulus. Subjects are often given a standard stimulus with an arbitrarily assigned number (often 10) before the start of experimental trials.

main effect

n. In an analysis of variance, the effect of an independent variable on a dependent variable across all values of the independent variable.

mainstreaming

n. The practice of placing students who are markedly above or below average in academic performance in the same classrooms with students who are in the average range in academic achievement.

maintenance rehearsal

n. The repeating of information such as a telephone number over and over again in an attempt to remember it. This is done without any thinking about the meaning of the information, which is referred to as an elaboration.

maintenance schedule

n. In operant conditioning, the frequency and conditions in which an established response is reinforced and so prevented from becoming extinct over time after it has been established, often with a different schedule of reinforcement.

major depression
n. A period of 6 or more months in which a person feels depressed, low in energy, worthless, and guilty most of the time; lacks interest and pleasure in daily activities; has disturbed sleep and/or appetite and psychomotor agitation or retardation; has diminished capacity to concentrate and indecisiveness; and thinks often about death and suicide.

major depressive disorder
n. A disorder characterized by two or more episodes of depressive episodes which are periods between 2 weeks and 6 months in which the person feels depressed, low in energy, worthless, and guilty most of the time; lacks interest and pleasure in daily activities; has disturbed sleep and/or appetite, psychomotor agitation or retardation; has diminished capacity to concentrate and indecisiveness; and thinks often about death and suicide.

major epilepsy
n. A chronic brain disorder characterized by uncontrolled electrical activity in the brain which produces full body convulsions, loss of consciousness, and loss of bodily control over bladder and bowels. Brain trauma is the most common known cause of epilepsy, but in many cases the cause is unknown. Also called grand mal or psychomotor epilepsy.

major tranquilizer
n. An archaic name for antipsychotic medications which emphasized the difference between them and anxiolytics, hypnotics, and sedatives, which were called minor tranquilizers.

maladaptive
adj. Interfering with optimal biological, economic, emotional, intellectual, occupational, or social functioning within a particular environment, culture, or set of circumstances.

maladjustment
n. The state of coping less than optimally in biological, economic, emotional, intellectual, occupational, or social functioning within a particular environment, culture, or set of circumstances.

mal de ojo
n. A mental disorder characterized by sleep disturbances, crying without apparent cause, diarrhea, fever, and vomiting found mostly in the Mediterranean area and most prevalent in children but sometimes occurring in grown women. It is commonly believed to be a culture-bound disorder. Also known as the evil eye.

male erectile disorder
n. The persistent or recurrent inability to maintain an adequate penile erection for the completion of sexual activity, which normally causes significant frustration and personal distress and interpersonal difficulties.

male orgasmic disorder
n. A disorder characterized by persistent or recurrent absence of or delay in orgasm after sexual arousal during sexual activity that would normally produce orgasm, which causes significant personal or interpersonal distress.

malingering
n. Intentionally pretending to have an illness or disability or exaggerating psychological or physical symptoms in order to gain rewards such as sympathy, attention, monetary compensation, or light work duties or to avoid something the person deems undesirable such as military service, criminal prosecution, or social responsibility.

malleus
n. One of the three ossicles of the auditory system. Because of the shape, it is also known as the hammer. It is attached to the tympanic membrane and connects with the second ossicle, the incus or anvil.   – A A

mammary glands
n. The glands in mammalian females that secrete milk. Also called breasts or teats.

mammillary body
n. Either of two bumps on the bottom of the brain at the end of the fornix resembling

breasts which are important to emotion, memory, and arousal and are part of the limbic system. Also spelled mamillary body.

MANCOVA ▶ *See* MULTIVARIATE ANALYSIS OF COVARIANCE

mandala
n. **1.** Any symmetrical geometric figure usually including a circle or square. **2.** In Jungian psychology, an archetype that was a representation of the unconscious with polarities balanced across an empty center which was the self. **3.** In Buddhism, there are mandalas which represent experience with a point of perception in the middle and a representation of experience or energies around it. **4.** In Hinduism, there are also many mandalas, which are representations of completion with a square often representing the four directions and a figure known in European culture as the star of David representing the universal interplay of male and female energies.

mania
n. **1.** A mental state characterized by abnormally high energy, low need for sleep, excessive uncoordinated motor activity and an elevated, expansive, or irritable mood, often with grandiosity, talkativeness, distractibility, excessive sexuality, drug use, or impulsive behavior. **2.** A preoccupation with or passion for a particular topic or activity.

mania, unipolar
n. A mental state characterized by abnormally high energy, low need for sleep, excessive uncoordinated motor activity and an elevated, expansive, or irritable mood, often with grandiosity, talkativeness, distractibility, excessive sexuality, drug use, or other impulsive behavior without a corresponding depressive period as occurs in bipolar I disorder.

manic bipolar disorder
n. A disorder characterized by abnormally high energy, low need for sleep, excessive uncoordinated motor activity, and an elevated, expansive, or irritable mood, often with grandiosity, talkativeness, distractibility,

excessive sexuality, drug use, or other impulsive behavior.

manic-depressive personality
n. An enduring pattern of psychological functioning and behavior characterized by the alternation of high energy, an elevated mood, egotism, and impulsive behavior with corresponding periods of depression including mental and physical slowing, sad mood, feelings of worthlessness and helplessness, and indecisiveness.

manic episode
n. A period in which a person has abnormally high energy, low need for sleep, excessive uncoordinated motor activity, and an elevated, expansive, or irritable mood, often with grandiosity, talkativeness, distractibility, excessive sexuality, drug use, or other impulsive behavior.

manifest anxiety
n. Overt arousal and visible acting out of internal feelings of stress.

Manifest Anxiety Scale
n. A self-report inventory of overt or conscious symptoms of anxiety. Also called the Taylor Manifest Anxiety Scale.

Mann-Whitney U test
n. A statistical measure test of the likelihood that two samples of ordinal or ranked data are drawn from the same population that makes no assumptions about the distribution of the populations involved.

MANOVA ▶ *See* MULTIVARIATE ANALYSIS OF VARIANCE

MAO inhibitors
n. A family of antidepressant drugs that operate by inhibiting the action of monoamine oxidase (MAO) in synaptic clefts by increasing the levels of the monoamine-based neurotransmitters serotonin, norepinephrine, and dopamine. Irreversible MAO inhibitors permanently bind to MAO and can cause dangerously high blood pressure if the person eats food high in tryptophan or tyramine.

Reversible MAO inhibitors only temporarily bind with MAO and so are less dangerous.

marginal group

n. Any identifiable group of people who have not been assimilated into the mainstream of a culture for cultural, economic, ethnic, medical, religious, social, or other reasons.

marginalization

n. Originally coined by sociologists, the term *marginalization* is used in acculturation psychology to refer to the phenomenon whereby a person maintains little connection to her/ his cultural group of origin and its traditions and engages in little association with any other cultural group and its traditions. Related terms include *deculturation* and *alienation*. In the work of Park (1928), Stonequist (1935), and others, marginalization is suggested to be most likely to occur to a cultural group that is subject to prejudice and discrimination of a sociopolitically dominant group. Members of the nondominant group begin to adopt the dominant group's negative attitudes toward their group, but discriminatory barriers prevent them from passing into the dominant group. Marginalization has often been exemplified by the experience of some colonized indigenous people who have been forced to abandon their cultural traditions and simultaneously been ostracized by the colonizing society. In this situation, a person may feel that she/he lives at the intersection of two cultures, not fully belonging to either group. Such a predicament is claimed to be linked to the experience of identity crisis and confusion, feelings of anomie or normlessness, and a sense of loneliness and homelessness. Faced with the tension of living in a marginalized situation, individuals may be at higher risk for psychological and physical distress, although empirical research has not unequivocally supported this assertion.

Indeed, a contrasting perspective argues that as a result of the greater individualization that results from relinquishing cultural group memberships, the marginal person may experience greater cognitive flexibility, bicultural competence, and less ethnocentrism. This description has some similarities to the notion of *integration*. Other scholars suggest that the liminal experience is related to greater engagement in activism and resistance to oppression by dominant cultural groups. Still others insist that the notion of deculturation, in the sense that one can be devoid of culture or "cultureless," is meaningless if one views culture as an interpersonal process that is an inherent dynamic of human life rather than as a repertoire of psychological traits and characteristics that can be "lost." It is likely some people would describe their experience as "life on the margins" of two or more cultures; it behooves acculturation researchers to articulate better the conditions under which such an experience promotes a negative sense of alienation, a positive feeling of self-actualization, or other patterns of adaptation.   – KN

marijuana

n. The plant species *Cannabis sativa*, whose leaves and flowers contain intoxicating cannabinoid chemicals and especially delta 9 tetrahydrocannabinol (THC), which produce mild euphoria, relaxation, and increased appetite and attention to sensory stimuli and inhibit memory when smoked or ingested. Some persons experience increased anxiety when using cannabis and hallucinations and other sensory distortions occur at high dose levels. Cannabis is not generally considered addictive. Commonly called marijuana, marihuana, or hemp, it is grown in many areas of the world for its fiber, which makes strong rope and woven products.

marital therapy

n. Any form of therapy in which married couples engage which is usually focused on improving communication and negotiating skills or other frustrations within the relationship. Also called marriage therapy or marriage counseling.

market research

n. The systematic and objective study of marketing mix variables (e.g., price, promotion, product, and placement), or any research conducted by a marketing organization. Marketing research may be either applied (intended to solve specific marketing-related problems) or basic (intended to advance knowledge), conducted in the field or the laboratory. The research may be exploratory, such as focus groups, case studies, or experience surveys; descriptive, such as surveys or observational research; or causal, experimental research. Market research is conducted by people in many fields of study, including psychology, sociology, anthropology, communications, and history.   – PTV

masculinity

n. The characteristics associated with a men in general which in cross-cultural studies include being a protector and being unemotional, strong, enduring, authoritative, active, dominant, critical, and aggressive. Specific cultures have additional social roles expected of men, and some emphasize some parts of the general masculine role more than do other cultures.

masculinity-femininity scale

n. Any scale which attempts to measure gender roles. **1.** The fifth scale on the Minnesota Multiphasic Personality Inventory (MMPI), which measures the degree to which people resemble homosexual male self-descriptions. **2.** The Mf Scale on the California Psychological Inventory, in which people are assessed as to the degree to which they resemble the self-descriptions of men and women. **3.** The Bem Sex Role Inventory, which measures masculinity and femininity as independent dimensions with the possibility of being high or low on both rather than polar opposites.

masking

n. Masking is an impairment of a person's awareness of a target (e.g., a letter or word) caused by the presentation of a mask (e.g., &&&&) close in time and near in location to the target. Theoretically, masking can occur in any sensory modality; but it is most frequently studied in vision and audition. In visual masking, there are several known forms, including energy masking, integration masking, interruption masking, metacontrast masking, and common-onset masking (or object-substitution masking). In auditory

masking, there are also several forms of masking by noise, including simultaneous, forward, backward, and central masking.   – DGr

▶ *See also* **BACKWARD MASKING** *and* **FORWARD MASKING**

masochism

n. **1.** The characteristic of being sexually aroused by stimulation most people would consider painful and especially the intentional infliction of pain in a sexual context. It often includes a desire to give up power and responsibility and to submit to another who has appropriately arousing intentions to dominate and/or inflict pain. **2.** In psychoanalysis, the tendency to bring shame, suffering, and humiliation on oneself as a result of guilt leading to self-hate and self-aggression. **3.** Commonly used about anyone who is self-defeating or maintains an abusive relationship or brings shame or punishment on himself/herself.

massed practice

n. In memory research, a summary term for attempting to memorize any material all at one time, as opposed to having several learning periods, which is called distributed practice.

mass hysteria

n. A rapid outbreak of emotional outbursts, suggestibility, and/or conversion symptoms in a crowd or large group.

masturbation

n. **1.** Manipulation of one's genitals for sexual pleasure. This is the most common form of sexual expression in human males, very common in human females. Attitudes toward and beliefs about masturbation vary widely across cultures. Most nonhuman mammals masturbate, as do some nonmammalian species. **2.** Manual manipulation of another's genitals for the purpose of sexual arousal or pleasure.

MAT

n. The Miller Analogies Test is a measure of intellectual ability which uses a graded series of items of increasing difficulty in which subjects must fill in a missing part of an analogy for each item. This has commonly been used in graduate school admissions.

matched-groups procedure

n. A research procedure in which two or more groups are selected on the basis of being the same on one or more variables so as to ensure that those variables do not have an effect on the observation of the relationship(s) between the independent variable(s) and the dependent variable(s).

matched pairs

n. A research procedure in which pairs of subjects are selected on the basis of being the same on one or more important variables and are then randomly assigned to one of two differently treated groups in an experiment. The purpose is to ensure that the variables on which the subjects are matched do not interfere with the effect of the independent variable on the dependent variable(s).

Matching Familiar Figures Test

n. An instrument designed to measure a cognitive dimension of reflection versus impulsivity in which subjects are shown a picture of a familiar object and are required to select which of six other pictures are identical to the original one. The latency and accuracy of the response are recorded. Those who are slower than median and above the median in accuracy are deemed reflective. Those who are quicker than the median and make more than the median number of errors are deemed impulsive. Those who are quicker than the median and make fewer errors than the median are called quick, and those who are slower and make more errors than the median are called slow. The test does not theoretically account for those who are in the quick and slow categories.

matching hypothesis

n. The idea that individuals are attracted to or join with persons of similar levels of physical attractiveness within a particular culture.

matching law

n. In operant conditioning, the idea that responses among several alternatives will be distributed according to the degree to which they are reinforced. Thus a response through which the subject has received 50% of its reinforcement will occur about 50% of the time, and a response through which a subject has received 20% of its reinforcement will occur about 20% of the time.

matching to sample

n. A family of experimental tasks in which a subject is required to select a test stimulus which is the same as a sample stimulus from among other stimuli. Variations have been introduced in the timing of the presentation of the stimuli, the number, and the type of both test and alternative stimuli in order to test a variety of hypotheses about discrimination and memory.

mate poaching

n. Attracting someone who is already in a romantic relationship with someone else.

materialism

n. Materialism has been defined in a variety of ways. However, such definitions all tend to describe materialism as the emphasis that one places on material possessions, as a central feature of one's existence, a means to happiness, and an indicator of personal success. Additionally, materialistic people have been described as greedy, possessive of their own possessions, and envious of other people's possessions. Although it is postulated that materialism does have some benefits, such as stimulating macroeconomic activity and helping people achieve happiness (in the short term), much research has examined the pitfalls of materialism. Such pitfalls include depletion of the Earth's resources and long-term individual dysfunction such as lower levels of life satisfaction and higher levels of depression. However, some research suggests that different people can be materialistic for different reasons, and it may be the reasons why individuals are materialistic that are associated with dysfunction. Research is thus starting to differentiate between functional materialism (such as providing for one's family) and dysfunctional materialism (such as the "need" to own multiple expensive sports cars). — ANC

maternal deprivation

n. Inadequate nurturing during infancy by the mother or other attachment figure which leads to disturbance in the expression of the attachment instinct. The nurturing can be inadequate in a number of ways, including loss of an attachment figure, lack of physical care, lack of attention or responsiveness to the needs of the infant, or expression of disgust, resentment, and/or inappropriate anger toward the child.

matrix, correlation

n. A square matrix whose margins are identical lists of variables which presents the correlations between each pair of variables in the cell which is the intersection of the row and column of a pair of variables. The left-to-right diagonal of such a matrix represents the correlation of a variable with itself, which would be 1 but is often filled with a reliability correlation of the variable involved.

maturation

n. Fulfillment of the inherent or natural processes of growth and development in any living thing.

maximal likelihood

n. In statistics, any procedure for predicting the value of one or more variables which is closest to the observed distribution of data of all possible predictions.

McGurk effect

n. The tendency of the human listener to combine visual and auditory information in understanding speech. Thus when the sound of a person saying the word *gay* is dubbed onto a videotape of a person saying the word *bay*, a person watching and hearing the dubbed tape is likely to combine the two sources of information and hear an intermediate word such as *day*.

McNemar test

n. In statistics, a form of chi-square test for dichotomous variables which tests whether the two possibilities are equally likely while making no assumptions about the population distribution. This test is often used when testing the effectiveness of a treatment in eliminating a disease.

mean

n. Any one of several measures of central tendency, the most common of which is the arithmetic mean, which is the sum of a set of numbers divided by how many numbers are in the set. ▶ *See also* **HARMONIC MEAN**

mean, arithmetic

n. The sum of a set of a finite set of numbers divided by how many numbers there are in the set.

mean deviation

n. The arithmetic mean of the differences between a set of observations and their arithmetic mean used to indicate degree of dispersion around a central point. This statistic is seldom used, as in many distributions it approaches 0.

mean, harmonic

n. An average calculated by taking the reciprocal of the arithmetic mean of the reciprocals of a group of numbers. Thus the harmonic mean of 1, 2, and 3 is equal to

$$\frac{1}{1} + \frac{1}{2} + \frac{1}{3} = \frac{1.8333}{3} = .6111, \frac{1}{.6111} = 1.636$$

mean length of utterance

n. (MLU) In linguistics, the arithmetic mean of the number of words in the average sentence or quasi-sentence in natural speech. It is often used as a measure of language development in children.

mean, sample

n. The arithmetic mean of a set of observations drawn from a population of possible observations.

means-end analysis

n. **1.** An approach to solving a problem that examines the difference between the present state and the desired state and attempts to find a way to reduce the difference between the two, often in a step-by-step manner. Sophisticated analyses allow a step further away from the desired state if it allows greater progress on successive steps. **2.** In artificial intelligence, the decomposition of problems into a series of goals and subgoals which either more closely approximate the goal or remove obstacles to closer approximation of the goal state. This is used in cases in which an exhaustive search of all possible courses of action would be too large for practical solution such as in chess playing programs.

mean square
n. The arithmetic mean of the squares of any set of numbers.

measurement
n. The process of assigning numbers to represent dimensions or aspects of perceived reality according to a system of rules.

measure of central tendency
n. A numerical index of the middle of a set of numbers around a central point such as mean, median, and mode.

medial forebrain bundle
n. (MFB) Either of a pair of nerve tracts which constitute the most important pleasure centers in the brain, which lie on each side of the hypothalamus and connect the ventral tegmentum to the nucleus accumbens, amygdala, septum, and prefrontal cortex.

medial geniculate nucleus
n. Either of a pair of bumps on the side of the thalamus which relay auditory information from the inferior colliculus to the auditory cortex.

median
n. The median is a measure of central tendency that is located at the center of a distribution of scores that have been ranked in numerical order. For example, the median in the distribution of ages 18, 18, 19, 23, and 24 is 19 because it occurs at the midpoint of the group of values. Half the values occur above and half occur below 19. If the distribution has an even number of scores, the median is the average of the two middle scores. For example, the median of 18, 18, 19, 23, 24,

and 27 is 21. The median is unaffected by extreme scores and is the best measure to use for skewed distributions, such as annual income, in which a small number of scores may be extremely high. For example, in the distribution of hourly wages $13, $15, $15, $17, and $350 the median would be $15 an hour.
– DS

median test
n. In statistics, a test of the likelihood that samples with two medians are drawn from the same population that does not depend on the distribution of the populations.

mediating variable
n. A mediating variable explains how or why two variables are related by specifying that the mediating variable transmits the effect of one variable to another variable. There is a temporal relation such that the initial variable is related to the mediating variable and then the mediating variable is related to the outcome variable. Mediating variables may be observed measures used in a statistical analysis, or they may be theoretical constructs that guide a research project. One of the difficulties of research on mediating variables is the development of accurate measures of theoretical mediating constructs.

Mediating variables are often considered once a relation between two variables is established. Here the mediating variable provides an interpretation of the relation between two variables by elucidating a process by which the initial variable is related to the mediating variable and the mediating variable is related to the outcome variable. Stimulus-organism-response models provided the first examples of mediating variables in psychology. These models hypothesized that a mediating variable in the organism translates the stimulus to the response. For example, mental processes mediate how exposure to information affects behavior. More recent applications of mediating variables are in treatment and prevention studies, where a manipulation is designed to change a mediating variable hypothesized to be causally related to the outcome variable. If the mediating variable is changed by the treatment program and the mediating variable is truly related to the outcome variable, then the program will affect the outcome variable. For example, a prevention program that changes norms about smoking may reduce smoking.

Mediating variable relations may be complicated. More than one mediating variable may explain the relation between the initial and outcome variable. A mediating process may consist of a long chain of variables that lead from the initial to the outcome variable. Mediating variables may be categorical (e.g., divorced or not) or continuous (e.g., attitudes, norms) variables. Mediation relations may differ at different time lags; for example, a mediation relation may be observed for daily measures but not for weekly measures.

The statistical assessment of mediating variables consists of statistical tests of the relation of the initial to mediating variable and the mediating variable to the outcome variable. Random assignment of participants to levels of the mediating variable helps clarify whether the mediating variable is related to the outcome variable. Generally, a program of research is necessary to provide convincing evidence for a mediating variable, including experiments, statistical analysis, clinical observations, and qualitative methods.

– DVM

medical model

n. The general approach to disease of Western medicine and science, which is the assumption that it is produced by specific causes whose removal will alleviate the disease. This is in contrast to holistic approaches, common in non-Western cultures, which understand disease as a set of imbalances in a system with multiple levels of cause and multiple possibilities of treatment.

meditation

n. **1.** Any process of training the mind through focusing on the senses, an object, or an internal thought, mantra, or image. There are two basic types of meditation: mindfulness meditations, which seek to increase attention to sensory experience, and transcending meditations, which seek to withdraw from sensory experience in order to attain a higher state of consciousness; both types take many forms.

2. The continuous and profound contemplation of a subject or an area of thought of a philosophic or scientific nature.

medulla

n. **1.** The central region of any organ. **2.** The medulla oblongata.

medulla oblongata

n. The bottom of the hindbrain at the top of the spinal cord between the pons and the cerebellum which connects the spinal cord to many brain centers and is involved in autonomic processes such as respiration, heartbeat, and blood pressure.

megalomania

n. An extreme form of grandiosity and self-centeredness in which all things are believed subservient to one's self and are seen only in relation to one's self. It is characteristic of mania, extreme narcissism, and paranoia.

Meissner's corpuscle

n. An ovate sense receptor concentrated in the skin of the genitals, fingertips, lips, nipples, palms, and soles of the feet, which are sensitive to pressure on the skin. It is constituted by a single, unmyelinated nerve cell which runs through the center of laminated structural cells surrounded by a capsule of connective tissue. Also called a tactile corpuscle and Wagner-Meissner's corpuscle.

melancholia

n. An archaic term for a depressed mood or a depressive disorder.

melatonin

n. A hormone produced when the pineal gland breaks down serotonin during the night which is involved in bodily cycles such as the sleep-wake and other diurnal cycles and seasonal changes in physiology. It also acts to inhibit sexual development in males before puberty and affects the menstrual cycle in females.

membrane

n. A layer of usually fibrous boundary tissue that encloses cells, lines organs, or otherwise creates boundaries within living organisms and must allow in and out only the materials appropriate for cell or organ functioning.

membrane potential
n. Any difference in electric charge between the inside and outside of a cell or other membrane. This is important in neurons, in which nerve impulses are created by a wave of depolarization when sodium and potassium ions switch sides of the neuron's membrane.

memory
n. **1.** Any relatively lasting storage of information in the brain, which is currently hypothesized to involve processes of encoding, storage, and retrieval of the information. This includes numerous kinds of information and different storage processes including that necessary for remembering a specific event, knowledge in general, and knowledge of how to do things like see, move in a coordinated way, and ride a bicycle. **2.** A specific recollection of an experience or some factual information. **3.** The hypothetical storage system or systems for information of different kinds.

memory code
n. A hypothesized form into which sensory and other information is transformed for storage.

memory, declarative
n. The process which underlies the ability to recall and verbalize information.

memory drum
n. An archaic experimental device used in memory experiments which consisted of a rotating cylinder with a cover which could expose a single word or image for a predetermined time interval so as to allow control of the learning exposure for a word or other item. This function has been replaced by computer displays.

memory, echoic
n. A hypothesized very-short-term memory for sound which allows storage of auditory information long enough for the auditory system to make sense out of it. Air pressure waves which constitute sound last for various periods of time, and the auditory system must store the first information of a sound to compare with later information of a sound so as to form a reasonably whole perception of the sound.

memory, episodic
n. The capacity to recall specific events.

memory, explicit
n. Aspects of memory that can be recalled at will from both episodic and semantic memory, as opposed to implicit memory for such things as how to ride a bicycle or speak one's native language.

memory, false
n. Recollections of events that have not actually occurred. In the retrieval of information and recoding into a form used in verbal communication, there are often inclusions of information which is not factually true, and in some cases there is little or no truth to the information in some memories. Memories can be influenced by more recent experience, and there is much controversy over some memories, particularly memories of childhood abuse by adults, which some researchers claim have been suggested or implanted by therapists or other persons.

memory, flashbulb
n. Biographical memories of important events that seem unusually clear and detailed, such as the moment when people first learned about the attack on the World Trade Center. Research has shown that belief in the clarity of these memories is unfounded, as the details of such memories have often been found to be erroneous.

memory, iconic
n. A hypothesized very-short-term memory store for visual information which allows the integration of visual information to complete a Gestalt of a scene.

memory, implicit
n. The storage and use of information which is not easily recollected and stated such as how to ride a bicycle or read this definition.

memory, long-term
n. A hypothesized information store in the brain which lasts indefinitely and has no limit on its capacity.

memory, recognition
n. **1.** The capacity to indicate accurately whether or not a particular item was included in a previously learned list, which is an easier task than recalling the items of such a list. **2.** The capacity to recognize a previously encountered face, person, object, event, situation, or piece of information.

memory, reconstructive
n. A form of recollection in which some parts of the information recalled are accurate and some parts of the information are inserted from other sources where recollection is missing the data. This seems to occur in most long, term memories for events.

memory, semantic
n. The storage of general information not tied to specific events such as how many stars are in the flag of the United States or what the word *penguin* means.

memory, short-term
n. A hypothesized information storage system of a limited capacity which allows material to be used in tasks requiring several seconds and to be repeated for maintenance, as in repeating a telephone number until it is dialed.

memory span
n. The length of a list of items an individual can recall without error immediately after presentation, which, for normal adults, is in the range of seven plus or minus two. This differs from trying to recall items from longer lists, which is often less than seven.

memory trace
n. A hypothetical physiological change in the brain that is the physical process of storing information.

memory, working
n. A hypothesized information storage system containing the information necessary for working on a particular task at a particular time. It is often used synonymously with *short-term memory*.

Mendelian
adj. Of or relating to the theories of Gregor Mendel, who first noticed that traits are inherited as whole and there are mathematical relationships governing dominant and recessive characteristics.

meninges
n. The three membrane layers which cover the brain and spinal column consisting of a fibrous outer dura mater, a middle layer called the arachnoid membrane, and the thin and transparent inner layer called the pia mater.

menopause
n. The cessation of a woman's fertility including a drastic lowering of estrogen production in the ovaries and cessation of menstrual cycles, which usually occurs over a period of several years called perimenopause and is complete around age 50. The perimenopausal period is often accompanied by hot flashes, heart palpitations, depression or anxiety, and mood swings. Also called the climacteric or change of life.

menses
n. The monthly cycle of a woman's sexual fertility and infertility in which an ovum is readied for fertilization and released by the ovary, the lining of the fallopian tubes and uterus engorge with blood and prepare to receive a fertilized ovum, and then both are shed through the openings of the uterus and vagina if no fertilization occurs. This monthly cycle is characteristic of humans and great apes; the females of other species undergo cycles called estrus which have different frequencies and usually do not involve the shedding of blood and the uterine lining. Also called menstruation.

mens rea
n. Latin for guilty mind or criminal intent, which is an element of some criminal statutes in some states.

menstrual cycle

n. The reproductive cycle of female anthropoid primates, including humans. Levels of hormones from the pituitary (luteinizing hormone [LH] and follicle-stimulating hormone [FSH]) and ovaries (estrogen and progesterone) rise and fall in feedback loops over the course of approximately a month. This controls the timing of fertility. Unlike mammalian females with the more common estrous cycle, females with menstrual cycles can copulate at any point during the cycle. Thus sexual receptivity is not bound to hormone levels or fertility. The cycle has effects on sexual desire and on a range of other behaviors, including some cognitive tasks, but these effects are very subtle.   – JMJ

menstruation

n. The monthly cycle of a woman's sexual fertility and infertility in which an ovum is readied for fertilization and released by the ovary, the lining of the fallopian tubes and uterus engorge with blood and prepare to receive a fertilized ovum, and then both are shed through the openings of the uterus and vagina if no fertilization occurs. This monthly cycle is characteristic of humans and great apes; the females of other species undergo cycles called estrus which have different frequencies and usually do not involve the shedding of blood and the uterine lining.

mental age ▶ *See* AGE, MENTAL

mental deficiency

n. The state of lacking normal levels of intellectual capacity. Also called mental retardation or developmental delay.

mental disorder

n. A recognizable pattern of personal distress, abnormal emotional reactions and behavior, cognitive impairment, and an increased risk of death or injury due to a presumed malfunction of the mind and the brain.

mental illness

n. A recognizable pattern of personal distress, abnormal emotional reactions and behavior, cognitive impairment, and an increased risk of death or injury due to a presumed malfunction of the mind and the brain.

mental imagery

n. **1.** The process of creating internal experiences of sensory and particularly of visual perception. **2.** The content of mental constructions of sensory experience. **3.** The study of mental processes by asking subjects to create mental images.

Mental Measurements Yearbook

n. Any of an irregularly published series of 12 books containing reviews of most published psychological tests and a large but noncomprehensive set of references for publications using the individual tests.

mental representation

n. The theoretical mental structure corresponding to information processing models of perception, memory, thinking, speech, and other mental functions.

mental retardation

n. The state of lacking normal levels of intellectual capacity. There are several levels, usually labeled mild (IQ 52–69), moderate (IQ 36–51), severe (IQ 20–35), and profound (IQ 19 and below). Mild retardation is often the low end of the normal curve of intelligence; lower levels of retardation are due to brain abnormalities. Also called mental deficiency or developmental delay.

mental retardation, mild

n. A range of intellectual deficiency usually defined by having an IQ in the range from 52 to 69. Persons in this range are usually able to function in routine lifestyles but are low in educational attainment and intellectual capacity.

mental retardation, moderate

n. A range of intellectual deficiency usually defined by having an IQ estimated to be in the range from 36 to 51. Persons with this level of impairment usually are unable to function independently but can learn daily hygiene and perform routine jobs under supervision.

mental retardation, profound

n. A range of intellectual deficiency usually defined by the IQ range 19 and below. Persons with this level of deficiency usually have significant brain deficiencies and are unable to walk, talk, and care for themselves and will die without constant nursing care.

mental retardation, severe

n. A range of intellectual deficiency usually defined by the IQ range 20–35. Persons with this level of deficiency usually have significant brain deficiencies and usually have poor coordination, making walking difficult; have some limited ability to communicate; have a little ability to care for themselves with intensive habit training; and will die without constant nursing care.

mental rotation

n. An experimental task in which subjects are asked to make judgments about visual images which require rotation from their presented position in order to make accurate judgments. There is an inference that the mind creates a visual image and rotates it to arrive at a correct answer based on the observation that the time it takes to respond correctly is proportional to the angle through which the object has to be rotated in order to make the correct judgment.

mental set

n. The temporary activation of a particular mental network in preparation for coping with a particular situation or task. This both makes routine tasks easier and makes perception or use of things outside the activated set more difficult.

mental state

n. The experiential and functional status of the mind at any given moment.

mental status examination

n. A comprehensive mental examination intended to include a global assessment of a subject's personality, cognitive, emotional, and behavioral states. This usually includes an interview, taking a history, psychological testing, and gathering all other sources of available information in order to make a diagnosis and a prognosis and formulate a treatment plan.

mental stimulation

n. The act or process of increasing the level of activity in the mind or the brain, usually through presenting novel or challenging stimuli to the subject, which has been found to be necessary to the normal mental and emotional development of most organisms and the maintenance of cognitive functioning in human old age.

mere exposure effect

n. The observation that familiar things tend to be liked better than unfamiliar things whether or not the subject is conscious of the familiarity; thus simply exposing a subject to a stimulus increases the likelihood of his or her liking the stimulus in the future.

mesencephalon

n. The midbrain, an inch-long region of the brain between the spinal cord and hindbrain on one end and the cerebrum on the other, is a major pathway for sensory and motor information. It is divided into the tectum, which contains the inferior and superior colliculi, which are major sensory pathways, and the cerebral peduncle, which is involved in motor coordination.

mesolimbic system

n. A system of dopaminergic neurons with cell bodies in the tegmentum of the midbrain and axon terminals in the limbic system which is believed to be a main route for pleasure and reward in the brain. It includes parts of the nucleus accumbens, amygdala, and olfactory tubercle.

messenger RNA

n. (mRNA) A short-lived form of ribonucleic acid that is formed as a mirror image of a strand of DNA in a cell nucleus and then, after inactive regions are removed, is used as a template by ribosomes to manufacture proteins in the cell. mRNA is broken down quickly after its use, which helps regulate protein production.

meta-analysis

n. Any statistical procedure in which the effect sizes of numerous studies are combined into a distribution of effect sizes used to gauge the likely size of the effect in general.

metacognition

n. Awareness of or knowledge about one's own thought processes and knowledge which allows conscious changes in mental strategy toward solving problems and understanding new things.

meta contrast

n. A form of backward masking in which a target stimulus, usually a dot, is presented briefly and then quickly followed by a nearby masking stimulus, often a circle around the dot, which has the effect of masking or distorting perception of the original stimulus. This demonstrates that backward masking is a cognitive, not a sensory process.

metamemory

n. Awareness or knowledge about one's own memory or knowing one knows. Thus one can answer a question like "Do you know your date of birth?" without recalling your date of birth.

metaphor

n. A form of speech in which a word or phrase is applied to another word or idea that it does not actually denote in order to convey a meaning difficult to convey otherwise. Thus one can say, "Life is a cabaret," which is not literally true but conveys meaning about a point of view on the nature of life, or "The brain is a computer," which is also not true but points out aspects of brain function one might not otherwise notice.

metaphysics

n. **1.** The branch of philosophy concerned with first principles or ultimate meaning. **2.** Any systematic description or explanation that goes beyond that which is amenable to observation by the senses, including their extension through quasi-sensory instrumentation.

metapsychology

n. The study of the basic principles and approaches of psychology.

methadone

n. A synthetic addicting drug of the opiate family which is relatively long-acting and often used as a substitute for heroin in treating heroin addiction.

methamphetamine

n. The most potent drug in the amphetamine family, which acts as a strong central nervous system stimulant, mimicking the effects of norepinephrine and dopamine. Methamphetamine raises heart rate and blood pressure, suppresses immune function and sleep, increases blood flow to skeletal muscles and away from the digestive tract and teeth, suppresses appetite, and produces feelings of energy and well-being, and, in high doses, euphoria. Prolonged use can result in anxiety, panic, acute paranoia, dental problems, and malnutrition. Amphetamines are widely and illegally used for staying awake and alert and for experiencing the euphoria high doses create. Methamphetamine is addicting in the traditional sense of producing tolerance and withdrawal. The withdrawal is due to an insufficiency of norepinephrine and dopamine in the brain, which results in depression, fatigue, and lack of motivation.

method of loci

n. A memory technique in which items to be remembered are associated with particular places or parts of places. Thus, to help remember material for a test, a student might associate one end of the blackboard with one part of the material, the middle of the blackboard with another part, and the other end of the blackboard with other material.

methodological behaviorism

n. An approach to psychology which concedes that the mind exists and that mental events are useful areas of inquiry but argues that such events can only be studied scientifically through their expression in observable behavior.

method, scientific

n. A process of investigation guided by the basic principles of skepticism and open-mindedness in which observations are used to generate testable theories which both account for previous observations and predict future observations. These hypotheses are then tested by further systematic observations, and the accuracy of the predictions is determined. These results are then used to generate further theories which can be tested, and the cycle is repeated as needed within a given area.

methylphenidate

n. Methylphenidate hydrochloride is a central nervous system stimulant which works by stimulating release of norepinephrine and dopamine and blocking their reuptake in the synaptic cleft. It is often prescribed to treat attention deficit–hyperactivity disorder and is sometimes used as an adjunct to antidepressants in treating depression and used to increase attention span in persons with brain damage, cancer, and dementia. Also called Ritalin.

microexpression

n. An extremely brief facial expression of emotion, often appearing for only a fraction of a second. These were originally discovered by the psychologist Paul Ekman as a sign of concealed or repressed emotions. Microexpressions are often, but not always, associated with deception, although there are many times in which microexpressions occur because of concealed feelings that are not necessarily lies. Contemporary work with microexpressions has shown that there are reliable individual differences in the ability to see microexpressions, and that the ability to see them can be systematically trained.

microsleep

n. A very brief period of sleep in a person who appears to be awake, usually lasting from 1 to about 30 seconds. This tends to occur during periods of fatigue when the person is attempting to perform boring or monotonous tasks such as driving a car or working as a guard and is exacerbated by alcohol and other depressant drugs.

midbrain

n. Brain area situated between the diencephalons (rostrally) and the pons (caudally). In the human brain it is a relatively small area approximately 2 cm long. The midbrain (also known as mesencephalon) forms with the pons and the medulla oblongata the brainstem. The dorsal surface of the midbrain forms the tectum. The floor of the midbrain is known as the tegmentum. The tegmentum is situated around the cerebral aqueduct (connection between the third and fourth ventricles). Two large neural pathways connecting the cerebral cortex and the brainstem and spinal cord are found in the ventral surface of the midbrain, known as the cerebral peduncles. The midbrain also contains the substantia nigra, a major component of the basal ganglia. Neurons of the substantia nigra use dopamine as a neurotransmitter and are involved in controlling movements. Parkinson's disease is associated with a degeneration of the dopaminergic neurons of the substantia nigra. The midbrain also contains the inferior and superior colliculi, both forming the corpora quadrigemina. Superior colliculi are involved in eye movements, and the inferior colliculi are the principal midbrain nucleus of the auditory pathway.   – AA

▶ *See also* **COLLICULUS**

middle ear

n. The portion of the auditory system from the eardrum to the oval window at the start of the cochlea, which includes the ossicles, which transfer and amplify sound, and the eustachian tube, which leads from the middle ear to the nasopharynx and equalizes the pressure inside and outside the eardrum.

Milgram experiment

n. Stanley Milgram's experiments on obedience to authority, conducted from 1960 to 1963 at Yale University, demonstrated that well-adjusted individuals can be driven to surprising acts of cruelty because of pressure from authority figures. The experimental paradigm consisted of a naïve participant asked to deliver increasingly painful electric shocks (none was ever actually given) to a confederate in the guise of a learning study. Despite audible sounds of discomfort and protests from the confederate, the experimenter repeatedly demanded that the participant continue delivering shocks. Although most observers believed that only a very few people would continue until the end of the experiment, 65% of participants delivered the full 450-volt shock levels in the original study. In follow-up studies, Milgram manipulated a number of factors and found that subtle contextual changes in the procedure (e.g., reducing the distance between subject and confederate, removing the experimenter from the room) substantially influenced rates of obedience. The experiments remain among the most famous and controversial in social psychology.   – JAV

military psychology

n. An applied area of psychology that studies leadership, assignment, evaluation, selection, training, and human-machine interfaces in military settings as well as dealing with mental health problems within the military and especially combat-related stress disorders.

Miller Analogies Test

n. (MAT) This is a measure of intellectual ability which uses a graded series of items of increasing difficulty in which subjects must fill in a missing part of an analogy for each item. This has commonly been used in graduate school admissions.

Millon Clinical Multiaxial Inventory

n. (MCMI III) A widely used self-report measure of psychopathology originally based on the theories of Theodore Millon and modified to conform to diagnostic categories in the DSM-IV-TR, which is intended for use in diagnosing psychological disorders. It includes 13 scales for personality disorders, 10 clinical syndrome scales, 3 modifying indices, and a 3-item validity scale that is of questionable utility. An innovation in the scoring of the MCMI III is the use of base rate information, which improves the diagnostic power of the test by lessening the frequency of false positive results.

mind

n. 1. A general term for mental, as opposed to physical, processes and contents. 2. Consciousness considered as an entity independent of physical conditions sometimes believed to exist before the birth of and to continue after the death of the body. 3. A particular kind of mentality, as in the mind of an assassin or the mind of a genius. 4. An explanatory entity used to account for the accomplishment of tasks not accounted for otherwise. 5. The sum of the operations of a brain. 6. An emergent property of increasing brain complexity. 7. The capacity to accomplish difficult tasks as in "She has a mind for mathematics." 8. *v.* To attend to.

mind/body problem

n. A concept extensively debated by the rationalist philosophers of the 17th century which became central to Descartes's theory of dualism: the separation of the soul/mind from the corporeal body. Today, the concept is revised as the mind/brain problem, since the brain is now recognized as the cognitive center of the body. At one pole, the monistic view is of one physical structure for the brain and mind, versus a dualistic nonphysical entity, the mind, separate from the physical entity of the brain. Most academic and research psychologists adopt an identity position: mental/psychological processes and brain/neural processes are identical, being merely differing and compatible approaches to the same phenomenon. In other words, mind is an aspect of the activity of the brain. Most of the issues in the resolution of this problem are concerned with levels of consciousness or awareness. The central questions for an academic psychologist are How does consciousness arise from the neural activity of the brain? Or, simply, what is consciousness? The central questions of the mind/body problem for the psychological practitioner are How do mind and body interrelate in health and in sickness? How can cognitive and/or psychological intervention aid in the process of healing, or assist in the maintenance of wellness?   – vs

mindfulness ▶ *See* MINDFULNESS/MINDLESSNESS

mindfulness/mindlessness

n. Mindfulness is an active state of mind characterized by novel distinction drawing. It is the phenomenological experience of engagement. Simply noticing or creating novelty situates us in the present and makes us sensitive to context and perspective. When in this state of mind, rules and routines may guide behavior, but they do not rigidly determine what we do. By contrast, mindlessness is an inactive state of mind characterized by reliance on distinctions and categories drawn in the past, where we are trapped in a rigid, single-minded perspective. As a result, we are insensitive to context and perspective, and, thus, we are insensitive to change. When mindless we are oblivious to not being in the present. The mindful act of noticing new things puts us in the present. We cannot have a phenomenological experience of our mindlessness, but often it is noticed in hindsight. Mindless behavior is rule and routine governed, rather than guided.   – EL

minimal audible pressure

n. The lowest level of air pressure change necessary for a person to hear sound at a particular tone.

minimal brain dysfunction

n. Inferred minor damage to the brain which does not appear on physical measures of the brain such as X-rays or MRIs but is evidenced by symptoms such as hyperactivity, impulsivity, emotional lability, distractibility, learning disability, or difficulty in learning appropriate social behavior.

Minnesota Multiphasic Personality Inventory

n. (MMPI) The most widely used self-report measure of personality and psychopathology in the world. It consists of either 550 or 567 true-false items to which the subject responds which are scored on scales of hypochondria, depression, hysteria, psychopathic deviancy, masculinity/femininity, paranoia, psychasthenia, schizophrenia, and hypomania as well as three or more response style scales. There are dozens of other scales which have been developed for special purposes from MMPI items, and recently a new set of 10 restructured clinical scales reflecting demoralization, somatic complaints, low positive emotions, cynicism, antisocial behavior, ideas of persecution, dysfunctional negative emotions, aberrant experiences, and hypomanic activation have come into widespread use. There is an adolescent form of the test, and the test was revised as the MMPI-2 in 1989.

minor depressive disorder

n. A mood disorder lasting more than 2 weeks characterized by fewer symptoms and less impairment than a major depression. Symptoms may include depressed mood, a belief one is helpless, diminished interest and pleasure in daily activities, feelings of worthlessness, inappropriate guilt, low energy level, psychomotor agitation or retardation, recurrent thoughts of death or suicide, sleep disturbance, and weight loss or gain.

minor epilepsy

n. A generalized seizure disorder which does not involve the motor cortex whose apparent symptoms are a short period of blank expression, ceasing of current activity, and unresponsiveness and amnesia for the seizure period, which typically lasts from 2 to 20 seconds. In some individuals the seizure is accompanied by jerky eye movements or aimless walking. Also called petit mal epilepsy and absence seizure.

minority group

n. A subgroup within any social group which is identified as being different from the group as a whole and which does not constitute a dominant plurality of the total group and is subject to discrimination and disadvantages. This subgrouping may be based on ethnicity, religion, economic status, caste, physical health, sexual preference, or any other difference the social group considers important.

minority group–affiliation hypothesis

n. The idea that bilingual minority group members behave according to the stereotypes the majority group has about the minority group when speaking in the minority group language but do not do so when speaking in the majority group language.

minority social influence

n. A form of social influence in which a minority consistently rejects a majority norm and persuades the majority to adopt the minority point of view or behavior pattern. This is sometimes considered the general process of innovation and evolution.

minor tranquilizer

n. Any of several types of drugs which have the effect of lowering anxiety level such as the benzodiazepines and some of the SSRIs, which are primarily used as antidepressants, fall into this category. Also called anxiolytics.

mirror drawing

n. A test of motor skills in which a person is asked to trace a shape such as a star or square while seeing his or her hand and the figure only in a mirror.

mirror writing

n. Writing in a way so that the letters and words are reversed as they would be seen in a mirror. This is characteristic of people with a perceptual disorder called strephosymbolia and has been used as a form of code as Leonardo da Vinci did in his notebooks. Also called palingraphia or retrographia.

misinformation effect

n. The misinformation effect is a memory error in which memory for an event is influenced by exposure to postevent misleading information. It has been found in numerous studies using a wide variety of materials (e.g., photographs of people, scenes, and objects).

In a typical study examining the misinformation effect, participants witness an event, and then some of the participants receive new misleading information while others do not. Participants are then asked about the event. It is typically found that the misleading information influences participants' responses and increases the likelihood that they will recall the misleading information as part of the original event.

Researchers have identified several factors that influence the misinformation effect such as age, the use of hypnosis, and the amount of time that passes between the presentation of the misleading information and the recall of the event.

While there is no controversy over the presence of the misinformation effect, there is much debate over its cause. Several explanations have been proposed: destructive updating, misinformation acceptance, source misattribution, and response bias.   – LMB

mitosis

n. The process of cell division in which a cell splits into two identical daughter cells with the same genetic makeup as the original cell which is characteristic of many single-celled animals as well as much growth in more complex organisms. It contrasts with meiosis, which is the division of cells into gametes or sex cells into two sperm or ova cells each with half the genetic material from the parent cell.

mnemonic

adj. Of or relating to memory or a technique to aid memory as in a mnemonic device.

mnemonic device

n. This is simply a strategy for enhancing memory. There are many different types of mnemonic devices. On example is imagery mnemonics. When one uses this strategy, he or she associates the information to be memorized with an image. For example, if being asked to memorize words, the individual creates a bizarre or memorable image he/she can associate with the word. Another example of this is called verbal elaboration. Here, when given pairs of words to memorize, one can create a sentence with both words that also creates an image. (e.g., when given the words *turkey* and *rock*, the individual thinks, "The turkey sat on the rock"). Another example of a mnemonic device is an acronym. Perhaps the most well known acronym is related to the lines of the treble staff, EGBDF. In order to remember the order of the letters, several phrases have been developed such as "Every Good Boy Deserves Fudge." These are just a few examples of the many different strategies that exist.   – EF

mnemonic trace

n. The hypothesized physical change in the brain which corresponds to memory. Also called an engram.

modality

n. **1.** A channel of sensory perception such as vision or hearing. **2.** A therapeutic process, technique, or approach.

modality effect

n. Any effect on perception or memory in which the sensory channel used to present the information has an effect on the processing of the information. As an example, in memorizing lists of words the first words are most likely to be remembered if the subject reads the list while the last words are most likely to be remembered if the list is heard.

mode

n. The mode is a measure of central tendency that is the most frequently occurring score in a distribution. For example, the mode in the distribution of exam grades 75, 70, 90, 75, and 80 is 75, since it is the value that occurs most often (twice, compared to the other scores, which each occur only once). A distribution with two scores that occur equally and most often is called bimodal, for example, 3, 7, 11, 3, 8, 7, and a distribution with two or more scores that occur equally and most often is termed multimodal. Among the advantages of using the mode to describe the center of a distribution are the relative ease of computation and the ability to use the mode with nominal level data. For example, taking a sample of students' favorite course, psychology would be the mode if it were reported more often than the other classes.   — DS

modeling

n. **1.** A technique used in several therapies in which the client changes through observing the therapist or another person enacting a desired form of behavior. **2.** The general process of learning through observation rather than action or reinforcement, which is important in much social learning.

model minority

n. The term *model minority* refers to minority groups whose members are widely *perceived* to have better than average educational attainment and socioeconomic achievement in the society. The qualities often attributed to a model minority include studious, hardworking, and family oriented and having high career achievements. For example, in the United States, Asian Americans are labeled as a "model minority" because this group is perceived to be more successful than other minority groups in terms of scholastic achievements and family income. However, researchers have criticized the seemingly positive "model minority" stereotypes for their failure to recognize and acknowledge the wide disparity within the model minority and the social and psychological problems that the group faces in mainstream society. These stereotypes may also widen the perceived gap between a model minority and other disadvantaged minorities and create or reinforce the impression that the problems other disadvantaged minorities face result from these groups' internal dispositions.   — MMC, CYC

moderate mental retardation

n. A level of intellectual deficiency usually defined by having an IQ estimated to be in the range from 36 to 51. Persons with this level of impairment usually are unable to function independently but can learn daily hygiene and perform routine jobs under supervision.

moderator variable

n. In statistics, a variable in a multiple regression that does not correlate with the dependent variable but improves the predictive power of the independent variables.

modus ponens

n. In logic, the idea that if the first part of a conditional statement is true, then the second part is also true. Thus if the statement "If X then Y" is true, then if we know that if X is true, we also know that Y is true. And so if the statement "Burning things are hot" is true and we know that a thing is burning, we also know that the thing is hot. Also called affirming the antecedent.

modus tollens

n. In logic, the idea that if the second part of a conditional statement is false, then the first part is also false. Thus if the statement "If X then Y" is true and if Y is not true, then we know that X is not true. And so if the statement "Burning things are hot" is true and we know that a thing is not hot, we also know that the thing is not burning. Also called affirming the antecedent and denying the consequent.

monaural

adj. **1.** Of or relating to one ear only. **2.** Of or relating to sound that is recorded on a single track and so the sound is the same no matter how many speakers it is played back from or how they are located. This usually results in a perception of the sound different from its original form as the cues we normally gain from interaural differences are absent in the recorded sound.

mongolism

n. An archaic name for a congenital condition characterized by mild to severe mental retardation, pleasant dispositions, a flat face, stubby fingers and toes, epicanthic folds in the eyes among non-Asians, tongue fissures, and unusual patterns of skinfolds on the palms of the hands and soles of the feet. It is caused by the presence of an extra chromosome 21 or in rare cases by an extra copy of chromosome 22 and is associated with an early onset of Alzheimer's disease. Also called Down syndrome.

monism

n. In philosophy, a point of view in which reality consists of only a single substance. In idealistic monism, mind is the only reality; in materialism, physical substance is the only reality; and in pantheism, God is the only reality. It is a denial of dualism, which, in Western thought, has supposed that mind and body are two separate kinds of reality.

monoamine

n. Any chemical compound that contains only one amine group, which is a nitrogen atom bonded to two hydrogen atoms. Psychologically important monoamines include the neurotransmitters dopamine, norepinephrine, and serotonin.

monoamine oxidase

n. (MAO) A hormone present in the mitochondrial membranes of almost all human tissues which metabolizes or breaks down monoamines such as the neurotransmitters dopamine, norepinephrine, and serotonin. There are A and B forms of MAO with the A form predominating in the brain and the B form predominating in the digestive tract.

monoamine oxidase inhibitor

n. Any of several drugs used as antidepressants whose mechanism of action is to inhibit monoamine oxidase, which is a hormone present in the mitochondrial membranes of almost all human tissues which metabolizes or breaks down monoamines such as the neurotransmitters dopamine, norepinephrine, and serotonin.

monochromatic vision

n. A form of color blindness in which the retina contains only one type of cone and the person is unable to distinguish different colors and so sees everything in shades of the same color. Also called monochromatism.

monochromatism

n. A form of color blindness in which the retina contains only one kind of cone and so the person is unable to distinguish different colors and so sees everything in shades of the same color. Also called monochromatic vision.

monocular

adj. Of or relating to a single eye, as in monocular vision, which lacks some of the depth and distance cues present in normal vision.

monocular cue

n. Any of several stimulus characteristics which are used to make inferences about distance and depth in perception by a single eye. These include size, interposition, linear perspective, accommodation, atmospheric perspective, and shading changes.

monogamy

n. **1.** A reproductive relationship in which a male and a female mate exclusively with one another. In the past this has been confused with pair bonding, in which couples of various species mate and cooperate in nest building or similar parenting activities but which genetic studies have found are often not monogamous. **2.** Marriage to only one spouse at a time.

monotonic
adj. Changing in only one direction as a variable that only increases or only decreases but does not reverse direction of change.

monozygotic
adj. Of or relating to a single fertilized embryo, as in monozygotic twins, who are genetically identical and are created when an embryo divides into halves which separate and each of which grows into a child.

monozygotic twins
n. Two genetically identical children born when an embryo divides into halves which separate and each of which grows into a child.

Monte Carlo method
n. In statistics, any technique which generates sequences of random numbers which are used as data in simulating a probabilistic process for which no algorithm is available. As an example, the tossing of a coin 10 times could be simulated by generating a random series of 1s and 0s in groups of 10 many times and then counting the relative frequency of 1s and 0s in the samples in order to estimate the distribution of outcomes likely were one actually to toss a fair coin 10 times.

Montessori method
n. An approach to early childhood and elementary education which assumes the child has an active will to learn and will learn in his or her own individual way and at his/her own pace if given the freedom to do so within a structured and protected environment. Individual freedom and choice with responsibility and practical limits are emphasized, and older children are urged to attempt cooperative projects as ways of learning.

mood
n. **1.** An affective state that persists from several minutes to several weeks which directs and colors perception, thought, and behavior. **2.** In linguistics, a category of verb form used to denote the speaker's attitude toward the statement. Thus a verb can indicate a command (imperative mood), a statement (indicative mood), a question (interrogative mood), or a conditional statement (subjunctive mood).

mood congruence
n. The degree to which a thought, action, or other occurrence fits in with a mood, especially in psychopathology. Thus weeping would be mood congruent with depression but not with mania.

mood-congruent memory
n. A memory which fits well with the mood of the person having the memory.

mood-dependent memory
n. An episodic memory which is recalled only when a person is in the same mood as when the original event occurred.

mood disorder
n. Any disorder whose chief characteristic is a prolonged emotional state which is independent of immediate events. This includes depressive disorders and bipolar disorders.

mood stabilizer
n. Drug which reduces the mania or hypomania in bipolar disorders and the sadness in both bipolar and depressive disorders. Lithium carbonate is the most commonly used mood stabilizer for bipolar disorders but is dangerous to use as its therapeutic dose is close to its lethal dose, and so close monitoring is necessary. The anticonvulsant drugs carbamazepine, valproic acid, and oxcarbazine are often used with bipolar II disorder and cyclothymic disorder. Anxiolytics are most commonly used as depressive mood stabilizers. Also called antimanics or antidepressives.

mood-state dependency
n. The characteristic of being affected by mood, as in mood-dependent memories or behavior.

moon illusion

n. The apparent difference in the size of the moon when it is near the horizon as opposed to when it is directly overhead. Also called the celestial illusion.

moral development

n. The process by which humans develop a code of values and ethical principles that guide decisions about right and wrong social behavior. There are two major models of moral development; the earlier model is advanced by classical psychoanalytic theory and the later model is a product of cognitive-developmental theory.

The psychoanalytic theory of moral development is part of the larger *psychosexual theory* of personality development proposed by Sigmund Freud. Psychosexual development posits that during the *phallic stage* between ages 3 and 6, children are preoccupied with securing the affections of the opposite-sex parent. This *Oedipal conflict* in boys and *Electra conflict* in girls is ultimately resolved by redirecting their attention toward the same-sex parent and learning to become more like that parent. This process of *identification* is held to be the basis for building the moral code of the child, and thus, the same-sex parent becomes the most critical influence in establishing values and principles.

The cognitive-developmental theory of moral development was proposed by Lawrence Kohlberg and derives from the general cognitive-developmental theories of Jean Piaget. Kohlberg proposes three levels of moral development labeled *preconventional*, *conventional*, and *postconventional*; each of these levels is further divided into two subordinate stages, resulting in six age-independent, sequential stages. In stage 1, good and bad acts are determined exclusively by their physical consequences: good behavior allows the person to avoid punishment from authorities. A more instrumental viewpoint emerges in stage 2, in which the person views acts as right if they are rewarding and satisfactory to the self and fair to others. Stage 3 moves the individual into the level of *conventional* morality, where maintenance of the social order is the primary aim. Acts that please others and conform to the expectations of the larger social group are seen as right by the person in stage 3. The need to abide by and respect the formal laws of the societal institutions characterizes stage 4. Acts are considered bad at stage 4 if they can lead to disorder and a breakdown of the larger social system. Stage 5 puts the individual at the level of *postconventional* morality, where rules and laws must become flexible to changing situations. Moral codes are no longer seen as absolute for the person in stage 5; some rules will be agreed upon less by members of different cultures while other rules will have more universal importance. Finally, in stage 6, there is a full recognition of basic and universal ethical principles that precede all formal laws and social contracts. An individual equipped with these principles will be capable of sound moral judgments in all situations regardless of whether a specific law or rule readily applies. The most common method for assessing an individual's level of moral development is to present vignettes that pose moral dilemmas. The solutions offered by the respondent and his or her justifications for those solutions yield insight into the level of moral reasoning. It has been claimed that Kohlberg's theory misses culture-specific moral principles (e.g., respect for older people, filial piety, harmony, nonviolence).   – JK

moral dilemma

n. A situation which appears to force an individual to choose between two or more strongly held beliefs about right and wrong.

morality

n. A code or system of right conduct against which real behaviors are judged.

moral obligation

n. A duty arising out of beliefs of right and wrong, which vary considerably from culture to culture.

moral realism (stage)

n. In Piagetian theory, the second stage of moral development, characteristic of children from about 5 to 10 years of age, in which they believe judgments are inherent in acts and that punishments will prevent the individual from repeating immoral acts.

Morgan's canon

n. The idea that we should interpret animal behavior as a function of the lowest possible level of mental organization instead of thinking about it in terms of human thinking, which leads to anthropomorphizing, or perceiving animals from a human-centered perspective. This idea is from C. Lloyd Morgan's textbook *Comparative Psychology* (1894), in which he wrote, "In no case may we interpret an action as the outcome of the exercise of higher psychical faculty, if it can be interpreted as the exercise of one which stands lower in the psychological scale." Also called Lloyd Morgan's canon.

Morita therapy

n. A Japanese approach to psychotherapy which focuses on mindfulness and moving from a focus on controlling emotion or symptoms to focusing on purposive action. In traditional Morita therapy, clients are first completely isolated and made to stay in bed, simply being mindful of what occurs without reading or other activity or distraction for about a week. In the next 4 to 7 days he or she is allowed up part of the time and allowed to perform light work in isolation while remaining mindful of what he/she is doing in each moment and keeping a journal of his/her experiences which he/she shares with a therapist and discusses in interviews which occur about every other day. This is followed by a period of 1 or 2 months in which he/she engages in more complex solitary work and then works with others while trying to maintain mindfulness of his/her actions and the needs of the situation. The final period of 1 to 4 weeks is occupied with commuting from the hospital to work and trying to integrate mindfulness and a focus on useful action into daily life while simply accepting anxiety and other emotions that arise in the course of living.

moron

n. An archaic term for a mildly retarded person.

Moro reflex

n. A reflex present in newborn infants in which, when startled, they open arms and legs wide and then contract them as if trying to hold on with their whole body. This reflex disappears in the first year of life.

morpheme

n. The smallest part of a word that carries meaning or performs a grammatical function is a *morpheme*. Morphemes are classified into two overarching types: free morphemes can appear alone; bound morphemes must be bound to another morpheme. Within the class of bound morphemes, derivational morphemes perform lexical operations, while inflectional morphemes have grammatical functions. For example, the derivational morpheme *–ly* in English is used to derive adverbs from adjectives (*happy, happily*), and the derivational morpheme *un-* negates the meaning of an adjective (*happy, unhappy*). Inflectional morphemes, responsible for marking grammatical relations among words, are a very small class in English, which includes plural *–s* and possessive *–'s* for nouns; comparative *–er* and superlative *–est* for adjectives; and third singular *–s*, past tense *–ed*, past participle *–en*, and present participle *–ing* for verbs. Spanish, a language with slightly more complex inflectional morphology, marks gender and number on nouns and adjectives and number, person, tense, and verb class on verbs.

— EMF

morphine

n. The primary drug in opium, which is a very powerful painkiller and sedative as well as being highly addictive.

morphology

n. Morphology is a component of the grammar of a language by which *morphemes* are combined to create words. As such, the morphology of a language dictates the internal structure of words and how such structure is generated, by means of morphological rules. There are morphological rules that relate a word to alternate forms of that word by affixing inflectional morphemes. For example, the verb *walk* is related to *walking, walked*, and *walks*, all different forms of the same verb. Other morphological rules serve to derive different words from existing words by affixing derivational morphemes or by combining free morphemes. For example, the verb *walk* is related to the noun *walker* by a derivational rule, and to the noun *Walkman* by a compounding rule.   – EMF

mortality salience

n. Mortality salience is a psychological state in which individuals consciously think about their own death. Jeff Greenberg, Tom Pyszczynski, and Sheldon Solomon first used the term in 1986 to refer to a state induced to assess hypotheses derived from terror management theory. The theory proposes that the fear of death motivates people to maintain faith in a culturally derived conception of reality, or cultural worldview, that imbues life with meaning and provides the possibility that they will live on in some way beyond their own death. Greenberg and colleagues proposed that, if the theory is correct, then when people think about their own death, that is, are in a state of mortality salience, they should become motivated to increase faith in and conformity to their own cultural worldview.

The first and most frequently used method to induce mortality salience is to ask participants to respond in writing to a questionnaire that includes the following two requests: "Please describe the emotions the thought of your own death arouses in you" and "Jot down, as specifically as you can, what you think will happen to you physically as you die and once you are physically dead." This method of inducing mortality salience was first used in a study in which municipal court judges were asked to read hypothetical case materials and recommend a bond for an alleged prostitute. The judges were randomly assigned to fill out the mortality salience questionnaire or not prior to recommending a bond. Judges led to experience mortality salience recommended a much higher bond than those not led to think of their own death. This finding supported terror management theory because it showed that mortality salience motivated the judges to uphold their worldview more

fervently by punishing someone who violated the morals of their worldview.

Since that first study, many studies have shown that mortality salience leads people to react favorably to those who support one's worldview and unfavorably to those who violate or criticize one's worldview. Additional research has found that mortality salience affects a wide range of judgments and behaviors that serve to preserve faith in either one's worldview or one's self-worth.

To date, over 250 studies have induced mortality salience using a variety of methods. Mortality salience has been induced by exposure to fear-of-death questionnaires, gory accident footage, a request to write one sentence about death, a word search task with death-related words embedded in it, and physical proximity to funeral homes and cemeteries. These mortality salient conditions have been compared to a wide range of control conditions in terms of their effects on a diverse variety of dependent variables indicative of increased terror management. These control conditions have reminded participants of neutral topics such as food and television and aversive topics such as failure, uncertainty, meaninglessness, pain, paralysis, general worries, upcoming exams, and social exclusion. In the vast majority of mortality salience studies, the findings have supported the specific role of thoughts of mortality.

Studies investigating the cognitive processes instigated by mortality salience have shown that mortality salience first leads people to distract themselves from thoughts of death. This is viewed as a set of proximal defenses which serve to remove these potentially threatening thoughts from consciousness. Once these thoughts have been removed from consciousness, they tend to remain on the fringes of consciousness, or high in accessibility. The distal defenses aroused by mortality salience, which bolster the participant's worldview or self-esteem, occur during this later time, when death-related thoughts are no longer in focal attention but are high in accessibility. Indeed, similar effects to the delayed effects of mortality salience have been shown to occur immediately in response to exposure to brief subliminal flashes of death-related words on a computer screen. Study participants are unaware of these subliminal primes, so they do not make mortality salient, but they have similar effects because they put death-related thoughts closer to consciousness.

Mortality salience research supports terror management theory by showing that thoughts about death outside consciousness motivate a wide range of judgments and behaviors to bolster individuals' faith in their worldview and self-worth. This work thereby suggests that mortality concerns contribute to nationalism, prejudice, and intergroup aggression, as well as prosocial behavior and cultural achievements.   – JG

mosaic Down syndrome

n. A congenital condition characterized by mild to severe mental retardation, pleasant disposition, a flat face, stubby fingers and toes, epicanthic folds in the eyes among non-Asians, tongue fissures, and unusual patterns of skinfolds on the palms of the hands and soles of the feet. It is caused by the presence of an extra chromosome 21 in some but not all of the body's cells. This occurs when there is an error in replicating chromosome 21 at some early stage of development so that an extra copy of the chromosome is produced and subsequently will be present in whatever portion of future cells develop from the original aberrant one.

motherese

n. Motherese (also *baby talk, infant-directed speech, caretaker speech*) is speech directed at infants and young children, altered in relatively systematic ways across speakers. Infant-directed speech tends to be produced with an overall higher pitch as well as with exaggerated pitch movements. Sentences uttered to infants generally consist of simplified structure (subject-verb-object utterances, without embedded clauses) and convey relatively simple meanings. Caretakers tend to engage in frequent use of diminutives (*doggie* in English, *perrito* in Spanish, for example) and in frequent repetition (*Look at the doggie. See the doggie? What a cute doggie!*). Motherese is not characterized by the presence of correction;

in fact, errors produced by children seldom are corrected, particularly if they involve form rather than meaning. While some aspects of motherese – the overall pitch differences in particular – are present across different cultures, caretakers of children across the world do not all uniformly alter speech directed at infants and young children. Furthermore, there are vast cross-cultural differences in caretaking behaviors; for example, children in some cultures are reared by older siblings rather than adults. That motherese is not universally available in all contexts where language is successfully acquired strongly suggests that it is not a necessary ingredient for first-language acquisition.   – EMF

motion aftereffect

n. The illusion that a stationary object is moving. After looking at a moving object for several seconds a stationary object will sometimes appear to be moving in the direction opposite to the thing that is actually moving. For instance, if an observer watches a long train go past and then sees a telephone pole behind the train, the telephone pole may appear to be moving toward the back of the train. Also called kinetic aftereffect and movement aftereffect.

motion, apparent

n. An illusion of motion created when two visual stimuli are displayed in rapid alternation close together. This phenomenon underlies the effects of neon signs with arrows that appear to move and movies and television, which show a series of still pictures in rapid succession with each frame changing slightly so that there appears to be continuous motion. Also called the phi effect.

motion detector

n. **1.** Any cell or system of cells which detects motion, as do many neurons in the visual system. **2.** An instrument such as radar which is capable of detecting the motion of an object.

motion parallax

n. A visual depth cue that occurs when an observer moves and the movement of faraway objects is less than that of nearby objects.

motion, stroboscopic

n. **1.** An illusion of motion created when visual stimuli are displayed in rapid alternation close together. This phenomenon underlies the effects of neon signs with arrows that appear to move and movies and television, which show a series of still pictures in rapid succession with each frame changing slightly so that there appears to be continuous motion. **2.** A false perception of stillness or unreal motion perceived when a moving object such as a rotating tire or fan blade is seen in a stroboscopic light and appears to turn backward or stand still.

motivate

v. **1.** To cause a desire or impulse to action. **2.** To function as a goal or incentive.

motivation

n. **1.** The hypothetical physio-mental force that leads humans and other animals to act. **2.** In learning theory, any situation which acts to punish or reinforce particular behavior. **3.** A willingness to make an effort in the pursuit of a goal. **4.** The process or action of convincing others to make an effort in the pursuit of a goal.

motivational research

n. Any of numerous lines of study which investigate the purposes or causes of behavior. This has been a central theme in research on consumer behavior and is central in many personality theories, such as psychoanalysis, analytic psychology, and personology.

motoneuron

n. Any neuron which connects to a muscle fiber and causes the contraction of the muscle when it fires. Also called an efferent neuron or a motor neuron.

motor aphasia

n. Acquired language disorder characterized by agrammatical, nonfluent, poorly articulated speech, composed by short utterances, which is produced with significant effort and due to a brain pathology involving the third frontal gyrus (Brodmann's 44 area) and surrounding areas. It is also known as Broca's aphasia, expressive aphasia, or efferent motor aphasia. Usually, the damage is located in the left hemisphere. Expressive language is basically composed by nouns with an evident decrease in grammatical elements (agrammatism). The expressive defect in speech has been named in different ways, but most frequently it is referred as apraxia of speech. Level of language understanding is superior to verbal production, although it is not completely normal because of the difficulties in grammatical understanding. Language repetition is abnormal: phonetic deviations, phonological paraphasias, simplification of complex syllables, and iterations are observed. Repeating grammatical elements is harder than repeating nouns. Verbal automatisms (e.g., to count) are better than spontaneous language; signing is also better than speaking. Pointing/naming is deficient, but pointing (e.g., show me the pencil) is notoriously superior to naming (e.g., what is the name of this object?). — AA

motor apraxia

n. Loss of the ability to produce purposeful, skilled movements as the result of brain pathology. This impairment in the production of learned (or skilled) movements is not due to weakness, paralysis, lack of coordination, or sensory loss. Three subtypes of motor apraxia are described: **(1)** limb kinetic apraxia, **(2)** ideokinetic or ideomotor apraxia, and **(3)** ideational apraxia. Limb kinetic apraxia is a loss of the kinetic components of engrams resulting in coarse or unrefined movements. Ideokinetic or ideomotor apraxia is a loss of the voluntary ability to perform learned movements. Ideational apraxia is an impairment of ideational (conceptual) knowledge resulting in loss of the conceptual linkage between tools and their respective actions as well as the ability to sequence correctly produced movements. Ideomotor apraxia can be divided according to the body segment where it is observed: face apraxia (ocular and oral apraxia), limb apraxia (upper limb apraxia and gait apraxia), and axial apraxia (body trunk apraxia). Other subtypes of motor apraxia have also been described, such as callosal apraxia, conceptual apraxia, and sympathetic apraxia.   – A A

▶ *See also* **APRAXIA**

motor area

n. Any area of the cerebral cortex which sends impulses, causing the initiation, coordination, or regulation of muscles. The precentral gyrus is the primary motor area.

motor cortex

n. Posterior part of the frontal lobe involved in organizing, controlling, and executing voluntary movements. It includes the primary motor cortex (Brodmann's area 4), the premotor cortex (basically Brodmann's area 6, but also Brodmann's areas 44, which includes Broca's area, and 8, the frontal eye field), and the supplementary motor area situated in the medial aspect of the cerebral hemispheres, although the supplementary motor area can also be included as premotor cortex.   – A A

▶ *See also* **PREMOTOR CORTEX** *and* **PRIMARY MOTOR CORTEX**

motor end plate

n. The end of a motor neuron which connects the neuron to a muscle fiber and which generates a small electric potential, causing the muscle fiber to begin to contract when an action potential travels down the axon to the end plate.

motor learning

n. Any increase in coordination or skill at any bodily motion or complex task, which usually comes about through integration of sensory and proprioceptive information over the course of practice. Motor learning through imagery and mental practice has been noted, but it usually is accompanied by small mimicry of muscle movement involved in the actual skill.

motor nerve

n. Any of a large number of nerves whose neuronal axons convey information from the motor cortex or the spinal cord to muscles or glands.

motor neuron

n. Any neuron which connects to a muscle fiber and causes the contraction of the muscle

when it fires. Also called an efferent neuron or a motoneuron.

motor unit

n. Any neuron which connects to a muscle fiber and causes the contraction of the muscle when it fires. Also called an efferent neuron or a motor neuron.

movement disorder

n. Any disorder which interferes with voluntary body movements, including all the aparaxias, dissociative movement disorder, and stereotypic movement disorder.

movement illusion

n. Any of numerous illusions of movement, including the phi phenomenon, the waterfall illusion, the kinetic effect, and numerous others.

movement parallax

n. A visual depth cue that occurs when an observer moves and the movement of faraway objects is less than that of nearby objects.

movement perception

n. The visual detection of object motion, which is accomplished by the magnocellular nerves with connections to centers in both the lateral geniculate nuclei and the visual cortex.

movement therapy

n. An approach to psychotherapy that uses dance, rhythmic exercise, and other forms of bodily movement to increase bodily awareness and so disrupts habitual patterns of withdrawal into unproductive rumination.

MRI

n. Magnetic resonance imaging, which uses a medical device for creating three-dimensional images of the body by measuring the reactivity of the hydrogen atoms in tissues to intense magnetic fields. The MRI is more accurate than computed tomography (CT) scanning and shows more tissue differences than do X-ray images.

mucous membrane

n. Any of numerous thin sheets of epithelial tissue and a deeper layer of connective tissue that secrete and are covered by mucus and absorb water, salt, and other dissolved chemicals, such as the linings of the nasal passages, lungs, digestive tract, urethra, and vagina.

Mullerian duct
n. Either of a pair of ducts that appear in female mammalian embryos and eventually develop into female sexual organs, including the fallopian tubes, uterus, and upper portion of the vagina.

Muller-Lyer illusion
n. A visual illusion in a line with outward-facing wedges at the ends appears longer than the same line with inward-facing wedges at the ends, for example, <--> >--<

multiculturalism
n. Multiculturalism is an ideology advocating that a society or organization should allow and include distinct cultural groups with equal status. Multiculturalism stands in sharp contrast with the ideology of monoculturalism (normative cultural unity or homogeneity), which historically was the norm in the European nation-state. Although the term *multiculturalism* is typically used to acknowledge the presence of the distinct cultures of immigrant groups, sometimes it can also be applied to acknowledge the presence of indigenous peoples in colonized nations.

Multiculturalism should also be differentiated from ideologies such as "assimilation" (the belief that cultural minorities should abandon their original culture and adopt the majority culture) and "melting pot" (when all minority cultural groups "melt" and are combined so that they lose their discrete elements and identities and yield a final product of uniform cultural consistency). The terms *cultural mosaic* and *salad bowl* (when different cultures are combined but do not merge together or result in a homogeneous culture), on the other hand, are often used as synonyms of *multiculturalism*, although more specifically the former refers to the results yielded from multicultural ideology.

Multiculturalism has been formally adopted as an official policy in nations such as Canada, Australia, and the Netherlands,

for reasons that vary from country to country. Multicultural policies influence the structures and decisions of governments to ensure that political and economic power and resources are allocated equitably to all the represented cultural groups. Examples of government-endorsed multicultural policies are dual citizenship; government support for media outlets (e.g., newspapers, television, radio) in the minority languages; support for cultural minority holidays, celebrations, and community centers; and acceptance of traditional and religious codes of dress and behavior in the public sphere (e.g., work, school). In the United States multiculturalism is not an official policy, although the government in recent years has moved toward acceptance of some multiculturalist policies (e.g., being able to take a driving exam in a number of languages, shaping of voting districts to facilitate proportional minority representation).

Multiculturalism is a controversial issue in some societies. Some political segments within the United States and some European nations view multiculturalism as a policy that undermines national unity, social integration, and even security. Conversely, the melting pot concept has also been greatly criticized as an idealized version of the assimilation process.

— VB-M

▶ *See also* **ACCULTURATION, BICULTURAL IDENTITY,** *and* **BICULTURALISM**

multicultural psychology
n. Multicultural psychology concerns all aspects of human behavior as it occurs where people from two or more cultural backgrounds encounter each other. Research in multicultural psychology is diverse, covering at least five broad areas of inquiry: (1) intergroup relations: what are the social antecedents and psychological consequences of cultural stereotyping (e.g., stereotype threat, race-based rejection sensitivity, culturally motivated prejudice, and discrimination), (2) acculturation and adjustment: how do individuals from a minority culture respond to the majority culture, and what are the health implications of the different response patterns? (3) mental representations of cultures: how are cultural and racial differences constructed and

negotiated, and what are the implications of cultural/racial essentialism for intercultural relations? (4) multicultural identity: how do individuals with extensive exposure to two or more cultures negotiate their multicultural identities? and (5) intercultural competence: what is intercultural competence and how can it be developed?   – CYC

multidimensional scaling
n. (MDS) A scaling procedure in which similarities in a data set are represented by spatial proximity, and differences are represented by distal spacing in an artificial space of any number of dimensions. MDS is often used as an alternative to factor analysis as it can use computations other than linear correlations to represent spatial dimensions.

multilevel random modeling
n. A mixed statistical procedure in which correlation matrices of relationships among variables are developed at each level of a categorical variable or variables. Also called hierarchical random modeling.

multimodal therapy
n. An outgrowth of behavior therapy in which the therapist assesses the client's behavior, affective responses, sensations, imagery, cognitions, interpersonal relationships, and need for drugs (the first letters of which form the acronym BASIC ID) in the belief that these modalities interact with one another so that changing one will alter the others. The therapist and client form an agreement on which are the most salient problems discovered in the initial assessment and begin trying to alter them in a more positive direction using procedures drawn from all areas of learning theory.

multiple choice
n. A form of test or task in which a subject is given three or more fixed options and forced to choose among them.

multiple correlation
n. A numerical index (usually symbolized by R) of the degree to which a target variable can be predicted by two or more predictor variables using a linear model.

multiple correlation coefficient
n. (R) A numerical index of the degree to which a target variable can be predicted by two or more predictor variables using a linear model. R ranges from 0 to 1 with 0 indicating no predictive power and 1 indicating perfect prediction.

multiple intelligences
n. Theoretical perspective that intelligence extends beyond the analytical, verbal, and quantitative abilities measured by traditional intelligence tests; rather, intelligence may be demonstrated through extraordinary skill or ability in a range of various areas of human potential. The theory of multiple intelligences was originally proposed by Dr. Howard Gardner, who specified eight areas of intelligence: linguistic, logical-mathematical, spatial, bodily-kinesthetic, musical, interpersonal, intrapersonal, and naturalist (added after the original proposal of seven intelligences). The theory of multiple intelligences has received considerable attention in educational settings for its potential to alter instructional techniques to educate a range of students who possess different types of intelligence more effectively. While the theory of multiple intelligences provides a unique theoretical and philosophical perspective for examining the construct of intelligence, it is criticized for the inability to measure multiple intelligences in a psychometrically sound fashion as well as concerns that the different intelligences specified by multiple intelligence theory are simply different cognitive styles rather than independent constructs.   – BJM

multiple linear regression analysis
n. A statistical procedure in which more than one predictor variable is correlated with a target variable as well as with the other predictor variables in order to form a linear model using a weighted sum of the predictor variables to predict values of the target variable.

multiple personality
n. The presence of two or more distinct personalities or identities in the same person who recurrently exchange control of the

person and who may have only some knowledge about each other and the history of the person involved.

multiple personality disorder

n. A disorder characterized by the presence of two or more distinct personalities or identities in the same person who recurrently exchange control of the person and who may have only some knowledge about each other and the history of the person involved. Also called dissociative identity disorder.

multiple regression

n. A statistical procedure in which more than one predictor variable is correlated with a target variable as well as with the other predictor variables in order to form a linear model using a weighted sum of the predictor variables to predict values of the target variable.

multiple sclerosis

n. (MS) A chronic and usually progressive disease in which there is inflammation of many small patches of the myelin sheathing of nerves in the brain and spinal cord which leads to destruction of the patch of sheathing and the nerve beneath it, disrupting the neural pathway in which the nerve lies. The symptoms of MS depend on which nerves are attacked by the disease. Often, the first symptom is disruption of vision, which can be followed by fatigue and weakness, particularly in the hands and feet, and numbness, stiffness, muscular spasms, bodily pain, incoordination, and difficulty in maintaining balance. Eventually the person loses control of the bladder and bowels, and most persons with the disease become depressed. Some victims also suffer cognitive impairment of various sorts. MS usually appears in early adulthood and has periods of remission followed by periods of further deterioration. It is difficult to predict the course of the disease in individuals, although the more different symptoms that appear early in the course of the disease the worse the prognosis. More than 10% of individuals die within the first 25 years of diagnosis. The causes of the disease are unknown, but some experts believe it to be an autoimmune disorder. It is more common in people of northern European ancestry and those who spend their childhood in colder climates.

multipolar neuron

n. Any nerve cell which has more than one dendrite.

multitrait-multimethod matrix

n. A tabular display of the correlations of several traits measured in several ways and all correlated with each other. The correlation of a trait measured in one way with itself is a measure of the reliability of the measure. The correlations between any measure of a trait and another measure of the same trait constitute measures of the convergent validity of both measures. The correlation of a trait with other traits measured the same way is a measure of the confounding effect due to similarity in measurement. Correlations between different traits measured differently are used to estimate discriminant validity.

multivariate

adj. Of or relating to the inclusion of more than one variable in a research design or statistical analysis.

multivariate analysis methods

n. Any of several statistical procedures that analyze the variance among multiple independent and multiple dependent measures.

multivariate analysis of covariance

n. (MANCOVA) A calculation of the ratios of within-group variance to between-group differences in more than one dependent variable in two or more groups defined by independent variables with the variance of another variable removed using regression techniques. This is used to test hypotheses about differences among the groups with the object of being able to attribute any such differences to effects of the independent variable(s) on the dependent variables.

multivariate analysis of variance

n. (MANOVA) A calculation of the ratios of within- to between-group differences in more

323

than one dependent variable in two or more groups defined by independent variables. This is used to test hypotheses about differences in the dependent variables between the groups with the object of being able to attribute any such differences to effects of the independent variables on the dependent variables.

multivariate statistics

n. Any of several mathematical procedures that analyze the variance among multiple independent and/or multiple dependent measures such as multiple regression, analysis of variance (ANOVA), analysis of covariance (ANCOVA), or multivariate analysis of variance (MANOVA).

Munchausen syndrome

n. A disorder characterized by repeatedly producing or feigning psychological or medical signs or symptoms in order to adopt a sick role. Also called factitious disorder.

Munchhausen syndrome by proxy

n. A disorder characterized by repeatedly producing or feigning psychological or medical signs or symptoms in another person in order to adopt a sick role by proxy. Also called factitious disorder by proxy.

Munsell color system

n. A numerical method of describing or specifying colors by means of hue, saturation, and brightness using three additive primary colors to specify hue, which has been widely adopted in science, art, and technology.

muscarinic receptor

n. A part of cholinergic transmission which is activated through a metabotropic route, necessarily slower than transmission at a nicotinic-ionic receptor site. Muscarinic receptor action requires a multiple-stage metabolic alteration involving a G-protein coupling to a second messenger, which may then open or close ionic channels in the neural membrane, leading to synaptic transmission. In addition, stimulation of a muscarinic receptor site may alter protein production within the neuron. Although nicotinic receptors are also found

in the brain, muscarinic receptors predominate in the brain and are also found in the heart. Atropine (similar to ophthalmological eye drops used to dilate the pupil) inhibits cholinergic muscarinic receptor sites.   – vs

muscle

n. A form of fibrous tissue that contracts when subject to electrical stimulation. This contraction causes pressure across joints that enables bodies to move. There are three types of muscle: smooth muscles, as in the lining of the intestines; skeletal muscles, which enable bodily movement; and cardiac muscle, which causes the blood to circulate.

muscle spindle

n. Any of the sensory nerves connected to intrafusal fibers that lie within muscles and send impulses toward the spinal cord and brain when the muscle is stretched.

music therapy

n. A method of psychotherapy in which clients use the performance of music as a way of relieving their psychological symptoms.

mutagen

n. Any substance or form of energy such as X-rays and gamma rays which causes a permanent change in the genetic material in a cell.

mutation

n. Any permanent change in the genetic information encoded in the DNA of a cell capable of being transmitted to offspring cells or, in the case of mutation in a sex cell, transmission to the next generation of organisms. Mutation is the process by which species change over time as some of the mutations produce offspring that are better adapted for survival in the particular environment in which the organism lives and so increase the chance individuals with that genetic form will survive and procreate.

mutism

n. The refusal or inability to speak, which may result from malformation or damage to the vocal apparatus, neurological areas involved in speech, congenital deafness which prevents learning speech, mental disorders, or decision not to speak, as is the case with some monastics and some angry persons.

myelencephalon
n. The medulla oblongata or the part of the fetal hindbrain that develops into the medulla oblongata.

myelin
n. The fat and protein which form sheathing around nerves which electrically insulates them from surrounding tissue, enabling more rapid transmission of nerve impulses, and gives portions of the brain and nerve tracts their typical off-white color.

myelin sheath
n. The sheath of fat and protein which forms around nerves which electrically insulates them from surrounding tissue, enabling more rapid transmission of nerve impulses, and gives portions of the brain and nerve tracts their typical off-white color.

Myers-Briggs Type Indicator
n. (MBTI) A personality inventory developed to measure Jungian polarities of introversion-extroversion, thinking-feeling, and sensing-intuiting, to which the polarity of judging-perceiving has been added. Subjects' responses are used to assign them to one or the other end of each polarity and then assigned to 1 of the 16 possible types formed by the four polarities. The MBTI is probably the most widely used personality measure in the world, in industrial, academic, and clinical applications.

myopia
n. Near-sightedness, or difficulty in clearly perceiving distant objects due to elongation of the eyeball, which results in light focusing in front of the retina instead of directly on it.

myostatic reflex
n. A reflex involving a single stretch receptor and a single efferent nerve fiber in which the stretching of a muscle causes contraction of the muscle which helps maintain posture. Also called stretch reflex.

myotonia
n. Prolonged rigidity or spasm of a muscle or part of a muscle.

myristin
n. A hallucinogenic drug found in nutmeg and mace which is structurally similar to mescaline and affects serotonin, norepinephrine, and dopamine receptors. It is also used as an herbal treatment for arthritis.

myth
n. Literally a true story, meaning ancient or traditional stories that contain significant cultural meanings often conveyed through supernatural characters or events.

myth of mental illness
n. A phrase coined by Thomas Szasz, who suggests that categories of mental illness are not disease entities but categories of socially inappropriate behavior and that psychiatry and clinical psychology are pseudoscientific social control institutions not much different from the Inquisition during the Middle Ages.

Naikan therapy
n. Naikan therapy is an intensive, systematic form of self-reflection (*Naikan* literally means "inside-looking" in Japanese) in which clients review three aspects of their relationship with each person they consider important in their lives: (1) the emotional or material support they received from that particular person, (2) the support they returned, and (3) the difficulties or suffering they caused the person. This form of therapy was developed in the 1950s by Ishin Yoshimoto (1916–1988) according to Buddhist principles such as the connectedness of all things, acceptance of

suffering, and giving. Distinct from some traditional Western therapies, the aim of Naikan in reflecting on past relationships is not to procure insight into the origins of maladaptive behaviors and symptoms, and it does not involve spontaneous free talking with a therapist. Rather, through a systematic reflection on their interrelatedness with and indebtedness to others, clients develop humility and gratitude in their relationships with both significant others and the larger world, fostering a positive sense of interconnectedness, trust, responsibility, and meaning.   – JWK, SAH

naïve psychology
n. **1.** The common beliefs of persons in any culture about the workings of the mind and their interaction with behavior. **2.** The way(s) a person unfamiliar with the science of psychology understands the mind and behavior, particularly in attribution theory.

naïve realism
n. The belief that perception of an object is direct knowledge of the nature of the object itself rather than a mental representation of the object subject to various limitations of the senses and interpretations and interpolations of the mind, as is the case in modern psychology and philosophy.

naïve scientist metaphor
n. The portrayal of the workings of the mind as like those of a naive scientist trying to understand the world guided by practicality, curiosity, and a willingness to use shortcuts if they work most of the time.

naloxone
n. A short-lived opiate antagonist often used to treat opiate overdoses. It binds to opiate receptors without having sedative or depressant effects, thus preventing opiates from binding to them. It can precipitate withdrawal symptoms in individuals addicted to opiates. Also known as naline.

naltrexone
n. A long-lived opiate antagonist that binds to opiate receptors without having sedative or depressant effects, thus preventing opiates from binding to them. It can precipitate withdrawal symptoms in individuals addicted to opiates. Since it prevents opiates from having their usual effects, it has been used as an adjunct to treatment for opiate addiction and has been used in the treatment of alcoholism as well.

narcissism
n. **1.** In common usage, excessive positive self-evaluation and lack of consideration for others. **2.** As a personality type, one given to grandiose evaluations of self, preoccupation with fantasies of success and power, exaggerated sense of entitlement, and an exploitative approach to others. **3.** In psychoanalysis, the focus of sexual desire on one's own body and sexual relations with others based on the similarity to one's own body.

narcissistic injury
n. Any injury to one's sense of self-worth or sense of entitlement but particularly important in infancy when one is dependent on others.

narcissistic libido
n. Sexual desire directed toward one's self which decreases in direct proportion to libido investment in another object.

narcissistic personality disorder
n. An enduring pattern of personal adjustment characterized by grandiosity, need for attention and admiration, and a lack of empathy. Individuals with this disorder believe that they are special, are exploitative in their approach to others, and are excessively envious of others while being preoccupied with fantasies of their own achievement and power.

narcolepsy
n. A disorder characterized by repeatedly falling into deep, refreshing sleep during waking hours and occasions of complete loss of muscle tone and the intrusion of rapid eye movement sleep into the transition between sleep and waking.

narcosis
n. Drug-induced sleep.

narcotic analgesic

n. Any sleep inducing drug that is used as a painkiller such as morphine. These include buprenorphine, codeine, dihydrocodeine, fentanyl, heroin, hydromorphone, laudanum, levorphenol, mepiridine, oxycodone, oxymorphone, paregoric, pentazocine, and propoxyphene.

national character

n. The modal personality type within a culture that most persons in that culture share to some degree. Perceptions of national character are often quite different from actual national character as quantified as the average of scores on measures of personality traits.

national stereotype

n. A perception of the average or modal personality traits of individuals in a particular nation or culture, which is often inaccurate.

nativism

n. The point of view that the capacity to perceive time and space, intellectual abilities, character, and thought patterns are born in the individual and minimally influenced by experience. Few persons now take an extreme position in the discussion over what and to what extent is the mind innately structured versus constructed in interaction with experience. Chomsky's ideas of a language acquisition device (LAD), cross-cultural studies of universal human expressions, and Jung's ideas of a collective unconscious are examples of partial nativism.

natural category

n. Any category that occurs in natural language or folk usage, as opposed to ad hoc categories or those constructed during scientific, technological, philosophical, or religious practices. This is sometimes confused with basic level categories, which are those categories that occur first in the development of natural languages and at which there is the most similarity within categories and the most dissimilarity between categories.

naturalistic fallacy

n. The supposition that what occurs in nature or is historically true is morally right. Thus since there have always been wars, war is morally good, or since there have always been poor people, society should organize itself in a way so as to ensure there are always some people who are poor.

naturalistic observation

n. A research methodology that collects descriptive data via observations of target phenomena occurring in their natural context (as opposed to laboratory research). Naturalistic research involves watching target behaviors, events, or phenomena without interference from the researcher; as such, naturalistic observation is one of the most common unobtrusive research methods. The goal of naturalistic observation is to observe and record target behaviors without influencing, controlling, or manipulating the situation. For example, a researcher interested in mating behavior may choose to observe individuals interacting at a dance to examine social interaction in an environment in which people do not know they are being studied. The advantage of this type of approach is that people are not influenced by the research environment; the disadvantage is that there are often ethical concerns with the observation and recording of behavior without the consent of the individuals being studied.   – BJM

natural killer cell

n. A kind of lymphocyte with many receptor varieties which reacts quickly to infection before the production of antigen-specific B and T lymphocytes takes place.

natural language

n. Any language that has evolved through common usage in a human society and has native speakers, as opposed to artificial languages such as those used by computers, or Esperanto, which was created as an easily learned amalgam of other languages.

natural selection

n. The process whereby some individuals of a species survive and procreate whereas others do not because of differences in genetic endowment. This leads to a greater abundance in the population of the genes from the surviving individuals than of those who do not survive. This is the process by which most evolution takes place.

nature-nurture

n. The controversy over the relative contributions of heredity and experience to the makeup of the individual. Environmentalists or constructionists emphasize the role of learning, while nativists emphasize the role of heredity.

near-death experience

n. (NDE) The thoughts, feelings, memories, and perceptions of persons during a short period in which they are close to dying and then return to normal functioning. Typically NDEs include a sense of separation or distance from one's body, sometimes with the ability to look at the body from above; a sense of equanimity; the perception of a quickly flashing set of images that encompass the meaning of one's life; and an entering into an unlimited space filled with light. Sometimes there is also a sense of the presence of a spiritual other.

near-sightedness

n. Difficulty in clearly perceiving distant objects due to elongation of the eyeball which results in light focusing in front of the retina instead of directly on it.

Necker cube

n. A line drawing of a transparent cube in which all lines and vertices are apparent which is ambiguous as to which two sides are in front of the other two sides and whether the view is from above or below the cube.

necromania

n. A preoccupation with dead bodies which causes distress to the individual or interferes with social adjustment within the individual's culture.

necrophilia

n. Recurrent sexual arousal by fantasies of, desire for, or actual sexual interaction with dead bodies.

need

n. **1.** Anything necessary for the survival of an organism. **2.** The desire for anything necessary for the survival of an organism **3.** A desire for some particular thing, activity, or state necessary to the experienced well-being of an organism, as in the need for creativity or play.

need-drive-incentive model

n. A theory of motivation that asserts that deprivation of physical necessities (need) produces motivational states (drive) which lead to behavior aimed at obtaining the missing things or conditions. The behavior can be either a simple or a complex path toward the desired objects.

need for achievement

n. An inferred drive to accomplish difficult tasks at a high standard of competence and overcoming all obstacles. A desire to master tasks, manipulate and control objects and other human beings, and to do so better than others are able to do. A desire to surpass one's previous accomplishments and to be recognized as better than others. It includes a need to increase one's self-esteem by the successful exercise of one's own talents.

need for affiliation

n. The desire to interact with and form attachments with others; to be part of a group and to be loyal to them.

need for closure

n. The need for closure is the desire for immediate and definite knowledge and the aversion toward the uncertainties associated with ambiguity.

The need for closure construct originates from lay epistemic theory, which has been developed by Arie Kruglanski to describe and highlight the role of motivation in everyday cognitive processes. The theory explains everyday cognition as a form of naïve science. Similarly to scientists, laypeople construe their judgments and beliefs by observing, by using these observations to generate hypotheses, and then by validating these hypotheses through matching with available evidence. As a result of these processes of hypothesis generation and hypothesis validation, a particular stimulus environment becomes disambiguated, thus affording judgment and action.

The process of disambiguation often requires considerable mental resources. As a consequence, motivation may play a role in when and how people will engage in the processing of particular stimulus information. The construct of need for closure is used to describe the motivational components of the cognitive process. Within the framework of lay epistemic theory, a distinction is made between specific and nonspecific closure motivation. Both of these types of closure are assumed to vary along a continuum with a strong need to attain closure on the one end versus a strong need to avoid closure on the other end of the continuum. The need for specific closure is used to describe the cognitive motivation of an individual who aims to obtain specific, desirable knowledge. This need for desirable knowledge may culminate in a biased search for information, favoring particular information over other information. The need for nonspecific closure refers to the tendency of an individual to obtain certainty by accepting any information, as opposed to remaining in a state of uncertainty and ambiguity. This tendency of nonspecific closure has been associated with quick adoption of particular beliefs or knowledge elements, a tendency referred to as "seizing," and a tendency to hang on to these beliefs fervently, referred to as "freezing." In the psychological literature, the need for closure has often been equated with the need for nonspecific closure.

The need for nonspecific closure may be elicited by a variety of factors. These factors pertain to the extent to which reaching closure is perceived to have greater benefits than avoiding closure. Reaching closure can be considered particularly beneficial when immediate action needs to be initiated or predictability is sought. Working under time pressure may thus be a particularly powerful instigator of the need for closure. Similarly, the need for closure may be enhanced when individuals perform particular tasks in particularly unpleasant environments. Moreover, being confronted with an informational overload, or being mentally fatigued and thus deprived of the resources to cope with incoming information, may induce the need for closure because reaching closure gratifies the situationally induced desire for predictability. Factors such as time pressure and mental fatigue that contribute to the need for closure have all been used in experimental settings to study the phenomenon.

The need for closure also varies across individuals. Research testing the psychometric properties of the need for cognitive closure scale has demonstrated stable personality differences in five subcomponents of the need for closure: a preference for order and structure, an emotional discomfort associated with ambiguity, an impatience and impulsivity with regard to decision making, a desire for security and predictability, and closed-mindedness. Finally, the need for cognitive closure has been shown to vary across cultures. Some cultures may value order and predictability to a greater extent than others.

Whether situationally induced, measured by means of a personality questionnaire, or studied by means of cross-cultural comparison, the need for closure has been shown to encompass a variety of implications for intrapersonal and interpersonal components of cognition. Research has shown that time pressure induces the seizing and freezing tendencies referred to earlier, producing pronounced primacy effects in impression formation and the tendency to base judgments on prevalent stereotypes and to assimilate numerical estimates to anchor values. Another line of research has shown that heightened need for closure increases the tendency to accept accessible attributions. Several studies have attempted to separate the seizing from the freezing tendency, both of which were assumed to emanate from a high need for closure. Consistently with need for closure theory, before participants were able to form a crystallized opinion, increased need for closure led to seizing expressed in the tendency to be quickly persuaded by an interaction partner. After participants crystallized an opinion, however, a heightened need for closure led to freezing expressed in a resistance to be persuaded.

In the domain of interpersonal perception, the need for closure has been linked to a decreased ability to take the perspective of an interaction partner, once the person "freezes" on his or her own perspective. This tendency has also been shown to affect the negotiation strategies of high versus low need for closure individuals. It has been found that individuals with high (vs. low) dispositional need for closure tend more to adhere to anchor values (alleged profits attained by others) in defining the minimal profits they themselves would accept, to make smaller concessions to their negotiation partners, to engage in less systematic information processing, and to base their negotiation behavior more on stereotyped perceptions of their opponents. Need for closure has also been associated with language use, particularly with regard to abstractness. Abstract language indicates a permanence of judgments across situations and hence a greater stability of closure. Consistently with the basis of lay epistemic theory, research supports the notion that people who have high need for closure use more abstract terms in their communications

On a group level, higher need for closure has been related to a variety of features of group dynamics that are especially conducive to creating and maintaining a consensually shared reality. Research has identified a number of these features, including pressures to opinion uniformity among group members, endorsement of an autocratic leadership and decision-making structure, intolerance of diversity in group composition, rejection of opinion deviates and extolment of conformists, in-group favoritism and out-group derogation, attraction to groups possessing strongly shared realities, conservatism and adherence to the group's norms, loyalty to one's in-group qualified by the degree to which it constitutes a "good" shared reality provider.

Generally, research on the need for closure continues to expand across domains of social psychology and across labs throughout the world. Taken together, lay epistemic theory and the construct of need for closure have demonstrated the fertility of jointly considering motivational and cognitive processes and of taking into account the full application potential of the motivated cognition movement in social psychology.   – MD, AK

need for cognition
n. Contemporary conceptions define the need for cognition as the general tendency to engage in and enjoy complex and effortful cognitive activity. The need for cognition has not always been conceived as such. Early work on the need for cognition defined it as a need to perceive one's world as simple and predictable. This definition of the need for cognition fits well with contemporary constructs such as the need for closure and the need for structure, intolerance of ambiguity, and closed-mindedness. However, the contemporary understanding of need for cognition is inversely related to these concepts. Rather than a tendency to aim for simplicity, the need for cognition is used to denote a tendency to value complexity in thought. This contemporary understanding is to a considerable extent inspired by the work of John Cacioppo and Richard Petty.

need for distinctiveness
n. The desire to be seen as different from others, usually in a positive way.

need for evaluation
n. A propensity to engage in evaluative cognitions, which differs from the need to think about things in general (need for cognition), and leads those high in this need to think more about their preferences and to form more opinions than those low in this need.

need for structure
n. The desire to have predictable experience or to impose order on oneself or some aspects of the world around oneself.

need hierarchy
n. The relative importance of things or states to the survival or well-being of an organism

at a particular time. Thus the need for oxygen is usually more important than the need for food or sex. A hypothesized general order of the relative importance of various motivations for living organisms.

need-hierarchy theory
n. **1.** Any theory which supposes that the behavior of humans or other organisms is well explained in terms of movement toward satisfaction of the most important unmet need in a set of needs ordered by relative importance. **2.** Maslow's hierarchy of needs. **3.** Murray's theory of regnant needs.

need-press
n. Motivational states that result from environmental circumstances as a bus moving rapidly toward us might result in a need to get out of the way.

need to belong
n. The desire to be socially included, accepted, and approved by others.

negative afterimage
n. The visual form which remains after a visual stimulus has been removed which has reversed patterns of light and dark.

negative feedback
n. **1.** Reactions to an action or a communication which express negative evaluation of the action or communication. **2.** In information processing, information about a system which results in the termination or lessening of a process so as to prevent the system from moving away from a point of equilibrium as a thermostat will turn off a heater when a preset temperature is reached.

negative priming
n. The interference by one stimulus in the perception of an ensuing stimulus. Thus showing a blank red field on a computer screen immediately before showing the word *blue* will cause subjects to take longer to read the word *blue*.

negative reference group
n. Any group of people with which an individual does not wish to be associated.

negative reinforcement
n. The reinforcement of a behavior by the removal or prevention of an aversive stimulus. Thus a dog can be conditioned to move from one side of a cage to another in order to escape or avoid an electrical shock.

negative symptoms of schizophrenia
n. Symptoms that are a *reduction* in the functioning of a typical healthy person. Note that *negative* refers to a reduction of an average functioning individual and not a "harmful or bad symptom" (symptoms by definition are detrimental). Negative symptoms in schizophrenia include anhedonia (a diminished ability to experience pleasure), avolition (apathy, or loss of drive or motivation), alogia (poverty of speech), flat affect (decreased expression but not experience of emotion), lack of self-care (such as not bathing), problems focusing or paying attention, and social isolation. In general these symptoms have been less responsive to typical antipsychotic medications.   – DGa

negative transfer
n. The interference in learning appropriate responses created by previous learning of different responses in similar circumstances. Thus, if one has learned to speak with casual familiarity with one's teachers and parents, one will be slower to learn to speak formally, as required in many legal and military situations.

negativity bias
n. The tendency for people to weigh negative information more heavily than positive information in making judgments about a person.

nemawashi
n. The broad-based consensus-building procedure that occurs within the Japanese *ringi* system of decision making.

neobehaviorism
n. **1.** Any form of behaviorism that differs from that of J. B. Watson. **2.** A form of psychological theory and research that focuses on stimuli and responses as data but allows mental concepts as explanations for the observable.

neocortex

n. Newer portion of the cortex found in the brain of mammals. It is about 2–5 mm thick and contains some 100 billon cells. The distinctive characteristic of neocortex (also known as neopallium or isocortex) is that it is composed by six different layers (numbered from I to VI). The neocortex is the type of cerebral cortex most recent in evolution. Archicortex and paleocortex (both referred as allocortex) are phylogenetically older and contain a lower number of layers. The neocortex contains the body of the neurons (gray matter). With evolution, the sulci (grooves) and gyri (wrinkles) increase, increasing the total area of the neocortex. It is assumed that the neocortex is crucial in complex forms of cognition, such as language, complex perception, and reasoning.   – A A

neo-Darwinism

n. Neo-Darwinism is the synthesis during the early decades of the 20th century of Darwin's original theory of natural selection, Mendelian genetics, and mathematical population genetics. Darwin's theory lacked a modern theory of genetics, which was provided around 1900, when Mendel's work entered the scientific mainstream. Mendel's work showed that genes were transmitted discretely between generations rather than as a result of blending the genes from the male and female. For example, a recessive gene transmitted from parent to child retains its characteristics in the offspring apart from mutations. The details of how Mendelian genetics could be integrated with natural selection and the inheritance of continuous traits were provided by the field of mathematical population genetics, beginning with the work of Ronald Fisher in 1918. Fisher developed a model in which continuous traits such as height or intelligence are influenced by many discrete genes, each with small effects which result in genetically based correlations between parents and offspring. This work revolutionized evolutionary science and led to a number of landmark publications: Fisher's *The Genetical Theory of Natural Selection*

(1930), Sewall Wright's *Evolution in Mendelian Populations* (1931), and J. B. S. Haldane's *The Causes of Evolution* (1932). Later work, notably Theodosius Dobzhansky's *Genetics and the Origin of Species* (1937), Ernst Mayr's *Systematics and the Origin of Species* (1942), G. G. Simpson's *Tempo and Mode in Evolution* (1944), and G. Ledyard Stebbins's *Variation and Evolution in Plants* (1950), applied neo-Darwinism to natural populations of plants and animals, resulting in what is often termed "the modern synthetic theory of evolution," or the modern synthesis.   – K M

neo-Freudian

adj. Of or relating to any psychological approach that has evolved from the psychoanalysis of Sigmund Freud but has altered or added to it in some way, usually by focusing on the individual and his or her relations with the external world. Neo-Freudian theorists include Erik Erikson, George Klein, Heinz Kohut, Karen Horney, and Margaret Mahler.

neologism

n. **1.** A newly coined word or phrase or a new use for an old word. Thus the new word *def* means "good" and the word *radical* has also been used to mean "good." **2.** The use of a nonsense word by a person with some form of aphasia, dementia, or psychosis.

Neonatal Behavioral Assessment Scale

n. (NBAS) A neonatal scale of development which assesses neurological and behavioral development from birth to 2 months of age. The scale consists of 14 neurological items and 26 behavioral items. Also called the neonatal Behavioral Assessment Scale and the Brazelton Neonatal Behavioral Assessment Scale.

neonatal development

n. All the progressive changes in body, mind, and behavior that occur in the first few weeks after birth.

neonate

n. An infant in the first few weeks of life.

nerve

n. A bundle of nerve cells running together in a branching path outside the central nervous system and usually encased in a myelin sheath. Nerves connect the brain with the rest of the body and may be afferent, efferent, or mixed in function.

nerve cell

n. An individual unit in the nervous system defined by a cell wall and consisting of a cell body, an axon, and one or more dendrites. The cell body carries out the biological maintenance of the cell and sums the electrical impulses which are received via the dendrites. The dendrite or dendrites act as receivers for impulses from other nerves and may form as many as 10,000 synaptic connections with the axons of other nerve cells. The axon is a single tree-shaped structure that carries electrical impulses from the cell body down its length, which varies between a fraction of a millimeter and several feet in length, and causes the release of neurotransmitters at the end of its many branches, which may connect with as many as 10,000 dendrites of other nerve cells. Also called a neuron.

nerve deafness

n. An inability to hear due to malfunction of the inner ear or the auditory nerve. By far the most common cause is death of hair cells in the cochlea caused by loud sounds.

nerve ending

n. The terminus of an axon that does not synapse with another neuron, including basket endings, flower-spray endings, free nerve endings, Krause end bulbs, and Meissner's corpuscles.

nerve fiber

n. The axon of a neuron; the elongated portion of the neuron that carries electrical impulses forward from the cell body.

nerve growth factor

n. (NGF) A hormone produced in smooth muscle cells that stimulates growth and development in spinal and sympathetic ganglia as well as playing a role in their maintenance.

nerve impulse

n. A wave of electrical depolarization which travels along the cell wall of a neuron or chain of neurons and is the chief means of transmitting information in the nervous system.

nerve pathway

n. **1.** A route through the nervous system of a neural impulse. **2.** A chain of neuronal connections that have a specific function within the nervous system.

nervous breakdown

n. A folk term for any mental illness that causes significant interference in daily living.

nervous system

n. The complex organization of neurons in the body that enables the senses, exercises control over bodily functioning, and is associated with mental events. It includes the brain, spinal cord, and peripheral nerves, which can be divided into the autonomic nervous system and the somatic nervous system.

network model

n. Any theory of psychological functioning which includes nodes connected to one or more other nodes by excitory and inhibitory pathways. The nodes are generally described as being mental representations of information and the links as representations of different kinds of associations among the nodes.

neuralgia

n. Pain along the course of a nerve or nerve tract caused by damage to or malfunction of the nerve, which is usually sharp, spasmodic, and recurrent.

neural imaging

n. The process of creating pictures of nerves and their functioning such as functional magnetic resonance imaging and electron microscopy.

neural mechanisms of learning

n. An interdisciplinary area of study seeking to identify the chemical and neural processes in all the many kinds of learning of which humans are capable. Such studies usually focus on axonic growth, dendritic branching, and the chemicals involved in memory at different brain sites.

neural network
n. 1. Any set of interconnected neurons in the central nervous system. 2. In cognitive science, a hypothesized organization of the mind in which there are semantic nodes connected by defined relationships. 3. A form of computer programming intended to model the mind in which programs create a structure of semantic nodes with defined relationships which alter to accommodate inherent structures of input data, thus modeling learning in the human brain.

neural network models
n. In cognitive science, a hypothesized organization of the mind in which there are semantic nodes connected by defined relationships.

neurasthenia
n. An archaic term for a mental condition in which the individual feels fatigued and weak, suffers from sleep disturbances, and often has miscellaneous neuralgias and joint stiffness without any obvious physical cause. Today the condition would be labeled as undifferentiated somatoform disorder.

neurilemma
n. Chains of Schwann cells making up the external myelin sheath of neurons in the peripheral nervous system. Also called neurolemma.

neuroanatomy
n. The study of the structure and function of the nervous system and all its constituent parts.

neurobiology
n. The study of the development, structure, function, biochemistry, and physiology of the nervous system.

neurochemistry
n. The study of the atomic, ionic, and molecular processes involved in the nervous system

and their use to describe and predict larger cellular or behavioral aspects of the functioning of the nervous system.

neurocognition
n. The study of the relationships between neural processes and thought processes.

neuroendocrine
adj. Of or relating to the processes of interaction between the central nervous system and the endocrine glands.

neuroendocrine system
n. Includes the hypothalamus, pituitary gland, and all endocrine glands, including the adrenal glands and the reproductive glands. The hypothalamus, in response to psychological and/or sensory influences, releases a hormone which stimulates the pituitary gland to activate other endocrine glands to produce their specific hormones.   – vs

neuroendocrinology
n. A scientific discipline which investigates the interaction of the central nervous system (CNS) and the autonomic nervous system (ANS) with the secretion of glandular hormones. Neurons in the CNS interact with the endocrine system via the pituitary gland, which directs the activity of the endocrine system. The pituitary gland and the parasympathetic and sympathetic divisions of the ANS respond to stimulation from the hypothalamus, regulator of homeostasis, and then signal the endocrine glands to increase or decrease hormonal output. When neuroendocrinologists study psychological stimulation such as emotional stress or pleasure, the term *psychoneuroendocrinology* is used.   – vs

neuroglia
n. Any tissue made up of glial cells, which are nonneural cells within the nervous system which provide structural support, nutrition, or other assistance to nerve cells. Two types of glial cells, oligodendrocites and Schwann cells, form the myelin sheath, which surrounds nerve tracts and increases the speed of impulse transmission. Other types of glial cells include astrocytes, which are star-shaped

cells which outnumber neural cells by 10 to 1 in the brain; microglia, which provide immune function in the brain; and ependymal cells, which line the walls of the ventricles within the brain.

neurohypophysis
n. Another name for the pituitary gland.

neuroimaging technique
n. Any process of creating pictures of nerves and their functioning such as functional magnetic resonance imaging and electron microscopy.

neuroleptic
adj. Of or relating to an ability to alter the functioning of the nervous system and most often applied to drugs used to treat psychotic disorders. Also called antipsychotic.

neurolinguistic programming
n. (NLP) A program of psychotherapy and personal growth which attempts to reprogram the mind in more useful ways using techniques which incorporate ideas borrowed from linguistics, cognitive psychology, and sensory awareness which has also found popularity in education and business management.

neurolinguistics
n. The study of the interaction between brain function and linguistic behavior, which often focuses on deficits in language due to damage to different brain areas.

neuromodulation
n. The process of regulating synaptic transmission of electrical impulses by means of modifying the concentrations of chemicals and/or the density of chemical receptors present in synapses. This is one of the mechanisms by which drugs produce tolerance.

neuromuscular disorder
n. Any of several disorders in which muscle coordination is adversely affected by trauma or disease in the nervous system, including muscular dystrophy, myasthenia gravis, and all the myopathies.

neuron
n. An individual unit in the nervous system defined by a cell wall and consisting of a cell body, an axon, and one or more dendrites. The cell body carries out the biological maintenance of the cell and sums the electrical impulses which are received via the dendrites. The dendrite or dendrites act as receivers for impulses from other nerves and may form as many as 10,000 synaptic connections with the axons of other nerve cells. The axon is a single tree-shaped structure that carries electrical impulses from the cell body down its length, which varies between a fraction of a millimeter and several feet in length, and causes the release of neurotransmitters at the end of its many branches, which may connect with as many as 10,000 dendrites of other nerve cells.

neuron receptor site
n. A point on the surface of a dendrite that has an electrochemical configuration which will cause certain neurotransmitters and other similarly shaped chemicals to bind to it temporarily. This changes the electrochemical state of the dendrite in ways which tend either to inhibit or to excite electrical impulses in the neuron of which the dendrite is a part.

neuropathic
adj. Of or relating to disease or dysfunction of the nervous system.

neuropathy
n. Disease or disorder of the nervous system.

neuropeptide
n. A short chain of amino acids produced in the nervous system and functioning as either a hormone or a nervous transmitter. These include endogenous painkillers such as the endorphins and enkephalins, hypothalamic releasing hormones, pituitary hormones such as growth hormone and prolactin, and general nervous system hormones such as substance P and neurotensin.

neurophysiology
n. The study of the structure and function of nerve cells, nerves, and nervous systems.

neuropsychological assessment

n. Cognitive evaluation approached from a clinical neuropsychology perspective. It includes the assessment of different cognitive areas such as attention, memory, language, visual-perceptual processing, constructive skills, praxis abilities, spatial abilities, and executive functions. Usually, neuropsychological assessment has one or several of the following purposes: (1) to pinpoint a patient's cognition frequently but not necessarily after an abnormal brain condition, in order to describe the pattern of impairments that may have occurred, that is, to pinpoint his/her current cognitive status; (2) to analyze current symptoms and signs, in order to identify fundamental syndromes; (3) to suggest potential underlying pathological processes; (4) to suggest rehabilitative and compensatory strategies; (5) to provide additional information for a differential diagnosis. Neuropsychological assessment instruments include test batteries, aimed to evaluate different cognitive domains (Halstead-Reitan Neuropsychological Test Battery) or different abilities in a particular domain (e.g., different linguistic abilities, such as verbal fluency, language understanding, language repetition, naming, e.g., Boston Diagnostic Aphasia Examination) and tests targeting a specific ability (e.g., Wisconsin Card Sorting).   – A A

neuropsychology

n. Study of the brain organization of cognition and behavior under normal and abnormal conditions. The major topics included in neuropsychology are aphasia, alexia, agraphia, acalculia, apraxia, amnesia, agnosia, visuo-perceptual impairments, executive functioning disorders, dementia, developmental disorders, and the like. Neuropsychology is in consequence the study of the brain organization of language (perception, memory, etc.) under normal and abnormal conditions. As in any scientific area, two major objectives can be distinguished: (1) a fundamental objective (i.e., acquiring knowledge and understanding the phenomena under study; in the case of neuropsychology, how cognition and behavior organization are

represented in the brain and how they can be impaired in cases of brain pathology) and (2) an applied objective (i.e., the use of this basic knowledge for assessment and rehabilitation in cases of brain pathology). Two major approaches in neuropsychology can be separated: experimental neuropsychology and clinical neuropsychology. Most neuropsychologists, however, work in clinical areas. Neuropsychological assessment and cognitive rehabilitation have represented the two major professional activities of clinical neuropsychologists.   – A A

neuroscience

n. An interdisciplinary approach to the study of the nervous system that includes anatomy, biochemistry, cognitive modeling, pharmacology, and physiology,

neurosis

n. A general and somewhat archaic term for any pervasive and enduring pattern of maladjustment that causes significant personal distress but does not involve psychotic features or stem from physiological problems. This includes anxiety disorders, personality disorders, somatoform disorders, dissociative disorders, some sexual disorders, eating disorders, some sleep disorders, impulse control disorders, and adjustment disorders.

neurotic

1. *n.* A person who suffers from a pervasive and enduring pattern of maladjustment that causes significant personal distress but does not involve psychotic features or stem from physiological problems. **2.** *adj.* Of or relating to neurosis.

neuroticism

n. **1.** The degree to which an individual chronically engages in dysfunctional emotional, behavioral, and cognitive actions. **2.** One of the putative "big five" dimensions of personality, which measures the frequency of experiencing negative emotions, tendency to interpret stimuli as threatening, social withdrawal, and a tendency to react with stress to minor frustrations at the high end and emotional stability and positive emotions at the low end.

neurotoxin

n. Any substance that causes temporary or permanent damage to or disrupts the function of any part of the nervous system. This includes many spider, insect, and snake venoms, as well as chemicals such as carbon monoxide, nicotine, and alcohol.

neurotransmitter

n. Any chemical that is released from an axon terminal of one neuron which attaches to a dendritic receptor site of another neuron and increases or decreases the chance of a wave of depolarization in the second neuron. Neurotransmitters include acetylcholine, dopamine, norepinephrine, serotonin, GABA, and glutamate.

Newman-Keuls test

n. A post hoc procedure in an analysis of variance in which group means are ranked and a t statistic is used to test the difference between the largest and smallest groups' means, the smallest and second largest, and so on, as long as significant differences are found.

nicotine

n. The psychoactive chemical in tobacco, which works by mimicking acetylcholine and triggering the release of dopamine, norepinephrine, and vasopressin. In low doses nicotine produces a stimulating effect with increased alertness and calmness while at higher doses it causes dizziness, diarrhea, vomiting, tremors, and paralysis and can cause death by paralyzing the diaphragm. In its common usage patterns nicotine is the most highly addictive drug.

nicotinic receptor

n. The site of action of acetylcholine at the neuromuscular junction, and at preganglionic synapses in the sympathetic nervous system. This receptor site is stimulated directly by ionic action, a more rapid level of activation than the slower metabotropic muscarinic receptor for acetylcholine. The ionic action opens channels in the neural membrane for a direct excitatory effect on neural transmission. Curare (South American arrow tip poison) inhibits nicotinic cholinergic receptor sites.   – vs

nictitating membrane

n. A thin transparent or semitransparent membrane beneath the eyelid that can be drawn across the eye to protect it without totally obscuring vision, which is present in a diverse group of animals including birds, reptiles, and mammals such as rabbits and cats.

night blindness

n. An inability to see in dim light. In some cases this is an inherited condition; in other cases it may be due to vitamin A deficiency or the death or degeneration of the retinal cones. Also called nyctalopia.

nightmare

n. A dream in which there is intense negative emotion, usually fear but sometimes anger, sadness, or disgust. People sometimes awaken abruptly in nightmares and continue feeling the emotion that occurred in the dream.

night terror

n. A disorder in which an individual experiences recurrent episodes in which he or she abruptly awakens from sleep feeling terrified and often screams upon awakening. Usually there is no memory of a dream, or if there is, it is a single image and there is often amnesia for the terror after a night's sleep. Also called sleep terror disorder.

night vision

n. Seeing in very dim light in which only the rods of the eyes are functioning as cones need a higher level of illumination to work. In night vision the center of the visual field is insensitive and there is no perception of color. Also called scotopia.

nirvana

n. In Buddhism, a state of being in which the individual is in complete contact with reality without conceptual distortion including no sense of self and no sense of desire for things to be other than they are. It is characterized by the cessation of passion, aggression, and ignorance; the end of the creation of mental cause and effect (karma); and a disinterested compassion (*maitri*) coupled with a gentle sense of humor.

nitric oxide

n. (NO) A colorless, odorless gas which easily separates into free radicals, sometimes acts as a neurotransmitter, is a vasodilator and a bronchodilator, and relaxes smooth muscles. It should not be confused with nitrous oxide (N_2O), or laughing gas, which is used as an anesthetic and for recreational purposes.

nocturnal emission

n. A sexual ejaculation that occurs during sleep, usually during dreams and during REM stage sleep. This is very common among young males in all cultures. Orgasms during sleep tend to occur less often and to begin several years later in females than males. Also known as a wet dream.

nodes of Ranvier

n. The regularly spaced gaps in the myelin sheath surrounding axon fibers in which the axon is exposed to ambient liquids. Nerve impulses in myelinated fibers pass very quickly because depolarization at one end of a myelinated section causes nearly instantaneous depolarization throughout the section so impulses jump from one node to another in a process called saltatory transmission. It is only at the nodes of Ranvier that there is actually an exchange of ions across the cell wall, which takes a small but significant amount of time.

noise, white

n. Short, random patterns of sound which have equal energy at all frequencies when averaged over time such as static heard on the radio when the radio is tuned between stations.

nominal scale

n. Nominal scales lack all three key scale properties: magnitude, equal intervals, and absolute zero. As such, nominal scales are simply a means of labeling or categorizing data but do not express any quantitative relationships among variables, categories, or values. For example, demographic data, such as sex, is often converted into a nominal scale for data entry by assigning the category 1 to men and 2 to women. These numbers serve solely as numerical labels; they do not represent a quantitative relationship between variables. The only appropriate mathematical calculations for nominal data are frequency and mode. — BJM

nomological network

n. A predictable pattern of interrelationships between theoretical constructs and observations which establish the construct validity of a test or measure.

nomological validity

n. A predictable pattern of interrelationships between theoretical constructs and observations which establish the construct validity of a test or measure.

nomothetic

adj. Of or relating to the formulation of general rules, as opposed to the study of individuals.

nonalcoholic Korsakoff's psychosis

n. Korsakoff's syndrome and Korsakoff's psychosis reflect a depletion of nutrients, notably a thiamine deficiency. This vitamin deficiency is most commonly caused by the poor diet of persons experiencing chronic alcoholism, but the lack of essential vitamins can have other explanations. For example, surgical patients on severely restricted diets, patients recovering from bariatric surgery, persons with severe pneumonia, and persons experiencing prolonged vomiting may all be at risk for malnutrition. Extended exposure to these conditions may result in the vitamin deficiencies found in patients with Korsakoff's syndrome.

The loss of memory experienced by persons with nonalcoholic Korsakoff's syndrome is similar to that experienced by those with alcohol causation. These individuals are all impaired in their ability to use their long-term memories and to remember the order of temporal events; they usually remain virtually unimpaired in other cognitive pursuits. — TJM

▶ *See also* **KORSAKOFF'S PSYCHOSIS** *and* **KORSAKOFF'S SYNDROME**

nondetermination, coefficient of

n. (k) An index of the variance between two variables not explained by their covariance. It is given by the formula $1 - r^2$ where r is the Pearson product-moment correlation between two variables, or $1 - R^2$ in a multiple regression. Also called the residual and the coefficient of alienation.

nondirectional test

n. A statistical test of the difference between means which does not specify which mean is expected to be larger, and so probability calculations are used which include both possibilities or both tails of a frequency distribution of probabilities. Also called a two-tailed test.

nondirective therapy

n. An approach to psychotherapy developed by Carl Rogers in which it is assumed that clients have inherent tendencies and capacities to grow and develop and will do so if freed of social judgment. And so the therapist provides a supportive environment and helps the client notice and clarify the matters the client raises without judging the client or attempting to fit his or her experience into a set of preconceptions. Also called client-centered therapy.

nondisjunction

n. In reproduction, the failure of chromosomal pairs to split into two pairs so that one of the daughter cells gets both chromosomal pairs and the other lacks one or more chromosomes.

nonequivalent groups design

n. A quasi-experimental research design in which individuals are not randomly assigned to groups, and existing or convenient groups which differ on an independent variable are selected, such as those in two hospitals or schools, or in different cultures. The groups are measured at the beginning and end of the treatment and compared with each other, but the comparisons are suspect as there are likely to be differences between the groups before the experiment which have an effect on the dependent variable, making group comparisons difficult to interpret.

nonessential amino acids

n. Any of a group of organic molecules containing both at least one amine (NH_2) and at least one carboxyl (COOH) group which can be synthesized within the body. Amino acids are the building blocks of which the body is largely composed.

nonfluent aphasia ▶ See MOTOR APHASIA

nonidentical twins

n. Two babies born of the same mother who shared their gestational period and were formed from the unions of two separate sperm and ova and generally share about half their genes. By contrast, identical twins are born of an embryo that splits in two and develops into two separate babies with identical genes. Also called fraternal twins.

nonintermittent reinforcement schedule

n. A process of reward in which each target behavior is rewarded regardless of the timing or sequence of the behaviors.

nonlinear

n. Any relationship between two variables whose graphic depiction is not a straight line and which cannot be expressed in the mathematical formula of the form $y = mx + b$.

nonparametric statistic

n. Any statistical test which does not make assumptions about the distribution of the population from which a sample has been drawn and is usually used with nominal and ordinal data. Common assumptions which nonparametric tests do not use are normal distribution and homogeneity of variance.

nonprobability sample

n. Any sample selected by a method other than a random process.

nonreactive measure

n. Any observation of behavior of which the subject is unaware and so is uninfluenced by the process of observation.

non-REM sleep

n. Any portion of sleep in which rapid eye movements do not occur. Rapid eye movements are characteristic of sleep during dream periods. Also called NREM sleep.

nonreversal shift

n. An experimental learning task in which subjects are first rewarded for selecting a certain type of stimulus such as a square instead of a circle, then the contingencies of reward are switched so that a characteristic that has been present but irrelevant, such as color, becomes the basis of receiving or not receiving a reward.

nonsense syllable

n. A string of three letters in a consonant-vowel-consonant pattern, such as *nug*, which does not form a word in the language being used. These are often used in memory and recognition tasks in part because they are assumed to be free of previous learning.

nontaster

n. A person who has no experience of taste when given a solution of propylthiouracil. About 25% of the population cannot taste propylthiouracil, an inability which is associated with generally poor taste perception and willingness to eat a wider than normal variety of foods.

nonverbal behavior

n. All overt actions other than those of language, and especially those judged to convey information about the intentions, emotions, or other aspects of the mental state of the individual. Facial expressions, postures, and gestures are particularly good information sources and often convey at least as much information as the verbal channel.

nonverbal communication

n. The conveyance of information through facial expression, gestures, postures, tone of voice, and other behavior, which is often more effective than is the verbal channel of communication among humans. Among humans and some animals, forms of nonverbal communication are learned and vary among cultures, subcultures, and other subgroupings of the species.

nonverbal hot spot

n. A term coined originally by Paul Ekman and Mark Frank to refer to any occurrence in which the messages sent in verbal and nonverbal signals are inconsistent with each other, or with the context. It is often used as a method for detecting lies. But a hot spot is not necessarily a sign of lying; rather, it is an indicator of areas of concealed thoughts or feelings.

nonverbal intelligence

n. Any capacity to learn or perform tasks other than through words. This is usually measured as performance intelligence on intelligence tests and correlates only moderately with verbal intelligence.

nonverbal intelligence tests

n. Any measure of mental capacity which does not use words as either the question or the response. These include tests such as putting a puzzle together, arranging pictures to form a coherent story, and perceiving relationships among complex patterns.

nonverbal leakage

n. Refers to the giving away of one's mental state or intention through nonverbal behaviors, which are often unnoticed. This term is often used to describe behavioral cues to lying.

nonverbal test

n. Any measure which does not use words as a query or a response.

noradrenaline

n. A largely excitory neurotransmitter of the catecholamine family synthesized from tyrosine in the adrenal glands and in the brainstem. It is important in maintaining alertness, physiological arousal, task performance, and physical exertion. Also known as norepinephrine.

noradrenergic

adj. Of or relating to the release or response to noradrenaline or norepinephrine.

norepinephrine

n. A largely excitory neurotransmitter of the catecholamine family synthesized from tyrosine in the adrenal glands and in the brainstem. It is important in maintaining alertness, physiological arousal, task performance, and physical exertion. Also known as noradrenaline.

norm

n. **1.** A generally accepted standard of behavior within a cultural or subcultural group. **2.** An average or usual range of values for a variable, as in the arithmetic mean of a group of test scores used as a standard for comparison.

normal curve

n. A theoretical and continuous probability distribution that is a function of the expected value and variance about the mean. The normal curve is approximated many times in nature in observations of probabilistic events such as random error in measurement. Also called a bell curve and the normal or Gaussian distribution.

normal distribution

n. A class of probability distributions that are depicted graphically as a unimodal (single-peak), symmetrical, bell-shaped density curve with the majority of scores in the middle of the distribution and fewer scores near the ends of the distribution (the ends of the curve extend to infinity). While the area under a normal distribution curve is always constant (equal to 1), the height and spread of the curve vary as a mathematical function of the mean and standard deviation. If data is drawn from a normally distributed population, 68% of the values are within one standard deviation of the mean, 95% are within two standard deviations, and 99.7% are within three standard deviations (this is known as the 68-95-99.7 rule or the empirical rule). As such, the vast majority of scores on a normal distribution will fall within three standard deviations from the mean. While there are many possible configurations for a normal distribution based on various means and standard deviations, a standard normal distribution always has a mean of 0 and a standard deviation of 1.   – BJM

normality

n. **1.** Conforming to that which is expected of the social, age, and cultural group of which one is a member. **2.** Free from mental disease or disorder. **3.** Lacking significant statistical difference from a norm.

normal probability plot

n. A theoretical and continuous probability distribution that is a function of the expected value and variance about the mean. The normal curve is approximated many times in nature in observations of probabilistic events such as random error in measurement. Also called a bell curve and the normal or Gaussian distribution.

normative

adj. **1.** Of or relating to standards or expected values as in obtaining a normative score on a test. **2.** Prescribing or establishing standards for comparison as in normative decision making.

normative reference group

n. Any group that is taken as a standard for self-comparison by an individual. Reference groups can be real or imagined, identifiable individuals who meet in one location, or statistical or theoretical entities defined across space or time by similarity on one or more variables. Thus a reference group might be all the members of a culture, a group of neighborhood children, or all those individuals across the world who are able to read Sumerian tablets or solve equations in tensor calculus.

norm group

n. A group used to establish a standard against which others are compared.

norm-referenced test

n. A standardized test that reports an individual's results in relationship to the performance of other test takers, rather than on the basis of a preset criterion (as is the case with a criterion-referenced test). Norm-referenced scoring is a direct reflection of the comparison of a given person's results to the results of the norm group. As such, the overall score is not important; rather, the key factor is examining an individual's performance in comparison to others. For example, a student who misses 50% of the questions on a norm-referenced test may still score high if most other students missed more than 50% of the questions. Norm-referenced tests may be referred to as "scaled" or "curved" because of the importance of relative position in scoring. In a norm-referenced test, performance of a given individual is calculated in direct comparison to that of the norm group.   – BJM

nose
n. The organ of olfaction containing two nostrils or nares through which air is normally inspired, olfactory epithelium containing olfactory receptors, and a septum which divides the air passages. The nose modulates the temperature and humidity of air as it passes toward the nasal cavities, which contain the sensory receptors.

nosology
n. The systematic classification and study of diseases and disorders.

nuclear family
n. A conception of the family as limited to two parents and their offspring. This is often considered the norm for family organization in Euro-American societies.

nuclear magnetic resonance
n. The rapid tilting and realignment of protons during exposure to high-frequency radiation in a strong magnetic field. This gives off enough energy to be detectable, and as different molecules react to and so emit different frequencies of energy, images can be made of tissues which have different levels of constituent molecules in magnetic resonance imaging (MRI).

nucleic acid
n. A long chain of molecules consisting of a nitrogenous base, a sugar, and one or more phosphate groups which makes up DNA and RNA, which contain genetic information and are necessary for the synthesis of proteins within cells.

nucleus
n. **1.** A core or essential part around which other parts are gathered or grouped. **2.** The ovate central compartment of most living cells, which contains the genetic material and controls the cell's metabolism, reproduction, and growth. **3.** In the nervous system, a mass of cell bodies with associated functions.

nucleus accumbens
n. Either of two masses of cell bodies in the basal forebrain where dopamine secreting neurons in the ventral tegment terminate, forming an important pathway in the brain's pleasure and reward system.

nuisance variable
n. A variable of no interest to an experimenter which may influence the relationship between dependent and independent variables, making interpretation of results less certain.

null hypothesis
n. The formal idea that any differences between groups in an experiment can be attributed to random variation, whose improbability is used as a demonstration that the difference between groups is likely to be due to experimental variables.

null hypothesis significance testing
n. Comparison of a test statistic to a preselected criterion value of the statistic to determine the acceptability of the null hypothesis. The significance level for rejection of the null hypothesis is set by convention usually at a probability of 5% or less.

number-completion test
n. A measure of intellectual ability in which a subject is given a sequence of numbers and required either to fill in a missing number or supply the next number in the sequence. Thus is the sequence 2, 4, 6, __, 10 the missing number is 8, and in the sequence 2, 3, 5, 7, ___. the missing number is 11.

nurturance

n. **1.** The provision of the physical and emotional factors required by a living thing for its well-being and growth. **2.** A hypothesized need or motivation to provide the physical and emotional factors required by another living thing for its well-being and growth.

nurture

n. The total of all environmental factors including physical care, emotional attachments, and upbringing style that contribute to the growth and development of an organism, as contrasted with the contribution of heredity (nature).

nyctalopia

n. An inability to see in dim light. In some cases this is an inherited condition; in other cases it may be due to vitamin A deficiency or the death or degeneration of the retinal cones. Also called night blindness.

nymphomania

n. A state of excessive and uncontrollable craving and seeking of sexual stimulation and gratification in a woman. Typically the woman frantically and somewhat indiscriminately pursues sexual activity without ever reaching orgasm or feeling satisfied.

nymphomaniac

n. A woman who suffers from insatiable craving and seeking of sexual stimulation and gratification; some women who have this condition never reach orgasm or feel sexually satisfied. This term has been applied to any woman who acts on normal sexual desires in sexually repressive cultures.

nystagmus

n. Rapid, involuntary, and rhythmic movement of the eyeballs. This may be caused by intoxication or malfunction in the brainstem, cerebellum, or vestibular system.

obedience

n. Acting in compliance with a command or other directive such as obeying the law.

obesity

n. A state of having a significant excess of adipose or fatty tissue. No exact division between being mildly overweight and being obese is generally accepted, but having 30% or more of body weight composed of fat would certainly be obese. Obesity is considered attractive and desirable in some cultures and repulsive in others. Obesity is correlated with numerous health problems, including cardiovascular disease, diabetes, gallstones, and some forms of cancer. Most obesity is the result of adopting a lifestyle which includes eating too much and exercising too little. Some obesity is due to organic problems such as hypothyroidism or damage to the amygdala, temporal lobe, or ventromedial nucleus of the hypothalamus.

object blindness

n. A type of visual agnosia in which there is a failure to recognize objects that are clearly seen.

object concept

n. In Piagetian psychology, the understanding that things are real, physical entities which move in the same space as the child and continue to exist after they leave the perceptual field. This understanding is believed to be lacking in young infants.

object constancy

n. The perceptual tendency to see objects as unchanging as the light reflected from them changes with movement, occlusion, and changes in illumination or distance. Thus, if we see a dog, it looks like the same dog if it turns around or is partially obscured by a bush or runs into a shadow despite the considerable variation in the patterns of light reflected from it which strike our retina. This is a very difficult capacity for artificial intelligence systems to mimic.

objectivism

n. The philosophical point of view which accepts that both physical and metaphysical aspects of the external world can be accurately assessed independently of individual or cultural perspectives, limitations, or bias.

object libido

n. The sexual energy or desire directed toward something or someone external to the self.

object of instinct

n. Any object toward which libido is directed and which satisfies the aim of the instinct when it is obtained. Thus a glass of ginger ale may be the object of an instinct whose aim is to relieve thirst. Also called instinctual object.

object permanence

n. In Piagetian psychology, the understanding that things continue to exist after they leave the perceptual field. This understanding is believed to be lacking in young infants and is a part of a mature object concept.

object recognition

n. The understanding that some thing is a particular thing or belongs to a particular category of things. Thus one might recognize one's own mother or recognize that a thing is a cat. This occurs in natural perception despite large variation in the sensory information received from the object at different times and in different circumstances and is a very difficult process for artificial information systems to duplicate.

object relations

n. In psychoanalysis, all of one's emotional connections to other people, things, activities, or ideas. This is a focus of ego psychology and object-relations theory but was a relatively minor part of Sigmund Freud's original theory.

object-relations theory

n. Any of several later developments in psychoanalysis in which relationships between self and the objects of the external world and the relationships among mental objects are taken as the most important aspects for understanding the individual.

object representation

n. **1.** In cognitive psychology, a hypothesized model of an object in the mind or in the brain. **2.** In psychoanalysis, the mental image of an object toward which desire or aggression may be felt.

object theory

n. Any of several later developments in psychoanalysis in which relationships between self and the objects of the external world and the relationships among mental objects are taken as the most important aspects for understanding the individual. Also called object-relations theory.

oblique rotation

n. In factor analysis, a solution in which the axes are correlated rather than orthogonal or at right angles to one another in a spatial representation of the factors.

oblique solution ▶ *See* **OBLIQUE ROTATION**

observational learning

n. Any relatively permanent change in behavior or thought which takes place after watching or otherwise sensing another being acting in some particular way. Also called vicarious learning.

observational method

n. Any scientific approach which involves recording information without interference with the subject or process under scrutiny. This approach is often used in developmental psychology, ethology, and social psychology.

observational study

n. Any research project that involves recording information without interference with the subject or process under scrutiny. This approach is often used in developmental psychology, ethology, and social psychology.

obsession

n. A recurrent and persistent thought, image, idea, or impulse that causes the person distress and seems intrusive and inappropriate and beyond one's will to stop. Obsessions are often quite frustrating as they seem alien to the self, and yet the person is unable to prevent or stop the thought process involved.

obsessive-compulsive disorder

n. A disorder characterized by (1) recurrent and persistent thoughts, images, ideas, or impulses that cause the person distress and seem intrusive and inappropriate and are beyond one's will to stop; they are often quite frustrating as they seem alien to the self, and yet the person is unable to prevent or stop the thought process involved. It is also characterized by (2) repetitive behaviors such as hand washing, checking things, or mental acts the person feels compelled to perform in response to an obsession and often with rigid rules intended to ward off distress or the occurrence of some dreaded event.

Occam's razor/Ockham's razor

n. Occam's razor is a logical principle attributed to the medieval philosopher William of Occam (or Ockham). The principle states that one should not make more assumptions than the minimum needed. This principle is also called the principle of parsimony, and it underlies scientific modeling and theory building. The principle also admonishes one to choose the simplest of a set of otherwise equivalent models of a given phenomenon. In any given model, Occam's razor helps us to "shave off" those concepts, variables, or constructs that are not essential to explain the phenomenon. By doing that, developing the model becomes easier, and there is less chance of introducing inconsistencies, ambiguities, and redundancies.

The principle is considered essential for model building because of what is known as the "underdetermination of theories by data." For a given set of observations, there is always an infinite number of possible models explaining the same data. This is because a model normally represents an infinite number of possible cases, of which the observed cases are only a finite subset. The nonobserved cases are inferred by postulating general rules covering both actual and potential observations.

For example, through two data points in a diagram one can always draw a straight line and induce that all further observations will lie on that line. However, one could also draw an infinite variety of the most complicated curves passing through those same two points, and these curves would fit the empirical data just as well. Only Occam's razor would in this case guide one in choosing the "straight" (i.e., linear) relation as the best candidate model. Similar reasoning can be used for *n* data points lying in any kind of distribution.

Occam's razor is especially important for universal models, such as those developed in general systems theory, mathematics, or philosophy, because there the subject domain is of an unlimited complexity. If one starts with overly complicated foundations for a theory that potentially encompasses the universe, the chance of producing any manageable model is greatly reduced. Moreover, the principle is sometimes the only remaining guideline when entering domains of such a high level of abstraction that no concrete tests or observations can decide between rival models. In mathematical modeling of systems, the principle can be made more concrete in the form of the principle of uncertainty maximization: from your data, induce that model which minimizes the number of additional assumptions. – TJM

occipital

adj. Of or relating to the back of the head, which is called the occiput.

occipital lobe

n. Either of the rearmost areas of the cerebral hemispheres, which are involved in visual perception.

occupational stress

n. A prolonged state of physical and mental arousal resulting from demands from one's job, which can lead to prolonged fatigue, loss of motivation, burnout, stress disorders, and the general adaptation syndrome.

occupational therapy

n. (OT) A method of treating mental disorders or medical conditions by performing or learning to perform useful activities of daily living, job functions, or recreation. This is often used in conjunction with medical and/or psychological treatment and is intended to help the person adjust or readjust to independent functioning.

Ockham's razor ▶ *See* OCCAM'S RAZOR/OCKHAM'S RAZOR

ocular dominance

n. The degree to which neural impulses from one eye cause more response in the visual cortex than does corresponding information from the other eye. This leads stimuli presented only to the dominant eye to be seen more clearly than information presented only to the nondominant eye, and the unified field of visual perception is usually that seen by the dominant eye with the information from the nondominant eye overlaying it.

oculomotor nerve

n. Either of the third pair of cranial nerves which control the muscles which move the eye, alter its shape to focus it, constrict the pupil to control the amount of light entering the eye, and control the eyelid. The oculomotor nerve leads from the eye muscles to several centers in the midbrain near the superior colliculus.

Oedipal phase

n. In psychoanalysis, the phase of development in which the primary form of pleasure is immature genital play, which leads little boys to fall in love with their mother and hate their father and leads little girls to fall in love with their mother and envy their father's possession of a penis. Also called the phallic phase.

Oedipus complex

n. In psychoanalysis, the third phase of development, in which primary pleasure is derived from immature genital play. In little boys this typically leads to desire to have sex with the mother, feelings of rejection when she does not comply, and feelings of envy and hatred toward the father, who is seen as the a rival for the mother. The little boy wishes to kill and castrate his father and projects these desires onto his father, leading to fear of castration. Eventually this set of conflicts is repressed and the energy redirected into becoming what the culture defines a man to be so the little boy can grow up and marry a girl like the girl who married his father. Little girls typically fall in love with their mother and want to have sex with her and are frustrated by the mother's rejection of sexual advances and so they envy their father and particularly his possession of a penis, which seems to have the power to make the mother love him. The little girl then resents her mother as she believes her father has castrated her and the mother should have prevented this and has betrayed her for love of the father. This set of conflicts is repressed at the end of the period, and the energy goes into fulfilling what the culture defines as a woman's role, and the little girl grows up with the unconscious intention of marrying a man so as to gain possession of the power of his penis.

olfaction

n. The sense of smell, which includes a set of chemical detectors located in the mucus linings of the nose and nasal passages and nerves leading back to the olfactory bulbs on the bottom of the cerebral cortex.

olfactory

adj. Of or relating to the sense of smell or the set of chemical detectors located in the mucus linings of the nose and nasal passages and nerves leading back to olfactory bulbs on the bottom of the cerebral cortex.

olfactory bulb

n. Small bump on the bottom of the cerebral cortex which receives the nerve fibers from nasal scent receptors, connects with the olfactory cortex and amygdala, and is the only sensory system which bypasses the thalamus.

olfactory cortex

n. Cortical areas involved in olfactory reception and processing. The olfactory bulb situated in the base of the frontal lobes is the nerve involved in conducting the olfactory information from the olfactory epithelium to the brain (I cranial nerve). Olfactory information is directed to the olfactory cortex, or piriform cortex, in the temporal lobes. The pirifom cortex is included in the rhinencephalon ("olfactory brain"). The function of the piriform cortex relates to olfactory recognition. Olfactory information is also directed to the amygdala and the hypothalamus by the accessory olfactory bulb.   – A A

olfactory epithelium

n. Areas in the mucus membrane which lines the nasal cavities where olfactory receptors are located.

olfactory lobe

n. An area on the bottom of the cerebral cortex containing the olfactory bulbs, olfactory tract, and olfactory cortex which processes the sense of smell and is closely connected with emotional response. Also called the rhinencephalon.

olfactory nerve

n. Either of the first pair of cranial nerves which connect the smell receptors in the nasal epithelium with the olfactory lobe in the cerebral cortex.

olfactory receptor

n. Any of the spindle-shaped neurons in the nasal epithelium that react to particular chemicals which enter the nose with the breath and generate the impulses involved in the sense of smell.

olfactory tract

n. The nerve fiber that originates in the receptor cells in the nasal epithelium, forms tracts, and runs to the olfactory lobe in the cerebral cortex carrying information which constitutes the sense of smell.

oligarchy

n. An organizational structure characterized by rule- or decision-making power of a few. Decisions are typically made by people "at the top," who impose their decisions on subordinates.

omega squared

n. (ω^2) In analysis of variance, the percentage or proportion of the variance of the dependent variable associated with the relationship between the independent variables and the dependent variable.

omnibus test

n. **1.** Any statistical test of significance in which there are more than two groups being compared, as is often the case in analysis of variance in which the F ratio for the whole procedure is an omnibus test. **2.** A test which contains subtests embedded in its items whose scores are combined in a total score.

omnipotence of thought

n. The belief that one's wishes, beliefs, or thoughts affect the course of the external world, which is often characteristic of young children's thought and psychoanalysis suggests underlies some aspects of animism, magic, and religion.

one-sample *t* test

n. A test of the hypothesis that a sample is drawn from a population whose mean and standard deviation are known.

one-tailed probability

n. In inferential statistics, the probability that one would find a result as extreme as or more extreme than that actually found in one direction from the mean if the null hypothesis were true. The *one-tailed (1-tailed) probability* refers to the appearance of one end of a probability distribution far from the mean which appears similar to a tail. Since the area under probability distributions, such as the normal curve, in one end or tail is half that in the two tails combined, then the probability of obtaining an extreme result is half that of a 2-tailed probability, and thus a 1-tailed test has twice the statistical power of a 2-tailed test in symmetrical probability distributions.

one-tailed test

n. In inferential statistics, a one-tailed (1-tailed) test is one that tests the null hypothesis that an observed result is less extreme in a particular direction from the mean than would occur by chance. So a difference from the mean in the other direction would be attributed to chance no matter how much it differed from the mean. The criterion for deciding what size difference from the mean is sufficiently large as to be not attributed to chance is conventional and usually set at 5% probability.

one-way analysis of variance

n. An analysis of variance with a single independent variable which is testing the hypothesis that three or more samples are drawn from the same population.

online processing

n. Any form of data analysis that occurs during a period of connection between two or more information processing systems. An ATM is an example of an online processor as it connects with the user's bank, and both conduct data processing while they are connected via telephone or other lines.

ontogeny

n. The biological origin and development of an individual, as opposed to a group or a species.

ontology

n. The study of origins, including the origin of existence, of knowledge, and of reality. Originally ontology focused on metaphysical speculation but in recent years has focused on questions about the meaning of questions about existence deriving from existential philosophy and hermeneutics.

open-ended question

n. Item format in which there are no predefined response options or response categories to guide an individual's answer to a question. Open-ended questions provide the opportunity for unrestricted responses in a respondent's own words that are uninfluenced by predetermined response alternatives. The purpose of open-ended questions, which are often used in interviews, is to gather individualized data in greater depth and detail. The benefit of open-ended questions is that they elicit a range of responses and encourage the exploration of unique perceptions, views, and interpretations. The drawback of open-ended questions is that the coding and interpretation of the large volume of qualitative data obtained may be time-consuming and/or subject to interpretive bias.   – BJM

openness to experience

n. Openness to experience is one of the dimensions of the five factor model. It contrasts individuals who are intellectual, imaginative, sensitive, and open-minded with those who are down-to-earth, insensitive, and conventional. Openness to experience has been the most controversial of the big five factors, with some scholars noting that it possesses a greater breadth of meaning than the other four. Some authors emphasize sophistication and refinement of interests. Others emphasize the creative and imaginative component of this cluster of traits. Still others identify the factor as *intellect*, focusing on intellectual interests, preference for deeper and more effortful cognition, and the factor's correlation with intelligence tests. Open individuals enjoy deeper, more effortful thought and are attracted to the theoretical. They show a preference for liberal, as opposed to conservative, positions on political issues. Among the positive correlates of openness are absorption, moral development, and accepting attitudes toward minority groups, Finally, openness to experience is a major predictor of creativity.
                                                                                      – SJD

operant

n. In operant conditioning, a single class of behaviors which produce a particular effect in the world, such as pressing a lever, which allows a food pellet to drop into a feeding tray. The lever may be pressed in many different ways, and so it is the effect of the lever's being pressed and releasing a food pellet which constitutes the operant rather than a description of the behaviors themselves.

operant aggression

n. A threat or attack on another carried out for the purpose of obtaining a goal other than causing harm to the object of the attack. Thus a dog may attack another dog in order to keep a bone for itself rather than with intent to harm the other dog. Also called instrumental aggression.

operant behavior

n. Any behavior which brings about a defined effect in the world. Thus pressing a lever which allows a food pellet to drop into a feeding tray is an operant behavior. The lever may be pressed in many different ways, and so it is the effect of the lever's being pressed and releasing a food pellet which makes it an operant behavior rather than a description of the behavior itself, which, in another situation, would not be an operant behavior if it did not produce the effect.

operant conditioning

n. A form of learning in which an organism learns to act so as to bring about certain effects in the world. Thus a cat may learn that if it meows loudly on the porch, the door will be opened and it can enter the house. Also called instrumental conditioning.

operant level

n. The baseline or frequency of occurrence of a set of behaviors before a schedule of reinforcement is attached to the set of behaviors. Thus a rat newly introduced to a test apparatus will randomly press a lever before the lever presses start delivering food.

operant response

n. Any single behavior of an organism which achieves a reinforcement.

operating characteristic

n. In signal detection theory, a curve on a graph which represents the accuracy of a receiver operating at different levels of detectability with the probability of a correct detection on the vertical axis and the probability of a false alarm on the horizontal axis.

operational definition

n. A detailed description of the measurements used to define an experimental procedure, concept, or variable. The operational definition explains precisely how a numeric value is assigned to relevant constructs in a study. Typically, the operational definition will describe all the necessary steps or components for replicating the measurement or procedure.   – BJM

operationalism

n. An archaic approach to science and psychology in which it was supposed that concepts derive their meaning solely from the operations used to measure them. Thus intelligence was what intelligence tests measure and heat was what thermometers measure without reference to any other understanding of the world.

operationalization

n. The construction of a procedure to measure a theoretical construct.

operational stage

n. In Piagetian psychology, either of the stages of intellectual development in which the child is able to represent a problem mentally and carry out mental tests of different approaches to the problem. The stage of concrete operations runs from about 7 to 11 years of age, and the stage of formal operations begins at about 12 years of age and is characteristic of adult thought.

operationism

n. An archaic approach to science and psychology in which it was supposed that concepts derive their meaning solely from the operations used to measure them. Thus intelligence was what intelligence tests measure and heat was what thermometers measure without reference to any other understanding of the world.

opiate

n. Any drug derived from the juice of the Asiatic poppy, including codeine, morphine, opium, and heroin, which have strong analgesic and moderate soporific effects.

opinion

n. An attitude, belief, or judgment that is held to be true without conclusive proof.

opinion poll

n. A measure of the attitudes, beliefs, or judgments of a number of a sample of people intended to represent those of the population from which the sample is drawn. Opinion polls may be taken orally in person or via the telephone, on the Internet, or in written form.

opponent process

n. Any of a number of mechanisms in which two submechanisms act in opposite directions, the sum of which is the product of the mechanism. Thus in the opponent process theory of color perception, it is assumed that there are sets of two color receptors which produce opposite sensations of color and the action of one inhibits the other.

opponent-process theory

n. Any hypothesized mechanism in which two submechanisms act in opposite directions, the sum of which is the product or output of the mechanism.

opponent-process theory of color vision

n. Any of several theories of color perception in which there are different kinds of color receptors which mutually inhibit each other. In the Hering theory there are three kinds of color receptors, red-green, blue-yellow, and black-white, in which the activation of one color receptor inhibits the activation of the other paired color.

opponent-process theory of motivation

n. The hypothesis that when any stimulus arouses an affective response, it also arouses its opposite but to a lesser degree, thereby reducing the intensity of the original affect so that emotion is a combination of the two. The secondary affect is supposed to be aroused more slowly, to be less intense, but to endure longer than the original one so that after an emotion occurs it is likely to be replaced by its opposite but at a markedly reduced intensity. Thus after experiencing joy we experience a letdown which is a subdued form of sadness.

optical illusion

n. Any of dozens of sorts of false visual images which can be produced through many physiological and psychological mechanisms.

optic chiasm

n. The point at which the branches of the optic nerve from each eye meet. The half of the neuronal fibers from the outer side of the retina in each nerve continue on the same side of the brain back toward the lateral geniculate nuclei, superior colliculus, and the optic cortex, while the half from the nasal side of the retina cross over and travel toward the opposite side of the cortex. The fibers cross in such a way that the receptors from the right side of the visual field send impulses to the left side of the brain, and vice versa.

optic disk

n. The part of the retina in which retinal nerve fibers gather into a bunch and leave the retina so that there are no light receptors in this area. This creates a blind spot in the visual field which we do not ordinarily perceive as receptors in the opposite eye cover each other's blind spot.

optic nerve

n. Either of the second cranial nerves which arise in the ganglion cells in the retina whose axons carry visual information back to the lateral geniculate nuclei, from which information is communicated to the superior colliculi and visual cortex.

optimal distinctiveness model

n. Brewer's optimal distinctiveness model is based on the premise that social identities are derived from a tension between the opposing needs for inclusion and distinctiveness. The need for inclusion involves individuals' desire for belonging and similarity to others, while distinctiveness involves the desire for individuation and uniqueness. This model describes the process by which individuals achieve a balance between these fundamental needs through the formation and activation of social identities. Within any social context, social categories exist that vary in their level of inclusiveness or size. According to the model, individuals select identities that provide a sense of inclusion in a larger collective but are exclusive enough to provide a basis for distinction from others (e.g., minority groups). Group identification and loyalty are hypothesized to be enhanced for optimal group identities where the needs for inclusion and differentiation are satisfied simultaneously.   – KAS, CLP

optimism

n. A tendency to expect the best possible outcome and to dwell on positive aspects of situations.

optimism, unrealistic

n. A person's underestimation of the likelihood that he or she will experience a negative event, such as a heart attack, in the future or overestimation of the likelihood that he or she will experience a positive event, such as winning the lottery, in the future. Most often, unrealistic optimism has been demonstrated by asking a representative sample of people to compare themselves to the average person in the population from which they are selected. For example, male college students may be asked to compare their own risk of failing to graduate to the risk of the average male student at the same educational institution. The college students could be asked to make a "direct comparison," for example, on a scale that ranges from "much below average" to "much above average," or they could be asked to make separate estimates for their own risk and the risk of the average student ("indirect comparison"). If the mean comparative risk judgment of the sample is significantly different from "average" (direct method), or if the means of the individuals' personal estimates are significantly different from the mean estimate they make for the "average student" (indirect method), this is evidence of a systematic bias in the risk judgments of the sample as a whole. One cannot say, however, that a particular individual is unrealistic, in the

absence of detailed information about both the factors that determine an individual's risk and the person's standing on these factors. Thus, a person who gives an optimistic judgment ("My risk is below average") is not necessarily being unrealistic.   – NW

oral character

n. In psychoanalysis, a personality fixated in the oral stage of development, which tends to be friendly, optimistic, generous, and dependent on others and to use oral pleasures such as eating, drinking, talking, and smoking to relieve anxiety.

oral personality

n. In psychoanalysis, a persistent pattern of adjustment fixated in the oral stage of development, which may be either oral receptive or oral aggressive. The oral passive personality tends to be fixated on oral pleasure and is friendly, optimistic, generous, and dependent on others, using oral pleasures such as eating, drinking, talking, and smoking to relieve anxiety. The oral aggressive personality tends to be fixated on oral frustration and tends to be easily frustrated, hostile, critical, envious, exploitative, and demanding.

oral stage

n. **1.** In Sigmund Freud's psychoanalysis, the first stage in personality development, in which the infant is focused on oral stimulation and pleasure through sucking, biting, chewing, and swallowing. Ego forms in this stage as the id's wishful thinking is incapable of dealing with frustration, and so frustrated energy is directed into the formation of a self that is capable of the beginnings of rational thought and planning. There is no conscience or superego in this stage. **2.** In Erik Erikson's epigenetic development cycle, this stage is characterized by the development of sensory organization and the necessity for establishing trust through predictable relationships with adult caregivers, which establish the basis for hope for the future.

orbitofrontal cortex

n. Prefrontal area situated above the orbit of the eyes. It is one of the three major divisions of the prefrontal cortex (dorsolateral, orbitofrontal, and medial). It receives projections from the dorsomedial nucleus of the thalamus. Damage in the orbitofrontal cortex is associated with nonspecific amnesia, difficulties in controlling attention, defects in planning behavior, disinhibition, and personality changes. — AA

▶ *See also* **PREFRONTAL CORTEX**

order effect

n. **1.** In repeated-measures experimental designs, the effect of different placement in the series of conditions on the relationship between independent and dependent variables. **2.** In memory experiments, the effect the place of an item in a list of items has on its likelihood of being recognized or recalled. Items first and last in the list tend to be remembered better than items in the middle of the list.

ordinal scale

n. A quantitative scale with magnitude but lacking equal intervals or an absolute zero; used primarily to rank or rate individuals or objects. Ordinal scales provide information about degrees of difference but do not provide any information about the meaning or amount of difference between rankings or ratings. The lack of equal intervals prevents the direct comparison of the difference measurement between any two points. For example, when runners complete a race, an ordinal scale is used to rank first, second, third, and fourth place, and so on, but the ranking does not tell you the difference between first and second places; nor can you assume that the first-place runner was four times as fast as the fourth-place runner. The ordinal rankings simply provide a measure of the degree of difference between runners. Because of the lack of equal intervals, the most appropriate calculations for ordinal scale data are mode, median, range, and percentile rank. — BJM

▶ *See also* **RATIO SCALE**

ordinary personology

n. In social cognition, the study of how people make inferences about one another.

organic disorder

n. Any bodily dysfunction or disease having an identifiable physical cause. An organic mental disorder is a functional impairment brought about by disease, damage, or physiological malfunction of the brain.

organizational centralization

n. A form of social order in which power and decision making for the whole group are exercised by a few persons, who tend to be the focus of communication in the group. This form of organization is associated with a lack of communication and difficulty in changing to meet new situations.

organizational climate

n. The general experience of being in a particular business or other social group from the point of view of those inside it. It is usually considered a subset of organizational culture.

organizational complexity

n. The degree to which a business or other social group is divided into differentiated units and levels.

organizational culture

n. The distinctive pattern of attitudes, behaviors, beliefs, customs, thoughts, and values shared by members of a business or other social group.

organizational justice

n. The perception of the degree to which a business or other social group is fair in its treatment of its employees or members, including both the procedures used for decision making and the allocation of benefits within the group.

organizational psychology

n. The branch of psychology that studies humans in the workplace and attempts to apply general psychological principles to workplaces to improve productivity and to improve working circumstances for those employed. I/O psychology stresses the study of motivation, group processes and organizational effectiveness, personnel selection, training, employee evaluation, and leadership.

organ of Corti
n. A liquid-filled chamber within the cochlea in the inner ear which contains hair cells which generate nerve impulses in reaction to sound. There are 15,000–20,000 hair cells which react as waves of pressure moves across their area; the length of the waves determines the pitch of the sound.

orgasm disorder
n. A persistent or recurrent delay of or inability to reach orgasm despite appropriate sexual stimulation and excitement which causes significant personal or interpersonal distress in either a male or a female.

orgasmic dysfunction
n. **1.** A persistent or recurrent delay of or inability to reach orgasm despite appropriate sexual stimulation and excitement which causes significant personal or interpersonal distress in either a male or a female.

orgasmic impotence
n. **1.** The persistent or recurrent inability to maintain an adequate penile erection for the completion of sexual activity which causes significant frustration and personal distress and interpersonal difficulties. Also called male erectile disorder.

orgone therapy
n. An approach to psychotherapy in which it is assumed that psychological problems arise from blockage in the flow of life energy due to habitual bodily tension (character armor). The natural expression of orgone energy is in orgasm, and sufficient orgasms would prevent the construction of character armor. Through a combination of verbal therapy and physical contact, the orgone therapist seeks to free the individual from his or her character armor and allow free movement of orgone ultimately into orgasm as well as better functioning in other areas of life. Some orgone therapists use an orgone box, a device consisting of outer layers of wood and inner layers of metal, which directs orgone inward and in which a person sits to allow his/her orgone to be reflected back to him/her as well as to have environmental orgone accumulate in the box.

orienting reflex
n. A quick response to an intense or rapidly changing stimulus involving moving of the head to look toward the stimulus as well as physiological arousal.

orienting response
n. A reflexive movement after an intense or rapidly changing stimulus involving moving of the head to look toward the stimulus as well as physiological arousal.

orthogonal
adj. **1.** Uncorrelated or at right angles to. **2.** In factor analysis, refers to a solution in which the axes are uncorrelated rather than oblique and at right angles to one another in a spatial representation of the factors.

orthogonal rotation
n. In factor analysis, a solution in which the axes are uncorrelated rather than oblique and at right angles to one another in a spatial representation of the factors.

orthogonal solution ▶ *See* **ORTHOGONAL ROTATION**

orthogonal trait
n. In a factor analysis matrix, any factor which is uncorrelated with any other factor.

orthography
n. **1.** The writing system of a language. **2.** The spelling of words within a system of writing.

orthomolecular therapy
n. The preservation of health and treatment of disease by varying the concentrations of substances normally present in the human body. This was popularized by Linus Pauling's work with vitamin C and the cold but has been found to have little or no usefulness in treating mental disorders.

orthopsychiatry

n. A multidisciplinary approach to preventive mental health that includes pediatricians, educators, nurses, social workers, psychiatrists, and psychologists. Orthopsychiatry tries to intervene before a problem arises or in its early stages so as to forestall its development into a full disorder by using educational, organizational, environmental, family, and individual interventions, usually in a cooperative team.

osmometric thirst

n. Thirst brought about by loss of cellular fluids, which increases osmotic pressure. Also called intracellular thirst and osmotic thirst.

osmoreceptor

n. A hypothesized mechanism in the hypothalamus that responds to changes in the serum levels of various bodily chemicals and particularly to salt. It is believed to be involved in the regulation of thirst and the secretion of vasopressin.

osmosis

n. The diffusion of molecules in solution through a semipermeable membrane which has different concentrations of the molecules on the two sides of the membrane.

ossicle

n. Small bone. Any small bone, such as the three tiny bones within the human ear.
                                                        – AA

ostracism

n. Ostracism is being ignored and excluded. The word *ostracism* derives from the Greeks, who used shards of clay (*ostraka*) to vote to exile members of their community, but the practice of ostracism appears to have been used since the appearance of social animals. Ostracism allows the group to remain strong and safe, either by permitting exclusion of burdensome members or by motivating ostracized individuals to correct their undesirable behaviors. Ostracism can be observed in all human enterprises, from ordinances passed down by the government to interpersonal ostracism in the home ("the silent treatment"). The impact of ostracism is initially painful and distressing. Then individuals are motivated to cope with the pain and the threat to their sense of belonging, self-esteem, control, and meaningful existence. Concerns for belonging and self-esteem lead to behaviors that garner favor from others; concerns for control and existence can result in antisocial and aggressive acts.   – KDW

Othello error

n. An error in attribution of the source or reason behind an emotion. When we observe emotion in others, we often make assumptions about the causes of that emotion with no rational basis. The actual cause of someone else's emotion, however, may be quite different from what one assumes. This is called Othello's error because in the Shakespearean play, Othello made a grave mistake in interpreting the source of his wife's fear and killed her.

Othello syndrome

n. Irrational or delusional jealousy; named after the character Othello in Shakespeare's play, who murders his innocent wife in a fit of jealousy brought about by hearing rumors that she has been unfaithful to him.

other directed

adj. Of or relating to individuals whose attitudes, beliefs, goals, and values are adopted from those around them instead of resulting from their personal experience. Also called outer directed.

other, significant

n. **1.** Any person who has a significant influence on a person's self-image. **2.** A spouse or other person with whom a person has a meaningful sexual relationship.

otolith

n. Any one of numerous small crystals of calcium carbonate embedded in the gelatinous walls of the vestibular system which move slowly with linear acceleration of the head and so stimulate hair cells, which move more rapidly with linear acceleration, including the acceleration of gravity. This forms an important part of our sense of balance.

ought self-guide

n. Self-guides are self-directive standards, which are a major source of people's emotions and motivation. They both directly prompt action as desired end states (i.e., goals to be attained) and, through their use in self-evaluation (i.e., standards to be met), arouse emotions that are themselves motivating. Ought self-guides represent a person's beliefs about his or her duties, responsibilities, and obligations.

Ought self-guides vary in strength. There are different modes of strong socialization that produce strong ought self-guides. Strong ought self-guides are produced by interactions with significant others that involve protection and safeguarding, as well as punishment and criticism for failure to meet an ought self-guide. Success and failure in meeting strong ought self-guides arouse different emotions. When people's representation of their actual self-representation is congruent with one of their ought self-guides, they experience quiescence-related emotions, such as feeling calm or relaxed. When people's representation of their actual self-representation is discrepant with one of their ought self-guides, they experience agitation-related emotions, such as feeling nervous or worried.

When strong ought self-guides predominate, people have a prevention focus on safety and security. They prefer to use vigilant strategic means to make decisions and perform tasks. They appraise the world and remember past events in terms of the absence of negative outcomes (nonlosses) and the presence of negative outcomes (losses).   – ETH

outbreeding

n. The practice of mating with individuals outside one's normal social group, clan, nationality, ethnicity, or breed. In animals this is often referred to as cross-breeding and tends to produce more healthy individuals, a result referred to as hybrid vigor. Also called exogamy.

out-group

n. Any social group which an individual identifies as one to which he/she does not belong, which is usually judged as inferior to the social group with which one identifies one's self.

out-group extremity effect

n. A cognitive distortion whereby individuals tend to overemphasize both positive and negative qualities of groups and members of groups with which they do not identify themselves. Thus some Euro-Americans tend to believe that all African-Americans have a superior sense of rhythm and are poor at academic tasks.

out-group homogeneity bias

n. A cognitive distortion in which humans have a tendency to ignore individual differences among members of groups to which they do not believe they belong as well as to ignore contrary evidence to their beliefs about the out-group.

out-group homogeneity effect ▶ *See* OUT-GROUP HOMOGENEITY BIAS

outlier

n. A data point which is outside the usual distribution in a set of measurements and differs significantly from all or almost all other data points. Outliers sometimes occur by chance and sometimes through measurement error and tend to have great influence on the mean and variance of a data set.

out-of-body experience

n. A sense of detachment from one's body and perception of one's body from a distance, usually above. It is characteristic of near-death experiences, some forms of intoxication, and some mental disorders such as dissociative disorders and schizophrenia.

outplacement counseling

n. Vocational and psychological assistance given persons whose employment has ended or will soon end to help them cope with the stress of the situation and to find new work.

oval window

n. An oval opening between the middle and inner ears which is covered with a thin membrane which transmits pressure changes from the stapes to the fluid in the cochlea.

ovarian follicle

n. Any one of numerous very small fluid-filled sacs in the ovary in which an ovum develops. At ovulation one sac in the ovary ruptures, releasing an ovum into the fallopian tube, where it may or may not be fertilized and turn into an embryo, while the ruptured follicle becomes part of the corpus luteum. Also called Graafian follicle.

ovary

n. Either of the two female reproductive organs which produce ova, or egg cells, as well as estrogen and progesterone hormones. In humans, they are ovate, being a little more than 1 inch long and 0.75 inch in diameter, and are located at the ends of the fallopian tubes, which connect them with the uterus. Approximately every 4 weeks a woman of breeding age produces one or rarely two ova at the ends of the fallopian tubes, where they may or may not be fertilized and move into the uterus.

overanxious disorder

n. A disorder characterized by excessive, unproductive, and uncontrollable worries, restlessness, likeliness to become fatigued, difficulty in concentrating, irritability, prolonged muscular tension, and sleep disturbance. Also called generalized anxiety disorder and overanxious disorder of childhood.

overconfidence effect

n. An experimental observation that most individuals have unwarranted certainty in the correctness of their beliefs and judgments.

overextension

n. The use of a single category name to denote a broader range of individual things than the word usually denotes, usually by small children or adults with a small vocabulary as in speaking a second language. Thus, small children will often call all furry animals *doggie* or *kitty* or all men *daddy*.

overgeneralization

n. In language development, the use of a grammatical rule beyond its normal range or in cases of linguistic irregularity. Thus a child who is just beginning to learn to add *-ed* to verbs to form the past tense may say *goed* for *went* or *throwed* for *threw*. Also called overregularization.

overjustification effect

n. A reduction in the frequency or intensity of an act after a new reward for performing the act is first introduced and then withdrawn. The supposition is that the new reward situation leads to a change in the person's internal justification for the act so it is focused on the new reward rather than the intrinsic rewards or previous rewards of the act.

overlearning

n. Continued practice in memory experiments after something has been learned to a criterion. Overlearning results in increased retention of the material. Also called overtraining.

overpathologizing

n. Misinterpreting culturally sanctioned behavior as expression of a pathological symptom.

overtone

n. A component of a complex tone which is an integer multiple of the fundamental frequency. Thus a tone with a frequency of 1,500 cycles per second is an overtone of a fundamental frequency of 500 cycles per second. Also called a harmonic.

ovum

n. An individual unfertilized female gamete or egg cell.

oxytocin

n. A hormone, produced in the hypothalamus and secreted by the posterior pituitary gland, which stimulates contractions of the uterus and delivery of milk from the mammary glands. Oxytocin levels in the blood are tripled in both males and females during orgasmic pleasure. It has been suggested that increases in oxytocin levels are associated with social attachment, pair bonding, and even improvements in spatial memory. Oxytocin, commonly called "the love hormone," is associated with caregiving and pair bonding in both humans and other mammals.   – vs

Pacinian corpuscle
n. A sensory nerve ending surrounded by several layers of connective tissue about the size and shape of a grain of rice, which is sensitive to pressure and vibration. Pacinian corpuscles are found in hairy skin, the sides of the fingers and palms, tendons, and abdominal membranes.

pain
n. An aversive experience usually associated with stimulation of free sensory nerve endings, nerve damage, or high-intensity sensory stimulation such as loud sounds or very bright flashes of light. It is associated with an increase in heart and respiration rate, narrowed attentional focus, pupil dilation, and facial grimacing. Pain is mediated by the brain so that the same stimulation may sometimes produce pain and at other times not. There are several types of pain specific receptors located throughout the body but concentrated in the skin, which respond to physical deformation, tension in the muscles or tendons, heat or cold, and chemical damage.

pain, acute
n. An aversive sensory experience which occurs rapidly or lasts only a short time, usually associated with stimulation of free sensory nerve endings, nerve damage, or high-intensity sensory stimulation such as loud sounds or very bright flashes of light.

pain, chronic
n. An aversive sensory experience which lasts a long period of time, usually associated with stimulation of free sensory nerve endings, nerve damage, or high-intensity sensory stimulation such as loud sounds or very bright flashes of light. Chronic pain is also associated with significant symptoms of stress.

pain coping strategy
n. A plan for an action, series of actions, or thought processes used in an attempt to deal with pain. These often include medication, diversion, exercise, heat, cognitive reappraisal, relaxation, meditation, and combinations of these.

pain pathway
n. Any of numerous nerve paths that carry the sensations of pain from nerve endings toward the central nervous system or efferent pathways that inhibit pain. Afferent pain fibers include myelinated fibers, which rapidly conduct pain information, and unmyelinated fibers, which are slow in conductance, which together form the ascending tracts connecting with the anterolateral system, the central gray matter, the reticular formation, the thalamus and hypothalamus, and the cingulate gyrus.

pain receptor
n. Any of the free nerve endings throughout the body that respond to mechanical deformation, heat or cold, chemical stimulation, or nerve damage.

pain threshold
n. The minimal level of a particular stimulus required for the experience of pain.

pain tolerance
n. **1.** The ability to continue normal functioning despite experiencing pain. **2.** In physiology experimentation, the upper threshold for voluntary experience of pain or the point at which subjects terminate the stimulation in an experiment involving pain.

paired-associate learning
n. An experimental procedure in which subjects are required to learn pairs of items usually so that they can recall one at a later time when the other is used as a cue.

paired comparison
n. **1.** In sensation research, a method of measuring some aspect of sensation in which pairs of stimuli are presented so that every stimulus is paired with every other stimulus and each

pair is judged on the aspect of the sensation under study. Thus one might make six pots of soup which differ only in how much salt is in the recipe and then ask people to taste each possible pair of the soups and say which they like better. This procedure can establish an ordinal scale of the dimension being measured so that in the example one can find out which soup each person likes best.

paired samples *t* test

n. A comparison of the mean of the differences in a set of number pairs divided by a measure of their deviance to a table of t statistics to decide whether the differences are likely to be due to chance. Also called related scores, dependent, or repeated-measures *t* test.

panel study

n. A research design in which a group of subjects is measured repeatedly over time in order to determine whether they change in the area under study. Also called a longitudinal study.

panel survey

n. A research design for measuring attitudes, opinions, judgments, or other variables of interest in which they are surveyed repeatedly over time using the same group of subjects.

panic attack

n. A brief, discrete period in which a person experiences intense fear or discomfort in the absence of any realistic danger coupled with an inability to act and often accompanied by trembling, shortness of breath, choking sensations, chest pain, nausea, dizziness, depersonalization, fear of insanity or death, and chills and fever.

panic disorder

n. A mental disorder characterized by repeated discrete periods in which the individual suffers attacks of intense fear often accompanied by palpitations, accelerated heart rate, sweating, trembling, shortness of breath, choking sensations, chest pain, nausea, dizziness or light-headedness, feelings of unreality or detachment, numbness, and hot or cold flashes along with persistent worries about having another attack or becoming insane, and changes in behavior related to the attacks.

paper-and-pencil tests

n. Paper-and-pencil tests in psychology are sometimes referred to as questionnaires, inventories, surveys, rating scales, or checklists. They are designed so that a person taking the test (respondent) is required to answer (endorse) one or more questions (items) on a paper form. Paper-and-pencil tests in psychology are used to measure, among other things, personality traits, vocational interests, educational achievement, mental disorders, job performance, and intellectual aptitudes. Such tests can easily be adapted for computerized administration, whereby the items are displayed and endorsed at a computer terminal.

The items in a paper-and-pencil test might be questions that, for example, ask the respondent to solve certain logic problems, describe some typical day-to-day behaviors, identify any symptoms of pathology, or indicate his or her preferences for different work activities. The response to each item can take the form of an open-ended written answer, a true-false response, a check mark beside one of several response alternatives, a circle on a 10-point rating scale, and so on.

Paper-and-pencil tests in psychology generally have multiple items measuring an attribute or construct. The items are considered to be parallel measures of the construct, so their endorsements can be summed to get a total score for the respondent. For example, a paper-and-pencil measure of quantitative ability might contain 50 arithmetic problems (e.g., $9 \times 7 =$ ___). A respondent's total quantitative ability score would be tallied as the number of correct answers out of 50. A measure of depression might present a list of 20 depressive symptoms (e.g., "I cry on most days"). A respondent's total depression score would be the number of symptoms checked out of 20.

A raw count of the number of items endorsed on a psychological test usually has little meaning in and of itself. It must be compared with the scores of other people on the test. Raw test scores, therefore, are typically reported in relation to the scores of a norm group, which can be defined as a large sample of respondents representative of the population for whom the test was designed.

Paper-and-pencil tests are to be contrasted with other forms of assessment in psychology. These include psychological interviews, direct behavior sampling, expert ratings, and physiological measures.   – SVP

▶ *See also* **PERSONALITY ASSESSMENT**

Papez circuit
n. One of the major pathways of the limbic system, which is chiefly involved in the cortical control of emotion as well as in storing memory and is circular in structure. The pathway includes connections from the hippocampus to the fornix to the mammillary bodies to the mammillothalamic tract to the anterior thalamic nucleus to the genu of the internal capsule to the cingulate gyrus to the cingulum to the parahippocampal gyrus to the entorhinal cortex to the perforant pathway and finally back to the hippocampus.

Papez's theory of emotion
n. Papez (1937) enhanced the Cannon theory by refining the neuroanatomical structures involved and introducing complex feedback paths of the Papez circuit. According to Papez, affective experience is the result of information flowing through the following loop: sensory apparatus to the hippocampus to the fornix to the mammillary bodies to the mammillothalamic tract to the anterior thalamic nucleus to the genu of the internal capsule to the cingulate gyrus to the cingulum to the parahippocampal gyrus to the entorhinal cortex to the perforant pathway and finally back to the hippocampus.

papilla
n. Any small biological projection, such as those on the tongue, including the vallate papillae, the fungiform papillae, and the folliate papillae, which contain taste buds at their bases, as well as the filiform papillae, which do not contain taste buds. There are also papillae on the skin, at the base of a hair or the root of a feather, or around the base of

a new tooth. A pimple or blister can be considered a papilla, and there are interdental papillae, the part of gingiva located between teeth, and in the kidney, inside the cheek, on or around the nipple, and on the eyelid around the inner corner of the eyes as well.

paradigm
n. **1.** A prototype, model, pattern, or general conceptual framework within which an approach to research in a particular area of study makes sense. **2.** The set of inflected forms of a word within a natural language such as all the forms of the French verb *to speak*: *je parle, tu parle, il parle, nous parlons, vous parlez, ils parlent.* **3.** An experimental procedure such as classical conditioning. **4.** A generally accepted point of view within a discipline at any one point in time, including its attitudes, beliefs, values, procedures, and techniques.

paradigm shift
n. A rapid and large shift in the general point of view within a science or an area of science such as those which occurred in theoretical physics around the turn of the 20th century with the publication of the theory of relativity and then again in the 1930s with the advent of quantum theories.

paradox
n. **1.** A logically valid argument based on accepted premises which yields a conclusion which contradicts some of the premises from which it was derived. **2.** A surprising result in science. **3.** A semantic paradox is one arising from a possible but contradictory use of words such as "This sentence is not true."

paradoxical intention
n. A psychotherapeutic technique in which the client is encouraged to engage intentionally in a neurotic symptom or unwanted behavior in the belief that doing so will increase the client's awareness of the action and its consequences as well as its absurdity and so reduce the behavior's frequency or the anxiety associated with it. Thus a person who has difficulty sleeping may be instructed to go to bed and try to stay awake as long as possible, or a person who washes his or her hands in an obsessive

way may be instructed to wash his or her hands much more than he/she already does.

paradoxical intervention

n. An action taken by a therapist in which the client is encouraged to engage intentionally in a neurotic symptom or unwanted behavior in the belief that doing so will increase the client's awareness of the action and its consequences as well as its absurdity and so reduce the behavior's frequency or the anxiety associated with it. Thus a person who has difficulty sleeping may be instructed to go to bed and try to stay awake as long as possible, or a person who washes his or her hands in an obsessive way may be instructed to wash his or her hands much more than he/she already does.

paradoxical sleep

n. A sleep stage during which rapid eye movements occur and dreams are frequent. Also called REM sleep.

paralanguage

n. The nonverbal aspects of oral communication including tone, voice quality, timing, loudness, inflection, and nonword noises such as hisses, hems and haws, sighs, whistles, grunts, and groans. The paralanguage has a large influence on the meaning of the verbal aspects of language and can reverse the meaning of words as in the case of sarcasm or contain most or all of the meaning of an utterance.

paralinguistics

n. The study of the nonverbal portion of spoken language including tone, voice quality, timing, loudness, inflection, and nonword noises such as hisses, hems and haws, sighs, whistles, grunts, and groans.

parallax

n. The differences in the apparent motion of objects when the observer moves so that the apparent movement of faraway objects is less than that of nearby objects. Thus if a person is walking down the street and is able to see the moon, the yards and houses will appear to move as he or she walks while the moon will appear stationary and a tall building in the distance will move only slightly.

parallel distributed processing

n. (PDP) In cognitive psychology, any of several approaches to learning and memory in which knowledge is encoded as connections between multiple, parallel nodes rather than in a single location or memory entity. This suggests that knowledge is distributed rather than local and is defined by a net of activation that has a particular spread. It includes artificial intelligence programs that use spreading nets of activation to model neural networks.

parallel forms

n. In testing, two equivalent forms of the same test. Also called alternate forms.

parallel forms reliability

n. The level of a test's measurement error determined by examining the consistency of the scores of two different tests constructed from the same content domain. Parallel forms reliability (also called alternate forms or equivalent forms reliability) is concerned with error due to item sampling. Specifically, parallel forms reliability is designed to examine the error variance that can be attributed to the selection of a specific item or subset of items for inclusion in a measure. To calculate parallel forms reliability, two equivalent forms of a test are developed to measure the same construct or attribute (the specific items on the tests are different, but the tests are designed to be equivalent in target, difficulty, structure, etc.); the two different versions of the test are then administered to the same group of people on the same day (counterbalancing the order of administration). The scores of the two tests are then correlated to determine the reliability coefficient. Correlation coefficients closer to 0 represent low reliability, while coefficients closer to 1 represent high reliability. While parallel forms reliability is a rigorous and valuable method of estimating a test's reliability, it is often shunned by test developers because of the constraints associated with developing an alternate version of the target test.   – BJM

parallel play

n. A form of children's play in which they play beside each other but do not coordinate their play. It is often considered an early form of social play, which tends to occur before more cooperative play.

parallel processing

n. **1.** Any computer setup in which there are two or more processors which work independently and simultaneously on different aspects of the same data analysis. **2.** In models of human mental functioning, it is any model which assumes that there are multiple simultaneous processes occurring which would account for the human capacity to carry on different cognitive functions at the same time.

parameter

n. A numerical characteristic of a population such as the mean or standard deviation, which may be estimated by computing the mean or standard deviation of a sample from the population.

parametric statistic

n. Any form of sampling or mathematical inference from a population whose parameters are known, assumed, or inferred to agree with a theoretical form as in a normal distribution.

paranoia

n. A general term for any form of illness characterized by delusions of persecution. This can include delusional disorder, persecutory type; paranoid schizophrenia; or paranoid personality disorder.

paranoid delusion

n. Any well-developed set of beliefs in which a person reasons logically from obviously false premises that he/she is being persecuted, conspired against, maligned, poisoned, or similarly attacked.

paranoid disorder

n. Any illness characterized by delusions of persecution. This can include delusional disorder, persecutory type; paranoid schizophrenia; or paranoid personality disorder.

paranoid personality disorder

n. An enduring pattern of adjustment in which the individual is pervasively distrustful and suspicious of others. This includes being suspicious without evidence that others are exploiting or harming her/him, being preoccupied with doubts of others' loyalty, being unwilling to confide in others because of suspicions about them, reading negative meanings into benign actions of others, being hypersensitive and holding grudges, believing others are attacking her/his character without reasonable evidence, and having unwarranted sexual suspiciousness of spouses or other significant others.

paranoid schizophrenia

n. A pervasive mental illness characterized by persecutory and/or grandiose delusions and auditory or other hallucinations of persecution, often in the presence of otherwise near-normal cognitive, perceptual, and affective functioning. The prognosis for this form of schizophrenia is better than for other forms, as is the capacity for independent living and vocational self-support.

paranormal

adj. **1.** Of or relating to any phenomena inexplicable by scientific principles. **2.** Referring to the transfer of information energy or matter in ways deemed impossible by the principles of science, as in extrasensory perception, prescience, or mental control of physical events.

paraphilia

n. Any form of recurring, intense sexual arousal, urges, or actions inconsistent with cultural norms usually involving nonhuman objects, suffering or humiliation, or children or other nonconsenting partners. For some individuals the paraphilia is their main or only mode of sexual expression; for most it is occasional or incidental to culturally normal sexual desires and expressions.

paraplegia

n. Paralysis of the legs and usually the lower part of the abdomen often due to injury to the lower part of the spinal cord.

parapsychology

n. The field of study like psychology that deals with communication that does not follow the laws of physics as presently understood. It includes extrasensory perception, clairvoyance, telekinesis, and telepathy. Research in the field has not been widely accepted, as findings have been weak, do not fit into any other established body of knowledge, and often have had glaring methodological flaws.

parasuicide

n. The infliction of self-injury that falls short of death and may or may not have death as a clear goal. Many suicidal attempts fall into this category, as does passive suicide.

parasympathetic nervous system

n. The portion of the autonomic nervous system that stimulates the smooth muscle systems in the body such as those in the digestive system and is associated with digestion, sleep and relaxation, sexual arousal and recuperation. It acts in a negatively reciprocal way with the sympathetic system, which prepares the body for large muscle activity as in the flight-or-fight syndrome. It includes the nerve fibers that leave the skull via the oculomotor, facial, glossopharyngeal, and vagus nerves, as well as the sacral nerves in the spinal cord.

parathyroid gland

n. Any of four small endocrine glands attached to the thyroid gland at the base of the neck which secrete parathyroid hormone, which controls the levels of calcium in the blood, digestive system, and bones.

parental ethnotheories

n. Parental cultural belief systems.

parental investment theory

n. Parental investment theory is an important middle-level theory in evolutionary psychology that makes predictions of sex-differentiated behavior. The basis for this theory is that it is common in nature for males and females to have asymmetrical patterns of parental investment. Among the mammals, the obligatory costs of reproduction are relatively high for females because reproduction requires a period of gestation and lactation, whereas the obligatory costs of reproduction for males are relatively minor. As a result, the higher-investing sex (females) becomes the limiting resource in mating. The prediction is that females will be discriminating maters, seeking investment and other resources such as emotional commitment and good genes from males. Mating is expected to be problematic for the low-investment sex, with the result that males must often compete with other males for access to females. Successful males have often been able to mate polygynously and to have access to younger, more desirable mates. This theory makes a number of predictions. Males and females are expected to have different patterns of sexual jealousy: Male sexual jealousy is predicted to be based on concern with paternity certainty because their partner's infidelity could lead them to invest in another man's children. On the other hand, female sexual jealousy is expected to center around concerns that her partner may develop an emotional relationship with another female and not continue to invest in their relationship. Males are also predicted to be more aggressive and more prone to risk taking because these behaviors have a greater potential payoff in terms of reproductive success. However, because females are the high-investment sex, mating for females is much less problematic, with the result that females are expected to pursue less risky behavior, to show a greater tendency toward fear, and to exhibit less aggression. Evolutionary psychologists have amassed considerable support for these hypotheses.   – KM

parent-child interaction

n. **1.** An instance of a reciprocal stimulation of a parent and their child resulting in mutual influence. **2.** The general category of relationships between parents and children.

parenting

n. All aspects of behavior by adults with children intended to protect, nurture, teach, discipline, and guide them.

parietal lobe

n. The portion of the brain in the middle of the side of the cerebral cortex separated from the frontal lobe by the central sulcus and from the temporal lobe by the lateral sulcus, and differentiated from the occipital lobe by a line from the preoccipital notch up to the parieto-occipital sulcus. The parietal lobe is involved in somatosensory functions including the sense of touch; the size, shape, and position of objects in space; speech perception; and integration of visual and bodily perceptions.

Parkinson's disease

n. Parkinson's disease is a disease of the nervous system characterized by trembling arms and legs, jaw tremors, muscle rigidity, unsteady balance, general slowing of voluntary movement, and sometimes speech impairments. Parkinson's disease is marked by the death of certain nerve brain cells. These cells are responsible for the production of dopamine, and the death of these cells results in reduced supplies of dopamine and subsequent loss of muscle control. Unfortunately, as these nerve cells continue to die off, the symptoms of Parkinson's disease worsen over time.

The precise cause of the atrophy and death of these cells is unknown, but researchers have proposed that a combination of genetic predispositions, mutations, and environmental toxins may be responsible for the onset of the disease. Researchers have noted that the disease is often mistaken as part of the normal aging process or may be misinterpreted as being symptomatic of other diseases. It often takes several years for an individual to develop new symptoms that might alert doctors that the patient is experiencing something more profound than the normal aging and loss of motor skills. The uncertainty of cause and delayed diagnosis add to the difficulty in understanding the onset, development, and treatment of the disease. Additionally, the disease does not present uniformly across individuals. The onset can be either sudden or slow, and the typical symptoms of motor difficulties are sometimes accompanied by symptoms of anxiety, depression, or impaired

reasoning. Occasionally, persons with Parkinson's disease later develop dementia.

Currently, Parkinson's disease can often be distinguished from other possible diagnoses on the basis of the patient's response to drug treatments. Persons with Parkinson's disease often respond more positively to the prescribed medications than do persons experiencing symptoms due to other causes. While none of the drugs provides a cure for Parkinson's disease, it has been possible for doctors to control the symptoms and slow decline.   – TJM

paroxetine

n. An anxiolytic and antidepressant medication commonly prescribed for depression, which works by selectively blocking serotonin reuptake. It tends to have calming or sedating effects on most patients, in contrast to most selective serotonin reuptake inhibitors (SSRIs), which tend to increase motor activity. Also called Paxil.

parsimony principle

n. The basic scientific principle that the simplest explanation is the best one. Simplicity is defined as a combination of making the fewest assumptions, supposing the existence of the fewest theoretical constructs, and supposing the fewest unobserved forces. Also called Occam's Razor or the economy principle.

part correlation

n. The correlation between two variables with the variance of a third variable removed from one but not both variables. Also called a semi-partial correlation.

partial correlation

n. The correlation of two variables with the variance of one or more other variables mathematically removed from the calculations.

partial reinforcement

n. An instrumental conditioning technique in which only some appropriate responses are rewarded, usually following either a ratio or interval schedule. Partial reinforcement is associated with more difficulty in establishing a response but more resistance to extinction when the response is no longer rewarded. Also called intermittent reinforcement.

partial-report technique

n. A procedure in memory studies in which only part of the learned information is tested. This has been used in studies of iconic memory, in which it was supposed that the memory store would decay before a full report could be produced, and in long-term memory studies, in which it was used to prevent contamination of original memory traces with those of subsequent testing.

participant

n. Any subject in any psychological study, including both experimental and control subjects.

participant observation

n. A research methodology that involves direct participation of the researcher within the context of the investigation. The goal of participant observation is to obtain detailed, intimate information about an environment, group, event, or experience. Through intensive involvement in the natural environment, the researcher is able to gain an in-depth perspective of phenomena or experiences that may not be easily observed by external evaluation. Generally, the researcher's role and purpose in the study are not obvious to others involved in the situation (so that others do not change their behavior as a function of the study). For example, a researcher interested in studying the psychological consequences of being homeless may immerse himself/ herself in the context and spend time living as a homeless person and observing the other homeless individuals in their environment. As with other unobtrusive observation research methods, there are concerns about the ethical implications of this approach. – BJM

participant observer

n. A researcher conducting participant observation research methodology. Being a participant observer requires simultaneously participating in a naturalistic context and monitoring and/or recording target behaviors

or phenomena. The goal of the participant observer is to obtain detailed, intimate information about an environment, group, event, or experience. Through intensive involvement in the natural environment, the participant observer is able to gain an in-depth perspective of phenomena or experiences that may not be easily observed by external evaluation. Generally, the participant observer's role and purpose in the study are not obvious to others involved in the situation (so that others do not change their behavior as a function of the study). For example, a participant observer interested in studying the psychological consequences of being homeless may immerse himself/herself in the context and spend time living as a homeless person and observing the other homeless individuals in their environment. – BJM

passionate love

n. **1.** A powerfully erotic attraction or attachment. **2.** A form of love involving passion and commitment but lacking intimacy in R. J. Sternberg's triangular theory of love.

passive-aggressive

adj. A characteristic of behavior that hostilely obstructs progress toward a goal while seeming to be innocuous, forgetful, incompetent, neutral, or accidental. It is characteristic of persons who feel hostile but powerless to express their hostility or opposition directly without experiencing severe negative consequences. Thus a private in the army may fail to warn a hated officer who is driving into a minefield.

passive-aggressive personality disorder

n. An archaic category of personality dysfunction included in the appendix of the DSM-IV-TR characterized by a pervasive and enduring pattern of dysphoria, ambivalence, negativism and discontent, passive resistance, disdain for authority, feelings of rejection and of being misunderstood, low empathy, and occasional explosions of hostile defiance followed by attempts at atonement. Also called negativistic personality disorder.

passive avoidance

n. Learning to refrain from emitting a particular response in order to avoid punishment in operant conditioning.

passive avoidance conditioning

n. The process of learning to refrain from emitting a particular response in order to avoid punishment in operant conditioning.

pastoral counseling

n. Psychotherapy or advice on adjustment to personal problems delivered by religious personnel to members of their religious group, which usually combines processes and perspectives of social science with the particular religious point of view of the practitioner.

path analysis

n. Path analysis is a multilevel strategy for analysis of complex interrelationships among variables of interest. There are a variety of specific statistical strategies that researchers use to conduct path analysis. One basic objective of path analysis is to uncover mediated relationships, that is to say, relationships between variables that are accounted for or explained by intermediary variables. In a sense, a mediated relationship between two variables is one that "passes through" a third variable. Mediated relationships exist when a significant proportion of a demonstrated overlap between two variables is accounted for by a mutual relationship with a third variable.

It is important to distinguish between *mediation* and a similar-sounding term with a very different meaning: *moderation*. Critics have pointed out instances where researchers have mistakenly used these two terms interchangeably. *Mediation*, one of the central aspects of path analysis, is about channeling relationships between other variables. *Moderation* is synonymous with interaction, which occurs when the influence of one variable upon another variable varies, depending on the value of a third variable. For example, an interaction would exist if a hypothetical relationship between viewing violent pornography and aggressive behavior depended on the sex of the participant in the following way: for

males, there is a relationship between viewing violent porn and subsequent aggressive behavior, and for females there is no relationship between violent porn and aggression.

Mediation can be quite complex; the simplest version of it exists in the abstract as follows: Mediation exists when a relationship between variable A and variable C is channeled through variable B in the following way: A is related to B, B is related to C, and the relationship between A and C is significantly reduced when variable B is added to the statistical model.

Here is a more concrete hypothetical example of mediation: There is a relationship established between university class attendance (A) and scores on the final exam of the course (C). Closer examination of this relationship shows that **(1)** attendance is associated with higher scores on periodic measures of understanding of course content (B), **(2)** understanding of course content is associated with final exam scores, and **(3)** the relationship between attendance and final exam scores is significantly reduced when understanding of course content is added to the model.

Relationships between variables, which are often referred to as path coefficients in path analysis, are presented in a few different ways. Path coefficients generally range from -1 to 1, similarly to correlation coefficients (often path analysis is conducted using multiple regression analysis, and the path coefficients are standardized beta weights). Researchers refer to the detailed analysis of path coefficients as decomposition of effects. There are three basic ways in which path coefficients are measured: total effects, direct effects, and indirect effects. The total effect is the overall relationship between one variable and another, variables A and C from the hypothetical example. That total effect can be decomposed into direct and indirect components.

The direct effect is the amount of the total relationship between A and C that is remaining or "left over" when the complete model is present, that is, when variable B enters the model in the hypothetical example. In order for mediation to be potentially present, the total effect will be reduced when the mediator variables are added to the model, resulting in a smaller direct effect compared to the total effect. The difference between the total effect and the direct effect is the indirect effect. The indirect effect is the portion of the relationship that is potentially mediated. In summary, total effect = direct effect + indirect effect.

In order for mediation to exist, most researchers require not only the presence of indirect effects, but also significant direct relationships between the primary variables and the mediator variables. To return to the abstract example, in order for mediation to exist, the total effect between A and C must be larger than the direct effect when B is added to the model (the difference between the total effect and the direct effect between A and C is called the indirect effect). In addition, for mediation to exist, A must have a significant relationship with B, and B must have a significant relationship with C.

To return to the concrete example, then, assume that the total effect path coefficient between class attendance (A) and final exam scores (C) is .65. When understanding of course content is added to the model, the direct effect path coefficient between attendance and final exam scores is .15. Therefore, the indirect effect path coefficient is .50 (total effect .65 minus direct effect .15 equals .50). In addition, there is a significant path of .53 between attendance and understanding of content, and also a path between understanding and final exam scores, .38. Because there is a significant indirect effect of .50 between attendance and final exam scores, and because there are direct relationships both between attendance and understanding and between understanding and final exam scores, we can conclude from our path analysis that the relationship between attendance and final exam scores is mediated by understanding of course content.

Path analysis can be conducted in a variety of ways, involving a variety of different types of variables and testing a variety of different types of hypotheses and/or research objectives. Sometimes path analysis will be used to test a theoretical model that results directly from prior research findings, and at other times it will be used as an exploratory tool based on a few basic a priori expectations about relationships among variables.

One of the advantages of path analysis is that it allows researchers to map complex interrelationships among variables. As psychological science progresses, there are corresponding increases to the complexity of psychological research models. Path analysis allows researchers to test complex interrelationships among varieties of variables in such a way that research begins more closely to approximate the very complex circumstances that exist in the real world. Many researchers believe that more complex research designs, which involve many variables and many interrelationships among those variables, are a necessary-but-difficult challenge for psychological researchers because only complex research has the potential to approximate the real world realistically.   – MWP

pathogenesis
n. The origin and process of development of a disease or disorder. Also called nosogenesis and pathogeny.

pathognomic
adj. Of or relating to the signs or symptoms indicative of particular disorders that distinguish it from other disorders.

pathological gambling
n. The inability to resist impulses to wager or bet in a pattern that causes significant discomfort and distress to the individual or the persons around her/him. This is one of many impulse-control disorders, all of which involve inability to resist an impulse to engage in a pattern of behavior the person knows is dysfunctional and feels unable to resist despite his or her best efforts to do so.

pathological liar
n. A person who persistently and compulsively says things they know to be untrue whether or not they gain advantage by doing so. This is common among persons who are intoxicated or have dementia or antisocial personality disorder.

pathological stealing

n. An inability to resist impulses to steal or shoplift despite absence of need for the stolen objects, conscious attempts to resist the impulse, and understanding that the habit of stealing has negative consequences. This is one of many impulse control disorders, all of which involve inability to resist an impulse to engage in a pattern of behavior the person knows is dysfunctional and feels unable to resist despite his or her best efforts to do so.

pattern discrimination

n. The capacity of organisms to respond differently to varying patterns of sensory stimuli in all sensory modalities.

pattern recognition

n. **1.** The ability of organisms to recognize patterns of stimuli and respond differently to them than to other patterns of stimuli. **2.** The classification and identification of patterns in data gathered by artificial intelligence systems, which are a central problem in the creation of robotic systems.

Pavlovian

adj. Of or relating to the person or ideas of Ivan Pavlov, a 19th-century physiologist who won a Nobel Prize for his studies of the digestive system and developed ideas about learning that have become known as classical conditioning.

Pavlovian conditioning

n. A type of learning in which a stimulus to which an organism does not initially respond (the conditioned stimulus [CS]) is paired in time and space with a stimulus which predictably produces a reflex response (the unconditioned stimulus [UCS]) so that the same reflex response begins to be predictably produced by exposure to the new (conditioned) stimulus. Also known as classical conditioning.

Peabody Picture Vocabulary Test

n. A measure of verbal ability for all persons over the age of $2\frac{1}{2}$ in which sets of four black-and-white drawings are presented to subjects, who have to select which of the four pictures is associated with words uttered by the tester.

There are 204 items on the test arranged in 17 groups of 12; administering the test takes roughly 15 minutes.

peace psychology

n. A branch of psychology that focuses on ending and preventing wars through nonviolent conflict resolution, reconciliation, and studying the causes, consequences, and prevention of war and other destructive forms of conflict.

peak experience

n. A short period in which one experiences an intense sense of unity, clarity, insight, sometimes ecstasy, and relaxation in which the person often feels that life has a new and more open perspective. In the past this has usually been considered a religious experience but more recently has been called a transient moment of self-actualization. Also called the oceanic feeling, satori, and being born again.

Pearson chi-square test

n. A set of tests used with categorical data in which the degree to which a data set fits a theoretical distribution is calculated. It is often called a goodness of fit test as it tests how well a distribution fits actual data or how well two data sets fit each other. For instance, a chi-square test of the proportion of ethnic groups in a sample can be compared to the distribution of the groups in the population as a way of thinking about the appropriateness of a sample to make inferences about the population. Also called chi-square test.

Pearson product-moment correlation

n. A numerical index of shared, linear relationship between two variables. The Pearson product-moment correlation is the most widely used correlation coefficient and is appropriate for use with ratio variables and with interval data. It shows relationship on a scale where 0 is no relationship, +1 is a perfect positive relationship, and −1 is a perfect negative relationship.

Pearson's correlation coefficient ▶ *See* **PEARSON PRODUCT-MOMENT CORRELATION**

pedophilia

n. Preferential sexual desire for, arousal by, and sexual interaction with prepubescent children. This has been criminalized in most industrialized cultures and is viewed variably in more traditional cultures. Some cultures believe it is the duty of the parental or grandparental generation to introduce children to sexuality, and this usually is accomplished by aunts, uncles, or great aunts and uncles rather than parents or grandparents.

peduncle

n. Any star-shaped biological structure, such as the cerebral and cerebellar peduncles, which are star-shaped neural formations.

peer group

n. **1.** Any group whose members have approximately equal status within some social context, which is usually defined by some characteristic such as location, age, sex, socioeconomic status, occupation, education, or avocation. **2.** A social group of children or adolescents who frequently associate together and who typically have significant influence on the enculturation of its members. **3.** The group of individuals with which a person identifies herself or himself.

peer rating

n. A numerical evaluation of an individual by other members of an identifiable group to which the person belongs.

peer relationship

n. Any relationship between individuals who regard themselves as equals or who are identifiable as similar on some important dimension.

peer review

n. The process of scientific review in which researchers read and critique each other's work, usually prior to publication or as a precondition to publication.

penetrance

n. In genetics, the degree to which the characteristic(s) associated with a particular form of a gene or allele is actually expressed in the living organism. Penetrance of an allele can vary from 100%, or complete penetrance, in the case of some dominant alleles, to some lesser proportion, depending on its interaction with its complementary allele and its physiological environment.

penis envy

n. In psychoanalysis, a girl's envy of the perceived power of a man's penis to make the mother love him instead of the girl. Girls try to overcome this envy by possessing the power of a man's penis through sex or marriage so as to obtain the mother's love, usually expressed as approval and given evidence by bearing a child.

perceived self

n. The total of an individual's conceptualizations about herself or himself which affect interpretation of sensory stimuli about the self and others' reactions to the person.

percentile score

n. More commonly called a percentile rank, a percentile score designates the percentage of scores that are lower than a specific score. Percentile scores go beyond simple ranking to take into consideration the number of scores in a group. Percentile rank is calculated by determining the ratio between the number of cases that fall below the target score and the total number of cases. Percentile scores are expressed as a percentage to indicate relative performance of a given score. Percentile scores must be interpreted with respect to the cases in the comparison sample. For example, in an Olympic race, a runner may finish 98th of 100 runners; this would mean that the runner's percentile rank is 2. But the runner is still likely to be quite fast in comparison to the general population; his or her percentile rank is simply low in this context as a result of the extraordinary ability of the comparison group.   – BJM

percept

n. The mental representation of a sensory object experienced or used by an organism, as distinguished from both the object itself and the pattern of energy the sensory system uses as a data source to create the percept.

perception

n. The process, product, or act of creating coherence from the patterns of energy impinging on sensory organs, which allows either consciousness of objects or states of the external world or the capacity to react differentially to them.

perception, binocular

n. The process, product, or act of combining information from two eyes to form a visual image or a mental representation of a visual scene, which allows the organism to respond differentially to it.

perception, subliminal

n. The process, product, or act of creating coherence from the patterns of energy impinging on sensory organs without consciousness of objects or states of the external world but with the capacity to react differentially based on the information from these processes.

perceptual constancy

n. The maintenance of a continuous perception of the characteristics of an object despite variation in the actual sensory information received from the object. Thus we can maintain our perception of a car as a constant whole despite the fact that part of it may be in shade, part may be unseen, and it may change as we walk around it.

perceptual field

n. **1.** In Gestalt psychology, the whole of the environment that an organism perceives at one moment of time. **2.** Generally, all the sensory information available at any point in time or the organism's consciousness of the environment at some point in time.

perceptual illusion

n. Any misperception of the external world brought about by the interaction of the particular structure of the perceived objects and the structure of the sensory system. ▶ *See also* **HORIZONTAL-VERTICAL ILLUSION, MULLER-LYER ILLUSION,** *and* **PONZO ILLUSION.**

perceptual memory

n. The long-term store of sensory information about particular objects such as people's faces or voices or food odors or tastes, which is remembered differently than general semantic knowledge. This is also differentiated from sensory memory, which is the very-short-term storage of large amounts of sensory information during percept formation.

perceptual-motor skill

n. Any particular ability to perform a task which involves the integration of sensory information with voluntary movement.

perceptual organization

n. The process or product of creating coherence in sensory information. Gestalt psychology created a list of laws of sensory organization, such as proximity coherence.

perceptual schema

n. Internal representation of the structure of sensory objects to which sensory data is compared and which is used as the basis of making inferences about unperceived aspects of the objects in the world.

perceptual set

n. **1.** A frame of reference or set of schemas that guide the interpretation of sensory information. **2.** A momentary readiness to interpret sensory data in a particular way elicited by the context in which perception takes place.

perfectionism

n. Perfectionism refers to a trait-based tendency to hold extremely high expectations of the self or others and to expect such performance from self or others in goal pursuit. Traditionally considered maladaptive, perfectionism has been linked to negative cognitive, affective, and behavioral outcomes (e.g., depression, anxiety). Recent arguments have countered that when high expectations motivate efforts toward high achievement or allow for enjoyment of success, perfectionism may be seen as an adaptive trait. Debate continues regarding the unidimensionality versus multidimensionality of perfectionism, as well as whether individuals showing this tendency should be identified as categorically perfectionistic (as opposed to the dimensional description of "having high levels of a perfectionistic attribute"). Current research often focuses on the sources and targets of perfectionistic expectations (e.g., from and/or toward self or other), as well as specific behaviors that may indicate perfectionism (e.g., a desire for organization or a marked fear of failure).   – CAD, ECC

performance anxiety
n. **1.** A generalized fear which occurs before one is required to perform a public act, which usually focuses on consequences of being unable to perform adequately. **2.** Fear by a man that he will be impotent when attempting sexual intercourse.

performance appraisal
n. A formal evaluation of an employee's job performance usually done by the employee's immediate supervisor on an annual or semiannual basis, which may employ quantitative ratings and usually includes feedback to the employee.

performance test
n. A test of ability requiring manipulation of objects rather than simply verbal or written responses.

peripheral cue
n. Environmental information which is used to select which of alternative interpretations of sensory data is most likely to be accurate. Thus if a person is holding a picture of her mother and says, "She is so kind," the holding of the picture is a peripheral cue that "She" is the mother.

peripheral nerve
n. Any nerve cell or fiber outside the brain and spinal cord.

peripheral nervous system
n. The system of nerves which collect information from and control the functioning of the body and which lie outside the brain and spinal cord. Almost all sensory data gathering and motor actions are performed by peripheral nerves.

peripheral vision
n. The perception of visual information outside the central focus of the eyes around the edges of the visual field. Peripheral vision is more accurate under low lighting conditions than is central or focal vision.

perlocutionary act
n. The act performed of causing an effect on others (such as alerting, persuading, or amusing), as distinct from the content of what is said or the form in which it is said (asking, ordering, pleading).

permissive parent
n. A father or mother who makes few demands on children and tends to avoid exercising control over children and encourage children to make their own choices. This is contrasted with authoritarian, authoritative, and neglecting parents.

persecution, delusion of
n. Any well-developed set of beliefs in which a person reasons logically from obviously false premises that he/she is being persecuted, conspired against, maligned, poisoned, or similarly attacked.

persecutory delusion
n. Any well-developed set of beliefs in which a person reasons logically from obviously false premises that he/she is being persecuted, conspired against, maligned, poisoned, or similarly attacked.

perseveration
n. **1.** In general, the repetition of an act after it has become inappropriate. **2.** Inappropriate repetition of behavior, often seen after frontal lobe brain damage. **3.** The continuation of a lower level of language performance after a developmental stage has been finished, as in the continuation of baby talk by school-age children. **3.** The inability to discontinue a behavior pattern when it is not successful, which is often characteristic of an inability to learn. **4.** The repetition of a learning experience so as to consolidate learning.

persistent vegetative state

n. A prolonged state in which there is minimal brain function, which usually includes maintenance of breathing but in which the person shows no responsiveness to stimuli or voluntary motion. Only a very small minority of persons regain normal function after entering a persistent vegetative state, and these are usually children.

persona

n. **1.** In Jungian psychology, a basic structure of mind which leads people to construct a social mask by enacting recognizable roles as well as to interpret other people's actions; it is a social mask used to cover a true and vulnerable self. **2.** Any assumed identity.

personal construct theory

n. The theory of George A. Kelly in which the individual is presented as an intuitive scientist who is constantly formulating and testing hypotheses whose basis forms the personal constructs which govern behavior and the individual's understanding of the world. Constructs are used by the individual to anticipate events and to formulate plans of action for the anticipated events. Personal construct therapy in which a person changes her/his behavior by changing her/his ideas or understanding of some parts of the world was derived from this theory.

personality

n. The dynamic organization within the individual of common traits, behavior patterns, values, interests, plans and motives, self-understanding and worldview, abilities, and emotional patterns that determine characteristic behavior and thought. All the systems within the individual that develop and interact to create the unique and shared characteristics of the person.

personality assessment

n. Some psychologists believe that human behaviors represent manifestations of underlying psychological attributes or traits. It is further believed that individuals differ in the extent to which they possess these attributes and, consequently, in the degree to which they engage in trait-relevant behaviors. Personality assessment is the enterprise of measuring individuals and quantifying their differential standing on these psychological characteristics.

Personality traits. Personality traits are hypothetical constructs. As such, they cannot be measured directly with electrical or mechanical instruments. Instead, the personality psychologist will infer the level of a trait within an individual by observing the effects of the trait on the person's behavior. The more of a trait that a person possesses, the more trait-relevant behaviors he or she is likely to display.

Consider a psychological attribute common to many theories of personality: extroversion. This trait is a hypothetical construct because it cannot be observed directly. Yet it has been proposed to be a veridical construct, having utility in describing and explaining consistencies in people's behaviors and in predicting future behaviors.

Personality traits are generally conceived of as forming normally distributed dimensions. Thus, for any particular trait, such as extroversion, humans are thought to vary along a continuum, ranging from low levels of the trait to high levels, with most people falling somewhere in the middle of the dimension. The task of personality assessment is to identify those people who are, for example, more extroverted and those who are less extroverted (i.e., more introverted).

Personality questionnaire. One way in which to assess degree of extroversion in a person might be to observe how talkative and friendly he or she is among a group of people. But there are two problems with this behavior sampling approach to personality assessment. The first is that the method is very resource intensive, requiring substantial time and effort to obtain individual difference scores on the traits of interest. The second problem is that the situations in which the person is observed are very limited and circumscribed, and the behaviors elicited therein might not be typical of the person's behaviors more generally.

Contemporary methods of personality assessment generally rely on questionnaires, inventories, checklists, and so on. A personality questionnaire comprises one or more personality scales, each of which is designed to quantify differences among people on a personality trait or construct. The rationale behind the personality questionnaire is that people can be trusted to describe their characteristic behaviors accurately. Furthermore, to the extent that a person's self-description includes behaviors that are exemplars of a particular trait, that trait is inferred to be part of his or her personality makeup.

The basic unit of the personality scale is the personality item. Typical personality scales have items that represent statements describing specific behaviors, behaviors that are considered to be exemplars of personality traits. To illustrate, an extroversion measure might contain the item "I am usually the life of a party." A person taking the questionnaire (respondent) might be asked to answer (endorse) the item as true or false. Alternatively, the response could take the form of choosing a number from a 5-point scale, where smaller numbers mean stronger disagreement with the statement and larger numbers mean stronger agreement. (Some personality questionnaires use single trait-defining adjectives as items instead of statements describing behaviors in situations. For example, an extroversion scale might instruct the respondent to rate the degree to which the term *outgoing* is characteristic of him or her.)

In the example item about being the life of a party, someone who endorses the statement (i.e., exemplar of extroversion) as true, or who agrees with the item, would be classified as being higher on the trait of extroversion than would someone who says false to the item or disagrees with the item. Note that an item measuring a trait might be reverse-keyed. This means that a person endorsing the item as false (or disagree) would be measured to be higher on the trait. An example of a reverse-keyed extroversion item would be "I prefer spending time alone rather than in a large group."

For obvious reasons, one would not generally measure a personality trait with only one behavior statement. Someone high in extroversion, for example, might paradoxically say false to the item "I go out of my way to talk to strangers" for any number of good reasons. A personality scale generally contains several such statements, and a respondent's attribute score is based on the sum or average of his or her endorsements of all the items in the scale. Statistically it can be shown that whereas any one item might grossly overestimate or underestimate the level of trait in a person, the overestimates tend to cancel the underestimates when several such items are averaged, resulting in a more accurate estimate of the person's true level of trait. In general, a scale with more items measuring a trait has better psychometric properties than does a scale with fewer items.

Problem of misrepresentation. One problem with using behavior statements in personality questionnaires is that there is no inherently right or wrong answer to an item. This means that someone can choose to endorse an item as true when, in fact, the more accurate description of the person would be false (or vice versa). Research in personality assessment has shown that some respondents routinely select questionnaire items' more socially desirable response options, regardless of their actual behaviors. The reason for such distortion is a motivation, of which the respondent may or may not be consciously aware, to present a favorable impression by earning high scores on desirable traits (e.g., responsibility) and low scores on undesirable traits (e.g., aggression). Another form of distortion involves misrepresenting oneself as high or low on a trait, regardless of its desirability, if there is a direct incentive to do so. For instance, someone applying for a job as an investigative journalist might be motivated to describe himself or herself as high in aggression.

This issue of misrepresentation in one's self-description presents a challenge to personality inventory designers. One solution to the problem of a respondent's trying to make a good impression is to avoid items that have strong desirability connotations. A solution to the more general problem of misrepresenting oneself as high or low on a trait, regardless of its desirability, is to use items that are not obviously related to the construct being assessed. This latter expedient is considered to be one of the advantages of the so-called empirical method of test construction. Using that method, items are selected for a personality scale based on their empirical ability to predict criteria related to the trait being measured, without regard to the manifest content of the items.

An example will illustrate the empirical method of personality scale construction and its relevance to misrepresentation. Suppose we are developing a questionnaire measure of extroversion and we administer the potential item "My favorite color is green" to a group of suspected extroverts (e.g., members of a debating club) and a group of suspected introverts (e.g., members of a chess club). If the one group endorses the item differently than does the other group, that item would be considered a candidate for our extroversion scale, simply because it predicts a relevant criterion of group membership. Now, someone attempting to fake high extrovert (or high introvert) on that item might be at a loss as to how to proceed. He or she would be unlikely to know whether the correct response is true or false because, although the item is statistically associated with the psychological attribute being measured, the content of the item has no ostensible link to extroversion. It should be mentioned that many assessment specialists reject the empirical method of personality scale construction, arguing that the only viable personality items are those whose content is both rationally and theoretically related to the constructs being assessed.

Other forms of personality assessment. Other paper-and-pencil methods of measuring personality are available that do not use behavior descriptive statements or adjectives as items. There is a whole class of personality instruments known collectively as projective tests. These include such measures as the Rorschach inkblot test, the Thematic Apperception Test, and the Incomplete Sentences Task. The assumption underlying projective tests is that a respondent's interpretation of an ambiguous stimulus is revealing of his or her personality dispositions. For example, the image a person sees in an inkblot may be indicative

of his or her level of anxiety. Or the story one makes up when asked to describe what is happening in a picture of two people talking could reveal the person's level of self-esteem.

Projective tests are thought to enjoy the advantage of being relatively immune to social desirability responding and other forms of motivated distortion. The reason is that respondents generally do not know which responses to give to the ambiguous stimuli if they are intent on misrepresenting their personality characteristics in a particular direction. A major disadvantage of projective tests is related to subjectivity in scoring and interpreting respondent protocols. Despite the fact that formal training procedures are typically required for the administration of such tests (arguably a disadvantage in itself), differences in the judgments of scorers can lead to disagreements among them, even when evaluating the same protocols. This problem then raises broader issues concerning the reliability and the validity of the resultant test scores.

Questionnaires, tests, and inventories are not the only ways in which personality has been assessed. Direct behavior observation has been recommended by some as being superior to self-report, paper-and-pencil measures of traits. As mentioned earlier, however, such direct observations are difficult to obtain in sufficient numbers to yield reliable estimates of personality trait scores. Moreover, the difference in the quality of assessments by direct observation versus self-report questionnaire might not justify the added cost of the former. Self-reports of behavior have sometimes been supplemented with other-reports. For example, an expert rater who is familiar with a person's real-life behaviors (e.g., close acquaintance, coworker, clinician) might be asked to describe that person on a standard personality questionnaire. Presumably, such other-reports are less susceptible to misrepresentation than are self-reports.

Some researchers believe that the best prospect for the future of personality assessment lies in the search for individual differences in quantifiable physical attributes. People high in extroversion, for example, have been found to differ in several material respects from those high in introversion (i.e., low in extroversion). Extroverts, compared to introverts, are more easily distracted from a problem, are more tolerant of pain, are worse at signal detection tasks, and have quicker physiological responsiveness but lower levels of cortical activity. One theory is that introverts and extroverts differ fundamentally in their levels of central nervous system arousal – a physiological state that is proposed to be genetically determined, the basis of most extroversion-related behavior differences, and potentially measurable by electro-mechanical instruments.   – SVP

▶ *See also* **PAPER-AND-PENCIL TESTS, RELIABILITY,** *and* **VALIDITY**

personality disorders

n. A pervasive and enduring pattern of dynamic psychophysical processes, subjective experience, perceptual distortion, and behavior which is markedly maladaptive within a culture. These patterns tend to develop before adulthood, persist in the face of punishment, and lead to personal unhappiness and interpersonal difficulties.

personality inventory

n. A questionnaire type of *personality test* that includes several scales to survey a particular domain of interest in personality. For example, several inventories are available to survey clinical conditions or psychopathology, such as the Personality Assessment Inventory (PAI) or the revised Minnesota Multiphasic Personality Inventory (MMPI-2). Existing taxonomies of normal personality differences have given rise to inventories that assess basic trait dimensions, such as the revised NEO Personality Inventory (NEO-PI-R), the Eysenck Personality Questionnaire (EPQ-R), and the Sixteen Personality Factor Questionnaire (16PF). Inventories are available to identify appropriate careers and occupations, such as the Strong Interest Inventory (SII) or the Campbell Interest and Skill Survey (CISS). Many inventories have a hierarchical structure of scores with the major scales being divided into subscales to facilitate more detailed interpretation of the results. A personality inventory may also contain scales

to evaluate the test taking style of the respondent, such as positive impression management or malingered psychopathology. Other scales are sometimes used to assess whether the respondent has adequate comprehension of the items or attended sufficiently to the items while selecting the responses. These more basic protocol validity measures use single items that are answered uniformly by cooperative respondents or pairs of items with similar or identical content. Computer programs are available for many major personality inventories that provide narrative interpretation reports.   – JK

personality, multiple

n. The presence of two or more distinct personalities or identities in the same person, who recurrently exchange control of the person and who may have only some knowledge about each other and the history of the person involved.

personality organization

n. The coordination, integration, and unification of the different, values, traits, behavior patterns, emotional patterns, plans and goals, and understandings of the world which make up an individual's basic individuality.

personality, split

n. The presence of two or more distinct personalities or identities in the same person, who recurrently exchange control of the person and who may have only some knowledge about each other and the history of the person involved.

personality test

n. A group of procedures designed to quantify or classify some aspect of personality in an individual. Personality tests are used for psychological research, clinical assessment, and psychodiagnosis and in screening and selection of job candidates for many occupations. Traditionally, personality tests have been grouped into two classes, labeled objective tests and projective tests. The term *objective test* generally refers to questionnaires, and the term *projective test* refers to a group of procedures that use an incomplete or ambiguous stimulus and an open-ended response format. However, contemporary experts in personality assessment increasingly recognize that the terms *objective* and *projective* are based on antiquated theories of how these tests operate and carry misleading connotations about the specific tests to which they refer. All personality tests may be considered more or less objective to the extent that they use a standardized method of administration and a reliable scoring procedure. Many tests also have norms based on a large sample of respondents who are representative of the population for which the test will be applied. Some personality tests do not have norms, restricting their usage to research purposes.

Questionnaire tests are the most commonly used procedure in personality assessment. This method uses a fixed list of adjectives, phrases, or statements, and the respondent judges how well each item describes his or her personality using a limited set of discrete response options (true/false; yes/no, etc.) or a Likert scale. The popularity of this method stems from the simplicity of scoring and the possibility of testing respondents in groups, via an Internet Web site, or by conventional mail. Most questionnaires are designed to be self-rated; however, several published questionnaires have separate versions that can be completed by third-party informants. Children's behavioral or personality characteristics are often assessed using rating scales completed by parents, teachers, or trained observers. Structured interview methods require a trained interviewer to select the response options to be scored based on the interviewee's responses to a fixed sequence of questions. The Rorschach Inkblot Method remains a commonly used test in clinical assessment and personality research, despite ongoing controversy about the empirical support for the validity of its scoring systems. Narrative techniques, or storytelling procedures, also have a long history in personality assessment; the Thematic Apperception Test and the Picture Story Exercise provide two common stimulus sets. Here the respondent is shown a drawing or photograph and asked to compose a story. The content and style of the story narrative can be used to score a wide variety of personality variables, such as needs and motives, defense mechanisms, or patterns of relating to others. There are several sentence completion procedures available that provide half-finished sentences to be completed by the respondent. These methods, like the narrative techniques, can provide rich qualitative data that suggest recurrent themes, and they can also yield quantitative scores to use for research or clinical applications. The Washington University Sentence Completion Test (WUSCT) is an example of a sentence completion procedure with a well-developed scoring system. Drawing techniques are another open-ended approach to personality assessment that may be used, especially with children, to gain insight into characteristics that the respondent may not be capable of judging or describing through explicit means.   – JK

▶ *See also* **EGO DEVELOPMENT**

personality theory

n. Any integrated set of constructs which attempts to understand the individual as a unit, including shared traits, behavior patterns, values, interests, plans and motives, self-understanding and worldview, abilities, and emotional patterns that determine characteristic behavior and thought.

personality trait

n. An enduring neuro-psychic structure that guides perception and reaction so that the individual has a moderately predictable pattern of behavior, beliefs, and emotional reactions which is inferred from consistency in behavior, belief, and emotional reaction. Traits can be used to predict and explain a significant fraction of the individual's behavior.

personality type

n. A category of human functioning into which humans can be sorted according to any of a number of theories including Carl Jung's theories of mental orientation and functions, Richard Sheldon's physique types, or Erich Fromm's character orientations.

personal project

n. An extended set of actions related to an individually selected goal which is derived from the basic personality of the individual in interaction with his or her unique environment and which can vary in meaningfulness, management style, social approval, likelihood of success, and stress or burden to the individual. Personal projects are a middle level of analysis in personality psychology between enduring traits and reactions to the immediate environment.

personal striving

n. A system of personal goals which involve a complex set of interrelated values and aims derived from them, some of which conflict with each other and some of which support each other.

personal unconscious

n. In Jungian theory, the relatively small portion of the unconscious which is unique to the individual and contains repressed, suppressed, weak, and forgotten memories, as well as individually created constellations of memories, feelings, thoughts, and perceptions which guide mostly conscious understanding which are called complexes and occasionally dominate the mind.

person-centered therapy

n. The therapy developed by Carl Rogers which assumes that each person lives in a reality of his or her own, has inherent drive to actualize his/her own unique potential, and will do so unless prevented by the need for the positive regard of significant other people. Conditional regard from important other persons leads an individual to have and to act on false beliefs about himself/herself, which lead to anxiety and poor choices in life. This nondirective therapy consists of the therapist's helping the client verbally explore the issues that the client selects by acknowledging the therapist understands what the client is expressing and does not condemn the client for his or her experience. This leads the client to acknowledge the parts of himself/herself that he/she has been ignoring or denying and thus gain better information with which to make choices.

personnel evaluation

n. The processes of rating the performance and worth to the organization of individuals employed by an organization.

personnel psychology

n. The branch of psychology that deals with the selection, placement, training, supervision, morale, evaluation, advisement, discipline, and promotion of persons employed by an organization.

personnel selection

n. The process of identifying and selecting candidates for particular jobs based on their suitability for the demands of the jobs, personal soundness, and likelihood of success on the job using a variety of empirical data and procedures as well as often using intuitive processes.

personology

n. The holistic study of individual human beings with a focus on their individual uniqueness and the totality of their mental and behavioral organization and especially their motivations.

person-situation debate

Definition. *n.* The person-situation debate was a controversial discussion that lasted two decades and dealt with the relative influence of both personal, internal factors (such as personality, thoughts, feelings, attitudes) and external, situational factors on a person's behavior. Some psychologists strictly believed that personality alone influenced behavior, while others thought that only the situation influenced behavior. Presently, it is generally accepted that both personality and the situation interact to produce behavior; thus both must be taken into account when attempting to predict behavior.

Explanation. Trait theories of personality psychology contend that each person possesses certain stable, identifying characteristics (i.e., personality traits) that make him or her who he/she is and that determine what he/she does. For example, a well-known personality trait is extroversion. A person may either be extroverted and outgoing or more shy and introverted. Personality traits influence behavior. Extroverted people tend to enjoy getting attention, meeting new people, and attending large gatherings. Introverted people are just the opposite: they tend to prefer small-group events, are more likely to be shy, and do not like to be the focus of attention. Various personality traits have been shown to predict such behaviors as helping, conformity, aggressiveness, and prejudiced behavior.

Knowledge of people's personalities does not allow the prediction of their behavior in all circumstances. If observed over time, people are bound to have inconsistencies in their behavior. For example, though an individual may have an introverted personality, the person may behave in an outgoing fashion around family members and close friends. Further, the person's job may require acting in an outgoing manner when he or she normally would not choose to do so. Therefore, it has been noted that the situation the person is in must also play a role in influencing behavior.

This observation that people behave differently in different situations resulted in a debate called the "person-situation controversy," which lasted two decades and involved the discussion of when personality versus the situation could be used to predict behavior better. Some psychologists (termed behaviorists) thought only the situation influences behavior. At the same time, other psychologists specializing in personality believed that internal personality characteristics had more influence on behavior. The eventual compromise was the determination that both personality and the situation influence behavior, though the relative effects of personality and the situation change with circumstances. There are certain conditions under which an individual's personality is more likely to influence his/her behavior than the situation he/she is in now. Such circumstances may involve situations when the individual is displaying a strong or dominant personality trait, when the situation is not putting any pressure on the individual to behave in a certain way, when the individual does not care about how his/her behavior fits into the situation,

or when the individual's behavior is being observed over time across several situations. When none of these conditions is met, the person is more likely to behave in a way that fits the current situation rather than his/her usual, personality-driven way of acting.

Carefully controlled experimental research allows the identification of the importance of the situation versus personality in the prediction of a person's behavior. After creating two or more different situations, the experimenter exposes each participant to one of the situations and then measures the participants' behavior. If the participants' behavior differs as a function of which situation they were exposed to, the experimenter determines that this situational difference does influence behavior. To determine the relative importance of the situation versus personality in determining behavior, the researcher can measure personality characteristics with personality scales and manipulate the situation to determine whether personality or the situation better predicts behavior. In general, it is important to have good measures of behavior as well as good measures of personality. There are many scales available for measuring various personality characteristics. Further, if one is trying to measure the way a person usually behaves, multiple people who know the individual well should be asked about his or her typical behavior. The behavior should also be something that can be observed directly, and it should be related to the personality characteristic of interest. The behavior should also be recorded across several situations.

Development and details. Some situations are more influential on behavior than are others. These situations may be those with which the person is less familiar or which may require more formal or specific behaviors. Examples of these types of situations are job interviews and church. In these types of situations there tend to be strong situational cues (there is an expectation for a certain type of behavior), and the individual's personality will tend to influence behavior less than those situational requirements. However, if the person is in a familiar situation (among family and friends), his/her personality is more likely to influence behavior. Consider how a person's behavior would differ if he/she were among friends compared to on a job interview. Even if the person is normally a relaxed, happy-go-lucky person, in an interview it is likely that he/she will be somewhat anxious and on edge. In a job interview, the person would also try to be as professional and polite as possible, while with friends, he/she might tease and make silly jokes. So knowledge of the person's happy-go-lucky personality would lead to the prediction of his/her behavior better when the person is among friends than in a more formal job interview setting. Similarly, while some people might have personality tendencies that lead them consistently to exhibit either helpful or aggressive behaviors, the situation can also influence their behavior, making that personality tendency more or less pronounced. For example, even a very helpful person may become unhelpful and dismissive if he/she is very busy or upset about something.

Some personality types also influence the person to react more or less to situational pressures. In effect, just having the specific personality characteristic makes the situation more or less influential on behavior. The trait of self-monitoring is one example of this type of personality characteristic that affects how influential the situation is. People who have a high level of this trait care a great deal about what other people think about their behavior and want to ensure that their behavior fits the situational demands. These people will be vigilant about monitoring and adjusting their own behavior so they fit in and will be accepted. Because of this constant monitoring, people who have a high level of this trait have a tendency to behave differently on the basis of situational cues. Their behavior is likely to be very different across various situations. People who have a low level of this trait, on the other hand, are not as concerned about fitting their behavior to the situation. These people's behaviors are more likely to be consistent across situations (around different groups of people), and these consistent behaviors are judged to be influenced by the person's personality.

Personality traits also exist in varying degrees. Some personality traits are stronger in some people than in others. For example, one person may be somewhat assertive, while another person may be domineering. When a personality trait is considered strong, or dominant, in a person, that personality trait is more likely to influence the person's behavior across various situations. A person could be very open to new experiences, and somewhat introverted. This person would be expected to be open to the new experiences present in many situations, but he/she would only be expected to be introverted some of the time. Personality traits can also be strong across individuals. An example of this is people's expressive traits, which are displayed in a person's speech, mannerisms, and gestures. Expressive traits are considered strong across individuals because most people tend to use the same types of ways to express themselves across different situations. A person with a very apathetic personality will generally speak in a very monotonous voice and seem bored or practically lifeless in his or her expressions no matter the situation. This is because the strong traits will influence behavior more than the situation. On the other hand, the situation has a greater influence on whether weak personality traits will be displayed. For example, people differ in how concerned they are with impressing others. Those people who are concerned with the impressions they make are more likely to behave differently around people they do not care about impressing (strangers) and those they do (their spouse's friends and family). Thus, the situation makes a difference in the behavior they display.

In addition, personality is a better predictor of behavior across multiple situations than in any one specific situation. In each specific situation, there could be some particular aspect of the situation that influences behavior dramatically. Looking at the way a person behaves on average (across situations) allows us a look at his/her personality and its relationship to the person's behavior. For example, a person who is conscientious may not remember to complete a particular assignment at one point in time, but over time the person's behavior will tend to be conscientious (e.g., usually gets homework done on time, attends class regularly, pays bills on time).

Overall, it turns out that personality and the situation are equally important in predicting behavior. The two have a similar overall influence on a person's behavior. Knowledge of either relationship (personality or the situation) with behavior allows researchers to predict behavior accurately approximately 70% of the time. Although both are important predictors of behavior, either can be more useful in particular instances. For example, it is more useful to use personality to predict a person's behavior across many situations (or how he/she will usually act). Personality is more likely to be a better predictor of behavior in specific situations if the personality characteristic is considered to be dominant in that person, if the situation is a comfortable one for the person, or if the person does not care what kind of impressions are being made. However, it is usually difficult to use personality to predict behavior in a specific situation because there could be some special aspect of that situation that causes the person to alter behavior radically. For example, even an extremely talkative person may be quiet at the library or at a funeral. The situation will play a greater role in the prediction of behavior if there are set social rules to follow or if the person is worried about the impression being made.

While it is true that the situation influences behavior, the individuals' personality has an effect on the situation as well. For example, people with certain types of personalities are drawn to certain situations over others. People with extroverted personalities are more likely to be drawn into very social situations. Being in particular situations also influences the behaviors people will exhibit. Being in a social situation allows a person to display more outgoing behaviors than being at the library. Behaving a certain way can also influence the situation. Behaving in an outgoing fashion tends to attract other people into conversation. Merely displaying outgoing behaviors may increase the likelihood that the person will display such behavior in the future (thus making his/her extroverted personality stronger). — VKP, LAB

person-situation interaction

n. Person-situation (P × S) interaction refers to the process whereby enduring personal qualities are expressed in some situations but not in others in a systematic and predictable manner over time. Therefore, a person's characteristic behavior, thoughts, and emotions are reflected in the interaction between the person and the specific situation. Put slightly differently, what is stable about people's personality is the consistency with which they respond to particular situations in particular ways.

Historically, this notion has emerged in reaction to trait theories of personality. Trait theories assume that personality dispositions are stable across situations and across time. Therefore, the stability of personality is reflected in the consistency with which people behave similarly across situations. According to this view, for example, an aggressive person should, on average, behave more aggressively than a person who is not aggressive across a wide range of situations and settings. Trait psychologists examine similarity clusters in the personality trait descriptions people use in everyday language to identify the structure of personality – a method of investigation known as the psycholinguistic approach. Over the last four decades, this approach has revealed that trait terms cluster into five groups reflecting individual differences in people's tendencies toward neuroticism (e.g., emotional stability vs. instability), conscientiousness (e.g., self-control vs. impulsivity), agreeableness (e.g., friendliness vs. unfriendliness), extroversion (e.g., high-energy, outgoing vs. low-energy, shy), and open-mindedness (e.g., conservative, rigid vs. cultured, open-minded). It is assumed that these traits express themselves in relatively stable behavior across situations. If person A is higher in extroversion (e.g., outgoing behavior) than person B at parties, he/she is expected to be higher than person B also in the office, when dealing with the boss, for example.

In the 1960s, however, research that examined people's behaviors across different situations found cross-situational consistency to be of relatively low magnitude. Although people did show some cross-situational consistency in their behavior, the consistency was much lower than what would be expected by laypeople's intuitions as well as by the trait models. Out of this research emerged the *personality paradox*: on the one hand, our intuitions say that there are stability and coherence to personality; on the other hand, the consistency of behavior across situations is not very high. The paradoxical question then is, Where is the locus of stability, consistency, and coherence in personality if not in cross-situational consistency?

It had been assumed until the late 1960s that the variability observed in people's behavior across situations reflected measurement error – random noise generated in the data by the unreliability of the methods used to measure behavior and personality. Thus, the situation was aggregated out by taking the average of people's behavior across situations to minimize this noise. Researchers who adopted the P × S perspective, however, raised the question of whether this variability could be systematic rather than random. They argued that the variability in a person's behavior across situations could be an expression of a stable underlying personality system, and there might be order in what seems to be chaos. P × S researchers refer to the variability of behavior across situations within a person as *if-then profiles* or *situation-behavior signatures* of personality: *If* Adam is with his elders, *then* he is outgoing, but with his peers then he is not. In contrast, *if* John is with his peers, *then* he is outgoing but not if he is with his elders.

Before this variability could be taken seriously as a viable expression of personality, however, it was necessary to demonstrate empirically that the profiles are stable across time. In other words, it needed to be demonstrated that Adam is more outgoing with his parents and teachers than with his friends and classmates every time he interacts with them. This issue was examined in a study of 6- to 11-year-old boys who resided in a summer camp. Their behavior was closely observed by counselors over many hours and many situations over the course of 6 weeks. The researchers identified five different kinds of "psychological" situations that happened frequently and in which boys' behavior (e.g., aggression, whining) was recorded: situations in which the child was positively approached by a peer (e.g., invitation to play), situations

in which the child was negatively approached by a peer (e.g., teasing), situations in which an adult praised the child, situations in which an adult gave a warning to child, and situations in which an adult actually punished the child. Thus, these situations varied along two dimensions: whether the interaction was positive or negative in nature and whether the interaction was with a same-status peer or a higher-status adult.

The counselors' observations indicated that each child showed a distinctive if-then profile. For example, whereas one child was verbally aggressive above the average when warned by adults but lower than average when approached prosocially by peers, another one was highest in comparison to others when approached positively by a peer, but not when warned by an adult. More importantly, when boys' if-then profiles for odd-numbered days of the camp were compared to their profiles on even-numbered days, the profiles were highly correlated and similar. Thus, situation-behavior profiles were found to be stable, reflecting each child's distinctive situation-behavior signature.

Researchers also studied whether people are sensitive to information about their own if-then profiles. In one study, they observed college students' conscientious behavior over time and across situations, asking questions such as "Is their room tidy at home?" and "Do they arrive for class on time?" The students were also asked whether they perceived themselves as a person who is consistent in his or her conscientious behavior. The question of interest was, Do students who perceive themselves to be consistently conscientious do so because their conscientious behavior is consistent across situations and across time (for example, always tidy in their room and on time to class, thus, exhibiting *cross-situational consistency*) or because their conscientious behavior varies across situations in a consistent manner (for example, *always* tidy in their room but *rarely* arrives on time for class, thus, exhibiting *if-then profile consistency*)? The researchers found that it is the latter type of consistency that gave rise to people's perceptions of stability in their own personality, explaining how people may have strong intuitions about the consistency and coherence of their personality even though they do not necessarily behave very consistently across situations.

Research suggests that people are also sensitive to information about how behavior may systematically vary across situations in describing others' personality. For example, analyses of people's spontaneous descriptions of personality revealed that people use statements that identify the situations in which people exhibit a certain behavior and those in which they do not (e.g., "John is *always* outgoing and friendly when around his friends but *never* gives a smile to his teachers"). People also seem to underscore the stability of these relationships in their language by using *certainty* modifiers such as *always, all the time*, or *never* that communicate the consistency with which others behave in certain ways in specific situations.

Thus, in recent social-cognitive reconceptualizations of personality that draw from these findings, the building units for the structure of personality are considered to be individuals' expectancies, beliefs, emotions, goals, values, encodings, and competencies. These units are organized into a unique network of interconnections that function as an organized whole. Personality differences are thought to arise from differences in the content of the units people have (e.g., one person may expect to be rejected whereas another may expect to be accepted all the time) and in the organization or connections they have among themselves. For example for Person X, a situation that involves a potential dating partner may bring to mind the expectation that rejection is about to occur. This expectation, in turn, may activate the need and desire to leave the situation, leading to withdrawal and avoidance. In Person Y, in contrast, the same rejection expectation may activate anger and resentment, leading to hostile behavior even before rejection actually occurs. Thus, the content of available units and the organization among those units within the personality system explain differences in behavior between people.

How does such a model explain if-then profiles? Of all the beliefs, goals, values, encodings, and feelings that a person can potentially experience at any given time, only those which are activated (i.e., brought to mind) in a given situation can influence subsequent behavior. Thus, as the individual moves differently across situations, different goals, expectations, beliefs, emotions, competencies, and different relations are activated in relation to these differing psychological conditions. However, the organization of relations among these units remains relatively stable and invariant across situations. Let us take our previous example. For Person Y, situations that involve potential dating partners activate expectations of rejection, which lead to thoughts and emotions that result in aggressive behavior. For this same person, however, situations that involve same-sex friends may inhibit rejection expectations and instead elicit feelings of trust and safety. In these situations, Person Y may not be aggressive at all; in fact he/she may very well be even more friendly than other people. Thus, Person Y's personality may reflect a distinctive if-then profile: "if with opposite sex-partners, then aggressive, but if with same sex-partners, then friendly." What remain stable, however, are the cognitive and affective mediating processes that generate these relationships: dating partner situations always activate rejection concerns, which are stably linked to aggressive behavioral scripts, whereas same-sex peer situations always activate a sense of safety, which always leads to greater friendly behavior. In this sense, the person and the situation function in tandem in a dynamic system: we can draw conclusions about personality not by factoring the situation out, but precisely by factoring the situation *in*.   – OA

perspective taking

n. The mental capacity to imagine a point of view different from one's own, usually either another person's point of view or a physically or intellectually different point of view.

perspectivism

n. Developed by William J. McGuire, perspectivism is an epistemological stance that combines pragmatist and postpositivist philosophy of science. It assumes a "tragic theory of knowledge" in which "all knowledge representations are imperfect but all catch some aspect of the known." Because all knowledge – including scientific knowledge – is conditionally true *from some perspective*, the task of the researcher is to generate, capture, and critically assess multiple hypotheses creatively by theoretically and empirically identifying their respective domains of applicability. The implication that hypothesis generation and exploration are as important as empirical confrontation led McGuire to the identification of dozens of methodological heuristics and guiding principles for the creative generation and rigorous assessment of hypotheses in psychology and related fields. What results is an expansive search for the enabling and boundary conditions of real phenomena situated in a world of multiple causes, effects, and mechanisms.   – CDH, JTJ

persuasion

n. The act or process of inducing another person or persons to change their ideas, beliefs, attitudes, or feelings about some topic or topics.

persuasive communication

n. Information conveyed with the intention of shaping another's point of view on a particular topic.

pervasive developmental disorders

n. A family of childhood disorders characterized by severe and encompassing impairment in multiple areas of mental development and especially in social perception, interaction, and communication. These include autistic disorder, Rett's disorder, childhood disintegrative disorder, and Asperger's disorder.

pessimism

n. Pessimism has been described as generalized negative outcome expectancies as well as a negative outlook on life. Evidence exists for unidimensional, bidimensional, and possibly multidimensional conceptualizations of pessimism (with optimism), and it is unclear whether optimism and pessimism are on a continuum or partially independent of each other. Research has linked pessimism to negative physiological and psychological outcomes

such as depressive symptoms and increased mortality, but several studies have failed to replicate those results. Additionally, pessimism may confer certain benefits. "Defensive pessimists" use pessimism to manage their mood and prepare for important events by setting low expectations and reflecting extensively on possible negative outcomes, and that strategy improves their performance. Studies have also suggested that compared with European Americans, Asian Americans have higher levels of pessimism, though pessimism may serve an adaptive function in Asian Americans by helping them to prepare for the worst.   – RC, ECC

petit mal

n. A form of epilepsy in which the individual's seizures do not involve gross muscle movements.

PET scan

n. Positron emission tomography. A method of creating images of the insides of bodies including the brain by means of computer analysis of the absorption of positron emitting radioactive chemicals ingested by or injected into subjects and then differentially absorbed by different tissues. This leads to interpretable spatial patterns of data received by arrays of positron receptors. This technique allows analysis of functioning of different tissues during different activities such as the absorption of the radioactive sugar fluorine-18 labeled 2-deoxyglucose, which is taken up by brain cells in proportion to their activity level.

phallic

adj. Of or relating to the penis; often used in psychoanalysis to refer to anything resembling a penis or associated with the penis such as power.

phallic phase

n. In psychoanalysis, the phase of development, beginning about age 3, in which children begin to focus on their genitals as the main source of sensory pleasure. Most boys and girls want to put the pleasure they derive from manipulating their genitals together with their mother, a desire that leads to conflict with their father, whom they see as a rival for their mother's love. This typically leads to castration anxiety for boys, in which they project their hatred and desire to castrate the father onto the father and fear he will castrate them. Eventually boys try to become like their father so they can induce someone like their mother to marry them. Little girls envy their father's possession of a penis and feel wounded and inadequate, blame their mothers for not preventing their fathers from castrating them, and eventually seek to become like their mothers so they can marry a man and thus possess the power of their husband's penis. The anxiety resulting from these conflicts eventually leads children to repress overt sexuality and enter the latency stage of development.

phallic stage
n. In psychoanalysis, the phase of development, beginning about age 3, in which children begin to focus on their genitals as the main source of sensory pleasure. Most boys and girls want to put the pleasure they derive from manipulating their genitals together with their mother, a desire that leads to conflict with their father, whom they see as a rival for their mother's love. This typically leads to castration anxiety for boys, in which they project their hatred and desire to castrate the father onto the father and fear he will castrate them. Eventually boys try to become like their father so they can induce someone like their mother to marry them. Little girls envy their father's possession of a penis and feel wounded and inadequate, blame their mothers for not preventing their fathers from castrating them, and eventually seek to become like their mothers so they can marry a man and thus possess the power of their husband's penis. The anxiety resulting from these conflicts eventually leads children to repress overt sexuality and enter the latency stage of development.

phallic symbol
n. Any object which bears some resemblance, either physical or nonphysical, to a penis, which is used as a replacement for a penis.

Thus in dreams a sexually repressed person may dream of a snake, tall slender trees, or the columns on the front of a building instead of a penis.

phallus
n. A penis or a symbolic representation of a penis.

phantom limb
n. The sensation that a missing arm or leg is still present, which is often experienced as pain or tingling in part or all of the missing limb. This may occur when spontaneous or random impulses in the nerve tracts that convey information from the limb reach the brain and the brain interprets them as it would were the limb still present.

pharmacology
n. The study of the effects of chemicals on the body and research into the best uses of chemicals to treat medical problems.

phenobarbital
n. $C_{12}H_{12}N_2O_3$. A long-acting barbiturate which acts as a central nervous system depressant, which is primarily used as an anticonvulsant in grand mal epilepsy. It was formerly often prescribed as a sedative or hypnotic. It has high overdose and addiction potential and so is less frequently used than in the past. Also called Luminal.

phenomenal self
n. The active perception of a person by himself/herself. The self as perceived is very changeable and seldom includes all the information that an objectivist account would include in a description of the individual.

phenomenological method
n. A research method in which data consists of an individual's record or description of his or her experience. In the pure form of the method, the experiential data is analyzed without reference to anything not experienced. In less pure forms, the experiential data is used to form hypotheses concerning objectivist theories concerning human function such as in rating the effectiveness of a

drug in blocking pain or the effectiveness of meditation in lifting depression.

phenomenology
n. The study of experience in its own terms without reference to any thing or theory which is not part of experience, as opposed to using experience as an adjunct to descriptions of objective data. Phenomenological analysis is the basis of existential psychology and person-centered therapy.

phenomenon
n. 1. Any single experience or observed event. 2. An odd or unusual event or individual. 3. Any object as perceived and understood by the mind, as opposed to the thing as it actually is.

phenothiazine
n. A family of older, antipsychotic drugs often referred to as typical antipsychotics, including Thorazine, Stelazine, Haldol, and Prolixin. These drugs caused a revolution in the treatment of schizophrenia when they were first used in the 1950s which led to a great reduction in the institutionalization of psychotic individuals. They work primarily by blocking dopamine D2 receptors and have serious side effects including tardive dyskinesia, extrapyramidal symptoms, and sedation and may cause brain damage with long-term usage.

phenotype
n. In genetics, the actual characteristics of an individual, which may differ from those of another individual with the same gene or set of genes for a particular characteristic and are presumed to be an expression of the genes in interaction with the environment.

phenylketonuria
n. (PKU) The presence of high levels of phenylketones (phenylpyruvic acid) in the urine due to an inherited inability to metabolize phenylalanine, which is caused by the absence of phenylalanine hydroxylase and leads to high levels of phenylalanine in the blood, which, in turn, cause severe mental retardation unless diet is controlled to prevent the ingestion of foods containing phenylalanine.

phi coefficient
n. A linear measurement of the degree of relationship between two dichotomous and randomly distributed variables which equals the product-moment correlation if the variables are coded using 0 and 1 for the dichotomous values.

philosophy of science
n. The branch of philosophy which examines science, the methods of science, scientific explanation, and the epistemology and ultimate meaning of the scientific approach.

phi phenomenon
n. An apparent movement from one location to the other, which is perceived when two lights quickly flash on and off near each other. This is common in lighted signs with rows of bulbs which rhythmically go on and off.

phobia
n. An irrational and persistent fear of a particular thing, event, or situation which is extreme enough to bother the individual and often leads to irrational acts of avoidance. This includes common irrational fears such as those of spiders, public speaking, flying, water, blood, particular animals, and people from other countries, cultures, or social groups.

phobia, simple
n. An irrational and persistent fear of a particular thing, event, or situation which is extreme enough to bother the individual and often leads to irrational acts of avoidance in the absence of any other diagnosis of psychological disorder.

phobia, social
n. An irrational and persistent fear of interaction with other people which is extreme enough to bother the individual and often leads to irrational acts of avoidance.

phobic anxiety
n. The irrational fear experienced by a person with a phobia or irrational fear when exposed to a feared thing, event, or situation.

phobic disorder

n. Any mental illness that involves an irrational and persistent fear of a particular thing, event, or situation which is extreme enough to bother the individual and often leads to irrational acts of avoidance. This is common in anxiety disorders such as panic disorder, generalized anxiety disorder, obsessive-compulsive disorder, and social anxiety disorder and is sometimes present in psychotic disturbances.

phoneme

n. A phoneme is an abstract mental representation of a sound or family of sounds. The collection of phonemes for a language is referred to as that language's phonemic inventory. Within a phonemic inventory, different phonemes are contrastive with respect to each other: replacing one with another in a word results in a change in meaning. Contrastive differences can be diagnosed by finding minimal pairs, pairs of words that differ only in terms of the two sounds in question: /t/ and /d/ are contrastively different in English (minimal pair: *bet, bed*), /t/ and the flap /R/ are contrastively different in Spanish (minimal pair: *pata* "duck," *para* "for"). Families of sounds that are not contrastively different in a language are called allophonic variants, or allophones, of the same underlying phoneme. Two allophones are in complementary distribution when the contexts in which one occurs differ from the contexts in which the other occurs. In English, the two allophones of /t/, aspirated [t?] and the flap [R], are in complementary distribution: flaps only occur intervocalically (between two vowels) as the onset consonants of unstressed syllables. Allophones of a single phoneme are usually perceived by native speakers of a language as belonging to the same category. For example, words such as *top, stop, baton, butter, beat* illustrate the range of English allophones for the phoneme /t/.   – EMF

phonemic restoration

n. The phonemic restoration effect is a phonological illusion informative about the processes involved in recovering phonological structure during language comprehension. In experiments eliciting phonemic restoration effects, listeners are asked to identify words presented alone or inside sentences. These words are presented with a segment of noise (white noise, coughs, clicks) or with a segment of silence replacing one or several phonetic segments. For example, the /s/ in the word *legislatures*, uttered inside a sentence, can be removed and replaced with a cough. Listeners to the altered utterance will perceive *legislatures* as intact and the cough as superimposed, or perhaps even displaced to the right or left of *legislatures*. Another robust phonemic restoration effect is induced by inserting silence in a word like *slit*, between the first two consonants. Listeners will hear *split*, even though the silence could have signaled other stop consonants, [t] or [k]. This second example emphasizes how phonotactic constraints are exploited during speech perception: the sequence [spl] is a phonotactically permissible onset in English, unlike [stl] and [skl].
     – EMF

▶ *See also* **PHONOLOGY**

phonemics

n. Phonemics is a term used to describe the study of phonemes and phoneme systems, a use of the term that is relatively obsolete. In the field of literacy, *phonemics* is sometimes used interchangeably with the more specific term *phonemic awareness*, the ability consciously to identify and distinguish between phonemes. Phonemic awareness, a highly reliable predictor of early reading ability, is assessed by testing a person's ability to blend, isolate, categorize, segment, and delete phonemes in words.   – EMF

phonetic alphabet

n. A phonetic alphabet is a set of symbols used to transcribe the sounds of natural languages. One such system, the International Phonetic Alphabet (IPA), was created in the late 1800s by a group of language instructors who founded the International Phonetic Association. The IPA categorizes its symbols – and, by extension, the sounds of natural languages – into vowel and consonant categories, distinguishing within these between place of articulation and other articulatory parameters. While the IPA is one of the most widely used systems for transcribing speech sounds, it is far from being the only system. The APA (American Phonetic Alphabet), for example, is used by many phoneticians who transcribe American English; it differs in the symbols and symbol sequences it uses to transcribe a handful of consonants and some of the vowels of the language. SAMPA (Speech Assessment Methods Phonetic Alphabet) and its variant X-SAMPA (Extended SAM Phonetic Alphabet) are phonetic alphabets that use only seven-bit ASCII characters to transcribe speech; they were created to facilitate transcriptions in computer contexts where the extended characters required by alphabets like the IPA are not available.

– EMF

▶ *See also* **ARTICULATION**

phonetics

n. Phonetics is a field of inquiry concerned with the study of speech sounds by examining the articulatory mechanisms involved in speech production (articulatory phonetics) and in speech perception (auditory phonetics) and the acoustic properties of the signal (acoustic phonetics). Other subfields of phonetics include clinical phonetics, experimental phonetics, and forensic phonetics. One outcome of the systematic study of phonetics has been the classification of speech sounds along a number of phonetic parameters, which predominantly have articulatory foundations with auditory consequences but also have acoustic signatures identifiable in the signal. Consonants are characterized phonetically on three dimensions: their voicing (whether they are produced with phonation), their place of articulation (where in the vocal tract they are produced: at the lips, teeth, palate, etc.), and their manner of articulation (how they are produced: with full or partial closure, with or without turbulence, etc.). Vowels are characterized on the basis of the position of the tongue along a horizontal (front, central, or back) and a vertical (high, mid, low) axis, as well as other parameters, including rounding, nasalization, rhoticity (r-coloring), and tenseness.   – EMF

▶ *See also* **ARTICULATION** *and* **VOCAL CORDS**

phonology

n. Phonology is the component of a language's grammar which licenses the sound structure for sentences, phrases, or words. Phonological structure consists of a sequence of *phonemes*, or contrastive sounds, related to each other hierarchically: consonants and vowels are grouped into syllables; syllables are grouped into prosodic words (or *phonological words*); prosodic words are grouped into intonational phrases; and so on. The phonology of a language specifies what sound sequences are allowed and disallowed within and between words, by *phonotactic constraints*. For example, neither *plarg* nor *tlarg* is a word in English, but the sequence of initial consonants in *tlarg* makes it an impossible word for the language. A language's phonology also specifies the *phonemic inventory*, the collection of distinctive sounds for that language. Finally, a language's phonology contains principles used to transform a phonological representation into its surfacing phonetic form. For example, in American English, the underlying phoneme /t/ at the end of the morpheme *write* surfaces, by phonological rule, as a flap [R] in *writing*, as an unaspirated stop [t] in *writes*, and possibly as unreleased [t?] in *write*.   – EMF

▶ *See also* **PHONEME** *and* **PROSODY**

photopigment

n. A chemical in the rod or cone of the eye which undergoes a change in state when struck by a photon, which then causes changes in the electrochemical state of the cell which may lead to generation of a neural impulse, causing us to see light. In the rods this chemical is known as rodopsin and the different kinds in cone cells are called iodopsins.

photoreceptor

n. A cell or mechanism which responds to the impingement of light in an organized way, such as the rods and cones in human eyes or the electrochemical processes in an electronic eye.

photosensitive epilepsy

n. A seizure disorder in which seizures are triggered by light, usually bright light or light with particular characteristics such as flashing at a particular rate.

phototaxis
n. Movement toward or away from light such as that of many plants which move toward sunlight. It is the most common form of tropism.

phototherapy
n. A treatment involving exposure to particular wavelengths of light. Many skin conditions are treated with ultraviolet or infrared light. Seasonal affective disorder (SAD) is often treated by exposure to bright white light, which leads to a suppression of melatonin production, which is associated with SAD.

phototropism
n. A movement toward or away from light such as that of many plants which move toward sunlight. It is the most common form of tropism.

phrenology
n. An archaic theory in which the shape of the skull was associated with personality and various abilities. It supposed that different brain areas governed different characteristics and abilities, and those that were strongest in a person would cause the skull to bulge outward while growing so that the resulting bumps indicated the strength of the ability or characteristic associated with the part of the brain beneath it.

phylogenesis
n. **1.** The evolutionary development of any group of organisms. **2.** A diagrammatic representation of the evolutionary development of a group of organisms showing theoretical linkages among different species.

phylogenetic
adj. Of or relating to the evolutionary development of any group of organisms.

phylogeny
n. The evolutionary process of development of a species or other group of organisms.

physical attractiveness
n. The degree to which an individual person or other organism fits criteria of desirability

defined by a culture or species. In humans, it has been found that there are both cultural and universal criteria for attractiveness.

physiological arousal
n. A bodily state of preparedness to act characterized by high levels of norepinephrine and adrenaline in the bloodstream, accelerated heart and respiration rates, elevated blood pressure, increased blood flow to the skeletal muscles and decreased flow to the inner organs, increased muscle tension, narrowed attention, and heightened emotionality.

physiological psychology
n. The branch of psychology that studies biological processes and their interaction with mental states and behavior with special emphasis on the central nervous system, neurochemical, and hormonal processes. It includes the fields of cognitive neuroscience, behavioral neuroscience, psychoneuroimmunology, and behavioral endocrinology.

physiology
n. The branch of science that studies the chemistry of biological processes and its interaction with function and behavior with special focus on processes of cell, tissue, and organ function.

physostigmine
n. An alkaloid extracted from the African Calabar bean which has strong cholinergic effects and is used in the treatment of glaucoma and as an antidote to overdoses of anticholinergic agents such as strychnine and atropine. Its use increases the activity of post nicotinic acid and muscarine pathways in the brain.

Piagetian
adj. Of or relating to the person, ideas, or works of Jean Piaget, a Swiss researcher who developed many theories about human epistemology and especially the structure and development of mind.

Piaget's theory
n. A set of ideas developed by the Swiss physiologist Jean Piaget, who suggested that the

human mind develops in a set of stages, which he called the sensorimotor, preoperational, concrete, operational, and formal operational stages, whose order is invariant across culture. The awareness of the continuous existence of an object when it is outside our sensory field develops during the sensorimotor period and is called object permanence. During the preoperational stage the child is self-centered and unable to see things from nonsensory points of view although rudimentary language and number concepts are learned. In the stage of concrete operations the child begins to think objectively about both the world and himself/herself and begins to use operations such as reversibility, conservation, and categorization about specific objects and situations. In the stage of formal operations these are extended into abstract thinking, hypothetico-deductive reasoning, and mature moral reasoning.

pica

n. An eating disorder of infancy and early childhood in which the child preferentially seeks out and eats specific nonnutritive substances such as dirt, hair, paint, plaster, or starch which may be due to calcium deficiency and can lead to poisoning such as lead poisoning if the child ingests lead-based paint or other toxic materials.

pidgin

n. Pidgins are languages that develop in contexts where speakers do not have a common language for communication. One language will serve as the lexifier, providing the bulk of the vocabulary. Early in its development, a pidgin will have highly variable structure, but as the pidgin stabilizes, so does its grammar. A defining characteristic of pidgins is that they are acquired as second languages. However, when children begin acquiring a pidgin as a first language – say, from caregivers who speak it to each other – the pidgin begins a transformation into a creole. Alternatively, pidgins can become obsolete if a different language takes over as the primary medium for communication. Common to pidgins is a tendency toward subject-verb-object canonical word order, no complex structure involving

embedded clauses, limited morphological processes, and a preference for syllables consisting of a nuclear vowel plus an optional onset consonant.   – EMF

pilot study

n. A preliminary version of a research project intended to test the practicality of the intended measures and procedures in the project and to suggest modifications to be used in the actual study.

pineal gland

n. A small cone-shaped gland on the wall of the third ventricle of the brain which secretes melatonin, which is involved in the rhythms of sleep, adjustments to seasonal light variations including seasonal affective disorder (SAD), and the onset of adolescence.

pinna

n. The external part of the ear. Also called auricle.

pivot grammar

n. The structure of language typically used by children during the stage in which most of their sentences have only two words such as "More milk" or "Open door" in which there is a pivot word which denotes action and another word (open word) which denotes the object of the action.

PKU

n. (phenylketonuria) The presence of high levels of phenylketones (phenylpyruvic acid) in the urine due to an inherited inability to metabolize phenylalanine, which is caused by the absence of phenylalanine hydroxylase and leads to high levels of phenylalanine in the blood, which, in turn, cause severe mental retardation unless diet is controlled to prevent the ingestion of foods containing phenylalanine.

placebo

n. An inactive substance substituted for a drug or a meaningless treatment substituted for an experimental treatment given to a control group during an experiment to prevent them and, sometimes, the experimenter from knowing they did not receive the treatment so they can be used as a comparison group for the group that actually received the treatment.

placebo effect

n. The change in functioning or behavior brought about by the administration of an inert substance or nonspecific treatment which seems to be caused by a belief that a subject has received a treatment. Thus a person who is given a sugar pill and is told it is a powerful sleeping pill may experience sleepiness after taking the pill, while a person who is not told it is a sleeping pill is unlikely to feel sleepy after taking the same kind of pill. Placebo effects account for a significant portion of the effectiveness of many medications and treatments.

planned behavior, theory of

n. The theory of planned behavior (TpB) is a model for predicting behaviors that are not necessarily within a person's control. There are five main components constituting the TpB. The theory states that an individual's *behavior* is best predicted from his/her *intention* of performing the behavior and his/her control over it. This behavioral intention must first be predicted from knowledge of the individual's *attitudes, subjective norms,* and *perceived behavioral* control for performing the behavior.   – VKP, LAB

planned comparison

n. A comparison of the means of two or more groups in an analysis of variance or regression analysis that has been planned prior to gathering the data. This is contrasted with post hoc comparisons.

planned test

n. A comparison of the means of two or more groups in an analysis of variance or regression analysis that has been planned prior to gathering the data. This is contrasted with post hoc comparisons.

plantar reflex

n. An involuntary extension and spreading of the toes when the sole is appropriately stroked

that is usually present in infants but largely disappears in older children and adults.

plasticity

n. Malleability, flexibility, or adaptability, especially as applied to the growth and development of neural and other tissue. This seems to be inherent in the expression of genetic forms and is assumed to be the basis for the differences observed between genotypes and phenotypes. It is also one of the processes by which the brain learns and develops sensory acuity.

platykurtic

adj. Of or relating to a distribution of scores that has more extreme scores and fewer scores near the median than a normal curve.

play therapy

n. Any of numerous forms of child therapy in which the child is given an opportunity to play, usually with a set of toys, clay, drawing materials, or sand tray, in the presence of a therapist who may or may not ask questions or otherwise direct the play. It is based on the assumption that the child's emotional life is reflected in his or her play and is an opportunity to discover new ways of coping with her/his problems. Play therapy is done both individually and in groups, and in groups it is assumed that the children in the group serve as a situation in which the child can explore forms of acting, thinking, and feeling with different feedback from that received in their home situations.

pleasant emotions

n. Any pattern of reaction to events that are believed by the individual to be positive with reference to him or her, as is experiencing those events. Happiness is basic positive emotion, and it is similar to a wide range of emotions such as satisfaction, glee, love, euphoria, and contentment that are also deemed pleasant.

pleasure center

n. Any of several brain centers which when stimulated in humans are associated with sensations of pleasure and which rats and other mammals will repeatedly self-stimulate if given the opportunity to do so. These include areas in the hypothalamus, nucleus accumbens, septum pellucidium, other portions of the limbic system, and the medial forebrain cluster.

pleasure-pain principle

n. In psychoanalysis, the basic motivation of human nature, which is to obtain the gratification of biological drives, is located in the id and through associations becomes attached to nonphysiological objects. As the person matures, behavior is governed more and more by the reality principle, which delays gratification of pleasure in order ultimately to obtain the most possible gratification through following complex plans for the future. Also called the pleasure principle.

pleasure principle

n. In psychoanalysis, the basic motivation of human nature, which is to obtain the gratification of biological drives, is located in the id and through associations becomes attached to nonphysiological objects. As the person matures, behavior is governed more and more by the reality principle, which delays gratification of pleasure in order ultimately to obtain the most possible gratification through following complex plans for the future. Also called the pleasure-pain principle.

point-biserial correlation

n. (Rb) A measure of relationship between a continuous variable and a dichotomous one scaled so that 0 indicates no relationship and +1 indicates a perfect positive relationship while −1 indicates a perfect inverse relationship.

point of subjective equality

n. The intensity of a comparison stimulus that is equally likely to be judged as less intense or more intense than the original stimulus by a particular subject.

Poisson distribution

n. A theoretical data distribution which gives the likelihood of occurrence of relatively rare events that are randomly distributed in time or space.

polarization

n. **1.** A difference in electric potential across a cell membrane such as occurs in nerve and muscle cells, whose depolarization leads to nerve impulses and contractions. **2.** A phenomenon in subgroups in which individuals' opinions grow more extreme when there is conflict between the subgroups or the attention of the groups focuses on the differences between the groups. **3.** A state of light transmission in which the light follows parallel paths within a plane.

politeness ideology

n. A belief system about the observance of accepted social patterns and especially patterns of linguistic interaction. These ideas are generally associated with the idea of face or public self-image and are variable among cultures, subcultures, and individuals of different status and familiarity.

politeness theory

n. The scientific investigation of the observance and nonobservance of accepted social patterns and especially patterns of linguistic interaction within and between cultures and subcultures. These ideas are generally associated with the idea of face or public self-image and are variable among cultures, subcultures, and individuals of different status and familiarity.

political participation

n. The degree to which an individual or group acts with an intention of influencing a government or other formalized social group.

political psychology

n. An interdisciplinary branch of psychology that studies political beliefs, attitudes, and participation and their interaction with the functioning of the mind.

Pollyanna effect

n. The tendency of people to have unrealistically positive expectations, to focus on positive information often to the exclusion of negative information, and to process positive information better than negative information.

polyandry

n. The social practice of having more than one husband or mate at the same time. This is uncommon in human cultural practice, is usually found in cultures in which there is matrilineal inheritance, but is not uncommon in animals.

polydipsia

n. Prolonged, excessive thirst, often without any physiological need for water. It sometimes occurs in diabetes mellitus but is more often of psychological origin.

polygamy

n. The practice of having more than one wife or mate at the same time, which has been the most common form of marriage across cultures and throughout history. It has occurred much more often than polyandry, the practice of having multiple husbands, or monogamy. It is also frequent among animals.

polygenic inheritance

n. Any characteristic passed from one generation to the next which is determined by more than one gene.

polygyny

n. The practice of having more than one wife or female mate at the same time but not allowing a woman multiple husbands, which has been the most common form of marriage across cultures and throughout history. It is also frequent among animals.

polysemy

n. The situation in which a word has more than one meaning in the same language. For instance, the word *kind* can mean either "benevolent" or "type."

pons

n. That portion of the brainstem above the medulla oblongata and below the midbrain, which is primarily an area of connection for nerve tracts running among different parts of the nervous system. It has some role in coordinating voluntary movement and maintaining balance.

Ponzo illusion

n.

A visual illusion in which two identical, parallel lines appear different in length when transected by converging lines.

population density

n. The number of people within a fixed area of land. Can be computed by determining the ratio between the number of people in an area and the size of the area. Population density has been shown to be an important factor in influencing human cultures; cultures will differ in the rules, norms, and ways of living created in an area with high population density as compared to one with low population density.

positive afterimage

n. A visual perception after the actual stimulus is gone which is usually in attenuated or altered form. A Hering, or positive, afterimage is a brief image similar to the original image but not as bright. In contrast, a Purkinje, or negative, afterimage is like a color negative image of the original in which light and dark are reversed and colors are seen as the ones complementary to the original ones. Thus an original image with blue in it will be seen as a yellow Purkinje image.

positive correlation

n. A linear relationship between two variables in which one increases as the other increases, as indicated by a positive number in a correlation coefficient.

positive feedback

n. **1.** Approval, praise, or acceptance received in response to a specific act. **2.** An information system arranged so that output data is input into the system in order to correct performance.

positive illusion

n. An unrealistically good evaluation, usually of the self, maintained in the face of contrary evidence.

positive logical determinism

n. A tendency to see contradictions as mutually exclusive categories, as either-or, yes-no, one-or-the-other types of categories.

positive psychology

n. Positive psychology is a newly christened approach that takes seriously as a subject matter those things that make life most worth living. The field was named in 1998 as one of the initiatives of Martin Seligman in his role as president of the American Psychological Association. Today's positive psychologists do not claim to have invented notions of happiness and well-being, to have proposed their first theoretical accounts, or even to have ushered in their scientific study. Rather, the contribution of contemporary positive psychology has been to provide an umbrella term for what had been isolated lines of theory and research and to make the argument that what makes life worth living deserves its own field of inquiry within psychology, at least until that day when all of psychology embraces the study of what is good along with the study of what is bad.   – CPe, NP

positive regard

n. Warmth, caring, and acceptance toward another individual, which is often regarded as a necessary condition for optimal human growth and development of self-worth in children and in therapy clients.

positive reinforcement

n. **1.** A reward or rewarding circumstance following an action which leads to the action's being more likely to be repeated. **2.** The act of rewarding particular behaviors.

positive symptoms of schizophrenia

n. Symptoms that are an *addition* in the functioning of a typical healthy person. Note that *positive* refers to added aspects of an average functioning individual and not a "good or helpful symptom" (symptoms by definition are detrimental). Positive symptoms in schizophrenia include hallucinations (a sensory perception in the absence of any external stimulus, for example, hearing voices) and delusions (fixed false beliefs). Occasionally disorganized symptoms in schizophrenia are classified as positive symptoms. They include disorganized speech and thinking (such as tangential, incoherent, or circumstantial speech) and disorganized behavior (such as odd or erratic behavior or gestures). In general positive symptoms (especially hallucinations and delusions) have been the most responsive to typical antipsychotic medications.   – DGa

positive transfer

n. A reduction in the effort or time necessary to learn something due to similar previous learning. Thus learning to conjugate one verb in a foreign language may make it easier to learn to conjugate other verbs in the same or similar languages.

positivism

n. Any of a number of philosophical approaches in which all ideas are based upon sensory experience subjected to empirical methods of verification.

positivism, logical

n. An archaic philosophy in which spirituality and ethics are rejected as meaningless and the assumption is made that the only meaningful statements that can be made are simple propositions which can be verified by observation. It was an important point of view in late 19th- and early 20th-century psychology in points of view such as behaviorism.

positron emission tomography

n. (PET) A method of creating images of the insides of bodies including the brain by means of computer analysis of the absorption of positron emitting radioactive chemicals ingested by or injected into subjects and then differentially absorbed by different tissues. This procedure leads to interpretable spatial patterns of data received by arrays of positron receptors. This technique allows analysis of functioning of different tissues during different activities such as the absorption of the radioactive sugar, fluorine-18 labeled 2-deoxyglucose, which is taken up by brain cells in proportion to their activity level.

postconventional morality

n. In Kohlberg's theory of moral development, this is the third and highest level of reasoning, characterized by a reliance on autonomous moral principles. Two stages compose this level of moral reasoning. In stage 5, social contract orientation, individuals base their moral judgments on the degree to which actions promote commonly agreed upon laws and rules. Unlike in earlier stages, rules are *not* obeyed simply to avoid punishment (stage 1) or to obey authority for authority's sake blindly (stage 4), but because they represent social contracts agreed upon by the larger society and are based on principles that benefit the greater majority. Rules are seen as flexible, depending on their continued utility. In stage 6, ethical principle orientation, moral reasoning is based on self-chosen ethical principles which are abstract, universal, and context free. These principles are maintained because they are ends in themselves, rather than means to an end. It has been argued that the postconventional level of morality can only be found in complex urban societies (both Western and non-Western). — MRTG

posterior probability

n. In statistical inference, the relative frequency of an event inferred from empirical evidence after its occurrence, which can then be used to predict future events.

postfigurative culture

n. A culture in which change is slow and socialization occurs primarily by elders' transferring their knowledge to their children. Elders hold the knowledge necessary for becoming a successful and competent adult.

post hoc test

n. A test of the equality of two or more means in an analysis of variance or multiple regression analysis that is decided upon after the data has been collected and examined.

postmodernism

n. Postmodernism refers to a family of late 20th-century intellectual and cultural movements that envision personhood, social life, truth, knowledge, and morality in ways that self-consciously diverge from "modernist" versions of these concepts. Postmodern psychologists (including social constructionists, discursive psychologists, and relational theorists) are influenced by postmodernist trends in literary criticism, philosophy, and sociocultural theory, as well as by the rise of global capitalism and rapid advances in communication technology. They call into question, and propose alternatives to, the constructs and methods used by "mainstream" psychologists. For example, they challenge the assertion that the individual mental and behavioral processes should be psychology's units of analysis, redirecting the focus of inquiry to the relational or discursive field. They also dispute the assumption that psychological concepts correspond to empirical realities, by demonstrating that psychological "truths" are inevitably embedded in social, cultural, and political frames. Finally, they criticize the claim that psychology functions in society to help foster greater individual freedom, arguing instead that psychologists often unwittingly reinforce inequality and intolerance. — SRK

postpartum depression

n. A period beginning shortly after the birth of a child in which a woman begins to have a depressed mood every day or almost every day, loses interest in normal pleasures, and may have sleep problems, marked change in diet, feelings of anxiety, low energy, and chronic fatigue despite sleeping, feelings of worthlessness or guilt, difficulty in concentrating, and thoughts of death or suicide. These symptoms usually disappear within a few weeks.

postsynaptic membrane

n. The dendritic membrane of a neuron adjacent to the axonic membrane of another neuron, which has chemical receptor sites for neurotransmitters released from the axon of the neuron beside it or preceding it in a neural tract.

postsynaptic neuron

n. A nerve cell which receives input from a particular other nerve cell in the form of neurotransmitters which are released by the other nerve cell and float across a synaptic gap.

postsynaptic potential

n. A change in the electric potential of the membrane of a nerve cell following reception of neurotransmitters from another nerve cell across the synaptic gap.

post-traumatic amnesia

n. Inability to store new information and/or retrieve previous information as a result of traumatic head injury. Head injury can be associated with coma, and post-traumatic amnesia becomes evident only when the patient can respond. Post-traumatic amnesia is associated with a diversity of cognitive impairments, including attention, perception, problem solving, and memory. After the head injury and once the patient can respond to questions, usually it is evident that he/she has not only significant anterograde amnesia (defect in acquiring new memories) but also retrograde amnesia (loss of previously acquired memories). As the patient improves, the duration of the retrograde amnesia shrinks to within a few hours, minutes, or seconds before the brain injury, and the anterograde amnesia also improves, as the patient becomes progressively capable of retaining some information. The duration of the post-traumatic amnesia has been used as a criterion of the head injury severity and in monitoring the course of traumatic brain injury. Mild head injury is associated with a post-traumatic amnesia shorter than 1 hour. Moderate traumatic brain injury includes a post-traumatic amnesia of 1 hour to 24 hours. Severe traumatic brain injury is associated with amnesia for more than 24 hours.   – AA

post-traumatic stress disorder

n. (PTSD) An anxiety disorder diagnosable according to the DSM-IV-TR. PTSD occurs in people who have experienced life-threatening events to which they respond with feelings of fear, helplessness, or horror. Examples of causal events include, but are not limited to, combat, childhood abuse, rape, other physical assaults, natural or human-caused disasters, and severe motor vehicle accidents. Not everyone who experiences a traumatic event will develop PTSD, but chances increase with more severe or repeated traumas. PTSD is marked by three distinct sets of symptoms: reexperiencing the trauma, avoiding reminders of the trauma, and experiencing increased physiological arousal. Reexperiencing symptoms may include intrusive thoughts or nightmares about the event, psychological or physiological reactivity when reminded of the event, and in its most severe form flashbacks in which the person feels as if he/she is reliving the event in the moment. Children may display reexperiencing symptoms by reenacting the trauma during play. Avoidance symptoms may include trying to avoid things that remind the person of the trauma and failing to remember parts of the trauma. Avoidance symptoms can also be marked by a lack of interest in activities, detachment from others, restricted emotions, and a sense of a foreshortened future. Arousal symptoms may include trouble sleeping or concentrating, irritability, hypervigilance in which the person is always on guard against future dangers, and an exaggerated startle response. For a diagnosis of PTSD, someone must have experienced a qualifying trauma and have at least one reexperiencing, three avoidance, and two arousal symptoms, and the symptoms must last for at least a month, causing significant personal distress or functional impairment. Symptoms of PTSD typically begin shortly after a trauma; however, they may have a delayed onset, not developing until years later.   – ABB

poverty of speech

n. An inability to generate spontaneous speech or varied or elaborate responses to questions. Patients with this symptom respond to open-ended questions (e.g., "Describe how your mood has been lately" or "Tell me about your childhood") almost entirely in very short phrases (e.g., "OK" or "It was good"). This symptom is also called alogia and is a common negative symptom of schizophrenia. These short responses are not thought to be motivated by a resistance to respond to open-ended questions (i.e., giving limited information as a way of preventing the interviewer from knowing more) but instead are thought to result from a lack of varied or spontaneous responses for whatever reason (e.g., being preoccupied with internal stimuli).   – DGa

power
n. 1. The capacity to control, decide, or influence. Social power is usually exercised by control of rewards and punishments, exercise of social roles endowed with rights or duties, and control of information. 2. In statistics, the likelihood of finding a positive result when there is actually a result there to find. 3. In mathematics, the number of times a number is multiplied by itself.

power distance
n. The degree of social acceptance of unequal distribution of capacity to control social events, groups, organizations, and societies as a whole. Cultures differ considerably in this dimension, as do smaller social groups.

practical intelligence
n. The capacity to deal with problems in everyday life through adapting one's behavior to the environment, altering the environment to meet one's needs better, or deciding to move to a new environment and selecting that new environment.

practice, distributed
n. A learning procedure in which practice is spread over time with nonpractice intervals between practice periods rather than in massed practice, in which all attempts to learn happen consecutively. Distributed learning has been found to be significantly more efficient than massed practice.

practice effect
n. Increased performance in learning tasks with repeated learning trials.

practice, massed
n. A learning procedure in which all attempts to learn occur consecutively with no time gaps between trials. Massed practice has been found to be significantly less time efficient than distributed learning.

Prader-Willi syndrome
n. A form of congenital mild to moderate mental retardation resulting from damage to or missing genes in chromosome 15, which results in short stature, weak muscles, underdeveloped sexual organs, preoccupation with eating, obesity, light and soft skin, pain insensitivity, and stubby fingers and toes. The syndrome is treated with human growth hormone.

pragmatics
n. In linguistics, the social and behavioral functioning of language communication such as word choice, situational differences in language, and the effect of verbal acts on the listener.

Pragnanz
n. In Gestalt psychology, the tendency of perceptual systems to form the best and simplest possible image or internal representation of an external object or information source from the data received.

precentral gyrus
n. The ridge on each side of the brain at the back of the frontal cortex immediately in front of the central sulcus, which is important in motor control of voluntary actions. Also called the motor cortex.

precocious development
n. Abnormally early appearance of skills or abilities usually not developed until later in maturation.

precognition
n. In parapsychology, the capacity to know future events before they occur.

preconscious
1. n. (Pcs) In psychoanalysis, thoughts, feelings, or memories which are not presently conscious but can easily be called into consciousness such as a person's telephone number or mother's first name. 2. adj. Of or relating to material which is not presently

conscious but can be readily called into consciousness.

preconventional morality

n. In Kohlberg's theory of moral development, this is the first and lowest level of reasoning, characterized by egocentric concerns and a focus on concrete consequences of actions. Two stages compose this level of moral reasoning. In stage 1, obedience/punishment orientation, children base their moral judgments on avoidance of physical punishment and unquestioning obedience to authority figures, particularly because of their ability to mete out physical punishment. In stage 2, individualism and exchange, also called instrumental relativism, children begin to understand that people hold multiple perspectives but judge morality of actions in terms of the practical benefits that can be gained by those behaviors. For instance, children will judge that actions are appropriate if concrete gains can be obtained. Children ages 4 to 10 are often considered to be in this level of moral reasoning.   – MRTG

predatory aggression

n. A form of aggression in which animals kill other animals for food.

prediction, statistical

n. The process of attempting to foretell the likelihood of future events on the basis of the relative frequency with which they have occurred in past observations.

predictive validity ▶ *See* VALIDITY, PREDICTIVE

predictor variable

n. A parameter used in a regression or other statistical analysis either to attempt to predict a future outcome or to create a model of relationships of variables.

predisposition

n. **1.** In genetics, a chromosomal configuration that makes the development of a particular trait likely in normal conditions of maturation. **2.** A likelihood of or susceptibility to development of a particular disease.

preference

n. **1.** The better liking or choice of one option over one or more other options. **2.** In learning theory, the relative frequency of two or more available responses.

prefigurative culture

n. A culture that is changing so rapidly that young people may be the ones to teach adults cultural knowledge.

prefrontal area ▶ *See* PREFRONTAL CORTEX

prefrontal cortex

n. Anterior part of the frontal lobes, located in front of the cortical motor areas (primary motor cortex and premotor cortex). From the cytoarchitectonic point of view, it is defined by the internal granular cortex; because of that, it is also referred to as the frontal granular cortex. Three major divisions are usually recognized: dorsolateral or convexital, orbitofrontal, and mesial prefrontal areas. This prefrontal cortical region has been related to complex cognition, planning behavior, controlling attention, and personality characteristics. These complex forms of cognition and behavior are referred to with the general term *executive functions*. Damage in the prefrontal cortex results in a diversity of impairments referred to as *dysexecutive syndrome*. Anatomically, the frontal lobes are the most evolved anterior areas of the brain and also late-maturating areas during ontogeny. Laterally, they are anterior to the Rolandic fissure and superior to the Sylvian fissure. Medially, they extend forward from the Rolandic fissure and the corpus callosum. It is the prefrontal cortex (Brodmann's areas 8, 11, 12, 24, 25, 32, 33, 46, and 47) that is thought to play a significant role in neurobehavioral syndromes.   – AA

▶ *See also* EXECUTIVE FUNCTIONS

prefrontal lobotomy

n. The surgical separation of the prefrontal lobes of the brain from the rest of the brain, which results in a chronic lack of motivation and self-direction and grossly flattened affective response. This was used early in the 20th century in attempts to cure a variety of problems such as chronic depression and psychosis and led to easily managed docility, although there was no evidence of its actual efficacy in treating any of the disorders for which it was used. Also called prefrontal leucotomy.

preganglionic
adj. Of or relating to efferent neurons in the sympathetic nervous system whose axons connect with a peripheral ganglion in the sympathetic nervous system.

prejudice
n. **1.** Any judgment arrived at before access to the information necessary to reach such a judgment. **2.** A set of negative attitudes and beliefs about a group of people which ignores within-group diversity and is resistant to contrary evidence.

preliterate
adj. **1.** Of or relating to any culture that has not developed a written language. **2.** Of or relating to a child who has not yet learned to read and write.

Premack principle
n. The idea that if any two behaviors are both possible in a given situation and differ in their probability of occurrence, then engaging in the more probable behavior will increase the likelihood of engaging in the less likely behavior in the future.

premenstrual dysphoric disorder
n. An emotional disorder in women characterized by cyclic periods of depressed mood, anxiety, marked affective variability, marked irritability, lethargy, sleep disturbance, decreased interest in normal activities, and a sense of being overwhelmed, whose symptoms begin the week before menstruation and disappear shortly after menstruation. Also called premenstrual syndrome.

premenstrual syndrome
n. An emotional disorder in women characterized by cyclic periods of depressed mood, anxiety, marked affective variability, marked irritability, lethargy, sleep disturbance,

decreased interest in normal activities, and a sense of being overwhelmed, whose symptoms begin the week before menstruation and disappear shortly after menstruation. Also called premenstrual dysphoric disorder.

premise
n. A stated idea assumed to be true from which a train of reasoning begins and which is usually necessary to reach a conclusion.

premotor cortex
n. Area in the frontal lobe situated in front of the primary motor area (Brodmann's area 4) and behind the prefrontal cortex. It corresponds in general to the Brodmann's area 6, but the Broca's area (Brodmann's area 44), the frontal eye field (Brodmann's area 8), and the supplementary motor area (in the medial aspect of the cerebral hemispheres) can also be regarded as premotor cortex. It is involved in organizing sequences of movements. The premotor cortex is a dysgranular cortex (transition between the granular prefrontal cortex and the agranular primary motor cortex).

— A A

▶ *See also* **MOTOR CORTEX** *and* **PRIMARY MOTOR CORTEX**

prenatal development
n. All growth and elaboration of organic structures in a fetus that takes place from the moment of conception until birth.

preoperational period
n. In Piagetian psychology, the second stage of intellectual development from approximately 2 to 6 years of age, during which the child is egocentric and gradually develops both linguistic and mathematical symbolic thinking, including the ideas of conservation, predicate thinking, and transductive reasoning. Near the end of this period a child begins to develop the capacity to understand events from others' points of view.

preoperational stage
n. In Piagetian psychology, the second stage of intellectual development from approximately 2 to 6 or 7 years of age, during which

the child is egocentric and gradually develops both linguistic and mathematical symbolic thinking, including the ideas of conservation, predicate thinking, and transductive reasoning. Near the end of this period a child begins to develop the capacity to understand events from others' points of view.

preoperational thought

n. Thought characteristic of children from 2 to 6 or 7 years of age, in which the child is egocentric and gradually develops both linguistic and mathematical symbolic thinking, including the ideas of conservation, predicate thinking, and transductive reasoning. Near the end of this period a child begins to develop the capacity to understand events from others' points of view.

presbyopia

n. An inability to focus on near objects, usually caused by a loss of elasticity in the lens of the eye due to aging. Acuity for distant objects is usually unimpaired as it requires less stretching of the lens in order to focus.

presenile dementia

n. A general and pervasive loss of cognitive functions such as judgment, memory, and language abilities which begins before 65 years of age.

press

n. In the motivational theories of Henry Murray, motivation that occurs as a result of environmental circumstances rather than internal processes of the organism or what the environment can do to and for the individual.

pressure receptor

n. Any of several kinds of nerve endings that respond to deformation of the shape of the skin or some internal organs.

presynaptic

adj. Of or relating to the portion of a nerve cell immediately before the synapse, which contains vesicles of neurotransmitters which can be released when the membrane potential depolarizes.

presynaptic neuron

n. Any nerve cell whose depolarization results in the release of neurotransmitters into a particular synapse.

pride

n. An experience of self-satisfaction that occurs when an individual positively evaluates himself/herself and believes others are similarly evaluating him or her. In U.S. culture, this is often connected with accomplishing goals but may be due to simply being perceived as having desirable characteristics.

primacy

n. Being first in a series.

primacy effect

n. The tendency for the first information encountered to be better remembered and to have a greater influence on an individual's perception of some person, event, or thing.

primal scene

n. In psychoanalysis, seeing one's parents engaging in sexual intercourse in reality or fantasy.

primary auditory cortex

n. A brain area in the posterior part of the superior temporal gyrus necessary for the conscious perception of sound. It receives input from the auditory thalamus, and damage to it results in subjective deafness although a person with an intact auditory thalamus may react to sounds he/she cannot hear.

primary colors

n. The colors blue, green, and red, from which all other colors can be made by adding various proportions of each colored light in human perception. Some researchers argue that yellow and violet should be added because of sensitivity peaks at those wavelengths in the human visual system. Magenta, cyan, and yellow are the basic colors used in mixing paints or other art materials, which is a subtractive process.

primary drive

n. An innate motivation to get something or do something which is little affected by circumstances. In contrast, secondary drives are acquired through learning.

primary emotion

n. The basic set of emotional responses of human beings, which commonly is held to include anger, contempt, disgust, fear, happiness, and sadness, which have been found to have panculturally recognized facial expressions.

primary memory

n. A hypothesized memory store that held only a few items for several seconds in memory theories that had a dual storage model and was supplanted by the term *short-term memory*.

primary mental abilities

n. The seven factors commonly resulting from factor analysis of intelligence test scores. These have been named *verbal comprehension, word fluency, number, spatial ability, associative memory, perceptual speed,* and *reasoning* on the basis of the content of the items most commonly correlated with each factor.

primary motor cortex

n. Anterior bank of the central fissure (precentral gyrus), corresponding to the Brodmann's area 4. It is the origin of the pyramidal motor system (voluntary movements) and contains the body cells of the pyramidal neurons (Betz cells); axons of these neurons descend through the internal capsule, forming the upper motor neuron of the corticobulbal and corticospinal pyramidal system. The primary motor cortex is arranged in such a way that its lower segment controls the movements of the upper part of the body (face, etc.), whereas the movements of the lower part of the body (knees, etc.) are controlled by the upper part and mesial aspects of the primary motor cortex. This cortical representation of the motor control in the primary motor cortex is known as the motor homunculus. Damage in the primary motor area results in contralateral motor difficulties (paresis or paralysis).   – A A

▶ *See also* **MOTOR CORTEX** *and* **PREMOTOR CORTEX**

primary reinforcement

n. A stimulus which increases the likelihood that an act immediately prior to the stimulus will increase in frequency and which seems not to have been acquired by learning but to be innate to the organism. As contrasted to a secondary reinforcement, which does not initially increase the likelihood of an act that precedes it but does so after having been paired with a primary reinforcement.

primary sex characteristic

n. A difference between male and female organisms in their genitals or gametes. These contrast with secondary sexual characteristics, such as facial hair, breast enlargement, body proportions, and tone of voice.

primary somatosensory cortex

n. Anterior part of the parietal lobe (Brodmann's areas 3, 1, and 2), situated behind the central fissure and anterior to the parietal association areas (Brodmann's areas 5, 7, 39, and 40). It receives information from the ventral posterior nucleus of the thalamus. It is the main receptive area for the sense of touch, kinesthesia (movement), and proprioception (body position). Primary somatosensory cortex contains a sensory representation of the different body areas; this body map is referred to as sensory homunculus. Damage in the primary somatosensory cortical area results in contralateral hypesthesia, difficulties in two-point discrimination, position sense impairments, tactile recognition defects, and similar types of body recognition disorders.   – A A

▶ *See also* **SOMATOSENSORY CORTEX**

primary visual cortex

n. Cortical area of projection of the visual information (V1). It corresponds to the striate cortex (Brodmann's area 17) situated in and around the calcarine fissure in the occipital lobe. It receives information from the lateral geniculate body of the thalamus through the optic radiation. Unilateral damage is associated with contralateral hemianopsia and bilateral damage with cortical blindness.   – A A

▶ *See also* **EXTRASTRIATE CORTEX** *and* **STRIATE CORTEX**

priming
n. Method used to determine whether one stimulus influences another. Typically, a prime word (e.g., *table*) influences the speed or reaction time at which one can access a related word, the target (e.g., *chair*). Priming facilitates cognitive processing for semantically related words. For example, a target word, *table*, is accessed faster after a related prime, *chair*, relative to an unrelated prime, *shoe*. Priming may also occur for words that are related in form such as overlapping sounds or letters. In some circumstances, form priming may actually inhibit target processing. Priming has implications for the organization of memory systems.   – EGS

principal-components analysis
n. A form of factor analysis in which the initial communality estimate is set to 1 for each variable in the analysis.

prisoner's dilemma
n. A game frequently used in game theory in which each player must choose between an option that maximizes his or her own gain at the expense of his/her fellow players and an option which returns a lesser but positive return for all players. The name of the game is derived from a police tactic of giving immunity or a reduced sentence to one member of a suspected criminal group who will testify against his/her alleged accomplices.

prisoner's dilemma game
n. A game frequently used in game theory in which each player must choose between an option that maximizes his or her own gain at the expense of his/her fellow players and an option which returns a lesser but positive return for all players. The name of the game is derived from a police tactic of giving immunity or a reduced sentence to one member of a suspected criminal group who will testify against his/her alleged accomplices.

private self
n. The part of the self that is known only by the individual himself/herself and is distinguished from the public self and the collective self.

proactive inhibition
n. A lessening or prevention of perception or learning due to the prior presentation of a similar stimulus to perceive or learn. Also called proactive interference.

proactive interference
n. A lessening or prevention of perception or learning due to the prior presentation of a similar stimulus to perceive or learn. Also called proactive inhibition.

probability
n. The likelihood that an event will occur, as opposed to all other possible alternative events.

probability, conditional
n. The likelihood an event will occur, given that another event has occurred.

probability curve
n. A graphic representation of the likelihood of occurrence of different values of a variable.

probability density
n. The likelihood of the outcome of an event falling within a given range.

probability distribution
n. A graphic representation in which the area below a curve at all points and along all segments represents the relative frequency of a variable that has a particular value or range.

probability function
n. A mathematical statement giving the relationship between each possible outcome of a situation and its likelihood of occurring.

probability, joint
n. The likelihood that two events will both occur at the same time.

probability matching
n. A form of learning in which an observer attempts to guess which of two or more choices is correct when each correct answer is randomly selected according to a predetermined probability. Humans generally learn to distribute their guesses in a way that matches

the probability distribution among choices, which may not be the optimal way to choose.

probability sample
n. A subset of a population selected by a random selection from the population so that each member of the population has a known probability of being chosen.

probability sampling
n. The technique of selecting a subset of a population by a random selection from the population so that each member of the population has a known probability of being chosen.

probability theory
n. The branch of mathematics which deals with the likelihood of different outcomes of events whose outcome is uncertain and modeled as random.

probe
n. 1. Anything that is used to examine or explore. 2. A question used to explore further in an interview. 3. In cognitive psychology, a cue used to investigate. 4. *v.* To penetrate in order to investigate or examine.

problem solving
1. *n.* Cognitive or behavioral processes used to discover solutions to difficulties or to achieve goals or subgoals. 2. *v.* Engaging in attempts to overcome or discover solutions to difficulties or to achieve goals or subgoals.

procedural justice
n. Methods and procedures, usually encoded in laws, which are assumed or intended to arrive at fair and impartial decisions.

procedural knowledge
n. Being able to do something, as opposed to knowing how to describe how to do something. Thus many people know how to ride a bicycle but may have difficulty in saying how it is done. Having the skill to accomplish something difficult.

procedural memory
n. Being able to do something that one has previously learned to do. This usually involves long-term retention of nonverbal information.

process
n. 1. A sequence of events or actions which leads to an alteration in the state of a system or situation. 2. In anatomy, a projecting part, as the axon is a neural process and the bumps on the backbone are spinous processes.

processing, parallel
n. Data manipulation in which two or more activities analyses are carried out simultaneously and independently as humans simultaneously see and hear and feel.

processing, sequential
n. Data manipulation which is carried out in single, usually rapid steps.

product-moment correlation coefficient
n. A numerical index of linear relatedness between two continuous variables scaled so that 0 indicates no relationship and +1 indicates a perfect positive relationship while –1 indicates a perfect inverse relationship.

professional ethics
n. The rules of socially acceptable conduct which members of a profession are expected to follow while engaging in professional practice.

profile analysis
n. A multivariate statistical analysis which compares individuals or groups on both the shape of the profile of their scores on several variables and the magnitude of their scores on the same variables.

profiling
n. 1. Construction of an outline of likely characteristics of an unknown criminal from the nature of the crime, characteristics of the victim, and evidence gathered at the crime scene. 2. In athletics, creating an outline of individual components of athletic performance and assessing the degree to which a particular athlete possesses each component.

programmed instruction

n. An approach to teaching in which the material to be taught is broken down into small steps, each of which is presented as a unit requiring a response from the subject, who proceeds to the next step only after correctly completing the present step.

progressive matrices test

n. A test of intelligence intended to be fair to persons with different cultural backgrounds and different educational opportunities. In the test the subject is presented with a series of matrices, each of which has a piece missing, and is required to select which of several possibilities would correctly complete the matrix. The matrices are presented in order of difficulty, and the test has been found to give scores which are correlated with standard intelligence tests and particularly with performance scores on those tests. There are several forms of the test.

projection

n. This primitive defense mechanism is the unconscious warding off of negative experiences or emotions (e.g., anger, hostility, sadness) by denying an experience, perceiving it in another person, and then seeing that negative experience as being directed back at the projector. For example, John is feeling very angry with Mary but is not consciously aware of his anger. Additionally, he is unconsciously very uncomfortable with his anger, perhaps worried about what he might do were he to identify with it. One way of dealing with this discomfort is to "turn the tables" and see Mary as angry with him. In this way he has projected his own feelings onto Mary and now sees the anger redirected at him. He now can deal with this (presumably) more manageable emotion since the anger is not influencing his behavior but someone else's.
— DGa

projective device

n. This is a personality test that is based on the projective hypothesis, which states that when presented with unfamiliar stimuli that are prone to a variety of interpretations, an individual will interpret the stimuli on the basis of his/her own needs, feelings, experiences, prior conditioning, thought processes, and so on. It may be noted that even though what a subject sees is assumed to be a reflection of personal qualities or characteristics, some responses may be more revealing than others. For example, if a person gives a very obvious typical response, less will be gained than if someone gives a very atypical response. The reliability and validity of these types of devices are questionable, and as with any test, they should only be used in conjunction with other measures as one piece of a comprehensive assessment. The Rorschach is perhaps the most widely known projective device, and the Thematic Apperception Test is also often used.
— EF

projective identification

n. In Kleinian analysis, a defensive fantasy in which an individual imagines part of himself/herself is split off and injected into an object, thus allowing the individual to control or harm it and so give the individual the illusion of control. This is similar to Sigmund Freud's ideas of the function of religion and people's beliefs about God.

projective technique

n. An approach to personality assessment techniques that consists of soliciting free responses to a fixed set of stimuli such as inkblots, pictures, incomplete sentences, or words. The underlying assumption is that subjects project the form of their personality into their responses, which can be analyzed to understand the personality of the subject.

projective test

n. Any of numerous personality tests which consist of a fixed set of stimuli such as inkblots, pictures, incomplete sentences, or words to which responses are solicited. The underlying assumption is that subjects project the form of their personality into their responses, which can be analyzed to understand the personality of the subject. Projective tests include the Rorschach and Holtzman inkblot tests, the Thematic Apperception Test, the Children's Apperception Test, the incomplete sentences blank, and numerous word association tests.

Projective tests are difficult to standardize and have doubtful reliability and therefore validity although they are widely used.

propaganda

n. Persuasive communication that intentionally distorts facts or selects only information supportive of its author's point of view for the purpose of exercising political control. It often contains emotionally provocative images which distract the hearer from relevant contrary information and belittlement of alternative points of view.

propositional knowledge representation

n. Any theoretical model of how the mind works which uses words, images, or relationships as the smallest unit of thought processes and in which these nodes are linked into a network by several kinds of relationships. Any thought in such a system is an activated portion of the network.

proprioception

n. The sense of bodily position relative to gravity, acceleration, and the position of one body part relative to others, all of which are important in balance, walking, and most voluntary actions.

prosocial behaviors

n. Prosocial behaviors are any actions intended to benefit or help another. These actions may include, but are not limited to, sharing, donating, volunteering, comforting, cooperating, and altruism. Prosocial behaviors are distinct from other types of positive social skills and characteristics (e.g., social support, attachment) and distinct from social competence, a broader construct that includes several types of social skills. It is also important to distinguish prosocial behaviors from theoretically related moral cognitions and emotions such as perspective taking, sympathy, moral reasoning, and social responsibility. While these constructs may explain helping actions, they are nonetheless distinct from prosocial behaviors. Interest in the study of prosocial behaviors has a long history across many academic disciplines, especially theology, philosophy, and the social sciences. Because prosocial behaviors are actions that are deemed desirable by society, there is tremendous interest in understanding this topic, and it has important social implications, including health, policy, education, and economic.

Assessments of prosocial behaviors have typically included global measures which measure how often a person may engage in a prosocial behavior across situations and personal motivations. Some scholars, however, have noted the usefulness of defining subtypes of prosocial behaviors. Prosocial behaviors that are defined as a product of the situation or personal motives, for example, may have unique correlates that are otherwise masked when implementing global measures. Some researchers have identified six such types of prosocial behaviors: altruism (selfless helping, usually intrinsically motivated by the primary desire to help others), public (helping in front of an audience, usually motivated by wanting to gain approval, respect from others, and self-worth), compliant (helping because it has been requested by another), emotional (helping under emotionally evocative circumstances), dire (helping in emergency situations), and anonymous (helping without the receiver's knowing the identity of the helper). Other unique types of prosocial behaviors studied by researchers have included affective/supportive (nurturance and caring), helpfulness (helping with household chores), volunteerism, service learning, and cooperative behaviors in children.

Some scholars have argued that some types of prosocial behaviors (e.g., altruism) are truly motivated by selfless motives such as empathy, sympathy, and internalized norms, values, and principles. Some scholars have debated that prosocial behaviors are primarily driven by egoistic motives such as money, social approval, and social power. Furthermore, it is likely these two motives may sometimes conflict in particular situations and might produce moral dilemmas. There is considerable research on altruism and prosocial behaviors, much of which focuses on situational factors such as characteristics of the victim, number of bystanders, mood, and ambiguousness of the need. This continues to be a hotly debated topic of research.

There appears to be a genetic and biological basis for prosocial tendencies in humans. For example, on the basis of twin studies, empathy appears to have a strong heritable component. Furthermore, empathy appears early in life, and individual differences in empathy remain stable over the life span. Although evidence on the heritability of prosocial behaviors is sparse, there is evidence that such behaviors appear early in life and remain stable over the life span. Moreover, a recent surge of studies have focused on the links among temperament, empathy, and prosocial behaviors, and these studies further support the notion of a biological basis for these prosocial tendencies. Negative affectivity (an aspect of temperament) in infancy, for example, has been linked to early childhood prosocial development. Other studies have shown that interactions among emotion regulation and moderate levels of affectivity are also related to more frequent prosocial behaviors. The accumulating evidence on the genetic and biological basis of prosocial tendencies also supports evolutionary theorists' assertions that prosocial tendencies are adaptive for human functioning.

Animal research has also supported evolutionary mechanisms for prosocial behavior. Three hypotheses have been proposed to explain the adaptiveness of prosocial behaviors: genetic similarly, kin selection, and reciprocal altruism. These hypotheses suggest that individuals engage in prosocial behaviors to increase reproductive success and fitness. Research with great apes and chimpanzees has accordingly demonstrated that these mammals exhibit a range of prosocial behaviors, including cooperation, nurturance, and altruistic-like behaviors. A neurophysiological mechanism that has also been supported by animal research includes the hypothalamic-pituitary-adrenal axis and frontal cortical functioning, which are associated with arousability and self-regulation. Early maternal care experiences do seem to impact later sensitivity to distress in research with rodents. Researchers have also speculated on the importance of central neuropeptides such as oxytocin and vasopressin in affiliative behaviors during mother-infant bonding and other positive social behaviors.

While young children are capable of expressing emotions associated with prosocial behaviors (e.g., concern for others, sorrow, sadness), the frequency of prosocial behaviors does change with age. In general, the frequency of prosocial behaviors increases into adolescence, with the greatest age increase found between preschool and adolescence. Smaller age increases have been found between infancy and preschool, childhood and adolescence, and throughout adolescence. However, recently, there is evidence that prosocial behaviors might decline slightly during adolescence. These age-related changes may be attributable to changes in sociocognitive and socioemotional skills, or they may be due to changes in the social context. For example, there is evidence that prosocial behaviors may increase as a result of increases in the social opportunities to engage in prosocial actions. These age increases, though, may be qualified by study characteristics such as study design (e.g., observational vs. paper-and-pencil measures) or the type of prosocial behavior being examined.

Regarding gender differences, researchers have typically found that girls engage in more prosocial behaviors than boys. These findings support gender socialization theorists, who maintain that girls, more than boys, are encouraged to exhibit nurturing and caring behaviors. These gender-specific experiences and their impact on prosocial behaviors also accumulate and intensify over time; accordingly, gender differences in prosocial behaviors have been found to be the greatest into adolescence. However, several reviews of gender differences in prosocial behavior have found that these differences may not be as evident once study characteristics are taken into account. For example, while women tend to engage in more nurturant types of prosocial behavior, men tend to engage in more instrumental (risky/chivalrous) forms of prosocial behavior. Thus, the type of prosocial behavior being examined is one factor that may affect the extent of gender differences reported.

Parents have been identified as key socializing agents of prosocial development during childhood. Parents can be models of desirable behavior, reinforce prosocial behaviors, encourage children in moral decision-making situations, or provide direct verbal messages such as beliefs or attitudes about prosocial behaviors. Researchers have found that prosocial development has been positively, but not consistently, related to authoritative (vs. authoritarian) parenting and parental support and attachment. Disciplining techniques such as the use of inductions and explanations have also been positively related to prosocial behaviors. For example, these parents often induce empathy and perspective taking by explaining how a child's actions may harm (or benefit) others. Moreover, explanations provide an opportunity to transmit parental moral values in an emotionally regulated manner. This emotionally regulated manner may be perceived by the child as appropriate, leading the child to accept a parental message more willingly. Conversely, children may be less likely to accept the same moral message if power assertion accompanies it, as situations involving power assertion are usually emotionally overarousing. Power assertion also may lead to fewer prosocial behaviors as parents who use this technique provide models of aggressive behaviors.

Siblings are another powerful socializing agent during childhood for the development of prosocial behaviors. For example, younger children not only learn about prosocial behaviors that older siblings may model, but they also learn about the consequences for engaging, or failing to engage, in prosocial behaviors. These older siblings may also offer opportunities for younger siblings to practice prosocial behaviors. This influence, however, may be dependent on younger siblings' social-cognitive abilities, emotional responsiveness, and emotion regulation skills. Researchers have also suggested that play contexts may be important training grounds for the expression of prosocial behaviors, as many of the prosocial behaviors observed among siblings have been during play.

Peers become increasingly important socializing agents of prosocial development into adolescence. Interacting with peers provides opportunities to engage in prosocial behaviors with socialization agents who are similar in social power and status, and to observe and practice new modes of providing instrumental help. Through social comparisons, children gain a deeper understanding of their moral self by exposure to differing perspectives on moral issues. In addition to family members, peers may offer sources of support and warmth which may facilitate prosocial development. Peers also provide reinforcements or punishers that can foster or diminish prosocial behaviors in children. Finally, engaging in prosocial behaviors may lead to better peer relationships as children who exhibit high levels of prosocial behaviors tend to have higher ratings of peer acceptance and status.

The media have also been studied as another socializing agent of prosocial behaviors. A number of studies in the 1970s demonstrated the strong influence of positive television and film models on prosocial behaviors. Overall, researchers have found that those observers who watched characters who engaged in prosocial acts (especially if they were physically, socially, or psychologically similar to the viewer) engaged in prosocial behaviors themselves in the future. Later studies revealed that the effect of prosocial television on behaviors is much stronger than the effect of antisocial television on future behaviors. Few studies examining media's effect on prosocial behaviors have been conducted since then, with fewer studies examining the effects of media popular with adolescents (e.g., magazines and novels) or types of interactive media (e.g., Internet, video games).

Individual differences in sociocognitive skills also have been studied in regard to prosocial behavior. Two of the most commonly studied sociocognitive skills are perspective taking and moral reasoning. Perspective taking, or understanding another's situation, has been theoretically linked to prosocial behaviors in that it has been thought that being able to understand another's plight may result in sympathy, which in turn may lead to engaging in helpful actions in order to relieve this person's distress. Alternatively, being able to understand another's situation may result in disequilibrium, and this disequilibrium may then cause behaviors that will reduce this state. Research on perspective taking and prosocial behaviors has generally been mixed. However, scholars have found the strongest relations between these two constructs when there is a match between the task characteristics, or when perspective taking is jointly studied with other influences on prosocial behaviors (e.g., sympathy, other related cognitive skills).

Moral reasoning, specifically, prosocial moral reasoning, is another common sociocognitive correlate of prosocial behaviors. *Prosocial moral reasoning* is defined as thinking about dilemmas in which one's needs are in conflict with the needs of others in the relative absence of formal laws or rules. This care-oriented moral reasoning is in contrast to moral reasoning that is justice oriented (e.g., Kohlberg), which has not been thought to be as strongly associated with prosocial behaviors. Prosocial moral reasoning has been theorized to increase in sophistication along with other age-related cognitive advances (e.g., abstract thinking, perspective taking). This higher-level reasoning, which is more other oriented and internalized, has been found by researchers to be related to higher levels of prosocial behaviors.

Despite the evidence for the biological basis of prosocial behaviors, there is abundant evidence that cross-cultural differences of prosocial behaviors exist. Moral socialization theorists have asserted that culture group differences in prosocial behaviors can arise from unique socialization experiences and unique culturally related ecological features. Some scholars have noted that those in collectivist societies (i.e., orientation and emphasis on group goals and needs) more frequently express cooperative behaviors than those in individualistic societies (i.e., orientation and emphasis on self-goals and needs). Furthermore, culture group differences in prosocial behaviors have been shown such that children in societies that are commonly assigned to primary caregiver roles and responsibilities engage in higher

levels of prosocial behaviors than children in other societies. These culture group differences in prosocial behaviors also appear to be a function of the characteristics of peers children commonly interact with and the degree to which they interact with and around adult figures. It is also likely that culture group differences in prosocial behaviors vary according to parenting practices and values unique to each society; however, much more research on culture group differences in prosocial behaviors is needed.   – GC, MM

prosody
n. Prosody refers to the suprasegmental tiers of the phonological structure of an utterance. Prosody therefore includes specifications related to *intonation* (realized acoustically in modulations of pitch), *rhythm* (with acoustic correlates in the duration of phonetic segments and periods of silence), and, to a certain extent, loudness (linked to the amplitude of the signal). Lexical stress is a prosodic phenomenon realized suprasegmentally. A word might consist of a sequence of consonants and vowels – say, [nunu]. These might be clustered into two rhythmic units, or syllables: [nu.nu]. Of these, perhaps the first syllable is uttered with higher pitch, longer duration, and greater amplitude and thus receives stress: ['nu.nu]. Prosodic phenomena may span more than one segment, more than one syllable, and more than one word. For example, speakers of American English use prosody to distinguish between interrogatives and declaratives and to disambiguate between certain types of structural ambiguities.   – EMF

▶ *See also* **INTONATION** *and* **RHYTHM**

prosopagnosia
n. Neurological disorder characterized by a partial or total inability to recognize faces. It is also known as face blindness and corresponds to a particular subtype of visual agnosia. Some patients with prosopagnosia are even unable to recognize their own face in photos or when looking at themselves in a mirror. Frequently, face recognition defects are accompanied by other types of

recognition impairments (recognizing cars, flowers, animals, etc.), though sometimes they appear to be relatively restricted to the identification of human faces. Patients with prosopagnosia know how a face is (that is, they know that a face includes two eyes, a nose, etc.) but fail in recognizing individual faces. Prosopagnosia has been proposed to be interpreted as a defect in recognizing the individual members (specific flowers, animals, faces, etc.) of a visual-perceptual category. Prosopagnosia is the result of brain pathology, usually involving the right fusiform gyrus (temporal-occipital) or both the right and left fusiform gyri. Prosopagnosia can result from a diversity of etiologies, including stroke, traumatic brain injury, or neurodegenerative diseases. Cases of developmental prosopagnosia have been described. It has been observed that people who have difficulties in social relations (e.g., autism, Asperger's syndrome) may have some difficulties in recognizing faces.   – AA

▶ *See also* **AGNOSIA**

prospect theory

n. A theory of decision making in which actual human preferences violate statistical utility (1) in being focused on the present situation instead of on their absolute gains and losses, (2) in overvaluing losses as opposed to gains and so showing risk aversion for gains but risk taking to avoid losses, and (3) in overvaluing low-probability events and undervaluing high-probability events.

Protestant work ethic

n. The idea that work and success in worldly affairs are both a moral duty and an indication of God's favor *for Christians.* The idea was developed by Max Weber, who associated it with the rise of capitalism in late medieval Europe in his book *The Protestant Ethic and Spirit of Capitalism.* The ethic has been used in later work to refer to an orientation in any group that emphasizes the moral duty of hard work and success as a sign of righteousness.

prototype

n. **1.** In concept formation, a best example of a category which may be a real thing or an abstracted idea of the category and to which all individual things are compared for judgment as to category membership. **2.** A first or early model of something which is later reproduced. **3.** An ideal or best example of a category.

proverbs test

n. Any test of intelligence, personality, or psychopathology which uses the interpretation of proverbs as items.

proxemics

n. The scientific study of personal space including territoriality and crowding. Both individuals and cultures have rules and preferences about the appropriate distance at which to carry on social interactions, and proxemics studies these in relationship to other cultural and personality characteristics.

proximal stimulus

n. The energy which reaches a sense organ from a sense object as opposed to the object itself. In vision, the proximal stimulus is the light striking the eye, and the distal stimulus is the object from which the light is reflected.

proximate compatibility principle

n. In control systems, the idea that information displays work best when a control for a variable is placed close to the information display for that variable, or the data and control efforts together create an emergent display that combines variable level with control effort.

proximity, law of

n. A Gestalt principle of sensory organization which suggests that in making sense of the world our senses group together things that appear close together in space. Thus in the following series of letters *ddd ddd ddd* there seem to be three groups because they are proximate, or near to, each other.

proximodistal

adj. Of or relating to the direction from the center of a body toward the extremities.

proximodistal development

n. A general principle of development in which organs and functions near the center of an organism develop before those farther from the center. In humans and similar vertebrates, development usually proceeds from the head outward, in what is called a *cephalocaudal* pattern of development.

proxy control

n. Refers to control by someone else for the benefit of oneself. This is a form of control that can be used when personal control – either direct or indirect – is not available or is inappropriate. Proxy controls are third-party interventions.

pseudobulbar palsy

n. A paralysis of voluntary movements of the face which leaves involuntary movements such as smiling, sneezing, and coughing unaffected resulting from damage to the corticobulbar nerve pathway.

pseudodementia

n. A deterioration of cognitive functions similar to those caused by brain damage in the absence of brain damage. This often occurs in severe depression and disappears as the depression diminishes.

pseudohermaphrodite

n. A condition in which a person has the internal sexual organs of one sex and external genitalia that resemble those of the other sex. Thus a genetic male with testes may also have a small penis, testes which do not descend into the scrotum, and a urethral opening on the underside of the penis. A pseudohermaphrodite who is a genetic female may have an enlarged clitoris and a labia majora that resembles a scrotum.

psychiatrist

n. A medical doctor who specializes in the treatment of psychopathology. Psychiatrists normally serve a multiple-year residency (number of years depending on the country) learning the specialization of psychiatry after completing normal medical training and most commonly focus on prescribing drugs for the treatment of mental disorders.

psychiatry

n. The medical specialty which focuses on diagnosing and treating psychopathology usually from a biological perspective.

psychic determinism

n. The theory that all behavior, thoughts, and emotions have some (often unconscious) meaning or reason for being; nothing is accidental or random. Psychic determinism is one of the central components of a psychoanalytic approach to human behavior. From this starting point every detail in human life, both large (e.g., choice of job, choice of partner, moral and political views) and small (e.g., dreams, slips of the tongue, forgetting someone's name), results from some unconscious drive or desire and is never the result of random occurrences. From this perspective, because so much of human motivation (e.g., hostile, aggressive, or sexual urges) is thought to be outside awareness, very few decisions in life are made with a truly rational conscious free will. Therefore, behavior is determined by one's unconscious.

– DGa

psychoactive

adj. Of or relating to having an effect on the functioning of the mind and the behavior which results from the functioning of mind.

psychoactive substance

n. Any chemical which has an effect on the functioning of the mind and the behavior which results from that mental functioning.

psychoanalysis

n. **1.** A form of psychotherapy developed by and based on the theories of Sigmund Freud in which the patient is required to say whatever comes to mind without hesitation or censure and gradually transfers feelings associated with these free associations onto the therapist. The therapist analyzes these remarks and overcomes resistance to the interpretations of the client by using the energies of the transference, which ultimately help the patient remake emotional decisions which have kept him or her functioning as if the present were a repetition of the past. **2.** More generally, the theories of Sigmund Freud and his followers.

psychoanalyst
n. A psychotherapist who uses the methods of psychoanalysis as his/her therapeutic approach. In the United States, becoming a psychoanalyst usually requires licensure as a psychiatrist or psychologist, personal psychoanalysis, and supervised practice in psychoanalysis.

psychoanalytic stages
n. The five stages of psychosexual development hypothesized by Sigmund Freud as part of his psychoanalytic theory. These include the oral stage, in which infants are focused on oral pleasure and in which the ego or sense of self and real world first develop; the anal stage, in which the child is focused on pleasure in the bowels and rectum and in which ego gains strength and the development of superego or morality begins; the phallic stage, in which the center of pleasure shifts to either the penis or the clitoris and children go through an immense conflict over love and sexuality whose resolution leads to the temporary repression of overt sexuality and thus entry into the latency period, in which sexual pleasure is indirect and the child usually seeks to emulate the same-sex parent; and finally the genital stage, in which puberty overcomes the repression of sexuality and the person must include mature sexual expression in his/her ideas of who he/she is and learn to love and work in ways culturally appropriate to his/her sex.

psychobabble
n. Superfluous, excessive, and largely meaningless use of psychological terms.

psychobiology
n. **1.** A biological approach to psychology which combines physiological and evolutionary perspectives with ideas about mental functioning. **2.** A holistic approach to psychology in which all normal and abnormal processes are assumed to have biological, sociological, and psychological aspects.

psychodrama
n. An approach to psychotherapy in which individuals create plays out of their internal conflicts and use the dynamics of the play format and the presence of others to resolve the conflicts. Usually the individual whose problem is being worked on serves as the lead actor while other clients act out other roles and the therapist acts as director.

psychodynamic
adj. Of or relating to the psychoanalytic approach in which unconscious motives are a focus.

psychodynamic therapy
n. Psychotherapy that is based on the theories of Sigmund Freud or one of their offshoots which attempts to help the client achieve insight into her/his unconscious motives and often seeks to find the childhood origins of present psychological conflicts and difficulties.

psychoendocrinology
n. The study of psychological and sensory influences which may initiate activity in the endocrine glands. Such activity may include the release of stress hormones from the adrenal glands and sex hormones from the ovaries or testes. – vs

psychogalvanic response
n. (GSR) A change in the level or degree to which the skin conducts electricity, which tends to decrease when subcutaneous muscles relax and increase when those muscles tense and is used as a crude estimate of general bodily tension. This has been used in crude and usually inaccurate attempts to create a lie detector.

psychogenesis
n. The origin and development of the individual's mind including his or her intelligence and abilities, personality, habits, and behavior patterns, and any disorders or disabilities he/she may have.

psychogenic
adj. Of or relating to an origin in the mind.

psychogenic amnesia

n. Loss of memory for personal history or specific events, which is assumed to be caused by mental processes rather than biological ones.

psychoimmunology

n. The study of the interaction of psychological stimulation and responses with immune system reactivity. It is recognized that the level of resistance to many immune disorders is affected by psychological states and traits. In particular, resistance to the common cold rhinovirus is heavily influenced by psychological states of emotional distress or exhaustion, anxiety, and feelings of well-being. The inverse effect may be demonstrated as well: decreased levels of immunity may have pronounced effects on emotional distress/ exhaustion, anxiety levels, and feelings of well-being.   – vs

psychokinesis

n. In parapsychology, the ability to move physical objects or control external events by mental effort.

psycholinguistics

n. Psycholinguistics is the psychological study of language. Although there are roots in psychological and linguistic studies in the late 1800s, the field as it is understood today emerged in the 1950s. Contemporary psycholinguistics is a merging of a number of scientific fields, including neuroscience, computer science, philosophy, sociology, and anthropology, in addition to psychology and linguistics. Psycholinguists study language skills in children and in adults, in both oral and written language, and in monolinguals and multilinguals.

One theme of psycholinguistics is the relationship between biology and language behavior. Early work correlated naturally occurring brain injuries due to strokes or accidents with resulting language impairments. In recent decades, brain-imaging techniques have sharpened our understanding of the brain regions associated with language.

A second theme is the relationship between language and thought. For example, languages use different methods of describing spatial arrays, and these differences influence the spatial behavior of language users. Although languages do not create or prevent thinking patterns, one's language experience may make it relatively easier or more difficult to think in certain ways.   – DWC

psychological dependence

n. The habitual use of a drug or other behavior pattern as a way of reducing anxiety without actually dealing with the problems of living such that removal of the drug or behavior pattern causes a marked increase in anxiety and usually ineffectual attempts to cope with the anxieties of daily life.

psychological disorder

n. A recognizable pattern of personal distress, abnormal emotional reactions and behavior, cognitive impairment, and an increased risk of death or injury due to a presumed malfunction of the mind and the brain.

psychological methods

n. The sum total of all the approaches to psychological research, including conceptual analysis, reliability and validity of measures, experimental design, and appropriate ways of collecting, analyzing, understanding, and interpreting psychological data, including the use of statistical techniques.

psychological refractory period

n. (PRP) A period of diminished responsiveness to a stimulus following reaction to a previous similar stimulus.

psychological science

n. The use of methods derived from physical sciences in explorations of the functioning of mind and the control of behavior.

psychological test

n. A standardized scale or set of scales used to measure an attribute of mind, usually composed of numerous individual items to which a subject is asked to respond. Criteria of psychological tests include the consistency of the scale in measuring (reliability) and the accuracy with which test scores reflect the actual psychological attribute the test is intended to measure (validity).

psychological warfare

n. **1.** Any attempt to gain advantage in a war by manipulating the minds of either side in the conflict or uninvolved parties to the benefit of one's own side. This includes morale boosting, propaganda, control of information, and attempts to change the attitudes of both sides in the war. **2.** A general application of techniques derived from the use of psychological methods in war to business or other relationships.

psychologism

n. **1.** The view that psychology is the most important form of intellectual investigation, from which all others are derived. **2.** An exaggeration of the importance of psychology or psychological concepts or variables. **3.** Any of several theoretical positions including the idea that logic is persuasive only because it fits the way that the human mind works, that knowledge originates in the workings of the mind and so only by understanding the way the mind works can one understand the origin of knowledge, that words mean what our ideas of words are, or that truth is a correspondence of the workings of the human mind and the external world.

psychologist

n. A person who is trained in psychological research or the clinical practice of psychology and is usually actively engaged in one of those fields. Such persons usually hold doctoral degrees in psychology and are required to have licenses to engage in clinical practice in most areas, although in some areas some activities are performed without doctoral degrees.

psychology

n. The study of the mind, including consciousness, perception, motivation, behavior, the biology of the nervous system in its relation to mind, scientific methods of studying the mind, cognition, social interactions in relation to mind, individual differences, and the application of these approaches to practical problems in organization and commerce and especially to the alleviation of suffering.

psychometric function

n. Any formal description of the functioning of some aspect of mind and especially as applied to perception. This is frequently used in describing relationships between stimuli and the perception of those stimuli.

psychometrics

n. A subdiscipline of psychology focusing on the measurement of individual differences across a range of human constructs (including attitudes, abilities, interests, beliefs, achievement, personality, and knowledge). Psychometric research aims to enhance the theoretical understanding of psychological assessment as well as create tests, instruments, and procedures to be utilized in an applied setting. Much of the emphasis in psychometrics is integrating theory and statistics to ensure that psychological tests and measurements are valid and reliable.   – BJM

psychomotor

adj. Of or relating to any relationship between bodily movement and the functioning of mind.

psychomotor agitation

n. Excessive motor movement not directed toward any goal that is characteristic of anxiety or tension. This often includes pacing; hand wringing; pulling at the hair, ear lobes, or clothing; jiggling limbs; or other fidgeting.

psychomotor epilepsy

n. A seizure disorder in which there is a complex set of psychological experiences, which may include illusory sensory experiences, paramnesias, and strong emotions, and which often is evidenced by repetitive motor movements such as tapping, grimacing, chewing, or swallowing but no convulsions typical of grand mal seizures. It was formerly called temporal lobe epilepsy as the focus for the seizures is most commonly in the temporal lobe.

psychoneuroimmunology

n. The study of the recursive interaction of psychological states, traits, and behavior on the substrates of neural function and endocrinology, and immune system responsivity. In the science of the early 20th century, it was assumed that the immune system operated independently of control or influence of other systems of the body. It was demonstrated, however, in the 1980s, that there are direct connections among the central nervous system (CNS), autonomic nervous system (ANS), and immune system, both structurally and chemically. Thus began the study of neuroimmunology, to which were soon added the recursive effects of psychological stimulation and responses on the interaction of the CNS, ANS, and immune responses. This recursive interaction is commonly known as the mind-body phenomenon. In wellness, illness, and especially oncology, practitioners often encourage their clients to imagine the immune system cells destroying their tumors or infections, and/or encourage clients to draw pictures of the immune cells in action as an aid to recovery.   – vs

psychopathology
n. **1.** The study of mental disorders, including their origin, diagnosis, symptoms, course, associated features, epidemiology, physical correlates, cultural meaning, and treatment. **2.** Any specific mental disorder.

psychopathy
n. An archaic term for a mental disorder characterized by lack of guilt and remorse, impulsiveness, rule breaking, and disregard for others which is prevalent among violent criminals who repeat their offenses and which was originally called moral imbecility.

psychopharmacology
n. The study of the effects of psychoactive drugs and other chemicals on the mind and body with a particular emphasis on using the drugs to alleviate mental disorders and suffering.

psychophysical function
n. A formal description of the relationships between stimulus characteristics and the perception of the stimuli.

psychophysics
n. The branch of psychology that studies the relationships between stimulus characteristics and the perception of those stimuli.

psychosexual development
n. In psychoanalytic theory, the origin and maturation of the mind as it develops, guided by the pursuit of sexual pleasure and constrained by reality. Psychoanalysis assumes all pleasure is sexual in nature and is focused in different organs in stages over the course of maturation, and the development of mind in each stage affects the course of future development as well as adult functioning.

psychosexual disorder
n. Any sexual disorder with mental rather than physical causes. Also called sexual and gender identity disorder.

psychosexual dysfunction
n. A repetitive or enduring problem in sexual function which has mental rather than physical causes. Also called sexual dysfunction.

psychosexual stage
n. Any of the five stages of development hypothesized by Sigmund Freud as part of his psychoanalytic theory. These include the oral stage, in which infants are focused on oral pleasure and in which the ego or sense of self and real world first develop; the anal stage, in which the child is focused on pleasure in the bowels and rectum and in which ego gains strength and the development of superego or morality begins; the phallic stage, in which the center of pleasure shifts to either the penis or the clitoris and children go through an immense conflict over love and sexuality whose resolution leads to the temporary repression of overt sexuality and thus entry into the latency period, in which sexual pleasure is indirect and the child usually seeks to emulate the same-sex parent; and finally the genital stage, in which puberty overcomes the repression of sexuality and the person must include mature sexual expression in his or her ideas of who he/she is and learn to love and work in ways culturally appropriate to his/her sex.

psychosis
n. **1.** An abnormal mental state in which a person's cognition is sufficiently disturbed so as to be unable to perceive reality in a

normal manner so that he/she has either hallucinations or bizarre delusions which he/she thinks are real as well as disturbances in affect. Disorders usually considered forms of psychosis include schizophrenia, schizophreniform disorder, schizoaffective disorder, delusional disorder, brief psychotic disorder, folie à deux, dementia, and drug-induced psychotic disorder. **2.** In older usage any mental disorder that grossly disturbs everyday functioning.

psychosocial
adj. Of or relating to both the mind and interaction with other people.

psychosocial stressor
n. Any life situation to which an individual reacts with unusually high levels of tension and anxiety, which increase the likelihood of both mental and physical pathology. Examples of psychosocial stressors include marriage conflict, divorce, death of a close friend or relative, isolation, poor relationships at work, loss of a job, change of residence, or severe illness or disability.

psychosomatic
adj. Of or relating to a belief that the mind is playing a role in creating physical illness or disability, as in studies relating stress to heart disease.

psychosomatic disorder
n. Any type of disorder in which mind and mental functioning affect physical functioning. Also called psychological factors affecting medical condition.

psychosomatic illness
n. Any physical disorder in which there has been a significant contribution by mind, as in stress or destructive habitual behavior patterns.

psychosomatic medicine
n. The branch of medical science which investigates the relationships between social, psychological, and behavioral factors and bodily processes in humans and treats psychological factors that affect medical conditions.

psychosurgery
n. Any brain surgery done with the intention of remediating psychological disorders. This has included temporal lobectomy for severe cases of epileptic lobe seizure disorder and, in the past, prefrontal leucotomy for schizophrenia and other disorders.

psychotherapist
n. Any person who provides treatment for mental disorders or adjustment problems by means of personal interaction with a client or group of clients or by other psychological means such as biofeedback or milieu control.

psychotherapy
n. The process of relieving mental disorders by psychological means. There are numerous therapeutic approaches, which use a wide variety of theoretical approaches and techniques.

psychotic
adj. Of or relating to being sufficiently disturbed in mental functioning as to lose touch with significant portions of reality via either hallucinations or delusions.

psychotic depression
n. A state of mind characterized by negative mood, low energy, loss of interest in usual activities, pessimism, unrealistically negative thoughts about self and the future, social withdrawal, and losing touch with significant portions of reality via either hallucinations or delusions.

psychotic disorder
n. Any disorder in which the person is sufficiently disturbed in mental functioning as to lose touch with significant portions of reality via either hallucinations or delusions. These disorders include schizophrenia, schizophreniform disorder, schizoaffective disorder, delusional disorder, brief psychotic disorder, folie à deux, dementia, and drug-induced psychotic disorder.

psychotomimetic
1. *adj.* Of or relating to the induction of hallucination. **2.** *n.* Any drug which causes

perception in the absence of the things perceived. Typically they also produce dream like alterations in thinking, mood, and perception. Most hallucinogens work by stimulating serotonin or catecholamine receptors. LSD (lysergic acid diethylamide), psilocybin, and dimethyl and diethyltriptamine (DMT, DET) primarily stimulate serotonin receptors, while mescaline, 3,4-methylenedioxyamphetamine (MDA), dimethoxymethylamphetamine (DOM), and 3,4-methylenedioxymethamphetamine (MDMA) work primarily via the catecholamine receptors. Hallucinogens have shown some promise in psychotherapy, but their use in the United States has been banned. Also called psychedelic drugs.

psychotropic
adj. Of or relating to having an effect on the functioning of the mind and the behavior which results from the functioning of mind.

psychotropic drug
n. Any chemical having an effect on the functioning of the mind and on behavior which results from the functioning of mind.

puberty
n. The period of time during which a child's sexual organs mature, secondary sexual characteristics develop, and the individual becomes capable of sexual reproduction.

puberty rite
n. Any form of initiation or age-specific behavior which a culture deems appropriate for persons moving from childhood to adulthood. Almost all cultures have such rites, and they vary tremendously from one culture to another. In most of the United States getting a driver's license is such a rite while among traditional Tiwi people of Australia radical circumcision and going walkabout were puberty rites.

public self
n. The self presented to other persons through actions, appearance, social interactions, and self-description, which varies depending on the audience. This is often contrasted with the private self and the collective self.

Pulfrich phenomenon
n. An optical illusion in which a pendulum swinging perpendicular to the line of sight appears to be moving in an ellipse if one eye is covered with a dark lens and the subject stares at the center of the pendulum's swing.

pulvinar
n. The pillow-shaped bulge on the posterior of the thalamus which receives input from the superior colliculi and the auditory, somatosensory, and visual cortex and is believed to be important in focusing visual attention.

punctuated equilibrium
n. The theory that evolution tends to proceed by means of short periods of rapid change in speciation followed by long periods of relatively little change.

punisher
n. Any stimulus that decreases the likelihood that the behavior that immediately precedes the stimulus will be repeated. Thus an electric shock given immediately after a rat or most other organisms press on a lever will reduce the chance that the bar will be pressed again by that organism.

punishment
n. The administration of a stimulus that decreases the likelihood that the behavior that immediately preceded the stimulus will be repeated. Thus an electric shock given immediately after a rat or most other organisms press on a lever will reduce the chance that the bar will be pressed again by that organism.

pupil
n. **1.** The opening through which light passes in order to enter the eye, the size of which is altered by a circle of muscle which constitutes the iris. **2.** A student.

pupillary reflex
n. An involuntary change in the size of opening in the pupil in response to changes in ambient light levels.

pure hue

n. **1.** Light all of a single wavelength. **2.** The perception produced by monochromatic light.

pure tone

n. **1.** Sound of a single wavelength of air pressure variation. **2.** The perception of sound produced by a single wavelength of air pressure level variation.

Purkinje cell

n. A large, flat nerve cell in the cerebellum which can have more than 100,000 connections with other cells and receives proprioceptive information from the body and makes connection with spinal nerves. Purkinje cells are important in coordinating voluntary muscle movements.

Purkinje figure

n. The image of the blood vessels in one's own retina which can occur when a bright light is shined into the eye from the side.

Purkinje-Sanson image

n. Any of three reflected images of a brightly lit object at which a subject is looking in a darkened room produced by the surface of the cornea and the front and back of the lens.

pursuit movement

n. A smooth tracking of an object by means of eye rotation which allows continuous visual fixation on the object.

pursuit rotor

n. A laboratory instrument used to test visual-motor coordination in which a small target is embedded in a disk whose movement the subject has to follow with a wand while the rotation speed of the object is varied either systematically or randomly.

putamen

n. A large reddish structure in the basal ganglia comprising a lateral portion of the lenticular nucleus which receives input from the motor cortex and which is believed to be involved in control of posture and voluntary movement.

puzzle box

n. A locked container in which an animal is placed which has an unlocking mechanism the animal must manipulate to get a reward or to get out of the box. The difficulty of the unlocking mechanism can be varied to create tasks of greater and lesser difficulty.

p-value

n. *P*-value, a very common concept in empirical research, refers to the statistical probability that an observed trend in the data (e.g., a relationship or difference) has occurred by chance alone. In a technical sense, the *p*-value is a statistical estimate of the likelihood, assuming a representative sample of data from the population at large, that a particular effect observed in the sample data resulted from chance sampling error. *P*-values can range from 0 (0%) to 1 (100%). By convention, researchers generally adhere to the guideline that an effect is statistically significant if the *p*-value is less than or equal to 5% ($p = .05$). Many researchers have come to question this convention for a variety of reasons. Since *p*-values fluctuate, depending on sample size, with a large enough sample, even a very minor variation or relationship in a data set will reach a *p*-value of less than .05. This has led to a blurring of the line between statistical significance and nonsignificance; sometimes research reports include discussion of "marginally significant" findings for effects with *p*-values ranging from .05 to .15.

    P-values are associated with type I error, the likelihood of falsely concluding that a trend exists in the population, and type II error, the likelihood of missing a trend in the data that exists in the population. Researchers can choose to be more conservative about type I errors by choosing a more stringent criterion level for decisions about the significance of *p*-values, also known as the alpha level. While the general convention is to set the alpha level at 5% ($p = .05$), sometimes researchers will set an alpha level at a more stringent level such as 1% ($p = .01$) or even .1% ($p < .001$) if the cost of a type I error is especially high. Statistical power is the likelihood of avoiding a type II error, or missing a signal that is present in the data. Because *p*-values are more sensitive with larger samples, the simplest way to boost the power of a study is to increase the sample size. – MWP

▶ *See also* **SIGNIFICANCE TEST** *and* **TYPE I** and **TYPE II ERROR**

Pygmalion effect

n. A form of self-fulfilling prophecy in which the expectations of a leader or person of high social status are fulfilled by his or her followers or social subordinates. Thus a teacher's expectations of his/her students tend to be reflected in student behavior such as performance on IQ tests and the expectations of managers to be reflected in the behavior of their subordinates.

Pygmalionism

n. **1.** Falling in love with one's own creation as in Greek myth Pygmalion fell in love with the statue of Aphrodite he had made. **2.** A sexual attraction to a statue, dressmaker's dummy, or similar facsimile of the human body.

pyramidal cell

n. A large nerve cell in the cortex shaped like a pyramid which typically has long dendritic branches near the surface of the cortex and a long, slender axon, which may be as long as a meter before ending in a dense bush of branches.

pyramidal tract

n. A set of nerve fibers composed mostly of pyramidal cells whose cell bodies are in the cortex and whose axons reach into the spinal column. Also called the corticospinal tract.

pyromania

n. A mental disorder characterized by a failure to resist impulses to set fires and watch them burn (beyond the normal human fascination with fire), an unusually strong interest in fire, increased tension when thinking about setting a fire, and then an orgasmlike pleasure and sense of release while setting the fire.

Q-methodology

n. A factor analytic technique in which persons rather than tests are analyzed. It has usually been used in conjunction with the Q sort.

Q sort

n. A method of description of a person or thing in which the describer sorts a deck of cards with adjectives or adjective phrases into piles from most descriptive to least descriptive, and the number of cards in the piles approximates a normal curve.

Quaalude

n. A synthetic sedative and hypnotic drug which depresses the cortex at moderate doses and the peripheral nervous system at higher doses. It has been widely used as a recreational drug and has caused many overdose deaths. Also called methaqualone.

quadriplegia

n. The paralysis of all four limbs. This is usually the result of injury to the upper spine. Also called tetraplegia.

qualitative research

n. Any scientific approach that does not use mathematical formulas to describe nature. This has traditionally included interviews, phenomenological analysis, psychoanalysis, content analysis, conversational analysis, critical theory, deconstruction, ethnology, focus groups, grounded theory, hermeneutics, protocol analysis, and theories of knowledge.

quality of life

n. The degree to which a person is able to enjoy being alive, which is related to physical and emotional health, economic sufficiency, social engagement, opportunity for self-expression and development, and the capacity to make decisions for oneself. In cases of deciding treatments for potentially fatal illness, it is often quantified as the expected quality of life times life expectancy.

quantitative psychology
n. **1.** All psychological approaches that use mathematics in order to describe the workings of mind and control of behavior. **2.** The area of psychology that studies the theory and practice of applying mathematics to problems of psychology.

quantitative research
n. Any scientific investigation that uses mathematics as a way of describing nature.

quartile
n. Any one-quarter of a distribution of scores or numbers. Thus the first quartile is the lowest 25% of the scores, et cetera.

quartile deviation
n. One-half of the distance between the first- and third-quartile boundaries, which is used as a measure of dispersion or scatter.

quasi-experiment
n. A study in which there is not random assignment of subjects to treatment groups but which is usually analyzed in the same way as an experiment. This method is used when it is difficult or impossible to assign subjects randomly.

quasi-experimental research
n. All studies in which there is not random assignment of subjects to treatment groups but which are usually analyzed in the same way as experiments. This method is used when it is difficult or impossible to assign subjects randomly.

questionnaire
n. Any list of questions or other items used to solicit information from people. These are widely used in attitude, health psychology, and personality research. Also called a self-report questionnaire.

quiet-biting attack
n. The complex but predictable pattern of behavior exhibited by predators stalking and killing their prey, which has been elicited in some species by stimulating the median forebrain bundle.

R

race
n. An inexact method of grouping people by ancestry whose categories vary from one locale to another and which usually includes people of recent European ancestry as one race, people of recent African ancestry as a race, and people from East Asia as a race and sometimes people whose ancestry was native to the Americas before European conquest as a fourth race. It should be noted that only about 6% of genetic variance is found within races with no genes accurately defining the races while each race has more variance within it than between it and other races. Racial categorization of individuals varies depending on the method of categorization.

race-based rejection sensitivity
n. Race-based rejection sensitivity (RS-race) is defined as a psychological process wherein a person anxiously expects, readily perceives, and intensely reacts to rejection on the basis of his or her race. This construct is one in a family of models emphasizing the notion that the anticipation of being stigmatized is an aversive, affectively charged experience.

When people are exposed to discrimination, mistreatment, or exclusion (i.e., rejection) on the basis of status characteristics such as race, they may develop anxious expectations that they may be similarly treated in the future. Discrimination does not have to be experienced personally in order for a person to expect similar treatment in the future. For instance, a person may develop anxious expectations of race-based rejection after having been unfairly targeted by police but may also develop such expectations from having seen other people of his/her race being treated in this way. When triggered, these anxious expectations place a person in a state of anticipatory threat, lowering the threshold, in turn, for perceiving the rejection. This state also prepares people to react intensely upon perceiving this outcome. Although first applied to race-based rejection, the process is applicable to other potentially stigmatized characteristics, such as gender, sexual orientation, or religion.

An important feature of the RS-race construct is its context specificity at two levels. On one level, the process is triggered only in situations that contain the potential for race-based rejection. As such, RS-race reflects the interaction between features of situations (potential for stigma) and persons (psychological processes). This distinguishes RS-race from broader constructs such as domain-general neuroticism. It also implies that even though a person may be concerned about being stigmatized, he or she can feel at ease given a safe, welcoming context. On another level, RS-race is context specific in that the triggers of the process for one group may not necessarily be the same as those of another. For instance, whereas RS-race may be triggered among African Americans at a roadblock where police are randomly pulling people over, this particular situation is less likely to trigger race-based rejection concerns among Asian Americans.

An *RS-race Questionnaire* designed specifically for African Americans assesses anxious expectations of race-based rejection across a number of situations relevant to this group. African Americans score higher overall on the measure than Asian Americans or Whites. Nevertheless, there is substantial within-group variability among African Americans; this variability highlights the within-group

diversity of experiences surrounding race – although some people anxiously expect rejection, others may more calmly expect acceptance. Individual differences in anxious expectations of race-based rejection have been linked to a higher frequency of perceiving racial discrimination and prejudice in a series of cross-sectional and longitudinal studies. People who score high on the RS-race questionnaire report greater feelings of rejection and alienation after a negative race-related experience than those who score low in RS-race.

Research suggests that RS-race can play a formative role in the experience of people entering predominantly or historically White institutions. It does so by influencing the quality of the relationships people form with institutional representatives and peers as well as the sense of belonging that people feel in the institution. In a study of African American college students, for example, RS-race was related to the trust and obligation students felt toward the university, as well as the discomfort experienced in interacting with professors. Consistently with a literature showing that concerns about belonging can disrupt people's ability to focus on their goals, RS-race was also shown to predict academic achievement negatively. These findings strongly suggest the need for educational and other institutions with a history of marginalizing groups of people on the basis of characteristics such as race or sex to attend to ways to foster a sense of inclusion among all their members.   – RM-D

race bias in testing

n. Concerns about race bias in testing are centered on the fact that specific ethnic groups consistently obtain lower average scores on traditional intelligence tests (as well as some other psychological tests). The differential scores have been attributed to environmental (i.e., education and schooling) and biological (i.e., genetic) factors as well as test bias as a result of inclusion of test questions that rely on specific cultural knowledge or language. Concerns over race bias in testing have led to the creation of various legal standards (i.e., the Civil Rights Act, which created the Equal

Employment Opportunity Commission [EEOC]) for guiding the use of psychological testing.   – BJM

race prejudice

n. A set of negative attitudes and beliefs about a group of people believed to constitute a race which ignores within-group diversity and is resistant to contrary evidence.

racial difference

n. **1.** Any difference attributed to groups of people identified as a race and believed to be held by all members of one group and not those of another such group. **2.** Any empirical difference between the averages on any measurable dimension between groups in or recently emigrated from a particular geographical area.

racial identity

n. Racial identity is a sense of collective identity based on an individual's perception of shared racial heritage with a particular racial group. Conceptions of race, as well as the specific racial groupings, vary across cultures and time. Most social scientists now contend that racial groupings are arbitrary and are derived from social conventions and customs embedded within specific historical contexts. As such, they maintain that race is best understood as a socially constructed variable rather than as taxonomy that is biologically meaningful. Although recent genetic studies have renewed the debate about the potential utility of racial groupings in biomedical research, psychology remains ambivalent regarding how, if at all, best to understand racial groupings as a psychological construct.

Less controversial is the notion that racial identity is a psychologically useful construct, although there remain disagreements over terminology and conceptualization. The concept of racial identity overlaps with ethnic identity. Although some scholars use the two terms interchangeably, there are some conceptual distinctions between racial identity and ethnic identity that have been noted. For example, Janet Helms has suggested that *race* has a clear meaning in the context of contemporary American society, whereas *ethnicity* is less clearly defined and is often used as a proxy for

racial classifications. Helms has also argued that racial identity centers around one's reaction to societal oppression based on race, whereas ethnic identity is based on a sense of a collective with others who share cultural characteristics such as religion and language.

Racial identity research has been most actively pursued within counseling psychology in the United States. It is generally concerned with the psychological implications of racial group membership, with the basic premise that in a society where racial categorization has social and political meanings, the development of a racial identity will occur in some form for everyone. The dominant theory of racial identity development was proposed in the early 1970s by William Cross, who argued that racial identity among African Americans can be understood as a developmental transformational process. According to Cross, the first stage is the pre-encounter stage, in which an African American individual has absorbed the racist beliefs, images, and values of the dominant culture without questioning. The second, the encounter stage, is precipitated by an event or a series of events that results in the individual's acknowledging that racism impacts his or her life. In the third, immersion/emersion stage, the individual desires to surround himself/herself with symbols of his or her racial identity and to learn about his/her history and share this experience with same-race peers while avoiding actively symbols of the White dominant culture. In the next, internalization stage, the individual has unlearned the internalized stereotypes about Blacks and holds a more secure racial identity such that he or she can begin to re-establish meaningful relationships with the members of the dominant society. In the final, internalization/commitment stage, the individual's positive racial identity translates into action for social change and a sense of commitment to the collective action on behalf of the racial group in selective alliances with members of the dominant society. Cross has termed this process of becoming Black psychologically *nigrescence.* Similar models of racial identity development have been proposed for other racial minority groups (including biracial individuals) in the United States.

Helms has argued that White Americans may also undergo development of positive White racial identity but that this entails coming to terms with their privileged status within society. According to Helms, white racial identity develops in six stages, starting with the contact stage, in which the individual has little or no awareness of the pervasiveness of racism. In the disintegration stage, the individual gains a growing awareness of, and discomfort with, racism and White privilege. In the third, reintegration, the individual may channel the guilt and anxiety felt during the previous stage to anger toward racial minority groups and blame them for the discomfort. The pseudoindependent stage is thought to follow, in which the individual no longer blames African Americans for racism and begins to disavow his or her own Whiteness in efforts to align with African Americans. Immersion/emersion is thought to involve the individual's search for positive White role models of antiracist behavior in an effort to redefine his/her racial identity. And in the final stage of autonomy, Helms describes the achievement of positive White identity that entails commitment to social change and a new sense of personal efficacy in multiracial settings.

Although these racial identity development models are presented as progressive stage models, theorists caution that the actual developmental processes are not always necessarily linear. Notably, Cross's (and other similar) racial identity development models have also been criticized for privileging a multicultural agenda as the desirable end stage of racial identity development and for lacking systematic empirical validation. Notwithstanding such challenges, racial identity theories have been applied to research, primarily in counseling and education. For example, scholars have examined the association between self-reported racial identity attitudes and multicultural competencies among mental health practitioners, especially among White counselors and trainees. Other research with racial minority individuals has examined the relationship between attitudes associated with specific racial identity stages and their experiences with racism and discrimination, self-esteem, friendship

patterns, and so on. Finally in a different line of scholarship that has not been linked specifically to racial identity development models, a series of social psychological studies have shown that making individuals' racial identity salient (through explicit or implicit priming) can affect their performance on a wide range of tasks from cognitive performance to visual search performance for Black or White faces.

– sok

racism
n. An irrational belief that some group of people identified as a race is in many ways inferior to another group of people which largely ignores within-group variance and is resistant to contrary information.

radial-arm maze
n. An experimental apparatus often used in learning experiments with mice and rats in which there are 6 to 12 narrow pathways leading away from a central area. The test animal is usually placed in the center of the apparatus and its movement observed to determine the pattern of its movement in different arms of the maze in relation to some independent variables.

random assignment
n. A process of deciding which subject or group in a study is included in which treatment condition such that all subjects or groups have an equal prior probability of being assigned to any particular treatment.

random effects model
n. In statistics, a model in which it is assumed that the differences within groups on the variables of interest are due to random sampling errors rather than to unobserved heterogeneity and that any such random differences are orthogonal to the variables of interest. Also called variance component model.

random error
n. Unpredictable variability in scores with no known cause which tends to fall into a normal curve whose mean is used to approximate a true score.

random factor

n. Any experimental variable whose levels are selected by a chance procedure within the experimental range of values.

random group

n. Any group of subjects selected by a chance process from a larger population of potential subjects. This procedure minimizes the chance that subject-related factors will affect the outcome of the study.

randomization

n. A process of assignment of subjects or treatments by means of a chance process so that there is no order or predictability in the assignments.

randomized blocks design

n. An experimental design in which subjects are selected on the basis of a variable or variables and then within each group a chance process is used to assign subjects to treatment conditions. Thus the variable or variables used to select groups become independent variables in the statistical analysis following the experiment.

randomized double-blind experiment

n. An experiment in which subjects are assigned by a chance process to treatment groups without either the subject or the experimenter knowing which treatment any subject receives. This is done to reduce the likelihood that the expectations of either subjects or experimenters will affect the outcome of the study so that comparisons between a treatment and a control group or between treatment groups are more likely to be due to the effects of the treatment.

random number table

n. A columnar presentation of numbers, usually of a fixed number of digits, which have been selected by a chance process so that there is no order or predictability in the numbers.

random sample

n. A set of items or individuals drawn from a larger population in which each member of the larger population has an equal opportunity for or probability of selection into the sample group. In a true random sample, there must be no systematic means by which individuals or items are selected for inclusion in the sample. A random sample is used to represent the larger population and allow researchers to generalize conclusions to the larger population in an efficient manner. For example, if a researcher were interested in examining the political views of students on a specific college campus, it would not be practical or efficient to survey every student on his or her position. Rather, the researcher would want to select a random sample of students, and then draw conclusions about the political views of the larger population based upon the responses of the sample. The accuracy of these conclusions depends upon the size of the sample relative to the size of the target population. When targeting a smaller population, one needs to sample a larger percentage to draw an accurate conclusion; when examining a large population, one needs to sample a smaller percentage to get the same level of accuracy.   – BJM

range

n. **1.** In statistics, the difference between the highest and the lowest number in a set of numbers. **2.** In biology, the geographical area in which an individual animal or a particular group of animals is likely to be found. **3.** In biology, the size of the geographical area in which an individual animal or a particular group of animals is likely to be found.

rank correlation

n. An index of the degree of relationship between two variables that consist of rank orderings. Also called the Spearman rank order correlation.

rank-difference correlation

n. An index of the degree of relationship between two variables that consist of rank orderings. Also called the Spearman rank correlation or Spearman rank order correlation.

ranked distribution

n. Any group of numbers arranged by order of magnitude.

Rankian psychology

n. The ideas and theories of Otto Rank (1884–1939), who supposed that each individual is a creative personality desiring to immortalize his or her self who needs to free himself/herself from the past and fully engage in experience so as to use his/her will to balance impulses and inhibitions in the creation that is the individual's life.

rank order

n. A list arranged according to the ordinal position of each item in relation to other items. Commonly used in nonparametric statistics, rank order implies that items within a list have been numerically (i.e., first, second, third, fourth) or qualitatively (i.e., worst, bad, good, better, best) sequenced. Rank order lists provide information on the relative position of an item within a larger grouping but do not provide information on the meaning of individual scores or the amount of difference between ranks. Because rank order indicates magnitude but not equal intervals, meaningful mathematical calculations are limited.   – BJM

rank-order correlation

n. An index of the degree of relationship between two variables that consist of rank orderings. Also called the Spearman rank order correlation.

raphe nuclei

n. A group of neuron clusters in the brainstem connecting the two halves of the medulla oblongata which release serotonin and have been associated with deep sleep.

rapid eye movement

n. A quick, unpredictable movement in which the two eyes are coordinated as if they were looking at something, which occurs with eyelids closed during a light stage of sleep and is associated with dreaming.

rapport

n. A sense of mutual understanding and communicative openness between two or more people. Rapport is often considered a necessary first step in psychotherapeutic relationships.

ratchet effect

n. The concept that humans continually improve on improvements, that they do not go backward or revert to a previous state. Progress occurs because improvements move themselves upward, similarly to the way a ratchet works. It is an important concept to explain the evolution and continued development of human culture.

rating scale

n. A measurement scale using categories or descriptive phrases to represent quantitative values; often used in social science research to measure attitudes, perceptions, or performance levels. For example, student course evaluations often use Likert-type rating scales which ask students to rate various dimensions of their course experience. A statement such as "I found the lectures relevant and informative" may be rated according to the following response options:

1. strongly agree
2. agree
3. neutral
4. disagree
5. strongly disagree

Alternatively, rating scales may utilize a category format which asks respondents to indicate their level of agreement on a numeric scale. Using a 10-point rating system, respondents may be asked "On a scale of 1 to 10, with 1 representing no jealousy and 10 representing extreme jealousy, how much jealousy would you feel if you saw your mate talking to another person of the opposite sex?" Regardless of whether the measurement is using a Likert or category type response option, rating scales assign numbers to represent the category descriptions. Despite the assignment of quantitative information, one must be careful in interpreting and manipulating rating scales as the numbers only provide ordinal data (which does not allow for mathematical calculations).

– BJM

rating scale, bipolar

n. A device intended to allow a subject to express his or her judgment numerically or spatially about a situation's or stimulus's relative position to two extremes of a single dimension.

rating scale, checklist

n. Test item format that provides a list of response options, characteristics, or target behaviors from which respondents indicate the relevance, presence, or applicability of each response option. As such, checklists require respondents to make a single, dichotomous choice for each response option by indicating whether the target criterion has been met or not met. For example, clinicians may use a behavioral checklist to indicate an individual's demonstration of various diagnostic criteria. Simple checklists do not provide any qualitative or value information for the degree to which each response option is met; rather, they are a simple indication of the presence or absence of the target criteria.
— BJM

ratio IQ

n. The original meaning of *intelligence quotient*, which was a summation of ability scores from which a measure of mental age was computed and then divided by chronological age: mental age/chronological age.

rational emotive behavior therapy

n. (REBT) A therapy in which it is assumed that thoughts, emotions, and behavior are aspects of an integrated system such that influencing one affects the others. It was a development of rational emotive therapy (RET), which placed more emphasis on the behavioral aspects of therapy than did the original RET. Both RET and REBT focus on recognizing automatic thoughts, which are often irrational, negative, and self-defeating, and altering them as a basic approach to therapy.

rational emotive therapy

n. A therapy in which it is assumed that thoughts, emotions, and behavior are aspects of an integrated system such that influencing one affects the others. It focuses on recognizing automatic thoughts, which are often irrational, negative, and self-defeating, and altering them as a basic approach to therapy.

rationality

n. The quality or state of being guided by logical thought.

rationality, bounded

n. An approach to understanding human judgment in which it is recognized that completely working out a logic for all actions in life is impossible because of limitations of information and processing capacity as well as not being worthwhile in turns of rewards achieved by doing so. Bounded rational approaches often use heuristics, or rules of thumb, to make choices which involve less information and less processing time and usually achieve correct results.

rationalization

n. A defense mechanism whereby the individual uses complicated (often circuitous) explanations in order to justify behavior. This defensive process happens outside conscious awareness and is thought to be a way of covering up a more painful unconscious reality. For example, a person may be in an abusive relationship but focus on the good aspects of the partner's behavior (e.g., "He is actually a really nice person when you get to know him") in order to justify staying in the relationship. The rationalization therefore serves to justify the behavior. Additionally, rationalization acts as a way of covering up other unconscious motivators (e.g., in the example rationalization allows the individual to focus on the positive aspects of the partner, as opposed to focusing on his/her own unconscious reasons for remaining in the relationship, such as feelings of being needy or dependent on the partner). – DGa

ratio reinforcement

n. A procedure in training in which a predetermined proportion of target behaviors are rewarded. Ratio reinforcement typically takes longer to establish a high likelihood of the target behavior than does continuous reinforcement, but, once established, the target behavior is more resistant to extinction than is that established through continuous reinforcement. Ratio reinforcement can be variable or remain the same over time.

ratio scale

n. A quantitative scale including all three key scale properties: magnitude, equal intervals, and an absolute zero. All mathematical calculations are appropriate for ratio data. For example, money or income is measured on a ratio scale. The absolute zero represents no money and $50 is twice as much as $25; there are equal intervals as the difference of a dollar means the same thing when comparing $1 to $2 or $100 to $101. The large number of available calculations with a ratio scale makes it one of the most useful measures of quantitative data.   – BJM

▶ *See also* **ORDINAL SCALE**

Raven's Progressive Matrices

n. A test of intelligence designed by John Raven which is intended to be fair to persons of different cultural backgrounds and those who have had different educational opportunities. In the test the subject is presented with a series of matrices, each of which has a piece missing, and the subject is required to select which of several possibilities would correctly complete the matrix. The matrices are presented in order of difficulty, and the test has been found to give scores which are correlated with standard intelligence tests and particularly with performance scores on those tests. There are several forms of the test.

raw data

n. Any piece of information in research in its original form before it is summarized, normalized, or converted into any other form.

raw score

n. A numerical result from a measurement in the first form in which it is recorded before it is summarized, normalized, or converted into any other form.

R correlation

n. A numerical index of the degree a target variable can be predicted by two or more predictor variables using a linear model. *R* ranges from 0 to 1 with 0 indicating no predictive power and 1 indicating perfect prediction.

reactance theory

n. The idea that in many circumstances people will seek to avoid having their choices or options limited by others or restore them when they have already been limited. This includes the notions that an attractive object becomes more attractive when access to it has been curtailed and that when a person feels pressured to choose a particular option, that option becomes less attractive and the person becomes more likely to choose in a direction against the experienced pressure.

reaction formation

n. A primitive defense mechanism in which the individual covers up painful unconscious realities by conveying and feeling the opposite emotional experience. For example, an individual may unconsciously feel anger and frustration toward his/her mother but feel that this anger is much too destructive to convey directly. In a complicated unconscious process the individual identifies only with positive experiences of his/her mother and conveys these experiences in a single-minded manner. Reaction formation is notable in that the conveyance of positive experience often appears too strong and lacks any depth or subtlety. As with most defense mechanisms, this process is unconscious: the individual using this defense mechanism is only aware of his or her positive experience and is oblivious to the more intensely negative unconscious experiences.   – DGa

reaction latency

n. The time which elapses between the onset of a stimulus and the behavioral reaction to it. Also called reaction time.

reaction potential

n. In Hull's learning theory, the probability that a particular stimulus will be followed by a particular response, which is the product of habit strength and drive strength.

reaction time

n. The time which elapses between the onset of a stimulus and the behavioral reaction to it. Also called reaction latency.

reactive attachment disorder

n. An age-inappropriate and markedly disturbed pattern of social relating in children under 5 years of age resulting from grossly inadequate parental care with inhibited and disinhibited types. The inhibited type involves excessive behavioral inhibition with hypervigilance, frozen watchfulness, and failure to feel comforted by contact with or ambivalence toward a parent or other attachment figure. In the disinhibited type the child shows indiscriminate sociability without appropriate attachment to his or her caregiver.

reactive depression

n. A state of mind characterized by negative mood, low energy, loss of interest in usual activities, pessimism, unrealistically negative thoughts about self and the future, and social withdrawal which occurs shortly after an emotionally traumatic event. Short states of depression are normal after personal losses of various sorts and are considered disorders only when they persist for long periods or significantly interfere with daily functioning, as in the various depressive disorders.

reactivity

n. **1.** The degree to which an object of study is affected by the process of being studied. **2.** In psychopathology, the tendency to exhibit pathological symptoms following stressful external events.

realistic conflict theory

n. Any conflict which occurs when there are two or more groups competing for limited resources. This is opposed to conflict over ideas or beliefs.

reality monitoring

n. The process or capacity to know the original source of remembered information and to discriminate experienced information from dreams, works of fiction, television, gossip, or other secondhand sources. Normal humans have been shown to lack this capacity in many circumstances, and the capacity decreases markedly in dementia and other mental disorders as well as intoxication. Also called source monitoring.

reality principle

n. In psychoanalysis, the governing process of the ego, which monitors the external world and attempts to satisfy the impulses of the id within the constraints imposed by the situation. The reality principle leads to the temporary suppression of some impulses in order to carry out long-term plans for achieving the greatest possible level of satisfaction available to the person.

reason

1. *n.* The capacity to think with normative rationality. **2.** *n.* A motive or explanation for a decision or course of action. **3.** *v.* To think in a linear manner, usually either inductively or deductively.

reasoned action, theory of

n. The theory of reasoned action (TRA) is a model for the prediction of people's behavior from knowledge of three characteristics: their intention to perform the behavior, their attitudes about the behavior, and subjective norms (other people's attitudes) about the behavior. First, the TRA states that a specific behavior can be predicted most directly from the person's intention to perform the behavior. Not surprisingly, people are most likely to perform a behavior when they intend to do it and least likely to perform a behavior when they do not intend to do it. Behavioral intention can be predicted from the person's attitudes and subjective norms (perceived attitudes of other people who are important to the person) toward the behavior.

— VKP, LAB

reasoning

n. **1.** Thinking in a linear and logical manner to draw conclusions from facts or the classification of things or events using general principles to infer order in the information. **2.** The particular sequence of ideas used to arrive at a conclusion.

rebound effect

n. A change in the opposite direction as a previous change in behavior or other process which occurs after a force has altered the course of behavior or other process from its usual pattern. Thus taking calcium carbonate reduces the level of acid in the stomach, an effect that is followed by an increase in acid production in the stomach, which increases acid level to above the normal level. When many organisms have a normal pattern of behavior prevented or suppressed through punishment, that pattern of behavior often shows an increase above expected levels when the situation allows or the punishment ceases.

recall

1. *v.* To remember specific information, as opposed to recognizing appropriate choices when they are presented. **2.** *n.* The capacity to remember specific information.

recategorization

n. The process of assigning a new classification to a thing or event. This is important in creative thinking, which often involves perceiving an unconventional use or perspective on something by classifying the thing according to its functional properties rather than its normative class. It is also important in information processing models, in which recategorization can allow flexibility as well as a check on programming structure.

receiver operating characteristic

n. (ROC) In signal detection theory, the relative proportion of correct identifications (hits) and incorrect identifications (false alarms). This is frequently represented as a curve relating the two probabilities as well as chance expectation, from which the signal-to-noise ratio is calculated and in which the sensitivity of the system is represented as d' (d prime), which is the area of the curve between the curve of performance and the line of chance expectation.

recency effect

n. The fact that it is easier to remember information recently learned than that learned a longer time ago.

receptive field

n. A region in space from which energy or stimulation is likely to result in a reaction in the nervous system. Thus light from one angle is more likely to stimulate a rod or cone in the retina than is light from other angles. And, similarly, a retinal ganglion cell is more likely to react to receptor stimulation in one region of the retina than in others.

receptor

n. Any cell in a sensory system that converts the energy of a stimulus into neural excitation. Thus the rods and cones in the eye convert the energy of light which strikes them into nerve impulses, and the hair cells in the cochlea convert air pressure changes into neural impulses in the perception of sound.

receptor potential

n. A change in the electric potential across the membrane of a sensory receptor resulting from a sensory stimulus which tends to change the likelihood of an action potential in an associated sensory neuron in either a positive or a negative direction. Also known as a generator potential.

receptor site

n. An area on a nerve or other cell that is chemically configured to interact with particular chemicals. In neurons the dendritic terminals have many receptor sites for neurotransmitters. Also called neuroceptor.

recessive gene

n. A segment of DNA which encodes for a particular trait that is expressed only if both chromosomes carry the same version of the DNA chain. If the DNA chain is matched with another version of the DNA segment, the other tends to be expressed and is called a dominant gene.

recessive trait

n. An inherited characteristic that appears in the phenotype only if it is inherited from both parents so that the DNA segments which encode for the characteristic are the same on both of the pair of chromosomes in the organism.

recidivism

n. The tendency or rate at which a convicted criminal is convicted of a new offense or a disease or mental disorder recurs.

recidivism rate

n. The proportion of convicted criminals who are convicted of a new offense or the proportion of individuals who have a disease or mental disorder who suffer from a recurrence.

reciprocal altruism

n. A form of relationship in which one individual helps in a way that is more beneficial to the individual receiving help than it is detrimental to the individual giving help and is extended only if the individual expects the other to help him or her in a similar situation at a later time. If the other fails to reciprocate, this failure is identified by the group, and then altruistic cooperation is withdrawn and the nonreciprocator is punished in some way. Thus, in vampire bats, a bat that has had a good feeding will sometimes regurgitate some of the blood it has drunk for another member of the colony that has not been able to feed. If the bat receiving blood does not reciprocate to other members of the colony when it has drunk plenty of blood, then the other bats expel it from the community.

reciprocal determinism

Definition. *n.* Reciprocal determinism is a concept involving three factors: a person's behavior, his or her personal internal factors or attributes (for example, personality), and his or her external environment. The concept of reciprocal determinism states that at any given time each of these three factors may be influencing the others or be influenced by them. More specifically, a person's behavior is influenced by internal factors as well as by the environment, the person's personal factors or attributes are also influenced by his or her behavior and by the environment, and the environment itself is influenced by the person's personal factors and behaviors.

Explanation. People and their environment interact in various ways. For instance, people select which environments they enter. In addition, people's attributes and their ways of looking at the world actually influence the way they interpret that environment. Consequently, two people in the same situation can interpret the environment in very different ways. For example, introverts may view attending a party as a somewhat stressful situation, while extroverts may find the same party to be relaxing and fun. This interpretation of the environment will affect the way these people behave. The extroverts may act open and friendly and thus attract potential new friends, whereas the introverts may appear unfriendly because they feel awkward, and therefore no one may approach them. In this case, the people's behaviors, which are based on their interpretations of the situation, can also influence the environment (the ways other people react toward them). This can further shape the people's future behaviors. (If no one is friendly toward the introverts at the party, they will be less likely to attend parties in the future). These behaviors may then influence the persons' personalities because if they engage in more and more introverted behaviors (such as avoid parties), they will become more committed to the perception that they are introverted. If people view themselves as more introverted, they will be more likely to practice introverted activities in the future and to avoid extroverted activities. On the other hand, extroverts will be likely to attend many parties and behave in a very outgoing way; this behavior may influence others to be more outgoing, and in this way the extrovert will have influenced the situation itself. People with different personalities, interests, and customs select different environments (different friends, jobs, neighborhoods, television shows, etc.). Though people select their environments on the basis of their preferences, the exposure to these environments continues to influence them and shape who they are. Reciprocal determinism is the concept of a never-ending cycle in which a person's personality and perceptions, his/her behavior, and his/her environment all influence each other. All of these elements affect and are affected by the others.

Development and details. At one time many psychologists (called behaviorists) believed that a person's behavior was influenced solely by external events in the environment. In essence, they believed that people had very little control over their behaviors; they were a product of their environment. However, this concept was considered to be too simplistic by other theorists. Social-cognitive psychologists thought behavior was a product of a person's interaction with his or her environment. Instead of the environment's being the sole influence on behavior, it was suggested that both the individual and the environment influence each other, as well as the behavior. Further it was noted that a person's behavior can also influence the individual and the environment. The interaction of all these factors was labeled *reciprocal determinism* because all of the factors influence (or determine) the others simultaneously.

− VKP, LAB

reciprocal inhibition

n. **1.** In behavior therapy, a technique for getting rid of an unwanted behavior by substituting a different and physiologically incompatible response for the original behavior. Thus anxious individuals are often taught to relax in situations in which they habitually feel anxious, and since relaxation and anxiety are incompatible, the anxiety tends to diminish or disappear as the relaxation response is learned. **2.** In neuroscience, a mechanism in which one reaction tends to inhibit other reactions. Thus in the retina if one receptor cell depolarizes after stimulation by light, it inhibits the receptors around it from also depolarizing. **3.** In cognitive science, the interference of one idea or memory in recollection or recognition of a similar idea or memory. **4.** In biology, a neural mechanism which restrains opposing muscle groups from contracting at the same time.

reciprocal inhibition therapy

n. A therapeutic technique for getting rid of an unwanted behavior by substituting a different and physiologically incompatible response for the original behavior. Thus anxious individuals are often taught to relax in situations in which they habitually feel anxious, and since relaxation and anxiety are physiologically incompatible responses, the

anxiety tends to diminish or disappear as the relaxation response is learned.

reciprocality principle

n. **1.** In neo-Jungian psychology, the idea that everything expresses itself as two polar opposites. **2.** In information processing, the idea that the generation of new artifact types is mediated by the transformation of relationships among agents, and the generation of new artifact types mediates the transformation of relationships among agents. **3.** In law, the idea that the courts of one country will recognize the legal proceedings of another country if that country recognizes the legitimacy of its legal proceedings.

reciprocity hypothesis

n. The idea that the magnitude of a sensation is equal to the intensity of a stimulus multiplied by its duration. Also called the reciprocity law.

recognition

n. **1.** In memory, the capacity to know that a particular stimulus has been previously learned when encountering something previously encountered. **2.** In general, a sense of familiarity upon encountering something that has been previously encountered. **3.** Praising or otherwise bestowing rewards, usually for achievement.

recognition memory

n. The capacity to know that a particular stimulus has been previously learned when presented with the previously learned information. This is distinguished from recall memory, which does not need to be cued by representing the learned material.

reconstructive memory

n. Reconstructive memory is the process by which we recall the past, assembling the past each time we remember. When we try to remember the past, we do not replay an event as a video camera might. Rather, we "reconstruct" what happened, sometimes by drawing inferences about what happened or piecing together information that seems plausible. The memory process comprises three essential stages: acquisition, retention, and retrieval. *Acquisition* refers to an individual's initial experience, when attention is devoted and the event is encoded in memory. *Retention* is the amount of time that elapses between the original event and recall. The final stage of the memory process is *retrieval* of the event. It is during retrieval that we construct a narrative of the event, filling in any gaps with logical details, thus reconstructing the event in a way that differs in some way from the original event. – TP, EFL

recovered memory
n. A memory, often traumatic, which has been recalled after not having been recalled for a long period, often years or decades, in which the individual was unaware or minimally aware of the material in the recovered memory. Given the reconstructive nature of memory for events, there is much debate as to the accuracy of recovered memories.

recruitment
n. **1.** The process of enlisting participants. **2.** In perception, the increase in the number of neurons which respond to a stimulus as it persists and especially if it increases in magnitude. **3.** In audition, a perceived increase in loudness of a stimulus as it crosses the threshold for perception, which is often characteristic of sensorineural hearing loss.

red-green color blindness
n. A form of color blindness in which red and green are not separated and which is usually caused by an absence of red-green cones in the retina. Also called deuteronopia.

reductionism
n. The process of classifying all phenomena in a limited set of categories, usually in an attempt to develop a comprehensive explanation for something. Thus mental events are sometimes said to be examples of biological processes, or numerous widely differing behaviors are said to be examples of acting out subconscious desires.

reductive interpretation
n. A dismissive term for psychoanalytic interpretations which causally explain in terms of unconscious forces, which, from a Jungian perspective, is not possible because of the teleological nature of human development.

reference group
n. Any group of people used as a mental reference frame for making judgments by an individual. Most people compare themselves to only a very small subset of all people when deciding about their own worth, characteristics, and appropriate behavior.

reference group effect
n. The idea that people make implicit social comparisons with others when making ratings on scales. That is, people's ratings will be influenced by the implicit comparisons they make between themselves and others, and these influences may make comparing responses across cultures difficult.

reference memory
n. **1.** The storage of general information not tied to specific events such as how many stars are in the flag of the United States or what the word *penguin* means. Also called semantic memory. **2.** In information processing, any part of actual or virtual memory referred to by a command.

referential communication task
n. **1.** An experimental situation used in psycholinguistic and communications studies in which a subject is required to select which of two or more objects are referred to or being described in a communication. **2.** An experimental situation used in psycholinguistic and communications studies in which a subject is required to describe an object and the accuracy of the description of the object being referred to is assessed.

reflex
n. An automatic, largely fixed response to a limited range of stimuli that is not learned and typically is quicker than would be the case were conscious processes involved, as in eye blink and patellar reflexes.

reflex arc
n. The neural circuit involved in reflexes usually composed of sensory nerves connecting to the

spinal column in which the sensory nerves connect with motor nerves, triggering the reflex.

reflex, conditioned
n. A reflexive response in the presence of a stimulus which did not originally evoke the response but which has been paired with an unconditioned stimulus until the stimulus provokes a response similar to the one originally evoked by the unconditioned stimulus. Thus if a dog hears a bell immediately before being fed, it will begin to salivate when it hears the bell without being fed; the salivation to the bell will be the conditioned reflex. Also called conditioned response.

refractory period
n. **1.** A short and variable period of time after orgasm in which sexual desire is not present and in which sexual response is limited. **2.** A short period after a neuron has been depolarized in which it does not depolarize again. **3.** A variable period of time after a particular behavior has occurred in which that behavior is unlikely to recur.

region of rejection
n. In statistics, the area of a frequency distribution of scores beyond the minimum that will lead to rejection of the null hypothesis.

regression
n. **1.** Generally a going backward, as in returning to a less mature level of behavior or thought. **2.** In psychoanalysis, a defense mechanism in which the person returns to an immature form of coping or an earlier psychosexual stage when the person feels overwhelmed by anxiety and his or her usual coping styles are insufficient. **3.** The creation of a linear model of prediction using one or more variables to predict another variable.

regression analysis
n. Any of several techniques of creating a linear model of prediction using one or more variables to predict another variable.

regression coefficient
n. A numerical weight assigned to one predictor variable in a regression equation.

regression, curvilinear
n. A type of polynomial regression that uses a linear model to fit a regression line to a curved set of data points. A curvilinear regression is used to depict the relation between variables when the regression equation is nonlinear. Curvilinear regression analysis tests various transformations of variables to find the best-fitting model.   – BJM

regression equation
n. A formal mathematical description of the use of weighted variables to predict another variable using a linear regression technique.

regression, linear
n. Any of several techniques of creating a linear model of prediction using one or more variables to predict another variable.

regression toward the mean
n. **1.** The tendency of an observation to be closer to the mean of a population than a prediction of the observation using a sample mean as a basis for prediction. **2.** The higher likelihood that an unlikely result will be followed by a more likely result. Thus if an athlete has an outstanding performance, his or her next performance is more likely to be close to the average than to be similarly outstanding. This is the basis for the gambler's fallacy in which chance events are believed to be self-correcting.

regression weight
n. A numerical index of the relative importance of one variable in a linear regression to the value of the prediction.

regret
Definition. n. Regret is a negative emotional state predicated on an upward, self-focused counterfactual inference. In other words, regret is an unpleasant feeling based on the recognition that one could have decided or acted differently so as to have produced a more desirable state of affairs.

Explanation. Regret is both a consequence and a determinant of decision making. If a decision produces a suboptimal outcome, the feeling of regret can make the subjective appraisal of that outcome seem even worse. This effect is an example of a contrast effect: the juxtaposition of an attained object (e.g., buying stock in General Electric) against a more favorable alternative (e.g., buying stock in Microsoft) makes the obtained object seem less favorable, by contrast. The experience of regret may, in turn, influence subsequent decisions in ways that may be problematic (i.e., regret may be a source of bias). The individual might become overly cautious and withdraw from similar situations entirely, or he or she might become overly likely to alter his/her decision-making strategy. People tend to be regret-averse: that means that they make suboptimal decisions just to prevent the possibility of subsequent regret (e.g., individuals prefer gambles in which they will not learn the outcome of nonchosen options). These observations have resulted in the view that value of attained objects and events depends not only on their objective properties, but also on the way they compare to alternatives that might have been attained.

Development and details

Functional basis of regrets. Regret was first understood in terms of its role as a bias in decision making. More recent theory has emphasized the functional nature of regret. That is, regret is largely useful in providing feedback on decisions and guiding subsequent corrective action. Like other negative emotions, then, regret is best understood in terms of its role in regulating behavior for overall benefit, with bias occurring relatively rarely against this functional backdrop. As such, regret seems to be strongest when there is further opportunity to correct problems or effect improvements. When the situation is closed to further modification (e.g., a basketball game is over; an initial stock offering is closed), regrets seem to be rapidly suppressed according to principles long understood under the rubric of cognitive dissonance theory. Nevertheless, severe regret has been associated with depression and as such has been the focus of intervention techniques informed by the cognitive-behavioral therapy (CBT) approach.

Regrets across the life span. The longest-lasting regrets are those that focus on inaction (i.e., actions that should have been taken), as opposed to regrets that focus on actions that should *not* have been taken. The specific content of regrets changes with age. Because opportunity changes across the life span (e.g., college students have more opportunity in the area of romance than do adults who have been married for decades; middle-aged workers have more opportunities in their careers than do those who have retired), the aspects of life in which people harbor their greatest regrets also change across the life span. For adult Americans, the top three areas of regret are, in order, education, career, and romance; for college students, the top areas of regret, in order, are romance, friendships, and education. Moreover, the nature of regrets changes in older adulthood. These older adults tend to experience "neutered regrets" which focus more on the actions of others than of themselves, most likely caused by the lower degree of opportunity in most domains toward the end of life.

Conclusion. Regret is a negative emotional state driven by an upward counterfactual thought, elicited by negative outcomes over which the individual has the opportunity for future correction. Regrets are highly functional, identifying the antecedents of negative events and supporting the formation of relevant behavioral intentions to prevent similar outcomes in the future.   – AS, NR

regulators

n. Nonverbal behaviors that are used to regulate the flow of speech in a conversation, such as tone of voice or facial expressions. These often signal that one speaker is finished talking and the other can start.

regulatory focus theory

n. Regulatory focus theory proposes that two distinct regulatory systems have developed to deal with two distinct survival concerns – nurturance and security. To survive, people (and other animals) receive support or nourishment from the environment (often provided by others) and protection from dangers in the environment (social and nonsocial dangers). When people succeed in satisfying a concern, they experience pleasure, and when they fail, they experience pain. Thus, both of these regulatory systems involve approaching pleasure and avoiding pain. To this extent, regulatory focus theory is consistent with the classic hedonic principle that people approach pleasure and avoid pain. The hedonic principle has been the dominant motivational principle across all areas of psychology and many other disciplines as well. Although consistent with the hedonic principle, regulatory focus theory goes beyond this principle by emphasizing the motivational significance of the *differences* in *the ways* actors approach pleasure and avoid pain when they regulate within the distinct nurturance and security systems.

Regulatory focus theory relates the nurturance motive to the development of *promotion focus* concerns with accomplishment, with fulfilling hopes and aspirations (ideals). It relates the security motive to the development of *prevention focus* concerns with safety, with meeting duties and obligations (oughts). People can succeed or fail to fulfill their promotion or prevention focus concerns, and, thus, for both promotion and prevention, they will experience pleasure from success and pain from failure. But the hedonic experience is not the end of the story. Regulatory focus theory predicts, and research has found, that the emotional and motivational consequences of success or failure are different in the promotion and prevention systems. When people are in the promotion focus system, they experience cheerfulness-related emotions after success (e.g., happiness, joy) and dejection-related emotions after failure (e.g., sadness, discouragement). This is true whether people are in a promotion focus from a chronic predisposition to be in that system or from a current situation activating that system. The pleasure of success and the pain of failure are different in the prevention focus system. They experience quiescence-related emotions after success (e.g., calmness, relaxation) and agitation-related emotions after failure (e.g., nervousness, tension). These emotional differences between promotion and prevention also apply to emotional appraisals. Individuals in a promotion focus more readily appraise objects and events along a cheerfulness-dejection dimension, whereas individuals in a prevention focus more readily appraise objects and events along a quiescence-agitation dimension.

Regulatory focus theory is especially concerned with the differences between promotion and prevention motivationally. Regulatory focus theory proposes that when people pursue goals, their *strategic preferences* are different in a promotion versus a prevention focus. The theory proposes that individuals in a promotion focus prefer to use *eager* strategies to pursue goals – strategies of advancement (a gain), which move the actor from a neutral (the status quo) to a positive state. In contrast, individuals in a prevention focus prefer to use *vigilant* strategies to pursue goals (a nonloss) – strategies of carefulness that stop the actor from moving from neutral to a negative state. What underlies this difference in strategic preferences? Individuals in a promotion focus experience positive and negative events in the world as gains and nongains, respectively, because their concerns are about accomplishments and aspirations. Strategic eagerness is also about ensuring gains and not wanting to miss gains, so eagerness fits a promotion focus. In contrast, individuals in a prevention focus experience positive and negative events in the world as nonlosses and losses, respectively, because their concerns are about safety and meeting obligations. Strategic vigilance is also about trying to be careful to ensure nonlosses and not wanting to commit mistakes that produce a loss, so vigilance fits a prevention focus.

Indeed, many studies have found that individuals in a promotion focus prefer to use eager strategies to pursue goals, whereas individuals in a prevention focus prefer to use vigilant strategies. There is also evidence that when an eager versus strategic approach to an achievement task is experimentally manipulated, individuals in a promotion focus perform better when instructed to use eager means than when instructed to use vigilant means, whereas the opposite is true for individuals in a prevention focus. Persuasive messages with an eager tone are more effective in changing attitudes when received by individuals in a promotion than a prevention focus, whereas the reverse is true for persuasive messages with a vigilant tone. The difference between a promotion focus on eager gains versus a prevention focus on vigilant nonlosses also influences the nature of in-group versus out-group bias. For individuals in a promotion focus, in-group members are treated with a positive bias ("promoting us"), but there is little bias regarding out-group members. In contrast, for individuals in a prevention focus, the out-group members are treated with a negative bias ("preventing them"), but there is little bias regarding in-group members.

Because of this difference in strategic preferences for people in a promotion versus a prevention focus, the motivational significance of success and failure is also very different in promotion versus prevention. When individuals succeed in a promotion focus, that increases their eagerness (experienced as high-intensity joy), and when they fail, that decreases their eagerness (experienced as low-intensity sadness). In contrast, when individuals succeed in a prevention focus, that reduces their vigilance (experienced as low-intensity calmness), and when they fail, that increases their vigilance (experienced as high-intensity nervousness).

This regulatory focus difference in the motivational significance of success and failure influences postperformance expectations as well. Optimism increases eagerness but reduces vigilance. Thus, after success on an initial trial of a task, individuals in a promotion state, more than individuals in a prevention state, should raise their expectations for the next trial (be optimistic) to maintain the strategic eagerness that sustains their focus. After failure on an initial trial, individuals in a prevention state, more than individuals in a promotion state, should lower their expectations for the next trial (be defensively pessimistic) to maintain the strategic vigilance that sustains their focus. Research has confirmed these predictions.

Regulatory focus differences in strategic approaches are especially likely to be revealed when there is a conflict between different choices or different ways to proceed on a task. One prevalent conflict is between being "risky" or being "conservative" when making a judgment or decision. When people are uncertain, they can take a chance and treat something as being correct that could actually be incorrect (a possible error of commission). Alternatively, they can be cautious and reject something as being incorrect that could actually be correct (a possible error of omission). Studies on memory and judgment have found that, when the status quo is satisfactory, individuals in a promotion focus are more risky than those in a prevention focus. There is also evidence that individuals in a promotion focus are more creative than those in a prevention focus and are also more willing to change and try something new when given the opportunity. This again suggests that under conditions of uncertainty (and a satisfactory status quo), individuals in a promotion focus, compared to individuals in a prevention focus, are more willing to consider new alternatives and not simply stick with the established state of affairs. There are benefits from the prevention strategic approach as well, however. Compared to promotion focus individuals, prevention focus individuals are more committed to their choices and are less likely to abandon them when obstacles arise.

There are other conflicts on which individuals in a promotion focus act differently than those in a prevention focus. One classic conflict on many tasks is between speed (or quantity) and accuracy (or quality). Individuals in a promotion focus emphasize speed more than accuracy, whereas individuals in a prevention focus emphasize accuracy more than speed. A third conflict concerns whether to represent objects or events in a more global and abstract manner or in a more local and concrete manner. There is evidence that individuals in a promotion focus are more likely to represent objects and events in a global and abstract manner (and as more temporally distant) than in a local and concrete manner, whereas the opposite is true for those in a prevention focus.

In sum, regulatory focus theory differs from the traditional emphasis on hedonic outcomes. Rather than outcomes, it considers the strategic and process differences of individuals making decisions and pursuing goals in a promotion versus a prevention focus. These strategic and process differences have been shown to have significant emotional and motivational effects on people's lives.

– ETH

rehearsal

n. **1.** A practice period for an approaching performance or test in which the material to be performed or tested is practiced. **2.** The repetition of information in order to learn it or hold it in memory for a longer period, as in repeating a phone number between the time of looking it up and the time it is dialed into the telephone.

reinforcement

n. **1.** In general, anything that strengthens something else. **2.** In classical conditioning, the presentation of an unconditioned stimulus immediately after presentation of a conditioned stimulus. **3.** In operant conditioning, any stimulus which makes a particular behavior more likely to occur. **4.** The process of making a behavior more likely to occur by rewarding the behavior or successive approximations of the behavior.

reinforcement, contingent

n. A reward or plan for rewarding that is conditional on something else, usually a particular set of behaviors. In learning theory, it is reinforcing a particular set of behavior. In management, it is any form of leadership in which rewards and penalties are used to increase worker productivity.

reinforcement, continuous

n. A plan for providing reward for target behavior in which a reward is provided for each instance of a target behavior.

reinforcement, differential

n. A technique in learning in which the frequency of some behaviors is increased by associating them with reinforcement while the frequency of other behaviors is decreased by lessening the frequency with which they are rewarded.

reinforcement gradient (effect)

n. The observation that the closer in time a reward is to a response, the more likely the response is to be repeated.

reinforcement, intermittent

n. Rewards in which not every occurrence of a target behavior is rewarded. There are many ways of creating intermittent reinforcement schedules, the most common of which are ratio and interval schedules. In ratio schedules a reward is issued after a certain number of responses, and in interval schedules a reward is given at the end of a period in which an appropriate response has occurred.

reinforcement, interval

n. A plan for increasing the likelihood of a particular behavior by providing a reward every time the target behavior occurs after the lapse of a predetermined time.

reinforcement, negative

n. A plan for increasing the likelihood of a target behavior by removing a noxious stimulus when the behavior occurs. Thus a dog can be conditioned to move from one side of a cage to another in order to escape or avoid an electrical shock.

reinforcement, noncontingent

n. A state in which the occurrence of rewards is unrelated to the behavior of an organism. This circumstance often leads to superstitious behavior and is often experienced by humans as markedly unpleasant.

reinforcement, positive

n. A plan for increasing the likelihood of a target behavior by associating it with a reward in time and space. Thus a dog can be positively reinforced for lying down when the owner says, "Lie down" if the order is followed by giving the dog a doggie treat.

reinforcement, ratio

n. A plan for increasing the likelihood of a target behavior by rewarding a predetermined proportion of the target behaviors. Ratio reinforcement typically takes longer to establish a high likelihood of the target behavior than does continuous reinforcement, but, once established, the target behavior is more resistant to extinction than is that established through continuous reinforcement. Ratio reinforcement can be variable or remain the same over time.

reinforcement schedule

n. In learning theory, a plan for which target responses will be rewarded. The most common schedules of reinforcement are continuous reinforcement, in which each instance of a target behavior is rewarded; interval reinforcement, in which the first instance of a target behavior after the elapse of a predetermined period is rewarded; and ratio reinforcement, in which a predetermined percentage of the target behaviors are rewarded.

reinforcement, social

n. A form of rewarding particular behaviors through positive interpersonal interactions such as recognition, praise, positive facial expressions, or touching.

reinforcement theory

n. Any coherent set of ideas attempting to explain the relationships between behavior and reward.

reinforcer

n. Anything which can be used to increase or decrease the likelihood of the appearance of a behavior when appropriately associated with the behavior in time and space.

reinforcer, conditioned

n. A response in the presence of a stimulus which did not originally evoke the response but which has been paired with an unconditioned stimulus until the stimulus provokes a response similar to the one originally evoked by the unconditioned stimulus. Thus if a dog hears a bell immediately before being fed, it will begin to salivate when it hears the bell without being fed; the salivation to the bell will be the conditioned response.

reinforcer, negative

n. The removal or prevention of an aversive stimulus which either is contingent upon a particular behavior or is intended to increase the likelihood of a particular behavior. Thus the removal of pain can negatively reinforce a dog's moving from one side of a cage to another.

reinforcer, positive

n. Anything which increases the likelihood of a behavior which immediately precedes the appearance of the thing. Thus food given to a hungry animal increases the likelihood of behavior which immediately precedes it.

reinforcer, primary

n. Anything which increases the likelihood of a behavior which immediately precedes the appearance of the thing by satisfying a biological need of the organism. Thus food given to a hungry animal increases the likelihood of behavior which immediately precedes it.

reinforcing stimulus

n. Anything that can be used to increase or decrease the likelihood of the appearance of a behavior when appropriately associated with the behavior in time and space.

rejection sensitivity

n. Rejection sensitivity (RS) is *a cognitive-affective processing disposition to expect rejection anxiously,* shaped by cognitive-social learning history and triggered in situations when either acceptance or rejection is possible. RS develops to help individuals previously hurt by frequent or severe rejection prepare for future rejection threat, by promoting efforts to detect it and then prevent, avoid, or defend the self against it. Yet the resulting behaviors are often maladaptive, involving excessive self-silencing, ingratiation, social withdrawal, and hostile overreactions that precipitate actual rejection by others. Rooted in attachment and interpersonal psychodynamic theories, this conceptualization of RS was introduced by Geraldine Downey and her colleagues to explain why some individuals tend to perceive readily and react strongly to potential rejection cues at a cost to their well-being and relationships. Research has linked RS with maladaptive responses both to potential rejection in personal relationships and to potential rejection based on membership in devalued social groups.   – KRB, GD

relationship

n. **1.** An emotional bond between people in which each person's actions affect the other and particularly one which lasts over time. **2.** Any covariance of any two things such that changes in one are reflected to some degree in the other although not necessarily causally linked. Thus there is a relationship between birth order and political affiliation although the relationship is imperfect and not necessarily causal.

relationship therapy

n. **1.** Any of numerous techniques for healing psychological discomfort or disorder in which the interactions of the client and therapist are held to be the therapeutic tool. **2.** A therapeutic approach which attempts to improve the relationship between two or more people, all of whom usually participate in the therapy.

relative deprivation

n. The subjective perception that the amount of a desirable resource a person has is less than is expected or deserved. This perception of deprivation is usually based on one's mental reference group – that is, by asking the question "What are people like me getting?" which involves judgments about the self as well as perceptions of others relative to the self. Research has suggested that a sense of deprivation can result from perceptions about self relative to the perceived peer group and from perceptions that a person's in-group gets less than other groups.

relative risk

n. The frequency of a disease or disorder in a group with a risk factor relative to those without the risk factor. Thus the relative risk of getting lung cancer among those who smoke cigarettes compared to those who do not smoke cigarettes is greater than 4 to 1.

relaxation therapy

n. The use of progressive relaxation or similar techniques as a method of treating anxiety and other disorders.

relaxation training

n. Any program in which a person is taught to relax his/her entire body by focusing on and then relaxing one muscle group at a time. Usually the relaxation is preceded by intentionally tensing the muscle group before relaxing it as a way of both becoming aware of the muscle group and learning to exercise voluntary control over it.

releaser

n. A set of stimuli that can serve to initiate a fixed action pattern in animals of a particular species in the appropriate circumstances. Thus graylag geese chicks will act to keep close to their mother when she moves away from them unless distracted by another stimulus.

reliability

n. The degree to which a measure of a psychological characteristic gives similar results under different conditions. If a bathroom scale indicates that a person weighs 150 lb. on Tuesday and 250 lb. on Thursday, we are likely to conclude that it is broken; its results are unreliable. Similarly, if a personality scale suggests that one is an extrovert on one day and an introvert on the next, we may suspect that the test is not fully reliable. There are several different kinds of reliability that must be distinguished, including internal consistency, retest, and interrater reliability. Establishing reliability is one of the first tasks in creating a psychological measure, because acceptable reliability is generally necessary for psychological measurement. However, reliability is not sufficient, because a reliable measure can be consistently wrong, like a scale that repeatedly reports a weight of 150 lb. for a person who actually weighs 250 lb.   – RRM

reliability, alternate forms

n. The level of a test's measurement error determined by examining the consistency of the scores of two different tests constructed from the same content domain. Alternate forms reliability (also called parallel forms or equivalent forms reliability) is concerned with error caused by item sampling. Specifically, alternate forms reliability is designed to examine the error variance that can be attributed to the selection of a specific item or subset of items for inclusion in a measure. To calculate alternate forms reliability, two equivalent forms of a test are developed to measure the same construct or attribute (the specific items on the tests are different, but the tests are designed to be equivalent in target, difficulty, structure, etc.); the two different versions of the test are then administered to the same group of people on the same day (counterbalancing the order of administration). The scores of the two tests are then correlated to determine the reliability coefficient. Correlation coefficients closer to 0 represent low reliability while coefficients closer to 1 represent high reliability. While alternate forms reliability is a rigorous and valuable method of estimating a test's reliability, it is often shunned by test developers because of the constraints associated with developing an alternate version of the target test.   – BJM

reliability coefficient

n. A numeric index which reflects the stability of a test score or the relative proportion of true score and random error within a test score. The most important coefficient of reliability is a test-retest correlation coefficient, which estimates the temporal stability of a test. Kuder-Richardson 20, coefficient alpha, and split-half reliability coefficients are all measures of the internal consistency of a test, which is important when unidimensionality is an issue or when the dimension being measured is not expected to have temporal stability, as in a mood scale. The alternate form, reliability correlation coefficient, is rarely used as it is difficult to ensure that alternate forms are actually equivalent.

reliability, interrater

n. The level of a test's measurement error attributed to differences in the ratings, scores, or observations provided by different evaluators of the same event or phenomenon. When using people to evaluate or observe an event, there may be differences between true scores and recorded scores caused by human error and/or perception; as such, interrater reliability (also called interscorer or interobsersver

reliability) is used to examine the extent to which different observers give consistent estimates, evaluations, or ratings of the same phenomenon. While there are various ways of calculating interrater reliability (such as percentage of agreement between raters or use of z score estimates of agreement), the most appropriate method for calculating interrater reliability is application of the kappa statistic, which reports interrater reliability as a proportion of complete agreement, taking into consideration corrections for chance agreement. Interrater reliability based on the kappa statistic ranges from 1 (perfect agreement) to –1 (less agreement than predicted by chance); kappa scores above 0.40 are generally considered satisfactory.   – BJM

reliability, item

n. The relative stability of answers to a particular item in a scale.

reliability, parallel forms

n. The level of a test's measurement error determined by examining the consistency of the scores of two different tests constructed from the same content domain. Parallel forms reliability (also called alternate forms or equivalent forms reliability) is concerned with error caused by item sampling. Specifically, parallel forms reliability is designed to examine the error variance that can be attributed to the selection of a specific item or subset of items for inclusion in a measure. To calculate parallel forms reliability, two equivalent forms of a test are developed to measure the same construct or attribute (the specific items on the tests are different, but the tests are designed to be equivalent in target, difficulty, structure, etc.); the two different versions of the test are then administered to the same group of people on the same day (counterbalancing the order of administration). The scores of the two tests are then correlated to determine the reliability coefficient. Correlation coefficients closer to 0 represent low reliability while coefficients closer to 1 represent high reliability. While parallel forms reliability is a rigorous and valuable method of estimating a test's reliability, it is often shunned by test developers because of the constraints associated with developing an alternate version of the target test.   – BJM

reliability, sampling

n. The process of selecting groups to gather information in order to estimate the consistency of a measurement of some aspect of a population.

reliability, scale

n. A measure of the consistency with which a device measures a particular variable. The most important measure of scale reliability is a test-retest correlation coefficient, which estimates the temporal stability of a test. Kuder-Richardson 20, coefficient alpha, and split-half reliability coefficients are all measures of the internal consistency of a scale, which is important when unidimensionality is an issue or when the dimension being measured is not expected to have temporal stability, as in a mood scale. The alternate forms reliability measure is rarely used as it is difficult to ensure that alternate forms are actually equivalent.

reliability, split-half

n. The level of a test's measurement error determined by examining the consistency of the scores of two halves of a given test. Split-half reliability is concerned with internal consistency. To calculate split-half reliability, the test is divided in half (division can be done by randomly selecting half the questions, dividing by the first and last half of the items, or by using the odd-even system of item selection), and then each half is scored separately. Unlike other measures of reliability that simply correlate the resultant scores, a simple correlation of the two halves would provide an underestimation of the overall test reliability (as reliability increases with more items). As such, the Spearman-Brown formula is applied to correct for the half-length; the Spearman-Brown formula adjusts the correlation calculations to estimate what the reliability would be if each half of the test had been the length of the entire test.   – BJM

reliability, temporal

n. The degree to which a scale measures consistently across time. This is usually measured in psychological scales using test-retest correlations.

reliability, test-retest ▶ *See* TEST-RETEST RELIABILITY

religion ▶ *See* RELIGION, PSYCHOLOGY OF

religion, psychology of

n. Psychology of religion is the discipline that studies religion and religious phenomena using psychological theories, concepts, and methods. Psychologists of religion try to understand the many ways that people express their faith through behavior (practices), belief (in the supernatural), and experience (emotions). A complete understanding of the psychological nature of human beings is impossible without a consideration of religion. It is our preoccupation with matters of the spirit that makes us uniquely human. Understanding when, under what conditions, and why religion does and does not shape human consciousness and action is among the major tasks of psychologists who study religion. Psychologically, religion (a) is a specific quest for meaning; (b) contributes to the strengthening of self-control; (c) is motivated by the need for unity, integration, and harmony; (d) satisfies the needs for attachment and social support as well as identity formation and belonging; and (e) promotes and reinforces altruistic tendencies.   – RAE

religious fundamentalism

n. Any tightly held set of religious beliefs that refer to some limited set of writings or ideas as the only basis for understanding all religious meaning and which are not subject to rational or experiential disconfirmation.

REM

n. (rapid eye movement) A quick, unpredictable movement in which the two eyes are coordinated as if they were looking at something, which occurs with eyelids closed during a light stage of sleep and is associated with dreaming.

remembering

n. **1.** The act or process of bringing to consciousness previous experiences or information. **2.** The process of storing information or of using previously acquired information.

reminiscence
n. The calling to mind of previous experience, usually of long past times and usually with a sense of fondness.

REM rebound
n. The tendency for both the proportion and total amount of time spent in rapid eye movement sleep to increase after sleep deprivation.

REM sleep
n. A period of relatively light sleep characterized by quick, unpredictable movement of the eyes in which the two eyes are coordinated as if they were looking at something, which occurs with eyelids closed during a light stage of sleep and is associated with dreaming.

repeated-measures analysis of variance
n. A statistical method for determining whether differences between two or more measurements of the same subjects and one or more other variables are due to chance variation or some other factor. This is accomplished by calculating the ratios of within-subjects and within-groups variance to between-group differences on a dependent variable and comparing the results to what would be expected were the results due to chance variation within a single population. This is used to test hypotheses about differences among the treatments with the object of being able to attribute any such differences to effects of the independent variable(s) on the dependent variable.

repetition blindness
n. The tendency of subjects being presented with a series of very brief stimuli to be less likely to detect a second presentation of one stimulus than presentation of a new stimulus. Thus if a subject is presented with the words *red blue yellow black red white* he/she is less likely to report the second occurrence of *red* than he/she would had *pink* or *green* been used instead.

repetition compulsion
n. The tendency to repeat unfinished or traumatic events in order to deal with them. The repetition can take the form of daydreams, storytelling, perception that present relationships are the same as old ones or emotional relations with a therapist that mirror those of childhood. In psychoanalytic theory, this is believed to be an attempt to deal with emotional conflicts from childhood and often takes the form of projections in therapy.

repetition effect
n. Repetition effect is facilitated (easier) processing resulting from repeated experience with a single task. For example, when a text is read twice, reading time tends to decrease and comprehension increases during the second reading because memory for the first reading makes the text easier to read a second time. Likewise, repeated study of a list of words improves memory for those words. Repetition effects can be considered a form of transfer benefit in that processes performed during the encounter (e.g., first reading or study session) transfer to the identical second encounter (e.g., second reading or study session).
– GER, FD

replicate
v. **1.** To perform an experiment or other study again in order to assure that the results originally obtained are not due to chance or some other extraneous factor. **2.** To produce exact copies of DNA or other living tissue during biological growth or reproduction. **3.** To make a copy of something.

replication
n. The process of performing an experiment or other study again in order to assure that the results originally obtained are not due to chance or some other extraneous factor. **2.** The process of producing exact copies of DNA or other living tissue during biological growth or reproduction. **3.** The process of making a copy of anything.

representation
n. **1.** The use of any one thing to stand for another thing. **2.** In cognitive psychology, the

mental or encoded form of information which stands for some sensation, perception, object, or other idea external to itself. **3.** In psychoanalysis, the use of a symbol to substitute for an unconscious idea, impulse, or object.

representativeness heuristic

n. A model of human decision making in which it is assumed people judge the likelihood that some thing A is in a class B by the similarity of A to B, which is insensitive to prior probabilities and sample size and misconstrues chance events. This leads to viewing chance as a self-correcting process, as in the gambler's fallacy, and an assumption that perceived rare events are normal so that regression to the mean is ignored.

representative sample

n. A sample that is selected to have characteristics similar to those of the larger target population on variables of interest to the study or investigation. A representative sample is selected by dividing the population into nonoverlapping and collectively exhaustive subpopulations or strata (the number of strata depends on the target of the study and the relevant grouping characteristics). Sample members are then selected from each stratum or subgroup in proportion to the population. The members of each stratum are pooled to form the overall representative sample.

– BJM

representative sampling

n. Representative sampling is a method of selecting members for a sample so that the relevant characteristics of the sample are similar to those of the larger target population. The population is divided into nonoverlapping and collectively exhaustive subpopulations or strata (the number of strata depends on the target of the study and the relevant grouping characteristics). Sample members are then randomly selected from each stratum or subgroup in proportion to the population. The members of each stratum are pooled to form the overall sample. For example, if you were interested in studying political attitudes on a specific college campus, you would want to ensure that your study sampled a representative number of freshmen, sophomores, juniors, and seniors. So, you would divide your population (all students) into strata (class levels) and randomly select your sample using representative numbers from each subgroup. Representative sampling is necessary for making valid inferences and generalizing conclusions to the target population.

– BJM

repressed gene

n. Any sequence of DNA whose replication has been blocked by the binding of a protein to an operator gene which prevents it from assembling proteins to replicate the gene.

repressed memory

n. In psychoanalysis, any recollection which has been pushed into or kept in the unconscious by the ego in order to prevent the emotion associated with it from disrupting the ego's plans.

repression

n. **1.** The forcible subjugation, exclusion, or checking of the progress of something by something else. **2.** In psychoanalysis, the exclusion of any impulse, memory, or idea from consciousness in order to protect the ego's plans from disruption by the impulses associated with the repressed material.

repression-sensitization scale

n. Any scale which measures the tendencies to react to stimuli classified as threatening by pushing them into the unconscious versus approaching and confronting the threatening stimuli directly, often using intellectualization and vigilance as polar opposites, so that a high score on sensitization requires a low score on repression, and vice versa.

repressor gene

n. An operator gene which acts to bind a protein to another operator gene so as to prevent the transcription and replication of a third gene.

Rescorla-Wagner theory

n. A formal theory describing classical conditioning in terms of the discrepancy between expectation, which is the sum of all previous conditioning, and actual experience. This formula for change in associative strength on any one trial is $V_A/n = L_A$ Bus$/n$ (Gus$/n - V_{ALL}/n)$, where V is the associative strength, A is the conditioned stimulus, n is the trial number, L is the learning rate parameter for the unconditioned stimulus, G is the asymptote of learning supported by the unconditioned stimulus, and V_{ALL}/n is the net associative strength of all stimuli present in the trial.

research

n. Any attempt to investigate some aspect of the universe systematically, usually by employing the scientific method.

research hypothesis

n. In statistics, the hypothesis that there is a difference between the means of different groups in an analysis of variance, implying that there is a relationship between levels of the independent variable and the dependent variable which is accepted when the null hypothesis that there is no difference between the different groups not due to chance is rejected. This is used as an alternative to the null hypothesis so that when the null hypothesis can be statistically rejected, it is not unreasonable to believe that there has been an effect produced by the independent variable on the dependent variable. Also called the alternative hypothesis.

research methodology

n. Any plan for systematically investigating some aspect of the universe, which usually employs the scientific method. There are numerous different ways of approaching any topic of interest, and the key is in selecting the one most likely to provide a clear answer to the question of interest.

reserpine

n. A drug derived from the *Rauwolfia serpentina* plant of Southeast Asia, which has been used to treat hypertension and anxiety but can cause severe acute depression. It works by depleting noradrenaline, dopamine, and serotonin from synaptic vesicles in the brain.

residential mobility

Definitions

1. The actual frequency with which individuals have changed their residence. It is known that the frequency with which individuals change their residence during their adulthood is associated with openness to experiences and less conscientiousness. Individuals in some professions (e.g., bankers, consultants) are more likely to change their residence than individuals in others (e.g., farmers).

2. The actual frequency with which individuals in a given neighborhood or society have changed their residence during a certain period of time. On the average, about 50% of individuals who live in the United States change their residence over a 5-year period. Some cities (e.g., Denver, Phoenix) have much higher residential mobility than others (e.g., Pittsburgh, Philadelphia).

3. The freedom with which individuals can change their residence as they wish. The degree to which individuals can choose the location of their residence at their own will. For instance, the United States is a high-mobility society because citizens have freedom to live wherever they want to. In contrast, 17th-century Japan was low in residential mobility because Japanese in the lowest caste (*eta* and *hinin*) at that time did not have the right to choose their place of residence.

The distinction between the first two definitions and the last definition is important because some societies are considered high in terms of one definition but low in the other. For instance, Denmark is high in residential mobility in terms of the right to choose the place of residence. However, it is low in terms of actual residential mobility, because many Danes choose to live in the same place for an extended period.

Operationalizations. Residential mobility at the individual level is often assessed by the number of times individuals changed their residence or the city/town of their residence. In contrast, residential mobility at the collective level is often assessed using census data, which provides the information regarding the proportion of people who lived in the same house as in the previous census data collection, the proportion of people who lived in the same county as in the previous census data collection, or the proportion of people who lived in the same state as in the previous census data collection at the various levels (ranging from neighborhood block to state).

– SOI, FM

residual

1. *n.* In statistics, the difference between an observation and a prediction of the observation using a mathematical model. 2. *n.* In statistics, the proportion of variance in a dependent or quasi-dependent variable not accounted for by experimental variables and usually attributed to random error. 3. *adj.* Denoting symptoms remaining after an acute attack of a disease or disorder has mostly subsided, as in residual symptoms of schizophrenia. 4. *n.* In general, anything remaining after some portion has been removed or used up.

residual schizophrenia

n. A form of schizophrenia characterized by affective flattening, deficits in fluency of speech and thought, and lack of motivation but lacking the delusions, hallucinations, and grossly disorganized speech, thought, and behavior which are characteristic of many forms of schizophrenia.

resistance

n. 1. In general, the process of standing against, opposing, or withstanding something or someone else. 2. In psychoanalysis, unconscious blocking of the movement of material from the unconscious to consciousness, especially during psychotherapy. 3. The ability of a biological organism to withstand an attack on it, especially as in withstanding a disease or drugs.

resistance stage

n. The second stage of the general adaptation syndrome, which is characterized by active coping with a stressor and stabilization at an elevated physiological state, including high blood pressure, rapid pulse rate, elevated serum noradrenaline level, and narrowed attentional focus, during which physiological resources are used up more rapidly than usual and may become depleted if the state is prolonged.

resistance to extinction

n. The degree to which nonreinforced behavior persists.

respect

n. The acknowledgment or recognition of the worth of another person in relation to that person's or his or her group's worldview and beliefs.

respondent conditioning

n. The learning theories of Ivan Pavlov in which only observable events such as stimulus conditions and change in responses are used to define and explore learning. The basic process of respondent conditioning is that a new or conditioned response (CR) replaces or appears in addition to an unconditioned response (UCR) when a conditioned stimulus (CS) is paired with an unconditioned stimulus (UCS) that is usually followed by the unconditioned response. In the classic experiment it was observed that when a bell was rung shortly before dogs were fed, the dogs soon began to salivate upon hearing the bell whether food was subsequently presented or not. So the UCR of salivating to UCS, food, had a CR of salivation to the bell added after pairing of the CS, bell, with the UCS, food. Also called classical conditioning or Pavlovian conditioning.

response

n. Any behavior which reliably occurs immediately after a stimulus or as a reaction to a stimulus.

response bias

n. A tendency to respond to questions or scale items in a particular way regardless of the content of the item or according to some variable the test is not intended to measure such as social desirability. For instance, many people will check the middle of a scale or select the middle answer on a multiple-choice test in preference to more extreme answers. In signal detection, some responders show a tendency to say yes or no regardless of the presence of a signal.

response class

n. A category of behaviors that are sorted into the same group by an observer, usually according to a predetermined assortment scheme. Thus hitting, kicking, biting, and pushing others may all be identified as instances of a category called aggression.

response competition

n. **1.** In many learning theories, a situation in which a stimulus activates more than one response so that the response which is strongest is enacted while the others are not. **2.** In cognitive psychology, the interference of one tendency to respond with the accuracy or speed of another response. Thus in the Stroop test it takes longer to read a word for a color if it is printed in a color different from the word as the recognition of the color of the ink interferes with reading the word, which is not the name of the color perceived.

response differentiation

n. The process of learning to react differently to stimuli that differ only slightly through a program of selective reinforcement, usually done in a series of steps requiring increasing stimulus discrimination.

response generalization

n. **1.** In learning theory, the observation that reinforcing some behaviors makes the likelihood of similar but unreinforced behaviors more likely. **2.** In general, the tendency of organisms to respond to novel stimuli with previously learned behavior, usually in muted form so that novel stimuli produce a gradient of response whose magnitude is proportional to the similarity of the novel stimuli to the learned stimulus.

response hierarchy

n. The order of a set of learned responses according to how likely they are to occur in the presence of a given stimulus or in a given stimulus situation.

response latency

n. The time delay between a stimulus and a response, which can be used as a measure

of the cognitive processing involved or the strength of the response conditioning.

response magnitude

n. The size, intensity, or duration of a response, which is often used as an indication of the strength of the conditioning of the response.

response probability

n. The relative frequency with which a given response occurs in a particular situation.

response rate

n. The frequency with which a particular response occurs within a given period.

response set

n. **1.** In psychometrics, a tendency to respond to the social desirability or demand characteristics of items rather than to their content or meaning. **2.** A tendency of an organism to respond in a particular way to a stimulus or series of stimuli, usually after having given a similar response and remaining mentally focused on the response.

response strength

n. A theoretical quantity which reflects the power of a bond between a stimulus and a response and determines response magnitude, duration, and probability in a given set of circumstances.

response style

n. In psychometrics, a tendency to select certain answers in a multiple-choice test or questionnaire regardless of the content of the items. Thus some persons' responses occur only in the middle three categories in a five- or seven-choice set while other persons' responses occur mostly in the extreme ranges of categories. Other persons seem to acquiesce and go along with what they perceive as the test makers' intent, and others pick what appear to be the most socially desirable responses.

response time

n. The time delay between a stimulus and a response, which can be used as a measure of the cognitive processing involved or the strength of the response conditioning.

responsibility attribution
n. Responsibility attribution takes place when the perceiver holds an actor or a collection of individuals responsible for a negative outcome. Responsibility and blame are assigned spontaneously when an actor adopts a counternormative conduct. Responsibility attribution is closely connected to causal attribution; individuals who cause a negative outcome are likely to be held responsible for it. The perceiver will also consider the actor's state of mind when determining responsibility; thus, more responsibility will be assigned to an actor who intended a negative outcome than to an actor who caused a negative outcome but did not intend it. Responsibility attribution may be motivated. For example, individuals who want to see the world as a just world may blame innocent victims for their mishaps. Some collectivist societies (e.g., Japan) practice collective responsibility attribution: perceivers may hold the group and/or the group leader responsible for a group member's misconduct.   – MMC, CYC

responsibility, diffusion of
n. A state in which an individual perceives her/his own moral obligation or duty as less than usual because it is shared by a group of people. This is the hypothesized cause of the bystander effect, in which bystanders' likelihood of acting to help after witnessing an accident, crime, or other incident depends on the number of other people who are also witnesses or are believed to be witnesses to the same incident.

resting potential
n. The size of the difference in electrical potential between the negatively charged inside and positively charged outside of a neuron or other excitable cell's membrane, which varies but is generally around 70 millivolts.

Restorff effect
n. The observation that memory for a distinctive item in a series of items will generally be better than for nondistinctive items in the same list. Also called the von Restorff effect.

retardation, mental
n. Significantly slowed or delayed intellectual development, which results in limitations in adaptive functioning, usually defined as having an IQ more than two standard deviations below average. Mild retardation is the IQ range about 50–55 to 70, depending on the IQ test used. Moderate retardation is the IQ range 35–40 to 50–55. Severe mental retardation is the IQ range 20–25 to 35–40. Profound mental retardation is the IQ range below 20 or 25. Also called developmental delay.

retardation, psychomotor
n. A slowing or inhibition of motor responses characterized by reduction in overall motor activity, slow speech with long pauses before speaking which are culturally inappropriate, and slow bodily movements which appear to reflect slowed mental processes. This is characteristic of some forms of major depression and some forms of schizophrenia.

reticular activating system
n. The portion of the small thick bundle of ascending and descending nerve fibers in the brainstem which connects the peripheral nervous system to the thalamus and other portions of the brain and which is thought to be important to the sleep-wake cycle, alertness, and general arousal level.

reticular formation
n. A small but thick band of neurons and neural fibers in the brainstem which extends from the medulla oblongata to the midbrain; has a wide net of connections, including the cortex, thalamus, cerebellum, and spinal cord; and is thought to be important to the sleep-wake cycle, alertness, and general arousal level, as well as posture and voluntary muscle activity.

retina
n. Several layers of cells which line the inside back of the eye, including the rod and cone cells, which are photoreceptors, and the horizontal, bipolar, amacrine, and ganglion cells, which partially process visual information

and send it out of the retina via the optic nerve.

retinal disparity

n. The difference in perception caused by the distance between the two eyes, which is used as a clue in depth perception. The two slightly different images of the two retinas are fused in the brain so we usually see only one image.

retinal image

n. The inverted image formed on the back of the retina by light reflected from the visual scene upon which the eye is focused, whose clarity depends on the momentary size of the pupillary opening, being sharper when the opening is smaller.

retributive justice

n. Retributive justice is a theory of criminal justice in which the criminal has created an imbalance in society that must be balanced by a proportional action against the criminal. This point of view has often been associated with harsh punishments such as cutting off the hand of the criminal and among Christian cultures with the biblical phrase "an eye for an eye and a tooth for a tooth." In some cultures and for some crimes the primary imbalance is economic, in others it is harm to persons, and in others it is harm to a theoretical entity such as family honor.

retrieval

n. The process of finding and taking back something. In memory storage, it is the process of finding and taking back information so it can be used in other processes, such as having memories or riding a bicycle in humans or computations in information systems.

retrieval cue

n. Environmental information that facilitates the retrieval of particular stored information. Thus seeing the word *mother* may facilitate memories mentally connected with one's own mother.

retroactive association

n. A memory link formed by presenting a neutral stimulus after an unconditioned stimulus.

This seldom results in formation of an association as the order of presentation prevents the neutral stimulus from having any signal value for the organism. Also called backward association.

retroactive facilitation

n. Increased performance on a task after learning a different but related task at a later time.

retroactive inhibition

n. Decreased performance on a task after learning a different but related task or other material at a later time.

retroactive interference

n. Inhibition of the recollection or use of previously learned material after learning new material.

retrograde amnesia

n. Defect in retrieving old memories. The individual who has retrograde amnesia becomes unable to recall the events that occurred and the knowledge that existed before the onset of the amnesia. It is generally associated with anterograde amnesia. Retrograde amnesia can impair both semantic memory (memories mediated through a semantic system, such as verbal memory) and episodic memory (memory for events), but procedural memory (skills and habits) is usually relatively better preserved. Retrograde amnesia is associated with damage of different structures of the so-called brain memory system, such as the hippocampus, but specific forms of retrograde amnesia (for example, retrograde amnesia for words or faces) can be found in cases of cortical damage. Diverse pathological conditions are associated with retrograde amnesia, such as traumatic head injury and brain infections. Retrograde amnesia usually follows a temporal gradient: remote memories are more easily accessible than events occurring just prior to the pathological condition.   – AA

▶ *See also* **AMNESIA**

retrospective study

n. A systematic examination of historical events seeking to explain the present situation in terms of the past. Most of the discipline of history is of this type, as are most case histories. Such research is not repeatable as are prospective studies and so is less relied upon than experimental studies in most scientific fields.

return of the repressed
n. In psychoanalysis, the idea that there is conservation of energy in the id such that no impulse that is pushed into the unconscious disappears and its energy seeks and eventually finds expression although often in a redirected form.

reuptake
n. The process of removing and storing molecules of neurotransmitters from the synaptic cleft, which is accomplished by transporter proteins in the presynaptic membrane. The molecules of neurotransmitters are then stored in vesicles in the axon terminal until they are released again during another nerve impulse.

reversal learning
n. A process of relearning in a discrimination learning task when the contingencies of reinforcement are changed so that a behavior which previously was less likely becomes the most likely one and the behavior that was previously the most likely becomes less likely than the new dominant behavior.

reversible figure
n. An ambiguous figure which most people can perceive as either of two objects and which tends to appear to change from one object to the other over time.

reward
1. v. To provide something of value to a person or animal that has behaved in a desirable way. 2. n. In learning theory, anything that increases the likelihood of the behavior which immediately precedes it.

rhodopsin
n. A photoreactive chemical found in retinal rods which changes shape when struck by a photon of appropriate energy and then causes the rod to hyperpolarize, sending an electrical impulse to the nerve and other cells to which it is connected. Chemically it is 11-*cis* retinal, which changes to all-*trans* retinal when struck by light. Rhodopsin bleaches out quickly at high ambient brightness levels and is responsible for night vision. Also called visual purple.

rhombencephalon
n. The third and rearmost of the bulges in the human embryonic brain, which develops into the cerebellum and brainstem. Also called the hindbrain.

rhythm
n. The rhythm of an utterance is the way its constituent parts are timed with respect to each other. Along with *intonation*, rhythm is a prosodic property of utterances. The most basic rhythmic units are moras (vowels or consonants in the rhyme of a syllable) and syllables (sequences of consonants and vowels obligatorily containing a nucleus, usually a vowel, flanked by an optional onset and/ or coda, usually consonants or consonant clusters). Syllables combine to create feet, in which one syllable receives more prosodic prominence than the rest. Bisyllabic feet are iambic (e.g., *portray*) or trochaic (e.g., *portrait*), depending on which syllable is more prominent. Languages can be classified into those whose lexical stock is predominantly iambic (e.g., French) or trochaic (e.g., English). Languages have been classified as mora-timed (e.g., Japanese), syllable-timed (e.g., Spanish), or stress-timed (e.g., English), though these categories are not yet well understood or empirically supported. Higher-order rhythmic units include pitch accents, signaled by increased pitch movement and duration, and intonational phrases, marked by intonational contours as well as by phrase-final lengthening and optional pausing. Certain structural ambiguities, like *We gave her dog biscuits*, can be disambiguated rhythmically, by pitch accenting different words and grouping them into different intonational phrases.   – EMF

ribonucleic acid
n. (RNA) A complex acidic chain of proteins in the nucleus of living cells that is necessary

for the synthesis of proteins, which is the primary way in which living things grow as well as being necessary for cell division and all forms of reproduction.

ribosomes

n. Tiny particles inside all living cells containing proteins and RNA which are the sites for protein synthesis and copying DNA in reproduction when stimulated by messenger RNA. They are found free floating in cytoplasm as well as attached to the endoplasmic reticulum.

rigidity

n. **1.** Resistance to change as in difficulty bending at the joint. **2.** A character trait which leads the individual to resist change in ways of thinking and acting which is associated with intolerance of ambiguity and many kinds of racial and ethnic prejudice.

ringi

n. The Japanese process of decision making, which involves circulating a proposal among all people who will be affected by it, addressing concerns and negative consequences raised by as many parties as possible, consulting on as broad a basis as possible about the proposal, and achieving consensus before the proposal is formally implemented.

risk

n. **1.** The likelihood that a negative event will occur, as in the risk of getting lung cancer if one smokes. **2.** An uncertain negative event as that one risks lung cancer if one smokes.

risk aversion

n. The tendency to avoid choices that entail a probability of aversive consequences regardless of the smallness of the probability or the probability of high reward.

risky shift

n. The observation that an individual is usually more willing to act in a manner that entails a chance of negative consequences in the company of others than he/she would while alone. This has been explained in numerous ways, including group polarization, social

comparisons, persuasive argument, and cultural valuing of risk takers.

Ritalin

n. Methylphenidate hydrochloride is a central nervous system stimulant, which works by stimulating release of norepinephrine and dopamine and blocking their reuptake in the synaptic cleft. It is often prescribed to treat attention deficit–hyperactivity disorder and is sometimes used as an adjunct to antidepressants in treating depression and in increasing attention in persons with brain damage, cancer, and dementia. Also called methylphenidate.

ritual behavior

n. **1.** Repeated actions that are intended to ward off or undo past actions or situations, which are common among persons with obsessive-compulsive disorder and schizophrenics. **2.** Culturally prescribed conduct, as in religious rituals or a bride's walking down the aisle with her father in U.S. weddings. **3.** Any established procedure and routine such as having a cup of coffee in the morning. **4.** Instinctive animal behavior, as in species-wide premating gestures or dances among many species of animals.

rivalry

n. A form of relationship in which two or more individuals act as if the others are antagonists in a competition.

RNA

n. Ribonucleic acid, a complex acidic chain of proteins in the nucleus of living cells that is necessary for the synthesis of proteins, which is the primary way in which living things grow as well as being necessary for cell division and all forms of reproduction.

Robbers' Cave study

n. A study carried out by Muzafer Sherif in which groups of 11-year-old boys were first put in groups and allowed to develop group cohesion and ritual, then placed in competition, and finally presented with an urgent problem which required both groups to solve in Robber's Cave State Park in Oklahoma.

The main findings of the study were that group situation tended to determine individual feelings and actions toward others, which were positive toward in-group members and negative toward out-group members in the competitive situation and then positive toward everybody in the group cooperation situation.

rod

n. An elongated kind of light receptor cell in the back of the retina which is concentrated in the periphery of the visual field and responds to low light levels and so is most important in night vision. Rods contain a chemical called rhodopsin, which changes shape when struck by a photon of appropriate energy, thus triggering an electrical impulse, which is carried from the rod cell to neurons and other nearby rods.

rod-and-frame test

n. An experimental apparatus used to measure people's accuracy in judging spatial orientation without visual clues, which has been called field independence. It consists of a long box with a hood which blocks visual perception outside the box at one end and a rod inside a square frame at the far end of the box, both of which can be rotated independently. The subject is presented with a series of preset alignments of the rod and frame and required to adjust the rod to a vertical position. The test measures accuracy in adjustment.

rod vision

n. Visual perception without the participation of cone cells in the retina, which is typically the case for humans under very dim lighting conditions such as at night without artificial illumination. In humans, rods are not present in the fovea, which corresponds to the center of the visual field, and so rod vision is more sensitive in the periphery, so that humans see better outside the center of their visual field in dim lighting conditions.

Rogerian

adj. Of or relating to Carl Rogers, his ideas, or the client-centered therapy he developed,

which has phenomenological and humanistic roots.

Rolandic fissure ▶ *See* CENTRAL FISSURE

role conflict

n. A state of being in which an organism experiences conflict between contrary behavioral patterns. Usually in humans this results from having more than one behavioral script and being uncertain which one to enact in a given situation. The existence or perception of contradictory expectations from others regarding how one should fulfill a social role.

Role overload. The existence or experience of such excessive demands and expectations of role incumbents that it is not feasible to meet them. This is the most debilitating problem people report in fulfilling roles.

Role ambiguity. The existence or experience of a lack of clarity regarding the definition of what others expect a role incumbent to do in order to fulfill a role.

Role Construct Repertory Test

n. A measure of the content of an individual's repertory of role *constructs*, which are the unique system of interconnected meanings that define a person's perceived relationships with other people. It requires the subject to compare and contrast successive sets of three significant people (e.g., my mother, my father, and myself) and decide on an important way in which two of the figures are alike, and different from the third. As an example, if prompted with the trio, a person might say, "I think my mother and I are feeling people, whereas my dad is more analytical." The dimension of feeling versus analyzing would then be considered one of the constructs that the person uses to understand and approach other people and to define her/his role in life. Presenting the test taker with many varying triads such as a best friend, a teacher, a romantic partner, an enemy, other family members, and one's ideal self, the test usually elicits the wide spectrum of personal constructs that constitute the subject's basic perspective on life and perceived role alternatives. Also called the Repertory Grid Test and the Reptest.

role model

n. An esteemed person, group, or imagined or fictional character that a person attempts to imitate in coping with life.

role playing

n. **1.** Acting out the behavior characteristic of emotionally significant people in one's life in an attempt to understand the people involved and the pattern of interactions perceived as typical of them better. **2.** Acting in accord with one's belief about one's self and one's social roles in life.

role reversal

n. **1.** A technique used to help individuals understand social interactions better, in which each person in a relationship acts as he/she believes the other typically does. **2.** A change in one's situation vis à vis another person in which social roles are reversed, as in an English teacher's taking an art class from a former student.

role transition

n. A change in the social role appropriate to an individual as a worker experiences when he/she retires or a student experiences when he/she graduates.

rolfing

n. An often painful process of physical manipulation developed by Ida Rolf in which a person's habitual patterns of muscular tension and posture are broken loose and the body realigned with gravity. Also known as structural integration.

romantic attachment

n. **1.** A relationship involving emotional connection which has a sexual and a passionate aspect. **2.** The emotional connection to a sexual partner or potential sexual partner.

romantic love

n. Romantic love is a historical construction, originally associated with knighthood and chivalry. This concept was recently developed and is considered to be a Western construction. Traditional stories of love portrayed it as a tragic and despairing emotion that drove lovers to accomplish daring deeds for their beloved; in theory, true love is the unattainable love that cannot be consummated. Through the centuries, the idea of romantic love developed, and the ideals of romantic love were modified. As arranged marriages declined, romantic love became the basis for choosing a partner. In the media today, romantic love is often portrayed as a feeling that allows partners to transcend past barriers imposed by differences in social class, race, religion, and sometimes even values.

— EWMA, CYC

rooting reflex

n. An unlearned, automatic relatively fixed response in newborn infants in which they turn their head back and forth and open and close their mouth when stroked on the cheek, which facilitates finding the nipple during breast feeding.

root mean square

n. The result of a process in which the mean of a set of numbers is subtracted from each number and the result squared, then the mean of the squares is calculated and the square root of that mean is taken. A standard deviation is an example of a root mean square.

Rorschach test

n. A personality test in which the subject is presented with inkblots and asked, "What might this be?" It was developed by Hermann Rorschach and includes 10 inkblots, some in black, white, and gray, and some in color. Responses are scored for form, color, movement, detail, thematic content and whether the whole figure is included, whether it is a popular response, and whether humans are present. It has been found to be lacking in reliability and so its use is declining. Another inkblot test, constructed by Wayne Holtzman, uses 30 inkblots and can be reliably scored, but its use has never grown widespread despite its psychometric advantage over the Rorschach test.

Rosenthal effect

n. The Rosenthal effect, named after the psychologist Robert Rosenthal and sometimes referred to as the Pygmalion effect, is the powerful influence of expectancies on human behavior. Rosenthal's research was originally conducted in educational settings in the 1960s, and the findings suggested powerful effects of teacher expectancies on student progress. The researchers randomly selected some students and (falsely) informed teachers that those students, who had ostensibly performed in the top 20% on a measure of intelligence, were "bloomers," who were likely to progress at an advanced rate. When researchers gathered intelligence data at a later point in time, those who had been identified as "bloomers" showed more improvements than those who had not.

Social psychologists have extensively studied the effects that expectations can have on the behavior of others in our social environments, an area of research known as self-fulfilling prophecy. Data from a variety of areas point to the powerful influence of expectancies, effects which are manifest in sometimes subtle verbal and nonverbal behavior toward others. Research has also shown that expectancies can influence others without our knowledge and that efforts to minimize or eliminate expectancy effects are met with limited success. In other words, even if we are aware that our expectancies have the potential to influence others, our efforts to prevent these effects are met with limited success. The double-blind procedure, in which both experimenters and participants are unaware of the researchers' objectives, is an effective and common way for researchers to avoid expectancy effects in their research.   — MWP

▶ *See also* **DEMAND CHARACTERISTICS**

Rosenzweig Picture-Frustration Study

n. A test of characteristic modes of responding to frustration. It consists of 24 cartoon drawings in which one person is saying something which is likely to be experienced as frustrating by the other person in the cartoon. The frustrated person in each cartoon has a blank voice bubble, whose content the test taker is supposed to supply. The test is then scored for direction of aggression (inward, outward, or repressed), type of aggression, obstacle dominance, ego defense, need persistence, and the degree to which the subject's score conforms to typical responses.

rostral

adj. Of, relating to, or situated toward the beak or anterior part of an organism or an organ.

rotary-pursuit procedure

n. A task for measuring hand-eye coordination in which a subject is required to follow the movement of a light or spot which revolves on a turntable with a stylus. Time on target or the number of hits is the usual measurement in the procedure. Also called a pursuit rotor task.

rotation

n. **1.** The turning of an object about one of its axes. **2.** In statistics, the movement of a mathematical function around the graphic origin, as in factor analytic procedures which rotate factors so as to maximize and minimize aspects of the relationships of the functions.

rotation, mental

n. The turning of a mental image on one of its axes. An experimental task in which subjects are asked to make judgments about visual images which require rotation from their presented position in order to make accurate judgments. There is an inference that the mind creates a visual image and rotates it to arrive at a correct answer based on the observation that the time required to respond correctly is proportional to the angle through which the object has to be rotated in order to make the correct judgment.

rote learning

n. Memorization through repetition and reproduction without regard to the meaning of the material or forming of mental connections from the material to other knowledge.

rote memory

n. Learning to repeat information without errors and without regard to its content, as in learning random numbers.

round window

n. A round membrane-covered opening in the cochlea at the border with the middle ear, which transmits pressure from the oval window to the basilar membrane, thereby creating pressure waves which stimulate hair cells, which transduce the pressure waves into patterns of neural impulses.

R squared

n. A numerical index of the proportion of total variance of a variable predicted or shared by two or more other variables. *R* squared varies from 0 to 1 with 0 indicating no shared variance and 1 indicating 100% of the variance of the target variable is shared or predicted by the other variables.

Rubin's figure

n. An ambiguous figure that is easily perceived as a goblet or as the profiles of two identical faces facing each other.

rubrospinal tract

n. A nerve tract that carries messages from the red nucleus in the brain to the spinal cord through which flexor muscles are stimulated to action and neurons to extensor muscles are inhibited.

Ruffini corpuscle

n. One kind of sensory nerve ending in hairy human skin and near the fingernails, which is believed to be partially responsible for perceptions of hand and finger position, motion perception, and skin stretching.

rule learning

n. The process of inferring regularities in experience, which can be applied as local laws of occurrence. This has been important in learning studies in which experimenters make up rules, create stimuli that follow those rules, and then see whether subjects learn them and how long it takes.

rumination

n. **1.** Pondering or contemplating ideas or memories for a longer period than is normal. Excessive rumination is characteristic of obsessive-compulsive disorder. **2.** The regurgitation, rechewing, and swallowing of food by grazing animals such as cows. **3.** The regurgitation, rechewing, and swallowing of or expectorating of food by humans, which is common among infants and profoundly retarded individuals and occurs occasionally in normal adults.

rumor

Definition. *n.* Rumor is unverified information in circulation among people attempting to make sense of an unclear situation or to manage threat or potential threat. Rumor is like news – in that it is often "new" (i.e., of current interest) and pertains to topics of importance or interest to people – but unlike news, in that it is never verified. A rumor's unstable foundation may or may not be salient to rumor discussants: that is, a rumor may be passed around as though it is a fact. Nonetheless, dubious or absent evidence is rumor's key distinguishing feature.

Functions and contexts. Rumors are typically discussed by people trying to make sense of an ambiguous situation or to manage a physical or psychological threat. An example of a sense making rumor in a school district setting: "I heard that the real reason the school superintendent was forced to step down was certain 'off-color' remarks she made to employees." Faced with a murky state of affairs in which the meaning of current events is not clear or the likelihood of future events is uncertain, people fill the information void with speculation, discussion, and evaluation. Such collective sense making attempts employ rumors as working hypotheses. Rumors also help people to manage physical threat, sometimes by warning them of how to avoid a potential future negative event, for example, "Get out of town now! A tsunami is headed this way!" More often rumors simply afford a psychological sense of control over the threat by helping people understand and interpret negative events, for example, "I heard that the department is being downsized despite strong profits this quarter because the new CEO wants short-term stock gains (so he can sell his own shares for a windfall before moving on) and doesn't care about long-term effects on the company." Rumors may also help manage threats to one's psychological sense of self, often by derogating groups with whom one is not associated; one way of building oneself up is to "put others down." An example of one such (false) rumor: "The Israeli government is behind the events of September 11, 2001: 4,000 Jews were told by the Israeli Secret Service not to show up for work at the World Trade Center that day." Rumors may, of course, perform more than one of these functions, as when we discuss rumors to make sense of a threatening situation in a way that derogates another social group. Thus, rumor is what people collectively do when they find themselves in an unclear or potentially threatening set of circumstances.

Comparison with gossip. Rumor is often confused with gossip, but there are important differences. Whereas rumor is unverified information circulated to make sense and manage threat, gossip is evaluative social chat about individuals that may or may not be verified. Gossip is idle chit-chat about an individual – typically not present – whose content is often slanderous and personal. Though an important social phenomenon, gossip talk is perceived as less serious, significant, and purposeful than rumor talk. It is part of a relaxed session of "shooting the breeze." A classic example: "Did you hear? Bill and Jennifer are an 'item'!" It matters not whether the statement is firsthand observation or remote speculation; it qualifies as gossip in either case. Thus, gossip may or may not be verified, but rumor is never verified. Gossiping to another person tends to strengthen the social bonds between the gossiper and the listener – the listener feels like a privileged "insider" – and at the same time weakens the social standing of the gossip target. Gossip therefore can be a type of aggression that often attacks another person's relationships and excludes the target from the group. Gossip also serves to convey and reinforce social norms of the group by way of comparison. The statement "Did you hear what Sally did at the Christmas party?" may laud or shame Sally's behavior – depending on the speaker's tone of voice. Though gossip is often negative, it performs a positive function in that it allows us to gain information about a larger group of people – albeit in a secondhand fashion – that would not be available if we were limited to firsthand interactions. "Johnny steals from people" is useful

social information if we are deciding whom to invite to a party. Finally, gossip is often entertaining – a mutual mood enhancer that again strengthens bonds of participants.

Comparison with urban legend. Urban (also called modern or contemporary) legends also differ from rumors in their characteristic content, function, and context. Whereas rumors are unverified claims circulated in a collective sense making effort, urban legends are entertaining stories containing themes related to the modern world that are often funny or horrible and usually teach a moral lesson. The urban legend first of all tells a story – it is a narrative with a background, plot, climax, and conclusion; a rumor is typically not so complex and is often a "one-liner." Urban legends are often entertaining and tell a morality tale; rumors are not set forth primarily to entertain or propagate norms. For example, when a teenage couple was unable to start their car after necking on a secluded country road, the boyfriend went for help, only to be found dead the next morning hanging upside down above the car, his fingernails scraping against the hood in a macabre fashion. Moral of the story: Don't park! Urban legends are stories about modern themes, such as automobiles, Coca-Cola®, and computers. In addition, an urban legend is characteristically *migratory*: that is, its details vary from time to time and from place to place. However, urban legends may instantiate as specific rumors. For example, stories about the thief who hid underneath a parked car at a shopping mall and – upon the return of the shopper – slashed her exposed ankles with a razor and stole her bags and car constitute a well-known urban legend. However, "I heard that a woman was slashed on the ankles by a robber at Jonestown Mall last Saturday night" would constitute a rumor.

Of course, these forms of informal human discourse sometimes do not fall neatly into one or the other category. Rumors sometimes possess a narrative structure and entertain. Passing a rumor may also endear the speaker to the listener, convey moral norms, and contain slander about an absent third party. Nebulous and intermediate forms do exist. On the whole, however, rumors, gossip, and urban legends tend to possess the divergent qualities discussed: rumors are unverified claims circulating during group sense making and threat management, gossip is evaluative social chat, and urban legends are entertaining narratives.

Types of rumors. Rumors have been categorized according to a number of different typologies. They have been grouped by *subject matter,* for example, racial, disaster, organizational, political, and product rumors. They have been classified according to the *rumor public* – the group through which the rumor circulates. For example, *internal* organizational rumors circulate among employees, vendors, and stockholders associated with an organization; *external* rumors circulate among the general public outside an organization. They have been classified by *object of collective concern* of the rumor public. For example, *pecking order* rumors are about changes in management structure and how they might affect job duties and compensation. *Stock market* rumors circulate among shareholders who want to profit from changing stock values. *Organizational change* rumors often concern whether or not the change will be effective and how it will affect working conditions. Perhaps the most common rumor typology is by motivational tension: *Dread* or *fear* rumors are about potential negative events (e.g., "I heard that 25 staff will be laid off"), whereas *wish* rumors are about desired positive events (e.g., "We are getting a Christmas bonus this year!"). *Wedge-driving* rumors derogate other groups (e.g., during World War II: "The Catholics are evading the draft" enjoyed audience among non-Catholics).

Effects of rumor. Rumors cause or materially contribute to a variety of outcomes. Rumors can have attitudinal effects such as sullying a company's reputation (e.g., "Corporation *x* contributes to the Church of Satan") or fostering hatred toward another group (e.g., "Ethnic Group *y* greeted the World Trade Center bombing with celebration"). Rumors also result in behavioral outcomes such as reducing sales (e.g., "Soft Drink Company *z* is owned by the Ku Klux Klan and puts a substance in their soda that makes Black men sterile"), fomenting a riot (e.g., rumors that

police caused the death by impalement of a native Australian by chasing him on his bicycle led to extensive rioting in Sydney), or fostering noninvolvement in disaster relief (e.g., rumors that water flooding New Orleans – after hurricane Katrina – was toxic prevented many workers from participating in rescue operations). Negative rumors in particular affect a variety of organizational attitudes and behaviors, including job satisfaction, organizational commitment, morale, trust in management, productivity, and intention to leave. For example, in a division of one large company, hearing negative rumors about management month after month led to significant increase in negative work attitudes and intentions. Rumors during organizational change are also associated with greater employee stress. Rumors also affect stock market trading behaviors. Experimental investigations have suggested that rumors draw investors away from profitable *buy-low-sell-high* trading strategies. And field studies confirm that the stock market is strongly responsive to rumors. Surprisingly, rumors can have these effects even though they are not believed. For example, disaster rumors circulating in 1934 after a catastrophic earthquake in India were not believed but were acted upon nevertheless.

Factors in rumor transmission. Several variables have been associated with rumor transmission. *Uncertainty* about a situation – being filled with questions about what current events mean or what future events will occur – leads to speculation and rumor as people try to understand their environment and predict what will happen in the future. *Anxiety* – an emotional state of dread concerning a potential negative event – promotes rumor discussion as people talk with one another in an attempt to thwart the dreaded negative event or to feel better about it by regaining a *psychological sense of control.* In addition, people tend to discuss *important* rumors – rumors that pertain to an outcome that is personally relevant to them. People also pass along rumors they *believe* more than those they disbelieve. Poorly managed manufacturing plant layoff situations in which employees are given minimal information provide an example of all these factors in action. Employees in such situations are naturally filled with uncertainty; the prospect of losing one's job is anxiety-provoking; the topic is an important one; employees often have no control over such decisions; and if trust is low, negative rumors about management are quite believable. Rumors in such situations are rife. Rumor transmission may also be viewed through a motivational lens. People often spread and discuss rumors in order to *find facts*, that is, to ascertain a true state of affairs in order to deal effectively with real or perceived threats and to make sense of ambiguity. Telling rumors is fundamentally a social act, however, and people may also spread them to *enhance their relationships*. "I heard that your university is excellent," for example, will tend to improve the teller-listener relationship. Finally, rumors may be told to *boost one's self-esteem*. Self-enhancing rumors typically do this by putting other groups down in order to build up one's own group in contrast – and by association, oneself.

Factors affecting rumor belief. At least four factors have been associated with belief in rumor. Not surprisingly, rumors in *agreement with one's currently held attitudes* are more likely to be believed than those that disagree. An example: rumors of government waste and special privilege during the rationing programs necessitated by World War II were more likely to be believed by those opposed to the Roosevelt administration than those in favor of it. Rumors that proceed from a *credible source* are more likely to be believed than those spread by a noncredible one. In a series of laboratory experiments, rumors about a murder were more likely to be believed when they were heard from someone close to the detective investigating the case than from an elderly busybody with no apparent connection to the case. *Repeated* hearing of a rumor is also associated with belief. After initial skepticism, a Wall Street stockbroker began to place greater credence in a false rumor that the Clinton White House was covering up the true nature of top aide Vince Foster's death; this occurred solely because he had heard it several times. Finally, *hearing a rumor denial* reduces belief in the rumor. In one experiment, denying rumors that admittance to a sought-after academic psychology program

would be tightened reduced belief in that rumor.

Rumor accuracy. Sometimes collectives are very good at ferreting out the facts – and sometimes they are very bad at it. For example, rumors circulating in established organizational grapevines tend to be accurate, but rumors following natural disasters tend to be fallacious. Several types of mechanisms have been identified in rumor accuracy. Cognitive mechanisms, such as the narrowing of attention, memory limits, and perceptual biases, tend to reduce accuracy during transmission. Student who *serially transmitted* rumors – passed them along a chain – tended to pass along parts of a rumor that were more consistent than inconsistent with stereotypes because stereotype-consistent information is easier to process. Motivational mechanisms, including fact finding, relationship enhancement, and self-enhancement motives, also play a part. Rumors spread by people intent on fact finding tend to become more accurate than those motivated by either relationship enhancement or self-enhancement. Situational features such as the ability to check on the veracity of the rumor tend to increase rumor accuracy. Soldiers in one World War II field study could ask superior officers whether rumors they heard were false; rumors circulating among this group were highly accurate. Group mechanisms, such as conformity, culture, and epistemic norms, also affect accuracy. In one observational study of rumors among prison inmates, rumors about who was "snitching" circulated until a consensus was reached, then conformity to that rumor was demanded. Rumors also tend to agree with the cultural axioms and ideas of the rumor public. Finally, social network mechanisms affect transmission and include interaction among participants and transmission patterns. Rumors transmitted serially with interaction between each teller-listener pair in one laboratory study were more accurate than those in which discussion was not permitted.

Managing rumor. Not all rumors are harmful, but those that are remain an object of interest to those interested in preventing or ameliorating such harm. Rumors can be successfully prevented and managed by reducing uncertainty and anxiety, reducing belief in rumor, or reducing dissemination. A sample of experienced public relations officers recommended rumor prevention strategies that *reduce uncertainty* and *enhance formal communications*. Strategies rated most highly in effectiveness include stating the values and procedures that will guide organizational change, explaining how decisions will be made, and – if true – confirming the rumor. Increasing trust was also rated highly; in independent research, *distrust* of management was strongly related to negative rumor transmission in a department facing radical downsizing. Rumor rebuttal – denying the truth of the rumor – is overall an effective rumor management strategy (given that the rumor is indeed false). It is also a more effective strategy than one commonly advocated by some business commentators: *no comment*. Presenting a no comment statement to experimental participants who had heard negative rumors about a food manufacturer raised their level of uncertainty and suspicion as much as simply hearing the rumor alone. Some variables moderate the effectiveness of rebuttals: rebuttals proceeding from a source perceived to be appropriate (i.e., knowledgeable regarding the rumor) and honest were most effective in reducing belief in a rumor. Indeed, trusted third-party sources of rebuttal are very effective. In addition, effective rebuttals assist the recipient in attaining a sense of control; for example, rebuttals can include specific actions the hearer can take in order to minimize potential harm from a dreaded negative event. Finally, effective rebuttals can include a rebuttal context that addresses why the rebuttal is being issued, for example, "A competitor is spreading false and malicious rumors, and that is why we are rebutting them today."

— NDF

rumor intensity formula

n. A mathematical function $R \sim i \times a$, where R is the intensity of a rumor, i is the importance of the information in the rumor, and a is the ambiguity or uncertainty associated with the rumor which attempts to describe the persistence of particular pieces of gossip. This was formulated by Gordon W. Allport and Leo Postman to describe war rumors during the Second World War.

runs test

n. In statistics, a test of the randomness of a sequence of binary or dichotomous data in which the observed number of consecutive, identical numbers or outcomes is compared with the amount expected by chance.

runway

n. **1.** A straight alley maze or a long straightaway in a maze. **2.** A paved landing strip for aircraft.

saccade

n. A quick movement of the eye from one fixation point to another which cannot be interrupted once began and which lasts 20 to 100 milliseconds, during which the eye is not sharply focused.

sacred values

n. Values considered to be nonnegotiable. They differ from normal values because they incorporate moral beliefs that drive action in ways dissociated from prospects for success. Across the world, people believe that devotion to core values (such as the welfare of their family and country or their commitment to religion, honor, and justice) is, or ought to be, absolute and inviolable. Such values outweigh other values, particularly economic ones.

sadism

n. **1.** The desire to inflict and practice of inflicting pain and humiliation on another as a way of gaining sexual arousal and pleasure derived from the marquis de Sade, who wrote on this subject in the late 1700s and early 1800s. **2.** Enjoyment of inflicting pain in nonsexual contexts as in police beating handcuffed prisoners or teachers humiliating students. **3.** In psychoanalysis, which views all pleasure as sexual, any form of aggressiveness, or expression of Thanatos, the death instinct, such as an infant's biting the nipple, is seen as sadistic.

sadomasochism
n. **1.** The most common form of sadism and masochism in which the same person desires both to inflict pain for sexual arousal as well as to experience pain and humiliation, which is sexually arousing. **2.** The sexual practice of using the infliction of pain or humiliation as a method of intensifying sexual desire.

salience
n. The protruding of something from the background, often used to denote the tendency of some stimulus to become figure to other stimuli's ground in a perceptual field.

sample
n. Any process which selects some but not all of a population, usually as a practical means of measurement. Thus in psychology a sample is usually a group of people drawn from the whole population of people who are included in a study.

sample bias
n. Any characteristic of a sample which is not similarly characteristic of the population from which it is drawn, thus rendering any conclusions drawn about the population inaccurate. Practically this is usually due to using samples of convenience or other sampling errors.

sample distribution
n. The distribution of scores in a particular sample on a particular variable.

sample, matched
n. Two or more subsamples selected to make the groups equivalent on one or more variables so as to prevent those variables from confounding other comparisons among the groups.

sample mean
n. The arithmetic mean of scores from a particular group on a particular variable.

sample, nonrepresentative
n. Any group or set of groups used in research which differ significantly from the population in some salient way.

sample, representative
n. A sample from the population that does not differ from the population in any significant way and can be accurately used to make generalizations about the population.

sample, time
n. The collection of research data at a given time, usually part of a larger sample including data from different times and usually using time as an independent variable.

sampling
n. The process of selecting a part of a population for measurement. Ensuring that the sample does not differ significantly from the population is an essential feature of good sampling; the most efficacious way of ensuring this is usually random sampling.

sampling, convenience
n. The most common procedure of selecting subjects for study in the field of psychology, in which anyone who is handy is selected for a study without regard for the representativeness of the subjects of the population to which generalizations are to be made.

sampling distribution
n. The theoretical distribution of a statistic assumed to be the scores on a particular variable from an infinite number of repeated samplings of a population.

sampling errors
n. **1.** Inaccuracies in inference from a sample to a population which occur because the sample differs from the population. **2.** Random differences in mean scores between different groups of subjects drawn from the same population.

sampling frame

n. A complete list of a population from which samples are drawn.

sampling, nonprobablitity

n. Any nonrandom approach to selecting a group from a population for inclusion in a research project.

sampling procedure

n. The process of selecting subjects for a research project.

sampling, random

n. A sampling procedure in which each item or individual in a population has an equal opportunity or probability of being selected for inclusion in the sample. The value of random sampling is that it creates a sample group from which conclusions can be generalized to the larger population; as such, it is an efficient means of representing the views, attitudes, or opinions of a large group of people. The accuracy of conclusions depends upon the size of the sample in relation to the size of the target population. When targeting a smaller population, one needs to sample a larger percentage to draw an accurate conclusion; when examining a large population, one needs to sample a smaller percentage to get the same level of accuracy.   – BJM

sampling, representative

n. Representative sampling is a method of selecting members for a sample so that the relevant characteristics of the sample are similar to those of the larger target population. The population is divided into nonoverlapping and collectively exhaustive subpopulations or strata (the number of strata depends on the target of the study and the relevant grouping characteristics). Sample members are then randomly selected from each stratum or subgroup in proportion to the population. The members of each stratum are pooled to form the overall sample. For example, if you were interested in studying political attitudes on a specific college campus, you would want to ensure that your study sampled a representative number of freshmen, sophomores, juniors, and seniors. So, you would divide your population (all students) into strata (class levels) and randomly select your sample using representative numbers from each subgroup. Representative sampling is necessary for making valid inferences and generalizing conclusions to the target population.   – BJM

sampling, snowball

n. A method of finding subjects for a study by asking existing subjects and subsequent subjects to find or recruit new subjects. This procedure is often associated with sample bias.

sampling, stratified

n. Stratified sampling is a method of selecting members for a sample so that the relevant characteristics of the sample are similar to those of the larger target population. The population is divided into nonoverlapping and collectively exhaustive subpopulations or strata (the number of strata depends on the target of the study and the relevant grouping characteristics). Sample members are then randomly selected from each stratum or subgroup in proportion to the population. The members of each stratum are pooled to form the overall sample. For example, if you were interested in studying political attitudes on a specific college campus, you would want to ensure that your study sampled a representative number of freshmen, sophomores, juniors, and seniors. So, you would divide your population (all students) into strata (class levels) and randomly select your sample using representative numbers from each subgroup. Stratified sampling is necessary for making valid inferences and generalizing conclusions to the target population.   – BJM

sampling without replacement

n. In statistics, the process of randomly selecting subjects for inclusion in a sample and then keeping each subject out of the population after measuring it so that there is no possibility that a subject may be selected more than once. This procedure allows the proportions of variables connected with individuals to vary across samplings as the removal of each individual may alter the relative proportions of variables within the population.

sampling with replacement

n. In statistics, the process of randomly selecting subjects for inclusion in a sample and
then returning each subject to the population after measuring it so that there is a possibility that a subject may be selected more than
once. These keeps the proportions of a variable within the population constant across
repeated samplings.

Sapir-Whorf hypothesis

n. The idea that the ways people perceive
the world and think are determined by their
language(s), and, having learned different
languages, people understand the world differently. Thus Edward Sapir and Benjamin
Whorf believed that monolingual Hopi speakers who have only one word for flying things
could not distinguish among birds, bats, and
butterflies. Subsequent research has not confirmed this strong version of the hypothesis,
but the notion that language has some guiding effect on thought and perception persists in more subtle effects on thinking and
perceiving.

satiation

n. **1.** The state of having a particular desire
completely fulfilled, as in eating until full. **2.**
In learning theory, the temporary absence
of reinforcing effect of something that often
serves as a reinforcer because of the repeated
presentation of the reinforcer. Thus food
ceases to be a reinforcer when the subject has
eaten all it desires.

satiety

n. The temporary state of having a desire
completely satisfied so that the desire has no
motivating force.

satiety center

n. The ventromedial nucleus in the hypothalamus, which has been associated with the
control of eating and sexual expression.

savings, method of

n. An experimental procedure for determining the amount of residual knowledge that
remains when a person or other animal is
unable to recall some information in which

the training necessary to relearn the material is compared to the amount of training
required to learn the material without previous exposure. Also known as method of
relearning.

scale

n. Any organized system for arranging items
or values in a progressive series, usually
related to magnitude or amount.

scale, interval

n. A quantitative scale with magnitude and
equal intervals but lacking an absolute zero.
The lack of an absolute zero allows interval
data to be added or subtracted to compare
differences at any point on the scale, but values cannot be multiplied or divided to create
meaningful ratios. The Fahrenheit scale is an
example of an interval scale as a 10-degree
difference at any point on the scale indicates
a consistent variance in temperature (equal
intervals), but there is no such thing as no
temperature (absolute zero). Appropriate
calculations of interval data include mean,
median, mode, range, and standard deviation.   – BJM

scale, nominal

n. Nominal scales lack all three key scale properties: magnitude, equal intervals, and absolute zero. As such, nominal scales are simply
a means of labeling or categorizing data but
do not express any quantitative relationship
among variables, categories, or values. For
example, demographic data, such as sex, is
often converted into a nominal scale for data
entry by assigning the category 1 to men and
2 to women. These numbers serve solely as
numerical labels and do not represent a quantitative relationship between variables. The
only appropriate mathematical calculations
for nominal data are frequency and mode.
                                               – BJM

scale, ordinal

n. A quantitative scale with magnitude, but
lacking equal intervals or an absolute zero,
used primarily to rank or rate individuals
or objects. Ordinal scales provide information about degrees of difference but do not

provide any information about the meaning or amount of difference between rankings or ratings. The lack of equal intervals prevents the direct comparison of the difference measurement between any two points. For example, when runners complete a race, an ordinal scale is used to rank first, second, third, and fourth place, and so on, but the ranking does not tell you the difference between first and second place; nor can you assume that the first-place runner was four times as fast as the fourth-place runner. The ordinal rankings simply provide a measure of the degree of difference between runners. Because of the lack of equal intervals, the most appropriate calculations for ordinal scale data are mode, median, range, and percentile rank.   – BJM

scale, ratio
n. A quantitative scale including all three key scale properties: magnitude, equal intervals, and an absolute zero. All mathematical calculations are appropriate for ratio data. For example, money or income is measured on a ratio scale. The absolute zero represents no money and $50 is twice as much as $25; there are equal intervals as the difference of a dollar means the same thing when comparing $1 to $2 or $100 to $101. The large number of available calculations with a ratio scale makes it one of the most useful measures of quantitative data.   – BJM

scale of measurement
n. An organized system for arranging individual measurements in a progressive series, usually related to magnitude or amount.

scale reliability
n. A measure of the consistency with which a device measures a particular variable. The most important measure of scale reliability is a test-retest correlation coefficient, which estimates the temporal stability of a test. Kuder-Richardson 20, coefficient alpha, and split-half reliability coefficients are all measures of the internal consistency of a scale, which is important when unidimensionality is an issue or when the dimension being measured is not expected to have temporal stability, as in a mood scale. The alternate forms reliability measure is rarely used as it is difficult to ensure that alternate forms are actually equivalent.

scaling
n. The process of creating an organized system for arranging variable values in a progressive series, usually related to magnitude or amount.

scapegoating
n. A group process in which a blameless and usually weak member of the group is made the target for expressing anxiety and anger that other members of the group experience. This often happens when the real source of frustration lies beyond the power of the group to attack or control.

scatter diagram
n. A graphical representation of all individual data points in a two-dimensional space of paired measurements on the two dimensions represented by the axes of the space.

scatterplot
n. A graphical representation of all individual data points in a two-dimensional space of paired measurements on the two dimensions represented by the axes of the space.

schedule of reinforcement
n. In learning theory, a plan for which responses will be rewarded. The most common schedules of reinforcement are continuous reinforcement, in which each instance of a target behavior is rewarded; interval reinforcement, in which the first instance of a target behavior after the elapse of a predetermined period is rewarded; and ratio reinforcement, in which a predetermined percentage of the target behaviors are rewarded.

Scheffe test
n. In statistics, a post hoc method for making all possible comparisons of linear combinations in an analysis of variance while controlling for type I error.

schema
n. **1.** An outline, often in graphic form. **2.** A mental representation of a thing, category, or

event and especially one that is self-structured for easy access in information processing. **3.** In cognitive therapy, a negative and irrational idea about the self which brings about erratic or ineffectual behavior and negative feelings and is not modified by contradictory information but which may be altered in a more realistic and effective way through conscious examination and reality testing.

schizoaffective disorder

n. A psychological illness characterized by both severe mood disturbance and psychosis. Thus a person with this disorder would have either mania or depression and delusions, hallucinations, disorganized thought and speech, or grossly disorganized or catatonic behavior.

schizoid personality

n. An enduring pattern of individual thought, behavior, and affect characterized by marked social withdrawal, minimal emotional reaction to social interactions, lack of interest in other people, and lack of satisfaction in relationships with other people. Thus the person prefers hobbies and occupations that do not involve others, prefers mechanical or abstract tasks, has a low sexual drive, and has a generally low level of pleasure in living.

schizoid personality disorder

n. A psychological maladjustment characterized by an enduring pattern of individual thought, behavior, and affect characterized by marked social withdrawal, minimal emotional reaction to social interactions, lack of interest in other people, and lack of satisfaction in relationships with other people. Thus the person prefers hobbies and occupations that do not involve others, prefers mechanical or abstract tasks, has a low sexual drive, and has a generally low level of pleasure in living.

schizophrenia, catatonic

n. A rare from of schizophrenia characterized by rigid immobility or marked abnormality of posture or movement in repeated patterns, mutism, echolalia, as well as disturbance in thought, affect, and responsiveness generally characteristic of schizophrenia. Marked social and occupational dysfunction is usually present.

schizophrenia, childhood

n. Schizophrenia beginning in childhood instead of the normal course, in which schizophrenia appears during late adolescence or early adulthood. In earlier times *childhood schizophrenia* was a broader term, which included autism and other pervasive developmental disorders. Marked social and occupational dysfunction is usually present.

schizophrenia, disorganized

n. A psychological disorder characterized by disorganized speech and thought, gross disturbances in behavior, and flat or inappropriate affect, as well as delusions and hallucinations. Marked social and occupational dysfunction is usually present.

schizophrenia, paranoid

n. A form of psychosis characterized by prominent bizarre delusions or auditory and other hallucinations with a relatively normal cognitive and affective functioning. Delusions are usually persecutory and grandiose, but other types may occur. Persons with this disorder exhibit emotions appropriate to their irrational beliefs about the world and so are often anxious, angry, and aloof and argue strenuously for the reality of their bizarre delusions. Marked social and occupational dysfunction is often present but less often than in other forms of schizophrenia.

schizophrenia, undifferentiated

n. A psychotic disorder characterized by delusions, hallucinations, and disorganized speech, thought, and behavior, as well as flat or inappropriate affect. Marked social and occupational dysfunction is usually present.

schizophrenic episode, acute

n. A relatively short period of intensified delusions, hallucinations, and disorganized speech, thought, and behavior, as well as flat or inappropriate affect. Marked social and occupational dysfunction is usually present.

schizophrenic thought disorder

n. A psychological disorder characterized by slow thinking, which may have bizarre or nonsensical content, loosening of associations, delusions, disturbance of speech and writing, and lack of affective content, which cause marked social and occupational dysfunction.

schizophreniform disorder

n. A psychotic disorder characterized by a short period (less than 1 month) of delusions, hallucinations, and disorganized speech, thought, and behavior, as well as flat or inappropriate affect. Marked social and occupational dysfunction may or may not occur.

schizophrenogenic

adj. Of or relating to the causation of schizophrenia. Schizophrenogenic factors contribute to but are not sufficient conditions for the development of the disease, as having a very stressful home life is schizophrenogenic, but most people who have stressful home lives do not develop schizophrenia.

schizophrenogenic parent

n. A parent whose behavior contributes to the development of schizophrenia. In the past it was thought that schizophrenia was caused by maladaptive parenting, but research has found parenting to be a minor but contributory factor in the development of the disease. Psychoanalytic theorists such as Sigmund Freud believed cold, domineering, insensitive, perfectionistic, overprotective, seductive, and morally rigid mothers caused schizophrenia. This idea has not been found to be correct in careful research.

schizotypal personality disorder

n. A psychological maladjustment characterized by an enduring pattern of individual thought, behavior, and affect characterized by acute social anxiety that does not usually diminish with familiarity and eccentric behavior and cognitive and perceptual distortions of social situations leading to pervasive social and interpersonal maladjustment. Ideas of reference are common, but delusions are not. Odd beliefs, unusual perceptual experiences, paranoid thinking, but not delusions are often present. Close relationships are unusual, and behavior is generally odd and peculiar as if the person did not take cultural appropriateness into account.

Scholastic Aptitude Test ▶ *See* SCHOLASTIC ASSESSMENT TEST

Scholastic Assessment Test

n. (SAT) A timed omnibus test of academic achievement including sections on reading and critical thinking, mathematics, and writing ability used by many colleges and universities as a criterion for admission. It also has many subtests in a variety of academic subject areas, which are widely used for class placement in colleges and universities and sometimes for advanced standing or college credits. Formerly known as the Scholastic Aptitude Test.

school psychologist

n. An individual usually with an advanced degree in psychology or educational psychology who applies the findings and methods of psychology in the field of education, usually working in schools. Testing is the primary function of the school psychologist, and they tend also to be involved in diagnosis, assessment, and treatment of behavioral problems of schoolchildren.

school psychology

n. The branch of psychology focused on the problems of schoolchildren and education, usually in primary and secondary schools. Testing is the primary function of school psychology, and it is also involved in learning theory and curriculum development, program assessment, and the diagnosis, assessment, and treatment of behavioral problems of schoolchildren.

Schwann cells

n. Nonneural cells within the nervous system which form the myelin sheath, which surrounds individual nerve cells and nerve tracts and increases the speed of impulse transmission.

scientific law

n. Any widely accepted idea derived from systematic observation or experimentation. The term is a misnomer, as there are no fixed laws or rules in science, only tentatively held theories and procedures subject to disproof and replacement.

461

scientific management
n. The application of scientific principles to the study of work conditions and worker efficiency such as ergonomics and incentives.

scientific method
n. The general procedure of discovering the nature of the universe and all things in it through systematic observation and experimentation guided by the attitudes of skepticism and open-mindedness. This is usually embodied in objective measurement and the search for reproducible results which can be used to make generalizations.

scientific psychology
n. All parts of psychology which follow the general procedure of discovering the nature of the mind and behavior through systematic observation and experimentation guided by the attitudes of skepticism and open-mindedness. This is usually embodied in objective measurement and the search for reproducible results which can be used to make generalizations.

scientific revolution
n. **1.** The historical shift in perspective that occurred in Euro-American cultures in the 16th through 18th centuries in which intellectual beliefs began to be guided more by observation and experimentation than by religious revealed truth and simple superstition. This transformation has never been completed, as belief in revealed truth and superstitions contradictory to fact continues, but the dominant perspective remains scientific for now. **2.** A marked shift in perspective within a particular field of scientific endeavor such as occurred in physics around the turn of the 20th century, when Newtonian physics was found to be inadequate and was superseded by relativistic and later quantum perspectives.

sclera
n. The tough opaque white outer covering of the eye, which gives the eye its shape and attaches to the muscles which move the eyeball in its socket.

scopolamine
n. A colorless liquid, $C_{17}H_{21}NO_4$, found in the henbane plant which acts as a central nervous system depressant by replacing acetylcholine at neural receptor sites. It has sedative effects and often causes amnesia so that little or nothing is remembered of the period in which it is effective. It has been used in low doses to combat motion sickness. Also called hyoscine.

score, raw
n. A numerical result from a measurement in the first form in which it is recorded before it is summarized, normalized, or converted into any other form.

score, standard
n. A numerical result which has had the average score subtracted from it and then been divided by the standard deviation of all scores.

score, transformed
n. Any numerical result which has been altered to another form, usually for ease of comparison, as in standard or normalized scores.

script
n. **1.** A theoretical mental representation of an outline of acts and their order and permutations which are entailed in a complex behavior, such as eating in a restaurant, going on a date, or having a marriage or career. **2.** A theoretical structured mental representation of the semantic relationships in everyday human situations. Also called script schema.

seasonal affective disorder
n. (SAD) A recurrent pattern of depression or bipolar disorder which regularly coincides with the seasons of the year. For example, many people in monsoon-type climates as in Oregon and Washington State have recurring depressions in the winter months when sunlight is markedly diminished.

secondary drive
n. A motivation that has been learned rather than being inherent in the organism.

secondary gain

n. In psychoanalytic theory, rewards brought about by neurotic behavior in addition to the internal rewards of decreased anxiety and the unconsciousness of emotional conflict.

secondary reinforcement

n. Anything which increases the likelihood of behavior which immediately precedes it which is acquired through learning and not inherent in the organism in its normal development.

secondary reinforcer

n. A stimulus which was originally neutral but has been paired with an unconditioned reinforcer and to which the subject has come to react in a manner similar to his or her reaction to the unconditioned reinforcer. Thus, when a particular voice is coupled with feeding a hungry animal, the animal will soon begin to seek and be rewarded by the sound of the voice alone.

secondary sexual characteristic

n. Any feature associated with biological sex but not directly tied to reproduction, such as facial hair, waist-to-hip ratio, and breast development.

second-order conditioning

n. In classical conditioning, the learning of a conditioned response by pairing a neutral stimulus with a conditioned stimulus.

second-signal system

n. In classical conditioning, stimuli that are generated within the organism and to which the organism reacts as it would to external stimuli, as in speech, language, ideas, and mental images.

secure attachment

n. **1.** In the strange situation experimental paradigm, the child acts comforted by the caregiver, uses the caregiver as a secure base from which to explore, and feels anxious at separation and comforted by contact when the caregiver returns. **2.** In adult attachment theory, an internal working model of relationships in which others are expected to be attentive, accepting, and generally responsive to the needs of the person, which allows the person to feel secure in his or her lovableness in developing sexual relationships and nurturing children.

sedative

1. *n.* Any drug which has a generally depressive effect on the central nervous system so that taking it results in calming and relaxation such as the benzodiazepines. Usually such drugs produce sleepiness at higher doses. **2.** *adj.* Of or relating to anything that calms or soothes a person or other organism.

sedative-hypnotic

n. Any central nervous system depressant that is used for calming at low doses and producing sleep at higher doses such as the barbiturates, chloral hydrate, the propradiols, and GHB.

seizure

n. **1.** An instance of excessive and uncontrolled electrical discharge by some of the neurons in the brain. When motor neurons are involved, it produces convulsions. **2.** An acute attack of any disease, especially those involving convulsions.

seizure disorder

n. A family of chronic brain disorders characterized by uncontrolled electrical activity in the brain, some of which produce convulsions, clouding of consciousness, unconsciousness, and various sensory and cognitive malfunctions, depending on which parts of the brain are involved. Brain trauma is the most common known cause of this disorder, but in many cases the cause is unknown. Also known as epilepsy.

selection

n. **1.** In genetics, the different survival rates of individuals of different genotypes which produce differences in populations over time. **2.** The process of choosing a person, thing, or action.

selection ratio

n. The proportion of a population actually picked for inclusion in a sample. In selecting personnel it is the proportion of applicants who are actually hired so that the lower the ratio the more an employer may take into account individual characteristics in the selection process.

selective attention
n. The focus of attention on some stimuli and not on others, resulting in a greater processing of the stimuli upon which the individual is focused.

selective breeding
n. The process of increasing the likelihood of certain traits in a population by controlling mating so that those with the desired characteristics and without the undesired ones increase as a proportion of the population. Thus a dairy farmer may mate the best milk producing cows with a bull whose mother was a high milk producer.

self
n. The whole of the individual, including all physical and mental processes and activities with his/her history of development as well as personal identity and experience. Different writers have stressed different aspects of self or used the word to mean more specific things. Thus Jung suggested there was an inherited structure or archetype called self, whose development was the goal of human life. Carl Rogers suggested there was an experiential self, which often conflicted with one's understanding of one's self, the latter of which is determined by experience, learning, and social pressure. Adler suggested the self was a self-serving concept used as a tool in one's chosen lifestyle. William James suggested self was used both as a source of agency and a target of appraisal. Karen Horney suggested that self is unique capacities for growth and development. Gordon Allport substituted the word *proprium* for *self* and suggested it was what is most personal and important in us. Edward Murray used the term mostly to mean our consciousness of our self.

self, actual
n. The person as he/she actually is rather than as he/she believes he/she is. In several branches of psychology it is believed that there are often differences between the way a person perceives and reacts to his/her experience and the way he/she believes he/she perceives and reacts. This is most likely to occur when a person believes it is socially desirable to be a way that he/she actually is not. For example, a person may believe he/she lacks sexual desire when he/she actually does react with arousal to sexual stimulation.

self-actualization
n. **1.** In humanistic psychology, the full use of all the talents, capacities, and potentialities of each individual. **2.** The process of striving toward a full realization of all the talents, capacities, and potentialities of each individual. **3.** The needs that emerge when physical, safety, love, and esteem needs have been sufficiently satisfied, which include but are not limited to beauty, justice, order, and unity.

self-affirmation theory
n. The theory that supposes that people are motivated to maintain positive views of themselves as competent, moral, emotionally stable and well-adjusted, and able to deal with the stresses of life. When confronted with negative information about the self, people feel uncomfortable and tend either to ignore it and affirm some other aspect of self or to find a way to resolve the inconsistency that allows them to maintain a positive sense of self.

self-appraisal ▶ *See* SELF-CONSTRUAL

self-awareness
n. **1.** The perception of one's self, including bodily sensations, actions, and mental processes, as an object of observation and analysis. **2.** The understanding that one exists as an individual, separate from other people, with private thoughts, feelings, and sensations.

self-blaming
n. The process of harassing one's self with criticism, usually involving holding one's self responsible for negative but not positive outcomes as well as finding one's self morally culpable and reproaching one's self whether it is reasonable to do so or not. The level of

self-blaming is partly a cultural phenomenon with some cultures valuing the tendency and others devaluing it.

self-categorization theory

n. (SCT) The study of the ways people include themselves in social categories along with the stereotyping and depersonalization such categories necessarily entail and the ways individuals cope with the uncertainty and contradictions of such categorization, the desire to enhance the self in doing so, and differences between self- and normative individual categorization.

self-complexity

n. The degree to which one's understanding of one's personal mental, physical, social, historical, and functional attributes is varied and acknowledges the variability, changeability, and contradictoriness of individual experience and behavior.

self-concept

n. The sum of one's idea about one's self, including physical, mental, historical, and relational aspects, as well as capacities to learn and perform. Self-concept is usually considered central to personal identity and change over time. It is usually considered partially conscious and partially unconscious or inferred in a given situation.

self-conscious emotions

n. A category of emotions that theoretically require some kind of evaluation of the self in their elicitation. These typically include pride, shame, guilt, embarrassment, jealousy, or envy.

self-consciousness

n. **1.** Excessive focus on the self and its characteristics from an observer's perspective in social situations, usually with a high degree of self-criticism, anxiety, and a tendency to panic along with a disruption in normal capacity to think clearly. **2.** The characteristic of thinking about one's self and one's attributes, including mental processes and other private experiences as well as public aspects of the self.

self-consistency

n. **1.** The regularity and integration of different aspects of one's mental and physical functioning. **2.** The compatibility or relative absence of internal contradictions in an idea or theory.

self-construal

n. A person's cognitive representations of one's own self (i.e., how a person defines his or her self). It has been shown that these representations are to a large part shaped and guided by culture and the social context in which the person is situated. Hazel Markus and Shinobu Kitayama have identified two types of self-construal, which vary in the degree to which individuals include the social world (such as family, coworkers, social groups to which one belongs) in their representation of the self. Specifically, the *independent self-construal* views the self as autonomous entity and separated from other people; emphasis is placed on one's uniqueness in relation to others; the self is defined in terms of an individual's traits and preferences, which guide individuals' behaviors consistently across situations. By contrast, *interdependent self-construal* includes important others (such as family or social groups one belongs to) as part of the self; emphasis is placed on connectedness with one's in-group; the needs and wishes of the group are often put before those of the individual; attention is given to fulfillment of role obligations and expectations and wishes of the in-group; individuals are expected to behave differently across situations that involve different social relations.

These two types of self-construal have different prevalence in individualist and collectivist cultures. Specifically, independent self-construal is more frequently endorsed by individuals in individualist cultures (typically North Americans and Australians), whereas the interdependent self-construal is more frequently endorsed by individuals in collectivist cultures (typically Japanese, Chinese, Koreans, and Indians). Moreover, there are also gender differences. Females are more likely than men to hold interdependent self-construal. It has been argued that these cross-cultural or gender differences are shaped by social institutions, norms, and practices within the culture. However, it is important to note that there are discernible variations within cultural groups. Moreover, Marilynn Brewer proposes that people, regardless of their cultural heritage, have the need to be connected to others and at the same time the need to be differentiated from others. To fulfill these two needs, individuals in all cultures may possess both independent self-construal, which meets the differentiation need, and interdependent self-construal, which meets the connectedness need. The immediate social context may make one need and its accompanying self-construal more salient than the other need and its accompanying self-construal.

Individual differences in self-construal can be assessed using questionnaires. Many such measures have been created. For example, in the scale created by Hazel Markus and Shinobu Kitayama, independent self-construal is measured by participants' extent of agreement with statements such as "I assert my opposition when I disagree strongly with the members of my group" "I act the same way no matter who I am with" "I enjoy being unique and different from others in many respects," whereas interdependent self-construal is measured by participants' extent of agreement with statements such as "I will stay in a group if they need me, even when I am not happy with the group" "It is important for me to maintain harmony within my group" "I often have the feeling that my relationship with others is more important than my own accomplishments" and "My happiness depends on the happiness of those around me." Scores on the independent self-construal items are often not correlated with those on interdependent self-construal items, suggesting that the two types of self-construal are orthogonal to each other. That is, individuals may endorse both self-contruals, predominantly one of the self-contruals, or none.

Many of the self-construal measures have been criticized for lack of internal reliability and consistency across measures. In particular, some measures include relational others (family members, coworkers) as the targets, whereas others focus on a collective (my group). The loci of the items across measures are also mixed: some items tap on the

characteristics of the self, others on agency or values. Participants may score low on one interdependence measure but high on another interdependence measure.

In face of this problem, Susan Cross and associates propose *relational interdependent self-construal*, which includes relational others (such as parents, spouse, children, coworkers) in the definition of the self. This type of interdependent self-construal is distinguished from the group-oriented interdependent self-construal that focuses on collectives (the social groups one belongs to). Cross and associates argue that the relational interdependent self-construal is more prevalent than the group-oriented interdependent self-construal in North America. Not differentiating these two types of interdependent self-construal would lead to erroneous underestimation of the prevalence of interdependent self-construal in North American culture.

Another related measure is designed by Arthur Aron, Elaine Aron, and associates. This measure involves presenting participants with a series of two circles. The two circles overlap to different extents across the scale. Participants are asked to imagine that one of the circles is their self and the other is a specific close other (e.g., mother) and select the figure that most reflects the extent of closeness or inclusiveness between them and that other person. The more individuals include a close other in the self, the less likely they are to differentiate between the self and the other in allocating resources, the more they tend to share the other's characteristics vicariously and tend to think about the other much as they think about the self.

Aside from assessing self-construal using questionnaires, researchers have activated (made salient) one or the other type of self-construal using experimental manipulations. For example, David Trafimow and associates have created two versions of a story about an ancient warrior. One story emphasizes the individual achievement of the warrior, while the other emphasizes the family prestige and loyalty of the warrior. Participants who read the former story generated more independent (vs. interdependent) self-construal subsequently than did the participants who read the latter story. Another widely used manipulation is created by Marilynn Brewer and Wendi Gardner. Participants were asked to circle the pronoun *I* or *we* in an essay to activate their personal self and social self, respectively. Subsequently, participants who circled *we* generated more interdependent self-construal than did participants who circled *I*. In short, these manipulations have shown that (a) individuals, regardless of their cultural heritage, possess both independent and interdependent self-construals, and (b) individuals' self-construals are amenable to change by situational primes.   – Y Y H

self-control

n. The capacity to command one's mental activities and overt behavior, especially so as to formulate and carry out plans despite environmental distractions and contrary impulses. The capacity to resist impulses for short-term pleasure in carrying out plans for longer-term satisfaction is often used as a measure of self- or ego control.

self-criticism

n. The evaluative examination of one's own mental processes and behavior. Overly harsh or negative evaluation of the self is associated with depression.

self-deception

n. The act of concealing some aspects of self from one's consciousness, particularly limitations or faults. It is seen as one of two dimensions of social desirability.

self-defeating prophecy

n. A prophecy that fails to occur because of the effects of having been stated. Thus a patient who is told that he may die of a heart attack may forestall it by dieting and exercising.

self-determination

n. The capacity to decide for one's self on the basis of inner guides such as beliefs, preferences, and attitudes rather than being coerced or feeling pressured to decide on the basis of others' beliefs, preferences, or attitudes. In existential theory, such choice is necessary to self-fulfillment.

self-disclosure

n. The revealing of one's inner experience or nonobvious facts about one's self to another person. This kind of revelation to a receptive listener has been found to be related to self-esteem and general good mental health, and it is key in most forms of psychotherapy.

self-discrepancy theory

n. Why do people react so differently emotionally to the same tragic event? More specifically, why is it that when people are emotionally overwhelmed by a severe setback in their life, such as the death of their child, the loss of their job, or the breakup of their marriage, some suffer from depression whereas others suffer from anxiety? Self-discrepancy theory was developed in an attempt to answer this question. Self-discrepancy theory proposes that even when people have the same specific goals, such as seniors in high school wanting to go to a good college or older adults wanting a good marriage, they often vary in the way they represent these goals. Some individuals represent their goals (or standards), called *self-guides* in self-discrepancy theory, as hopes or aspirations – *ideal* self-guides. Other individuals represent their self-guides as duties or obligations – *ought* self-guides. According to self-discrepancy theory, it is the difference between failing to meet one's ideals versus failing to meet one's oughts that provides the key to unlock the mystery of why people react differently emotionally to the same negative life event.

Self-discrepancy theory proposes that when a negative life event happens to someone, it is represented as saying something about his or her current state – his or her *actual self* now. Individuals compare their actual self to a self-guide – "Compared to the kind of person I want to be (e.g., going to a good college, having a good marriage), how am I doing?" People suffer emotionally when there is a discrepancy between their actual self and a self-guide – a *self-discrepancy*. When the actual self is discrepant from an ideal self-guide, people feel sad, disappointed, discouraged – dejection-related emotions that relate to depression. When the actual self is discrepant from an ought self-guide, people feel nervous, tense, and worried – agitation-related emotions that relate to anxiety. According to self-discrepancy theory, then, people's vulnerabilities to different kinds of emotional suffering depend on which type of self-guide is emphasized in their self-regulation – dejection/depression suffering when ideals are emphasized and agitation/anxiety suffering when oughts are emphasized.

Research with clinically depressed and clinically anxious patients has found support for these proposals about emotional vulnerabilities. Discrepancies between patients' actual selves and their ideal self-guides predict their suffering from depression more than they predict their suffering from anxiety disorders, whereas discrepancies between patients' actual selves and their ought self-guides predict their suffering from anxiety disorders more than they predict their suffering from depression. Because some individuals have actual-self discrepancies from both their ideal and their ought self-guides, one or the other kind of discrepancy can be made temporarily more active by exposing them either to words related to an ideal they possess or to an ought they possess. When such "priming" of either an ideal or an ought occurs in an experiment, participants whose actual-ideal discrepancy is activated suddenly feel sad and disappointed and fall into a depression-like state of low activity (e.g., talk more slowly). In contrast, participants whose actual-ought discrepancy is activated suddenly feel nervous and worried and fall into an anxiety-like state of high activity (e.g., talk more quickly).

What is the psychological mechanism that underlies these predictions? Self-discrepancy theory proposes that different emotions are associated with different psychological situations that people experience. That is, the psychological situations produced by success or failure to meet your ideals are different from the psychological situations produced by success or failure to meet your oughts. Specifically, when events are related to ideal self-guides (i. e., to someone's hopes and aspirations), individuals experience success as the presence of a positive outcome (a gain), which is a happy experience, and they experience failure as the absence of positive outcomes

(a nongain), which is a sad experience. In contrast, when events are related to ought self-guides (i.e., someone's beliefs about his or her duties and obligations), individuals experience success as the absence of a negative outcome (a nonloss), which is a relaxing experience, and they experience failure as the presence of a negative outcome (a loss), which is a worrying experience. Consistently with this underlying logic of the theory, several studies have found that individuals with strong ideals are especially sensitive to events reflecting the absence or the presence of positive outcomes (gains and nongains), whereas individuals with strong oughts are especially sensitive to events reflecting the presence or absence of negative outcomes (nonlosses and losses).

What kind of parenting is likely to result in children's having strong ideal self-guides, and what kind of parenting is likely to result in children's having strong ought self-guides? In answering these questions, self-discrepancy theory relies on the basic idea that self-regulation in relation to ideal self-guides involves experiencing successes in the world as the presence of positive outcomes (gains) and failures as the absence of positive outcomes (nongains), whereas self-regulation in relation to ought self-guides involves experiencing successes as the absence of negative outcomes (nonlosses) and failures as the presence of negative outcomes (losses). When children interact with their parents (or other caretakers), the parents respond to the children in ways that make the children experience one of these different kinds of psychological situations. Over time, the children respond to themselves as their parents respond to them, producing the same specific kinds of psychological situations, and this develops into the kind of self-guide (ideal or ought) that is associated with those psychological situations.

What pattern of parenting, then, predicts the development of strong ideal self-guides in children? It is when parents combine bolstering (when managing success) and love withdrawal (when disciplining failure). Bolstering occurs, for instance, when parents encourage the child to overcome difficulties, hug and kiss him or her when he/she succeeds, or set up opportunities for the child to engage in success activities – it creates an experience of the presence of positive outcomes in the child. Love withdrawal occurs, for instance, when parents end a meal when the child throws some food, take away a toy when the child refuses to share it, stop a story when the child is not paying attention – it creates an experience of the absence of positive outcomes in the child. What pattern of parenting predicts the development of strong ought self-guides in children? It is when parents combine prudence (when managing success) and punitive/critical behavior (when disciplining failure). Prudence occurs, for instance, when parents "child-proof" the house, train the child to be alert to potential dangers, or teach the child to "mind your manners" – it creates an experience of the absence of negative outcomes in the child. Punitive/critical behavior occurs, for instance, when parents play roughly with the child to get his or her attention, yell at the child when he or she does not listen, criticize the child when he or she makes a mistake – it creates an experience of the presence of negative outcomes. There is evidence supporting these predictions that bolstering plus love withdrawal parenting is associated with developing strong ideals, and prudence plus critical/punitive parenting is associated with developing strong oughts.

Self-discrepancy theory does not only distinguish between ideal and ought self-guides. It also distinguishes between whose viewpoint or standpoint on the self is taken in the self-regulation. Individuals' self-regulation could be from their own independent viewpoint or standpoint – "What are my own goals and standards for myself?" Self-discrepancy theory refers to this standpoint as the *own* standpoint. Alternatively, individuals' self-regulation could be from the standpoint of a significant person in their life, such as their father or mother – "What are my mother's goals and standards for me?" Self-discrepancy theory refers to this standpoint as the *significant other* or simply *other* standpoint. The theory proposes that there are individual differences in whether it is discrepancies from independent self-guides or discrepancies from significant other self-guides that

underlie individuals' emotional vulnerabilities. As predicted, individual differences have been found in whether it is discrepancies from independent self-guides or discrepancies from significant other self-guides that most determine emotional vulnerabilities. In particular, it has been found that, in North America at least, discrepancies from independent self-guides are a more important determinant of emotional vulnerabilities for males than for females, whereas discrepancies from significant other self-guides are more important for females than for males.

Self-discrepancy theory has practical significance. For example, a new method of clinical treatment for depression and for anxiety, called *self-system therapy*, is based on self-discrepancy theory, and this new therapy has been shown to help some patients more than standard drug treatment or cognitive-behavioral therapy. There is also evidence that discrepancies of the actual self from ideal self-guides are a vulnerability factor for bulimic eating disorders, whereas discrepancies from ought self-guides are a vulnerability factor for anorexic eating disorders. What self-discrepancy theory highlights is that it is not simply individuals' specific goals that are critical. Instead, what determines the quality of our emotional and motivational lives is our more general concerns, our viewpoints on how the world works – is it a world of gains that we hope for (ideals) or a world of non-losses that it is our duty to assure (oughts)?

– ETH

self-effacement

n. **1.** The process of making one's self less obvious to others, as in modesty or humility. **2.** A neurotic coping strategy based on a need to restrict life practices to within narrow borders and to live as inconspicuously as possible in which one idealizes compliance, dependence, and selfless love of another.

self-efficacy

n. Perceived self-efficacy is concerned with people's beliefs in their ability to influence events that affect their lives. This core belief is the foundation of human motivation, performance accomplishments, and emotional well-being. Unless people believe they can produce desired effects by their actions, they have little incentive to undertake activities or to persevere in the face of difficulties. Perceived efficacy operates in three different forms. In individual efficacy, people bring their influence to bear on their own functioning and on environmental events. However, in many spheres of functioning, people do not have direct control over conditions that affect their lives. They exercise proxy efficacy by influencing others who have the resources, knowledge, and means to act on their behalf to secure the outcomes they desire. People do not live their lives in isolation. Many of the things they seek are achievable only by working together through interdependent effort. In the exercise of perceived collective efficacy, they pool their knowledge, skills, and resources and act in concert to shape their future.   – A B

self-enhancement

n. Self-enhancement relates to a motive to protect, maintain, and promote a class of emotional states called feelings of self-worth. These emotional states include positive and negative emotions (e.g., pride and shame). The self-enhancement motive calls attention to the fact that people prefer to feel proud of themselves rather than ashamed of themselves.

Self-enhancement biases. *n.* Psychological motives do not reveal themselves directly. Instead, we infer their existence by analyzing how people behave in specifiable situations. If we find that behavior is consistently biased in a particular direction, we assume an underlying motive is at work. With respect to the self-enhancement motive, three behaviors are relevant: (a) The way people evaluate themselves, (b) the manner in which they approach and process self-relevant information; and (c) the way they respond when circumstances threaten their feelings of self-worth. In the following sections, I show how these behaviors support the existence of the self-enhancement.

Self-enhancing self-evaluations. Self-evaluations provide the most obvious example of a self-enhancement bias. Suppose you randomly select a group of people and ask each person how honest he/she is compared to most other people. Logically, approximately half of the respondents should say they are more honest than others and half should say they are less honest than others. This does not occur. Instead, the vast majority of your sample will say they are more honest than most other people (a tendency known as the "better than most" effect). Insofar as most people cannot be more honest than most other people, assessments of this sort are said to be illusory.

The better than most effect occurs for a wide range of attributes. For example, people think they are more caring than others, more deserving than others, more insightful than others, and fairer than others. They also believe they drive better than others, are happier than others, and have more satisfying interpersonal relationships than do others.

The bias also includes people we care about or associate with. When making social evaluations, people appraise their friends, family, and fellow group members more positively than they appraise most other people. In fact, the bias even extends to inanimate objects. People evaluate their initials, birth dates, and possessions in overly positive terms. In short, things that are mine or ours are evaluated more positively than things that are yours or theirs.

Considering how common the better than most effect is, you might think that people are aware they are biased. Think again! Instead, most people believe they are less biased than are other people. For example, when discussing politics, we believe our opinions are well supported by facts, but other people's opinions are driven by ideology. We also believe our judgments are less distorted by greed, self-aggrandizement, or personal gain than are other people's judgments, and that we are open-minded and impartial but other people are narrow-minded and prejudiced.

Numerous processes produce the better than most effect. Perhaps the most important one is that traits are inherently ambiguous. Consider, for example, what it means to be honest. Does it mean you always tell your friends what you really think about their new hairstyle and clothes, that you never lie on your income tax, or always correct a waiter when he forgets to charge you for some item? Each of these examples is indicative of honesty, but none is essential. This opens the door for individuals to define honesty in ways that cast them in a favorable light. Most people take advantage of this opportunity. They define traits in ways that allow them to believe they possess many positive and few negative traits. For example, a person who is lithe and quick defines athletic ability in terms of speed and balance; a person who is beefy and muscular defines athletic ability in terms of power and strength. In this manner, each believes she is more athletic than the other.

Self-enhancement biases in the processing of personal information. People also process feedback in a self-enhancing way. First, they avidly approach positive feedback but reluctantly seek negative feedback. This pattern ensures that most of the feedback they receive will be positive. Most people also uncritically accept positive feedback but carefully scrutinize and refute negative feedback, show better memory for positive feedback than negative feedback, interpret ambiguous feedback as more positive than negative, and introspect about themselves in ways that enable them to believe they possess many positive qualities and few negative ones.

People also accept responsibility for their successes but deflect responsibility for their failures, a phenomenon known as the self-serving bias in causal attributions. To illustrate, when students do well on a test, they readily credit their ability. When they do poorly on a test, they blame the professor for asking tricky questions or excuse their performance by citing an illness, bad mood, or poor study skills. This pattern enables them to maintain overly positive beliefs in their ability even in the face of failure.

In some cases, individuals will even sabotage their own performance by actively creating an impediment to success. For example, a student may fail to study for an exam or an athlete may fail to practice before an upcoming competition. Although these so-called self-handicapping strategies make success less likely, they give people a ready-made excuse for failure. To illustrate, if a student who fails to study for an exam does poorly, he/she blames the poor performance on a lack of preparation, thereby evading the conclusion that he/she lacks ability. And if he/she happens to succeed, lack of effort provides even stronger evidence of high ability. After all, only a veritable genius could succeed when saddled with the impediment of insufficient preparation.

Self-enhancement biases following threats to self-worth. People cannot always avoid receiving negative feedback about themselves. For some of us, years of struggling with the most basic of household repairs provide irrefutable evidence that we lack mechanical ability. When this occurs, individuals create acknowledged pockets of incompetence by readily admitting to possessing the limitation in question, to the point that they may even exaggerate the extent of their deficiency. At the same time, they call on a host of reserve self-enhancement strategies to minimize the damage this admission does to their overall feelings of self-worth.

First, they minimize the attribute's importance. A person who is all thumbs in the woodshop but has a green thumb in the garden tends to regard mechanical ability as less important than gardening skills. The reverse is true for someone who is more accomplished at building boats than growing plants. By derogating the importance of qualities they lack, individuals are able to accept a limitation and still ensure that its negative impact on their self-worth is minimal. In a similar vein, individuals tend to exaggerate the commonality of their deficiencies. Although they believe their skills are rare and distinctive (e.g., few people can solve crossword puzzles as quickly as I can), they believe their deficiencies are ordinary and common (e.g., most people do not know a sparkplug from a piston). Viewing one's shortcomings as common softens the negative impact of an accepted deficiency.

Downward social comparison provides another means of neutralizing negative feedback. This strategy involves comparing oneself with others who are worse off than one. For example, a student who receives a D in a course can console himself/herself by comparing with those who failed the class. By focusing on those who are even more disadvantaged, one's own situation looks good in comparison. Alternatively, one can augment self-worth by emphasizing one's association with those who are relatively advantaged on some dimension. This strategy is known as "basking in reflected glory." To illustrate, one study found that students are more likely to use the pronoun *we* when discussing a football game their university team had won than when talking about a game their team had lost (e.g., we won; they lost). Moreover, this tendency was most apparent after the students had first experienced a personal failure. Emphasizing one's association with successful others allows individuals to succeed vicariously, even in situations in which they have personally failed.

A final strategy that may be used to offset negative feedback regarding one aspect of the self is to exaggerate one's worth in other aspects of the self. To illustrate, an individual who has recently been rebuffed by a lover may offset this blow to self-worth by exaggerating his/her athletic prowess. This process, known as self-affirmation, has been shown to provide a powerful antidote to a wide range of negative experiences that threaten feelings of self-worth. In fact, simply reminding oneself that one holds many fine values or has many fine qualities is sometimes sufficient to neutralize the impact of negative feedback.

When looking over all of these various strategies, it is important to note that they can all be used somewhat interchangeably. If one strategy does not work to restore feelings of self-worth, individuals will simply turn to another. The specific means by which self-enhancement occurs is thus far less important than the commitment to restore it. This is why psychologists believe an underlying motive drives all of these behaviors. If one strategy is thwarted or ineffective, individuals simply turn to another to help them feel better about themselves.

Assessing the accuracy of people's self-views. Self-enhancement biases are also revealed when we assess the accuracy of people's self-views. Considering all of the feedback people receive in life, you might think we all have a pretty good idea of what we are like. There is some evidence for accuracy in domains of low importance (e.g., people are reasonably accurate about how tidy they are), but there is not much evidence for accuracy in domains of high importance. For example, people's judgments of their intelligence, attractiveness, and likability are only weakly correlated with the judgments of neutral, unbiased observers. A low correlation does not mean no one is accurate, only that, on average, people are just as likely to be accurate as inaccurate.

People are also biased when they predict their future. For the most part, they are overly optimistic. They believe their future will be much brighter than base rate data can justify. For example, although the current divorce rate is a bit over 50%, only 25% of newlyweds believe there is any chance they will not stay married for life. These estimates arise, in part, because couples view their relationship in unrealistically positive terms. They believe their love is stronger than other people's love, and that the problems that beset other people's relationships, such as poor communication skills or incompatible interests, pose less of a threat to their own relationship.

These biases extend to other areas of life as well. Across a wide range of good and bad outcomes, people believe their lives will be better than other people's lives. For example, people believe they are more likely than their peers to have a gifted child, own their own home, or live to a ripe old age. Conversely, they believe they are less likely than their peers to experience negative events, such as having a serious automobile accident, being a crime victim, or becoming depressed. Insofar as everyone's future cannot logically be rosier than everyone else's, the extreme optimism individuals display is illusory.

Cross-cultural issues. Many, though not all, psychologists believe that self-enhancement needs are universal. Across cultures, people the world over are motivated to feel good about themselves rather than bad about themselves. At the same time, cultures clearly influence how the motive is satisfied and expressed, and many of the biases we have been discussing are more prevalent in America, Canada, and the countries of Western Europe than they are in some East Asian countries, such as

China and Japan. The most likely explanation for these cultural differences is that Western cultures encourage people to think of themselves in highly positive terms, whereas East Asian cultures emphasize humility and interconnectedness with others rather than bluster and bravado.

Self-esteem and self-enhancement biases. Across cultures, many of the self-enhancement biases I have reviewed are greatly reduced or entirely absent among low-self-esteem people or those who are depressed. This association has led some theorists to speculate that self-enhancement biases promote psychological well-being. Others have argued that people are better served by knowing what they are really like, and that self-enhancement is a disguised form of narcissism.

Although there is evidence on both sides of the matter, most of the evidence shows that positive self-evaluations are generally beneficial, provided that the degree of distortion is mild. People who think they are better than they really are, exaggerate their ability to bring about desired outcomes, and are unrealistically optimistic about their future are happier, have more satisfying friendships and romantic relationships, are more productive and creative in their work, and are better able to cope and grow with life's challenges than are people with more realistic self-views. In short, rather than knowing the truth about themselves, individuals seem to be better off thinking they are slightly better than they really are.   – JDB

self-esteem

n. The degree to which one's attitude toward, opinions about, and evaluation of one's own body, history, mental processes, and behavior are positive. Self-esteem is related to many aspects of thought, emotion, and behavior and is often considered a central part of understanding an individual.

self-evaluation maintenance theory

n. The self-evaluation maintenance (SEM) model attempts to capture some of the dynamics underlying our reaction to the performance of others, particularly close others. Sometimes the outstanding performances

of close others make us feel good. Albert beams with pride when he tells us that his friend Bob is selected as the first chair in the school orchestra. Other times the outstanding performance of close others can be quite negative. In spite of Albert's forced smile, he recognizes some very negative feelings in himself when he learns that his friend Charlie made the starting football team. In both cases Albert was outperformed by a friend, yet his responses to those performances were totally opposite in character. How might we understand this?

The SEM model starts with the assumption that people want to feel good about themselves: that is, they want to maintain a positive self-evaluation. The model further assumes that the *performance* of others, particularly *close others*, is consequential to self-evaluation. The *self-relevance* of a performance domain is also an important determinant of our response to another's performance. For each of us, it is important to be successful in a few particular areas but not so important to be particularly good in many other areas. In a word, some performance domains are more *relevant* to our self-definition than are other areas. For example, Albert plays the piano but does not think of himself as a musician. Music is low in relevance for him. On the other hand, he cares very much about his performance on the football field. Football is high in relevance.

The outstanding performance of others affects us through two separate processes: the *comparison process* and the *reflection process*. The more self-relevant is a particular domain the more important is the comparison process (relative to the reflection process). When a friend or relative performs better in a highly self-relevant domain, then self-evaluation is likely to suffer by comparison. Such threat via comparison will produce negative feelings. On the other hand, if the performance domain is low in self-relevance, then the reflection process is likely to be more important (relative to the comparison process). The outstanding performance of a friend or relative in a low-relevance domain can boost self-evaluation via "basking in reflected glory." Such basking will produce positive feelings.

473

Research on the SEM model. Research on the SEM model focuses on three variables that can be measured and/or manipulated: (1) another's *performance* relative to the self. The effects we noted make sense only if the other outperforms the self. One will not suffer by comparison if one is not outperformed. And there is little to be gained by basking in the reflected glory of someone whose performance is mediocre. A second variable is closeness. *Closeness* refers to the extent to which self and other are "connected" to one another. The connection can be affective, as friends are closer than strangers; it can be genetic, as relatives are closer than strangers. The connection can even result from the changing context. Two women, even strangers, will be closer to one another in a class with 20 men than in a class with 20 other women. Two people from Asheville, North Carolina, will be closer to one another in Dallas, Texas, than in Asheville. Closeness is important because it intensifies the comparison and reflection experience. For example, we are less likely to compare ourselves to people with whom we have little or no connection, and the results of such comparison are likely to be less extreme. The same is true for reflection. One can almost see the pride and feel the reflected joy when the mother introduces her son: "Meet my son the doctor." All of those feelings are absent when the mother introduces a person to whom she has little connection: "Meet John Smith the doctor." The third variable that is either measured or manipulated in SEM research is the *relevance* of the performance domain to one's own self-definition. As noted, relevance is crucial because it determines the relative importance of the reflection and comparison process. When the performance domain is highly relevant, then the good performance of a close other is likely to result in comparison and a threat to self-evaluation; when the performance domain is low in personal relevance, then the good performance of a close other is likely to result in reflection and a boost to self-evaluation.

Predictions. The underlying assumption of the SEM model is that people behave in ways that tend to maintain a positive self-evaluation. This assumption allows predictions regarding performance, closeness, and relevance. If any two of these variables are fixed, then one can make unambiguous predictions regarding behavior that will impact the third variable. Let us focus on what happens to each of the three variables in turn when the other two variables are fixed.

Often we can affect the *performance* of another person. We can facilitate his/her performance by helping, or we can hinder his/her performance by creating difficulties that he/she must overcome. When will we help and when will we hinder the performance of another? The SEM model suggests that the answer depends on the relevance of the performance domain and the closeness of the other: When relevance is high, self will suffer via comparison to another who performs well, particularly if that other person is psychologically close. If we wish to maintain a positive self-evaluation, then, perhaps surprisingly, when relevance is high, we may be *less* motivated to help a close other, such as a friend, than a distant other, such as a stranger. On the other hand, low relevance creates the opportunity to bask in the reflected glory of another's good performance, particularly if that other is close. This leads to the expectation that when relevance is low, we will be more motivated to enhance the performance of a close other than the performance of a distant other.

An experiment conducted by Tesser and Smith tested these predictions. Each participant was required to take a friend to the laboratory and each session included two friendship pairs. The pairs were strangers to one another. Each participant, in turn, was required to guess target words on the basis of clues given by the other three players. Each of the three other players anonymously selected clues from a list of clues graded for difficulty. The experimenter selected from among these clues on each round of the task. Half of the participants were in a high-relevance condition. They were led to believe that performance on the task was related to such traits as verbal ability and intelligence; participants in the low-relevance condition were told that is spite of the verbal nature of the game, research had shown that it was unrelated to such traits as verbal ability and intelligence. In sum, each participant had an opportunity to affect the performance of a friend and of a stranger on a task that was either high or low in relevance. If he/she wanted to facilitate the other's performance, he/she could give clues that made it easy to guess the target word; if he/she wanted to hinder the other's performance, he/she could select difficult clues. The results were just as predicted by the SEM model. When the task was highly relevant, participants were more helpful (gave easier clues) to a stranger than they were to their friend; when the task was low in relevance, people were more helpful to their friend than to the stranger.

What about *closeness*? When will we want to be more connected to another? When will we try to cut the ties that connect us? The SEM model predicts that the answers to these questions depend on the state of the other two variables, relevance and performance. When relevance is high, the comparison process is prepotent. A better-performing other is threatening. Since closeness intensifies this threat, the better another's performance, the greater the motivation to reduce closeness. When relevance is low, the reflection process is prepotent. When another outperforms us, there is an opportunity for reflection, particularly when the other is close. Thus, the model predicts that when relevance is low, the better the other's performance the greater the motivation to increase closeness.

This prediction was tested by Pleban and Tesser. There were two participants in each session; a real participant and a participant who worked for the experimenter posing as a real participant. At the beginning of the session participants received a list of topics such as movies, current events, hunting and fishing, and American history. For each topic they independently and privately indicated how knowledgeable they were and the extent to which it was important for them to be particularly knowledgeable. These ratings served as an index of the personal relevance of each domain. The two participants then participated in a "college bowl" quiz on one of the topics. For half of the real participants, the topic was one that they

indicated was highly relevant; for the others, it was a topic that was low in relevance. The experimenter asked topical questions. The speed and correctness of the answers by each participant determined his/her score. By prearrangement, the person posing as a participant outperformed some of the participants and did not outperform the others. Finally, participants went into a second room to fill out additional questionnaires. The posed participant always entered the second room first and always sat in the same seat. The experimenter surreptitiously literally measured how close the real participant sat to the posed participant. The SEM prediction was confirmed. When the college bowl quiz was on a high-relevance topic, the better the performance of the posed participant, the farther away from the posed participant the real participant sat. When the college bowl quiz was on a topic of low relevance, the better the posed participant's performance, the closer to the posed participant the real participant sat.

Relevance. Can the performance of another affect the way we think about ourselves? Can it increase or decrease the importance of a performance domain to our own self-definition? The SEM model suggests that it can. If we claim a performance domain to be self-relevant, then we are likely to suffer by the better performance of another, particularly a close other. So, the better another's performance the more we should be motivated to reduce the self-relevance of the performance domain, and this should be particularly the case when the other person is psychologically close.

Tesser and Paulhus tested this prediction. Pairs of participants were scheduled for the same session. To vary closeness, half of the participants were told that they were scheduled at the same time because previous information indicated that they were very similar to one another; the remaining participants were told that they were scheduled for the same session because they had almost nothing in common. Their task was to work on a new personality measure, a dimension called "Cognitive Perceptual Integration" or CPI (CPI is a fictitious dimension invented so that participants had no prior standing on it). The participants then worked on a computer task that purported to measure CPI. Then they were given feedback on the CPI test: half the participants were told that they outperformed the other; half were told that the other outperformed them. They then indicated the personal importance of CPI in an interview and on a questionnaire. Finally, each participant was left alone in a booth waiting. In the booth were two binders: one contained biographies of people high in CPI; the other contained biographies of people low in CPI. The experimenter surreptitiously measured the amount of time participants read about people high in CPI relative to the amount of time they read about people low in CPI. Again the SEM model predictions were validated. Participants who believed that they were outperformed by the other participant said that CPI was less important to them and spent less time reading the high-CPI biographies than participants who believed that they outperformed their partner. Importantly, this relationship was more pronounced when the partner was described as similar (close) rather than dissimilar.

SEM and emotions. The SEM model does a powerful job of predicting overt behavior. Often these overt changes in behavior are associated with recognizable emotions. For example, Tesser and Collins found that when people are asked to recall their feelings when outperformed by another, they recall anger, disgust, envy, frustration, jealousy, sadness, and shame. This is particularly the case when the performance domain is relevant to the self. On the other hand, outperforming another leads to the recollection of emotions like happiness, hope, and pride. Again, this is particularly the case when the performance domain is relevant to the self.

Sometimes the feelings that we experience in connection with a close other's outstanding performance are not clearly recognized. Indeed they may not even be consciously processed. For example, Tesser, Millar, and Moore videotaped the faces of people given feedback regarding the better or poorer performance (compared to

the self) of either a friend or a stranger on a task that was either high or low in relevance. Participants rated their mood in connection with these patterns of feedback. Videotapes of the face were also taken because positive and negative feelings can be distinguished in facial expressions and because such feelings may be available for viewing even when they are fleeting and even when the person is unaware of them. The findings from the study are too complicated to describe completely here. However, the point to be made is that the emotions rated from the facial displays more closely followed even the subtle predictions of the SEM model than did the self-rated emotions.

Why is there a disconnect between what the body indicates and verbal self-reports? Self-reports are more vulnerable to at least two biases: social desirability and "naïve theories." For example, it may be socially undesirable to admit or even to believe that one feels bad upon learning that a friend did well. Such reports may be suppressed or perhaps even repressed. Also, since feelings in real situations are often complex, fleeting and unrecognizable, our naïve theories of how we are likely to feel can guide our verbal responses. For example, we might think that it is likely that we experience positive emotions when we do well and negative emotions when we do poorly; positive emotions when friends do well and negative emotions when they do poorly. Such theories have a grain of truth, but they lack the subtlety of prediction embodied in a formal model such as the SEM model.

The extended SEM model. The extended SEM model was developed by Beach and Tesser in order to recognize the impact of committed relationships on SEM dynamics. The original SEM model focused on the actor's concern with maintaining his or her own self-evaluation. However, people in committed relationships must be concerned with maintaining the relationship as well. And one's partner is subject to the same SEM dynamics as the self. Outperforming a committed partner in a domain that is highly self-relevant may be personally satisfying, but if the domain is also relevant to the partner, it can threaten the partner and, ultimately, the relationship. Thus, the joy associated with doing well on a relevant activity will be muted by the potential threat to one's partner and to the relationship. On the other hand, outperforming a partner on a task that has little self-relevance to the partner provides the partner with the opportunity to bask. In this case, both members of the dyad can take joy in the outcome.

This analysis has at least two important implications. First, in committed relationships one's response to a performance inequality will be determined not only by the relevance to the self but also by the relevance to one's partner. Second, if people are motivated to maintain their own self-evaluation and to help protect the self-evaluation of their partner, then we would expect to find a *complementary* distribution of relevance and performance in committed relationships. In domains where there are consistent, noticeable differences in performance, relevance should be high for the better-performing partner; relevance should be low for the poorer-performing partner. Such a distribution provides for positive affective outcomes for both partners via comparison and via reflection.

Several empirical studies using married couples have confirmed both expectations. (1) When marital partners perform on the same task, then the affective response of each partner is determined by own relative performance, relevance to self, *and* relevance to partner. (2) The kind of complementary distribution of performance and relevance described also tends to emerge between marital partners. Moreover, the greater the reported marital satisfaction the more pronounced is this complementary distribution.   – AT

self-fulfilling prophecy

n. Any prediction which comes true as a result of having been made. Thus a teacher who believes her/his students are intelligent will behave so as to have them learn more while a teacher who believes they are dull will teach so that they learn less.

self-guides

n. Self-guides are self-directive standards. These self-directive standards are a major source of people's emotions and motivation, particularly ideal self-guides representing a person's hopes, wishes, and aspirations and ought self-guides representing a person's beliefs about his or her duties, responsibilities, and obligations. They both directly prompt action as desired end states (i.e., goals to be attained) and, through their use in self-evaluation (i.e., standards to be met), arouse emotions that are themselves motivating.

Self-guides vary in strength. Socialization is a major determinant of self-guide strength. Through interacting with significant others, individuals develop self-other contingency knowledge regarding which kinds of self-attributes others respond to positively and which kinds others respond to negatively. There are four features of socialization that strengthen the self-other contingency knowledge underlying self-guides: (1) frequency of exposure to messages about self-other contingency, (2) consistency of messages, (3) clarity of messages, and (4) significance of messages (i.e., association with important outcomes). There are different modes of strong socialization that produce either strong ideal self-guides or strong ought self-guides. Strong ideal self-guides are produced by interactions with significant others that involve bolstering and supportiveness, as well as love withdrawal for failure to meet an ideal self-guide. Strong ought self-guides are produced by interactions with significant others that involve protection and safeguarding, as well as punishment and criticism for failure to meet an ought self-guide.

When self-guides are strong from socialization, they have high chronic accessibility. They predominate in self-regulation for years. Self-guides can also have high accessibility momentarily by being activated or primed in a particular situation. Success and failure in meeting different strong self-guides arouse different emotions. When people's representation of what they are currently like, that is, their actual-self representation, is congruent with or matches one of their ideal self-guides, they experience cheerfulness-related emotions, such as feeling happy or joyful. When people's representation of their actual self-representation is discrepant (a mismatch) with one of their ideal self-guides, they experience dejection-related emotions, such as feeling sad or discouraged. When people's representation of their actual self-representation is congruent with one of their ought self-guides, they experience quiescence-related emotions, such as feeling calm or relaxed. When people's representation of their actual self-representation is discrepant with one of their ought self-guides, they experience agitation-related emotions, such as feeling nervous or worried.

The motives of people also differ, depending on which type of strong self-guide predominates. When strong ideal self-guides predominate, people have a promotion focus on accomplishment and advancement. They prefer to use eager strategic means to make decisions and perform tasks. They appraise the world and remember past events in terms of the presence of positive outcomes (gains) and the absence of positive outcomes (non-gains). When strong ought self-guides predominate, people have a prevention focus on safety and security. They prefer to use vigilant strategic means to make decisions and perform tasks. They appraise the world and remember past events in terms of the absence of negative outcomes (nonlosses) and the presence of negative outcomes (losses).

There are trade-offs, that is, benefits and costs, to having strong self-guides. On the one hand, individuals with strong self-guides are highly motivated to attain those desired end states and are generally more successful in attaining them. Thus, individuals with strong self-guides generally have fewer discrepancies between their actual self and their self-guides. On the other hand, individuals with strong self-guides are highly motivated to evaluate themselves in relation to these self-guides and to have strong emotional reactions to their success or failure in meeting these self-guides. Thus, individuals with strong self-guides generally suffer more emotionally from whatever discrepancies they do have. — ETH

self-handicapping

n. The creation of an excuse for failure by imposing a limitation on oneself. Thus a student who believes he/she is not going to get a good grade on a test may fail to study for the test, thus having an excuse for failure.

self-identity ▶ *See* IDENTITY

self-image ▶ *See* SELF-CONSTRUAL

self-interest

n. One's individual benefit or advantage in any form; often used monetarily.

selfish gene

n. A way of describing individual genes as if they were self-interested in competition with other genes for replication and multiplication. This simplification of natural selection ignores organism and population levels of selection, in which large groups of genes are simultaneously selected, and the dependence of some genes on others for their biological utility.

self-looking glass concept

n. An understanding of oneself from other people's perceptions and evaluations rather than one centered on one's own experience.

self-monitoring

Definition. n. Self-monitoring refers to a person's typical level of being sensitive to, and behaving in line with, signals provided in any given situation. For example, people are expected to behave quite differently during a church service than at the ice cream social following the service. Most people are aware of the expected behavior in each of these situations and adjust their behavior accordingly. In other words, they understand that they should sit still and remain silent through the majority of the church ceremony but become animated and talkative at the social. This suggests that most people possess some basic level of the ability to self-monitor.

However, people differ in the likelihood they will respond to more subtle clues. Some individuals (known as high self-monitors) are extremely sensitive to signals provided in a situation and consistently change their behavior to make the best possible impression on others. Conversely, some individuals (known as low self-monitors) rarely adjust their behavior to fit such sensitive cues provided in a situation, choosing to use their own preferences to guide the way they behave across situations. High self-monitors can be thought of as "social chameleons" while low self-monitors can be thought of as consistent individuals.

Development and details. The idea that individuals vary in the extent to which they monitor their social behavior was introduced in 1974 by the social psychologist Mark Snyder. At this time, Snyder introduced a 25-item true/false personality test to determine whether individuals tended to be high or low self-monitors. In the course of determining whether the test was measuring a real personality characteristic, it was administered to different groups of people who would be believed to possess traits expected of high versus low self-monitors. In particular, it was administered to actors and patients in mental health institutions. As expected, actors received scores identifying them as extremely high self-monitors, because they are skilled in adopting various personas and changing their behavior in front of audiences. Also as expected, individuals in mental health institutions received scores identifying them as extremely low self-monitors, as they were likely to have been institutionalized because of their failure to behave in line with social expectations over many situations.

Although the original self-monitoring test was administered to individuals at the extremes of the self-monitoring spectrum, most people in more typical populations can be identified as high or low self-monitors to a lesser extent. For example, items on the self-monitoring scale to which a high self-monitoring person is likely to agree include "I would probably make a good actor" and "I may deceive people by being friendly when I really dislike them," while a low self-monitoring individual is likely to agree with statements such as "I can only argue for ideas which I already believe" and "I would not change my opinions (or the way I do things) in order to please someone or win his or her favor." It is

important to note that although in the presented examples being a low self-monitor may appear to be better (more honest, etc.) than being a high self-monitor, self-monitoring is neither a particularly good nor bad attribute. Having either high or low self-monitoring tendencies can be beneficial in different situations. So, for example, high self-monitors tend to be socially sensitive (which tends to be a good attribute), whereas low self-monitors can be somewhat rigid.

The self-monitoring concept has been a useful tool for psychologists who try to predict behavior. Social psychologists have long believed that attitudes predict behavior, and some research has supported this notion. However, in actuality, it is not always possible to predict behavior just by knowing a person's attitudes. Consider the behavior of volunteering to help a community organization. If asked, most people would indicate a positive attitude toward volunteering (for example, they believe it is important to volunteer some free time for charitable causes). However, only a small percentage of those expressing this attitude are likely to sign up for volunteer work.

Not surprisingly, researchers who have asked participants to complete the self-monitoring instrument have found that attitudes of low self-monitors (which tend to be stable because they are driven by internal factors) are more likely to predict behavior than are attitudes of high self-monitors (which tend to change as a function of the social situation). Therefore, a low self-monitoring individual may be more likely to volunteer if he or she indicates a positive attitude toward volunteering than a high self-monitor, whose attitude may be more subject to change. One possible reason for this may be that low self-monitors are simply more aware of their attitudes because they refer to them more frequently than do high self-monitors, who are more likely to refer to the social cues surrounding them when describing their preferences.

This does not mean that high self-monitors are not capable of behaving in a manner consistent with their attitudes. For example, if they are told that attitudes should predict behavior, then they are more likely to behave in line with a previously stated attitude. However, this demonstrates the fact that high self-monitoring individuals tend to look to a social situation to determine their behavior, in that they realize they would not be perceived positively by others if their behavior did not reflect their attitude.

Examples. The self-monitoring personality characteristic is important in a variety of real-world situations, including advertising and interpersonal relationships. For example, advertisers aim to interest different types of individuals in purchasing a product. Not surprisingly, low self-monitors are interested in products that are advertised to be of high quality and to perform reliably well according to their purpose. On the other hand, high self-monitors tend to respond more favorably to advertisements suggesting that owning a particular product will improve their image. For example, low self-monitoring consumers are likely to respond well to an advertisement touting a particular brand of car as being the most reliable form of transportation, while high self-monitoring consumers are likely to respond well to an advertisement claiming that owning a particular car will make others "take notice" of them when they are driving it.

In addition, individuals exhibiting different levels of self-monitoring differ in the type of information they use when selecting individuals to work with, become friends with, and date. High self-monitors place a greater emphasis on the physical appearance of a potential job applicant when deciding whom to hire than do low self-monitors. Further, they are more likely to believe they can pretend to be interested in a potential romantic partner, and they are more skilled at recognizing when another individual is merely trying to flatter them through praise. Alternatively, individuals scoring low on the self-monitoring scale tend to select potential workers on the basis of how they perceive their personalities. Further, they select friends and romantic partners on the basis of common values and experience deeper, longer-lasting relationships.
— AEC, LAB

Self-Monitoring Scale
n. A 25-item true-false scale intended to predict the degree to which individuals differ in the degree to which they watch others to see how they are being evaluated and conform their behavior to fit the desires of others. Low scorers on the test are believed to act more from inner feelings and beliefs than do high scorers.

self-perception
n. A person's experience of himself/herself and beliefs about himself/herself including physical, behavioral, and mental aspects derived from reflection on his or her experience of the self, both independently of others and in relation to others.

self-perception theory
n. A theory that supposes that people have limited access to their own attitudes, beliefs, opinions, characteristics, and mental states and so make inferences about themselves from observing themselves rather than reporting directly from those processes. It is often used as an alternative to cognitive dissonance in explaining social behavior.

self-presentation
n. The management of the impressions one makes on others by means of enacting identifiable roles so that others will see him or her in the ways in which he/she would like to be thought of by the individual or group with whom he/she is interacting. This is often used as an explanation for the observation that any individual's behavior changes when interacting with different people.

self-psychology
n. A neo-psychoanalytic approach to psychology elaborated by Heinz Kohut, which is primarily concerned with the experience of self in social relationships; it suggests that relationships, particularly with caregivers in infancy, are responsible for mental health and neurosis and empathic connection. Relationships, rather than analysis, are emphasized in therapy.

self-reference effect
n. (SRE) A term coined by Rogers, Kuiper, and Kirker (1977) referring to the advantage

in recall or recognition enjoyed by material encoded with respect to the self, compared to material analyzed for its orthographic, phonemic, or semantic properties. Within the framework of a "depth of processing" view of memory, the SRE was interpreted as indicating that the self was a highly, perhaps uniquely, elaborate knowledge structure. The SRE procedure has also been employed in neuroimaging studies that sought to locate the neural substrates of the self and self-referent processing. Unfortunately, subsequent research revealed that a similar advantage was obtained for material encoded with respect to other people. More critically, the SRE proved to be an artifact of organizational activity incidental to self-referent processing. The self may be a highly elaborate cognitive structure, but this is not demonstrated by the SRE.   – JFK

self-regulation

n. The process of exercising control over one's body and mind through self monitoring the aspects of concern and then acting so as to obtain the desired outcomes. Thus a person who wants to become less anxious in social situations may learn relaxation techniques, monitor his/her anxiety levels in different social situations, and practice relaxation in those situations so as to lower the anxiety until his/her habitual pattern of response is altered to a satisfying degree.

self-reinforcement

n. Self-reinforcement entails motivation and regulation of one's behavior through self-directed consequences. Self-reinforcement is rooted in personal standards of merit against which people judge their performances.

Self-reinforcement operates mainly through its motivational function. In the case of tangible self-motivators, people induce themselves to do things they would otherwise put off or avoid altogether by making tangible rewards conditional on given performance attainments. Self-evaluative reactions to one's performances serve as even more influential guides and regulators of one's behavior. The self-evaluative incentives take the form of anticipated self-satisfaction for attainments that fulfill valued standards and discontent with substandard performances. Human behavior is governed by the interplay of extrinsic and self-evaluative consequences. External outcomes are most likely to wield influence when they are compatible with self-evaluative ones. People experience conflicts of outcomes when they are rewarded for behavior they personally devalue. Another type of conflict arises when individuals are punished for activities they value highly. The relative strength of external and self-evaluative outcomes determines whether given courses of actions are pursued or abandoned.   – AB

self-report data

n. Any information gathered that reflects individuals' opinions about themselves. Attitude scales and most personality tests use self-reports as their data source, as do scales which measure personal reactions which are not observable by others, such as pain scales and taste preferences.

self-schema

n. **1.** In cognitive therapy, an idea about the self which may be negative and irrational and thus bring about ineffectual or self-defeating behavior and negative feelings; it is sometimes not modified by contradictory information but may be altered in a more realistic and effective way through conscious examination and reality testing. **2.** An organized mental representation of the self structured so as to make it readily accessible in information processing.

self-selected groups design

n. A quasi-experimental plan for research in which subjects select the groups to which they belong or the treatment to which they will be subjected, often using preexisting groups. Comparisons are made between group means on a dependent variable; however, causal attributions based on the comparisons are questionable because of the increased likelihood that intervening variables affect the relationships between independent and dependent variables, as with other nonrandom methods of group assignment.

self-selected sample

n. Any group of research subjects who choose to participate rather than being randomly chosen; the subjects are likely to be different in some important aspects from individuals who do not choose to participate, making interpretation of results problematic.

self-serving biases

n. Self-serving biases are a collection of motivated cognitive strategies that allow an individual to feel good about himself/herself, either for preservation of the positive view of the self or as a reaction to a threat to self-esteem. Examples of self-serving biases include attributing one's successes to the self and one's failures to external sources, perceiving oneself as being more responsible for a successful project than other group members, and perceiving oneself as better than average on desirable traits or characteristics.

— EWMA, CYC

▶ *See also* **BASKING IN REFLECTED GLORY, SELF-ESTEEM, SELF-HANDICAPPING,** *and* **UNREALISTIC OPTIMISM**

self-system

n. In the theories of Harry Stack Sullivan, the stable aspects of the personality resulting from early childhood interactions with parents and other older persons in which socially desirable ideas and actions tend to be retained and socially disapproved actions and thoughts blocked out.

self-verification theory

n. Self-verification theory proposes that once people develop firmly held beliefs about themselves, these self-views become important in their efforts to make sense of their world and guide behavior. People therefore come to prefer that others see them as they see themselves (e.g., those who see themselves as relatively dominant, intelligent, or unsociable want others to see them as such). Among people with positive self-views, the desire for self-verification works together with another important motive, the desire for positive, self-enhancing evaluations. In contrast, for those with negative self-views (including those with low self-esteem and depression), their desire for self-verification will encourage them to seek negative evaluations. When self-verification strivings override self-enhancement strivings, people with negative self-views will seek and embrace negative evaluations, a tendency that may cause them to foreclose possibilities that would lead to happier, more satisfying lives.

— WBS

semantic differential

n. A procedure for measuring the connotative meaning of words, ideas, or attitudes in which subjects are asked to rate the object under consideration on a series of 7-point polar scales, such as good-bad, active-passive, and strong-weak. Factor analytic studies of meaning suggest that there are three basic dimensions of affective meaning, which have been called valuation, activity, and potency, as in the scales mentioned.

semantic encoding

n. A theoretical mental transformation of experiential data into nodes or units of meaning, as opposed to perceptual characteristics.

semantic feature

n. A term adopted in the componential analysis approach to semantics to refer to a minimal contrastive element of a word's meaning. For example, the words *man*, *woman*, *boy*, and *girl* can be represented as a combination of features "male," "adult," and "human" (man: +MALE, +ADULT, +HUMAN). It is a compact and visual way of representing meaning, but it cannot provide an exhaustive description of the meaning of any word. It only accounts for those aspects which are in systematic opposition to other words in a given set.

The idea that word meanings can be represented via simpler concepts is also adopted in the natural semantic metalanguage approach developed by Anna Wierzbicka and Cliff Goddard. It proposes an inventory of 65 empirically tested indefinable human concepts, which can be used to formulate reductive paraphrases of word meanings in any language. The use of semantic primes like *someone, people, thing, do, good, bad, feel, because, words,* and *say* has enabled the meanings of terms from numerous semantic domains to be described successfully.   – AG

semantic generalization

n. A form of generalization in classical conditioning in which a conditioned stimulus is generalized to other stimuli on the basis of meaning rather than perceptual characteristics. Thus if a person learns to react to the word *red* written on a card with a particular response, he/she is likely to react similarly but with diminished magnitude to a red-colored card.

semantic memory

n. **1.** The capacity to recall or use general knowledge divorced from the circumstances in which it was learned. **2.** The capacity to recall or use the meanings of words.

semantic priming

n. Altering the reaction of subjects to a target stimulus by presenting a stimulus with a related meaning immediately prior to presenting the target stimulus.

semantics

n. Semantics is the study of meaning in language. In the logical tradition, semantics concerns the relationship between linguistic expressions and the phenomena in the world to which they refer and considers the conditions under which such expressions can be regarded as true or false. The linguistic or conceptual tradition, on the other hand, refers to the meaning of an expression as a structured idea or "concept" in the mind of the person using that expression. Studies in linguistic semantics demonstrate that there exists considerable cross-linguistic variation in the conceptual content of the lexicon, especially in areas such as emotions, values, speech acts, motion, and artifacts. However, it is also possible to identify a set of universal meanings (or semantic primes) which are found across all languages. Semantic studies create a window onto conceptualization and cognition and provide valuable findings for cultural and cross-cultural psychology, psycholinguistics, bilingualism, and cognitive linguistics.   – AG

▶ *See* **SEMANTIC FEATURE**

seminal vesicles

n. The two pouches about 3 inches long in human males which secrete and store most of the fluid in ejaculate and are located between the bladder and the rectum and connected to the ejaculatory duct of the prostate gland. The fluid secreted by the seminal vesicles contains proteins, enzymes, fructose, and other nutrients. The fructose provides nutrient energy for the spermatozoa as they travel through the female reproductive system to the ovaries.

semiotics

n. The study of signs in both verbal and non-verbal forms and the ways they communicate meaning among humans, including facial expressions, personal distance, touching, gestures, and kinesics, as well as oral and written language structures.

semipartial correlation

n. The correlation of two variables with the variance of one or more other variables mathematically removed from only one of the variables. Also called part correlation.

semipermeable membrane

n. Any thin tissue which forms a boundary between biological structures and through which some material can pass and other material cannot pass. Typically some ions can diffuse through the barrier while other ions and larger particles cannot cross it. Thus nerve cell membranes are semipermeable, allowing different proportions of sodium and potassium ions into the cell and creating an electric potential or electrical difference across the membrane, which creates an electrical impulse when the permeability changes in a wave like motion.

senile dementia ▶ *See* **DEMENTIA**

senile plaque

n. Senile plaques, also known as amyloid or neuritic plaques, are concentrations of amyloid protein and dead nerve cells in the brain. This buildup interrupts the communication between neurons and healthy brain cells, disrupting the brain's proper functioning.

Senile plaques develop naturally with increasing age, but persons with Alzheimer's disease develop significantly more senile plaques. These plaques often collect in areas of the brain responsible for memory and learning, partially explaining the memory loss evident among persons with Alzheimer's disease. Because of the correlation between age and increasing numbers of plaques, it is possible to develop a threshold of Alzheimer's disease likelihood. The presence of even a few plaques in a middle-aged adult may strongly suggest the presence of Alzheimer's disease. Conversely, many more plaques must exist in the brain of an elderly person to justify the diagnosis of Alzheimer's disease. — TJM

sensation
n. **1.** The subjective experience of the stimulation of a sensory organ by an appropriate source of energy, such as light striking the eye or a stick touching the skin. **2.** The process of gathering information through the sensory organs. **3.** An exciting event.

sensation seeking
n. The tendency to search out exciting or thrilling experiences whose strength differs measurably among individuals in many cultures.

sense modality
n. Each of the channels through which human beings gain information about the world around them as well as about themselves, including sight, hearing, smell, taste, and several varieties of touch, including pressure, pain, temperature, and body position or kinesthesis and equilibrium.

sense organ
n. Any biological structure which gathers information from the world and transmits it to the central nervous system, such as the eye or the ear.

sensitization
n. A process of making a sensory organ or the mind more likely to react to a stimulus from a given class of stimuli, usually after repeated exposure to the class of stimuli. Thus

regularly stretching muscles while noticing the sensations of stretching makes one more sensitive to sensations in the muscles, and learning to tell different kinds of birds apart makes one more likely to notice birds in general.

sensorimotor
adj. Of or relating to the portions of the cortex that process and integrate information from the senses with motor impulses guided by feedback.

sensorimotor cortex
n. The areas of cerebral cortex immediately in front of and behind the central sulcus in each hemisphere which are central in controlling voluntary movement and processing bodily sensations.

sensorimotor intelligence
n. In Piagetian psychology, knowledge gained through experience of the senses and motor interaction with objects in the external world, which characterizes the child's understanding in the first 2 years of life. During this period the child learns to adapt motor behavior to sensory input to accomplish his or her goals.

sensorimotor process
n. **1.** Any bodily movement initiated by environmental stimuli. **2.** The integration of vestibular and other sensory data to guide and control bodily movements.

sensorimotor stage
n. In Piagetian psychology, the first 2 years of life, in which knowledge is gained through experience of the senses and motor interaction with objects in the external world, during which the child learns to adapt motor behavior to sensory input to accomplish his or her goals.

sensory
adj. Of or relating to the channels through which humans or other organisms gain information about themselves and the world around them, including but not limited to vision, hearing, taste, touch, and smell.

sensory adaptation

n. A reduction in the responsiveness of a sensory cell, organ, or system following prolonged or intense stimulation. Thus the eye is less able to see dimly lit objects after exposure to bright light.

sensory cortex

n. In a general sense, cortical areas involved in receiving and processing sensory information, roughly corresponding to the retro-Rolandic cortex. In a more restricted sense, cortical areas involved in receiving and processing somatosensory information, roughly corresponding to the parietal lobe.   — A A

▶ *See also* **PRIMARY SOMATOSENSORY CORTEX** *and* **SOMATOSENSORY CORTEX**

sensory deprivation

n. The absence or marked reduction of input to the senses as would occur floating in a warm pool in a dark, silent room. In the absence of stimulation, the senses eventually seem to create false sensations in the form of hallucinations, delusions, and excessive reaction to small stimuli.

sensory information store

n. A hypothetical memory for data in each sensory channel which has a large capacity and a very short duration but which allows the integration of sensory input over short periods, thus enhancing clarity of perception and allowing selection of some information for further processing.

sensory memory

n. A hypothetical data storage in each sensory channel which has a large capacity and a very short duration but allows the integration of sensory input over short periods, thus enhancing clarity of perception and allowing selection of some information for further processing.

sensory nerve

n. Any neural pathway that conveys information from a sense organ to the central nervous system, such as the optic nerve.

sensory neuron

n. Any nerve cell that receives input from sensory receptor cells and sends information from the receptor toward the central nervous system.

sensory preconditioning

n. A form of classical conditioning in which two neutral stimuli, A and B, first are paired repeatedly, then one of the stimuli, A, is paired with an unconditioned stimulus such that a conditioned response comes to be evoked by it. If the stimulus B also evokes the conditioned response, then sensory preconditioning has occurred. Thus if a dog first is exposed to the pairing of a bright red light and a bell and later conditioned to salivate to the bell, if the red light also evokes salivation, then sensory preconditioning has occurred.

sensory projection area

n. Any area of the cerebral cortex to which information from the senses is directed. Thus the precentral gyrus of the brain is the most important projection area for bodily sense, the occipital lobe for vision, and a part of the superior temporal gyrus for hearing.

sensory register

n. A hypothetical data storage in each sensory channel which has a large capacity and a very short duration but allows the integration of sensory input over short periods, thus enhancing clarity of perception and allowing selection of some information for further processing. Also called sensory memory.

sensory threshold

n. The minimal magnitude a stimulus must reach in order to be reported as present 50% of the time by a subject. Thus a sound must reach a certain intensity before a person can hear it. Thresholds differ from person to person.

sentiment

n. Thoughts concerning feelings or emotions that are attached to objects or people. Thinking about a dog, for example, which one feels attached to and positive about may be a sentiment.

separation

n. Following the terminology proposed by John Berry, *separation* refers to a pattern of psychological acculturation in which one values the retention of the original cultural characteristics and identity and avoids contact with a new cultural group and the adoption of its cultural characteristics. This strategy for dealing with sustained intercultural contact can be initiated by the individual or imposed on the individual by the new cultural group with which he/she has contact. In the latter case the pattern is termed *segregation*.   – KN

separation anxiety

n. The normal state of alarm and arousal with nonspecific fears that children experience when faced with separation from their parent or other caregiver from the ages of 6 months to 3 years of age. It is most intense in the second 6 months of life and persists at lower levels beyond 3 years. Attachment theory deems this to be part of the attachment system which helps children maintain proximity to their caregivers and so increase the likelihood of their survival.

separation anxiety disorder

n. A psychological disorder of young children characterized by recurrent and excessive distress when faced with separation from an attachment figure such as a parent or leaving the home, persistent worry about losing the attachment figure, reluctance to go to school or otherwise be separated from an attachment figure, and being afraid to be alone or to go to sleep without an attachment figure. Children with this disorder also tend to have nightmares about being separated and to develop physical symptoms such as headaches or stomachaches when separated from attachment figures.

separation-individuation

n. In the object-relations theory of Margaret Mahler, the stage of development and process whereby infants begin to develop an understanding of themselves as an entity separate and independent of their mother and with a sense of autonomy.

serial anticipation method

n. A form of cued recall in verbal learning in which a subject is shown one word and asked to provide the next word in a list and then shown the correct word so that each trial has both test and training components. It is also used in paired associate learning, in which the subject attempts to recall the paired word when cued with the stimulus word and is then shown the correct word after responding.

serial learning

n. Any task that requires learning a list and recalling it in the correct order, as actors must learn their lines in correct order.

serial order effect

n. The observation that the first and last items in a learned list of items tend to be more accurately recalled than those in the middle of the list. Also called serial position effect.

serial position curve

n. A U-shaped graphical representation showing the relative frequency with which items in different positions on an item list are recalled. It usually has the position of an item on the horizontal axis and the likelihood or frequency with which it is remembered on the vertical axis.

serial position effect

n. The observation that the first and last items in a learned list of items tend to be more accurately recalled than those in the middle of the list.

serial processing

n. **1.** An approach to data processing in computer programming in which each task is accomplished one after another with no overlap in processing, as opposed to parallel processing, in which multiple tasks are being computed simultaneously. **2.** A kind of model of mental processes in humans or other animals which uses the serial processing idea from computer programming as a basic structure.

serial recall

n. Memory for items in a particular order, as the alphabet is usually recalled from *A* to *Z*.

serial reproduction

n. A technique for studying memory in which a person is read or told a short story or sees a picture and then tells the story to or draws it from memory for a second person, who then tells or draws it for a third person, and so on. At the end of the sequence, errors in the retelling or redrawing are recorded and analyzed. Usually some aspects of the story or picture are overemphasized while others are omitted and some elements simply added.

serotonergic

adj. Of or relating to the release of serotonin or the capacity to become excited by serotonin in nervous systems.

serotonin

n. A common neurotransmitter synthesized from the amino acid L-tryptophan. It is important in the raphe nucleus, reticular activating system, and most parts of the central nervous system, as well as in the digestive system and in the smooth muscles of the respiratory and cardiovascular systems. It has been implicated in arousal, emotion, sleep, appetite, pain, and the regulation of reflexes. Lack of serotonin is associated with sleep disorders, and selective serotonin reuptake inhibitors have been found to reduce anxiety and depression. Very high levels of serotonin as occur after ingesting LSD are associated with hallucinations and other psychedelic experiences. Also called 5-hydroxytryptamine.

serotonin reuptake inhibitor

n. Any of a family of drugs which selectively block several kinds of serotonin reuptake mechanisms, causing a rise in the levels of serotonin floating in the synaptic clefts at these sites. They are used as anxiolytics and antidepressants and include Prozac, Zoloft, Celexa, Lexapro, Luvox, Paxil, and Dapoxetine.

set point

n. **1.** A natural state of equilibrium to which biological systems tend to return if not prevented from doing so, as in the body's normal temperature of 98.6 degrees Fahrenheit. Some theorists have suggested that body weight has a set point and dieting causes only short-term weight loss in more than 95% of obese persons because the body adapts to the temporary shortage of food by slowing metabolism and then increasing consumption once the diet ends. **2.** The desired outcome in an information processing system such as the desired temperature on a thermostat.

set, response

n. **1.** In testing, a bias in which there is a tendency to answer in a systematic way that is unrelated to item content, such as using only the middle range of responses on a multiple-choice test or marking mostly true answers on a true-false scale. **2.** In general, a list of all possible or past responses from among which a response to a present situation is chosen, as in a basketball point guard's tendency to move to her/his right instead of the left when dribbling the ball.

seven plus or minus two

n. The normal item capacity of short-term memory. That is, most people can remember about seven items at a time for several seconds, although in some cases they will remember as many as nine and as few as five. Also called magic number seven.

severe mental retardation

n. The state of being markedly below normal in intellectual capacity so that measured IQ is four or five standard deviations below the mean in the range from 20 to 35. This is almost always due to brain malformation or trauma.

sex

n. **1.** The characteristics associated with reproductive status as male or female and especially sexual organs. Most people and complex animals can be classified clearly as belonging to one or the other sex, but a minority of all species are ambiguous in their biological sexuality and some species can switch from one sex to the other. **2.** The activities and processes associated with reproduction and with erotic pleasure in general as in having sex.

sex change

n. The process of changing an individual's body from hermaphroditic to primarily one sex or to change an individual who is primarily one sex to the other, which is usually accomplished by a combination of surgery and hormonal supplements.

sex characteristics, primary

n. The reproductive organs associated with one biological sex or the other, the most prominent organs of which are testes and a penis in the male and ovaries, a vagina, and a uterus in the female.

sex characteristics, secondary

n. Any feature associated with biological sex but not directly tied to reproduction, such as facial hair, tone of voice, waist-to-hip ratio, and breast development.

sex chromosome

n. A strand of DNA and proteins that carries the genetic predisposition to be male or female. They are often referred to as X and Y chromosomes as the shape of the female version looks like an X under a powerful microscope while the male version looks like a Y. All people have at least one X chromosome, and females have two X chromosomes while males have an X chromosome from their mother and a Y chromosome from their father.

sex difference

n. Any average or usual difference between male and female organisms. Primary and secondary sexual characteristics are the most obvious such differences, and many small differences in internal structures have been found to be correlated with sex. Instinctive and culturally learned behaviors also usually differ between males and females, although there is almost always overlap and anomaly in these behaviors among complex organisms. There is much debate as to which sex differences and how much of observed sex difference are due to genetic predisposition and which and how much to environmental influence and, in the case of humans, how much is individual choice.

sex role

n. The behaviors and patterns of activities in which those identified as men and women in a given culture may engage that are directly related to biological differences and the process of reproduction, as opposed to gender role, which refers to the gender-specific behaviors prescribed by their culture. Among humans there is clearly some interaction between biological sex and sex role, although many cultures have alternative forms of sex identities in which individuals of one biological sex enact many of the roles characteristic of or assigned to the other sex.

sex role development

n. The process of developing the behaviors and patterns of activities in which those identified as men and women in a given culture may engage that are directly related to biological differences and the process of reproduction. This usually results from an interaction of biological maturation, the expectations of the culture in which an individual is raised, and the individual's personal observations, understandings, and attempts to integrate them all with his or her understanding of the self.

sex role stereotype

n. A relatively stable and often oversimplified belief people have about what is usual and appropriate for individuals identified as a member of one sex or the other. Studies have shown cross-cultural agreement in such stereotypes, although cultures differ on the values placed on the different characteristics.

sex therapy

n. The treatment of sexual disorders, which is usually accomplished through a combination of information giving, psychological counseling, sensate focus, and behavioral training appropriate to the particular sexual dysfunction. Medications are available for some problems such as erectile dysfunction.

sexual abstinence
n. The avoidance of sexual interaction.

sexual anomaly
n. **1.** An abnormality of the reproductive system, such as presence of both male and female genitalia or the absence of complete genitalia. These conditions can come about through genetic abnormality; prenatal or postnatal poisoning, as by pesticides or herbicides such as Agent Orange; or other developmental problems. **2.** Any sexual paraphilia.

sexual deviation
n. Any sexual behavior significantly different from the norms within a culture or subculture. Within the mainstream culture of the United States this includes voyeurism, fetishism, bestiality, masochism, necrophilia, transvestitism, sadism, and exhibitionism, although all of these excepting necrophilia are within the mainstream of other cultures.

sexual dimorphism
n. The characteristic of some species including humans of having noticeable bodily differences between males and females.

sexual harassment
n. Any offensive behavior, including verbal and nonverbal behavior, that is perceived as an unwelcome sexual advance or demand. It can also refer to any unwelcome behavior that is directed toward a person because of his or her sex. The unwelcome behavior often interferes with daily routines and creates an intimidating, hostile, or offensive work environment.

sexual identity
n. A person's understanding of himself/herself as a sexual being, including awareness and recognition of biological sex roles, as a man is aware that he has the potential to impregnate women and knows the necessary behaviors, and a woman is aware of her capacity to bear children and has knowledge about behaviors that lead to pregnancy. Sexual identity is usually meant to include sexual orientation and personal affiliation with some aspects of cultural gender roles.

sexuality
n. **1.** The desire for and capacity to enjoy sexual pleasure. **2.** The activities and mental processes involved in giving and receiving sexual pleasure as well as enabling reproduction. **3.** In psychoanalysis, all forms of pleasure and especially those involving bodily stimulation. **4.** The particular sexual character or potency of an individual or culture.

sexual orientation
n. The moderately stable preference of the individual for some potential sexual partners over others, as a heterosexual would prefer a partner of the opposite sex, a homosexual would prefer a person of the same sex, and a bisexual might have no such preference.

sexual pain disorder
n. In both men and women, a recurrent or persistent pain in the genitals before, during, or after sexual intercourse which significantly interferes with normal sexual or interpersonal functioning which is called dyspareunia or, in women only, vaginismus, which is involuntary and uncomfortable contraction of the perineal muscles around the outside of the vagina when something is inserted in the vagina and which interferes with normal sexual or interpersonal functioning.

sexual preference
n. The moderately stable tendency of the individual for some potential sexual partners over others, as a heterosexual would choose a partner of the opposite sex, a homosexual would choose a person of the same sex, and a bisexual might choose either on different occasions.

sexual response cycle
n. The cycle of arousal (or excitement), plateau, orgasm, and resolution which is characteristic of sexual response in both men and women. The arousal phase is the first stage, which can result from any mental or physical stimulation. It is characterized by bodily

preparation for intercourse. In both sexes the arousal phase results in an increase in heart rate, breathing rate, and blood pressure. The nipples become erect in almost all women and the majority of men. Vasocongestion, or a reddening of the skin of the breasts, upper chest, and lower neck, occurs in most women and some men and typically lasts throughout the cycle. An increase in muscle tone occurs both voluntarily and involuntarily among both sexes. The external anal sphincter may also contract upon contact. It has been observed that the degree of the sex flush can predict the intensity of orgasm to follow. The sex flush typically disappears soon after orgasm occurs. In males, arousal phase includes erection of the penis, which may be lost and regained repeatedly. The testicles draw in and the scrotum can tense and thicken. In females the breasts very slightly increase in size, the labia tend to swell and spread, and the clitoris swells as the penis does. Vaginal lubrication is produced by the vasocongestion of the vaginal walls, the uterus elevates, and the inner two-thirds of the vagina expand. The plateau phase is the period of sexual excitement prior to orgasm, during which most sexual activity occurs. During this phase, the male urinary bladder closes and prevents urine from mixing with semen, muscles at the base of the penis begin steady rhythmic contraction, and seminal fluid begins to drip from the head of the penis. At this stage in females the areola and labia further increase in size, the clitoris withdraws slightly, and further lubrication is produced. The tissues of the outer third of the vagina swell considerably, and the muscles of the vagina wall tighten, reducing the diameter of the opening of the vagina. Orgasm is the conclusion of the plateau phase and consists of waves of pleasure along with short cycles of muscle contraction and relaxation in the lower pelvic muscles for both sexes, and women also have uterine and vaginal contractions. In men orgasm usually includes ejaculation of seminal fluid and the cessation of sexual desire. The resolution phase occurs after orgasm and is characterized by a deep sense of relaxation and return of all the physical symptoms of arousal to normal. Some individuals of both sexes experience a refractory period in which sexual excitement does not occur, and some find sexual stimulation temporarily aversive, although this is more common in males and women are often capable of multiple consecutive orgasms while only a minority of males can do so. The refractory period is variable and can last as long as 24 hours but is usually much shorter with appropriate stimulation.

sexual sadism

n. A paraphilia in which sexual arousal occurs as the result of inflicting physical or mental pain on another person as a means of exercising control over him or her. There is a gradation of sadism as many people enjoy exercising control and inflicting mild pain on their partners as in love bites or spanking, which are common sexual practices. Inflicting pain on a nonconsenting person or in a way that is not enjoyed by the other person or that causes marked personal distress or interpersonal problems becomes a sexual disorder.

sexual selection

n. An evolutionary mechanism in which males and females with particular characteristics are more successful in attracting mating partners, breeding, and rearing offspring, leading to an increase in those characteristics within a population. This is thought to be a cause of sexual dimorphism.

sexual violence

n. Physical force exerted for the purpose of violating, damaging, or abusing another person in a sexual context including rape, forcible sodomy, and sexual assault of all sorts.

shadow

n. In Jungian psychology, the archetype embodying the sexual and aggressive animal heritage of human beings which tends to be denied by the conscious mind and is sometimes projected onto disliked others.

shadowing

n. A task in cognitive psychology in which a person repeats aloud what he/she hears at the same time that he/she hears it. It has been used in studies of attention in dichotic listening tasks and in studies in which the effects of distracters are investigated.

shaman

n. A spiritual leader or priest in a small culture not usually respected by larger cultures. Shamanism involves an immense variety of traditional beliefs and practices which vary in different cultures. As in Christian and other larger cultures, shamans are often consulted to intercede with supernatural powers to heal the sick, obtain good fortune, or otherwise intervene in human affairs. The position of shamans is often a hereditary one in which the craft is passed from father to son or other close family member.

shamanism

n. Any of an immense variety of traditional beliefs and practices in small cultures, which vary considerably among cultures and are usually rejected and derided by larger cultures. As in Christian and other larger cultures, shamanism often involves intercession with supernatural powers to heal the sick, obtain good fortune, or otherwise intervene in human affairs.

shame

1. *n.* A markedly unpleasant emotion experienced when one has been exposed to the others as in some way deficient, which usually includes a strong sense of self-consciousness and desire to hide. **2.** *n.* A markedly unfortunate incident, as in the statement "It is a shame that child was killed by lightning." **3.** *v.* To expose a deficiency of others in a public way, thus subjecting them to the scorn or derision of others.

sham rage

n. Extreme and unfocused anger in response to any prominent stimulus regardless of its desirability which is characteristic of animals whose cerebrum, septum pellucidum, or ventromedial thalamus has been severely damaged or removed or in which the connection between the hypothalamus and pituitary gland has been severed. It has also been observed in humans with massive brain damage from carbon monoxide poisoning and from severe hypoglycemic shock.

shape constancy

n. The process by which perception of an object remains the same while the sensory data received from the object changes, as when we walk past a mailbox and the mailbox is perceived as maintaining a regular shape although the image from it that falls on our retina is rarely regular and changes markedly with our position.

shaping

n. In operant conditioning, the elicitation of a new behavior by reinforcing successive approximations of the behavior.

shared reality theory

n. The idea that our experience of reality is primarily a social or cultural construction jointly held by members of a particular social group, culture, or subculture.

Sheldon's constitutional psychology

n. The psychology of William H. Sheldon, who suggested that there were three basic breeds of humans called somatotypes in which body form and character are interrelated. The three somatotypes are endomorph, mesomorph, and ectomorph. Sheldon suggested these come about because of the dominance of the inner, middle, or outer portion of the embryonic tube as the individual matures. The inside of the embryonic tube matures into the inner organs of the body, and a person dominated by this physique tends to be soft, spherical, and dominated by the digestive process. The character of endomorphs tends to be warm, sociable, relaxed, tolerant, and affectionate, and they tend to grow fat because of their appreciation of food. Mesomorphs are dominated by the growth of the middle portion of the embryonic tube, which matures into muscle and bone. They tend to have wide shoulders, narrow waists, and a larger proportion of muscle in their bodies than the other somatotypes. The character of mesomorphs is active, aggressive, risk taking, callous, and dominant. Ectomorphs are dominated by the development of the outside of the embryonic tube, which develops into the skin and nervous system. They tend to be tall and skinny with a low muscle mass. The character of ectomorphs tends to be oversensitive, inhibited, tense, and avoidant, with a wish for concealment. Most humans are crossbreeds of the somatoypes as most dogs are crossbreeds, and so most people show a mixture of the body and personality traits associated with the different somatotypes, depending on their particular mix of somatotypes.

shock therapy
n. The intentional induction of convulsions through sending low-voltage electrical current through the head or administering insulin or other drugs, which is used to treat severe depression. The effectiveness of this treatment for most disorders has been widely questioned, and it has been found to be seldom useful except in some cases of intractable depression. Also called electroconvulsive therapy (ECT) and convulsive therapy.

short-term memory
n. A hypothesized information storage system of a limited capacity which allows material to be used in tasks requiring several seconds and to be repeated for maintenance, as in repeating a telephone number until it is dialed.

shyness
n. The trait or experience of being anxious, inhibited, and self-conscious in real or imagined social settings.

sibling
n. A brother or sister with the same parents.

sibling rivalry
n. Competition among brothers and sisters for dominance, attention, and affection from the parents; for the resources of the family; and for recognition and status in the world external to the family.

Sidman avoidance
n. An experimental procedure in which a brief shock or another aversive stimulus is given to a subject at fixed intervals without a warning signal whenever the subject does not engage in a specified action. If the subject engages in the specified action, then the shock is postponed for a fixed period.

Sidman avoidance conditioning
n. An experimental procedure in which a brief shock or another aversive stimulus is given to a subject at fixed intervals without a warning signal whenever the subject does not engage in a specified action. If the subject engages in the specified action, then the shock is postponed for a fixed period.

signal detection theory
n. A psychophysical approach to measuring the process of detecting signals of various strengths in the presence of noise. It assumes that both internal and external noise interferes with the detection of signal stimuli and that the receiver of the signals sets a stimulus magnitude level for deciding as to the presence of a signal, which determines the number of hits, misses, false alarms, and false positives that will occur at any given signal-to-noise ratio.

signal-to-noise ratio
n. The ratio of the magnitude of noise to the magnitude of a signal in a signal detection system.

significance ▶ *See* P-VALUE *and* SIGNIFICANCE TEST

significance level ▶ *See* P-VALUE *and* SIGNIFICANCE TEST

significance test
n. A significance test is a statistical analysis of whether or not a particular trend or effect exists in the population at large. The conventional test of significance is a determination of the probability that a trend in the data has been observed by chance, specifically whether that probability is 5% or less. Traditionally, significance testing has been a dichotomous yes or no decision. Many researchers have begun to question conventional significance testing, and many have adopted less rigid approaches to statistical significance. An emerging movement

in research is to examine closely the magnitude of trends in the data, which are commonly referred to as effect sizes. While effect sizes and significance tests are not necessarily at odds with each other, many argue that effect sizes are more meaningful than traditional dichotomous significance tests. The American Psychological Association has adopted a stance in favor of reporting and discussing effect size estimates alongside significance tests, and many editors of scholarly journals have begun to require that research reports include effect size estimates in addition to traditional significance tests. — MWP

▶ *See also* P-VALUE

significant difference

n. In statistics, a difference between two models which is unlikely to be due to chance and beyond a conventional limit on the acceptability of differences, which is usually set at 1 chance in 20.

significant other

n. **1.** Any person who has a significant influence on a person's self-image. **2.** A spouse or other person with whom a person is in a meaningful sexual relationship.

sign language

n. In a spoken language, a signal containing structural information is transmitted acoustically: decoded auditorily, encoded using the vocal apparatus. In a *sign language*, in contrast, structural information is transmitted via gestures that are decoded visually and encoded using hand shape, position, and movement, along with facial expressions and head and body position. Sign languages have full-fledged lexicons as well as complex grammars whose operations are based on principles subsumed under *universal grammar*. Signs can be combined into complex strings, as words are combined into sentences in spoken languages. Sign languages also have a prosodic component, to combine signs into phrases and separate phrases from each other, indicated by synchronous upper face markers (eyebrows, eye blinks) and head position or body orientation. — EMF

▶ *See also* AMERICAN SIGN LANGUAGE

sign stimulus

n. A set of stimuli that can serve to initiate a fixed action pattern in animals of a particular species in the appropriate circumstances. Thus graylag geese chicks will act to keep close to their mother when she moves away from them unless distracted by another stimulus. Also called releaser.

sign test

n. In statistics, a nonparametric test of the similarity in two sets of paired numbers in which each number is compared to the median, and the sign, positive, negative, or neutral, is recorded. The numbers of similar signs in the sets are compared to what would be expected by chance, and the null hypothesis that there is no difference between the groups is rejected when too many of the signs are dissimilar.

sign tracking

n. In learning theory, movement toward a stimulus that has been paired with a primary reinforcer.

silent pause

n. A moment in an ongoing conversation during which no party speaks. The meaning and usage of silent pauses vary considerably among language cultures and subcultures. In some it is taken as a sign of weakness and in others as a sign of strength or wisdom; it can be used as a sign of agreement or disagreement and many other things.

similarity-attraction hypothesis

n. The idea that we like people who are similar to us in characteristics as well as those who agree with our opinions.

similarity grouping law

n. The observation that in perceptual organization elements of a scene that appear similar tend to be grouped together so that the sequence XXXoooXXX appears to be three groups of things.

simple correlation

n. A mathematical index of linear association between two variables scaled so that 0 indicates no relationship and +1 indicates a perfect positive relationship while −1 indicates a perfect inverse relationship.

simple schizophrenia
n. One of the four main types of schizophrenia in Kraepelin's system of classification, which has the symptoms of social withdrawal, low motivation and initiative, and apathy which would today be called flattened affect. This system has been supplanted by the APA's DSM-IV-TR and the International Classification of Diseases (ICD), which use different and changing systems of classification.

simultaneous conditioning
n. In classical conditioning, a conditioning technique in which the conditioned and unconditioned stimuli are presented at the same time.

simultaneous matching to sample
n. A learning technique in which the subject is presented with a target stimulus and two or more other stimuli at the same time and must choose the target which matches the sample stimulus.

single blind
n. A research design in which the subject does not know which of the experimental treatments he/she receives.

single-blind study
n. A research project in which the subject does not know which of the experimental treatments he/she receives.

single-case design
n. Any of a large family of possible plans for a study used when there is only one individual involved. These almost always involve multiple observations over time, often with alternating treatments and baselines.

single-case experiment
n. Any of a large family of possible plans for a controlled study used when there is only one individual involved. These almost always involve multiple observations over time, often with alternating treatments and baselines.

single-subject research designs
n. Any of a large family of possible plans for a study used when there is only one individual involved. These almost always involve multiple observations over time, often with alternating treatments and baselines.

situational attribution
n. When attempting to explain a person's behavior (what is referred to in psychology as making an attribution for the person's behavior), a situational attribution is made when it is assumed that the person has behaved in such a way because of something very specific to the situation the person was in (rather than influenced by some part of his or her personality or other internal factors). Situational attributions are a special case of external attributions, and the two concepts are often confused. An external attribution refers to anything outside the person that is thought to influence the person's behavior. For example, if a student gets a bad grade on an exam, a person might make an external attribution like the following: "The student did poorly on the exam because life is not fair" or "It was just bad luck." These external attributions are due to something completely outside any person's control. A situational attribution is a specific case of an external attribution in that the cause of the behavior is outside the person's control. However, rather than explaining behavior as generally unfair or unlucky, situational attributions single out an element in the specific situation that caused the behavior. In the circumstances in the example, a person might make the following situational attribution: "The student did so poorly on the test because the teacher does not like him and graded him unfairly." In this instance the attribution is considered situational because it is due to something specific to that situation (the teacher's evaluating the student unfairly) rather than some general enduring quality about the world (which would be an external attribution).
— VKP, LAB

situational factor
n. Any environmental circumstance that may affect the outcome of a research project.

situational lay theories

n. Lay theories (also referred to as implicit, naïve, or intuitive theories) are the underlying beliefs about objects, people, or events that help to define an individual's subjective reality. Situational lay theories are lay theories that have been recently or temporarily activated in an individual's mind by cues in the environment.

Evidence from research in social, cognitive, and clinical psychology indicates that individuals with different lay theories often construe the same stimulus or event in strikingly different manners. For example, research by Carol Dweck and colleagues has focused on *entity theorists* (who hold that human attributes such as intelligence and moral character are largely fixed over time and across situations) and *incremental theorists* (who hold that such qualities are malleable and cultivable). Studies have shown that entity theorists (relative to incremental theorists) are more prone (a) to attribute an actor's behavior to underlying traits, (b) to attribute their own behavior to underlying traits, (c) to apply stereotypes to group members, and (d) to expect actors to display high behavioral consistency. These differences in attribution have been shown to underlie noteworthy differences in achievement motivation and person judgment. Importantly, these effects have been found whether the entity and incremental theories were assessed as chronic, personality structures (using the Implicit Theories Questionnaire) or were temporarily manipulated in the laboratory.

Lay theories have been situationally manipulated in several ways. In several studies, researchers randomly assigned participants to read one of two stimulus articles, ostensibly taken from a current psychology journal. One article touted the entity position by describing new longitudinal research indicating that personality attributes remain fixed from childhood through adulthood. The other touted the incremental position by describing research showing that personality attributes are malleable over time. Other researchers have manipulated the entity and incremental theories by having participants study a set of proverbs reflecting the entity view (e.g., "You can't teach an old dog new tricks") or the incremental view (e.g., "It's never too late to learn"). With both methods, those who were given the entity theory prime tended to make person judgments consistent with the entity theory and those given the incremental theory prime made judgments consistent with the incremental theory.

The finding that lay theories can be situationally manipulated has important implications. First, it appears that, at least in the short term, a person's chronic theory may be superseded. This implies relatively simple intervention strategies to reduce some of the maladaptive effects of the entity theory. Second, it suggests that people often hold simultaneous, contradictory assumptions about their world. The particular theory an individual will use to guide cognition is often determined by incidental features present in the environment. Thus, by studying the influence of environmental cues on the activation of lay theories, researchers may gain a fuller understanding of basic processes in human reasoning.   —JP

Sixteen Personality Factor Questionnaire

n. (16PF) A self-report personality inventory designed by Catell with 16 scales derived from factor analytic studies finding five main personality factors and 16 facets of the factors. The five main factors are extroversion, independence, tough-mindedness, anxiety, and self-control; the 16 factors are warmth, vigilance, reasoning, abstractedness, emotional stability, privateness, dominance, apprehension, liveliness, openness to change, rule-consciousness, self-reliance, social boldness, perfectionism, sensitivity, and tension. There are also three validity scales: impression management, infrequency, and acquiescence. Also called the 16 Personality Factor Inventory.

size constancy

n. The understanding that objects do not change their size when the retinal image of them grows or shrinks, as in moving toward or away from an object.

size-weight illusion

n. The perceptual tendency of human beings to judge weight by the size of an object while largely ignoring its density so that a larger object will be judged heavier than a smaller object of the same weight when they are picked up.

skewness

n. The degree to which a distribution of scores is asymmetrical around its median.

skin conductance response

n. A change in the level or degree to which the skin conducts electricity, which tends to decrease when subcutaneous muscles relax and increase when those muscles tense and is used as a crude estimate of general bodily tension. This has been used in crude and usually inaccurate attempts to create a lie detector. Also known as galvanic skin response.

Skinner box

n. An operant conditioning chamber containing a lever or key which a small animal can operate in order to obtain food from an automatic device and sometimes another device as well.

Skinnerian

adj. Of or relating to the operant conditioning theories of B. F. Skinner.

Skinnerian conditioning

n. Operant conditioning in which an organism learns to operate on the environment in order to obtain reinforcement, which may be obtained through a variety of actual behaviors as long as they accomplish a specified task, rather than engaging in a behaviorally specific response, as is true in classical conditioning.

skin sense

n. Any of the capacities of the skin to gather information and conduct it to the central nervous system, including awareness of pressure, pain, hot, and cold.

sleep

n. A periodic state characterized by reduced or absent consciousness, muscular relaxation, low arousal level, and general unresponsiveness to most stimuli. This state of being has five distinctive patterns of brain activity and sometimes includes dreams.

sleep apnea

n. A disorder characterized by cessation of breathing during sleep. Obstructive sleep apnea is due to the temporary blockage of the upper airway by mucus or tissue of the airway, which can be congenital or due to obesity. Usually breathing resumes with a loud snore and sometimes with bodily jerks. It results in daytime sleepiness, which can become severe and is associated with heart disease, memory loss, lethargy, irritability, mood changes, lowered sexual drive and capacity, and reduction of intellectual ability. Obstructive sleep apnea is usually treatable using a Continuous Positive Air Pressure (CPAP) machine to maintain an open airway during sleep. Central sleep apnea results from brain disease or trauma in the brainstem, which causes interruptions in the signals from the brain to the diaphragm.

sleep disorders

n. Any of a family of disorders involving disturbance of sleep for an extended period or on a frequent basis which cause significant personal distress or interfere with daily functioning. These include primary insomnia, which is difficulty falling asleep or staying asleep or having sleep that does not bring about a feeling of restedness; hypersomnia, which is excessive sleepiness which involves either sleeping for prolonged periods or falling asleep during the waking part of a person's daily cycle; narcolepsy, in which the person falls asleep at unpredictable and inopportune times; sleep apnea, in which the person temporarily stops breathing during sleep, which can markedly disrupt sleep; circadian rhythm sleep disorder, in which sleep is disrupted as a result of sleep schedule changes or a mismatch between internal and external schedules; nightmare disorder, in which nightmares frequently wake the subject; sleep terror disorder, in which the individual frequently awakens during the night feeling terrified for no apparent reason; and sleepwalking disorder, in which the person frequently walks while asleep.

sleeper effect

n. The research finding that the effect of a persuasive message often increases over time and especially so if the person scrutinizes the message and finds evidence that the argument in the message is flawed. Over time the flawed argument tends to be forgotten and the original message better remembered so that the message has greater effect long after it has been received than is true immediately afterward.

sleep-onset insomnia

n. A frequent, recurrent difficulty in falling asleep at the appropriate time in an individual's daily sleep-wake cycle.

sleep spindle

n. Spindle-shaped electroencephalogram patterns of about 15 Hz sometimes recorded during the second stage of sleep.

sleep-wake cycle

n. The daily pattern of falling asleep and waking up which most higher organisms follow. These patterns can be quite variable both among species and within a species and are variable among cultures as well.

sleepwalking

n. Walking or engaging in other complex motor tasks while asleep. This becomes a disorder if it recurs frequently and causes distress and dysfunction in a person's daily activities.

slip of the tongue

n. A slip of the tongue (also called *speech error, Freudian slip, lapsus linguae, spoonerism*) is an unintentional error occurring during speech production. In a famous example, the president of the Austrian Parliament said, "I take notice that a full quorum of members is present and herewith declare the sitting closed!" It is tempting to interpret errors such as this as revealing aspects of the struggle between *id* and *ego*, as proposed by Sigmund Freud (*Psychopathology of Everyday Life*, 1901). However, these errors are more insightful about the operation and sequencing of language production routines. The study of speech error corpora has revealed that slips

of the tongue never result in ungrammatical or impossible strings, and that errors are subject to the phonological, morphological, and syntactic principles of the language in which they are produced. Some errors, such as the one quoted, involve exchanges between related words (*closed* and *open*) and thus presumably happen at the early stage of lexical access. Others involve the exchange of two morphemes within a sentence, such as *There are too many churches in our minister,* where *church* and *minister* are exchanged, an error suggesting a separate stage in production during which inflectional morphemes are added at structurally appropriate positions. Other slips involve exchanges between phonemes, such as *a smuck in the tid,* where the intended expression was *a stick in the mud,* and thus are seen as reflecting a stage during which phonological representations are built.   – EMF

slow-to-warm-up

n. A type of temperament in which infants need time to make transitions in activity and experiences. Though they may withdraw initially or respond negatively, given time and support they will adapt and react positively.

slow-wave sleep

n. Deep sleep characterized by large, slow (1–3 Hz) brain waves on an electroencephalograph which seems to eliminate feelings of fatigue and is controlled by serotonin levels in the brainstem.

small group

n. **1.** A collection of 10 or fewer subjects in a research project whose responses are compared to the responses of other groups treated differently. **2.** A collection of 4–12 people who meet in a face-to-face situation in order to learn about group processes, enhance their communication skills, or engage in therapy together.

small group research

n. A small group may be defined as 3 to 12 persons who interact with each other and influence each other in order to achieve an objective or goal. We set the minimal size at 3 because pairs (dyads) are typically considered apart from small group research in areas such as negotiation and bargaining, and the maximal size at 12 because groups larger than 12 tend to divide or be divided into subgroups.

Small groups serve many purposes. Perhaps the most important, and clearly the most researched, is task performance, such as a scientific research team solving a problem, a jury making a decision, or a football team running a play. Small groups are settings for member learning, such as elementary students in classroom groups or college students in discussion groups. Small groups distribute resources, such as a team of middle managers determining salary raises, or figure skating judges rating the performance of the skaters. Small groups legitimize decisions, behavior, and language usage, such as a jury acting for society in determining guilt or innocence, middle school students deciding what clothing styles are "cool" or unspeakably "retro," or the United States Supreme Court determining the meaning of "equal protection under the laws." Small groups are a source of pleasure and enjoyment, in games, music, family reunions, dinner table conversations, and the countless interactions of small groups at home, school, work, and play. However, the majority of experimental research on small groups has studied group performance.

Theory and research on small groups distinguishes (a) the group task, (b) group structure, (c) group process, and (d) group product. The group task is what the group is attempting to do, such as solve a problem, make a decision, play a game, or operate a complex machine. Group structure includes member characteristics such as beliefs, competences, interests, and preferences; roles, such as leader or ordinary member; and norms, the assumed beliefs and expected behavior of the group members, such as norms of courtesy and considering the pros and cons of proposed alternatives. Group processes basically entail who says what when how to whom with what effect, as in both classical rhetoric and the lead paragraph of a contemporary newspaper article. The group product is the collective output or performance of the group on the task, which achieves or fails to achieve the group goal or objective to some degree.

Four dimensions have been distinguished in small group theory and research. The first dimension is *cooperative, mixed-motive, and competitive interaction.* In cooperative interaction all group members share the same goal or objective and share equally in the rewards and punishments of achieving or failing to achieve the goal, such as a small scientific research team conducting a successful or unsuccessful experiment, or the three *Apollo 13* astronauts attempting to return safely to Earth after the explosion of an oxygen tank in their spacecraft. In competitive interaction one group desires to defeat the other, such as two football or basketball teams. Such groups and teams engage in cooperative interaction within the group and competitive interaction between the groups. In mixed-motive interaction the group members are motivated both to cooperate with each other and to compete with each other for differential rewards, as in the social dilemmas we consider later.

A second dimension distinguishes *cognitive versus physical group tasks.* Cognitive tasks include group memory, problem solving, and decision making. Physical tasks include digging a ditch, pulling a rope, or participating in athletics. Although all group tasks entail both cognitive and physical elements, such as three engineering students building a robot, a string quartet, or a basketball team, the majority of research on small group performance has used tasks whose requirements and objectives are primarily cognitive.

A third dimension distinguishes *intellective and judgmental tasks.* Intellective tasks have a correct solution within some mathematical, logical, or verbal conceptual system, such as mathematical problems, logical reasoning problems, or crossword puzzles. On intellective tasks one or more group members who know a correct answer may demonstrate it to the incorrect members, who have sufficient understanding of the conceptual system to recognize and accept a correct answer. Judgmental tasks are evaluative, behavioral, or aesthetic judgments and preferences for which no objectively correct demonstrable answer exists, such as whether George Washington or Abraham Lincoln was a greater president, Mozart or Beethoven a greater composer, blackberry or raspberry a tastier jam, or the defendant innocent or guilty in a jury trial. On intellective tasks the objective for the group is to obtain the correct answer, whereas on judgmental tasks the objective for the group is to achieve consensus on some response (a hung jury that fails to render a verdict has failed to achieve the objective of a jury). Again this is a continuous dimension rather than a dichotomy, but the tasks used in experimental research tend to fall at either the intellective or judgmental end of the dimension.

A fourth dimension distinguishes *the number of group members that are necessary for a collective response*. On *conjunctive* tasks all group members must succeed for the group to succeed, such as a team of mountain climbers roped together, The Great Wallendas performing a human pyramid on a high wire, or a team of neurological surgeons removing an extensive cranial tumor. On *disjunctive* tasks only one group member needs to succeed for the group to succeed, such as three students attempting to solve a high school geometry problem or a family at dinner trying to recall the name of a distant relative. Conjunctive and disjunctive tasks define the end points of a dimension of the number of members that is necessary for a group decision. This is often formalized by constitutions and bylaws, such as unanimity in jury decisions for capital cases or simple majority to pass a motion in Robert's Rules of Order for Parliamentary Procedure.   – PRL

smell
n. **1.** The olfactory sense or the sensory capacity to detect the presence of certain chemicals in the air. **2.** The presence of some chemicals in the air which are detectable by the olfactory sense.

smooth muscle
n. The muscles found in the digestive system, in blood vessels, around the eyeballs, around hair follicles, and in internal organs with the exception of the heart. Smooth muscles lack the striations of skeletal muscles; are generally under the control of the autonomic nervous system, which usually moves them in slow, rhythmic contractions; and can maintain tension for long periods without fatigue.

snowball sample
n. A group of subjects for a study obtained by asking existing subjects and subsequent subjects to find or recruit new subjects. This procedure is often associated with sample bias.

SOA
n. Stimulus onset asynchrony The time between the start of one stimulus and the start of the next stimulus, which is usually of importance in masking experiments.

sociability
n. The characteristic of liking to be around other people and actively seeking out friends, lovers, other companions, and social relationships in general.

social adjustive function
n. The utility of an attitude or belief system in facilitating social interactions in general and creating group cohesion in particular. Thus members of a group find comfort in the company of persons with a similarity in beliefs and create mental separation from persons who do not share their beliefs.

social anxiety
n. A generalized fear of social rejection or failure and self-consciousness in the presence of others which often leads to an avoidance of social interactions.

social anxiety disorder
n. A severe and persistent fear of acting in a way which will invite embarrassment and humiliation in social or performance situations so that the person avoids the situations even knowing the fears to be unreasonable, thus causing distress and dysfunction in the person's daily living. Also called social phobia.

social approval
n. The expression of positive evaluation by people of a person or event or idea including praise, compliments, rewards, and envy.

social axioms
n. General, context-free beliefs generally held within a culture or subculture which are central to an individual's thinking and adjusting to her/his social environment, including understanding others' behavior.

social behavior
n. **1.** Any action performed by a social animal in the presence of others of its species. **2.** Any human action in which there is a real or imagined audience. **3.** The communication, cooperation, altruism, and grouping together which define the social nature of a species.

social category
n. Any group of people defined by culturally recognized criteria such as Caucasians, conservatives, and wage earners.

social change
n. Any alteration in one or more significant aspects or relationships within a culture or subculture such as the alteration of U.S. society by the advent of personal computers and similar devices or the movement of the majority of the population in the United States from rural to urban settings during the latter part of the 19th and early 20th centuries.

social class
n. Any large group within a society that share an economic level and usually have similar status, prestige, power, customs, and values within the society.

social cognition
n. Several definitions of social cognition have been proposed. They generally converge on the view that social cognition is the study of (a) the factors that influence the acquisition, representation, and retrieval of information of the sort that is transmitted in a social context and (b) the influence of these processes on judgments and behavior. Subareas of social cognition, each of which focuses on a different stage of information processing, address the comprehension of information in terms of previously formed concepts and knowledge; the organization of information in memory and the construction of complex mental representations of the persons, objects, and events to which it pertains; the retrieval of the information from memory; the rules for construing and integrating the implications of different pieces of information; and the transformation of subjective inferences into overt judgments and behavior decisions.
— RSW

social cognitive neuroscience
n. The field of science that attempts to understand social processes from the point of view of brain functioning.

social cognitive theory
n. An approach to understanding people through the perspective of the interactions of people's thoughts and social behavior.

social comparison theory
n. The idea that people evaluate their personal characteristics relative to those of particular other people, who are called one's reference group.

social conflict
n. **1.** A hostile or antagonistic clash between different social groups. **2.** Any opposition of the interests of two or more social groups whether or not there is any actual overt conflict.

social constructionism
n. The idea that perception, memory, and other complex cognitive functions are actively built up by the individual in ways largely determined by the culture and language in which a person is raised and somewhat by the contemporary social milieu. It is further supposed that there is no point of view, including scientific ones, which has universal validity.

social contagion
n. The rapid spread of ideas, attitudes, and behaviors through crowds of people and other social animals.

social Darwinism
n. The belief that social position reflects one's biological fitness and that societies evolve

through the survival of the fittest and are hampered by the survival of those who are not successful within the context of the society. This point of view was rejected by Charles Darwin but gained widespread popularity in Great Britain and the United States and was used to justify economic deprivation of the poor, including starving them to death, and unbridled accumulation of wealth by those able to exploit the laissez-faire economic system of the time. It was also later used as the theoretical basis for the eugenics movements in the United States, Great Britain, and Nazi Germany, in which sterilization of those deemed by the wealthy and powerful including doctors to be unfit members of society was considered a good thing.

social desirability
n. **1.** The degree to which a person, thing, or action is positively valued within a particular culture or subculture. **2.** A bias in self-presentation that leads people to behave in ways they believe will be positively valued within a particular culture or subculture, which reduces the validity of self-reports and many types of psychological questionnaires, tests, and experimental procedures.

social development
n. The gradual acquisition of language, interpersonal understanding, and culturally appropriate behavior patterns which make up cultural competence in a given society.

social dilemma
n. **1.** The conflict between individual desires and the benefit or desires of others in many situations. **2.** In gaming theory, a game set up so that an individual benefits most if he/she acts selfishly while others act for the good of the group, while all lose if everyone acts selfishly and all benefit moderately if all act for the good of the group.

social distance scale
n. A method of measuring intergroup attitudes by asking what distances would be acceptable for members of other groups such as within the country or as potential marriage partners.

social emotions ▶ see SELF-CONSCIOUS EMOTIONS

social exchange
n. Any social interaction in which two or more enter into a symbolic or real transaction with another person.

social exchange theory
n. The point of view which sees social interactions as exchanges of both tangible and intangible rewards and punishments. Within this view people are believed to act to maximize their gains and minimize their losses though mostly remaining within cultural norms of reciprocity and equity.

social facilitation
n. The observation that the mere presence of others increases the productivity of workers in many circumstances. This effect is particularly noticeable with relatively simple and well-learned tasks that do not require intense concentration, and productivity may decline as the tasks are more demanding and less well learned.

social identity theory
n. **1.** The point of view which supposes that people's understanding and valuation of themselves as well as most of their behavior derive from the attitudes and actions of those people around them with whom they identify themselves. **2.** Any social psychological theory that supposes that others influence both the public and the private sense of self.

social impact theory
n. An understanding of social influence that supposes that persuasion, conformity, compliance, and obedience are obtained by a combination of (1) the social strength of the person exerting control relative to the person being controlled, (2) the proximity of the two people both physically and psychologically, (3) the directness of the influence, that is, how many sources and targets of influence there are in a given situation. This is often expressed in the equation Impact = $f(SIN)$, where S = social strength, I = immediacy, and N = number of sources of influence.

social influence

n. **1.** The capacity to bring about change in another's thoughts, feelings, or behavior. **2.** The process of bringing about change in another's thoughts, feelings, or behavior.

social information processing

n. An approach to understanding interpersonal interactions by breaking them into parts and examining the interaction of the parts. The parts are (a) encoding social clues, (b) mentally representing and interpreting the cues, (c) selecting desired outcomes, (d) searching memory for possible social responses or formulation of new response possibilities, (e) selecting a response, and (e) acting out selected responses while monitoring their effects.

social intelligence

n. **1.** The set of abilities which allow an individual to adapt to the people around him or her through experience so as most easily to meet their needs and contribute to the well-being of the society of all people. **2.** Emotional intelligence, which includes the capacities to perceive, appraise, and express one's own emotions effectively as well as to understand others' emotions and make use of that information in guiding one's own behavior.

social interaction

n. Any process of mutual or reciprocal action or influence among organisms, including but not limited to cooperation, competition, conflict, simple recognition, status influence, role playing, and group processes.

social isolation

n. The state of being cut off from or having limited social interactions with others or with a particular group of others of one's own species.

socialization

n. Socialization is the process by which an individual learns and internalizes the rules and patterns of behavior of her/his culture, particularly in childhood but continuing through adulthood. This involves learning and mastering societal and cultural norms, attitudes, values, and belief systems, as well as the particular skills needed for daily living and performance of the person's cultural economic functions.

socialization agents

n. The people, institutions, and organizations that exist to help ensure that socialization occurs.

social justice

n. The idea that there is moral imperative in any society to give each member of the society fair treatment and a just share of the goods and benefits of the society. There are many ideas about what constitutes fair treatment and a just share of the goods and benefits of the society.

social learning

n. **1.** The processes by which an individual acquires the capacities and knowledge necessary to cope with life successfully in a particular culture. **2.** In learning theory, the process of acquiring socially effective behaviors including through observational learning.

social learning theory

n. Social learning theory is a collection of theories that share the common goal of describing and explaining how the social environment influences individuals' behavior and how individuals affect their social environment. These bidirectional effects are believed to occur on a more or less continuous basis and to change dynamically as behavior and context change and evolve over time. This process is sometimes referred to as dynamic reciprocal determinism. Social learning theories differ fundamentally from psychodynamic theories, in which individuals' behavior is viewed as being influenced by psychic forces outside their control, and classic behaviorist approaches, in which behavior is considered to be controlled solely by environmental stimulus conditions. In social learning theories, individuals are seen as agentic and active in their planning and pursuit of life goals and in thinking about themselves, others, and the world. Early social learning theories were advanced in the 1950s and 1960s by psychologists such as Albert Bandura (e.g., social modeling of aggressive behavior) and Julian Rotter (e.g., locus of control). These early theories paved the way for later, more cognitively oriented approaches to understanding social behavior and personality, social cognitive theories.   – WGS

social loafing

n. Social loafing refers to a group phenomenon in which individuals are less motivated and exert less effort when working collectively than when working coactively (side by side, but independently) or individually. Collective efforts are those in which individuals pool their contributions to form a single group product. Working collectively reduces motivation because the individual contributions are relatively unidentifiable, are likely to be redundant with others' contributions, and are perceived to be insufficiently connected to the final outcome. Social loafing is likely to be greater with larger, less cohesive groups who work on uninteresting tasks. Social loafing has been documented worldwide but is reduced in collectivistic cultures, for females, and for groups that are highly cohesive. Working harder collectively – social compensation – occurs when working on an important group task that reflects on the self and when there is doubt that the others will contribute adequately. Then, individuals are more motivated and work harder collectively than coactively.   – KDW

socially desirable responding

n. Tendencies to give answers on questionnaires that make one look good.

social mobility

n. The ability of individuals to move in status from one generation to another, or during their lifetime. *Upward mobility* refers to the change from one's socioeconomic status to a higher status, whereas *downward mobility* refers to the change from one's socioeconomic status to a lower status. Changes in social status may be due to changes to an individual's wealth, income, occupation, education, or some other social variable. The ancient Chinese imperial examinations provided opportunities for upward social mobility. Individuals from any social class were given the chance to become a high-ranking government official. Society does not always provide opportunities for mobility.

During the feudal era social mobility was extremely low. Educational opportunities are often tied with social mobility. In a society high in social mobility, higher education is available to people regardless of individuals' socioeconomic backgrounds. In a society low in social mobility, higher education is often limited to privileged individuals.   – SOI, FM

social movement

n. Any deliberate and organized attempt by a group of people to alter the structure or functioning of a culture. Such movements usually begin as ad hoc organizations which embody the aspirations and frustrations of a group of individuals, who gradually become conscious of the sharedness of their hopes and frustrations and organize in an escalating series of face-to-face meetings, which eventually expand to more public forms of communication. In the Internet age this appears to be expanding to include virtual movements.

social network

n. **1.** The set of interdependent relationships a person or group has with others. **2.** Sometimes used specifically for either personal or working relationships, as in the emotional support one gets from one's social network or the set of mutually beneficial contacts a business person has.

social network analysis

n. A quantitative method of measuring the set of relationships a person or group has with others, usually expressed in terms of mathematical ties among social nodes. Relationships can include ideas, airline routes, financial exchange, friendship, kinship, biases, conflict, trade, sexual relations, and transmission of diseases or genes, values, or Web links.

social norm

n. Consensual standards within a culture as to expected, prescribed, and proscribed behavior for persons of particular status within the culture. Standards of behavior and belief can be implicit or explicit, and their violation usually causes irritation and anxiety in other people, although most cultures have rebel roles or classifications and those in these groups are expected to violate some standards but not others and may serve as scapegoats for the culture.

social perception
n. The process of gathering and interpreting information about other people and group processes including noticing behaviors and inferring motives.

social phobia
n. A severe and persistent fear of acting in a way which will invite embarrassment and humiliation in social or performance situations so that the person avoids the situations even knowing the fears to be unreasonable, thus causing distress and dysfunction in the person's daily living.

social power
n. The capacity to influence or control others' behavior, beliefs, and emotional reactions, which can be accomplished by reward, punishment, a consensual right to demand obedience, compliance to perceived expertise, or the status of the influencer in the identity of others; thus a movie star may influence people who want to be like her or him and so imitate him/her.

social projection
n. The tendency to expect similarities between oneself and others.

social psychologist
n. Social psychologists study the influence that other people (actual, implied, or imaginary) have on human behavior and mental processes. In the latter part of the 20th century, social psychologists began borrowing heavily from the methods and findings of cognitive psychologists, forming the dominant social psychological perspective known as social cognition. Some of the major areas of study within social psychology are attraction, obedience, conformity, persuasion,

attitudes, prejudice, aggression, person perception, and applied social psychology.
– MWP

social psychology
n. The branch of psychology that specializes in studying processes of social interaction among humans including ways the thoughts, feelings, and beliefs of the individual are affected by the real or imagined presence of others. This includes study of attitudes, affiliation, mass communication, compliance, conformity, cross-cultural issues, authority, social roles and status, interpersonal attraction, group processes, social attribution, altruism, and nonverbal communication.

social reinforcement
n. Any behavior by others which increases the likelihood that the act immediately before it or referred to by it will be repeated.

social relations model
n. A theoretical and statistical method for decomposing interpersonal perceptions into perceiver, target, and relationship effects. Perceiver effects are the general point of view of the perceiver, as evidenced by her/his ratings of all people on a dimension. Target effects are the way the target is perceived by people in general. Relationship effects acknowledge the unique perception of this target by this perceiver.

social role
n. Any recognizable pattern of behavior within a given culture involving rights, expectations, obligations, and duties which a particular individual is expected, encouraged, and sometimes trained to perform in suitable situations. As in the cast of a play, each person in social interactions has a part or parts that others expect of him or her and he/she expects of himself/herself. This can involve formal long-term roles such as mother, doctor, or real estate agent or short-term and situational roles such as sympathetic friend, bully, or peacemaker.

social stigma
n. A severe and enduring form of social disapproval of personal, behavioral, or social

characteristics that often leads to formal or informal punishment and partial exclusion from a culture or subculture. One source of stigma is physical deformity, such as bodily malformation, or disease, as in having a humpback or leprosy. A second source is the behavioral or personal characteristics of the individual, as in child molesters, drug addicts, or, in the United States, supporters of Islamic terrorists. A third source is belonging to a disfavored social or ethnic group, as Jews have traditionally been persecuted by Christians, African Americans are still stigmatized in the United States, and Christians and Buddhists were stigmatized by the Taliban when they ran Afghanistan. All three forms of stigma are found in most large cultures to some extent.

social stratification

n. The hierarchical structure of power, prestige, and economic benefits within a culture or subculture or the emergence or creation of such a hierarchy.

social striving

n. **1.** The observation that in many circumstances individuals work harder in the presence of others than they do when working alone. **2.** A motivation to or attempt by an individual to raise his or her position in society through successful work, social connection, or any other method.

social support

n. Giving assistance or emotional support to others and especially in situations of stress. It often involves simply establishing rapport with a person in a stressful situation but may include the provision of protection or material support or any other form which leaves the recipient with a sense of connection, belonging, and being valued by another.

society

n. **1.** An enduring and interdependent group of people whose members share cultural, political, and economic institutions and similar values, social rules, and mores and usually live close together, although some such groups are mobile, in which case they tend to share ranges or territories. **2.** A group of interdependent nonhuman animals residing closely together.

sociobiology

n. Sociobiology is a synthesis of data and theory related to the biological basis of social behavior that originated with the publication in 1975 of *Sociobiology: The New Synthesis* by E. O. Wilson. Sociobiology focused on animal societies, their population structure, forms of communication, and the physiological and genetic basis of the adaptations underlying social behavior. Sociobiology also drew extensively from the literature on population genetics, life history theory (the theory of the determinants of age-graded fertility and survivorship), ethology (i.e., the study of animal behavior from an evolutionary perspective), and behavioral ecology (i.e., the study of how behavior is adapted to ecological context). At the level of theory, sociobiology is an heir of the neo-Darwinian synthesis among evolution by natural selection, Mendelian genetics, and population genetics. At the core of sociobiology is W. D. Hamilton's theory of inclusive fitness, showing that genes are selected for their beneficial effects not only on the reproductive success of individuals but also on their relatives. Indeed, the fundamental theoretical problem of sociobiology is the problem of altruism: why would animals sometimes sacrifice their own fitness for the benefit of others? According to Wilson, the answer was inclusive fitness: animals increase their own inclusive fitness by helping their relatives, even at a cost to themselves. In addition, sociobiology drew on the theoretical contributions of Robert Trivers, particularly parental investment theory and parent-offspring conflict theory.

Wilson's synthesis led to a deluge of theoretical and empirical research in the social behavior of animals based on inclusive fitness models and the other theoretical strands of sociobiology. This research has continued unabated and has confirmed the power of the sociobiological synthesis.

The main controversy over sociobiology has resulted from attempts to understand human behavior and social structure in terms of the sociobiological synthesis. Wilson himself envisioned the humanities and social sciences as eventually being subsumed as branches of biology in a unified science of human behavior. In fact, research on humans stemming from the theoretical insights of sociobiology has continued apace. This movement has led to journals, books, and academic societies devoted to the study of evolution and human behavior, including evolutionary psychology, human ethology, human behavioral ecology, evolutionary sociology, political science, and evolutionary perspectives in literature and the arts.   – KM

▶ *See also* **EVOLUTIONARY PSYCHOLOGY** *and* **PARENTAL INVESTMENT THEORY**

sociocultural perspective

n. **1.** Within the social sciences, any perspective which emphasizes or takes into account the importance of environmental factors to the development of humans and their behavior, thoughts, and feelings. **2.** In developmental psychology, the view that the cognitive development of children is guided by adults interacting with the children in culturally determined times, places, and manners. This is opposed to the view that children simply unfold their natural pattern of cognitive development if given opportunity free of outside constraint. **3.** Those points of view shared by most persons within a particular society or culture.

socioeconomic status

n. (SES) The relative level of economic resources and prestige of an individual or group within the hierarchy of a particular culture. Members of one level usually share similar incomes, education levels, types of occupations, places of residence, and sometimes ethnic or religious backgrounds.

sociogram

n. A pictorial representation of interrelationships in a group of people, usually with persons or groups represented as a geometric shape (circle, square, triangle) whose spatial arrangement and lines connecting them with other persons or groups represent kinds or amounts of relationship, such as feelings of liking, desire to work together, or status.

sociolinguistics

n. The field of study which examines interaction between social factors and language form and use, especially as related to social class, status, age, gender, and ethnic group, using techniques borrowed from both linguistics and sociology. It studies how the language an individual uses changes depending upon the person he/she is speaking to and how groups use language differently, including developing their versions of the base language or mixtures of language among groups with more than one language.

sociology

n. The science which examines human societies and how they develop, organize, formalize and change structures; create patterns of cooperation, competition, and avoidance among individuals and groups; and organize and are affected by the economic activity of the society; and how the social roles which guide the behavior of individuals within the groups are created by the social organization.

sociopath

n. An archaic term for a person who ignores the rights of others, has no conscience, and generally acts impulsively and self-centeredly independently of the perspectives of his or her culture and the needs of people around him/her. The contemporary term for this pattern of characteristics is *antisocial personality disorder.*

sociopathic personality

n. An archaic term for a person who ignores the rights of others, has no conscience, and generally acts impulsively and self-centeredly independently of the perspectives of his or her culture and the needs of people around him/her. The contemporary term for this pattern of characteristics is *antisocial personality disorder.*

sociopathy

n. The cognitive style and behavioral patterns of persons suffering from antisocial personality disorder, including ignoring the rights of others, having no conscience, and generally acting impulsively and self-centeredly independently of the perspectives of their culture and the needs of people around them.

sodium channel

n. Proteins in cell membranes that conduct sodium ions through a cell's plasma membrane. In excitable cells such as neurons, sodium channels are responsible for the rising phase of action potentials as they change permeability and allow the exchange of sodium and potassium ions, which causes the waves of electricity that flow down the neuron. Also called voltage-gated sodium channel.

sodium pump (sodium-potassium pump)

n. Within the neuron, an electrolytic balance must be attained for normal neural transmission to occur. To obtain this electrical (ionic) and chemical balance, some sodium ions (Na^+) must be relocated through the cell membrane from the intracellular portion of a neuron to the extracellular space by an active mechanism, the sodium-potassium pump. The pump obtains energy to supply this transport from the breakdown of adenosine triphosphate (ATP) produced by the mitochondria in the cell. The sodium-potassium pump exchanges intracellular sodium ions for extracellular potassium ions (K^+), to obtain the necessary cellular balance. This transport is expensive, requiring up to 40% of the neuron's metabolic resources, indicating the importance of this active transport for neural transmission.   – vs

soma

n. **1.** The physical body. **2.** The cell body of a neuron. **3.** A plant regarded as holy by several ancient European societies. **4.** The drug used to tranquilize the masses of people in Aldous Huxley's futuristic novel *Brave New World*.

somatic

adj. **1.** Of or relating to the body as distinct from the mind (psychic). **2.** Arising in the body or cells of the body, as in somatic mutations.

somatic disorder

n. An illness or disease arising in the body, as opposed to a behavioral or psychological disorder.

somatic nervous system

n. The part of the central nervous system outside the brain, consisting of afferent and efferent nerves which gather information from and control the movements of the skeletal muscles, as opposed to the brain and autonomic nervous system.

somatization

n. The conversion of a psychological process to a bodily manifestation, as in the physiological reactions and behaviors associated with anxiety up to development of ulcer and heart disease as a result of chronic emotional states.

somatization disorder

n. A family of psychological disturbances which produce bodily manifestations which cause significant distress and interfere with the daily functioning of the sufferer. This includes somatization disorder, in which the individual has a recurring pattern of multiple, clinically significant complaints for which physical causes cannot be found and which are judged by the clinician to be due to psychological factors; undifferentiated somatoform disorder, in which there are persistent complaints of chronic fatigue, loss of appetite, or gastrointestinal, genitourinary, or other symptoms without obvious physical cause and attributed by a clinician to psychological factors; conversion disorder, in which voluntary or sensory nerve functioning is impaired (such as numbness or paralysis of a body part) without apparent physical cause and attributed by a clinician to psychological factors; pain disorder, in which a specific pain interferes with daily functioning and becomes the focus of the person's life without sufficient physical cause and is attributed by a clinician to psychological factors; and hypochondriasis, in which a person is incapacitated by multiple fears of having a disease based on misinterpretation of bodily symptoms that are not allayed by medical opinions to the contrary.

somatoform disorders

n. A family of psychological disturbances which produce bodily manifestations which cause significant distress and interfere with the daily functioning of the sufferer. This includes somatization disorder, in which the individual has a recurring pattern of multiple, clinically significant complaints for which physical causes cannot be found and which are judged by the clinician to be due to psychological factors; undifferentiated somatoform disorder, in which there are persistent complaints of chronic fatigue, loss of appetite, or gastrointestinal, genitourinary, or other symptoms without obvious physical cause and attributed by a clinician to psychological factors; conversion disorder, in which voluntary or sensory nerve functioning is impaired (such as numbness or paralysis of a body part) without apparent physical cause and attributed by a clinician to psychological factors; pain disorder, in which a specific pain interferes with daily functioning and becomes the focus of the person's life without sufficient physical cause and is attributed by a clinician to psychological factors; and hypochondriasis, in which a person is incapacitated by multiple fears of having a disease based on misinterpretation of bodily symptoms that are not allayed by medical opinions to the contrary.

somatoform pain disorder

n. A psychological disturbance whose main symptom is bodily pain, which interferes with daily functioning and becomes the focus of the person's life without sufficient physical cause and is attributed by a clinician to psychological factors.

somatosensory association area

n. Most of the postcentral gyrus in the front part of the parietal lobe, which is believed to integrate information from bodily sense and is associated with bodily consciousness and produces bodily sensations when electrically stimulated. Also known as the somatosensory cortex.

somatosensory cortex

n. The region of the cerebral cortex where the somatic (sensation from the body – touch, pain, pressure, temperature, proprioception, etc.) sensory information is projected and processed. It can be further divided into the primary somatosensory area and somatosensory association area. The primary somatosensory area corresponds to the anterior part of the parietal lobe (postcentral gyrus), roughly the Brodmann's areas 3, 1, and 2. Body information is projected in an up-down way (lower part of the body goes to the upper part; upper part of the body to the lower part); this cortical map of the general body sensitivity is sometimes referred to as the sensory homunculus. The primary somatosensory area receives information from the ventrolateral nucleus of the thalamus. Damage in this cortical area is associated with hypoesthesia, two-point discrimination defects, and similar deficits in using somatosensory information. The somatosensory association cortex includes the Brodmann's areas 5, 7, 39, and 40. These cortical association areas further process the somatosensory information. – AA

▶ *See also* **PRIMARY SOMATOSENSORY CORTEX**

somatotype

n. Any of the three basic body/mind types described by William Sheldon in his constitutional psychology, which includes the mesomorph, whose body is dominated by muscle and bone and whose character is aggressive and domineering; the endomorph, whose body is dominated by internal organs and character is dominated by seeking comfort and sociability; and the ectomorph, whose body is dominated by the skin and nervous system and whose character is nervous, intellectual, and withdrawing.

sound pressure level

n. (SPL) The absolute intensity of a sound in decibels relative to the standard of 10^{-16} watts per square centimeter, which is just below the human capacity to hear at 1,000 hertz, which is about two octaves above middle C on a piano. A sound of 100 dB SPL is 100 watts per square centimeter above the standard. Because 3 dB corresponds to a factor of 2 in SPL, a sound at 6 dB SPL is twice as loud as a sound at 3 dB SPL and half as loud as a sound at 9 dB SPL.

source amnesia

n. Memory defect in which certain information can be recalled, but it is impossible to recall the source or origin of that information (i.e., source memory: memory for the broad contextual aspects surrounding the memory of an event). Source amnesia is considered as an explicit memory (declarative) disorder, particularly an episodic memory deficit. Source memory is affected by aging more than fact or event memory. Source memory has been related to the frontal lobe and medial temporal lobe structures.   – AA

▶ *See also* **AMNESIA** *and* **MEMORY**

spaced practice

n. A learning procedure in which practice is spread over time with nonpractice intervals between practice periods rather than in massed practice, in which all attempts to learn happen consecutively. Distributed learning has been found to be significantly more efficient than massed practice. Also known as distributed practice.

span of apprehension

n. The maximal number of units that can be perceived in a single sensory moment. It is usually measured by having subjects report the number of items they can identify after a single short exposure to an array of items.

spastic paralysis

n. The chronic contraction of a muscle or a group of muscles due to damage or disease to the motor cortex.

spatial ability

n. The capacity to integrate perceptual and cognitive abilities so as to orient and move around, to create working mental models of size and distance relationships so as mentally to rotate objects, read maps, and make correct deductions about the relative positions and sizes of objects in space.

spatial cognition

n. The mental processes involved in perceiving, representing, operating on, and communicating about space. Research in spatial cognition includes – but is not necessarily limited to – research in the areas of spatial memory, spatial reasoning, navigation, spatial language, and mental rotation. Spatial cognition is researched extensively in both human and other animal populations.
– ARS, MRO

spatial discrimination

n. The ability to make decisions about spatial information within one's environment. It involves the ability to differentiate between two or more locations within space using either egocentric or allocentric spatial information. Discrimination using egocentric information uses body position while discrimination using allocentric information bases the decision on external landmarks. Spatial discrimination tasks are used to study spatial memory, spatial abilities, the role of the hippocampus, and general cognitive functioning. For example, a spatial discrimination task may involve rats learning which arm of a multiple-armed maze will have food on the basis of the spatial organization of the arms.
– MRO, ARS

spatial perspective taking

n. The capacity to make correct deductions about size and distance relationships of objects from a location other than one's own.

spatial summation

n. The process by which a postsynaptic neuron combines the stimulation from multiple dendritic connections with presynaptic neurons so as to produce a graded potential in itself, which is often greater than would be the case if a single dendritic connection were stimulated.

Spearman-Brown formula

n. A correction for reliability correlations to account for the reduction in the correlation due to attenuation in the length of the scale by splitting it in half.

Spearman rank correlation

n. A numerical index of the degree of relationship between two variables that consist of rank orderings. Also called rho.

Spearman rank correlation coefficient

n. A numerical index of the degree of relationship between two variables that consist of rank orderings.

Spearman's rho

n. A numerical index of the degree of relationship between two variables that consist of rank orderings. Also called Spearman rank correlation.

speciation

n. The process by which species develop and vary from one another. It is theorized that two populations of an existing species begin to include more and more genetic differences due to different survival contingencies in their environments, and eventually these differences reach a magnitude such as to preclude fertile interbreeding, at which time there are two separate species.

species

n. Among sexual animals or plants requiring fertilization, any group of organisms that can interbreed and produce fertile offspring. Among nonsexual plants and animals such grouping is by inference on the basis of physical similarities or genetic similarity.

species-specific

adj. Of or relating to something that is characteristic of a single species.

species-specific behavior

n. A pattern of behavior that is characteristic of most members of a species or most members of one sex of a species and which is different from the behavior of other, similar species. Such behaviors are typically unlearned and manifest in all members of a species in appropriate circumstances and stages of maturity.

specific developmental disorder

n. In DSM III but not in DSM-IV-TR, a delay in developing some particular and circumscribed ability or area of functioning which is not attributable to mental retardation, such as autism. These are classified as learning disorders, motor skills disorders, and communications disorders in DSM IV and DSM IV-TR.

specific hunger

n. A desire or craving for a specific food or nutrient which typically occurs when the body is deficient in a nutrient which the food contains, as a salt-deficient athlete may crave potato chips for their saltiness.

specific learning disability

n. Any of the family of difficulties of acquiring skills including reading disorder, mathematics disorder, disorder of written expression, and learning disorder not otherwise specified.

spectrum

n. **1.** The range of any variable from highest to lowest. **2.** The entire range of particle energies and wavelengths in electromagnetic radiation, of which visible light is a portion. **3.** The various colors of the rainbow.

spectrum, visual

n. The range of electromagnetic radiation with wavelengths from about 400 to 700 nanometers, which can be seen by the normal human eye. Some other species see markedly different wavelengths of electromagnetic radiation. Some butterflies and bumblebees, for instance, see ultraviolet light.

speech accommodation theory

n. **1.** The idea that people both consciously and unconsciously change their style of speech (accent, rate, types of words, etc.) and nonverbal communication, usually in the direction of that used by the other(s) with whom they are communicating and their understanding of the social situation in which the speech occurs. **2.** The research which examines and analyzes such changes.

speech act

n. In pragmatics, an individual verbal utterance described in terms of the content of the utterance, the intention of the speaker, and the effect of the utterance on the listener. An utterance also involves a locutionary act and can involve an illocutionary act or a perlocutionary act.

speed-accuracy trade-off

n. The observation that there is some point in increasing the rapidity with which a task is being accomplished at which accuracy in performance begins to diminish. So there is then a choice as to whether to speed up performance further, sacrificing accuracy, or to maintain a moderate pace so as to maintain accuracy at the sacrifice of further speed.

spinal canal

n. The tunnel through the middle of the vertebrae through which the spinal cord runs.

spinal cord

n. The large tract of nerves which runs from the base of the brain down through the holes in the vertebrae to the lumbar region of the spine, where it branches into numerous smaller nerve tracts in the cauda equina. It includes afferent and efferent tracts as well as numerous ganglia at each level. It is covered by the meninges and has 31 pairs of major fibers that emerge from it.

spinal nerve

n. Any of the 31 pairs of nerves that originate in the gray matter of the spinal cord and emerge from between the vertebrae containing both afferent and efferent fibers for the skeletal muscles, the skin, and the autonomic nervous system. The spinal nerves are numbered from the top with 8 pairs emerging at the cervical level, 12 pairs at the thoracic level, 5 pairs at the lumbar level, 5 pairs in the sacrum, and 1 in the coccyx.

spinal reflex

n. Any behavioral arc of sensory information and efferent action that passes through a ganglion in the spine but does not include the brain in the process, as in some aspects of posture and walking.

spinal root

n. The connection between a spinal nerve and the spinal cord, which consists of a dorsal root joining the sensory fibers to the cord in the rear part of the spinal cord and a ventral root joining the efferent fibers to the spinal cord in the front part of the spinal cord.

spinothalamic tract

n. Two large sensory nerve tracts running up the spinal cord to the thalamus, which carry touch, pressure, pain, and temperature sensation to the brain.

split brain

n. Any brain in which the cerebral hemispheres have been partially disconnected by cutting the corpus callosum, which is the largest of the three major connections between the two sides of the cortex. A few humans have had surgery to accomplish this in order to forestall severe epileptic seizures, which increase each time they cross the corpus callosum. It has also been done in numerous laboratory animals, in order to study the mostly independent functioning of the two halves of the cerebral cortex.

split-brain research

n. **1.** Any study conducted on a brain in which the cerebral hemispheres have been partially disconnected by cutting the corpus callosum, which is the largest of the three major connections between the two sides of the cortex. It has largely found that the two halves of the brain have both shared and specialized functions in humans. In men more than in women, the left hemisphere is more active and quick to process verbal material and the right is better at spatial processing.

split-brain technique

n. The process cutting the corpus callosum, which is the largest of the three major connections between the two sides of the cortex of brain, which partially disconnects the right and left cerebral hemispheres. A few humans have had surgery to accomplish this in order to forestall severe epileptic seizures, which increase each time they cross the corpus callosum. It has also been done in numerous laboratory animals in order to study the mostly independent functioning of the two halves of the cerebral cortex.

split-half correlation

n. The calculation of a product-moment correlation between a set of scores on any two halves of a test so as to estimate the test's internal consistency reliability. This procedure has been supplanted by using Kuder-Richardson formula 20 for true-false or right-wrong test formats and by Cronbach's alpha coefficient for multiple-choice tests, both of which are the average of all possible split-half reliability coefficients corrected for attenuation.

split-half reliability

n. The level of a test's measurement error determined by examining the consistency of the scores of two halves of a given test. Split-half reliability is concerned with internal consistency. To calculate split-half reliability, the test is divided in half (division can be done by randomly selecting half the questions, dividing by the first and last half of the items, or using the odd-even system of item selection), and then each half is scored separately. Unlike other measures of reliability that simply correlate the resultant scores, a simple correlation of the two halves would provide an underestimation of the overall test reliability (as reliability increases with more items). As such, the Spearman-Brown formula is applied to correct for the half-length; the Spearman-Brown formula adjusts the correlation calculations to estimate what the reliability would be if each half of the test had been the length of the entire test.   – BJM

split personality

n. A disorder characterized by the presence of two or more distinct personalities or identities in the same person, who recurrently exchange control of the person and who may have only some knowledge about each other and the history of the person involved. Also called dissociative identity disorder.

splitting

n. A primitive defense mechanism whereby the individual deals with conflicting emotions (i.e., ambivalence) by identifying strongly with one side of the emotional experience only. For example, an individual may unconsciously feel frustration at his father as well as love and connection. Unconsciously this individual may feel that these two emotions are unable to coexist and specifically

fear that feeling any frustration may eliminate the positive feelings of love. The solution is to temporarily identify only with one emotional experience at a time. The result is a vacillation between idealization and devaluation of others and seeing the world in "black and white" terms or as "all good or all evil." As with most defense mechanisms, this process is unconscious; the individual using this defense mechanism is only aware of his or her current strong emotional experience and is oblivious to other complicated feelings.
                                        – DGa

spontaneous recovery

n. The reappearance of a conditioned response after it has been extinguished and after a rest period has elapsed.

spontaneous self-concept

n. Spontaneous self-concept is the self-concept researchers infer from individuals' spontaneous descriptions of themselves. When individuals are asked to describe themselves freely, they tend to define themselves using characteristics that would distinguish the self from others in the immediate context. Accordingly, individuals will construct different spontaneous self-concepts in different social contexts. The notion of spontaneous self-concept highlights the constructive and contextualized nature of the self – different characteristics of the self-concept are recruited to define who one is in response to different features of the social situation.
                                     – YHK, CYC

spontaneous trait inference

n. Spontaneous trait inference is the process of inferring personality traits about other people without intending to do so, and usually without even being aware of doing so. When you read, "The secretary solved the mystery halfway through the book," you probably infer that the secretary is clever. If you see a student kick a puppy out of his way in his rush across campus, it is hard to escape the impression that the student is cruel. These are examples of spontaneous trait inferences (STIs), and the process that produces them is called spontaneous trait inference (STI).

More than two decades of research show that whenever most people comprehend information about someone else that could be used to infer a personality trait, they make an inference, even if they do not intend to form an impression. These "implicit impressions" persist and influence subsequent judgments and interactions, even (or particularly) when people do not realize they have made them. They seem to be a ubiquitous feature of our social life. They are a major component of what is often called "intuition" about others. There is nothing to guarantee the accuracy of these impressions, and the presence of individual and cultural differences in STI about the same events ensures that some perceivers must be inaccurate.

Spontaneous trait inferences (STIs) may refer to the person doing the action, or to the action itself. Solving the mystery halfway through the book is clever behavior. So what evidence is there that STIs refer to the actor, in this case, the secretary? When we make inferences intentionally, we know what they refer to, because we have intentions to make them about something. But when they are unintended, how can we tell what they refer to (as distinct from what they are based upon)? There are two lines of evidence that show they are about actors (in addition, perhaps, to being about behaviors).

Traits are not the only things about other people that are inferred spontaneously. There is now evidence that, given the right information, we infer other people's goals and intentions, their social category memberships and the stereotypes associated with them, their emotions, and our evaluations of them. We spontaneously infer the causes of natural and human-caused events and aspects of other people's situations. We spontaneously infer counterfactuals, that is, alternative scenarios to those we actually observe. And we spontaneously develop expectancies and emotions about others, often based on their unrecognized similarity to significant others (i.e., important people whom we know well). This latter phenomenon, called social cognitive transference, has been studied extensively by Susan Andersen. Future research will no doubt extend this list.

Some people are more likely to infer STIs, and everyone is more likely to do it at some times rather than others. Perceivers' temporary states such as moods, thoughts, goals, or questions can make particular STIs more likely, when perceivers encounter relevant information about others. For example, if you were thinking about honesty (rather than rudeness) and learned that an actor told his friend that she has bad breath, you might spontaneously infer that the actor was *honest* rather than *rude*. Or if you were curious about what kind of situation an actor was in, rather than what kind of person he was, you might spontaneously interpret fearful behavior as evidence that the actor was in a frightening situation rather than a fearful person. That is, ambiguous behavior can be spontaneously disambiguated by perceivers' temporary mental states. And most behavior is ambiguous in one way or another.

Relatively stable personality differences can also affect STI. For example, authoritarian perceivers spontaneously interpret many behaviors differently than nonauthoritarians do. Those with high "personal need for closure" are more likely to make STIs, perhaps because they prefer to categorize others in trait terms. Those with repressive coping styles differ from others in their likelihood of inferring negative and threatening traits.

There are also cultural and social class differences in STIs. Those in individualistic cultures (as well as more individualistic perceivers within U.S. culture) make STIs more readily than those from collectivistic cultures. The best evidence for this is found in a study of Latino and Anglo college students in Texas, using the lexical decision procedure described earlier. Middle- and upper-middle-class Americans make STIs more readily than working- and lower-class Americans.   – JSU

▶ *See also* **PRIMING**

spoonerism

n. A slip of the tongue in which two sounds are unintentionally transposed in a way to give a different meaning to the utterance, which is sometimes humorous as in saying "The weight of rages will press hard upon the employer" instead of "The rate of wages will press hard upon the employer." Or in saying "A well-boiled icicle is a joy to ride" instead of "A well-oiled bicycle is a joy to ride."

sports psychology
n. The field of psychology that studies and applies the findings of psychology to the field of sports, usually with the aim of enhancing the performance of athletes.

spreading activation
n. **1.** In physiology, the hypothesis that activation of one neuron spreads to other neurons, either increasing or decreasing their likelihood of activation. **2.** In cognitive psychology, an increase in the activity of one node in a hypothetical neural or semantic network increases the activity level of adjacent nodes.

spreading depression
n. A wave of markedly lower activity among brain neurons accompanied by relatively strong negative electrical potential, which, in the cerebral cortex and hippocampus, is associated with migraine headaches. This may be induced by electrical stimulation of the brain or the application of a salt solution such as potassium chloride to the brain.

spurious correlation
n. **1.** A correlation between two variables which is due to relationships of both variables to a third variable rather than to a causal connection between the two variables. **2.** A correlation in a data set which is characteristic of the sample from which it is calculated but not true of the population in general.

SQ 3R method
n. An acronym for a five-step method of study in which the student surveys, questions, reads, recites, and reviews a set of material to be learned.

S-R learning
n. An approach to understanding the acquisition of behaviors in which it is presumed that behavior occurs as a response to a stimulus. In classical conditioning, the learning is a connection between a particular response and a novel stimulus associated with an

unconditioned stimulus. In instrumental conditioning, it is between a discriminative stimulus and the response.

S-R psychology
n. An archaic form of psychology that conceptualizes behavior in terms of the relationship between a stimulus and a response. In classical conditioning, the learning is a connection between a particular response and a novel stimulus associated with an unconditioned stimulus. In instrumental conditioning, it is between a discriminative stimulus and the response.

S-R theory
n. A psychological viewpoint which conceptualizes behavior in terms of the relationship between a stimulus and a response. In classical conditioning, the learning is a connection between a particular response and a novel stimulus associated with an unconditioned stimulus. In instrumental conditioning, it is between a discriminative stimulus and the response.

S-S learning
n. A neo-behavioral approach to learning that suggests that there are stimulus-to-stimulus connections developed through exposure to a link between two stimuli associated in time and space which occur independently of any overt behavior of the learning organism.

stabilized retinal image
n. An image on the retina that does not move as quickly as the eyes move as the receptor cells in the retina take time to respond to new stimuli and are responsive to change rather than fixed stimuli. This is important in vision as the eyes are nearly constantly moving a small amount, and without a stabilized image vision would be constantly fuzzy.

stage of concrete operations
n. In Piagetian psychology, the period of cognitive development which occurs during middle childhood (7–11 years of age) in which children become less ego centered, the capacity to see things from a different point of view begins to develop, and children begin

to think logically about concrete objects and about those objects in particular situations.

stage of formal operations

n. In Piagetian psychology, the period of cognitive development which occurs during late childhood, starting at about age 11, in which children begin to develop adult forms of thought, including hypothetico-deductive reasoning, in which the person can remember abstract ideas and tentatively apply them to specific situations; scientific inductive reasoning, in which generalizations based on multiple observations can be formed; and reflective abstraction, in which memory can be searched and the information from it used to create new ideas which have not been learned.

stages of sleep

n. The four distinct patterns of electroencephalographic recordings characteristic of human sleep over the course of a night. Stage 1, the initial stage, is characterized by relaxation and slow, irregular, low-amplitude brain waves at about 4–6 cycles per second. The second stage of sleep is characterized by sleep spindles, which are variable in amplitude bursts at about 14–18 cycles per second. The third stage of sleep is characterized by a mixture of large-amplitude, slow brain waves of about 1–4 cycles per second interspersed with sleep spindles which are similar to those in the second stage. The fourth stage of sleep, called deep sleep, is characterized by high-amplitude, slow brain waves without the spindle activity of the third stage of sleep. Many people cycle through the four sleep stages in about 90 minutes and have several such cycles in a night's sleep. Rapid eye movement (REM) sleep, characterized by many rapid eye movements and often dreaming, is sometimes considered a fifth stage of sleep, although it typically occurs during other stages, particularly during the first and second stages in the latter half of a night's sleep and at other times of high fatigue.

stage theory

n. Any theory in which sequential and somewhat independent processes occur. Examples include Freud's stages of psychosexual development, Erikson's epigenetic cycle of ego development, and Piaget's stages of cognitive development.

stage theory of memory

n. An early formulation of the processes of memory in cognitive psychology in which information first enters one of several sensory stores which have a high but unspecified capacity in relatively unprocessed form and for periods less than about 1 second. Some of this information from sensory storage is then transferred to short-term memory, which has a capacity of about seven plus or minus two items and lasts from a few seconds up to about 30 seconds and allows more information processing to occur. The long-term memory is the third and final stage, in which an unlimited amount of information is stored on a somewhat permanent basis and is capable of being recalled or used with appropriate cuing.

stalking

n. The legal definition of what constitutes stalking varies across the United States. However, most agree that stalking constitutes a willful, repetitive, and obsessional pattern of following or harassing behaviors that engender fear in the victim. Unwanted pursuit of the victim, spying, surreptitious observation, and surveillance behaviors are prototypical acts of stalking. However, a variety of other "less severe" behaviors such as repeatedly leaving unwanted phone messages, sending unwanted e-mails or letters, or delivering unwanted gifts can also result in violation of the victim's sense of safety and/or privacy. There is a continuum of stalking behaviors, which varies along several dimensions: the severity of the behavior perpetrated and the degree to which the victim is aware that the behavior is taking place. Stalking perpetrators are not homogeneous and can range from individuals who have never formerly met their victim (e.g., celebrity stalkers), to individuals who are stalking a potential love interest or a coworker, to perpetrators who currently are or have been in a consensual romantic relationship with the victim. One common time

for stalking to occur is during relationship dissolution. Former intimate partners are the most common perpetrators of stalking behaviors; these stalkers may also be the most dangerous as there is a higher than expected co-occurrence of stalking, harassment, and the perpetration of domestic violence.
— JL-R, KMW

standard deviation
n. The square root of the average of the squared differences from the mean of a set of numbers.

standard error
n. The average amount of random error expected in a score or other data set, which is calculated as the standard deviation of the data set divided by the square root of the sample size.

standard error of measurement
n. The average amount of random error expected in a score, which is calculated as the standard deviation of the set of scores divided by the square root of the sample size.

standard error of the mean
n. The average amount of random error expected in the mean of a sample drawn from a population, which is calculated as the standard deviation of the data set divided by the square root of the sample size.

standardization
n. **1.** In testing, the process of creating procedures for administration and scoring as well as norms for interpreting the test relative to a population. **2.** In general, the process of creating normal procedures or routine for a process.

standardization group
n. The sample of subjects used to represent the population in creating norms in psychological testing.

standardization sample
n. The group of subjects used to represent the population in creating norms in psychological testing.

standardized regression coefficient
n. The slope of the regression line associated with each predictor variable in a regression equation. Also called a beta weight.

standardized test
n. A test that is uniformly administered, scored, and interpreted according to defined standards. Generally, scores are norm-referenced (using a representative sample) to provide a basis for comparing test results. Because the test is administered, scored, and interpreted according to specific guidelines, the results can be effectively compared across a range of populations, settings, and times. As such, standardized testing is commonly used in academic, vocational, and clinical settings.
— BJM

standard score
n. A raw score from which the mean of scores has been subtracted and the result divided by the standard deviation of scores.

Stanford-Binet intelligence scale
n. An intelligence test originally devised by Alfred Binet to select schoolchildren who needed special attention, then modified by Lewis Terman for use in the United States and most recently revised in 2003 by Gale Roid. It is intended for use with individuals from age 3 to 89 and yields verbal, nonverbal, and full-scale deviation IQs with an average of 100 and a standard deviation of 15. It also has scores for fluid reasoning, knowledge, quantitative reasoning, visual-spatial processing, and working memory, as well as the five verbal and five nonverbal subtests. It is the second-most-widely-used test of intelligence.

stapes
n. The stirrup-shaped small bone (ossicle) in the middle ear that is one of three connected bones which transmit sound to the oval window.

startle reflex
n. A bodily reflexive jerk, without cognitive mediation, to a sudden, unexpected stimulus. This reflex is present even in neonates. The

stimulus may be a touch, noise, bright light, or other sudden change in the environment. The startle reflex may be accompanied by an array of sympathetic nervous system responses such as the release of adrenaline and an increase in heart rate.

Researchers use a heightened or prolonged startle reflex to measure fear/anxiety levels associated with increased activity in the amygdala, a regulator of fear/anxiety. Treatment with benzodiazepines such as diazepam (Valium) or alcohol reduces exaggerated anxiety startle responses, leading to the possibility of abuse of either drug.

startle response ▶ *See* STARTLE REFLEX

state anxiety
n. A temporary period of fearful mood that has a vague or no specific focus accompanied by bodily arousal which is not usual to the person experiencing it.

state-dependent learning
n. Acquisition of information which occurs in a nonnormal biological condition or environmental situation which is better remembered in similar conditions than when the organism is in a normal or different condition or situation.

state-dependent memory
n. Acquisition of information which occurs in a nonnormal biological condition or environmental situation which is better remembered in similar conditions than when the organism is in a normal or different condition or situation.

statement analysis
n. A technique for evaluating the truthfulness of verbal contents and statements, originally developed in Europe and widely used since the 1950s. It is based on the assumption that truthful and nontruthful statements differ in several ways, both qualitatively and quantitatively.

State-Trait Anxiety Inventory
n. (STAI) A 40-item self-report assessment device for anxiety with separate scales for immediate (state) and chronic (trait) anxiety symptoms.

statistic
n. Any mathematical description of any aspect of a data set, relations among parts of the data set, or prediction of the value of an aspect of a theoretical population from a data set.

Statistical Analysis System
n. (SAS) A group of integrated computer programs for performing a wide variety of statistical analyses on data sets.

statistical artifact
n. An overgeneralization or illogical application of a statistical procedure so as to present an erroneous or distorted view of the population parameter from which a data set is drawn.

statistical association
n. The degree of predictability of one variable when the value of another variable is known.

statistical control
n. The use of statistical analysis to reduce the error introduced in an analysis by variables which are not of interest in the study. Thus if one were interested in the relationship between two personal variables and were concerned that social desirability might be a factor in self-reports, then a measure of tendency to respond in a socially desirable way to self-reports could be given along with measures of the personal variables and a regression performed examining the relationship between the two personal variables with the variance of social desirability removed.

statistical error
n. Any distortion or error in conclusions drawn from a statistical procedure due to sampling, measurement, or treatment errors.

statistical inference
n. The process of generalizing from the results of a statistical analysis of sample data to estimate population parameters.

statistical interaction

n. Any situation in statistical analysis in which the relationship between two variables is different at different levels of a third variable.

statistically significant result

n. A research finding which cannot be reasonably attributed to random or chance processes.

statistical method

n. Any approach to the analysis of data which employs a mathematical description of the data or uses probability to estimate population parameters from sample data.

Statistical Package for the Social Sciences

n. The Statistical Package for the Social Sciences (SPSS) is a statistical software package very commonly used by researchers. SPSS offers a spreadsheet-type data format similar in layout to Microsoft Excel. SPSS is capable of many different data manipulations and sophisticated statistical tests. Early versions of SPSS required researchers to have some basic programming ability in order to run statistical analyses. More contemporary versions have a much more user-friendly point-and-click menu, though it is still possible to direct the software manually through text commands.

— MWP

statistical power

n. Statistical power is the probability of avoiding a type II error or missing a signal that is present in the data. Type II error is most likely with small sample sizes and small effect sizes. Statistical power is a serious concern for researchers because they generally want to be confident that their statistical analyses will enable them to see the trends that are present in their data. Increasing the sample size is the most common way of increasing statistical power. Psychologists have developed precise ways of calculating necessary sample size to ensure adequate statistical power. When planning a research study, psychologists often consult statistical power tables to determine the optimal sample size for detecting a trend they expect

to find in their data. Power tables require researchers to estimate the magnitude of the effect they expect to find. Power tables can also be used to illustrate, post hoc, the likelihood that a type II error occurred in a given research study. By looking at the magnitude of effects and sample sizes in prior research, psychologists can determine the likelihood that an effect was missed in a given study.

— MWP

▶ *See also* **TYPE II ERROR**

statistical reliability

n. A mathematical measurement of the consistency or accuracy of a measurement or a measurement procedure.

statistical significance

n. Statistical significance refers to a decision about whether a trend observed in sample data exists in the population at large. By convention, researchers usually adhere to a decision criterion of $p = .05$ for determining statistical significance. Statistical significance does not necessarily indicate practical significance: if a trend in the data is "significant" from a statistical standpoint, that significance indicates only that a relationship observed in the sample is likely to exist in the population at large. In many cases, effects that are statistically significant are of such small magnitude that they lack any practical meaning or implications. One emerging trend in psychological research is to examine carefully the magnitude of trends in the data, known as effect sizes, alongside traditional significance tests.

— MWP

▶ *See also* **P-VALUE** *and* **SIGNIFICANCE TEST**

statistical test

n. Any of numerous mathematical procedures used to test the likelihood of the correctness of an empirical hypothesis.

statistics

n. The branch of mathematical science that seeks to describe data or to make inferences about populations from data in determining the accuracy of empirical hypotheses.

statistics, correlational

n. The branch of the mathematical description of data samples that uses linear models of the relationships among variables to predict future relationships among the variables.

statistics, descriptive

n. The branch of mathematics that uses numerical indexes and graphic representations to summarize or present data.

statistics, inferential

n. The branch of mathematical science concerned with making predictions about population parameters using sample characteristics as a basis.

stem-and-leaf display

n. A graphical method of presenting data in which the first digit or two digits serve as a stem or category for a table and the remaining digits (leaves) are listed in order beside the stems so that the whole resembles a sideways histogram. Hence the data list 100, 102, 117, 117, 118, 128, 129, 130 would be presented thus:

```
10 0 2
11 7 7 8
12 8 9
13 0
```

stereogram

n. A stereogram is any visual pattern that contains binocular disparity. Because human observers view the world with two frontally oriented eyes, each retina receives a different perspective view of environmental objects and surfaces. The small differences between the two eyes' retinal images are referred to as binocular disparities. Traditionally, stereograms were viewed using a stereoscope. Charles Wheatstone invented the mirror stereoscope and in 1838 published the first stereograms depicting 3-D objects. The stereograms used today are typically presented using computers. In the early 1960s Bela Julesz developed computer-generated random-dot stereograms. These stereograms are unique in that the depicted 3-D objects and surfaces are defined only by the pattern of binocular disparities.

No monocularly visible object contours or outlines are present within either individual eye's retinal image. In modern psychological research, random-dot stereograms are usually preferred because the depicted objects and scenes are defined only by binocular disparity.   – JFN

stereoscope

n. Any device that presents slightly different views of the same scene to each eye so that the brain fuses the images into a single one with the illusion of depth.

stereoscopic illusion

n. The fusion in the brain of two flat images of the same scene from slightly different points of view, which creates a false sense of depth.

stereoscopic vision

n. Normal human vision in which the images from each eye are fused in the brain into a single image which is three-dimensional, allowing inferences about depth not possible with a single two-dimensional view.

stereotactic instrument

n. A complex set of frameworks, clamps, and instruments for holding the head and surgical instruments in precise alignment with the brain, which is used in brain surgery in order to increase the precision with which the surgery is performed.

stereotaxic

adj. Of or relating to the active movement of an organism in response to touch or contact with a solid surface.

stereotaxic surgery

n. An operative procedure involving cutting, electrically stimulating, or otherwise altering the brain using a stereotactic instrument to hold the head and brain steady and to guide the instruments used precisely.

stereotaxis

n. The active movement of an organism in reaction to touch or other direct contact with a solid surface.

stereotyped behavior

n. A fixed pattern of behavior that does not alter with differing circumstances, as is characteristic of some forms of bigotry and compulsive acts in humans and is usual with instinctive behavior in other animals.

stereotypes

n. Stereotypes, prejudice, and *discrimination* are frequently used interchangeably in public discourse, and even in some social scientific scholarship. Furthermore, there is no universally agreed upon definition for any of these phenomena. Although this entry discusses the definition of stereotypes in more depth later, it is important to point out that, despite differences in definition, most social psychologists view stereotypes as beliefs, prejudice as an attitude or affect, and discrimination as some sort of behavior. Although related to one another, sometimes causally, beliefs, attitudes, and behaviors are also clearly distinguishable from one another. A stereotype is not the same as either prejudice or discrimination. It is a belief, not an attitude or behavior.

Furthermore, and perhaps even more surprisingly, there is little evidence strongly linking stereotypes to either prejudice or discrimination. A small number of studies have correlated stereotypes with prejudice, but those studies consistently find only a weak relation between them. Even less research has examined the relationship between stereotypes and discriminatory behavior. Although there is very little evidence that stereotypes cause discrimination (or vice versa), this is because little evidence has addressed this issue. It remains possible, therefore, that future research will show a powerful cause-and-effect relationship between stereotypes and discrimination. It is also possible that there are specific conditions under which stereotypes are strongly related to prejudice and discrimination. If so, as of this writing, they have yet to be discovered.

Many laypeople and social scientists alike assume that stereotypes are inherently inaccurate. One of the most effective ways to dismiss a person's claim about a group (e.g., "They are [bad drivers, rich, smart, dumb, aggressive, etc.]") is to declare, "That's just a stereotype." To accuse someone of "stereotyping" is to accuse him or her of doing something bad, unjustified, unfair, and inaccurate. There are, however, serious problems inherent in defining stereotypes as inaccurate.

Stereotype should be defined in a neutral manner, one which does not provide a false and unjustified "resolution" of the accuracy issue by definition. A simple, broad, inclusive, pragmatic, and coherent definition is, Stereotypes are beliefs about groups. This allows for all sorts of possibilities not explicitly stated. Stereotypes may or may not be accurate and rational, be widely shared, be conscious, be rigid, exaggerate group differences, assume group differences are essential or biological, cause or reflect prejudice, cause biases and self-fulfilling prophecies. It is good that this definition does not specify these things. Rather than foreclosing answers to questions regarding the nature of stereotypes by definition, it leaves them open for empirical investigation.

Stereotypes are nothing more than people's beliefs about groups. They are much like other beliefs. Sometimes they are reasonable, rational, and useful and make a lot of sense. At other times, they are irrational and inaccurate and do not make much sense. Although stereotypes can and do lead to a wide range of biases in memory, judgment, and perception, in general, those biases tend to be quite modest. Nonetheless, research has identified conditions under which stereotypes do have some powerful effects, and it is under these conditions that stereotypes are most likely to play a significant role in prejudice and discrimination.

            – LJ

stereotype threat

n. A person's fear that her/his behavior will confirm an existing negative generalization about her/his ethnic or other group, which sometimes incapacitates performance and causes the negative expectation to turn into a self-fulfilling prophecy.

stereotyping

n. Stereotyping refers to the use of stereotypes to judge other people. It typically refers to using stereotypes to judge a particular person. If, for example, people rate the intelligence of a student from a lower-social-class background less favorably than they rate the intelligence of a student from a higher-social-class background, despite identical academic performance on identical tests, people's social class stereotypes would appear to be influencing and biasing their judgments of these particular students. The primary questions addressed by research on stereotyping have been (1) What types of influences do stereotypes exert on how we judge individuals? (2) To what extent do people rely on stereotypes versus individuating information when judging other people? (3) Under what conditions are people more or less likely to rely on stereotyping when judging other people?

Perceiver, target, and individuating information: Some necessary jargon. Everyone in social interaction both perceives other people and is a target of other people's perceptions. Nonetheless, in order to have a comprehensible discussion of the role of stereotypes in person perception, it is necessary to distinguish the perceiver from the target. The perceiver is the person holding and possibly using a stereotype to judge the target, who is, potentially, a target of stereotyping. Thus, despite the fact that everyone is both perceiver and target, this discussion, as do most on stereotypes and person perception, relies on the artificial but necessary distinction between perceiver and target.

What is the alternative to stereotyping? It is the use of *individuating information* – judging individual targets, not on the basis of stereotypes regarding their group, but, instead, on the basis of their personal, unique, *individual* characteristics. *Individuation*, therefore, is judging a person as a unique individual, rather than as a member of a group, and *individuating information* refers to the unique personality, behaviors, attitudes, accomplishments, and so on, of a particular target.

There are two broadly separable ways in which stereotypes can influence the way people perceive a particular target. *Biases* occur when stereotypes influence perception, evaluation, memory, and judgment. Biases

alter the way a *perceiver* judges a target but do not necessarily directly affect the target. *Self-fulfilling prophecies*, however, occur when the stereotype influences perception because it first alters targets' actual behavior (which is then perceived accurately).

Not all influences of stereotypes on judgment are unjustified. In many situations, it is reasonable, appropriate, and justified for people to use their expectations as a basis for making predictions about particular individuals and for "filling in the blanks" when faced with unclear or ambiguous situations. First, consider a nonsocial example. In the Northern Hemisphere, it is usually much warmer in July than in January. People are, therefore, doing something quite reasonable if they expect any particular July day to be warmer than any particular January day. This is a reasonable expectation, despite the fact that, sometimes, daytime highs in January are warmer than nighttime lows in July.

This basic principle – that an accurate belief can lead to an expectation that is as accurate as possible under the circumstances – is just as true for social beliefs, such as stereotypes, as it is for nonsocial beliefs. So, if without any additional, relevant individuating information, if people expect any given woman to be shorter than any given man, or if they expect any given doctor to be wealthier than any given janitor, or if they expect any given Latino-American adult to have completed less education than any given Asian-American adult, they are similarly simply being as reasonable and rational (and as accurate) as possible, in the absence of specific relevant information about each target.

Similarly, accurate beliefs can often be appropriately used to "fill in the blanks" when perceiving ambiguous situations. For example, people interpret a fidgety interviewee to be "nervous" if they believe the interview is about sex, but "bored" if they think it is about international economics. So, if people find out that both a member of a pacifist group and an Al Qaeda member "attacked" the United States, they are simply being reasonable if they use their beliefs about pacifists and Al Qaeda members (their stereotypes) and assume that the antiwar activist's attack was a verbal critique of U.S. policies, but the Al Qaeda attack was something much more dangerous.

Only a very small number of studies have examined whether stereotypes increase or reduce the accuracy of perceptions and judgments, but what they find is most interesting. If the stereotype itself is accurate, stereotyping (i.e., using the stereotype to judge an individual) will often increase the accuracy of those judgments, at least in the absence of perfectly clear and relevant individuating information. (When individuating information is perfectly clear and relevant, people should rely exclusively on it for making judgments – as, in fact, most research shows they do). On the other hand, when the stereotype is inaccurate, stereotyping *reduces* the accuracy of person perception judgments. For practical purposes, therefore, of eliminating unfair biases and maximizing accuracy, an important starting point is simply understanding how and when stereotypes enhance or reduce the accuracy of person perception.

Conclusions. Stereotyping occurs in a wide variety of ways. Stereotypes influence people's perceptions, judgments, and evaluations of, attributions and memory for, and interactions with other people. Stereotyping is most likely to occur when targets' behavior or attributes are unavailable or unclear. However, people also easily discard their stereotypes when judging others, at least when they have clear, individualized information about those others. Although there are conditions under which stereotypes can strongly influence person perception, in general, such influence is weak, fragile, and fleeting, largely because, in general, people rely heavily on individuating information when it is available. ▶ *See also* **STEREOTYPES**

stereotypy

n. Any persistent repetition of a behavior pattern such as habitual gestures or expressions in normal individuals and repeated phrases, sounds, or movements in persons having autistic disorder, obsessive-compulsive disorder, and some forms of schizophrenia.

stimulus

n. **1.** Any energy that is sufficient and appropriate in form as to activate a sensory receptor. **2.** In conditioning, anything that elicits a response.

stimulus control

n. The degree to which behavior is guided by the environment. The behaviorist point of view suggests that all behavior is under the control of the environment, while more cognitive positions hold that mental processes are more important than stimulus conditions.

stimulus, discriminative

n. An environmental signal that is received by an organism and used to choose responses so that response with the discriminative stimulus is different from response without it.

stimulus equivalence

n. **1.** In behaviorism, the state of being in which two or more similar environmental energies or objects are followed by identical behavior of an individual organism. **2.** In general, the failure of an organism to discriminate between two sources of perceptual energy.

stimulus generalization

n. The process of reacting to a variety of stimuli with the same behavior with which one has reacted to another stimulus in the past. Typically the magnitude of the reaction is a linear function of the similarity between new and old stimuli.

stimulus, neutral

n. An environmental signal to which an organism does not respond with any behavior measured or noticed by an experimenter.

stimulus onset asynchrony

n. The time between the start of one stimulus and the start of the next stimulus, which is usually of importance in masking experiments.

stimulus, reinforcing

n. Anything that can be used to increase or decrease the likelihood of the appearance of a behavior when appropriately associated with the behavior in time and space.

stimulus-response

n. A model of learning in which the basic learning unit is a particular response to a particular stimulus.

stimulus-response learning

n. A model of learning in which the basic learning unit is a particular response to a particular stimulus.

stimulus-response psychology

n. The study of behavior within the confines of a conditioning model so that all explanations are learned responses to particular stimuli.

stimulus-response theory

n. All the various ideas about learning and psychology in general that limit explanations to learning particular responses to particular stimuli.

stimulus-stimulus learning

n. Any form of learning in which one stimulus is associated with another stimulus instead of with a particular response.

stirrup

n. One of the small bones of the middle ear, which together convey sound to the oval window of the cochlea.

stochastic

adj. Of or relating to a random process that has a probability distribution which is somewhat predictable but whose particular occurrence cannot be precisely predicted.

Stockholm syndrome

n. A psychological condition in which a hostage identifies with her/his captors and shows loyalty and affection toward them.

strabismus

n. A misalignment of the eyes making binocular fixation and vision impossible. In strabismus, either an individual with strabismus has double vision or the brain blocks out the

vision of one eye so the person has monocular vision, making depth perception less accurate. Also called hypertropia.

stranger anxiety

n. The observation that normal children become more anxious in the presence of unfamiliar people and especially adults shortly before the age of 1 year than they were as young infants and that this anxiety gradually recedes between the ages of one and three.

strange situation

n. An experimental arrangement and procedure in which a 9' by 9' room with two doors and three chairs and a standard set of toys is used as a setting to investigate the attachment behavior of infants. The standard procedure is for the caregiver with the infant to be greeted by an experimenter, be shown into the room, and be seated, encouraging the child to play with the toys. A stranger to the child enters and leaves the room, the mother leaves and returns twice, and the stranger is left alone with the infant in a standard series of events designed to stress the child mildly so as to observe the infant's reactions and relationship with the caregiver.

strategic processing

n. The ability to control and select one's own cognitive activities in a reflective, goal-oriented way so as to use one's available mental processing capacities most efficiently in a given task. This involves the metacognitive abilities to notice one's own cognitive processes, to evaluate whether one is performing optimally, and to alter them at will.

strategic self-presentation

n. The process of managing the impression one makes on others, usually through a combination of ingratiation, self-promotion, and intimidation.

stratified random sample

n. A sample that is selected to have characteristics similar to those of the larger target population on variables of interest to the study or investigation. A stratified random sample is selected by dividing the population into nonoverlapping and collectively exhaustive subpopulations or strata (the number of strata depends on the target of the study and the relevant grouping characteristics). Sample members are then randomly selected from each stratum or subgroup in proportion to the population. The members of each stratum are pooled to form the overall sample.   – BJM

stream of consciousness
n. **1.** The dynamic flow or succession of experiences including sensations, thoughts, fantasies, emotions, and images of which our consciousness is composed. **2.** A writing style describing or imitating the stream of consciousness.

stress
n. **1.** A prolonged state of psychological and physiological arousal leading to negative effects on mood, cognitive capacity, immune function, and physical health. **2.** An emphasis placed on a syllable or word by saying it more loudly and deliberately than surrounding words and by drawing out its sound slightly longer than usual.

stressor
n. Any environmental circumstance to which the organism reacts with prolonged physiological arousal.

stretch reflex
n. The involuntary contraction of a muscle in response to a sudden stretching of the muscle, which is important in maintaining balance.

striate cortex
n. Primary visual area (V1) located in the calcarine fissure of the occipital lobe (Brodmann's area 17). It receives information from the lateral geniculate body of the thalamus through the optic radiation. The different points of the primary visual area clearly correspond to specific segments in the retina (retinotopic organization). Damage in the right or left primary visual area results in contralateral hemianopia. Complete, bilateral lesions of the occipital lobes produce cortical blindness.   – AA

▶ *See also* **EXTRASTRIATE CORTEX** *and* **PRIMARY VISUAL CORTEX**

striate muscle
n. Any of the skeletal muscles which appear striped to the eye.

stroke
n. A blockage or breaking of a blood vessel in the brain, resulting in a reduced blood supply to a part of the brain which can rapidly cause cell death in the brain, which has a high need for oxygen and other nutrients. Also known as an infarct or cerebrovascular accident.

Strong-Campbell Interest Inventory
n. An older form of the Strong Interest Inventory.

Strong Interest Inventory
n. A widely used test of vocational interest for adolescents and adults which includes Holland's 6 general occupational themes; 25 basic occupational interest scales; 211 occupational scales normed on successful and longtime workers in a particular job or field which predict work adjustment in those fields; 4 personal style scales; and 3 administrative indices, which are used to detect invalid protocols or unusual response styles.

Strong Vocational Interest Blank
n. An older form of the Strong Interest Inventory.

Stroop effect
n. The interference in reading a color name which occurs when the color name is printed in an ink of a different color. This is an example of response interference effect.

Stroop test
n. A test of response interference in which the time it takes to read a color name printed in an ink of a different color is compared to the time it takes to read the same color name in black ink or ink of the same color and to name a color from a bar of the color. Also called the Stroop color-word interference test.

structural equation modeling

n. A set of statistical procedures for measuring the effect of latent variables in the relationships among other, observed variables so as to make causal inferences about them when the latent variables cannot be measured directly.

structuralism

n. **1.** The scientific study of experience through a systematic examination of introspection. This began in the late 1800s under the leadership of Edward Titchener and Wilhelm Wundt and was the method employed in the first psychology laboratory. **2.** A multidisciplinary approach to linguistics, textual analysis, social anthropology, human psychology, and culture which is based on the analysis of linguistic signs and their functional relationships to each other, which was popularized by Ferdinand de Saussure in the 1960s.

structured personality test

n. Any instrument intended to measure the enduring style of personal adjustment of the individual in which the format of the inquiries and items is predetermined and limited, unlike projective tests, in which responses are more free form. This includes such tests as the California Psychological Inventory, the Minnesota Multiphasic Personality Inventory, the NEO Personality Inventory, and the Myers-Briggs Type Inventory.

structure-of-intellect model

n. A model of intelligence that imagines that there are five operations, six products, and five content types of intellect for a total of 150 factors or aspects of intelligence. The five operations are cognition, memory, divergent production, convergent production, and evaluation. The six products are units, classes, relations, systems, transformations, and implications. The five content types are symbolic, content, behavioral, auditory, and visual.

Student-Newman-Keuls procedure

n. A post hoc comparison of all pairs of means in a one-way analysis of variance which has high statistical power but does not provide confidence intervals and does not control type I error. Also known as the Newman-Keuls test.

stuttering

n. A disturbance in the fluency and time patterning of speech characterized by repetition of sounds or syllables, drawing out of some sounds, inappropriate pauses within words, interjections of inappropriate sounds in words, obvious blocking of intended speech, word substitutions, and excess physical tension during speech.

subconscious

adj. Below or out of consciousness, as in thought or other metal processes occurring without the knowledge of the thinker.

subcortical

adj. Of or relating to the nervous system below the cerebral cortex.

subject (research)

n. Any living participant in a research study whose reactions to the conditions of the study are a source of data for the study. Also known as a research participant.

subjective contour

n. An illusory border or edge in an image which is inferred by the observer but not actually present in the image.

subjective culture

n. People in each culture (defined by the conjunction of language, location, and history) have a characteristic way of viewing their social environment. Culture is to society what memory is to individuals, so it consists of what has worked in the past, has helped a group adjust to its environment, and thus was worth transmitting to future generations.

Subjective culture includes *shared* ideas, theories, and political, religious, scientific, economic, and social standards for judging events in the environment. Subjective culture can be contrasted with *material culture:* the tools, dwellings, foods, clothing, pots, machines, roads, bridges that are widely used in a culture.

Subjective culture includes also shared memories, ideas about correct and incorrect behavior, stereotypes, and the way members of the culture value entities in their environment. Categorizations, associations among the categories, role definitions, values, and value orientations (e.g., are humans intrinsically "good" or "bad"?) are also elements of subjective culture.   – HTT

subjective norms

Definition. n. Subjective norms are a person's perceptions of what the people who are important to him or her think about his/her performing a specific behavior. In other words, subjective norms are a function of a person's evaluation of whether different people or groups of people approve or disapprove of his/her performing a behavior and how much the person is motivated to comply with those people's wishes. A person is likely to perform a behavior that important others approve of because he/she may feel subtle social pressure to conform to their wishes.

Explanation. As mentioned, subjective norms refer to a person's perceptions of what important others' attitudes are about his or her performing a behavior. For example, college students are confronted with the choice of skipping class rather than attending class regularly. When deciding whether or not to skip class, a student may consider what parents, teachers, and other students think about his/her skipping class. The student would probably determine that parents and teachers would disapprove of skipping class. However, perhaps friends in the class skip frequently, and they encourage the student to skip too. In this case, if peer attitudes matter more to the student than the attitudes of parents and teachers, the student would have positive subjective norms about skipping class. On the other hand, if the student's parents agree to pay for school only if the student regularly attends class, or if the teacher disapproves of skipping class and deducts points, the student is more likely to have negative subjective norms for skipping class. Also, if the student is involved in a group project in class, and the other students' grades are dependent on this student's contribution, peers will likely disapprove of the student's skipping class and the student is more likely to have negative subjective norms for doing so.

Development and details. Subjective norms play a key role in two closely related theories – the theory of reasoned action (TRA) and the theory of planned behavior (TpB). These theories are widely used to understand and predict a person's behavior. While social scientists once believed that knowledge of a person's attitudes about a behavior was sufficient to allow the prediction of that behavior, inconsistent research findings forced these scientists to reevaluate their position. Although people's attitudes influence what they do, what their friends and other important people in their lives think (subjective norms) also influences what they do. The TRA takes this influence into account and states that attitudes *and* subjective norms must be used to predict a person's intention for performing a behavior, and this behavioral intention can then be used to predict whether the actual behavior will be carried out. The addition of the subjective norms element does improve prediction of behavior. The TpB is similar to the TRA except it adds that perceived control over the behavior must also be used to predict intentions (in addition to attitudes and subjective norms), and then the intentions can be used to predict behavior.

While subjective norms are considered generally to improve the accuracy of behavioral predictions, this is not *always* the case. There are certain types of people who are less influenced by subjective norms. For example, picture someone who would be considered a loner. When making decisions regarding the performance of behaviors, this type of person is probably less likely to have important others in his/her life and less likely to consider what other people think about his/her performing the behavior. Also, some people (called low self-monitors) do not care as much about what other people think about their behaviors. These low self-monitors have been found to behave in a consistent manner across situations, regardless of who is present or what other people think about their behavior.

                  – VKP, LAB

subjective well-being

n. An overall personal impression of the quality of one's life at a particular point in time, sometimes unrelated to the impression of others of one's objective state.

subjectivity

n. The process of making judgments based on personal experience, intuition, and interpretations rather than in terms of social definitions, culturally consensual viewpoints, or attempts at objectivity, as in science.

sublimation

n. A defense mechanism which converts unconscious negative drives and desires into positive and productive behavior. In classical psychoanalytic terms, our impulse is to fulfill the wishes of the id (often sexual and aggressive urges). However, through the reality principle, the ego transforms these urges and energies to fit appropriately within the larger societal context. From this perspective all choices that are appropriate and expected within society, both large (e.g., choosing a career or a partner) and small (e.g., keeping one's house tidy, creative endeavors), are thought of as sublimations of base desires. This process is unconscious; the individual using this defense mechanism is only aware of his or her choices and decisions and is completely unaware of the urges that have been transformed. Sublimation is the ultimate goal of the ego and is therefore thought to be the most positive defense mechanism in both the short and the long term.   – DGa

subliminal

adj. Of or relating to stimuli to which the individual responds but of which the individual is not conscious.

subliminal influence

n. Any stimulus or set of stimuli affecting behavior or mental processes of whose presence the individual is unaware.

subliminal perception

n. The process of reacting to stimuli of which the subject has no awareness.

subliminal stimulus

n. Any environmental energy source or event affecting behavior or mental processes of whose presence the individual is unaware.

substance abuse

n. The recurrent use of a drug or other substance in a way that interferes with daily functioning, repeatedly endangers the individual user, or causes the user recurrent legal problems, although the use of the substance causes repeated social or interpersonal problems.

substance-induced disorders

n. Substance tolerance disorder, substance withdrawal disorder, and other mental disorders caused by use of a drug or other substance.

substance P

n. An 11-member neurotransmitter in the central and peripheral nervous systems which mediates pain in the dorsal horn of the spinal column, causes smooth muscles to contract in response to pain and mast cells to secrete histamine, as well as serving as a vasodilator in blood vessels.

substance-related disorders

n. A family of disorders caused by abusing a drug or other substance, side effects of taking a drug, and exposure to toxic substances such as mercury.

substance use disorders

n. Any maladaptive pattern of using a drug or other substance including dependence disorders, substance abuse disorders and substance tolerance disorders, substance withdrawal disorders, and other substance-induced disorders.

substantia nigra

n. A dark-colored area in the midbrain below the thalamus with many dopamine-releasing neurons whose axons project into the striata which is involved in motor control and implicated in Parkinson's disease.

subtractive color mixture

n. A form of color mixing as in paint in which the addition of new colors absorbs more light and so reduces the wavelengths of light reflected, as opposed to additive color mixtures as in mixing colored lights, in which the mixture contains more light waves than the original.

subtractive counterfactual

n. A form of imagining in which a person thinks about what did happen and removes some of the factual aspects of it and then thinks about what might have happened, as in "If only my brother had not smoked, then he would not have gotten lung cancer and would still be alive."

subtyping

n. **1.** In social psychology, the process of creating a new category within a stereotype when experience disconfirms the stereotype, which allows preservation of the stereotype with a new subcategory. Thus if a person has a stereotype of African-Americans as lazy and sees an African-American neighbor getting up at 6 o'clock to go jogging every morning, he/she may create a subtype of athletic African Americans so as to maintain the stereotype and account for the new information. **2.** In computer programming, the creation of a subclassification in a program that will serve as a member of the superordinate class in some circumstances but not others as duck or robin might be a subclass of the class birds and treated as birds in some contexts and not in others.

successive approximations, conditioning by

n. A process of training an organism to perform a particular behavior by reinforcing behavior that is closer to the desired behavior than was past behavior and requiring a closer approximation for each successive reinforcement.

sudden infant death syndrome

n. (SIDS) The sudden and unexpected death of a healthy infant for no apparent reason. There is no certain cause, although sleep apnea has been blamed and low-birth-weight and premature babies are somewhat more susceptible than full-term and normal-weight babies. Also called crib death.

suffix effect

n. A special case of the serial position effect in which memory impairment is brought about when words presented at the end of a list being memorized are not included in the list to be memorized.

suggestibility

n. **1.** The degree to which a person uncritically accepts the ideas, attitudes, or actions of another person. **2.** A characteristic of a hypnotized person.

sum of squares

n. The figure obtained by adding up the squared differences from the mean of a group of numbers:

$$SS = \Sigma(X - Xmean).$$

sundowning

n. The tendency of individuals with dementia to have their symptoms worsen late in the day. Sometimes also applied to other institutionalized persons.

sunk costs

n. Previously made and unrecoverable investments of time, energy, or money in a particular decision or enterprise. Often used in decision theory as well as in economics.

superego

n. In psychoanalysis, the conscience, which consists of introjected ideals and moral prescriptions from the parents, mostly in early childhood, and other admired adults through later life. The superego restricts the actions of the ego and mostly confines them within the limits imposed by society in the form of parents and other admired older persons in the child's life, but the ego tries to trick or circumvent the superego and find ways of expressing morally proscribed impulses.

superior colliculus

n. Either of two small bumps below the pineal gland near the bottom of the brain which receive a large tract of neural fibers from the optic nerve and connect both with the lateral geniculate nucleus and the tectospinal tract, which is involved in startle reactions and orienting movement of the head toward visual stimuli.

superior olivary nucleus

n. A collection of neurons in the pons which receive information from the cochlear nuclei and function to help locate sound via the time differences in auditory input from the two ears. Also called the superior olivary complex.

superior temporal gyrus

n. The ridge on the top of the temporal gyrus just below the lateral sulcus which contains the primary auditory cortex and Wernicke's area, which is necessary for the understanding of speech.

superstition

n. Any belief which is not subject to critical scrutiny and disconfirmation by evidence, including many beliefs about supernatural phenomena such as ghosts, werewolves, or crossing fingers to ward off evil.

superstitious behavior

n. Any behavior pattern that results from random or accidental reinforcement such as a rat's licking its paws before pressing a lever which delivers food and then licking its paws before pushing the bar on future occasions.

supplementary motor area

n. A part of area 6 of the precentral gyrus that is involved in planning complex movement, often involving both hands, with reference to memory rather than to visual stimuli. This brain area appears late in brain evolution, appearing in many monkey brains but lacking in brains of some other mammals.

suppression

n. The deliberate and conscious pushing of unwanted material from the mind, as in thought-stopping techniques. In psychoanalysis, suppressed material enters the preconscious and is distinct from repression, which is an unconscious process of relegating material to the unconscious.

suprachiasmatic nucleus

n. A small region on each side of the hypothalamus above the optic chiasm which receives input directly from the retina from an accessory optic tract which sends information to the pineal gland and is involved in daily body cycles or circadian rhythms.

surface structure

n. In Chomskian transformational grammar, the actual form of an utterance as it is said or written, as opposed to the deep structure or intended meaning of the utterance. The deep structure is modified by the processes of transformational grammar, following grammatical rules into one of many possible surface structures.

surgency

n. The personality trait of cheerfulness, spontaneity, sociability, and responsiveness in Cattell's factor analytic system of personality.

surprise

n. The emotion which results from a violation of expectations or perception of novelty in the environment and which is one of the six basic facial expressions of emotion. Surprise results when one is confounded with the unexpectedness of circumstances.

survey research

n. Survey research is a rigorous quantitative methodology employed by social scientists to collect information that can be used to estimate the characteristics of defined populations and/or test research hypotheses. The varieties of survey research are highly diverse. Both cross-sectional and longitudinal, or panel, survey designs are common. Although most surveys are of individuals, many other units of analysis are also examined, including social networks, discrete and random events, and various organizational structures, such as businesses, hospitals, schools, and political jurisdictions. More complex, multilevel survey research, in which information is collected and organized at two or more levels (e.g., from surveys of both employers and employees), is also becoming commonplace. Survey research is routinely conducted using a variety of different modes, including face-to-face and telephone interviews and self-administered mail and Web-based questionnaires. Types of phenomena commonly measured via survey research include the behaviors, attitudes, opinions, and other qualities of the individuals or units being studied.   – TPJ

surveys

n. Surveys involve systematically gathering information by asking questions. Surveys typically involve questioning individuals but can also involve organizations or institutions. Survey questions can be asked in telephone or in-person interviews or via self-administered questionnaires completed on paper or on an Internet Web site. Surveys typically involve gathering data from a subsample of a larger population (often with the goal of surveying a representative sample). Questions asked in a survey are also usually standardized (i.e., questions are asked in the same way to each respondent), and responses to survey questions are typically quantified into categories for aggregation and analysis.
                                                  – ALH

survival analysis

n. Any statistical procedure for estimating the time until an event such as death or the failure of a machine occurs. Also known as reliability theory in engineering and duration analysis in economics.

survival of the fittest

n. A slogan describing an aspect of evolution by natural selection in which the organisms best fitted to an ecological niche are most likely to survive long enough to produce viable offspring. The term was coined by Herbert Spencer and used to justify cruelty and indifference to others in Victorian society and later times.

survivor guilt

n. A sense of remorse for the fate of people who die and of failure to have done enough to prevent their deaths in persons who have lived through a life-threatening situation in which others did not. This is common among those who live through catastrophic events such as the 9/11 attacks and among the families of people who die of disease related to genetic predispositions. Most such persons ask the question Why me? repeatedly without finding a satisfactory answer.

susto

n. A belief that the soul has left the body, resulting in apathy, fatigue, headaches, digestive difficulties, weight loss, muscle aches, sleep disturbance, and low self-esteem. This is a psychological disorder usually found among persons from Latin American countries including emigrants from those countries. Also called *chibih*, *espanto*, *pasmo*, *perdida del alma*, and *tripa ida*.

syllabary

n. A syllabary is a phonetic writing system whose symbols (graphemes) represent syllables or moras. A syllable is a rhythmic unit consisting of a cluster of segments inside a word, including an obligatory vowel (the nucleus) and optional consonants in onset (prenuclear) or coda (postnuclear) position. The Hiragana and Katakana writing systems used to write Japanese are syllabaries.
                                                  – EMF

syllogism

n. A form of deductive reasoning in which a major and a minor proposition assumed to be true are used to reach a conclusion, as in "All men are mortal. Bob is a man. Therefore Bob is mortal." There are 256 possible forms of syllogism, and only 24 are held to be true in the field of logic.

Sylvian fissure ▶ *See* LATERAL FISSURE

symbiosis

n. In biology, the living together of two distinct species. It is most commonly used to describe the situation in which both species benefit from living together as humans benefit from having *Lactobacillus* in their gut which allows them to digest milk, while drinking milk feeds the *Lactobacillus*. The term may also include situations in which there is benefit to only one of the species involved and it is either harmful or neutral to the other species and some situations in which it is harmful to both species, as in competition.

symbol

n. **1.** Anything that is used to represent something else, as a number may represent quantity, a flag may represent a country, and a smile may represent assent or agreement. **2.** In psychoanalysis, an image which represents something else, as a bear may represent a feared father or a cigar may represent a penis. **3.** A standard pictorial device used to convey information and usually a warning, as $\otimes$ denotes "do not cross."

symbol-digit test

n. A measure of ability in which a person is given lists of symbols and corresponding numbers and must then translate the list into numbers while being timed. The number of correct translations within a fixed time interval is the measure of ability.

symbolic interactionism

n. Symbolic interactionism is an intellectual tradition in sociology and social psychology. Inspired by the early writings of Blumer, Cooley, and Mead, this tradition seeks to understand individual social behaviors through a systematic analysis of how human beings make sense of each other's actions on the basis of the meanings and implications these actions have for social interactions. Symbolic interactionism emphasizes negotiation and transformation of meanings in the social interactions through the interpretive use of language and other symbols. From this perspective, self-knowledge is constructed by appraising what other people think of the self and then integrating these perceptions into the self-image.
         − YHK, CYC

symbolic representation

n. The process of encoding experience or data into abstract forms in the mind or in a computer program. Words and numbers are two forms of symbolic representations, and there is much debate about the actual forms of mental symbols.

symbolization

n. **1.** The process of encoding one thing into an abstract representation of it, as a circle may be used to represent the moon. **2.** In social learning theory, the ability to think about one's behavior in words and images.

symbolizing three dimensions in two

n. A theory of perception that suggests that people in Western cultures focus more on representations on paper than do people in other cultures and in particular spend more time learning to interpret pictures.

symbol-substitution test

n. Any test that requires subjects to translate one set of symbols into another, as in the symbol-digit test commonly used as a part of IQ tests.

sympathetic apraxia

n. Apraxia observed in patients with anterior left hemisphere damage associated with right hemiparesis. Because of the right hemiparesis, praxis can only be tested in the left hand. In consequence, the patient presents simultaneously two different motor defects: paresis in the right hand and apraxia in the left. Sympathetic apraxia is frequently found in motor aphasias.   − AA

▶ *See also* **APRAXIA**

sympathetic branch

n. The portion of the autonomic nervous system which tends to prepare the body for action when aroused and is opposed to the parasympathetic nervous system, which calms the body and prepares it for rest and digestion.

sympathetic nervous system

n. (SNS) The division of the autonomic nervous system, which tends to be associated with catabolism, the expenditure of energy, in contrast with the parasympathetic system, which is associated with anabolism, the storage of energy. When the SNS is stimulated, blood flow to skeletal muscles is increased and epinephrine levels are raised, leading to an increase in heart rate and blood sugar levels, as well as piloerection (goose bumps).

    Preganglionic neurons are cholinergic: they release acetylcholine, which binds to nicotinic receptor sites, leading to a rapid, brief response. Some of these neurons also release acetylcholine to muscarinic metabotropic receptor sites, leading to a slow response or even inhibition of response, depending on the type of stimulation. When the SNS motor neurons emerge from thoracic and lumbar levels of the spinal cord, they are then organized into a chain of sympathetic ganglia which lies along the spinal cord to coordinate appropriate responses.

A portion of the SNS not organized into the sympathetic ganglia is the medulla of the adrenal gland, which secretes adrenaline (epinephrine) in response to sympathetic preganglionic stimulation.

Postganglionic SNS neurons are adrenergic, sending axons directly to enervate their target organs.   – vs

symptom
n. **1.** A subjective complaint by an individual to a doctor or psychotherapist. **2.** A departure from normal condition or functioning which may be a sign of an underlying disease or disorder. **3.** Anything that is taken as an indication of something else, as a rising national debt may be a symptom of war.

symptom formation
n. **1.** The process by which a sign of underlying disorder or disease is produced by the disorder or disease or a reaction to it. **2.** In psychoanalysis, the expression of the anxiety from a repressed impulse in a behavioral or somatic form.

symptom substitution
n. In psychoanalysis, the appearance of a new complaint or expression of repressed anxiety that occurs when one complaint or expression has disappeared but the underlying conflict which is the source of anxiety has not been resolved.

synapse
n. The narrow gap between the axon terminal of one nerve cell and a dendritic receptor site of another nerve cell (or between a neuron and a muscle cell) across which neurotransmitters float to propagate nerve impulses

from one neuron to the next. Electrical depolarization in the axon causes vesicles holding chemical neurotransmitters to move to the cell wall and release their transmitter chemical into the cleft between the two cells. The chemical transmitter then floats across the gap between cells and attaches to specialized receptor sites in the dendrite, causing the opening of ion channels, which results in an exchange of sodium and potassium ions across the dendritic cell wall, which alters the local electric potential of the cell wall and may lead to a wave of depolarization in this neuron, which would then lead it to stimulate as many as 50,000 other neurons to which it is connected.

synaptic button
n. The bulbous end of an axon at the junction with another neuron. Also called a terminal button and *bouton synaptique* in French.

synaptic cleft
n. The narrow gap between an axon terminal and the postsynaptic membrane of a dendrite filled with salty water across which neurotransmitters must float in order to propagate neural impulses.

synaptic gap
n. The narrow cleft between an axon terminal and the postsynaptic membrane of a dendrite filled with salty water across which neurotransmitters must float in order to propagate neural impulses.

synaptic receptor
n. A specialized site on the postsynaptic membrane of a neuron or muscle specialized to react to chemical neurotransmitters.

synaptic reuptake
n. The active process by which proteins in presynaptic membranes remove neurotransmitter chemicals from the water in the synaptic cleft and store them in vesicles.

synaptic terminal
n. The bulbous end of an axon at the junction with another neuron.

synaptic transmission

n. The process of chemical transmission of an electric impulse across the water-filled gap between nerve cells.

synaptic vesicle

n. A small saclike structure in synaptic terminals that holds neurotransmitter chemicals and releases them when electrically stimulated by a nerve impulse.

syncope

n. A brief lapse in consciousness (commonly called fainting). The cause is a transient loss of cerebral oxygenation, which may result from a variety of external and/or internal events. These events may include stimulation of the vagus nerve, which affects parasympathetic control, slowing the heart rate and decreasing the availability of oxygen to the brain. Also, a parasympathetic rebound from sympathetic activity in the abdominal viscera (a vaso-vagal phenomenon) may produce syncope. Extreme temperature, emotional stress, or hypoglycemia may also induce syncope. Syncope may be prevented or minimized by lying down flat or by sitting with the head between the knees. It is possible that the acupressure point for fainting, pressure applied between the upper lip and nostrils, may also prevent or minimize syncope. The use of an ammonia inhalant capsule may revive a person who is fainting or has just fainted.   – VS

synesthesia

n. A sensory experience resulting from stimulation of a different body part or a different sense from the one experienced by the subject, as in seeing music as a flow of colors. This is a common experience when taking LSD or other hallucinogenic drugs.

synonym

n. Two words with similar or identical meanings are *synonyms*. For example, *volume* and *tome* are synonyms for the word *book*; *student* and *disciple* are synonyms for the word *pupil*. Arguably, details of the origins of words, as well as their additional senses (e.g., *book* can be a noun or a verb; *pupil* can refer to a student or to the opening in the iris of the eye), mean that no two words can be perfectly synonymous. Additional terminology provides more detailed ways for describing relations between words with similar meanings. For instance, *plant* is a hypernym for *flower* (or *tree*, *bush*, etc.) and *tulip* (or *rose*, *dahlia*, etc.) is a hyponym to *flower*.   – EMF

▶ *See also* **HOMOGRAPH**

syntactic aphasia

n. One of the four subtypes of aphasia proposed by Henry Head, who suggested a fourfold classification of aphasia into verbal, syntactic, nominal, and semantic. Syntactic aphasia in general corresponds to what is usually referred as Broca's aphasia. Patients with this type of language defect have difficulties in using the morphosyntactic rules of the language and apraxia of speech. It is usually associated with damage in the left posterior frontal lobe, the brain area named *Broca's area* (Brodmann's area 44).   – AA

syntactic processing

n. Syntactic processing, or *parsing*, is the process of recovering syntactic structure from a perceived string of words. Linguistic signals – written, acoustic, or gestural – are first decoded into a string of linearly ordered lexical items. The syntactic processor must determine the hierarchical relations between these lexical items. It does so generally in a left-to-right fashion, following a handful of heuristics, or *parsing strategies*, by which it builds the simplest structure. Parsing strategies are grounded on limitations imposed by the cognitive architecture, including working memory limitations. Evidence for the existence of parsing strategies has come from garden path sentences, like *The horse raced past the barn fell.* In such sentences, the initial analysis built by the syntactic processor (here, taking *raced* to be the main verb of the sentence) turns out to be incorrect (*raced* is really the participle of an omitted verb in a reduced relative clause; cf. *The horse that was raced past the barn fell*). Garden path sentences are difficult to process because their correct structure violates a parsing strategy, that is, a principle of syntactic processing.   – EMF

syntax

n. Syntax is the component of a language's grammar that licenses sentence structure, by means of a set of principles that generate the set of well-formed sentences in that language. Syntactic relationships between words in sentences are not simply linear (in a sentence like *Augustine dates Beatrice*, the subject *Augustine* precedes the verb *dates*, which precedes the object *Beatrice*). Instead, syntactic relationships are hierarchical: the two adjacent words *dates Beatrice* are related in a way that *Augustine dates* are not. The syntax of a language plays three fundamental roles in determining the structural relations between words. First, by the application of phrase structure rules, the syntax generates basic sentence structures consisting of a subject (noun phrase) and a predicate (verb phrase), as well as any obligatory heads (e.g., nouns or verbs) plus any obligatory or optional arguments (e.g., direct object noun phrases or prepositional phrases). Second, basic sentence structures are combined by the syntax to create complex sentences containing subordinate clauses, such as sentences with relative clauses (*I know Augustine, who dates Beatrice*) or with sentential complements (*I know that Augustine will date Beatrice*). Third, the syntax contains principles which license the movement of constituents within sentences, to obtain constructions such as questions (*Who does Augustine date?*).

— EMF

▶ *See also* **DEEP STRUCTURE**

synthetic language

n. **1.** An artificial language such as those used in computer programs, as opposed to natural languages, which have evolved in and are spoken by persons of particular cultures. **2.** In linguistics, a language which tends to express multiple meanings with a single word, as opposed to isolating languages, in which there is a single meaning per word although in practice languages vary along a continuum of morpheme-to-word ratios.

systematic desensitization

n. A therapeutic procedure used to lessen phobic and other anxious reactions involving learning relaxation techniques followed by graded systematic exposure to the anxiety-producing stimuli, which leads to acquisition of a competing response (relaxation) in the presence of the anxiety-producing object, which lessens emotional and physical reactivity to the stimulus.

System C

n. A system descriptive language used in computer programming, such as C^{++}, which enables simulation of concurrent processes including communication between the processes.

system justification theory

n. Societies differ in the manner and extent of differentiation between groups and the forms of inequality that prevail. Social institutions and hierarchies are maintained in part through attitudes and belief systems that justify them. *System justification* refers to the social psychological tendency to defend, justify, and uphold aspects of the social status quo, even if it was arrived at arbitrarily or if a different system would better meet people's interests.

System justification researchers propose that there is an abstract system-justifying goal that underlies people's motivation to maintain the status quo. This goal is a powerful determinant of thoughts, feelings, and behaviors, because it satisfies several social and psychological needs, including *epistemic* needs for consistency, certainty, and meaning and *existential* needs to manage threat and distress.

From the perspective of the disadvantaged, justifying the system perpetuates their own deprivation and therefore works against their personal and collective interests. People system justify because attaining this goal serves the palliative function of reducing the anxiety, guilt, dissonance, discomfort, and uncertainty that result from being part of an unequal and possibly unjust system. The net result of system justification is social and political acquiescence.

— JVT, JTJ

systems analysis

n. The process of breaking down complex processes into component parts which can be modeled by a computer program, as is common in cognitive psychology.

systems theory

n. An approach to industrial psychology, family therapy, and group dynamics in which the functions and patterns of interaction of the parts are the focus of analysis and intervention.

System X

n. A supercomputer that comprises 1,100 Apple Power Mac G5 computers, which was the first supercomputer to achieve a speed of 10 teraflops, in 2003.

T

taboo

1. *adj.* Forbidden, prohibited or strongly condemned morally. **2.** *n.* A prohibition against particular behaviors, things, or persons based on religious or moral grounds although sometimes expanded to include social or legal grounds as well, as it is taboo to remove lava rocks from the Hawaiian Islands as they are the property of Madam Pele, who will cause misfortune for anyone who removes them.

tabula rasa (blank slate)

n. Term originated by the 17th-century philosopher John Locke. Locke's idea was that an infant is born with its mind/brain a total blank slate, upon which is written its life experience. One variant of this nurture-only approach was B. F. Skinner's mid-20th-century description of the mind/brain as a "black box" which receives the conditioning and reinforcements of an individual's life. This position postulates that nurture, not nature (i.e. genetics and biology), is responsible for the personal, social, and cognitive development of the person. Today, the commonly accepted position among psychologists is that nature and nurture are inextricably interwoven, each continuously contributing to human development over the entire life span.   – vs

tachistoscope

n. Any of several arrangements of instruments which expose visual stimuli for brief measured amounts of time which usually have divided fields of vision so that material can be presented to each eye independently.

tachycardia

n. A very rapid heartbeat, usually considered a sign of extreme arousal, anxiety, or physical pathology.

tacit communication

n. The transfer of information between people without verbal, obvious, or overt efforts at transferring the information, as in reaching an unspoken agreement.

tacit knowledge

n. Information possessed by a person or other organism of which the possessor is not aware and which cannot be articulated or directly expressed.

tactical self-enhancement

n. The idea that people of different cultures all self-enhance but choose to do so in different ways, that is, tactically.

tactile receptor

n. Any of the nerve endings having receptors located in the skin, including those for pressure, texture, vibration, temperature, and pain.

tactual

adj. Of or relating to the sense of touch or contact with the skin.

Taijin-kyofu-sho

n. Taijin-kyofu-sho (TKS), a form of anxiety, literally means symptoms (*sho*) of fear (*kyofu*) of interpersonal relations (*taijin*). While TKS varies on a continuum from common, short-lived adolescent social anxiety to DSM-IV-TR-type social phobia to delusional TKS to social phobia with schizophrenia, it is typically classified dichotomously (offensive vs. non-offensive). Nonoffensive TKS patients experience feelings of humiliation and believe that people have negative opinions of them (egocentric). Nonoffensive TKS symptoms primarily include competition for approval from others, fear of blushing (*sekimen-kyofu*), tremors, and/or stiff facial expressions. Offensive TKS patients feel guilt that their behaviors or appearances will offend or bring shame on others, causing those other people to avoid them (allocentric). Offensive TKS symptoms are primarily distorted cognitions manifested by a desire for acceptance, fear of eye-to-eye contact (*jikoshisen-kyofu*), socially inappropriate gaze orientation, fear of emission of offensive body odors (*jikoshu-kyofu*), and/or fear of exposing others to their deformed bodies (*shubo-kyofu*).   – DLD

tandem reinforcement

n. Rewards that are contingent on the satisfaction of two independent sets of conditions without any signal as to when one has been satisfied. An example of this is a combination of a fixed ratio and a variable interval schedule in which an organism is rewarded every time it performs a specific act at least three times within a period of approximately 30 seconds.

tandem reinforcement schedule

n. A plan for rewarding particular behavior contingent on the satisfaction of two independent sets of conditions without any signal as to when one has been satisfied. An example of this is a combination of a fixed ratio and a variable interval schedule in which an organism is rewarded every time it performs a specific act at least three times within a period of approximately 30 seconds.

tantrum

n. **1.** A sudden outburst or fit of childish rage, which typically occurs between the ages of 2 and 4 years of age. **2.** Adult behavior resembling such childish fits of unreasonable rage.

tardive dyskinesia

n. Involuntary tremors, jerky displacement of the facial or limb muscles, and stereotyped or rhythmic motions of the tongue, fingers, or other extremities, usually resulting from the long-term use of antipsychotic medication and/or damage to the basal ganglia. It is often a permanent effect of long-term use of antipsychotic medications.

task difficulty

n. The amount of effort, use of resources, and likelihood of failure associated with a particular piece of work.

task-oriented

adj. **1.** Being focused on and motivated to accomplish a particular piece of work. **2.** Having the character trait of preferring work to other activities, including persistence, endurance, and goal-oriented effort, as well as valuing the expected products of those activities.

task relevance

n. The perceived pertinence or applicability of a given piece of work either to a larger job or to the goals and motivations of the individual performing it.

taste

n. **1.** The chemical sense of detecting molecules dissolved in liquid placed on the tongue, including sensations of salt, sweet, sour, and bitter and the unlimited number of sensations possible when combined with olfactory and tactile senses. **2.** The experience of any combination of sweet, sour, salt, and bitterness mixed with olfactory and tactile sensations, as in the taste of a chocolate bar. **3.** Preference style, as in a taste for French provincial furniture.

taste aversion

n. **1.** A fixed, intense dislike for a particular taste resulting in a turning away from it. **2.** A thing for which one has a fixed, intense dislike.

taste aversion learning

n. A special case of learning which often occurs in a single trial in which a food which is soon followed by vomiting becomes aversive to the organism. Also called the Garcia effect and taste aversion conditioning.

taste bud

n. Any of about 5,000–9,000 small balloon-shaped structures on the tongue and in other parts of the mouth and larynx containing several dozen taste receptor cells in the interior, which send microvilli out through a hole in the apex which sample the liquid they encounter and generate either sweet, sour, bitter, or salt sensations.

taste cell

n. Any of about 350,000 neuroreceptor cells in the mouth, throat, or larynx which convert certain chemicals dissolved in liquid into a sensation of sweet, sour, bitter, or salt, depending on the type of taste cell. Each kind of taste cell acts to inhibit the impulses from other types of cells. The number of these cells varies widely among individuals and declines with age.

taster (PROP)

n. An individual with the hereditary capacity to taste propylthiouracil, a usually bitter-tasting chemical used as a drug to treat hypothyroidism. This characteristic is present in about 75% of the adult population.

taste receptor

n. Any of about 350,000 neuroreceptors in the mouth, throat, or larynx, which convert certain chemicals dissolved in liquid into a sensation of sweet, sour, bitter, or salt, depending on the type of taste cell.

tau (Kendall's)

n. A measure of association between two pairs of rankings such that no association = 0 and perfect association =1 using the formula

$$Tau = \frac{4p}{n(n-1)} - 1$$

where n = the number of pairs and p = the sum of the rankings greater than a particular ranking to the right of the ranking, when one variable is ordered by the other variable.

taxis

n. A hereditary reflexive movement toward or away from a particular class of stimuli which differs from a tropism in that the organism has bodily motility. Thus some flagellate protozoa move toward light in taxis, while some plants have a tropism in which their leaves turn toward light but lack the ability to move their

entire being through space. Positive taxis is movement toward a stimulus, while negative taxis is movement away from a stimulus.

taxonomy

n. **1.** Any organized system of classification. **2.** The science of classification, as in biological or etymological taxonomy.

Taylor Manifest Anxiety Scale

n. A widely used 50-item true-false scale consisting of a list of symptoms of anxiety, each of which a subject admits or denies.

t distribution

n. A theoretical distribution of scores defined by sampling from the population of scores of (Mean$_{sample}$ – Mean$_{population}$)/standard deviation$_{sample}$, which is widely used in hypothesis testing. Also called Student's t distribution.

teaching machine

n. Any device for presenting a learner with a program of instruction structured to include reading or observable material, problems, or questions to check understanding of each segment of material and the provision of feedback as to correctness of response to the problems or questions.

tectorial membrane

n. A soft tissue in the organ of Corti in which the ends of hair cells are embedded. Also called Corti's membrane.

tegmentum

n. A central part of the midbrain and pons below the tectum containing many motor pathways descending to the spinal cord and sensory pathways ascending to the thalamus, as well as the red nucleus, the occulomotor nucleus, and the subthalamic nucleus. Also called the tegmentum mesencaphali.

telegraphic speech

n. A term used in the context of agrammatic oral expression to describe the use of short, deficiently constructed utterances, lacking morphosyntactic requirements (e.g., articles, prepositions, auxiliaries, verb endings), by patients with Broca's or transcortical motor aphasia. Patients with telegraphic or agrammatic expression speak in halting, nonfluent, efforful speech, relying on the most meaning-carrying words (i.e., verbs, nouns, and adjectives) as in "Girl eat apple" or "Eat apple" for "The girl is eating/ate/has eaten the apple."

– JGC

telekinesis

n. The capacity to move physical bodies by using the mind or by supernatural beings, which has been attributed to many religious figures, magicians, and shamans.

teleology

n. The point of view that many phenomena are best understood in terms of their purpose rather than in causal terms. Thus Carl Jung suggested we could best understand human beings by understanding what individuals are in the process of developing into rather than in terms of their situation and history.

telepathy

n. The communication of information across space or time without discoverable physical processes, which has been claimed by or attributed to many religious figures, magicians, and shamans.

television violence

n. The observation of numerous acts of violence through the medium of television as occurs thousands of times during the childhoods of most children in the United States and many other countries. This has been an area of controversy: many studies show that such exposure both desensitizes individuals to violence and provides role models for the expression of violence, and other studies question the controls of such studies.

temperament

n. **1.** The basic character of the person present at birth from which personality develops. It is usually assumed to include energy level, responsiveness, and exploratory drive. **2.** Basic differences in character among non-human animals which tend to have similar dimensions to human temperament.

temperature sense

n. The aspect of the somatosensory sense in the skin and some internal organs which reacts to contact with anything significantly above or below mean body temperature.

temporal avoidance conditioning

n. A learning paradigm in which animals are taught to escape experiencing an aversive stimulus by engaging in a specified behavior within each of a series of specified periods. Also known as Sidman avoidance conditioning.

temporal discounting

n. Temporal discounting (also called delay discounting) is the tendency for behavioral decisions to be relatively uninfluenced by consequences that are deferred in time. All potential courses of action have consequences that are beneficial (rewards) or detrimental (costs), and their subjective value fuels choices among competing courses of action. Delay reduces the subjective value of a consequence, resulting in reduced impact on current action.

For example, a person with cash in hand may choose to save it or spend it now. Saving may generate sizable deferred benefits (e.g., retirement income), while an extravagant purchase today generates immediate but lesser pleasures. Temporal discounting renders this choice between large and small rewards difficult, because the psychological impact of the former is diluted under delay. This is true even for persons who can describe the value of the delayed consequences (e.g., how important it is to be well funded in old age) because the factors that affect choice are not necessarily the ones that drive awareness.

Two features are central to problems associated with temporal discounting. First, many situations require choice between one course of action with smaller-sooner consequences and another with larger-later consequences. Second, unit for unit, immediate consequences, which are relatively unaffected by discounting, have greater impact on choice than delayed ones.

When action prevails in service of short-term consequences, we say that an individual has behaved impulsively or shown a failure of the will. When action prevails in service of deferred consequences, we say that the individual has exhibited self-control. Yet all individuals act impulsively at times, in part because larger rewards are discounted proportionally more than smaller ones. For reasons that are beyond the scope of the present discussion, this effect has two implications. First, it exacerbates the subjective superiority of smaller-sooner consequences. Second, it assures that the temptation of small, immediate rewards is most pronounced when they are imminent. In the latter case, a decision to break one's diet is more likely when the dessert cart is rolled past the restaurant table than during the half-hour drive to the restaurant prior to dinner, even though the long-term benefits of healthy eating remain the same in the two cases.

Individuals differ in the extent to which they discount delayed outcomes. Children discount more than do adults, and some cultural differences have been detected (e.g., Americans were found to discount more than natives of China or Japan). Overall, research suggests a population distribution that is skewed away from extreme impulsiveness, with those at the impulsive tail of the distribution at risk for a variety of clinical and social problems. Especially strong discounting of delayed rewards has been found in academic procrastinators, pathological gamblers, substance abusers, and persons with attention deficit–hyperactivity disorder – all classes of individuals who are regarded as excessively impulsive. Additionally, consistently with the notion that good social interactions require some tolerance for temporary imbalances in social exchange, individuals who deeply discount delayed rewards do poorly in some social situations.

Temporal discounting is described by a hyperbolic function that approximates the form of $SV = A/(1 + kD)$. The subjective value (SV) of a consequence is its objective amount (A) or size discounted as a function of the length of the delay (D) until the consequences occur. This function is negatively decelerating, meaning that subjective value decreases quickly under brief delays and then changes relatively little as delays become more extended. That is, even brief delays have pronounced discounting effects. The fitted parameter k is a measure of how quickly subjective value decreases under delay, with larger values implying greater impulsiveness. Thus, k differs across groups of individuals (e.g., substance abusers vs. normal controls) and also may vary across circumstances.

Two common situational influences on temporal discounting have been observed. First, rewards are discounted more deeply than equal-sized costs – that is, their effects are weaker in the face of delay – providing one possible basis for the well-known tendency of unpleasant events to be more psychologically potent than pleasant ones. Second, the same person may show different degrees of temporal discounting for consequences of different types. One individual may, for instance, deeply discount money rewards but not outcomes related to good health; another may show the opposite pattern. Thus, to speak of an individual as impulsive or not oversimplifies matters. The cause of domain effects is not known, but there is some evidence that experience can affect discounting tendencies. For example, discounting of money rewards appears to change with rates of inflation in the local economy, which is a measure of how quickly money loses its value over time. Perhaps analogously, substance abusers discount outcomes related to obtaining drugs especially steeply. In this latter case, it is possible that experience with drug taking (e.g., exposure to withdrawal symptoms) creates this tendency, although it is also possible that individuals already equipped with the tendency are simply at special risk of substance abuse problems.

A temporal discounting analysis predicts several hedges against impulsive choice. Here is one illustration. *Precommitment* consists of locking in a course of action before the temptation of smaller-sooner outcomes becomes imminent. Compare two dieters shopping for food. Shopper A purchases food in person at the market, while Shopper B orders groceries through an online service that delivers the next day. Both must choose between items that taste good now (smaller-sooner rewards) but adversely affect weight and items that taste worse but promote healthy weight (larger-later rewards). Both shoppers can eat items as soon as they are purchased. For Shopper A, this means that buying occurs when the power of smaller-sooner rewards to tempt is near its undelayed, undiscounted maximum. Shopper B, however, benefits from the fact that all consequences are discounted under delay. The delay to delivery may reduce the subjective value of fattening foods to the point where better items are chosen for purchase, and without fattening foods in the pantry, Shopper B is likely to eat better.   – TSC

temporal lobe

n. One of the four large divisions of the cerebral cortex located on the lower side of each hemisphere, which is separated from the frontal and parietal lobes by the lateral sulcus and contains structures concerned with memory, hearing, speech perception, sexual and other social behavior, and some visual perception.

temporal lobe epilepsy

n. A form of brain seizure in the temporal lobe of the cortex characterized by a partial or complete loss of consciousness or alternatively by automatic, abnormal, or violent behavior without loss of consciousness. Such attacks are often preceded by unusual experiences such as an aura, déjà vu, a sense that things are not real or are unfamiliar, a strange odor, or hallucinations.

temporal lobe seizure

n. A burst of uncontrolled electrical activity in the temporal lobe of the cortex characterized by a partial or complete loss of consciousness or alternatively by automatic, abnormal, or violent behavior without loss of consciousness. Such attacks are often preceded by unusual experiences such as an aura, déjà vu, a sense that things are not real or are unfamiliar, a strange odor, or hallucinations.

temporal summation

n. A process characteristic of sensory neurons in which a subthreshold postsynaptic potential lasts long enough for one or more subsequent potentials to add to its effect, thus creating a depolarization sufficient to propagate down the axon, causing the release of neurotransmitters into the synaptic cleft which affect postsynaptic cells.

tendon reflex

n. The involuntary contraction of a muscle caused by the activation of Golgi tendon organs which occurs when a tendon is stretched, as in the familiar knee-jerk reaction when the patellar tendon is struck.

tension reduction

n. A lessening of the experience of strain or state of pressure. Occasionally used to mean drive reduction.

teratogen

n. Any agent that causes abnormalities in the development of a fetus including drugs such as alcohol, infections such as German measles, or exposure to X-rays.

terminal button

n. The bulbous end of an axon at the junction with another neuron. Also called a synaptic button and *bouton synaptique* in French.

terminal reinforcement

n. The final reinforcement in a series in which reinforcements are received for partial completion of a task as a student's grades and credit for completion for a class are given after the class ends.

territoriality

n. **1.** The marking and exclusion of most members of the same species from a specific geographic area by an animal or group of animals as a pride of lions defends its territory against invasion by other lions. **2.** The characteristic of seeking control of a geographical area.

terror management theory

n. A set of ideas suggesting that the control of death-related thinking and anxiety is the primary function of human society and the basic motivation in all human thinking and behavior. It asserts that high self-esteem and perceiving the self as a member of a powerful and stable society are the most successful ways of warding off death anxiety and avoiding recognition of their own mortality.

testable hypothesis

n. Any conjecture about anything that is reasonably subject to empirical verification.

test anxiety

n. Tension and worry about taking a test.

test battery

n. A series of subtests that are designed to measure different abilities, traits, or subjects that are related components of a broader skill, ability, or characteristic. All of the subtests of a test battery are normed on the same sample. Test takers may be given a complete test battery, or specific subtests from a battery may be selected for specific purposes. For example, the Aviation Selection Test Battery (ASTB) is used in military training programs to predict the likelihood of success for students in aviation officer training. The complete test battery contains six subtests measuring math, reading, mechanical comprehension, spatial apperception, aviation/nautical information, and aviation supplemental information. Students complete various subtests to determine their placement in training programs.

– BJM

test bias

n. In psychometrics, the property of unequally estimating the true scores of some of the individuals who are tested. In slope bias the test more accurately predicts the scores of some groups of individuals than others. In intercept bias one group of individuals consistently and inaccurately scores higher or lower than another group of individuals with the level of the characteristic being measured.

test item

n. Any individual question, problem, or statement to which a subject must respond in taking a test.

test-retest method

n. Method of determining the level of measurement error of a test by examining the consistency of test scores from multiple administrations of the same measure. Test-retest reliability utilizes time sampling to evaluate the error associated with administering a test on two or more different occasions. To calculate test-retest reliability, a test must be administered to the same group of people on at least two separate, specified occasions; then the correlation of the scores from the two testing sessions is calculated to determine the reliability coefficient. Correlation coefficients closer to 0 represent low reliability while coefficients closer to 1 represent high reliability. Test-retest reliability estimates are only meaningful when the target of the measurement is stable. For example, constructs such as intelligence are assumed to be stable and thus should not change much from one testing session to another, while other characteristics, such as reading ability, are not stable and are likely to change dramatically from age 5 to age 7. When interpreting test-retest reliability data, one must ensure that changes in test scores are not due to random variations in testing conditions or the impact of carryover effects, practice effects, and reactivity.

– BJM

test-retest reliability

n. The level of a test's measurement error, determined by examining the consistency of test scores from multiple administrations of the same measure. Test-retest reliability utilizes time sampling to evaluate the error associated with administering a test on two or more different occasions. To calculate test-retest reliability, a test must be administered to the same group of people on at least two separate, specified occasions; then the correlation of the scores from the two testing sessions is calculated to determine the reliability coefficient. Correlation coefficients closer to 0 represent low reliability while coefficients closer to 1 represent high reliability. Test-retest reliability estimates are only meaningful when the target of the measurement is stable. For example, constructs such as intelligence are assumed to be stable and thus should not change much from one testing session to another, while other characteristics, such as reading ability, are not stable and are likely to change dramatically from age 5 to age 7. When interpreting test-retest reliability data, one must ensure that changes in test scores are not due to random variations in testing conditions or the impact of carryover effects, practice effects, and reactivity.   – BJM

tests and measurement

n. The field of psychology that examines the processes and procedures of creating, administering, and interpreting evaluative devices such as personality and IQ tests.

tetrachoric correlation

n. A product-moment correlation calculated using the column and row totals in a 2 x 2 contingency table which estimates the value of a correlation of the two variables were they continuous.

tetrahydrocannabinol

n. (THC) The major active ingredient in marijuana, which produces most of the hallucinogenic and sedative effects for which the drug is typically smoked. Also known as delta-9-tetrahydrocannabinol.

T-group

n. A small group of people, usually between 6 and 12 in number, who use their interactions as a learning experience in order to increase understanding of group and interpersonal dynamics and leadership and communication skills, including sensitivity to nonverbal communications and others' varying points of view. This kind of group is to be distinguished from therapy groups that focus on healing mental disorders and encounter groups that focus on personal growth. Also known as training group.

thalamus

n. Either of a pair of golf-ball-size hemispheres of gray matter in the diencephalon, below the cortex and forming the lateral walls of the third ventricle. It contains all of the nerve pathways between the cerebral cortex and the spinal cord as well as numerous nuclei for sensory, motor, visual, somatosensory, autonomic, and associative processes.

Thanatos

n. **1.** In later versions of psychoanalysis, the instinct to destroy one's self and die, which is usually turned outward in the form of aggression toward others. The existence of this instinct was supposed by Sigmund Freud after he had been traumatized by witnessing the horrors of World War I and runs counter to his earlier tendency to make his theories fit well within an understanding of the theory of evolution, in which instincts would make survival and procreation more likely rather than less likely. **2.** The Greek god of death.

Thematic Apperception Test

n. A projective test in which subjects are asked to make up stories about 30 provocative pictures in which they detail the motivations of all the persons in the picture as part of their stories. There is no one standard way of scoring the test, and those that have been used have had variable reliability. Despite this, the use of this test in research studies has been widespread, although its use in clinical work has been minor in recent years.

theory

n. **1.** In science, a testable set of hypotheses attempting to describe or explain a particular set of phenomena systematically or to predict new phenomena that will occur in a particular set of circumstances. **2.** In general, a conjecture or opinion on any topic.

theory of mind

n. The understanding each person has about his or her own and other people's experience and mental processes, which is usually intuitive and some of which is explicit and some of which is implicit. Inferences and predictions based on this make mutual understanding possible and enable our complex social interactions. Most people begin to exhibit some understanding of their own and others' mental workings around age 4, but it appears markedly lacking in individuals with autism and in some cases of mental retardation and psychosis. There is no agreement about which, if any, nonhuman animals have a theory of mind.

theory of planned behavior ▶ *See* **PLANNED BEHAVIOR, THEORY OF**

theory of reasoned action ▶ *See* **RESONED ACTION, THEORY OF**

therapeutic alliance
n. The implicit and largely intuitive cooperative working relationship between a therapist and a client based on trust, commitment to the relationship, and empathy.

therapeutic community
n. **1.** An intentional living setting residents enter in order to facilitate recovery from mental disorders, addictions, or other problems through open group discussions of daily life and its conflicts as well as more traditional therapy as an adjunct. **2.** Any treatment facility in which the setting and interactions with the other residents are part of the treatment.

therapist
n. Any person who works to treat physical or mental disorders with any of the dozens of varieties of physical and verbal methods.

therapy
n. Any process, other than surgery, intended to treat a mental or physical disorder or disability.

thermoregulation
n. All the processes of physiological and behavioral response by which organisms regulate their body temperatures, including panting, sweating, seeking shade or sunlight, increasing or decreasing physical activity, as well as making postural adjustments, such as an elephant's holding its ears away from its body.

think aloud technique
n. A preliminary approach to investigating mental processes involved in a task or other activity in which a subject is asked to describe audibly his or her thought processes while he/she is performing a task or engaging in the activity of interest. It has been found useful in many areas, including problem solving, judgments under conditions of uncertainty, and efficiency studies.

thinking
n. **1.** The stream of consciousness and all its contents including silent vocalizations, emotions, images, and the perception of the external and internal worlds. **2.** The processes which underlie behavior and all the phenomena of experience. **3.** Any product of the mind, such as judgments, attitudes, knowledge, opinions, and beliefs.

thinking, convergent
n. Any process of problem solving that applies learned methods or solutions to a problem.

thinking, critical
n. A form of problem-centered thinking in which the person consciously reflects on a task and mentally tests potential solutions for their possibility, efficiency, costs, likely problems, and their likelihood of success.

thioridazine
n. A relatively weak antipsychotic drug of the family of older, antipsychotic drugs often referred to as typical antipsychotics. It works primarily by blocking dopamine D2 receptors; it has serious side effects, including tardive dyskinesia, extrapyramidal symptoms, and sedation, and may cause blindness or brain damage with high doses or with long-term usage. Also called thioridazine chloride and Mellaril.

thirst
n. **1.** The desire to drink. **2.** A high concentration of salts in bodily tissues leading to increased osmotic pressure, which activates a specialized center in the thalamus known as the thirst center, which increases motivation to take in fluid.

Thorazine
n. One of a family of older, antipsychotic drugs often referred to as typical antipsychotics including Stelazine, Haldol, and Prolixin. These caused a revolution in the treatment of schizophrenia when they were first used in the 1950s which led to a great reduction in the institutionalization of psychotic individuals. They work primarily by blocking dopamine D2 receptors and have serious side effects, including tardive dyskinesia, extrapyramidal

symptoms, and sedation, and may cause brain damage with long-term usage. Also called chlorpromazine.

Thorndike-Lorge list

n. A list of word frequencies of the 30,000 most commonly used English words compiled by Edward Thorndike and Irving Lorge from a wide variety of written texts in 1944.

Thorndike puzzle box

n. A locked container in which an animal is placed which has an unlocking mechanism the animal must manipulate either to get a reward or to get out of the box. The difficulty of the unlocking mechanism can be varied to create tasks of greater and lesser difficulty. Invented by Edward Thorndike to study animal learning.

Thorndike's laws of learning

n. Three generalizations concerning the acquisition of stimulus-response links suggested by Edward Thorndike. The law of effect suggests that rewarded behavior tends to be repeated. The law of exercise suggests that the bonds between a stimulus and a response are strengthened by practice and weakened by the passage of time in which they are not practiced. The law of readiness suggests that previously learned responses can be chained into more complex sets of behavior if doing so will satisfy a goal.

thought broadcasting

n. The delusion that one's thoughts are heard by other people so that one has no privacy in the mind.

thought disorder

n. Any psychological disorder leading to abnormal processes of thought, including delusions, hallucinations, dulled or exaggerated affect, ideas of reference, flight of ideas, or perseveration, which are typical of schizophrenia and relatively severe disorders.

thought disturbance

n. Any abnormal processes of thought, including delusions, hallucinations, dulled or exaggerated affect, ideas of reference, flight of

ideas, or perseveration, which are typical of neuroses or psychoses.

thought experiment

n. The imaginary design and execution of an experiment including the outcome. Also called gedanken experiment.

thought insertion

n. The delusion that a thought has been injected into one's mind by an outside source and does not actually belong to one's self.

thought withdrawal

n. The delusion that some outside force is removing ideas, images, memories, or other contents from one's mind.

three-color theory

n. A conceptualization of the process of human color perception which suggests that all perceived hues are combinations of three basic hues: blue, green, and red. This theory has largely been supported by modern physiology and expanded by the idea of opponent processes among the different visual receptors. Also called the Young-Helmholtz theory.

threshold

n. The lowest level of a sensory stimulus or a change in the intensity of a stimulus which a subject can reliably report. Originally psychophysicists believed there was some absolute level which corresponded with human consciousness which defined this limit, but close study revealed variability in subject responses, which were partially random, partially dependent on the instructions given to the subject, and partially dependent on previous observation of stimuli. Subsequent study revealed that there is a gradual onset of stimulus detection which can be described using signal detection methods which give probabilities of response to a stimulus at different intensities or levels of the stimulus. Also called a limen.

Thurstone scale

n. An archaic measure of positive versus negative attitude toward some target constructed by the following method. First a large pool of statements relevant to the topic is composed; they are then rated by a panel of judges on a 9- or 11-point scale where 1 is very negative and 9 or 11 is very positive. The mean and central tendency of the judges' ratings are calculated, and two or more items with a mean close to each number with narrow dispersion are selected for each point on the scale. The scale is administered to subjects who are asked to mark the statements with which they agree. The score on the scale is the median of the endorsed items.

thymine
n. $C_5H_6N_2O_2$ is one of the four bases of which all DNA is composed. Also known as 5-methyluracil.

tic disorder
n. A family of disorders involving rapid, unpredictable, recurrent, and stereotyped motor movement including vocalizations. Included in this group are Tourette's disorder, chronic motor or vocalization disorder, transient tic disorder, and similar disorders which do not fit neatly into any category.

tightness versus looseness
n. A polar dimension of a cultural group with rigid adherence to cultural norms on one end and flexible adherence to norms on the other end. Cultures that are tight tend to be homogeneous, aggressive toward other cultures, and punitive toward those who transgress the norms. Loose cultures tend to be more heterogeneous in membership and to value originality, creativity, risk taking, and inclusiveness and to be tolerant toward other cultures and toward individuals who transgress norms.

timbre
n. The timbre of a sound refers to the sound's tonal quality. A clarinet and a piano playing the same note – a signal that will have the same fundamental frequency – are perceived as having the same tone yet as sounding very different. Likewise, two different speakers producing the same vowel at approximately the same pitch are also perceived as different

speakers, as their timbre may be describable as being nasal, breathy, hoarse, tremulous, and so on. Timbre is a property of sounds judged subjectively and linked to multiple dimensions, which are generally described by examining the distribution of spectral energies (sourced in the fundamental frequency and the resulting harmonics of the signal). In speech, timbre or vocal quality is related to the configuration of the vocal tract, the anatomy of the larynx, and the speaker's vocal habits; these characteristics are sometimes related to a particular culture or social register. — EMF

time out
n. **1.** A technique for punishing undesired behavior by removing the individual exhibiting the behavior from the situation, which disrupts the pattern of reinforcement and usually punishes the individual by isolating him or her from others as well as from normal levels of external stimulation. This is in widespread use in schools in the United States. **2.** In operant conditioning, a time interval in which a particular behavior is either prevented or not reinforced.

time perception
n. An awareness of duration or a hypothesized capacity to use duration information in a task.

time pressure
n. Time pressure constitutes an experimental technique used to investigate the strategic use of cognitive resources. It is often used in the domains of basic cognition, judgment and decision making, and social cognition.

Asking participants in an experimental setting to perform a task under a stringent deadline has been shown to entail profound implications for basic cognitive and judgmental processes. Time pressure forces individuals to consider relatively few pieces of information to reach a judgment, to use simple heuristics to process information more effectively, and to rely on incomplete information to form a judgment. As a result, time pressure is often used as a technique to study the strategies people employ to balance informational gains and the costs of cognitive effort optimally. These balance processes culminate in specific biases. Such biases may consist of failing to adjust from initial anchors, overestimating the role of salient information in the formation of a judgment, or basing one's judgment on intuitions rather than rational considerations. The effects of time pressure have been depicted as an enhanced need for nonspecific closure, representing a desire for immediate and definite knowledge and aversion to the uncertainties associated with ambiguity. In the area of social cognition, the need for nonspecific closure, often induced by means of time pressure manipulations, has been shown to lead to enhanced reliance on preexisting categories, culminating in stereotypical perception and often decreased tolerance for opinion deviates.

An ongoing debate within the study of cognitive resource limitation concerns the extent to which the manipulation of time pressure fundamentally alters the decision-making process. Some have argued that time pressure forces individuals to rely on an intuitive knowledge system based on primitive associative processing, whereas more extensive deliberation can be described in terms of formal logical processes. The notion of dual processes of judgment has been questioned, however. Opponents of the dual process view maintain that time pressure may limit the amount and type of information the individual is able to process, yet it does not necessarily affect the cognitive process itself.

Time pressure can also be considered an occupational and societal phenomenon that constitutes a significant source of stress and hence entails a number of negative psychological and physical consequences. Considerable attention has been paid to this phenomenon. Its dynamic should not be confused with the cognitive understanding of time pressure described.   — MD, AK

time sample
n. A series of observations of the same subjects or situations across time or in a fixed order.

time series
n. A sequence of observations of the same subjects or situations in a succession or in a fixed order.

time-series analysis
n. A set of procedures used to analyze a sequence of observations of the same subjects or situations.

tinnitus
n. A hearing disorder in which the affected individual hears noises which are not present in the environment. This can be due to infections of the ear, damage or disease of the receptor cells, drug effects, or epilepsy. Auditory hallucinations are not included in this category.

tip-of-the-tongue phenomenon
n. The temporary experience of knowing something but not being able to recall it to consciousness or to say it, as in knowing the name of one's mother and for a period of time being unable to recall or say it.

tit for tat strategy
n. In game theory, a bargaining or programming approach in which there is initial cooperation followed by a response in kind to whatever the other party does. Cooperation is met with cooperation and competition with competition. It is one way of simulating reciprocal altruism.

T-maze
n. A simple maze in which there is an alley leading to two arms perpendicular to the original alley shaped like the letter *T* and only one choice of direction to take.

toilet training
n. The process of learning to control one's bowels and bladder and to void them only into a toilet or other appropriate place or the process of teaching such self-control to another person.

token
n. **1.** Any sign, symbol, or object representing something else, as a nod is a token of

agreement in many cultures. **2.** A small object that can be exchanged for goods or services, as in a token economy. **3.** In linguistics, an instance or concrete example of the use of a word, as opposed to the word itself.

token economy

n. A behavioral training program in which desired behavior is rewarded by giving tokens which can be accumulated and exchanged for goods, services, or privileges. This is a widely used technique in controlled institutions in the United States.

token reward

n. A small object with little or no intrinsic value which can be exchanged for desired goods, services, or privileges.

tolerance

n. **1.** The capacity to endure differences from expectations with equanimity. **2.** The range of permissible deviations from norms or standards. **3.** A homeostatic reaction to the continued presence of a drug or other stimulus such that it takes more of the drug or other stimulus to obtain the same level of reaction as first obtained.

tolerance, drug

n. A homeostatic reaction to the continued presence of a drug such that more of the drug is required to obtain the same level of reaction first obtained by a given dose of the drug. Tolerance along with another homeostatic reaction, withdrawal, is a criterion for drug addiction.

tolerance of ambiguity

n. The ability to consider ambiguous stimulus information in an open manner. Although this definition applies to both social and nonsocial stimulus information, the concept of tolerance of ambiguity is primarily studied in social, organizational, and clinical contexts. Intolerance of ambiguity is closely linked to psychological constructs such as closed-mindedness, need for closure, and the authoritarian personality. In contemporary psychology, tolerance of ambiguity is frequently associated with the ability to adjust to new social and cultural environments.

The basis for research on (in)tolerance of ambiguity was established by the research of Frenkel-Brunswik, whose work and thinking are closely tied to Adorno's work on the authoritarian personality. Both the authoritarian personality and the notion of tolerance of ambiguity emerged in the early 1950s in order to explain the rise and popularity of Nazi ideology. According to Frenkel-Brunswik, the intolerance of ambiguity (rather than tolerance of ambiguity) played a critical role in this process. She described intolerance of ambiguity as a general personality variable with manifestations in both social and cognitive domains.

Frenkel-Brunswik described individuals with intolerance of ambiguity as especially prone to engage in black-and-white thinking, to think in terms of certainty rather than probability, and to be rigid in their thoughts even when flexibility is required. These tendencies were also observed on a social level, where intolerance of ambiguity was associated with a preference for clear role patterns between the sexes, between parents and their children, and in interpersonal interaction in general. Frenkel-Brunswik also typified individuals intolerant of ambiguity as having strong fervor with regard to upholding cultural norms, and as feeling especially disturbed when these norms are violated. Obedience to authority, discipline, obsession with morality, and conformity were also characteristics mentioned. As many of her contemporaries did, Frenkel-Brunswik traced the origins of the personality type to early childhood. Building on psychoanalysis, she argued that intolerance of ambiguity originates from an unconscious experience of emotional conflict regarding how to approach and perceive one's parents, either with hostility or with reverence.

Since Frenkel-Brunswik's introduction of the concept of intolerance of ambiguity, it has received considerable research attention, in various countries and domains of psychology. A number of attempts have been made to measure the construct adequately. These attempts have resulted in a personality approach to intolerance of ambiguity, which treats it as a stable personality trait that can be measured by means of questionnaires or projective tests. In this context, a 16-item scale developed by Budner in the mid-1960s is most commonly used. Others have taken a more basic, cognitive approach, identifying the intolerance of ambiguity by means of perceptual tasks, whereby tendencies to use simple categories to order stimulus information and unease with ambiguous stimuli are taken as indicators of greater intolerance of ambiguity.

Intolerance of ambiguity has been studied with regard to its relevance for understanding prejudice and has been applied in clinical and organizational settings. Research has provided evidence for the negative consequences of the construct in all domains, although results tend to vary across studies. In the social domain, intolerance of ambiguity has indeed been found to correlate with measures of ethnocentrism and authoritarianism. In clinical settings, intolerance of ambiguity as a personality trait was found to be associated with hysteria, obsessive behavior, and, to a lesser extent, anxiety. In organizational contexts, intolerance of ambiguity has in some studies been found to reduce job satisfaction directly, although other studies have shown that the construct only predicts reduced job satisfaction if the employee experiences role ambiguity. Further, tolerance of ambiguity has been associated with an increased tendency to seek feedback from managers. Interest in research on tolerance of ambiguity has grown considerably as a result of Hofstede's research demonstrating the relevance of the construct for understanding variations in behavior across cultures. This research has led to the insight that national cultures show variation in the extent to which members are willing to tolerate uncertainty, and this variation is argued to account for specific cultural phenomena, as well as a more general receptivity toward foreign influences including expatriate workers.

These research findings highlight the appeal of the concept of tolerance of ambiguity among a very diverse group of psychologists.

It has been argued that the breadth of application of the construct may in large part account for its continuing popularity.

– MD, AK

tomography

n. (CT or CAT scan) A process of generating a three-dimensional set of images of a person or object's internal structure by using a series of axial X-rays whose images are then connected or filled in using imaging software so as to present computer images that appear whole to the viewer. It is very useful in diagnostic imaging, where it is difficult for a person mentally to fill in between numerous single X-ray images to understand the three-dimensional situation.

tone

n. **1.** A sound that has only one wavelength in it. **2.** The subjective perception of different wavelengths of sound pressure waves. **3.** The emotional reaction evoked by something. **4.** In linguistics, differences in pitch that denote grammatical meanings.

tone deafness

n. A partial or total incapacity to distinguish different wavelengths or pitches of sound. Also called asonia.

top-down processing

n. An approach to the analysis of new information based on previously stored information so that new information is compared to stored patterns derived from old information for confirmation or disconfirmation of a match, or the applications of general rules, assumptions, or presuppositions to new information. Also called conceptually driven processing.

topography

n. **1.** The science which studies and describes surfaces, as in map making including the mapping of internal organs. **2.** In psychoanalysis, the division of the mind into conscious, preconscious, and unconscious areas.

topological psychology

n. An approach to the study of the mind in which mental and social phenomena are described in terms of their distance from and attraction or repulsion toward other phenomena which are within the life space through which an individual moves. This system of description is seldom used in contemporary psychology.

Total Quality Management

n. An approach to running a business concern which requires that all workers engage in a process of identifying all the internal and external needs of the production process and make a commitment to continuous improvement in the quality and productivity of each unit, meeting each of the needs, all of which is statistically monitored for performance.

Tourette's disorder

n. A tic disorder characterized by rapid, unpredictable, recurrent, and stereotyped motor movements including one or more vocalizations. The number, frequency, complexity, and severity of the tics tend to change over time and are unpredictable.

Tower of Hanoi

n. A puzzle used in studies of problem solving in which three or more doughnut-shaped disks are stacked on any of three posts and the subject is required to move the disks one at a time from wherever they begin to one post, with the largest disk on the bottom and the smallest on top, without ever placing a larger disk on top of a smaller disk. Additional disks and posts may be added in order to make the task more difficult.

trace conditioning

n. A form of classical conditioning in which a conditioned stimulus is presented and after a time delay an unconditioned stimulus is presented. Eventually the unconditioned stimulus is likely to produce the conditioned response, suggesting that a memory trace from the conditioned stimulus lasts over the time delay.

trainable mentally retarded

1. *adj.* Of or relating to persons who are mentally retarded and capable of being taught to care for themselves and engage in

relatively simple vocational occupations. **2.** *n.* Individuals with IQ in the range from 35 to 49 who generally do not benefit from formal education but are capable of being taught to care for themselves and engage in relatively simple vocational occupations.

traits

n. Relatively stable individual differences in consistent patterns of behavior. Although traits are a central concept in personality, theorists disagree about the extent to which they refer to structures in the brain that determine behavior versus useful descriptions of behavior patterns with no causal status. The five factor theory of traits suggests that there are five basic traits that capture the major dimensions on which all human traits vary. ▶ *See also* **BIG FIVE PERSONALITY TRAITS**

trait anxiety

n. The enduring characteristic of being above average in levels of arousal and generalized fearfulness.

trait approach

n. An approach to personality that describes individuals in terms of several measurable dimensions of individual differences in patterns of attention, intention, and behavior.

trait negativity bias

n. The observed tendency of people to weigh traits considered negative more heavily in overall estimates of character than they do traits considered positive.

trait psychology

n. An approach to psychology that describes individuals in terms of several measurable dimensions of individual differences in patterns of attention, intention, and behavior.

tranquilizer

n. Any drug used to produce calming. Most original tranquilizers were depressants such as the diazepines, whose calming effects occurred at a lower dose than the dose required to produce sedation or sleep. Newer tranquilizers such as the SSRI family of drugs produce calming largely without sedation. Antipsychotic medications are sometimes called major tranquilizers.

transactional analysis

n. (TA) An approach to psychology that characterized ego states as like those of a child, a parent, or an adult which tended to play roles in interactions associated with each ego state. The adult ego state is associated with introjections of our parents and other authority figures from our childhood, which role we tend to act out in the parent ego state. The child ego state is feeling and perspectives from our own childhood, which we act out in that ego state. The adult state is a reasonable and effective state dealing with present situations. Each person has a plan for his/her life which is called a life script and involves a succession of social roles. A game is a repeated behavior pattern of adopting a child or parent ego state and behaving in that role largely outside the awareness of the adult ego state. In the game of Rapo, for instance, a client, Anika, may enter a child state, run her hand up her therapist's pant leg and fondle him, later claim that she was innocent of any sexual motivation, then switch to a parent role and blame the therapist for being seductive without her adult ego state realizing she has been playing a game.

transcendental meditation

n. A form of Hindu meditation in which a person sits with eyes closed and repeats a mantra while excluding everything except the mantra from the mind for 20 minutes twice a day. This generally produces a sense of calmness and is claimed to allow access to deeper levels of mind and, ultimately, access to cosmic consciousness.

transcription

n. **1.** The writing down of verbal materials, as in tapes of therapy sessions or court proceedings. **2.** The process of reproducing DNA in which messenger RNA forms into complementary patterns to the DNA and then directs synthesis of a copy of the DNA by assembling chains of nucleic bases in the appropriate order to produce a nearly exact copy of the DNA. Over the course of many such replications small fragments tend to be lost from the ends of the DNA strands, a process which is a primary cause of aging.

transducer

n. A biological structure or artificial device that converts energy from one form to another, as the eye converts light energy into patterns of electrical impulses in the central nervous system.

transduction

n. The process of converting or transforming energy from one form into another. Thus automobiles convert the energy stored in chemical bonds first into heat, then into mechanical power which moves the vehicle, and the ear converts the energy of sound pressure waves into patterns of electrical impulses in the central nervous system.

transfer-appropriate processing

n. Encoding data into a form that is usable by a specific information processing system.

transfer benefit

n. Transfer benefits refer to experience with one task that facilitates processing in a subsequent task. For example, transfer occurs when reading one text (about alligators) helps the reader understand a second text (about crocodiles). Likewise, if two math problems require similar solutions, solving the first problem might facilitate solving the second problem. Evidence for transfer benefits includes reduced processing time for the second text or problem, as well as improved comprehension for the second text or problem. When experience with one task inhibits processing in a subsequent task, this represents negative transfer (e.g., reading one text slows processing of a second text). This might occur if the first text contradicts the second text.

— GER, FD

transference

n. The unconscious feelings toward one person from the past redirected or *transferred* to another in the present (e.g., meeting someone who unconsciously reminds you of your father and interacting with that person in ways you would normally interact with your father). Transference is more generally defined as the interpretation of ambiguous (usually interpersonal) cues based on one's upbringing or attachment. In psychotherapy, transference refers specifically to the patient's interpretation of the therapist's behavior, based on the patient's early attachment to primary caregivers. A patient is said to have a *positive transference* if he or she sees the therapist's behavior and interpretations as positive or benevolent and is said to have a *negative transference* if he/she sees the therapist's behavior and interpretations as negative or harmful. In long-term psychoanalytic psychotherapy, it is common for a patient to have both positive and negative transferences over the course of treatment. – DGa

transfer of training

n. The effect of previous learning on new learning, which may enhance, retard, or have no effect on the new learning. Solving new problems or performing new tasks is easier if they can be solved or accomplished without new effort in analysis. If the patterns learned in old solutions or tasks lead us to think or act in ways that are not helpful in the new tasks and especially if they prevent us from noticing new possibilities, then the transfer of training makes matters harder.

transfer RNA

n. A soluble chain of ribonucleic acid that transports specific amino acids to a limited number of appropriate sites during protein synthesis in the cytoplasm of living cells.

transformational grammar ▶ *See* GENERATIVE GRAMMAR

translocation Down syndrome

n. A congenital condition caused when a piece of chromosome 21 breaks off and sticks to chromosome 14 which accounts for 3–5% of all Down syndrome cases. It is characterized by mild to severe mental retardation, pleasant disposition, a flat face, stubby fingers and toes, epicanthic folds in the eyes among non-Asians, tongue fissures, and unusual patterns of skinfolds on the palms of the hands and soles of the feet and is associated with an early onset of Alzheimer's disease.

transmitter

n. Any instrument, device, or process that encodes information and sends it to a receiver. Several chemicals, such as serotonin, norepinephrine, and dopamine, serve as neurotransmitters in that they transmit electricity across the synaptic cleft, or gap between nerve cells.

transsexual

n. A person who clearly has the anatomical features of one sex and feels his or her body should be that of the other sex, especially in two-gender cultures. These individuals tend to dislike their genitals and wish to live as the other sex. Many cultures have social roles in which these persons are considered normal and sometimes as a gender independent of the male and female genders in most Western cultures.

transsexualism

n. The state of having a clear biological sex and persistently wishing to be a member of the other sex coupled with a dislike for one's genitals. Many cultures have social roles in which these persons are considered normal and sometimes as a gender independent of the male and female genders in most Western cultures.

transvestic fetishism

n. A sexual disorder in which a person's sexual arousal occasioned by wearing the clothing of the other gender causes acute personal or interpersonal distress and significantly interferes with daily functioning. This is different from cross-dressing, which does not cause distress or interfere with daily living, which is simply a sexual preference.

transvestism

n. The wearing of clothing deemed appropriate for the other or another gender within a culture or subculture. Also called cross-dressing.

tranylcypromine

n. A monoamine oxidase (MAO) inhibitor drug used as an antidepressant or anxiolytic, which is chemically related to amphetamines and stimulates dopaminergic systems more than other MAO inhibitors.

trauma

n. **1.** Any event which inflicts physical damage on the body or severe shock on the mind or both. Being the victim of a serious car accident, assault, rape, or false prosecution is likely to produce shock in an individual with lasting mental consequences just as being injured in some way inflicts damage to the body. **2.** The damage inflicted by a traumatic event, as in the head trauma caused by a car accident or the stress caused by being falsely prosecuted.

traumatic shock

n. The partial or complete collapse of normal autonomic and voluntary mental and physical processes following a sudden drop in blood pressure, injury to the spinal cord or central nervous system, a severe allergic reaction, or intense psychological stress.

traveling wave

n. Any wave which progressively transfers its energy along a boundary in the direction in which it is traveling, and especially a sound wave which displaces the basilar membrane in the inner ear at different points, depending on the wavelength of the sound which causes it.

tremor

n. An involuntary trembling of the hand or other part of the body. This is often due to neurological problems such as side effects of antipsychotic medication, brain damage caused by prolonged alcohol abuse, or insufficient blood supply to the brain.

trial-and-error learning

n. The kind of learning in which an organism is faced with a novel situation and tries one behavior after another in an apparently random fashion until something works. In successive trials or similar situations the behavior

which worked tends to appear earlier in the sequence of behavior and to be repeated more often.

trial, extinction

n. An instance of presenting an organism with a stimulus previously paired with either an unconditioned stimulus or a reinforcement without the unconditioned stimulus or reinforcement.

trial, learning

n. An instance in which an organism is presented with an unconditioned stimulus and a potential conditioned stimulus or an instance in which an organism has the opportunity to act to attain a reinforcement.

triangular theory of love

n. A psychological description of romantic relationships in which passion, commitment, and intimacy are the three basic dimensions and a particular relationship may have any combination of or all of the three. Passion without the other two is called infatuation. Intimacy without the other two is called friendship. Commitment without the other two is called a vacuous relationship. Companionate love is a relationship characterized by high levels of intimacy and commitment but lacking passion. Romantic love is a relationship characterized by high levels of passion and intimacy but lacking commitment. Fatuous love is a relationship with high levels of passion and commitment but lacking intimacy. Consummate love is a relationship with high levels of all three aspects.

triarchic theory of intelligence

n. An approach to understanding cognitive abilities which assumes there are three main types of ability, analytical ones, creative ones, and practical ones, which are moderately distinct and somewhat independent and are applied to experience to adapt to, shape, and select environments. The theory also suggests that individuals vary in the kinds of experience to which they apply different components of their intelligence and in the ways they apply the components of their abilities to different parts of experience.

trichotillomania

n. An impulse control disorder in which a person repeatedly pulls out small tufts of his or her own hair, producing pleasure or release of tension, which causes significant personal distress to the person or impairment in daily functioning.

trichromacy

n. The property of visual light in which any hue can be created by the combination of red, blue, and green light or by any other three colors as long as they are widely separated on the color spectrum.

trichromatic theory

n. A conceptualization of the process of human color perception which suggests that all perceived hues are combinations of three basic hues, blue, green, and red, for which there must be specific sensory receptors whose combined activity gives rise to all perceptions of hue. This theory has largely been supported by modern physiology and expanded by the idea of opponent processes among the different visual receptors. Also called the Young-Helmholtz theory.

tricyclic antidepressant

n. Any of a family of antidepressant drugs characterized by a basic molecular structure of three carbon rings. They act by blocking the reuptake of serotonin, dopamine, and norepinephrine, thereby increasing the overall activity of the brain at sites utilizing those neurotransmitters. Side effects can include dry mouth, blurred vision, constipation, and difficulty in urination. Examples of tricyclics include Elavil, Tofranil, Pamelor, and Sinequan.

tricyclic drug

n. Any drug characterized by a basic molecular structure of three carbon rings; most frequently used to refer to tricyclic antidepressants.

trigeminal lemniscus

n. A long, ascending neural pathway reaching from the tongue and jaws to the thalamus.

trigeminal nerve

n. The fifth cranial nerve, which includes both sensory and motor pathways between the tongue and jaws and the thalamus, which controls movements of the jaws and tongue in chewing and speaking.

trigeminal neuralgia

n. Recurrent, sharp spasmodic pain of the fifth cranial nerve, which is felt in the jaws and tongue.

trigram

n. **1.** Any three-letter nonsense word, many of which are used in memory and other sorts of perceptual and cognitive experiments. **2.** A three-line symbol indicating any of 64 mixtures of masculine and feminine used in the I Ching to symbolize the nature of a situation.

trisomy 18

n. A genetic disorder caused by the presence of three copies of chromosome 18 attributed to the nondisjuncture of chromosomes 17 and 18 in an egg or sperm cell. Most fetuses who have this abnormality spontaneously abort, and those that are born seldom live more than a few weeks. They usually have a small, abnormally shaped head with a small mouth and jaw, low-set ears, clenched fists with overlapping fingers, and a rounded foot bottom. Also called Edwards syndrome.

trisomy 21

n. A genetic disorder caused by the presence of an extra copy of chromosome 21, which is present in about 85% of cases of Down syndrome. Most individuals who have this abnormality will be mentally retarded, usually in the mild to moderate range of retardation. Physical symptoms include almond-shaped eyes with an epicanthic fold, a single transverse crease instead of the normal double crease in the palm, short limbs, poor muscle tone, and a protruding tongue.

tritanopia

n. A rare form of partial color blindness in which affected individuals lack light-sensitive pigment in the cones sensitive to blue light, causing confusion between blue and green hues.

troland

n. A unit for the intensity of light striking the retina which is a function of pupil size and ambient light. 1 troland is equal to the retinal illumination produced by viewing a surface illuminated by 1 lumen per square meter entering through a pupil with an area of 1 square millimeter.

trophic hormone

n. Any of a group of pituitary hormones that regulate the secretions of other endocrine glands, including thyroid stimulating hormone, adrenocorticotropic hormone, follicle stimulating hormone, and luteinizing hormone. Also called tropic hormone.

Troxler effect

n. The subjective fading of a stimulus in the periphery of vision when vision is fixated steadily elsewhere but attention is focused on the stimulus object, which has been attributed to adaptation in the rods involved in the portion of the retina receiving stimulation from the object. Also called Troxler fading.

trust versus mistrust

n. The developmental task in the oral-sensory stage in Erik Erikson's epigenetic cycle of self-development which runs from birth to about 1 year of age. In learning to make sense of the sensory world around it, the infant must acquire a belief in the possibility of need satisfying relationships, which Erikson called basic trust. Achievement of this basic trust leads to hope that needs can be met even if temporarily frustrated and so gives emotional strength to the ego's plans for the future. Basic mistrust, the other possibility, is a failure to establish a belief in the possibility of satisfying relationships, which leads to social withdrawal and despair. Infants develop a mistrust of the world when there is a failure of their efforts to interact with the world to produce significant need satisfaction, as when they are severely neglected. Mistrust-trust is not an all-or-none phenomenon, and infants who have complete mistrust tend to die or lack contact with reality, while those with mostly mistrust with a little admixture of trust tend to be shy, hypersensitive to rejection, and suspicious. Infants who develop mostly trust with some skepticism of others tend to have a greater capacity to grow and deal with the world in realistic ways.

tryptophan

n. An essential amino acid which is a precursor to the neurotransmitter serotonin and vitamin B_3, which is present in dairy products, chicken meat, pineapples, and bananas. It is essential in cell metabolism and DNA repair.

T score

n. A scaled score distribution with a mean of 50 and a standard deviation of 10. Many score sets are converted to T scores for ease of understanding by persons not sophisticated in statistics using the formula (Score − mean score/ Standard deviation of scores) × 10 + 50.

t test

n. A family of tests of the hypothesis that two group means are equal when the test statistic follows the t distribution. Usually one of these tests is used to detect differences in the means of two groups.

Tukey honestly significant difference test

n. A test of differences between group means in an analysis of variance which takes into account the increase in obtaining a false positive result when making multiple comparisons. The Tukey test is calculated as

$$Dmin = t(\sqrt{MSError} / \sqrt{SampleSize})$$

where *Dmin* is the minimal difference between group means needed to infer a population difference, *t* is the critical value of Student's *t* statistic with appropriate degrees of freedom and alpha level, MSError is the mean square of the within-group errors, and Sample Size is the sample size per cell. It is more conservative than Fisher's LSD test but less conservative than the Scheffe procedure.

Tukey-HSD test ▶ *See* **TUKEY HONESTLY SIG-NIFICANT DIFFERENCE TEST**

tumescence

n. Swelling or the state of being swollen as the penis or clitoris swells when engorged with blood during sexual excitement.

tuning fork

n. A fork-shaped piece of steel with two tines which vibrates with a nearly pure tone of a given pitch when struck.

tunnel vision

n. **1.** A defect in vision such that a person lacks a significant portion of his or her peripheral vision so his/her capacity to see is like always looking through a dark tunnel. This can be caused by glaucoma, retinosa pigmentosa, or bilateral injury to visual centers in the brain. **2.** Being narrow-minded so that a person cannot recognize things outside his/her own limited perspective or set of concepts.

Turing machine

n. A Turing machine is an abstract, mathematically well-defined finite state machine described by the British mathematician Alan M. Turing in 1937. Basically, it consists of (a) an infinitely extensible tape divided into cells marked by a symbol of a finite alphabet or a blank symbol, (b) a head performing reading and writing operations on the tape, and (c) a transition function. Given the current state of the machine and the symbol under the head, the transition function tells the machine (i) the next state it should go to, (ii) the next symbol it should write, and (iii) the direction in which the tape should move. The tape moves back and forth under the head one (and only one) cell at a time. Following Turing's idea, researchers in cognitive science and artificial intelligence have envisioned that the human mind itself may be represented as a Turing machine.   – A K

Turing test

n. The Turing test invented by the British mathematician Alan M. Turing in 1950 gauges whether an artificial symbol-processing system (e.g., a computer program) is intelligent.

The basic idea behind the test is whether an observer engaged in non-face-to-face conversation with both the symbol-processing system and a human by means of teletype machine (or, more recently, chat room) can distinguish one from the other. As Turing theorized it, if the system can so effectively simulate human responses that 30% of observers during a 5-minute test cannot reliably discern whether they are dealing with a computer or a person, then the system passes the test. According to Turing, any artificial system capable of passing the test should be considered capable of human intelligence.   – A K

▶ *See also* **ARTIFICIAL INTELLIGENCE**

Turner's syndrome

n. A genetic defect in women in which part or all of one of the X chromosomes is missing. This can lead to infertility, failure of the genitals to develop, short stature, webbing of the neck, and an IQ that is slightly below average. Also called XO syndrome.

twenty statements test

n. A self-report measure in which the person is given a sheet of paper on which the phrase "I Am" followed by 20 blank spaces is printed and asked to fill in the blank spaces. This is generally used as a rough assessment of a person's self-identity and has been used to examine cross-cultural differences in independent and interdependent self-construal. There is no standard scoring procedure and so no empirical estimates of the reliability or validity of the test.

twilight vision

n. Visual perception in very dim light in which only the rods of the eyes are functioning as cones need a higher level of illumination to work. The center of the visual field is insensitive and there is no perception of color in very dim lighting. Also called night vision and scotopic vision.

twins, dizygotic

n. Two people born of the same mother within a very short time of one another who developed from two different fertilized eggs which shared the prenatal environment.

twins, monozygotic

n. Two genetically identical individuals who developed when a fertilized egg split into two separate fetuses and gestated at the same time in the uterus and are born within a short time of one another.

twin study

n. A research design in which pairs of twins are compared, usually to compare the relative contributions of heredity and postnatal development. A frequently used design compares the similarities of fraternal and identical twins on a dimension of interest in an attempt to control for environmental similarities, which is at best partially successful as families are different for each person in them.

two-alternative forced-choice task

n. An experimental setup in which a subject is asked to select between a pair of predetermined alternatives in each trial. A true-false test is an example of this task. This setup is often used in signal detection tasks in which the subject is asked to select which of two time intervals contained a signal.

two-factor theory of emotion

n. An approach to emotion in which it is hypothesized that emotion consists of physiological arousal and an interpretation of that arousal in terms of a situation to which the subject attributes her/his arousal.

two-point threshold

n. The smallest distance between two points of stimulation on the skin at which people can tell they are being touched in two separate places.

two-process learning theory

n. The point of view which suggests that classical and operant conditioning are two separate learning systems. In classical conditioning, an organism is responding to antecedent conditions; in operant conditioning, the organism is responding to consequences or subsequent conditions.

two-sample t test

n. A test of the hypothesis that two group means are equal using Student's t statistic, in which the difference in the means is divided by the standard error of the difference.

two-tailed probability

n. In inferential statistics, the probability that one would find a result as extreme or more extreme than that actually found if the null hypothesis were true. The description *two-tailed* (2-tailed) refers to the appearance of the ends of a probability distribution far from the mean which appear similar to a tail. Since the area under probability distributions, such as the normal curve, in one end or tail is half that in the two tails combined, then the probability of obtaining an extreme result is twice that of a 1-tailed probability and so a 2-tailed test has half the statistical power of a 1-tailed test in probability distributions.

two-tailed test

n. In inferential statistics, a two-tailed (2-tailed) test is one that tests the null hypothesis that an observed result is less extreme in difference from the mean than would occur by chance. So a result either greater or lesser than the mean will be determined to be due to chance if it is larger than the a priori criterion. The criterion for deciding what size difference from the mean is sufficiently large as to be not attributed to chance is conventional and usually set at 5% probability.

two-way avoidance conditioning

n. Learning to move away from a stimulus that has previously been paired with an aversive stimulus such as electric shock in an experimental apparatus that has two areas between which the organism can move and in which either side may be electrified.

tympanic membrane

n. A membrane separating the outer ear from the inner ear which vibrates to communicate sound to the ossicles of the middle ear. Also known as the eardrum.

type A personality

n. An enduring pattern of adjustment characterized by chronic expressed hostility which predisposes individuals who have it to coronary heart disease. The original formulation of type A included competitiveness, high achievement motivation, status insecurity, and impatience, which have not been found to be associated with coronary heart disease.

type B personality

n. An enduring pattern of adjustment that is below average in expression of hostility, impatience, and frustration and tends to be easygoing and relaxed and not to crave status advancement.

type fallacy

n. The tendency of human beings to assign people or things to mental categories such as classifying someone as neurotic, extroverted, or open to experience, which tends to create mental separation among people while most people actually fall close to average on these and most dimensions of individual difference.

type I error

n. Type I error is the likelihood of falsely concluding that a trend in sample data is actually present in the population at large. Sometimes referred to as making a "false alarm," type I errors are sometimes very costly, depending on the situation and the implications to be drawn from the research findings. Traditionally, the statistical cutoff point

for making a type I error is a probability of 5% or less that a trend in the data occurred by chance alone, though researchers may choose a more conservative decision point (or alpha level) if the cost of type I errors is high.

— MWP

▶ *See also* P-VALUE, SIGNIFICANCE TEST, *and* STATISTICAL SIGNIFICANCE

type II error

n. ype II error is the likelihood of missing a trend that exists in the data. Sometimes referred to as "missing the signal," type II errors are especially problematic when (a) the sample size is small and (b) the magnitude of the effect is small. Type II error is directly linked to statistical power, which is the likelihood of avoiding type II errors. The simplest way for a researcher to reduce the likelihood of type II errors (i.e., to increase statistical power) is to increase the sample size. Generally speaking, sample size is inversely related to type II error rates: the larger the sample size, the smaller the likelihood of type II errors.

— MWP

▶ *See also* STATISTICAL POWER

tyrosine

n. An amino acid the body synthesizes from phenylalanine, which is the chemical precursor to the neurotransmitters dopamine, norepinephrine, and epinephrine, as well as the pigment melanin and the thyroid hormone thyroxin.

ultimate attribution error
n. An overly positive evaluation of the group to which one belongs and a denigration of other groups through converging cognitive errors. Negative acts by one's in-group members are attributed to circumstances while positive acts are attributed to stable personal characteristics among group members. Negative acts by out-group members are assumed to characteristics of the whole out-group and attributable to basic character while positive acts by out-group members are dismissed as attributable to the situation and not characteristic of the group. Also known as group serving bias.

ultimatum game
n. In gaming theory, a two-person game in which a prize is split by the two players: one player is allowed to suggest a division of the prize and then the second player either accepts or rejects the suggested division. If the second player accepts the prize, then the prize is split as suggested, and if the second player rejects the split, then neither of the two players receives anything. Second players tend to reject offers of less than about a third of the prize even though they get nothing if they reject and report they believe such a division unfair, while in classical gaming theory they should accept an offer even as low as a penny as something better than nothing. Number one players usually offer much more than a penny and often offer 50%.

ultradian rhythm
n. Any biological cycle longer than a day, such as human menstruation or the alteration of the daily wake/sleep cycle in bears or other animals that hibernate.

ultraviolet
n. The part of the electromagnetic spectrum between 0.5 nanometer and about 390–400 nanometers which cannot be seen by the human eye but can be seen by some butterflies,

fish, bumblebees, and other organisms. This is the radiation in sunlight that causes both suntan and sometimes skin cancer and is mostly absorbed by glass and plastic.

umwelt
n. The experience of being in and involved in the physical and biological world around one's self. This includes one's experience of needs, the character of the landscape, and there being some things that are possible and others that are not possible, such as walking down a path, as opposed to walking through a brick wall.

unbalanced bilingual
n. An individual who speaks two languages but one of them better than the other; the category includes most or all bilinguals as equal ability in more than one language is uncommon.

uncertainty
n. **1.** The state of not knowing something or being unable to predict something with great accuracy or high probability. **2.** The state of not having made a decision or of holding judgment in abeyance.

uncertainty avoidance
n. **1.** The intolerance of ambiguity and uncertainty, which is hypothesized to bring about a need for formal rules and for following them. **2.** A cognitive style with a preference for thinking in conventional or preconceived patterns, which contrasts with an uncertainty preference, in which new ideas and experiences are preferred and explored. **3.** A values dimension that differentiates cultures from each other: some cultures are high on uncertainty avoidance, adopting rituals to avoid the anxiety of the unknown, while some are low.

uncertainty principle
n. In quantum physics, the idea, introduced by Werner Heisenberg in 1927, that it is impossible to measure both the position and the momentum of a subatomic particle at the

same time because of the fact that all known methods of measurement of one of these quantities will change the other in unpredictable ways. The implied suggestion that thinking in terms of cause and effect may not be the best way of understanding the workings of the world has also been of influence in other sciences, including psychology.

uncertainty reduction

n. The process of obtaining more information about other people or events through observation and communication as a means of improving ability to predict and explain their behavior or outcomes. Uncertainty reduction theory supposes that initial relationships between individuals are more rule governed and used to gain information about the other person which reduces the anxiety associated with uncertainty. This allows the people to relax and enter a more personal phase of relationship in which their communication and behavior are less rule governed.

unconditional positive regard

n. In Rogerian theory, an unaffected valuing, caring for, and interest in another individual which is not dependent on the other's feelings, attitudes, or behavior and which is conducive to reclaiming ignored parts of the self, reforming distorted self-concepts, and self-actualization. It is an attitude which a therapist must possess in order to be helpful to clients; it is also characteristic of a good parent's relationship to his or her child and is used by the child to form a healthy conception of the self.

unconditional response

n. (UCR, UR) Any behavior that occurs in the absence of specific conditioning for it. Hypothetically it may be inherited or instinctual, but in a practical sense it is anything not known to have been learned. In Pavlov's original experiments with dogs, the UCR was the salivating of a dog when being fed. Also known as unconditioned response or unconditioned reflex.

unconditional stimulus

n. (UCS, US) Any stimulus that elicits a particular response without being taught that

response. In Pavlov's original experiments with dogs, the UCS was the food for which the unconditioned response was salivating when fed. Also known as unconditioned stimulus.

unconditioned reflex

n. (UR) Any behavior that occurs in the absence of specific conditioning for it. Hypothetically it may be inherited or instinctual, but in a practical sense it is anything not known to have been learned. In Pavlov's original experiments with dogs, the UR was the salivating of a dog when being fed. Also known as unconditioned response or unconditional response.

unconditioned reinforcer

n. In operant conditioning, anything which can be used to increase or decrease the likelihood of the appearance of a behavior when appropriately associated with the behavior in time and space.

unconditioned response ▶ *See* UNCONDITIONAL RESPONSE

unconditioned stimulus ▶ *See* UNCONDITIONAL STIMULUS

unconscious

1. *adj.* Of or relating to any process or content of the mind of which the individual is not aware at a particular moment in time. **2.** *n.* In Freudian psychology, the region of the mind which contains actively repressed materials such as memories, impulses, desires, and conflicts which are not accessible for the conscious portion of the mind. **3.** *n.* In Jungian psychology, the unconscious is divided into the collective unconscious, which contains the inherited structures and potentialities of mind, and the personal unconscious, which contains weak and repressed memories, thoughts, and feelings as well as personal ways of understanding created by the individual during his/her lifetime in the form of complexes. **4.** *n.* In general usage, any part of the mind outside the awareness of the individual.

unconscious drive

n. Any motivational force or energy outside the awareness of the individual. These are usually considered repressed in psychoanalytic theory but may be simply not recognized or not attended to in most forms of psychology.

unconscious ideation

n. Any thought process outside the awareness of the individual.

unconscious inference

n. The supposition that perception is influenced by conclusions about sensory data using the perceiver's general knowledge of the world and previous experience with similar sensory information. Thus, when we see a common cat up close we judge it to be smaller than a lion viewed at a distance even though the light reflected from the nearby cat casts a larger image on our eye than does the distant lion.

unconscious memory

n. **1.** In cognitive psychology, the capacity to use information from past experience while having no conscious recollection of the information. **2.** In psychoanalytic and psychodynamic psychologies, repressed or weak memories which the person is unable to recall to awareness.

underextension

n. An inappropriate failure to generalize the use of a word to all appropriate objects or situations, characteristic of a child's speech in the second year of life. For example, a child may speak as though *mother* means only her/his particular mother.

underpathologizing

n. Attributing pathological symptoms to normative cultural differences.

undifferentiated schizophrenia

n. A psychotic disorder characterized by delusions, hallucinations, and disorganized speech, thought, and behavior, as well as flat or inappropriate affect. Marked social and occupational dysfunction is usually present.

undimensionality

n. The quality of having a single statistical factor.

unfolding technique

n. A scaling procedure which differentiates between a subject's own preferences about a stimulus dimension and judgments about the relative position of stimuli along that dimension. In this technique subjects are asked to make relative comparisons of pairs of stimuli along a dimension as well as to select their own preference or ideal on that dimension. The subject's judgments about each stimulus are summed to give each a place on the dimension and the dimension folded at the subject's ideal point to produce a scale in which the subject's ideal is at one end and the two extremes of the original dimension are at or near the other end of this new individual preference dimension. This allows inferences about the relative preferences of subjects among stimuli not near each other on the original (joint) dimension. Also called the Coombs unfolding technique.

unidimensionality

n. The quality of having a single statistical factor.

unidimensional scaling

n. Any procedure which produces a measuring device having a single factor in it. In psychological measurement, these procedures would include scales developed using cluster analysis, factor analysis, Thurstone equal appearing interval scaling or paired comparison scaling, Guttman cumulative scaling and Likert summative scaling procedures.

uninvolved parents

n. A style of parenting in which parents are often too absorbed in their own lives to respond appropriately to their children and may seem indifferent to them.

unipolar depression

n. Any depressive disorder that occurs without periods of mania or hypomania.

unipolar neuron

n. A sensory neuron in the skin that has a single extension from the cell body which branches in one direction to become the axon, sending impulses toward the spinal column and in another direction to act as the dendrite, which receives messages from a sensory transducer in the skin. Also called monopolar neurons.

univariate

adj. Relating to having a single dimension of variability.

univariate statistics

n. The branch of statistics devoted to analyzing the relationships between one or more independent variables and a single dependent variable.

universal

1. *adj.* Of or relating to all possible individuals, as in all people or all living things. **2.** *n.* In cross-cultural psychology or cultural anthropology, any aspect of human behavior or aspect of culture that is true of all cultures; for example, the occurrence of puberty is universal although different cultures deal with it differently. **3.** *n.* In linguistics, a grammatical rule or other linguistic feature found in all natural languages. **4.** *n.* In psychology, a psychological process found in all humans or members of a specific group. **5.** *n.* In logic, a proposition that is always true, a widely held idea, or a concept considered axiomatic.

universal grammar

n. The term *universal grammar* (UG) describes the set of universal principles that license the grammars of all languages. Knowledge of these principles is argued to be innate, part of the human genetic endowment. Acquisition of a language-specific grammar therefore involves using input to determine the language-specific settings of the universal principles dictated by UG for the particular language being learned. For example, UG licenses languages that form questions by movement of the question (or wh-) element to the beginning of the sentence (such as English), as well as languages where the wh-element remains in situ (such as Chinese). However, forming questions, say, by flipping the linear order of words in a sentence falls beyond the range of languages licensed by UG. Arguments for the existence of UG rely on evidence from language acquisition: children acquire a highly complex linguistic system in a relatively brief amount of time, without explicit instruction and from impoverished input that vastly underrepresents what they eventually know about their language. Proponents of UG have proposed that children are able to learn such a complex system because most of it is available to them a priori, from birth.   — EMF

universals (universality)

n. **1.** In psychology, any cognitive forms or functions that appear in all people (or all members of another species) in all cultures and environments, but which may be given form by the culture or environment, such as parental care for infants. **2.** In linguistics, a feature of all known human languages such as words and sentences. **3.** In philosophy, either an essence, such as dogness that allows us to recognize a dog as a dog, or a proposition that is true in all possible contexts without creating a contradiction.

universals, linguistic ▶ *See* **LINGUISTIC UNIVERSALS**

unobtrusive measure

n. Any measurement taken without the awareness of the subject and without this awareness's affecting the dimension being measured. Thus using a telephoto lens to capture images of people's gestures might be an unobtrusive way of measuring them while being obviously near at hand recording their behavior would probably be an obtrusive measurement, which might affect the way individuals acted.

unpackaging studies

n. Studies that unpackage the contents of the global, unspecific concept of culture into specific, measurable psychological constructs and examine their contribution to cultural differences.

unpleasant affect

n. A transient response to a stimulus that is subjectively disliked, including anger, fear, disgust, and contempt and in some cases surprise.

unrealistic optimism

n. Unrealistic optimism is the belief that positive events are more likely to happen to the self than others, while negative events are more likely to happen to others, compared to the self. At least in Western cultural contexts, unrealistic optimism has been found to be related to higher self-esteem.   – EWMA, CYC

up-and-down method

n. A method in psychophysics in which the limits of perceptual accuracy are discovered by presenting a series of stimuli ordered from strongest to weakest or weakest to strongest and the limen threshold is determined by the intensity of the stimulus at which responses change. For difference thresholds, the absolute difference between a stimulus and a comparison stimulus is adjusted up when the difference is not perceived or down when the difference is perceived until the difference at which response change is found. Also known as the staircase method.

upper threshold

n. **1.** The maximal intensity of a stimulus that can be perceived without causing pain or damage to the subject. **2.** In difference perception, the smallest increase in size or intensity of a stimulus which the subject can detect.

uracil

n. $C_4H_4N_2O_2$, One of the four bases which form all RNA; it corresponds to thymine in DNA, into which it is transformed during DNA synthesis. It is commonly found in many organic tissues, absorbs light, and readily pairs with adenine and reacts with many chemicals because of its unsaturated structure.

urethral eroticism

n. Sexual arousal by and sexual interest in the process or sensation of urination.

urolagnia

n. Sexual arousal by urine or the process or sensations of urination. This may involve watching or drinking one's own or another's urine or urinating or being urinated upon during sexual activity.

urophilia

n. A psychological disorder in which a person is sexually aroused by thoughts about or the action of forcing a minor or nonconsenting partner to urinate or be urinated on during sexual interactions.

utilitarian function of an attitude

n. The part an attitude plays in gaining rewards and avoiding punishments. Thus a person might come to have a positive attitude about something because expressing that attitude leads to inclusion and other social benefits.

utility

n. **1.** The degree to which an object or event is valued by or gives happiness to an individual. **2.** The degree to which a course of action or strategy results in gains rather than losses. **3.** The character, fact, or quality of serving a purpose; for example, a nail has utility in holding boards together. **4.** In biology, the effectiveness of a characteristic in the survival and/or procreation of an individual or species. **5.** In industrial psychology, the increase or decrease in profit to the business from a program, decision, or other course of action. **6.** An organization that provides a specific service or commodity to a community, such as a water company or a bus service.

utility theory

n. In the psychology of decision making or game theory, any coherent set of ideas trying to describe the ways in which courses of action are being chosen.

utricle

n. A fluid-filled sac in the vestibule of the inner ear which is part of the sense of bodily position. It contains mechanoreceptors called hair cells which respond to acceleration and deceleration and which are used to detect both bodily motion and body position. The nerves serving the mechanoreceptors do not adapt over time, so that if a person is standing up, the person does not lose over time the ability to know he/she is standing up, as a person will cease hearing a continuing sound over time.

A relatively brief amount of time, without explicit instruction, and from impoverished input that vastly under-represents what they eventually know about their language.

Proponents of UG have proposed that children are able to learn such a complex system because most of it is available to them *a priori*, from birth.

vacuum activity
n. In ethology, the performance of a fixed action pattern in the absence of the stimulus or releaser which normally is the occasion for performance of that behavior. This is supposed to be the result of a buildup of motivation which eventually seeks release without normal external stimulus for its release.

vagina
n. A muscular canal leading from the labial opening to the uterus in female mammals. The interior of the vagina is lined with mucus membrane which is kept moist by secretions from Bartholin's glands located on each side of the vaginal opening, facilitating intercourse, whose failure to secrete lubricant is a cause of dyspareunia, or painful intercourse.

vaginismus
n. A sexual dysfunction in which the muscles of the vagina contract spasmodically before or during intercourse leading to pain and sometimes preventing intercourse, causing personal discomfort and relationship problems.

vagus nerve
n. Either of the pair of tracts of the 10th cranial nerve which receives sensory input from the linings of the digestive tract and the external ear and controls motor functions of the mouth and tongue, the heart, the lungs, and the digestive tract.

valence
n. **1.** In field theory, the positive or negative subjective value of a person, thing, or event in the individual's life space. **2.** In motivation, the anticipated satisfaction of an outcome.

validation
n. **1.** The act or process of verifying the truth of an idea, or the accuracy with which a measure measures what it is intended to measure. **2.** In client-centered therapy, the process of acknowledging the experience of another person.

validity
n. A statistical indicator of the extent to which a measure accurately reflects the target construct or phenomenon, or the extent to which logical conclusions can be drawn from the available data. In essence, validity examines whether a test, assessment, or study effectively measures what it was designed to measure. If a measure is valid, it is assumed that it is also reliable, although the converse is not true. While there are a number of types of validity, all emphasize various threats to the meaningfulness of the measurement and the conclusions drawn from it.   — BJM

validity coefficient
n. A numerical index of the degree to which a test measures what it is intended to measure, as opposed to reflecting extraneous variables and random error. A test-criterion correlation coefficient is the most usual and important coefficient. In cases in which a theoretical single dimension is being measured, the coefficient alpha can be used as a measure of validity.

validity, concurrent
n. Concurrent validity is the extent to which a measure or test score is correlated with another criterion measure that is occurring within the same time interval. Concurrent validity is most relevant when using one measure as a substitute for another. For example, students who successfully pass a College Level

Examination Program (CLEP) test receive college credit in exchange for their test score. As such, high concurrent validity between the CLEP test scores and grades in the relevant class provides evidence that the CLEP test is a valid substitute for taking the class. Because concurrent validity relies on the correlation between a measure and an external criterion, the terms *concurrent validity* and *criterion validity* are often used interchangeably. – BJM

validity, congruent

n. Congruent validity is the relationship between a measure and a known valid and reliable measure of the same construct. A measure that has a strong positive correlation with a previously validated test has high congruent validity with that test. Congruent validity emphasizes intertest correlations and emphasizes the logical coherence between new and known measures. – BJM

validity, construct

n. Construct validity is the extent to which a measure assesses the relevant underlying theoretical construct it is designed to measure. For example, if you are measuring intelligence, you would want to ensure that your measure effectively assesses the domain captured by intelligence yet is not influenced by other factors such as gender, language, or culture. Construct validity is established via the compilation and integration of multiple sources of evidence relying on both convergent and discriminant validity. Construct validity is demonstrated when there is evidence that the test measures what it is designed to measure as shown via correlations with similar constructs or tests (convergent validity), and evidence that the test does not measure unrelated or irrelevant constructs (discriminant validity). Construct validity relies on the clear operational definition of relevant terms, concepts, and measurable indicators. – BJM

validity, content

n. Content validity is the extent to which test items match or align with the target topic, performance, or content domain. Content validity relies on the ability of test items to measure the full content domain implied by the construct label, a task that can be particularly challenging when determining the criteria necessary to represent the full domain of abstract psychological constructs. For example, if one were developing a measure of self-esteem, content validity would focus on the extent to which test items effectively measure all aspects relevant to self-esteem. Generally, content validity is established via expert analysis relevant to the target construct. For example, the content validity of a subject test on the Scholastic Aptitude Test may be established by a committee of teachers who can provide expert analysis of the relevance of the items to measure all relevant subject factors. – BJM

validity, convergent

n. Convergent validity, a type of construct validity, is the extent to which one measure of a construct correlates with other measures of the same construct. For example, a researcher examining the validity of a short-form test of intelligence would want to examine the correlation between scores obtained from the short-form intelligence test and scores from established, accepted intelligence tests (such as the Wechsler or Stanford-Binet series). The convergence of scores from various tests attempting to measure the same theoretical construct provides evidence of convergent validity. – BJM

validity, convergent and discriminant

n. In testing, the degree to which a measure is correlated with other measures of the same variable and uncorrelated with measures of conceptually independent variables. It is often considered a form of concept validity.

validity, criterion

n. Criterion validity examines the relationship between a target measure and known, accepted criteria of the same (or a very similar) construct. For example, the criterion validity of a self-report measure of introversion may examine the correlation of self-report scores with actual behavior in social situations; a high correlation would provide support for the criterion validity of the self-report introversion measure. Ideally, the criteria used for comparison will be direct and objective; when direct measures of the target phenomenon are not available, similar constructs may be used as a basis to compare qualities such as the strength or direction of the correlation. Criterion validity may examine the correlation of a measure with future performance (called predictive validity) or with a current, similar measure (called concurrent validity). Because of the overlap between criterion and concurrent validity, these terms are often used interchangeably.   – BJM

validity, discriminant

n. Discriminant validity, a type of construct validity, is the extent to which a measure can effectively differentiate among various theoretical constructs. In essence, measures of different constructs should not be so highly correlated that they appear to measure the same thing. Discriminant validity is determined by examining the correlation of a measure across various indicators. For example, a measure of clinical depression would want to show that it could effectively differentiate between depression and anxiety. Low correlations provide evidence for discriminant validity.   – BJM

validity, ecological

n. **1.** The accuracy with which research findings correspond to the external world. Research is often focused on one or a few variables that represent only part of reality. Hence, the onus is on researchers to show that their data are relevant to the external world. **2.** The degree of agreement between perception of an object and the way the object actually is.

validity, external

n. External validity examines the extent to which conclusions drawn from a single study or target sample can be accurately generalized to the larger population, other populations, alternate settings, or alternate periods. External validity is concerned with unique factors that may have influenced the results of a particular study that would prevent findings from generalizing to other groups. As such, external validity may be negatively influenced by interactions between the way subjects are

selected and their assignment to groups, unintentional effects of pretesting, unique factors of the research setting, participant reactance, or the cumulative impact of repeated measures. External validity is limited when samples or observations are selected or assigned in a nonrandom fashion; as such, external validity is generally low for case studies or single-subject methodology. External validity is increased through the use of randomization, replication, and extension.   – BJM

validity, face

n. In testing, face validity relates to the degree to which the test resembles the variable being measured. Sometimes used to denote the degree to which a test includes all aspects of the variable which the test intends to measure.

validity, incremental

n. Incremental validity is the extent to which a test adds to the predictive validity already provided by other measures. Incremental validity is driven by the belief that use of multiple information sources increases the validity of the assessment. Incremental validity can be enhanced via use of clear, precise operational definitions of the full content domain; integration of multiple items utilizing alternate formats; use of test items that represent single components; and reduction of complex constructs into their basic components.   – BJM

validity, internal

n. Internal validity refers to the accuracy of causal research conclusions in which changes in outcome measures can be attributed solely to the experimental manipulation rather than unintended, covert, or extraneous variables. As such, internal validity in between-group studies examines whether changes in the dependent variable are solely a product of independent variable manipulations; internal validity in single-subject research emphasizes the extent to which changes in subject behavior can be attributed to treatment interventions. Generally, discussions of internal validity are limited to experimental research that attempts to draw cause-effect conclusions, but descriptive research may also discuss internal validity in terms of study quality (i.e., operational definitions, research design, sample, measurement, etc.). Studies with low internal validity are subject to a number of potential biases that may influence outcomes or results. Specifically, internal validity can be negatively impacted by subject maturation in repeated measures or longitudinal studies, pretest effects, changes in measurement methods, statistical regression, participant mortality, or participant selection.

              – BJM

validity, predictive

n. Predictive validity is the extent to which a measure or test score can predict future performance or behavior on a theoretically relevant construct. Predictive validity is obtained by examining the correlation between a given measure and a known outcome. For example, one may theorize that scores obtained from standardized tests taken in high school (such as the Scholastic Aptitude Test [SAT]) should be a predictor of success in college. The predictive validity of the standardized tests could be obtained by examining the correlation of SAT scores with the grade-point average of college graduates; a high correlation between these two measures would provide evidence for the predictive validity of the standardized tests.   – BJM

validity scale

n. **1.** Any scale on a self-report inventory or other test designed to detect any form of invalid responding on the part of the test-taker. This is usually done through adding scales to assess the number of rare answers, claims of unusual virtue or pathology, response inconsistency, defensiveness, or blank or multiply answered items on the self-report. **2.** The L, F, K, ?, TRIN, VRIN, and Fb scales on the MMPI.

value

n. **1.** A trans-situational goal that serves as a guiding principle in the life of a person or group (e.g., kindness, creativity). Values motivate and justify behavior and serve as standards for judging people, actions, and events. **2.** Any moral, political, social, economic, aesthetic, or spiritual preference. **3.** Primarily in economics, any quality of an object that gives it worth.

value expressive function of an attitude

n. In social psychology, strongly held attitudes are important to our self-concept, which we defend, in part, by expressing these attitudes, thus demonstrating our self-concept to others. This is widely used in marketing, in which an advertisement may describe a threat to one's self-concept and then propose buying a particular product as a way of demonstrating the strongly held attitude and so defending self-concept.

value system

n. The moral, political, social, economic, aesthetic, and spiritual ethics of a person or group of people as well as their interactions.

variability

n. The characteristic of undergoing change over time, across circumstances, or among members of a group. In statistics, this is estimated using various measures of dispersion, most commonly the standard deviation.

variable

n. Any scale for observations that vary over time, over circumstance, or between subjects, which is usually operationally defined in a research study. Dependent variables are usually outcome variables, while independent variables are those controlled or created by the experimenter in order to see what effects changes on these variables will have on the dependent variables.

variable, dependent ▶ *See* DEPENDENT VARIABLE

variable, independent ▶ *See* INDEPENDENT VARIABLE

variable interval reinforcement

n. In conditioning, a scheme for rewarding an organism whenever a set but changing period of time has elapsed during which a target behavior occurred. Habits established by such a scheme are very resistant to extinction but hard to establish.

variable-interval schedule ▶ *See* **VARIABLE INTERVAL REINFORCEMENT**

variable, intervening

n. **1.** Any variable not measured or controlled in a research study that affects the outcome variable and renders interpretation of variation in the dependent variable problematic. **2.** In learning theory, a theoretical variable which affects the relationship between independent and dependent variables and which is inferred from the observed relationships between independent and dependent variables.

variable, mediator

n. Any changeable quantity or condition which affects the relationship between any two or more other variables.

variable, moderator

n. A variable that influences the relationship between two other variables. For example, performance on a task may be related to one's attitudes about the task, but only under conditions of low (but not high) stress. In this case stress moderates the relationship between attitudes and performance.

variable ratio reinforcement

n. In conditioning. a scheme of reward in which a changing percentage of the occurrences of target behaviors is rewarded. Habits established by such a scheme are very resistant to extinction but are hard to establish.

variable-ratio schedule ▶ *See* **VARIABLE RATIO REINFORCEMENT**

variance

n. **1.** In statistics, a measure of dispersion calculated by taking the mean of the squared differences of scores from the mean score in a sample. **2.** In general, the degree to which differences are present in a set of data. Thus there can be variance in church attendance both between members and for a single member over time.

variance, between-group

n. In statistics, the portion of total variation in a data set that is not attributable to variation within groups but is supposed to be due to the differing experimental conditions to which different groups are subjected.

variance, within-group

n. In statistics, a measure of dispersion calculated by taking the mean of the squared differences of scores from the mean of one sample or one group within a larger study. This is calculated as one of the components of variance in analysis of variance (ANOVA).

vascular dementia

n. Any significant loss in cognitive function due to cerebrovascular disease; usually there are small strokes which cause very small, scattered areas of cell death in the brain. The particular symptoms depend on which brain areas accumulate areas of dead cells. Also called multi-infarct dementia.

vasocongestion

n. A localized swelling caused by increased blood flow and blood pressure in a limited area. Examples include erection of sexual tissues during sexual excitement, swelling of mucus membranes during allergic reactions, and face flushing during strong emotions.

vasoconstriction

n. A narrowing of the blood vessels usually resulting in lessened blood flow to a localized area, sometimes raising blood pressure. Stimulant drugs such as the amphetamines and methylphenidate cause vasoconstriction.

vasodilation

n. A widening of blood vessels resulting in increased blood flow to a localized area, which is usually accompanied by lower blood pressure.

vasomotor

adj. Of or relating to the smooth muscles in the walls of blood vessels which tighten to cause vasoconstriction and relax to cause vasodilation, in response to drugs, hormones, or nerves that serve to cause tension or relaxation in these muscles.

vasopressin

n. A hormone produced in the hypothalamus and stored in the pituitary gland which regulates water retention in the body and blood pressure by acting to constrict blood vessels. It may also act as a neurotransmitter in the brain and is particularly active in memory functioning.

ventral anterior nucleus

n. A cluster of nerve cells in the lower front part of the thalamus which receives inputs from the globus pallidus and the substantia nigra and sends projections into the premotor cortex and the frontal cortex.

ventral lateral nucleus

n. A cluster of nerve cells in the thalamus which receives inputs from the globus pallidus, the substantia nigra, and the cerebellum and sends projections into the motor cortex and premotor cortex. Also called the ventrolateral nucleus.

ventral posterior nucleus

n. A cluster of nerve cells on each side of the thalamus behind the ventral lateral nucleus, which is organized as a virtual map of the body with a disproportionate amount of space for the face and tongue. It receives input from the medial lemniscus, the trigeminal tract, and the ascending gustatory lemniscus and projects onto the somatosensory cortex and the ascending reticular activating system.

ventral root

n. Either of the inner columns of the spinal cord which carry motor nerves from the central nervous system and spinal ganglia toward the muscles.

ventricle

n. A cavity in the body such as the lower, contracting chambers of the heart or the four large, interconnected, and fluid-filled cavities in the brain, including the two lateral ventricles and the third and fourth ventricles.

ventromedial hypothalamic syndrome

n. A behavior pattern caused by experimental damage to the ventromedial nucleus on both sides of the hypothalamus in which the subject animal first has an acute phase in which it becomes hyperactive and eats without control for about 24 hours. This is follwed by an active phase of overeating resulting in gross obesity, followed by a static phase in which obesity is maintained but the animal ceases to seek food, is picky about what it will eat, and will seldom work for food or endure shocks for food when hungry as will normal animals. Also called hypothalamic hyperphagia.

ventromedial hypothalamus

n. The lower middle part of the hypothalamus on each side of the brain, which controls feelings of satiation after eating and is involved in the control of anger and aggression.

verbal behavior

n. Any action involving words including speaking, hearing, spoken language, reading, and writing. This phrase is often used by learning theorists attempting to describe or explain language from a purely observational point of view using only the ideas of operant conditioning without reference to mental processes.

verbal conditioning

n. The process of learning a particular language act described from a behavioristic point of view; usually described as the increase or decrease of particular actions after their pairing with particular stimuli.

verbal intelligence

n. The ability to learn language including vocabulary and grammar and to use it effectively in communication, memory, understanding, and problem solving. This is one of the two main factors measured in traditional tests of intelligence and an important component of crystallized intelligence.

verbal learning

n. **1.** Any acquisition of knowledge about language, its content, forms, and uses. This phrase is often used by learning theorists attempting to describe or explain language from a purely observational point of view using only the ideas of operant conditioning without reference to mental processes or modern linguistic theory. **2.** The study of a limited aspect of memory, including that for word lists, nonsense word lists, and paired word associates and occasionally for solving word problems.

verbal overshadowing effect

n. The observation that describing a previously seen face or other complex stimulus impairs recognition of the stimulus.

verbal protocol

n. The recorded speech of a person describing his or her thoughts about what he/she is doing or trying to do and the problems he/she encounters, usually recorded while he/she is attempting to solve a problem and used to understand the mental processes involved in problem solving.

vertical icicle plot

n. In statistics, a graphical representation of the successive steps of a cluster analysis in which steps of the analysis are shown on the vertical axis and cases or individuals on the horizontal axis.

vertigo

n. A word in common usage, which refers to a feeling of dizziness, light-headedness, and/or loss of balance. These sensations may be caused by a variety of changes in a person's motion, position, rotation, or equilibrium. Vertigo may be episodic or chronic; chronicity most often results from injury or infection in the middle or inner ear. Vertigo is also known as vestibulitis, indicating the role of the vestibular system (the inner ear mechanism for sensing position, movement, and balance). Vertigo may be accompanied by nausea and vomiting. Vertigo may be relieved by specific head movement exercises, acupuncture, or motion sickness medication such as meclizine.   – vs

vestibular nerve

n. The branch of the vestibulocochlear nerve carrying information used in the maintenance of balance or equilibrium and orientation, which runs from the inner ear to the brainstem.

vestibular sense

n. The capacity to know one's body position and to maintain balance, which results from the movement of hair cells in the inner ear, which are moved by acceleration, causing impulses that flow to the brainstem and cerebellum via the vestibular branch of the vestibulocochlear nerve.

vestibule

n. A small bodily cavity at the entrance to a larger cavity, such as the vestibule of the inner ear, which is the fluid-filled chamber between the three canals of the inner ear and the cochlea and contains the utricle and saccule; or the vaginal vestibule, which is the opening between the labia minora at the entrance to the vagina and into which the urethra and greater vestibular glands open.

VI

n. An abbreviation for *variable interval*, as in *variable interval schedule of reinforcement.*

vibratory sense

n. The capacity to detect small back-and-forth movements which is accomplished by touch receptors in the skin.

vicarious learning

n. Vicarious learning refers to the acquisition of attitudes, values, emotional proclivities, and styles of behavior by observing other people's behavior and its consequences for them. Vicarious learning through social modeling serves diverse functions. In addition to fostering the acquisition of knowledge, competencies, and new styles of behavior, modeling influences can have strong motivational effects. Seeing others gain desired outcomes by their actions creates outcome expectancies that function as positive incentives, whereas seeing others punished for certain actions creates negative outcome expectancies that function as disincentives. People are easily aroused by the emotional expressions of others. Observers can learn emotional dispositions toward persons, places, or things that have been associated with modeled emotional experiences. During the course of their daily lives, people have direct contact with only a

small sector of the physical and social environment. Consequently, their conceptions of social reality are heavily influenced by the symbolic modeling in the mass media.
— AB

Vienna circle

n. A group of mathematicians, philosophers, and logicians working in and around the city of Vienna in the 1920s and 1930s who believed that the only knowledge resulted from experience and that logical analysis using symbols was the best approach to understanding the world. This school of thought became known as logical positivism. The group called itself the Ernst Mach Society and included Maritz Schlick, Kurt Gödel, Marcel Natkin, Theodore Radakovic, and Rudolf Carnap.

Viennese school

n. Any of three approaches to psychology originating in Vienna, including the first school, based on the theories of Sigmund Freud; the second school, based on the theories of Alfred Adler; and the third school, based on the ideas of Victor Frankl.

vigilance

n. The state of being alert and watchful of the environment or a particular part of the environment. This is usually measured experimentally using reaction time or the likelihood of detecting a signal. In ethology and social psychology, vigilance includes increased alertness toward particular sorts of important environmental or social situations, such as watching for predators or the behavior of status rivals.

Vineland Adaptive Behavior Scales

n. A test battery intended to assess an individual's social competence with measures of communication, daily living skills, socialization, and motor skills. A structured interview or a set of rating scales filled out by a parent or caregiver is scored to diagnose dementia, brain injury, autism, mental retardation, or other developmental disabilities. The recent form of the scales can be used for newborns to persons aged 90.

Vineland Social Maturity Scale ▶ *See* VINELAND ADAPTIVE BEHAVIOR SCALES

violence

n. Alternative definitions exist for describing the essence of violence; definitions differ particularly in their scope. Traditionally, definitions describe physical actions perpetrated with the deliberate intention of harming, violating, or damaging the victim. While historically the term *violence* has been used to refer to physical actions alone, there is a shift toward including abusive types of psychological and sexual actions within the definition.

Types of violence include individual and collective or group violence. Extreme cases of individual violence include murder, aggravated or physical assault, and rape. Extreme cases of group violence include ethnic cleansing, terrorism, and war. Controversy exists as to which lesser harmful events constitute violence, as well as whether events perpetrated against nonhuman entities, including animals and property, ought to be considered as acts of violence.

The term is also increasingly applied to oppressive social structures like the caste system or slavery (structural violence) and conditions like poverty or the prison system (institutional violence). Psychologists tend to focus on two approaches to study violence: prediction of violence and control of violence. The latter includes treatment of violence offenders and legal responses.   — HLa

visceroreceptor

n. Any sensory nerve ending in the digestive system.

visible spectrum

n. The range of electromagnetic radiation which the human eye is able to detect, ranging from about 390 to 740 nanometers in wavelength.

vision

n. **1.** The capacity to detect light and perceive objects reflecting light. **2.** A spiritual or religious experience involving perceiving religious figures or objects and events invisible to others. **3.** A visual hallucination. **4.** A picture in the mind of something not present in the external world.

vision, achromatic

n. The capacity to detect light and perceive objects reflecting light, but lacking the capacity to perceive either hue or saturation.

vision, binocular

n. The capacity to perceive objects reflecting light using the difference in the images on the two retinas to form three-dimensional representations.

vision, chromatic

n. The capacity to detect the hue and saturation of light, especially in the perception of objects reflecting light.

vision, monocular

n. The capacity to perceive objects reflecting light with a single eye and without using the difference in the images on two retinas to form three-dimensional perceptions.

vision, peripheral

n. The capacity to detect light and perceive objects in the area of the visual field more than about 10 degrees away from the point of focus. In most people the visual field extends about 180 degrees horizontally and about 140 degrees vertically when both eyes are normally functioning.

vision, stereoscopic

n. Normal human vision in which the images from each eye are fused in the brain into a single image which is three-dimensional, allowing inferences about depth not possible with a single two-dimensional view.

vision, theories of

n. Any coherent set of observations and hypotheses about the nature of the capacity to detect light and perceive objects reflecting light.

visual accommodation

n. The process of tightening and relaxing the ciliary muscles, which changes the shape of the lens in the eye to allow the image of an object of focus to be sharpened on the retina. Tightening the muscles flattens the lens so that the images of distant objects become clearer, while relaxing the muscles thickens the lens so that the images of near objects become sharper.

visual acuity

n. The degree of clarity or sharpness with which an image can be created on the retina by light reflected from an object.

visual adaptation

n. The several processes of change in the functioning of the perception of light and objects reflecting light after prolonged exposure to the light. As an example, the retinal rods are soon depleted of photopigment and become unresponsive after exposure to bright light. Visual adaptation includes chromatic, dark, light, and prism adaptations, as well as transient tritanopia.

visual aftereffect

n. Any perception of light or an object reflecting light that follows and is a result of a previous perception. An instance is the perception of an illusory blue image after staring at a yellow object for several seconds.

visual angle

n. The size of a seen object measured by the number of degrees of the visual field through which it extends, which is determined by both the size of the object and its distance from the eye. As an instance, if you hold your thumb about 2.5 cm in front of your eye, your thumb will cover about 90 degrees of your visual field, whereas if you hold it at arm's length, it will cover around 1 degree of your visual field.

visual aphasia

n. An incapacity to read in a person who has previously learned to read. This is usually caused by brain trauma in the left angular gyrus near the junction between the occipital and temporal lobes. Also known as alexia and word blindness.

visual association cortex ▶ *See* **EXTRASTRIATE CORTEX**

visual capture

n. The dominance of the sense of sight over other senses so that plausible visual images are perceived as the location of touch or sound whenever the source of the touch or sound is not too distant from what is seen. Thus if an object appears to touch the skin in one location but actually touches it a half-inch from where it is seen as touching, the person will report the touch at the point which is seen rather than at the point of actual touch. Similarly, in a theater the sound appears to come from the movie screen rather than from the location of hidden speakers.

visual cliff

n. An experimental apparatus used to investigate depth perception in infants and small animals in which a clear surface covers a checkerboard pattern which goes to an edge and extends down a side to a lower level, as does a tablecloth draped over the edge of a table and onto the floor. Infants and young animals are placed near the edge, and their willingness to move over the edge is used to infer whether or not they are capable of perceiving depth.

visual cortex

n. Cortical area involved in visual information reception and processing. It includes the primary visual area or striate cortex (Brodmann's area 17) and visual association areas or extrastriate cortex (Brodmann's areas 18 and 19).   – A A

▶ *See also* **EXTRASTRIATE CORTEX** *and* **STRIATE CORTEX**

visual disparity

n. The difference in the images on the two retinas of a single object, which is used as a cue to form three-dimensional perceptions. Also called binocular disparity and retinal disparity.

visual dominance

n. **1.** The tendency of the image from one eye to be seen in preference to the image from the other eye. **2.** The tendency to perceive the world as seen, rather than as heard, felt, smelled, or tasted when the information

of the senses is in conflict. Thus, if an object appears to touch the skin in one location but actually touches it a half-inch from where it is seen as touching, the person will report the touch at the point which is seen rather than at the point of actual touch. Similarly, in a theater the sound appears to come from the movie screen rather than from the location of hidden speakers.

visual field

n. The space which is seen at any one time. In most people the visual field extends about 180 degrees horizontally and about 140 degrees vertically when both eyes are normally functioning.

visual fixation

n. **1.** The point at which the center of the retina, the fovea, is pointed. **2.** The act or process of focusing the eyes at a particular point or object.

visual hallucination

n. The visual perception of an image or scene not present, caused by a mental or physical disorder or intoxication, as with LSD, and usually believed to be real by the person perceiving it.

visual illusion

n. Any of dozens of sorts of incorrect visual impressions which can be produced through many physiological and psychological mechanisms. Some visual illusions are normal and caused by the working processes of the visual system, such as in the figure ⊥ where the vertical line appears to be longer than the horizontal line when both are the same length. Other visual illusions are caused by damage to the visual system, as when a person sees two or more images of the same object or continues to see an object after it has gone. Also called optical illusion.

visual image

n. **1.** An optically formed representation of an object or scene, such as the image projected by the lens of the eye onto the retina. **2.** The subjective experience of seeing something. **3.** A subjective experience or mental representation of an object or scene in the absence of that object or scene, usually formed by memory or constructed by imagination.

visual induction
n. The effect of one part of a visual scene or the visual field on other parts of it. As an example, a blue color patch will be seen differently if it is between two yellow patches than if it is between two black patches.

visual memory
n. The capacity to remember what has been seen in the form of virtual images in the mind.

Visual-Motor Gestalt Test
n. A test in which subjects copy nine line drawings as accurately as possible onto a blank sheet of paper. The test is used as a screening instrument for brain damage in adults and for developmental problems in children, as well as occasionally for psychological disorders such as depression. Also called the Bender Visual-Motor Gestalt Test.

visual perception
n. **1.** The capacity to detect light and perceive objects reflecting light. **2.** The processes whereby sight occurs or is experienced.

visual pigment
n. A chemical in the rod or cone of the eye which undergoes a change in state when struck by a photon, which then causes changes in the electrochemical state of the cell, which in turn may lead to generation of a neural impulse causing us to see light. In the rods this chemical is known as rhodopsin; the different kinds in cone cells are called iodopsins.

visual purple
n. A photoreactive chemicals found in retinal rods, which changes shape when struck by a photon of appropriate energy, which then causes the rod to hyperpolarize, sending an electrical impulse to the nerve and other cells to which it is connected. Rhodopsin bleaches out quickly at high ambient brightness levels and is responsible for night vision. Also called rhodopsin.

visual receptor
n. A cell that converts the energy of light into neural excitation. Thus the rods and cones in the eye convert the energy of light which strikes them into nerve impulses, which ultimately result in the experience of seeing objects. Also called a photoreceptor.

visual search
n. **1.** The process of detecting a particular object among other objects using the eyes. **2.** An experimental task in which the characteristics of the target object and various distracter objects are varied to investigate effects and make inferences about the processes involved in visual perception. The game Find Waldo is a nonexperimental example of a visual search task.

visuomotor priming
n. The process of facilitating or inhibiting a motor action by presenting a visual image immediately before the motor action. Thus, if the motor task is picking up a glass of water, then presenting an image of a vertical metal bar about the same diameter as the glass immediately before picking up the glass will make it faster to pick up the glass. If the subject is shown an image of a horizontal bar immediately before picking up the upright glass, there will be an inhibitory effect on picking up the glass.

vitalism
n. The idea that there is a life force which cannot be explained in terms of physical sciences such as physics and chemistry, usually including the idea that the life force is self-determining in some way and suggesting the failure of the physical and biological sciences fully to explain life itself. The idea of libido in Freud's psychology is sometimes viewed as a form of vitalism, as is the teleological principle in Jung's writings. Vitalism is gradually being replaced in academic thought by the idea of emergent properties in which new aspects emerge that are not necessarily inferable from the parts of a complex system as it existed at a prior moment in time.

vitamin therapy

n. The idea that mental disorders and physical diseases are a result of the lack or oversupply of specific chemicals in the body and can be treated by supplying chemicals to bring about a correct balance. Thus it has been suggested that vitamin C could cure the common cold as colds were a family of diseases resulting, in part, from inadequate functioning of the immune system due to the presence of too many free radicals which could be treated by vitamin C. Also called orthomolecular therapy.

vitreous humor

n. The thick, clear liquid filling most of the eyeball between the lens and the retina.

vocal cords

n. The vocal cords (also *vocal folds*) are two folds of flesh housed in the larynx and surrounding the *glottis*. Muscles in the larynx pull the vocal cords apart (abduct) during breathing, opening the glottis and allowing air to enter and escape from the lungs through the trachea. During phonation (in the production of voiced sounds, such as vowels and voiced consonants), the vocal cords move together (adduct). The increased subglottal pressure forces air through the vocal cords, causing them to move apart. The rush of air at the same time decreases pressure, by Bernoulli's principle, moving the vocal cords together again. This cycle takes place in rapid sequence – on average, 125 Hz (cycles per second) in adult males, 200 Hz in females, 300 Hz in children; these differences are linked to differences in the size of the larynx, the length and mass of the vocal cords, and the length of the vocal tract. The result of the cyclical opening and closing of the vocal folds is voicing, or phonation, in speech production or singing: a fundamental frequency is generated that will be modulated as it travels through the vocal tract. — EMF

vocal folds

n. A pair of membranes vaguely resembling lips which stretch across the larynx whose opening is called the glottis. The vibration of the vocal folds by air passing from the lungs is the mechanism by which people speak and make other sounds. The amount of tension on the folds regulates the tone of the sound produced. The sounds from the vocal folds are amplified by resonation in the cavities of the chest, throat, mouth, nose, and sinus. Also called vocal cords.

vocal tract

n. All the structures involved in speaking or singing, including the laryngeal cavity, the vocal cords (or folds), the glottis, the pharynx, the mouth, and the nasal cavities, as well as the resonating chambers of the chest.

vocational aptitude test

n. Any test of ability, interest, or personality used to predict success in a particular occupation. Such tests are often constructed of varied tests of the abilities assumed to be central to successful performance in the occupation.

vocational counseling

n. The process of assisting a person to find an appropriate job or career through testing, personal interviews, and discussions of the nature and qualifications for particular jobs and their intersection with the interests, abilities, and training of the individual.

vocational interests

n. Any general or specific curiosity, preference for, or concern with an area that is found to be or deemed to be characteristic of persons who are successful in particular occupations. Thus the Strong Vocational Interest Blank scores persons on their similarity in preferences, interests, and activities to persons who are successful in a variety of careers.

voice box

n. A colloquial name for the larynx.

voiceprint

n. A graphic representation of the tones and cadences of human speech, which has been used in attempts to identify individuals but has not generally been found to be satisfactorily reliable. It has also been used in the study of speech characteristics.

volley theory of hearing

n. The idea that no individual nerve in the auditory nerve tract responds to every sound stimulus but that some group of cells responds to each stimulus so that in a succession of sound waves some respond to the first wave, some to the second, some to the third, up to some *n*th repetition of the wave. This creates waves of response that match the waves of sound, allowing the perception of sounds whose time period is too fast for an individual cell to respond to each wave. Nerve cells can respond at most between 500 and 100 times per second, and yet we can hear sounds at up to about 20,000 cycles per second because of the partial response pattern of auditory nerve cells.

volume color

n. The characteristic of color distributed throughout the volume of a transparent object, such as color that is distributed throughout water with a dye in it. Also called bulky color.

volumetric thirst

n. Thirst caused by a loss of extracellular liquid through bleeding or vomiting. Also called extracellular thirst and hypovolemic thirst.

voluntary muscle

n. Any of the muscles of the body connected to the skeleton which can be controlled at will by the individual.

vomeronasal organ

n. A narrow horizontal channel ending in a pouch on each side of the septum in each nostril containing chemoreceptors that are especially responsive to sex pheromones in many animals. They are present in humans but are very small, and their function is unknown.

von Osten's horse

n. A horse which was famous in the early 1900s for being able to give the correct answer to any question its owner asked of it by tapping its hooves on the ground. It was eventually found that Clever Hans could only answer questions to which his owner knew the answer and only when he could see his owner. It was eventually assumed by scientists that the owner was unconsciously giving Hans subtle cues. This story has been used ever since that time as an example of reaching false conclusions by overlooking important variables in research. Also known as Clever Hans.

von Restorff effect

n. The observation that in remembering lists of items, the items that are most distinctive will be best remembered. As an instance, if a list of words is printed in black ink except for one word printed in blue ink, the word in blue ink is more likely to be remembered.

voodoo death

n. The death of a person after a curse by a voodoo priest or sorcerer. This has been observed primarily among members of the cultures of Haiti, Africa, Australia, and some islands in the Caribbean Sea and Pacific Ocean in which there is a strong belief in the power of such curses. No satisfactory mechanism for the deaths has been discovered by science, although they are widely supposed to be due to the power of suggestion.

voting

n. The act of choosing by indicating one's preference for a person or course of action.

voting paradox

n. If a vote of preference is held with three choices, *x*, *y*, and *z* with three voters, suppose one person has a preference for *x*, *y*, and *z* in that order; the second voter chooses *z*, *y*, and *x* in that order; and the third voter chooses *y*, *z*, and *x* in that order. Then *x* is preferred by two to one to *y*, *y* is preferred by two to one to *z*, and *z* is preferred by two to one to *x*. Also called Condorcet's paradox.

vowel

n. Any of the letters *a*, *e*, *i*, *o*, *u*, or *y* or the sounds they represent, which are voiced by an unobstructed flow of air through the glottis and the vocal tract.

voyeurism

n. A disorder in which a person has a recurrent and intense desire to watch unsuspecting and nonconsenting persons who are naked, disrobing, or engaging in sexual activity.

vulva

n. The external female genitals including the labia majora, labia minora, clitoris, and vestibule of the vagina. Also called the pudenda.

Vygotsky blocks

n. A set of 32 blocks of differing color, width, height, and shape used in a test of concept formation with children. The blocks were developed by L. S. Sakharov and widely used by Lev Vygotsky. In Vygotsky's research, the subject is asked to sort the blocks into categories using nonsense words written on the bottom of the blocks but not explained to the subject. One word usually refers to tall, wide blocks; another to low, wide blocks; a third to tall, thin blocks; and the last to low, thin blocks, and color and shape are irrelevant to the coding scheme. The subject is then asked the meaning of the nonsense words, and younger and older children differ in their explanations: younger children give complex or unworkable convoluted explanations and adolescents begin to give coherent conceptual definitions.

Wada test

n. A test for determining the separate functioning of the two cerebral hemispheres in which a drug, usually sodium amytal, is injected into one of the internal carotid arteries, which take blood to one side of the cerebrum, and then testing the person's abilities with the functions of one side of the cerebrum depressed. This test is primarily used before brain surgery, typically temporal leucotomy for intractable epilepsy.

Walden Two

n. Title of a novel by Burrhus F. Skinner in which a managing elite control the contingencies of reinforcement within an isolated community so that all members will want to behave in ways which are good for the community and derivatively for themselves.

Wallerian degeneration

n. The disintegration of a nerve fiber after destruction of an axon segment downstream away from the cell body. The muscles or other cells innervated by the destroyed axon typically atrophy. Axons sometimes grow back after such destruction, with regrowth depending on the extent of damage and the distance between the cell body and the enervated tissue. In research, degeneration is sometimes brought about intentionally in order to track the path of an axon.

water-jar problem

n. Any of a large set of problems asking how to obtain a specific amount of water from three or more jugs having a specific capacity. For instance, a subject might be asked how to obtain 10 quarts using a jug that holds 12 quarts, one that holds 5 quarts, and one that holds 1 quart. Also called water jug problem.

Watsonian

adj. Of or relating to the theories of James B. Watson, who was an early advocate of the behavioral point of view in psychology, conducted studies in comparative psychology, and was the first to conduct market research applying psychological methods.

wavelength

n. The distance between peaks of successive waves measured in the direction of propagation in any medium. Wavelength is equal to the speed of the wave divided by its frequency. The wavelengths of light visible to humans extend from violet at about 380 nanometers to red at about 760 nanometers. The wavelengths of sounds that humans can hear range from about 1.7 meters to about 21.5 meters.

Weber-Fechner law

n. The idea that to increase a subjective perception of a stimulus a fixed amount, the absolute intensity of the stimulus must increase exponentially, following the formula $s = k \log I$ (where *s* is the sensory magnitude, *k* is a constant and *I* is the physical intensity of the stimulus).

Weber fraction

n. The ratio of a just noticeable difference (JND) between two stimuli to the intensity of one of them. The absolute amount of change needed for a person to notice a difference changes with the intensity of the stimulus so that a bright light needs to change more than a dim light for a person to notice a change in brightness.

Weber's law

n. The idea that there is a constant relationship between the intensity of a stimulus and the amount of change in the stimulus needed for a human observer to detect the change, as expressed in the formula $\Delta I / I = k$ (where *I* is the physical intensity of a stimulus, ΔI is a change in physical intensity, and *k* is a constant).

Wechsler Adult Intelligence Scale

n. (WAIS) A general battery of intelligence or ability tests first derived from the U.S. Army general ability tests and last revised in 1997. It generates a verbal IQ, a performance IQ, and a full-scale or composite IQ with a mean of 100 and a standard deviation of 15 so that about 68% of all subjects score between 85 and 115. It includes subtests of general information, verbal comprehension, arithmetic, similarities, vocabulary, short-term memory (digit span), letter-number sequencing, picture completion, digit symbol, block design,

matrix reasoning, picture arrangement, symbol search, and object assembly. Composite scores can also be computed for verbal comprehension, perceptual organization, working memory, and processing speed.

Wechsler-Bellevue scale

n. An intelligence test battery devised by David Wechsler using U.S. Army Alpha and Beta tests as a basis while he was employed at Bellevue Hospital in New York City. The battery has subsequently been revised several times and was the basis for the contemporary Wechsler Scales of Intelligence.

Wechsler Individual Achievement Test

n. (WIAT) An omnibus measure of educational achievement for children aged 4 to 19 which is intended to diagnose learning disabilities and to assist in interventions with individual students who are having trouble in school. It consists of nine tests including word reading, pseudoword reading, reading comprehension, spelling, written expression, numerical operations, mathematical reasoning, and oral expression and generates content area scores in reading, mathematics, written language, and language.

Wechsler Intelligence Scale for Children

n. (WISC, WISC III) A set of tests for children from ages 6 to 16, devised to predict general capacity to learn and particularly the capacity to learn in standard American educational settings. The tests do not require the child to have the ability to read or write in order to complete the test. They yield verbal, performance, and full-scale IQs, as well as scores on subtests of general information, similarities, arithmetic, vocabulary, comprehension, memory for digits, picture completion, coding, arranging pictures in order to tell a story, block design, object assembly, mazes, symbol search, and indices of verbal comprehension, freedom from distractibility, perceptual organization, and a processing speed factor.

Wechsler Intelligence Tests

n. Any of several measures of intelligence developed originally by David Wechsler and subsequently revised by others. These include the Wechsler Adult Intelligence Scale (WAIS), the Wechsler Intelligence Scale for Children (WISC), and the Wechsler Preschool and Primary Scale of Intelligence (WPPSI). The Wechsler Memory Scales (WMS) and the Wechsler Individual Achievement Test (WIAT) are intended to discriminate between intelligence and specific learning problems. Adaptations of the Wechsler tests exist for many countries and languages.

Wechsler Memory Scale

n. A collection of memory tests intended to assess memory in persons over the age of 16 for comparison with general intellectual functioning. It includes 18 subtests from which indexes for auditory immediate memory, visual immediate memory, immediate memory, auditory delayed memory, visual delayed memory, auditory reception delayed, general memory, and working memory are derived. It was normed in conjunction with the WAIS-III on a national stratified sample in the United States.

Wechsler Preschool and Primary Scale of Intelligence

n. (WPPSI) An intelligence test for children between the ages of 30 months and 7 years, 3 months of age which was most recently revised in 2002 for the United States. It includes measures for information, vocabulary, word reasoning, similarities, comprehension, and picture naming in the verbal section and picture completion, picture concepts, block design, object assembly, matrix reasoning, symbol search, and coding in the performance section of the test. The test yields an index of general language ability and processing speed score, as well as verbal, performance, and full-scale IQ scores which have a mean of 100 and a standard deviation of 15.

Weltanschauung

n. A worldview or general understanding of the universe and the place of humans in the world. This worldview can be that of an individual, a culture, or a subculture, and it serves as the basis for the development of material and intellectual aspects of culture as well as providing a base of common understanding facilitating communication among those holding the worldview.

Wernicke-Korsakoff syndrome

n. A chronic debilitation with lesions in the brain due to thiamine deficiency, usually occasioned by long-term alcoholism. These lesions are often located in the midbrain, cerebellum, and diencephalon and first produce ataxia, acute confusion, gaze palsy, and nystagmus. In later stages damage occurs throughout the brain and particularly in the mammillary bodies and dorsomedial nuclei, leading to memory loss, deterioration of executive functions, and dementia.

Wernicke's aphasia

n. Language disorder characterized by fluent speech, paraphasias (wrongly produced words), and language understanding defects. Different names, such as *sensory aphasia*, *receptive aphasia*, and *central aphasia*, have been used to refer to this particular type of language disorder. In Wernicke's aphasia spontaneous language is abundant and sometimes excessive. Grammatical structure is acceptable, although an excessive number of grammatical elements – sometimes wrongly selected – can be observed (so-called paragrammatism). Prosody and articulation are correct. There is a significant decrease in the number of meaningful words, potentially resulting in an "empty speech." Paraphasias (incorrect words) and neologisms (newly constructed words) are usually abundant. Paraphasias can be due to errors in phoneme sequences (phonological paraphasias) and to errors in the selection of the words (verbal paraphasias). Sometimes language is abundant but completely nonunderstandable. This type of language is referred as jargon aphasia (or jargonaphasia). Language understanding is abnormal. In extreme cases, the patient simply does not understand anything; more frequently, there is a certain level of language understanding, limited to high-frequency words and simple sentences. Language understanding is not steady but fluctuates. Some patients who have Wernicke's aphasia have difficulties in discriminating phonemes, particularly acoustically similar phonemes. Verbal memory defects are routinely observed.

– AA

▶ *See also* **AUDITORY AGNOSIA, AUDITORY CORTEX, AUDITORY PERCEPTION, CENTRAL DEAFNESS, JARGON APHASIA, WERNICKE'S AREA,** *and* **WORD DEAFNESS**

Wernicke's area

n. Wernicke's area coresponds to the auditory association area involved in language recognition, usually found in the left hemisphere. In 1874 Wernicke described that damage in the left temporal lobe resulted in a language defect (aphasia) characterized by difficulties in language understanding, word-finding deficits, paraphasias (wrongly produced words), and disturbances in verbal memory, whereas language production was fluent, grammar was preserved (and even overused), and no associated speech defects (dysarthria) were observed. This type of aphasia is usually known as Wernicke's aphasia, or sensory aphasia, or receptive aphasia. Wernicke's area is considered to be the brain area responsible for Wernicke's aphasia. Nonetheless, Wernicke's aphasia is a rather variable syndrome, and the limits of Wernicke's area are controversial. Different authors describe Wernicke's area not completely coincidentally: some authors only include the posterior part of the superior temporal gyrus (Brodmann's area 22); some authors include the superior and middle temporal gyri; and others even include the angular gyrus of the parietal lobe in Wernicke's area. – AA

Wernicke's encephalopathy

n. A chronic debilitation from lesions in the brain due to thiamine deficiency, usually occasioned by long-term alcoholism. These lesions first produce ataxia, acute confusion, gaze palsy, and nystagmus. In later stages damage occurs throughout the brain and particularly in the mammillary bodies and dorsomedial nuclei, leading to memory loss, deterioration of executive functions, and dementia. Acute phases of the disease can be treated by administration of thiamine, but deterioration continues in the case of alcohol abuse despite thiamine treatment.

Werther syndrome

n. Suicide following the example of the suicide of a public figure which tends to occur in a cluster when the suicide of the public figure is extensively covered in the public media.

white matter

n. The off-white tissue of the brain and spinal cord which is given its hue by the myelin sheaths that insulate nerve fibers, as opposed to the gray appearance of nerve cell bodies and unmyelinated nerve fibers.

white noise

n. Sound composed of a random mixture of all frequencies within a range.

Whitten effect

n. The synchronization of the estrus cycle of females living in a group which typically occurs only when a male is present or nearby and is supposed to be due to pheromones. This effect has been observed in humans, mice, rats, goats, hamsters, cows, sheep, and several other mammalian species. Also called the male mouse effect.

whole object

n. In Kleinian analysis, the mother or another person or object which serves to satisfy the sexual instinct of an infant or other person, as opposed to the part object, such as the mother's breast, upon which the infant is focused.

whole report technique

n. An experimental procedure in which a subject attempts to recall all of the parts of a presented stimulus such as a word list. This has been employed in studies of iconic memory, as opposed to partial report techniques, in which a particular line or other part of a stimulus is reported.

whole-word method

n. A method of teaching children to read in which they are encouraged to recognize words instead of reading the letters and sounding out the word, as is done in most schools in the United States.

Whorfian hypothesis

n. The idea that the ways people perceive the world and think is determined by their language(s); having learned different languages, people understand the world differently. Thus Benjamin Whorf believed that monolingual Hopi speakers who have only one word for flying things would less readily distinguish among birds, bats, and butterflies than speakers of English. Subsequent research has not confirmed this strong version of the hypothesis, but the notion that language has subtle guiding effects on thought and perception persists. Also known as the Sapir-Whorf hypothesis.

Wilcoxon matched pairs test

n. A nonparametric test of the similarity of two distributions in which the differences between pairs of scores are found and then ranked. If there is no difference between the distributions, the two sums of the ranks of the positive and negative differences should be nearly equal. The statistic is calculated by the formula

$$\frac{n(n-1)/4 - T}{\sqrt{n(n+2)(2n+1)/24}}$$

where *T* is the smaller of the two summed ranks and *n* is the number of pairs in the sample.

Wilcoxon rank-sum test

n. A nonparametric test of the similarity of two distributions in which the absolute difference between pairs of scores is found and then ranked, and the ranks of the positive and negative differences are summed. If there is no difference between the distributions, the two sums should be nearly equal. The statistic is calculated by the formula

$$\frac{n(n-1)/4 - T}{\sqrt{n(n+2)(2n+1)/24}}$$

where *T* is the smaller of the two summed ranks and *n* is the number of pairs in the sample.

wild boy of Aveyron

n. A boy of about 8–12 years of age who had been living without human contact until discovered by a group of hunters in the forest near Aveyron, France, in 1798 and studied by Jean-Marie Gaspard Itard. He is considered a classical example of a feral child and was unable to speak a human language, wore no clothes, had numerous scars from fights with wild animals on his body, and appeared to know nothing of human culture. Some French doctors examined him and concluded he was a mentally deficient child deserted by his parents. He learned to speak only two words, *milk* and *Oh God*, but learned behaviorally with kind treatment. There has been much debate as to whether he was actually genetically deficient or had missed a critical period for learning language in early childhood.

Williams syndrome

n. A rare genetic defect of chromosome 7 which leads to a deficit in the production of elastin, a protein which gives strength and elasticity to blood vessels. Persons who have this syndrome have delayed physical development and often have features resembling those of elves or pixies, hoarse voices, abnormal sensitivity to noise, and elevated serum calcium level and are prone to cardiovascular problems. Persons with this syndrome also tend to be mentally delayed in some areas but normal in social skills, verbal ability, and musical skills. Also called hypercalcimea syndrome.

willpower

n. A hypothetical mental force which allows a person to overcome temptation and moral laxity and to carry out his or her intentions.

windigo

n. **1.** A predator that prefers human prey in Algonquin mythology. **2.** A culture-bound mental disorder in which a person of the Algonquin culture believes he or she is possessed by a windigo spirit and becomes depressed and violent with a desire to eat human flesh.

win-shift, lose-stay strategy

n. The inferred strategy of subjects in two-choice gaming situations in which they change their choice when it is rewarded and repeat the same decision when it is punished or not rewarded.

win-stay, lose-change strategy
n. The inferred strategy of subjects in two-choice gaming situations in which they keep making the same choice when it is rewarded and change their choice if it is punished or not rewarded.

WISC ► *See* WECHSLER INTELLIGENCE SCALE FOR CHILDREN

Wisconsin Card Sorting test
n. A test of problem solving and ability to alter one's mental set, using 128 cards with geometric shapes in different colors and different numbers. On each trial the subject is asked to sort a card into one of four piles headed by an example card and is told only if the choice is wrong or right but not the rule which the tester has decided upon to determine correctness. After the subject makes 10 consecutive correct choices the principle of correctness is changed and the reactions of the subject observed.

Wisconsin General Test Apparatus
n. An experimental device for testing monkey learning and perception, which consists of a presentation tray and a movable screen which separates the monkey's cage from the experimenter. On each trial an object or set of objects are placed on the tray with a piece of food underneath one of them, and the monkey is allowed to select one object and gets the food if he/she chooses correctly.

wish fulfillment
n. In psychoanalysis, the satisfaction, usually in a dream or fantasy, of an unconscious desire disguised by imagining an associated set of images.

withdrawal effect
n. Any experienced discomfort or bodily imbalance which results from the sudden absence of a drug or other substance to whose presence the body has become accustomed.

withdrawal symptom
n. Any experienced discomfort or bodily imbalance which results from the sudden absence of a drug or other substance to whose presence the body has become accustomed.

within-group variance
n. The differences on a dependent variable among members of a group seen as identical or given identical treatments in an analysis of variance design.

within-subject comparison
n. A contrasting of performance on the same measure by an individual on different occasions, usually under circumstances of different experimental treatment.

within-subjects design
n. An experimental plan in which the performance of the same subjects is contrasted across different experimental treatments.

Wolffian duct
n. Either of a pair of small passageways in the developing embryo which will turn into male gonads if supplied with adequate testosterone during development and which atrophy and disappear if not supplied with testosterone. These are contrasted with the Mullerian ducts, which turn into female gonads with the proper balance of female hormones and which disappear in males during the course of normal development.

word-association test
n. Any of numerous measures of personality, pathology, and mental deficiency in which a subject is asked to respond as quickly as possible with the first word that comes to mind, and reaction time as well as the content of the response are analyzed. This measure was first devised by Carl Jung in order to investigate the mental functioning of schizophrenics. Reliability and validity for this measure are largely lacking, although many clinicians claim it gives considerable insight into clients.

word blindness
n. A colloquial term for alexia or inability to read or recognize words.

word-building test
n. A task employed in studies of cognition in which a subject is given a set of letters and asked to combine them into as many words as possible, usually within a fixed time.

word completion task

n. An experimental chore in which subjects are given a cue such as *cl* and asked to supply the missing letters to make an entire word.

word deafness

n. Neuropsychological syndrome characterized by severe difficulties in understanding spoken language, with sparing written language understanding and language production. Patients who have this disorder can hear, but they cannot discriminate the language sounds (phonemes). When a clear and overt dissociation between oral and written language understanding is observed, frequently the term *pure word deafness* is used. Because of the preserved ability to understand written language, it can be interpreted as an auditory processing defect (verbal auditory agnosia). Word deafness has been regarded either as a subtype of Wernicke's aphasia, as an independent aphasic disorder, or just as one of the underlying disturbances in Wernicke's aphasia. Some phoneme discrimination defects are usually found in cases of Wernicke's aphasia and left temporal lobe damage, but cases of pure word deafness are extremely unusual. Reported cases have found a left or bilateral superior temporal lobe pathology including the Heschl's gyrus or the auditory projection to this region. Word deafness is most frequently caused by cerebrovascular accidents or head injuries, with left or bitemporal cortico-subcortical lesions. Although it is assumed that the auditory recognition defect is limited to language, testing of nonlinguistic sound comprehension and music usually has found a more pervasive auditory agnosia. In cases of unilateral pathology, significant recovery has been observed over time.   – A A

word-form dyslexia

n. A form of learning disability in which the individual is not able to recognize whole words but must sound them out each time they are read.

word fragment completion

n. An experimental task in which subjects are given a cue such as *cl* from a previously learned word and asked to supply the missing letters to make the entire word. Thus a subject might have previously learned the word *claw* and memory for this would be tested by asking him or her to complete the word from the fragment.

word salad

n. A collection of spoken words without any apparent meaning or coherent order, often uttered by florid schizophrenics or others with markedly disturbed thought processes.

word-stem completion task

n. An experimental task in which subjects are given a cue such as *cl* from a previously learned word and asked to supply the missing letters to make the entire word. Thus a subject might have previously learned the word *claw* and memory for this would be tested by asking him or her to complete the word from the fragment.

word superiority effect

n. The faster recognition of letters when presented as part of a word than when presented alone. Thus if a subject sees rapid presentations of stimuli and is asked to determine whether the letter *x* is present, it will be easier for him or her to assess the presence of the letter *x* accurately if it is imbedded in the word *next* than if it is presented by itself. This is an interesting finding in research on reading in which it had been assumed that individual letter recognition was the process by which reading occurs.

work group

n. Any group of three or more persons whose primary reason for meeting is to complete a task or set of tasks. The interactions, cohesion, and performance of such groups have been topics of intensive study in social and organizational psychology.

working hypothesis

n. A formalized tentative theory or proposition subject to further testing and revision.

working memory

n. Working memory refers to the temporary storage of information that is currently being used in a cognitive task. The concept emerged from studies of a related but simpler concept, short-term memory. The distinction may be clarified by comparing two memory tasks. In a simple span test, which is often used to assess short-term memory, individuals are given a series of items (e.g., digits). A person's memory span is the number of items that can be reliably recalled in the correct order.

In contrast, a complex span test requires participants to retain some information while performing another cognitive task. For example, an individual is asked to perform the following arithmetic calculations while also retaining the corresponding word:

$$(5 \times 5) + 1 = 26 \qquad \text{cat}$$
$$(8/4) + 7 = 9 \qquad \text{truck}$$

The complex memory span is the number of words remembered while successfully performing the second task.

Complex span scores predict verbal SAT scores in college students as well as young children's reading and academic success. In contrast, the simple span score is not correlated with such tasks. The key difference is that complex scan tests require individuals to perform storage and processing functions simultaneously, whereas simple span tests are based on storage only. It is thought that working memory consists of a limited pool of resources, and that storage and processing functions compete for resources.   – DWC

working self-concept

n. The self as experienced by the individual in a given moment of time, thus acknowledging the variability of self-concept over time, the susceptibility of the self-concept to outside influence, and the partial use of the self-concept repertoire at any one point in time.

working through

n. In psychotherapy, the process of remembering, analyzing and coming to emotional terms with a memory or other psychological issue so that the person is free to deal with present life without being distracted by the memory or issue.

work psychology

n. A general term for occupational, industrial, and organizational psychology, as well as ergonomics and human factors design.

worldview ▶ *See* **CULTURAL WORLDVIEW**

WPPSI ▶ *See* **PRIMARY SCALE OF INTELLIGENCE** *and* **WECHSLER PRESCHOOL**

writing disorder

n. Any sensory, motor, or cognitive problem that prevents a person from learning to express language in graphic form.

Würzburg school

n. A point of view in psychology from 1894 until 1915 which was developed in Würzburg, Germany, by Oswald Külpe and his associates, which rejected the idea that consciousness was composed primarily of images and studied intangible aspects such as attention, judgment, meaning, and aesthetic response, which may be conscious but have no imaginal aspect.

Xanax

n. A brand name for alprazolam, which is one of a family of addictive central nervous system depressant drugs which are used to treat anxiety, sleeping problems, and seizure disorders and relieve symptoms of alcohol withdrawal. They are frequently prescribed to depressed individuals because the overdose potential is low, as it requires more than a thousand normal doses to be fatal to an average adult. This group includes chlordiazapoxide, alprazolam, bromazepam, clonazepam, clorazepate, diazepam (Valium), estazolam, flurazepam, lorazapam, midazolam, oxazepam, quazepam, temaze-pam, and triazolam.

xanthopsia

n. A visual disorder in which everything appears yellow. It can be temporarily induced by staring at a blue screen for several moments and is sometimes a symptom of jaundice and can be caused by digitalis poisoning. Also called chromatopsia.

X chromosome

n. A female sex chromosome, one copy of which is present in all the cells of a male's body and two copies of which are present in all cells in a female's body. It gets its name for its shape, which roughly approximates the letter *X*, as opposed to the male sex chromosome, which roughly resembles the letter *Y*.

xenophobia

n. An abnormal fear of strangers or people from different countries, cultures, subcultures, ethnicities, social classes, or any other identifiably different social group. In both humans and other animals, it is often associated with territoriality, and those perceived as intruders are met with hostility and sometimes physical aggression.

XXX syndrome

n. A randomly occurring genetic defect in which a female has three instead of two female chromosomes. Most individuals who have this disorder have no negative symptoms and are not diagnosed. The most common effects are being taller than and having an IQ that averages about 10 points lower than siblings; a moderate increase in the probability of learning disabilities is also associated with the syndrome.

XXY syndrome

n. A genetic disorder of males characterized by the presence of an extra X, or female sex, chromosome in all the cells of the body. Such males usually have very small testes, do not produce sperm, have enlarged breasts, and produce follicle stimulating hormone. Behavioral problems are common among boys with this disorder, and it is not known whether they are due to the genetic abnormality or the difficulty in social adjustment caused by being physically different from other boys. Also called Klinefelter syndrome.

XYY syndrome

n. A genetic disorder in which a male has two copies of the male sex chromosome instead of one. Most males who have this syndrome are normal, and their chromosomal abnormality is not detected. It has been associated with being taller and more active than siblings, and there is moderate correlation with learning disorders and an IQ about 10 points lower, on average, than that of siblings.

Y

Yates' correction for continuity

n. A method for correcting for the discrete nature of data, often used in 2x2 chi-square tests, needed because the chi-square distribution is continuous. It is most often used in 2x2 chi-square tests when a frequency of less than 5 occurs in a cell and is accomplished by subtracting .5 from the difference in each cell. This correction reduces the likelihood of a false positive result but also increases the likelihood of type II error.

Y chromosome

n. The male sex chromosome, one of which is present in all the cells of a male's body and which females do not have. It gets its name for its shape, which roughly approximates the letter *Y*, as opposed to the female sex chromosome, which roughly resembles the letter *X*.

yellow-sightedness

n. A visual disorder in which everything appears yellow. It can be temporarily induced by staring at a blue screen for several moments and is sometimes a symptom of jaundice and can be caused by digitalis poisoning. Also called chromatopsia.

yellow spot
n. A small yellow spot in the retina of the eye in which cones are highly prevalent, which contains the fovea, which appears yellow from the outside. Also called macula lutea.

Yerkish
n. An artificial written language using geometric shapes on computer keyboards for words, which has been used in experiments attempting to teach language to nonhuman primates.

yoga
n. **1.** Any of several schools of stretching exercises which have been found conducive to reduction in many medical problems and are either derived from or are a part of Hindu spiritual traditions. **2.** The Hindu religion, which seeks union of the individual with the universal soul or atman.

yoked control
n. An experimental methodology in which subjects of two experimental groups are paired, and both are given the same treatment but one subject of each pair of subjects is given either no control over the situation or a different test from the experimental subjects. It is used to ensure identical treatment of two groups of subjects.

young girl/old woman figure
n. An ambiguous picture which can alternately be perceived as the face of a young woman wearing a hat or an old woman wearing a scarf.

Young-Helmholtz theory
n. A theory of color vision in which it is supposed that there are three color receptors sensitive to different parts of the light spectrum corresponding to the colors blue, green, and red. It was supposed that combinations of these produced all the colors perceived and the combination of all three receptors produced a perception of white. This theory was independently propounded by Thomas Young and Hermann von Helmholtz.

Z

Z
n. A normally distributed set of scores with an average of 0 and a standard deviation of 1 often used as a transformation of other data sets, in which the difference between a score and the mean score is found and divided by the standard deviation to produce a z score distribution.

Zanforlin illusion
n. An illusion in which a line drawn between the outsides of two circles appears to be longer than a line of the same length which crosses the two circles before joining them.

Zeigarnik effect
n. The observation that problems which have been interrupted and not completed are better remembered than those which have been vcompleted. The effect tends to be temporary and dependent on the type of task.

Zeitgeber
n. An environmental cue such as a sunrise used to activate or calibrate circadian and other biological rhythms.

zeitgeist
n. The spirit of the times; used to denote a shared mentality or worldview common to a particular era in a particular culture.

Zen Buddhism
n. A school of Buddhism which began in about the sixth or seventh century C.E. in China and later in Japan, Korea, and Vietnam, which emphasizes direct experience through meditation (*zazen*) and the

using of everyday life as a part of mindfulness practice. It is part of Mahayana Buddhism, which suggests that compassion is inherent but covered up by the illusion of desire, in which most people spend most of their lives mired.

Zener cards

n. A set of 25 cards on the face of which is printed a circle, cross, square, star, or wavy lines, used for research in the area of extrasensory perception. Also called ESP cards.

zenith distance

n. The direction of a point or object in the visual field relative to a point directly overhead.

zero population growth

n. **1.** A balance between births and deaths in a group of animals such that the population remains stable. **2.** A slogan used by birth control advocates to point out the negative effects on the environment of human population growth.

zero-sum game

n. Any game in which the gains and losses of the various players add up to 0 so that for every gain by one player there is an equal loss by other players. The term is often used in economic discussions.

zeta

n. A measure of the linearity of a relationship on which a regression analysis has been performed.

Zipf curve

n. A graphical representation of the frequency with which something occurs and the total number of things which can occur such as the choice of words in a natural language.

Zipf's law

n. **1.** The observation that in natural languages there is a power relation between frequency of use and rank such that the most common word is used about twice as often as the second most common word, which is used about twice as often as the fourth most

common word, and so on. **2.** The suggestion that there is an equilibrium between uniformity and diversity.

Zollner illusion

n. A visual illusion in which several parallel lines appear to converge and diverge when crossed with short lines uniformly at 45-degree angles to the original line set.

Zoloft

n. The brand name for sertraline hydrochloride, which acts as a selective serotonin reuptake inhibitor and is currently the most widely used antidepressant and antianxiety drug in the United States.

zone of proximal development

n. In the sociocultural developmental theories of Lev Vigotsky, the actual level of ability of a child in any particular area and the level at which he or she could achieve with the help of guidance from an adult or more knowledgeable child.

zooerasty

n. The practice of having sexual intercourse with nonhuman animals. Also called bestiality.

zoosemiotics

n. The study of animal communication systems.

z score

n. A transformed score which has had the average of a set of scores subtracted from it and the result divided by the standard deviation of the original set of scores. Also called a standard score.

z transformation

n. The process of converting scores into standard scores.

Zurich school

n. The group of early followers of Carl Jung based in Zurich after Jung's split with Sigmund Freud and his followers, which was called the Vienna school.

9454

Zwaardemaker olfactometer

n. A glass tube open on both ends, one of which was inserted in the nostril while the other was connected to a tube filled with a measured amount of a substance to be smelled. The amount of the substance to be smelled was controlled by the length of the Zwaardemaker tube.

Zwaardemaker smell system

n. A classification system for describing odors in which there are nine primary odors, ethereal, aromatic, fragrant, ambrosiac, allaceous, empyreumatic, hircine, foul, and nauseous, which were hypothesized to serve as the basis for all odors as the primary colors combine to form all the hues humans can perceive.

zygote

n. A fertilized ovum with two half-sets of chromosomes, one-half contributed by the mother and one-half by the father, which normally divides into an embryo which grows into an infant.